Mastering
Borland Delphi 2005

Mastering

Borland® Delphi™ 2005

Marco Cantù

SYBEX®

San Francisco   London

Publisher: Joel Fugazzotto

Acquisitions Editor: Tom Cirtin

Developmental Editor: David Clark

Production Editor: Leslie E.H. Light

Technical Editor: Brian Long

Copyeditor: Sally Engelfried

Compositor: Chris Gillespie, Happenstance Type-O-Rama

Proofreaders: Nancy Riddiough, Jim Brook, Candace English

Indexer: Ted Laux

Cover Designer/Illustrator: Design Site

An earlier version of this book was published under the title *Mastering Delphi 7* © 2003 SYBEX Inc.

Library of Congress Card Number: 2004117987

ISBN: 0-7821-4342-3

To Lella, the love of my life,
Benedetta and Jacopo, our love come to life.

Acknowledgments

This eighth edition of *Mastering Delphi* follows the ninth release of a Delphi development environment by Borland, a revolution started in the winter of 1995. As it has for many other programmers, Delphi has been my primary interest throughout these years; and writing, consulting, teaching, and speaking at conferences about Delphi have absorbed more and more of my time, leaving other languages and programming tools in the dust of my office. Because my work and my life are quite intertwined, many people have been involved in both, and I wish I had enough space and time to thank them all as they deserve. Instead, I'll just mention a few particular people and say a warm thank you to the entire Delphi community (especially for the Spirit of Delphi 1999 Award I was happy to share with Bob Swart).

The first official thanks are to the Borland programmers and managers who made Delphi possible and continue to improve it: Danny Thorpe, Allen Bauer, Mark Edington, Jim Tierney, Steve Trefethen, Corbin Dunn, Chris Hesik, Ramesh Theivendran, Jesper Hogstrom, and all the others I have not had a chance to meet. I'd also like to give particular thanks to my friends at Borland's Developer Relations: Borland living icon David Intersimone, John Kaster, Anders Ohlsson, and Karen Giles. Other friends have worked at Borland in the past, including Charlie Calvert, Steve Teixeira, and Zack Urlocker.

The next thanks are to the Sybex editorial and production crew, many of whom I don't even know. Special thanks go to Leslie Light, Tom Cirtin, Sally Engelfried, and David Clark; I'd also like to thank in particular Joel Fugazzotto, who keeps believing in my book projects.

This edition of *Mastering Delphi* has had a very detailed and scrupulous review from Delphi guru Brian Long (www.blong.com). His highlights and comments have improved the book in all areas: technical content, accuracy, examples, and even readability and grammar. Thanks a lot, once more! Brian also contributed a chapter, as did Malcolm Groves (www.malcolmgroves.com) of Borland Australia.

Previous editions also had special contributions by Tim Gooch, Giuseppe Madaffari, Guy Smith-Ferrier, Nando Dessena, John Bushakra, Jim Gunkel, Chad Hower, and Robert Leahey. Many improvements to the text and sample programs were suggested by technical reviewers of past editions (Danny Thorpe, Juancarlo Anez, Ralph Friedman, Tim Gooch, and Lino Tadros) and in other reviews over the years by Bob Swart and Steve Tendon. Uberto Barbini helped me write *Mastering Kylix 2* and some of his ideas also ended up affecting this book.

Special thanks go to my friends Bruce Eckel, Andrea Provaglio, Norm McIntosh, Joanna Pooley, Ray Konopka, Mark Miller, Cary Jensen, Chris Frizelle, Michael Lant, Joanna Carter, Jim Cooper, Mike Orriss, Dan Miser, my coworker Paolo Rossi, and the entire Italian D&D Team (www.delphiedintorni.it). Also, a very big thank you to all the attendees of my Delphi programming courses, seminars, and conferences in Italy, the United States, France, the United Kingdom, Singapore, the Netherlands, Germany, and Sweden.

My biggest thanks go to my wife Lella, who had to endure yet another book-writing season, to our daughter Benedetta and our son Jacopo, who would have rather played with Daddy's computer than see me working on it. Their liveliness (and that of our puppy dog Lillo) and the care they deserve provided very good reasons to stay away from working enough hours each day, although it also engendered many late night sessions and early wake-ups. Many of our friends provided healthy breaks in the work, along with our parents, brothers, sisters, and their families (including our eight nieces and nephews—Matteo, Andrea, Giacomo, Stefano, Andrea, Pietro, Elena, and Sara).

Finally, I would like to thank all of the people, many of them unknown, who enjoy life and help to build a better world. If I never stop believing in the future and in peace, it is because of them.

Contents at a Glance

Contents

Introduction

Year 2005 has seen the introduction of a brand new version of Delphi and the celebration of Delphi's tenth anniversary. The product, in fact, officially debuted on February 14th, 1995, as you can see on my personal Delphi anniversary celebration web page at www.marcocantu.com/delphibirth.

About a year before that Zack Urlocker first showed me a yet-to-be-released product code-named Delphi and I immediately realized that it would change my work—and the work of many other software developers. I used to struggle with C++ libraries for Windows, and Delphi was and still is the best combination of object-oriented programming and visual programming not only for the Win16 (when it was introduced) and Win32 APIs, but also for the Linux operating system and the Microsoft .NET Framework.

Delphi 2005 builds on this tradition and on the solid foundations of the VCL, but it is also a revolutionary release with a completely redesigned Integrated Development Environment (IDE), a significantly extended object-oriented programming language, and the inclusion of many Borland developer tools covering the entire software development lifecycle. Even more significant and unique in the industry, it has the ability not only to target both Win32 and .NET from a single IDE, but also to build programs for both platforms using the same source code.

Delphi development covers almost all areas: simple standalone programs, graphics processing, database development, client/server and multitier business applications, intranet and Internet solutions, XML and web services. Whether you are looking for control and power, fast productivity, or an enjoyable developer experience, you'll be able to accomplish all this with Delphi and the abundance of techniques and tips presented in this book.

Nine Versions and Counting

Some of the original Delphi features that attracted me were its form-based and object-oriented approach, its extremely fast compiler, its great database support, its close integration with Windows programming, and its component technology. But the most important element was the Object Pascal language (now called the Delphi language), which is the foundation of everything else.

Delphi 2 was even better! Among its most important additions were these: the Multi-Record Object and the improved database grid, OLE Automation support and the variant data type, full Windows 95 support and integration, the long string data type, and Visual Form Inheritance. Delphi 3 added to this the code insight technology, DLL debugging support, component templates, the TeeChart, the WebBroker technology, component packages, ActiveForms, and an astonishing integration with COM, thanks to interfaces.

Delphi 4 gave us the AppBrowser editor, new Windows 98 features, improved OLE and COM support, extended database components, and many additions to the core VCL classes, including support for docking, constraining, and anchoring controls. Delphi 5 added to the picture many more improvements of the IDE, extended database support with specific ADO and InterBase datasets, an improved version of MIDAS (now called DataSnap) with Internet support, translation capabilities, the concept of frames, and new components.

Delphi 6 added to all these features support for Linux cross-platform development with the Component Library for Cross-Platform (CLX, now dropped), an extended run-time library, the dbExpress database engine, web services and exceptional XML support, the powerful WebSnap development framework, more IDE enhancements, and a number of components and classes.

Delphi 7 made some of these newer technologies more robust with improvement and fixes (SOAP support and DataSnap come to mind) and offered support for newer technologies (like Windows XP themes or UDDI), but it most importantly made readily available an interesting set of third-party tools: the RAVE reporting engine, the IntraWeb web application development technology, and the ModelMaker design environment.

Delphi 8 for the Microsoft .NET Framework opened up a brand new world by providing the first Borland compiler for the Pascal/Delphi language not targeting the Intel CPU, but rather the .NET CIL platform. All of the most relevant features of the .NET Framework are supported and often extended, including ADO.NET, WinForms, and most notably ASP.NET. Delphi 8 also introduced some of the application lifecycle management technologies bought by Borland, such as StarTeam and Caliber.

Now Delphi 2005 encompasses all these features, providing a single IDE for both Win32 and .NET development, and supporting multiple programming language including Delphi and C#. Delphi is still a strong player in the RAD field but has now also entered the Model Driven Architecture (MDA) world with its ECO framework. As I already mentioned, Delphi 2005 features a redesigned IDE with countless new features and many handy coding helpers as well as having an extended programming language for both Win32 and .NET.

Mastering Delphi, over the Years

With its first edition released shortly after the original version of Delphi, the series of Mastering Delphi books has had a rather long history as well, and quite a successful one. In addition to several editions in the U.S. and a large number of translations (into over 15 different languages), the book has also received a few awards:

◆ *Mastering Delphi 3* won the *Delphi Informant* Magazine Readers Choice Award 1997.

◆ I won the 1999 edition of the Spirit of Delphi Award issued by Borland.

◆ *Mastering Delphi 5* won the *Delphi Informant* Magazine Readers Choice Award 2000.

◆ *Mastering Delphi 6* won the *Delphi Informant* Magazine Readers Choice Award 2002.

◆ *Mastering Delphi 7* won the *Delphi Informant* Magazine Readers Choice Award 2003.

The Structure of the Book

Delphi is a great tool, but it is also a complex programming environment that involves many elements. This book will help you master Delphi programming, including the Delphi language, its library of components, its database and client/server support, and Internet and web development, spanning across Win32 and .NET for each of these topics.

You do not need in-depth knowledge of any of these areas of the product to read this book, but you do need to know the basics of programming. Having some familiarity with Delphi will help you considerably, particularly after the introductory chapters. The book starts covering its topics in depth immediately; much of the introductory material from previous editions has been removed. Some of this material (including an introduction to the Pascal language and one on Delphi programming) is available on my website, as discussed in Appendix A.

The book is divided into four parts:

◆ Part 1, "Foundations," introduces new features of the Delphi 2005 Integrated Development Environment (IDE) in Chapter 1, discusses the two target platforms (Win32 and .NET) in Chapter 2, then moves to the Delphi language (in Chapters 3 and 4) and to the run-time library (in Chapter 5) and Visual Component Library (in Chapters 6, 7 and 8), ending with an overview of the .NET Framework Class Library (in Chapter 9).

◆ Part 2, "Delphi Object-Oriented Architectures," covers refactoring, unit testing, the architecture of dynamic Delphi applications, COM and the interoperability of .NET with COM and Win32.

◆ Part 3, "Delphi Database-Oriented Architectures," covers plain database access, in-depth coverage of the data-aware controls, client/server programming, dbExpress, InterBase, ADO, ADO.NET, and multitier architectures with DataSnap and ADO.NET remoting techniques. The last chapter in this part covers the Enterprise Core Objects (ECO) architecture.

◆ Part 4, "Delphi and the Internet," first discusses Internet protocols HTTP and HTML, then moves on to specific areas of web development technologies: WebBroker, WebSnap, IntraWeb, and ASP.NET. The last two chapters cover XML and the development of web services.

As this brief summary suggests, the book covers topics of interest to Delphi users at nearly all levels of programming expertise and for almost all areas of Delphi programming. I've tried to skip reference material almost completely and focus instead on techniques for using Delphi effectively. Because Delphi provides extensive online documentation, to include lists of methods and properties of components in the book would not only be superfluous, it would also make it obsolete as soon as the software changes slightly. I suggest that you read this book with the Delphi Help files at hand so you'll have reference material readily available.

However, I've done my best to allow you to read the book away from a computer if you prefer. Screen images and the key portions of the listings should help in this direction (even if listings are very limited compared to the thousands of lines of code of the projects discussed in the book). The book uses just a few conventions to make it more readable. All the source code elements, such as keywords, properties, classes, and functions, appear in `this font`, and code excerpts are formatted as they appear in the Delphi editor, with boldfaced keywords and italic comments and strings.

Free Source Code on the Web

This book focuses on examples. After the presentation of each concept you'll find a working program example (sometimes more than one) that demonstrates how the feature can be used. All told, there are over 300 examples presented in the book, most of which are available for both Win32 and .NET. These programs are available in a single zipped file of slightly over 3MB on both Sybex's website (www.sybex.com) and my website (www.marcocantu.com). Most of the examples are quite simple and focus on a single feature. More complex examples are often built step-by-step, with intermediate steps including partial solutions and incremental improvements.

NOTE   Some of the database examples also require you to have the Delphi sample database files installed; they are part of the default Delphi installation. Others require the InterBase EMPLOYEE sample database (as well as the InterBase server, of course). A few of the web examples require a web server installed.

On my website there is also an HTML version of the source code, with full syntax highlighting, along with a complete cross-reference of keywords and identifiers (class, function, method, and property names, among others). The cross-reference is an HTML file, so you'll be able to use your browser to easily find all the programs that use a Delphi keyword or identifier you're looking for (not a full search engine, but close enough).

The directory structure of the sample code is quite simple. Basically, each chapter of the book has its own folder, with a subfolder for each example (e.g., 05\FilesList). In the text, the examples are simply referenced by name (e.g., FilesList).

NOTE   Be sure to read the source code archive's readme file, which contains important information about using the software legally and effectively.

How to Reach the Author

If you find any problems in the text or examples in this book, both the publisher and I would be happy to hear from you. In addition to reporting errors and problems, please give us your unbiased opinion of the book and tell us which examples you found most useful and which you liked least. There are several ways you can provide this feedback:

- On the Sybex website (www.sybex.com), you'll find updates to the text or code as necessary. To comment on this book, click the Contact Sybex link and then choose Book Content Issues. This link displays a form where you can enter your comments.

- My own website (www.marcocantu.com) hosts further information about the book and about Delphi, where you might find answers to your questions. The site has news and tips, technical articles, free online books (outlined in Appendix A), white papers, Delphi links, and my collection of Delphi components and tools (covered in Appendix B).

- I have also set up a newsgroup section specifically devoted to my books and to general Delphi Q&A (but Borland's own newsgroup will generally provide you with better and faster feedback). Refer to my website for a list of the newsgroup areas and for the instructions to subscribe to them (my newsgroups are totally free, but require a login password). You can browse my groups over the Web along with Borland's most relevant Delphi groups on a site I manage, http://delphi.newswhat.com. The area devoted to my books, in particular, can be found at:

    http://delphi.newswhat.com/geoxml/forumlistthreads?
      groupname=marcocantu.com.books

- Finally, you can reach me via e-mail at marco.cantu@gmail.com (you can write in English or in Italian). For technical questions, please try using the newsgroups first, as you might get answers earlier and from multiple people. My mailbox is usually overflowing and, regretfully, I cannot reply promptly to every request, particularly if they don't relate to the book but are merely Delphi development requests.

Part 1

Foundations

In this section:

- ◆ Chapter 1: Introducing Borland Developers Studio 3.0
- ◆ Chapter 2: The Platforms: Win32 and Microsoft .NET
- ◆ Chapter 3: The Delphi Programming Language
- ◆ Chapter 4: The Delphi Language for .NET
- ◆ Chapter 5: DelphiWin32 Run-Time Library
- ◆ Chapter 6: Architecture of the Visual Component Library (VCL)
- ◆ Chapter 7: Working with Forms
- ◆ Chapter 8: Building the User Interface with VCL (for Win32 and .NET)
- ◆ Chapter 9: Delphi.NET Run-Time Library and the Framework Class Library

Chapter 1

Introducing Borland Developer Studio 3.0

In a visual programming tool such as Delphi, the role of the integrated development environment (IDE) is at times even more important than the programming language. If you are coming to Delphi 2005 from Delphi 7 or earlier, you will notice that Delphi 2005 provides a completely rewritten IDE based on a newer and more open architecture. Programmers used to the Delphi IDE, which never changed very radically between Delphi 1 and Delphi 7, will take a little time to get used to the new IDE. That's why in this chapter I'm mostly offering some tips and suggestions for developers who've already used past versions of Delphi—although I'll also cover new features and a few traditional Delphi features that are not well known or obvious to newcomers. There is some introductory material, but this chapter is not a step by step tutorial on using each and every feature of the Delphi IDE because in such a rich environment that could easily take hundreds of pages.

If you *are* a beginning programmer, don't be afraid. The Delphi IDE is quite intuitive to use. Delphi itself includes a manual with a tutorial that introduces the development of Delphi applications. The Delphi 2005 IDE was already introduced in Borland's C#Builder and in Delphi 8 for the Microsoft .NET Framework, which is why Borland Developers Studio (BDS) in Delphi 2005 is labeled as version 3.0.

Editions of Delphi

Before delving into the details of the Delphi programming environment, let's take a side step to underline two key ideas. First, there isn't a single edition of Delphi; there are many of them. Second, any Delphi environment can be customized. For these reasons, Delphi screens you see illustrated in this chapter may differ from those on your own computer. Here are the current editions of Delphi:

- ◆ The Professional edition is the real entry-level version, aimed at professional developers with limited needs, particularly in the areas of database connectivity and web development. The Professional edition includes all the basic features, database programming support (without the complete support for client/server development), basic web server support (WebBroker), and some of the external tools.

- ◆ The Enterprise edition is aimed at developers building complete business applications. It includes full database support, all of the XML and advanced web services technologies, internationalization support, three-tier architectures, and many add-on tools. Some chapters of this book cover features included only in Delphi Enterprise; I try to identify these sections but refer to the Delphi Feature Matrix document on Borland's website (`www.borland.com/delphi`) for more details. Notice that in the past it has happened that while providing updates, Borland has added features to the lower versions, making my aim for accuracy in this area quite difficult to achieve.

◆ The Architect edition adds to the Enterprise edition extra support for many of the Borland Application Lifetime Management (ALM) tools, such as StarTeam and Caliber, and for Enterprise Core Object (ECO). The ECO framework is an environment for building applications that are driven at run time by a UML model and are capable of mapping their objects both to a database and to the user interface, thanks to a plethora of advanced components. See Chapter 18 for more details.

NOTE   In past versions of Delphi, there was also a Personal edition aimed at Delphi newcomers, with limitations in the feature set (such as a lack of database programming support) and in the rights to distribute applications written with it. In the past this was either a free (or very cheap) download or was bundled with magazines. At the time of this writing, a Personal edition of Delphi 2005 has not been released, and it is not clear whether Borland will create one.

Aside from the different editions available, there are ways to customize the Delphi environment. In the screen illustrations throughout the book, I've tried to use a standard user interface (as it comes out of the box); however, I have my preferences, of course, and I generally install many add-ons, which may be reflected in some of the screen shots.

An Overview of the IDE

Having briefly looked at the various editions of Delphi, it is time to start focusing on its integrated development environment (IDE). There are many things to cover, even for experienced Delphi programmers, because the Delphi 2005 IDE has a large number of new features.

An IDE with Multiple Personalities

Besides having multiple editions, the Borland Developers Studio IDE also has multiple *personalities*. Borland uses the term *personality* to indicate that a single IDE can be used for working with different programming languages and for targeting different platforms. In other words, you don't have to run one IDE for Win32 development and another one for .NET development. Instead you can run a single IDE and open projects of different types and possibly even create project groups containing projects of different types and compile them all with a single command.

Out of the box, Delphi 2005 has three personalities:

◆ The Delphi for Win32 personality, which allows you to keep developing programs for the standard Win32 platform.

◆ The Delphi for .NET personality, which allows you to move existing Delphi VCL applications to the .NET architecture or write specific WinForms and ASP.NET applications.

◆ The C# personality, which is for .NET only and is based on Microsoft's compiler but is not really covered in this Delphi book.

To figure out the current personality you are working with, the IDE shows a small icon in a specific toolbar (clicking it opens the About box), as just shown.

The IDE is quite flexible, and more personalities can be added by Borland and possibly also by third-party developers (if Borland discloses some more internal information about this process). Shortly after releasing Delphi 2005, Borland announced their intention to make available the old VCL-based C++Builder as an extra personality, although at the time of this writing no time frame and no feature sets have been specified.

NOTE   Another foreseeable option is the integration of a Delphi for Linux personality, something you can almost already achieve by using Simon Kissel's CrossKylix tool (`http://crosskylix.untergrund.net`).

An IDE for .NET and ALM

You might wonder why Borland choose to create a brand new IDE instead of simply updating the existing one. There are probably multiple reasons, including the fact that the Delphi 7 IDE project was rooted back in the early days of Delphi, and it was about time for an overall update of the user interface and probably also for a better internal architecture.

Certainly one of the core reasons for designing a new IDE was the need to fully support .NET while also keeping Win32 features. In particular, the IDE hosts the .NET run time for integrating the .NET SDK designers (like the WinForms designer and the ASP.NET designer). Other IDE features, however, rely on .NET. For example, all of the refactoring support (discussed in Chapter 11) is based on the CodeDOM architecture that's part of the .NET Framework.

Another driving reason for a new design of the IDE comes from the evolution of Borland as a company. Instead of focusing on tools for coding the applications, Borland now has tools embracing the overall software development process, from requirements analysis to UML design, from development to optimization, deployment, and testing. This approach was earlier touted as Application Lifetime Management (ALM) and is now extended and expanded into a strategy Borland calls Software Delivery Optimization (SDO).

Regardless of the global name, what's relevant for Delphi developers is that the new IDE was designed to host many other tools built from different departments within Borland. The Architect edition of Delphi 2005, in fact, includes:

◆ The StarTeam client, supporting not only version control but complete management of the development process and products, with strong tools for developer collaboration and offering integration with all of the other tools of the ALM suite.

◆ The Caliber client for managing requirements.

◆ The Together UML modeling tool, supporting the ECO framework and partially usable to create and maintain UML diagrams for your custom Delphi code.

◆ OptimizeIt, used to check for bottlenecks in your .NET applications.

◆ A Web Deployment Wizard for ASP.NET and IntraWeb applications.

This book is focused on Delphi, so I'll only marginally touch on these ALM topics, some of which require detailed information to be understood (a few pages wouldn't be useful) and are not included in the Professional and Enterprise editions of Delphi that are the primary targets of this book.

Notice, anyway, that the IDE is written mostly in Delphi itself, with portions in other languages. It is relevant to notice that most of the new VCL components have been added because Borland needed them in the IDE itself, as you'll see in Chapter 6.

Partial Installations

Delphi comes with three personalities, but if you don't need to use them all (for example, you don't care about C# or don't need Win32 support anymore), you can install only some of the personalities or remove them afterward. At the time of this writing, it was reported that partial installations add some instability to the IDE, so you might still choose to install everything even if you don't need to use all of the features.

Notice that the BDS IDE uses demand loading, meaning that it loads only the core of each personality when it starts, delaying the loading of other needed assemblies and packages to the time you actually start using a specific feature (like the first time you work with a VCL application). This means that personalities you install but don't use do not put a lot of burden on the IDE at run time.

Even if you install only the Delphi Win32 personality, the IDE still needs to rely on .NET for some of its features (like refactoring, as I mentioned earlier). It is technically possible to use Delphi 2005 for Win32 development on a computer without the .NET run time installed but only if you choose to disable those features.

Finally, notice that you can also fully disable .NET support—that is, use Delphi 2005 without having .NET installed on your computer. This is not officially supported by Borland but seems to work, although I really don't recommend it because refactoring is one of my favorite features of Delphi 2005! Also, this operation seems to make the help system totally unusable. However, if you are interested, you can see the detailed instructions on the website `http://delphi2005.cjb.net`.

What is relevant in any case is that you can indeed remove some of the packages or assemblies used by the IDE if you know you are not going to use those features. For example, you can remove Together or StarTeam support, saving some load time. These are the registry entries you want to look at (at your own risk, as editing the registry can create troubles on your system):

```
HKEY_CURRENT_USER\Software\Borland\BDS\3.0\Known IDE Assemblies
HKEY_CURRENT_USER\Software\Borland\BDS\3.0\Known IDE Packages
```

Starting the IDE with Multiple Configurations

On a related note, consider that it is also possible to set up different sets of registry entries for Delphi 2005, choosing which one to use at each execution by means of a command line parameter. This means you can create a stripped down version of Delphi but also keep the full version ready to use.

Technically, Delphi has an undocumented command line parameter, -r, which you can use to specify the base registry key to use. For example, create a shortcut like this (provided you have a default installation path):

```
"C:\Program Files\Borland\BDS\3.0\Bin\bds.exe" -rSmall
```

The first time you run it, Delphi creates a brand new set of registry keys, using default settings from:

```
HKEY_LOCAL_MACHINE\SOFTWARE\Borland\BDS\3.0
```

and copying them into:

```
HKEY_CURRENT_USER\Software\Borland\Small\3.0
```

In other words, the name you provide replaces the BDS name in the registry tree. If you don't want to start with brand new settings but edit your current configuration, export the standard Borland\ BDS\3.0 registry key, edit it to change the key name, and reimport it in the registry.

In addition to this -r parameter (which already worked in past version of Delphi but was not documented, and still isn't officially mentioned), there are other command line parameters you can use when starting Delphi 2005. For example, the -hm parameter (Heap Monitor) displays in the title bar the amount of memory allocated by the IDE itself and updates this information at idle time. Another interesting parameter is -ns (No Splash): it disables the display of the splash screen.

Welcome to Delphi 2005

As you run the IDE, your starting point will be the Welcome page, as you can see in Figure 1.1. The Welcome page is a pane hosting Internet Explorer and allowing you to view some relevant information and browse the Web as well. It has four areas: below the toolbar there are some buttons for common tasks (like opening projects and files), on the left there is a menu with local and online links, on the right is a list of recent projects, and underneath that is the Headlines area.

FIGURE 1.1

Delphi 2005 Welcome
page with the
Getting Started
offline information

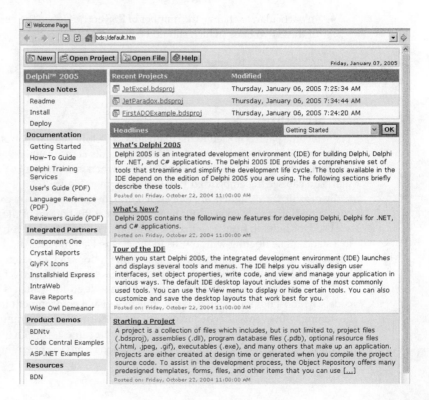

In the Headlines area you can choose among a set of Borland-related RSS feeds, which get updated automatically and provide up to date information on given areas of Delphi. The most relevant feeds for Delphi developers are the Delphi section of Borland Developer Network and the Borland blogs. Of course, the feeds are totally customizable, as is the overall structure of the Welcome page and its menu. Before I offer you a list of customization tips, however, let me point out that I prefer using a full-blown browser (and possibly not Internet Explorer) for browsing the Web and a RSS-specific program for keeping in touch with blog writers.

In any case, if you want to customize this page, you can modify some of its configuration files available in the BDS\3.0\Welcomepage folder:

◆ The overall page structure is defined in the file default.htm.

◆ The file xml/menuBar.xml defines the links on the left of the page, and you can easily provide your own entries.

◆ The file xml/defaultProviders.xml defines the list of RSS feeds. Notice that there are some ready-to-use entries that are commented in the file, such as a list of Borland bloggers; simply remove those comments to get more RSS feed options right away.

◆ The css folder contains the Cascading Style Sheet files you can change to customize the fonts and the colors of the page.

◆ In particular, to change the number of RSS entries, open the rss.js file and modify the second of these two lines (which should be line 249):

```
// limit to 10 entries displayed on welcome page
if (maxItems > 10)
```

IDE Structure

The Welcome page is hosted in the main area of Delphi 2005, which is also used by the editor and the designers. Designers let you work with components at the visual level (such as when you place a button on a form) or at a nonvisual level (such as when you place a DataSet component on a data module). You can see the embedded Win32 VCL form in Figure 1.2.

By default, the designers are embedded into the main pane; you can switch from a designer to the corresponding source code editor using the tabs at the bottom of the page (while the tabs at the top are used for moving from a source file to another). If you prefer, you can display the VCL designers in a stand-alone floating window, as in the classic Delphi IDEs, disabling the Embedded designer check box in the Environment Options/Delphi Options/VCL Designer section of the Options dialog box available on the Tools menu. Notice that this setting takes effect only after restarting the IDE.

The same main pane of the IDE also hosts the code editor, which is where you write Delphi (or C#) code. The most obvious way to write code in a visual environment involves responding to events, beginning with events attached to operations performed by program users, such as clicking a button or selecting an item from a list box. You can use the same approach to handle internal events, such as events involving database changes or notifications from the operating system.

FIGURE 1.2

The Delphi 2005 IDE with an embedded VCL Form Designer

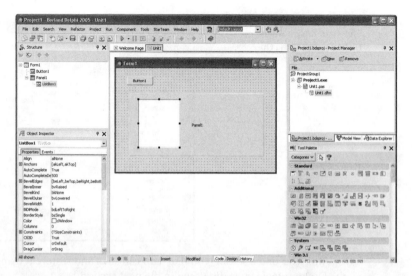

Most Delphi programmers start by writing mainly event-handling code. As they become more knowledgeable, they move to writing their own classes and components and often end up spending most of their time in the editor rather than the visual designers. Because this book covers more than visual programming and tries to help you master the entire power of Delphi, as the text proceeds you'll see more code and fewer forms.

Going back to the structure of the Delphi 2005 IDE, notice that on the left and right side of the main pane (see again Figure 1.2) there are several other windows hosting various panes. By default on the left there are the Structure View and the Object Inspector; on the right a single tabbed windows hosts the Project Manager, the Data Explorer, and the Model View Designer; while the right bottom area is taken by the Tool Palette. Another window at the bottom of the IDE generally hosts compiler results, search results, and a refactoring preview. This window is displayed when necessary. There are also dozens of other windows used by the IDE, including a number of debugger views.

If you come from Delphi 7 or previous versions, you'll notice that though the layout is quite different, the content of these panes looks familiar. For example, the Structure View is similar to the Object Tree View of Delphi 7, while the Tool Palette replaces the Components Palette. At the same time, these two windows can host other information as well, like the code structure in case of the Structure View and code snippets in case of the Tool Palette. In the BDS IDE, most panes are more flexible and host different content depending on what the user is doing, particularly which main window one is working on (visual designer, editor, UML viewer, and so on).

Of course, you can rearrange everything as you like, moving windows and panes around, keeping them floating or hooked to a side of the IDE, or even using the pin button to make them slide into view by moving the mouse over them. Notice that the main Environment Options page of the Options dialog box (displayed in Figure 1.3) has a check box that, if disabled, prevents Delphi windows from automatically docking with each other. (I mention this setting because it is one I always change from the default, along with the Show Compiler Progress check box on the same page.)

FIGURE 1.3

The main Environment Options page of the Options dialog box

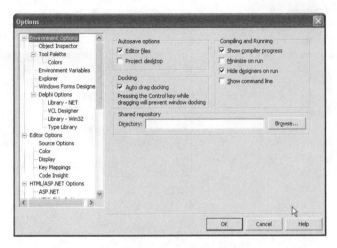

After you find a setting you like, you can save and restore it using the buttons and combo box of the Desktop toolbar, as discussed in the next section.

Desktop Settings

Programmers can customize the Delphi IDE in various ways—typically, opening many windows, arranging them, and docking them to each other. However, you'll often need to open one set of windows at design time and a different set at debug time. Similarly, you might need one layout when working with forms and a completely different layout when writing components or low-level code using only the editor. Rearranging the IDE for each of these needs is a tedious task.

For this reason, Delphi lets you save a given arrangement of IDE windows (called a *desktop*) with a name and restore it easily. You can also make one of these configurations your default debugging setting, so that it will be restored automatically when you start the debugger. All these features are available in the Desktops toolbar and in the View ➢ Desktops menu.

Desktop setting information is saved in DST files (stored in Delphi's bin directory), which are INI files in disguise. If you open one of them you'll find they are easily readable.

About Menus

The main Delphi menu bar is an important way to interact with the IDE, although you'll probably accomplish most tasks using shortcut keys, shortcut menus, and toolbar buttons. The menu bar doesn't change much in reaction to your current operations: you need to click the right mouse button for a full list of the operations you can perform on the current window or component. Notice that the menu bar can change considerably depending on third-party tools and wizards you've installed.

A relevant menu added to Delphi in recent editions is the Window menu in the IDE. This menu lists the open floating windows and dialog boxes. The Window menu is really handy, because windows often end up behind others and can be hard to find. You can control the alphabetic sort order of this menu using a setting in the Windows Registry: look for the Sort Window Menu string key (under Borland\BDS\3.0\Main Window). This registry key uses a string (in place of Boolean values), where '–1' and 'True' indicate true, and '0' and 'False' indicate false.

The To-Do List

A feature Delphi has had for quite some time but that is probably still underused is the to-do list. This is a list of tasks you still have to do to complete a project—it's a collection of notes for the programmer (or programmers; this tool can be very handy in a team). Although the idea is not new, the key concept of the to-do list in Delphi is that it works as a two-way tool.

You can add or modify to-do items by adding special TODO comments to the source code of any file of a project; you'll then see the corresponding entries in the list. In addition, you can visually edit the items in the list to modify the corresponding source code comment. For example, here is how a to-do list item might look in the source code:

```
procedure TForm1.FormCreate(Sender: TObject);
begin
  // TODO -oMarco: Add creation code
end;
```

All of these special comments are displayed in the To-Do List window, which can also be used to edit them with its Edit To-Do Item dialog. Figure 1.4 shows a code snippet, a floating To-Do List (by default it is conveniently hooked to the bottom of the IDE), and that same snippet in its own editor.

The exception to this two-way rule is the definition of project-wide to-do items. You must add these items directly to the list. To do that, you can either use the Ctrl+A key combination in the To-Do List window or right-click in the window and select Add from the shortcut menu. These items are saved in a special file with the same root name as the project file and a .TODO extension. See the ToDoTest demo for an example, which includes the previous code snippet.

FIGURE 1.4

The To-Do list with some source code and the corresponding editor

You can use multiple options with a TODO comment. You can use −o (as in the previous code excerpt) to indicate the owner (the programmer who entered the comment), the −c option to indicate a category, or simply a number from 1 to 5 to indicate the priority (0, or no number, indicates that no priority level is set). For example, using the Add To-Do Item command on the editor's shortcut menu (or the Ctrl+Shift+T shortcut) generated this comment:

```
{ TODO 2 -oMarco : Button pressed }
```

Delphi treats everything after the colon—up to the end of the line or the closing brace, depending on the type of comment—as the text of the to-do item.

Finally, in the To-Do List window you can check off an item to indicate that it has been done. The source code comment will change from TODO to DONE. You can also change the comment in the source code manually to see the check mark appear in the To-Do List window.

One of the most powerful elements of this architecture is the main To-Do List window, which can automatically collect to-do information from the source code files as you type them, sort and filter them, and export them to the Clipboard as plain text or an HTML table. All these options are available in the context menu of the To-Do List.

Extended Search Results

Another pane generally displayed on the bottom of the IDE is the Messages window. It displays both compiler messages and search results. Even if simple to use, this window has several improvements over past versions of Delphi. Since Delphi 7 you have been able to display search results in a different tabs so they do not interfere with compiler messages as they did in the past. Second, every time you do a different search you can request that Delphi show the results in a different page, so the results of previous search operations remain available.

In Delphi 2005 you can also use a check box in the Find Text dialog box to group the search results by source code file, which often results in a more manageable search result if there are many hits. You can press the Alt+Page Down and Alt+Page Up key combinations to cycle through the tabs of this window. (The same commands work for other tabbed views, but not all of them.)

The Delphi Editor

At first sight of Delphi 2005, you realize that the Delphi editor has changed considerably (unless you have used Delphi 8, of course). The first difference is that the editor window is not floating anymore, although you can easily open a floating editor window with the View ➤ New Edit Window command. Other relevant changes include the display of source code line numbers (you can disable this), the icons on the side you can use to fold elements of the source code, support for various file formats, and more, as discussed in the following sections.

As you'd expect from an IDE with multiple personalities, you can use Delphi 2005 to edit different types of files, including source code in Delphi and C# as well as other languages like C++ and VB.NET and other source files like JavaScript, SQL, XML, HTML, and XSL. XML and HTML editing is based on DTDs, which help with syntax highlighting and code completion.

The editor settings on each file (including the behavior of keys like Tab) depend on the extension of the file being opened. You can configure these settings for each file format in the Editor Options/ Source Options page of the Options dialog box, displayed in Figure 1.5. This feature has been extended and made more open so you can even configure the editor by providing a DTD for

XML-based file formats or by writing a custom wizard that provides syntax highlighting for other programming languages. Another feature of the editor, code templates, is now language specific (your predefined Delphi templates will make little sense in HTML or C#).

The Delphi editor allows you to work on several files at once, using a "notebook with tabs" metaphor. You can jump from one page of the editor to the next by pressing Ctrl+Tab (or Ctrl+Shift+Tab to move in the opposite direction). You can drag-and-drop the tabs with the unit names in the upper portion of the editor to change their order so that you can use a single Ctrl+Tab to move between the units you are working on at any given time. The editor's shortcut menu has also a Pages command, which lists all the available pages in a submenu (a handy feature when many units are loaded). Notice that many edit windows also have bottom tabs to move among different views like Code, Design, and History. You can move along these views with Alt+Page Up and Alt+Page Down.

Several options affect the editor, as you can see in the Editor Options section of the Options dialog box in Figure 1.5. However, you have to go to the Environment Options page to set the editor's AutoSave feature. This option forces the editor to save all of your source code files each time you run the program, preventing data loss in the (rare) case the program crashes badly in the debugger.

Delphi's editor provides many commands, including some that date back to its WordStar emulation ancestry (of the early Turbo Pascal compilers). I won't discuss the various settings of the editor because they are quite intuitive and are described in the online help.

TIP   Remember that using the Cut and Paste commands is not the only way to move source code. You can also select and drag words, expressions, or entire lines of code. In addition, you can copy text instead of moving it by pressing the Ctrl key while dragging.

FIGURE 1.5
The multiple languages supported by the Delphi IDE can be associated with various file extensions in the Editor Options/Source Options page of the Options dialog box.

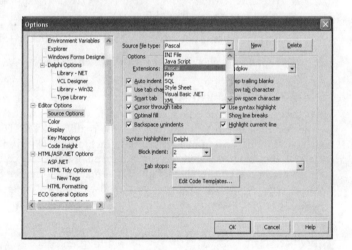

Delphi 2005 Code Folding and Regions

Delphi allows you to fold (or collapse) any declaration, including class declarations, methods, or entire sections such as the implementation section of a unit. What's relevant and the main reason this feature was introduced, though, is that you can define custom collapsible regions using the $REGION and $ENDREGION directives (which look like compiler directives but are actually ignored by the compiler).

For example, in the RegionsTest program, I've written the following code:

```
{$REGION 'extra code'}
// this is code you want to hide by default
procedure TestMessage;
begin
  ShowMessage ('Test');
end;
{$ENDREGION}
```

When you open the file with this code, by default, you'll see this section folded with a caption corresponding to the string provided in the $REGION directive, as I've shown next:

```
24  {$R *.nfm}
25
26⊞ extra code
35
36⊟procedure TForm1.Button1Click(Sender: TObject);
37  begin
38    TestMessage;
39  end;
```

You can enable or disable folding with the BDS/3.0/Editor/Options/Enable Elisions registry key and determine the automatic collapsing of region blocks in files you open with BDS/3.0/Editor/Options/Auto Collapse Region Blocks. There are also some new shortcut keys you can use with regions and folding, including:

- Toggling folding with Ctrl+Shift+K+O (which requires a manual refresh of the edit window when you restore the folding option)
- Collapsing or expanding the nearest block with Ctrl+Shift+K+E and K+U
- Expanding all code blocks with Ctrl+Shift+K+A

Source Code Files Encoding

In the past, the Delphi editor allowed you to work only with ANSI source code files. While this is still the default, the code editor now works internally with the UTF-8 encoding and supports saving and converting files in a number of formats, including UTF-8 and UTF-16 with Little and Big Endian mode. You can use the File Format submenu of the editor context menu to change the file format.

You can also control the default file format by adding the BDS\3.0\Editor\Options\DefaultFile-Filter registry key. For example, you can use the string Borland.FileFilter.UTF8ToUTF8 to use UTF8 encoded files by default.

Delphi 2005 Code Snippets

Another new feature of the IDE is the support for code snippets. There have been other ways in the past to define reusable blocks of source code (like code templates that you can still display with the Ctrl+J keystroke), but code snippets collected in the Tool Palette are much simpler and more intuitive to use.

If fact, using the Tool Palette you can easily arrange snippets in multiple categories, drag them from one category to the other, and also create a new code snippet by selecting some source code and dragging the mouse while keeping the Alt key pressed. To select a code snippet without having to drag it to the code editor, you can select the Tool Palette with Ctrl+Alt+P, type the initial letter of the snippet to filter it, and press the Enter key to paste it to the current edit position.

Code snippets are saved in the file `CodeSnippets.xml` in the `BDS\3.0\Objrepos` folder so that they can be easily moved from one computer to another and shared with other developers. Notice there is also an HtmlSnippets.xml file for snippets for the HTML editor.

As much as I like this feature, there is one thing I'd like to see improved. The code snippets in the Tool Palette are best managed by turning the captions on, while I prefer working with components with no captions. However, the setting for captions is unique to the entire palette, so what I'd like is not available. In any case, considering that captions are displayed as you start filtering the palette (by selecting it with Ctrl+Alt+P and starting to type), I tend to end up keeping the captions disabled.

Code Insight

For several versions now, the Delphi editor has had a set of helpers to simplify code writing, collectively known as Code Insight and based on a continuous parsing of the source code you write and the library and system units you refer to. This means that if your code has too many syntax errors these features cannot really work.

Delphi 2005 sees the introduction of two new features of this family, namely Help Insight and Error Insight, which complement the other Code Insight features discussed in the following sections. You can enable, disable, and configure each of Code Insight features in the corresponding page of the Options dialog box.

NOTE Delphi 2005 includes a number of Refactoring tools, which is another set of features based on code parsing. They are so relevant that I'm going to cover them in a separate and lengthy section in Chapter 10.

CODE COMPLETION

Code completion allows you to choose the property or method of an object simply by looking it up on a list or by typing its initial letters. To activate this list, you just type the name of an object, such as `Button1`, then add the dot, and wait. To force the display of the list, press Ctrl+spacebar; to remove it when you don't want it, press Esc. Here is an example:

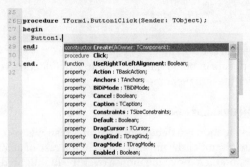

As you begin typing, the list filters its content according to the initial portion of the element you've inserted. Another feature is that in the case of functions with parameters, parentheses are included in the generated code, and the parameters list hint (called code parameters) is displayed immediately. Code completion also lets you look for a proper value in an assignment statement. When you type `:=`

after a variable or property and press Ctrl+spacebar, Delphi will list all the other variables or objects of the same type, plus the objects having properties of that type.

While the list is visible, you can right-click it to change the order of the items, sorting either by scope or by name; you can also resize the window. Even experienced programmers often don't know that code completion also works within class definitions. If you press Ctrl+spacebar, you'll get a list of virtual methods you can override (including abstract methods), the methods of the interfaces implemented by the class, the base class properties, and eventually system messages you can handle. Simply selecting one (or several of them at once) will add the proper method (or all of the selected methods) to the class declaration. In this particular case, the code completion list allows multiple selection.

TIP Delphi 2005 can display Help Insight information on the currently selected symbol of the code completion list.

CODE TEMPLATES

This feature lets you insert one of the predefined code templates, such as a complex statement with an inner begin...end block. Code templates must be activated manually by pressing Ctrl+J to show a list of all of the templates. If you type a few letters (such as a keyword) before pressing Ctrl+J, Delphi will list only the templates starting with those letters.

You can add custom code templates, in the Editor Options/Source Options page of the Options dialog box, and you can even import and export them (notice that they are saved in the DELPHI32.DCI text file). However, with the advent of code snippets in Delphi 2005 I doubt many people will actively keep using code templates.

CODE PARAMETERS

While you are typing a function or method, code parameters display the data type of the function's or method's parameters in a hint or Tooltip window. Simply type the function or method name and the open (left) parenthesis, and the parameter names and types appear immediately in a pop-up hint window:

```
26  procedure TForm1.Button1Click(Sender: TObject);
27  begin
28    Button1.ContainsControl()
29  end;                          Control: TControl
30
```

To force the display of code parameters, you can press Ctrl+Shift+spacebar. As a further help, the current parameter appears in bold type, and multiple overloaded versions that do not match are removed as you enter the initial parameters.

TOOLTIP EXPRESSION EVALUATION

Tooltip expression evaluation is a debug-time feature. It shows you the value of the identifier, property, or expression that is under the mouse cursor. In the case of an expression, you typically need to select it in the editor and then move the mouse over the highlighted text.

ERROR INSIGHT

A new Code Insight feature of Delphi 2005 is Error Insight. This works in two different ways. The first is that as you type code that Delphi doesn't understand, it marks it with a red squiggle, as word processors do for misspelled words. As you move the mouse over the words with a red squiggle, you'll see a short description of the error, as shown below:

```
26  procedure TForm1.Button1Click(Sender: TObject);
27  begin
28    Buton1
29    Undeclared identifier 'Buton1'
30
31  end;
```

Another feature of Error Insight is the detailed description of all of the errors of a unit displayed at the top of the Structure View while editing code. At times you'll see errors appear in the Structure View only by adding components to a form, like in this example:

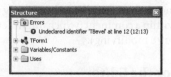

In such a case the problem lies in the fact that when the component is added Delphi doesn't also add a reference to its unit. This operation takes place only as you save the code or compile it. That's why saving the unit is the simplest way to get rid of similar *fake* errors.

HELP INSIGHT

Help Insight shows a summary help window as you move the mouse over a symbol or select an entry in the code completion window. Help Insight looks for an XML file hosting information regarding the symbol (type, field, method…).

```
53  begin
54    enum := aList.GetEnumerator;
55              ArrayList.GetEnumerator Method
56
57              Returns an enumerator for the entire
58              System.Collections.ArrayList.
59
60              Returns
61              An System.Collections.IEnumerator for the
62              entire System.Collections.ArrayList.
```

There are similar XML files for Win32 packages and .NET assemblies. If it doesn't find the proper XML file or this file doesn't list the symbol, the Help Insight engine displays the internal symbol information, like the type itself, the method parameters, and the return value without really providing much extra information.

The Help Insight window is a small version of Internet Explorer. Its output depends on the `HelpInsight.xsl` XSL transformation file used to turn the core XML data into proper HTML and the `HelpInsight.css` file used to determine the color and fonts of the display. Both files are stores in the `Objrepos` folder of Delphi 2005 (again by default Borland\BDS\3.0). If you want to customize the user interface of Help Insight, you can edit the CSS file.

NOTE Editing the XSL file is slightly more complex; this topic is introduced in Chapter 22.

Sync Edit

Another new Delphi 2005 feature worth its own section is Synchronized Editing, or Sync Edit. Every time you select a block of code, you'll see a small icon with two pencils appearing in the gutter on the side of the editor. By selecting this icon or pressing Ctrl+Shift+J, you activate Sync Edit mode:

```
procedure TForm3.Button1Click(Sender: TObject);
51  var
52     enum: IEnumerator;
53  begin
54     enum := aList.GetEnumerator;
55     while enum.MoveNext do
56        Listbox1.Items.Add(enum.Current.ToString);
57  end;
```

The editor will highlight repeated words with a box. You can select one of the repeated words with the mouse or even more easily by pressing the Tab key, and start typing to edit each of the occurrences at the same time.

Notice that Sync Edit is not fully syntax based but is only a smart search and replace mechanism, so it might pick up a word within a comment (which might actually be what you want, if the comment refers to a local variable you're modifying).

The Structure View for the Editor

When the editor is active, the Structure View window lists all the types, variables, and routines defined in a unit, plus other units appearing in `uses` statements. It might also list the unit errors, as discussed earlier. For complex types, such as classes, the Structure View can list detailed information, including a list of fields, properties, and methods. All the information is updated as soon as you begin typing in the editor.

You can use the Structure View to navigate in the editor. If you double-click one of the entries in the Structure View, the editor jumps to the corresponding declaration. You can also modify variables, properties, and method names directly in the Structure View. However, this is not as flexible as using the Rename refactoring.

You have full control of the information layout of the Structure View, but how this works is far from intuitive. You can configure the Structure View for the editor by using the corresponding Environment Options/Explorer page of the Options dialog box (see Figure 1.6). Oddly, this page has retained a name similar to the name this feature had in Delphi 7, Code Explorer.

FIGURE 1.6
You can configure the Structure View for the editor in the Explorer page of the Options dialog box.

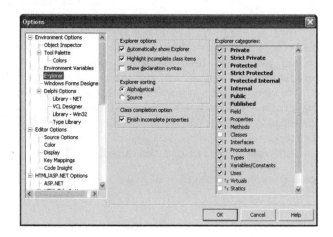

When you deselect one of the Explorer Categories items on the right side of this page of the dialog box, the Structure View doesn't remove the corresponding elements from view—it simply adds the node in the tree. For example, if you deselect the Uses check box, Delphi doesn't hide the list of the used units from the Structure View; on the contrary, the used units are listed as main nodes instead of being kept in the Uses folder. I generally disable the Types, Classes, and Variables/Constants selections.

Because each item of the Structure View tree has an icon marking its type, arranging by field and method seems less important than arranging by access specifier. My preference is to show all items in a single group, because this arrangement requires the fewest mouse clicks to reach each item.

Selecting items in the Structure View provides a handy way of navigating the source code of a large unit—when you double-click a method in the Structure View, the focus moves to the definition in the class declaration.

Browsing in the Editor

As you move the mouse over a symbol in the editor, you see either Help Insight or Tooltip Symbol Insight, indicating where the identifier is declared. You can turn this feature into a navigational aid called *code browsing*. When you hold down the Ctrl key and move the mouse over the identifier, Delphi creates an active hyperlink to the definition. These links are displayed with the blue color and underline style that are typical of links in web browsers, and the pointer changes to a hand whenever it's positioned on the link.

For example, you can Ctrl+click the TLabel identifier to open its definition in the VCL source code. As you select references, the editor keeps track of the various positions you've jumped to, and you can move backward and forward among them—again, as in a web browser—using the Browse Back and Browse Forward buttons in the Browser toolbar or the keystrokes Alt+Left arrow or Alt+Right arrow. You can also click the drop-down arrows near the Back and Forward buttons of the toolbar to view a detailed list of the lines of the source code files you've already jumped to, for more control over the backward and forward movement.

How can you jump directly to the VCL source code if it is not part of your project? The editor can find not only the units in the Search path (which are compiled as part of the project), but also those in Delphi's Debug Source, Browsing, and Library paths. These directories are searched in the order I just listed, and you can set them in the Directories/Conditionals page of the Project Options dialog box and in the Environment Options/Delphi Options/Library - Win32 or Library - NET pages of the Options dialog box. By default, Delphi adds the VCL source code directories in the Browsing path of the environment.

Class Completion

Delphi's editor can also help by generating some source code for you, completing what you've already written. This feature is called *class completion*, and you activate it by pressing the Ctrl+Shift+C key combination. Adding an event handler to an application is a fast operation, because Delphi automatically adds the declaration of a new method to handle the event in the class and provides you with the skeleton of the method in the implementation portion of the unit. This is part of Delphi's support for visual programming.

Newer versions of Delphi simplify life in a similar way for programmers who write a little extra code behind event handlers. This code-generation feature applies to general methods, message-handling methods, and properties. For example, if you type the following code in the class declaration

```
public
  procedure Hello (MessageText: string);
```

and then press Ctrl+Shift+C, Delphi will provide you with the definition of the method in the implementation section of the unit, generating the following lines of code:

```
{ TForm1 }
procedure TForm1.Hello(MessageText: string);
begin
end;
```

This feature is really handy compared with the traditional approach of many Delphi programmers, which is to copy and paste one or more declarations, add the class names, and finally duplicate the begin...end code for every method copied. Class completion also works the other way around: you can write the implementation of the method with its code directly and then press Ctrl+Shift+C to generate the required entry in the class declaration.

The most important and useful example of class completion is the automatic generation of code to support properties declared in classes. For example, if you type in a class

```
property Value: Integer;
```

and press Ctrl+Shift+C, Delphi will turn the line into

```
property Value: Integer read fValue write SetValue;
```

Delphi will also add the SetValue method to the class declaration, provide a default implementation for it, and declare the data field in the class. You'll find more on properties in Chapter 3.

Other Editor Shortcut Keys

The editor has many more shortcut keys that depend on the editor style you select. Here are a few of the lesser-known shortcuts:

◆ Ctrl+E activates the incremental search. You can press Ctrl+E and then directly type the word you want to search for without having to go through a special dialog box and clicking the Enter key to do the actual search.

◆ Ctrl+Shift+I indents multiple lines of code at once. The number of spaces used is set by the Block Indent option in the Editor page of the Editor Options dialog box. Ctrl+Shift+U is the corresponding key for unindenting the code.

◆ Ctrl+O+U toggles the case of the selected code; you can also use Ctrl+K+E to switch to lowercase and Ctrl+K+F to switch to uppercase.

◆ While holding down the Alt key, you can drag the mouse to select rectangular areas within the editor, not just consecutive lines and words.

Editor History

In the past, Delphi kept a single backup copy of the previous version of each source code file. This meant that by saving a modified file twice you'd lose the previous version of the code, unless you had a backup copy or a source code versioning system. Delphi 2005 adds a rather flexible local history for each file. You determine how many versions to keep (the default is 10) and Delphi saves them in a hidden __history subfolder under the folder hosting the source code file.

You can control this setting using the Create Backup Files check box and the File Backup Limit edit box of the main Editor Options page of the Options dialog box. Delphi creates a physical file for each version, naming them like this:

```
ForInDotNetForm.pas.~1~
ForInDotNetForm.pas.~2~
```

You can reopen these files with any editor or browse them from the History page of the editor. This pane has three further subpanes:

◆ The Contents page (see Figure 1.7) shows a combo box with each file (PAS and designer files) and, for the selected files, a list of versions in the main window. The selected version is displayed in a viewer (which is not an editor, as you cannot type in it). Notice that the list shows both local versions and versions stored in a Versions Control System, if you've installed one and are using it for the files of the project.

FIGURE 1.7

The Contents page of the History for a source code file

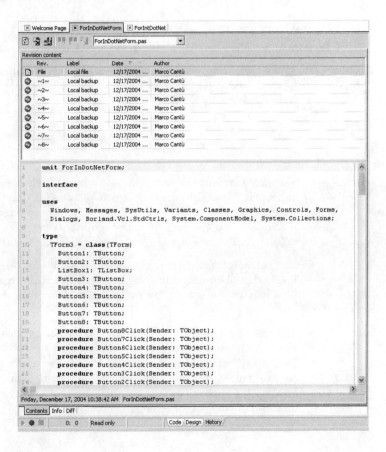

◆ The Info page is mostly to interact with a Versions Control System, as it shows a description of the version and other information not relevant for local backup files.

◆ The Diff page allows you to pick any two versions (including the editor buffer still not saved to a file) and compare them with a simple differencing view. Both here and in the Contents page you can copy lines from an older version and paste them into the edit buffer.

Notice also that local versioning comprises designer files, like DFM files for VCL applications. In this pane you can reactivate an older version of a file with the Revert command. As designer files (like DFM files) have almost no Undo capability, you can use the History to actually Undo unwanted changes to a DFM file.

NOTE When I need to compare two Delphi units, including the local backups produced by Delphi 2005, I invariably use Beyond Compare—www.scootersoftware.com—a superb, low-cost file comparison utility written in Delphi and capable of understanding even binary DFM files.

Other New Editor Features

There are many other brand new features in the editor worth mentioning briefly. Here is a summary:

◆ As you type or move around the code, the editor shows matching parentheses and quotes. This long-awaited feature is a time saver when you have code with many nested parentheses, as shown below:

```
procedure TestMessage;
begin
    MessageBox ('Test ' + DateToStr (IncMonth (Now)));
end;
```

◆ The macro toolbar at the left of the status bar at the bottom of the editor can be used to record and replay identical sequence of keystrokes. This feature was already available in the past with the corresponding shortcut keys (Ctrl+Shift+R for recording, Ctrl+Shift+P for play). Editor macros can be useful for performing multistep operations over and over again, such as reformatting source code or arranging data more legibly in the source code.

◆ You can show the actual new line separator used by the source code files (like the carriage return, line feed combination) by turning the Show line breaks registry setting to True in one of the BDS\3.0\Editor\Source Options subfolders. I find this handy when moving files to or from Linux and Kylix.

◆ The editor now saves the bookmarks you set along with other project desktop settings. This means the bookmarks are persisted between editing sessions, unlike in past versions of Delphi. By the way, bookmarks are created using Ctrl+Shift plus a number key from 0 to 9, as you'll see in a "gutter" margin on the side of the editor. To jump back to the bookmark, press the Ctrl key plus the number key. There is no way to see a list of active bookmarks unless you install a third-party plug in (including my very own Cantools Wizard discussed in Appendix B).

♦ Finally, one of my favorite new features is the Toggle Comment command, which is used to add or remove the // comment from the current line of source code or all of the selected source code lines at once. This feature is activated by pressing the Ctrl key plus the *physical '/'* key. By *physical*, I mean the low-level keyboard key, which generally changes on foreign keyboards. For example, on my Italian keyboard I have to use Ctrl+ù. Luckily enough, the context menu of the editor shows the actual key on the side of the Toggle Comment option.

The Designers

As Delphi is a Visual Development Environment, you don't spend all of your time writing code: another key activity is interacting with the visual designers. The most classic designer in Delphi is the VCL Form Designer, but Delphi 7 already had other VCL designers for data modules and frames, plus a number of custom HTML related designers (for example in WebSnap and IntraWeb). Delphi 2005 adds a minor variation to the theme (the VCL for .NET designers) and also embeds the designers from the .NET SDK: the WinForms designer and the ASP.NET designer. This last designer is hosted within a sophisticated HTML designer that Borland has added to Delphi.

In this section I'll give you some hints for working with the VCL Form Designer in Delphi 2005 only because this still tends to be the most popular designer. Specific sections of the book will cover other designers when discussing the related technologies.

Delphi's Form Designer is a visual surface where you can place components. Contrary to past versions of Delphi, in which you had to click on the Component Palette to select a component and then on the form to place it, in Delphi 2005 you can really drag and drop a component from the Tool Palette to the Form Designer.

You can select a component directly with the mouse in the Form Designer, use the instance list of the Object Inspector, or use the Structure View, which is particularly handy when a control is behind another one or is very small. You can see the Structure View for a form with a few components in Figure 1.8. If one control covers another completely, you can use the Esc key to select the parent control of the current one. Press Esc one or more times to select the form, or press and hold Shift while you click the selected component. Doing so will deselect the current component and select the form by default.

FIGURE 1.8

The VCL Form Designer and the related Structure View

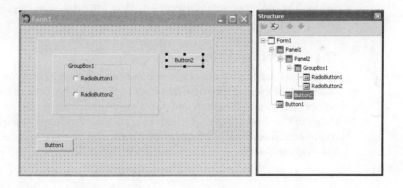

There are two alternatives to using the mouse to set the position of a component. You can either set values for the Left and Top properties, or you can use the arrow keys while holding down Ctrl. Using arrow keys is particularly useful for fine-tuning an element's position (when the Snap To Grid option is active), as is holding down Alt while using the mouse to move the control. If you press Ctrl+Shift along with an arrow key, the component will move only at grid intervals. By pressing the arrow keys while you hold down Shift, you can fine-tune the size of a component. Again, you can also do this with the mouse and the Alt key.

To align multiple components or make them the same size, you can select them and set the Top, Left, Width, or Height property for all of them at the same time. To select several components, click them with the mouse while holding down the Shift key; or, if all the components fall into a rectangular area, drag the mouse to "draw" a rectangle surrounding them. To select controls inside a container (say, the buttons inside a panel), drag the mouse within the panel while holding down the Ctrl key—otherwise, you move the panel. When you select multiple components, you can also set their relative position using Delphi 2005's Align toolbar, or you can keep using the Alignment dialog box (with the Align command of the designer context menu) or the Alignment Palette (accessible through the View ➢ Alignment Palette menu command). When you've finished designing a form, you can use the Lock Controls command of the Edit menu to avoid accidentally changing the position of a component.

Among its other features, the Form Designer offers some additional information and hints:

◆ The designer will show the name of a nonvisual component if you turn on the Show Component Captions check box in the Environment Options/Delphi Options/VCL Designer page of the Options dialog box. This setting is disabled by default.

◆ As you move the pointer over a component, the hint shows you the name and type of the component. If extended hints are enabled (in the same settings page) you'll also see details about the control's position, size, tab order, and more.

◆ As you resize a control, the hint shows the current size (the Width and Height properties). As you move a component, the hint indicates the current position (the Left and Top properties).

In a VCL application all the visual operations you do are saved in a DFM (Delphi Form Module) or NFM (.NET Form Module) file, which by default uses a text format (it used to be a binary format, an option still available). Having designer files stored as text lets you operate more effectively with version-control systems. Notice anyway that .NET designers typically generate initialization source code instead of separate designer files.

The Object Inspector

To see and change properties of components placed on a form (or another designer) at design time, you use the Object Inspector. Compared to the early versions of Delphi, the Object Inspector has a number of extended features and also a more modern look and feel. One of the recent features is the ability of the Object Inspector to expand component references in place. Properties referring to other components are displayed in a different color and can be expanded by selecting the + symbol on the left. You can then modify the properties of that other component without having to select it.

A related but little known feature lets you select the component referenced by a property. To do this, double-click the property value with the left mouse button while pressing the Ctrl key. For example, if you have a MainMenu component in a form and you are looking at the properties of the form in the Object Inspector, you can select the MainMenu component by moving to the Menu property of the form and Ctrl+double-clicking the value of this property. Doing so selects the main menu indicated as the value of the property in the Object Inspector.

Here are some other tips related to the Object Inspector:

♦ The instance list at the top of the Object Inspector shows the type of the object and allows you to choose a component. You might remove this list to save some space, considering that you can select components in the Structure View.

♦ You can optionally view read-only properties in the Object Inspector. Of course, they are grayed out.

♦ The drop-down list for a property can include graphical elements. This feature is used for properties such as Color and Cursor and is particularly useful for the ImageIndex property of components connected to an ImageList.

♦ When you are working with a WinForms application, notice that the Object Inspector might show designer verbs at the bottom, which are like the extra items of the context menu of a component added by component editors. Another feature of the Object Inspector for WinForms alone is the display of a very short description of the current property at the bottom on the Inspector's window.

NOTE A new feature of the Object Inspector of Delphi 2005 is the support for Unicode characters. This support is available also for Win32 components that use WideStrings (now supported as published properties).

Delphi includes the idea of *property categories*, activated by the Arrange option of the Object Inspector's shortcut menu. If you set this option, properties are arranged by group rather than listed alphabetically, with each property possibly appearing in multiple groups. Categories have the benefit of reducing the complexity of the Object Inspector. You can use the View submenu from the shortcut menu to hide properties of given categories, regardless of the way they are displayed (that is, even if you prefer the traditional arrangement by name, you can still hide the properties of some categories).

The Structure View for Designers

Delphi 5 introduced a TreeView for data modules, which Delphi 6 extended into an Object TreeView available for every designer. This feature was not available in Delphi 8, but it is now integrated in the Structure View, which also merges the functionality previously part of the Code Explorer, as I discussed earlier.

The Structure View for a designer shows all the components and objects on the form in a tree representing their relations. The most obvious is the parent/child relation: if you place a panel on a form, a button inside the panel, and a button outside the panel, the tree will show one button under the form and the other under the panel, as already shown in Figure 1.8.

Besides parent/child, the Structure View shows other relations, such as owner/owned, component/subobject, and collection/item, plus various specific relations, including dataset/connection and data source/dataset relations. Here, you can see an example of the structure of a menu in the tree:

The Structure View is particularly useful when working with collection properties and the database tables fields at design time. You can drag components within the Structure View—for example, moving a component from one container to another. With the Form Designer, you can do so only with cut-and-paste techniques. Moving instead of cutting provides the advantage that any connections among components are not lost, as happens when you delete the component during the cut operation.

Right-clicking any element of the Structure View displays a shortcut menu similar to the component menu you get when the component is in a form (and in both cases, the shortcut menu may include items related to the custom component editors). You can even delete items from the tree.

Copying and Pasting Components

An interesting feature of the Form Designer is the ability to copy and paste components from one form to another or to duplicate a component in the form. During this operation, Delphi duplicates all the properties, keeps the connected event handlers and, if necessary, changes the name of the control (which must be unique in each form).

You can also copy components from the Form Designer to the editor and vice versa. When you copy a component to the Clipboard, Delphi also places the textual description there. You can even edit the text version of a component, copy the text to the Clipboard, and then paste it back into the form as a new component. For example, if you place a button on a form, copy it, and then paste it into an editor (which can be Delphi's own source-code editor or any word processor), you'll get the following description:

```
object Button1: TButton
  Left = 152
  Top = 104
  Width = 75
  Height = 25
  Caption = 'Button1'
  TabOrder = 0
end
```

Now, if you change the name of the object, its caption or its position, for example, or if you add a new property, these changes can be copied and pasted back to a form. Here are some sample changes:

```
object Button1: TButton
  Left = 152
  Top = 104
  Width = 75
  Height = 25
  Caption = 'My Button'
  TabOrder = 0
  Font.Name = 'Arial'
end
```

Copying this description and pasting it into the form will create a button in the specified position with the caption *My Button* in an Arial font.

To use this technique, you need to know how to edit the textual representation of a component, what properties are valid for that particular component, and how to write the values for string properties, set properties, and other special properties. When Delphi interprets the textual description of a component or form, it might also change the values of other properties related to those you've changed, and it might change the position of the component so that it doesn't overlap a previous copy. Of course, if you write something that's completely incorrect and try to paste it into a form, Delphi will display an error message indicating what has gone wrong.

You can also select several components and copy them all at once, either to another form or to a text editor. This approach might be useful when you need to work on a series of similar components. You can copy one to the editor, replicate it a number of times, make the proper changes, and then paste the whole group into the form again.

Managing Projects

Delphi's multitarget Project Manager works on a project *group*, which can have one or more projects under it. For example, a project group can include a DLL and an executable file or multiple executable files. As I've already mentioned, a project group can contain projects pertaining to different personalities (.NET and Win32, C# and Delphi). Moreover, all open VCL packages will show up as projects in the Project Manager view, even if they haven't been added to the project group.

Figure 1.9 shows the Project Manager with a simple project group, including the two examples of the current chapter (a Win32 program and a .NET VCL application). As you can see, the Project Manager is based on a tree view, which shows the hierarchical structure of the project group, the projects, and all the forms and units that make up each project. In a .NET project you see a references folder indicating the required assemblies.

If the Project Manager toolbar is very simple, its context menus can be very handy. For example, on a project you can see a large number of options, as shown in Figure 1.9. The shortcut menu is context-sensitive; its options depend on the selected item and can even be customized by installing build tools (see the next section) or by using the Delphi Tools API. There are menu items to add a new or existing project to a project group, to compile or build a specific project, and to open a unit.

FIGURE 1.9
Delphi's multitarget
Project Manager with
the context menu for
a project

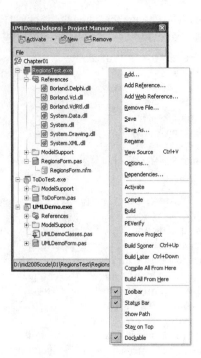

FIGURE 1.9
Delphi's multitarget
Project Manager with
the context menu for
a project

Of all the projects in the group, only one is active; this is the project you operate on when you select a command such as Project ➢ Compile or Ctrl+F9. The Project menu has two commands you can use to compile or build all the projects of the group. When you have multiple projects to build, you can set a relative order by using the Build Sooner and Build Later commands. These two commands basically rearrange the projects in the list.

TIP   The Project Manager context menu allows you to compile projects beginning with a given one, using the Make All From Here or Build All From Here command.

In Delphi 2005 the project group can host almost any file, including INI files, text files, XML configuration files, and almost anything else because projects have more extended configuration files than they used to have. To add these extra files and projects or source code files, you can drag them from the Windows Explorer onto the Project Manager window.

Tools and Build Tools

Since the early days of Delphi it has been possible to add menu items to the Tools menu by using the Tools ➢ Configure Tools command. This is a helper for calling external programs, as you can pass as parameters the current project name or the project folder, using special purpose macros. For example, you can open the Explorer window for the project folder by setting up a new Tools entry with the proper program and a parameter based on macros like $PATH($PROJECT).

What is new in Delphi 2005 though, is the ability to integrate external tools in the Project Manager with the Tools ➢ Build Tools command. The menu to invoke a Build Tool, in fact, appears in the context menu of the corresponding node of the Project Manager. If you add an entry to the list, you'll see that you have to specify one or more extensions (a default extension plus other extensions). After the name that will appear in the menu, I used *.exe for the default extension and *.dll for the other extensions and entered the following value of the Command Line field:

```
"C:\Program Files\Microsoft.NET\SDK\v1.1\Bin\PEVerify.exe"
 $PATH$TARGETNAME$EXT
```

This adds a new menu entry for every EXE or DLL (as you can see in Figure 1.9). Calling such an external program is considered part of the build process, and the output of the external output is redirected in the standard compiler messages pane.

Project Files

Unlike past versions of Delphi, each project has the classic project source code file (DPR), which is a Pascal source code file in disguise, plus an extended project file, with the extension BDSPROJ (Borland Developer Studio Project).

This file has compilation information like past configuration files but also includes the personality. In fact, by looking at the source code files alone, Delphi might have a hard time figuring out, for example, if a project is a VCL for Win32 or VCL for .NET application. Listing 1.1 includes a reduced version of the BDSPROJ project file for an example of this chapter. As you can see, this file uses the XML format.

LISTING 1.1:   A reduced version of the ToDoTest.bdsproj file

```xml
<?xml version="1.0" encoding="utf-8"?>
<BorlandProject>
  <PersonalityInfo>
    <Option>
      <Option Name="Personality">Delphi.Personality</Option>
      <Option Name="ProjectType"></Option>
      <Option Name="Version">1.0</Option>
      <Option Name="GUID">
        {6B0317A4-7530-455D-B260-C98B30192B7C}</Option>
    </Option>
  </PersonalityInfo>
  <Delphi.Personality>
    <Source>
      <Source Name="MainSource">ToDoTest.dpr</Source>
    </Source>
    <FileVersion>
      <FileVersion Name="Version">7.0</FileVersion>
    </FileVersion>
    <Compiler>
      <Compiler Name="A">8</Compiler>
      <Compiler Name="B">0</Compiler>
      ...
      <Compiler Name="DuplicatesIgnored">True</Compiler>
    </Compiler>
    <Linker>
```

```
      <Linker Name="MapFile">0</Linker>
      <Linker Name="OutputObjs">0</Linker>
      ...
      <Linker Name="ExeDescription"></Linker>
    </Linker>
    <Directories>
      <Directories Name="OutputDir"></Directories>
      ...
      <Directories Name="UsePackages">False</Directories>
    </Directories>
    <Parameters>...</Parameters>
    <Language>...</Language>
    <VersionInfo>...</VersionInfo>
    <VersionInfoKeys>... </VersionInfoKeys>
  </Delphi.Personality>
</BorlandProject>
```

NOTE   Speaking of project files, Delphi 2005 suggests as a default location for projects and their files the Borland Studio Projects folder under the MyDocuments virtual folder. However, the default project folder can be modified by adding an extra registry key under the Globals key. The new string key should be called DefaultProjectsDirectory.

DELPHI 2005 PROJECT UPGRADE WIZARD

When you open an existing Delphi project, the BDSPROJ file doesn't exist. This file is created by the Project Upgrade Wizard, which is invoked every time you open a DPR Delphi project file that doesn't have an associated BDSPROJ file.

The Upgrade Wizard prompts you to choose whether to keep the project as a Win32 project or move it to .NET:

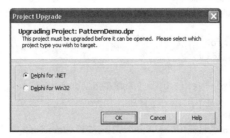

If you have already upgraded a project but you need to change the project personality or have both a Win32 and a .NET project, there is no apparent way to invoke the wizard again. The trick in this case is to delete or temporarily rename the BDSPROJ file. To upgrade a project to both Delphi personalities, you can also open it once, save it with a new name, and then open it again.

THE PROJECT SOURCE FILE

What doesn't change much from version to version is the project source code file, which (as I already mentioned) is a Pascal source code file. You can see this file with the Project ➢ View Source menu command. In a VCL Win32 app, the project source file for a new project looks like this:

```
program Project1;

uses
  Forms,
  Unit1 in 'Unit1.pas' {Form1};

{$R *.res}

begin
  Application.Initialize;
  Application.CreateForm(TForm1, Form1);
  Application.Run;
end.
```

A .NET application adds to such a file some directives to refer to the required assemblies, plus some assembly attributes. This is the source code of a brand new VCL for the .NET application (not one upgraded from a Win32 program), in which I've omitted the many comments and a few lines with declarations and global attributes:

```
program Project2;

{%DelphiDotNetAssemblyCompiler
  '$(SystemRoot)\microsoft.net\framework\
  v1.1.4322\System.dll'}

uses
  System.Reflection,
  System.Runtime.CompilerServices,
  SysUtils, Forms,
  Unit1 in 'Unit1.pas' {Form1};

{$R *.res}

{$REGION 'Program/Assembly Information'}
[assembly: AssemblyDescription('')]
[assembly: AssemblyVersion('1.0.*')]
{$ENDREGION}

[STAThread]
begin
  Application.Initialize;
  Application.CreateForm(TForm1, Form1);
  Application.Run;
end.
```

As you can see, the actual code is really identical, and the Win32 versions can be easily compiled under .NET, provided you add the STAThread attribute declaration for the main program. Finally, if you go for a WinForms application under .NET, you'll end up with a project source code file like this (where I've *completely* omitted declarations and assembly attributes):

```
program Project1;

{%DelphiDotNetAssemblyCompiler
  '$(SystemRoot)\microsoft.net\framework\
  v1.1.4322\System.dll'}

uses
  System.Reflection,
  System.Runtime.CompilerServices,
  System.Windows.Forms,
  WinForm in 'WinForm.pas' {WinForm.TWinForm:
    System.Windows.Forms.Form};

{$R *.res}

[STAThread]
begin
  Application.Run(TWinForm.Create);
end.
```

Project Group Files

Delphi saves the project groups with the .bdsgroup (Borland Developer Studio Group) extension. This is completely different from the past .bpg (Borland Project Group) format, which was a makefile in disguise. The new project group file is another XML file, similar in scope to a project file. Listing 1.2 shows an example:

LISTING 1.2:   The project group file Chapter01.bdsgroup

```
<?xml version="1.0" encoding="utf-8"?>
<BorlandProject>
  <PersonalityInfo>
    <Option>
      <Option Name="Personality">Default.Personality</Option>
      <Option Name="ProjectType"></Option>
      <Option Name="Version">1.0</Option>
      <Option Name="GUID">
        {394C2198-774A-4280-B54E-1F769076DD33}</Option>
    </Option>
  </PersonalityInfo>
  <Default.Personality>
    <Projects>
```

```
        <Projects Name="RegionsTest.exe">
          RegionsTest\RegionsTest.bdsproj
        </Projects>
        <Projects Name="ToDoTest.exe">
          ToDoTest\ToDoTest.bdsproj
        </Projects>
        <Projects Name="Targets">
          RegionsTest.exe ToDoTest.exe
        </Projects>
      </Projects>
      <Dependencies/>
    </Default.Personality>
  </BorlandProject>
```

Project Options

The Project Manager doesn't provide a way to set similar options for two different projects at one time. Instead, you can invoke the Project Options dialog from the Project Manager for each project. The first page of Project Options (Forms) lists the forms that should be created automatically at program startup and the forms that are created manually by the program. The next page (Application) is used to set the name of the application and the name of its Help file and to choose its icon. Other Project Options choices relate to the Delphi compiler and linker, version information, and the use of run-time packages.

There are two ways to set compiler options. One is to use the Compiler page of the Project Options dialog. The other is to set or remove individual options in the source code with the compiler directives, where you replace X with the option you want to set. This second approach is more flexible because it allows you to change only an option for a specific source-code file or even for just a few lines of code. The source-level options override the compile-level options.

All project options are saved automatically with the project, in the .bdsproj file. Delphi also saves the compiler options in another format in a CFG file for command-line compilation. These files have similar content but a different format: the dcc command-line compiler cannot use .bdsproj files, but needs the .CFG format.

Another alternative for saving compiler options is to press Ctrl+O+O (press the O key twice while keeping Ctrl pressed). This key combination inserts, at the top of the current unit, compiler directives that correspond to the current project, as in the following snippet taken from a .NET application:

```
{$A-,B-,C+,D+,E-,F-,G+,H+,I+,J-,K-,L+,M-,N+,O+,P+,Q-,R-,S-,T-,
  U-,V+,W-,X+,Y+,Z1}
{$MINSTACKSIZE $00001000}
{$MAXSTACKSIZE $00100000}
{$IMAGEBASE $00400000}
{$APPTYPE GUI}
{$WARN SYMBOL_DEPRECATED ON}
{$WARN SYMBOL_LIBRARY ON}
{$WARN SYMBOL_PLATFORM ON}
```

Looking at Source Code Files

I just listed some files related to the development of a Delphi application, but I want to spend a little time covering their actual format. The fundamental Delphi files are Pascal source code files. The bold, italic, and colored text you see in the editor depends on syntax highlighting, but it isn't saved with the file. It is worth noting that there is a single file for the form's whole code, not just small code fragments.

TIP In the listings in this book, I've matched the bold syntax highlighting of the editor for keywords and the italic for strings and comments.

For a VCL form, the Pascal file contains the form class declaration and the source code of the event handlers. As I mentioned, the values of the properties you set in the Object Inspector are stored in a separate form description file (with a .DFM or .NFM extension).

The DFM file is by default a text representation of the form. The simplest way to open the textual description of a form is to select the View As Text command on the shortcut menu in the Form Designer. This command closes the form, saving it if necessary, and opens the DFM file in the editor. You can later go back to the form using the View As Form command on the shortcut menu in the editor window.

You can edit the textual description of a form, although you should do so with extreme care. As soon as you save the file, it will be parsed to regenerate the form. If you've made incorrect changes, compilation will stop with an error message; you'll need to correct the contents of your DFM file before you can reopen the form. For this reason, you shouldn't try to change the textual description of a form manually until you have good knowledge of Delphi programming.

TIP In the book, I often show you excerpts of DFM files. In most of these excerpts, I show only the relevant components or properties; generally, I have removed the positional properties, the binary values, and other lines providing little useful information to avoid wasting precious space in the book.

Beyond Delphi Programming

Despite the name, Delphi 2005 is not only a Delphi programming tool. In fact, out of the three default personalities, only two of them use the Delphi language, while the other is based on the C# language.

Moreover, Delphi 2005 embeds a totally different model, based on Model Driven Architecture (MDA) and powered by ECO and the UML designers provided by the integration of the Together modeling technology. ECO supports both C# and Delphi as languages and both .NET WinForms and ASP.NET as platforms.

Another relevant area of the IDE, which is not strictly related to Delphi, is the design time support for databases. For the first time, the Delphi IDE allows you to create tables and other database entities and to work with RDBMS metadata quite extensively.

In the following sections I'll briefly introduce these three topics, some of which are also covered in other chapters of the book.

C# in Delphi 2005

Because this is not just a book on Delphi 2005 but specifically one on the Delphi language, I don't plan on discussing in any depth the C# personality of the IDE. However, it is relevant to mention it at least in this chapter, which is devoted to the IDE.

The C# personality of Delphi 2005 represents the second version of C#Builder, the Borland product that marked the introduction of the Borland Developer Studio. As I mentioned earlier, Borland hasn't written a compiler for C#, but the IDE uses the one part of the .NET SDK and is provided by Microsoft. This is the same C# compiler used by Microsoft's Visual Studio.

If you are interested in C#, notice that Delphi 2005 fully supports it, including visual designer for both WinForms and ASP.NET applications. You can also easily create C# Console applications and others, as shown in the C# Projects page of the New Items dialog box, which you can display by selecting the File ➤ New ➤ Other menu item, as shown in Figure 1.10.

The C# language is fully supported by the IDE, with syntax highlighting, Code Insight, and even Together UML visualization, complete ECO support, database integration, and much more.

FIGURE 1.10

The C# Projects page of the New Items dialog box

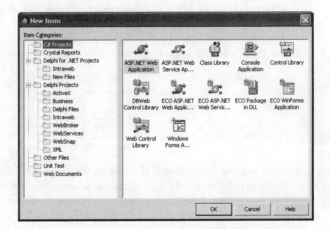

The UML Designer

Over the last few years, the Unified Modeling Language (UML) has become more and more popular. Delphi's first attempt to support UML was the inclusion of the ModelMaker tool in Delphi 7. If you liked ModelMaker, it is still available as a separate tool (see www.modelmakertools.com for more details).

Since that time, Borland has invested more heavily in the development process and UML. In particular, Borland bought TogetherSoft, a company that specializes in UML tools. The most interesting feature of Together technology is that the UML diagrams are generated directly from the source code: editing the diagrams is immediately reflected in the code, while working on the code causes the diagrams to change on the fly. The diagramming technology is based on an internal model that is continuously updated and is visible in the Model View pane:

NOTE Together technology is based on Java, which is why Delphi 2005 needs the .NET J# SDK to work properly.

Together technology has full support for languages like Java and C#, while it still has limited support for the Delphi language. In practice, you can use view package and class diagrams for Delphi code, but you cannot edit those diagrams to change the source code. What you can do is arrange the diagrams visually and annotate them.

Package diagrams are used to depict the overall structure of a project with the list of units and the classes they define, as shown next for the simple UMLDemo example:

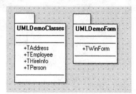

What is more interesting is the automatic generation of class diagrams, which list the fields and methods of the classes and also show the relationship among classes. The classes of the UML-DemoClasses unit, for example, include inheritance (from TPerson to TEmployee) and reference (from TPerson to TAddress, from TEmployee to THireInfo, and from TEmployee to itself). As you can see in Figure 1.11, I've also added a textual note with a link.

FIGURE 1.11
Some classes in a UML diagram generated automatically from a Delphi unit.

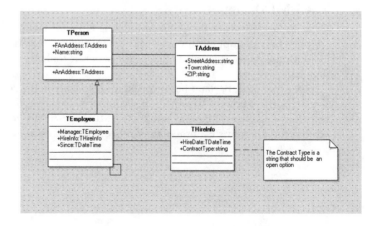

An exception to the limited editing capabilities of UML class diagrams for the Delphi language is the use of the Enterprise Core Objects (ECO) technology, which has full editing support for its specific diagrams, as you'll see in Chapter 18.

IDE Database Tools

As I mentioned earlier, another new design-time tool is the Data Explorer. This is the first technology for working on database definitions embedded in Delphi (without resorting to third-party tools, of course).

The Data Explorer works with all of the Borland Data Providers (BDP) for ADO.NET and is a .NET-specific technology. However, nothing forbids you from using the Data Explorer to change metadata of a database you plan on working with in a Win32 application or a .NET application based on a different data access technology.

Data Explorer allows you to create and manage database connections and to manipulate metadata (like creating, altering, and dropping tables). When you select a table you can expand its detailed structure (fields, indexes, and so on) in the Data Explorer window, but you can also view the data from the table in the main Delphi pane, as you can see in Figure 1.12.

Another main pane allows you to edit the structure of a database table visually, as you can see next:

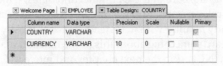

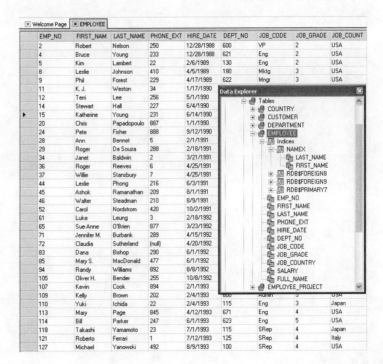

FIGURE 1.12

The Data view and the Data Explorer

One of the most powerful features of the Data Explorer is the ability to copy tables (both the meta-data and the actual data) from a database to another, which can be from a different vendor altogether. Delphi should be able to adapt its table creation commands and the data format to the target database.

This data copying technique and most of the other features used by the Data Explorer are surfaced also in the components part of the specific support for ADO.NET based on the BDP, which is covered in some detail in Chapter 16.

What's Next?

This chapter presented an overview of the new and more advanced features of the Delphi programming environment, now called Borland Developer Studio. I've tried to cover the most relevant features of the IDE, offering tips and suggestions about some lesser-known features that were already available in previous Delphi versions.

I didn't provide a step-by-step description of the IDE, partly because it is generally simpler to begin *using* Delphi than it is to read about how to use it. Moreover, there is a detailed Help file describing the environment and the development of a new simple project, and you might already have some exposure to one of the past versions of Delphi or a similar development environment.

Before delving into the core of the Delphi technologies, which are the platforms Delphi 2005 targets, I have another relevant area to cover. I won't cover the Win32 platform in a lot of detail, as most developers are already familiar with it. Instead, I'll focus mostly on .NET because many Delphi developers might have heard something about this new Microsoft platform but not know the details. If you are already fluent in .NET, skip the next chapter and move to Chapters 3 and 4, which cover the Delphi programming language.

Chapter 2

The Platforms: Win32 and Microsoft .NET

Unless you've been living on a desert island for the past few years, you've probably already heard of Microsoft .NET architecture, what it is, and why it matters. However, Microsoft operating systems are still based on a low-level API (Application Programming Interface), which is not going away any time soon. In between the C API and the .NET architecture, there is another technology, Microsoft's COM (Component Object Model).

In this chapter I'll try to guide you from Win32 through COM to .NET, giving you a technical overview of the multiple platforms provided by Microsoft in its ubiquitous operating systems. Having only a limited amount of space, I'm going to skip some in-depth technical details (particularly of the older technologies), while still trying to be as precise as I can. As I'll cover Win32 and COM very briefly here, this is mostly an introduction to .NET, and it certainly won't be complete.

My aim here is only to help you understand .NET from the Delphi perspective and for you to gain enough knowledge to understand Delphi language changes and other related features. Given some striking similarities between Delphi and .NET, it is generally easier for Delphi programmers to understand .NET if you compare those features, looking behind the new name to discover a technology you are already familiar with, even if in a different (at times more primitive) form.

NOTE If this chapter offers only an overview of many topics, following chapters will provide more details of the various technologies discussed here, at least those relevant for Delphi programmers. For example, Chapters 4 and 9, which cover the language and the runtime libraries, and Chapter 11, which covers application architectures and the use of libraries, packages, and assemblies, will offer more insight on the Win32 and .NET architectures, in addition to showing practical Delphi examples using these technologies.

The Win32 API

The development of software on the Windows operating system is based on a set of C language API functions. At the beginning, there were three libraries of 16-bit functions (Kernel, User, and GDI) that were later replaced by a much larger set of 32-bit API function libraries (with those three libraries still playing a central role in today's Windows).

While originally conceived as an object-oriented architecture, the Win32 API is a flat C-language API made of global functions you call that provide a reference (called *handle*) of the system object you are referring to. A handle can refer to a window, a control, a menu item, a memory block, a file, or almost any other entity used by the system. The communication from the system back to your application takes place through *callback functions*: you provide the memory address of the function (a function pointer) to

Windows, and the system will call it when appropriate. Most of these calls provide you with some information, technically called a Windows message, regarding why your function was called. Messages provide the most relevant communication system and play such a central role in Windows that it is often called a message-based operating system.

NOTE   If you have never seen a plain vanilla Windows API application written in Pascal or C, the PlainAPI example of the current chapter provides one. It is a simple program written in plain Pascal (without using classes) but has all of the low-level windows creation code and a window procedure callback with a couple of message handlers. A lot of code even for a trivial task.

When all of this was conceived back in the mid-1980s, OOP languages were still seldom used, so everything was mapped to functions with a heavy use of pointers, a technique very prone to error. From a more modern (and object-oriented) perspective, such a system has severe limitations, which over the years were overcome in two different ways.

OOP Class Libraries

OOP languages used for Windows development introduced class libraries sitting on top of the Windows API. Originally these libraries, like the C++ Object Windows Library (OWL) from Borland and the C++ Microsoft Foundation Class (MFC) library, required rather lengthy and difficult coding. This is why the alternative approach of hiding the complexity with a simplified and visual development tool like Visual Basic was very successful, even if developers lost full control of the operating system features.

The original idea Delphi pushed was to combine the RAD approach with a full-featured class library called Visual Component Library (VCL). This made Delphi almost as easy to use as Visual Basic but as powerful as a C++ compiler with a good class library. In Delphi you can, at one end of the scale, create a simple application by dropping components to a form (without writing any actual code) and, at the opposite end of the scale, write all of the code without using any visual component. Not that you'll often see these two extreme cases, but there are situations for which a visual approach is better, while in others a more OOP approach delivers a better and more flexible architecture. As the more OOP approach means you'll generally have to write more code, this usually makes sense for larger and more complex applications.

NOTE   The architecture of the VCL is discussed in Chapter 6.

As is the case with the C++ class libraries, windows and standard controls in Delphi are encapsulated in classes, like TForm or TEdit. Unlike those libraries, however, handling events is as simple as connecting a handler method to the event, and even writing a new custom component is relatively simple (specifically if compared to the early versions of Visual Basic). The VCL classes shield you from low-level details of the Windows API such as window procedures, message handling, handle allocation, and so forth. Still, all of these low-level features are available if you want to customize the library itself or some of its components.

If all of this sounds very positive, there is a relevant limitation to this approach: all you do in Delphi is available only to other developers using the same tool. The interoperability with other languages and class libraries is very limited. Even sharing strings with a library can be troublesome, as Delphi strings are quite different from the Win32 API PChar pointers. This is why a native solution of the platform can be a good idea, providing a benefit also to Delphi programmers.

COM to the Rescue

The Windows platform itself introduced object-oriented capabilities with the Component Object Model. This architecture comprised and extended the original OLE (Object Linking and Embedding) technology and offered many features, ranging from a visual component model (ActiveX, intended for use within other development environments but also from web browsers) to a business object and database access architecture based on MTS (Microsoft Transaction Server).

COM technology can be used for sharing objects among applications written in different programming languages. Programmers can use an Interface Definition Language (IDL) or a Type Library for sharing a language-independent definition of the classes implemented by a server.

NOTE   COM programming in Delphi for Win32 (and bridging COM and .NET solutions) is discussed in Chapter 12.

COM is a binary object model: you share compiled components. This happens to be one of the sources of problems, because even slightly different implementation of the type system can hamper an effective cross-language use (with Type Libraries not being mandatory or at times not so clearly defined). Moreover, every server is responsible for allocating and freeing the memory for the objects with the help of a reference-counting mechanism that is far from robust.

Another problem with COM is that everything is based on GUIDs, which are used to identify even interfaces and classes, and these IDs are generally made available to other applications by storing them in the registry. There are other limitations in COM and even more in DCOM, the distributed version of COM that never took off substantially.

Two enhanced versions of COM, COM+ and MTS, provided some help, but for the system to address the new computing needs (and the threat posed to Microsoft by competing platforms like Java) it was clear that COM needed to be redesigned. Also, Microsoft's long-term goal with COM or a similar architecture was to use it as a replacement of the old Windows API and as the foundation of a new object-oriented operating system the company has dreamed of since the early 1990s.

Efforts in this direction took quite some time and many radical shifts, but the final result of rewriting COM is the .NET Framework, a rather different solution which has very little in common with the starting point but which is mostly positive, as you'll soon see.

As Win32 and COM are the architectures of the past and are now considered obsolete technologies by Microsoft (even if they're still actively used in the present and the focus of a large portion of this book), I'll devote most of this chapter to what Microsoft considers the architecture of the future.

What Is Microsoft .NET?

A few years ago, Microsoft started to promote its new vision of the future of computing, focusing on its .NET initiative, a technical framework clouded by a large marketing initiative. By attaching the ".NET" label to each and every of its products, while apparently trying to push a "common vision," Microsoft ended up confusing its own users. After acknowledging this mistake, the company narrowed the use of the .NET moniker to its core technology: the .NET virtual machine (or CLR—Common Language Runtime) and the .NET Framework with its SDK (or Software Development Kit).

Before we get to the technical details, it is important to understand why Microsoft put (and still puts) a considerable effort into this technology, which is basically given away for free. You can download the .NET SDK and start to develop new applications for it at no cost (just use Notepad or a free programmer's editor and use the command line to invoke the free C# and VB.NET compilers included in the .NET SDK).

.NET "Marketing" Goals

Let me first try to focus on what the "literature" (more or less Microsoft-independent) says are the key reasons Microsoft moved to .NET:

The Component Infrastructure of .NET is better than the one provided by COM The ActiveX technology is, in effect, cumbersome, uselessly complex, and error-prone. Over the last few years, new component architectures have emerged that equate the concepts of classes and components, simplifying their construction and use. Delphi and Java are two notable examples that use this approach. .NET is following.

.NET offers language integration and real multilanguage support With its robust and complete type system and a common object model, various .NET languages map their OOP constructs to the system. In contrast, COM had only a limited language independence based on an obscure IDL and simpler Type Libraries, which were mainly added for the sake of VB developers but are not fully used even by the core Windows system.

.NET supports Internet and intranet interoperability While DCOM was inherently insecure since it was impossible to use it through a firewall, .NET uses and supports SOAP. However, you don't need .NET to use SOAP, as Delphi 7 (and Kylix 3) developers know—not to mention those in the Java camp.

.NET offers simplified development and simplified deployment Compared to COM, this is only too easy to say. .NET doesn't use GUIDs in the registry, there is no DLL Hell, and the installation is mostly done by copying a set of files to a folder (called *xcopy installation*). The term "DLL Hell" describes the situation of two applications requiring different versions of a DLL, and often different versions of an ActiveX. This is indeed a Windows problem, but its frequency varies with the development tool you use. Delphi developers seldom bump into this issue because you can build an executable file that includes the code of Borland's and the third party's components. This is something you cannot do if you use ActiveX controls, a technology other development tools rely on more heavily.

.NET means reliability and security As .NET code can be verified for type safety and security and executed in a sandbox, you can have fine-tuned code access security (that is, you can determine who is allowed to execute a given piece of code, as opposed to Windows traditional resource access control, which allows conditioned access to given resources) so you should expect fewer viruses and a safer Internet experience. This is partially the promise of Java and partially a nonissue since it's the browser or the mail program that need to be secured, not the applications you buy for your own company needs! Of course, a secure architecture will make people willing to download code from the Web, which is one of Microsoft's goals with .NET.

In other words, Microsoft realized that COM wasn't really a suitable model, particularly to address the fact that Windows is perceived as unsafe. So they took ideas from Java, Delphi, and other languages and systems to define a model better than COM and of other existing architectures. They implemented the model only on their own Windows operating system and made sure this architecture is much more reliable and safer than the current Windows technology.

My point is that .NET is actually a very sound set of technologies that solve a lot of programmers' problems. However, it is important to keep in mind that it was designed to solve Microsoft's own problems (and push the Windows client and server platforms).

Why .NET?

Let's get back to beginning and try to figure out why Microsoft has made and is making this considerable effort (in R&D and marketing terms). This is my own short list of reasons; it's supported by many articles, but you can certainly disagree with it.

Regain developers' confidence   A core idea is that Microsoft realized that after many years it has at least partially lost the confidence and support of the developer community. Java, the open source movement, the communities around the many Internet scripting languages (like Perl and Python), and in part even the Delphi community tend to be anti-Microsoft as they regard the value of platform-independence quite highly. To regain the developer community, there was nothing better they could do than to make available a set of top-quality technologies, low-cost IDEs, and free developer support and add to the mix lots of books and technical material. This has amounted to a great advantage for the developers, since now those focused on Microsoft technologies undeniably have a much better platform to target.

Push enterprise development on Windows   Microsoft has always had difficulties in doing this but was slowly starting to succeed—until the widespread use of Java and other technologies in large enterprises and telecommunication companies eroded their efforts even further.

Convince users to upgrade   They do this by enticing them to run applications based on the latest operating system features. Versions 1 and 2 of .NET are free add-ons for an existing operating system. In the future, Microsoft will try to persuade developers to use new features of the .NET platform that will work only on newer operating systems; for example, most of the announcements related to the Avalon User Interface framework indicate it will be available also for Windows XP but will be optimized only for Longhorn (the next version of Windows).

Move Microsoft Windows everywhere   They want Windows on handheld devices, watches, portable phones, and appliances. Microsoft virtually owns the desktop, but this is less and less the only relevant computing platform, and it is one too stable and mature to allow the growth Microsoft is used to. Consider portable phones. There are countries in which there are two, three, five times more portable phones than computers; before you say they are much less powerful, consider that they are becoming—and will become more and more—the way to access information (Internet, e-mail, financial or sport news, and even TV). Despite its efforts, Microsoft's role in phones is limited. Even in the segment of traditional handhelds, they took years to reach the market share of Palm OS in terms of new sales, although not in terms of installed user base. On yet another segment, the XBox console is having a tough time competing with the Sony PlayStation. Having a common runtime to let programs run on all of these heterogeneous platforms could be a very strong weapon for Microsoft and could really lure developers to the .NET Framework.

Push Microsoft Windows on company servers and web servers   At the opposite end, on the web farm/data center side, Microsoft is trying to unseat Linux and Apache from their current key role. Not only is this difficult for Microsoft, but Linux is also slowly gaining inroads on the desktop, so Microsoft knows it needs to move ahead on the technology side (not only on the marketing side) as fast as possible. Microsoft's push on servers is particularly strong with SQL Server, which is slowly turning from a database tool into a server operating system of its own, with the capability of hosting .NET managed code written in any .NET language for the stored procedures, managing XML data and SOAP calls, and integrating seamlessly with IIS (Microsoft web server).

Now let's get back to the technical side and focus on the technologies at the heart of the Microsoft .NET Framework: the virtual machine (or CLR) and the intermediate language.

VES: Virtual Execution System

The first element to consider as we start to focus on the .NET technology is the virtual machine at the heart of the new Microsoft architecture. The most compact definition of the core .NET technology is that of a *Virtual Execution System* (VES) or *virtual machine* or *virtual execution environment*. These terms imply that the program being executed is not physically bound to a given CPU and hardware architecture but that there is a software layer that emulates a computer that's generally a much higher level than the physical one. Instead of running machine code, the computers appears to execute a higher level set of instructions, generally called *intermediate code* or *bytecode*, while .NET uses the specific term of *common intermediate language* (CIL).

This approach is far from new in computing. In the early 1980s there was a very well known version of the Pascal language (UCSD Pascal) based on an intermediate pcode that allowed the same program to run on different hardware and operating systems (incompatible PCs, CP/M, DOS, and the like). The system was very successful, and the overall idea was highly regarded. Even Microsoft, in the first versions of its application software (the Multiplan spreadsheet, the first versions of Word for DOS), used a pcode-based architecture to make the programs more portable to slightly different PCs. However, at that time speed was a major issue, and assembly language programs like Lotus 1-2-3 could easily beat Multiplan performance-wise (which also resulted in a widely different market share).

Getting closer to today, the most relevant architecture based on bytecode is the Java architecture, which (in many areas) was used as a starting point in the specification and development of the .NET architecture. Java source code gets compiled into bytecode, which is interpreted by the Java Virtual Machine (JVM) executing it. To increase the speed, most recent JVMs include a just-in-time (JIT) compiler, which performs the transformation of the bytecode into specific machine code only the first time a method is executed. Another key feature of Java is that there are many JVMs for different operating systems and by different vendors. Although the mantra "compile once, run everywhere" is more a promise than a reality, the cross-platform support is certainly one of Java's goals.

The Virtual Execution System of .NET resembles the one implemented in Java but focuses more on efficiency, making the JITter a key and compulsory element of the architecture. The CIL code is never interpreted but is always compiled (the first time each method is executed) before being executed to the physical CPU.

There are other features to a VES besides the way it interprets or compiles its intermediate and abstract code representation. These systems generally offer a sophisticated runtime environment that supports the management of the objects' lifetime (often including a garbage collector for disposing of "used" objects), includes a rich set of data types with detailed runtime type information, provides the dynamic loading of program portions (or modules), and offers a large high-end class library to support development. In summary, at the heart of .NET there is a virtual machine that manages types and executes intermediate code (CIL) with the support of a very rich runtime environment called CLR, as you'll see later on. Unlike COM, which provides binary data types (or components), .NET types are described in an intermediate language and are implemented by the virtual machine. The actual machine-level implementation of types is determined at run time (and can change on different implementation platforms), and therefore is independent from the high-level programming language used to code the type (or component). Moreover, the objects' lifetime is completely managed by the runtime, saving developers a lot of effort.

CIL: Common Intermediate Language

The Common Intermediate Language (CIL) is the language of the virtual computer .NET emulates; it is the intermediate representation produced by compiling source code in languages like C#, Delphi.NET, or VB.NET. CIL is at the heart of .NET and is probably its single most important feature.

NOTE   CIL was originally called MSIL (Microsoft Intermediate Language) but was later renamed when Microsoft proposed the language for standardization to Ecma International. CIL is now a part of the Ecma standard #335, and ISO standard 23271:2003, called CLI (Common Language Infrastructure), documented at www.ecma-international.org. Although Microsoft fully controls the standardization process, making it far from open, this is still very relevant because a third party can come up with a custom and legal implementation of the standard (such as what is happening with the Mono project, www.go-mono.com, and the DotGNU project, www.dotgnu.org). Note also that Borland representatives sit on the Ecma standards committee.

Compared to other similar bytecodes or intermediate languages, CIL has a few notable features:

◆ The CIL code is verifiable for type safety. This means a program (such as PEVerify, included in the .NET SDK) can analyze the code and figure out if it is safe. A program (or a module) is safe if a memory location is invariably considered of a given type and interpreted in a single way and if there are no memory leaks and dangling references, no buffer overruns, no pointers used to access memory at random, and many other features like these.

◆ CIL code is compact. Most CIL operand instructions are typeless, so most of the instruction set can be encoded in only 1 byte. For example, operations like ADD, SUB, MUL, DIV, AND, and OR can operate on multiple different data types; how they behave depends on the values on the top of the stack (that is, their parameters).

◆ CIL uses a stack-based architecture. To perform an ADD operation (on two operands) the pseudo-code would be something like:

```
PUSH operand1
PUSH operand2
ADD
```

This last operation pops the parameters off stack and pushes the result on the stack. This is like the reverse-polish notation used in the past by pocket calculators, particularly those from Hewlett-Packard.

◆ CIL is self documenting, so that multiple languages can interoperate. There are actually two sides to this equation: CIL is very readable, and compiled modules on .NET include lots of metadata. This makes it possible for an IDE (like Delphi) to import a module and easily make available all of the module classes and their public methods. To call these public methods there is no need for header translations or type library interpretations. The module also makes available the internal structure of the classes to let you inherit new classes from these classes. The drawback of this openness is that code can be reverse engineered with a very limited effort. There are, as you'd expect, obfuscation tools that scramble the compiled code to make it less readable and more complex to reverse engineer, but the core architecture cannot be changed altogether.

As an example, you can look at a very simple CIL code fragment. This is the result of compiling the TryIL example, which has the following Pascal code:

```
var
   x, y, z: integer;
begin
   x := 10;
   y := 33;
   z := x + y;
```

In the corresponding compiled IL code, shown next, you can see the declaration of the three local int32 variables (.locals), the loading of the two constant values (10 and 33) to the stack (ldc.i4.s) and their storage in the 0 and 1 locations (stloc), and the loading of the two local variables on the stack and their addition (add), followed by the storage in the third local variable:

```
.method public static void TryIL() cil managed
{
   .entrypoint
   // Code size       54 (0x36)
   .maxstack  3
   .locals init (int32 V_0,
            int32 V_1,
            int32 V_2)
   ...
   IL_0006:  ldc.i4.s   10
   IL_0008:  stloc.0
   IL_0009:  ldc.i4.s   33
   IL_000b:  stloc.1
   IL_000c:  ldloc.0
   IL_000d:  ldloc.1
   IL_000e:  add
   IL_000f:  stloc.2
   ...
   IL_0035:  ret
} // end of method TryIL::TryIL
```

The actual code of the example also has calls to writeln and readln that make the IL more complex than I want to cover here.

CLS: Common Language Specification

The Common Language Specification (CLS) defines the common ground among all of the .NET programming languages. It defines features like identifier rules, naming conventions, type relationship linkage, and the like. CLS compliance is important to obtain full interoperability between modules of code in different languages and implies type safety.

Notice that CLS is more restrictive than CIL, which allows you to use non-CLS constructs. Delphi for .NET includes a number of non-CLS–compliant features that produce proper CIL code (which is also verifiable) other languages might not be able to deal with. For example, Delphi classes can have multiple overloaded constructors with different parameters (as can any other CLS compliant .NET language), but it can also have multiple *named* constructors with the same parameters.

NOTE   I'll discuss this issue again in Chapter 4 while covering some of the non-CLS–compliant Delphi language features.

CLR: Common Language Runtime

If CIL defines the execution statements, the language of the virtual machine, the CLR defines the execution environment and support that the virtual machines makes available to applications. The CLS defines an abstract object model; the CLR implements it. Another implementation of the same abstract model is the open source Mono project (`www.go-mono.com`), available for different operating systems including Windows and Linux.

NOTE   Technically speaking, the CLR is a superset of the CLI, the Common Language Infrastructure standardized by Ecma International and now ISO, along with the CIL language (available at `www.ecma-international.org`, as mentioned earlier).

The CLR defines a base `Object` class, which is the base class of the .NET Framework Class Library (FCL). From the Delphi perspective, as you will see in many places in this book, the connection between the Delphi language and the CLR is based on the correspondence between the core CLR class (`System.Object`) and the Delphi common base class (`TObject`). This is defined in Delphi for .NET System unit with the statement:

```
type
  TObject = System.Object;
```

There is much more to this issue, including class helpers, but I'm getting ahead of myself. Wait until Chapter 9 for a full coverage of the base `System.Object` class.

CLR IDENTIFIERS

CLR supports Unicode identifiers based on the UTF8 characters set. UTF8 represents the entire set of Unicode characters using variable-length characters. Base ASCII characters use a single byte, while extended characters use a 2-byte or 4-byte representation. This allows for non-ASCII characters within identifiers for classes, methods, properties, and so on. Of course, you cannot have a space, punctuation, or iconography symbols within a CLR-compliant identifier.

Having said this, it is important to note that the first version of Delphi for .NET (that is, Delphi 8 for .NET) didn't support Unicode identifiers, while Delphi 2005 fully supports them both on the .NET and on the Win32 platforms, as the UnicodeIdentifiers example of Chapter 4 demonstrates.

The .NET Compile Cycle and the JIT

The compilation of a program in the .NET environment is quite different from the classic Win32 compilation cycle. The classic compilation of a C language source file, for example, produces an object file (usually .obj) made of machine code. The linker binds a number of these .obj files together into an executable. Delphi on Win32 uses a slightly different approach: when you compile a Delphi unit you get a .dcu file including both machine code and a greater amount of symbol information for the compiler. This makes statements much faster than C language includes and makes the linking operation a breeze. By the way, the linker generally strips the symbol information unless you are building a package, in which case the linker places the code in the .bpl library file and the symbol information in a separate .dcp file.

In .NET, when you compile a C# language module, you get both CIL code (not machine code, of course) and symbol information. Unlike Delphi on Win32, the symbol information is not removed from the application (or assembly) you are building. When you compile a Delphi source file for .NET, the dccil compiler produces a .dcuil file, again with CIL code and symbol information. However, the symbol information is in a proprietary Delphi format. The linker, instead, produces modules with IL and CLR-compliant symbol information.

The fact that .NET assemblies and executables always include full symbol information has many effects, some positive and some negative:

◆ .NET executable files tend to be larger because of the symbol information (even if CIL is compact). Since the system library code remains external to your program (as it happens with Delphi packages but without having to distribute anything to the end users), applications are often tiny, so that you'll more than balance the *fat* caused by symbol information.

◆ By looking to the symbol information, you have more chances of reverse engineering the code of a "compiled" module. Actually, in this respect CIL plays a major role!

◆ By including symbol information it is possible to write programs that integrate with or extend a compiled module without the need to have its source code. This is particularly relevant for using libraries of classes and components.

Once the program is compiled, at execution time a significant role is played by the loader. When .NET loads the program, the run time also loads the referenced assemblies (more or less as in Win32), then determines the class memory layouts (because the physical representation of types depends on the actual CPU the program is executed on), creates stubs (or "placeholders") for each method of each class, and jumps to the module entry point (that is, to the first stub to be executed).

Now when the system reaches a method stub, the Just-In-Time (JIT) compiler transforms CIL opcodes into machine code instructions, replacing the method stub with the actual compiled code. At this point the system runs the natively compiled code. The compiled code of the method is kept in memory (and exclusively in memory) for any subsequent execution of the same method. The compiled code is discarded only if the program is terminated and executed again or if the system is low on memory (as the compiled code cannot be saved to the swap file for security reasons) or if the program is running on a very small device with severe memory constraints.

NOTE   The rule is that machine code generated by the JIT compiler is never cached to disk in any way, for security and efficiency reasons.

Since I'm mentioned reverse engineering, I think it is worth looking at what Lutz Roeder's Reflector can do with converting a compiled assembly (written in Delphi for .NET or any other .NET language) in a Delphi source code file. If you remember the TryIL example mentioned earlier in this chapter (see "An Example of CIL") you can see source code very similar to the original by opening it in Reflector, as shown in Figure 2.1.

As you have seen, at the heart of the CLR there is a Just-In-Time compiler, also called JIT compiler, JIT, or JITter. I've already stated that no code can be executed (or interpreted) in .NET until the JIT compiler has converted the IL code in the native machine code of the CPU the program is running on.

One of the relevant features of the JIT compiler is that it performs a number of optimizations. Some of the optimizations provided by the JIT compiler are similar (but not identical) to those of the Delphi Win32 compiler, like constant folding, loop induction variables, register variables, variable lifetime analysis, common subexpression elimination, and stack frame elimination. Another relevant feature of the JIT compiler, function call inlining, is also now available in the Delphi compiler.

NOTE   Function call inlining is a very powerful feature and has been available in languages like C++ for many years now. Because Delphi 2005 introduces this feature at the compiler level for both Win32 and .NET, I'll cover it in the next chapter.

FIGURE 2.1

Lutz Roeder's Reflector displaying the reverse engineered source code of the TryIL demo

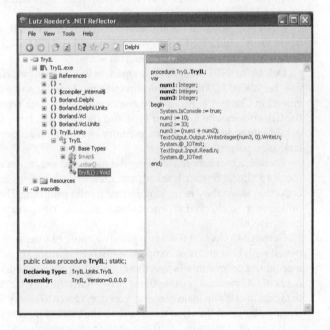

While general optimizations can also be performed by traditional compilers, an advantage of the JIT compiler is that is can potentially optimize the code for a specific CPU. With a regular Win32 executable you have to stick with a standard set of statements most Intel-compatible CPUs have. However, a JIT compiler can also provide specific optimization for a Pentium 4, use MMX or AMD instructions, and even work with 64-bit platforms and non-Intel CPUs. In the future, Microsoft plans to introduce profile based re-optimization, that is, a JIT compiler that adapts itself to the type of functionality that gets executed most in a given program. For example, if a particular branch of a condition is most often chosen, the CPU can be instructed to optimize the execution of that branch.

You have seen that in the default compilation cycle in .NET the JIT compiler is invoked on the method call after the program is loaded. An optional alternative, used by small devices, is to compile on install. This is done using the NGEN application of the .NET SDK. Contrary to what you might believe, with this approach the application execution speed can be slower than normal JITted code due to indirect method calls and the fact that inter-assembly calls cannot be optimized when each assembly is individually precompiled.

Managed Execution Model and Garbage Collection

The CIL code executed in the Virtual Execution System (VES) is generally described as *managed* code, as the CLR manages the objects and the types used in the code. To contrast this definition, Win32 code is described as *unmanaged* code. It is technically possible to mix managed and unmanaged code in a program. This is done exclusively by Managed C++, while all other .NET languages generate managed code.

Managed code that has tight type requirements on CIL code and the objects and primitive types being used is indicated as *safe code*. Managed code is the CIL output of the compiler; safe code depends on the actual statements you write.

Delphi for .NET compiles managed code, which is by default safe code. That is, it is safe unless you use the $UNSAFECODE compiler directive to allow for some limited unsafe pointer operations, as discussed in Chapter 4. As already mentioned, since data types are specified in the instruction stream, the CIL code can be tested for type and memory safety by inspection with tools like PEVerify. To obtain safe code, pointer tricks, memory overlays, and other type mutilations of the traditional Pascal language are prohibited.

There are two benefits to using the managed execution model. The first and most obvious is that memory allocations are tracked, and memory allocations are freed up automatically with a garbage collection when they're no longer used by the program. The second and less obvious is that security policies can be checked at process load, module load, and method call boundaries automatically and transparently.

Garbage Collection (GC) is typically a topic of intense debate among programmers—this happened with Java and now happens with .NET. Critics argue such a system will invariably slow down a program, programmers lose their control, programs will use too much memory, and so on. Proponents of GC systems counter these issues with the core fact that programmers have one less problem to tackle, and it's an insidious one: you don't have to worry about memory leaks, dangling references, freeing objects at the right time, and all the related memory issues.

However, if memory management becomes simpler, it is important to know there are relevant differences in behaviors programmers are used to. For example, you still have to worry about asking components to release external resources. In the CLR, objects don't have destructors any more but they have finalizers, which are called by the garbage collector when an object is collected.

C# destructors implement finalizers and their call becomes *nondeterministic* because you don't know when and if (in case a program terminates) they are executed. That's why finalizers are seldom used in .NET. The deterministic release of external resources is generally accomplished using the dispose pattern (an implementation of the IDisposable interface's single method Dispose). Many .NET classes protect the Dispose method and surface it through the public Close method you need to call when you end using the object.

In Delphi the situation is different. Delphi destructors implement IDisposable.Dispose and not a finalizer. Delphi's Free method invokes IDisposable.Dispose. This is covered in more detail in Chapter 4.

On the other hand, although even a properly designed GC system might need a little extra memory (because objects are destroyed after some time and not right away), its performance in allocation and its overall memory management can far exceed a classic memory manager. Coming from a Delphi background, there are memory segmentation issues that will disappear in Delphi for .NET, ending up (in same cases) with a better and more compact memory structure, along with faster allocations.

Knowing the GC and how it works at times helps you write better code for it. This is nice, but partially defeats the purpose of a GC, which is to let the programmer work freely ignoring memory issues. It is also hard to have the final word on how the GC works, and even official descriptions from Microsoft don't agree on all of the details.

In short, the garbage collector in .NET uses a multigenerational architecture. Every object (except the very large ones—over 85 KB) is allocated on a small heap called generation 0. When this first heap is full, the system performs an analysis of the live objects, discarding those not referenced any more and promoting the remaining active objects of generation 0 to a second large heap called generation 1. To move these objects the system needs to be able to change the related references, something possible only on a fully managed system.

Later on, when the generation 1 heap is full, the same process is repeated with a larger heap called generation 2. Objects moved to this third memory area will last the lifetime of the application. The concept behind the generational approach, in fact, is that programs tends to use a huge number of very short-lived objects (that in the best situations will never even reach generation 1) and a smaller number of long-lived objects you can afford to keep around even more time than you actually need them.

You might be skeptical (as I was at the beginning), but this system ends up working very well, on average much better than Delphi's own memory manager. (Although to be honest, there are also third-party add-in memory managers for Delphi that do work much better than the predefined one, which is okay for most users but far from optimized.)

CTS: The Common Type System

What the .NET CLR manages and knows how to manage is a set of types shared among the different .NET languages. This common set of types is part of the Common Language Specification (CLS). The CLS-compliant types define the commonality between .NET programming languages. Languages can pick a subset of the CLS types and also provide extra non CLS-compliant types or features.

The actual .NET implementation of the CLS type system is called Common Type System (CTS). The CTS defines primitive types and complex types, particularly the structure of objects. The CTS can be extended, making classes non CLS-compatible (something you'll generally want to avoid, particularly if you need to work across languages).

The CTS defines two totally separate families of types: value types in which the variable or field holds the actual value (like an integer) and reference types in which the variable or field holds an address in the managed heap. This is a reference to a memory location hosting the data, as also happens for objects in Delphi for Win32. Unlike unmanaged Win32, however, an address in a managed heap can be changed automatically during memory compaction by the GC, as described earlier. The next two sections explore the two areas of the type system.

CTS: Value Types

The most distinctive feature of value types is that they live in local memory: local variables of value types live only on the stack; data fields of value types use memory of the object hosting them.

Value types cannot be null, as they must always hold some data (possibly zero). Value types can be passed to methods by value (generally the default) or by reference (using the var keyword in Delphi).

Value types include the most basic elements of the type system:

◆ Primitive types (characters, integer and floating point numbers, dates and time values, and so on). Notice that when needed, primitive types can be boxed into objects; that is, the CLR can automatically create an object hosting a value type so that you can have a uniform way to refer to any data type when needed.

◆ Enumerations, which in Delphi work similarly to their Win32 version, although an enumeration that comes from a referenced assembly has to be qualified by its type. In C#, enumerations are considered a new concept, at least for C-derived languages.

◆ Records, or structures, to use the C# jargon. These are much richer than in Delphi for Win32, as records can have methods and constructors like classes do and even implement interfaces. Records also support overloaded operators.

◆ Custom value types that inherit from System.ValueType and are sealed (which means you cannot further inherit from them). These include the new TDateTime type, the Variant type, and a few others covered in Chapter 5.

NOTE   I'll cover most of the value types (particularly primitive types and records) in more detail in Chapter 4, specifically how they are defined and managed in Delphi for .NET.

CTS: Reference Types

Unlike value types, reference types live only on the heap. To be more precise, a variable of a reference type is, as the name implies, a reference to a dynamic memory location. A local method variable of a reference type doesn't hold the object data on the stack, it holds *only* a reference to the object data. The data is allocated (something you often have to do manually!) on the heap and kept around until some time after there are no references to it. Reference types are managed by the GC, while value types are not. Their managed nature and the extra dereferencing required to access them make reference types such as classes less efficient than value types such as records.

Reference types can be null; that is, a reference might not refer to any object. Reference type parameters are generally passed by value, as you are already passing the reference to the actual object, which can be modified by the method being called. You can also pass an object reference by reference (using a var parameter in Delphi) if you want to be able to alter the reference itself. On the other hand, the only thing you can to simulate pass-by-value parameters is to make a copy of the data to another similar object and use that other object so that the original will never be modified.

Reference types include all objects but also strings and dynamic arrays. This is similar to what happens in Delphi for Win32, with the huge difference that in Win32 you have to manually free the objects from memory.

Class types in .NET support properties, methods, and events (the so-called PME approach), as in Delphi. Implementation differences include the fact that properties must have getter and setter methods (and cannot be mapped directly to fields) and that events allow multicast semantics (which means that a single event can have multiple handler methods assigned). Again, you'll see more details in Chapter 4.

Namespaces and Assemblies

With so many developers building libraries and applications for .NET, there is a fair chance that type names might conflict. For this reason, .NET introduces the idea of a namespace, a logical container of types. Namespaces do not have any physical manifestation; in fact, an assembly can contribute to multiple namespaces, and multiple assemblies can contribute to a single namespaces.

NOTE In Delphi 2005, namespaces are defined by omitting the last portion of a dot-separated unit name. A unit called Marco.Test.Code belongs to the Marco.Test namespace. Nondotted unit name use is the default project namespace, if any. I'll cover this topic in more detail in Chapter 4.

What Is an Assembly?

If namespaces are logical containers of types, the physical containers are called assemblies. The term *assemblies* is used in .NET to denote Portable Executable (PE) files containing managed code and metadata. Assemblies can be distributed in the forms of a DLL or an EXE file. Note that unlike in Win32, assemblies referenced by other assemblies generally come in the form of a DLL, while assemblies you execute directly use the .exe format.

NOTE Technically, you can reference an executable assembly and link to its types. However, the smart linker is off for DLLs (and Delphi Win32 packages) and on for EXEs, so care must be taken when linking to EXEs that what you want is actually there. This somewhat explains the presence of the RuntimeRequiredAttribute attribute in WinForms form units. It's a Borland attribute that ensures the referenced type is compiled into the EXE.

Where a traditional DLL includes compiled code, and a COM server library contains compiled code plus an optional type library describing the server interface, a .NET assembly must include the compiled CIL code and compulsory symbol information. This means that you can inspect the types included in an assembly by browsing its metadata (and also the actual code as IL, or you can reverse engineer it to view it as source code).

An assembly can consist of multiple binary files in the PE format, but this is quite rare and also impossible with Delphi for .NET without tinkering at the IL level. Technically an assembly is a collection of modules, which are defined in .NET as "internal clumps of code and complete symbol info." Most languages create a module for each source code file. This is similar to what Delphi for .NET does, creating a .dcuil file for each compiled unit. Interestingly enough, Delphi .dcu files included symbol information since the first version.

From the Delphi point of view an assembly is like a package, an extended library hosting components (see Chapter 11 for more on Delphi packages in Win32 and assemblies in .NET). On one side, in fact, to create a new .NET assembly you define a package. On the other side, Delphi treats CLR assemblies written in other languages as if they were packages.

As you add an assembly to the reference list of a project (or use the -lu<name> command-line directive), Delphi reads the metadata of the assembly and creates an import file for it with the dcpil extension. These .dcpil files are symbol files with no actual code, like .dpc files created when you produce a package. The .dcpil files are used by the compiler to optimize the way it refers to the types defined in that assembly.

The .dcpil file contains enough info for binding against the assembly and for code completion. One of the reasons for this extra step is that loading data every time from the assembly would be too slow. One of the advantages is that if you have the .dcpil file you can compile and link your application against an assembly even without having the assembly installed on the machine where you compile. This potentially allows you to build programs against different versions of .NET (even if they are not installed on your computer).

NOTE   The .dcpil files in Delphi 8 were dependent on a specific version of the target assemblies and included more than its public interface. This caused quite a few troubles when Microsoft released the update 1 to .NET 1.1 and Borland had to release the update 3 of Delphi 8 to fix the problem. Delphi 2005 binds symbol names rather than version-specific metadata token values to avoid a similar problem in the future.

A .NET application is linked against multiple assemblies—at least the core assemblies that make up the .NET runtime are. A core difference between assemblies/packages produced in Delphi and other .NET assemblies is that in the former case you can choose whether to link the Delphi units (.dcuil) into your executable file or refer to the external assembly at run time. This works exactly as in Delphi for Win32 with run time packages.

Binding and Loading Assemblies

As with DLLs, the assemblies your application is linked against must be available on the computer where you run the program. The core .NET assemblies will already be there, at least if the target computer has the .NET runtime (of the proper version) installed on it. If your programs use other assemblies, you'll have to deploy them along with the program (a missing assembly will prevent your program from starting).

Now the question becomes: where does the .NET runtime look when loading assemblies? It depends if the assembly is a private assembly or a shared assembly. Private assemblies are application specific and often deployed along with the application. Shared assemblies are system wide and are deployed to the Global Assembly Cache (GAC). Of course, the .NET system assemblies are shared assemblies.

Now let's look at assembly loading in the two cases. Similarly to DLL loading on Win32, the .NET system looks for a private assembly in the same folder of the program (or library), in a subfolder with same name of the assembly, or in the location indicated in a local configuration file. This allows you to have a single subfolder (in this case called `local_lib`) hosting a number of private assemblies:

```
<configuration>
  <runtime>
    <assemblyBinding
      xmlns="urn:schemas-microsoft-com:asm.v1">
      <probing privatePath="local_lib"/>
    </assemblyBinding>
  </runtime>
</configuration>
```

Unlike Win32, a shared assembly is not found on a single system folder or a directory on the path but within a complex data structure known as the Global Assembly Cache (GAC). Relevant differences include that you can have multiple versions of the same library (with the same DLL filename), shared assemblies are versioned, and they are signed (hence much safer).

Assembly Versioning and the GAC

One of the most annoying problems with Win32 development, particularly in the COM area, is the so-called "DLL Hell." This term, used mostly by VB developers, describes the problems you have when different applications need to work with different versions of the same ActiveX control. In Delphi this issue was never as relevant because you can compile component code into your executable file and you tend to use native VCL controls, which do not need to be installed on the registry. Many DLL conflicts are possible also in Delphi, but the issue is less relevant than with other Win32 development tools.

To provide a robust solution to this problem, assemblies on .NET have sophisticated support for versioning. A program (or another assembly) refers to a specific version of the dependent assemblies in the manifest portion of its compiled file, a setting you can override using an external manifest file. This way, if a new (potentially incompatible) version of the assembly is installed on the computer, your program by default will keep using the version it knows about.

The version of an assembly is made of four numbers (such as 1.2.0.1) and a culture, which is the general term to indicate language and locale-specific settings. This means you can have multiple versions of the assemblies with a different number or the same number but a different culture. Most system assemblies (and most assemblies installed in the GAC, which are code-containing assemblies) are marked as culture neutral, meaning they don't have a specific culture but only a version number. You can see this by opening the GAC folder in Explorer, as in Figure 2.2. Satellite assemblies, on the other hand, contain things that are specific for a given culture.

FIGURE 2.2

The GAC in Explorer

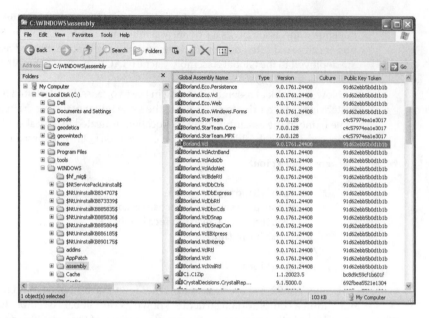

Notice that although Explorer shows the installed assemblies as if they were in a single folder, this is not actually the case. In practice the system creates a folder for each version, using the version, culture, and strong name for the intermediate folder. For example, for the Borland.Delphi assembly the GAC structure looks like this:

```
Assembly
  GAC
    Borland.VCL
      7.1.1523.17956__91d62ebb5b0d1b1b
        Borland.Delphi.dll
        __AssemblyInfo__.ini
      9.0.1761.24408__91d62ebb5b0d1b1b
        Borland.Delphi.dll
        __AssemblyInfo__.ini
```

The final portion of the preceding folder name is its public key token. An assembly can be placed in the GAC only if it has a strong name. This is a combination of a key used to sign the assembly and a hash code of the assembly content. Developers can obtain a public/private key pair using the share name utility of the .NET SDK (sn.exe). Using the private portion of the key, they can sign the assembly, adding the public portion in the assembly itself, so that the CLR at load time can check the hash and figure out if anyone has tampered with the file—that is, physically modified it. In that case the assembly would have a new strong name. As you link your applications against such a strong name, if a malicious user (or Trojan program) replaces the assembly, your program won't use this "new" version unless specifically instructed to do so in a manifest file. Applications can be saved in directories that are write-protected from the user, so that fake manifests cannot be created there. Once your assembly has a strong name you can use the Global Assembly Cache Utility, gacutil.exe, to install it.

As you add a reference to an assembly in a Delphi for .NET application, the IDE will pick up the version information and add it to its configuration. The project file itself will include a comment like this (on a single line):

```
{%DelphiDotNetAssemblyCompiler
  '$(SystemRoot)\microsoft.net\framework\
  v1.1.4322\System.Data.dll'}
```

while the project configuration file (.bdsproj) will include a more detailed reference like:

```
<File
  FileName="$(SystemRoot)\microsoft.net\framework\
    v1.1.4322\System.Data.dll"
  ContainerId="DelphiDotNetAssemblyCompiler"
  ModuleName="System.Data"
  AssemblyName="system.data"
  Version="1.0.5000.0"
  LinkUnits="False"/>
```

Dynamic Assembly Loading

In addition to being bound to a program at link time, assemblies can also be loaded dynamically by an application. You can find the support required for this operation in the System.Reflection. Assembly class of the .NET Framework. I'll cover this issue in more details and provide an actual example in Chapter 11.

A specific case of dynamically loaded assemblies is that of satellite assemblies. These special assemblies contain only resource data (strings, icons, and so on) and are loaded at run time to complement an actual assembly based on user locale in conjunction with the culture specifier in the strong name. In other words, the assembly can use the resources of the satellite assemblies instead of its own version to provide, for example, a translation without deploying a copy of the entire assembly with the compiled code.

This is very similar to Delphi translation support, which are based on resource packages you can manage with the front end available in the IDE, called Internal Translation Manager or the stand-alone External Translation Manager you can distribute to a professional translator. Delphi IDE tools have been extended to also support the .NET platforms and the development of satellite assemblies.

What's Next

In this chapter we explored the foundations of the platforms Delphi 2005 supports (in particular the .NET platform). This was a summary of the features of the platform, as one could easily write an entire book covering .NET core technologies (and there are many good ones already). Moreover, it was an introduction tailored to the perspective of Delphi programmers.

Now, it is time to start looking into the language and the runtime libraries used by Delphi. Because the language has evolved and there are differences between the Win32 and the .NET version of the Delphi language, Chapter 3 gives an overview of the standard and common features, while Chapter 4 addresses the .NET version of the language. I'll also provide you with more details in Chapter 4 on Delphi's .NET support, covering some of the .NET features already discussed in this chapter from the specific perspective of the Delphi language.

Chapter 3

The Delphi Programming Language

The Delphi development environment is based on an object-oriented extension of the Pascal programming language previously known as Object Pascal. Recently, Borland started to refer to the language as "the Delphi language." Most modern programming languages support *object-oriented programming* (OOP). OOP languages are based on three fundamental concepts: encapsulation (usually implemented with classes), inheritance, and polymorphism (or late binding). Although you can write Delphi code without understanding the core features of its language, you won't be able to master this environment until you fully understand the programming language.

NOTE   Due to space constraints and the fact that the language hasn't changed much in recent years, in this chapter you'll find only a very fast-paced introduction to the language. You can read the more detailed description from past editions of this book on my website (see Appendix A for details).

The following topics are covered in this chapter: classes and objects; encapsulation (private and public); using properties, constructors, objects and memory; inheritance; virtual methods and polymorphism; type-safe down-casting (run-time type information); interfaces, working with exceptions, class references, and the `for..in` loop; and inlining.

Core Language Features

The Delphi language is an OOP extension of the classic Pascal language, which Borland pushed forward for many years with its Turbo Pascal compilers. The syntax of the Pascal language is known to be quite verbose and arguably more readable than, for example, the C language. Its OOP extension follows the same approach, delivering the same power of the recent breed of OOP languages, from Java to C#.

Even the core language is subject to continuous changes, but few of them will affect your everyday programming needs. In Delphi 6, for example, Borland added support for several features more or less related to the development of Kylix, the Linux version of Delphi:

◆ A new directive for conditional compilation (`$IF`)

◆ A set of hint directives (`platform`, `deprecated`, and `library`, of which only the first is used to any extent) and the `$WARN` directive used to enable or disable them and many other warnings

◆ A `$MESSAGE` directive to emit custom information (including hints, warnings, and errors) among compiler messages

Delphi 7 added three additional compiler warnings: unsafe type, unsafe code, and unsafe cast. These warnings are emitted in case of operations that you won't be able to use to produce safe managed code on the Microsoft .NET platform.

Another change relates to unit names, which can now be formed from multiple words separated by a dot, as in the `marco.test` unit, saved in the `marco.test.pas` file. This feature helps support namespaces and more flexible unit references in Delphi for .NET, as we'll see in the next chapter.

Delphi 2005 adds to the core Pascal language Unicode identifiers a new looping statement, the `for..in` loop, and an optimization directive and feature, inlining. These two topics are covered at the end of the chapter because the discussion is partially based on other concepts that will be described first.

COMPILER VERSIONS

If you need to maintain compatibility with older versions of Delphi, you can use the VER170 define to check for the compiler version in an IFDEF conditional directive or an $IF directive like {$IF Defined(VER170)}. Even better, use the newer CompilerVersion compiler-defined constant in an IF conditional directive. You can also check the RTLVersion constant. These two constants are set to 17.00 in the initial release of Delphi 2005; they are both set to 16.00 in Delphi 8 for .NET; and they are both set to 15.00 in Delphi 7 and 7.01.

To distinguish between the Win32 and the .NET compiler, you can test the presence of the CLR, CIL, or MANAGEDCODE symbols or the WIN32 or MSWINDOWS symbols, as in:

```
{$IF Defined(CLR)}
...
{$IFEND}
```

Classes and Objects

Delphi is based on OOP concepts and in particular on the definition of new class types. The use of OOP is partially enforced by the visual development environment because for every new form defined at design time, Delphi automatically defines a new class. In addition, every component visually placed on a form is an object of a class type available in or added to the system library.

NOTE   The terms *class* and *object* are commonly used and often misused, so let's be sure we agree on their definitions. A class is a user-defined data type, which has a state (its representation or internal data) and some operations (its behavior or its methods). An object is an instance of a class or a variable of the data type defined by the class. Objects are actual entities. When the program runs, objects take up some memory for their internal representation. The relationship between object and class is the same as the one between variable and type.

As in most other modern OOP languages (including Java and C#), in Delphi a class-type variable doesn't provide the storage for the object but is only a pointer or reference to the object in memory.

Before you use the object, you must allocate memory for it by creating a new instance or by assigning an existing instance to the variable:

```
var
  Obj1, Obj2: TMyClass;
begin
  // assign a newly created object
  Obj1 := TMyClass.Create;
  // assign to an existing object
  Obj2 := ExistingObject;
```

The call to `Create` invokes a default constructor available for every class, unless the class redefines it (as described later). To declare a new class data type in Delphi with some local data fields and some methods, use the following syntax:

```
type
  TDate = class
    Month, Day, Year: Integer;
    procedure SetValue (m, d, y: Integer);
    function LeapYear: Boolean;
  end;
```

NOTE The convention in Delphi is to use the letter *T* as a prefix for the name of every class you write and every other type (*T* stands for Type). This is just a convention—to the compiler, *T* is just a letter like any other—but it is so common that following it will make your code easier for other Delphi developers to understand. When programming for the .NET Framework, some developers tend to omit the initial *T*, as the CLS naming rules ban prefixing letters for classes and this convention is not used in other .NET languages. Other Delphi developers still prefer to keep the initial *T* as a marker that the class originated in Delphi.

A method is defined with the *function* or *procedure* keyword, depending on whether it has a return value. Inside the class definition, methods can only be declared; they must be then defined in the *implementation* portion of the same unit. In this case, you prefix each method name with the name of the class it belongs to using dot notation:

```
procedure TDate.SetValue (m, d, y: Integer);
begin
  Month := m;
  Day := d;
  Year := y;
end;

function TDate.LeapYear: Boolean;
begin
  // call IsLeapYear in SysUtils.pas
  Result := IsLeapYear (Year);
end;
```

TIP If you press Ctrl+Shift+C while the cursor is within the class definition, the Class Completion feature of the Delphi editor will generate the skeleton of the definition of the methods declared in a class.

This is how you can use an object of the previously defined class:

```
var
  ADay: TDate;
begin
  // create an object
  ADay := TDate.Create;
  try
    // use the object
    ADay.SetValue (1, 1, 2000);
    if ADay.LeapYear then
      ShowMessage ('Leap year: ' + IntToStr (ADay.Year));
  finally
    // destroy the object
    ADay.Free;
  end;
end;
```

Notice that ADay.LeapYear is an expression similar to ADay.Year, although the first is a function call and the second a direct data access. You can optionally add parentheses after the call of a function with no parameters. You can find the previous code snippets in the source code of the Dates1 example; the only difference is that the program creates a date based on the year provided in an edit box.

NOTE The previous code snippet uses a try/finally block to ensure the destruction of the object even in the case of exceptions in the code. You can find an introduction to the topic of exceptions later in this chapter. Notice that calling Free on objects of this class in .NET is a do-nothing operation: because your class has no specific destructor to implement as IDisposable.Dispose method, the compiler won't bother calling Dispose when you call Free.

More on Methods

There is a lot more to say about methods. Here are some short notes about the features available in Delphi:

- Delphi supports method *overloading*. This means you can have two methods with the same name, provided that you mark the methods with the overload keyword and that the parameter lists of the two methods are sufficiently different. By checking the parameters, the compiler can determine which version you want to call.

- Methods can have one or more parameters with default values. If these parameters are omitted in the method call, they will be assigned the default value.

- Within a method, you can use the Self keyword to access the current object. When you refer to local data of the object, the reference to Self is implicit. For example, in the SetValue method of the TDate class listed earlier, you use Month to refer to a field of the current object, and the compiler translates Month into Self.Month.

◆ You can define class methods marked by the class keyword. A class method doesn't have an object instance to act upon, because it can be applied to an object of the class or to the class as a whole. Delphi for Win32 doesn't (currently) have a way to define class data, while Delphi for .NET does so using class var sections, as you'll see in the next chapter. In Win32 you can mimic this functionality by adding global data in the implementation portion of the unit defining the class.

◆ By default, methods use the register calling convention: (simple) parameters and return values are passed from the calling code to the function and back using CPU registers, instead of the stack. This process makes method calls much faster.

◆ You can now use inlining to optimize the execution of a method, although you may gain little and risk a code bloat situation. More on this topic in the "Inlining" section at the end of this chapter.

Creating Components Dynamically

To emphasize the fact that Delphi components aren't much different from other objects (and also to demonstrate the use of the Self keyword), I've written the CreateComps example. This program has a form with no components and a handler for its OnMouseDown event, which I've chosen because it receives as a parameter the position of the mouse click (unlike the OnClick event). I need this information to create a button component in that position. Here is the method's code:

```
uses
  StdCtrls;

procedure TForm1.FormMouseDown (Sender: TObject;
  Button: TMouseButton; Shift: TShiftState; X, Y: Integer);
var
  Btn: TButton;
begin
  Btn := TButton.Create (Self);

  Btn.Left := X;
  Btn.Top := Y;
  Btn.Width := Btn.Width + 50;
  Btn.Caption := Format ('Button at %d, %d', [X, Y]);
  Btn.Parent := Self;
end;
```

The effect of this code is to create buttons at mouse-click positions, as you can see in Figure 3.1. In the code, notice in particular the use of the Self keyword as both the parameter of the Create method (to specify the component's owner) and the value of the Parent property. I'll discuss these two elements (ownership and the Parent property) in Chapter 4.

FIGURE 3.1

The output of the Create-Comps example, which creates Button components at run time

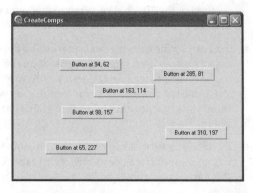

When writing code like this, you might be tempted to use the Form1 variable instead of Self. In this specific example, that change wouldn't make any practical difference; but if there are multiple instances of a form, using Form1 is a logical error. In fact, if the Form1 variable refers to the first form of that type being created, then by clicking in another form of the same type, the new button will always be displayed in the first form. The button's Owner and Parent will be Form1, not the form the user has clicked. In general, referring to a particular instance of a class when the current object is required is bad OOP practice.

Encapsulation

A class can have any amount of data and any number of methods. However, for a good object-oriented approach, data should be hidden, or *encapsulated*, inside the class using it. When you access a date, for example, it makes no sense to change the value of the day by itself. In fact, changing the value of the day might result in an invalid date, such as February 30. Using methods to access the internal representation of an object limits the risk of generating erroneous situations, because the methods can check whether the date is valid and refuse to modify the new value if it is not. Encapsulation is important because it allows the class writer to modify the internal representation in a future version.

The concept of encapsulation is often indicated by the idea of a black box. You don't know about the internals: you only know how to interface with the black box or use it regardless of its internal structure. The "how to use" portion, called the *class interface*, allows other parts of a program to access and use the objects of that class. However, when you use the objects, most of their code is hidden. You seldom know what internal data the object has, and you usually have no way to access the data directly. Of course, you are supposed to use methods to access the data, which is shielded from unauthorized access. This is the object-oriented approach to a classical programming concept known as *information hiding*. However, in Delphi there is the extra level of hiding, through properties, as you'll see later in this chapter.

Delphi implements this class-based encapsulation, but it still supports the classic module-based encapsulation using the structure of units. Every identifier that you declare in the interface portion of a unit becomes visible to other units of the program, provided there is a uses statement referring back to the unit that defines the identifier. On the other hand, identifiers declared in the implementation portion of the unit are local to that unit.

Private, Protected, and Public

For class-based encapsulation, the Delphi language has three access specifiers: private, protected, and public. A fourth, published, controls run-time type information (RTTI) and design-time information (as discussed in more detail in Chapter 5), but it gives the same programmatic accessibility as public. Here are the three *classic* access specifiers and the two new ones introduces in Delphi 2005:

- The private directive denotes fields and methods of a class that are not accessible outside the unit that declares the class.

- The new strict private directive denotes fields and methods that can be accessed only by methods of the same class and not by other classes in the same unit.

- The protected directive is used to indicate methods and fields with limited visibility. Only the current class and its inherited classes can access protected elements. More precisely, only the class, subclasses, and any code in the same unit as the class can access protected members, which opens up to a trick discussed in the sidebar "Accessing Protected Data of Other Classes (or, the "Protected Hack")" later in this chapter. We'll discuss this keyword again in the section "Protected Fields and Encapsulation."

- The new strict protected directive denotes fields and methods accessible by the class and the inherited classes but not to other classes in the same unit.

- The public directive denotes fields and methods that are freely accessible from any other portion of a program as well as in the unit in which they are defined.

Generally, the fields of a class should be private and the methods public. However, this is not always the case. Methods can be private or protected if they are needed only internally to perform some partial computation or to implement properties. Fields might be declared as protected so that you can manipulate them in inherited classes, although this isn't considered a good OOP practice.

WARNING Original Delphi access specifiers only restricted code outside a unit from accessing certain members of classes declared in the interface section of your unit. This meant that if two classes were in the same unit, there was no protection even for their private fields. With the new strict private and strict protected specifiers of Delphi 2005, however, you can obtain a stronger protection, like most other OOP languages have.

As an example, consider this new version of the TDate class:

```
type
  TDate = class
  private
    Month, Day, Year: Integer;
  public
    procedure SetValue (y, m, d: Integer); overload;
    procedure SetValue (NewDate: TDateTime); overload;
    function LeapYear: Boolean;
    function GetText: string;
    procedure Increase;
  end;
```

You might think of adding other functions, such as GetDay, GetMonth, and GetYear, which return the corresponding private data, but similar direct data-access functions are not always needed. Providing access functions for each and every field might reduce the encapsulation and make it harder to modify the internal implementation of a class. Access functions should be provided only if they are part of the logical interface of the class you are implementing.

Another new method is the Increase procedure, which increases the date by one day. This calculation is far from simple, because you need to consider the different lengths of the various months as well as leap and nonleap years. To make it easier to write the code, I'll change the internal implementation of the class to Delphi's TDateTime type for the internal implementation. The class definition will change to the following (the complete code is in the DateProp example):

```
type
  TDate = class
  private
    fDate: TDateTime;
  public
    procedure SetValue (y, m, d: Integer); overload;
    procedure SetValue (NewDate: TDateTime); overload;
    function LeapYear: Boolean;
    function GetText: string;
    procedure Increase;
  end;
```

Notice that because the only change is in the private portion of the class, you won't have to modify any of your existing programs that use it. This is the advantage of encapsulation!

NOTE The TDateTime type is a floating-point number. The integral portion of the number indicates the number of days since 12/30/1899, the same base date used by OLE Automation and Microsoft Win32 applications. (Use negative values to express previous years.) The decimal portion indicates the time as a fraction. For example, a value of 3.75 stands for the second of January 1900, at 6:00 A.M. (three-quarters of a day). To add or subtract dates, you can add or subtract the number of days, which is much simpler than adding days with a day/month/year representation.

When Private Is Really Private

For CLR compatibility, Borland has added to Delphi 2005 two more access specifiers to Win32 compiler (matching Delphi 8 .NET compiler), strict private and strict protected. These correspond to the CLR private and protected specifiers and behave as you might expect, which means that other classes within the same unit cannot access strict private symbols of a class and can access strict protected symbols only if they inherit from that class.

As an example of the syntax and error messages you'll get, see the ProtectedPrivate demo in this chapter's code. The demo has a couple of classes and code using them, and you can experiment with it by changing the access specifiers. The base class code is the following (listed here only to show the exact syntax):

```
type
  TBase = class
  strict private
    one: Integer;
```

```
strict protected
  two: integer;
end;
```

There are a couple of things to notice. The first is that the error message you'll get when you try to access an inaccessible member is quite readable ("Cannot access protected symbol TBase.two"), while in the past it used to be very cryptic ("Undeclared identifier"). The second and less relevant element is that the syntax of this feature has changed since the original Delphi for .NET preview distributed with Delphi 7 and discussed in *Mastering Delphi 7*. The preliminary syntax was `class private` and is now replaced with `strict private`.

Encapsulating with Properties

Properties are a very sound OOP mechanism, or a well-thought-out application of the idea of encapsulation. Essentially, you have a name that hides its implementation details. This allows you to modify the class extensively without affecting the code using it. A good definition of properties is that of *virtual fields*. From the perspective of the user of the class that defines them, properties look exactly like fields, because you can generally read or write their value. For example, you can read the value of the `Caption` property of a button and assign it to the `Text` property of an edit box with the following code:

```
Edit1.Text := Button1.Caption;
```

It looks like you are reading and writing fields. However, properties can be directly mapped to data, as well as to access methods, for reading and writing the value. When properties are mapped to methods, the data they access can be part of the object or outside of it, and they can produce side effects, such as repainting a control after you change one of its values. Technically, a property is an identifier that is mapped to data or methods using a `read` and a `write` clause. For example, here is the definition of a `Month` property for a date class:

```
property Month: Integer read FMonth write SetMonth;
```

To access the value of the `Month` property, the program reads the value of the private field `FMonth`; to change the property value, it calls the method `SetMonth` (which must be defined inside the class, of course).

Different combinations are possible (for example, you could also use a method to read the value or directly change a field in the `write` directive), but the use of a method to change the value of a property is common. Here are two alternative definitions for the property, mapped to two access methods or mapped directly to data in both directions:

```
property Month: Integer read GetMonth write SetMonth;
property Month: Integer read FMonth write FMonth;
```

Often, the actual data and access methods are private (or protected), whereas the property is public. For this reason, you must use the property to have access to those methods or data, a technique that provides both an extended and a simplified version of encapsulation. It is an *extended* encapsulation because not only can you change the representation of the data and its access functions, but you can also add or remove access functions without changing the calling code. A user only needs to recompile the program using the property.

TIP When you're defining properties, take advantage of the extended Class Completion feature of Delphi's editor, which you activate with the Ctrl+Shift+C key combination. After you write the property name, type, and semicolon, press Ctrl+Shift+C, and Delphi will provide you with a complete definition, a field of the right type named with an F prefix, and an implementation of the setter method that assigns its value parameter to the field. Write **Get** in front of the name of the field identifier after the read keyword, and you'll also have a getter method with almost no typing.

PROPERTIES FOR THE *TDATE* CLASS

As an example, I've added properties for accessing the year, the month, and the day to an object of the TDate class discussed earlier. These properties are not mapped to specific fields, but they all map to the single fDate field storing the complete date information. This is why all the properties have both getter and setter methods:

```
type
  TDate = class
  public
    property Year: Integer read GetYear write SetYear;
    property Month: Integer read GetMonth write SetMonth;
    property Day: Integer read GetDay write SetDay;
```

Each of these methods is easily implemented using functions available in the DateUtils unit (more details in Chapter 5). Here is the code for two of them (the others are very similar):

```
function TDate.GetYear: Integer;
begin
  Result := YearOf (fDate);
end;

procedure TDate.SetYear(const Value: Integer);
begin
  fDate := RecodeYear (fDate, Value);
end;
```

The code for this class is available in the DateProp example. The program uses a secondary unit for the definition of the TDate class to enforce encapsulation and creates a single-date object that is stored in a form variable and kept in memory for the lifetime of the main form, which almost corresponds to the entire execution of the program. Using a standard approach, the object is created in the form OnCreate event handler and destroyed in the form OnDestroy event handler. The program form (see Figure 3.2) has three edit boxes and buttons to copy the values of these edit boxes to and from the properties of the date object.

FIGURE 3.2
The DateProp example's form

WARNING   When writing the values, the program uses the SetValue method instead of setting each of the properties. Assigning the month and the day separately can cause you trouble when the month is not valid for the current day. For example, suppose the day is currently January 31, and you want to assign to it February 20. If you assign the month first, this part of the assignment will fail, because February 31 does not exist. If you assign the day first, the problem will arise when doing the reverse assignment. Due to the validity rules for dates, it is better to assign everything at once.

ADVANCED FEATURES OF PROPERTIES

Properties have several advanced features I'll focus on in future chapters. Specifically, in Chapter 5 I'll cover the TPersistent class, RTTI, and streaming. Here is a short summary of these more advanced features:

♦   The write directive of a property can be omitted, making it a *read-only* property. The compiler will issue an error if you try to change the property value. You can also omit the read directive and define a *write-only* property, but that approach doesn't make much sense and is used infrequently.

♦   The Delphi IDE gives special treatment to *design-time* properties, which are declared with the published access specifier and generally displayed in the Object Inspector for the selected component. You'll find more on the published keyword and its effect in Chapter 5.

♦   An alternative is to declare properties, often called *run-time only* properties, with the public access specifier. These properties can be used in program code.

♦   You can define *array-based* properties, which use the typical notation with square brackets to access an element of a list. For example, the Strings property of the TStrings class is an array property, which is used indirectly by all *string list–based* properties, such as the Lines of a list box.

♦   Properties have special directives, including stored and default, which control the *component streaming system* (introduced in Chapter 5).

NOTE   You can usually assign a value to a property or read it, and you can even use properties in expressions, but you cannot always pass a property as a parameter to a procedure or method. This is because a property is not a memory location, so it cannot be used as a var or out parameter; it cannot be passed by reference. This problem arises, for example, when you try to increment a numeric property by passing it to Inc.

Encapsulation and Forms

One of the key ideas of encapsulation is to reduce the number of global variables used by a program. A global variable can be accessed from every portion of a program. For this reason, a change in a global variable affects the whole program. On the other hand, when you change the representation of a class's field, you only need to change the code of some methods of that class and nothing else. Therefore, we can say that information hiding refers to *encapsulating changes*.

Let me clarify this idea with an example. When you have a program with multiple forms, you can make some data available to every form by declaring it as a global variable in the interface portion of the unit of one of the forms:

```
var
   Form1: TForm1;
   nClicks: Integer;
```

This approach works, but the data is connected to the entire program rather than a specific instance of the form. If you create two forms of the same type, they'll share the data. If you want every form of the same type to have its own copy of the data, the only solution is to add it to the form class:

```
type
   TForm1 = class(TForm)
   private
      nClicks: Integer;
   end;
```

ADDING PROPERTIES TO FORMS

The previous class uses public data, so for the sake of encapsulation, you should instead change it to use private data and data-access functions. An even better solution is to add a property to the form. Every time you want to make some information about a form available to other forms, you should use a property, for all the reasons discussed in the section "Encapsulating with Properties." To do so, change the field declaration of the form (in the previous code) by adding the keyword `property` in front of it, and then press Ctrl+Shift+C to activate Code Completion. Delphi will automatically generate all the extra code you need.

The complete code for this form class is available in the FormProp example and illustrated in Figure 3.3. The program can create multi-instances of the form (that is, multiple objects based on the same form class), each with its own click count.

NOTE Adding a property to a form doesn't add to the list of the form properties in the Object Inspector. To obtain this effect you need to write a wizard to register a custom module designer used as base class for the design-time form.

FIGURE 3.3
Two forms of the
FormProp example
at run time

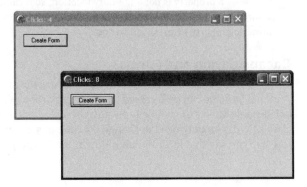

In my opinion, properties should also be used in form classes to encapsulate the access to the components of the form. For example, if you have a main form with a status bar used to display some information (and with the `SimplePanel` property set to True) and you want to modify the text from a secondary form, you might be tempted to write

```
Form1.StatusBar1.SimpleText := 'new text';
```

This is a standard practice in Delphi, but it's not a good one because it doesn't provide any encapsulation of the form structure or components. If you have similar code in many places throughout an application and you later decide to modify the user interface of the form (for example, replacing `StatusBar` with another control or activating multiple panels), you'll have to fix the code in many places. The alternative is to use a method or, even better, a property to hide the specific control. This property can be defined as

```
property StatusText: string read GetText write SetText;
```

with `GetText` and `SetText` methods that read from and write to the `SimpleText` property of the status bar (or the caption of one of its panels). In the program's other forms, you can refer to the form's `StatusText` property; and if the user interface changes, only the setter and getter methods of the property are affected.

NOTE   See Chapter 6 for a detailed discussion of how you can avoid having published form fields for components, which will improve encapsulation. But don't rush there: the description requires a good knowledge of Delphi, and the technique discussed has a few drawbacks.

Constructors

So far, to allocate memory for objects, I've called the `Create` method. This is a *constructor*—a special method that you can apply to a class to allocate memory for an instance of that class and to initialize its state to a known default. The instance is returned by the constructor and can be assigned to a variable for storing the object and using it later. Before the constructor code executes, all the data of the new instance is set to zero. If you want your instance data to start out with specific values, then you need to write a custom constructor to do that.

Use the `constructor` keyword in front of your constructor. Although you can use any name for a constructor, you should stick to the standard name, `Create`. If you use a name other than `Create`, the `Create` constructor of the base `TObject` class will still be available, but a programmer calling this default constructor might bypass the initialization code you've provided because they don't recognize the name.

By defining a `Create` constructor with some parameters, you replace the default definition with a new one and make its use compulsory. For example, after you define

```
type
  TDate = class
  public
    constructor Create (y, m, d: Integer);
```

you'll only be able to call this constructor and not the standard Create:

```
var
  ADay: TDate;
begin
  // Error, does not compile:
  ADay := TDate.Create;
  // OK:
  ADay := TDate.Create (1, 1, 2000);
```

The rules for writing constructors for custom components are different. The reason is that in this case you have to override a virtual constructor. Overloading is particularly relevant for constructors, because you can add multiple constructors to a class and call them all Create; this approach makes the constructors easy to remember and follows a standard path provided by other OOP languages in which constructors must all have the same name. As an example, I've added to the class two separate Create constructors: one with no parameters, which hides the default constructor; and one with initialization values passed as parameters. The constructor with no parameter uses as the default value today's date (as you can see in the complete code of the DataView example):

```
type
  TDate = class
  public
    constructor Create; overload;
    constructor Create (y, m, d: Integer); overload;
```

NOTE   In Delphi for .NET, every constructor must properly initialize its base class, and it should do this first thing because many operations are disallowed until the base class constructor is called, with the relevant exception of accessing its own instance data. The base class initialization is accomplished by calling one of its constructors prefaced with the inherited keyword (see later in the "Overriding and Redefining Methods" section for more info on this keyword). Since every class inherits from TObject, the call to inherited Create becomes more or less compulsory in every constructor. If you make a habit of also doing this in Win32, it won't really harm you, and your code will be easier to port to .NET.

Destructors and the *Free* Method

In the same way that a class can have a custom constructor, it can have a custom destructor—a method declared with the destructor keyword called Destroy. Just as a constructor call allocates memory for the object, a destructor call frees the memory after running through the finalization code of the destructor of the class and its ancestor classes. Destructors are needed only for objects that acquire *external* resources in their constructors or during their lifetime. You can write custom code for a destructor, generally overriding the default Destroy destructor, to let an object execute some cleanup code before it is destroyed.

Destroy is a virtual destructor of the TObject class. You should never define a different destructor, because objects are usually destroyed by calling the Free method, and this method calls the Destroy virtual destructor of the specific class (virtual methods will be discussed later in this chapter).

`Free` is a method of the `TObject` class, inherited by all other classes. The `Free` method basically checks whether the current object (`Self`) is not `nil` before calling the `Destroy` virtual destructor. `Free` doesn't set the object reference variable to `nil` automatically; this is something you should do yourself! The object doesn't know which variables may be referring to it, so it has no way to set them all to `nil`.

Delphi has a `FreeAndNil` procedure you can use to free an object and set its reference to `nil` at the same time. Call `FreeAndNil(Obj1)` instead of writing the following:

```
Obj1.Free;
Obj1 := nil;
```

NOTE   There's more on this topic in the section "Destroying Objects Only Once" later in this chapter.

Delphi's Object Reference Model

In some OOP languages, declaring a variable of a class type creates an instance of that class. Delphi, instead, is based on an *object reference model*. The idea is that a variable of a class type, such as the TheDay variable in the preceding ViewDate example, does not hold the value of the object. Rather, it contains a reference, or a *pointer*, to indicate the memory location where the object has been stored. You can see this structure depicted in Figure 3.4.

The only problem with this approach is that when you declare a variable, you don't create an object in memory (which is inconsistent with all other variables except dynamic arrays and explicit pointer variables, confusing new users of Delphi); you only reserve the memory location for a reference to an object. Object instances must be constructed manually, at least for the objects of the classes you define. Instances of the components you place on a form are constructed automatically by the Delphi library.

You've seen how to create an instance of an object by applying a constructor to its class. Once you have created an object and you've finished using it, you need to dispose of it (to avoid filling up memory you don't need any more, which causes what is known as a *memory leak*). This can be accomplished by calling the `Free` method. As long as you create objects when you need them and free them when you're finished with them, the object reference model works without a glitch. The object reference model has many consequences with regard to assigning objects and managing memory, as you'll see in the next two sections.

NOTE   Obviously this does not apply to .NET development, because the CLR provides automatic garbage collection of unreachable objects, as discussed in Chapters 2 and 4.

FIGURE 3.4
A representation of the structure of an object in memory, with a variable referring to it

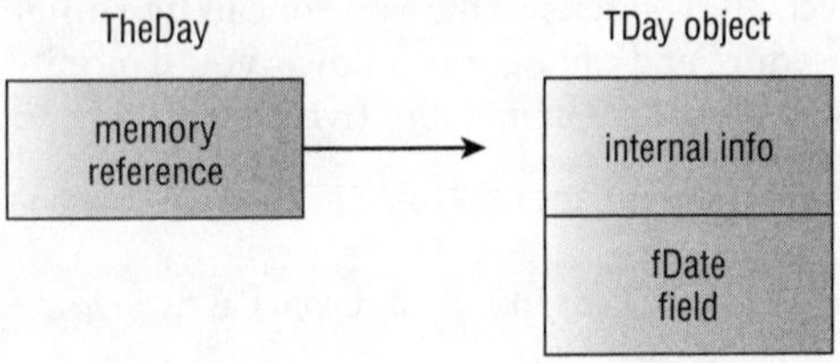

Assigning Objects

If a variable holding an object only contains a reference to the object in memory, what happens if you copy the value of that variable? Suppose you write the BtnTodayClick method of the ViewDate example in the following way:

```
procedure TDateForm.BtnTodayClick(Sender: TObject);
var
  NewDay: TDate;
begin
  NewDay := TDate.Create;
  TheDay := NewDay;
  LabelDate.Caption := TheDay.GetText;
end;
```

This code copies the memory address of the NewDay object to the TheDay variable (as shown in Figure 3.5); it doesn't copy the data of one object into the other. In this particular circumstance, this is not a very good approach—you keep allocating memory for a new object every time the button is clicked, but you never release the memory of the object the TheDay variable was previously pointing to.

This specific issue can be solved by freeing the old object, as in the following code (which is also simplified, without the use of an explicit variable for the newly created object):

```
procedure TDateForm.BtnTodayClick(Sender: TObject);
begin
  TheDay.Free;
  TheDay := TDate.Create;
```

The important thing to keep in mind is that, when you assign an object to another object, Delphi copies the reference to the object in memory to the new object reference. You should not consider this a negative: in many cases, being able to define a variable referring to an existing object can be a plus. For example, you can store the object returned by accessing a property and use it in subsequent statements, as this code snippet indicates:

```
var
  aButton: TButton;
begin
  aButton := aForm.FindComponent ('Button1'); ;
  // now use the aButton reference to the form button
```

The same thing happens if you pass an object as a parameter to a function: you don't create a new object, but you refer to the same one in two different places in the code. For example, by writing this procedure and calling it as follows, you'll modify the Caption property of the Button1 object, not of a copy of its data in memory (which would be totally useless):

```
procedure CaptionPlus (Button: TButton);
begin
  Button.Caption := Button.Caption + '+';
```

```
end;

// call...
CaptionPlus (Button1)
```

This means that the object is being passed by reference without the use of the var keyword and without any other obvious indication of the pass-by-reference semantic, which also confuses new-comers. What if you really want to change the data inside an existing object so that it matches the data of another object? You have to copy each field of the object, which is possible only if they are all public, or you have to provide a specific method to copy the internal data. Some classes of the VCL have an Assign method, which performs this copy operation. To be more precise, most of the VCL classes that inherit from TPersistent but do not inherit from TComponent have the Assign method. Other TComponent-derived classes have this method but raise an exception when it is called.

In the DateCopy example, I've added an Assign method to the TDate class and called it from the Today button, with the following code:

```
procedure TDate.Assign (Source: TDate);
begin
  fDate := Source.fDate;
end;

procedure TDateForm.BtnTodayClick(Sender: TObject);
var
  NewDay: TDate;
begin
  NewDay := TDate.Create;
  TheDay.Assign(NewDay);
  LabelDate.Caption := TheDay.GetText;
  NewDay.Free;
end;
```

FIGURE 3.5

A representation of the operation of assigning an object reference to another object. This is different from copying the actual content of an object to another.

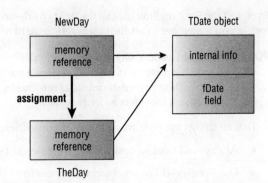

Objects and Memory

Memory management in Delphi is subject to three rules, at least if you allow the system to work in harmony without access violations and without consuming unneeded memory:

♦ Every object must be created before it can be used.

♦ Every object must be destroyed after it has been used.

♦ Every object must be destroyed only once.

Whether you must perform these operations in your code or can let Delphi handle memory management for you depends on the model you choose among the different approaches provided by Delphi. Delphi supports three types of memory management for dynamic elements:

♦ Every time you create an object explicitly in your application code, you should also free it (with the only exception of objects that are used through interface references). If you fail to do so, the memory used by that object won't be released for other objects until the program terminates.

♦ When you create a component, you can specify an owner component, passing the owner to the component constructor. The owner component (often a form) becomes responsible for destroying all the objects it owns. In other words, when you free a form, it frees all the components it owns. So, if you create a component and give it an owner, you don't have to remember to destroy it. This is the standard behavior of the components you create at design time by placing them on a form or data module. However, it is mandatory that you choose an owner that you can guarantee will be destroyed; for example, forms are generally owned by the global Application objects, which is destroyed by the VCL library when the program ends.

♦ When Delphi's RTL allocates memory for strings and dynamic arrays (which are reference types like objects), it will automatically free the memory when the reference goes out of scope. You don't need to free a string: when it becomes unreachable, its memory is released. For more information about strings in Delphi, see the references in Appendix A.

DESTROYING OBJECTS ONLY ONCE

If you call the Free method (or call the Destroy destructor) of an object twice, you get an error. However, if you remember to set the object reference to nil, you can call Free twice with no problem.

NOTE   You might wonder why you can safely call Free if the object reference is nil, but you can't call Destroy. The reason is that Free is a known method at a given memory location, whereas the virtual function Destroy is determined at run time by looking at the type of the object—a very dangerous operation if the object no longer exists.

To sum things up, here are a couple of guidelines:

♦ Always call Free to destroy objects instead of calling the Destroy destructor.

♦ Use FreeAndNil or set object references to nil after calling Free unless the reference is going out of scope immediately afterward.

In general, you can also check whether an object reference is `nil` by using the `Assigned` function. The following two statements are equivalent in most cases:

```
if Assigned (ADate) then ...
if ADate <> nil then ...
```

Notice that these statements test only whether the pointer is not `nil`; they do not check whether it is a valid pointer. If you write the following code, the test will be satisfied, and you'll get an error on the line with the call to the object method:

```
ToDestroy.Free;
if ToDestroy <> nil then
  ToDestroy.DoSomething;
```

It is important to realize that calling `Free` doesn't set the object reference to `nil`.

Inheriting from Existing Types

You'll often need to use a slightly different version of an existing class. For example, you might need to add a new method or slightly change an existing one. If you copy and paste the original class and then modify it (certainly a terrible programming practice, unless there is a specific reason to do so), you'll duplicate your code, bugs, and headaches. Instead, in such a circumstance you should use a key feature of OOP: *inheritance*.

To inherit from an existing class in Delphi, you only need to indicate that class at the beginning of the declaration of the new class. For example, this is done each time you create a new form:

```
type
  TForm1 = class(TForm)
  end;
```

This definition indicates that the TForm1 class inherits all the methods, fields, properties, and events of the TForm class. You can call any public method of the TForm class for an object of the TForm1 type. TForm, in turn, inherits some of its methods from another class, and so on, up to the TObject base class. In other words, TForm1 is a superset of TForm, which in turn extends its base classes.

As an example of inheritance, you can derive a new class from TDate and modify its GetText function. You can find this code in the Dates unit of the NewDate example:

```
type
  TNewDate = class (TDate)
  public
    function GetText: string;
  end;
```

To implement the new version of the GetText function, I used the FormatDateTime function, which uses (among other features) the predefined month names available in Windows; these names depend on the user's regional and language settings. (Many of these regional settings are copied by

Delphi into constants defined in the library, such as LongMonthNames, ShortMonthNames, and many others.) Here is the GetText method, where 'dddddd' stands for the long date format:

```
function TNewDate.GetText: string;
begin
  GetText := FormatDateTime ('dddddd', fDate);
end;
```

TIP Using regional information, the NewDate program automatically adapts itself to different Windows user settings. If you run this program on a computer with regional settings referring to a language other than English, it will automatically show month names in that language. To test this behavior, you just need to change the regional settings. Notice that regional-setting changes immediately affect the running programs.

Once you have defined the new class, you need to use this new data type in the code of the form of the NewDate example, defining the TheDay object of type TNewDate and creating an object of this new class in the FormCreate method. You don't have to change the code with method calls because the inherited methods still work exactly in the same way; however, their effect changes, as the new output demonstrates (see Figure 3.6).

Protected Fields and Encapsulation

The code of the GetText method of the TNewDate class compiles only if it is written in the same unit as the TDate class. In fact, it accesses the fDate private field of the ancestor class. If you want to place the descendant class in a new unit, you must either declare the fDate field as protected or add a protected access method in the ancestor class to read the value of the private field.

Many developers believe that the first solution is always the best because declaring most of the fields as protected will make a class more extensible and will make it easier to write inherited classes. However, this approach violates the idea of encapsulation. In a large hierarchy of classes, changing the definition of some protected fields of the base classes becomes as difficult as changing some global data structures. If 10 derived classes are accessing this data, changing its definition means potentially modifying the code in each of the 10 classes.

In other words, flexibility, extension, and encapsulation often become conflicting objectives. When this happens, you should try to favor encapsulation. If you can do so without sacrificing flexibility, that will be even better. Often this intermediate solution can be obtained by using a virtual method, a topic I'll discuss in detail in the section "Late Binding and Polymorphism." If you choose not to use encapsulation in order to obtain faster coding of the inherited classes, then your design might not follow the object-oriented principles.

FIGURE 3.6

The output of the New-Date program, with the name of the month and day depending on Windows regional settings

ACCESSING PROTECTED DATA OF OTHER CLASSES (OR, THE "PROTECTED HACK")

You've seen that in Delphi, the private and protected members of a class are accessible to any functions or methods that appear *in the same unit as the class*. For example, consider this class (part of the Protection example):

```
type
  TTest = class
  protected
    ProtectedData: Integer;
  end;
```

Once you place this class in its own unit, you won't be able to access its protected portion from other units directly. Accordingly, if you write the following code

```
var
  Obj: TTest;
begin
  Obj := TTest.Create;
  Obj.ProtectedData := 20;  // won't compile
```

the compiler will issue an error message, "Undeclared identifier: 'ProtectedData.'" At this point, you might think there is no way to access the protected data of a class defined in a different unit. However, there is a way. Consider what happens if you create an apparently useless derived class, such as the following:

```
type
  TTestHack = class (TTest);
```

Now, if you make a direct cast of the object to the new class and access the protected data through it, this is how the code will look:

```
var
  Obj: TTest;
begin
  Obj := TTest.Create;
  TTestHack (Obj).ProtectedData := 20; // compiles!
```

This code compiles and works properly, as you can see by running the Protection program. How is it possible for this approach to work? Well, if you think about it, the TTestHack class automatically inherits the protected fields of the TTest base class, and because the TTestHack class is in the same unit as the code that tries to access the data in the inherited fields, the protected data is accessible. As you would expect, if you move the declaration of the TTestHack class to a secondary unit, the program will no longer compile.

Now that I've shown you how to do this, I must warn you that violating the class-protection mechanism this way is likely to cause errors in your program (from accessing data that you really shouldn't), and it runs counter to good OOP technique. However, there are times when using this technique is the best solution, as you'll see by looking at the VCL source code and the code of many Delphi components. Two examples that come to mind are accessing the Text property of the TControl class and the Row and Col positions of the DBGrid control. These two ideas are demonstrated by the TextProp and DBGridCol examples, respectively. (These examples are quite advanced, so I suggest that only programmers with a good background in Delphi programming read them at this point in the text—other readers might come back later.) Although the first example shows a reasonable example of using the typecast *cracker*, the DBGrid example of Row and Col is a counterexample—it illustrates the risks of accessing bits that the class writer chose not to expose. The row and column of a DBGrid do not mean the same thing as they do in a DrawGrid or StringGrid (the base classes). First, DBGrid does not count the fixed cells as actual cells (it distinguishes data cells from decoration), so your row and column indexes will have to be adjusted by whatever decorations are currently in effect on the grid (and those can change on the fly). Second, the DBGrid is a virtual view of the data. When you scroll up in a DBGrid, the data may move underneath it, but the currently selected row might not change.

This technique—declaring a local type only so that you can access protected data members of a class—is often described as a *hack*, and it should be avoided whenever possible. The problem is not accessing protected data of a class in the same unit but declaring a class for the sole purpose of accessing protected data of an existing object of a different class! The danger of this technique is in the hard-coded typecast of an object from a class to a different one.

A variation of it is to use an interposer classes, that is, declare an inherited class with the same name of the class for which you want to access protected properties. With this technique (which is still a hack) you can avoid the type cast. This is demonstrated by the DBGridCol example. Using an interposer class for accessing protected properties and methods is still a hack, but it's a nicer one than using the direct cast.

Inheritance and Type Compatibility

Pascal is a strictly typed language. This means that you cannot, for example, assign an integer value to a Boolean variable, unless you use an explicit typecast. The rule is that two values are type-compatible only if they are of the same data type, or (to be more precise) if their data type refers to a single type definition. To simplify your life, Delphi makes some predefined types assignment compatible: you can assign an Extended to a Double and vice versa, with automatic promotion or demotion (and potential accuracy loss).

WARNING If you redefine the same data type in two different units, the types won't be compatible, even if their names are identical. A program using two equally named types from two different units will be a nightmare to compile and debug.

There is an important exception to this rule in the case of class types. If you declare a class, such as TAnimal, and derive from it a new class, say TDog, you can then assign an object of type TDog to a variable of type TAnimal. You can do so because a dog is an animal! As a general rule, you can use an object of a descendant class any time an object of an ancestor class is expected. However, the reverse is not legal; you cannot use an object of an ancestor class when an object of a descendant class is expected. To simplify the explanation, here it is again in code terms:

```
var
  MyAnimal: TAnimal;
  MyDog: TDog;
begin
  MyAnimal := MyDog;  // This is OK
  MyDog := MyAnimal;  // This is an error!!!
```

Late Binding and Polymorphism

Pascal functions and procedures are usually based on *static* or *early binding*. This means that a method call is resolved by the compiler and linker, which replace the request with a call to the specific memory location where the function or procedure resides (the routine's address). OOP languages allow the use of another form of binding, known as *dynamic* or *late binding*. In this case, the actual address of the method to be called is determined at run time based on the type of the instance used to make the call.

This technique is known as *polymorphism* (a Greek word meaning "many forms"). Polymorphism means you can call a method and apply it to a variable, but which method Delphi actually calls depends on the type of the object the variable relates to. Delphi cannot determine until run time the class of the object the variable refers to because of the type-compatibility rule discussed in the previous section. The advantage of polymorphism is being able to write simpler code, treating disparate object types as if they were the same and getting the correct run-time behavior.

For example, suppose that a class and an inherited class (let's say TAnimal and TDog) both define a method, and this method has late binding. You can apply this method to a generic variable, such as MyAnimal, which at run time can refer either to an object of class TAnimal or to an object of class TDog. The actual method to call is determined at run time, depending on the class of the current object.

The PolyAnimals example demonstrates this technique. The TAnimal and TDog classes have a Voice method that outputs the sound made by the selected animal, both as text and as sound (using a call to the PlaySound API function defined in the MMSystem unit). The Voice method is defined as virtual in the TAnimal class and is later overridden, when you define the TDog class, by the use of the virtual and override keywords:

```
type
  TAnimal = class
  public
    function Voice: string; virtual;

  TDog = class (TAnimal)
  public
    function Voice: string; override;
```

The effect of the call MyAnimal.Voice depends. If the MyAnimal variable currently refers to an object of the TAnimal class, it will call the method TAnimal.Voice. If it refers to an object of the TDog class, it will instead call the method TDog.Voice. This happens only because the function is virtual (you can experiment by removing this keyword and the override keyword in the TDog class and recompiling).

The call to MyAnimal.Voice will work for an object that is an instance of any descendant of the TAnimal class, even classes that are defined in other units—or that haven't been written yet! The compiler doesn't need to know about all the descendants in order to make the call compatible with them; only the ancestor class is needed. In other words, this call to MyAnimal.Voice is compatible with all future TAnimal inherited classes.

NOTE   This is the key technical reason why object-oriented programming languages favor reusability. You can write code that uses classes within a hierarchy without any knowledge of the specific classes that are part of that hierarchy. In other words, the hierarchy—and the program—is still extensible, even when you've written thousands of lines of code using it. Of course, there is one condition: the ancestor classes of the hierarchy need to be designed very carefully.

In Figure 3.7, you can see an example of the output of the PolyAnimals program. By running it, you'll also hear the corresponding sounds produced by the PlaySound API call.

FIGURE 3.7
The output of the
PolyAnimals example

Overriding and Redefining Methods

As you have just seen, to override a late-bound method in a descendant class, you need to use the override keyword. Note that this can take place only if the method was defined as virtual (or dynamic) in the ancestor class. Otherwise, if it is a static method, there is no way to activate late binding, other than to change the code of the ancestor class.

The rules are simple: a method defined as static remains static in every inherited class, unless you hide it with a new virtual method having the same name. A method defined as virtual remains late-bound in every inherited class (unless you hide it with a static method, which is quite a foolish thing to do). There is no way to change this behavior because of the way the compiler generates different code for late-bound methods.

To redefine a static method, you add a method to an inherited class having the same parameters or different parameters from the original one, without any further specifications. To override a virtual method, you must specify the same parameters and use the override keyword:

```
type
  TMyClass = class
    procedure One; virtual;
    procedure Two; {static method}
  end;

  TMyDerivedClass = class (MyClass)
```

```
  procedure One; override;
  procedure Two;
end;
```

Typically, you can override a method two ways: replace the method of the ancestor class with a new version, or add more code to the existing method. This can be accomplished by using the `inherited` keyword to call the same method of the ancestor class. For example, you can write:

```
procedure TMyDerivedClass.One;
begin
  // new code
  ...
  // call inherited procedure MyClass.One
  inherited One;
end;
```

When you override an existing virtual method of a base class, you must use the same parameters. When you introduce a new version of a static method in a descendant class, you can declare it with the parameters you want. In fact, this will be a new method unrelated to the ancestor method of the same name—they only happen to use the same name. Here is an example:

```
type
  TMyClass = class
    procedure One;
  end;

  TMyDerivedClass = class (TMyClass)
    procedure One (S: string);
  end;
```

NOTE   Using the class definitions just given, when you create an object of the TMyDerivedClass class, you can call its One method with the string parameter but not with the parameter-less version defined in the base class. If this is what you need to do, it can be accomplished by marking the redeclared method (the one in the derived class) with the `overload` keyword. If the method has different parameters than the version in the base class, it becomes effectively an overloaded method; otherwise it replaces the base class method. Notice that the method doesn't need to be marked with `overload` in the base class. However, if the method in the base class is virtual, the compiler issues the warning "Method 'One' hides virtual method of base type 'TMyClass.'" To avoid this message and to instruct the compiler more precisely on your intentions, you can use the `reintroduce` directive. If you are interested in this advanced topic, you can find this code in the Reintr example and experiment with it further.

Virtual versus Dynamic Methods

In Delphi, there are two ways to activate late binding. You can declare the method as virtual, as you have seen, or declare it as dynamic. The syntax of the `virtual` and `dynamic` keywords is exactly the same, and the result of their use is also the same. What is different is the internal mechanism used by the compiler to implement late binding.

Virtual methods are based on a *virtual method table* (VMT, also known as a *vtable*), which is an array of method addresses. For a call to a virtual method, the compiler generates code to jump to an address stored in the *n*th slot in the object's virtual method table. VMTs allow fast execution of the method calls, but they require an entry for each virtual method for each descendant class, even if the method is not overridden in the inherited class.

Dynamic method calls, on the other hand, are dispatched using a unique number indicating the method, whose address is stored in a class only if the class defines or overrides it. The search for the corresponding function is generally slower than the one-step table lookup for virtual methods. The advantage is that dynamic method entries only propagate in descendants when the descendants override the method.

Message Handlers

A late-bound method can be used to handle a Windows message, too, although the technique is somewhat different. For this purpose Delphi provides yet another directive, `message`, to define message-handling methods, which must be procedures with a single var parameter. The `message` directive is followed by the number of the Windows message the method wants to handle.

For example, the following code allows you to handle a user-defined message, with the numeric value indicated by the `wm_App` Windows constant:

```
type
  TForm1 = class(TForm)
    ...
    procedure WMApp (var Msg: TMessage);
      message wm_App;
  end;
```

NOTE In Win16 days, custom messages started at `wm_User`. Later Microsoft reserved some of these values for the operating system itself. For this reason in Win32 the advice is to start custom messages from `wm_App`.

The name of the procedure and the type of the parameters are up to you, although there are several predefined record types for the various Windows messages (in the `Messages` or `Borland.Vcl` `.Messages` unit). You could later generate this message, invoking the corresponding method, by writing:

```
PostMessage (Form1.Handle, wm_App, 0, 0);
```

This technique can be extremely useful for veteran Windows programmers who know all about Windows messages and API functions. You can also dispatch a message immediately by calling the SendMessage API or the VCL `Perform` method.

Abstract Methods

The `abstract` keyword is used to declare methods that will be defined only in inherited classes of the current class. The `abstract` directive fully defines the method; it is not a forward declaration. If you try to provide a definition for the method, the compiler will complain. Classes having one or more abstract methods are generally called abstract classes. Delphi 2005 allows you also to add the abstract directive to a class as a whole. In the .NET compiler this turns the class into an abstract class, even if it has no abstract method, while in the Win32 compiler it seems to have no effect at all.

In Delphi's Win32 compiler, you can create instances of abstract classes. However, when you try to do so, Delphi issues the warning message "Constructing instance of <class name> containing abstract method <methodname>." (The method name part has been added in Delphi 2005.) If you happen to call an abstract method at run time, Delphi will raise an exception, as demonstrated by the AbstractAnimals example (an extension of the PolyAnimals example), which uses the following class:

```
type
  TAnimal = class
  public
    function Voice: string; virtual; abstract;
```

NOTE   Most other OOP languages use a stricter approach: you cannot generally create instances of classes containing abstract methods. The same happens in Delphi for .NET, as you'll see in the next chapter in an example called AbstractAnimalsNet.

You might wonder why you would want to use abstract methods. The reason lies in the use of polymorphism. If class TAnimal has the virtual method Voice, every inherited class *can* redefine it. If it has the abstract method Voice, every inherited class *must* redefine it.

In early versions of Delphi, if a method overriding an abstract method called inherited, the result was in an abstract method call. Since Delphi 6, the compiler has been enhanced to notice the presence of the abstract method and skip the inherited call. This means you can safely use inherited in every overridden method, unless you specifically want to disable executing some code of the base class.

Sealed Classes and Final Methods

In the .NET Framework, as in the Java architecture, there is a way to prevent further inheritance from a class completely (for the entire class) or partially for some of its virtual methods. *Sealed classes* are classes you cannot further inherit from, while final methods are virtual methods you cannot further override in inherited classes.

These features are also available in Delphi 2005 on the Win32 compiler. This is the syntax of a sealed class (taken from the SealedAndFinal example):

```
type
  TDeriv1 = class sealed (TBase)
    procedure A; override;
  end;
```

Trying to inherit form, it causes the error, "Cannot extend sealed class TDeriv1." This is the syntax of a final method:

```
type
  TDeriv1 = class (TBase)
    procedure A; override; final;
  end;
```

Inheriting from this class and overriding the A method causes the compiler error, "Cannot override a final method."

Now, you might ask yourself what the rationale is behind these related concepts. It seems that the more relevant issue is protection. You might want to disallow others from inheriting from your classes in general, and in particular you'll want to disallow others from inheriting from security/ cryptography classes. In my opinion these features should be used sparingly in a library to let developers inherit from the available classes as much as possible. However, looking at Microsoft's class library for .NET (the FCL), it seems there are too many sealed classes and too many virtual methods shortcutted with final.

By looking at the .NET literature you'll see references to the fact that a virtual final method can be made very efficient by the system, as it basically boils down to a (slightly faster) nonvirtual call. This is the reason behind the same features offered by the Java language. However, in Java this efficiency consideration makes perfect sense as all methods are virtual by default. In C# or Delphi, you can instead write plain (nonvirtual) methods, which seems a better idea than declaring a virtual method and disabling its key capability for performance reasons.

In any case, when you distribute .NET assemblies you make many classes available to other developers, which might be a good reason for limiting their use. In the Win32 compiler most of the reasons for using sealed classes and final methods don't apply, but still, having this feature available in some special cases might be handy (though I've never found a very good example!).

Nested Types and Nested Constants

Delphi traditionally allows you to declare new classes in the interface section of a unit, allowing other units of the program to reference them, or in the implementation section, where they are accessible only from methods of other classes of the same unit or from global routines implemented in that unit after the class definition. Delphi 2005 adds another possibility, namely the declaration of a class (or any other type) within another class. As any other member of the class, the nested class and other nested types can have a restricted visibility (say, private or protected). Relevant examples of nested types include enumerations used by the same class and support classes.

A related syntax allows you to define a nested constant, a constant value associated with the class (again usable only internally if private or from the rest of the program if public). As an example, consider the following declaration of a nested class (extracted form the NestedClass unit of the Nested-Types demo):

```
type
  TOne = class
  private
    someData: Integer;
  public
    // nested constant
    const foo = 12;
    // nested type
    type TInside = class
    public
      procedure InsideHello;
    private
      Msg: string;
    end;
  public
```

```
    procedure Hello;
  end;

procedureTOne.Hello;
var
  ins: TInside;
begin
  ins := TInside.Create;
  ins.InsideHello;
  writeln ('constant is ' + IntToStr (foo));
end;

procedureTOne.TInside.InsideHello;
begin
    someData := 22;
    writeln ('internal call');
end;
```

The nested class can be used directly within the class (as demonstrated in the listing) or outside the class (if it is declared in the public section), but with the fully qualified name TOne.TInside. The *full name* of the class is used also in the definition of the method of the nested class, in this case TOne.TInside. This method of the nested class has full access to the data of the hosting class, including its private data. The hosting class can have a field of the nested class type right after you've declared the nested class (see the complete code of the NestedClass demo for an example).

How would you benefit from using a nested class in the Delphi language? The concept is commonly used in Java to implement event handlers and makes sense in C# where you cannot have a class hidden inside a unit. In Delphi nested classes are the only way you can have a field of the type of another private class (or inner class) without adding it to the global name space and making it available.

If the internal class is used only by a method, you can obtain the same effect by declaring the class within the implementation portion of the unit. But if the inner class is referenced in the interface section of the unit (for example because it is used for a field or a parameter), it must be declared in the same interface section and will end up being visible. The trick of declaring such a field of a generic or base type and then casting it to the specific (private) type is much less clean than the use of a nested class. Anyway, it is important to have this feature in the language for compatibility with the .NET world.

NOTE Later in this chapter there is a practical example in which nested classes come in handy, namely the implementation of a custom iterator for a for..in loop.

Type-Safe Down-Casting

The Delphi type-compatibility rule for descendant classes allows you to use a descendant class where an ancestor class is expected. As I mentioned earlier, the reverse is not possible. Now, suppose the TDog class has an Eat method, which is not present in the TAnimal class. If the variable MyAnimal refers to a dog, it should be possible to call the function. But if you try and the variable is referring to another class, the compiler will issue an error because the type of MyAnimal hasn't got an Eat method. By making an explicit typecast, you could cause a nasty run-time error (or worse, a subtle memory overwrite problem) because the compiler cannot determine whether the type of the object is correct and the methods you are calling actually exist.

To solve the problem, you can use techniques based on *run-time type information* (RTTI, for short). Essentially, because each object "knows" its type and its parent class, you can ask for this information with the `is` operator (or in some peculiar cases using the `InheritsFrom` method of `TObject`). The parameters of the `is` operator are an object and a class type, and the return value is a Boolean:

```
if MyAnimal is TDog then ...
```

The `is` expression evaluates as True only if the `MyAnimal` object is currently referring to an object of class `TDog` or a type descendant from `TDog`. This means that if you test whether a `TDog` object is of type `TAnimal`, the test will succeed. In other words, this expression evaluates as True if you can safely assign the object (`MyAnimal`) to a variable of the data type (`TDog`).

Now that you know for sure that the animal is a dog, you can make a safe typecast (or type conversion). You can accomplish this direct cast by writing the following code:

```
var
  MyDog: TDog;
begin
  if MyAnimal is TDog then
  begin
    MyDog := TDog (MyAnimal);
    Text := MyDog.Eat;
  end;
```

This same operation can be accomplished directly by the second RTTI operator, `as`, which converts the object only if the requested class is compatible with the actual one. The parameters of the `as` operator are an object and a class type, and the result is an object converted to the new class type. You can write the following snippet:

```
MyDog := MyAnimal as TDog;
Text := MyDog.Eat;
```

If you only want to call the `Eat` function, you might also use an even shorter notation:

```
(MyAnimal as TDog).Eat;
```

The result of this expression is an object of the `TDog` class data type, so you can apply to it any method of that class. The difference between the traditional cast and the use of the `as` cast is that the second approach raises an exception if the object type is incompatible with the type you are trying to cast it to. The exception raised is `EInvalidCast` (exceptions are described at the end of this chapter).

To avoid this exception, use the `is` operator and, if it succeeds, make a plain typecast (in fact, there is no reason to use `is` and `as` in sequence, doing the type check twice):

```
if MyAnimal is TDog then
  TDog(MyAnimal).Eat;
```

NOTE In .NET you cannot perform a hard cast from a type to another. Every cast is checked at run time for safety reasons. In Delphi for .NET the `as` cast keeps working as you are used to, while the `direct` cast returns `nil` in case of a type mismatch. More details in the next chapter.

Both RTTI operators are very useful in Delphi because you often want to write generic code that can be used with several components of the same type or even of different types. When a component is passed as a parameter to an event-response method, a generic data type is used (TObject), so you often need to cast it back to the original component type:

```
procedure TForm1.Button1Click(Sender: TObject);
begin
  if Sender is TButton then
    ...
end;
```

This is a common technique in Delphi, and I'll use it in examples throughout the book. The two RTTI operators, is and as, are extremely powerful, and you might be tempted to consider them as standard programming constructs. Although they are indeed powerful, you should probably limit their use to special cases. When you need to solve a complex problem involving several classes, try using polymorphism first. Only in special cases, where polymorphism alone cannot be applied, should you try using the RTTI operators to complement it. *Do not use RTTI instead of polymorphism.* This is bad programming practice, and it results in slower programs. RTTI has a negative impact on performance because it must walk the hierarchy of classes to see whether the typecast is correct. As you have seen, virtual method calls require just a memory lookup, which is much faster.

NOTE   Run-time type information (RTTI) involves more than the is and as operators. You can access detailed class and type information at run time, particularly for published properties, events, and methods. You'll find more on this topic in Chapter 5.

Using Interfaces

When you define an abstract class to represent the base class of a hierarchy, you can come to a point at which the abstract class is so abstract that it only lists a series of virtual functions without providing any implementation. This kind of *purely abstract class* can also be defined using a specific technique: an interface. For this reason, we refer to these classes as *interfaces*.

Technically, an interface is not a class, although it may resemble one. Interfaces are not classes because they are considered a totally separate element with distinctive features:

◆ Interface type objects in Delphi for Win32 are reference-counted and automatically destroyed when there are no more references to the object. This mechanism is similar to the way Delphi for Win32 manages long strings and makes memory management almost automatic.

◆ A class can inherit from a single ancestor class, but it can implement multiple interfaces.

◆ Just as all classes descend from TObject, all interfaces descend from IInterface, forming a totally separate hierarchy.

NOTE   In early versions of Delphi the base interface class was IUnknown, but Delphi 6 introduced a new name for it—IInterface—to mark even more clearly the fact that this language feature is separate from Microsoft's COM (which uses IUnknown as its base interface).

It is important to note that interfaces support a slightly different OOP model than classes. Interfaces provide a less restricted implementation of polymorphism. Object reference polymorphism is based around a specific branch of a hierarchy. Interface polymorphism works across an entire hierarchy. Certainly, interfaces favor encapsulation and provide a looser connection between classes than inheritance. Notice that the most recent OOP languages, from Java to C#, have the notion of interfaces.

Here is the syntax of the declaration of an interface (which, by convention, starts with the letter *I*):

```
type
  ICanFly = interface
    ['{EAD9C4B4-E1C5-4CF4-9FA0-3B812C880A21}']
    function Fly: string;
  end;
```

This interface has a GUID (Globally Unique Identifier) called Interface Identifier (IID)—a numeric ID following its declaration and based on Windows conventions. You can generate these identifiers by pressing Ctrl+Shift+G in the Delphi editor.

NOTE   Although you can compile and use an interface without specifying a GUID for it, you'll generally want to generate the GUID because it is required to perform interface querying or dynamic as typecasts using that interface type. The whole point of interfaces is (usually) to take advantage of greatly extended type flexibility at run time; so, compared with class types, interfaces without GUIDs are not very useful. Notice though, that in Delphi for .NET the interface GUIDs are not needed at all but can be kept for source compatibility reasons.

Once you've declared an interface, you can define a class to implement it:

```
type
  TAirplane = class (TInterfacedObject, ICanFly)
    function Fly: string;
  end;
```

The RTL already provides a few base classes to implement the basic behavior required by the IInterface interface. For internal objects, use the TInterfacedObject class I've used in this code.

You can implement interface methods with static methods (as in the previous code) or with virtual methods. You can override virtual methods in inherited classes by using the override directive. If you don't use virtual methods, you can still provide a new implementation in an inherited class by redeclaring the interface type in the inherited class, rebinding the interface methods to new versions of the static methods. At first sight, using virtual methods to implement interfaces seems to allow for smoother coding in inherited classes, but both approaches are equally powerful and flexible. However, the use of virtual methods affects code size and memory.

NOTE   The compiler has to generate stub routines to fix up the interface call entry points to the matching method of the implementing class and to adjust the Self pointer. The interface method stubs for static methods have to adjust Self and jump to the real method in the class. The interface method stubs for virtual methods are much more complicated, requiring about four times more code (20 to 30 bytes) in each stub than the static case. Also, adding more virtual methods to the implementing class just bloats the virtual method table (VMT) that much more in the implementing class and all its descendants. An interface already has its own VMT, and redeclaring an interface in descendants to rebind the interface to new methods in the descendant is just as polymorphic as using virtual methods, but it's much smaller in code size.

Now that you have defined an implementation of the interface, you can write some code to use an object of this class, through an interface-type variable:

```
var
  Flyer1: ICanFly;
begin
  Flyer1 := TAirplane.Create;
  Flyer1.Fly;
end;
```

As soon as you assign an object to an interface-type variable, Delphi automatically checks to see whether the object implements that interface, using the as operator. You can explicitly express this operation as follows:

```
Flyer1 := TAirplane.Create as ICanFly;
```

NOTE   The compiler generates different code for the as operator when used with interfaces or with classes. With classes, the compiler introduces run-time checks to verify that the object is effectively "type-compatible" with the given class. With interfaces, the compiler sees at compile time that it can extract the necessary interface from the available class type, so it does. This operation is like a "compile-time as," not something that exists at run time.

Whether you use the direct assignment or the as statement, Delphi does one extra thing: it calls the _AddRef method of the object (defined by IInterface). The standard implementation of this method, like the one provided by TInterfacedObject, is to increase the object's reference count. At the same time, as soon as the Flyer1 variable goes out of scope, Delphi calls the _Release method (again part of IInterface). The TInterfacedObject's implementation of _Release decreases the reference count, checks whether the reference count is zero, and, if necessary, destroys the object. For this reason, the previous example doesn't include any code to free the object you've created.

In other words, in Delphi, objects referenced by interface variables are reference-counted, and they are automatically de-allocated when no interface variable refers to them any more.

WARNING   When using interface-based objects, you should generally access them only with object references or only with interface references. Mixing the two approaches breaks the reference counting scheme provided by Delphi and can cause memory errors that are extremely difficult to track. In practice, if you've decided to use interfaces, you should probably use exclusively interface-based variables. If you want to be able to mix them, disable the reference counting by writing your own base class instead of using TInterfacedObject.

Working with Exceptions

Another key feature of Delphi is its support for *exceptions*. Exceptions make programs more robust by providing a standard way for notifying and handling errors and unexpected conditions. Exceptions make programs easier to write, read, and debug because they allow you to separate the error-handling code from your normal code, instead of intertwining the two. Enforcing a logical split between code and error handling and branching to the error handler automatically makes the actual logic cleaner and clearer. You end up writing code that is more compact and less cluttered by maintenance chores unrelated to the actual programming objective.

At run time, Delphi libraries raise exceptions when something goes wrong (in the run-time code, in a component, or in the operating system). From the point in the code at which it is raised, the exception is passed to its calling code, and so on. Ultimately, if no part of your code handles the exception, the VCL handles it by displaying a standard error message and then trying to continue the program by handling the next system message or user request.

The whole mechanism is based on four keywords:

try   Delimits the beginning of a protected block of code.

except   Delimits the end of a protected block of code and introduces the exception-handling statements.

finally   Specifies blocks of code that must always be executed, even when exceptions occur. This block is generally used to perform cleanup operations that should always be executed, such as closing files or database tables, freeing objects, and releasing memory and other resources acquired in the same program block.

raise   Generates an exception. Most exceptions you'll encounter in your Delphi programming will be generated by the system, but you can also raise exceptions in your own code when it discovers invalid or inconsistent data at run time. The `raise` keyword can also be used inside a handler to *re-raise* an exception; that is, to propagate it to the next handler.

TIP   Exception handling is no substitute for proper control flow within a program. Keep using `if` statements to test user input and other foreseeable error conditions. You should use exceptions only for abnormal or unexpected situations.

Program Flow and the *finally* Block

The power of exceptions in Delphi relates to the fact that they are "passed" from a routine or method to the caller, up to a global handler (if the program provides one, as Delphi applications generally do), instead of following the standard execution path of the program. The real problem you might have is not how to stop an exception but how to execute code even if an exception is raised.

Consider this code, which performs some time-consuming operations and uses the hourglass cursor to show the user that it's doing something:

```
Screen.Cursor := crHourglass;
// long algorithm...
Screen.Cursor := crDefault;
```

In case there is an error in the algorithm (as I've included on purpose in the TryFinally example's event handlers), the program will break, but it won't reset the default cursor. This is what a `try/finally` block is for:

```
Screen.Cursor := crHourglass;
try
  // long algorithm...
finally
  Screen.Cursor := crDefault;
end;
```

When the program executes this function, it always resets the cursor, regardless of whether an exception (of any sort) occurs.

This code doesn't handle the exception; it merely makes the program robust in case an exception is raised. A try block can be followed by either an except or a finally statement, but not by both of them at the same time; so, if you want to also handle the exception, the typical solution is to use two nested try blocks. You associate the internal block with a finally statement and the external block with an except statement, or vice versa as the situation requires. Here is the skeleton of the code for the third button in the TryFinally example:

```
Screen.Cursor := crHourglass;
try
  try
    // long algorithm...
  finally
    Screen.Cursor := crDefault;
  end;
except
  on E: EDivByZero do ...
end;
```

Every time you have some finalization code at the end of a method, you should place the code in a finally block. You should always, invariably, and continuously (how can I stress this more?) protect your code with finally statements to avoid resource or memory leaks in case an exception is raised.

TIP   Handling the exception is generally much less important than using finally blocks, because Delphi can survive most exceptions. Too many exception-handling blocks in your code probably indicate errors in the program flow and possibly a misunderstanding of the role of exceptions in the language. In the examples in the rest of the book, you'll see many try/finally blocks, a few raise statements, and almost no try/except blocks.

Exception Classes

In the exception-handling statements shown earlier, you caught the EDivByZero exception, which is defined by Delphi's RTL. Other such exceptions refer to run-time problems (such as a wrong dynamic cast), Windows resource problems (such as out-of-memory errors), or component errors (such as a wrong index). Programmers can also define their own exceptions; you can create a new inherited class of the default exception class or one of its inherited classes:

```
type
  EArrayFull = class (Exception);
```

When you add a new element to an array that is already full (probably because of an error in the logic of the program), you can raise the corresponding exception by creating an object of this class:

```
if MyArray.Full then
  raise EArrayFull.Create ('Array full');
```

This `Create` constructor (inherited from the `Exception` class) has a string parameter to describe the exception to the user. You don't need to worry about destroying the object you have created for the exception, because it will be deleted automatically by the exception-handler mechanism.

The code presented in the previous excerpts is part of a sample program called Exception1. Some of the routines have been slightly modified, as in the following `DivideTwicePlusOne` function:

```
function DivideTwicePlusOne (A, B: Integer): Integer;
begin
  try
    // error if B equals 0
    Result := A div B;
    // do something else... skip if exception is raised
    Result := Result div B;
    Result := Result + 1;
  except
    on EDivByZero do
    begin
      Result := 0;
      MessageDlg ('Divide by zero corrected.', mtError, [mbOK], 0);
    end;
    on E: Exception do
    begin
      Result := 0;
      MessageDlg (E.Message, mtError, [mbOK], 0);
    end;
  end; // end except
end;
```

In the Exception1 code, there are two different exception handlers after the same `try` block. You can have any number of these handlers, which are evaluated in sequence.

Using a hierarchy of exceptions, a handler is also called for the inherited classes of the type it refers to, as any procedure will do. For this reason, you need to place the broader handlers (the handlers of the ancestor `Exception` classes) at the end. But keep in mind that using a handler for every exception, such as the previous one, is not usually a good choice. It is better to leave unknown exceptions to Delphi. The default exception handler in the VCL displays the error message of the exception class in a message box and then resumes normal program operation. You can modify the normal exception handler with the `Application.OnException` event or the `OnException` event of the Application-Events component, as demonstrated in the ErrorLog example in the next section.

Another important element of the previous code is the use of the exception object in the handler (see `on E: Exception do`). The reference E of class `Exception` refers to the exception object passed by the `raise` statement. When you work with exceptions, remember this rule: You raise an exception by creating an object and handle it by indicating its type. This has an important benefit because, as you have seen, when you handle a type of exception, you are really handling exceptions of the type you specify as well as any descendant type.

DEBUGGING AND EXCEPTIONS

When you start a program from the Delphi environment (for example, by pressing the F9 key), you'll generally run it within the debugger. You can also run it independently of the debugger using Ctrl+Shift+F9. When you run a program in the debugger and an exception is encountered, the debugger will suspend the program by default. This result is normally what you want, of course, because you'll know where the exception took place, and you can see the call of the handler step by step. You can also use Delphi's Stack Trace feature to see the sequence of function and method calls that caused the program to raise an exception.

In the case of the Exception1 test program, however, this behavior will confuse a programmer not well aware of how Delphi's debugger works. Even if the code is prepared to properly handle the exception, the debugger will stop the program execution at the source code line closest to where the exception was raised. Then, moving step by step through the code, you can see how it is handled.

If you just want to let the program run when the exception is properly handled, without stopping in the debugger, you can disable that specific exception, either manually in the Language Exceptions page of the Debugger section of the Environment Options dialog box or by using the proper check box displayed in Delphi 2005 when an exception is encountered:

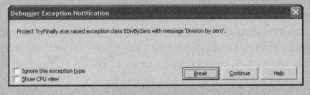

Logging Errors

Most of the time, you don't know which operation will raise an exception, and you cannot (and should not) wrap each and every piece of code in a try/except block. The general approach is to let Delphi handle all the exceptions and eventually pass them to you by handling the OnException event of the global Application object. You can do so rather easily with the ApplicationEvents component.

In the ErrorLog example, I've added to the main form an instance of the ApplicationEvents component and written a handler for its OnException event:

```
procedure TFormLog.LogException(Sender: TObject; E: Exception);
var
  Filename: string;
  LogFile: TextFile;
begin
  // prepares log file
  Filename := ChangeFileExt (Application.Exename, '.log');
  AssignFile (LogFile, Filename);
  if FileExists (FileName) then
    Append (LogFile) // open existing file
```

```
else
  Rewrite (LogFile); // create a new one
try
  // write to the file and show error
  Writeln (LogFile, DateTimeToStr (Now) + ':' + E.Message);
  if not CheckBoxSilent.Checked then
    Application.ShowException (E);
finally
  // close the file
  CloseFile (LogFile);
  end;
end;
```

NOTE   The ErrorLog example uses the text file support provided by the traditional Turbo Pascal Text-File data type. You can assign a text file variable to an actual file and then read or write it. You can find more on TextFile operations in the free material covered in Appendix A.

In the global exceptions handler, you can write to the log, for example, the date and time of the event and also decide whether to show the exception as Delphi usually does (executing the ShowException method of the TApplication class). By default, Delphi executes ShowException only if no OnException handler is installed. In Figure 3.8, you can see the ErrorLog program running and a sample exceptions log open in the Delphi IDE.

FIGURE 3.8

The ErrorLog example and the log it produces

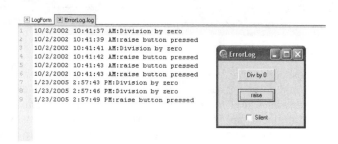

Exceptions and Constructors

There is a slightly more advanced issue surrounding exceptions, namely what happens when an exception is raised within the constructor of an object. Not all Delphi programmers know that in such a circumstance the destructor of that object (if available) will be called.

This is relevant to know, because it implies that a destructor might be called for a partially initialized object. Taking for granted that internal objects exist in a destructor because they are created in the constructor might get you in some dangerous situations in case of actual errors (that is, raising another exception before the first one is handled).

This also implies that the proper sequence for a `try-finally` should be (as you'll often see in code):

```
AnObject := aClass.Create;
try
  // use the object...
finally
  AnObject.Free;
end;
```

In fact, if the constructor fails, the object destructor will be called anyway, while if another method call fails within the `try` block, you destroy the object in the `finally` section.

NOTE In Delphi 2005, something similar also happens for the special `AfterDestruction` and `BeforeConstruction` methods, a pseudo-constructor and destructor introduced many years back for C++Builder compatibility (but seldom used in Delphi). Similarly to what happens with the plain constructor and destructor, if an exception is raised in the `AfterDestruction`, `BeforeConstruction` is called (and also the plain destructor, of course). This behavior fixes a long-standing asymmetry that could have easily misled developers.

Class References

The next language feature I'll discuss in this chapter is the use of *class references*, which implies the idea of manipulating classes themselves within your code. The first point to keep in mind is that a class reference isn't an object; it is a reference to a class type. A class reference type determines the type of a class reference variable. Sound confusing? A few lines of code will make this concept a little clearer.

Suppose you have defined the class `TMyClass`. You can now define a new class reference type, related to that class:

```
type
  TMyClassRef = class of TMyClass;
```

Now you can declare variables of both types. The first variable refers to an object, the second to a class:

```
var
  AnObject: TMyClass;
  AClassRef: TMyClassRef;
begin
  AClassRef := TMyClass;
  AnObject := TMyClass.Create;
```

You may wonder what class references are used for. In general, class references allow you to manipulate a class data type at run time. You can use a class reference in any expression where the use of a data type is legal. There are not many such expressions, but the few cases are interesting, like the creation of an object. You can rewrite the last line of the previous code as follows:

```
AnObject := AClassRef.Create;
```

This time, you apply the `Create` constructor to the class reference instead of to an actual class; you use a class reference to create an object of that class.

Class reference types wouldn't be as useful if they didn't support the same type-compatibility rule that applies to class types. When you declare a class reference variable, such as `MyClassRef`, you can then assign to it that specific class and any inherited class. So if `TMyNewClass` is an inherited class of `TMyClass` my class, you can also write:

```
AClassRef := TMyNewClass;
```

Delphi declares a lot of class references in the run-time library and the VCL, such as the following:

```
TClass = class of TObject;
TComponentClass = class of TComponent;
TFormClass = class of TForm;
```

In particular, the `TClass` class reference type can be used to store a reference to any class you write in Delphi, because every class is ultimately derived from `TObject`. The `TFormClass` reference is used in the source code of most Delphi projects. The `CreateForm` method of the `Application` object requires as a parameter the class of the form to create:

```
Application.CreateForm(TForm1, Form1);
```

The first parameter is a class reference; the second is a variable that stores a reference to the created object instance.

When you have a class reference, you can apply to it the class methods of the related class. Considering that each class inherits from `TObject`, you can apply to each class reference some of the methods of `TObject`, as you'll see in Chapter 5.

NOTE   Although class references are not part of the .NET CLS specification, they can be used in Delphi for .NET almost as in traditional Delphi for Win32. The code behind the scenes changes considerably, though. Again, more on this .NET issue in the next chapter.

Creating Components Using Class References

What is the *practical* use of class references in Delphi? Being able to manipulate a data type at run time is a fundamental element of the Delphi environment. When you add a new component to a form by selecting it from the Component Palette, you select a data type and create an object of that data type. (Actually, that is what Delphi does for you behind the scenes.) In other words, class references give you polymorphism for object construction.

To give you a better idea of how class references work, I've built an example named ClassRef. The form displayed by this example has three radio buttons, placed inside a panel in the upper portion of the form. When you select one of these radio buttons and click the form, you'll be able to create new components of the three types indicated by the button labels: radio buttons, push buttons, and edit boxes.

To make this program run properly, you need to change the names of the three components. The form must also have a class reference field, declared as `ClassRef: TControlClass`. It stores a new data type every time the user clicks one of the three radio buttons, with assignments like `ClassRef :=` `TEdit`. The interesting part of the code is executed when the user clicks the form. Again, I've chosen the `OnMouseDown` event of the form to hold the position of the mouse click:

```
procedure TForm1.FormMouseDown(Sender: TObject; Button: TMouseButton;
  Shift: TShiftState; X, Y: Integer);
var
  NewCtrl: TControl;
  MyName: String;
begin
  // create the control
  NewCtrl := ClassRef.Create (Self);
  // set the position
  NewCtrl.Left := X;
  NewCtrl.Top := Y;
  // compute the unique name (and caption)
  Inc (Counter);
  MyName := ClassRef.ClassName + IntToStr (Counter);
  Delete (MyName, 1, 1);
  NewCtrl.Name := MyName;
  // now set the parent and show it
  NewCtrl.Parent := Self;
  NewCtrl.Visible := True;
end;
```

The first line of the code for this method is the key. It creates a new object of the class data type stored in the `ClassRef` field. You accomplish this by applying the `Create` constructor to the class reference. Now you can set the value of the `Parent` property, set the position of the new component, give the component a name (which is automatically used also as the value of `Caption` or `Text`), and make it visible. You can see an example of the output of this program in Figure 3.9.

FIGURE 3.9
An example of the output of the ClassRef program

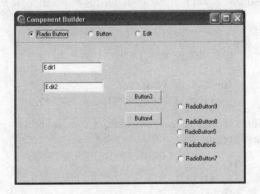

NOTE For polymorphic construction to work, the base class type of the class reference must have a virtual constructor. If you use a virtual constructor (as in the example), the constructor call applied to the class reference will call the constructor of the type that the class reference variable *currently refers to*. But without a virtual constructor, your code will call the constructor of *fixed class type* indicated in the class reference declaration. Virtual constructors are required for polymorphic construction in the same way that virtual methods are required for polymorphism.

The *for..in* Loop

Microsoft's Visual Basic has always had a specific loop construct for cycling all of the elements of a collection, called *for each*. The same idea was later introduced in C#, and partially in the .NET Framework itself. Not that IL has a similar feature in itself, but the framework class library promotes the idea of iterating over a container with a specific interface (IEnumerator) and a standard coding pattern. The .NET IEnumerator interface has two methods:

◆ MoveNext gets you to the first or following element of the enumeration, returning a Boolean value indicating whether you are at the end of the list (notice that this method has to be called before accessing the first item and returns False after the last item has already been used, in a fashion reminiscent of the BofCrack and EofCrack of Delphi's TDataSet).

◆ Current returns the current element of the enumerator.

The standard coding pattern used to access to this interface is to have a while loop iterating on the MoveNext call. You can code this pattern in Delphi for .NET as follows (see the ForInDotNet example):

```
var
  enum: IEnumerator;
begin
  enum := aList.GetEnumerator;
  while enum.MoveNext do
    Listbox1.Items.Add(enum.Current.ToString);
```

With the advent of Delphi 2005, Borland has decided to better support this coding style. But instead of sticking with the .NET implementation, it has opened it up for both the .NET and the Win32 compilers and made it available for much more than just iterating across container classes.

You can now write the previous code as follows:

```
var
  Obj: TObject;
begin
  for Obj in aList do
    Listbox1.Items.Add(Obj.ToString);
```

But you can also use enumerators in many other cases, like for strings or sets. Here is an example based on strings:

```
var
  s: string;
  ch: Char;
begin
  s := 'Hello world';
  for ch in s do
    Listbox1.Items.Add(ch);
```

If you stick to the Win32 compiler, the `for..in` loop can be used to access to the elements of the following data structures (all also available on .NET):

◆ Characters in a string (see previous code)

◆ Active values in set (see the ForInDotNet demo for an example)

◆ Items in a static or dynamic array, including two-dimensional arrays

◆ Objects referenced by classes with `GetEnumerator` support

Specifically, if you examine the `GetEnumerator` support for classes, this is available in a number of VCL "container" classes, including `TList` and `TStringList`. Each `TComponent` implements an enumerator on its owned components (see Chapter 5 for a discussion of components ownership, although the topic was already mentioned toward the start of this chapter). So, for example, in a VCL form you can write the following code (again from the ForInDotNet demo):

```
var
  C: TComponent;
begin
  for C in Self do
    ListBox1.Items.Add (C.Name);
```

What is very relevant, though, is that you can implement the `GetEnumerator` support in any of your classes in which it makes sense. What the compiler does is resolve the `for..in` loop with calls to specifically named methods that must be available. The class you want to iterate on (the container) must provide a `GetEnumerator` method, and the object returned by this method must provide a `Next` method and a `Current` property. The type of the `Current` property determines the type of the element that must be used by the loop.

Although this is not necessary, it seems a good idea to implement the enumerator support class as a nested type, as in the following class that stores a range of numbers and allows iterating on them:

```
type
  TNumbersRange = class
  public
  type
    TNumbersRangeEnum = class
    private
      nPos: Integer;
      fRange: TNumbersRange;
    public
      constructor Create (aRange: TNumbersRange);
      function MoveNext: Boolean;
      function GetCurrent: Integer;
      property Current: Integer read GetCurrent;
    end;
  private
    FnStart: Integer;
    FnEnd: Integer;
  public
    function GetEnumerator: TNumbersRangeEnum;
```

```
      procedure set_nEnd(const Value: Integer);
      procedure set_nStart(const Value: Integer);
      property nStart: Integer read FnStart write set_nStart;
      property nEnd: Integer read FnEnd write set_nEnd;
    end;
```

The GetEnumerator method creates the object of the nested type that stores status information for iterating on the data:

```
function TNumbersRange.GetEnumerator: TNumbersRangeEnum;
begin
  Result := TNumbersRangeEnum.Create (Self);
end;


constructor TNumbersRange.TNumbersRangeEnum.
  Create(aRange: TNumbersRange);
begin
  inherited Create;
  fRange := aRange;
  nPos := fRange.nStart - 1;
end;
```

Finally the enumerator methods provide access to the data and movement to the following value:

```
function TNumbersRange.TNumbersRangeEnum.GetCurrent: Integer;
begin
  Result := nPos;
end;


function TNumbersRange.TNumbersRangeEnum.MoveNext: Boolean;
begin
  Inc (nPos);
  Result := nPos <= fRange.nEnd;
end;
```

After all of this work, you can now use the for..in loop to iterate on the values of the range object:

```
var
  aRange: TNumbersRange;
  I: Integer;
begin
  aRange := TNumbersRange.Create;
  aRange.nStart := 10;
  aRange.nEnd := 23;

  for I in aRange do
    ListBox1.Items.Add (IntToStr (I));
```

Inlining

Inlining is a new feature of Delphi 2005 available on both Delphi compilers, although the story of this feature is quite peculiar. First of all, however, let me explain what inlining is. Generally, when you call a method, the compiler generates some code to let your program jump to a new execution point. This implies setting up a stack frame and doing a few more operations and might requite a dozen machine instructions. However, the method you execute might be very short, possibly even an access method that sets or returns some private field. In such a case, it makes a lot of sense to copy the actual code to the call location, avoiding the stack frame setup and everything else. By removing this overhead, your program can run faster, particularly when the call takes place in a tight loop executed thousands of times.

For some very small functions, the resulting code might even be smaller, as the code pasted in place might be smaller than the code required for the function call. However, notice that if a longer function is inlined and this function is called in many different places in your program, you might experiment a code bloat, which is an unnecessary increase in the size of the executable file.

The .NET platform supports inlining as a native feature, although inlining in .NET is not very aggressive and is applied only for very short method bodies (with a large number of language constructs that will disable it). Delphi 2005 adds this feature to both platforms, meaning that on .NET you have two different places (the Delphi compiler and the CLR) where a method can be inlined. This is relevant because, for example, the CLR inlining is disabled for any class inherited from Marshal ByRef (or TPersistent), which means it is disabled for most of the classes in the Delphi libraries and large portions of your code.

In Delphi you can ask the compiler to inline a method (or a global function) with the inline directive, placed after the method (or function) declaration. It is not necessary to repeat this declaration in the method definition (the method body). Always keep in mind that the inline directive is only a hint to the compiler, which can decide that the function is not a good candidate for inlining and skip your request (without warning you in any way). The compiler might also inline some of the calls of the function but not all of them after an analysis of the calling code and depending on the status of the $INLINE directive at the calling site. This directive can assume three different values (notice that this feature is independent from the optimization compiler switch):

♦ With default value, {$INLINE ON}, inlining is enabled for the functions marked by the inline directive.

♦ With {$INLINE OFF} you can suppress inlining in a program, in a portion of a program, or for a specific call site, regardless of the presence of the inline directive in the functions being called.

♦ With {$INLINE AUTO} the compiler will generally inline the functions you mark with the directive, plus automatically inline very short functions. Watch out, because this directive can cause code bloat.

There are many functions in the Delphi RTL that have been marked as inline candidates. For example, the Max function of the Math unit has definitions like:

```
function Max(const A, B: Integer): Integer; overload; inline;
```

To test the actual effect of inlining this function, I've written the following loop in the InliningTest example:

```
var
  ttt: TTimeTest;
  I, J: Integer;
begin
  J := 0;
  ttt := TTimeTest.Create;
  try
    for I := 0 to LoopCount do
      J := Max (I, J);
    memo1.Lines.Add ('Max ' + ttt.Elapsed +
      '[' + IntToStr (J) + ']');
  finally
    FreeAndNil (ttt);
  end;
```

In this code, the TTimeTest class is a very simple class that uses the system time (through the Now function) to get the initial time in the constructor and compute how much time has passed in the Elapsed method (see the source code for more details). The form has two buttons both calling this code, but one of them has inlining disabled at the call site (and a slightly different output). With one hundred million interactions, on my computer I get the following results:

```
Max 290[100000000]
Off 610[100000000]
```

which means that inlining more than doubles the execution speed! The same program does a second test with the Length function. As this is one of the so called "compiler magic" functions, it cannot be inlined. However, replacing it with a similar function with code like:

```
function LengthInline (const s: AnsiString): Longint; inline;
begin
  Result := integer(S);
  if Result <> 0 then
    Result := PInteger(Result-4)^;
end;
```

will again more than double its speed:

```
Length 591[1300000013]
Inline 239[1300000013]
```

NOTE   The use of the const parameter, which is generally relevant only for strings, can speed up the inlined code, as it can help the compiler produce better code. Consider it as an optimization suggestion for the compiler in case of inlining. The Max function shown earlier has it, like most of the RTL inlined functions.

The Delphi compiler doesn't define a clear cut limit on the size of a function to allow inlining it or a specific list of constructs (`for` or `while` loops, conditional statements) that would prevent inlining. However, since inlining a large function provides little advantage but exposes you to the risk of some real disadvantages, you should avoid it.

A limitation is that the method or function cannot reference identifiers (such as types, global variables, or functions) defined in the implementation section of the unit, as they won't be accessible in the call location. However, if you are calling a local function, which happens to be inlined as well, then the compiler will accept your request to inline your routine.

A drawback is that inlining requires more frequent recompilations of units, as when you modify an inlined function: the code of each of the calling sites will need to be recompiled as well. Within a unit, you might write the code of the inlined functions before calling them. Place them at the beginning of the implementation section. Delphi uses a single pass compiler, so it cannot paste in the code of a function it hasn't compiled yet.

Within different units, you need to specifically add other units with inlined functions to your `uses` statements, even if you don't call those methods directly. Suppose your unit A calls an inlined function defined in unit B. If this function in turn calls another inlined function in unit C, your unit A needs to refer to C as well. If not, you'll see a compiler warning indicating the call was not inlined due to the missing unit reference. A related effect is that functions are never inlined when there are circular unit references (through their implementation sections).

What's Next?

In this chapter, we discussed the foundations of object-oriented programming (OOP) in Delphi. We considered the definition of classes and the use of methods, encapsulation, and memory management, as well as some more advanced concepts such as properties and the dynamic creation of components. Then we moved to inheritance, virtual and abstract methods, polymorphism, safe typecasting, interfaces, exceptions, and class references.

Toward the end of the chapter we also explorer two generic features of the compiler, not particularly tied to OOP but brand new in Delphi 2005, the `for..in` loop and inlining.

This is certainly a lot of information if you are a newcomer. But if you are fluent in another OOP language or if you've already used past versions of Delphi, you should be able to apply the topics covered in this chapter to your programming.

Understanding the secrets of Delphi's language and library is vital to becoming an expert Delphi programmer. That's why the next chapter will keep delving into the language but from a specific point of view: how the Delphi language adapts itself for .NET and how it changed to support this new platform. After this, we'll get back to the Win32 world with an overview of the Delphi run-time library (mainly a collection of functions, with little OOP involved). Chapter 5, in fact, will give you more information about the language, discussing features related to the structure of the Delphi class library, such as the effect of the `published` keyword and the role of events.

Chapter 4

The Delphi Language for .NET

The transition from Delphi 7 to Delphi 8 for the Microsoft .NET Framework and Delphi 2005 has marked the most significant set of changes Borland has made to the Object Pascal (or Delphi) language since the first version of Delphi came to light in 1995. There are several reasons for these changes, but the most significant is certainly the need to obtain a high degree of compatibility with the underlying architecture of the Microsoft .NET Framework, which in turn makes the Delphi language compatible with other .NET languages.

On one hand, obtaining full language-features compatibility with other .NET languages is critical to being fully interoperable so that programmers using other languages can use assemblies and components written in Delphi while Delphi programmers have all of the features of the .NET libraries immediately available. On the other hand, having an existing implementation (at the CIL level) of a number of core language features has made Borland's job of updating the language somewhat easier.

This chapter describes not only the changes Borland has made to the Delphi language to adapt it to .NET, but also how existing language features now rely on capabilities of this platform. We are going to explore changes introduced to the language since Delphi 7, with the exception of a few features (such as the new access specifiers, final methods, and sealed classes) that are shared with the Win32 version of the language and that I already discussed in the previous chapter.

The Delphi Language on Microsoft .NET

As I've already discussed in the previous chapter, the Delphi language is a very modern OOP language, with an object model much closer to C# and Java than to C++. In Delphi, objects are invariably allocated on the heap; there is a single base class for all of the classes you define, features like properties and interfaces are built into the language, and RAD capabilities are based on the simple idea that components are classes with a rich RTTI.

Delphi actually did introduce some features that were also ported to other languages. In particular, the original Turbo Pascal and Delphi chief architect was Anders Hejlsberg, who later moved to Microsoft to become a key architect of the .NET Framework and the C# language (his title at Microsoft is something like "Distinguished Engineer and Chief C# Language Architect"). His influence (and the Delphi influence) is clearly visible on a number of features of C# and .NET. The reason for underscoring this fact is not so much to point out how good Delphi is, but rather to make it understandable that Delphi is a natural fit for .NET: the Delphi language has been moved to .NET much more easily than most other languages (including VB.NET and C++).

One of the positive effects of this easy migration is that your code maintains a high degree of compatibility from Win32 projects to .NET projects written with Delphi 2005. In fact, one of the advantages of Delphi is that you can compile your code (often the same source code files) on different platforms: Win32, .NET, and (with more limitations) even Linux.

NOTE   Migration concerns and backward compatibility have been a key goal of Borland when working on the Delphi for .NET project. This concern has been one of the driving forces, as you'll see in a while when I cover units and namespaces. Code portability has been looked after almost maniacally: as you'll see later in this chapter, even some low-level common hacks, like the one used for protected data access, have been made available on the new platform, despite the fact they violate almost all of the rules of .NET safety.

The other relevant thing to mention is that although both traditional Delphi and its new .NET incarnation lack some language features of C# or Java, they do provide many constructs not found in those other languages. For example, Delphi for .NET is one of the few languages that supports enumerated sets (a feature not supported by VB.NET or C#) and class helpers, not to mention class reference types and virtual constructors. I'll cover all of those features in this chapter, but first, I need to cover how the Delphi language adapts to .NET.

Good Old Units

One of the relevant differences between the Delphi language and the C# language is that the latter is a pure OOP language, a term used to indicate that all the code must be inside methods, rooting out global functions (or procedures). The same happens, of course, in the underlying .NET object model. The Delphi language, instead, allows for both an OOP programming paradigm and a procedural one, such as C++.

I don't want to enter a technical dispute whether a pure OOP language is any better than an OOP language that also supports procedural programming. Some developers (myself included) find it quite awkward to see libraries with classes not meant to be instantiated and used only to access class functions. Other developers think it's a great move to apply scope to functionality rather than arbitrarily looking for one out of a large number of global functions.

Globals and the Fake Unit Class

Moving Delphi to .NET, Borland had to find a way to maintain the existing model with global functions, procedures, and data. This effect is obtained by creating a "fake" class for each unit and adding global procedures and functions to it as if they were class methods and global data as if it was class data. For example, the UnitTestDemo program has a unit with a single global function, *Foo*:

```
unit Marco.Test;

interface

function Foo: string;

implementation
```

```
function Foo: string;
begin
  Result := 'foo';
end;

end.
```

By adding this function to a program, compiling it, and inspecting it with Reflector, you can see (in the output below and in Figure 4.1) that Delphi generates a Test fake class with the Foo class method (see the static keyword) within the `Marco.Units` namespace:

```
.namespace Marco.Units
{
  .class public auto ansi sealed beforefieldinit Test
        extends [mscorlib]System.Object
  {
    ...
    .method public static string  Foo() cil managed
    {...}
  }
}
```

NOTE This is quite different from Delphi 8, which generates a Unit fake class within the `Marco.Test` namespace, also hosting regular classes for the unit. The Delphi 2005 implementation is more namespace friendly, as it allows for multiple units to contribute to a single namespace and also helps insulate Delphi-specific features (like globals inside fake *unit* classes) from other .NET languages by storing those in a separate namespace.

FIGURE 4.1
The output of Reflector for the UnitTestDemo program shows how Delphi global procedures are encapsulated in fake classes.

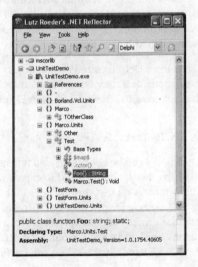

Units as Namespaces, Almost

The other relevant way in which units are used is that they do become namespaces. This is why you can have units with long names using the dot notation (something that was actually already available in Delphi 7, even if much less useful).

In Delphi 8 a compiled assembly had as many namespaces as there were units in its source code. In Delphi 2005 (in the .NET compiler) a unit name using the dot notation belongs to a namespace equal to its name minus the last portion, the portion after the last dot. In other words, the `Marco.Test` unit will add its definitions to the `Marco` namespace. If the unit name uses doesn't use the dot notation, Delphi will use the namespace indicated in the Default Namespace project option.

The UnitTestDemo program has a second unit, `Marco.Other`, contributing a class (`TOtherClass`) to the same `Marco` namespace:

```
.namespace Marco
{
  .class public auto ansi beforefieldinit TOtherClass
        extends [mscorlib]System.Object
  {...}
}
```

It is remarkable that Borland has achieved this without changing the language syntax or the way Delphi developers write their code. This approach is not as open ended as the C# approach, in which you specifically declare a namespace, but it allows code to be easily portable from Delphi for Win32 and back. It is a very good step forward from the Delphi 8 solution, which really constrained namespaces to equal units, with the negative effect of making people write some very large units or making it weird to use Delphi-coded assemblies from C# and other .NET languages.

NOTE   By removing the last portion of the unit name from the namespace, Borland has exposed Delphi programmers to the risk of duplicated identifiers. In fact, while it is legitimate (even if not suggested) in Delphi to have two classes with the same name if they are in two different units, if the name of these units differs only in the last portion, you'll end up with a namespace with a duplicate type name, something the compiler will not currently warn you about.

Similarly, from Delphi code you can access CLR namespaces and namespaces defined by other assemblies exactly as if they were native units by using the `uses` clause, but you keep using the unit name when referring to other *local* units or Delphi-generated assemblies that you have a DCPIL file for:

```
uses
    System.IO.Text, System.Web, Marco.Test;
```

Notice that this can be confusing as `uses` statements refer to namespaces defined by assemblies compiled with other languages and to classic units for any assembly (even from third parties) compiled with Delphi. A related difference is that the system namespace contains large numbers of classes, while a single Delphi unit is limited to a few classes to remain manageable.

A particular source of confusion comes from the fact that there is a System unit (the core RTL unit) in Delphi for Win32 and a System namespace (the core .NET namespace) in Delphi for .NET, and you refer to both with `uses System`. You can partially avoid the confusion because you refer to specific namespaces under the System namespace, as in the examples above; also consider that on .NET Delphi the core RTL unit is now called Borland.Delphi.System.

Regarding namespaces and units, it's important to notice that Delphi classic Win32 library units, like SysUtils or Classes, have been prefixed with the Borland.Vcl name. So in theory when porting an existing project you should modify lines like:

```
uses
   Classes, SysUtils;
```

into

```
uses
   Borland.Vcl.Classes, Borland.Vcl.SysUtils;
```

However, Delphi 2005 allows you to indicate a namespace prefix (or a list of project namespaces), like Borland.Vcl, so you can omit the first portion of the declaration and the compiler will pick up the correct unit anyway. In practice, you can add a list of namespace prefixes in the Directories/Conditionals page of the Project Options dialog box. The same effect can be obtained with the -ns compiler flag, such as -nsBorland.Vcl. This approach eliminates the tedious use of the IFDEF directives Delphi programmers had to deal with for compatibility between Delphi and Kylix or between the VCL and CLX libraries on Windows alone.

NOTE The Delphi 2005 help file, in the Language Reference section, mentions a multi-unit namespace capability one should be able to activate with a semicolon-delimited uses statement (uses <namespace> in 'unit1;unit2'). As far as I can guess, this was only an idea and never actually existed, but the description slipped in the help file. Similarly, in the Delphi 8 help file there was a reference to unit aliases (with a uses <unitname> as <alias> construct), a feature never actually added to the compiler.

Unit Initialization and Class Constructors

In the context of how units are adapted to a pure OOP structure, a relevant change relates to the initialization and finalization sections of a unit, which are "global" potions of code executed (in Delphi for Win32) at the start and termination of a program in a deterministic order given by the sequence of inclusion (uses statements).

In Delphi for .NET, units become fake classes and the initialization code becomes a class static method (see the section "Class Data and Class Static Methods" in this chapter) that is invoked by the class constructor (see the "Class Constructors" section). As class constructors are automatically invoked by the CLR before each class is used, the resulting behavior is similar to what you were used to. The only difference, which is very relevant, is that there is no deterministic order of execution for the various class constructors in a program. That is, the order of execution of the various initialization sections is not known and can change for different executions of the program.

As an example, consider this initialization section (again taken from the UnitTestDemo example) that sets a value for a global variable:

```
initialization
   startTime := Now;
```

Compiling this code adds to the unit class a static method with the same name of the unit (Marco.Test), which calls Borland.Vcl.Units.SysUtils::Now() and saves the result in the startTime local variable with a call to this method from the class constructor (.cctor), as the following IL snippets show:

```
.method public static void  Marco.Test() cil managed
{
  // Code size       7 (0x7)
  .maxstack  1
  .locals init ([0] valuetype [Borland.Delphi]
    Borland.Delphi.TDateTime startTime)
  IL_0000:  call        valuetype [Borland.Delphi]
    Borland.Delphi.TDateTime [Borland.VclRtl]
    Borland.Vcl.Units.SysUtils::Now()
  IL_0005:  stloc.0
  IL_0006:  ret
} // end of method Test::Marco.Test


.method private hidebysig specialname rtspecialname static
  void   .cctor() cil managed
{
  // Code size       36 (0x24)
  .maxstack  1
  ... // more IL code omitted
  IL_001e:  call        void Marco.Units.Test::Marco.Test()
  IL_0023:  ret
} // end of method Unit::.cctor
```

Identifiers

Identifiers in a programming language are used to name any new element you introduce, from local variables to new types, from methods to properties. The standard rule on identifiers in the Delphi language allows you to use any uppercase or lowercase letter (Delphi is not case sensitive), the underscore character, or a digit (but you cannot start the identifier with a digit). The second rule is you cannot use a reserved word as an identifier. This rule is now amended in case you *qualify* the identifier, as explained in the next section. Another relevant new feature of Delphi 2005 is the support for extended Unicode characters in identifiers.

Qualified Identifiers

With multiple languages and a single CLR, chances are that a reserved symbol of a language will be legitimately used by programmers using another language. In the past, this would have made it very hard to refer to that symbol from the code. Delphi for .NET introduces special symbol, the ampersand (&) that you can use as a prefix for any reserved word, to legitimately use it as an identifier. This is called a *qualified identifier*.

To be more precise, the & allows you to access CLR-defined symbols (or other symbols in general, whenever they are defined) but won't allow you to declare identifiers within Delphi code that violate

Delphi's own syntax rules ("& is for access only, not declaration" as Borland says). For example, you can use & when referring to a class type imported from an assembly that is named the same as a reserved word but not when defining the name of a new class. I'd say this makes a lot of sense.

Two classic examples are the use of the System.Type type and the use of the Label class of the WinForms library. As the type and label words are reserved in the Delphi language, you can either use the full namespace to indicate them or prefix them with the &. The following declarations are identical:

```
type1: System.Type;
type2: &Type;
Label1: System.Windows.Forms.Label;
Label2: &Label;
```

NOTE   Although this is less relevant, the & character in front of a keyword (or any identifier, for that matter) can also be used on the Win32 compiler of Delphi 2005, not only the .NET compiler.

Unicode Identifiers

The CLR definition of an identifier is different from the classic Delphi definition. Although in both cases identifiers must start with a letter (or an underscore) and be followed by letters and numbers (or the underscore), the difference is that letters for the CLR include all Unicode characters. Technically the CLR uses the UTF8 Unicode encoding.

Delphi 8 introduced the use of Unicode for source code files (something the Delphi 2005 offers as well), but was short of supporting Unicode (UTF8) identifiers. Delphi 2005 fixes the problem, offering complete Unicode support and making the language even more CLS compliant. In fact, Delphi 8's problem of working with an assembly that was written in another .NET language and that used Unicode identifiers has now been solved.

Notice that Unicode identifiers are available both on the .NET and the Win32 compilers of Delphi 2005. You can find two simple demos of Unicode identifiers in the UnicodeIdentifiers folder, one for .NET and the other for Win32. Both demos are console applications and include code like:

```
var
  CantùName: string;
begin
  CantùName := 'Marco Cantù';
  writeln (CantùName);
```

Although the Win32 version has problems with the accented letter in the output, they both accept the accented letter in the identifier.

Base Data Types

Contrary to what happened in the past, when the Delphi language base data types had to partially adapt to the underlying CPU (for example, in relation to the handling of floating point numbers), now the language must comply with the Common Type System specification indicated in the CLI. Of course, most of the base data types are still there, and others have been built by Borland on top of what's available.

The CLR makes a clear distinction between two different families of data types, value types and reference types:

- Value types are allocated directly on the stack. When you copy or assign a value type, the system will make a complete copy of all of its data. Value types include the primitive data types (integer and floating point numbers, characters, Boolean values) and records.

- Reference types are allocated on the heap and garbage collected. Reference types include anything else, from objects to strings, from dynamic arrays to class metadata.

Primitive Types

The .NET CLR defines quite a few "primitive types," which are not natively mapped to objects but a direct representation of data. The internal layout of the data for some of these types is not fixed, as it can change with the target CPU and operating system version, for example, on a 32-bit or 64-bit CPU. The CLR primitive types are mapped to corresponding Delphi types, as Table 4.1 highlights.

What you can notice is that not all Delphi types have a CLR equivalent. You are recommended not to use those types if you want your classes to be usable by other .NET languages and to be fully CLS-compliant. Feel free to use them *inside* a program and for compatibility with existing Delphi code, but whenever possible stick to the types with a direct CLR mapping.

If you don't trust me, the data here is taken from the output of the PrimitiveList program. The program passes as parameters to the PrintDelphiType function a long list of Delphi types, occasionally with a comment. The function uses Delphi's RTTI and the system reflection to print out to the console the Delphi and CLR type names. (Reflection in .NET is an extended form of analysis of the rich RTTI available in an assembly, introduced in Chapter 2 and also demonstrated in the "Attributes, or RTTI to the Extreme" section toward the end of this chapter.) Here is the relevant code:

```
procedure PrintDelphiType (tInfo: TTypeInfo;
  strComment: string = '');
begin
  write (tInfo.DelphiTypeName);
  write (' - ');
  write (tInfo.ToString);
  writeln (' ' + strComment);
end;

// snippet from main program
begin
  writeln ('');
  writeln ('generic size');
  PrintDelphiType (typeInfo (Integer));
  PrintDelphiType (typeInfo (Cardinal),
    'declared as Cardinal');

  writeln ('');
  writeln ('specific size: signed ');
  PrintDelphiType (typeInfo (ShortInt));
  PrintDelphiType (typeInfo (SmallInt));
  PrintDelphiType (typeInfo (LongInt));
  PrintDelphiType (typeInfo (Int64));
```

In the output of this program you'll be able to see the internal RTL name of the type for the Delphi .NET compiler and for the .NET run time itself. Of course, you can extend a similar program to explore how other native and custom data types are handled by the Delphi compiler.

TABLE 4.1: Mapping of Delphi and CLR Base Data Types

CATEGORY	DELPHI TYPE	CLR TYPE
Generic size	Integer	System.Int32
	Cardinal (equals LongWord)	System.UInt32
Signed	ShortInt	System.SByte
	SmallInt	System.Int16
	Integer	System.Int32
	Int64	System.Int64
Unsigned	Byte	System.Byte
	Word	System.UInt16
	LongWord	System.UInt32
Floating point	Single	System.Single
	Double	System.Double
	Extended	
	Comp (equals Int64, deprecated)	System.Int64
	Currency	
	Decimal	System.Decimal
	Real (equals Double)	System.Double
char	Char	System.Char
	WideChar (equals Char)	System.Char
boolean	Boolean	System.Boolean
	ByteBool	
	WordBool	
	LongBool	

NOTE   The old Real48 type, representing 6-byte floats and already deprecated in the last few versions of Delphi, is not available any more. Not being directly mapped to a supported FPU type of the Pentium-class CPUs, its implementation was slow in Delphi for Win32 and is not part of Delphi for .NET. The Real type, instead, is directly mapped by the compiler to Double.

Boxing Primitive Types

Primitive types can be boxed into object wrappers to *convert* them into objects:

```
var
  n1: Integer;
  o1: TObject;
begin
  n1 := 12;
  o1 := TObject (n1);
```

The last statement looks like a cast (something that would be illegal in .NET), but since it is a value type being *converted*, the system will actually perform a box operation. This is very handy in a number of cases, including the possibility of using object container classes to hold primitive types along with objects. Boxing introduces the notion that an object reference can host anything (including a primitive value) and gives you the ability to apply some of the predefined methods of the base Object class (like the ToString method) to any value. For example, this code won't make sense in Delphi for Win32 (even if the cast from an Integer to a TObject would indeed compile, its effect would be totally different: that is, storing the numeric value as the address of the object!):

```
var
  n1: Integer;
  str: string;
begin
  n1 := 12;
  str := TObject (n1).ToString;
```

Of course, you could argue that a pure object-oriented language should root out the use of primitive types and make use of objects for everything (as Smalltalk, the father-of-all-OOP-languages, does), but efficiency reasons demand keeping primitive types close to the system. As a simple test, the BoxingDemo application saves the intermediary value of a computation in an integer boxed in an object, with the time it takes to box and unbox it far exceeding the time taken for the computation (which, in this extreme case, involves only adding numbers). Similarly, I'd expect an IntToStr call to be much faster than boxing the value into an object and than applying to ToString method to it.

The other operation demonstrated by the application is the definition of a list of objects accepting boxed elements and based on Delphi own container classes:

```
var
  list: TObjectList;
  i: Integer;
begin
  list := TObjectList.Create;
  list.Add(TObject (100));
```

```
list.Add(TObject ('hello'));
list.Add (button3);

for i := 0 to list.Count - 1 do
begin
  Memo1.Lines.Add (list[i].ToString);
end;
```

Running this code, the program adds to the memo the following output:

```
100
hello
Button3 [Borland.Vcl.StdCtrls.TButton]
```

Delphi Enumerated and Set Types

Enumerated types and sets are commonly used in Delphi and have been available in the Pascal language since its inception. A form of strictly-typed enumerations is available in the C# language (while it was not in the C language) and is part of the CLR types system. This means that Delphi enumerations are mapped to corresponding CLR features, as you can see by inspecting compiled code.

For example, the definition of this enumeration from the Borland.Delphi.System unit:

```
TTextLineBreakStyle = (tlbsLF, tlbsCRLF);
```

gets transformed in the following "compiled" definition in IL, which looks like an enumeration class (marked as sealed) that inherits from System.Enum and has a single value (a short unsigned integer) and two literal constants:

```
[ENU] TTextLineBreakStyle
.class public auto ansi sealed
extends [mscorlib]System.Enum
[STF] tlbsCRLF : public static literal valuetype
  Borland.Delphi.System.TTextLineBreakStyle
[STF] tlbsLF : public static literal valuetype
  Borland.Delphi.System.TTextLineBreakStyle
[FLD] value__ : public specialname rtspecialname unsigned int8
```

What all these means is that enumerated types in Delphi are fully CLS complaint. The Delphi set type, on the other hand, is not commonly found in many other programming languages, which is why the CLR has no clue about sets and why they are not CLS-compliant. Delphi for .NET implementation of sets is based on the following declaration, plus some compiler magic:

```
type
  _TSet = array of Byte;
```

In other words, it is not recommended to use sets in method parameters or as the type of properties you intend to be used by other .NET languages.

Records on Steroids

Another relevant family of value types is represented by structures in C# jargon, or records as they are called in Delphi. Records have always been part of the language, but in this version they gain a lot of new ground because they can now have methods associated with them (and even operators, as you'll see later on in this chapter).

A record with methods is somewhat similar to a class: the most relevant difference (besides the lack of inheritance and polymorphisms) is that record type variables use local memory (of the stack frame they are declared onto or the object they are part of), they are passed as parameters to functions by value by default (without a parameter modifier like var) making a copy, and they have a "value copy" behavior on assignments. This contrasts with class type variables that must be allocated on the dynamic memory heap, are passed by references, and have a "reference copy" behavior on assignments (thus copying the reference to the same object in memory).

For example, when you declare a record variable on the stack, you can start using it right away, without having to call its constructor. This means record variables are leaner (and more efficient) on the memory manager and garbage collector than regular objects, as they do not participate in the management of the dynamic memory. These are the key reasons for using records instead of objects for small and simple data structures.

```
type
  TMyRecord = record
  private
    one: string;
    two: Integer;
    three: Char;
  public
    procedure Print;
    constructor Create (aString: string);
    procedure Init (aValue: Integer);
  end;
```

A record can also have a constructor, but the record constructors must have parameters (if you try with Create() you'll get the error message "Parameterless constructors not allowed on record types." Why Borland imposed this limitation is far from clear to me, as you still have to manually call the constructor, optionally passing parameters to it (you cannot use the constructor as a type conversion, something you can use the Implicit and Explicit operators for, as discussed later). Here is a sample snippet:

```
var
  myrec: TMyRecord;
begin
  myrec := TMyRecord.Create ('hello');
  myrec.Print;
```

This constructor syntax has been added to make record usage consistent with class initialization calls (even dynamic arrays can now use constructors, so you can notice a theme). Using the preceding syntax doesn't affect the initialization portion of the CIL code. In this respect, it is a better idea to use a plain initialization method rather than a constructor to assign multiple (initial) values to a record structure.

NOTE   From Borland Object Pascal days, Delphi for .NET has left out the *object* type definition, which predated Delphi and was introduced in the days of Turbo Pascal with Objects. They left it out because .NET provides extended records (with methods) that are value types and sit on the stack or in the container type exactly like objects defined with the *object* keyword in past versions of Delphi. This is another deprecated language feature that few Delphi programmers use, so its absence should not constitute a big roadblock.

Delphi for .NET still allows you to define either a *record* or a *packed record*. The difference is traditionally related to 16-bit or 32-bit alignment of the various fields, so that a byte followed by an integer might end up taking up 32 bits even if only 8 are used. This is because accessing the following integer value on the 32-bit boundary makes the code faster to execute.

In Delphi for .NET two syntaxes produce structures marked in the IL as *auto* (for a plain record) or *sequential* (for a packed record). Auto tells the CLR to lay out the record data as efficiently as it likes in a completely unpredictable memory layout, as it will often rearrange the fields in memory. Sequential tells the CLR to lay each field out in the order specified without padding them to specific boundaries. Thereby, if you serialize a record (stream it to disk) using a binary formatter, you get the same layout you would historically using a packed record.

Records or Classes

Because there are classes in the language, you might wonder, what's the rationale for also having records with methods? Aside from the lack of many advanced features of classes, the key difference between records and classes relates to the way they use memory.

The bytes needed for the storage of the fields of a record comes from *local* memory: (i) the stack if the record variable is a local variable, or (ii) the memory of the hosting data structure if the record is inside another type (an array, another record, a class...). On the other hand, a class variable or field is just a reference to the memory location where the class is held. This means classes need a specific memory allocation, their data blocks participate in the memory management (including the garbage collector), and they must eventually be reclaimed by the GC. Records just sit there on their own and cost much less to allocate, manage, and free.

Another relevant difference is in the way records are copied or passed as parameters. In both cases the default is to make a full copy of the memory block representing the record. Of course, you can use var or const record parameters to modify this default behavior. On the contrary, assigning or passing an object is invariably an operation on the references to the objects: it's the reference that is copied or passed around.

To get an idea of the performance differences among using objects and records, I added to the RecordsDemo example, mentioned earlier, two units that are extremely similar but use the two different approaches. The brute force code I've written uses a temporary record or object inside routines that are called a million times:

```
function ComputeDistance1: Double;
var
  pt1: TRecordPoint;
  pt2: TRecordPoint;
begin
  pt1 := TRecordPoint.Create (10, 20);
  pt2 := TRecordPoint.Create (20, 40);
  Result := pt1.Distance(pt2);
```

```
  end;

  function ComputeDistance: Double;
  var
    pt1, pt2: TClassPoint;
  begin
    pt1 := TClassPoint.Create (10, 20);
    pt2 := TClassPoint.Create (20, 40);
    Result := pt1.Distance(pt2);
  end;
```

The greatest difference depends on the weight of the actual algorithm (I had to remove the calls to random() I originally used as they slowed down things too much) and the amount of data of the structures. The current result of the RecordsDemo test on my computer gives a relative average speed of 360 ms for records against 540 ms for classes. The difference is a savings of 180 ms over 2 million memory allocations. This means that in a computationally intensive operation the difference is certainly noticeable, while in most other cases it will be almost unnoticeable.

So the difference from records to classes boils down to the fact that you might save one line of code of memory allocation, which you might still need to replace with a call to an initialization method.

Delphi's New Predefined Records

The presence of a sophisticated record type definition and of the operator overloading has led Borland to change a lot of predefined Delphi types into records. Notable examples are the types Variant, DateTime, and Currency.

The Variant type in particular represents another data type not part of the CLR foundations that Borland has been able to redefine on top of the available CLR features without affecting the syntax and the semantics of the existing code. The implementation of the Variant type on .NET differs heavily from that of Win32, but your code (at least the higher level code) won't be affected.

I'll cover these Borland predefined data types in Chapter 5, which is devoted to Delphi Classic RTL.

NOTE   Considering the relevant changes on the Variant data type, it should come as no surprise that the TVarData type has disappeared and the VarUtils unit is no longer present. Notice also that in a few circumstances you'll need to add a reference to the Variants unit for some existing Delphi programs to recompile under Delphi for .NET.

Reference Types

Objects are the most obvious examples of a reference type, but strings and dynamic arrays are part of the same category as well (which is not much different from what Delphi programmers were used to, apart from the garbage collection support).

NOTE   Some details on the garbage collector were already discussed in Chapter 2; a discussion on how this affects Delphi object destruction appears later in this chapter in "Free and Destroy in the Garbage Collected World."

Strings

Considering that Delphi long strings are allocated on the heap and that they are reference counted and use the copy-on-write technique, .NET strings will be quite familiar. There are a few differences, though. The first is that strings on .NET use UTF16 Unicode characters; that is, each character is represented with 16 bits of data (2 bytes). This is transparent, as when you index into a string looking for a given character, the index will be that of the character, not that of the byte (the two concepts are usually identical in Delphi for Win32). Of course, using UTF16 means that the strings will use on average twice as much memory as in Delphi for Win32 (that is, unless you used the widestring type on Win32).

As the array indexes refer to characters and not bytes, so the Length function returns the number of characters, not the number of bytes. The effect is that you can keep scanning a string writing:

```
for I := 1 to Length (str) do
  writeln (IntToStr (I) + ':' + str[I]);
```

If you want to know the actual size of a string you should use the expression:

```
Length(AString) * SizeOf(Char)
```

which doesn't take into account the trailing NULL character and other size information added to the string by the system.

The PrimitiveList program tells you, again, that the available Delphi string types have the mappings to CLR types visible in Table 4.2.

Another relevant issue is that strings in .NET are immutable. This means that string concatenation is slow when done with the classic + sign (and the already obsolete AppendStr routine is now gone). This slowness is due to the fact that a new string has to be created in memory, copying the contents of the two strings being added even if the effective result is to add some more characters to one of the strings. To overcome this slow implementation, the .NET Framework provides a specific class for string concatenation called StringBuilder.

TABLE 4.2:   Delphi and CLR String Types

CATEGORY	DELPHI TYPE	CLR TYPE
strings	string	System.String
	AnsiChar	
	ShortString	
	AnsiString	
	WideString	System.String

For example, if you have a procedure like the following `PlainStringConcat` that creates a string with the first 20,000 numbers, you should instead re-implement it using a `StringBuilder` object, as in the following `UseStringBuilder` function:

```
function PlainStringConcat: Integer;
var
  str: string;
  i, ms: Integer;
  t: tDateTime;
begin
  t := Now;
  str := '';
  for I := 1 to 20000 do
  begin
    str := str + IntToStr (i) + ' - ';
  end;
  ms := trunc (MilliSecondSpan(Now, t));
  writeln (str[100]);
  Result := ms;
end;
```

```
function UseStringBuilder: Integer;
var
  st: StringBuilder;
  str: string;
  i, ms: Integer;
  t: tDateTime;
begin
  t := Now;
  st := StringBuilder.Create;
  for I := 1 to 20000 do
  begin
    st.Append (IntToStr (i) + ' - ');
  end;
  str := st.ToString;
  ms := trunc (MilliSecondSpan(Now, t));
  writeln (str[100]);
  Result := ms;
end;
```

If you run the StringConcatSpeed demo that includes the two preceding functions (plus a third based on Delphi's `TStringList` class), you'll see the time taken by each of the two approaches, and the difference will be striking! This is the output (you should try it out with different ranges of the `for` loop counter):

```
String builder: 19
Plain concat: 10235
```

This means that the string builder takes a few milliseconds, while the string concatenation takes about 10 seconds. This code is also slower because it impacts the GC, as thousands of strings are allocated in the GC heap, probably filling the first memory area (Gen0) a few times and causing GC sweeps to occur. Another negative effect, though is that at the end there will doubtless be a whole bunch of orphaned strings in the GC heap waiting for the next GC sweep to occur. The moral of this story is that you have to get rid of all of the lengthy string concatenations in your code using either a `StringBuilder` or `TStringList`. The `TStringList` is a little slower (it takes almost twice as much time as the `StringBuilder`, which seems acceptable for most tasks) but has the advantage of maintaining your code compatible with Delphi for Win32. You can certainly obtain the same compatibility by writing a `StringBuilder` class for Delphi for Win32, but using a string list seems a better approach to me if you need backward compatibility.

Finally, notice that in Delphi for .NET using a `const` parameter when passing strings is not relevant, while it is in Delphi for Win32. This is reasonable, as strings are immutable and need no reference counting, and reference counting is exactly what is skipped for string parameters declared as `const`. However, for compatibility you might still want to also use `const` for string parameters that do not change on .NET, as this causes no harm whatsoever.

NOTE   In the .NET FCL (and, consequently, also in Delphi's RTL), every object has a string representation, available by calling the `ToString` virtual method. System library classes already define a string representation, while you can plug in your own code for your custom classes. This is covered in more detail and with an example in Chapter 9, focusing on the RTL in .NET.

Using Unsafe Types

In Delphi for .NET the use of pointers and other unsafe types is not totally ruled out. However, you'll need to mark the code as unsafe and go to a lot of trouble to obtain something you could easily and better achieve on the Win32 platform. In other words, although I'm going to show you a few tricks in this section, I'm not at all recommending the use of these techniques; quite the contrary—I'd rather discourage you from using them, unless you really need to do so!

WARNING   These features are mostly undocumented and not very reliable. This section is therefore by nature incomplete and should be understood as a description of some experiments in progress, not as reliable working code.

As a general rule, notice that you can ask the Delphi for .NET compiler to permit the generation of unsafe code with the directive:

```
{$UNSAFECODE ON}
```

After you've used this directive, you can mark global routines or methods with the `unsafe` directive. The application you'll produce will be a legitimate .NET application, possibly managed, but certainly not safe. Running it through PEVerify should fail.

I've mentioned PEVerify (here and in Chapter 2), but let me recap its features. The CLR needs a type-safe execution of CIL code to enforce the security of the overall .NET virtual machine. Code that is not verifiably type safe cannot run in the CLR unless you set specific security policies. In other words, type safety verification is not mandatory for managed code, but it is crucial to enforce assembly isolation and security.

The PEVerify tool helps you determine whether the IL code of the assemblies you've created and its associated metadata meet type safety requirements. PEVerify is a command-line tool you can invoke from the Project Manager of the Delphi IDE by adding it to your Build Tools for the .EXE and .DLL extensions, as demonstrated in Chapter 1.

NOTE   When declaring an unsafe method, you mark the method with this directive in the method definition of the implementation section, not in the method declaration (within the class definition) of the interface section. The exception to this is if the method takes unsafe types as parameters, in which case the unsafe directive goes in the method declaration.

Variant Records

Let's start with variant records. These are data structures with fields that can assume different data types depending either on a given field (as in the following example, taken from the UnsafeTest project), or in an undetermined way:

```
type
  TFlexi = record
  public
    value: integer;
    case test: Boolean of
      true: (c1: Char; c2: Char);
      false: (n: Integer);
  end;
```

If you compile this code, the compiler issues the warning "Unsafe type Tflexi," which is certainly correct. You can use it in a method like the following, which saves data using one format (the 'a' and 'b' characters) and retrieves it with another (the 6,422,625 number):

```
procedure UseVariantRecord;
var
  flexi: TFlexi;
begin
  writeln ('using variant record');
  flexi.test := true;
  flexi.c1 := 'a';
  flexi.c2 := 'b';
  flexi.test := false;
  writeln (IntToStr (flexi.n));
end;
```

Notice that this works even without marking the procedure unsafe or marking the module as such. The most relevant rule for variant records in Delphi for .NET is that you cannot use reference types (managed data) in the overlapping portion of the type. So if you try the following data structure:

```
type
  TFlexi2 = record
```

```
public
  value: integer;
  case test: Boolean of
    true: (s: string);
    false: (n: Integer);
end;
```

as soon as you try to use a local variable of this type, at run time you'll get a CLR exception like "Could not load type UnsafeTest.TFlexi2 from assembly UnsafeTest (...) because it contains an object field at offset 5 that is incorrectly aligned or overlapped by a non-object field."

Untyped Parameters

Another risky technique is the use of untyped parameters in procedures. Here is an example (again from the UnsafeTest project) that works:

```
procedure UnsafeParam (var param);
begin
  writeln (tObject(param).ToString);
end;

var
  test: string;
  n: Integer;
  obj: TObject;
begin
  test := 'foo';
  UnsafeParam (test);
  n := 23;
  UnsafeParam (n);
  obj := TObject.Create;
  UnsafeParam (obj);
```

In this case, you'll get the output you'd expect (and no compile time warning or run-time error):

```
foo
23
System.Object
```

Before you get too surprised by this behavior, notice that the compiler generates a method with the following signature:

```
.method public static void UnsafeParam(object& param) cil managed
```

The parameter if this method is an object passed by reference (& in IL is like var in Pascal), which means the compiler uses objects and boxing to *simulate* an undefined type.

Allocating Memory with New

Finally, you cannot use GetMem, FreeMem, or ReallocMem anymore. They have been removed from the standard routines. You can still use New, but only when allocating a dynamic array. In fact, if you try to use New in another context, you'll get the compiler error message "NEW standard function expects a dynamic array type identifier." Here is an example (again from the UnsafeTest project) of this usage:

```
type
  arrayofchar = array of Char;
var
  ptest2: arrayofchar;
begin
  ptest2 := New (arrayofchar, 100);
```

Using the PChar Type

Another issue relates to the use of PChar pointers. If you simply try using the PChar type, the compiler will stop with an error indicating that "Unsafe pointer variables, parameters or consts only allowed in unsafe procedure." This is solved by using the unsafe directive to mark the procedure or method.

But the actual question is, what exactly can you do with a PChar? It appears that you can do very little. This is an example (again in the UnsafeTest project) that uses a PChar to refer to a character in the array just declared and modify it:

```
procedure testpchar; unsafe;
var
  ptest: PChar;
begin
  ptest := @ptest2 [5];
  ptest^ := 'd';
  writeln (ptest2 [5]);
end;
```

The code does work as expected, but it is hard to tell why you might want to use it rather than accessing the dynamic array directly. PChar support is available mostly for moving old code across.

A related technique is the use of the GCHandle class of .NET, a sort of parent of the Object class, which allows you to "pin down" an object and get a pointer to its memory location to work with, while the CLR guarantees that the object won't be moved in memory (for example, as a result of a garbage collection). There is some code introducing this technique in the UnsafeTest project, but nothing really interesting for now.

The *file of* Type Is Gone

Very few of the traditional Pascal and Delphi types are missing in Delphi for .NET. A notable absence, albeit seldom used, is the file of <type> construct of the traditional Pascal language. This is a very old construct and is now generally replaced by the use of streams and RTTI-based objects persistence.

DYNAMIC ARRAY CONSTRUCTORS

Although this is not directly related to unsafe code, there is a feature very similar to allocating memory with New. It is a little known fact that since Delphi 7 you have been able to initialize a dynamic array by providing the initial values to the array and using the same notation of a class constructor. This works in both Win32 and .NET.

The notation actually borrows the Create name. Here is a code snippet (again from the UnsafeTest project):

```
type
    arrayofchar = array of WideChar;
var
    ptest3: arrayofchar;
begin
    // initialize a dynamic array with actual values
    ptest3 := arrayofchar.Create ('o', 'i', 'u');
    // display the third (array is zero based)
    writeln ('ptest3[2]: ' + ptest3[2]);
```

Type Casts on the Safe Side

The Delphi language tends to force developers to use the type system in an appropriate way. By treating the base data types as different entities (if you compare it, for example, with the C language), programs tend to be better written and more readable. For example, an enumeration is not the same as an integer, an integer is not type-compatible with a character, and so on.

Still, the Delphi language allows you to code a direct type cast, imposing your own rule on top of what the compiler generally allows you to do. When there is direct cast, the Delphi compiler for Win32 gives up (provided that the sizes match, as you can't cast a char to a LongInt). So you can cast an object into an object of another type because all references are of the same size, and you can cast an object reference to an integer (holding the address of the memory location of the object, not the object's data), and the like. These are *unsuggested* and *unsafe* practices, but they are somewhat frequent in Delphi.

As .NET CLR has a high regard for type safety (a precondition for having a safe application), some of the direct type cast capabilities you are used to don't apply any more, or they apply in a different way. The first example is when you cast an object to a class type different from its own. While in Delphi for Win32 the cast is always allowed (optionally ending up with a nonsense piece of code), Delphi for .NET treats any cast among class types as if they were done with the as operator. This means that any cast among classes is checked for type compatibility, with the rule that an object of an inherited class is compatible with each of its base class types.

Safe casts are slower than direct casts, but they are certainly safer. Where Delphi for .NET has a syntax to express the two types of casts, they are both converted into safe code (the as cast):

```
anotherObject := TAnotherClass (anObject); // safe direct cast
anotherObject := anObject as TAnotherClass; // safe as cast
```

If these two lines both perform a safe cast, their effect is actually different! In case of failure, the direct cast sets the result to nil, whereas the as cast raises an exception.

NOTE Delphi syntax for typecasts works the opposite of the corresponding C# syntax. In C# the as cast returns nil in case of incompatibility, while the direct cast raises an exception. Because Delphi's as typecast has raised an exception since Delphi 1, Borland decided not to change its behavior simply because of an opposite convention in a much newer language.

You can test the different behavior of the two casts statements by running the AsAndCast demo program, which has the following code snippet:

```
mem := TMemoryStream.Create;
str := TStringStream.Create;
try
  // str := mem as TStringStream; // line 1
  str := TStringStream (mem); // line 2
  writeln ('no exception');
except
  writeln ('error');
end;

if Assigned (str) then
  writeln ('assigned')
else
  writeln ('not assigned');
```

Comment either one of the two casts (in the lines marked line 1 and line 2) and run the program to see the relevant difference. The type cast notation always implements an automatic safe cast, the only exception being the case in which the compiler spots the use of the protected hack, as discussed later in "The Protected Hack Still Works!"

A totally different case is the cast of a primitive type (let's say an integer) to a class type. Instead of a cast involving the value of the reference (as on Win32), you end up with the boxing of the native value:

```
anObject := TObject (aNumber);
```

Thus you obtain an actual object (not just a fake reference), which is a new object containing the value you are casting. This value can be unboxed (or cast back) to the original native type, with a notation like:

```
aNumber := Integer (anObject);
```

As this is a controlled cast, casting to an integer a regular object (not a boxed integer) will cause an error. This breaks the existing Delphi code, which formally allows you to cast any object to an integer to extract the value of the reference. Of course, this was not a good way to write code in the first place, so you shouldn't really complain!

I won't even touch on the idea of casting object references to pointers and possibly even manipulating those pointers, as almost none of the pointer operations are allowed in a safe and managed .NET application.

Finally, notice that you can define custom type casts, or custom data type conversions, with the Implicit and Explicit operators (see the later section "Operators Gain New Ground").

Classes Gain New Ground

To fully support the class model of the CLR, Borland had to tweak the Delphi language in a few ways, including making changes to classes. Although most of the traditional features of classes were left unchanged, there are a few relevant new features. The most notable are the visibility rules definitions becoming more in line with other languages, the support for nested types, and concept of class helpers.

Access Specifiers

As I've already covered in the last chapter in the section "When Private is Really Private," Delphi recently introduced on both .NET and Win32 the new strict private and strict protected access specifiers to better comply with the CLS. These new specifiers correspond to the CLR private and protected specifiers and behave as you'd expect.

In fact, to maintain source code compatibility with Win32 code, the behavior of the private and protected keywords has not changed to match C# or other languages. This means your existing code taking advantage of this feature will keep working. The only change is that Delphi's protected access specifier is mapped to the CLR family or assembly access specifier. In other words, Delphi's protected specifier works as usual within an assembly but reverts to private across assembly boundaries. Table 4.3 lists correspondences between Delphi and the CLR.

TABLE 4.3:   Delphi and CLR Access Specifiers

DELPHI	CLR
private	assembly
strict private	private
protected	famorassem (family or assembly)
strict protected	family
public	public
published	public

THE PROTECTED HACK STILL WORKS!

Longtime Delphi programmers certainly know that there is a trick allowing you access to any protected data of another class, even if this class is declared in a different unit. This trick, often called the *protected hack*, is described in the last chapter.

One of the key elements of the protected hack is the ability to cast an object of a class to its fake subclass, something the CLR won't allow you to do (see the previous section "Cast on the Safe Side"). However, if the compiler recognizes you are using the protected hack (that is, when it notices a weird typecast to an empty subclass to access a protected member), it ignores the cast but lets you access the protected member anyway.

This is demonstrated by the ProtectedHack demo, which has a class with a protected member:

```
type
  TTest = class
  protected
    ProtectedData: Integer;
  public
    PublicData: Integer;
    function GetValue: string;
  end;
```

The main form uses the protected hack to access to the data, as follows:

```
type
 TTestHack = class (TTest);

procedure TForm1.Button2Click(Sender: TObject);
var
  Obj: TTest;
begin
  Obj := TTest.Create;
  Obj.PublicData := 10;
  TTestHack(Obj).ProtectedData := 20;
  ShowMessage (Obj.GetValue);
```

The generated IL code (in the following listing) shows that the compiler skips the type cast and produces the same code for the access to the public and protected data:

```
.method public instance void  Button2Click(object Sender)
          cil managed
{
  // Code size       40 (0x28)
  .maxstack  2
  .locals init ([0] class TestClass.TTest Obj)
  IL_0000:  newobj     instance void TestClass.TTest::.ctor()
  IL_0005:  stloc.0
  IL_0006:  ldloc.0
  IL_0007:  ldc.i4.s   10
  IL_0009:  stfld      int32 TestClass.TTest::PublicData
  IL_000e:  ldloc.0
  IL_000f:  ldc.i4.s   20
  IL_0011:  stfld      int32 TestClass.TTest::ProtectedData
  IL_0016:  ldloc.0
  IL_0017:  call       instance string
          TestClass.TTest::GetValue()
```

```
IL_001c:  call        void
          Borland.Vcl.Dialogs.Unit::ShowMessage(string)
IL_0021:  ldloc.0
IL_0022:  call        instance void TestClass.TTest::Free()
IL_0027:  ret
} // end of method TForm1::Button2Click
```

The only limitation is that, according to the rules mentioned in the previous section, the use of the protected hack is limited to a single assembly. If the unit that defines the base class is contained by a different assembly, the code will not work.

Class Data and Class Static Methods

Delphi has always allowed the declaration of class methods, that is, methods not bound to a specific object but to a class as a whole. A long-awaited feature of the Delphi language relates to the introduction of class data; that is, data shared among all objects of the class.

NOTE By the way, not all Delphi programmers know that within class methods you can indeed use the Self keyword, but that refers to the class itself, not an instance as it happens with regular methods.

It was possible to simulate this construct in past versions of Delphi by using global variables hidden in the implementation section of a unit, but this was far from a neat way of writing the code and sometimes caused troubles with derived classes. The introduction of class data adds to Delphi a feature that most other OOP languages share. How do you declare class data? Simply by pre-pending the class var keywords combination to the declaration:

```
type
  TMyData = class
  private
    class var
      CommonCount: Integer;
  public
    class function GetCommon: Integer;
```

Actually, class var introduces a block of one or more declarations. In addition to declaring class data, you can also define class properties and static class methods.

NOTE Class data is not available on the Delphi 2005 Win32 compiler (although class static methods are). I decided to cover class static methods in this chapter anyway, as they wouldn't be particularly useful on Win32 (due to the lack of class data, as they are often used together). Notice also that class properties mapped to static class methods (but not to class data, of course) have been introduced in the Win32 compiler by Delphi 2005, although they do not seem to work as expected: it seems impossible to apply them to a class instead of a regular object.

Class static methods have been introduced for compatibility to the CLS, as Delphi code could use class methods to express a very similar concept. Because there are relevant implementation differences, Borland decided to have two separate features in the language. The differences are that class static methods have no references to their own class (no *self* referring to the class itself) and cannot be virtual. On the positive side, they can be used to define class properties.

One of the reasons this difference is relevant is that, unlike Delphi's class methods, static methods can be used for Windows callbacks, as they are functionally equivalent to global procedures. Of course, Delphi for Win32 never needed this feature, as it allows the definition of global procedures not bound to classes.

Here is some sample code to highlight the syntax, taken from the ClassStatic example:

```
type
  TBase = class
  private
    class var
      fMyName: string;
  public
    class procedure One;
    class procedure Two; static;

    class function GetMyName: string; static;
    class procedure SetMyName (Value: string); static;
    class property MyName: string
      read GetMyNamxe write SetMyName;
  end;
```

Class properties in .NET are properties mapped to class static methods, but in Delphi you can also map them to class data (in this case the compiler will automatically generate the *missing* method as happens for plain properties and is discussed in the section "Properties" later in this chapter). For example, this Delphi declaration:

```
class property MyName: string
  read FMyName write SetMyName;
```

is mapped to the following CLS-compliant metadata:

```
.property instance string MyName()
{
  .custom instance void [System]
    System.ComponentModel.BrowsableAttribute::.ctor(bool) =
    ( 01 00 00 00 00 )
  .set void ClassStatic.TBase::set_MyName(string)
  .get string ClassStatic.TBase::get_MyName()
} // end of property TBase::MyName
```

Class Constructors

In addition to standard constructors used to allocate an object of a class and optionally initialize its data, .NET introduces the idea of a class constructor, a sort of class static method called automatically by the CLR to initialize a class. In fact, the class constructor executes before the class is referenced or used in the program.

A class can have only one class constructor:

```
type
    TMyTestClass = class
    strict private
      class constructor Create;
```

The effect of this code is a special method called `.cctor` (class constructor, as opposed to plain constructors internally called `.ctor`), as the following IL declaration shows:

```
.method private specialname rtspecialname static
        void  .cctor() cil managed
```

As mentioned earlier (in the "Good Old Units" section), the class constructors in .NET can be considered a replacement for Delphi initialization sections. They are generated by the Delphi compiler for the fake unit class when an initialization section is used.

Again, as mentioned, the key difference is that the call sequence of the various class constructors within a program is nondeterministic, so you cannot rely on a class constructor being called before another one gets executed. If you have similar dependencies, you'll have to move them off to the initial code of the project itself or some other global place where you can control the sequence of execution. At times, though, since class constructors are guaranteed to be called before a class is used, you can fine-tune your existing code to guarantee that the sequence you are looking for is followed. For example, if an initialization section uses a class from another unit, you know that the class constructor of that other unit is executed first.

Abstract Classes

You saw in the last chapter that Delphi's Win32 compiler allows you to instantiate an abstract class issuing only a warning. However, in Delphi for .NET, instantiating an abstract class is an error, as you can figure out by the AbstractAnimalsNET example, a slight variation of the AbstractAnimals example discussed in Chapter 3.

As mentioned, Delphi for .NET also allows an entire class to be declared as abstract, even though it does not contain any abstract virtual methods. You do this simply by adding the `abstract` keyword to the class declaration, as in the following case:

```
TAnotherAnimal = class abstract
    end;
```

Trying to create an instance with the following useless code:

```
with TAnotherAnimal.Create do
    Free;
```

will result in a compile-time error. This means you can mark a class as abstract to prevent the compiler from creating any object for it.

Class Helpers

When Borland started working on Delphi for .NET, one of the problems that surfaced was the need to somewhat reconcile Delphi's own base classes (such as TObject, Exception) with the corresponding classes of the .NET Framework. After some research, they came out with a somewhat astonishing trick called class helpers. A class helper is nothing but a way to pretend that some methods and properties are part of a class you have no power to modify, while in fact they are hosted by a different class. In other words, you can add a special class, the helper, that adds methods to an existing one (methods or class data only, but no instance data). This way you'll be able to apply the new method to an object of that other class, even if that class has no clue about the existence of the method.

If this is not clear, and it is probably not, let's look at an example (taken from the ClassHelperDemo project):

```
type
  TMyObject = class
  private
    Value: Integer;
    Text: string;
  public
    procedure Increase;
  end;

  TMyObjectHelper = class helper for TMyObject
  public
    procedure Show;
  end;
```

The preceding code declares a class and a helper for this class. This means that on an object of type TmyObject, you can call the method(s) of the class as well as each of the methods of the class helper:

```
Obj := TMyObject.Create;
Obj.Text := 'foo';
Obj.Show;
```

The helper method becomes part of the class and can use Self as any other method to refer to the current object (of the class it helps because class helpers are not instantiated), as this code demonstrates:

```
procedure TMyObjectHelper.Show;
begin
  WriteLn (Text + ' ' + IntToStr (Value) + ' -- ' +
    ClassName + ' -- ' + ToString);
end;
```

Finally, notice that a helper method can override the original method. In the code I've added a Show method both to the class and to the helper, but only one of the helpers gets called!

Of course, it makes very little sense to declare a class and an extension to the same class using the class helper syntax in the same unit or even in the same program. What can be interesting, however, is the ability to extend a class defined in an external assembly (and possibly even written in another language). Borland itself uses class helpers heavily in Delphi's RTL to extend standard .NET classes and integrate with .NET RTL support.

For example, a Delphi traditional `TObject` class has a `ClassName` method. In Delphi for .NET `TObject` is an alias of `System.Object`, which would prevent you from calling the `ClassName` method on your objects. However, by defining a class helper for the `TObject` class, Delphi makes it possible for you to call `ClassName` on any .NET objects, even those not originating in Delphi itself. This is the code you can find in System.pas:

```
TObjectHelper = class helper for TObject
public
  procedure Free;
  function ClassType: TClass;
  class function ClassName: string;
  class function ClassNameIs(const Name: string): Boolean;
  class function ClassParent: TClass;
  class function ClassInfo: System.Type;
  class function InheritsFrom(AClass: TClass): Boolean;
  class function MethodAddress
    (const AName: string): TMethodCode;
  class function MethodName(ACode: TMethodCode): string;
  function FieldAddress(const AName: string): TObject;
  procedure Dispatch(var Message);
end;
```

(More details about `TObjectHelper` implementation are in Chapter 9, which covers the Delphi RTL.) Given this declaration, you can not only call the helper methods on any object of classes you compile with Delphi, but also call them to any object written in any language and created by assemblies you hook to your code. This includes containers and contained objects, WinForms, and ASP.NET controls and just about any object in the system.

NOTE   Just in case you are thinking of mimicking this behavior in another language, consider that (as far as I know) Borland has filed for patents on the class helper technology.

According to Delphi's R&D members, the main rule is that class helpers should be used to bind the core classes of the library to new platforms while maintaining compatibility with existing code. Class helpers should *not* be used as a general language construct for developing applications or components. However, not only RTL libraries, but also the higher-level ECO framework uses class helpers extensively.

NOTE   My impression is that class helpers could be used to circumvent some of the security features based on the language. For example, you can modify a sealed class with a helper, and you can also replace an existing method. True, the additional features will be available only from your code...but still, these issues might be part of the "do not abuse" warning from Borland.

There are a few more rules that apply to class helpers. Class helper methods can have different access specifiers, can be class methods or virtual methods (which can be overridden—the compiler adds an interface behind the scenes), and can have extra constructors, class variables, properties, or class operators. The only features they lack are instance data.

Finally, notice that class helpers are now available also in the Win32 compiler, as you can see in the ClassHelpersWin32 example, almost identical to its .NET counterpart. However, on Win32 class helpers are less relevant, as in this environment you don't have an external class library to integrate with.

Properties

Properties in Delphi for .NET maintain the core features they have had since Delphi 1. The only relevant difference is in how they are translated to .NET code and how you can use them from other .NET languages. In fact, the CLS states that properties must be mapped to getter and setter methods and not directly to fields, as in Delphi. For this reason the Delphi for .NET compiler creates the methods for you if your code maps the properties directly to data. As there is a specific convention for naming the setter and getter methods (respectively, `set_` and `get_` followed by the name of the property), if you don't follow it the compiler will add methods with the correct names, which will call the methods you've written. Finally, notice that, unlike Delphi for Win32, the visibility of the getter and setter methods must match that of the property: if the property is public the methods must be public as well.

The following is a sample class with two properties. The first property (One) was *completed* automatically by the Delphi editor after writing the declaration `property One: string` and typing Ctrl+Shift+C. In this case, Delphi for .NET uses the `set_One` method name instead of the traditional Delphi name `SetOne`. The second property was written manually with a getter and a setter method (again generated by class completion). Here is the class code (from the PropertyDemo example):

```
type
  TMyClass = class
  public
    FOne, FTwo: string;
    procedure set_One(const Value: string);
    function GetTwo: string;
    procedure SetTwo(const Value: string);
  public
    property One: string read FOne write set_One;
  published
    property Two: string read GetTwo write SetTwo;
  end;
```

If you now compile this code and inspect it with Reflector, you can find out a couple of interesting things. First, the property One is mapped to two methods, one written in the code and the other generated by the compiler:

```
.property instance string One()
{
  .custom instance void [System]
    System.ComponentModel.BrowsableAttribute::.ctor(bool) =
    ( 01 00 00 00 00 )
  .get instance string PropertyDemo.TMyClass::get_One()
  .set instance void PropertyDemo.TMyClass::set_One(string)
} // end of property TMyClass::One
```

This is easily visible in the output of Reflector, which shows the two methods under the property node, as you can see in Figure 4.2. Now let's look at the method synthesized by the compiler, which is almost identical to one generated by hand:

```
.method public hidebysig specialname instance string
        get_One() cil managed
{
```

```
     // Code size       9 (0x9)
     .maxstack  1
     .locals init ([0] string Result)
     IL_0000:  ldarg.0
     IL_0001:  ldfld       string PropertyDemo.TMyClass::FOne
     IL_0006:  stloc.0
     IL_0007:  ldloc.0
     IL_0008:  ret
   } // end of method TMyClass::get_One
```

Now let's look a the second property. The first difference is that the `BrowsableAttribute` is set to true as an effect of the published declaration (more on this as we discuss attributes later in this chapter), but what I want to point out is the methods the property is mapped to are not those in the declaration!

```
  .property instance string Two()
  {
    .custom instance void [System]
      System.ComponentModel.BrowsableAttribute::.ctor(bool) =
      ( 01 00 01 00 00 )
    .get instance string PropertyDemo.TMyClass::get_Two()
    .set instance void PropertyDemo.TMyClass::set_Two(string)
  } // end of property TMyClass::Two
```

FIGURE 4.2
Reflector clearly shows
the access methods used
by the properties, in this
example for the TMyClass
class of the Property-
Demo program.

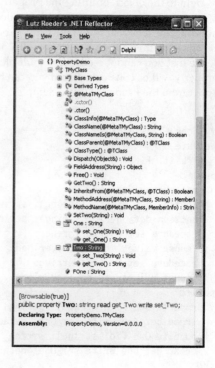

Again, the compiler does a few things behind the scenes. It doesn't change the method names, but it generates another method, get_Two, that calls GetTwo:

```
.method public hidebysig specialname instance string
        get_Two() cil managed
{
  // Code size        9 (0x9)
  .maxstack  1
  .locals init ([0] string Result)
  IL_0000:  ldarg.0
  IL_0001:  call        instance string
                        PropertyDemo.TMyClass::GetTwo()
  IL_0006:  stloc.0
  IL_0007:  ldloc.0
  IL_0008:  ret
} // end of method TMyClass::get_Two
```

The same happens with set_Two calling SetTwo.

Indexers or Array Properties

Since its first release, Delphi has always supported the idea of array properties that receive as a parameter a value passed among square brackets. We've also always enjoyed the possibility of marking one of the array properties of a class as *default* so that it can be referenced applying the square brackets right to the object, omitting the property name.

The C# language has a very similar idea, called an indexer, with a significant difference: you can have multiple indexers (that is, default array properties) for a single class, based on a different types of index. To match this feature, Delphi for .NET adds support for overloading the default array property. Notice that you cannot really have multiple array properties (if you try, only the last default array property will be considered), but you can have multiple definitions of a single property (as in this snippet from the PropertyDemo example):

```
type
  TMySecondClass = class
    private
      strList: TStringList;
    public
      constructor Create;
      function get_One(I: Integer): string; overload;
      function get_One(Id: string): string; overload;
      procedure set_One(I: Integer;
        const Value: string); overload;
      procedure set_One(Id: string;
        const Value: string); overload;
    public
      property One [I: Integer]: string
        read get_One write set_One; default;
      property One [Id: string]: string
        read get_One write set_One; default;
  end;
```

This means you can use both versions of the One default property simply by specifying different types of parameters within square brackets:

```
sc := TMySecondClass.Create;
sc ['text'] := 'hello';
writeln (sc [0]);
```

Applying Constructors to Instances

In past versions of Delphi, constructors could be used in two different scenarios: (i) you could use them in the traditional object creation mode by applying them to a class type, or (ii) you could use them in initializer mode by applying them to existing objects:

```
anObject := aClass.Create; // (i) object creation
anObject.Create; // (ii) object (re)initialization
```

In Delphi for .NET, you cannot apply a constructor to an instance anymore because the underlying execution environment doesn't support this feature. The effect of this change is quite positive, though. Applying a constructor to an instance is a classic error in Delphi, an error for which the compiler might at most issue a warning, because there is a legitimate use of the syntax. Now, with that use being illegal, the compiler will issue an error and will almost always be correct! In fact, 99 percent of the times you apply a constructor to an instance, you are typing the wrong code (this percentage is true for myself at least, and I still mistype constructor calls even after so many years of Delphi coding).

Calling Inherited Constructors

Delphi for .NET marks a clear departure from the traditional Delphi implementation of constructors. Delphi used to be one of the few OOP programming languages that didn't require you to initialize base classes in the constructor of an inherited class, opening up the possibility for errors and odd behaviors. Now Delphi for .NET enforces this rule. In the constructor of an inherited class you must call the base class constructor, and you must call it before touching any inherited field or calling any method of the base class.

For example, the following trivial code doesn't compile any more:

```
type
  TMyClass = class
  private
    fValue: Integer;
  public
    constructor Create;
  end;

constructor TMyClass.Create;
begin
  fValue := 10;
end;
```

Instead, it gives the error message: "'Self' is uninitialized. An inherited constructor must be called." In fact, the TMyClass class inherits from TObject, so it is bound to the same rule of any other class. This is quite unfortunate, as the `TObject.Create` constructor is basically useless. To compile the constructor you need to add a new line with the inherited constructor call, like:

```
constructor TMyClass.Create;
begin
  fValue := 10;
  inherited Create;
end;
```

In fact, you can use instance fields before the base class constructor call. Considering that there are restrictions on what you can do before initializing the base class, the preferred way of coding the constructor is to write the `inherited Create` call as the first thing, although in this case it is not required:

```
constructor TMyClass.Create;
begin
  inherited Create;
  fValue := 10;
end;
```

Free and Destroy in the Garbage Collected World

One of the features of the .NET platform (as in the Java platform) that gets the most enthusiastic supporter and angry opponents is garbage collection. I don't want to get into this discussion here but only address a specific issue related to the management of external resources. Although the garbage collector will automatically reclaim unused memory, there might be other operations you want to do when you no longer need an object, such as closing a database connection or freeing a file handle or a GDI resource.

In Delphi for Win32, you generally don't need to free a file handle as long as you destroy the object wrapping it, such as a `TFileStream` object. This library class has a destructor that frees the external resource for you, but only if and when you call `Free` on the object. Something similar happens on .NET, as FCL library classes (and also Borland's RTL and VCL classes) provide a way to release external resources in an automatic way.

The problem is that in a system that uses a garbage collector, you don't know when the memory of the object is going to be released, as an object may be destroyed a long time after it is no longer referenced by anything else. This might keep the external resources locked much longer than necessary. To account for this situation, .NET provides for two different options for disposing external resources. The nondeterministic `Finalize` method (defined in `System.Object`) is called, if implemented, just before the GC destroys the object. Programmers are advised to keep its usage to a minimum because this technique impacts negatively on the GC. The deterministic `Dispose` method (of the `IDisposable` interface) is called, if implemented, by the program after it has finished using the object.

This second solution is based on a specific pattern: any class needing resource cleanup should implement the `IDisposable` interface, which has only one method, `Dispose`. So you'll have to add this method to your classes, if needed. You must also consider that this method must be called either directly in the code you write or by a container class you add the object to (but not all container classes call `IDisposable.Dispose`).

It is important to consider that in .NET you don't have the notion of a destructor, because the object is destroyed automatically by the GC, but you do have these notions of the object finalization and of the disposing of object resources. Because OOP languages have the notion of a destructor though, different .NET languages can make different choices. Here, of course, I'll focus on what Delphi does.

In Delphi for .NET, the `Destroy` destructor is used by the compiler to implement `IDisposable.Dispose`. So if you have existing code in your destructor to take care of any external resources, you can keep Win32 the destructor code as it is. Of course, this method won't free the memory anymore, but it will do anything else that is necessary. However, as you don't need to free other objects from memory, you might want to remove some of the code of your destructors.

On the other hand, calls to `Free` are routed to calls of `IDisposable.Dispose`, so the old code that frees an object still works and still make sense if an object needs to be disposed (which is not true for every object). Again, you don't need to free the memory of the objects as in Win32 because the GC takes care of that for you. If a destructor (and a call to `Free`) in Win32 does both a finalization and memory reclamation, the Delphi for .NET implementation uses similar code to perform only the finalization portion.

The overall result is that most of your existing Delphi code still works, adapting itself properly to the correct .NET behavior, which is quite different.

NOTE If you write a destructor `Destroy` and forget the `override` keyword, you'll get an odd error message saying "Unsupported language feature: 'destructor.'" The reason for the message is that the Delphi overridden `Destroy` destructor has been hijacked to implement the dispose pattern, while any other attempt to add a traditional destructor fails. Destructors are not supported to do the same thing as they used to, although destructors other than `Destroy` are seldom used in Delphi.

Technically, if you write a Delphi destructor in .NET, like:

```
type
  TMyClass = class
  public
    destructor Destroy; override;
```

you'll end up with the following IL, indicating that the class implements `System.IDisposable`:

```
.class public auto ansi beforefieldinit TMyClass
  extends [mscorlib]System.Object
  implements [mscorlib]System.IDisposable
```

In turn, the `Destroy` method becomes an implementation to `Dispose`:

```
.method public newslot virtual instance void
  Destroy() cil managed
{
  .override [mscorlib]System.IDisposable::Dispose
```

NOTE If you look with more care into the code of the destructor, you'll notice that it sets a `Disposed_` Boolean field. This is a hidden field added to the class by the compiler. This field is checked upon entering the destructor to avoid re-executing it, thus making sure that the cleanup code is only executed once.

As in Delphi for Win32, you never call `Destroy` directly to dispose objects properly; you call `Free` instead. `Free` invokes the (virtual) destructor. In Delphi for .NET the call to `Free` has been redirected to a call to the `Dispose` method of the `IDisposable` interface, thereby invoking your deterministic cleanup routine that was defined like a traditional Delphi destructor:

```
procedure TObjectHelper.Free;
begin
  if (Self <> nil) and (Self is IDisposable) then
  begin
    if Assigned(VCLFreeNotify) then
      VCLFreeNotify(Self);
    (Self as IDisposable).Dispose;
  end;
end;
```

NOTE A curiosity: thanks to class helpers, you can also call `Free` on FCL objects or other objects written in C#. Regarding C#, it is also interesting to notice that the destructors are actually overrides of `Finalize`, the nondeterministic cleanup option. What's curious is that Microsoft advises against using `Finalize` whenever possible, due to performance issues.

Again, this means that to dispose external resources in a timely manner, if there are any, you can keep using `try-finally` blocks like:

```
var
  MyObj: TMyObj;
begin
  MyObj := TMyObj.Create;
  try
    // use MyObj
  finally
    MyObj.Free;
  end;
```

It is true that you don't need this code if the `TMyObj` class has nothing to dispose of, but since you generally don't know how an object is implemented, you might want to write code like this anyway. In fact, if an object doesn't implement the dispose pattern, the call to `Free` is a no-op.

Class References and Metaclasses

I already covered class references in the last chapter, discussing the standard Delphi (for Win32) implementation. Class references are a specific feature of the Delphi language, so it shouldn't surprise you that the .NET Framework doesn't have the same concept. As usual, Delphi for .NET retains the syntax for class references, and most of their behavior stays the same as well (including the call of virtual constructors on them and their support for virtual class methods). However, behind the scenes the implementation changes considerably.

In Delphi for .NET, for each class (let's call one TMyClass), the compiler creates both a class and a metaclass (called by default something like @MetaTMyClass) inherited from the generic TClass metaclass. The compiler also defines a constant static instance of the metaclass.

NOTE   Delphi class references (or metaclasses) are not CLS compliant: they are not intended for use by other .NET languages. The same holds for virtual constructors.

However, the Delphi for .NET compiler cannot impose the presence of a specific metaclass for classes not compiled by Delphi and imported from assemblies written in other languages. In this case the compiler creates an instance of a generic TClass metaclass, passing the CLR type to the constructor. This way, Delphi for .NET can simulate Delphi metaclass behaviors for any .NET class, although the code is not as efficient as the class-specific metaclasses generated by the compiler.

By the way, note that internally TClass uses an instance of the type System.RuntimeTypeHandle rather than the more obvious (but less memory efficient) System.Type.

In practice, class helpers of both types work smoothly, as the ClassReferences example shows. Here is a snippet:

```
type
  TMyDataClass = class of TMyData;
  TDotNetClass = class of ArrayList;
var
  aClass: TMyDataClass;
  anotherClass: TDotNetClass;
begin
  aClass := TMyData;
  anotherClass := ArrayList;
```

What's relevant for this example is to inspect the IL code of the two preceding assignment statements:

```
IL_0006:  ldsfld    class ClassReferences.TMyData/@MetaTMyData
ClassReferences.TMyData/@MetaTMyData::@Instance
IL_0011:  call      class Borland.Delphi.@TClass
Borland.Delphi.Units.System::@GetMetaFromHandle(valuetype
[mscorlib]System.RuntimeTypeHandle)
```

You can see that in the first case the compiler generates the nested class TMyData/@MetaTMyData and uses it, while in the second case it uses the generic @TClass data type. Similarly the following statements:

```
writeln (aClass.ClassName);
writeln (anotherClass.ClassName);
```

compile to IL code including these calls:

```
  IL_001d:  call      string ClassReferences.TMyData::ClassName(class
ClassReferences.TMyData/@MetaTMyData)
  IL_0038:  call      string Borland.Delphi.TObjectHelper::ClassName(class
Borland.Delphi.@TClass)
```

Interfaces Are Now "Pure"

At the time of its introduction in the early versions of Delphi, the interface type was considered by most programmers strictly a COM-related technique. This was also due to some implementation decisions within Delphi's RTL. With the introduction of each new version of Delphi, the relationship between the concept of interface and COM has increasingly reduced. For example, recent versions of Delphi introduced the IInterface base interface (a formal replacement of IUnknown) and helper classes and routines in general RTL units (instead of the COM/ActiveX units).

NOTE I'm definitely a big fan of the use of interfaces as a sound OOP technology. Chapter 3 shows some ways to benefit from interfaces, but Chapter 11, where I cover dynamic architectures, really shows the power of this technique.

In Delphi for .NET, COM is basically gone, so it should come as no surprise that some relevant implementation details of interfaces have changed as well. First of all, the definition of IInterface is still available but quite different, as it now has an *empty* definition:

```
// in System.pas (Win32)
type
  IInterface = interface
    ['{00000000-0000-0000-C000-000000000046}']
    function QueryInterface(const IID: TGUID; out Obj):
      HResult; stdcall;
    function _AddRef: Integer; stdcall;
    function _Release: Integer; stdcall;
  end;

// in Borland.Delphi.System.pas (.NET)
type
  IInterface = interface
  end;
```

This means that the reference counting for interfaces is gone—something that should come as no surprise with a run time that uses garbage collection—but it also means the type checking is not based on QueryInterface anymore but on specific compiler/run-time features. The side effect of this change is that you don't need to decorate interfaces with GUIDs any more for the type checking to work properly as required in previous versions of Delphi.

Correspondingly, the TInterfacedObject class has an empty implementation:

```
type
  TInterfacedObject = TObject;
```

These changes imply that interfaces are now completely a language feature, with no connection whatsoever to COM or anything else. The .NET run time fully supports interfaces (and the run time and the FCL uses them quite extensively), so Delphi for .NET embraces this approach.

Does it mean that interfaces work better in Delphi for .NET than they do in Delphi for Win32? Having garbage collection on interface objects is definitely very handy, as it is far from trivial to free objects in Delphi for Win32 when you don't access them exclusively via interfaces.

However, there are also some interesting features of interfaces in Delphi for Win32 that didn't make it over to .NET. In particular, dynamic aggregation of interfaces (that is, the use of the `implements` keyword for interfaces) is not supported in Delphi for .NET. This is quite bad, as dynamic aggregation allows you to share a common implementation of the interface methods between separate classes supporting the same interface.

As a sample of the use of interfaces in Delphi for .NET, you can look at the InterfaceTest demo. Its secondary unit has an interface with a few methods and a property. When declaring the property I found out that for .NET compatibility you should follow very precise rules, even more than for object properties. This is how Delphi likes it:

```
type
  ISimple = interface (IInterface)
    procedure ShowMessage;
    function Compute (a, b: Integer): Integer;
    function get_Value: Integer;
    procedure set_Value (Value: Integer);
    property Value: Integer read get_Value write set_Value;
  end;
```

Notice the lowercase names for the `get` and `set` methods and the underscore before the property name. If you don't follow this convention you'll get hints like:

```
[Hint] Property accessor GetValue should be get_Value
[Hint] Case of property accessor method ISimple.Get_Value should be ISimple.get_Value
```

These hints, which can be suppressed, help you write CLS-compatible code. If you fail do so, other .NET languages won't be able to use the property. Some of them (like VB.NET and C#) will still allow you to use the property or call the getter and setter accessor methods directly, but some .NET languages might not allow any access at all.

NOTE   If you look at the interfaces used by .NET, however, it seems that they avoid the problem altogether by *not* using properties inside interfaces and instead using only custom `set` and `get` methods written in many inconsistent ways...

Notice that the behavior of the Delphi compiler with properties inside interfaces (you'll get a compiler hint) is quite different from properties inside classes. In this case, as discussed earlier in the section "Properties," the compiler adds to your code the CLS-compliant methods generating code for
them. This ensures CLS compatibility, at the cost of extra code (and also generally slower code). With
interfaces, the automatic generation would make no sense, as you would have to implement multiple
versions of the same method.

As an experiment, I've added a GUID (or to be more precise an IID, an interface ID) to the interface
as follows:

```
type
  ISimple = interface (IInterface)
    ['{6F1B5589-3987-4665-9C4F-630287760BE9}']
```

Unlike Delphi 8, this declaration is converted by the compiler into the corresponding Guid attribute. The effect is identical to writing:

```
type
  [Guid('6F1B5589-3987-4665-9C4F-630287760BE9')]
  ISimple = interface (IInterface)
```

This attribute is what you need for COM interoperability in .NET (notice, in fact, you'll need to use the System.Runtime.InteropServices namespace for the Guid attribute to work).

Operators Gain New Ground

Another brand new addition to the Delphi language is the concept of operator overloading; that is, the ability to define your own implementation for doing standard operations (addition, multiplication, comparison, and so on) on your data types. Operator overloading can be used on both records and classes, although the general advice is to use it only on value types. The idea is that you can implement an add operator (a special Add method) and then use the + sign to call it.

To define an operator you use class operator (by reusing existing reserved words, Borland managed to have no impact on existing code). The term *class* here relates to class methods, as operators like class methods have no Self parameter, no current object. After the directive you write the operator's name, such as Add:

```
type
  TPointRecord = record
  public
    class operator Add (a, b: TPointRecord): TPointRecord;
```

The operator Add is than called with the + symbol, as you'd expect. So what are the available operators? Basically the entire set of operators of the language shown in Table 4.4, as you cannot define brand new language operators.

TABLE 4.4:   Delphi for .NET Operators

GROUP	OPERATORS
Cast Operators	Implicit, Explicit
Unary Operators	Positive, Negative, Inc, Dec, LogicalNot, BitwiseNot, Trunc, Round
Comparison Operators	Equal, NotEqual, GreaterThan, GraterThanOrEqual, LessThan, LessThenOrEqual
Binary Operators	Add, Subtract, Multiply, Divide, IntDivide, Modulus, ShiftLeft, ShiftRight, LogicalAnd, LogicalOr, LogicalXor, BitwiseAnd, BitwiseOr, BitwiseXor

In the code calling the operator, you do not use these names but use the corresponding symbol. This allows fields or methods within your code to have a name that would otherwise conflict. For example, you can still use a class with an Add method and add an Add operator to it.

When you define these operators, you spell out the parameters, and the operator is applied only if the parameters match exactly. To add two values of different types, you'll probably have to specify two Add operations, as each operand could be the first or second entry of the expression. In fact, the definition of operators provides no automatic commutativity. Moreover, you have to indicate the type very precisely, as automatic type conversions don't apply. Many times this implies overloading the overloaded operator and providing multiple versions with different types of parameters.

There are two special operators you can define, Implicit and Explicit. The first is used to define an implicit type cast (or silent conversions), which should be perfect and not lossy. The second, Explicit, can be invoked only with an explicit type cast from a variable of a type to another given type. Together these two operators define the casts that are allowed to and from the given data type. Notice that both the Implicit and the Explicit operators can be overloaded based on the function return type, which is generally not possible for overloaded methods. In case of a type cast, in fact, the compiler knows the expected resulting type and can figure out which is the typecast operation to apply.

As an example, the OperatorsOver demo includes both a record with a few operators and a class with similar ones:

```
type
  TPointRecord = record
  private
    x, y: Integer;
  public
    procedure SetValue (x1, y1: Integer);
    class operator Add (a, b: TPointRecord): TPointRecord;
    class operator Explicit (a: TPointRecord): string;
    class operator Implicit (x1: Integer): TPointRecord;
  end;

type
  TPointClass = class
  private
    x, y: Integer;
  public
    procedure SetValue (x1, y1: Integer);
    class operator Add (a, b: TPointClass): TPointClass;
    class operator Explicit (a: TPointClass): string;
  end;
```

Here is the trivial implementation of the methods of the record:

```
class operator TPointRecord.Add(a, b:
  TPointRecord): TPointRecord;
begin
  Result.x := a.x + b.x;
  Result.y := a.y + b.y;
end;
```

```
class operator TPointRecord.Explicit(a: TPointRecord): string;
begin
  Result := Format('(%d:%d)', [a.x, a.y]);
end;

class operator TPointRecord.Implicit(x1: Integer):
  TPointRecord;
begin
  Result.x := x1;
  Result.y := 0;
end;
```

Using such a record is quite straightforward, as you can write code like this (remember that record variables don't need an explicit allocation):

```
procedure TForm1.Button1Click(Sender: TObject);
var
  a, b, c: TPointRecord;
begin
  a.SetValue(10, 10);
  b := 30;
  c := a + b;
  ShowMessage (string(c));
end;
```

The second assignment (*b*) is done using the implicit operators, due to the lack of a cast, while the ShowMessage call uses the cast notation to activate an explicit type conversion. Consider also that the operator Add doesn't modify its parameters; rather it returns a brand new value. This is a general rule of operators overloading in Delphi for .NET, which applies also to classes. In this second case, however, you'll have to create—allocate—a new object:

```
class operator TPointClass.Add(a, b: TPointClass): TPointClass;
begin
  Result := TPointClass.Create;
  Result.x := a.x + b.x;
  Result.y := a.y + b.y;
end;
```

NOTE   In a presentation I attended, Danny Thorpe, Delphi Chief Scientist, suggested that "while it is valid syntax to define operators on class types, it seems significant that there is not one class in the entire .NET Framework that implements operators. Stick with records until we find out why." Most other .NET experts agree and also suggest to always overload Equal and NotEqual and make sure exceptions are not generated by their behavior. Consider also that operator overloading does not cater to polymorphism, so it fits better with the sealed nature of value types such as records than with classes.

A little known fact is that it is technically possible to call an operator using its fully qualified internal name (like &op_Addition), prefixing it with an &, instead of using the operator symbol. For example, you can rewrite the records sum as follows (see the demo for the complete listing):

```
c := TPointRecord.&&op_Addition(a, b);
```

although I can see very few marginal cases in which you might want to do so. (The entire purpose of defining operators is to be able to use a friendlier notation than a method name, not an uglier one as the preceding direct call.)

Delphi's RTL has been rewritten to take advantage of records with methods and operators. You'll see examples of operator overloading in the Currency type and DateTime type (in Borland.Delphi .System, the .NET version of the Win32 System unit) and in the complex numbers implementation you can find in the Borland.Vcl.Complex unit.

Finally, notice that the rules related to the resolution of calls involving operators are different than the traditional rules involving methods. With automatic type promotions there's the chance that a single expression will end up calling different versions of an overloaded operator and cause ambiguous calls. For this reason, most of the automatic type promotions are disabled for operators.

Attributes, or RTTI to the Extreme

The concept of attributes represents probably the single most relevant innovation of the .NET run time and the C# language (it's also one of the few ideas that didn't come from Java). Attributes in .NET represent RTTI to the extreme. In fact, just as in Delphi you can declare a property as published so you can access it at run time using RTTI techniques, in .NET you can decorate properties, methods, classes, and any other entity with attributes you can later query for at run time.

A published property in a Delphi class compiled with the $M+ directive (inherited from a class compiled with this directive, like TPersistent) generates RTTI or metadata for its published methods and properties and their types. The huge difference is that in .NET the metadata is manufactured for all members of all classes, and you can add additional custom metadata by decorating types, methods, parameters, or the assembly with attributes. There are already many predefined attributes in the FCL, and the system is extensible for building custom attributes, since attributes are simply classes rooted from a given base class.

Technically, in Delphi for .NET (as in other .NET languages) attributes are listed within square brackets immediately before the item to which the attribute is applied, like this (where the attribute is applied to a class):

```
type
  [ExtraAttribute]
  TFoo = class
    ...
  end;
```

NOTE An exception to the position of the attribute is possible using attribute scope modifiers such as assembly: or result:. Another less frequent attribute scope modifier is module:, which in Delphi can be aliased using a unit: scope modifier. An example of its usage is for the Delphi RunTimeRequired attribute as in: [unit:RunTimeRequired (typeof(…))].

The attribute name is generally shortened by removing the standard `Attribute` prefix, so you can write the previous attribute as [`Extra`]. An attribute can have parameters of two types, positional parameters or named parameters, which are declared as in the following code snippet (in this case the attributes are applied to a method):

```
TFoo = class
  [Positional (22)][Named (param1=12)]
  procedure Test;
end;
```

To see examples of the use of attributes, you can open the source code of any Delphi for .NET projects file (with the exclusion of console applications). Here you'll see many attributes applied to the assembly itself and the treading model attribute (usually [`STAThread`]) applied to the project source code, right before its `begin` statement. Most of the other attributes are usually *hidden* in a custom region titled "Program/Assembly Information," so you'll have to expand this region to see the attributes. This is a portion from a project file of an example discussed earlier in this chapter:

```
program UnitTestDemo;
...

{$REGION 'Program/Assembly Information'}
[assembly: AssemblyDescription('')]
[assembly: AssemblyConfiguration('')]
[assembly: AssemblyCompany('')]
...
[assembly: AssemblyVersion('1.0.*')]
...
{$ENDREGION}

[STAThread]
begin
  Application.Initialize;
  Application.CreateForm(TForm1, Form1);
  Application.Run;
end.
```

Declaring Custom Attributes

As I mentioned, you can define a new type of attribute, a new attribute class. This has to be a class inheriting from `TCustomAttribute` (which in turn is an alias of `System.Attribute`). The following is a simple code snippet showing the code of a custom attribute class with a positional parameter (the parameter of the constructor) and a names parameter (a public property):

```
type
  TMyCustomAttribute = class(TCustomAttribute)
  private
    FValue : Integer;
    FDescription: string;
```

```
public
  constructor Create (aValue: Integer);
  function GetValue: Integer;
  property Description: string
    read FDescription write FDescription;
end;

constructor TMyCustomAttribute.Create(aValue: Integer);
begin
  inherited Create;
  FValue := aValue;
end;

function TMyCustomAttribute.GetValue: Integer;
begin
  Result := FValue;
end;
```

This is how you can use this attribute to mark a class and a method, in this case also providing a value for the named parameter. Notice again that you can use the short form (the class name without the final attribute) or the complete form:

```
type
  [TMyCustom(17)]
  TFoo = class
  public
    [TMyCustomAttribute(22, description='some text')]
    Data : Integer;
  end;
```

The instance data and the class definition are now marked with the attribute:

```
.class public auto ansi beforefieldinit TFoo
  extends [mscorlib]System.Object
{
  .custom instance void
    CustomAttribute.TMyCustomAttribute::.ctor(int32) = (...)
  ...
  .field public int32 Data
  {
    .custom instance void
      CustomAttribute.TMyCustomAttribute::.ctor(int32) =
        (..., Description=string("some text") )
  }
```

Inspecting Attributes with Reflection

Adding attributes to declarations, as you did earlier, is completely useless by itself. It becomes interesting as soon as there is some other code you have written or part of the .NET libraries that looks for those specific attributes and behaves accordingly.

This means that other code typically acts only on classes or methods marked with a given attribute, eventually considering the attribute parameters. In the NetAttributes example this is accomplished by two routines, ShowCustomAttributes and ShowAttribs, shown next. The first routine receives as parameter a type, outputs the type name, and then extracts from the type the list of attributes of type TMyCustomAttribute (or a compatible derived class). This list, the array of Object returned by the GetCustomAttributes method, is passed to the second routine, which displays the attribute name (of the first attribute of the list) and grabs the value of its parameter. As you asked for TMyCustomAttribute attributes, the cast to this type is indeed correct. Back to the ShowCustomAttributes routine, it repeats the process of displaying the type name, the member type, and the eventual attribute for each of the type members, methods, and data.

```delphi
procedure ShowCustomAttributes (aType: System.Type);
var
  members : array of System.Reflection.MemberInfo;
  I: Integer;
  mtypes: System.Reflection.MemberTypes;
begin
  write (aType.Name);
  ShowAttribs (aType.GetCustomAttributes
    (TMyCustomAttribute.ClassInfo, True));
  writeln;

  members := aType.GetMembers;
  for I := 0 to High(members) do
  begin
    mtypes := members[i].MemberType;
    write (aType.Name + ':' + members[i].Name +
      ' (' + TObject(mtypes).ToString + ')');
    ShowAttribs (members[i].GetCustomAttributes
      (TMyCustomAttribute.ClassInfo, True));
    writeln; // new line
  end;
end;

procedure ShowAttribs (attribs: array of System.Object);
begin
  // show only the first one...
  if Length (attribs) > 0 then
  begin
    write (' ---> ' + attribs[0].ToString);
    write ('(' + IntToStr ((attribs[0] as TMyCustomAttribute).
      CustomValue) + ')' );
  end;
end;
```

The effect of this code is that a call in the main module over an object of the TFoo type, like:

```
ShowCustomAttributes (Foo.GetType);
```

(or over the TFoo type itself) produces an output like:

```
TFoo ---> CustomAttribute.TMyCustomAttribute(17)
TFoo:Data (Field) ---> CustomAttribute.TMyCustomAttribute(22)
TFoo:GetHashCode (Method)
TFoo:Equals (Method)
TFoo:ToString (Method)
TFoo:Free (Method)
(more output omitted)
```

Multicast Events

In its first incarnation, Delphi introduced events as most development tools use them nowadays. An event in Delphi provides a way to hook an external method to an object, thus modifying the object's behavior through delegation (instead of customizing its class through inheritance). For example, the code a button executes when it is clicked is not written in the button class, but the button delegates to a method of another object, usually the form hosting the button.

Technically, in Delphi an event is a property with a method pointer type, that is, a reference to a method of an object. Java took a different approach, but .NET uses an architecture similar to Delphi's, with a key extension: an event can have multiple handlers attached to it. The term generally used to indicate this behavior is *multicast events*.

Delphi for .NET actually supports both traditional unicast and the new multicast events, depending on the components you are working with. The classic event semantics is still supported through := assignments; the new multicast semantics use the Include() and Exclude() standard procedures, overloaded, to operate on events (these functions were used in the past solely to operate on *sets*). As a comparison, C# uses the += and -= operators of the C language.

```
Include (Button1.Click, Button1Click)
```

In general, you'll stick to the traditional approach when working with VCL.NET, while the multicast technique is necessary when integrating with .NET native framework. To better support interoperability, though, the standard Delphi read/write events also now support the add/remove semantic of .NET for compatibility with the CLR (for example, to let C# code use *traditional* Delphi objects), although the actual behavior will be a single assignment.

As a simple demo, I created a WinForms application with a button and a listbox in it where the button has a Click event handler set up at design-time that adds a string to the list box (see Figure 4.3 for the form at design time). The custom initialization code in the FormLoad event handler adds a second handler for the Click event of the button:

```
procedure TWinForm1.TWinForm1_Load(
  sender: System.Object; e: System.EventArgs);
begin
  Include (Button1.Click, AnotherHandler);
end;
```

FIGURE 4.3
The form of the Multi-
CastForm example at
design time.

For this to work, I manually added to the form class a method with the classic event handler signature used on WinForms, as well as the following code (similar to the code of the Button1_Click handler added at design time):

```
procedure TWinForm1.AnotherHandler(
   sender: TObject; e: System.EventArgs);
begin
   ListBox1.Items.Add ('AnotherHandler');
end;
```

After running the program, press the button and you'll see two lines added to the list box, one by each of the two handlers associated with the Click event of the button.

NOTE   The order in which multicast events are called is not guaranteed and should not be assumed.

What's Next

In this chapter we explored lots of details of the many language changes introduced by Borland to let Delphi fully support the .NET CLR and its type system. We covered features like records with methods, operator overloading, object destruction in a garbage collected environment, attributes, events, and many others.

Along with the previous chapter, this material should give you a fast-paced introduction to the language and its OOP features for Win32 and .NET. The next step will be to look into the support for core language features provided by the run-time library, the native classic Delphi RTL and .NET core libraries. This will be the topic of the next few chapters, along with an introduction to the component and visual controls libraries of the Delphi VCL and of the .NET Framework class library (FCL).

Chapter 5

Delphi Win32 Run-Time Library

As with any programming language, Delphi has a run-time library that provides core services and features to developers. Portions of Delphi's RTL date back to the Turbo Pascal days and are based on global functions and procedures. Other areas of the RTL define the core classes of the Delphi library, starting with the common base class TObject.

In this chapter, we'll explore a selection of relevant global RTL functions, focusing particularly on new functions introduced in the latest versions of Delphi for Win32 (Delphi 7 and Delphi 2005). Most of the pages of the chapter, though, are devoted to the library's core classes as well as to some standard programming techniques such as the definition of events. We'll explore some commonly used classes such as lists, string lists, collections, and streams. We'll spend most of our time exploring the content of the Classes unit, but we'll also examine other core units of the library.

Although most of the material covered in this chapter applies to both Win32 and .NET programming, this chapter includes only limited coverage of the .NET version of the Delphi run-time library, as this will be described, along with the native RTL of .NET, in Chapter 9. In this chapter I'll indicate only those relevant differences between Win32 and .NET that are worth considering even if you don't need .NET support right away.

This chapter covers the following topics: an overview of the RTL and relevant Delphi RTL functions; the TObject class; showing class information at run time; TPersistent and published; the TComponent base class and its properties; components and ownership; events; lists, container classes, and collections; and streaming.

The Units of the RTL

In the early days of Delphi, the RTL was made of two core units, System.pas and SysUtils.pas, which are still available today. The first is the core RTL and includes a lot of compiler-magic functions (functions that need special treatment by the compiler). The core RTL is automatically included in any compilation. SysUtils, conversely, is simply a collection of many routines (global functions and procedures) related to many different areas. In the most recent versions of Delphi, Borland added new units devoted to specific purposes (like StringUtils.pas or DateUtils.pas) to make the RTL more manageable. In any case, notice that you'll find the traditional functions in the same units they've always been in, but the new functions appear in specific units. For example, new functions related to dates are now in the DateUtils unit, but to avoid incompatibilities with existing code, previously existing date functions have not been moved out of SysUtils.

A little fine-tuning has also been applied to reduce the minimum size of an executable file, which is at times enlarged by the unwanted inclusion of global variables or initialization code.

In the following sections you'll find a list of the RTL units in Delphi, including all the units available (with the complete source code) in the Source\Win32\Rtl\Sys subfolder of the Delphi directory and some of those available in the subfolder Source\Win32\Rtl\Common.

I'll give a short overview of the role of each unit and an overview of the groups of functions included. I'll also devote more space to the newer units. I won't provide a detailed list of the functions included because the online help includes similar reference material. However, I picked a few interesting or little-known functions, and I will discuss them shortly.

Notice that in general there have been very few changes in the core RTL units from Delphi 7 to Delphi 2005 on the Win32 side. The most relevant changes relate to the support for inlining, as many RTL functions have now been marked inline.

The System Unit in Win32

System is the core unit of the RTL and is automatically included in any compilation (through an automatic and implicit uses statement referring to it). If you try adding the unit to the uses statement of a program, you'll get the following compile-time error:

```
[Error] Identifier redeclared: System
```

In Delphi for Win32, the System unit includes, among other things:

◆ The TObject class, which is the base class of any class defined in the Delphi language, including all the classes of the VCL. (This class is discussed later in this chapter.)

◆ Many interfaces, including IInterface (the base interface), IInvokable (to support SOAP-based invocation), IUnknown (the base COM interface), and IDispatch (the base COM late-binding interface), as well as the simple IInterface implementation class TInterfacedObject.

◆ Some variant support code, including the variant type constants, the TVarData record type, and the TVariantManager type; a large number of variant conversion routines; and variant record and dynamic array support (for more information see Appendix A).

◆ Many base data types, including pointer and array types and the TDateTime type described in Chapter 3.

◆ Memory allocation routines, such as GetMem and FreeMem, and the actual memory manager defined by the TMemoryManager record and accessed by the GetMemoryManager and SetMemoryManager functions. The GetHeapStatus function returns a THeapStatus data structure. Two global variables (AllocMemCount and AllocMemSize) hold the number and total size of allocated memory blocks.

◆ Package and module support code, including the PackageInfo pointer type, the GetPackageInfoTable global function, and the EnumModules procedure (package internals are discussed in Chapter 11).

◆ A rather long list of global variables, including the Windows application instance MainInstance; IsLibrary, indicating whether the executable file is a library or a stand-alone program; `IsConsole`, indicating console applications; `IsMultiThread`, indicating whether there are secondary threads; and the command-line string `CmdLine`. (The unit also includes `ParamCount` and `ParamStr` for easy access to command-line parameters.)

◆ Thread-support code, with the `BeginThread` and `EndThread` functions; file support records and file-related routines; wide string and OLE string conversion routines; and many other low-level and system routines (including a number of automatic conversion functions).

RECENT CHANGES IN THE SYSTEM UNIT

I just described some interesting features of the System unit in the previous section. Most of the changes made over the last few years relate to making the core RTL more cross-platform portable, replacing Windows-specific features with generic implementations shared by Delphi and Kylix. Along this line, there are new names for interface types, totally revised support for variants, new pointer types, dynamic array support, and functions to customize the management of exception objects.

NOTE   If you read the source code of `System.pas`, you'll notice some heavy use of conditional compilation, with many instances of `{$IFDEF LINUX}` and `{$IFDEF MSWINDOWS}` used to discriminate between the two operating systems. Notice that for Windows, Borland uses the MSWINDOWS define to indicate the entire platform because WINDOWS was used in 16-bit versions of the OS (and contrasts with the symbol WIN32).

For example, an addition for compatibility between Linux and Windows relates to line breaks in text files. The `DefaultTextLineBreakStyle` variable affects the behavior of routines that read and write files, including most text-streaming routines. The possible values for this global variable are tlbsLF (the default in Kylix) and tlbsCRLF (the default in Delphi). The line-break style can also be set on a file-by-file basis with `SetTextLineBreakStyle` function.

Similarly, the global `sLineBreak` string constant has the value #13#10 in the Windows version of the IDE and the value #10 in the Linux version. Another change is that the System unit now includes the TFileRec and TTextRec structures, which were defined in the SysUtils unit in earlier versions of Delphi.

FASTCODE IN DELPHI 2005

The System unit of Delphi 2005 has very limited changes on the Win32 side. One of these changes is that it uses a couple of contributions from the FastCode project, an open source project aimed at writing more efficient versions of the core Delphi routines. In particular, there is a new assembly implementation of `FillChar` and of the internal `__lldiv`. Moreover, in the SysUtils unit, there is a FastCode implementation of the `CompareText` function.

NOTE   You can find more about the FastCode project, by Dennis Kjaer Christensen, on `http://dennishomepage.gugs-cats.dk/FastCodeProject.htm`. It is very relevant that Borland accepted these contributions, even if only a handful, because it is a welcome change in Borland policy toward the Delphi community.

EXECUTABLE SIZE UNDER THE MICROSCOPE

While touching up the RTL, Borland engineers were able to trim a little "fat" out of each and every Delphi application. Reducing the minimum program size by a few KB seems odd, given all the bloated applications these days, but it is a good service to developers. In some cases, even a few KB (multiplied by many applications) can reduce size and eventually download time.

As a simple test, I built the MiniSize program, which is not an attempt to build the smallest possible program, but rather an attempt to build a very small program that does something interesting: it reports the size of its own executable file. All of the example code is as follows:

```
program MiniSize;

uses
  Windows;

{$R *.RES}

var
  nSize: Integer;
  hFile: THandle;
  strSize: String;

begin
  // open the current file and read the size
  hFile := CreateFile (PChar (ParamStr (0)),
    0, FILE_SHARE_READ, nil, OPEN_EXISTING, 0, 0);
  nSize := GetFileSize (hFile, nil);
  CloseHandle (hFile);

  // copy the size to a string and show it
  SetLength (strSize, 20);
  Str (nSize, strSize);
  MessageBox (0, PChar (strSize), 'Mini Program', MB_OK);
end.
```

The program opens its own executable file after retrieving its name from the first command-line parameter (ParamStr (0)), extracts the size, converts it into a string using the simple Str function, and shows the result in a message. The program does not have top-level windows. Moreover, I use the Str function for the integer-to-string conversion to avoid including SysUtils, which defines all of the more complex formatting routines and would impose a little extra overhead.

If you look at past versions, Delphi 5 compiled this program to 18,432 bytes, Delphi 6 reduced it to 15,360 bytes, and Delphi 7 produced a file of 15,872 bytes. In Delphi 2005 for Win32, the size of the compiled program grows slightly to 16,384. By replacing the long string with a short string and modifying the code a little, you can trim the program further, to less than 10 KB. (You'll end up removing the string support routines as well as the memory allocator, which is possible only in programs using exclusively low-level calls.) You can find both versions in the source code of the example file. In Delphi 2005 for .NET, the size depends on how you link the system unit (as discussed in Chapter 9) because it can change from 12 KB (with the external borland.Delphi.dll) to 28 KB (with system code linked in the executable).

What is really important, in my opinion, is the size of full-blown Delphi applications based on run-time packages. A simple test with a do-nothing program, the MiniPack example, shows an executable size of 17,408 bytes in Delphi 7, down to the same 16,384 bytes in Delphi 2005 for Win32 and 8,704 bytes in Delphi for .NET.

The SysUtils and SysConst Units

The SysConst unit defines a few constant strings used by the other RTL units for displaying messages. These strings are declared with the resourcestring keyword and saved in the program resources. Like other resources, they can be translated by means of the Integrated Translation Manager or the External Translation Manager.

The SysUtils unit is a collection of system utility functions of various types. Unlike other RTL units, it is largely an operating system–dependent unit. The SysUtils unit has no specific focus and includes a bit of everything, from string management to locale and multibyte-characters support to the Exception class and several other derived exception classes to a plethora of string-formatting constants and routines. In particular, later in this chapter we'll focus on some of the unit's file management routines.

Some features of SysUtils are used every day by every programmer, such as the IntToStr or Format string-formatting functions; other features are lesser known, such as the Windows version information global variables. These indicate the Windows platform (Window 9x or NT/2000/XP), the operating system version and build number, and the service pack installed. They can be used as in the following code, extracted from the WinVersion example:

```
case Win32Platform of
  VER_PLATFORM_WIN32_WINDOWS: ShowMessage ('Windows 9x');
  VER_PLATFORM_WIN32_NT: ShowMessage ('Windows NT');
end;

ShowMessage ('Running on Windows: ' +
  IntToStr (Win32MajorVersion) + '.' +
  IntToStr (Win32MinorVersion) + ' (Build ' +
  IntToStr (Win32BuildNumber) +
  ') ' + #10#13 + 'Update: ' + Win32CSDVersion);
```

The second code fragment produces a message like the one in the following graphic (of course, on the operating system version you have installed):

Another little-known feature of this unit is the TMultiReadExclusiveWriteSynchronizer class—probably the VCL class with the longest name. Borland has defined a much shorter alias name for the class: TMREWSync (the two classes are identical). This class supports multithreading; it allows you to work with resources that can be used by multiple threads at the same time for reading (multiread) but must be used by a single thread when writing (exclusive-write). This means writing cannot begin until all the reading threads have terminated.

NOTE   The multiread synchronizer is unique in that it supports recursive locks and promotion of read locks to write locks. The main purpose of the class is to allow multiple threads easy, fast access to read from a shared resource but still allow one thread to gain exclusive control of the resource for relatively infrequent updates. Delphi includes other synchronization classes, declared in the SyncObjs unit (available under Source/Win32/Rtl/Common) and closely mapped to operating system–synchronization objects (such as events and critical sections in Windows).

LITTLE-KNOWN SYSUTILS FUNCTIONS

Over the last few versions, Delphi has added some new functions within the SysUtils unit. One of these areas relates to Boolean-to-string conversion. The BoolToStr function generally returns '–1' and '0' for true and false values. If the second optional parameter is specified, the function returns the first string in the TrueBoolStrs and FalseBoolStrs arrays (by default 'True' and 'False'):

```
BoolToStr (True) // returns '-1'
BoolToStr (False, True) // returns 'False' by default
```

The reverse function is StrToBool, which can convert a string containing either one of the values of the two Boolean arrays mentioned or a numeric value. In the latter case, the result will be true unless the numeric value is zero. You can see a simple demo of the Boolean conversion functions in the StrDemo example, later in this chapter.

Other functions recently added to SysUtils relate to floating-point conversions to currency and date time types: you can use FloatToCurr and FloatToDateTime to avoid an explicit typecast. The TryStrToFloat and TryStrToCurr functions try to convert a string into a floating-point or currency value and will return False in case of error instead of generating an exception (as the classic StrToFloat and StrToCurr functions do).

The AnsiDequotedStr function, which removes quotes from a string, matches the AnsiQuoteStr function. Speaking of strings, there is support for wide strings, with a series of routines including WideUpperCase, WideLowerCase, WideCompareStr, WideSameStr, WideCompareText, WideSameText, and WideFormat. All of these functions work like their AnsiString counterparts.

Three functions (TryStrToDate, TryEncodeDate, and TryEncodeTime) try to convert a string to a date or encode a date or time without raising an exception, similar to the Try functions previously mentioned. In addition, the DecodeDateFully function returns more detailed information, such as the day of the week, and the CurrentYear function returns the year of today's date.

A portable, friendly, overloaded version of the GetEnvironmentVariable function uses string parameters instead of PChar parameters and is definitely easier to use than the original Win32 API version based on PChar pointers:

```
function GetEnvironmentVariable(Name: string): string;
```

Other functions relate to interface support. Two overloaded versions of the little-known Supports function allow you to check whether an object or a class supports a given interface. The function corresponds to the behavior of the is operator for classes and is mapped to the QueryInterface method. Here's an example:

```
var
  W1: IWalker;
  J1: IJumper;
begin
  W1 := TAthlete.Create;
  // more code...
  if Supports (w1, IJumper) then
  begin
    J1 := W1 as IJumper;
    Log (J1.Walk);
  end;
```

SysUtils also includes an IsEqualGUID function and two functions for converting strings to GUIDs and vice versa. The function CreateGUID has been moved to SysUtils as well, to make it available on Linux (with a custom implementation, of course).

Finally, more features were added in recent versions to improve cross-platform support. The AdjustLineBreaks function can now do different types of *adjustments* to carriage-return and line-feed sequences, and new global variables for text files have been introduced in the System unit, as described earlier. The FileCreate function has an overloaded version in which you can specify file-access rights *the Unix way*. The ExpandFileName function can locate files (on case-sensitive file systems) even when their cases don't exactly correspond. The functions related to path delimiters (backslash or slash) have been made more generic than in earlier versions of Delphi and renamed accordingly. (For example, the old IncludeTrailingBackslash function is now better known as IncludingTrailingPathDelimiter.)

Speaking of files, Delphi 7 added to the SysUtils unit the GetFileVersion function, which reads the version number from the version information optionally added to a Windows executable file.

EXTENDED STRING FORMATTING ROUTINES

Most of Delphi's string formatting routines use global variables to determine decimal and thousand separators, date/time formats, and so on. The values of these variables are first read from the system (Windows regional settings) when a program starts, and you are free to override each of them. However, if the user modifies the Regional Settings in Control Panel while your program is running, the program will respond to the broadcast message by updating the variables, probably losing your hard-coded changes.

If you need different output formats in different places within a program, you can take advantage of the new set of overloaded string formatting routines; they take an extra parameter of type

TFormatSettings, including all the relevant settings. For example, there are now two versions of Format:

```
function Format(const Format: string;
  const Args: array of const): string; overload;
function Format(const Format: string; const Args: array of const;
  const FormatSettings: TFormatSettings): string; overload;
```

Tens of functions have this new extra parameter, which is then used instead of the global settings. However, you can initialize it with the default settings of the computer on which your program is running by calling the new GetLocaleFormatSettings function.

LOCALE OPTIONS IN DELPHI 2005 SYSUTILS

In Delphi there are different functions for working with different locales. For example, you can call SameText or AnsiSameText depending on whether you want a plain implementation or one based on Windows ANSI encoding. In Delphi 2005, there are now overloaded versions of the base functions that accept a locale setting as parameter, such as:

```
function SameText(const S1, S2: string;
  LocaleOptions: TLocaleOptions): Boolean; overload;
```

In turn, this function calls either SameText or AnsiSameText. The advantage of this approach is that you can move from one version to the other by changing a setting of your application, optionally even at run time, rather than having to modify the code and recompile it. By the way, the TLocaleOptions enumeration comprises only two possible values, loUserLocale (used to call the ANSI version of the function) and loInvariantLocale (used to call the standard version).

Another advantage of this change is a more consistent naming, as you can avoid having the Ansi prefix for function names. A similar change, apparently going in the same direction, is the availability of a set of functions without the Ansi prefix in the StrUtils units. These StrUtils functions, however, are identical to their Ansi counterparts.

NOTE   Most of the ANSI versions of the string functions have been marked as obsolete in Delphi for .NET. This is another reason to use the plain versions whenever possible.

The Math Unit

The Math unit hosts a collection of mathematical functions: about 40 trigonometric functions, logarithmic and exponential functions, rounding functions, polynomial evaluations, almost 30 statistical functions, and a dozen financial functions.

Describing all the functions of this unit would be rather tedious, although some readers are probably very interested in Delphi's mathematical capabilities. For this reason and because the Math unit is almost unchanged since Delphi 6, I will focus on a handful of functions that are confusing (like the rounding functions) or little known (like the IfThen function).

A handy feature of the Math unit is the availability of an overloaded IfThen function, which returns one of two possible numbers depending on a Boolean expression. (A similar function is also available for strings.) You can use it, for example, to compute the minimum of two values:

```
nMin := IfThen (nA < nB, na, nB);
```

NOTE   The IfThen function is similar to the ?: operator of the C ,C++, and C# languages. I find it handy because you can replace a complete if/then/else statement with a much shorter expression, writing less code and often declaring fewer temporary variables.

Another set of useful functions relates to comparisons. Floating-point numbers are fundamentally inexact; a floating-point number is an approximation of a theoretical real value. When you do mathematical operations on floating-point numbers, the inexactness of the original values accumulates in the results. Multiplying and dividing by the same number might not return exactly the original number but one that is very close to it. The SameValue function allows you to check whether two values are close enough in value to be considered equal. You can specify how close the two numbers should be or let Delphi compute a reasonable error range for the representation you are using. (This is why the function is overloaded.) Similarly, the IsZero function compares a number to zero, with the same "fuzzy logic."

The RoundTo function allows you to specify the rounding digit—allowing, for example, rounding to the nearest thousand or to two decimals:

```
RoundTo (123827, 3);   // result is 124,000
RoundTo (12.3827, -2); // result is 12.38
```

WARNING   The RoundTo function uses a positive number to indicate the power of 10 to round to (for example, 2 for hundreds) or a negative number for the number of decimal places. This is exactly the opposite of the Round function used by spreadsheets such as Excel.

ROUNDING HEADACHES

Delphi's classic Round function and the RoundTo function (which allows you to specify the rounding digit—allowing, for example, rounding to the nearest thousand or to two decimals) are mapped to the CPU/FPU rounding algorithms. (Notice, by the way, FPU rounding configuration is not available on .NET.) By default, Intel CPUs use *banker's rounding*, which is also the type of rounding typically found in spreadsheet applications.

Banker's rounding is based on the assumption that when you're rounding numbers that lie exactly between two values (the .5 numbers), rounding them all up or all down will statistically increase or reduce the total amount (of money, in general). For this reason, the rule of banker's rounding indicates that .5 numbers should be rounded down or up depending on whether the number (without decimals) is odd or even. This way, the rounding will be balanced, at least statistically. You can see an example of the output of banker's rounding in Figure 5.1, which shows the output of the Rounding example I built to demonstrate different types of rounding.

The program also uses another type of rounding provided by the Math unit in the SimpleRoundTo function, which uses *asymmetric arithmetic rounding*. In this case, all .5 numbers are rounded to the upper value. However, as highlighted in the Rounding example, the function doesn't work as expected when rounding to a decimal digit (that is, when you pass a negative second parameter). In this case, due to the representation errors of floating-point numbers, the rounding trims the values; for example, it turns 1.15 into 1.1 instead of the expected 1.2. The solution is to multiply the value by 10 before rounding, round it to zero decimal digits, and then divide it, as demonstrated in the sample program:

```
SimpleRoundTo (d * 10, 0) / 10
```

FIGURE 5.1
The Rounding example
demonstrates banker's
rounding and arith-
metic rounding.

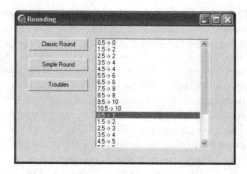

The ConvUtils and StdConvs Units

The ConvUtils unit contains the core of the conversion engine. The engine doesn't include any definition of actual measurement units; instead, it has a series of core functions for end users. The key
function is the conversion call, the `Convert` function. You simply provide the amount, the units it
is expressed in, and the units you want it converted into. The following converts a temperature of
31 degrees Celsius to Fahrenheit:

```
Convert (31, tuCelsius, tuFahrenheit)
```

An overloaded version of the `Convert` function lets you convert values that have two units, such
as speed (which has both a length unit and a time unit). For example, you can convert miles per hour
to meters per second with this call:

```
Convert (20, duMiles, tuHours, duMeters, tuSeconds)
```

A predefined set of measurement units is provided in the StdConvs unit. This unit has conversion
families and an impressive number of values, as shown in the following reduced excerpt:

```
// Distance Conversion Units
// basic unit of measurement is meters
cbDistance: TConvFamily;

duAngstroms: TConvType;
duMicrons: TConvType;
duMillimeters: TConvType;
duMeters: TConvType;
duKilometers: TConvType;
```

This family and the various units are registered in the conversion engine in the initialization section of the unit, providing the conversion ratios (saved in a series of constants, such as
`MetersPerInch` in the following code):

```
cbDistance := RegisterConversionFamily('Distance');
duAngstroms := RegisterConversionType(cbDistance, 'Angstroms', 1E-10);
duMillimeters := RegisterConversionType(cbDistance,
  'Millimeters', 0.001);
```

To test the conversion engine, I built a generic example (ConvDemo) that allows you to work with the entire set of available conversions. The program fills a combo box with the available conversion families and a list box with the available units of the active family, as you can see in its source code. A user can enter two measurement units and an amount in the corresponding edit boxes on the form, as you can see in Figure 5.2. To make the operation faster, the user can select a value in the list and drag it to one of the two Type edit boxes. The dragging support is described in the following sidebar "Simple Dragging in Delphi."

FIGURE 5.2
The ConvDemo example
at run time

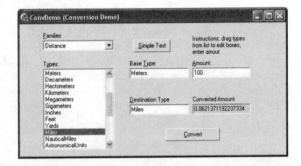

SIMPLE DRAGGING IN DELPHI

The ConvDemo example, built to show how to use the conversion engine, uses an interesting technique: dragging. You can move the mouse over the list box, select an item, and then, keeping the left mouse button pressed, drag the item over one of the edit boxes in the center of the form.

To accomplish this functionality, I had to set the DragMode property of the list box (the source component) to dmAutomatic and implement the OnDragOver and OnDragDrop events of the target edit boxes (the two edit boxes are connected to the same event handlers, sharing the same code). In the first method, the program indicates that the edit boxes always accept the dragging operation, regardless of the source. In the second method, the program copies the text selected in the list box (the Source control of the dragging operation) to the edit box that fired the event (the Sender object). Here is the code for the two methods:

```
procedure TForm1.EditTypeDragOver(Sender, Source: TObject;
  X, Y: Integer; State: TDragState; var Accept: Boolean);
begin
  Accept := True;
end;


procedure TForm1.EditTypeDragDrop(Sender, Source: TObject;
  X, Y: Integer);
begin
  (Sender as TEdit).Text := (Source as TListBox).Items
    [(Source as TListBox).ItemIndex];
end;
```

If distance, speed, temperature conversions, and the like are not interesting enough for you, consider that the conversion types provided serve only as a demo; you can fully customize the engine by providing the measurement units you are interested in, as shortly described in the next section.

CUSTOM CONVERSIONS

As soon as I saw this engine, I thought about using it for converting currencies. This is not exactly the same as converting measurement units, because currency rates change constantly. In theory, you can register a conversion rate with Delphi's conversion engine. From time to time, you check the new rate of exchange, unregister the existing conversion, and register a new one.

To make a simpler currency conversion example, past editions of this book introduced conversions between Euros and older European currencies. The EuroConv example is now a little dated, so I won't discuss it in depth here, although it is still available among the code examples for this chapter. The example teaches how to register any new measurement unit with the engine by declaring variables for the family and the specific units, defining constants for the conversion rates, and registering the family and the various currencies. Here are some code snippets from the example:

```
interface

var
  cbEuroCurrency: TConvFamily;
  cuEUR: TConvType;
  cuDEM: TConvType; // Germany

implementation

const
  DEMPerEuros = 1.95583;

initialization
  // Euro Currency's family type
  cbEuroCurrency := RegisterConversionFamily('EuroCurrency');

  cuEUR := RegisterConversionType(cbEuroCurrency, 'EUR', 1);
  cuDEM := RegisterConversionType(cbEuroCurrency,
    'DEM', 1 / DEMPerEuros);
```

In the EuroConv example, I added to the unit with the conversion rates a custom EuroConv function that does the conversion with the proper rounding required by the Euro conversion rules.

The DateUtils Unit

The DateUtils unit is a collection of date- and time-related functions. It includes functions for picking values from a TDateTime variable or counting values from a given interval, such as

```
// pick value
function DayOf(const AValue: TDateTime): Word;
function HourOf(const AValue: TDateTime): Word;
```

```
// value in range
function WeekOfYear(const AValue: TDateTime): Integer;
function HourOfWeek(const AValue: TDateTime): Integer;
function SecondOfHour(const AValue: TDateTime): Integer;
```

There are also functions for computing the initial or final value of a given time interval (day, week, month, year), including the current date, and for range checking and querying; for example:

```
function DaysBetween(const ANow, AThen: TDateTime): Integer;
function WithinPastDays(const ANow, AThen: TDateTime;
  const ADays: Integer): Boolean;
```

Other functions cover incrementing and decrementing by each of the possible time intervals, encoding and "recoding" (replacing one element of the TDateTime value, such as the day, with a new one), and doing "fuzzy" comparisons (approximate comparisons where a difference of a millisecond will still make two dates equal). Overall, DateUtils is quite interesting and not terribly difficult to use.

The StrUtils Unit

The StrUtils unit adds a number of string-related functions to those available in SysUtils, including string comparison functions. There are functions based on a *soundex* algorithm (AnsiResembleText) and others that provide lookup in arrays of strings (AnsiMatchText and AnsiIndexText), substring location, and text replacement (including AnsiContainsText and AnsiReplaceText).

NOTE *Soundex* is an algorithm that compares names based on how they sound rather than how they are spelled. The algorithm computes a number for each word sound, so that by comparing two such numbers you can determine whether two names sound similar. The system was first applied in 1880 by the U.S. Bureau of the Census; it was patented in 1918 and is now in the public domain. The soundex code is an indexing system that translates a name into a four-character code consisting of one letter and three numbers. More information is available at www.nara.gov/genealogy/coding.html.

In addition to comparisons, other functions provide a two-way test (the nice IfThen function, similar to the one you already saw for numbers), duplicate and reverse strings, and replace substrings. Most of these string functions were added as a convenience to Visual Basic programmers migrating to Delphi.

I used some of these functions in the StrDemo example, which also uses some of the Boolean-to-string conversions defined within the SysUtils unit. The program is little more than a test for a few of these functions. For example, it uses the soundex comparison between the strings entered in two edit boxes. The program also showcases the AnsiMatchText and AnsiIndexText functions after filling a dynamic array of strings (called strArray) with the values of the strings inside a list box. If you look at the source code, notice in particular the use of the IfThen function in cases like:

```
ShowMessage (IfThen (nMatch >= 0,
  'Matches the string number ' + IntToStr (nMatch), 'No match'));
```

Delphi 2005 adds to the StrUtils unit a second set of functions that are named without the initial Ansi. The code of these functions doesn't change at all; only the name is different. The reason seems to be call consistency, as described earlier in the section "Locale Options in Delphi 2005 SysUtils."

FROM *POS* TO *POSEX*

The PosEx function, available since Delphi 7, is handy to many developers and is worth a brief mention. When searching for multiple occurrences of a string within another one, a classic Delphi solution was to use the Pos function and repeat the search over the remaining portion of the string. For example, you could count the occurrences of a string inside another string with code like this:

```
function CountSubstr (text, sub: string): Integer;
var
  nPos: Integer;
begin
  Result := 0;
  nPos := Pos (sub, text);
  while nPos > 0 do
  begin
    Inc (Result);
    text := Copy (text, nPos + Length (sub), MaxInt);
    nPos := Pos (sub, text);
  end;
end;
```

The PosEx function allows you to specify the starting position of the search within a string, so you don't need to waste time by altering the original string. Thus the previous code can be simplified in the following way:

```
function CountSubstrEx (text, sub: string): Integer;
var
  nPos: Integer;
begin
  Result := 0;
  nPos := PosEx (sub, text, 1); // default
  while nPos > 0 do
  begin
    Inc (Result);
    nPos := PosEx (sub, text, nPos + Length (sub));
  end;
end;
```

Both code snippets are used in a trivial way in the StrDemo example discussed earlier.

The New WideStrUtils Unit

Along with the StrUtils unit, Delphi 2005 introduces a new support unit for Unicode and wide string operations. As you'd expect, the unit hosts new routines for supporting the WideString type. They include a set of routines for direct allocation and copy operations plus replacement functions for plain string functions available in other units, like:

- WideQuotedStr (corresponding to QuotedStr in the SysUtils unit)
- WideStringReplace (corresponding to StringReplace in the SysUtils unit)
- WideReplaceStr (corresponding to ReplaceStr in the StrUtils unit)

Most of the routines in the unit, despite the unit name, are meant to support strings with 8 bits per character based on the UTF8 encoding, with functions like:

```
function UTF8LowerCase(const S: UTF8string): UTF8string;
function UTF8UpperCase(const S: UTF8string): UTF8string;
function IsUTF8String(const s : UTF8String): Boolean;
function HasExtendCharacter(const s : UTF8String): Boolean;
function HasUTF8BOM(S : TStream) : boolean; overload;
procedure ConvertStreamFromAnsiToUTF8(Src, Dst : TStream;
  cp : integer = CP_ACP);
```

The Types Unit

The Types unit holds data types common to multiple operating systems. The types defined here are simple and include, among others, the TPoint, TRect, and TSmallPoint record structures plus their related pointer types.

WARNING   You will have to update old Delphi programs that refer to TRect or TPoint by adding the Types unit in the uses statement; otherwise they won't compile.

The Variants and VarUtils Units

Variants and VarUtils are two units that were introduced in Delphi 6 to host the variant-related portion of the library. The Variants unit contains generic code for variants. Functions include generic variant support, variant arrays, variant copying, and dynamic array to variant array conversions. In addition, the TCustomVariantType class defines customizable variant data types.

The Variants unit is totally platform independent and uses the VarUtils unit, which contains OS-dependent code. In Win32, this unit uses the system APIs to manipulate variant data; in .NET (and in Kylix), it uses custom code provided by the RTL library.

A specific area that has seen significant improvement in recent versions of Delphi is the ability to control the behavior of variant implementations, particularly comparison rules. To determine whether a *null* value can be compared with other values, you can set the NullEqualityRule and NullMagnitudeRule global variables (in Delphi for .NET class data fields of the Variant type), each of which assumes one of the following values:

ncrError   Any type of comparison causes an exception to be raised, because you cannot compare an undefined value.

ncrStrict   Any type of comparison always fails (returning False), regardless of the values.

ncrLoose   Equality tests succeed only among null values (a null is different from any other value). In comparisons, null values are considered empty values or zeros.

Other settings, like NullStrictConvert and NullAsStringValue, control how conversion is accomplished in case of null values. I suggest that you carry out your own experiments using the VariantComp example available with the code for this chapter. As you can see in Figure 5.3, this program has a form with a RadioGroup you can use to change the settings of the NullEqualityRule and NullMagnitudeRule global variables, along with a few buttons to perform various comparisons.

FIGURE 5.3

The form of the VariantComp example at design time

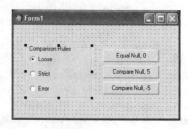

NOTE A special case of variants is represented by custom variants, a technique that allows you to define new data type that overloads standard arithmetic operators. Having actual operator overloading, as in the .NET compiler, makes much more sense, as the custom variant implementation is very difficult to work with and quite slow at run time.

The DelphiMM and ShareMem Units

The DelphiMM and ShareMem units relate to memory management. The standard Delphi memory manager is declared in the System unit. The DelphiMM unit defines an alternative memory manager library to be used when passing strings from an executable to a DLL (a Windows dynamic linking library), both built with Delphi. This memory manager library is compiled by default in the `Borlndmm.dll` library file you'll have to deploy with your program.

The interface to this memory manager is defined in the ShareMem unit. You must include this unit (it's required to be the first unit) in the projects of both your executable and library, as described in more detail in Chapter 11.

NOTE In Delphi for .NET there is no custom memory management and there are no DelphiMM and ShareMem units, as the CLR provides memory management and garbage collection by default.

While I'm on the topic of memory managers, notice that the one provided by Delphi for Win32 is for general purposes and doesn't suit each and every application; the memory hungry ones in particular can cause fragmentation. There are third-party memory managers that can help in these special circumstances.

Managing Files with SysUtils

To access files and file information, you can generally rely on the standard functions available in the SysUtils unit. Relying on these fairly traditional Pascal libraries makes your code easily portable among quite different operating systems (although you'll have to carefully consider the differences in the file system architectures, particularly case sensitivity on the Linux platform).

For example, the FilesList example uses the `FindFirst`, `FindNext`, and `FindClose` combination to retrieve from within a folder a list of files that matches a filter (an example of the output appears in Figure 5.4).

The following code adds the filenames to a list box called `lbFiles`:

```
procedure TForm1.AddFilesToList(Filter, Folder: string;
  Recurse: Boolean);
var
```

```
    sr: TSearchRec;
begin
  if FindFirst (Folder + Filter, faAnyFile, sr) = 0 then
  try
    repeat
      lbFiles.Items.Add (Folder + sr.Name);
    until FindNext(sr) <> 0;
  finally
    FindClose(sr);
  end;
```

If the Recurse parameter is set, the AddFilesToList procedure gets a list of subfolders by examining the local files again:

```
if (sr.Attr and faDirectory) = faDirectory then
  sList.Add (sr.Name);
```

Finally, the program uses an interesting technique to ask the user to select the initial directory for the file search by calling the SelectDirectory procedure (see Figure 5.5):

```
if SelectDirectory ('Choose Folder', '', CurrentDir) then ...
```

FIGURE 5.4

An example of the output of the FilesList application

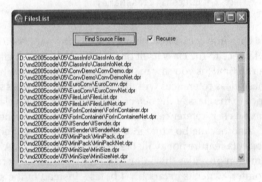

FIGURE 5.5

The dialog box of the SelectDirectory procedure displayed by the FilesList application

The *TObject* Class

As mentioned earlier, a key element of the System unit is the definition of the TObject class, which is the *mother of all Delphi classes*. Every class in the system inherits from the TObject class, either directly (if you specify TObject as the base class), implicitly (if you indicate no base class), or indirectly (when you specify another class as the ancestor). The entire hierarchy of classes in a Delphi program has a single root. So you can use the TObject data type as a replacement for the data type of any class type in the system, according to the type compatibility rules covered in Chapter 3.

For example, components' event handlers usually have a Sender parameter of type TObject. This simply means that the Sender object can be of any class because every class is ultimately derived from TObject. The typical drawback of such an approach is that to work on the object, you need to know its data type. In fact, when you have a variable or a parameter of the TObject type, you can apply to it only the methods and properties defined by the TObject class itself. If this variable or parameter happens to refer to an object of the TButton type, for example, you cannot directly access its Caption property. The solution to this problem lies in the use of the safe down-casting or run-time type information (RTTI) operators (is and as) discussed in Chapter 3.

You can also call for any object the methods defined in the TObject class. For example, the ClassName method returns a string with the name of the class. Because it is a class method (see Chapter 3 for details), you can apply it both to an object and to a class. Suppose you have defined a TButton class and a Button1 object of that class, then the following statements have the same effect:

```
Text := Button1.ClassName;
Text := TButton.ClassName;
```

On some occasions you need to use the name of a class, but it can also be useful to retrieve a class reference to the class itself or to its base class. The class reference allows you to operate on the class at run time (as you saw in the preceding chapter), whereas the class name is just a string. You can get these class references with the ClassType and ClassParent methods. The first returns a class reference to the class of the object; the second returns a class reference to the object's base class. Once you have a class reference, you can pass it to other methods or call a constructor on it.

Another method that might be useful is InstanceSize, which returns the run-time size of an object (a feature not available in Delphi for .NET). Although you might think that the SizeOf global function provides this information, that function actually returns the size of an object reference—a pointer, which is invariably 4 bytes—instead of the size of the object itself.

In Listing 5.1, you can find the complete definition of the TObject class extracted from the System unit. In addition to the methods I've already mentioned, notice InheritsFrom, which provides a test that's similar to the is operator but can also be applied to classes and class references (the first argument of is must be an object).

NOTE   The ClassInfo method returns a pointer to the internal run-time type information (RTTI) of the class, introduced later in this chapter.

These methods of TObject are available for objects of every class because TObject is the common ancestor class of every class. Here is how you can use these methods to access class information:

```
procedure TSenderForm.ShowSender(Sender: TObject);
begin
  Memo1.Lines.Add ('Class Name: ' + Sender.ClassName);
  if Sender.ClassParent <> nil then
```

```
    Memo1.Lines.Add ('Parent Class: ' + Sender.ClassParent.ClassName);
    Memo1.Lines.Add ('Instance Size: ' + IntToStr (Sender.InstanceSize));
  end;
```

The code checks to see whether the ClassParent is nil in case you are using an instance of the TObject type, which has no base type.

LISTING 5.1:   The definition of the *TObject* class (in the System RTL unit for Win32)

```
type
  TObject = class
    constructor Create;
    procedure Free;
    class function InitInstance(Instance: Pointer): TObject;
    procedure CleanupInstance;
    function ClassType: TClass;
    class function ClassName: ShortString;
    class function ClassNameIs(const Name: string): Boolean;
    class function ClassParent: TClass;
    class function ClassInfo: Pointer;
    class function InstanceSize: Longint;
    class function InheritsFrom(AClass: TClass): Boolean;
    class function MethodAddress(const Name: ShortString): Pointer;
    class function MethodName(Address: Pointer): ShortString;
    function FieldAddress(const Name: ShortString): Pointer;
    function GetInterface(const IID: TGUID; out Obj): Boolean;
    class function GetInterfaceEntry(const IID: TGUID):
      PInterfaceEntry;
    class function GetInterfaceTable: PInterfaceTable;
    function SafeCallException(ExceptObject: TObject;
      ExceptAddr: Pointer): HResult; virtual;
    procedure AfterConstruction; virtual;
    procedure BeforeDestruction; virtual;
    procedure Dispatch(var Message); virtual;
    procedure DefaultHandler(var Message); virtual;
    class function NewInstance: TObject; virtual;
    procedure FreeInstance; virtual;
    destructor Destroy; virtual;
  end;
```

This ShowSender method is part of the IfSender example. The method is connected with the OnClick event of several controls: three buttons, a check box, and an edit box. When you click each control, the ShowSender method is invoked with the corresponding control as sender (more on events in Chapter 6). One of the buttons is a Bitmap button, an object of a class derived from TButton. You can see an example of the output of this program at run time in Figure 5.6.

FIGURE 5.6

The output of the IfSender example

You can use other methods to perform tests. For example, you can check whether the Sender object is of a specific type with the following code:

```
if Sender.ClassType = TButton then ...
```

You can also check whether the Sender parameter corresponds to a given object with this test:

```
if Sender = Button1 then...
```

Instead of checking for a particular class or object, you'll generally need to test the type compatibility of an object with a given class; that is, you'll need to check whether the class of the object is a given class *or* one of its derived classes. Doing so lets you know whether you can operate on the object with the methods defined for the class. This test can be accomplished using the InheritsFrom method, which is also called when you use the is operator. The following two tests are equivalent:

```
if Sender.InheritsFrom (TButton) then ...
if Sender is TButton then ...
```

NOTE The definition of the TObject class on Delphi for .NET is quite different from its Win32 counterpart, although most of the existing methods are still there. TObject, in fact, is an alias of System.Object with helper classes filling some of the gaps, as introduced in Chapter 4. Chapter 9 will provide more information on this issue.

Showing Class Information

I extended the IfSender example to show a complete list of base classes of a given object or class. Once you have a class reference you can add all of its base classes to the ListParent list box with the following code:

```
with ListParent.Items do
begin
  Clear;
  while MyClass.ClassParent <> nil do
  begin
    MyClass := MyClass.ClassParent;
```

```
      Add (MyClass.ClassName);
    end;
  end;
```

You'll notice that I use a class reference at the heart of the `while` loop, which tests for the absence of a base class (so that the current class is `TObject`). Alternatively, I could have written the `while` statement in either of the following ways:

```
while not MyClass.ClassNameIs ('TObject') do...
while MyClass <> TObject do...
```

The code in the `with` statement referring to the `ListParent` list box is part of the ClassInfo example, which displays the list of base classes and some other information about a few components of the VCL (basically those on the Standard page of the Component Palette). These components are manually added to a dynamic array holding classes and declared as

```
private
  ClassArray: array of TClass;
```

When the program starts, the array is used to show all the class names in a list box. Selecting an item from the list box triggers the visual presentation of its details and its base classes, as you can see in the program output in Figure 5.7.

NOTE   As a further extension of this example, you can create a tree with all the base classes of the various components in a hierarchy. I've done that in one of my CanTools wizards (see Appendix B for details).

FIGURE 5.7
The output of the
ClassInfo example

The *TPersistent* Class

The first core class of the Delphi library we'll look at is `TPersistent`, which is quite a strange class: it has very little code and almost no direct use, but it provides a foundation for the entire idea of visual programming. You can see the definition of the class in Listing 5.2.

As the name implies, this class handles persistency—that is, saving the value of an object to a stream to be used later to re-create the object in the same state and with the same data. Persistency is a key element of visual programming. In fact, at design time in Delphi you manipulate actual objects that are saved to DFM files and re-created at run time when the specific component container—form or data module or frame—is created.

LISTING 5.2: The definition of the *TPersistent* class from the Classes unit for Win32

```
{ $M+}
TPersistent = class(TObject)
private
  procedure AssignError(Source: TPersistent);
protected
  procedure AssignTo(Dest: TPersistent); virtual;
  procedure DefineProperties(Filer: TFiler); virtual;
  function  GetOwner: TPersistent; dynamic;
public
  destructor Destroy; override;
  procedure Assign(Source: TPersistent); virtual;
  function  GetNamePath: string; dynamic;
end;
```

NOTE Everything I say about DFM files also applies to NFM files, the file extension used by VCL.NET applications. The format is identical and the extension difference is not relevant, as you can compile a VCL.NET application with forms still based on the traditional DFM extension.

Streaming support is not embedded in the TPersistent class but is provided by other classes that target TPersistent and its descendants. In other words, you can "persist" with Delphi default streaming only objects of classes inheriting from TPersistent. One of the reasons for this behavior is the fact that the class is compiled with a special option turned on, {$M+}. This flag activates the generation of extended RTTI information for the published portion of the class.

Delphi's streaming system doesn't try to save the in-memory data of an object, which would be complex because of the many pointers to other memory locations and would be totally meaningless when the object was reloaded. Instead, Delphi saves objects by listing the values of all properties in the published section of the class. When a property refers to another object, Delphi saves the name of the object or the entire object (with the same mechanism), depending on its type and relationship with the main object. For a comparison with other approaches, see the sidebar "Object Streaming versus Code Generation."

The only method of the TPersistent class that you'll generally use is the Assign procedure, which can be used to copy the actual value of an object. In the library, this method is implemented by many noncomponent classes but by very few components. Most descendant classes reimplement the virtual protected AssignTo method called by the default implementation of Assign.

Other methods include DefineProperties, used for customizing the streaming system and adding extra information (pseudo-properties), and the GetOwner and GetNamePath methods, used by collections and other special classes to identify themselves to the Object Inspector.

The *published* Keyword

Delphi has four directives specifying data access: public, protected, private, and published. I covered the first three in Chapter 3, so now it's time to look at what published means. For any published field, property, or method, the compiler generates extended RTTI information so that Delphi's run-time environment or a program can query a class for its published interface. For example, every

Delphi component has a published interface that is used by the IDE, in particular the Object Inspector. A proper use of published items is important when you write components. Usually, the published part of a component contains no fields or methods, just properties and events.

When Delphi generates a form (or a data module or frame), it places the definitions of its components and methods (the event handlers) in the first portion of its definition, before the `public` and `private` keywords. These fields and methods in the initial portion of the class are published. The default keyword is `published` when no special keyword is added before an element of a component class.

To be more precise, `published` is the default keyword only if the class was compiled with the $M+ or {$TYPEINFO ON} compiler directive or is descended from a class compiled with $M+. This directive is used in the `TPersistent` class, so most classes of the VCL and all the component classes default to `published`. However, noncomponent classes in Delphi (such as `TStream` and `TList`) are compiled with $M- and default to public visibility.

The methods used to handle events in the IDE (and in DFM files) should be published, and the fields corresponding to your components in the form should be published to be automatically connected with the objects described in the DFM file and created along with the form. (Later in this chapter I'll discuss the details of this situation and the problems it generates.)

OBJECT STREAMING VERSUS CODE GENERATION

The approach used by the Delphi VCL is different from the approach used by other visual development tools and languages. In WinForms applications the effect of the definition of a form inside an IDE is the generation of the Delphi or C# source code used to create the components and set their properties. Setting properties in an inspector affects the source code. You've already seen that in Delphi VCL or VCL.NET applications you can write code to generate the components instead of relying on streaming, but because there is no specific support in the IDE you'll have to write that code manually.

Each of the two approaches has advantages and disadvantages. When generating source code (as in WinForms), you have more control over what goes on and the exact sequence of creation and initialization. When working with forms files (as in VCL and VCL.NET), Delphi reloads objects and their properties but delays some assignments until a later fix-up phase, to avoid the problems of references to not-yet-initialized objects. This process is more complex, but it is so hidden that it becomes simpler for the programmer.

One advantage of the Delphi approach is that the DFM files can be translated into different languages without affecting the source code; in WinForms you should export all strings to resources and translate those, but this is not a perfect solution as you often need to change component size and positions when using longer or shorter captions. Another difference is that Delphi embeds the component's graphic in the DFM file instead of referring to external files. Doing so simplifies deployment (because everything ends up in the executable file) but can also make the executable much bigger.

Accessing Properties by Name

The Object Inspector displays a list of an object's published properties, even for components you've written. To do this, it relies on the RTTI information generated for published properties. Using some advanced techniques, an application can retrieve a list of an object's published properties and use them.

Although this capability is not very well known, in Delphi it is possible to access properties by name simply by using the string with the name of the property and then retrieving its value. Access to the RTTI information of properties is provided through a group of undocumented subroutines, part of the TypInfo unit.

WARNING These subroutines were undocumented in past versions of Delphi, so Borland remained free to change them. However, from Delphi 1 to Delphi 2005, changes were very limited and related only to supporting new features, with a high level of backward compatibility. Over the years, Borland added many more goodies and a few "helper" routines that are officially promoted (although they are still not fully documented in the Help file and are explained only with comments provided in the unit).

Rather than explore the entire TypInfo unit here, we will look at only the minimal code required to access properties by name. For this purpose, you can use the handy GetPropValue function, which returns a variant with the value of the property and raises an exception if the property doesn't exist. To avoid the exception, you can call the IsPublishedProp function first. You simply pass to these functions the object and a string with the property name. A further optional parameter of GetPropValue allows you to choose the format for returning values of properties of any set type (either a string or the numeric value for the set). For example, you can call

```
ShowMessage (GetPropValue (Button1, 'Caption'));
```

This has the same effect as calling ShowMessage, passing as parameter Button1.Caption. The only real difference is that this version of the code is much slower because the compiler generally resolves normal access to properties in a more efficient way. The advantage of the run-time access is that you can make it very flexible, as in the following RunProp example.

This program displays in a list box the value of a property of any type for each component of a form. The name of the property you are looking for is provided in an edit box. Being able to type the property name in the edit box makes the program very flexible. In addition to the edit box and the list box, the form has a button to generate the output and some other components added only to test their properties. When you click the button, the following code is executed:

```
uses
  TypInfo;

procedure TForm1.Button1Click(Sender: TObject);
var
  I: Integer;
  Value: Variant;
begin
  ListBox1.Clear;
  for I := 0 to ComponentCount -1 do
  begin
    if IsPublishedProp (Components[I], Edit1.Text) then
    begin
      Value := GetPropValue (Components[I], Edit1.Text);
      ListBox1.Items.Add (Components[I].Name + '.' +
        Edit1.Text + ' = ' + string (Value));
    end
```

```
    else
      ListBox1.Items.Add ('No ' + Components[I].Name + '.' +
        Edit1.Text);
  end;
end;
```

ACCESSING PUBLISHED FIELDS AND METHODS

As I mentioned, three different declarations make sense in the published section of a class: fields, methods, and properties. In your code, you'll generally refer to published items as you refer to public ones, that is, by referring to the corresponding identifiers in the code. In some special cases though, it is possible to access published items at run time by name. I'll discuss dynamic access to properties in the section "Accessing Properties by Name"; here, I'll introduce possible ways of interacting at run time with fields and methods. The TObject class has three interesting methods for this area: MethodAddress, MethodName, and FieldAddress.

The first function, MethodAddress, returns the memory address of the compiled code (a sort of function pointer) of the method passed as parameter in a string. By assigning this method address to the Code field of a TMethod structure and assigning an appropriate object to the Data field, you can obtain a complete method pointer. At this point, to call the method you must cast it to the proper method pointer type. Here is a code fragment highlighting the key points of this technique:

```
var
  Method: TMethod;
  Evt: TNotifyEvent;
begin
  Method.Code := MethodAddress ('Button1Click');
  Method.Data := Self;
  Evt := TNotifyEvent(Method);
  Evt (Sender); // call the method
end;
```

Delphi uses similar code to assign an event handler when it loads a DFM file because these files store the name of the methods used to handle the events, whereas the components store the method pointer. The second method, MethodName, does the opposite transformation, returning the name of the published method at a given memory address. This method can be used to obtain the name of an event handler, given its value, something Delphi does when streaming a component into a DFM file.

Finally, the FieldAddress method of TObject returns the memory location of a published field, given its name. Delphi uses this method to connect components created from the DFM files with the fields of their owner (for example, a form) having the same name.

Note that these three methods are seldom used in "normal" programs but play a key role in making Delphi work. They are strictly related to the streaming system. You'll need to use these methods only when writing extremely dynamic programs, special-purpose wizards, or other Delphi extensions.

Figure 5.8 shows the effect of clicking the Fill List button while using the default Caption value in the edit box. You can try it with any other property name. Numbers will be converted to strings by the variant conversion. Objects (such as the value of the Font property) will be displayed as memory addresses.

WARNING Do not regularly use the TypInfo unit instead of polymorphism and other property-access techniques. Use base-class property access first, or use the safe as typecast when required, and reserve RTTI access to properties as a last resort. Using TypInfo techniques makes your code slower, more complex, and more prone to human error; in fact, it skips the compile-time type-checking.

FIGURE 5.8

The output of the Run-Prop example, which accesses properties by name at run time

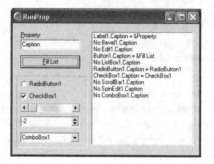

Lists and Container Classes

It is often important to handle groups of components or objects. In addition to using standard arrays and dynamic arrays, a few VCL classes represent lists of other objects. These classes can be approximately divided into three groups: simple lists, collections, and containers.

Simple lists and containers are detailed in the following sections. Collections define a homogeneous list of objects and are implemented in the TCollection and TCollectionItem classes.

NOTE On Delphi for .NET, in addition to the native containers, you can also use the native FCL collection classes, like the very handy ArrayList and many others. These are covered in Chapter 9. Of course, if you want to write code compatible with Delphi for Win32, you should stick with Delphi native lists and containers.

Lists and String Lists

Lists are represented by the generic list of objects, TList, and by the four lists of strings for standard and wide strings (16-bits per character):

♦ TList defines a list of pointers, which can be used to store objects of any class. A TList is more flexible than a dynamic array because it can be expanded automatically simply by adding new items to it. An advantage of a dynamic array over a TList is that the dynamic array allows you to indicate a specific type for contained objects and perform the proper compile-time type checking. Another advantage is the automatic memory reclamation for the dynamic array.

♦ TStrings is an abstract class to represent all forms of string lists, regardless of their storage implementations. This class defines an abstract list of strings. For this reason, TStrings objects are used only as properties of components capable of storing the strings themselves, such as a list box. TStringList, a derived class of TStrings, defines a list of strings with their own storage. You can use this class to define a list of strings in a program.

♦ New in Delphi 2005 are the TWideStrings and TWideStringList classes, corresponding to the previous two classes but based on the WideString type instead of the plain string type. The two sets of classes have almost identical methods, with very limited differences. This means you can easily move existing code from a plain string list class to a wide string list class, although they do not inherit from each other.

All of the string list object classes have both a list of strings and a list of objects associated with the strings. These classes have a number of different uses. For example, you can use them for dictionaries of associated objects or to store bitmaps or other elements to be used in a list box.

The two classes of string lists also have ready-to-use methods to store or load their contents to or from a text file: SaveToFile and LoadFromFile. To loop through a list, you can use a simple for statement based on its default property as if the list were an array, or you can use the new for..in loop as all of these classes provide enumerators.

NOTE   Oddly enough, the new wide string lists do not provide an enumerator to support the for..in syntax, while the traditional string lists do. What you can do is inherit your own custom class from those and provide enumeration support.

All these lists have a number of methods and properties. You can operate on lists using the array notation ([and]) both to read and change elements. There is a Count property as well as typical access methods such as Add, Insert, Delete, Remove; search methods (for example, IndexOf); and sorting support. The TList class has an Assign method that, in addition to copying the source data, can perform set operations on the two lists, including *and*, *or*, and *xor*.

To fill a string list with items and later check whether one is present, you can write code like this:

```
var
  sl: TStringList;
  idx: Integer;
begin
  sl := TStringList.Create;
  try
    sl.Add ('one');
    sl.Add ('two');
    sl.Add ('three');
    // later
    idx := sl.IndexOf ('two');
    if idx >= 0 then
      ShowMessage ('String found');
  finally
    sl.Free;
  end;
end;
```

NAME-VALUE PAIRS

The TStrings class has always had another nice feature: support for name-value pairs. If you add to a list a string like 'lastname=john', you can then search for the existence of the pair using the IndexOfName function or the Values array property. For example, you can retrieve the value 'john' by calling Values ['lastname'].

You can use this feature to build much more complex data structures such as dictionaries and still benefit from the possibility of attaching an object to the string. This data structure maps directly to initialization files and other common formats.

Delphi 7 further extended the possibilities of name-value pair support by allowing you to customize the separator, beyond the equal sign, using the NameValueSeparator property. In addition, the ValueFromIndex property gives you direct access to the value portion of a string at a given position; you no longer have to extract the name-value manually from the complete string using a cumbersome (and extremely slow) expression:

```
str := MyStringList.Values [MyStringList.Names [I]]; // old
str := MyStringList.ValueFromIndex [I]; // new
```

USING LISTS OF OBJECTS

I wrote an example focusing on the use of the generic TList class. When you need a list of any kind of data, you can generally declare a TList object, fill it with the data, and access the data while casting it to the proper type. The ListDemo example demonstrates this approach and also shows its pitfalls. The form has a private variable, holding a list of dates:

```
private
  ListDate: TList;
```

This list object is created when the form itself is created:

```
procedure TForm1.FormCreate(Sender: TObject);
begin
  Randomize;
  ListDate := TList.Create;
end;
```

A button on the form adds a random date to the list (of course, I included the unit containing the date component in the project built in the previous chapter):

```
procedure TForm1.ButtonAddClick(Sender: TObject);
begin
  ListDate.Add (TDate.Create (1900 + Random (200), 1 + Random (12),
    1 + Random (30)));
end;
```

When you extract the items from the list, you have to cast them back to the proper type, as in the following method, which is connected to the List button (you can see its effect in Figure 5.9):

```
procedure TForm1.ButtonListDateClick(Sender: TObject);
var
  I: Integer;
begin
```

```
  ListBox1.Clear;
  for I := 0 to ListDate.Count - 1 do
    Listbox1.Items.Add ((TObject(ListDate [I]) as TDate).Text);
end;
```

This traditional code can now be replaced with the following `for..in` loop (see Chapter 3 for more information on this new language feature):

```
var
  Pt: Pointer;
begin
  ListBox1.Clear;
  for Pt in ListDate do
    Listbox1.Items.Add ((TObject(Pt) as TDate).Text);
```

At the end of the code, before you can do an `as` downcast, you first need to hard-cast the pointer returned by the `TList` into a `TObject` reference. This kind of expression can result in an invalid type-cast exception, or it can generate a memory error when the pointer is not a reference to an object.

TIP   If there were no possibility of having anything but date objects in the list, extracting it with a static cast rather than an `as` cast would be more efficient. However, when there's even a remote chance of having a wrong object, I suggest using the `as` cast.

To demonstrate that things can indeed go wrong, I added one more button, which adds a `TButton` object to the list by calling `ListDate.Add(Sender)`. If you click this button and then update one of the lists, you'll get an error. Finally, remember that when you destroy a list of objects, you should destroy all of the list's objects first. The ListDemo program does this in the form's `FormDestroy` method (again a `for..in` loop):

```
procedure TForm1.FormDestroy(Sender: TObject);
var
  Pt: Pointer;
begin
  for Pt in ListDate do
    TObject(Pt).Free;
  ListDate.Free;
end;
```

FIGURE 5.9
The list of dates shown by
the ListDemo example

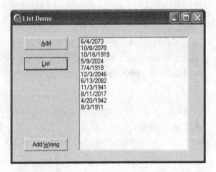

STRING LISTS IN DELPHI 2005

There a few new features related to string lists in Delphi 2005. I've already mentioned the support for enumerators and the availability of wide string lists. The other feature is a more flexible support for custom line breaks (beyond the use of the `sLineBreak` constant), through the new `LineBreak` property.

In addition to working with different line breaks, this property can be used to split a string with substrings divided by a separator into multiple strings of a string list. The classic Delphi code is to use `StringReplace` to add a separator and then copy the string in the `Text` property of the string list:

```
strTest := 'one|two|three';
strTest := StringReplace (strTest, '|', sLineBreak, [rfReplaceAll]);
slist.Text := strTest;
```

The new, alternative version you can write in Delphi 2005 is to set a proper line break symbol. The code below is actually significantly faster:

```
strTest := 'one|two|three';
sList.LineBreak := '|';
slist.Text := strTest;
```

Container Classes

Recent versions of Delphi include a series of container classes, defined in the Contnrs unit. The container classes extend the `TList` classes by adding the idea of ownership and by defining specific extraction rules (mimicking stacks and queues) or sorting capabilities.

The basic difference between `TList` and the new `TObjectList` class, for example, is that the latter is defined as a list of `TObject` objects, not a list of pointers. Even more important, however, is the fact that if the object list has the `OwnsObjects` property set to True, it automatically destroys an object when it is replaced by another one and destroys each object when the list itself is destroyed.

Here's a list of the container classes:

◆ The `TObjectList` class (already described) represents a list of objects, eventually owned by the list itself.

◆ The inherited class `TComponentList` represents a list of components, with full support for destruction notification (an important safety feature when two components are connected using their properties; that is, when a component is the value of a property of another component).

◆ The `TClassList` class is a list of class references.

◆ The classes `TStack` and `TObjectStack` represent lists of pointers and objects, from which you can only extract elements starting from the last one you've inserted. A stack follows LIFO order (last in, first out). The typical methods of a stack are `Push` for insertion, `Pop` for extraction, and `Peek` to preview the first item without removing it. You can still use all the methods of the base class, `TList`.

◆ The classes `TQueue` and `TObjectQueue` represent lists of pointers and objects from which you always remove the *first* item you've inserted (FIFO: first in, first out). The methods of these classes are the same as those of the stack classes, but they behave differently.

WARNING   Unlike TObjectList, the TObjectStack and TObjectQueue classes do not own the inserted objects and will not destroy those objects left in the data structure when it is destroyed. You can simply Pop all the items, destroy them once you're finished using them, and then destroy the container.

ENUMERATING CONTAINERS IN DELPHI 2005

Unlike the simpler list classes, the container classes defined in the Contnrs unit do *not* provide specific enumerators for the new for..in syntax. Technically, they do support enumerators because their base classes support it. For example, because TObjectList inherits from TList, you can enumerate an object list. But (and this is a *huge* limitation) the base class enumerator returns a pointer, defeating the entire idea of having a list of TObject elements and reducing the low-level type casts. I certainly don't like to write code like this (extracted from the ForInContainer demo):

```
var
  anObjectList: TObjectList;
  pt: Pointer;
begin
  anObjectList := TObjectList.Create;
  ...
  for pt in anObjectList do
    ShowMessage (TObject(pt).className);
```

A CONTAINERS DEMO

To demonstrate the use of the container classes, I modified the earlier ListDate example into the Contain example. First, I changed the type of the ListDate variable to TObjectList. In the FormCreate method, I modified the list creation to the following code, which activates the list ownership:

```
ListDate := TObjectList.Create (True);
```

At this point, you can simplify the destruction code because applying Free to the list will automatically free the dates it holds.

I also added to the program a stack and a queue object, filling each of them with numbers. One of the form's two buttons displays a list of the numbers in each container, and the other removes the last item (displayed in a message box):

```
procedure TForm1.btnQueueClick(Sender: TObject);
var
  I: Integer;
begin
  ListBox1.Clear;
  for I := 0 to Stack.Count - 1 do
  begin
    ListBox1.Items.Add (IntToStr (Integer (Queue.Peek)));
    Queue.Push(Queue.Pop);
  end;
  ShowMessage ('Removed: ' + IntToStr (Integer (Stack.Pop)));
end;
```

By clicking the two buttons, you can see that calling Pop for each container returns the last item. The difference is that the TQueue class inserts elements at the beginning, and the TStack class inserts them at the end.

HASHED ASSOCIATIVE LISTS

The set of predefined container classes includes TBucketList and TObjectBucketList. These two lists are associative, which means that for each item they have a key and an actual entry. The key is used to identify the items and search for them. To add an item, you call the Add method with two parameters: the key and the data. When you use the Find method, you pass the key and retrieve the data. The same effect is achieved by using the Data array property, passing the key as parameter.

These lists are based on a hash system. The lists create an internal array of items, called *buckets*, each having a sublist of list elements. As you add an item, its key value is used to compute the *hash* value, which determines the bucket to which the item should be added. When searching for the item, the hash is computed again, and the list immediately grabs the sublist containing the item and searches for it there. This process makes for very fast insertion and searches, but only if the hash algorithm distributes the items evenly among the various buckets and if there are enough different entries in the array. When many elements can be in the same bucket, searching is slower.

For this reason, as you create the TObjectBucketList and TBucketList, you can specify the number of entries for the list by using the parameter of the constructor and choosing a value between 2 and 256. The value of the bucket is determined by taking the first byte of the pointer (or number) passed as the key and doing an and operation with a number corresponding to the entries.

NOTE   I don't find this algorithm very convincing for a hash system, but replacing it with your own implies you are only overriding the BucketFor virtual function and that you must eventually change the number of entries in the array by setting a different value for the BucketCount property.

Another interesting feature, not available for lists, is the ForEach method, which allows you to execute a given function on each item contained in the list. You pass the ForEach method a pointer to your data and a procedure that receives four parameters: your custom pointer, each key and object of the list, and a Boolean parameter you can set to False to stop the execution. In other words, these are the two signatures:

```
type
  TBucketProc = procedure(AInfo, AItem, AData: Pointer;
    out AContinue: Boolean);

function TCustomBucketList.ForEach(AProc: TBucketProc;
  AInfo: Pointer): Boolean;
```

NOTE   In addition to these containers, Delphi includes a THashedStringList class, which inherits from TStringList. This class has no direct relationship with the hashed lists and is defined in a different unit, IniFiles. The hashed string list has two associated hash tables (of type TStringHash), which are completely refreshed every time the content of the string list changes. So this class is useful only for reading a large set of fixed strings, not for handling a list of strings changing often over time. On the other hand, the TStringHash support class seems to be quite useful in general cases and has a good algorithm for computing the hash value of a string.

Type-Safe Containers and Lists

Containers and lists have a problem: They are not type-safe, as I've shown in both examples by adding a button object to a list of dates. To ensure that the data in a list is homogeneous, you can check the type of the data you extract before you insert it, but as an extra safety measure you might also want to check the type of the data while extracting it. However, adding run-time type checking slows a program and is risky—a programmer might fail to check the type in some cases.

To solve both problems, you can create specific list classes for given data types and fashion the code from the existing TList or TObjectList class (or another container class). There are two approaches to accomplishing this:

♦ Derive a new class from the list class and customize the Add method and the access methods, which relate to the Items property. This is also the approach used by Borland for the container classes, which all derive from TList.

♦ Create a brand-new class that contains a TList object and map the methods of the new class to the internal list using proper type checking. This approach defines a wrapper class, a class that "wraps" around an existing one to provide a different or limited access to its methods (in this case, to perform a type conversion).

NOTE   Delphi container classes use static overrides to perform simple type conversions (parameters and function results of the desired type). Static overrides are not the same as polymorphism; someone using a container class via a TList variable will not be calling the container's specialized functions. Static override is a simple and effective technique used mostly when the signatures of the methods in the various classes are different, but it has one very important restriction: the methods in the descendant should not do anything beyond simple typecasting because you have no guarantee the descendant methods will be called. The list might be accessed and manipulated using the ancestor methods as much as by the descendant methods, so their operations must be identical. The only difference is the type used in the descendant methods, which allows you to avoid extra typecasting.

I implemented both solutions in the DateList example, which defines lists of TDate objects. In the code that follows, you'll find the declaration of a support enumerator and of the two classes, the inheritance-based TDateListI class and the wrapper class TDateListW:

```
type
  // support enumerator
  TDateListEnumerator = class (TListEnumerator)
  public
    function GetCurrent: TDate;
    property Current: TDate read GetCurrent;
  end;

  // inheritance-based
  TDateListI = class (TObjectList)
  protected
    procedure SetObject (Index: Integer; Item: TDate);
    function GetObject (Index: Integer): TDate;
  public
    function GetEnumerator: TDateListEnumerator;
```

```
    function Add (Obj: TDate): Integer;
    procedure Insert (Index: Integer; Obj: TDate);
    property Objects [Index: Integer]: TDate
      read GetObject write SetObject; default;
  end;

  // wrapper based
  TDateListW = class(TObject)
  private
    FList: TObjectList;
    function GetObject (Index: Integer): TDate;
    procedure SetObject (Index: Integer; Obj: TDate);
    function GetCount: Integer;
  public
    constructor Create;
    destructor Destroy; override;
    function GetEnumerator: TDateListEnumerator;
    function Add (Obj: TDate): Integer;
    function Remove (Obj: TDate): Integer;
    function IndexOf (Obj: TDate): Integer;
    property Count: Integer read GetCount;
    property Objects [Index: Integer]: TDate
      read GetObject write SetObject; default;
  end;
```

Obviously, the first class is simpler to write—it has fewer methods, and they just call the inherited ones. The good thing is that a TDateListI object can be passed to parameters expecting a TList. The problem is that the code that manipulates an instance of this list via a generic TList variable will not be calling the specialized methods because they are not virtual and might end up adding to the list objects of other data types.

Instead, if you decide not to use inheritance, you end up writing a lot of code; you need to reproduce every one of the original TList methods, simply calling the methods of the internal FList object. The drawback is that the TDateListW class is not type compatible with TList, which limits its usefulness. It can't be passed as parameter to methods expecting a TList.

Both of these approaches provide good type checking. After you've created an instance of one of these list classes, you can add only objects of the appropriate type, and the objects you extract will naturally be of the correct type. This technique is demonstrated by the DateList example. This program has a few buttons, a combo box to let a user choose which of the lists to show, and a list box to show the list values. The program stretches the lists by trying to add a button to the list of TDate objects. To add an object of a different type to the TDateListI list, you can convert the list to its base class, TList. This might happen accidentally if you pass the list as a parameter to a method that expects an ancestor class of the list class. In contrast, for the TDateListW list to fail, you must explicitly cast the object to TDate before inserting it, something a programmer should never do:

```
  procedure TForm1.ButtonAddButtonClick(Sender: TObject);
  begin
    ListW.Add (TDate(TButton.Create (nil)));
    TList(ListI).Add (TButton.Create (nil));
    UpdateList;
  end;
```

The UpdateList call triggers an exception, displayed directly in the list box, because I used an as typecast in the custom list classes. A wise programmer should never write the previous code. To summarize, writing a custom list for a specific type makes a program much more robust. Writing a wrapper list instead of one that's based on inheritance tends to be a little safer, although it requires more coding.

Finally, let me point out the enumerator, which inherits from the base TList class enumerator and overrides it by including a typecast to the proper data type in the GetCurrent function:

```
function TDateListEnumerator.GetCurrent: TDate;
begin
  Result := TObject (inherited GetCurrent) as TDate;
end;
```

This is relevant not only because it makes the code type-safe, but also because it allows us to use the correct data type in the for..in loop:

```
var
  D: TDate;
begin
  for D in ListW do
    ListBox1.Items.Add(D.GetText);
```

NOTE Version 2 of .NET will support generic types (or templates, to use the C++-language name), a technique used to solve specifically the problems of having lists and containers fine-tuned for a specific data type for internal objects. A future version of Delphi is expected to support this feature too. For the time being, instead of rewriting wrapper-style list classes for different types, you can use my List Template Wizard. See Appendix B for details.

Streaming

Another core area of the Delphi class library is its support for streaming, which includes file management, memory, sockets, and other sources of information arranged in a sequence. The idea of streaming is that you move through the data while reading it, much like the Read and Write functions traditionally used by the Pascal language.

The *TStream* Class

The VCL defines the abstract TStream class and several inherited classes. The base class, TStream, has just a few properties and you'll never create an instance of it, but it has an interesting list of methods you'll generally use when working with derived stream classes.

The TStream class defines two properties, Size and Position. All stream objects have a specific size (which generally grows if you write something after the end of the stream), and you must specify a position within the stream where you want to either read or write information.

Reading and writing bytes depends on the actual stream class you are using, but in both cases you don't need to know much more than the size of the stream and your relative position in the stream to read or write data. In fact, that's one of the advantages of using streams. The basic interface remains the same whether you're manipulating a disk file, a binary large object (BLOB) field, or a long sequence of bytes in memory.

In addition to the Size and Position properties, the TStream class also defines several important methods, most of which are virtual and abstract. (In other words, the TStream class doesn't define what these methods do; therefore, derived classes are responsible for implementing them.) Some of these methods are important only in the context of reading or writing components within a stream (for instance, ReadComponent and WriteComponent), but some are useful in other contexts, too. In Listing 5.3, you can find the declaration of the TStream class, extracted from the Classes unit.

LISTING 5.3:   The public portion of the definition of the *TStream* class

```
TStream = class(TObject)
public
  // read and write a buffer
  function Read(var Buffer; Count: Longint):
    Longint; virtual; abstract;
  function Write(const Buffer; Count: Longint):
    Longint; virtual; abstract;
  procedure ReadBuffer(var Buffer; Count: Longint);
  procedure WriteBuffer(const Buffer; Count: Longint);

  // move to a specific position
  function Seek(Offset: Longint; Origin: Word):
    Longint; overload; virtual;
  function Seek(const Offset: Int64; Origin: TSeekOrigin):
    Int64; overload; virtual;

  // copy the stream
  function CopyFrom(Source: TStream; Count: Int64): Int64;

  // read or write a component
  function ReadComponent(Instance: TComponent): TComponent;
  function ReadComponentRes(Instance: TComponent): TComponent;
  procedure WriteComponent(Instance: TComponent);
  procedure WriteComponentRes(const ResName: string;
    Instance: TComponent);
  procedure WriteDescendant(Instance, Ancestor: TComponent);
  procedure WriteDescendantRes(
    const ResName: string; Instance, Ancestor: TComponent);
  procedure WriteResourceHeader(const ResName: string;
    out FixupInfo: Integer);
  procedure FixupResourceHeader(FixupInfo: Integer);
  procedure ReadResHeader;

  // properties
  property Position: Int64 read GetPosition write SetPosition;
  property Size: Int64 read GetSize write SetSize64;
end;
```

The basic use of a stream involves calling the ReadBuffer and WriteBuffer methods, which are very powerful but not terribly easy to use. The first parameter is an untyped buffer in which you can pass the variable to save from or load to. For example, you can save into a file a number (in binary format) and a string with this code:

```
var
  stream: TStream;
  n: integer;
  str: string;
begin
  n := 10;
  str := 'test string';
  stream := TFileStream.Create ('c:\tmp\test', fmCreate);
  stream.WriteBuffer (n, sizeOf(integer));
  stream.WriteBuffer (str[1], Length (str));
  stream.Free;
```

An alternative approach is to let specific components save or load data to and from streams. Many VCL classes define a LoadFromStream or a SaveToStream method, including TStrings, TStringList, TBlobField, TMemoField, TIcon, and TBitmap.

Specific Stream Classes

Creating a TStream instance makes no sense because this class is abstract and provides no direct support for saving data. Instead, you can use one of the derived classes to load data from or store it to an actual file, a BLOB field, a socket, or a memory block. Use TFileStream when you want to work with a file, passing the filename and some file access options to the Create method. Use TMemoryStream to manipulate a stream in memory and not an actual file.

Several units define TStream-derived classes. The Classes unit includes the following classes:

◆ THandleStream defines a stream that manipulates a disk file represented by a file handle.

◆ TFileStream defines a stream that manipulates a disk file (a file that exists on a local or network disk) represented by a filename. It inherits from THandleStream.

◆ TCustomMemoryStream is the base class for streams stored in memory, but it is not used directly.

◆ TMemoryStream defines a stream that manipulates a sequence of bytes in memory. It inherits from TCustomMemoryStream.

◆ TStringStream provides a simple way to associate a stream to a string in memory so that you can access the string with the TStream interface and also copy the string to and from another stream.

◆ TResourceStream defines a stream that manipulates a sequence of bytes in memory and provides read-only access to resource data linked into the executable file of an application (the DFM files are an example of this resource data). It inherits from TCustomMemoryStream.

Stream classes defined in other units include the following:

◆ TBlobStream defines a stream that provides simple access to database BLOB fields. There are similar BLOB streams for database access technologies other than the BDE, including TSQLBlobStream and TClientBlobStream. (Notice that each type of dataset uses a specific stream class for BLOB fields.) All these classes inherit from TMemoryStream.

◆ TOleStream defines a stream for reading and writing information over the interface for streaming provided by an OLE object.

◆ TWinSocketStream provides streaming support for a socket connection.

Using File Streams

Creating and using a file stream can be as simple as creating a variable of a type that descends from TStream and calling components' methods to load content from the file:

```
var
  S: TFileStream;
begin
  if OpenDialog1.Execute then
  begin
    S := TFileStream.Create (OpenDialog1.FileName, fmShareDenyWrite);
    try
      Memo1.Lines.LoadFromStream (S);
    finally
      S.Free;
    end;
  end;
end;
```

As you can see in this code, the Create method for file streams has two parameters: the name of the file and a flag indicating the requested access mode. In this case, you want to read the file, so you use the fmOpenRead flag or fmShareDenyWrite flag.

NOTE   To limit concurrent access to a file, you can use the fmShareDenyWrite mode, when you're simply reading data from a shared file, and the fmShareExclusive mode, when you're writing data to a shared file. There is a third parameter in TFileStream.Create called Rights. This parameter is used to pass file access permissions to the Linux file system when the access mode is fmCreate (that is, only when you are creating a new file). This parameter is ignored on Windows.

A big advantage of streams over other file access techniques is that they're very interchangeable, so you can work with memory streams and then save them to a file, or you can perform the opposite operations. This might be a way to improve the speed of a file-intensive program. Here is a snippet of a file-copying function to give you another idea of how you can use streams:

```
procedure CopyFile (SourceName, TargetName: String);
var
  Stream1, Stream2: TFileStream;
begin
  Stream1 := TFileStream.Create (SourceName, fmShareDenyWrite);
```

```
try
  if FileExists (TargetName) then
    Stream2 := TFileStream.Create (TargetName, fmShareExclusive)
  else
    Stream2 := TFileStream.Create (TargetName, fmCreate);
  try
    Stream2.CopyFrom (Stream1, Stream1.Size);
  finally
    Stream2.Free;
  end
finally
  Stream1.Free;
end
end;
```

Another important use of streams is to handle database BLOB fields or other large fields directly. You can export such data to a stream or read it from one by calling the SaveToStream and LoadFromStream methods of the TBlobField class.

NOTE   Delphi 7 streaming support added a new exception base class, EFileStreamError. Its constructor takes as parameter a filename for error reporting. This class standardizes and largely simplifies the notification of file-related errors in streams.

The *TReader* and *TWriter* Classes

By themselves, the VCL stream classes don't provide much support for reading or writing data. In fact, stream classes don't implement much beyond simply reading and writing blocks of data. If you want to load or save specific data types in a stream (and don't want to perform a great deal of type-casting), you can use the TReader and TWriter classes, which derive from the generic TFiler class.

Basically, the TReader and TWriter classes exist to simplify loading and saving stream data according to its type, not just as a sequence of bytes. To do this, TWriter embeds special signatures into the stream that specify the type for each object's data. Conversely, the TReader class reads these signatures from the stream, creates the appropriate objects, and then initializes those objects using the subsequent data from the stream.

For example, I could have written out a number and a string to a stream:

```
var
  stream: TStream;
  n: integer;
  str: string;
  w: TWriter;
begin
  n := 10;
  str := 'test string';
  stream := TFileStream.Create ('c:\tmp\test.txt', fmCreate);
  try
    w := TWriter.Create (stream, 1024);
    try
      w.WriteInteger (n);
```

```
      w.WriteString (str);
   finally
      w.Free;
   end;
finally
   stream.Free;
end;
```

This time the file will include the extra signature characters, so I can read back this file only by using a TReader object. For this reason, using TReader and TWriter is generally confined to component streaming and is seldom applied in general file management.

Streams and Persistency

In Delphi, streams play a considerable role in persistency. For this reason, many methods of TStream relate to saving and loading a component and its subcomponents. For example, you can store a form in a stream by writing

```
stream.WriteComponent(Form1);
```

If you examine the structure of a Delphi DFM file, you'll discover that it's really just a text file that contains a notation. Inside this file, you'll find the component information for the form (or data module or frame) and for each of the components it contains. As you would expect, the stream classes provide two methods to read and write this custom resource data for components: WriteComponentRes to store the data and ReadComponentRes to load it.

For an in-memory experiment (not involving DFM files) though, using WriteComponent is generally better suited. After you create a memory stream and save the current form to it, the problem is how to display it. You can do this by transforming the form's binary representation to a textual representation. Even though the Delphi IDE saves DFM files in text format by default, the representation used in a form resource compiled into an application is a binary format.

The IDE can accomplish the form conversion, generally with the View as Text command of the Form Designer, as well as in other ways. The Delphi Bin directory also contains a command-line utility, CONVERT.EXE. Within your own code, the standard way to obtain a conversion is to call the specific VCL methods. There are four functions for converting to and from the internal object format obtained by the WriteComponent method:

```
procedure ObjectBinaryToText(Input, Output: TStream); overload;
procedure ObjectBinaryToText(Input, Output: TStream;
   var OriginalFormat: TStreamOriginalFormat); overload;
procedure ObjectTextToBinary(Input, Output: TStream); overload;
procedure ObjectTextToBinary(Input, Output: TStream;
   var OriginalFormat: TStreamOriginalFormat); overload;
```

Four different functions, with the same parameters and names containing the name *Resource* instead of *Binary* (as in ObjectResourceToText), convert the resource format obtained by WriteComponentRes. A final method, TestStreamFormat, indicates whether a DFM is storing a binary or textual representation.

In the FormToText program, I used the `ObjectBinaryToText` method to copy the binary definition of a form into another stream, and then I displayed the resulting stream in a memo, as you can see in Figure 5.10. Here is the code of the two methods involved:

```pascal
procedure TformText.btnCurrentClick(Sender: TObject);
var
  MemStr: TStream;
begin
  MemStr := TMemoryStream.Create;
  try
    MemStr.WriteComponent (Self);
    ConvertAndShow (MemStr);
  finally
    MemStr.Free
  end;
end;

procedure TformText.ConvertAndShow (aStream: TStream);
var
  ConvStream: TStream;
begin
  aStream.Position := 0;
  ConvStream := TMemoryStream.Create;
  try
    ObjectBinaryToText (aStream, ConvStream);
    ConvStream.Position := 0;
    MemoOut.Lines.LoadFromStream (ConvStream);
  finally
    ConvStream.Free
  end;
end;
```

FIGURE 5.10

The textual description of a form component displayed inside itself by the FormToText example

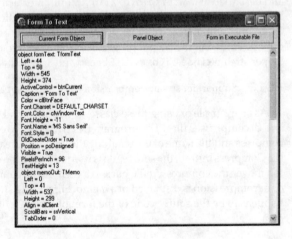

Notice that by repeatedly clicking the Current Form Object button you'll get more and more text, and the text of the memo is included in the stream. After a few times, the entire operation will become extremely slow, until the program seems to be hung up. In this code, you see some of the flexibility of using streams—you can write a generic procedure that you can use to convert any stream.

NOTE   It's important to stress that after you've written data to a stream, you must explicitly seek back to the beginning (or set the Position property to 0) before you can use the stream further— unless you want to append data to the stream, of course.

Another button, labeled Panel Object, shows the textual representation of a specific component, the panel, passing the component to the WriteComponent method. The third button, Form in Executable File, performs a different operation. Instead of streaming an existing object in memory, it loads in a TResourceStream object the design-time representation of the form—that is, its DFM file—from the corresponding resource embedded in the executable file:

```
procedure TFormText.btnResourceClick(Sender: TObject);
var
  ResStr: TResourceStream;
begin
  ResStr := TResourceStream.Create(hInstance, 'TFORMTEXT', RT_RCDATA);
  try
    ConvertAndShow (ResStr);
  finally
    ResStr.Free
  end;
end;
```

By clicking the buttons in sequence (or modifying the form of the program), you can compare the form saved in the DFM file to the current run-time object.

Compressing Streams with ZLib

A feature introduced in Delphi 7 was the official support for the ZLib compression library (available and described at www.gzip.org/zlib). A unit interfacing ZLib has been available for a long time on Delphi's CD, but now it is included in the core distribution and is part of the VCL source (the ZLib and ZLibConst units). In addition to providing an interface to the library (which is a C library you can directly embed in the Delphi program, with no need to distribute a DLL), Delphi defines a couple of helper stream classes: TCompressStream and TDecompressStream.

NOTE   Support for stream compression with ZLib is not available in Delphi for .NET.

As an example of using these classes, I wrote a small program called ZCompress that compresses and decompresses files. The program has two edit boxes in which you enter the name of the file to compress and the name of the resulting file, which is created if it doesn't already exist. When you click the Compress button, the source file is used to create the destination file; clicking the Decompress button moves the compressed file back to a memory stream. In both cases, the result of the compression or decompression is displayed in a memo. Figure 5.11 shows the result for the compressed file (which happens to be the source code of the form of the current program).

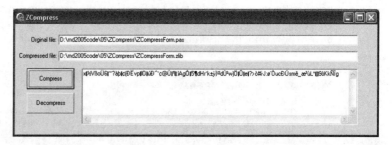

To make the code of this program more reusable, I wrote two routines for compressing or decompressing a stream into another stream. Here is the code:

```
function CompressStream (aSource, aTarget: TStream);
var
  comprStream: TCompressionStream;
begin
  comprStream := TCompressionStream.Create(clFastest, aTarget);
  try
    comprStream.CopyFrom(aSource, aSource.Size);
    Result := comprStream.CompressionRate;
  finally
    comprStream.Free;
  end;
end;


procedure DecompressStream (aSource, aTarget: TStream) ;
var
  decompStream: TDecompressionStream;
  nRead: Integer;
  Buffer: array [0..1023] of Char;
begin
  decompStream := TDecompressionStream.Create(aSource);
  try
    // aStreamDest.CopyFrom (decompStream, size) doesn't work
    // properly as you don't know the size in advance,
    // so I've used a similar "manual" code
    repeat
      nRead := decompStream.Read(Buffer, 1024);
      aTarget.Write (Buffer, nRead);
    until nRead = 0;
  finally
    decompStream.Free;
  end;
end;
```

As you can see in the code comment, the decompression operation is slightly more complex because you cannot use the CopyFrom method: you don't know the size of the resulting stream in advance. If you pass 0 to the method, it will try to get the size of the source stream, which is a TDecompressionStream. However, this operation causes an exception because the compression and decompression streams can be read only from the beginning to the end and don't allow for seeking the end of the file.

WRITING A CUSTOM STREAM CLASS

In addition to using the existing stream classes, Delphi programmers can write their own stream classes and use them in place of the existing ones. To accomplish this, you need only specify how a generic block of raw data is saved and loaded, and the VCL will be able to use your new class wherever you call for it. You may not need to create a brand-new stream class to work with a new type of media; you may only need to customize an existing stream. In that case, all you have to do is write the proper read and write methods.

As an example, I created a class to encode and decode a generic file stream. Although this example is limited by its use of a totally dumb encoding mechanism, it fully integrates with the VCL and works properly. The new stream class simply declares the two core reading and writing methods and has a property that stores a key:

```
type
  TEncodedStream = class (TFileStream)
  private
    FKey: Char;
  public
    constructor Create(const FileName: string; Mode: Word);
    function Read(var Buffer; Count: Longint): Longint; override;
    function Write(const Buffer; Count: Longint): Longint; override;
    property Key: Char read FKey write FKey;
  end;
```

The value of the key is added to each of the bytes saved to a file and subtracted when the data is read. Here is the complete code of the Write and Read methods, which uses pointers quite heavily:

```
constructor TEncodedStream.Create(const FileName: string; Mode: Word);
begin
  inherited Create (FileName, Mode);
  FKey := 'A'; // default
end;

function TEncodedStream.Write(const Buffer; Count: Longint): Longint;
var
  pBuf, pEnc: PChar;
  I, EncVal: Integer;
begin
  // allocate memory for the encoded buffer
  GetMem (pEnc, Count);
```

```pascal
  try
    // use the buffer as an array of characters
    pBuf := PChar (@Buffer);
    // for every character of the buffer
    for I := 0 to Count - 1 do
    begin
      // encode the value and store it
      EncVal := (Ord (pBuf[I]) + Ord(Key)) mod 256;
      pEnc [I] := Chr (EncVal);
    end;
    // write the encoded buffer to the file
    Result := inherited Write (pEnc^, Count);
  finally
    FreeMem (pEnc, Count);
  end;
end;


function TEncodedStream.Read(var Buffer; Count: Longint): Longint;
var
  pBuf, pEnc: PChar;
  I, CountRead, EncVal: Integer;
begin
  // allocate memory for the encoded buffer
  GetMem (pEnc, Count);
  try
    // read the encoded buffer from the file
    CountRead := inherited Read (pEnc^, Count);
    // use the output buffer as a string
    pBuf := PChar (@Buffer);
    // for every character actually read
    for I := 0 to CountRead - 1 do
    begin
      // decode the value and store it
      EncVal := ( Ord (pEnc[I]) - Ord(Key) ) mod 256;
      pBuf [I] := Chr (EncVal);
    end;
  finally
    FreeMem (pEnc, Count);
```

```
    end;
  // return the number of characters read
  Result := CountRead;
end;
```

The comments in this rather complex code should help you understand the details. I used this encoded stream in a demo program called EncDemo. The form of this program has two memo components and three buttons, as you can see in the following graphic:

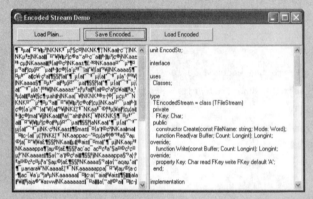

The first button loads a plain text file in the first memo; the second button saves the text of this first memo in an encoded file; and the third button reloads the encoded file into the second memo, decoding it. In this example, after encoding the file, I reloaded it in the first memo as a plain text file on the left, which of course is unreadable.

Because the encoded stream class is available, the code of this program is very similar to that of any other program using streams. For example, here is the method used to save the encoded file (you can compare its code to that of earlier examples based on streams):

```
procedure TFormEncode.BtnSaveEncodedClick(Sender: TObject);
var
  EncStr: TEncodedStream;
begin
  if SaveDialog1.Execute then
  begin
    EncStr := TEncodedStream.Create(SaveDialog1.Filename, fmCreate);
    try
      Memo1.Lines.SaveToStream (EncStr);
    finally
      EncStr.Free;
    end;
  end;
end;
```

What's Next?

As you have seen in this chapter, the Delphi run-time library has a large number of routines and a few root classes that play a considerable role and which you should learn to leverage to the maximum possible extent. I have provided only a summary of the RTL, not a complete overview (which would take too much space). Some programmers tend to become expert on the components they use every day, and this is important; but without understanding the core classes (and ideas such as streaming), you'll have a tough time grasping the full power of Delphi.

In this chapter we focused on Win32, although most of the RTL features discussed here are also available in the RTL of Delphi for .NET. There are some changes though, and a second RTL is provided by Microsoft (the core classes of the .NET Framework Class Library or FCL). All of this is covered in the Chapter 9.

Of course, the real power of Delphi lies in the fact that its class library is a component library. That's why in the next few chapters we'll first focus on the TComponent class and then move along with an analysis of the architecture of the Visual Component Library, or VCL.

Chapter 6

Architecture of the Visual Component Library (VCL)

Now that you've been introduced to the Delphi environment and have seen an overview of the Delphi language and the base elements of the run-time library, you are ready to delve into the foundations of the component library and the development of the user interface of applications. This is really what Delphi is about. Programming using components is a key feature of this development environment.

Delphi comes with a large number of ready-to-use components. I won't describe every component in detail, examining each of its properties and methods; if you need this information, you can find it in the Help system. The aim of this chapter and those following is to show you how to use some of the advanced features offered by the Delphi predefined components to build applications and to discuss specific programming techniques.

I'll start with an in-depth analysis of the TComponent class, followed by coverage of the core visual classes (particularly TControl). Then I'll examine the various visual components, because choosing the right basic controls will often help you get a project underway more quickly. This chapter covers components and ownership, events in Delphi components, and the TControl and TWinControl classes. There is also an overview of the standard components, information on basic and advanced menu construction, system menu modification, and graphics in menus and list boxes.

NOTE   Everything discussed here and in the next chapter applies both to the VCL for Win32 and the VCL for .NET. In fact, unlike the core RTL, the VCL is almost identical in Win32 and .NET. That's why there is no specific chapter devoted to the VCL for .NET and only notes on relevant differences and specific usage suggestions in the chapters discussing the VCL for both platforms. Moreover, most of the examples in this chapter also have a .NET version.

The *TComponent* Class

If the TPersistent class is more important than it seems at first sight, the key class at the heart of Delphi's component-based class library is TComponent, which inherits from TPersistent (and from TObject). The TComponent class defines many core elements of components; however, it is not as complex as you might think because the base classes and the language already provide most of what's needed.

I won't explore all the details of the TComponent class, some of which are more important for component designers than they are for component users. I'll just discuss ownership (which accounts for some public properties of the class) and the two published properties of the class, Name and Tag.

Ownership

One of the core features of the TComponent class is the definition of ownership. When a component is created, it can be assigned an owner component, which will be responsible for destroying it. So every component can have an owner and can also be the owner of other components.

Several public methods and properties of the class are devoted to handling the *two sides* of ownership. Here is a list, extracted from the class declaration (in the Classes unit of the VCL):

```
type
  TComponent = class(TPersistent, IInterface,
    IInterfaceComponentReference)
  public
    constructor Create(AOwner: TComponent); virtual;
    procedure DestroyComponents;
    function FindComponent(const AName: string): TComponent;
    procedure InsertComponent(AComponent: TComponent);
    procedure RemoveComponent(AComponent: TComponent);

    property Components[Index: Integer]: TComponent read GetComponent;
    property ComponentCount: Integer read GetComponentCount;
    property ComponentIndex: Integer
      read GetComponentIndex write SetComponentIndex;
    property Owner: TComponent read FOwner;
```

If you create a component and give it an owner, it will be added to the list of components (InsertComponent), which is accessible using the Components array property. The specific component has an Owner and knows its position in the owner components list, with the ComponentIndex property. Finally, the owner's destructor will take care of the destruction of the object it owns by calling DestroyComponents. A few more protected methods are involved, but this should give you the overall picture.

It's important to emphasize that component ownership can solve many of your applications' memory management problems, if used properly. When you use the Form Designer or Data Module Designer of the IDE, that form or data module will own any component dropped on it. At the same time, you should generally create components with a form or data module owner, even in your code. In these circumstances you need only remember to destroy the component containers (form or data module) when they are not needed anymore; you can forget about the components they contain. For example, you delete a form to destroy all the components it contains at once, which is a major simplification compared to having to remember to free each and every object individually. On a larger scale, forms and data modules are generally owned by the Application object, which is destroyed by the VCL shutdown code and frees all of the component containers (forms and data modules), which in turn free the components they contain.

THE COMPONENTS ARRAY AND THE COMPONENTS ENUMERATOR

The Components property can also be used to access one component owned by another—let's say, a form. This property can be very handy (compared to using a specific component directly) for writing generic code, acting on all or many components at a time. For example, you can use the following code to add to a list box the names of all a form's components (this code is part of the ChangeOwner example presented in the next section):

```
var
  I: Integer;
begin
  ListBox1.Items.Clear;
  for I := 0 to ComponentCount - 1 do
    ListBox1.Items.Add (Components [I].Name);
```

This code uses the `ComponentCount` property, which holds the total number of components owned by the current form, and the `Components` property, which is the list of owned components. When you access a value from this list, you get a value of the `TComponent` type. For this reason, you can directly use only the properties common to all components, such as the `Name` property. To use properties specific to particular components, you have to use the proper type-downcast (`as`).

In Delphi 2005, you can obtain the same effect with the simpler and more readable `for..in` construct, as already discussed and demonstrated in Chapter 3: the previous code can be written as:

```
var
  aComp: TComponent;
begin
  ListBox1.Items.Clear;
  for aComp in Self do
    ListBox1.Items.Add (aComp.Name);
```

The new `GetEnumerator` function is the only new feature of the `TComponent` class in this release of Delphi.

NOTE   In Delphi some components are also component containers: the GroupBox, Panel, PageControl, and, of course, Form components. When you use these controls, you can add other components inside them. In this case, the container is the parent of the components (as indicated by the `Parent` property), and the form is their owner (as indicated by the `Owner` property). You can use the `Controls` property of a form or group box to navigate the child controls, and you can use the `Components` property of the form to navigate all the owned components, regardless of their parent.

Using the `Components` property or the enumerator, you can always access each component of a form. If you need access to a specific component, however, instead of comparing each name with the name of the component you are looking for, you can let Delphi do this work by using the form's `FindComponent` method. This method simply scans the `Components` array looking for a name match. More information about the role of the `Name` property for a component is in the section "The Name Property."

CHANGING THE OWNER

You have seen that almost every component has an owner. When a component is created at design time (or from the resulting DFM file), its owner will invariably be its form. When you create a component at run time, the owner is passed as a parameter to the `Create` constructor.

`Owner` is a read-only property, so you cannot change it. The owner is set at creation time and should generally not change during the lifetime of a component. To understand why you should not change a component's owner at design time nor freely change its name, read the following discussion.

Be warned that the topic covered is not simple; if you're just beginning with Delphi, you might want to come back to this section at a later time.

To change the owner of a component, you can call the `InsertComponent` and `RemoveComponent` methods of the owner itself, passing the current component as parameter. However, you cannot apply these methods directly in a form's event handler, as I attempt to do here:

```
procedure TForm1.Button1Click(Sender: TObject);
begin
  RemoveComponent (Button1);
  Form2.InsertComponent (Button1);
end;
```

This code produces a memory access violation because when you call `RemoveComponent`, Delphi disconnects the component from the form field (`Button1`), setting it to `nil`. (I talk more about form fields in the section "Removing the Form Fields.") The solution is to write a procedure like this:

```
procedure ChangeOwner (Component, NewOwner: TComponent);
begin
  Component.Owner.RemoveComponent (Component);
  NewOwner.InsertComponent (Component);
end;
```

This method (extracted from the ChangeOwner example) changes the owner of the component. It is called along with the simpler code used to change the parent component; the two commands combined move the button *completely* to another form, changing its owner:

```
procedure TForm1.ButtonChangeClick(Sender: TObject);
begin
  if Assigned (Button1) then
  begin
    // change parent
    Button1.Parent := Form2;
    // change owner
    ChangeOwner (Button1, Form2);
  end;
end;
```

The method checks whether the `Button1` field still refers to the control because, while moving the component, Delphi will set `Button1` to `nil`. You can see the effect of this code in Figure 6.1.

To demonstrate that the owner of the `Button1` component actually changes, I added another feature to both forms. The List button fills the list box with the names of the components each form owns, using the procedure shown in the previous section. Click the two List buttons before and after moving the component, and you'll see what happens behind the scenes. As a final feature, the `Button1` component has a simple handler for its `OnClick` event, to display the caption of the owner form:

```
ShowMessage ('My owner is ' +
  ((Sender as TButton).Owner as TForm).Caption);
```

FIGURE 6.1
In the ChangeOwner
example, clicking the
Change button moves
the Button1 component
to the second form.

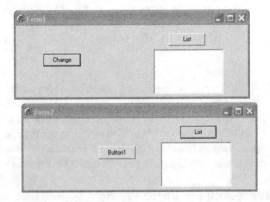

The *Name* Property

Every component in Delphi should have a name. The name must be unique within the owner component, which is generally the form into which you place the component. This means an application can have two different forms, each with a component that has the same name, although you might want to avoid this practice to prevent confusion. It is generally better to keep component names unique throughout an application.

Setting a proper value for the Name property is very important. Usually the name of a component has a prefix with the component type; this makes the code more readable and allows Delphi to group components in the combo box of the Object Inspector, where they are sorted by name.

Three important elements are related to a component's Name property:

◆ At design time, the value of the Name property defines the name of the form field in the declaration of the form class. This is the name you'll generally use in the code to refer to the object. For this reason, the value of the Name property must be a legal Delphi language identifier (it must have no spaces and begin with a letter, not a number).

◆ If you set a control's Name property before changing its Caption or Text property, the new name is often copied to the caption. That is, if the name and the caption are identical, then changing the name will also change the caption.

◆ Delphi uses the name of the component to create the default name of the methods related to its events. If you have a Button1 component, its default OnClick event handler will be called Button1Click unless you specify a different name. If you later change the name of the component, Delphi will modify the names of the related methods accordingly. For example, if you change the name of the button to MyButton, the Button1Click method automatically becomes MyButtonClick.

As mentioned earlier, if you have a string with the name of a component, you can get its instance by calling the FindComponent method of its owner, which returns nil if the component is not found. For example, you can write

```
var
  Comp: TComponent;
begin
```

```
Comp := FindComponent ('Button1');
if Assigned (Comp) then
  with Comp as TButton do
    // some code...
```

NOTE   Delphi also includes a FindGlobalComponent function, which finds a top-level component (a form or data module) that has a given name. FindGlobalComponent calls one or more
installed functions, so in theory you can modify the way the function works. However, because
FindGlobalComponent is used by the streaming system, I strongly recommend against installing
your own replacement functions. If you want a customized way to search for components on other
containers, simply write a new function with a custom name.

Removing the Form Fields

Every time you add a component to a form, Delphi adds an entry for it, along with some of its properties, to the DFM file. To the source code file, Delphi adds the corresponding field in the form class
declaration. This field of the form is a reference to the corresponding object, as is any class-type variable in Delphi. When the form is created, Delphi loads the DFM file and uses it to re-create all the components and set their properties back to the design-time values, saved in the DFM file itself. Then it
connects the new object with the form field corresponding to its Name property. This is why you can
use the form field to operate on the corresponding component in your code.

For this reason, it is possible to have a component without a name. If your application will not
manipulate the component or modify it at run time, you can remove the component name from the
Object Inspector. Examples include a static label with fixed text, a menu item, or even more obviously,
menu item separators. By blanking out the name, you remove the corresponding element from the
form class declaration. Doing so reduces the size of the form object (by only 4 bytes, the size of the
object reference) and reduces the DFM file by not including a useless string (the component name).
Reducing the DFM file size also implies reducing the final executable file size, even if only slightly.

WARNING   If you remove component names, make sure to leave at least one named component of
each class used on the form so the smart linker and the streaming system will link in the required
code for the class and recognize it from the DFM file. For example, if you remove from a form all the
fields referring to TLabel components, when the system loads the form at run time, it will be
unable to create an object of an unknown class and will issue an error indicating that the class is not
available. As you'll see in the next section, you can call the RegisterClass or RegisterClasses
routines to avoid such an error.

You can also keep the component name and manually remove the corresponding field of the form
class. Even if the component has no corresponding form field, it is created anyway, although using it
(through the FindComponent method, for example) will be a little more difficult.

Hiding the Form Fields

Many OOP purists complain that Delphi doesn't really follow the encapsulation rules, because all the
components of a form are mapped to public fields and can be accessed from other forms and units.
Fields for components are listed in the first unnamed section of a class declaration, which has a
default visibility of published. However, Delphi does that only as a default to help beginners learn
to use the Delphi visual development environment quickly. A programmer can follow a different

approach and use properties and methods to operate on forms. The risk, however, is that another programmer on the same team might inadvertently bypass this approach, directly accessing the components if they are left in the published section. The solution, which many programmers don't know about, is to move the components to the private portion of the class declaration.

As an example, I made a simple form with an edit box, a button, and a list box. When the edit box contains text and the user clicks the button, the text is added to the list box. When the edit box is empty, the button is disabled. This is the code of the HideComp example:

```
procedure TForm1.Button1Click(Sender: TObject);
begin
  ListBox1.Items.Add (Edit1.Text);
end;

procedure TForm1.Edit1Change(Sender: TObject);
begin
  Button1.Enabled := Length (Edit1.Text) <> 0;
end;
```

I list these methods only to show you that in a form's code, you usually refer to the available components, defining their interactions. For this reason, it seems impossible to get rid of the fields corresponding to the component. However, you can hide them, moving them from the default published section to the private section of the form class declaration:

```
TForm1 = class(TForm)
  procedure Button1Click(Sender: TObject);
  procedure Edit1Change(Sender: TObject);
  procedure FormCreate(Sender: TObject);
private
  Button1: TButton;
  Edit1: TEdit;
  ListBox1: TListBox;
end;
```

Now, if you run the program you'll get in trouble: the form will load, but because the private fields are not initialized, the events will use nil object references. Delphi usually initializes the published fields of the form using the components created from the DFM file. What if you do it yourself with the following code?

```
procedure TForm1.FormCreate(Sender: TObject);
begin
  Button1 := FindComponent ('Button1') as TButton;
  Edit1 := FindComponent ('Edit1') as TEdit;
  ListBox1 := FindComponent ('ListBox1') as TListBox;
end;
```

It will *almost* work, but it generates a system error, similar to the one discussed in the previous section. This time, the private declarations will cause the linker to link in the implementations of those classes; the problem is, the streaming system needs to know the names of the classes in order to locate the class reference needed to construct the components while loading the DFM file.

The final touch you need is registration code to tell Delphi at run time about the existence of the component classes you want to use. You should do this before the form is created, so I generally place this code in the initialization section of the unit:

```
initialization
  RegisterClasses ([TButton, TEdit, TListBox]);
```

The question is, is this really worth the effort? You obtain a higher degree of encapsulation, protecting the components of a form from other forms (and other programmers writing them). Replicating these steps for every form can be tedious, so I wrote a wizard to generate the code for me on the fly. The wizard is far from perfect because it doesn't handle changes automatically, but it is usable. See Appendix A for more information about how to get it. For a large project built according to the principles of object-oriented programming, I recommend you consider this or a similar technique.

The Customizable *Tag* Property (on Win32 and .NET)

The Tag property is strange because it has no effect at all. It is merely an extra memory location, present in each component class, where you can store custom values. The kind of information stored and the way it is used is completely up to you.

It is often useful to have an extra memory location to attach information to a component without needing to define it in your component class. Technically, the Tag property stores a long integer so that, for example, you can store the entry number of an array or list that corresponds to an object. Using typecasting, you can store in the Tag property a pointer, an object reference, or anything else that is 4 bytes wide. A programmer can associate virtually anything with a component using its tag. You'll see how to use this property in several examples in future chapters.

These hard casts are possible (although they are dangerous) on Win32. In the VCL for .NET, the Tag property is instead defined of the type TTag, which is an alias of the type variant (which in turn is an alias of System.Object). There are actually several other internal differences for the TComponent class in the VCL for .NET, as discussed in the next section.

NOTE   The .NET Framework class library uses a Tag property defined of the System.Object type. However, this is not defined at the components class level, but at the controls class level for Win-Forms applications.

The *TComponent* Class in the VCL for .NET

Similar to what happens for its base classes, TObject and TPersistent, the TComponent class in Delphi for .NET is also mapped to the corresponding class of the FCL framework with a class helper for reducing the interface differences to a bare minimum:

```
type
  TComponent = System.ComponentModel.Component;
  TComponentHelper = class helper (TPersistentHelper) for TComponent...
```

The situation in this case, however, is slightly different from the base class helpers, as the implementation of the TComponent interface, including the ownership, also requires some support data, something class helpers do not provide (as they can introduce only methods and properties). The trick Borland uses in this case is to piggyback on the Site property of the Component class by defining a fake component site attached to the component and providing the proper data. The data is defined in the TComponentSite class:

```
type
  TComponentSite = class(TObject, IDisposable,
    ISite, IServiceProvider, IContainer)
  private
    FDesignMode: Boolean;
    FComponent: IComponent;
    FName: string;
    FTag: TTag;
    FComponents: TList;
    FFreeNotifies: TList;
    FDesignInfo: Longint;
    FComponentStyle: TComponentStyle;
    FComponentState: TComponentState;
    FOwner: TComponent;
  ...
```

An object of this support class is created at the first call to the GetSiteObject protected method provided by TComponentHelper class. This method, in turn, is called by the implementation of most VCL-compatible methods, such as the simple

```
procedure TComponentHelper.SetTag(Value: TTag);
begin
  GetSiteObject.FTag := Value;
end;
```

Using this technique, the VCL for .NET reintroduces most of the classic methods of the TComponent class, as the class helpers have the following public interface:

```
type
  TComponentHelper = class helper (TPersistentHelper) for TComponent
  public
    constructor Create(AOwner: TComponent); overload; virtual;
    procedure DestroyComponents;
    procedure Destroying;
    function ExecuteAction(Action: TBasicAction): Boolean; virtual;
    function FindComponent(const AName: string): TComponent;
    procedure FreeNotification(AComponent: TComponent);
    procedure RemoveFreeNotification(AComponent: TComponent);
    function GetEnumerator: TComponentEnumerator;
    function GetParentComponent: TComponent; virtual;
    function GetNamePath: string; override;
    function HasParent: Boolean; virtual;
    procedure InsertComponent(AComponent: TComponent);
    procedure RemoveComponent(AComponent: TComponent);
    procedure SetParentComponent(Value: TComponent); virtual;
    procedure SetSubComponent(IsSubComponent: Boolean);
```

```
function UpdateAction(Action: TBasicAction): Boolean; virtual;
function IsImplementorOf(const I: IInterface): Boolean;
function ReferenceInterface(const I: IInterface;
  Operation: TOperation): Boolean;
class procedure ChangeComponentName(Instance: TComponent;
  const NewName: string); static;
class procedure SetComponentParent(Instance: TComponent;
  Parent: TComponent); static;

property Components[Index: Integer]: TComponent read GetComponents;
property ComponentCount: Integer read GetComponentCount;
property ComponentIndex: Integer
  read GetComponentIndex write SetComponentIndex;
property ComponentState: TComponentState read GetComponentState;
property ComponentStyle: TComponentStyle read GetComponentStyle;
property DesignInfo: Longint
  read GetDesignInfo write SetDesignInfo;
property Owner: TComponent read GetSelfOwner;
published
property Name: TComponentName read GetName write SetName
  stored False;
property Tag: TTag read GetTag write SetTag;
end;
```

There isn't a better example of this behavior than to open existing Delphi VCL code and compile it under the VCL for .NET, an operation which will generally require fixes in many details but not in the core code structure. Just to verify a couple of things discussed here, I wrote a simple demo with code working both on the System.ComponentModel.Component core and the TComponent class helper.

In the ComponentTestNet example, you can find, for example, code like this:

```
// it is a System.Component
ShowMessage ((Sender as TComponent).ToString);
// it is a VCL TComponent
ShowMessage ((Sender as TComponent).Owner.ClassName);
```

The example also includes the use of the Tag property as a variant, with code not compatible with the VCL for Win32; some code to dynamically create components via class references that works as usual, although this can be quite surprising for .NET experts as it departs from standard .NET coding; and sample usage of the Container property of the component, a role played in Delphi by the TComponentSite class introduced earlier, as this code shows:

```
// show the number of components in the owner/container
ShowMessage (IntToStr ((Sender as Component).
  Container.Components.Count));
// display the container name/description
ShowMessage (((Sender as Component).Container as TObject).ToString);
```

NOTE   As the TComponent class is an alias of the Component class of the FCL, Delphi automatically adds the System.ComponentModel namespace that defines this class to units of new VCL forms. Although it is not necessary to add it to forms ported from the VCL for Win32, doing it allows you to use specific features of that base class not found in the VCL.

Events

Now that I've discussed the TComponent class, I need to introduce one more element of Delphi. Delphi components are programmed using PME: properties, methods, and events. Methods and properties should be clear by now, but you haven't yet learned about events. The reason is that events don't imply a new language feature but are simply a standard coding technique. An event is technically a property—the only difference is that it refers to a method (a method pointer type, to be precise) instead of other types of data.

Events in Delphi

When a user does something with a component such as click it, the component generates an event. Other events are generated by the system in response to a method call or a change to one of that component's properties (or even a different component's). For example, if you set the focus on a component, the component currently having the focus loses it, triggering the corresponding event.

Technically, most Delphi events are triggered when a corresponding operating system message is received, although the events do not match the messages on a one-to-one basis. Delphi events tend to be higher-level than operating system messages, and Delphi provides a number of extra intercomponent messages.

From a theoretical point of view, an event is the result of a request sent to a component or control that can respond to the message. Following this approach, to handle the click event of a button, you would need to derive a new class from the TButton class and add the new event handler code inside the new class.

In practice, creating a new class for every component you want to use is too complex to be a reasonable solution. In Delphi, a component's event handler usually is a method of the form that holds the component, not of the component itself. In other words, the component relies on its owner, the form, to handle its events. This technique is called *delegation*, and it is fundamental to the Delphi component-based model. This way, you don't have to modify the TButton class unless you want to define a new type of component; you can simply customize its owner to modify the behavior of the button.

NOTE   As you'll see in the next section, events in Delphi are based on pointers to methods. This is not different from the .NET idea of delegates. What's relevant, however, is that .NET uses multicast events, that is, the fact that you can have multiple delegates attached to a single event, which are all invoked when the event *fires*. This is not supported in the VCL.NET for compatibility reasons, but as you saw in Chapter 4, this feature is available in Delphi for .NET and fully exploited in its WinForms support.

Method Pointers

Events rely on a specific feature of the Delphi language: *method pointers*. A method pointer type is like a procedural type but one that refers to a method. Technically, a method pointer type is a procedural type that has an implicit Self parameter. In other words, a variable of a procedural type stores the address of a function to call, provided it has a given set of parameters. A method pointer variable stores two addresses: the address of the method code and the address of an object instance (data). The address of the object instance will show up as Self inside the method body when the method code is called using this method pointer.

NOTE The structure of a method pointer variable explains the definition of Delphi's generic TMethod type, a record with a Code field and a Data field. In Delphi for .NET, the TMethod record has been expanded with several methods, including a handy Invoke method.

The declaration of a method pointer type is similar to that of a procedural type, except that it has the keywords of object at the end of the declaration:

```
type
  IntProceduralType = procedure (Num: Integer);
  IntMethodPointerType = procedure (Num: Integer) of object;
```

When you have declared such a method pointer type, you can declare a variable of this type and assign to it a compatible method—a method that has the same signature (parameters, return type, calling convention)—of another object.

In Delphi for .NET the of object suffix is irrelevant, as all routines compile to methods. The distinction between a procedure pointer and a method pointer is nonexistent in .NET.

When you add an OnClick event handler for a button, Delphi does exactly that. The button has a method pointer type property named OnClick, and you can directly or indirectly assign to it a method of another object, such as a form. When a user clicks the button, this method is executed, even if you have defined it inside another class.

What follows is a sketch of the code Delphi uses to define the event handler of a button component and the related method of a form:

```
type
  TNotifyEvent = procedure (Sender: TObject) of object;

  MyButton = class
    OnClick: TNotifyEvent;
  end;

  TForm1 = class (TForm)
    procedure Button1Click (Sender: TObject);
    Button1: MyButton;
  end;

var
  Form1: TForm1;
```

Now, inside a procedure, you can write

```
MyButton.OnClick := Form1.Button1Click;
```

The only real difference between this code fragment and the VCL code is that OnClick is a property name, and the data it refers to is called FOnClick. An event that shows up in the Events page of the Object Inspector is nothing more than a property of a method pointer type. This means, for example, that you can dynamically modify the event handler attached to a component at design time or even build a new component at run time and assign an event handler to it.

Events Are Properties

I've already mentioned that events are properties. To handle an event of a component, you assign a method to the corresponding event property. When you double-click an event value in the Object Inspector, a new method is added to the owner form and assigned to the proper event property of the component.

It is possible for several events to share the same event handler or change an event handler at run time. To use this feature, you don't need much knowledge of the language. In fact, when you select an event in the Object Inspector, you can click the arrow button to the right of the event name to see a drop-down list of compatible published methods—methods having the same signature of the method pointer type. Using the Object Inspector, it is easy to select the same method for the same event of different components or for different compatible events of the same component.

Just as you added some properties to the TDate class in Chapter 3, you can add an event. The event in this example is very simple. It is called OnChange, and it can be used to notify the user of the component that the date value has changed. To define an event, you simply define a property corresponding to it and add some data to store the method pointer the event refers to. These are the new definitions added to the class, available in the DateEvt example:

```
type
  TDate = class
  private
    FOnChange: TNotifyEvent;
    ...
  protected
    procedure DoChange; dynamic;
    ...
  public
    property OnChange: TNotifyEvent read FOnChange write FOnChange;
    ...
  end;
```

The property definition is simple. A user of this class can assign a new value to the property and, hence, to the FOnChange private field. The class doesn't assign a value to this FOnChange field; the user of the component does the assignment. The TDate class simply calls the method stored in the FOnChange field when the value of the date changes. Of course, the call takes place only if the event property has been assigned. The DoChange method (declared as a dynamic method as is traditional with event-firing methods) makes the test and the method call:

```
procedure TDate.DoChange;
begin
  if Assigned (FOnChange) then
    FOnChange (Self);
end;
```

The DoChange method in turn is called every time one of the values changes, as in the following method:

```
procedure TDate.SetValue (y, m, d: Integer);
begin
  fDate := EncodeDate (y, m, d);
  // fire the event
  DoChange;
```

If you look at the program that uses this class, you can simplify its code considerably. First, add a new custom method to the form class:

```
type
  TDateForm = class(TForm)
    ...
    procedure DateChange(Sender: TObject);
```

The method's code simply updates the label with the current value of the TDate object's Text property:

```
procedure TDateForm.DateChange;
begin
  LabelDate.Caption := TheDay.Text;
end;
```

This event handler is then installed in the FormCreate method:

```
procedure TDateForm.FormCreate(Sender: TObject);
begin
  TheDay := TDate.Init (2003, 7, 4);
  LabelDate.Caption := TheDay.Text;
  // assign the event handler for future changes
  TheDay.OnChange := DateChange;
end;
```

This seems like a lot of work. Was I lying when I told you the event handler would save you some coding? No. Now, after you've added some code, you can forget about updating the label when you change some of the object data. For example, here is the handler of the OnClick event of one of the buttons:

```
procedure TDateForm.BtnIncreaseClick(Sender: TObject);
begin
  TheDay.Increase;
end;
```

The same simplified code is present in many other event handlers. Once you have installed the event handler, you won't have to remember to update the label continually. That eliminates a significant potential source of errors in the program. Also note that you had to write some code at the beginning because this is not a component installed in Delphi but simply a class. With a component, you select the event handler in the Object Inspector and write a single line of code to update the label—that's all.

Traditional Sections of VCL

Delphi programmers used to refer to the sections of the VCL with names Borland suggested in its original documentation—names that became common afterward for different groups of components. Technically, component classes inherit from the TComponent class, which is one of the root classes of the hierarchy, as you can see in Figure 6.2. The TComponent class inherits from the TPersistent class; the role of these two classes will be explained in the next section.

In addition to components, the library includes classes that inherit directly from TObject and from TPersistent. These classes are collectively known as *Objects* in portions of the documentation, a rather confusing name. These noncomponent classes are often used for values of properties or as utility classes used in code; not inheriting from TComponent, these classes cannot be used directly in visual programming.

NOTE To be more precise, noncomponent classes cannot be made available in the Component Palette and cannot be dropped directly into a form, but they can be visually managed with the Object Inspector as subproperties of other properties or items of collections of various types. So, even noncomponent classes are often easily used when interacting with the Form Designer.

The component classes can be further divided into two main groups: controls and nonvisual components.

Controls All the classes that descend from TControl. Controls have a position and a size on the screen and show up in the form at design time in the same position they'll have at run time. Controls have two different subspecifications—window-based or graphical—that I'll discuss in more detail in later in this chapter.

Nonvisual components All the components that are not controls—all the classes that descend from TComponent but not from TControl. At design time, a nonvisual component appears on the form or data module as an icon with a caption below it (the caption is optional on forms and frames). At run time, some of these components may become visible (for example, the standard dialog boxes are displayed after invoking a method), and others are always invisible (for example, the database table component).

TIP You can simply move the mouse cursor over a control or component in the Form Designer to see a Tooltip with its name and class type (and some extended information). You can also use an environment option, Show Component Captions, to see the name of a nonvisual component under its icon.

FIGURE 6.2
A graphical representation of the main groups of VCL components

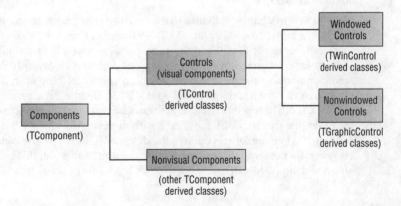

VCL Considerations

As I briefly discussed in Chapter 2, Delphi's VCL is a class library used to wrap the windows and controls provided by the Win32 API. The VCL includes wrappers of the native Windows controls (like buttons and edit boxes), the common controls (like TreeViews and ListViews), plus a bunch of native Delphi controls bound to the Windows concept of a window. In addition, a TCanvas class wraps the basic graphic calls, so you can easily paint on the surface of a window.

NOTE   Past editions of Delphi included a second visual library, called VisualCLX, which was a wrapper of the Qt (pronounced "cute") library. This library was meant for compatibility with Kylix/Linux version of CLX and has now been dropped from the product.

The VCL offers an object-oriented abstraction on top of a low-level API, as the Windows API is still bound to its C-language legacy and to a message-based system from 1985 (when Windows was released). The same is still also true for VCL for .NET and WinForms, as Microsoft's new platforms don't have a native management of windows and controls and still rely on the good-old Windows API.

DFM (AND NFM)

As you create a form at design time, it is saved to a form definition file. Traditional VCL applications use the DFM extension, which stands for Delphi form module. Delphi for .NET uses the NFM extension, which stands for .NET form module. In both cases, a form module is the result of streaming the form and its components. The format of DFM and NFM files, which can be based on a textual or binary representation, is identical.

The reason for having two different extensions doesn't lie in internal compiler tricks or incompatible formats. It is merely an indication to programmers and the IDE of the type of components you should expect to find within that definition (this indication is *not* included in the file).

If you want to convert a DFM file into an NFM file, you can simply rename the file, but nothing prevents you from using DFM files in a VCL.NET application. However, the opposite is not true because of the problems with the uses statements, as you'll see at the end of the next section.

WARNING   When you work on a VCL for a .NET form that is based on a DFM file, the Delphi IDE will show the VCL for Win32 components in the Tool Palette. Although there are very few differences, some might be annoying. As an example of the troubles that might happen you can refer to the examples that use the XmlDocument component in Chapter 22.

USES STATEMENTS

As you saw in Chapter 4, thanks to the default project name space, the uses statements do not need to change between a VCL and a VCL.NET application. When you place new components in the VCL.NET designer, it will add the corresponding unit with a complete name, like Borland.Vcl. StdCtrls; you can remove the Borland.Vcl prefix and leave only the final part if you want to keep the source code compatible with the Win32 counterpart. However, this happens only for a new form with an NFM extension, not if you open a DFM file in a .NET project.

A VCL.NET form will also list System.ComponentModel in its uses clause, making it impossible to recompile it as is in VCL for Win32. Although you can remove this reference, the system will keep adding it when the form is open in the designer (unless you use conditional compilation), even if it is generally not required for recompiling the unit. But again, this behavior happens only for a new form with an NFM extension, not for a VCL.NET form saved in a DFM file.

TControl and Derived Classes

One of the most important derived classes of TComponent is TControl, which corresponds to visual components. This base class defines general concepts, such as the position and the size of the control, the parent control hosting it, and more. For an actual implementation, though, you have to refer to its two derived classes, TWinControl and TGraphicControl. Here are their key features:

Window-based controls (also called windowed controls) Visual components based on an operating-system window. A TWinControl in VCL has a window handle, which is a number referring to an internal Windows structure. From a user perspective, windowed controls can receive the input focus and can contain other controls. This is the biggest group of components in the Delphi library. You can further divide windowed controls into two groups: wrappers of native controls of Windows and custom controls, which generally inherit from TCustomControl.

Graphical controls (also called nonwindowed controls) Visual components not based on an operating-system window. Therefore, these components have no handle, cannot receive the focus, and cannot contain other controls. They inherit from TGraphicControl and are painted by their parent control, which sends them mouse-related and other events. Examples of nonwindowed controls are the Label and SpeedButton components. There are just a few controls in this group, which were critical to minimizing the use of system resources in the early days of Delphi (on 16-bit Windows). Using graphical controls to save Windows resources is still useful on Win9*x*/Me, which has pushed the system limits higher but hasn't fully gotten rid of them (unlike Windows NT-based operating systems, including 2000, XP, and 2003).

TControl and Derived Classes in .NET

While TComponent and base classes are mapped to specific FCL classes and use class helpers to reintroduce the methods programmers are used to (that is, to keep their source code compatible while changing platforms), TControl and derived classes remain in the VCL for Win32 and the VCL for .NET.

The reason is simple: while the Delphi RTL merges with the core FCL classes, the visual portion of the VCL sits on the side of WinForms, the FCL equivalent. Both VCL and WinForms provide visual controls and forms that wrap Windows API calls. The two libraries are similar in scope in the set of components they provide and even in the names of their properties.

However, they are different enough in naming and some base concepts to make it hard to convert existing VCL code to WinForms or map everything with class helpers or similar techniques. For example, WinForms makes no use of DFM files; its designer simply generates initialization source code. This is a huge difference.

In short, in Delphi for .NET you can choose between using VCL.NET or WinForms. You can also partially merge the two (for example, you can use WinForms controls in a VCL.NET application after the generation of a wrapper using the VCL.NET import wizard, much like using ActiveXs in Win32 Delphi), but this should be far from a standard approach. I will provide a (limited) comparison of the two libraries, highlighting some reasons to choose one over the other only after I've introduced WinForms in Chapter 9.

Parent and Controls

The Parent property of a control indicates which other control is responsible for displaying it. When you drop a component into a form in the Form Designer, the form will become both parent and owner of the new control. But if you drop the component inside a Panel, ScrollBox, or any other *container* component, this will become its parent, whereas the form will still be the owner of the control.

When you create the control at run time, you'll need to set the owner (using the Create constructor's parameter), but you must also set the Parent property or the control won't be visible. If you assign the Parent property as the last operation, or as the close-to-last property assignment, you'll stop possible flicker through multiple redraws caused by changing other property values.

Like the Owner property, the Parent property has an inverse. The Controls array lists all the controls parented by the current one, numbered from 0 to ControlCount - 1. You can scan this property to operate on all the controls hosted by another control, potentially using a recursive method that operates on the controls parented by each subcontrol.

Properties Related to Control Size and Position

Some of the properties introduced by TControl and common to all controls are those related to size and position. The position of a control is determined by its Left and Top properties, and its size is specified by the Height and Width properties. Technically, all components have a position, because when you reopen an existing form at design time, you want to be able to see the icons for the nonvisual components in exactly the position you've placed them. This position is visible in the form file.

TIP When you change any of the positional or size properties, you end up calling the single SetBounds method, so any time you need to change two or more of these properties at once, calling SetBounds directly will speed up the program. Another method, BoundsRect, returns the rectangle bounding the control and corresponds to accessing the properties Left, Top, Height, and Width.

An important feature of the position of a component is that, like any other coordinate, it always relates to the client area of its parent component (indicated by its Parent property). For a form, the client area is the surface included within its borders and caption (excluding the borders themselves). It would be messy to work in screen coordinates, although some ready-to-use methods convert the coordinates between the form and the screen and vice versa.

However, the coordinates of a control are always relative to the parent control, such as a form or another *container* component. If you place a panel in a form and a button in a panel, the coordinates of the button relate to the panel and not to the form containing the panel. In this case, the parent component of the button is the panel.

Activation and Visibility Properties

You can use two basic properties to let the user activate or hide a component. The simpler is the Enabled property. When a component is disabled (when Enabled is set to False), some visual hint usually indicates this state to the user. At design time, the "disabled" property does not always have an effect; but at run time, disabled components are generally grayed.

For a more radical approach, you can completely hide a component, either by using the corresponding Hide method or by setting its Visible property to False. Be aware, however, that reading the status of the Visible property does not tell you whether the control is actually visible. If the container of a control is hidden, even if the control is set to Visible, you cannot see it. For this reason, you can read the value of the run-time, read-only Showing property to determine whether the control is really potentially visible to the user; that is, if it is visible, its parent control is also visible, the parent control of the parent control is also visible, and so on. Still, the control might be outside the parent's client area so that a user cannot really see it.

Fonts

The Color and Font properties are often used to customize the user interface of a component. Several properties are related to the color. The Color property itself usually refers to the background color of the component. There is also a Color property for fonts and many other graphical elements. Many components also have ParentColor and ParentFont properties, indicating whether the control should use the same font and color as its parent component, which is usually the form. You can use these properties to change the font of each control on a form by setting only the Font property of the form itself.

When you set a font, either by entering values for the attributes of the property in the Object Inspector or by using the standard font selection dialog box, you can choose one of the fonts installed in the system. The fact that Delphi allows you to use all the fonts installed on your system has both advantages and drawbacks. The main advantage is that if you have a number of nice fonts installed, your program can use any of them. The drawback is that if you distribute your application these fonts might not be available on your users' computers.

If your program uses a font that your user doesn't have, Windows will select some other font to use in its place. A program's carefully formatted output can be ruined by the font substitution. For this reason, you should rely on standard Windows fonts (such as MS Sans Serif, System, Arial, Times New Roman, and so on).

Colors

There are various ways to set the value of a color, including double-clicking the value in the Object Inspector to get a color change dialog. The type of this property is TColor, which isn't a class type but just an integer type. For properties of this type, you can choose a value from a series of predefined name constants or enter a value directly. The constants for colors include the classics clBlue, clSilver, clWhite, clGreen, clRed, as well as many exotic colors like clLawnGreen or clSkyBlue. As a better alternative, you can use one of the colors used by the system to denote the status of given elements.

VCL includes predefined Windows colors such as the background of a window (clWindow), the color of the text of a highlighted menu (clHighlightText), the active caption (clActiveCaption), and the ubiquitous button face color (clBtnFace).

Another option is to specify a TColor as a number (a 4-byte hexadecimal value) instead of using a predefined value. If you use this approach, you should know that the low 3 bytes of this number represent RGB color intensities for blue, green, and red, respectively. For example, the value $00FF0000 corresponds to a pure blue color, the value $0000FF00 to green, the value $000000FF to red, the value $00000000 to black, and the value $00FFFFFF to white. By specifying intermediate values, you can obtain any of 16 million possible colors.

However, instead of specifying these hexadecimal values directly, you should use the Windows RGB function, which has three parameters, all ranging from 0 to 255. The first indicates the amount of red, the second the amount of green, and the last the amount of blue. Using the RGB function generally makes programs more readable than using a single hexadecimal constant. RGB is *almost* a Windows API function; it is defined by the Windows-related units and not by Delphi units, but a similar function does not exist in the Windows API. The highest-order byte of the TColor type is used to indicate which palette should be searched for the closest matching color, but palettes are too advanced a topic to discuss here. (Sophisticated imaging programs also use this byte to carry transparency information for each display element on the screen.)

Regarding palettes and color matching, note that Windows sometimes replaces an arbitrary color with the closest available solid color, at least in video modes that use a palette. This is always the case with fonts, lines, and so on. At other times, Windows uses a dithering technique to mimic the requested color by drawing a tight pattern of pixels with the available colors.

The *TWinControl* Class

In Windows, most elements of the user interface are windows. From a user standpoint, a window is a portion of the screen surrounded by a border that has a caption and usually a system menu. But technically speaking, a window is an entry in an internal system table, often corresponding to an element visible on the screen that has some associated code. Most of these windows have the role of controls; others are temporarily created by the system (for example, to show a pull-down menu). Still other windows are created by the application but remain hidden from the user and are used only as a way to receive a message (for example, nonblocking sockets use windows to communicate with the system).

The common denominator of all windows is that they are known by the Windows system and refer to a function for their behavior; each time something happens in the system, a notification message is sent to the proper window, which responds by executing some code. Each window of the system has an associated function (generally called its *window procedure*), which handles the various messages the window is interested in.

In Delphi, any TWinControl class can override the WndProc method or define a new value for the WindowProc property. Interesting Windows messages, however, can be better tracked by providing specific message handlers. Even better, VCL converts some of these lower-level messages into events. In short, Delphi allows you to work at a high level to make application development easier, but it still allows you to go low-level when required.

Notice also that creating an instance of a TWinControl-based class doesn't automatically create its corresponding Window handle. Delphi uses a lazy initialization technique, so that the low-level control is created only when required—generally as soon as a method accesses the Handle property. The set method for this property calls HandleNeeded the first time, which eventually calls CreateHandle and so on, eventually reaching CreateWnd, CreateParams, and CreateWindowHandle (the sequence is complex, and you don't need to know it in detail). At the opposite end, you can keep an existing (perhaps invisible) control in memory but destroy its window handle to save system resources.

Opening the Component Toolbox

So, you want to write a Delphi application. You open a new Delphi project and find yourself faced with a large number of components. The problem is that for every operation, there are multiple alternatives. For example, you can show a list of values using a list box, a combo box, a radio group, a string grid, a list view, or even a tree view if there is a hierarchical order. Which should you use? That's difficult to say. There are many considerations, depending on what you want your application to do. For this reason, I provided a highly condensed summary of alternative options for a few common tasks.

NOTE For some of the controls described in the following sections, Delphi also includes a data-aware version, usually indicated by the DB prefix. As you'll see in Chapter 13, the data-aware version of a control typically serves a role similar to that of its "standard" equivalent, but the properties and the ways you use it are often quite different. For example, in an Edit control you use the Text property, whereas in a DBEdit component you access the Value of the related field object.

The Text Input Components

Although a form or component can handle keyboard input directly using the OnKeyPress event, this isn't a common operation. Windows provides ready-to-use controls you can use to get string input and even build a simple text editor. Delphi has several slightly different components in this area.

THE EDIT COMPONENT

The Edit component allows the user to enter a single line of text. You can also display a single line of text with a Label or a StaticText control, but these components are generally used only for fixed text or program-generated output, not for input.

The Edit component uses the Text property, whereas many other controls use the Caption property to refer to the text they display. The only condition you can impose on user input is the number of characters to accept. If you want to accept only specific characters, you can handle the OnKeyPress event of the edit box. For example, you can write a method that tests whether the character is a number or the Backspace key (which has an ordinal value of 8). If it's not, you change the value of the key to the null character (#0) so that it won't be processed by the Edit control and will produce a warning beep:

```
procedure TForm1.Edit1KeyPress(Sender: TObject; var Key: Char);
begin
  // check if the key is a number or backspace
  if not (Key in ['0'..'9', #8]) then
  begin
    Key := #0;
    Beep;
  end;
end;
```

THE LABELEDEDIT CONTROL

A LabeledEdit is an Edit control with a label attached to it. The label appears as a property of the compound control, which inherits from TCustomEdit.

This component is very handy because it allows you to reduce the number of components on your forms, move them around more easily, and have a more consistent layout for all of the labels of an entire form or application. The EditLabel property is connected with the subcomponent, which has the usual properties and events. Two more properties, LabelPosition and LabelSpacing, allow you to configure the relative positions of the two controls.

NOTE This component has been added to the ExtCtrls unit to demonstrate the use of subcomponents in the Object Inspector.

THE MASKEDIT COMPONENT

To customize the input of an edit box further, you can use the MaskEdit component. It has an EditMask property, which is a string that indicates whether each character should be uppercase, lowercase, a number, or other similar conditions. You can see the editor for the EditMask property here:

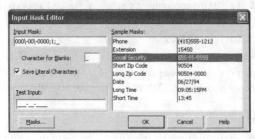

The Input Mask Editor allows you to enter a mask, but it also asks you to indicate a character to be used as a placeholder for the input and to decide whether to save the *literals* present in the mask, together with the final string. For example, you can choose to display the parentheses around the area code of a phone number only as an input hint or to save them with the string holding the resulting number. These two entries in the Input Mask Editor correspond to the last two fields of the mask (separated by semicolons).

TIP Clicking the Masks button in the Input Mask Editor lets you choose predefined input masks for different countries.

THE MEMO AND RICHEDIT COMPONENTS

The controls discussed so far allow a single line of input. The Memo component, by contrast, can host several lines of text but (on the Win95/98 platforms) still retains the 16-bit Windows text limit (32 KB) and allows only a single font for the entire text. You can work on the text of the memo line by line (using the Lines string list) or access the entire text at once (using the Text property).

If you want to host a large amount of text or change fonts and paragraph alignments in the VCL, you should use the RichEdit control, a Win32 common control based on the RTF document format. You can find an example of a complete editor based on the RichEdit component among the sample programs that ship with Delphi. (The example is named RichEdit too.)

The RichEdit component has a DefAttributes property indicating the default styles and a SelAttributes property indicating the style of the current selection. These two properties are not of the TFont type, but they are compatible with fonts, so you can use the Assign method to copy the value, as in the following code fragment:

```
procedure TForm1.Button1Click(Sender: TObject);
begin
  if RichEdit1.SelLength > 0 then
  begin
    FontDialog1.Font.Assign (RichEdit1.DefAttributes);
    if FontDialog1.Execute then
      RichEdit1.SelAttributes.Assign (FontDialog1.Font);
  end;
end;
```

Selecting Options

Two standard Windows controls allow the user to choose different options. Two other controls let you group sets of options.

THE CHECKBOX AND RADIOBUTTON COMPONENTS

The first standard option-selecting control is the *check box*, which corresponds to an option that can be selected regardless of the status of other check boxes. Setting the AllowGrayed property of the check box allows you to display three different states (selected, not selected, and grayed), which alternate as a user clicks the check box.

The second type of control is the *radio button*, which corresponds to an exclusive selection. Two radio buttons on the same form or inside the same radio group container cannot be selected at the same time, and one of them should always be selected (as programmer, you are responsible for selecting one of the radio buttons at design time).

THE GROUPBOX COMPONENTS

To host several groups of radio buttons, you can use a GroupBox control to hold them together, both functionally and visually. To build a group box with radio buttons, simply place the GroupBox component on a form and then add the radio buttons to the group box, as in the following example:

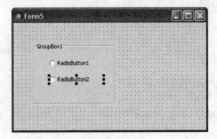

You can handle the radio buttons individually, but it's easier to navigate through the array of controls owned by the group box. Here is a small code excerpt to get the text of a group's selected radio button:

```
var
  I: Integer;
  Text: string;
begin
  for I := 0 to GroupBox1.ControlCount - 1 do
    if (GroupBox1.Controls[I] as TRadioButton).Checked then
      Text := TRadioButton(GroupBox1.Controls[I]).Caption;
```

THE RADIOGROUP COMPONENT

Delphi has a similar component that can be used specifically for radio buttons: the RadioGroup component. A RadioGroup is a group box with some radio buttons inside it. The difference is that these internal radio buttons are managed automatically by the container control. Using a radio group is generally easier than using a group box because the various items are part of a list, as in a list box. This is how you can get the text of the selected item:

```
Text := RadioGroup1.Items [RadioGroup1.ItemIndex];
```

Another advantage is that the RadioGroup component can automatically align its radio buttons in one or more columns (as indicated by the Columns property), and you can easily add new choices at run time by adding strings to the Items string list. By contrast, adding new radio buttons to a group box is quite complex.

Lists

When you have many selections, radio buttons are not appropriate. To avoid cluttering the user interface, the usual number of radio buttons is no more than five or six; when you have more choices, you can use a list box or one of the other controls that displays lists of items and allows the user to select one of them.

THE LISTBOX COMPONENT

The selection of an item in a list box uses the Items and ItemIndex properties as in the earlier code shown for the RadioGroup control. If you need access to the text of selected list box items often, you can write a small wrapper function like this:

```
function SelText (List: TListBox): string;
var
  nItem: Integer;
begin
  nItem := List.ItemIndex;
  if nItem >= 0 then
    Result := List.Items [nItem]
  else
    Result := '';
end;
```

Another important feature is that the ListBox component lets you choose between allowing only a single selection, as in a group of radio buttons, or allowing multiple selections, as in a group of check boxes. You make this choice by specifying the value of the MultiSelect property. There are two kinds of multiple selections in Windows and Delphi list boxes: *multiple selection* and *extended selection*. In the first case, a user selects multiple items simply by clicking them; in the second case, the user can use the Shift and Ctrl keys to select multiple consecutive or nonconsecutive items, respectively. The two alternatives are determined by the status of the ExtendedSelect property. The lesser known Shift+F8 keystroke puts you into selection mode, and then you can use the cursor keys to locate an item and the spacebar to select it; pressing Shift+F8 again gets out of this mode.

For a multiple-selection list box, a program can retrieve information about the number of selected items with the SelCount property, and it can determine which items are selected by examining the Selected array. This array of Boolean values has the same number of entries as the list box. For example, to concatenate all the selected items into a string, you can scan the Selected array as follows:

```
var
  SelItems: string;
  nItem: Integer;
```

```
begin
  SelItems := '';
  for nItem := 0 to ListBox1.Items.Count - 1 do
    if ListBox1.Selected [nItem] then
      SelItems := SelItems + ListBox1.Items[nItem] + ' ';
```

THE COMBOBOX COMPONENT

List boxes take up a lot of screen space, and they offer a fixed selection—that is, a user can choose only from among the items in the list box and cannot enter any choice the programmer did not specifically foresee.

You can solve both problems by using a ComboBox control, which combines an edit box and a drop-down list. The behavior of a ComboBox component changes a lot depending on the value of its Style property:

◆ The csDropDown style defines a typical combo box, which allows direct editing and displays a list box on request.

◆ The csDropDownList style defines a combo box that does not allow editing (but uses the keystrokes to select an item).

◆ The csSimple style defines a combo box that always displays the list box below it.

Note also that accessing the text of the selected value of a ComboBox is easier than doing so for a list box because you can simply use the Text property. A useful and common trick for combo boxes is to add a new element to the list when a user enters some text and presses the Enter key. The following method first tests whether the user has pressed that key by looking for the character with the numeric (ASCII) value of 13. It then tests to make sure the text of the combo box is not empty and is not already in the list (if its position in the list is less than zero). Here is the code:

```
procedure TForm1.ComboBox1KeyPress(
  Sender: TObject; var Key: Char);
begin
  // if the user presses the Enter key
  if Key = Chr (13) then
    with Sender as TComboBox do
      if (Text <> '') and (Items.IndexOf (Text) < 0) then
        Items.Add (Text);
end;
```

Among others, Delphi includes two specific events for the combo box: the OnCloseUp event corresponds to the closing of the drop-down list and complements the OnDropDown event; the OnSelect event fires only when the user selects something in the drop-down list, as opposed to typing in the edit portion.

Another nice feature is the AutoComplete property. When it is set, the ComboBox component (as well as the ListBox) automatically locates the string nearest to the one the user is entering, suggesting the final part of the text. The core of this feature is implemented in the TCustomListBox.KeyPress method. Delphi 2005 adds an AutoCompleteDelay property to both components to let you determine how fast the auto completion will take place.

THE CHECKLISTBOX COMPONENT

Another extension of the list box control is represented by the CheckListBox component, a list box with each item preceded by a check box:

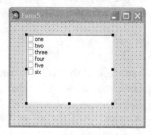

A user can select a single item in the list but can also click the check boxes to toggle their status. This makes the CheckListBox a very good component for multiple selections or for highlighting the status of a series of independent items (as in a series of check boxes).

To check the current status of each item, you can use the Checked and State array properties (use the latter if the check boxes can be grayed). The ItemEnabled array property can be used to enable or disable each item of the list.

TIP   Most of the list-based controls share a common and important feature: each item in the list has an associated 32-bit value, usually indicated by the TObject type. This value can be used as a tag for each list item, and it's very useful for storing additional information along with each item. This approach is connected to a specific feature of the native Windows list box control, which offers 4 bytes of extra storage for each list box item. You'll use this feature in the ODList example later in this chapter.

THE EXTENDED COMBO BOXES: COMBOBOXEX AND COLORBOX

The ComboBoxEx (where *ex* stands for extended) is the wrapper of a new Win32 common control that extends the traditional combo box by allowing images to appear next to the items in the list. You attach an image list to the combo box, and then select an image index for each item to display. The effect of this change is that the simple Items string list is replaced by a more complex collection, the ItemsEx property. I'll use the ComboBoxEx control in the RefList2 example in Chapter 7.

TIP   Since Delphi 7, the ComboBoxEx component has had the AutoCompleteOptions property, enabling the combo box to respond to user keystrokes.

The ColorBox control is a version of the combo box specifically aimed at selecting colors. You can use its Style property to choose which groups of colors you want to see in the list (standard color, extended colors, system colors, and so on).

THE LISTVIEW AND TREEVIEW COMPONENTS

If you want an even more sophisticated list, you can use the ListView common control, which will make the user interface of your application look familiar. This component is slightly more complex to use, as described in the section "ListView and TreeView Controls" later in this chapter. Other alternatives for listing values are the TreeView common control, which shows items in a hierarchical output, and the StringGrid control, which shows multiple elements for each line.

If you use the common controls in your application, users will already know how to interact with them, and they will regard the user interface of your program as more up to date. TreeView and List-View are the two key components of Windows Explorer, and you can assume that many users will be familiar with them—even more so than with the traditional Windows controls

NOTE   Both the ListView and the TreeView component in Delphi 2005 define an enumerator for iterating on all of their items or nodes.

THE VALUELISTEDITOR COMPONENT

Delphi applications often use the name-value structure natively offered by string lists, which I discussed in Chapter 5. Delphi has a version of the StringGrid component (technically a TCustomDrawGrid descendant class) specifically geared toward this type of string lists. The ValueListEditor has two columns in which you can display and let the user edit the contents of a string list with name-value pairs, as you can see in Figure 6.3. This string list is indicated in the Strings property of the control.

The power of this control lies in the fact that you can customize the editing options for each position of the grid or for each key value, using the run-time-only ItemProps array property. For each item, you can indicate:

◆   Whether it is read-only

◆   The maximum number of characters of the string

◆   An edit mask (eventually requested in the OnGetEditMask event)

◆   The items in a drop-down pick list (eventually requested in the OnGetPickList event), as demonstrated by the first item of the example

◆   The display of a button that will show an editing dialog box (in the OnEditButtonClick event, which the example handles with a message box)

FIGURE 6.3
The NameValues example uses the ValueListEditor component, which shows the name-value or key-value pairs of a string list, also visible in a plain memo.

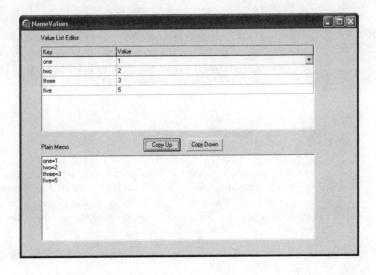

Needless to say, this behavior resembles what is generally available for string grids and the DBGrid control, as well as the behavior of the Object Inspector.

The `ItemProps` property must be set up at run time by creating an object of the `TItemProp` class and assigning it to an index or a key of the string list. To have a default editor for each line, you can assign the same item property object multiple times. In the example, this shared editor sets an edit mask for up to three numbers:

```
procedure TForm1.FormCreate(Sender: TObject);
var
  I: Integer;
begin
  SharedItemProp := TItemProp.Create (ValueListEditor1);
  SharedItemProp.EditMask := '999;0; ';
  SharedItemProp.EditStyle := esEllipsis;

  FirstItemProp := TItemProp.Create (ValueListEditor1);
  for I := 1 to 10 do
    FirstItemProp.PickList.Add(IntToStr (I));

  Memo1.Lines := ValueListEditor1.Strings;
  ValueListEditor1.ItemProps [0] := FirstItemProp;
  for I := 1 to ValueListEditor1.Strings.Count - 1 do
    ValueListEditor1.ItemProps [I] := SharedItemProp;
end;
```

You must repeat similar code in case the number of lines changes—for example, by adding new elements in the memo and copying them to the value list:

```
procedure TForm1.ValueListEditor1StringsChange(Sender: TObject);
var
  I: Integer;
begin
  ValueListEditor1.ItemProps [0] := FirstItemProp;
  for I := 1 to ValueListEditor1.Strings.Count - 1 do
    if not Assigned (ValueListEditor1.ItemProps [I]) then
      ValueListEditor1.ItemProps [I] := SharedItemProp;
end;
```

NOTE Reassigning the same editor twice causes trouble, so I assigned the editor only to the lines that didn't already have one.

Another property, `KeyOptions`, allows you to let the user edit the keys (the names), add new entries, delete existing entries, and allow for duplicated names in the first portion of the string. Oddly enough, you cannot add new keys unless you also activate the edit options, which makes it hard to let the user add extra entries while preserving the names of the basic entries.

Ranges

Finally, you can use a few components to select values in a range. Ranges can be used for numeric input and selecting an element in a list.

THE SCROLLBAR COMPONENT

The stand-alone ScrollBar control is the original component of this group, but it is seldom used by itself. Scroll bars are usually associated with other components, such as list boxes and memo fields, or associated directly with forms. In these cases, the scroll bar can be considered part of the surface of the other components. For example, a form with a scroll bar is actually a form that has an area resembling a scroll bar painted on its border, a feature governed by a specific Windows style of the form window. By *resembling*, I mean that it is not technically a separate window of the ScrollBar component type. These "fake" scroll bars are usually controlled in Delphi using two specific properties of the form and the other components hosting them: VertScrollBar and HorzScrollBar.

THE TRACKBAR AND PROGRESSBAR COMPONENTS

Direct use of the ScrollBar component is quite rare, especially with the TrackBar component available in Windows, which lets a user select a value in a range. Among Win32 common controls is the companion ProgressBar control, which allows the program to output a value in a range, showing the progress of a lengthy operation. These two components are visible here:

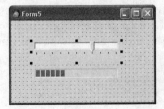

THE UPDOWN COMPONENT

Another related control is the UpDown component, which is usually connected to an edit box so that the user can either type a number in it or increase and decrease the number using the two small arrow buttons. To connect the two controls, you set the Associate property of the UpDown component. Nothing prevents you from using the UpDown component as a stand-alone control, displaying the current value in a label or in some other way.

THE PAGESCROLLER COMPONENT

The Win32 PageScroller control is a container allowing you to scroll the internal control. For example, if you place a toolbar in the page scroller and the toolbar is larger than the available area, the Page-Scroller will display two small arrows on the side. Clicking these arrows will scroll the internal area. This component can be used as a scroll bar, but it also partially replaces the ScrollBox control.

THE SCROLLBOX COMPONENT

The ScrollBox control represents a region of a form that can scroll independently from the rest of the surface. For this reason, the ScrollBox has two scroll bars used to move the embedded components. You can easily place other components inside a ScrollBox, as you do with a panel. In fact, a ScrollBox is basically a panel with scroll bars to move its internal surface, an interface element used in many Windows applications. When you have a form with many controls and a toolbar or status bar, you might use a ScrollBox to cover the central area of the form, leaving its toolbars and status bars outside of the scrolling region. By relying on the scroll bars of the form, you might allow the user to move the toolbar or status bar out of view (which would be a very odd situation).

Commands

The final category of components is not as clear-cut as the previous ones and relates to commands. The basic component of this group is the TButton (or *push button*, in Windows jargon). More than stand-alone buttons, Delphi programmers use buttons (or TToolButton objects) within toolbars (in the early ages of Delphi, they used speed buttons within panels). Nice additions to Delphi 2005 are the new ButtonGroup and CategoryButtons components, which provide a custom way to group buttons and options, as the Delphi IDE does for the Palette window.

DELPHI 2005 BUTTONGROUP AND CATEGORYBUTTONS

It is common to use a toolbar to host a set of buttons. However, the toolbar component is not very flexible in how it allows you to arrange those buttons aside from the classic single row. Moreover, toolbars tend to be associated with the topmost area of a window and are generally used to execute a command more than a select an element.

That's why I like the introduction of the new ButtonGroup component and the ButtonGroup collection component (that is, the CategoryButtons component). The first is a holder of a set of pseudo-buttons, more or less like a RadioGroup hosts pseudo radio buttons. A ButtonGroup, in fact, has an Items collection hosting the actual buttons. Adding a new button is a matter of adding an entry to the collection:

```
with ButtonGroup1.Items.Add do
    Caption := 'btn' + IntToStr (ButtonGroup1.Items.Count);
```

A ButtonGroup is quite flexible in its user interface: you can have buttons as large as the component (with the gboFullSize value in the ButtonOptions property), you can use images from an Image-List, you can have captions (gboShowCaptions option), possibly along with the images, and you can pick various other graphical settings. As you set the ButtonWidth and ButtonHeight properties, or simply resize the control at runtime, the group container will adjust itself to display the buttons in multiple rows and columns, eventually adding a vertical scrollbar. I added a couple of buttons to the BtnGroups demo (see Figure 6.4) so that you can play directly with some of these settings at run-time.

The ButtonGroup component is also the foundation of the CategoryButtons component, which is the exact component used in the IDE for the Tool Palette. A CategoryButtons component has a Categories collection, each item of which is similar (but not identical) to a ButtonGroup and has a collection of button Items. The CategoryButtons components supports background gradients, vertical or horizontal captions, expanding and collapsing categories, and each feature you see in the Palette window of the IDE.

A very simple example is visible in the bottom part of Figure 6.4. Again, there are many options you can set to modify the user interface of this control, or even to let the users customize it to their preference. Instead of going over these details, my question here is how can you use this component, other than creating something like a palette? Although I haven't had many chances to use these two components yet, my impression is that they can come in handy in many cases in which a user can select from among a large number of options, settings, documents, and the like. In this respect, it is relevant to notice that you can handle the OnClick event of each of these buttons or handle the single OnButtonClicked event of the control hosting the buttons, with the code depending on the Button parameter.

FIGURE 6.4
The BtnGroup demo has a sample of each component discussed in this section.

MENU COMMANDS

In addition to buttons and similar controls, the other key technique for issuing commands is the use of menu items, part of the *pull-down* menus attached to forms' main menus or local *pop-up* menus activated with the right mouse button.

Menu- or toolbar-related commands fall into different categories depending on their purpose and the feedback their interface provides to the user:

Commands   Menu items or buttons used to execute an action.

State-setters   Menu items or buttons used to toggle an option on and off to change the state of a particular element. The menu items of these commands usually have a check mark to their left to indicate that they are active (you can automatically obtain this behavior using the AutoCheck property). Buttons are generally painted in a *pressed down* state to indicate the same status (the ToolButton control has a Down property).

Radio items   Menus items that display a bullet and are grouped to represent alternative selections, like radio buttons. To obtain radio menu items, set the RadioItem property to True and set the GroupIndex property for the alternative menu items to the same value. In a similar fashion, you can have groups of toolbar buttons that are mutually exclusive.

Dialog openers   Items that cause a dialog box to appear. They are usually indicated by an ellipsis (…) after the text.

MENU ACCELERATORS AND SHORTCUT KEYS

A common feature of menu items is that they contain an underlined letter, generally called an accelerator or a *hot key*. This letter, which is often the first letter of the text, can be used to select the menu with the keyboard. Pressing Alt plus the underlined key selects the corresponding pull-down menu. By pressing another underlined key on that pull-menu, you issue a command.

Of course, each element of the menu bar must have a different underlined character. The same is true for the menu items on a specific pull-down menu. (Obviously, menu items on different pull-down menus can have the same underlined letter.) To indicate the underlined key, you simply place an ampersand (&) before it, as in "Save &As..." or "&File." In these examples, the underlined keys would be A for Save As and F for File. If you don't set these accelerators, Delphi can provide them automatically for you if you set the AutoHotkeys property of the menu to maAutomatic (which is the default).

Menu items generally have another feature: shortcut keys. When you see the shorthand description of a key, or key combination, beside a menu item, it means you can press those keys to give that command. Although giving menu commands with the mouse is easier, it tends to be somewhat slow, particularly for keyboard-intensive applications, since you have to move one of your hands from the keyboard to the mouse. Pressing Alt and the underlined letter might be faster, although it still requires two operations. Using a shortcut key usually involves pressing a special key and another key at the same time (such as Ctrl+C). Windows doesn't display the corresponding pull-down menu, so this results in a faster internal operation, too.

In Delphi, associating a shortcut key with a menu item (pull-down menus cannot have a shortcut key) is very easy. You simply select a value for the ShortCut property, choosing one of the standard combinations, Ctrl or Shift plus almost any key.

NOTE　There's a trick you can use to add shortcut keys to a program without adding a real menu. Create a pop-up menu with the proper shortcut keys, connect it to a form (by setting the PopupMenu property of the form), and set the Visible property of all of its items to False. A user will never see the menu, but the shortcuts will work.

COMMANDS AND ACTIONS

As you'll see in Chapter 8, modern Delphi applications tend to use the ActionList component or its ActionManager extension to handle menu and toolbar commands. In short, you define a series of action objects and associate each action object to a toolbar button and/or a menu item. You can define the command execution in a single place and also update the user interface simply by targeting the action; the related visual control will automatically reflect the status of the action object.

THE MENU DESIGNER

If you just need to show a simple menu in your application, you can place a MainMenu on the form. As you do this, the MainMenu component will be automatically connected to the Menu property of the form. If you add a PopupMenu component on the form, connect it to the related form property to enable it. In both cases, double-click one of the two menu components to fire up the Menu Designer, shown in Figure 6.5. You add new menu items and provide them with a Caption property, using a hyphen (-) to separate caption menu items.

Delphi creates new components for each menu item you add. To name each component, Delphi uses the caption you enter and appends a number (so that *Open* becomes Open1). After removing spaces and other special characters from the caption, if nothing is left Delphi adds the letter *N* to the name. Finally it appends the number. Thus menu item separators are called N1, N2, and so on. Knowing what Delphi tends to do by default, you should edit the name first so you end up with a sensible component naming scheme.

FIGURE 6.5
Delphi's Menu Designer
in action

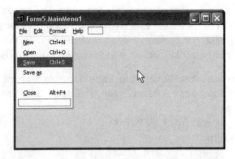

To obtain a more modern-looking menu, you can add an image list control to the program, hosting a series of bitmaps, and connect the image list to the menu using its Images property. You can then set an image for each menu item by setting the proper value of its ImageIndex property. The definition of images for menus is quite flexible—you can associate an image list with any specific pull-down menu (and even a specific menu item) using the SubMenuImages property. Having a specific smaller image list for each pull-down menu instead of a single large image list for the entire menu allows for more run-time customization of an application.

TIP   Creating menu items at run time is so common that Delphi provides some ready-to-use functions in the Menus unit. The names of these global functions are self-explanatory: NewMenu, NewPopupMenu, NewSubMenu, NewItem, and NewLine. The components returned by these functions have no owner, so you need to destroy them when you don't need them anymore.

Delphi 2005 has made it possible to make the menu designer even more flexible: a TMainMenu derived component can override the CreateMenuItem method returning a subtype of the TMenuItem type, with properties that will show up in the Object Inspector as expected.

POP-UP MENUS AND THE *ONCONTEXTPOPUP* EVENT

The PopupMenu component is typically displayed when the user right-clicks a component that uses the given pop-up menu as the value for its PopupMenu property. However, in addition to connecting the pop-up menu to a component with the corresponding property, you can call its Popup method, which requires the position of the pop-up in screen coordinates. The proper values can be obtained by converting a local point to a screen point with the ClientToScreen method of the local component, which is a label in this code fragment:

```
procedure TForm1.Label3MouseDown(Sender: TObject;
  Button: TMouseButton; Shift: TShiftState; X, Y: Integer);
var
  ScreenPoint: TPoint;
begin
  // if some condition applies...
  if Button = mbRight then
  begin
    ScreenPoint := Label3.ClientToScreen (Point (X, Y));
    PopupMenu1.Popup (ScreenPoint.X, ScreenPoint.Y)
  end;
end;
```

An alternative approach is to use the OnContextPopup event. This event fires when a user right-clicks a component—exactly what I traced previously with the test if Button = mbRight. The advantage is that the same event is also fired in response to a Shift+F10 key combination, as well as the shortcut-menu key of some keyboards. You can use this event to fire a pop-up menu with little code:

```
procedure TFormPopup.Label1ContextPopup(Sender: TObject;
  MousePos: TPoint; var Handled: Boolean);
var
  ScreenPoint: TPoint;
begin
  // add dynamic items
  PopupMenu2.Items.Add (NewLine);
  PopupMenu2.Items.Add (NewItem (TimeToStr (Now),
    0, False, True, nil, 0, ''));
  // show popup
  ScreenPoint := ClientToScreen (MousePos);
  PopupMenu2.Popup (ScreenPoint.X, ScreenPoint.Y);
  Handled := True;
  // remove dynamic items
  PopupMenu2.Items [4].Free;
  PopupMenu2.Items [3].Free;
end;
```

This example adds some dynamic behavior to the shortcut menu, adding a temporary item that indicates when the pop-up menu is displayed. This result is not particularly useful, but it illustrates that if you need to display a plain pop-up menu, you can easily use the PopupMenu property of the control in question or one of its parent controls. Handling the OnContextPopup event makes sense only when you want to do some extra processing.

The Handled parameter is preinitialized to False, so that if you do nothing in the event handler, the normal pop-up menu processing will occur. If you do something in your event handler to replace the normal pop-up menu processing (such as popping up a dialog or a customized menu, as in this case), you should set Handled to True and the system will stop processing the message. You'll rarely set Handled to True, however, because you'll generally use the OnContextPopup event to dynamically create or customize the pop-up menu and then let the default handler show the menu.

The handler of an OnContextPopup event isn't limited to displaying a pop-up menu. It can perform any other operation, such as directly displaying a dialog box. Here is an example of a right-click operation used to change the color of the control:

```
procedure TFormPopup.Label2ContextPopup(Sender: TObject;
  MousePos: TPoint; var Handled: Boolean);
begin
  ColorDialog1.Color := Label2.Color;
  if ColorDialog1.Execute then
    Label2.Color := ColorDialog1.Color;
  Handled := True;
end;
```

All the code snippets from this section are available in the simple CustPop example.

Control-Related Techniques

Now that you have a general overview of the most commonly used Delphi controls, I'll devote some space to discussing generic core techniques not related to a specific component. I'll cover the input focus, control anchors, the use of the splitter component, and the display of fly-by hints. Of course, these topics don't include everything you can do with visual controls, but they provide a starting point for exploration and get you up and running with some of the most common techniques.

Handling the Input Focus

Using the TabStop and TabOrder properties available in most controls, you can specify the order in which controls will receive the input focus when the user presses the Tab key. Instead of setting the tab order property of each component of a form manually, you can use the shortcut menu of the Form Designer to activate the Edit Tab Order dialog box, shown in Figure 6.6.

In addition to these basics settings, it is important to know that each time a component receives or loses the input focus, it receives a corresponding OnEnter or OnExit event. This allows you to fine-tune and customize the order of the user operations. Some of these techniques are demonstrated by the InFocus example, which creates a typical password-login window. Its form has three edit boxes with labels indicating their meaning, as shown in Figure 6.7. At the bottom of the window is a status area with prompts guiding the user. Each item needs to be entered in sequence.

FIGURE 6.6
The Edit Tab Order
dialog box

FIGURE 6.7
The InFocus example
at run time

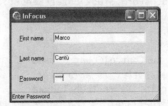

For the output of the status information, I used the StatusBar component with a single output area (obtained by setting its SimplePanel property to True). Here is a summary of the properties for this example. Notice the & character in the labels, indicating a shortcut key, and the connection of these labels with corresponding edit boxes (using the FocusControl property):

```
object FocusForm: TFocusForm
  ActiveControl = EditFirstName
  Caption = 'InFocus'
  object Label1: TLabel
```

```
      Caption = '&First name'
      FocusControl = EditFirstName
    end
    object EditFirstName: TEdit
      OnEnter = GlobalEnter
      OnExit = EditFirstNameExit
    end
    object Label2: TLabel
      Caption = '&Last name'
      FocusControl = EditLastName
    end
    object EditLastName: TEdit
      OnEnter = GlobalEnter
    end
    object Label3: TLabel
      Caption = '&Password'
      FocusControl = EditPassword
    end
    object EditPassword: TEdit
      PasswordChar = '*'
      OnEnter = GlobalEnter
    end
    object StatusBar1: TStatusBar
      SimplePanel = True
    end
  end
```

The program is simple and performs only two operations. The first is to identify in the status bar the edit control that has the focus. It does this by handling the controls' OnEnter event, using a single generic event handler to avoid repetitive code. In the example, instead of storing extra information for each edit box, I checked each control of the form to determine which label is connected to the current edit box (indicated by the Sender parameter):

```
procedure TFocusForm.GlobalEnter(Sender: TObject);
var
  I: Integer;
begin
  for I := 0 to ControlCount - 1 do
    // if the control is a label
    if (Controls [I] is TLabel) and
      // and the label is connected to the current edit box
      (TLabel(Controls[I]).FocusControl = Sender) then
    begin
      // remove the & used for the accelerator key
      StatusBar1.SimpleText := 'Enter ' + StripHotKey (
        TLabel(Controls[I]).Caption);
    end;
end;
```

The form's second event handler relates to the first edit box's OnExit event. If the control is left empty, it refuses to release the input focus and sets it back before showing a message to the user. The methods also look for a given input value, automatically filling the second edit box and moving the focus directly to the third one:

```
procedure TFocusForm.EditFirstNameExit(Sender: TObject);
begin
  if EditFirstName.Text = '' then
  begin
    // don't let the user get out
    EditFirstName.SetFocus;
    MessageDlg ('First name is required', mtError, [mbOK], 0);
  end
  else if EditFirstName.Text = 'Admin' then
  begin
    // fill the second edit and jump to the third
    EditLastName.Text := 'Admin';
    EditPassword.SetFocus;
  end;
end;
```

Control Anchors

To let you create a nice, flexible user interface with controls that adapt themselves to the current size of the form (a feature described as "geometry management"), Delphi allows you to determine the relative position of a control with the Anchors property. Before this feature was introduced, every control placed on a form had coordinates relative to the top and bottom, unless it was aligned to the bottom or right side. Aligning is good for some controls but not all of them, particularly buttons.

By using anchors, you can make the position of a control relative to any side of the form. For example, to anchor a button to the bottom-right corner of the form, you place the button in the required position and set its Anchors property to [akRight, akBottom]. When the form size changes, the distance of the button from the anchored sides is kept fixed. In other words, if you set these two anchors and remove the two defaults, the button will remain in the bottom-right corner.

On the other hand, if you place a large component such as a Memo or a ListBox in the middle of a form, you can set its Anchors property to include all four sides. This way the control will behave as an aligned control, growing and shrinking with the size of the form, but there will be some margin between it and the form sides.

TIP Anchors, like constraints, work both at design time and at run time. You should set them up as early as possible to benefit from this feature while you're designing the form as well as at run time.

As an example of both approaches, you can try the Anchors application, which has two buttons in the bottom-right corner and a list box in the middle. As shown in Figure 6.8, the controls automatically move and stretch as the form size changes. To make this form work properly, you must also set its Constraints property; otherwise, if the form becomes too small, the controls can overlap or disappear.

FIGURE 6.8

The controls of the An-
chors example move and
stretch automatically as
the user changes the size
of the form. No code is
needed to move the con-
trols, only proper use of
the Anchors property.

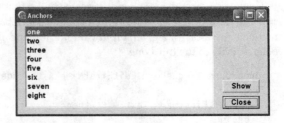

If you remove all the anchors or two opposite ones (for example, left and right), the resize operations will cause the control to *float* in the form. The control keeps its current size, and the system adds
or removes the same number of pixels on each side of it. This anchor can be defined as centered,
because if the component is initially in the middle of the form it will keep that position. If you want
a centered control you should generally use both opposite anchors so that if the user makes the form
larger the control size will grow as well. In the case just presented, making the form larger leaves a
small control in its center.

Using the Splitter Component

There are several ways to implement form-splitting techniques in Delphi, but the simplest approach
is to use the Splitter component, found in the Additional page of the Tool Palette. To make it more
effective, the splitter can be used in combination with the `Constraints` property of the controls it
relates to. As you'll see in the Split1 example, this technique allows you to define maximum and minimum positions for the splitter and the form. To build this example, place a ListBox component in a
form and align it to the left; then add a Splitter component that's also aligned to the left, a second left-
aligned ListBox, another left-aligned Splitter, and finally a third ListBox component aligned to the client areas. The form also has a simple toolbar based on a panel.

By simply placing these two splitter components, you give your form the complete functionality
of moving and sizing the controls it hosts at run time. The `Width`, `Beveled`, and `Color` properties of
the splitter components determine their appearance, and in the Split1 example you can use the toolbar
controls to change them. Another relevant property is `MinSize`, which determines the minimum size
of the form's components. During the splitting operation (see Figure 6.9), a line marks the final position of the splitter, but you cannot drag this line beyond a certain limit. The behavior of the Split1 program is not to let controls become too small. An alternative technique is to set the new `AutoSnap`
property of the splitter to True. This property will make the splitter hide the control when its size goes
below the `MinSize` limit.

I suggest you try using the Split1 program so that you'll fully understand how the splitter affects
its adjacent controls and the other controls of the form. Even if you set the `MinSize` property, a user
can reduce the size of the program's entire form to a minimum, hiding some of the list boxes. If you
test the Split2 version of the example, you'll get better behavior. In Split2, I set some `Constraints` for
the ListBox controls:

```
object ListBox1: TListBox
  Constraints.MaxHeight = 400
  Constraints.MinHeight = 200
  Constraints.MinWidth = 150
```

FIGURE 6.9

The Split1 example's Splitter component determines the minimum size for each control on the form, even those not adjacent to the splitter.

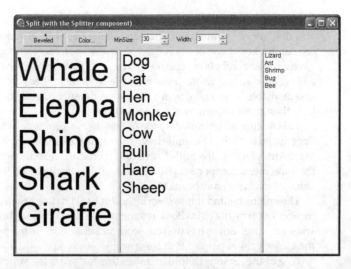

The size constraints are applied only as you resize the controls, so to make this program work satisfactorily you have to set the ResizeStyle property of the two splitters to rsUpdate. This value indicates that the controls' positions are updated for every movement of the splitter, not only at the end of the operation. If you select the rsLine or the new rsPattern value instead, the splitter simply draws a line in the required position, checking the MinSize property but not the constraints of the controls.

TIP When you set the Splitter component's AutoSnap property to True, the splitter will completely hide the neighboring control when the size of that control is below the minimum set for it in the Splitter component.

HORIZONTAL SPLITTING

You can also use the Splitter component for horizontal splitting instead of the default vertical splitting. Basically, you place a component on a form, align it to the top, and then place the splitter on the form. By default, the splitter will be left aligned. Choose the alTop value for the Align property, and you're done. You can see a form with a horizontal splitter in the SplitH example. This program has two memo components into which you can open a file, and it has a splitter dividing them, defined as follows:

```
object Splitter1: TSplitter
  Cursor = crVSplit
  Align = alTop
  OnMoved = Splitter1Moved
end
```

The program features a status bar, which keeps track of the current height of the two memo components. It handles the OnMoved event of the splitter (the only event of this component) to update the text of the status bar. The same code is executed whenever the form is resized:

```
StatusBar1.Panels[0].Text := Format ('Upper Memo: %d - Lower Memo: %d',
  [MemoUp.Height, MemoDown.Height]);
```

Accelerator Keys

You don't need to enter the & character in the Caption of a menu item, which provides an automatic accelerator key if you omit one. Delphi's automatic accelerator-key system can also figure out if you have entered conflicting accelerator keys and fix them on the fly. This doesn't mean you should stop adding custom accelerator keys with the & character because the automatic system simply uses the first available letter and doesn't follow the default standards. You might also find better mnemonic keys than those chosen by the automatic system.

This feature is controlled by the AutoHotkeys property, which is available in the main menu component and in each of the pull-down menus and menu items. In the main menu, this property defaults to maAutomatic; in the pull-downs and menu items, it defaults to maParent, so the value you set for the main menu component will be used automatically by all the subitems, unless they have a specific value of maAutomatic or maManual.

The engine behind this system is the RethinkHotkeys method of the TMenuItem class and the companion InternalRethinkHotkeys method. There is also a RethinkLines method, which checks whether a pull-down has two consecutive separators or if it begins or ends with a separator. In all these cases, the separator is automatically removed.

One of the reasons Delphi includes this feature is the support for translations. When you need to translate an application's menu, it is convenient if you don't have to deal with the accelerator keys, or at least if you don't have to worry about whether two items on the same menu conflict. Having a system that can automatically resolve similar problems is definitely an advantage. Another motivation was Delphi's IDE. With all the dynamically loaded packages that install menu items in the IDE main menu or in pop-up menus and with different packages loaded in different versions of the product, it's next to impossible to get nonconflicting accelerator-key selections in each menu. That is why this mechanism isn't a wizard that does static analysis of your menus at design time; it was created to deal with the real problem of managing menus created dynamically at run time.

WARNING   This feature is certainly handy, but because it is active by default, it can break existing Delphi code written quite some time ago. For example, I had a program that used the caption in the code, and the extra & broke my code. The change was quite simple, though: All I had to do was to set the AutoHotkeys property of the main menu component to maManual.

Using the Fly-by Hints

Another common element in toolbars is the *Tooltip*, also called *fly-by hint*—text that briefly describes the button currently under the cursor. This text is usually displayed in a yellow box after the mouse cursor has remained steady over a button for a set amount of time. To add hints to a group of buttons or components, simply set the ShowHints property of the parent control to True and enter some text for the Hint property of each element. You might want to enable the hints for all the components on a form or all the buttons of a toolbar or panel.

If you want to have more control over how hints are displayed, you can use some of the properties and events of the Application object. This global object has, among others, the following properties:

Property	Defines
HintColor	The background color of the hint window
HintPause	How long the cursor must remain on a component before hints are displayed

Property	Defines
HintHidePause	How long the hint will be displayed
HintShortPause	How long the system should wait to display a hint if another hint has just been displayed

For example, a program might allow a user to customize the hint background color by selecting a specific color with the following code:

```
ColorDialog.Color := Application.HintColor;
if ColorDialog.Execute then
  Application.HintColor := ColorDialog.Color;
```

As an alternative, you can change the hint color by handling the OnShowHint property of the Application object. This handler can change the hint's color for specific controls. The OnShowHint event is used in the CustHint example described in the next section.

CUSTOMIZING THE HINTS

Just as you can add hints to an application's toolbar, you can add hints to forms or to the components of a form. For a large control, the hint will show up near the mouse cursor. In some cases, it is important to know that a program can freely customize how hints are displayed. One thing you can do is change the value of the properties of the Application object, as I mentioned in the middle of the last section. To obtain more control over hints, you can customize them even further by assigning a method to the application's OnShowHint event. You need to either hook up this event manually or—better—add an ApplicationEvents component to the form and handle its OnShowHint event.

The event handler method has some interesting parameters, such as a string with the hint's text, a Boolean flag for its activation, and a THintInfo structure with further information, including the control, the hint position, and its color. The parameters are passed by reference, so you have a chance to change them and also modify the values of the THintInfo structure; for example, you can change the position of the hint window before it is displayed.

This is what I did in the CustHint example, which shows the hint for the label at the center of its area:

```
procedure TForm1.ShowHint (var HintStr: string; var CanShow: Boolean;
  var HintInfo: THintInfo);
begin
  with HintInfo do
    // if the control is the label show the hint in the middle
    if HintControl = Label1 then
      HintPos := HintControl.ClientToScreen (Point (
        HintControl.Width div 2, HintControl.Height div 2));
end;
```

The code retrieves the center of the generic control (the HintInfo.HintControl) and then converts its coordinates to screen coordinates, applying the ClientToScreen method to the control.

You can further update the CustHint example in a different way. The form's ListBox control has some rather long text items, so you might want to display the entire text in a hint while the mouse moves over the item. Setting a single hint for the list box won't do, of course.

A good solution is to customize the hint system by providing a hint dynamically corresponding to the text of the list box item under the cursor. You also need to indicate to the system which area the hint belongs to, so that by moving over the next line a new hint will be displayed. You accomplish this by setting the `CursorRect` field of the `THintInfo` record, which indicates the area of the component that the cursor can move over without disabling the hint. When the cursor moves outside this area, Delphi hides the hint window. Here is the related code snippet I added to the `ShowHint` method:

```
else if HintControl = ListBox1 then
begin
  nItem := ListBox1.ItemAtPos(
    Point (CursorPos.x, CursorPos.Y), True);
  if nItem >= 0 then
  begin
    // set the hint string
    HintStr := ListBox1.Items[nItem];
    // determine area for hint validity
    CursorRect := ListBox1.ItemRect(nItem);
    // display over the item
    HintPos := HintControl.ClientToScreen (Point(
      0, ListBox1.ItemHeight * (nItem - ListBox1.TopIndex)));
  end
  else
    CanShow := False;
end;
```

The resulting effect is that each line of the list box appears to have a specific hint, as shown in Figure 6.10. The hint position is computed so that it covers the current item text, extending beyond the list box border.

FIGURE 6.10

The ListBox control of the CustHint example shows a different hint, depending on which list item the mouse is over.

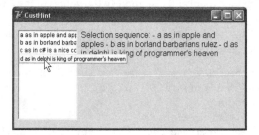

Owner-Draw Controls and Styles

In Windows, the system is usually responsible for painting buttons, list boxes, edit boxes, menu items, and similar elements. Basically, these controls know how to paint themselves. As an alternative, however, the system allows the owner of these controls, generally a form, to paint them. This technique, available for buttons, list boxes, combo boxes, and menu items, is called *owner-draw*.

In the VCL, the situation is slightly more complex. The components can take care of painting themselves in this case (as in the `TBitBtn` class for bitmap buttons) and possibly activate corresponding events. The system sends the request for painting to the owner (usually the form), and the form forwards the event back to the proper control, firing its event handlers.

Most of the Win32 common controls have support for the owner-draw technique, generally called *custom drawing*. You can fully customize the appearance of a ListView, TreeView, TabControl, PageControl, HeaderControl, StatusBar, or ToolBar. The ToolBar, ListView, and TreeView controls also support *advanced* custom drawing, a more fine-tuned drawing capability introduced by Microsoft in the latest versions of the Win32 common controls library.

The downside to owner-draw is that when the Windows user interface style changes in the future (and it always does), your owner-draw controls that fit in perfectly with the current user interface styles will look outdated and out of place. Because you are creating a custom user interface, you'll need to keep it updated yourself. By contrast, if you use the standard output of the controls, your applications will automatically adapt to a new version of such controls.

OWNER-DRAW MENU ITEMS

VCL makes the development of graphical menu items quite simple compared to the traditional approach of the Windows API: you set the OwnerDraw property of a menu item component to True and handle its OnMeasureItem and OnDrawItem events. In the OnMeasureItem event, you can determine the size of the menu items. This event handler is activated once for each menu item when the pulldown menu is displayed and has two reference parameters you can set: Width and Height. In the OnDrawItem event, you paint the actual image. This event handler is activated every time the item has to be repainted. This happens when Windows first displays the items and each time the status changes; for example, when the mouse moves over an item, the item should become highlighted.

To paint the menu items, you must consider all the possibilities, including drawing the highlighted items with specific colors, drawing the check mark if required, and so on. Luckily, the Delphi event passes to the handler the Canvas where it should paint, the output rectangle, and the status of the item (selected or not). In the ODMenu example, I handle the highlighted color but skip other advanced aspects (such as the check marks). I set the OwnerDraw property of the menu and wrote handlers for some of the menu items. To write a single handler for each event of the three color-related menu items, I set their Tag property to the value of the color in the OnCreate event handler of the form. This makes the handler of the items' OnClick event quite straightforward:

```
procedure TForm1.ColorClick(Sender: TObject);
begin
  ShapeDemo.Brush.Color := (Sender as TComponent).Tag
end;
```

The handler of the OnMeasureItem event doesn't depend on the actual items but uses fixed values (unlike the handler of the other pull-down). The most important portion of the code is in the handlers of the OnDrawItem events. For the color, you use the value of the tag to paint a rectangle of the given color, as you can see in Figure 6.11. Before doing this, however, you have to fill the background of the menu items (the rectangular area passed as a parameter) with the standard color for the menu (clMenu) or the selected menu items (clHighlight):

```
procedure TForm1.ColorDrawItem(Sender: TObject; ACanvas: TCanvas;
  ARect: TRect; Selected: Boolean);
begin
  // set the background color and draw it
```

```
    if Selected then
      ACanvas.Brush.Color := clHighlight
    else
      ACanvas.Brush.Color := clMenu;
    ACanvas.FillRect (ARect);
    // show the color
    ACanvas.Brush.Color := (Sender as TComponent).Tag;
    InflateRect (ARect, -5, -5);
    ACanvas.Rectangle (ARect.Left, ARect.Top, ARect.Right, ARect.Bottom);
  end;
```

The three handlers for this event of the Shape pull-down menu items are all different, although they use similar code:

```
procedure TForm1.Ellipse1DrawItem(Sender: TObject; ACanvas: TCanvas;
  ARect: TRect; Selected: Boolean);
begin
  // set the background color and draw it
  if Selected then
    ACanvas.Brush.Color := clHighlight
  else
    ACanvas.Brush.Color := clMenu;
  ACanvas.FillRect (ARect);
  // draw the ellipse
  ACanvas.Brush.Color := clWhite;
  InflateRect (ARect, -5, -5);
  ACanvas.Ellipse (ARect.Left, ARect.Top, ARect.Right, ARect.Bottom);
end;
```

FIGURE 6.11
The owner-draw menu
of the ODMenu example

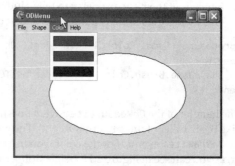

A LISTBOX OF COLORS

As you have just seen for menus, list boxes have an owner-draw capability, which means a program can paint the items of a list box. The same support is provided for combo boxes. To create an owner-draw list box, you set its Style property to lbOwnerDrawFixed or lbOwnerDrawVariable. The first value indicates that you will set the height of the list box items by specifying the ItemHeight property and that this will be the height of every item. The second owner-draw style indicates a list box with items of different heights; in this case, the component will trigger the OnMeasureItem event for each item to ask the program for their heights.

In the ODList example, I'll stick with the first, simpler approach. The example stores color information along with the list box items and then draws the items using those colors (instead of using a single color for the whole list).

The DFM file of every form, including this one, has a TextHeight attribute, which indicates the number of pixels required to display text. You should use this value for the list box's ItemHeight property. An alternative solution is to compute this value at run time, so that if you later change the font at design time, you don't have to remember to set the height of the items accordingly.

NOTE   I've just described TextHeight as an attribute of the form, not a property. It isn't a property, but a local value of the form. If it is not a property, you might ask, how does Delphi save it in the DFM file? The answer is that Delphi's streaming mechanism is based on properties plus special property clones created by the DefineProperties method.

Because TextHeight is *not* a property, although it is listed in the form description, you cannot access it directly. Studying the VCL source code, I found that this value is computed by calling a private method of the form: GetTextHeight. Because it is private, you cannot call this function. Instead, you can duplicate its code (which is quite simple) in the FormCreate method of the form after selecting the font of the list box:

```
Canvas.Font := ListBox1.Font;
ListBox1.ItemHeight := Canvas.TextHeight('0');
```

Next you add some items to the list box. Because this is a list box of colors, you should add color names to the Items of the list box and the corresponding color values to the Objects data storage related to each list item. Instead of adding each of the values separately, I wrote a procedure to add new items to the list:

```
procedure TODListForm.AddColors (Colors: array of TColor);
var
  I: Integer;
begin
  for I := Low (Colors) to High (Colors) do
    ListBox1.Items.AddObject (
      ColorToString (Colors[I]), TObject(Colors[I]));
end;
```

This method uses an open-array parameter, an array of an undetermined number of elements of the same type. For each item passed as a parameter, you add the name of the color to the list, and you add its value to the related data by calling the AddObject method. To obtain the string corresponding to the color, you call the Delphi ColorToString function. It returns a string containing either the corresponding color constant, if any, or the hexadecimal value of the color. The color data is added to the list box after casting its value to the TObject data type (a 4-byte reference), as required by the AddObject method.

TIP   In addition to ColorToString, which converts a color value into the corresponding string with the identifier or the hexadecimal value, the Delphi StringToColor function converts a properly formatted string into a color.

In the ODList example, this method is called in the form's `OnCreate` event handler (after the height of the items has been set):

```
AddColors ([clRed, clBlue, clYellow, clGreen, clFuchsia, clLime,
   clPurple, clGray, RGB (213, 23, 123), RGB (0, 0, 0), clAqua,
   clNavy, clOlive, clTeal]);
```

The code used to draw the items is not particularly complex. You simply retrieve the color associated with the item, set it as the color of the font, and then draw the text:

```
procedure TODListForm.ListBox1DrawItem(Control: TWinControl;
   Index: Integer; Rect: TRect; State: TOwnerDrawState);
begin
   with Control as TListbox do
   begin
     // erase
     Canvas.FillRect(Rect);
     // draw item
     Canvas.Font.Color := TColor (Items.Objects [Index]);
     Canvas.TextOut(Rect.Left, Rect.Top, Listbox1.Items[Index]);
   end;
end;
```

The system already sets the proper background color, so the selected item is displayed properly even without any extra code on your part. Moreover, the program allows you to add new items by double-clicking the list box:

```
procedure TODListForm.ListBox1DblClick(Sender: TObject);
begin
   if ColorDialog1.Execute then
     AddColors ([ColorDialog1.Color]);
end;
```

If you try using this capability, you'll notice that some colors you add are turned into color names (one of the Delphi color constants), whereas others are converted into hexadecimal numbers.

ListView and TreeView Controls

In the earlier section "Opening the Component Toolbox," I introduced the various visual controls you can use to display lists of values. The standard list box and combo box components are very common, but they are often replaced by the more powerful ListView and TreeView controls. These two controls are part of the Win32 common controls stored in the `ComCtl32.DLL` library.

A Graphical Reference List

When you use a ListView component, you can provide bitmaps both indicating the status of the element (for example, the selected item) and describing the contents of the item in a graphical way.

To connect the images to a list or tree, you need to refer to the ImageList component you've already used for the menu images. A ListView can have three image lists: one for the large icons (the `LargeImages` property), one for the small icons (the `SmallImages` property), and one for the state of the items (the `StateImages` property). In the RefList example, I set the first two properties using two different ImageList components.

Each item of the ListView has an `ImageIndex`, which refers to its image in the list. For this technique to work properly, the elements in the two image lists should follow the same order. When you have a fixed list view, you can add items to it using Delphi's ListView Item Editor, which is connected to the `Items` property. In this editor, you can define items and subitems. The subitems are displayed only in the detailed view (when you set the vsReport value of the `ViewStyle` property) and are connected with the titles set in the `Columns` property:

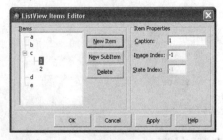

In my RefList example (a simple list of references to books, magazines, CD-ROMs, and websites), the items are stored to a file because users of the program can edit the contents of the list, which are automatically saved as the program exits. This way, edits made by the user become persistent. Saving and loading the contents of a ListView is not trivial, because the `TListItems` type doesn't have an automatic mechanism to save the data. As an alternative approach, I copied the data to and from a string list, using a custom format. The string list can then be saved to a file and reloaded with a single command.

The file format is simple, as you can see in the following saving code. For each list item, the program saves the caption on one line, the image index on another line (prefixed by the @ character), and the subitems on the following lines, indented with a tab character:

```
procedure TForm1.FormDestroy(Sender: TObject);
var
  I, J: Integer;
  List: TStringList;
begin
  // store the items
  List := TStringList.Create;
  try
    for I := 0 to ListView1.Items.Count - 1 do
    begin
      // save the caption
      List.Add (ListView1.Items[I].Caption);
      // save the index
      List.Add ('@' + IntToStr (ListView1.Items[I].ImageIndex));
      // save the subitems (indented)
      for J := 0 to ListView1.Items[I].SubItems.Count - 1 do
        List.Add (#9 + ListView1.Items[I].SubItems [J]);
    end;
    List.SaveToFile (
```

```
        ExtractFilePath (Application.ExeName) + 'Items.txt');
  finally
    List.Free;
  end;
end;
```

The items are then reloaded in the `FormCreate` method:

```
procedure TForm1.FormCreate(Sender: TObject);
var
  List: TStringList;
  NewItem: TListItem;
  I: Integer;
begin
  // stops warning message
  NewItem := nil;
  // load the items
  ListView1.Items.Clear;
  List := TStringList.Create;
  try
    List.LoadFromFile (
      ExtractFilePath (Application.ExeName) + 'Items.txt');
    for I := 0 to List.Count - 1 do
      if List [I][1] = #9 then
        NewItem.SubItems.Add (Trim (List [I]))
      else if List [I][1] = '@' then
        NewItem.ImageIndex := StrToIntDef (List [I][2], 0)
      else
      begin
        // a new item
        NewItem := ListView1.Items.Add;
        NewItem.Caption := List [I];
      end;
  finally
    List.Free;
  end;
end;
```

The program has a menu you can use to choose one of the different views supported by the List-View control and to add check boxes to the items, as in a CheckListBox control. You can see some combinations of these styles in Figure 6.12.

Another important feature, which is common in the detailed or report view of the control, lets a user sort the items on one of the columns. In the VCL, this technique requires three operations. First, you set the `SortType` property of the ListView to stBoth or stData. In both cases the ListView will sort based not on the captions but by calling the `OnCompare` event for each two items it has to sort.

FIGURE 6.12

Different examples of the output of a ListView component in the RefList program, obtained by changing the ViewStyle property

Second, because you want to sort on each of the columns of the detailed view, you also handle the OnColumnClick event (which takes place when the user clicks the column titles in the detailed view, but only if the ShowColumnHeaders property is set to True). Each time a column is clicked, the program saves the number of that column in the form class's nSortCol private field:

```
procedure TForm1.ListView1ColumnClick(Sender: TObject;
  Column: TListColumn);
begin
  nSortCol := Column.Index;
  ListView1.AlphaSort;
end;
```

Then, in the third step, the sorting code uses either the caption or one of the subitems according to the current sort column:

```
procedure TForm1.ListView1Compare(Sender: TObject;
  Item1, Item2: TListItem; Data: Integer; var Compare: Integer);
begin
  if nSortCol = 0 then
    Compare := CompareStr (Item1.Caption, Item2.Caption)
  else
    Compare := CompareStr (Item1.SubItems [nSortCol - 1],
      Item2.SubItems [nSortCol - 1]);
end;
```

The type of the Data parameter of this event (and the related handler) is different in VCL for .NET, where the method must be written:

```
procedure TForm1.ListView1Compare(Sender: TObject;
  Item1, Item2: TListItem;
  Data: TTag; var Compare: Integer);
```

As the program doesn't use the Data parameter in the code, it can be made compatible with a couple of IFDEF statements surrounding the method declaration and definition.

The final features I added to the program relate to mouse operations. When the user left-clicks an item, the RefList program shows a description of the selected item. Right-clicking the selected item sets it in edit mode, and a user can change it (keep in mind that the changes will automatically be saved when the program terminates). Here is the code for both operations in the OnMouseDown event handler of the ListView control:

```
procedure TForm1.ListView1MouseDown(Sender: TObject;
  Button: TMouseButton; Shift: TShiftState; X, Y: Integer);
var
  strDescr: string;
  I: Integer;
begin
  // if there is a selected item
  if ListView1.Selected <> nil then
    if Button = mbLeft then
    begin
      // create and show a description
      strDescr := ListView1.Columns [0].Caption + #9 +
        ListView1.Selected.Caption + #13;
      for I := 1 to ListView1.Selected.SubItems.Count do
        strDescr := strDescr + ListView1.Columns [I].Caption + #9 +
          ListView1.Selected.SubItems [I-1] + #13;
      ShowMessage (strDescr);
    end
    else if Button = mbRight then
      // edit the caption
      ListView1.Selected.EditCaption;
end;
```

Although it is not feature-complete, this example shows some of the potential of the ListView control. I also activated the "hot-tracking" feature, which lets the list view highlight and underline the item under the mouse. The relevant properties of the ListView can be seen in its textual description:

```
object ListView1: TListView
  Align = alClient
  Columns = <
    item
      Caption = 'Reference'
      Width = 230
    end
    item
      Caption = 'Author'
      Width = 180
    end
    item
      Caption = 'Country'
      Width = 80
    end>
```

```
    Font.Height = -13
    Font.Name = 'MS Sans Serif'
    Font.Style = [fsBold]
    FullDrag = True
    HideSelection = False
    HotTrack = True
    HotTrackStyles = [htHandPoint, htUnderlineHot]
    SortType = stBoth
    ViewStyle = vsList
    OnColumnClick = ListView1ColumnClick
    OnCompare = ListView1Compare
    OnMouseDown = ListView1MouseDown
  end
```

This program is quite interesting, and I'll further extend it in Chapter 7 by adding a dialog box.

A Tree of Data

Now that you've seen an example based on the ListView, let's examine the TreeView control. The TreeView has a user interface that is flexible and powerful (with support for editing and dragging elements). It is also standard, because it is the Windows Explorer user interface. There are properties and various ways to customize the bitmap of each line or each type of line.

NOTE   Delphi TreeView component encapsulates the corresponding Win32 Common Control. This control has some severe limitations when working on large sets of nodes. That's why there are TreeView components that do not use the standard control but are built from scratch to provide more flexibility and a much better performance. The most popular of these components is Mike Lischke's Virtual TreeView, available on www.soft-gems.net/VirtualTreeview. This open source component is licensed under MPL and LGPL.

To define the structure of the TreeView nodes at design time, you can use the TreeView Items Editor:

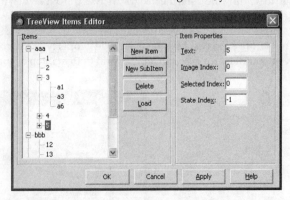

In this case, however, I decided to load the TreeView data at startup, in a similar way to the last example.

The Items property of the TreeView component has many member functions you can use to alter the hierarchy of strings. For example, you can build a two-level tree with the following lines:

```
var
  Node: TTreeNode;
begin
  Node := TreeView1.Items.Add (nil, 'First level');
  TreeView1.Items.AddChild (Node, 'Second level');
```

Using the Add and AddChild methods, you can build a complex structure at run time. To load the information, you can again use a StringList at run time, load a text file with the information, and parse it.

However, because the TreeView control has a LoadFromFile method, the DragTree example uses the following simpler code:

```
procedure TForm1.FormCreate(Sender: TObject);
begin
  TreeView1.LoadFromFile (
    ExtractFilePath (Application.ExeName) + 'TreeText.txt');
end;
```

The LoadFromFile method loads the data in a string list and checks the level of each item by looking at the number of tab characters. (If you are curious, see the TTreeStrings.GetBufStart method, which you can find in the ComCtrls unit in the VCL source code included in Delphi.) The data I prepared for the TreeView is the organizational chart of a multinational company, as you can see in Figure 6.13.

Instead of expanding the node items one by one, you can also use the File ➤ Expand All menu of this program, which calls the FullExpand method of the TreeView control or executes the equivalent code (in this specific case of a tree with a root item):

```
TreeView1.Items [0].Expand(True);
```

In addition to loading the data, the program saves the data when it terminates, making the changes persistent. It also has a few menu items to customize the font of the TreeView control and change some other simple settings. The specific feature I implemented in this example is support for dragging items and entire subtrees. I set the DragMode property of the component to dmAutomatic and wrote the event handlers for the OnDragOver and OnDragDrop events.

FIGURE 6.13

The DragTree example after loading the data and expanding the branches

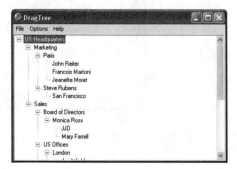

In the first of the two handlers, the program makes sure the user is not trying to drag an item over a child item (which would be moved along with the item, leading to an infinite recursion):

```
procedure TForm1.TreeView1DragOver(Sender, Source: TObject;
  X, Y: Integer; State: TDragState; var Accept: Boolean);
var
  TargetNode, SourceNode: TTreeNode;
begin
  TargetNode := TreeView1.GetNodeAt (X, Y);
  // accept dragging from itself
  if (Source = Sender) and (TargetNode <> nil) then
  begin
    Accept := True;
    // determines source and target
    SourceNode := TreeView1.Selected;
    // look up the target parent chain
    while (TargetNode.Parent <> nil) and (TargetNode <> SourceNode) do
      TargetNode := TargetNode.Parent;
    // if source is found
    if TargetNode = SourceNode then
      // do not allow dragging over a child
      Accept := False;
  end
  else
    Accept := False;
end;
```

The effect of this code is that (except for the particular case you need to disallow) a user can drag a TreeView item over another item. Writing the code for moving the items is simple, because the Tree-View control provides support for this operation through the TTreeNode class's MoveTo method:

```
procedure TForm1.TreeView1DragDrop(Sender, Source: TObject;
  X, Y: Integer);
var
  TargetNode, SourceNode: TTreeNode;
begin
  TargetNode := TreeView1.GetNodeAt (X, Y);
  if TargetNode <> nil then
  begin
    SourceNode := TreeView1.Selected;
    SourceNode.MoveTo (TargetNode, naAddChildFirst);
    TargetNode.Expand (False);
    TreeView1.Selected := TargetNode;
  end;
end;
```

NOTE   Among the demos shipping with Delphi is an interesting one showing a custom-draw Tree-View control. The example is in the CustomDraw subdirectory.

Custom Tree Nodes

Recent versions of Delphi added a few features to the TreeView controls, including multiple selection (see the MultiSelect and MultiSelectStyle properties and the Selections array), improved sorting, and several new events. The key improvement, however, is letting the programmer determine the class of the tree view's node items. Having custom node items implies the ability to attach custom data to the nodes in a simple, object-oriented way. To support this technique, there is a new AddNode method for the TTreeItems class and a new specific event, OnCreateNodesClass. In the handler for this event, you return the class of the object to be created, which must inherit from TTreeNode.

This is a very common technique, so I built an example to discuss it in detail. The CustomNodes example doesn't focus on a real-world case, but it shows a rather complex situation in which two different custom tree node classes are derived one from the other. The base class adds an ExtraCode property mapped to virtual methods, and the derived class overrides one of these methods. For the base class, the GetExtraCode function simply returns the value; for the derived class, the value is multiplied to the parent node value. Here are the classes and this second method:

```
type
  TMyNode = class (TTreeNode)
  private
    FExtraCode: Integer;
  protected
    procedure SetExtraCode(const Value: Integer); virtual;
    function GetExtraCode: Integer; virtual;
  public
    property ExtraCode: Integer read GetExtraCode write SetExtraCode;
  end;

  TMySubNode = class (TMyNode)
  protected
    function GetExtraCode: Integer; override;
  end;

function TMySubNode.GetExtraCode: Integer;
begin
  Result := fExtraCode * (Parent as TMyNode).ExtraCode;
end;
```

With these custom tree node classes available, the program creates a tree of items, using the first type for the first-level nodes and the second class for the other nodes. Because you have only one OnCreateNodeClass event handler, the program uses the class reference stored in a private field of the form (CurrentNodeClass of type TTreeNodeClass):

```
procedure TForm1.TreeView1CreateNodeClass(Sender: TCustomTreeView;
  var NodeClass: TTreeNodeClass);
begin
  NodeClass := CurrentNodeClass;
end;
```

The program sets this class reference before creating nodes of each type—for example, with code like the following:

```
var
  MyNode: TMyNode;
begin
  CurrentNodeClass := TMyNode;
  MyNode := TreeView1.Items.AddChild (nil, 'item' + IntToStr (nValue))
    as TMyNode;
  MyNode.ExtraCode := nValue;
```

Once the entire tree has been created, when the user selects an item, you can cast its type to TMyNode and access the extra properties (as well as methods and data):

```
procedure TForm1.TreeView1Click(Sender: TObject);
var
  MyNode: TMyNode;
begin
  MyNode := TreeView1.Selected as TMyNode;
  Label1.Caption := MyNode.Text + ' [' + MyNode.ClassName + '] = ' +
    IntToStr (MyNode.ExtraCode);
end;
```

This is the code used by the CustomNodes example to display the description of the selected node in a label, as you can see in Figure 6.14. Note that when you select an item within the tree, its value is multiplied for that of each parent node. There are certainly easier ways to obtain this effect, but having a tree view with item objects created from different classes of a hierarchy provides an object-oriented structure upon which you can base some very complex code.

FIGURE 6.14

The CustomNodes example has a tree view with node objects based on different custom classes, thanks to the OnCreateNodesClass event.

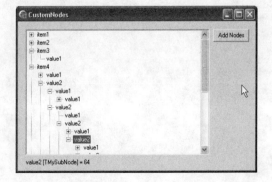

What's Next?

In this chapter, we explored the foundations of the library traditionally available in Delphi for building user interfaces: the VCL. I discussed the TControl class, its properties, and its most important derived classes. I also explored a few differences of its .NET counterpart, VCL for .NET. Later on in

Chapter 9, we'll also explore the native control library of the .NET Framework, generally called WinForms.

In this chapter we explored some of the basic components available in Delphi. These components correspond to the standard Windows controls and some of the common controls, and they are extremely common in applications. You also saw how to create main menus and pop-up menus and how to add extra graphics to some of these controls.

The next step is to explore in depth the structure of forms, dialog boxes, frames, and related topics like the visual form inheritance and the MDI architecture. This will happen in Chapter 7. We'll then see other elements of a complete user interface, discussing action lists and the Action Manager, and building some simple but complete examples in Chapter 8.

Chapter 7

Working with Forms

If you've read the previous chapters, you should now be able to use Delphi's visual components to create the user interface for your VCL applications. Now let's turn our attention to another central element of development in Delphi: forms. You have used forms since the initial chapters, but I've never described in detail what you can do with a form, which properties you can use, or which methods of the TForm class are particularly interesting.

This chapter looks at some of the properties and styles of forms and at sizing and positioning them, as well as form scaling and scrolling. I'll introduce applications with multiple forms (including some info on the MDI architecture), the use of dialog boxes (custom and predefined ones), frames, and visual form inheritance. I'll also devote some time to input on a form from both the keyboard and the mouse.

Delving into applications with multiple forms, the chapter also covers the global Application and Screen objects. In addition, I'll mention advanced topics like the use of interfaces for forms and the interposer classes trick.

This chapter covers form styles and border styles, mouse and keyboard input, direct form painting and special effects, positioning and scrolling forms, creating and closing forms, modal and modeless dialog boxes and forms, creating secondary forms dynamically, and predefined dialog boxes. It also covers the Application, Screen, and Mouse global objects, MDI applications, visual form inheritance, frames, and interfaces.

NOTE   This chapter covers forms in VCL for Win32 and VCL for .NET. For an introduction to forms in the WinForms library, which is part of the .NET FCL, refer to Chapter 9.

The *TForm* Class

Forms in Delphi are defined by the TForm class, which is included in the Forms unit of VCL. The TForm class is part of the windowed-controls hierarchy, which starts with the TWinControl. Throughout this chapter, I'll present some interesting techniques related to forms. I'll begin by presenting a technique for *not* defining the form of a program at design time, using the TForm class directly, and then explore a few interesting properties of the form class.

I'll also point out a few differences between VCL forms and VCL.NET forms. I built a .NET version for most of the examples, hosted in the same folder as the Win32 counterpart and sharing the exact same source code (but different project files).

Using Plain Forms

Delphi developers tend to create forms at design time, which implies deriving a new class from the base class and building the content of the form visually. This is certainly a reasonable standard practice, but it is not compulsory to create a descendant of the TForm class to show a form, particularly if it is a simple one.

Consider this case: suppose you have to show a rather long message to a user, and you don't want to use the simple predefined message box because it will look too large and won't provide scroll bars. You can create a form with a memo component in it and display the string inside the memo. Nothing prevents you from creating this form in the standard visual way, but you might consider doing this in code, particularly if you need a large degree of flexibility.

The DynaForm example is somewhat extreme as it has no form defined at design time but includes a unit with this function:

```
procedure ShowStringForm (str: string);
var
  form: TForm;
begin
  Application.CreateForm(TForm, form);
  form.caption := 'DynaForm';
  form.Position := poScreenCenter;
  with TMemo.Create (form) do
  begin
    Align := alClient;
    Scrollbars := ssVertical;
    ReadOnly := True;
    Color := form.Color;
    BorderStyle := bsNone;
    WordWrap := True;
    Text := str;
    Parent := form;
  end;
  form.Show;
end;
```

In this example I created the form by calling the Application global object's CreateForm method (a feature commonly used by Delphi applications in the code of the project source file and discussed later in this chapter) because the form is indeed the main form; other than that, this code does dynamically what you generally do with the Form Designer. Writing this code is undoubtedly more tedious, but it does allow a greater deal of flexibility because any parameter can depend on external settings.

The previous ShowStringForm function is not executed by an event of another form because there are no traditional forms in this program. Instead, it is called by the project's source code. The effect of running the DynaForm program is a strange-looking form filled with random characters—it isn't terribly useful in itself, but it underscores the idea:

Having the source code instead of a DFM file is also the .NET WinForms approach, but in that case you inherit a custom form class and use a designer to define those source code statements.

The Form Style

The FormStyle property allows you to choose between a normal form (fsNormal) and the windows that make up a Multiple Document Interface (MDI) application. In this case, you'll use the fsMDIForm style for the MDI parent window—that is, the frame window of the MDI application—and the fsMDIChild style for the MDI child window. To learn more about the development of an MDI application, see the section "Creating MDI Applications" later in this chapter.

A fourth option is the fsStayOnTop style, which determines whether the form must always remain on top of all other windows (except for any that also happen to be "stay-on-top" windows). To create a top-most form (a form whose window is always on top), you need only set the FormStyle property, as indicated earlier. This property has two different effects, depending on the kind of form you apply it to:

- ◆ The main form of an application will remain in front of every other application (unless other applications have the same top-most style). This behavior makes sense only for special-purpose alert programs.

- ◆ A secondary form will remain in front of any other form in the application it belongs to. The windows of other applications are not affected. This approach is often used for floating toolbars and other forms that should stay in front of the main window.

The Border Style

Another important property of a form is its border style. The BorderStyle property refers to a visual element of the form, but it has a much more profound influence on the *behavior* of the window. You can assign six different values to this property:

- ◆ bsSizeable (the default value) corresponds to a Windows style known as *thick frame*. When a main window has a thick frame around it, a user can resize it by dragging its border.

- ◆ bsDialog defines a form with the typical dialog-box frame that doesn't allow resizing. When you select this value, the VCL changes the standard form behavior to make it look like a dialog box. For example, the items on its system menu are different, and the form will ignore some of the elements of the BorderIcons set property.

- ◆ bsSingle creates a main window that's not resizable. Many games and applications based on windows with controls (such as data-entry forms) use this value, simply because resizing these forms makes no sense.

◆ bsNone is used only in very special situations and inside other forms. You'll seldom see an application with a main window that has no border or caption.

◆ bsToolWindow and bsSizeToolWin are related to the specific Win32 extended style ws_ex_ ToolWindow, which turns the window into a floating toolbox with a small title font and close button. You should not use this style for the main window of an application.

NOTE   At design time, the traditional Delphi floating form designer always shows the border style using the default bsSizeable value of the BorderStyle property, while the embedded form designer of Delphi 2005 shows the proper border style you have selected.

To test the effect and behavior of the different values of the BorderStyle property, I wrote a program called Borders. The main form of this program contains a radio group and a button. The secondary form has no components.

The program code is simple. When you click the button, a new form is dynamically created, depending on the item selected in the radio group:

```
uses
  Second;

procedure TForm1.BtnNewFormClick(Sender: TObject);
var
  NewForm: TForm2;
begin
  NewForm := TForm2.Create (Application);
  NewForm.BorderStyle := TFormBorderStyle (BorderRadioGroup.ItemIndex);
  NewForm.Caption := BorderRadioGroup.Items[BorderRadioGroup.ItemIndex];
  NewForm.Show;
end;
```

This code uses a trick: it casts the number of the selected item into the TFormBorderStyle enumeration. This technique works because I gave the radio buttons the same order as the values of the TFormBorderStyle enumeration. The BtnNewFormClick method then copies the text of the radio button to the caption of the secondary form.

Setting More Window Styles

The border style and border icons are indicated by two different Delphi properties, which you can use to set the initial value of the corresponding user interface elements. You have seen that in addition to changing the user interface, these properties affect the behavior of a window. It is important to know that in VCL, these border-related properties and the FormStyle property primarily correspond to different settings in the *style* and *extended style* of a window. These two terms reflect two parameters of the CreateWindowEx API function Delphi uses to create forms.

It is important to acknowledge this fact because Delphi allows you to modify these two parameters freely by overriding the CreateParams virtual method:

```
public
  procedure CreateParams (var Params: TCreateParams); override;
```

This is the only way to use some of the peculiar window styles that are not directly available through form properties. For a list of window styles and extended styles, see the help under the topics "CreateWindow" and "CreateWindowEx." You'll notice that the Win32 API has styles for these functions, including those related to tool windows.

To show you how to use this approach, I wrote the NoTitle example, which lets you create a program with a custom caption. First you must remove the standard caption but keep the resizing frame by setting the corresponding styles:

```
procedure TForm1.CreateParams (var Params: TCreateParams);
begin
  inherited CreateParams (Params);
  Params.Style := (Params.Style or ws_Popup) and not ws_Caption;
end;
```

To remove the caption, you need to change the overlapped style to a pop-up style; otherwise, the caption will simply remain there. To add a custom caption, I placed a label aligned to the upper border of the form and a small button on the far end. You can see this effect at run time in Figure 7.1.

To make the fake caption work, you have to tell the system that a mouse operation on this area corresponds to a mouse operation on the caption. You can do so by intercepting the wm_NCHitTest Windows message, which is frequently sent to Windows to determine where the mouse is. When the hit is in the client area and on the label, you can pretend the mouse is on the caption by setting the proper result:

```
procedure TForm1.WMNCHitTest (var Msg: TWMNCHitTest);
  // message wm_NcHitTest
begin
  inherited;
  if (Msg.Result = htClient) and (Msg.YPos <
      Label1.Height + Top + GetSystemMetrics (sm_cyFrame)) then
    Msg.Result := htCaption;
end;
```

The GetSystemMetrics API function used in this listing queries the operating system about the vertical thickness (cy) in pixels of the border around a window with a caption but that is not resizable. It is important to repeat this query every time (and not cache the result) because users can customize most of these elements by using the Appearance page of the Display options (in Control Panel) and other Windows settings. The small button has a call to the Close method in its OnClick event handler. The button is kept in its position even when the window is resized by using the [akTop,akRight] value for the Anchors property. The form also has size constraints so that a user cannot make it too small, as described in the "Form Constraints" section later in this chapter.

FIGURE 7.1
The NoTitle example has no real caption, only a fake one made with a label.

Direct Form Input

Now that we've discussed some special capabilities of forms, I'll move to a very important topic: user input in a form. If you decide to make limited use of components, you might write complex programs as well, receiving input from the mouse and the keyboard. In this chapter, I'll only introduce this topic.

Supervising Keyboard Input

Generally, forms don't handle keyboard input directly. If a user has to type something, your form should include an edit component or one of the other input components. If you want to handle keyboard shortcuts, you can use those connected with menus (possibly using a hidden pop-up menu).

At other times, however, you might want to handle keyboard input in particular ways for a specific purpose. In these cases, you can turn on the form's KeyPreview property. Then, even if you have some input controls, the form's OnKeyPress event will always be activated for any character-input operation (system and shortcut keys excluded). The keyboard input will then reach the destination component, unless you stop it in the form by setting the character value to zero (not the character 0, but the value 0 of the character set, a control character indicated as #0).

The example I built to demonstrate this approach, KPreview, has a form with no special properties (not even KeyPreview), a radio group with four options, and some edit boxes, as you can see in Figure 7.2. By default the program does nothing special, except when the various radio buttons are used to enable the key preview:

```
procedure TForm1.RadioPreviewClick(Sender: TObject);
begin
  KeyPreview := RadioPreview.ItemIndex <> 0;
end;
```

Now you'll begin receiving the OnKeyPress events, and you can do one of the three actions requested by the three special buttons in the radio group. The action depends on the value of the ItemIndex property of the radio group component. This is the reason the event handler is based on a case statement:

```
procedure TForm1.FormKeyPress(Sender: TObject; var Key: Char);
begin
  case RadioPreview.ItemIndex of
    ...
```

In the first case, if the value of the Key parameter is #13, which corresponds to the Enter key, you disable the operation (setting Key to zero) and then mimic the activation of the Tab key. You can do this many ways, but the technique I chose is quite particular: I sent the CM_DialogKey message to the form (calling the Perform method of the VCL that invokes the form's window procedure directly), passing the code for the Tab key (VK_TAB):

```
1: // Enter = Tab
  if Key = #13 then
  begin
    Key := #0;
    Perform (cm_DialogKey, VK_TAB, 0);
  end;
```

NOTE The cm_DialogKey message is an internal, undocumented Delphi message. There are a few of these undocumented messages, and it's quite interesting to build advanced components for them and to use them for special coding, but Borland never describes them.

To type in the form's caption, the program adds the character to the current Caption. There are two special cases. When the Backspace key is pressed, the last character of the string is removed (by copying to the Caption all the characters of the current Caption but the last one). When the Enter key is pressed, the program stops the operation by resetting the ItemIndex property of the radio group control. Here is the code:

```
2: // type in caption
begin
  if Key = #8 then // backspace: remove last char
    Caption := Copy (Caption, 1, Length (Caption) - 1)
  else if Key = #13 then // enter: stop operation
    RadioPreview.ItemIndex := 0
  else // anything else: add character
    Caption := Caption + Key;
  Key := #0;
end;
```

Finally, if the last radio item is selected, the code checks whether the character is a vowel (by testing for its inclusion in a constant "vowel set"). In this case, the character is skipped altogether:

```
3: // skip vowels
if UpCase(Key) in ['A', 'E', 'I', 'O', 'U'] then
  Key := #0;
```

FIGURE 7.2
The KPreview program
at design time

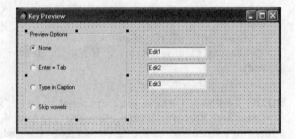

Getting Mouse Input

When a user clicks one of the mouse buttons over a form (or over a component), Windows sends the application messages. Delphi defines events you can use to write code that responds to these messages. The two basic events are OnMouseDown, received when a mouse button is clicked, and OnMouseUp, received when the button is released. Another fundamental system message is related to mouse movement: OnMouseMove. Although it should be easy to understand the meaning of the three messages—down, up, and move—you may wonder how they relate to the OnClick event you have often used up to now. You have used the OnClick event for components, but it is also available for the form. Its general meaning is that the left mouse button has been clicked and released on the same window or component.

Another difference between the OnMouse*XX* and OnClick events is that the latter relates only to the *left* mouse button. Most of the mouse types connected to a Windows PC have two mouse buttons, and some even have three. Usually you refer to these buttons as the left mouse button (generally used for selection), the right mouse button (for accessing shortcut menus), and the middle mouse button (seldom used).

Nowadays most new mouse devices have a button wheel instead of the middle button; users typically use the wheel for scrolling (causing an OnMouseWheel event), but they can also press it (generating the OnMouseWheelDown and OnMouseWheelUp events). Mouse wheel events are automatically converted into scrolling events.

TIP　A user should always be able to use any Windows application without the mouse. This is not because some users may not have a mouse connected, but rather because using the mouse tends to be slower, specifically for repetitive tasks of applications you use often. For these reasons, set up a proper tab order for controls, remember to add accelerator keys for buttons and menu items for keyboard selection, and define shortcut keys for menu commands.

THE PARAMETERS OF THE MOUSE EVENTS

All the lower-level mouse events have the same parameters: the usual Sender parameter, a Button parameter indicating which of the three mouse buttons has been clicked (mbRight, mbLeft, or mbCenter), the Shift parameter indicating which of the *mouse-related virtual keys* (the *shift-state modifiers* Alt, Ctrl, and Shift, plus the three mouse buttons) was pressed when the event occurred; and the x and y coordinates of the position of the mouse in *client area* coordinates of the current window.

Using this information, it is simple to draw a small circle in the position of a left mouse button–down event:

```
procedure TForm1.FormMouseDown(Sender: TObject;
    Button: TMouseButton; Shift: TShiftState; X, Y: Integer);
begin
  if Button = mbLeft then
    Canvas.Ellipse (X-10, Y-10, X+10, Y+10);
end;
```

NOTE　To draw on the form, you use a special property: Canvas. A TCanvas object has two distinctive features: it holds a collection of drawing tools (such as a pen, a brush, and a font) and it has some drawing methods, which use the current tools. The kind of direct drawing code in this example is not correct, because the on-screen image is not persistent; moving another window over the current one will clear its output. The next example demonstrates the Windows "store-and-draw" approach.

Dragging and Drawing with the Mouse

To demonstrate a few of the mouse techniques discussed so far, I built an example based on a form without any components. The program is called MouseOne. It displays the current position of the mouse in the form's Caption:

```
procedure TMouseForm.FormMouseMove(Sender: TObject;
  Shift: TShiftState; X, Y: Integer);
```

```
begin
  // display the position of the mouse in the caption
  Caption := Format ('Mouse in x=%d, y=%d', [X, Y]);
end;
```

You can use this feature of the program to better understand how the mouse works. Perform this test: run the program (this simple version or the complete one) and resize the windows on the desktop so that the form of the MouseOne program is behind another window and inactive but with the title visible. Now move the mouse over the form, and you'll see that the coordinates change. This behavior means the OnMouseMove event is sent to the application even if its window is not active; mouse messages are always directed to the window under the mouse. The only exception is the mouse capture operation, which I'll discuss in this same example.

In addition to showing the position in the title of the window, the MouseOne example can track mouse movements by painting small pixels on the form if the user keeps the Shift key pressed (again, this direct painting code produces nonpersistent output):

```
procedure TMouseForm.FormMouseMove(Sender: TObject; Shift: TShiftState;
  X, Y: Integer);
begin
  // display the position of the mouse in the caption
  Caption := Format ('Mouse in x=%d, y=%d', [X, Y]);
  if ssShift in Shift then
    // mark points in yellow
    Canvas.Pixels [X, Y] := clYellow;
end;
```

The most interesting feature of this example is its direct mouse-dragging support. Contrary to what you might think, Windows has no system support for dragging, which is implemented in VCL by means of lower-level mouse events and operations. (I discussed an example of dragging in Chapter 6.) In VCL, forms cannot originate dragging operations, so you are obliged to use the low-level approach. The aim of this example is to draw a rectangle from the initial position of the dragging operation to the final one, giving users visual clues about the operation they are doing.

The idea behind dragging is quite simple. The program receives a sequence of button-down, mouse-move, and button-up messages. When the button is pressed, dragging begins, although the real actions take place only when the user moves the mouse (without releasing the mouse button) and when dragging terminates (when the button-up message arrives). The problem with this basic approach is that it is not reliable. A window usually receives mouse events only when the mouse is over its client area; so if the user presses the mouse button, moves the mouse onto another window, and then releases the button, the second window will receive the button-up message.

There are two solutions to this problem. One (seldom used) is mouse clipping. Using a Windows API function (ClipCursor), you can force the mouse not to leave a certain area of the screen. When you try to move it outside the specified area, it stumbles against an invisible barrier. The second and more common solution is to capture the mouse. When a window captures the mouse, all the subsequent mouse input is sent to that window. This is the approach I used for the MouseOne example.

The example's code is built around three methods: FormMouseDown, FormMouseMove, and FormMouseUp. Clicking the left mouse button over the form starts the process, setting the fDragging Boolean field of the form (which indicates that dragging is in action in the other two methods). The method also uses a TRect variable that keeps track of the initial and current position of the dragging. Here is the code:

```
procedure TMouseForm.FormMouseDown(Sender: TObject;
  Button: TMouseButton; Shift: TShiftState; X, Y: Integer);
begin
  if Button = mbLeft then
  begin
    fDragging := True;
    Mouse.Capture := Handle;
    fRect.Left := X;
    fRect.Top := Y;
    fRect.BottomRight := fRect.TopLeft;
    dragStart := fRect.TopLeft;
    Canvas.DrawFocusRect (fRect);
  end;
end;
```

An important action of this method is the call to the SetCapture API function, obtained by setting the Capture property of the global object Mouse. Now, even if a user moves the mouse outside the client area, the form still receives all mouse-related messages. You can see that behavior by moving the mouse toward the upper-left corner of the screen; the program shows negative coordinates in the caption.

TIP   The global Mouse object allows you to get global information about the mouse, such as its presence, type, and current position; it also lets you set some of its global features. This global object hides a few API functions, making your code simpler and more portable.

When dragging is active and the user moves the mouse, the program draws a dotted rectangle corresponding to the mouse's position. The program calls the DrawFocusRect method twice. The first time this method is called, it deletes the current image, thanks to the fact that two consecutive calls to DrawFocusRect reset the original situation. After updating the position of the rectangle, the program calls the method a second time:

```
procedure TMouseForm.FormMouseMove(Sender: TObject; Shift: TShiftState;
  X, Y: Integer);
begin
  // display the position of the mouse in the caption
  Caption := Format ('Mouse in x=%d, y=%d', [X, Y]);
  if fDragging then
  begin
    // remove and redraw the dragging rectangle
    Canvas.DrawFocusRect (fRect);
    if X > dragStart.X then
      fRect.Right := X
    else
      fRect.Left := X;
    if Y > dragStart.Y then
      fRect.Bottom := Y
```

```
      else
        fRect.Top := Y;
      Canvas.DrawFocusRect (fRect);
    end
    else
      if ssShift in Shift then
        // mark points in yellow
        Canvas.Pixels [X, Y] := clYellow;
  end;
```

The DrawFocusRect function doesn't draw rectangles with a negative size, so the code of the program has been fixed (as you can see in the previous code) by comparing the current position with the initial position of the dragging, saved in the dragStart point. When the mouse button is released, the program terminates the dragging operation by resetting the Capture property of the Mouse object (which internally calls the ReleaseCapture API function) and by setting the value of the fDragging field to False:

```
procedure TMouseForm.FormMouseUp(Sender: TObject; Button: TMouseButton;
  Shift: TShiftState; X, Y: Integer);
begin
  if fDragging then
  begin
    Mouse.Capture := 0; // calls ReleaseCapture
    fDragging := False;
    Invalidate;
  end;
end;
```

The final call, Invalidate, triggers a painting operation and executes the following OnPaint event handler:

```
procedure TMouseForm.FormPaint(Sender: TObject);
begin
  Canvas.Rectangle (fRect.Left, fRect.Top, fRect.Right, fRect.Bottom);
end;
```

This makes the output of the form persistent, even if you hide it behind another form. Figure 7.3 shows a previous version of the rectangle and a dragging operation in action.

FIGURE 7.3

During a dragging operation, the MouseOne example uses a dotted line to indicate the final area of a rectangle.

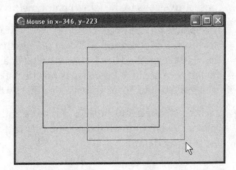

Painting on Forms

Why do you need to handle the OnPaint event to produce proper output, and why can't you paint directly over the form canvas? It depends on Windows' default behavior. As you draw on a window, Windows does *not* store the resulting image. When the window is covered, its contents are usually lost.

The reason for this behavior is simple: to save memory. Windows assumes it's "cheaper" in the long run to redraw the screen using code than to dedicate system memory to preserving the display state of a window. It's a classic memory-versus-CPU-cycles trade-off. A color bitmap for a 600 × 800 image at 256 colors requires about 480 KB. By increasing the color count or the number of pixels, you can easily reach 4 MB of memory for a 1280 ×1024 resolution at 16 million colors.

In the event that you want to have consistent output for your applications, you can use two techniques. The general solution is to store enough data about the output to be able to reproduce it when the system sends a *painting* requested. An alternative approach is to save the output of the form in a bitmap while you produce it by placing an Image component over the form and drawing on the canvas of this image component.

The first technique, painting, is the common approach to handling output in most windowing systems, aside from particular graphics-oriented programs that store the form's whole image in a bitmap. The approach used to implement painting has a very descriptive name: *store and paint*. When the user clicks a mouse button or performs any other operation, you need to store the position and other elements; then, in the painting method, you use this information to paint the corresponding image.

This approach lets the application repaint its whole surface under any of the possible conditions. If you provide a method to redraw the contents of the form, and if this method is automatically called when a portion of the form has been hidden and needs repainting, you will be able to re-create the output properly.

Because this approach takes two steps, you must be able to execute these two operations in a row, asking the system to repaint the window—without waiting for the system to ask for a repaint operation. You can use several methods to invoke repainting: Invalidate, Update, Repaint, and Refresh. The first two correspond to the Windows API functions, and the latter two were introduced by Delphi:

◆ The Invalidate method informs Windows that the entire surface of the form should be repainted. The most important point is that Invalidate does *not* enforce a painting operation immediately. Windows stores the request and responds to it only after the current event has finished being handled (unless you call Application.ProcessMessages or Update) and as soon as no other events are pending in the system. Windows deliberately delays the painting operation because it is one of the most time-consuming operations. At times, with this delay, it is possible to paint the form only after multiple changes have taken place, avoiding multiple consecutive calls to the (slow) paint method.

◆ The Update method asks Windows to update the contents of the form, repainting it immediately. However, this operation will take place only if there is an *invalid area*. This happens if the Invalidate method has just been called or as the result of an operation by the user. If there is no invalid area, a call to Update has no effect. For this reason, it is common to see a call to Update just after a call to Invalidate as is done by the two Delphi methods Repaint and Refresh.

◆ The Repaint method calls Invalidate and Update in sequence. As a result, it activates the OnPaint event immediately. A slightly different version of this method, called Refresh, calls Repaint by default.

When you need to ask the form for a repaint operation, you should generally call `Invalidate`, following the standard Windows approach. Doing so is particularly important when you need to request this operation frequently, because if Windows takes too much time to update the screen, the requests for repainting can be accumulated into a simple repaint action. The `wm_Paint` message in Windows is a low-priority message; if a request for repainting is pending but other messages are waiting, the other messages are handled before the system performs the paint action.

On the other hand, if you call `Repaint` several times, the screen must be repainted each time before Windows can process other messages; because paint operations are computationally intensive, this behavior can make your application less responsive. Sometimes, however, you want the application to repaint a surface as quickly as possible. In these less-frequent cases, calling `Repaint` is the way to go.

NOTE Another important consideration is that during a paint operation Windows redraws only the so-called *update region*, to speed up the operation. For this reason, if you invalidate a portion of a window, only that area will be repainted. To accomplish this, you can use the `InvalidateRect` and `InvalidateRegion` functions. This feature is a double-edged sword; it is a powerful technique that can improve speed and reduce the flickering caused by frequent repaint operations, but it can also produce incorrect output. A typical problem occurs when only some of the areas affected by the user operations are modified, while others remain as they were even if the system executes the source code that is supposed to update them. If a painting operation falls outside the update region, the system ignores it as if it were outside the visible area of a window.

Unusual Graphical Techniques: Alpha Blending, Color Key, and the Animate API

One of the recent Delphi features related to forms is support for new Windows APIs that affect the way forms are painted. *Alpha blending* allows you to merge the content of a form with what's behind it on the screen—functionality you'll rarely need, at least in a business application. The technique is more interesting when applied to a bitmap (with the new `AlphaBlend` and `AlphaDIBBlend` API functions) than to a form. In any case, by setting the `AlphaBlend` property of a form to True and giving to the `AlphaBlendValue` property a value lower than 255, you'll be able to see in transparency what's behind the form. The lower the `AlphaBlendValue`, the more the form will *fade*.

Another unusual Delphi feature is the `TransparentColor` Boolean property, which allows you to indicate a transparent color that will be replaced by the background, creating a sort of hole in a form. The actual transparent color is indicated by the `TransparentColorValue` property.

Finally, you can use a native Windows technique, *animated display*, which is not directly supported by Delphi (beyond the display of hints). For example, instead of calling the `Show` method of a form, you can write

```
Form3.Hide;
AnimateWindow (Form3.Handle, 2000, AW_BLEND);
Form3.Show;
```

Notice you have to call the `Show` method at the end for the form to behave properly. You can also obtain a similar animation effect by changing the `AlphaBlendValue` property in a loop. The `AnimateWindow` API can also be used to control how the form is brought into view, starting from the center (with the `AW_CENTER` flag) or from one of its sides (`AW_HOR_POSITIVE`, `AW_HOR_NEGATIVE`, `AW_VER_POSITIVE`, or `AW_VER_NEGATIVE`), as is common for slide shows. You can apply this same function to windowed controls, obtaining a fade-in effect instead of the usual direct appearance.

Position, Size, Scrolling, and Scaling

Once you have designed a form in Delphi, you run the program and expect the form to show up exactly as you prepared it. However, a user of your application might have a different screen resolution or want to resize the form (if this is possible, depending on the border style), eventually affecting the user interface. I've already discussed (mainly in Chapter 6) some techniques related to controls, such as alignment and anchors. Here I'll specifically address elements related to the form as a whole.

In addition to differences in the user system, there are many reasons to change Delphi defaults in this area. For example, you might want to run two copies of the program and avoid having all the forms show up in exactly the same place. I've collected many other related elements, including form scrolling, in this portion of the chapter.

The Form Position

You can use a few properties to set the position of a form. The Position property indicates how Delphi determines the initial position and size of the form. The default poDesigned value indicates that the form will appear where you designed it, using the positional (Left and Top) and size (Width and Height) properties of the form.

Some of the other choices (poDefault, poDefaultPosOnly, and poDefaultSizeOnly) depend on an operating system feature: using a specific flag, Windows can position and/or size new windows using a cascade layout. The poScreenCenter value displays the form in the center of the screen, with the size you set at design time. This is a common setting for dialog boxes and other secondary forms.

Another property that affects the initial size and position of a window is its *state*. You can use the WindowState property at design time to display a maximized or minimized window at startup. Of course, you can maximize or minimize a window at run time, too; changing the value of the WindowState property to wsMaximized or wsNormal produces the expected effect. Setting the property to wsMinimized, however, creates a minimized window that is placed over the Taskbar, not within it, which is the expected action for a secondary form! The solution to this problem is to call the Minimize method of the Application object. There is also a Restore method in the TApplication class that you can use when you need to restore a form, although usually the user will perform this operation using the system menu's Restore command.

Snapping to the Screen

Forms since Delphi 7 have two additional properties. The Boolean ScreenSnap determines whether the form should be *snapped* to the display area of the screen when it is close to one of its borders. The integer SnapBuffer determines the distance from the borders considered *close*.

Although not a particularly astonishing feature, it's handy to let users snap forms to a side of the screen and take advantage of the entire screen surface; it's particularly handy for applications with multiple forms visible at the same time. Do not set too high a value for the SnapBuffer property (something as large as your screen), or the system will become confused!

The Size of a Form and Its Client Area

At design time, there are two ways to set the size of a form: by setting the value of the Width and Height properties or by setting the ClientHeight and ClientWidth properties or by dragging its borders, which modifies all four of the previously mentioned properties. The ClientHeight and ClientWidth refer to the size of the internal area of the form, the surface you can use to place components on it.

Setting the client area you need, the form size changes accordingly. Constraints, however, are based on the nonclient size, which causes issues when moving a form from Windows 2000 to Windows XP in the default big caption theme.

TIP In Windows, you can also create output and receive input from the nonclient area of the form— that is, its border. Painting on the border (other than writing to the caption) and getting input when you click it are complex issues. If you are interested, look in the Help file at the description of such Windows messages as wm_NCPaint, wm_NCCalcSize, and wm_NCHitTest and the series of nonclient messages related to the mouse input, such as wm_NCLButtonDown.

Form Constraints

When you choose a resizable border for a form, users can generally resize the form as they like, including maximizing it to full screen. Windows informs you that the form's size has changed with the wm_Size message, which generates the OnResize event. OnResize takes place after the size of the form has already been changed. Modifying the size again in this would be silly. A preventive approach is better suited to this problem.

Delphi provides a specific property for forms and for all controls: the Constraints property. Setting the subproperties of the Constraints property to the proper maximum and minimum values creates a form that cannot be resized beyond those limits. Here is an example:

```
object Form1: TForm1
  Constraints.MaxHeight = 300
  Constraints.MaxWidth = 300
  Constraints.MinHeight = 150
  Constraints.MinWidth = 150
end
```

Notice that when you set up the Constraints property, it has an immediate effect even at design time.

If you need to change constraints at run time, you can also consider using two specific events, OnCanResize and OnConstrainedResize. The first of the two can also be used to disable resizing a form or control in given circumstances.

Scrolling a Form

When you build a simple application, a single form might hold all the components you need. As the application grows, however, you may need to squeeze in the components, increase the size of the form, or add new forms. If you reduce the space occupied by the components, you might add the capability to resize them at run time, possibly splitting the form into different areas. If you choose to increase the size of the form, you might use scroll bars to let the user move around in a form that is bigger than its visible portion on the screen.

Adding a scroll bar to a form is simple. In fact, you don't need to do anything—if you place several components in a big form and then reduce its size, a scroll bar will be added to the form automatically, as long as you haven't changed the value of the AutoScroll property from its default of True.

Along with AutoScroll, forms have two properties, HorzScrollBar and VertScrollBar, which you can use to set several properties of the two TFormScrollBar objects associated with the form. The Visible property indicates whether the scroll bar is present, the Position property determines the initial status of the scroll thumb, and the Increment property determines the effect of clicking one of the arrows at the ends of the scroll bar. The most important property, however, is Range.

The Range property of a scroll bar determines the virtual size of the form, not the range of values of the scroll bar. Suppose you need a form that will host several components and will therefore need to be 1000 pixels wide. You can use this value to set the "virtual range" of the form, changing the Range of the horizontal scroll bar.

The Position property of the scroll bar will range from 0 to 1000 minus the current size of the client area. For example, if the client area of the form is 300 pixels wide, you can scroll 700 pixels to see the far end of the form (the thousandth pixel).

To better understand the specific case I just discussed, you can refer to the Scroll1 example, which has a virtual form 1000 pixels wide. I set the range of the horizontal scroll bar to 1000:

```
object Form1: TForm1
  HorzScrollBar.Range = 1000
  VertScrollBar.Range = 305
  AutoScroll = False
  OnResize = FormResize
  ...
```

The interesting part of the example is the presence of a toolbox window displaying the status of the form and its horizontal scroll bar. This is obtained by handling the OnResize event and directly intercepting the wm_HScroll message. Refer to the program code for more details.

The scroll bar's Range property represents the "virtual range" of the form. The scroll bar is automatically removed from the form when the client area of the form is big enough to accommodate the virtual size; when you reduce the size of the form, the scroll bar is added again.

This feature becomes particularly interesting when the AutoScroll property of the form is set to True. In this case, the extreme positions of the right-most and lower controls are automatically copied into the Range properties of the form's two scroll bars.

Creating and Closing Forms

Up to now I have ignored the issue of form creation. You know that when the form is created, you receive the OnCreate event and can change or test some of the initial form's properties or fields. The statement responsible for creating the form is in the project's source file:

```
begin
  Application.Initialize;
  Application.CreateForm(TForm1, Form1);
  Application.Run;
end.
```

To skip the automatic form creation, you can either modify this code or use the Forms page of the Project Options dialog box (see Figure 7.4). In this dialog box, you can decide whether the form should be automatically created. If you disable automatic creation, the project's initialization code becomes the following:

```
begin
  Applications.Initialize;
  Application.Run;
end.
```

FIGURE 7.4

The Forms page of the Delphi Project Options dialog box

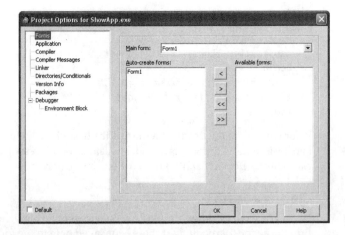

If you now run this program, nothing happens. It terminates immediately because no main window is created. The call to the application's CreateForm method creates a new instance of the form class passed as the first parameter and assigns it to the variable passed as the second parameter.

Something else happens behind the scenes. When CreateForm is called, if there is currently no main form, the current form is assigned to the application's MainForm property. For this reason, the form indicated as Main Form in the dialog box shown in Figure 7.4 corresponds to the first call to the application's CreateForm method (that is, when several forms are created at startup).

The same holds for closing the application. Closing the main form terminates the application, regardless of the other forms. If you want to perform this operation from the program's code, call the Close method of the main form, as you've done several times in past examples.

Form Creation Events

Regardless of the manual or automatic creation of forms, when a form is created, you can intercept many events. Form-creation events are fired in the following order:

1. OnCreate indicates that the form is being created.

2. OnShow indicates that the form is being displayed. In addition to main forms, this event happens after you set the Visible property of the form to True or call the Show or ShowModal method. This event is fired again if the form is hidden and then displayed again.

3. OnActivate indicates that the form becomes the active form within the application. This event is fired every time you move from another form of the application to the current one.

4. Other events, including OnResize and OnPaint, indicate operations always done at startup but then repeated many times.

As you can see in the previous list, every event has a specific role apart from form initialization, except OnCreate, which is guaranteed to be called only once as the form is created.

However, there is an alternative approach to adding initialization code to a form: overriding the constructor. This is usually done as follows:

```
constructor TForm1.Create(AOwner: TComponent);
begin
  inherited Create (AOwner);
  // extra initialization code
end;
```

Before the call to the Create method of the base class, the properties of the form are still not loaded and the internal components are not available. For this reason the standard approach is to call the base class constructor first and then do the custom operations.

Closing a Form

When you close the form, the OnCloseQuery event is called. In this event, you can ask the user to confirm the action, particularly if there is unsaved data in the form. Here is an example of the code you can write:

```
procedure TForm1.FormCloseQuery(Sender: TObject; var CanClose: Boolean);
begin
  if MessageDlg ('Are you sure you want to exit?', mtConfirmation,
      [mbYes, mbNo], 0) in [mrNo, mrCancel] then
    CanClose := False;
end;
```

If OnCloseQuery indicates that the form should still be closed, the OnClose event is called. The third step is to call the OnDestroy event, which is the opposite of the OnCreate event. In Win32 OnDestroy is generally used to de-allocate objects related to the form and free the corresponding memory, while in .NET it can be used to make the internal objects drop their unmanaged resources by calling Dispose or Free.

So what is the use of the intermediate OnClose event? In this method, you have another chance to avoid closing the application, or you can specify alternative "close actions." The method has an Action parameter passed by reference. You can assign the following values to this parameter:

caNone   The form is not allowed to close. This corresponds to setting the CanClose parameter of the OnCloseQuery method to False.

caHide   The form is not closed, just hidden. This makes sense if there are other forms in the application; otherwise, the program terminates. This is the default for secondary forms.

caFree   The form is closed, freeing its memory, and the application eventually terminates if this is the main form. This is the default action for the main form and the action you should use when you create multiple forms dynamically (if you want to remove the windows and destroy the corresponding Delphi object as the form closes).

caMinimize   The form is not closed but only minimized. This is the default action for MDI child forms.

NOTE   When a user shuts down Windows, the OnCloseQuery event is activated, and a program can use it to stop the shutdown process. In this case, the OnClose event is not called even if OnCloseQuery sets the CanClose parameter to True.

Dialog Boxes and Other Secondary Forms

When you write a program, there is no significant difference between a dialog box and another secondary form, aside from the border, the border icons, and similar user-interface elements you can customize.

What users associate with a dialog box is the concept of a *modal window*—a window that takes the focus and must be closed before the user can move back to the main window. This is true for message boxes and usually for dialog boxes, as well. However, you can also have nonmodal—or *modeless*— dialog boxes.

So if you think dialog boxes are just modal forms, you are on the right track but your description is not precise. In Delphi (as in Windows), you can have modeless dialog boxes and modal forms. You must consider two different elements: the form's border and its user interface determine whether it looks like a dialog box; the use of two different methods (Show and ShowModal) to display the secondary form determines its behavior (modeless or modal).

Adding a Second Form to a Program

To add a second form to a VCL for Win32 application, you can use the File ➤ New ➤ Form – Delphi for Win32 menu command or use the New Items dialog box (File ➤ New ➤ Other).

If you have two forms in a project, you can use the View Form or View Unit button on the Delphi toolbar to navigate through them at design time. You can also choose which form is the main one and which forms should be automatically created at startup using the Forms page of the Project Options dialog box. This information is reflected in the source code of the project file.

TIP   Secondary forms are automatically created in the project source-code file depending on the status of the Auto Create Forms & Data Modules check box of the Environment Options/Delphi Options/VCL Designer page of the Options dialog box. Although automatic creation is the simplest and most reliable approach for novice developers and quick-and-dirty projects, I suggest that you disable this check box for any serious development. When your application contains hundreds of forms, they shouldn't all be created at application startup. Create instances of secondary forms when and where you need them, and free them when you're done.

Once you have prepared the secondary form, you can set its Visible property to True, and both forms will show up as the program starts. In general, the secondary forms of an application are left "invisible" and are then displayed by calling the Show method (or setting the Visible property at run time). If you use the Show function, the second form will be displayed as modeless, so you can move back to the first form while the second is still visible. To close the second form, you might use its system menu or click a button or menu item that calls the Close method. As you've just seen, the default close action (see the OnClose event) for a secondary form is simply to hide it, so the secondary form is not destroyed when it is closed. It is kept in memory (again, not always the best approach) and is available if you want to show it again.

Creating Secondary Forms at Run Time

Unless you create all the forms when the program starts, you'll need to check whether a form exists and create it if necessary. The simplest case occurs when you want to create multiple copies of the same form at run time. In the MultiWin example, I did this by writing the following code:

```
with TForm3.Create (Application) do
  Show;
```

Every time you click the button, a new copy of the form is created. Notice that I don't use the Form3 global variable, because it doesn't make much sense to assign this variable a new value every time you create a new form object. The important thing, however, is not to refer to the global Form3 object in the code of the form or in other portions of the application. The Form3 variable will invariably be a pointer to nil. My suggestion in such a case is to remove it from the unit to avoid any confusion.

TIP In the code of a form that can have multiple instances, you should never explicitly refer to the form by using the global variable Delphi sets up for it. For example, suppose that in the code for TForm3 you refer to Form3.Caption. If you create a second object of the same type (the class TForm3), the expression Form3.Caption will refer to the caption of the form object referenced by the Form3 variable, which might not be the current object executing the code. To avoid this problem, refer to the Caption property in the form's method to indicate the caption of the current form object, and use the Self keyword when you need a specific reference to the object of the current form. To avoid any problem when creating multiple copies of a form, I suggest removing the global form object from the interface portion of the unit declaring the form. This global variable is required only for the automatic form creation.

When you create multiple copies of a modeless form dynamically, remember to destroy each form object as is it closed, by handling the corresponding event:

```
procedure TForm3.FormClose(Sender: TObject; var Action: TCloseAction);
begin
  Action := caFree;
end;
```

Failing to do so will result in a lot of memory consumption because all the forms you create (both the windows and the Delphi objects) will be kept in memory and hidden from view.

CREATING SINGLE-INSTANCE SECONDARY FORMS

Now let's focus on the dynamic creation of a form in a program that requires only one copy of the form at a time. Creating a modal form is quite simple because the dialog box can be destroyed when it is closed, with code like this:

```
var
  Modal: TForm4;
begin
  Modal := TForm4.Create (Application);
  try
    Modal.ShowModal;
  finally
    Modal.Free;
  end;
```

Because the ShowModal call can raise an exception, you should write it in a try block followed by a finally block with a call to the Free method. Usually the try block also includes code that initializes the dialog box before displaying it and code that extracts the values set by the user before destroying the form. The final values are read-only if the result of the ShowModal function is mrOK, as you'll see in the next example.

The situation is a little more complex when you want to display only one copy of a modeless form. You have to create the form, if it is not already available, and then show it:

```
if not Assigned (Form2) then
  Form2 := TForm2.Create (Application);
Form2.Show;
```

With this code, the form is created the first time it is required and then kept in memory, visible on the screen or hidden from view. To avoid using up memory and system resources unnecessarily, you'll want to destroy the secondary form when it is closed. You can do that by writing a handler for the OnClose event:

```
procedure TForm2.FormClose(Sender: TObject; var Action: TCloseAction);
begin
  Action := caFree;
  // important: set pointer to nil!
  Form2 := nil;
end;
```

After you destroy the form, the global Form2 variable is set to nil, which contradicts the rule set earlier for forms with multiple instances; but as this is a single-instance, it is the exact opposite case. Without this code, closing the form would destroy its object, but the Form2 variable would still refer to the original memory location. At this point, if you try to show the form once more with the btnSingleClick method shown earlier, the if not Assigned() test will succeed because it checks whether the Form2 variable is nil. The code fails to create a new object, and the Show method (invoked on a nonexistent object) will result in a system memory error.

As an experiment, you can generate this error by removing the last line of the previous listing. As you have seen, the solution is to set the Form2 object to nil when the object is destroyed so that properly written code will "see" that a new form must be created before using it. Again, experimenting with the MultiWin example can prove useful to test various conditions. (I haven't shown any screens from this example because the forms it displays are totally empty except for the main form, which has three buttons.)

NOTE   Setting the form variable to nil makes sense—and works—if there is to be only one instance of the form present at any given instant. If you want to create multiple copies of a form, you'll have to use other techniques to keep track of them. Also keep in mind that in this case you cannot use the FreeAndNil procedure because you cannot call Free on Form2—you should not destroy the form before its event handlers have finished executing.

Modal Forms and the New *PopupMode*

There is a long-standing problem in the VCL (and partially in Windows) that causes some modal forms and message boxes to be displayed behind their parent window. This problem became relevant in Windows XP, due to internal changes in the operating system. The reason for this problem is that there is actually no parent form for a main window, only a possible reference to a pop-up parent that Delphi did not always handle properly. This pop-up parent is the window behind the current one in the z-order, the order forms are stacked on the screen.

In Delphi 2005, VCL forms have two new properties you can use to solve this problem (in case you see it in your own programs):

◆   The PopupMode property indicates the "pop-up" behavior of the form. This property determines how the form handles the WS_POPUP style of the form window. Notice that if you set the value to pmAuto, the VCL recreates the form on a ShowModal call. Use pmExplicit for tool palettes and nonmodal floating windows.

◆   The PopupParent property indicates the parent form on the z-order stack. This works somewhat like a stay-on-top window, but with better programmatic control.

Creating a Dialog Box

I stated earlier in this chapter that a dialog box is not very different from other forms. To build a dialog box instead of a form, you just select the bsDialog value for the BorderStyle property. With this simple change, the interface of the form becomes like that of a dialog box, with no system icon and no Minimize and Maximize boxes. Of course, such a form has the typical thick dialog box border, which is nonresizable.

Once you build a dialog box form, you can display it as a modal or modeless window using the two usual show methods (Show and ShowModal). Modal dialog boxes, however, are more common than modeless ones. This is the reverse of forms; modal forms should generally be avoided because a user won't expect them.

The Dialog Box of the RefList Example

In Chapter 6, you explored the RefList program, which used a ListView control to display references to books, magazines, websites, and more. In the RefList2 version, I added to the basic version a dialog box that's used for two different purposes: adding new items to the list and editing existing items.

The only particularly interesting feature of this form is the use of the ComboBoxEx component, which is attached to the same ImageList used by the ListView control of the main form. The drop-down items of the list, used to select a type of reference, include both a textual description and the corresponding image.

As I mentioned, this dialog box is used in two different cases. The first takes place as the user selects File ➢ Add Items from the menu:

```
procedure TForm1.AddItems1Click(Sender: TObject);
var
  NewItem: TListItem;
begin
  FormItem.Caption := 'New Item';
  FormItem.Clear;
  if FormItem.ShowModal = mrOK then
  begin
    NewItem := ListView1.Items.Add;
    NewItem.Caption := FormItem.EditReference.Text;
```

```
    NewItem.ImageIndex := FormItem.ComboType.ItemIndex;
    NewItem.SubItems.Add (FormItem.EditAuthor.Text);
    NewItem.SubItems.Add (FormItem.EditCountry.Text);
  end;
end;
```

In addition to setting the proper caption for the form, this procedure initializes the dialog box because you are entering a new value. If the user clicks OK, however, the program adds a new item to the list view and sets all its values. To empty the dialog's edit boxes, the program calls the custom Clear method, which resets the text of each edit box control:

```
procedure TFormItem.Clear;
var
  I: Integer;
begin
  // clear each edit box
  for I := 0 to ControlCount - 1 do
    if Controls [I] is TEdit then
      TEdit (Controls[I]).Text := '';
end;
```

Editing an existing item requires a slightly different approach. First, the current values are moved to the dialog box before it is displayed. Second, if the user clicks OK, the program modifies the current list item instead of creating a new one. Here is the code:

```
procedure TForm1.ListView1DblClick(Sender: TObject);
begin
  if ListView1.Selected <> nil then
  begin
    // dialog initialization
    FormItem.Caption := 'Edit Item';
    FormItem.EditReference.Text := ListView1.Selected.Caption;
    FormItem.ComboType.ItemIndex := ListView1.Selected.ImageIndex;
    FormItem.EditAuthor.Text := ListView1.Selected.SubItems [0];
    FormItem.EditCountry.Text := ListView1.Selected.SubItems [1];

    // show it
    if FormItem.ShowModal = mrOK then
    begin
      // read the new values
      ListView1.Selected.Caption := FormItem.EditReference.Text;
      ListView1.Selected.ImageIndex := FormItem.ComboType.ItemIndex;
      ListView1.Selected.SubItems [0] := FormItem.EditAuthor.Text;
      ListView1.Selected.SubItems [1] := FormItem.EditCountry.Text;
    end;
  end;
end;
```

You can see the effect of this code in Figure 7.5. The code used to read the value of a new item or modified item is similar. In general, you should try to avoid this type of duplicated code and perhaps place the shared code statements in a method added to the dialog box. In this case, the method could receive as parameter a TListItem object and copy the proper values into it.

NOTE What happens internally when the user clicks the OK or Cancel button in the dialog box? A modal dialog box is closed by setting its ModalResult property to a non-mrNone value, and it returns the value of this property. You can indicate the return value by setting the ModalResult property of the button. When the user clicks the button, its ModalResult value is copied to the form, which closes the form and returns the value as the result of the ShowModal function.

FIGURE 7.5

The dialog box of the RefList2 example used in edit mode. Notice the ComboBoxEx graphical component in use.

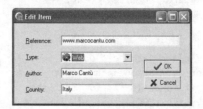

A Modeless Dialog Box

The second example of dialog boxes shows a more complex modal dialog box that uses the standard approach as well as a modeless dialog box. The main form of the DlgApply example has five labels with names, as you can see in Figure 7.6 and in the source code of the example.

If the user double-clicks a name, the program displays a modal dialog box with a list of names to choose from. If the user clicks the Style button, a modeless dialog box appears, allowing the user to change the font style of the main form's labels. The LabelDoubleClick method selects the Caption of the current label (indicated by the Sender parameter) in the list box of the dialog and then shows the modal dialog box. If the user closes the dialog box by clicking OK and a list item is selected, the selection is copied back to the label's caption:

```
procedure TForm1.LabelDoubleClick(Sender: TObject);
begin
  with ListDial.Listbox1 do
  begin
    // select the current name in the list box
    ItemIndex := Items.IndexOf (Sender as TLabel).Caption);
    // show the modal dialog box, checking the return value
    if (ListDial.ShowModal = mrOk) and (ItemIndex >= 0) then
      // copy the selected item to the label
      (Sender as TLabel).Caption := Items [ItemIndex];
  end;
end;
```

The modeless dialog box, by contrast, has a lot of coding behind it. The main form displays the dialog box when the Style button is clicked (notice that the button caption ends with three dots to indicate that it leads to a dialog box), by calling its Show method. You can see the dialog box running in Figure 7.6.

FIGURE 7.6

The three forms (a main form and two dialog boxes) of the DlgApply example at run time

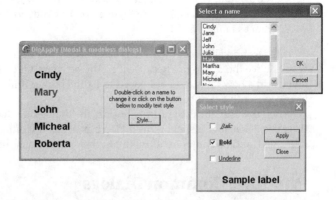

If the user clicks one of the check boxes in this modeless dialog box, the style of the sample label's text at the bottom changes accordingly. You accomplish this by adding or removing the specific flag that indicates the style, as in the following OnClick event handler:

```
procedure TStyleDial.ItalicCheckBoxClick(Sender: TObject);
begin
  if ItalicCheckBox.Checked then
    LabelSample.Font.Style := LabelSample.Font.Style + [fsItalic]
  else
    LabelSample.Font.Style := LabelSample.Font.Style - [fsItalic];
end;
```

When the user clicks the Apply button, the program copies the style of the sample label to each of the form's labels rather than considering the values of the check boxes:

```
procedure TStyleDial.btnApplyClick(Sender: TObject);
begin
  Form1.Label1.Font.Style := LabelSample.Font.Style;
  Form1.Label2.Font.Style := LabelSample.Font.Style;
  ...
```

As an alternative, instead of referring to each label directly, you can look for it by calling the FindComponent method of the form, passing the label name as a parameter, and then casting the result to the TLabel type. The advantage of this approach is that you can create the names of the various labels with a for loop:

```
procedure TStyleDial.btnApplyClick(Sender: TObject);
var
  I: Integer;
begin
  for I := 1 to 5 do
    (Form1.FindComponent ('Label' + IntToStr (I)) as TLabel).
      Font.Style := LabelSample.Font.Style;
end;
```

TIP The btnApplyClick method can also be written by scanning the Controls array in a loop, as I've done in other examples. I decided to use the FindComponent method here to demonstrate a different technique.

This second version of the code is certainly slower because it has more operations to do, but you won't notice the difference because it is still very fast. Of course, this approach is also more flexible; if you add a new label, you only need to fix the higher limit of the for loop, provided all the labels have consecutive numbers.

When the user clicks the Apply button, the dialog box does not close—only the Close button has this effect. Consider also that this dialog box needs no initialization code because the form is not destroyed, and its components maintain their status each time the dialog box is displayed.

Windows Common Dialogs

In addition to building your own dialog boxes, Delphi allows you to use some default dialog boxes of various kinds. The Delphi Component Palette contains a page of dialog box components. Each of these dialog boxes—known as *Windows common dialogs*—is defined in the system library ComDlg32.DLL.

I have already used some of these dialog boxes in several examples in the previous chapters, so you are probably familiar with them. Basically, you need to put the corresponding component on a form, set some of its properties, run the dialog box (with the Execute method returning a Boolean value), and retrieve the properties that have been set while running it.

NOTE Delphi 2005 adds an overloaded version of Execute with a Handle parameter. This is used in the DoExecute internal methods of most common dialogs. The plain and traditional Execute function now calls the other Execute, passing the handle of the active window of the application (Application.ActiveFormHandle). This code was introduced to support better z-order and redirector windows (see the end of this section).

To help you experiment with these dialog boxes, I built the CommDlgTest program. I'll highlight some key and nonobvious features of the common dialog boxes and let you study the source code of the example for the details:

◆ The Open Dialog Component can be customized by setting different file extension filters using the Filter property, which has a handy editor and can be assigned a value directly with a string like Text File (*.txt)|*.txt. Another useful feature lets the dialog check whether the extension of the selected file matches the default extension, by checking the ofExtensionDifferent flag of the Options property after executing the dialog. Finally, this dialog allows multiple selections by setting its ofAllowMultiSelect option. In this case you can get the list of selected files by looking at the Files string list property.

◆ The SaveDialog component is used in similar ways and has similar properties, although of course you cannot select multiple files.

◆ The OpenPictureDialog and SavePictureDialog components provide similar features but have a customized area of the dialog that shows a preview of an image. It makes sense to use these components only for opening or saving graphical files.

◆ The new (in Delphi 2005) OpenTextFileDialog and SaveTextFileDialog components provide another extension with a combo box asking for the text format.

◆ The FontDialog component can be used to show and select all types of fonts, fonts usable on both the screen and a selected printer (WYSIWYG), or only TrueType fonts. You can show or hide the portion related to the special effects and obtain other different versions by setting its `Options` property. You can also activate an Apply button by providing an event handler for its `OnApply` event and using the fdApplyButton option.

◆ The ColorDialog component is used with different options to show the dialog fully open at first or to prevent it from opening fully. These settings are the cdFullOpen or cdPreventFullOpen values of the `Options` property.

◆ The Find and Replace dialog boxes are truly modeless dialogs, but you have to implement the find and replace functionality yourself, as I did partially in the CommDlgTest example. The custom code is connected to the buttons of the two dialog boxes by providing the `OnFind` and `OnReplace` events.

The *Application* Object

I've mentioned the `Application` global object on multiple occasions, but because this chapter focuses on the structure of Delphi applications, it is time to delve into the details of this global object and its corresponding class. `Application` is a global object of the `TApplication` class, defined in the Forms unit and created in the Controls unit. The `TApplication` class is a component, but you cannot use it at design time. Some of its properties can be directly set in the Application page of the Project Options dialog box; others must be assigned in code.

To handle its events, Delphi includes a handy ApplicationEvents component. In addition to allowing you to assign handlers at design time, the advantage of this component is that it allows for multiple handlers. If you simply place an instance of the ApplicationEvents component in two different forms, each of them can handle the same event, and both event handlers will be executed. In other words, multiple ApplicationEvents components can chain the handlers.

Some of these application-wide events, including `OnActivate`, `OnDeactivate`, `OnMinimize`, and `OnRestore`, allow you to keep track of the status of the application. Other events are forwarded to the application by the controls receiving them, such as `OnActionExecute`, `OnActionUpdate`, `OnHelp`, `OnHint`, `OnShortCut`, and `OnShowHint`. Finally, there is the `OnException` global exception handler we used in Chapter 3, the `OnIdle` event used for background computing, and the `OnMessage` event, which fires when a message is posted to any of the windows or windowed controls of the application.

Although its class inherits directly from `TComponent`, the `Application` object has a window associated with it. The application window is hidden from sight but appears on the Taskbar. This is why in a new Delphi project the main form has a caption like *Form1* but the corresponding Taskbar button has a caption like *Project1*.

The window related to the `Application` object—the application window—serves to keep together all the windows of an application. The fact that all the top-level forms of a program have this invisible owner window, for example, is fundamental when the application is activated. When your program's windows are behind other programs' windows, clicking one window in your application will bring all of that application's windows to the front. In other words, the unseen application window is used to connect the application's various forms. (The application window is not *hidden*, because that would affect its behavior; it simply has zero height and width and therefore is not visible.)

TIP In Windows, the Minimize and Maximize operations are associated by default with system sounds and a visual animated effect. Applications built with Delphi produce the sound and display the visual effect by default.

When you create a new, blank application, Delphi generates code for the project file that includes the following:

```
begin
  Application.Initialize;
  Application.CreateForm(TForm1, Form1);
  Application.Run;
end.
```

As you can see in this standard code, the `Application` object can create forms, setting the first one as the `MainForm` (one of the `Application` properties) and closing the entire application when this main form is destroyed. The program execution is enclosed in the Run method, which embeds the system loop to process system messages. This loop continues until the application's main window (the first window you created) is closed.

The Windows message loop embedded in the Run method delivers the system messages to the proper application windows. A message loop is required by any Windows application, but you don't need to write one in Delphi because the `Application` object provides a default loop.

In addition to performing this main role, the `Application` object manages a few other interesting areas:

♦ Hints (discussed at the end of Chapter 6)

♦ The help system, which includes the ability to define the type of help viewer (a topic not covered in detail in this book)

♦ Application activation, minimization, and restoration

♦ A global exceptions handler, as discussed in the ErrorLog example of Chapter 3

♦ General application information, including the `MainForm`, executable filename and path (`ExeName`), Icon, and `Title` that are displayed in the Windows Taskbar and when you scan the running applications with the Alt+Tab keys

TIP To avoid a discrepancy between the two titles, you can change the application's title at design time. If the caption of the main form changes at run time, you can copy it to the title of the application with this code: `Application.Title := Form1.Caption`.

In most applications, you don't care about the application window apart from setting its `Title` and icon and handling some of its events. However, you can perform some other simple operations. Setting the `ShowMainForm` property to False in the project source code indicates that the main form should not be displayed at startup. Inside a program, you can use the `Application` object's `MainForm` property to access the main form.

NOTE There is no better proof that a window exists for the `Application` object than to display it, as in the ShowApp example. As you can see in its source code, this programs uses the `SetWindowLong` API to change the style of this window and the `SetWindowPos` API to resize it.

Activating Applications and Forms

To show how the activation of forms and applications works, I wrote a self-explanatory example called ActivApp. This example has two forms. Each form has a Label component (LabelForm) used to display the form's status. The program uses text and color to indicate this status information, as the handlers of the first form's OnActivate and OnDeactivate events demonstrate:

```
procedure TForm1.FormActivate(Sender: TObject);
begin
  LabelForm.Caption := 'Form1 Active';
  LabelForm.Color := clRed;
end;

procedure TForm1.FormDeactivate(Sender: TObject);
begin
  LabelForm.Caption := 'Form1 Not Active';
  LabelForm.Color := clBtnFace;
end;
```

The second form has a similar label and similar code.

The main form also displays the status of the entire application. It uses an ApplicationEvents component to handle the Application object's OnActivate and OnDeactivate events. These two event handlers are similar to the two listed previously; the only difference is that they modify the text and color of a second label on the form and that one of them makes a beep.

If you run this program, you'll see whether this application is active and, if so, which of its forms is active. By looking at the output (see Figure 7.7) and listening for the beep, you can understand how Delphi triggers each of the activation events.

FIGURE 7.7

The ActivApp example shows whether the application is active and which of the application's forms is active.

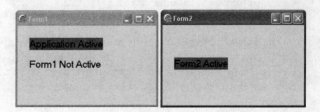

Processing Mouse Activation in Delphi 2005

When you select with the mouse an inactive form or a form of an inactive application, it receives a specific Windows activation message followed by the specific message caused by the mouse operation. So if you click a button to activate an application, not only do you obtain this effect, but you also press the button and execute the corresponding action. This might not be what every user expects, although some will be okay with this behavior.

To modify this standard VCL behavior, you could try handling the wm_MouseActivate windows message, but Delphi 2005 adds a specific ready-to-use event in the TControl class and publishes it in any inherited control, including forms. By *intercepting* this event you can *eat* the mouse message and stop it from reaching its target. The only trouble is that if you stop the mouse-activate event every time, you'll also stop requests received when the form and application are already active. In other words, your code needs to check for the activation state of form and application (as discussed in the previous section) and eventually stop the message flow.

The FormMouseActivate example shows how you can handle this event in a form:

```
procedure TForm11.FormMouseActivate(Sender: TObject;
  Button: TMouseButton; Shift: TShiftState;
  X, Y, HitTest: Integer; var MouseActivate: TMouseActivate);
begin
  if not Application.Active or not Active then
    MouseActivate := maActivateAndEat
  else
    MouseActivate := maDefault;
end;
```

Notice that if you run this program, when it is not active and you click the Close button of the form, it will be activated but not closed. I like this, but if you want a different behavior you can check the value of the HitTest parameter (see again the NoTitle application for an example of the use of a hit test).

Tracking Forms with the *Screen* Object

We have already explored some of the properties and events of the Application object. Other interesting global information about an application is available through the Screen object, whose class is TScreen. This object holds information about the system display (the screen size and the screen fonts) and about the current set of forms in a running application. For example, you can display the screen size and the list of fonts by writing:

```
Label1.Caption := IntToStr (Screen.Width) + 'x' +
  IntToStr (Screen.Height);
ListBox1.Items := Screen.Fonts;
```

The Screen object also reports the number and resolution of monitors in a multimonitor system. Right now, however, I will focus on the list of forms held by the Screen object's Forms property, the top-most form indicated by the ActiveForm property, and the related OnActiveFormChange event. Note that the forms the Screen object references are the forms of the application and not those of the system.

These features are demonstrated by the Screen example, which maintains a list of the current forms in a list box. This list is updated each time a new form is created, an existing form is destroyed, or the program's active form changes. One of the key portions of the program is the form's OnCreate event handler, which fills the list the first time and then connects a handler to the OnActiveFormChange event:

```
procedure TMainForm.FormCreate(Sender: TObject);
begin
  FillFormsList (Screen);
  // set the secondary form's counter to 0
  nForms := 0;
  // set an event handler on the screen object
  Screen.OnActiveFormChange := FillFormsList;
end;
```

The code used to fill the main form list box (part of the FillFormsList method) is the following:

```
for I := 0 to Screen.FormCount - 1 do
  FormsListBox.Items.Add (Screen.Forms[I].ClassName + ' - ' +
    Screen.Forms[I].Caption);
```

WARNING It is very important not to execute this code while the main form is being destroyed. As an alternative to testing whether the list box is set to nil, you could test the form's ComponentState for the csDestroying flag. Another approach is to remove the OnActiveFormChange event handler before exiting the application; that is, handle the main form's OnClose event and assign nil to Screen.OnActiveFormChange.

Figure 7.8 shows the output of this program when some secondary windows have been created. Each secondary form has a Close button and an OnClose event handler that sets the Action parameter to caFree so that the form is destroyed when it is closed. This code doesn't update the list of the windows properly. The system moves the focus to another window first, firing the event that updates the list and destroys the old form only after this operation.

The first idea I had to update the windows list properly was to introduce a delay, posting a user-defined Windows message. Because the posted message is queued and not handled immediately, if you send it at the last possible moment of the secondary form's life, the main form will receive it when the other form is destroyed. The trick is to post the message in the secondary form's OnDestroy event handler. The handler of this message refreshes the list of forms:

```
public
  procedure ChildClosed (var Message: TMessage); message wm_App;

procedure TMainForm.ChildClosed (var Message: TMessage);
begin
  FillFormsList (Screen);
end;
```

The problem is that if you close the main window before closing the secondary forms, the main form exists but its code can no longer be executed: you need to post the message only if the main form is not closing. But how do you determine whether the form is closing? One way is to add a flag to the TMainForm class and change its value when the main form is closing, so that you can test the flag from the code of the secondary window.

FIGURE 7.8
The output of the Screen example with some secondary forms

This is a good solution—so good that the VCL already provides similar functionality with the ComponentState property and its csDestroying flag. Therefore, you can write the following code:

```
procedure TSecondForm.FormDestroy(Sender: TObject);
begin
  if not (csDestroying in MainForm.ComponentState) then
    PostMessage (MainForm.Handle, wm_App, 0, 0);
end;
```

With this code, the list box always lists all the forms in the application.

The Screen2 version of the program includes an alternative and much more Delphi-oriented solution. The trick is to consider that every time a component is destroyed, it tells its owner about the event by calling the Notification method defined in the TComponent class. Because the secondary forms are owned by the main form, as specified in the NewButtonClick method's code, you can override this method and simplify the code by far (see the Screen2 folder for this version's code):

```
procedure TMainForm.Notification(AComponent: TComponent;
  Operation: TOperation);
begin
  inherited Notification(AComponent, Operation);
  if (Operation = opRemove) and Showing and (AComponent is TForm) then
    FillFormsList;
end;
```

NOTE   If the secondary forms were not owned by the main form, you could have used the FreeNotification method to get the secondary forms to notify the main form when they were destroyed. FreeNotification receives as parameter the component to notify when the current component is destroyed. The effect is a call to the Notification method that comes from a component other than the owned components. FreeNotification is generally used by component writers to safely connect components on different forms or data modules.

Creating MDI Applications

An MDI (Multiple Document Interface) application is made up of several forms that appear inside a single main form. This was a common approach for an application's structure that has become less and less common over the years. MDI has been replaced by SDI applications (in which every document has its own stand-alone form) or a tabbed interface (in which different documents are in different tabbed pages and not floating in a container like in MDI).

The MDI structure gives programmers several benefits automatically. For example, Windows handles a list of the child windows in one of an MDI application's pull-down menus, and specific Delphi methods activate the corresponding MDI functionality to tile or cascade the child windows. The following is the technical structure of an MDI application in Windows:

◆ The main window of the application acts as a frame or a container.

◆ A special window, known as the *MDI client,* covers the whole client area of the frame window. This MDI client is one of the Windows predefined controls, just like an edit box or a list box.

◆ There are generally one or more child windows of the same or different kinds. These child windows are not placed in the frame window directly, but each is defined as a child of the MDI client window, which in turn is a child of the frame window.

Frame and Child Windows in Delphi

Delphi makes it easy to develop MDI applications. You only need to set the FormStyle property of the main form to fsMDIForm and the same property of a secondary form to fsMDIChild. Set these two properties in a simple program and run it, and you'll see the two forms nested in the typical MDI style. Generally, however, you don't have a single child form created at startup but a way to add more forms dynamically.

An important feature to add to an MDI program is a Window pull-down menu, which you specify as the value of the form's WindowMenu property. This pull-down menu will automatically list all the available child windows. (Of course, you can choose any other name for the pull-down menu, but Window is the standard.)

To make this program work properly, you can add a number to the title of any child window when it is created:

```
procedure TMainForm.New1Click(Sender: TObject);
var
  ChildForm: TChildForm;
begin
  WindowMenu := Window1;
  Inc (Counter);
  ChildForm := TChildForm.Create (Self);
  ChildForm.Caption := ChildForm.Caption + ' ' + IntToStr (Counter);
  ChildForm.Show;
end;
```

Now suppose you want to close some of these child windows: clicking their Close boxes minimizes them! Delphi by default minimizes the MDI child windows when you try to close them, because hiding them (as it does with secondary forms) would keep them listed in the Window menu. To change this default, set the Action parameter of the OnClose event of the child windows to caFree.

The MdiDemo Example

I built an example to demonstrate most of the features of a simple MDI application. MdiDemo is a full-blown MDI text editor because each child window hosts a Memo component and can open and save text files. The child form has a Modified property that indicates whether the text of the memo has changed (it is set to True in the handler of the memo's OnChange event). Modified is set to False in the Save and Load custom methods and is checked when the form is closed (prompting the user to save the file).

The example's main form is based on an ActionList component. The actions are available through some menu items and a toolbar, as shown in Figure 7.9. You can see the details of the ActionList in the example's source code; I'll focus on the code of the custom actions. More details on the ActionList components are available in the next chapter.

One of the actions is the ActionFont object, which has both an OnExecute handler (which uses a FontDialog component) and an OnUpdate handler (which disables the action—and hence the associated menu item and toolbar button—when there are no child forms):

```
procedure TMainForm.ActionFontExecute(Sender: TObject);
begin
  if FontDialog1.Execute then
    (ActiveMDIChild as TChildForm).Memo1.Font := FontDialog1.Font;
```

```
  end;

  procedure TMainForm.ActionFontUpdate(Sender: TObject);
  begin
    ActionFont.Enabled := MDIChildCount > 0;
  end;
```

The action named New creates the child form and sets a default filename. The Open action calls the ActionNewExecute method prior to loading the file:

```
  procedure TMainForm.ActionNewExecute(Sender: TObject);
  var
    ChildForm: TChildForm;
  begin
    Inc (Counter);
    ChildForm := TChildForm.Create (Self);
    ChildForm.Caption :=
      LowerCase (ExtractFilePath (Application.Exename)) + 'text' +
      IntToStr (Counter) + '.txt';
    ChildForm.Show;
  end;

  procedure TMainForm.ActionOpenExecute(Sender: TObject);
  begin
    if OpenDialog1.Execute then
    begin
      ActionNewExecute (Self);
      (ActiveMDIChild as TChildForm).Load (OpenDialog1.FileName);
    end;
  end;
```

The file loading is performed by the form's Load method. Likewise, the child form's Save method is used by the Save and Save As actions, as you can see in the source code.

FIGURE 7.9

The MdiDemo program uses a series of pre-defined Delphi actions connected to a menu and a toolbar.

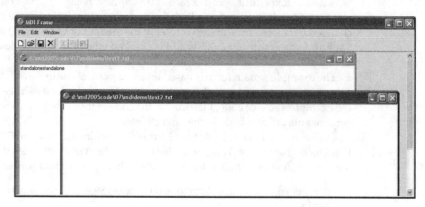

The MdiMulti Example

If you wish to use the MDI architecture (something I don't really encourage), you'll find it interesting to look at the MdiMulti example, which has many extra features, including:

◆ Child windows of different kinds (that is, based on different child forms).

◆ Child forms with a main menu that merges with the main form menu; this is obtained with the appropriate setting for the GroupIndex property of the various pull-down menus.

◆ A *subclassed* MDI Client window to obtain a background with a tiled image. Subclassing is a Windows technique for modifying the behavior of a predefined form, like the MDI Client.

Visual Form Inheritance

When you need to build two or more similar forms, possibly with different event handlers, you can use dynamic techniques, hide or create new components at run time, change event handlers, and use if or case statements. Or you can apply the object-oriented techniques, thanks to visual form inheritance. In short, instead of creating a form based on TForm, you can inherit a form from an existing form, adding new components or altering the properties of the existing components. But what is the advantage of visual form inheritance?

It mostly depends on the kind of application you are building. If the program has multiple forms, some of which are very similar or simply include common elements, then you can place the common components and the common event handlers in the base form and add the specific behavior and components to the inherited classes. For example, if you prepare a standard base form with a toolbar, a logo, default sizing and closing code, and the handlers of some Windows messages, you can then use it as the base class for each of the application's forms.

You can also use visual form inheritance to customize an application for different clients without duplicating any source code or form definition code—you inherit the specific versions for a client from the standard forms. Remember, the main advantage of visual inheritance is that you can later change the original form and automatically update all the derived forms. This is a well-known advantage of inheritance in object-oriented programming languages, but there is a beneficial side effect: polymorphism. You can add a virtual method in a base form and override it in an inherited form. Then you can refer to both forms and call this method for each of them.

NOTE   Delphi includes another feature that resembles visual form inheritance: frames. In both cases, you can work at design time on two versions of a form/frame. However, in visual form inheritance, you define two different classes (base class and derived class), whereas with frames, you work on a class and an instance. Frames are discussed in detail later in this chapter.

Inheriting from a Base Form

The rules governing visual form inheritance are simple, once you have a clear idea of what inheritance is. Basically, an inherited form has the same components as the base form as well as some new components. You cannot remove a component of the base class, although (if it is a visual control) you can make it invisible. What's important is that you can easily change properties of the components you inherit.

If you change a property of a component in the inherited form, any modification of the same property in the base form will have no effect. Changing other properties of the component will affect the inherited versions, as well. You can resynchronize the two property values by using the Revert to Inherited local menu command in the Object Inspector. You can do the same thing by setting the two properties to the same value and recompiling the code. After modifying multiple properties, you can resynchronize them all to the base version by applying the Revert to Inherited command from the component's local menu.

In addition to inheriting components, the new form inherits all the methods of the base form, including the event handlers. You can add new handlers in the inherited form and also override existing handlers.

To demonstrate how visual form inheritance works, I built a simple example called VFI. To build it, first start a new project and add four buttons to its main form. Then select File ➢ New ➢ Other and choose the Inheritable Items page of the proper section (depending on the personality of your active project) of the New Items dialog box (see Figure 7.10).

In the New Items dialog, you can choose the form from which you want to inherit. The new form has the same four buttons. Here is the initial textual description of the new form:

```
inherited Form2: TForm2
  Caption = 'Form2'
end
```

And here is its initial class declaration, where you can see that the base class is not the usual TForm but the base class form:

```
type
  TForm2 = class(TForm1)
  private
    { Private declarations }
  public
    { Public declarations }
  end;
```

Notice the presence of the inherited keyword in the textual description; also notice that the form has some components, although they are defined in the base class form. If you move the form and add the caption of one of the buttons, the textual description changes accordingly:

```
inherited Form2: TForm2
  Left = 313
  Top = 202
  Caption = 'Form2'
  inherited Button2: TButton
    Caption = 'Beep...'
  end
end
```

Only the properties with a different value are listed (and by removing these properties from the textual description of the inherited form, you can reset them to the value of the base form, as I mentioned earlier). I changed the captions of most of the buttons, as you can see in Figure 7.11.

Each of the first form's buttons has an OnClick handler with simple code. The first button shows the inherited form by calling its Show method; the second and third buttons call the Beep procedure; and the last button displays a message.

FIGURE 7.10
The New Items dialog
box allows you to create
an inherited form.

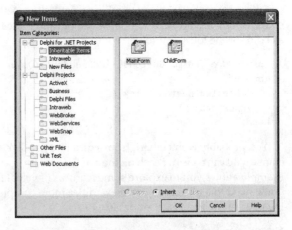

FIGURE 7.11
The two forms of the VFI
example at run time

In the inherited form you should first remove the Show button because the secondary form is already visible. However, you cannot delete a component from an inherited form. An alternative solution is to set the component's Visible property to False—the button will still be there, but it won't be visible (as you can guess from Figure 7.11). The other three buttons will be visible but with different handlers. If you select the OnClick event of a button in the inherited form (by double-clicking it), you'll get an empty method that's slightly different from the default one, because it includes the inherited keyword. This keyword stands for a call to the corresponding event handler of the base form. This keyword is always added by Delphi, even if the handler is not defined in the base class (and this is reasonable, because it might be defined later) or if the component is not present in the base class (which doesn't seem like a great idea to me). It is simple to execute the base form's code and perform some other operations:

```
procedure TForm2.Button2Click(Sender: TObject);
begin
  inherited;
  ShowMessage ('Hi');
end;
```

This is not the only choice. Alternatively, you can write a new event handler and not execute the base class's code, as I did for the VFI example's third button. To accomplish this, simply remove the inherited keyword.

Still another choice includes calling a base-class method after some custom code has been executed, calling it when a condition is met, or calling the handler of a different event of the base class, as I did for the fourth button:

```
procedure TForm2.Button4Click(Sender: TObject);
begin
  inherited Button3Click (Sender);
  inherited;
end;
```

You probably won't inherit from a different handler often, but you must be aware that you can. Of course, you can consider each method of the base form as a method of your form and call it freely. This example allows you to explore some features of visual form inheritance, but to see its true power you'll need to look at real-world examples more complex than this book has room to explore. Next, I want to show you *visual form polymorphism*.

NOTE   Visual form inheritance doesn't work nicely with collections: you cannot extend a collection property of a component in an inherited form. This limitation prevents the practical use of a series of components like toolbars or ListViews with details. Of course, you can use those components in the base or inherited form, but you cannot extend the elements they contain because they are stored in a collection. A solution to this problem is to avoid assigning these collections at design time and instead use a run-time technique. You'll still use form inheritance, but you'll lose the *visual* portion of it. If you try to use the Action Manager component, you'll find you cannot even inherit from a form hosting it. Borland disabled this feature because it would cause you too much trouble.

Polymorphic Forms

If you add an event handler to a form and then change it in an inherited form, there is no way to refer to the two methods using a common variable of the base class because the event handlers use static binding by default.

Confusing? Here is an example, which is intended for experienced Delphi programmers. Suppose you want to build a bitmap viewer form and a text viewer form in the same program. The two forms have similar elements, a similar toolbar, a similar menu, an OpenDialog component, and different components for viewing the data. So, you decide to build a base-class form containing the common elements and inherit the two forms from it, as you can see in the PoliForm example.

The main form contains a toolbar panel with a few buttons, a menu, and an open dialog component. The two inherited forms have only minor differences, but they feature a new component: either an image viewer (TImage) or a text viewer (TMemo). They also modify the settings of the OpenDialog component to refer to different types of files.

The main form includes some common code to handle the Close button and show an About box, while the handler of the Load button displays an error message. The File ➢ Load command, instead, calls another method:

```
procedure TViewerForm.Load1Click(Sender: TObject);
begin
  LoadFile;
end;
```

This method is defined in the TViewerForm class as a virtual abstract method (so that the class of the base form is an abstract class), so you must redefine it in the inherited forms. The code for this LoadFile method in the image viewer form is as follows:

```
procedure TImageViewerForm.LoadFile;
begin
  if OpenDialog1.Execute then
    Image1.Picture.LoadFromFile (OpenDialog1.Filename);
end;
```

The other inherited class has similar code, which loads the text into the memo component. The project has one more form, a main form with two buttons, that reloads the files in each of the viewer forms. The OnCreate event handler of the main form creates the secondary forms of the two inherited classes, and saves them to a polymorphic array:

```
FormList [1] := TTextViewerForm.Create (Application);
FormList [2] := TImageViewerForm.Create (Application);
for I := 1 to 2 do
  FormList[I].Show;
```

The array of forms is used to load a new file in each viewer form when one of the two buttons is clicked. The handlers of the two buttons' OnClick events use different approaches:

```
// ReloadButton1Click
for I := 1 to 2 do
  FormList [I].ButtonLoadClick (Self);

// ReloadButton2Click
for I := 1 to 2 do
  FormList [I].LoadFile;
```

The second button calls a virtual method, and it works without any problem. The first button calls an event handler and always reaches the generic TFormView class (displaying the error message of its ButtonLoadClick method). This happens because the method is static, not virtual.

To make this approach work, you can declare the ButtonLoadClick event handler method of the TFormView class as virtual and declare it as overridden in each of the inherited form classes, as you do for any other virtual method:

```
type
  TViewerForm = class(TForm)
    procedure ButtonLoadClick(Sender: TObject); virtual;
  public
    procedure LoadFile; virtual; abstract;
  end;

type
  TImageViewerForm = class(TViewerForm)
    procedure ButtonLoadClick(Sender: TObject); override;
  public
    procedure LoadFile; override;
  end;
```

This trick really works, although it is never mentioned in the Delphi documentation. This ability to use virtual event handlers is what I mean by visual form polymorphism. In other (more technical) words, you can assign a virtual method to an event property, which will take the address of the method according to the instance available at run time.

Understanding Frames

A frame is similar to a form, but it defines only a portion of a window, not a complete window. The interesting element of frames is that you can create multiple instances of a frame at design time, and you can modify the class and the instance at the same time. Thus frames are an effective tool for creating customizable composite controls at design time—something close to a visual component-building tool.

In visual form inheritance, you can work on both a base form and a derived form at design time, and any changes you make to the base form are propagated to the derived one (unless you have overridden the property or event in the descendant form class). With frames, you work on a class (as usual in Delphi), but you can also customize one or more instances of the class at design time. When you work on a form, you cannot change a property of the TForm1 class for a specific instance of only that form and not the others at design time. With frames, you can.

Once you realize you are working with a class and one or more of its instances at design time, there is nothing more to understand about frames. In practice, frames are useful when you want to use the same group of components in multiple forms within an application. In this case, you can customize each instance at design time. You could already do this with component templates, but component templates were based on the concept of copying and pasting components and their code. You could not change the original definition of the template and see the effect every place it was used. With frames (and, in a different way, with visual form inheritance), changes to the original version (the class) are reflected in the copies (the instances).

Let's discuss a few more elements of frames with an example called Frames2. This program has a frame with a list box, an edit box, and three buttons with code operating on the components. The frame also has a bevel aligned to its client area because frames have no border. Of course, the frame has also a corresponding class, which looks like a form class:

```
type
  TFrameList = class(TFrame)
    ListBox: TListBox;
    Edit: TEdit;
    btnAdd: TButton;
    btnRemove: TButton;
    btnClear: TButton;
    Bevel: TBevel;
    procedure btnAddClick(Sender: TObject);
    procedure btnRemoveClick(Sender: TObject);
    procedure btnClearClick(Sender: TObject);
  private
    { Private declarations }
  public
    { Public declarations }
  end;
```

Unlike a form, however, you can add the frame to a form. I used two instances of the frame in the example (as you can see in Figure 7.12) and modified the behavior slightly. The first instance of the frame has the list box items sorted. When you change a property of a component of a frame, the DFM file of the hosting form will list the differences, as it does with visual form inheritance:

```
object FormFrames: TFormFrames
  Caption = 'Frames2'
  inline FrameList1: TFrameList
    Left = 8
    Top = 8
    inherited ListBox: TListBox
      Sorted = True
    end
  end
  inline FrameList2: TFrameList
    Left = 232
    Top = 8
    inherited btnClear: TButton
      OnClick = FrameList2btnClearClick
    end
  end
end
```

As you can see from the listing, the DFM file for a form that has frames uses a specific DFM keyword, `inline`. The references to the modified components of the frame, however, use the `inherited` keyword, although this term is used with an extended meaning. In this case, `inherited` doesn't refer to a base class you are inheriting from, but to the class from which you are instancing (or inheriting) an object. It is a good idea, though, to use an existing feature of visual form inheritance and apply it to the new context. This approach lets you use the Revert to Inherited command of the Object Inspector or of the components on the frame to cancel the changes and get back to the default value of properties.

FIGURE 7.12

Two instances of a frame at design time in the Frames2 example

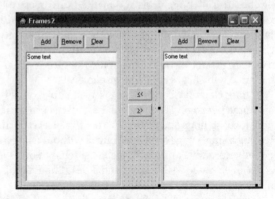

Notice also that unmodified components of the frame class are not listed in the DFM file of the form using the frame, and the form has two frames with different names but the components on the two frames have the same name. These components are not members of the form but are part of the frame. This implies that the form has to reference those components through the frame, as you can see in the code for the buttons that copy items from one list box to the other:

```
procedure TFormFrames.btnLeftClick(Sender: TObject);
begin
  FrameList1.ListBox.Items.AddStrings (FrameList2.ListBox.Items);
end;
```

Finally, in addition to modifying properties of any instance of a frame, you can change the code of any of its event handlers. If you double-click one of the frame's buttons while working on the form (not on the stand-alone frame), Delphi will generate this code for you:

```
procedure TFormFrames.FrameList2btnClearClick(Sender: TObject);
begin
  FrameList2.btnClearClick(Sender);
end;
```

The line of code automatically added by Delphi corresponds to a call to the inherited event handler of the base class in visual form inheritance. This time, however, to get the default behavior of the frame you need to call an event handler and apply it to a specific instance: the frame object itself. The current form doesn't include this event handler and knows nothing about it. Whether you leave this call in place or remove it depends on the effect you are looking for.

TIP   Because the event handler has some code, leaving it as Delphi generated it and saving the form won't remove it as usual. It isn't empty! Instead, to omit the default code for an event, you need to add at least a comment to it to avoid the system removing it automatically.

Frames and Pages

When a dialog box has many pages full of controls, the code underlying the form becomes very complex because all the controls and methods are declared in a single form. In addition, creating all these components (and initializing them) might delay the display of the dialog box. Frames don't reduce the construction and initialization time of equivalently loaded forms; quite the contrary, because loading frames is more complicated for the streaming system than loading simple components. However, using frames, you can load only the visible pages of a multipage dialog box, reducing the *initial* load time, which is what the user perceives.

Frames can solve both of these issues. You can easily divide the code of a single complex form into one frame per page. The form will host all the frames in a PageControl. This approach yields simpler, more focused units and makes it easier to reuse a specific page in a different dialog box or application. Reusing a single page of a PageControl without using a frame or an embedded form is far from simple. (For an alternative approach, see the sidebar "Forms in Pages.")

As an example of this approach, I built the FramePag example. It has some frames placed inside the three pages of a PageControl, as you can see in Figure 7.13 in the Structure View on the side of the design-time form. All the frames are aligned to the client area, using the entire surface of the tab sheet (the page) hosting them. Two of the pages have the same frame, but the two instances of the frame have some differences at design time. The Frame3 frame in the example has a list box populated with a text file at startup, and it has buttons to modify the items in the list and save them to a file. The filename is placed in a label so you can easily select a file for the frame at design time by changing the Caption of the label.

Being able to use multiple instances of a frame is one of the reasons this technique was introduced, and customizing the frame at design time is even more important. Because adding properties to a frame and making them available at design time requires some customized and complex code, it is a good idea to use a component to host these custom values. You have the option of hiding these components (such as the label in this example) if they don't pertain to the user interface.

In the example, you need to load the file when the frame instance is created. Because frames have no OnCreate event, your best choice is probably to override the CreateWnd method. Writing a custom constructor doesn't work because it is executed too early—before the specific label text is available. In the CreateWnd method, you load the list box content from a file.

NOTE When questioned about the issue of the missing OnCreate event handler for frames, Borland R&D members have stated that they could not fire it in correspondence with the wm_Create message because it happens with forms. The creation of the frame window (as is true for most controls) is delayed for performance reasons. More trouble occurs in the case of inheritance among forms holding frames, so to avoid problems, this feature has been disabled—programmers can write the code they deem reasonable.

FIGURE 7.13
Each page of the Frame-Pag example contains a frame, thus separating the code of this complex form into more manageable chunks.

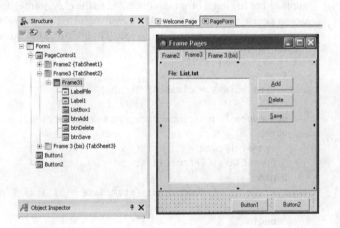

Multiple Frames with No Pages

Another approach avoids having to create all the pages along with the form hosting them by leaving the PageControl empty and creating the frames only when a page is displayed. When you have frames on multiple pages of a PageControl, the windows for the frames are created only when they are first displayed, as you can see by placing a breakpoint in the creation code of the previous example.

As an even more radical approach, you can get rid of the page controls and use a TabControl. Used this way, the tab has no connected tab sheets (or pages) and can display only one set of information at a time. For this reason, you must create the current frame and either destroy the previous one or hide it by setting its Visible property to False or calling the new frame's BringToFront. Although this sounds like a lot of work, in a large application this technique can be worth it because of the reduced resource and memory usage you can obtain.

To demonstrate this approach, I built the FrameTab example, which is similar to the previous one but is based on a TabControl and dynamically created frames. The main form has a TabControl with one page for each frame:

```
object Form1: TForm1
  Caption = 'Frame Pages'
  OnCreate = FormCreate
  object Tab: TTabControl
    Anchors = [akLeft, akTop, akRight, akBottom]
    Tabs.Strings = ( 'Frame2' 'Frame3' )
    OnChange = TabChange
  end
end
```

I gave each tab a caption corresponding to the name of the frame, because I'll use this information to create the new pages. When the form is created, and whenever the user changes the active tab, the program gets the tab's current caption and passes it to the custom ShowFrame method. The method's code checks whether the requested frame already exists (frame names in this example follow the Delphi standard of having a number appended to the class name) and then brings it to the front. If the frame doesn't exist, the method uses the frame name to find the related frame class, creates an object of that class, and assigns a few properties to it. The code makes extensive use of class references and dynamic creation techniques:

```
type
  TFrameClass = class of TFrame;

procedure TForm1.ShowFrame(FrameName: string);
var
  Frame: TFrame;
  FrameClass: TFrameClass;
begin
  Frame := FindComponent (FrameName + '1') as TFrame;
  if not Assigned (Frame) then
  begin
    FrameClass := TFrameClass (FindClass ('T' + FrameName));
    Frame := FrameClass.Create (Self);
    Frame.Parent := Tab;
    Frame.Visible := True;
    Frame.Name := FrameName + '1';
  end;
  Frame.BringToFront;
end;
```

To make this code work, remember to add a call to RegisterClass in the initialization section of each unit defining a frame.

FORMS IN PAGES

Although you can use frames to define the pages of a PageControl at design time, I generally use other forms at run time. This approach leaves me with the flexibility of having the pages defined in separate units (and DFM files) but at the same time allows me to also use those forms as stand-alone windows. In addition, I avoid having to live with the subtly different behaviors of frames.

Once you have a main form with a page control and one or more secondary forms to display in it, all you have to do is write the following code to create the secondary forms and place them in the pages:

```
var
    Form: TForm;
    Sheet: TTabSheet;
begin
    // create a tabsheet within the page control
    Sheet := TTabSheet.Create(PageControl1);
    Sheet.PageControl := PageControl1;
    // create the form and place it in the tabsheet
    Form := TForm2.Create (Application);
    Form.BorderStyle := bsNone;
    Form.Align := alClient;
    Form.Parent := Sheet;
    Form. Visible := True;
    // activate and set title
    PageControl1.ActivePage := Sheet;
    Sheet.Caption := Form.Caption;
end;
```

You can find this code in the FormPage example, but this is all the program does. For an actual application based on forms inside pages, see the RWBlocks demo in Chapter 14.

Base Forms and Interfaces

You have seen that when you need two similar forms in an application, you can use visual form inheritance to inherit one from the other or both of them from a common ancestor. The advantage of visual form inheritance is that you can use it to inherit the visual definition: the DFM. However, this is not always required.

At times, you might want several forms to exhibit a common behavior or respond to the same commands without having any shared component or user interface elements. Using visual form inheritance with a base form that has no extra components makes little sense to me. I prefer instead to define my own custom form class inherited from TForm and then manually edit the form class declarations to inherit from this custom base form class instead of the standard one. If you only need to define shared methods or override TForm virtual methods in a consistent way, defining custom form classes can be a good idea.

INI FILES AND THE REGISTRY IN DELPHI

To save information about the status of an application in order to restore it the next time the program is executed, you can use the explicit support Windows provides for storing this kind of information. ini files, the old Windows standard, are once again the preferred way to save application data. The alternative is the Registry, which is still quite popular. Delphi provides ready-to-use classes to manipulate both.

THE *TINIFILE* CLASS

For ini files, Delphi has a TIniFile class. Once you have created an object of this class and connected it to a file, you can read and write information to it. To create the object, you need to call the constructor, passing a filename to it, as in the following code:

```
var
  IniFile: TIniFile;
begin
  IniFile := TIniFile.Create (strPath + 'myprogram.ini');
```

There are two choices for the location of the ini file. If you list only the ini filename (something I strongly discourage you from doing), it will end up in the Windows directory. If you pass a full path, generally using the application folder extracted from the program name as in the FormIntf example, this is where the ini file will end up.

ini files are divided into sections, each indicated by a name enclosed in square brackets. Each section can contain multiple items of three possible kinds: strings, integers, or Booleans. The TIniFile class has three Read methods, one for each kind of data: ReadBool, ReadInteger, and ReadString. There are also three corresponding methods to write the data: WriteBool, WriteInteger, and WriteString. Other methods allow you to read or erase a whole section. In the Read methods, you can also specify a default value to be used if the corresponding entry doesn't exist in the ini file.

THE *TREGISTRY* AND *TREGINIFILE* CLASSES

The Registry is a hierarchical database of information about the computer, software configuration, and user preferences. Windows has a set of API functions to interact with the Registry; you basically open a key (or folder) and then work with subkeys (or subfolders) and values (or items), but you must be aware of the structure and the details of the Registry.

Delphi provides two approaches to using the Registry. The TRegistry class provides a generic encapsulation of the Registry API, whereas the TRegIniFile class provides the interface of the TIniFile class but saves the data in the Registry. This class is the natural choice for portability between ini-based and Registry-based versions of the same program. When you create a TRegIniFile object, your data ends up in the current user information, so you'll generally use a constructor like this:

```
IniFile := TRegIniFile.Create ('Software\MyCompany\MyProgram');
```

By using the TIniFile and the TRegIniFile classes offered by the VCL, you can move from one model of local and per-user storage to the other. Not that I think you should use the Registry much, because having a centralized repository for the settings of each application was an architectural error—even Microsoft acknowledges this fact (without really admitting the error) by suggesting, in the Windows 2000 Compatibility Requirements, that you no longer use the Registry for applications settings and instead go back to using ini files.

Using a Base Form Class

A simple demonstration of this technique is available in the FormIntf demo; it also showcases the use of interfaces for forms. In a new unit called SaveStatusForm, I defined the following form class (with no related DFM file—instead of using the New Form command, create a new unit and type the code in it):

```
type
  TSaveStatusForm = class (TForm)
  protected
    procedure DoCreate; override;
    procedure DoDestroy; override;
  end;
```

The two overridden methods are called at the same time as the event handler so you can attach extra code (allowing the event handler to be defined as usual). Inside the two methods, you load or save the form position in an ini file of the application, in a section marked with the form caption. Here is the code for the two methods:

```
procedure TSaveStatusForm.DoCreate;
var
  Ini: TIniFile;
begin
  inherited;
  Ini := TIniFile.Create (
    ChangeFileExt(Application.ExeName, '.ini'));
  Left := Ini.ReadInteger(Caption, 'Left', Left);
  Top := Ini.ReadInteger(Caption, 'Top', Top);
  Width := Ini.ReadInteger(Caption, 'Width', Width);
  Height := Ini.ReadInteger(Caption, 'Height', Height);
  Ini.Free;
end;

procedure TSaveStatusForm.DoDestroy;
var
  Ini: TIniFile;
begin
  Ini := TIniFile.Create (ChangeFileExt(Application.ExeName, '.ini'));
  Ini.WriteInteger(Caption, 'Left', Left);
  Ini.WriteInteger(Caption, 'Top', Top);
  ...
```

Again, this is a simple common behavior for your forms, but you can define a complex class here. To use this as a base class for the forms you create, let Delphi create the forms as usual (with no inheritance) and then update the form declaration to something like the following:

```
type
  TFormBitmap = class(TSaveStatusForm)
    Image1: TImage;
    OpenPictureDialog1: TOpenPictureDialog;
    ...
```

Simple as it seems, this technique is very powerful because all you need to do is change the definition of your application's forms to refer to this base class. If even this step is too tedious because you might want to change this base class in your program at some point, you can use an extra trick: "interposer" classes.

AN EXTRA TRICK: INTERPOSER CLASSES

In contrast to Delphi VCL components, which must have unique names within their owner, Delphi classes in general must be unique only within their unit. Thus you can have two different units defining a class with the same name. This technique looks weird at first sight but can be useful.

I read about a technique called "interposer classes" mentioned in an old issue of *The Delphi Magazine*. It suggested replacing standard Delphi class names with your own versions that have the same class name. This way, you can use Delphi's form designer and refer to Delphi standard components at design time but use your own classes at run time.

The idea is simple. In the SaveStatusForm unit, you can define the new form class as follows:

```
type
  TForm = class (Forms.TForm)
  protected
    procedure DoCreate; override;
    procedure DoDestroy; override;
  end;
```

This class is called TForm, and it inherits from TForm of the Forms unit (this last reference is compulsory to avoid a kind of recursive definition). In the rest of the program, you don't need to change the class definition for your form but simply add the unit defining the interposer class (the SaveStatusForm unit in this case) in the uses statement *after* the unit defining the Delphi class. The order of the units in the uses statement is important, and it is the reason some people criticize this technique—because it is difficult to know what is going on. I have to agree: I find interposer classes handy at times (more for components than for forms), but their use makes programs less readable and at times harder to debug.

Using Interfaces

Another technique, which is slightly more complex but even more powerful than the definition of a common base form class, is to create forms that implement specific interfaces. You can have forms that implement one or more of these interfaces, query each form for the interfaces it implements, and call the supported methods.

As an example (available in the same FormIntf program I began discussing in the last section), I defined a simple interface for loading and storing:

```
type
  IFormOperations = interface
    ['{DACFDB76-0703-4A40-A951-10D140B4A2A0}']
    procedure Load;
    procedure Save;
  end;
```

Each form can optionally implement this interface, as in the following `TFormBitmap` class:

```
type
  TFormBitmap = class(TForm, IFormOperations)
    Image1: TImage;
    OpenPictureDialog1: TOpenPictureDialog;
    SavePictureDialog1: TSavePictureDialog;
  public
    procedure Load;
    procedure Save;
  end;
```

The example code includes the Load and Save methods, which use the standard dialog boxes to load or save the image. (In the example's code, the form also inherits from the `TSaveStatusForm` class.)

When an application has one or more forms implementing interfaces, you can apply a given interface method to all the forms supporting it with code like this (extracted from the main form of the FormIntf example):

```
procedure TFormMain.btnLoadClick(Sender: TObject);
var
  i: Integer;
  iFormOp: IFormOperations;
begin
  for i := 0 to Screen.FormCount - 1 do
    if Supports (Screen.Forms [i], IFormOperations, iFormOp) then
      iFormOp.Load;
end;
```

Consider a business application in which you can synchronize all the forms to the data of a specific company or a specific business event. Also consider that, unlike inheritance, you can have several forms that implement multiple interfaces with unlimited combinations. This is why using such an architecture can improve a complex Delphi application a great deal, making it much more flexible and easier to adapt to implementation changes.

What's Next?

In this chapter, we explored some important form properties. Now you know how to handle the size and position of a form, how to resize it, and how to get mouse input and paint over it. You know more about dialog boxes, modal forms, predefined dialogs, MDI forms, and many other techniques, including the funny effect of alpha blending. Understanding the details of working with forms is critical to proper use of Delphi, particularly for building complex applications (unless, of course, you're building services or web applications with no user interface).

We also explored the overall structure of a Delphi application and covered the role of two global objects: `Application` and `Screen`. I also discussed MDI development and a few advanced features of forms, such as visual form inheritance and frames.

The next chapter concludes my "VCL trilogy" and covers techniques for building effective user interfaces, including the use of pages and tabs and docking support and more on actions and the Action Manager architecture.

Chapter 8

Building the User Interface with VCL (for Win32 and .NET)

In Chapter 6, I discussed the core concepts of the TControl class and its derived classes in the VCL library. Then, I provided a rapid tour of the key controls you can use to build a user interface, including editing components, lists, range selectors, and more. In this chapter, I'll discuss other controls used to define the overall design of a form, such as the PageControl and TabControl. I'll then introduce toolbars and status bars, including some slightly advanced features. This will give you the foundation material for the rest of the chapter, which covers actions and the Action Manager architecture.

Modern Windows applications usually have multiple ways of giving a command, including menu items, toolbar buttons, shortcut menus, and so on. To separate the actual commands a user can give from their multiple representations in the user interface, Delphi uses the concept of *actions*. In recent Delphi versions, this architecture has been extended to make the construction of the user interface on top of actions totally visual. You can now also let program users customize this interface easily, as in many other professional programs. Finally, Delphi 7 added to the visual controls supporting the Action Manager architecture a better and more modern UI, supporting the XP look and feel. On Windows XP, you can create applications that adapt themselves to the active theme, thanks to a lot of new internal VCL code.

This chapter covers multipage forms, pages and tabs, ToolBars and StatusBars, themes and styles, actions and ActionLists, predefined actions in Delphi, the ControlBar component, docking toolbars and other controls. The Action Manager architecture is also described.

Multiple-Page Forms

When you need to display a lot of information and controls in a dialog box or a form, you can use multiple pages. The metaphor is that of a notebook: using tabs, a user can select one of the possible pages. You can use two controls to build a multiple-page application in Delphi:

◆ The PageControl component has tabs on one side and multiple pages (similar to panels) covering the rest of its surface. There is one page per tab, so you can simply place components on each page (a TabSheet object) to obtain the proper effect both at design time and at run time. The TabSheet (or page) is not a stand-alone component; you create a TabSheet at design time by using the shortcut menu of the PageControl or at run time by using methods of the same control.

◆ The TabControl has only the tab portion but offers no pages to hold the information. It is a container like a panel with a set of tabs on a side. In this case, to mimic the *page change* operation you can either use one component and change its content or different components and bring one to front, or you can place different forms within the TabControl surface to simulate the pages at run time.

◆ The TabSet component is another set of tabs, like the TabControl, but it is not a container. If you hook it on one side for the form hosting it, you'll generally use the remaining portion of the form (or part of it) for the *simulated* tab content. An alternative solution is to combine a TabSet with a Panel to obtain something even more similar to a TabControl. The main difference between a TabSet and a TabControl is in the user interface. The TabSet is not based on the Win32 common control and for this reason is quite flexible in its UI, particularly with the tsModernTabs and tsSoftTabs values for the `Style` property.

◆ The DockTabSet is an extension of the TabSet component that has extra support for hosting *pinned* forms, like the IDE does. This component and the TabSet, in fact, are extensively used by Delphi 2005 itself.

NOTE Until Delphi 7, the TabSet component was part of the Win 3.1 compatibility components. Delphi still includes in this the Notebook and TabbedNotebook components. In 32-bit versions of Delphi, the TabbedNotebook component is implemented using the Win32 PageControl internally, to reduce the code size and update the look.

In the last chapter you saw a few examples of the use of tabs and pages to host frames and forms. Here I'll show you a few more examples and provide some extra details on the use of those components.

PageControls and TabSheets

As usual, instead of duplicating the help system's list of properties and methods for the PageControl component, I built an example that stretches the control's capabilities and allows you to change its behavior at run time. The example, called Pages, has a PageControl with three pages and the structure shown in Listing 8.1.

LISTING 8.1:   The PageControl of the Pages example

```
object PageControl1: TPageControl
  ActivePage = TabSheet1
  Align = alClient
  Images = ImageList1
  MultiLine = True
  object TabSheet1: TTabSheet
    Caption = 'Pages'
  end
  object TabSheet2: TTabSheet
    Caption = 'Tabs Size'
  end
  object TabSheet3: TTabSheet
    Caption = 'Tabs Text'
  end
```

FIGURE 8.1

The first sheet of the
PageControl of the Pages
example at design time
with its shortcut menu

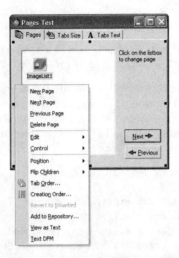

Notice that the tabs are connected to the bitmaps provided by an ImageList control and that some controls use the Anchors property to remain at a fixed distance from the right or bottom borders of the form. Even if the form doesn't support resizing (this would have been far too complex to set up with so many controls), the positions can change when the tabs are displayed on multiple lines (simply increase the length of the captions) or on the left side of the form.

Each TabSheet object has its own Caption, which is displayed as the sheet's tab. At design time, you can use the shortcut menu to create new pages and to move between pages. You can see the shortcut menu of the PageControl component in Figure 8.1, together with the first page. This page holds a list box and a small caption, and it shares two buttons with the other pages.

If you place a component on a page, it is available only in that page. How can you have the same component (in this case, two bitmap buttons) in each page, without duplicating it? Simply place the component on the form outside the PageControl (or before aligning it to the client area), and then move it in front of the pages, calling the Bring To Front command from the control shortcut menu (at design time). The two buttons I placed in each page can be used to move back and forth between the pages and are an alternative to using the tabs. Here is the code associated with one of them:

```
procedure TForm1.BitBtnNextClick(Sender: TObject);
begin
  PageControl1.SelectNextPage (True);
end;
```

The other button calls the same procedure, passing False as its parameter to select the previous page. There is no need to check whether you are on the first or last page because the SelectNextPage method considers the last page to be the one before the first and will move you directly between those two pages.

Now let's focus on the first page again. It has a list box, which at run time will hold the names of the tabs. If a user clicks an item in this list box, the current page changes. This is the third method available to change pages (after the tabs and the Next and Previous buttons). The list box is filled in the FormCreate method, which is associated with the OnCreate event of the form and copies the caption of each page (the Pages property stores a list of TabSheet objects):

```
for I := 0 to PageControl1.PageCount - 1 do
  ListBox1.Items.Add (PageControl1.Pages[I].Caption);
```

The second page hosts two edit boxes (connected with two UpDown components), two check boxes, and two radio buttons, as you can see in Figure 8.2. The user can input a number (or choose it by clicking the up or down buttons with the mouse or pressing the Up or Down arrow key while the corresponding edit box has the focus), check the boxes and the radio buttons, and then click the Apply button to make the changes:

```
procedure TForm1.BitBtnApplyClick(Sender: TObject);
begin
  // set tab width, height, and lines
  PageControl1.TabWidth := StrToInt (EditWidth.Text);
  PageControl1.TabHeight := StrToInt (EditHeight.Text);
  PageControl1.MultiLine := CheckBoxMultiLine.Checked;
  // show or hide the last tab
  TabSheet3.TabVisible := CheckBoxVisible.Checked;
  // set the tab position
  if RadioButton1.Checked then
    PageControl1.TabPosition := tpTop
  else
    PageControl1.TabPosition := tpLeft;
end;
```

With this code, you can change the width and height of each tab (remember that 0 means the size is computed automatically from the space taken by each string). You can choose to have either multiple lines of tabs or two small arrows to scroll the tab area, and you can move the tabs to the left side of the window. The control also lets you place tabs on the bottom or on the right, but this program doesn't allow that because it would make the placement of the other controls quite complex.

You can also hide the last tab on the PageControl, which corresponds to the TabSheet3 component. If you hide one of the tabs by setting its TabVisible property to False, you cannot reach that tab by clicking the Next and Previous buttons, which are based on the SelectNextPage method. Instead, you should use the FindNextPage function, which will select that page even if the tab won't become visible. A call of FindNextPage method is shown in the following new version of the Next button's OnClick event handler:

```
procedure TForm1.BitBtnNextClick(Sender: TObject);
begin
  PageControl1.ActivePage := PageControl1.FindNextPage (
    PageControl1.ActivePage, True, False);
end;
```

The last page has a memo component, again with the names of the pages (added in the FormCreate method). You can edit the names of the pages and click the Change button to change the text of the tabs, but only if the number of strings matches the number of tabs:

```
procedure TForm1.BitBtnChangeClick(Sender: TObject);
var
```

```
  I: Integer;
begin
  if Memo1.Lines.Count <> PageControl1.PageCount then
    MessageDlg ('One line per tab, please', mtError, [mbOK], 0)
  else
    for I := 0 to PageControl1.PageCount -1 do
      PageControl1.Pages [I].Caption := Memo1.Lines [I];
  BitBtnChange.Enabled := False;
end;
```

Finally, the last button, Add Page, allows you to add a new tab sheet to the PageControl, although the program doesn't add any components to it. The (empty) tab sheet object is created using the Page-Control as its owner, but it won't work unless you also set the PageControl property. Before doing this, however, you should make the new tab sheet visible. Here is the code:

```
procedure TForm1.BitBtnAddClick(Sender: TObject);
var
  strCaption: string;
  NewTabSheet: TTabSheet;
begin
  strCaption := 'New Tab';
  if InputQuery ('New Tab', 'Tab Caption', strCaption) then
  begin
    // add a new empty page to the control
    NewTabSheet := TTabSheet.Create (PageControl1);
    NewTabSheet.Visible := True;
    NewTabSheet.Caption := strCaption;
    NewTabSheet.PageControl := PageControl1;
    PageControl1.ActivePage := NewTabSheet;
    // add it to both lists
    Memo1.Lines.Add (strCaption);
    ListBox1.Items.Add (strCaption);
  end;
end;
```

FIGURE 8.2

The second page of the example can be used to size and position the tabs. Here you can see the tabs on the left of the page control.

TIP Whenever you write a form based on a PageControl, remember that the first page displayed at run time is the page you were in before the code was compiled. For example, if you are working on the third page and then compile and run the program, it will start with that page. A common way to solve this problem is to add a line of code in the FormCreate method to set the PageControl or notebook to the first page. This way, the current page at design time doesn't determine the initial page at run time.

An Image Viewer with Owner-Draw Tabs

Every time you need multiple pages that all have the same type of content, instead of replicating the controls in each page, you can use a TabControl (or a TabSet) and change its contents when a new tab is selected. This is what I did in the multiple-page bitmap viewer example called BmpViewer. The image that appears in the TabControl of this form, aligned to the whole client area, depends on the selection in the tab above it (as you can see in Figure 8.3).

At the beginning, the TabControl is empty. After selecting File ➢ Open, the user can choose various files in the File Open dialog box, and the array of strings with the names of the files (the Files property of the OpenDialog1 component) is added to the tabs (the Tabs property of TabControl1):

```
procedure TFormBmpViewer.Open1Click(Sender: TObject);
begin
  if OpenDialog1.Execute then
  begin
    TabControl1.Tabs.AddStrings (OpenDialog1.Files);
    TabControl1.TabIndex := 0;
    TabControl1Change (TabControl1);
  end;
end;
```

After you display the new tabs, you have to update the image so that it matches the first tab. To accomplish this, the program calls the method connected with the OnChange event of the TabControl, which loads the file corresponding to the current tab in the image component:

```
procedure TFormBmpViewer.TabControl1Change(Sender: TObject);
begin
  Image1.Picture.LoadFromFile (TabControl1.Tabs [TabControl1.TabIndex]);
end;
```

FIGURE 8.3
The interface of the bitmap viewer in the Bmp-Viewer example. Notice the owner-draw tabs.

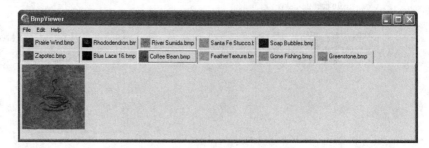

This example works unless you select a file that doesn't contain a bitmap. The program will warn the user with a standard exception, ignore the file, and continue its execution.

The program also lets you paste the bitmap on the Clipboard and copy the current bitmap to it. Clipboard support is available in Delphi via the global Clipboard object defined in the ClipBrd unit. For copying or pasting bitmaps, you can use the Assign method of the TClipboard and TBitmap classes. For the details of the Clipboard support in this example, refer to the source code.

One of the special features of the example is that the TabControl has the OwnerDraw property set to True. This means the control won't paint the tabs (which will be empty at design time) but will instead have the application do this by calling the OnDrawTab event. In its code, the program displays the text vertically centered, using the DrawText API function. The text displayed is not the entire file path but only the filename. Then, if the text is not *None*, the program reads the bitmap the tab refers to and paints a small version of it in the tab itself. To accomplish this, the program uses the TabBmp object, which is of type TBitmap and is created and destroyed along with the form. The program also uses the BmpSide constant to position the bitmap and the text properly:

```
procedure TFormBmpViewer.TabControl1DrawTab(Control: TCustomTabControl;
  TabIndex: Integer; const Rect: TRect; Active: Boolean);
var
 TabText: string;
 OutRect: TRect;
begin
  TabText := TabControl1.Tabs [TabIndex];
  OutRect := Rect;
  InflateRect (OutRect, -3, -3);
  OutRect.Left := OutRect.Left + BmpSide + 3;
  DrawText (Control.Canvas.Handle, PChar (ExtractFileName (TabText)),
    Length (ExtractFileName (TabText)), OutRect,
    dt_Left or dt_SingleLine or dt_VCenter);
  if TabText = 'Clipboard' then
    if Clipboard.HasFormat (cf_Bitmap) then
      TabBmp.Assign (Clipboard)
    else
      TabBmp.FreeImage
  else
    TabBmp.LoadFromFile (TabText);
  OutRect.Left := OutRect.Left - BmpSide - 3;
  OutRect.Right := OutRect.Left + BmpSide;
  Control.Canvas.StretchDraw (OutRect, TabBmp);
end;
```

NOTE   The preceding DrawText call doesn't work in .NET, as this API call requires a string instead of a PChar parameter for the output text. For this reason, the source code of the example has an IFDEF directive.

The program also has support for printing the current bitmap after showing a page preview form in which the user can select the proper scaling. This extra portion of the program that I built for earlier editions of the book is not discussed in detail, but I left the code in the program so you can examine it.

The User Interface of a Wizard

Just as you can use a TabControl without pages, you can also take the opposite approach and use a PageControl without tabs. For example, this can be useful for the development of the user interface of a wizard dialog box. In a wizard, you direct the user through a sequence of steps, one screen at a time, and at each step you typically offer the choice of proceeding to the next step or going back to correct input entered in a previous step. Instead of tabs that can be selected in any order, wizards typically offer Next and Back buttons to navigate. Next is context sensitive, while Back can be implemented using a stack of visited pages. The example is called WizardUI and is relatively simple, so I won't discuss it in detail here.

The core idea is to create a series of pages in a PageControl and set the TabVisible property of each TabSheet to False (while keeping the Visible property set to True). Because most of the programs' labels show HTTP addresses, a user can click a label to open the default browser showing that page. You accomplish this by extracting the HTTP address from the label and calling the ShellExecute function:

```
procedure TForm1.LabelLinkClick(Sender: TObject);
var
  Caption, StrUrl: string;
begin
  Caption := (Sender as TLabel).Caption;
  StrUrl := Copy (Caption, Pos ('http://', Caption), 1000);
  ShellExecute (Handle, 'open', PChar (StrUrl), '', '', sw_Show);
end;
```

This method is hooked to the OnClick event of many labels on the form, which have been turned into *links* by setting the Cursor to a hand. This is one of the labels:

```
object Label2: TLabel
  Cursor = crHandPoint
  Caption = 'Main site: http://www.borland.com'
  OnClick = LabelLinkClick
end
```

The ToolBar Control

To create a toolbar, Delphi includes a specific component that encapsulates the corresponding Win32 common control. This component provides a toolbar with its own buttons, and it has many advanced capabilities. You place the component on a form and then use the component editor (the shortcut menu activated by a right-click) to create buttons and separators.

The toolbar is populated with objects of the TToolButton class. These objects have a fundamental property, Style, which determines their behavior:

- The tbsButton style indicates a standard pushbutton.

- The tbsCheck style indicates a button with the behavior of a check box, or that of a radio button if the button is grouped with the others in its block (determined by the presence of separators).

- The tbsDropDown style indicates a drop-down button (a sort of combo box). The drop-down portion can be easily implemented in Delphi by connecting a PopupMenu control to the DropdownMenu property of the control.

- The tbsSeparator and tbsDivider styles indicate separators with no or different vertical lines (depending on the Flat property of the toolbar).

To create a graphic toolbar, you can add an ImageList component to the form, load some bitmaps into it, and then connect the ImageList with the Images property of the toolbar. By default, the images will be assigned to the buttons in the order they appear, but you can change this behavior quite easily by setting the ImageIndex property of each toolbar button. You can prepare further ImageLists for special button conditions and assign them to the DisabledImages and HotImages properties of the toolbar. The first group is used for the disabled buttons; the second is used for the button currently under the mouse.

NOTE   In a nontrivial application, you will generally create toolbars using an ActionList or the Action Manager architecture, discussed later in this chapter. In this case, you'll attach little behavior to the toolbar buttons, because their properties and events will be managed by the action components. Moreover, you'll end up using a toolbar of the specific TActionToolBar class.

The RichBar Example

As an example of the use of a toolbar, I built the RichBar application, which has a RichEdit component you can operate by using the toolbar. The program has buttons for loading and saving files, for copy and paste operations, and for changing some of the attributes of the current font.

I won't cover the many details of the RichEdit control's features, which I briefly discussed in Chapter 6, nor discuss the details of this application, which has quite a lot of code. All I'll do is focus on features specific to the ToolBar used by the example and visible in Figure 8.4. This toolbar has buttons, separators, and even a drop-down menu and two combo boxes (discussed in the next section).

The various buttons implement features, including opening and saving text files—the program asks the user to save any modified file before opening a new one to avoid losing any changes. The file-handling portion of the program is quite complex, but it is worth exploring because many file-based applications will use similar code. More details are available in the file RichBar File Operations.rtf with the source code for this example, a file you can open with the RichBar program itself.

FIGURE 8.4
The RichBar example's toolbar. Notice the drop-down menu.

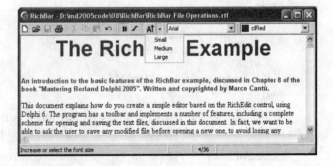

In addition to file operations, the program supports copy and paste operations and font management. The copy and paste operations don't require an interaction with the VCL Clipboard object because the component can handle them with simple commands like these:

```
RichEdit.CutToClipboard;
RichEdit.CopyToClipboard;
RichEdit.PasteFromClipboard;
RichEdit.Undo;
```

It is a little more advanced to know when these operations (and the corresponding buttons) should be enabled. You can enable Copy and Cut buttons when some text is selected, in the OnSelectionChange event of the RichEdit control:

```
procedure TFormRichNote.RichEditSelectionChange(Sender: TObject);
begin
  tbtnCut.Enabled := RichEdit.SelLength > 0;
  tbtnCopy.Enabled := tbtnCut.Enabled;
end;
```

The copy operation cannot be determined by an action of the user because it depends on the content of the Clipboard, which is also influenced by other applications. One approach is to use a timer and check the Clipboard content from time to time. A better approach is to use the OnIdle event of the Application object (or the ApplicationEvents component). Because the RichEdit control supports multiple Clipboard formats, the code cannot simply look at those but should ask the component itself, using a low-level feature not surfaced by the Delphi control:

```
procedure TFormRichNote.ApplicationEvents1Idle(Sender: TObject;
  var Done: Boolean);
begin
  // update toolbar buttons
  tbtnPaste.Enabled := RichEdit.Perform (em_CanPaste, 0, 0) <> 0;
end;
```

Basic font management is given by the Bold and Italic buttons, which have similar code. The Bold button toggles the relative attribute from the selected text (or changes the style at the current edit position):

```
procedure TFormRichNote.BoldExecute(Sender: TObject);
begin
  with RichEdit.SelAttributes do
    if fsBold in Style then
      Style := Style - [fsBold]
    else
      Style := Style + [fsBold];
end;
```

Again, the current status of the button is determined by the current selection, so you'll need to add the following line to the RichEditSelectionChange method:

```
tbtnBold.Down := fsBold in RichEdit.SelAttributes.Style;
```

A Menu and a Combo Box in a Toolbar

In addition to a series of buttons, the RichBar example has a drop-down menu and a couple of combo boxes, a feature shared by many common applications. The drop-down button allows selection of the font size, and the combo boxes allow rapid selection of the font family and the font color. This second combo is built using a ColorBox control.

The Size button is connected to a PopupMenu component (called SizeMenu) using the DropdownMenu property. A user can click the button, firing its OnClick event as usual, or select the drop-down arrow, open the pop-up menu (see Figure 8.4 again), and choose one of its options. This case has three possible font sizes, per the menu definition:

```
object SizeMenu: TPopupMenu
  object Small1: TMenuItem
    Tag = 10
    Caption = 'Small'
    OnClick = SetFontSize
  end
  object Medium1: TMenuItem
    Tag = 16
    Caption = 'Medium'
    OnClick = SetFontSize
  end
  object Large1: TMenuItem
    Tag = 32
    Caption = 'Large'
    OnClick = SetFontSize
  end
end
```

Each menu item has a tag indicating the actual size of the font, activated by a shared event handler:

```
procedure TFormRichNote.SetFontSize(Sender: TObject);
begin
  RichEdit.SelAttributes.Size := (Sender as TMenuItem).Tag;
end;
```

NOTE   In the VCL for .NET, to use the Tag property effectively you need to add the Variants unit to the uses clause; otherwise you'll see an error like "Incompatible types: 'Integer' and 'Variant'."

The ToolBar control is a full-featured control container, so you can take an edit box, a combo box, and other controls and place them directly inside the toolbar. The combo box in the toolbar is initialized in the FormCreate method, which extracts the screen fonts available in the system:

```
ComboFont.Items := Screen.Fonts;
ComboFont.ItemIndex := ComboFont.Items.IndexOf (RichEdit.Font.Name)
```

The combo box initially displays the name of the default font used in the RichEdit control, which is set at design time. This value is recomputed each time the current selection changes, using the font of the selected text, along with the current color for the ColorBox:

```
procedure TFormRichNote.RichEditSelectionChange(Sender: TObject);
begin
  ComboFont.ItemIndex :=
    ComboFont.Items.IndexOf (RichEdit.SelAttributes.Name);
  ColorBox1.Selected := RichEdit.SelAttributes.Color;
end;
```

When a new font is selected from the combo box, the reverse action takes place. The text of the current combo box item is assigned as the name of the font for any text selected in the RichEdit control:

```
RichEdit.SelAttributes.Name := ComboFont.Text;
```

A Simple Status Bar

Building a status bar is even simpler than building a toolbar. Delphi includes a specific StatusBar component based on the corresponding Windows common control. This component can be used almost like a panel when its `SimplePanel` property is set to True. In this case, you can use the `SimpleText` property to output some text. The real advantage of this component, however, is that it allows you to define a number of subpanels by activating its `Panels` property editor. (You can also display this property editor by double-clicking the status bar control or perform the same operations using the Structure View.) Each subpanel has its own graphical attributes, which you can customize using the Object Inspector. Another feature of the status bar component is the "size grip" area added to the lower-right corner of the bar, which is useful for resizing the form. This is a typical element of the Windows user interface, and you can partially control it with the `SizeGrip` property (it auto-disables when the form is not resizable).

A status bar has various uses. The most common is to display information about the menu item currently selected by the user. In addition, a status bar often displays other information about the status of a program: the position of the cursor in a graphical application, the current line of text in a word processor, the status of the lock keys, the time and date, and so on. To show information on a panel, you use its `Text` property, generally in an expression like this:

```
StatusBar1.Panels[1].Text := 'message';
```

In the RichBar example, I built a status bar with three panels for command hints, the status of the Caps Lock key, and the current editing position. The StatusBar component of the example actually has four panels—you need to define the fourth in order to delimit the area of the third panel. The last panel is always large enough to cover the remaining surface of the status bar.

TIP   Again, for more detail about the RichBar program, see the RTF file in the example's source code. Also, because the hints will be displayed in the first panel of the status bar, I could have simplified the code by using the AutoHint property. I showed the more detailed code so you can customize it.

The panels are not independent components, so you cannot access them by name, only by position as in the preceding code snippet. A good solution to improve the readability of a program is to define a constant for each panel you want to use and then use these constants when referring to the panels. This is my sample code:

```
const
  sbpMessage = 0;
  sbpCaps = 1;
  sbpPosition = 2;
```

In the first panel of the status bar, I want to display the toolbar button's hint message. The program obtains this effect by handling the application's OnHint event, again using the ApplicationEvents component and copying the current value of the application's Hint property to the status bar:

```
procedure TFormRichNote.ApplicationEvents1Hint (Sender: TObject);
begin
  StatusBar1.Panels[sbpMessage].Text := Application.Hint;
end;
```

By default, this code displays in the status bar the same text of the fly-by hints, which aren't generated for menu items. You can use the Hint property to specify different strings for the two cases by writing a string divided into two portions by a separator: the pipe (|) character. For example, you might enter the following as the value of the Hint property:

```
'New|Create a new document'
```

The first portion of the string, New, is used by fly-by hints, and the second portion, Create a new document, by the status bar.

TIP   When the hint for a control is made up of two strings, you can use the GetShortHint and GetLongHint methods to extract the first (short) and second (long) substring from the string you pass as a parameter, which is usually the value of the Hint property.

The second panel displays the status of the Caps Lock key, obtained by calling the GetKeyState API function, which returns a state number. If the low-order bit of this number is set (that is, if the number is odd), then the key is pressed. I decided to check this state when the application is idle, so the test is executed not only every time a key is pressed, but also as soon as a message reaches the window (in case the user changes this setting while working with another program). I added to the ApplicationEvents1Idle handler a call to the custom CheckCapslock method, implemented as follows:

```
if Odd (GetKeyState (VK_CAPITAL)) then
  StatusBar1.Panels[sbpCaps].Text := 'CAPS'
else
  StatusBar1.Panels[sbpCaps].Text := '';
```

Finally, the program uses the third panel to display the current cursor position (measured in lines and characters per line) every time the selection changes. Because the CaretPos values are zero-based (that is, the upper-left corner is line 0, character 0), I added one to each value to make them more reasonable for a casual user:

```
procedure TFormRichNote.RichEditSelectionChange(Sender: TObject);
begin
```

```
// update the position in the status bar
StatusBar.Panels[sbpPosition].Text := Format ('%d/%d',
   [RichEdit.CaretPos.Y + 1, RichEdit.CaretPos.X + 1]);
end;
```

Windows XP Themes

With the release of Windows XP, Microsoft introduced a new, separate version of the common controls library. The old library is still available for compatibility reasons, so that a program running on XP can choose which of the two libraries it wants to use. The new common controls library's main difference is that is doesn't have a fixed rendering engine but relies on the XP theme engine and delegates the user interface of the controls to the current theme.

The VCL fully supports themes, due to a lot of internal code and to the themes management library originally developed by Mike Lischke. Some of these new rendering features are used by the visual controls of the Action Manager architecture, independently of the operating system you are running on. However, full theme support is available only on an operating system that has this feature—at the moment, Windows XP and Windows 2003.

Even on XP, Delphi applications use the traditional approach by default. To support XP themes, you must include a manifest file in the program. You can do so in multiple ways:

♦ Place a manifest file in the same folder as the application. This is an XML file indicating the identity and the dependencies of the program. The file has the same name as the executable program with an extra .manifest extension at the end (as in MyProgram.exe.manifest). You can see a sample of such a file in Listing 8.2.

♦ Add the same information in a resource file compiled within the application. You have to write a resource file that includes a manifest file. The VCL has a WindowsXP.res compiled resource file, which is obtained by recompiling the WindowsXP.rc file available among the VCL source files. The resource file includes the sample.manifest file, again available among the VCL source files.

♦ Use the XpManifest component, which Borland has added to further simplify this task. As you drop this do-nothing component into a program's form, Delphi will automatically include its XPMan unit, which imports the VCL resource file mentioned earlier.

WARNING When you remove the XpManifest component from an application, you also have to delete the XPMan unit from the uses statement manually—Delphi won't do it for you. If you fail to do so, even without the XpManifest component, the program will still bind in the manifest resource file. Using the unit is what really matters, which makes me wonder why Borland chose to create the component instead of simply providing the unit or the related resource file. By the way, the component has no visible icon in Delphi 2005.

As a demo, I added the manifest file from Listing 8.2 to the folder of the Pages example discussed at the beginning of this chapter. By running it on Windows XP with the standard XP theme, you'll obtain output similar to that shown in Figure 8.5. You can compare this to Figure 8.2, which display the same program executed without the manifest.

LISTING 8.2:   A sample manifest file (*pages.exe.manifest*)

```xml
<?xml version="1.0" encoding="UTF-8" standalone="yes"?>
<assembly xmlns="urn:schemas-microsoft-com:asm.v1" manifestVersion="1.0">
  <assemblyIdentity version="1.0.0.0" processorArchitecture="X86"
    name="Pages.exe" type="win32" />
  <description>Mastering Delphi Demo</description>
  <dependency>
    <dependentAssembly>
      <assemblyIdentity type="win32"
        name="Microsoft.Windows.Common-Controls"
        version="6.0.0.0" processorArchitecture="X86"
        publicKeyToken="6595b64144ccf1df" language="*" />
    </dependentAssembly>
  </dependency>
</assembly>
```

FIGURE 8.5

The Pages example uses the current Windows XP theme, as it includes a manifest file (compare this with Figure 8.2).

The ActionList Architecture

Delphi's event architecture is very open: you can write a single event handler and connect it to the `OnClick` events of a toolbar button and a menu. You can also connect the same event handler to different buttons or menu items because the event handler can use the `Sender` parameter to refer to the object that fired the event. It's a little more difficult to synchronize the status of toolbar buttons and menu items. If you have a menu item and a toolbar button that each toggle the same option, then every time the option is toggled, you must both add the check mark to the menu item and change the status of the button to show it as pressed.

To help manage the situation, Delphi includes an event-handling architecture based on actions. An *action* (or command) both indicates what operation to perform when a menu item or button is clicked and determines the status of all the elements connected to the action. The connection of the action with the user interface of the linked controls is very important and should not be underestimated because it is where you can get the real advantages of this architecture.

There are many players in this event-handling architecture. The central role is certainly played by the action objects. An action object has a name, like any other component, and other properties that will be applied to the linked controls (called *action clients*). These properties include the Caption, the graphical representation (ImageIndex), the status (Checked, Enabled, and Visible), and the user feedback (Hint and HelpContext). There is also the ShortCut and a list of SecondaryShortCuts, the AutoCheck property for two-state actions, the help support properties, and a Category property used to arrange actions in logical groups.

The base class for all action objects is TBasicAction, which introduces the abstract core behavior of an action without any specific binding or connection (not even to menu items or controls). The derived TContainedAction class introduces properties and methods that enable actions to appear in an Action List or Action Manager. The further-derived TCustomAction class introduces support for the properties and methods of menu items and controls that are linked to action objects. Finally, there is the derived ready-to-use TAction class.

Each action object is connected to one or more client objects through an ActionLink object. Multiple controls, possibly of different types, can share the same action object, as indicated by their Action property. Technically, the ActionLink objects maintain a bidirectional connection between the client object and the action. The ActionLink object is required because the connection works in both directions. An operation on the object (such as a click) is forwarded to the action object and results in a call to its OnExecute event; an update to the status of the action object is reflected in the connected client controls. In other words, one or more client controls can create an ActionLink, which registers itself with the action object.

For client controls you connect with an action, you should not set the properties that have a corresponding property in the action itself, because the action will override the property values of the client controls. For this reason, you should generally write the actions first and then create the menu items and buttons you want to connect with them. Note also that when an action has no OnExecute handler, the client control is automatically disabled (or grayed), unless the DisableIfNoHandler property is set to False.

The client controls connected to actions are usually menu items and various types of buttons (pushbuttons, check boxes, radio buttons, speed buttons, toolbar buttons, and the like), but nothing prevents you from creating new components that hook into this architecture. Component writers can even define new actions and new link action objects. In addition to a client control, some actions can also have a target component. Some predefined actions hook to a specific target component. Other actions automatically look for a target component in the form that supports the given action, starting with the active control.

Finally, the action objects are held by an ActionList or ActionManager component, the only class of the basic architecture that shows up on the Component Palette. The action list receives the execute actions that aren't handled by the specific action objects, firing the OnExecuteAction. If even the action list doesn't handle the action, Delphi calls the OnExecuteAction event of the Application object. The ActionList component has a special editor you can use to create several actions, as you can see in Figure 8.6.

In the editor, actions are displayed in groups, as indicated by their Category property. By simply setting this property to a new value, you instruct the editor to introduce a new category. These categories are basically logical groups, although in some cases a group of actions can work only on a specific type of target component. You might want to define a category for every pull-down menu or group them in some other logical way.

FIGURE 8.6

The ActionList component editor, with a list of predefined actions you can use

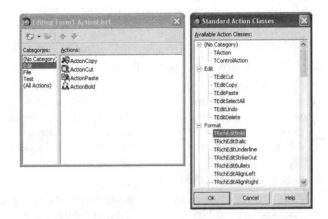

Predefined Actions

With the ActionList and the Action Manager editor, you can create a new action or choose one of the existing actions registered in the system. These are listed in a secondary dialog box, as shown in Figure 8.6. There are many predefined actions, which can be divided into logical groups:

File actions   Include open, save as, open with, run, print setup, and exit.

Edit actions   Illustrated in the next example. They include cut, copy, paste, select all, undo, and delete.

RichEdit actions   Complement the edit actions for RichEdit controls and include bold, italic, underline, strikeout, bullets, and various alignment actions.

MDI window actions   Already demonstrated in Chapter 7, where we examined the Multiple Document Interface approach. They include all the most common MDI operations: arrange, cascade, close, tile (horizontally or vertically), and minimize all.

Dataset actions   Relate to database tables and queries and will be discussed in Chapter 13. There are many dataset actions, representing all the main operations you can perform on a dataset. Delphi 7 added to the core dataset actions a group of actions specifically tailored to the ClientDataSet component, including apply, revert, and undo. I'll talk more about these actions in Chapter 13 (where I'll cover database programming in general and the ClientDataSet component in particular) and Chapter 14 (in which I'll discuss updating database data).

Help actions   Allow you to activate the contents page or index of the Help file attached to the application.

Search actions   Include find, find first, find next, and replace.

Tab and page control actions   Include previous page and next page navigation.

Dialog actions   Activate color, font, open, save, and print dialogs. In Delphi 2005 there is a new standard action that opens the BrowseForFolder dialog box.

List actions   Include clear, copy, move, delete, and select all. These actions let you interact with a list control. Another group of actions, including static list, virtual list, and some support classes, allows the definition of lists that can be connected to a user interface. More on this topic is in the section "Using List Actions" toward the end of this chapter.

Internet actions   Include browse URL, download URL, and send mail actions.

Tools actions   Include only the dialog to customize the action bars.

In addition to handling the OnExecute event of the action and changing the status of the action to affect the client controls' user interface, an action can handle the OnUpdate event, which is activated when the application is idle. This gives you the opportunity to check the status of the application or the system and change the user interface of the controls accordingly. For example, the standard Paste-Edit action enables the client controls only when the Clipboard contains some text.

Actions in Practice

Now that you understand the main ideas behind this important Delphi feature, let's try an example. The program is called Actions, and it demonstrates a number of features of the action architecture. I began building it by placing a new ActionList component in its form and adding the three standard edit actions and a few custom ones. The form also has a panel with some speed buttons, a main menu, and a Memo control (the automatic target of the edit actions). Listing 8.3 is the list of the actions extracted from the DFM file.

LISTING 8.3:   The actions of the Actions example

```
object ActionList1: TActionList
  Images = ImageList1
  object ActionCopy: TEditCopy
    Category = 'Edit'
    Caption = '&Copy'
  end
  object ActionCut: TEditCut...
  object ActionPaste: TEditPaste...
  object ActionNew: TAction
    Category = 'File'
    Caption = '&New'
    OnExecute = ActionNewExecute
  end
  object ActionExit: TAction...
  object NoAction: TAction
    Category = 'Test'
    Caption = '&No Action'
  end
  object ActionCount: TAction
    Category = 'Test'
    Caption = '&Count Chars'
    OnExecute = ActionCountExecute
    OnUpdate = ActionCountUpdate
  end
```

```
  object ActionBold: TAction...
  object ActionEnable: TAction
    Category = 'Test'
    Caption = '&Enable NoAction'
    OnExecute = ActionEnableExecute
  end
  object ActionSender: TAction...
end
```

All these actions are connected to the items of a MainMenu component, and some of them are also connected to the buttons of a Toolbar control. Notice that the images selected in the ActionList component affect the actions in the editor only. In order for the ImageList images to show up in the menu items and toolbar buttons, you must also select the image list in the MainMenu and in the Toolbar components.

The three predefined actions for the Edit menu don't have associated handlers, but these special objects have internal code to perform the related action on the active edit or memo control. These actions also enable and disable themselves, depending on the content of the Clipboard and on the existence of selected text in the active edit control. Most other actions have custom code, except the NoAction object; because it has no code, the menu item and the button connected with this command are disabled, even if the Enabled property of the action is set to True.

I've added to the example and to the Test menu another action that enables the menu item connected to the NoAction object:

```
procedure TForm1.ActionEnableExecute(Sender: TObject);
begin
  NoAction.DisableIfNoHandler := False;
  NoAction.Enabled := True;
  ActionEnable.Enabled := False;
end;
```

Setting Enabled to True produces the effect for only a short time, unless you set the Disable-IfNoHandler property as discussed in the previous section. Once you do this operation, you disable the current action because there is no need to issue the same command again.

This is different from an action you can toggle, such as the Edit ➢ Bold, for which I've set the AutoCheck property set to True so that it doesn't need to change the status of the Checked property in code:

```
procedure TForm1.ActionBoldExecute(Sender: TObject);
begin
  with Memo1.Font do
    if fsBold in Style then
      Style := Style - [fsBold]
    else
      Style := Style + [fsBold];
end;
```

The `ActionCount` object has very simple code, but it demonstrates an `OnUpdate` handler; when the memo control is empty, it is automatically disabled. You can obtain the same effect by handling the `OnChange` event of the memo control itself, but in general it might not always be possible or easy to determine the status of a control simply by handling one of its events. Here is the code for the two handlers of this action:

```
procedure TForm1.ActionCountExecute(Sender: TObject);
begin
  ShowMessage ('Characters: ' + IntToStr (Length (Memo1.Text)));
end;


procedure TForm1.ActionCountUpdate(Sender: TObject);
begin
  ActionCount.Enabled := Memo1.Text <> '';
end;
```

Finally, I added a special action to test the action event handler's sender object and get some other system information. In addition to showing the object class and name, I added code that accesses the action list object. I did this mainly to show that you can access this information and how to do it:

```
procedure TForm1.ActionSenderExecute(Sender: TObject);
begin
  Memo1.Lines.Add ('Sender class: ' + Sender.ClassName);
  Memo1.Lines.Add ('Sender name: ' + (Sender as TComponent).Name);
  Memo1.Lines.Add ('Category: ' + (Sender as TAction).Category);
  Memo1.Lines.Add (
    'Action list name: ' + (Sender as TAction).ActionList.Name);
end;
```

You can see the output of this code in Figure 8.7, along with the user interface of the example. Notice that the `Sender` is not the menu item you selected, even if the event handler is connected to it. The `Sender` object, which fires the event, is the action, which intercepts the user operation.

Finally, keep in mind that you can also write handlers for the events of the ActionList object itself, which play the role of global handlers for all the actions in the list and for the `Application` global object, which fires for all the actions of the application. Before calling the action's `OnExecute` event, Delphi activates the ActionList's `OnExecute` event and the `Application` global object's `OnActionExecute` event. These events can look at the action, eventually execute some shared code, and then stop the execution (using the `Handled` parameter) or let it reach the next level.

If no event handler is assigned to respond to the action, either at the action list, application, or action level, then the application tries to identify a target object to which the action can apply itself.

NOTE   When a standard action is executed, it searches for a control to play the role of the action target by looking at the active control, the active form, and other controls on the form. For example, edit actions refer to the currently active control (if they inherit from `TCustomEdit`), and dataset controls look for the dataset connected with the data source of the data-aware control having the input focus. Other actions follow different approaches to find a target component, but the overall idea is shared by most standard actions.

FIGURE 8.7

The Actions example, with a detailed description of the Sender of OnExecute event of an action

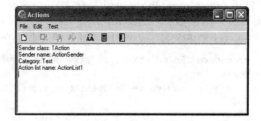

The Toolbar and ActionList of an Editor

Earlier in this chapter, I built the RichBar example to demonstrate the development of an editor with a toolbar and a status bar. Of course, I should have also added a menu bar to the form, but doing so would have created quite a few troubles in synchronizing the status of the toolbar buttons with those of the menu items. A very good solution to this problem is to use actions, as I do in the MdEdit1 example discussed in this section.

The application is based on an ActionList component, which includes actions for file handling and Clipboard support with code similar to the RichBar version. The font type and color selections are still based on combo boxes, so they don't involve actions—the same is true for the drop-down menu of the Size button. The menu, however, has a few extra commands, including one for character counting and one for changing the background color. These commands are based on actions, and the same is true for the three new paragraph justification buttons (and menu commands).

One of the key differences in this new version is that the code never refers to the status of the toolbar buttons but eventually modifies the status of the actions. In other cases I've used the actions' `OnUpdate` events. For example, the `RichEditSelectionChange` method doesn't update the status of the Bold button, which is connected to an action with the following `OnUpdate` handler:

```
procedure TFormRichNote.acBoldUpdate(Sender: TObject);
begin
  acBold.Checked := fsBold in RichEdit.SelAttributes.Style;
end;
```

Similar `OnUpdate` event handlers are available for most actions, including the counting operations (available only if there is some text in the RichEdit control), the save operation (available if the text has been modified), and the cut and copy operations (available only if some text is selected):

```
procedure TFormRichNote.acCountcharsUpdate(Sender: TObject);
begin
  acCountChars.Enabled := RichEdit.GetTextLen > 0;
end;
```

```
procedure TFormRichNote.acSaveUpdate(Sender: TObject);
begin
  acSave.Enabled := Modified;
end;
```

In the older example, the status of the Paste button was updated in the OnIdle event of the Application object. Now that you're using actions you can convert it into yet another OnUpdate handler (or, even better, use the corresponding predefined action):

```
procedure TFormRichNote.acPasteUpdate(Sender: TObject);
begin
  acPaste.Enabled := SendMessage (RichEdit.Handle, em_CanPaste, 0, 0) <> 0;
end;
```

The three paragraph-alignment buttons and the related menu items work like radio buttons: they're mutually exclusive, and one of the three options is always selected. For this reason, the actions have the GroupIndex set to 1, the corresponding menu items have the RadioItem property set to True, and the three toolbar buttons have their Grouped property set to True and the AllowAllUp property set to False. (They are also visually enclosed between two separators.)

This arrangement is required so that the program can set the Checked property for the action corresponding to the current style, which avoids unchecking the other two actions directly. This code is part of the OnUpdate event of the action list because it applies to multiple actions:

```
procedure TFormRichNote.ActionListUpdate(Action: TBasicAction;
  var Handled: Boolean);
begin
  // check the proper paragraph alignment
  case RichEdit.Paragraph.Alignment of
    taLeftJustify: acLeftAligned.Checked := True;
    taRightJustify: acRightAligned.Checked := True;
    taCenter: acCentered.Checked := True;
  end;
  // checks the caps lock status
  CheckCapslock;
end;
```

Finally, when one of these buttons is selected, the shared event handler uses the value of the Tag set to the corresponding value of the TAlignment enumeration to determine the proper alignment:

```
procedure TFormRichNote.ChangeAlignment(Sender: TObject);
begin
  RichEdit.Paragraph.Alignment := TAlignment ((Sender as TAction).Tag);
end;
```

Toolbar Containers: The ControlBar

Most modern applications have multiple toolbars, at times hosted by a specific container. Delphi has two ready-to-use toolbar containers:

- The CoolBar component is a Win32 common control introduced by Internet Explorer and used by some Microsoft applications. This component is now seldom used even by Microsoft and has had a few troubles (including incompatible versions in different common control libraries) that have discouraged its use. That's why it is not covered in this book.

- The ControlBar component is totally VCL based with no dependencies on external libraries. This is the suggested component to use if you need a toolbars container and is covered in this section.

Both components can host ToolBar controls as well as some extra elements such as combo boxes and other controls. A toolbar can also replace the menu of an application, as you'll see later.

The ControlBar is a control container, and you build it by placing other controls inside it, as you do with a panel (there is no list of **Bands** in it). Every control placed in the bar gets its own dragging area or *grabber* (a small panel with two vertical lines on the left of the control). Even a stand-alone button placed in a ControlBar gets a grabber:

For this reason, you should generally avoid placing specific buttons inside the ControlBar and instead add containers with buttons inside them. Rather than using a panel, you should use one ToolBar control for every section of the ControlBar. The MdEdit2 example is another version of the demo I developed to discuss the ActionList component earlier in this chapter. I grouped the buttons into three toolbars (instead of a single one) and left the two combo boxes as stand-alone controls. All these components are inside a ControlBar so a user can arrange them at run time, as you can see in Figure 8.8.

The following snippet of the DFM listing of the MdEdit2 example shows how the various toolbars and controls are embedded in the ControlBar component:

```
object ControlBar1: TControlBar
  Align = alTop
  AutoSize = True
  ShowHint = True
  PopupMenu = BarMenu
  object ToolBarFile: TToolBar
    Flat = True
    Images = Images
    Wrapable = False
    object ToolButton1: TToolButton
      Action = acNew
    end
    // more buttons...
  end
  object ToolBarEdit: TToolBar...
  object ToolBarFont: TToolBar...
  object ToolBarMenu: TToolBar
    AutoSize = True
    Flat = True
    Menu = MainMenu
  end
  object ComboFont: TComboBox
    Hint = 'Font Family'
    Style = csDropDownList
    OnClick = ComboFontClick
  end
  object ColorBox1: TColorBox...
end
```

FIGURE 8.8
The MdEdit2 example at
run time while a user is
rearranging the toolbars
in the control bar

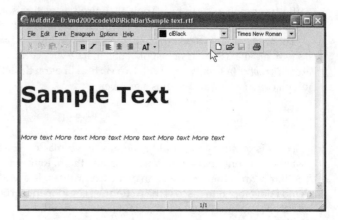

To obtain the standard effect, you have to disable the edges of the controls placed in the ToolBar
and set their style to flat. Sizing all the controls alike so that you obtain one or two rows of elements
of the same height is not as easy as it might seem at first. Some controls have automatic sizing or various constraints. In particular, to make the combo box the same height as the toolbars, you have to
tweak the type and size of its font. Resizing the control itself has no effect.

The ControlBar also has a shortcut menu that allows you to show or hide each of the controls currently inside it. Instead of writing code specific to this example, I implemented a more generic (and
reusable) solution. The shortcut menu, called `BarMenu`, is empty at design time and populated when
the program starts:

```
var
  I: Integer;
  mItem: TMenuItem;
begin
  // populate the control bar menu
  for I := 0 to ControlBar.ControlCount - 1 do
  begin
    mItem := TMenuItem.Create (Self);
    mItem.Caption := ControlBar.Controls [I].Name;
    mItem.Tag := Integer (ControlBar.Controls [I]);
    mItem.OnClick := BarMenuClick;
    BarMenu.Items.Add (mItem);
  end;
```

The `BarMenuClick` procedure is a single event handler used by all the menu items; it uses the `Tag`
property of the `Sender` menu item to refer to the element of the ControlBar associated with the item
in the `FormCreate` method:

```
procedure TFormRichNote.BarMenuClick(Sender: TObject);
var
  aCtrl: TControl;
begin
  aCtrl := TControl ((Sender as TComponent).Tag);
  aCtrl.Visible := not aCtrl.Visible;
end;
```

Finally, the OnPopup event of the menu is used to refresh the check mark of the menu items:

```
procedure TFormRichNote.BarMenuPopup(Sender: TObject);
var
  I: Integer;
begin
  // update the menu check marks
  for I := 0 to BarMenu.Items.Count - 1 do
    BarMenu.Items [I].Checked := TControl (
      BarMenu.Items [I].Tag).Visible;
end;
```

A Menu in a Control Bar

If you look at the user interface of the MdEdit2 application in Figure 8.8, you'll notice that the form's menu appears inside a toolbar, hosted by the control bar, below the application caption. All you have to do to accomplish this is set the toolbar's Menu property. You must also remove the main menu from the form's Menu property (keeping the MainMenu component on the form) to avoid having two copies of the menu on screen.

Delphi's Docking Support

Another feature available in Delphi is support for *dockable* toolbars and controls. In other words, you can create a toolbar and move it to any side of a form, or even move it freely on the screen, undocking it. However, setting up a program properly to obtain this effect is not as easy as it sounds.

Delphi's docking support is connected with container controls, not only with forms. A panel, a ControlBar, and other containers (technically, any control derived from TWinControl) can be set up as dock targets by enabling their DockSite property. You can also set the AutoSize property of these containers so they'll show up only if they hold a control.

To be able to drag a control (an object of any TControl-derived class) into the dock site, simply set its DragKind property to dkDock and its DragMode property to dmAutomatic. This way, the control can be dragged away from its current position into a new docking container. To undock a component and move it to a special form, you can set its FloatingDockSiteClass property to TCustomDockForm (to use a predefined stand-alone form with a small caption).

All the docking and undocking operations can be tracked by using special events of the component being dragged (OnStartDock and OnEndDock) and the component that will receive the docked control (OnDockOver and OnDockDrop). These docking events are very similar to Delphi dragging events.

There are also commands you can use to accomplish docking operations in code and to explore the status of a docking container. Every control can be moved to a different location using the Dock, ManualDock, and ManualFloat methods. A container has a DockClientCount property, indicating the number of docked controls, and a DockClients property, which is an array of these controls.

Moreover, if the dock container has the UseDockManager property set to True, you'll be able to use the DockManager property, which implements the IDockManager interface. This interface has many features you can use to customize the behavior of a dock container, including support for streaming its status. As you can see from this brief description, docking support in Delphi is based on a large number of properties, events, and methods—more features than I have room to explore in detail. The next example introduces the main features you'll need.

Docking Toolbars in ControlBars

The MdEdit2 example, already discussed, includes docking support. The program has a second ControlBar at the bottom of the form that accepts dragging one of the toolbars in the ControlBar at the top. Because both toolbar containers have the AutoSize property set to True, they are automatically removed when the host contains no controls. I also set the AutoDrag and AutoDock properties of both ControlBars to True.

I had to place the bottom ControlBar inside a panel, together with the RichEdit control. Without this trick, the ControlBar, when activated and automatically resized, kept moving below the status bar, which isn't the correct behavior. In the example, the ControlBar is the only panel control aligned to the bottom, so there is no possible confusion.

To let users drag the toolbars out of the original container, you once again (as stated previously) set their DragKind property to dkDock and their DragMode property to dmAutomatic. The only two exceptions are the menu toolbar, which I decided to keep close to the typical position of a menu bar, and the ColorBox control, because unlike the combo box this component doesn't expose the DragMode and DragKind properties. (In the example's FormCreate method, you'll find code you can use to activate docking for the component, based on the "protected hack" discussed in Chapter 3.) The Fonts combo box can be dragged, but I don't want to let a user dock it in the lower control bar. To implement this constraint, I used the control bar's OnDockOver event handler by accepting the docking operation only for toolbars:

```
procedure TFormRichNote.ControlBarLowerDockOver(Sender: TObject;
  Source: TDragDockObject; X, Y: Integer; State: TDragState;
  var Accept: Boolean);
begin
  Accept := Source.Control is TToolbar;
end;
```

WARNING   Dragging a toolbar directly from the upper control bar to the lower control bar doesn't work. The control bar doesn't resize to host the toolbar during the dragging operation, as it does when you drag the toolbar to a floating form and then to the lower control bar. This is a bug in the VCL, and it is very difficult to circumvent. As you'll see the next example, MdEdit3 works as expected even if it has the same code: it uses a different component with different VCL support code!

When you move one of the toolbars outside of any container, Delphi automatically creates a floating form; you might be tempted to set it back by closing the floating form. This doesn't work because the floating form is removed along with the toolbar it contains. However, you can use the shortcut menu of the top-most ControlBar, also attached to the other ControlBar, to show this hidden toolbar.

The floating form created by Delphi to host undocked controls has a thin caption, the so-called *toolbar caption*, which by default has no text. For this reason, I added some code to the OnEndDock event of each dockable control to set the caption of the newly created form into which the control is docked. To avoid a custom data structure for this information, I used the text of the Hint property (not used in this example) for these controls to provide a suitable caption, as you can see in Figure 8.9:

```
procedure TFormRichNote.EndDock(Sender, Target: TObject;
  X, Y: Integer);
begin
  if Target is TCustomForm then
```

```
      TCustomForm(Target).Caption := GetShortHint((
        Sender as TControl).Hint);
  end;
```

Another extension of the example (which I didn't do) might add dock areas on the two sides of the form. The only extra effort this would require would be a routine to turn the toolbars vertically instead of horizontally. Doing so requires switching the Left and Top properties of each button after disabling the automatic sizing.

FIGURE 8.9
The MdEdit2 example allows you to dock the toolbars (but not the menu) at the top or bottom of the form or to leave them floating.

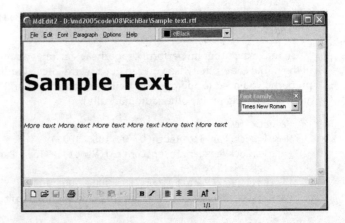

CONTROLLING DOCKING OPERATIONS

Delphi provides many events and methods that give you a lot of control over docking operations, including a dock manager. To explore some of these features, try the DockTest example, a test bed for docking operations shown in Figure 8.10. The program handles the OnDockOver and OnDockDrop events of a dock host panel to display messages to the user, such as the number of controls currently docked:

```
procedure TForm1.Panel1DockDrop(Sender: TObject;
  Source: TDragDockObject; X, Y: Integer);
begin
  Caption := 'Docked: ' + IntToStr (Panel1.DockClientCount);
end;
```

In the same way, the program handles the main form's docking events. The controls have a shortcut menu you can invoke to perform docking and undocking operations in code, without the usual mouse dragging, with code like this:

```
procedure TForm1.menuFloatPanelClick(Sender: TObject);
begin
  Panel2.ManualFloat (Rect (100, 100, 200, 300));
end;
```

```
procedure TForm1.Floating1Click(Sender: TObject);
var
  aCtrl: TControl;
begin
  aCtrl := Sender as TControl;
  // toggle the floating status
  if aCtrl.Floating then
    aCtrl.ManualDock (Panel1, nil, alBottom)
  else
    aCtrl.ManualFloat (Rect (100, 100, 200, 300));
end;
```

To make the program perform properly at startup, you must dock the controls to the main panel in the initial code; otherwise you can get a weird effect. Oddly enough, for the program to behave properly, you need to add controls to the dock manager and also dock them to the panel (one operation doesn't trigger the other automatically):

```
// dock memo
Memo1.Dock(Panel1, Rect (0, 0, 100, 100));
Panel1.DockManager.InsertControl(Memo1, alTop, Panel1);
// dock listbox
ListBox1.Dock(Panel1, Rect (0, 100, 100, 100));
Panel1.DockManager.InsertControl(ListBox1, alLeft, Panel1);
// dock panel2
Panel2.Dock(Panel1, Rect (100, 0, 100, 100));
Panel1.DockManager.InsertControl(Panel2, alBottom, Panel1);
```

The example's final feature is probably the most interesting and the most difficult to implement properly. Every time the program closes, it saves the current docking status of the panel, using the dock manager support. When the program is reopened, it reapplies the docking information, restoring the window's previous configuration. Here is a simplified version of the code you might write for saving and loading:

```
procedure TForm1.FormDestroy(Sender: TObject);
begin
  if Panel1.DockClientCount > 0 then
    Panel1.DockManager.SaveToStream (FileStr);
end;

procedure TForm1.FormCreate(Sender: TObject);
begin
  Panel1.DockManager.LoadFromStream (FileStr);
  Panel1.DockManager.ResetBounds (True);
end;
```

This code works fine as long as all controls are initially docked. When you save the program, if one control is floating, you won't see it when you reload the settings. However, because of the initialization code inserted earlier, the control will be docked to the panel anyway and will appear when you drag away the other controls. Needless to say, this is a messy situation. For this reason, after loading the settings, I added this further code:

```
for i := Panel1.DockClientCount - 1 downto 0 do
begin
  aCtrl := Panel1.DockClients[i];
  Panel1.DockManager.GetControlBounds(aCtrl, aRect);
  if (aRect.Bottom - aRect.Top <= 0) then
  begin
    aCtrl.ManualFloat (aCtrl.ClientRect);
    Panel1.DockManager.RemoveControl(aCtrl);
  end;
end;
```

The complete listing includes more commented code that I used while developing this program; you might use it to understand what happens (which is often different from what you expect!). Briefly, the controls that have no size set in the dock manager (the only way I could figure out they are not docked) are shown in a floating window and are removed from the dock manager list.

If you look at the complete code for the `OnCreate` event handler, you'll see a lot of complex code, just to get a plain behavior. You could add more features to a docking program, but to do so you should remove other features because some of them might conflict. Adding a custom docking form breaks features of the dock manager. Automatic alignments don't work well with the docking manager's code for restoring the status. I suggest you take this program and explore its behavior, extending it to support the type of user interface you prefer.

NOTE   Remember that although docking panels make an application look nice, some users are confused by the fact that their toolbars might disappear or be in a different position than they are used to. Don't overuse the docking features, or some of your inexperienced users may get lost.

FIGURE 8.10
The DockTest example
with three controls
docked in the main form

Docking to a PageControl

Another interesting feature of PageControls is their specific support for docking. As you dock a new control over a PageControl, a new page is automatically added to host it, as you can easily see in the Delphi environment. To accomplish this, you set the PageControl as a dock host and activate docking for the client controls. This technique works best when you have secondary forms you want to host. Moreover, if you want to be able to move the entire PageControl into a floating window and then dock it back, you'll need a docking panel in the main form.

This is what I've done in the DockPage example, which has a main form with the following settings:

```
object Form1: TForm1
  Caption = 'Docking Pages'
  object Panel1: TPanel
    Align = alLeft
    DockSite = True
    OnMouseDown = Panel1MouseDown
    object PageControl1: TPageControl
      ActivePage = TabSheet1
      Align = alClient
      DockSite = True
      DragKind = dkDock
      object TabSheet1: TTabSheet
        Caption = 'List'
        object ListBox1: TListBox
          Align = alClient
        end
      end
    end
  end
  object Splitter1: TSplitter
    Cursor = crHSplit
  end
  object Memo1: TMemo
    Align = alClient
  end
end
```

Notice that the Panel has the UseDockManager property set to True and that the PageControl invariably hosts a page with a list box because when you remove all the pages the code used for automatic sizing of dock containers might cause you trouble. The program has two other forms with similar settings (although they host different controls):

```
object Form2: TForm2
  Caption = 'Small Editor'
  DragKind = dkDock
  DragMode = dmAutomatic
  object Memo1: TMemo
    Align = alClient
  end
end
```

You can drag these forms onto the page control to add new pages to it, with captions corresponding to the form titles. You can also undock each of these controls and even the entire PageControl. The program doesn't enable automatic dragging, which would make it impossible to switch pages; instead, the feature is activated when the user clicks the area of the PageControl that has no tabs—that is, on the underlying panel:

```
procedure TForm1.Panel1MouseDown(Sender: TObject; Button: TMouseButton;
  Shift: TShiftState; X, Y: Integer);
begin
  PageControl1.BeginDrag (False, 10);
end;
```

You can test this behavior by running the DockPage example, which Figure 8.11 depicts. Notice that when you remove the PageControl from the main form, you cannot directly dock the other forms to the panel, as this is prevented by specific code within the program (simply because at times the behavior won't be correct).

FIGURE 8.11

The main form of the DockPage example after some forms have been docked to the page control on the left

Delphi 2005 New Docking Components

Delphi 2005 provides many low-level changes in the docking support, with a number of bug fixes particularly related to the DockManager, the internal data structure hosting dock information for controls (panels in particular) that have the UseDockManager property set to True.

As already mentioned in the section on TabControls, Delphi 2005 has a revamped TabSet component and a brand new DockedTabSet component. Contrary to what you might think at first, this is not a TabSet automatically hosting pages. This TabSet works with a companion container control (indicated in the DestinationDockSite property) and lists the *pinned* pages. What it automatically provides is a way to enlarge the *pinned* pages with an animated effect.

As there is some action involved, nothing can explain this behavior better than an example. To build the DockTabTest program I placed in a form a DockTab aligned to the bottom, a panel aligned to the client, and another panel aligned to the top and hosting two command buttons. The target panel and the DockTab component are connected by means the of the DestinationDockSite property of the DockTab.

By default, the DockTab component has its DockSite property active, which means by docking a control or form to the DockTab you'll actually dock it to the panel in pinned *mode* (more about this later) and connect it to the DockTab. I don't think this is generally the behavior you want, which is why I disabled this property and activated the DockSite and UseDockManager properties of the target panel, Panel1. This is a summary of the core properties of the two components:

```
object DockTabSet1: TDockTabSet
  Height = 25
  Align = alBottom
  ShrinkToFit = True
  SoftTop = True
  Style = tsModernTabs
  DockSite = False
  DestinationDockSite = Panel1
end
object Panel1: TPanel
  Align = alClient
  BevelOuter = bvNone
  DockSite = True
  TabOrder = 1
end
```

The program has two other forms you can create and dock automatically by pressing the toolbar buttons:

```
procedure TFormDockTab.btnOtherMemoClick(Sender: TObject);
begin
  if not Assigned (FormMemo) then
    FormMemo := TFormMemo.Create (Application);
  FormMemo.Show;
  FormMemo.ManualDock(Panel1);
end;
```

There is some extra code in these forms to handle their destruction, but this is all. What is relevant is that they have the DragKind property set to dkDock and the DragMode property set to dmAutomatic.

What is the effect of this program? If you press the two buttons, both forms will be hosted in the panel (see Figure 8.12, top) with the DockTab apparently not involved. If you click one of the pins, that form will be *pinned* to the DockTab and will be displayed with an animation when you select the corresponding tab. If you *pin* both forms, they'll show up in the DockTab (see Figure 8.12, bottom) and will be displayed alternatively, with an animation collapsing the active one and expanding the other.

The ActionManager Architecture

You have seen that actions and the ActionList component can play a central role in the development of Delphi applications because they allow a much better separation of the user interface from the actual code of the application. The user interface can now easily change without impacting the code too much. The drawback of this approach is that a programmer has more work to do. To create a new menu item, you need to add the corresponding action first, then move to the menu, add the menu item, and connect it to the action.

FIGURE 8.12

Two forms docked to a panel (top) and pinned to a DockTab (bottom)

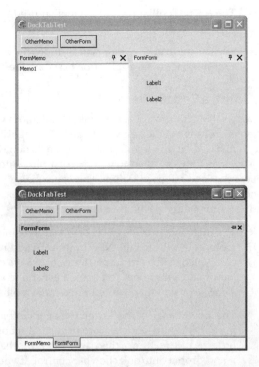

To solve this issue, and to provide developers and end users with some advanced features, Delphi provides an architecture based on the ActionManager component, which largely extends the role of actions. The ActionManager has a collection of actions as well as a collection of toolbars and menus tied to them. The development of these toolbars and menus is completely visual: you drag actions from a special component editor of the ActionManager to the toolbars to create the buttons you need. Moreover, you can let the end user of your programs do the same operation, rearranging their toolbars and menus beginning with the actions you provide them.

In other words, using this architecture allows you to build applications with a modern user interface, customizable by the user. The menu can show only the recently used items (as many Microsoft programs do), and it allows for animation and more.

This architecture is centered on the ActionManager component, but it also includes a few other components found at the end of the Additional page of the palette:

♦ The ActionManager component is a replacement for the ActionList (but can also use one or more existing ActionLists).

♦ The ActionMainMenuBar control is a toolbar used to display the menu of an application based on the actions of an ActionManager component.

♦ The PopupActionBar component lets your pop-up menus follow the same user interface as your main menus. (This component didn't ship in Delphi 7 but was available as a separate download; now it is part of Delphi 2005).

◆ The ActionToolBar control is a toolbar used to host buttons based on the actions of an Action-Manager component.

◆ The CustomizeDlg component includes the dialog box you can use to let users customize the user interface of an application based on the ActionManager component.

Building a Simple Demo

Because this architecture is mostly visual, a demo is worth more than a general discussion (although a printed book is not the best way to discuss a highly visual series of operations). To create a sample program based on this architecture, drop an ActionManager component on a form and double-click it to open its component editor. Notice that this editor is not modal, so you can keep it open while doing other operations in Delphi. This same dialog box is also displayed by the CustomizeDlg component, although with some limited features (for example, the addition of new actions is disabled).

The editor's three pages are as follows:

◆ The first page provides a list of visual containers of actions (toolbars or menus). You add new toolbars by clicking the New button. To add new menus, you have to add the corresponding component to the form, open the `ActionBars` collection of the ActionManager, select an action bar or add a new one, and hook the menu to it using the `ActionBar` property. These are the same steps you follow to connect a new toolbar to this architecture at run time.

◆ The second page of the ActionManager editor is very similar to the ActionList editor, providing a way to add new standard or custom actions, arrange them in categories, and change their order. A nice feature of this page, though, is that you can drag a category or a single action from it and drop it onto an action bar control. If you drag a category to a menu, you obtain a pull-down menu with all the category items; if you drag it to a toolbar, each of the category's actions gets a button on the toolbar. If you drag a single action to a toolbar, you get the corresponding button; if you drag it to the menu, you get a direct menu command, which is something you should generally avoid.

◆ The last page of the ActionManager editor allows you (and optionally an end user) to activate the display of recently used menu items and to modify some of the toolbars' visual properties.

The AcManTest program is an example that uses some of the standard actions and a RichEdit control to showcase the use of this architecture (I didn't write any custom code to make the actions work better, because I wanted to focus only on the Action Manager for this example). You can experiment with it at design time or run it, click the Customize button, and see what an end user can do to customize the application (see Figure 8.13).

In the program, you can prevent the user from doing some operations on actions. Any specific element of the user interface (a `TActionClient` object) has a `ChangedAllowed` property that you can use to disable modify, move, and delete operations. Any action client container (the visual bars) has a property to disable hiding itself (`AllowHiding` by default is set to True). Each Action-Bar `Items` collection has a `Customizable` option you can turn off to disable all user changes to the entire bar.

FIGURE 8.13

Using the CustomizeDlg component, you can let a user customize the toolbars and the menu of an application by dragging items from the dialog box or moving them around in the action bars.

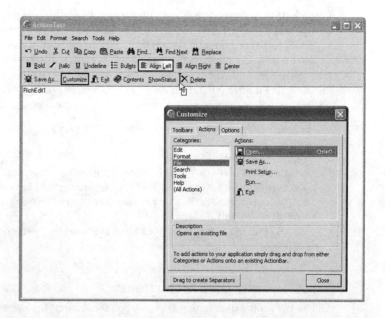

TIP When I say ActionBar I don't mean the visual toolbars containing action items; I mean the items of the `ActionBars` collection of the ActionManager component, which in turn has an `Items` collection. The best way to understand this structure is to look at the subtree displayed by the Structure View for an ActionManager component. Each `TActionBar` collection item has a `TCustomActionBar` visual component connected, but not the reverse (so, for example, you cannot reach this `Customizable` property if you start by selecting the visual toolbar). Due to the similarity of the two names, it can take a while to understand what the Delphi help is referring to.

To make user settings persistent, I connected a file (called `settings`) to the `FileName` property of the ActionManager component. When you assign this property, you should enter the name of the file you want to use; when you start the program, the file will be created for you by the ActionManager. The persistency is accomplished by streaming each ActionClientItem connected with the ActionManager. Because these action client items are based on the user settings and maintain state information, a single file collects both user changes to the interface and usage data.

Because Delphi stores user setting and status information in a file you provide, you can make your application support multiple users on a single computer. Simply use a file of settings for each of them (under the MyDocuments or MySettings virtual folder) and connect it to the ActionManager as the program starts (using the current user of the computer or after some custom login). Another possibility is to store these settings over the network, so that even when a user moves to a different computer, the current personal settings will move along with them.

In the program I decided to store the settings in a file stored in the same folder as the program, assigning the relative path (the filename) to the ActionManager's `FileName` property. The component will fill in the complete filename with the program folder, easily finding the file to load. However, the file includes among its data its own filename with an absolute path. So, when it is time to save the file, the operation may refer to an older path. This prevents you from copying this program with its settings to a different folder (for example, this is an issue for the AcManTest demo). You can reset the `FileName` property after loading the file. As a further alternative, you could set the filename at run time in the form's `OnCreate` event. In this case you also have to force the file to reload because you are assigning it after the ActionManager component and the ActionBars have already been created and initialized. However, you might want to force the filename after loading it, as just described:

```
procedure TForm1.FormCreate(Sender: TObject);
begin
  ActionManager1.FileName :=
    ExtractFilePath (Application.ExeName) + 'settings';
  ActionManager1.LoadFromFile(ActionManager1.FileName);
  // reset the settings file name after loading it (relative path)
  ActionManager1.FileName :=
      ExtractFilePath (Application.ExeName) + 'settings';
end;
```

Least Recently Used Menu Items

Once a file for the user settings is available, the ActionManager will save the user preferences into it and use it to track the user activity. This is essential to letting the system remove menu items that haven't been used for some time and making them available in an extended menu using the same user interface adopted by Microsoft, as you can see next:

The ActionManager doesn't just show the least recently used items; it allows you to customize this behavior in a precise way. Each action bar has a `SessionCount` property that keeps track of the number of times the application has been executed. Each ActionClientItem has a `LastSession` property and a `UsageCount` property that tracks user operations. Notice, by the way, that a user can reset all this dynamic information by using the Reset Usage Data button in the customization dialog.

The system calculates the number of sessions the action has gone unused by computing the difference between the number of times the application has been executed (`SessionCount`) and the last session in which the action has been used (`LastSession`). The value of `UsageCount` is used to look up in the `PrioritySchedule` how many sessions the items can go unused before they are removed. In other words, the `PrioritySchedule` maps the usage count with a number of *unused* sessions. By modifying the `PrioritySchedule`, you can determine how quickly the items are removed if they are not used.

You can also prevent this system from being activated for specific actions or groups of actions. The `Items` property of the ActionManager's `ActionBars` has a `HideUnused` property you can toggle to disable this feature for an entire menu. To make a specific item always visible regardless of the actual usage, you can also set its `UsageCount` property to –1. However, the user settings might override this value.

To help you better understand how this system works, I added a custom action (`ActionShowStatus`) to the AcManTest example. The action has the following code that saves the current Action Manager settings to a memory stream, converts the stream to text, and shows it in the memo (refer to Chapter 5 for more information about streaming):

```
procedure TForm1.ActionShowStatusExecute(Sender: TObject);
var
  memStr, memStr2: TMemoryStream;
begin
  memStr := TMemoryStream.Create;
  try
    memStr2 := TMemoryStream.Create;
    try
      ActionManager1.SaveToStream(memStr);
      memStr.Position := 0;
      ObjectBinaryToText(memStr, memStr2);
      memStr2.Position := 0;
      RichEdit1.Lines.LoadFromStream(memStr2);
    finally
      memStr2.Free;
    end;
  finally
    memStr.Free;
  end;
end;
```

The output you obtain is the textual version of the `settings` file automatically updated at each execution of the program. Here is a small portion of this file, including the details of one of the pull-down menus and plenty of comments:

```
item // File pulldown of the main menu action bar
  Items = <
    item
      Action = Form1.FileOpen1
      LastSession = 19 // was used in the last session
      UsageCount = 4 // was used four times
    end
    item
      Action = Form1.FileSaveAs1 // never used
    end
    item
      Action = Form1.FilePrintSetup1
      LastSession = 7 // used some time ago
      UsageCount = 1 // only once
    end
    item
      Action = Form1.FileRun1 // never used
    end
```

```
    item
      Action = Form1.FileExit1 // never used
    end>
  Caption = '&File'
  LastSession = 19
  UsageCount = 5 // the sum of the usage count of the items
end
```

Porting an Existing Program

If this architecture is useful, you'll probably need to redo most of your applications to take advantage of it. However, if you're already using actions (with the ActionList component), this conversion will be much simpler. The ActionManager has its own set of actions but can also use actions from another ActionManager or ActionList. The ActionManager's `LinkedActionLists` property is a collection of other containers of actions (ActionLists or ActionManagers), which can be associated with the current ActionManager. Associating all the various groups of actions is useful because you can let a user customize the entire user interface with a single dialog box.

If you hook external actions and open the ActionManager editor, you'll see in the Actions page a combo box listing the current ActionManager plus the other action containers linked to it. You can choose one of these containers to see its set of actions and change their properties. The All Actions option in this combo box allows you to work on all the actions from the various containers at once; however, I've noticed that at startup it is selected but not always *effective*. Reselect it to see all the actions.

As an example of porting an existing application, I extended the program built throughout this chapter into the MdEdit3 example. This example uses the same action list as the previous version, but it's hooked to an ActionManager that has the extra customize property to let users rearrange the user interface. Unlike the earlier AcManDemo program, the MdEdit3 example uses a ControlBar as a container for the action bars (a menu, three toolbars, and the usual combo boxes) and has full support for dragging them outside the container as floating bars and dropping them into the lower ControlBar.

To accomplish this, I only had to modify the source code slightly to refer to the new classes for the containers (`TCustomActionToolBar` instead of `TToolBar`) in the `ControlBarLowerDockOver` method. I also found that the ActionToolBar component's `OnEndDock` event passes as parameter an empty target when the system creates a floating form to host the control, so I couldn't easily give this form a new custom caption (see the form's `EndDock` method).

Using List Actions

In this section, I add an extra example showing how to use a rather complex group of standard actions: the list actions. List actions comprise two different groups. Some of them (such as move, copy, delete, clear, and select all) are normal actions that work on list boxes or other lists. The VirtualListAction and StaticListAction, however, define actions providing a list of items that will be displayed in a toolbar as a combo box.

The ListActions demo highlights both groups of list actions; its ActionManager has five actions displayed on two separate toolbars. This is a summary of the actions (I omitted the action bars portion of the component's DFM file):

```
object ActionManager1: TActionManager
  ActionBars.SessionCount = 1
  ActionBars = <...>
```

```
object StaticListAction1: TStaticListAction
  Caption = 'Numbers'
  Items.CaseSensitive = False
  Items.SortType = stNone
  Items = <...>
  OnItemSelected = ListActionItemSelected
end
object VirtualListAction1: TVirtualListAction
  Caption = 'Items'
  OnGetItem = VirtualListAction1GetItem
  OnGetItemCount = VirtualListAction1GetItemCount
  OnItemSelected = ListActionItemSelected
end
object ListControlCopySelection1: TListControlCopySelection
  Caption = 'Copy'
  Destination = ListBox2
  ListControl = ListBox1
end
object ListControlDeleteSelection1: TListControlDeleteSelection
  Caption = 'Delete'
end
object ListControlMoveSelection2: TListControlMoveSelection
  Caption = 'Move'
  Destination = ListBox2
  ListControl = ListBox1
end
end
```

The program also has two list boxes in its form, which are used as action targets. The copy and move actions are tied to these two list boxes by their ListControl and Destination properties. The delete action automatically works with the list box having the input focus.

The StaticListAction defines a series of alternative items in its Items collection. This is not a plain string list, because any item also has an ImageIndex that lets you add graphical elements to the control displaying the list. You can, of course, add more items to this list programmatically. However, if the list is highly dynamic, you can also use the VirtualListAction. This action doesn't define a list of items but has two events you can use to provide strings and images for the list: OnGetItemCount allows you to indicate the number of items to display, and OnGetItem is then called for each specific item.

WARNING The OnGetItem event of the TVirtualListAction class has a Pointer type parameter passed by reference. In the VCL for .NET the same parameter is of the System.Object type. To handle this different signature, you can use conditional compilation (as the source code of this example does) or go for separate projects (DFM and NFM, with different Delphi source code files). There are very few of these incompatibilities in the VCL for .NET, but they are annoying. The IDE, in fact, doesn't behave properly with IFDEFs in the designer-related source code, like event handlers.

In the ListActions demo, the VirtualListAction has the following event handlers for its definition, producing the list you can see in the active combo box in Figure 8.14:

```
procedure TForm1.VirtualListAction1GetItemCount(
  Sender: TCustomListAction; var Count: Integer);
begin
  Count := 100;
end;

procedure TForm1.VirtualListAction1GetItem(Sender: TCustomListAction;
  const Index: Integer; var Value: String;
  var ImageIndex: Integer; var Data: Pointer);
begin
  Value := 'Item' + IntToStr (Index);
end;
```

NOTE I originally thought the virtual action items were requested only when needed for display, making this a virtual list. Instead, all the items are created right away. You can prove it by enabling the commented code in the `VirtualListAction1GetItem` method (not included in the previous listing), which adds to each item the time its string is requested.

Both the static list and the virtual list have an `OnItemSelected` event. In the shared event handler, I wrote the following code to add the current item to the form's first list box:

```
procedure TForm1.ListActionItemSelected(Sender: TCustomListAction;
  Control: TControl);
begin
  ListBox1.Items.Add ((Control as TCustomActionCombo).SelText);
end;
```

FIGURE 8.14
The ListActions application has a toolbar hosting a static list and a virtual list.

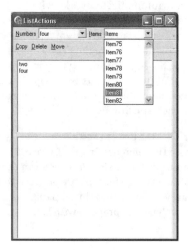

In this case, the sender is the custom action list, but the `ItemIndex` property of this list is not updated with the selected item. However, by accessing the visual control that displays the list, you can obtain the value of the selected item.

What's Next?

In this chapter, I introduced the use of actions, the actions list, and Action Manager architectures. As you saw, this is an extremely powerful architecture to separate the user interface from your application code, which uses and refers to the actions and not the menu items or toolbar buttons related to them. The recent extension of this architecture allows users of your programs to have a lot of control and makes your applications resemble high-end programs without much effort on your part. The same architecture is also very handy for designing your program's user interface, regardless of whether you give this ability to users.

I also covered some user-interface techniques, such as docking toolbars and other controls. You can consider this chapter the first step toward building professional applications. We will take other steps in the following chapters, but you already know enough to make your programs look similar to some best-selling Windows applications, which may be very important for your clients.

Now that I've devoted three chapters to the VCL for Win32 and .NET, let me focus on a specific .NET issue: the development of visual applications based on the WinForms portion of the Framework Class Library (FCL). This is the topic of the next chapter, along with the description of other portions of the FCL. Later, we'll get back to other VCL-related topics, such as the architecture of database applications (in Chapter 13 and beyond).

Chapter 9

Delphi .NET Run-Time Library and the Framework Class Library

In the last few chapters (from Chapter 5 to Chapter 8) I covered Delphi's run-time library (RTL) and Visual Component Library (VCL), mostly from the perspective of Win32 development. I have mentioned differences between Win32 and .NET solutions and provided code examples for both platforms, but I have devoted almost no space to .NET-specific technologies in this area.

This chapter fills that gap, covering three separate topics. In the first part, I emphasize some relevant changes to the Delphi RTL for .NET support. In the second part, I cover the native library of .NET, discussing some of the core classes of the Framework Class Library (FCL), globally indicated as Base Class Library (BCL). In the third part, I offer an overview of the native forms and controls library, called WinForms, and compare it to the VCL.

I have limited my coverage of the FCL (both in the BCL and WinForms areas) to how it relates specifically to Delphi. There are entire books devoted to these topics, so I recommend referring to more specialized sources if you are looking for in-depth and complete coverage of the classes of these libraries.

The Run-Time Library of Delphi for .NET

The starting point for this chapter is an analysis of differences in the run-time library of Delphi for .NET compared to Delphi for Win32. Borland made a considerable effort to make the low-level procedures and core classes of Delphi for .NET extremely compatible with their Win32 counterparts. However, even if class declarations didn't change, their actual implementation often changed considerably.

In some cases, Delphi uses class helpers to merge the interface of standard Delphi classes (like TObject or TComponent) to their .NET counterparts (System.Object or System.ComponentModel.Component). Whenever possible, core Delphi RTL classes for .NET wrap an available class of the FCL.

The System Unit in Delphi for .NET

From Delphi for Win32 to Delphi for .NET, a significant number of changes have been made to the system unit, more than to most other units of the RTL. Most of the changes are related to a totally different implementation, and Borland has made a huge effort to obtain a large degree of compatibility with existing Delphi code.

As you already saw in Chapter 4, the TObject type is now declared as an alias of the System.Object type, the core class of the .NET Framework. You also saw how by using a class helper (TObjectHelper) Borland was able to re-introduce most of the standard method of the TObject class to the System.Object class. This means that these methods are available for any class, including those not compiled in Delphi for .NET.

Not every feature of TObject could be moved to .NET, though. Here is a short comparison of the methods, divided in groups:

◆ The class-related methods (ClassType, ClassName, ClassNameIs, ClassInfo, ClassParent, and InheritsFrom) are still available and work the same.

◆ The methods used to work at the low-level with internal memory locations (MethodAddress, MethodName, and FieldAddress) are available but are quite different as they are not based on pointers anymore.

◆ The low-level object construction and destruction methods (InitInstance, Cleanup Instance, NewInstance, and FreeInstance) are gone, along with the second-level constructor and destructor (AfterConstruction and BeforeDestruction).

◆ Also gone are the Interface-related methods (GetInterface, GetInterfaceEntry, and GetInterfaceTable) and the SafeCallException method.

◆ You cannot use InstanceSize any more, as the size of an object is determined by the run time at load time and not by the compiler. Making any assumption on the size of an object in .NET is a bad design decision, as your code won't be portable to other .NET platforms other than those based on Win32.

◆ The virtual Dispatch method is still available, although it has an untyped parameter (var Message), while the DefaultHandler virtual method is not there anymore.

◆ Finally, the Free method is available, although it now invokes the IDisposable.Dispose method instead of the destructor, as discussed at length in Chapter 4.

By being an alias of System.Object, the TObject class gains new methods like Equals, GetHashCode, ToString, and GetType. This will be discussed later in this chapter in the section about the base classes of the FCL in the section "The *System.Object* Class."

In addition to the declaration of TObject, there are many other differences between the Win32 System unit and the .NET Borland.Delphi.System unit, some of which are listed here:

◆ The TClass class reference is quite different, as already covered in Chapter 4.

◆ The Exception class has been moved here from SysUtils and is now an alias of the .NET System.Exception class.

◆ The IInterface base interface has no methods (as reference counting doesn't apply on .NET, and query interface can be managed directly by the CLR during cast operations).

◆ The Assigned function has a GCHandle parameter, while on Win32 it has an untyped parameter.

◆ There is a large set of custom attribute types.

◆ Records are now used for some plain data types, including AnsiString, Currency, and TDateTime. These records have several methods and define operators, including conversion operators.

◆ Similarly, the TMethod record now has a few methods.

◆ Memory manager support and all memory-related functions have been removed.

The Delphi Run Time: Borland.Delphi.DLL

Another relevant difference compared to the past versions of Delphi is that on .NET the language comes with a run-time DLL. In Win32, the core run time (defined in the System unit) is compiled into each and every executable file, regardless of the fact you use run-time packages. This run time has a very limited overhead, particularly if you don't use all of its features such as variant support functions, which are linked into the executable file only if they are actually used.

The linking of the Delphi run time in the executable takes place by default also on .NET. However, on this platform you can request the use of an external Delphi run time, which is available in the Borland.Delphi.DLL library. This DLL is quite small (99.5 KB), and it is added to the GAC by the Delphi installer. You can add a copy to your target compilation folder by using the Copy Local command of the project menu, after selecting this assembly in the References list.

When you build general Delphi applications, you don't need to use and deploy this DLL, as you can use the Link in Units options to have a single executable file. The use of this external library is required when you build a library assembly and want to give it to other developers. You might also want to use it because keeping the run time outside of the program trims its size.

For example, the MiniSizeNet program discussed in Chapter 5, which is the smallest application you can build, shrinks from 28 KB to 12 KB, although these numbers are smaller than average as this is the extreme case of a minimal application.

Borland.VclRtl Routines

As is true with the run-time packages making up the Win32 VCL, the Delphi library can be split in two portions, a run-time library of global routines and low-level classes (like those covered in Chapter 5) and the visual component library per se (detailed in Chapter 6). The same happens in Delphi for .NET, with a Borland.VclRtl assembly and Borland.Vcl assembly. What is relevant is that while you have seen that the VCL portion is virtually unchanged (as it works in parallel to the .NET Framework classes), the RTL portion is integrated with the FCL.

Still, the overall approach used by the Delphi RTL is different from the FCL, as Delphi defines hundreds of global routines. (See Chapter 4 for details on how global routines are mapped to static methods of *compiler-generated* unit classes by the Delphi for .NET compiler.) The reason Borland had to follow this path (regardless of what OOP purists might think of it) is for backward compatibility with existing Delphi code.

In fact, there are units of the RTL that are almost unchanged, including (among others) the ConvUtils, DateUtils, Math, StrUtils, and SyncObjs units of the Borland.Vcl namespace. Many other units see limited changes:

Borland.Vcl.Types   Defines the TPoint, TSize and TRect records that in .NET have many methods and constructors.

Borland.Vcl.Variants and Borland.Vcl.VarConv   Offer a similar interface, although their implementation is totally different, as it was based on specific Win32 support (part of the COM architecture). For the same reason, the VarUtils unit is now missing. Notice you have to manually add the Borland.Vcl.Variants unit (or simply Variants with the default namespace set to Borland.Vcl) to the uses statements of programs using variants, as the variant type has been removed from the core system support.

There are also a few new RTL units:

Borland.Vcl.Complex   Defines a complex record type as a complete example of operators overloading. It supersedes the (still existing) Borland.Vcl.VarCmplx unit, which uses custom variants to obtain a similar effect with a much less polished technique.

Borland.Vcl.Convert   Defines the TConvert record, which offers support for the IComparable and IConvertible .NET interface for the conversion engine defined in the ConvUtils unit.

Borland.Vcl.WinUtils   Includes support functions that replace or complement Windows API calls like MakeObjectInstance and AllocateHWnd; defines a few conversion routines from Delphi standard data types to .NET data types like conversions from native buffers to array and from bytes the corresponding structure; global data access including HInstance and GetCmdShow.

Finally, missing units include DelphiMM and ShareMem.

WINDOWS API DECLARATIONS IN BORLAND.VCL.WINDOWS

The Borland.VCL.Windows unit, along with other similar units, provides an interface to the classic Win32 API from within a .NET application. The definitions of these APIs are quite different, as in one case:

```
// Win32 definition
function SetFocus; external user32 name 'SetFocus';
// .NET definition
[DllImport(user32, CharSet = CharSet.Ansi, SetLastError = True,
  EntryPoint = 'SetFocus')]
function SetFocus; external;
```

The DLLImport attribute is used to implement PInvoke (or Platform Invoke), the call of unmanaged DLL functions implemented in standard Win32 DLLs. The attribute provides the information needed to make a proper call. Although they are mapped to the same physical layer (the Windows core DLLs), the declaration of these APIs in .NET is typically different from their Win32 counterpart.

Calls from a managed application to Win32 unmanaged functions, in fact, are subject to both compilation rules and run-time checks by the CLR. For example, all of the parameters must be type safe on the CLR side. That's why all the PChar string parameters are now defined of the type string (which is a wide string!). At the time of the call, the CLR will marshal the parameters appropriately, converting them back and forth from one format to the other.

NOTE   You can find more information on PInvoke, Inverse PInvoke, and other related topics in Chapter 12.

In most cases, the changes you have to apply to the source code are limited, like removing the PChar cast from your call to pass the string parameter directly. The problem this poses is that it is not trivial to have single calls to the Win32 that you can compile with single source code on Win32 and .NET.

Here are two code snippets taken from examples discussed in the previous chapters. In the first, the IFDEF directive wraps the entire API call; in the second, it wraps only the specific parameter:

```
// from the MiniPack example, Chapter 5
{$IFDEF WIN32}
hFile := CreateFile (PChar (ParamStr (0)),
  0, FILE_SHARE_READ, nil, OPEN_EXISTING, 0, 0);
{$ENDIF}
```

```
{$IFDEF CLR}
hFile := CreateFile (ParamStr (0),
  0, FILE_SHARE_READ, nil, OPEN_EXISTING, 0, 0);
{$ENDIF}

// from the BmpViewer example, Chapter 8
DrawText (Control.Canvas.Handle,
  {$IFDEF WIN32}PChar (FileName),{$ENDIF}
  {$IFDEF CLR}FileName,{$ENDIF}
  Length (FileName),
  OutRect, dt_Left or dt_SingleLine or dt_VCenter);
```

Another case that makes some difference in the API declaration on Win32 and .NET is that Win32 APIs often allow a single parameter to be of different types, depending on the value of other parameters. The CreateWindow API is a classic example, in which a single parameter is used to pass the handle of the main menu or the ID of an MDI child window. Another example is that of APIs that accept in the same parameter either a string or an integer, as in the case of FindResource. As there are multiple combinations for this parameter, the declaration becomes:

```
function FindResource(hModule: HMODULE;
  lpName, lpType: string): HRSRC; overload;
function FindResource(hModule: HMODULE;
  lpName: string; lpType: Integer): HRSRC; overload;
function FindResource(hModule: HMODULE;
  lpName, lpType: Integer): HRSRC; overload;
function FindResource(hModule: HMODULE;
  lpName: Integer; lpType: string): HRSRC; overload;
```

Another frequent case is the use of pointers to data structures that can be nil. Now that the pointers are replaced with records (value types that cannot be null), you need an overloaded version to pass the empty parameter:

```
function InvalidateRect(hWnd: HWND;
  const lpRect: TRect; bErase: BOOL): BOOL; overload;
function InvalidateRect(hWnd: HWND;
  lpRect: IntPtr; bErase: BOOL): BOOL; overload;
```

BORLAND.VCL.SYSUTILS

Another unit with many changes is SysUtils, which in Delphi 2005 has been improved in the Win32 version also. Specific .NET features added to this unit include date format conversions between Delphi string format and the CLR string format (ConvertDelphiDateTimeFormat and ConvertClrDateTimeFormat) and the Win32 API replacements for thread-safe increment and decrement (InterlockedIncrement and InterlockedDecrement, and also InterlockedExchange).

In Delphi for .NET, SameStr replaces CompareMem, file handles are based on System.IO.FileStream, and FileRead and FileWrite routines have type-safe overloads.

Finally, all direct memory management and pointer-based routines are missing, including AllocMem, PChar-based (null-terminated) string functions, and AppendStr (which was already deprecated in Delphi 7).

Borland.VclRtl Classes

Most of the classes of the RTL retain the same interface, although in some cases the implementation changes considerably. Some of the units of the Borland.Vcl namespace that are almost identical are Contnrs, HelpIntfs, IniFiles, and Registry.

There is very little COM support left, so the ComObj and ActiveX units have little content left, while ComServ, VCLCom, and StdVCL are gone (along with CorbaVcl and the ZLib unit defining stream compression).

Many relevant implementation changes imply the use of a .NET support class instead of a native implementation. As an example you can consider the TMask class (in Borland.Vcl.Mask) in Delphi for .NET is a wrapper of the class `System.Text.RegularExpressions.RegEx`, discussed later in the section "Regular Expressions."

BORLAND.VCL.CLASSES

The core classes of Delphi's RTL are defined in the Classes unit (or Borland.Vcl.Classes). In many relevant cases these classes maintain interface compatibility but have been rewritten to take advantage of corresponding classes of the .NET library. Table 9.1 shows a list of these correspondences.

Other commonly used classes defined in this unit, including `TCollection`, `TStrings`, and `TStringList`, have not changed. It is worth noticing that stream classes have corresponding classes in the FCL, and that some of the Delphi streams are mapped to them. In particular, the `TCLRStream Wrapper` is the base stream class that implies mapping to CLR streams. In Delphi for .NET, classes like the `TFileStream` class inherit from `TCLRStreamWrapper`. There is also a `TStreamToCLRStream` class you can use to do the opposite operation, that is, wrap a Delphi stream in a CLR stream. Stream classes have many new overloaded read and write methods for type safety.

Another group of classes uses class helpers to integrate with the FCL while maintaining compatibility with existing code. This is particularly relevant for the `TPersistent` and `TComponent` classes:

```
type
  TPersistent = System.MarshalByRefObject;
  TPersistentHelper = class helper (TObjectHelper)
    for TPersistent

  TComponent = System.ComponentModel.Component;
  TComponentHelper = class helper (TPersistentHelper)
    for TComponent
```

TABLE 9.1:   Some of the Delphi for .NET RTL Classes That Wrap Corresponding FCL Classes

DELPHI "WRAPPER" CLASS	.NET FCL CLASS
TList	System.Collections.ArrayList
TThread	System.Threading.Thread
TCLRStreamWrapper (THandleStream)	System.IO.Stream

For the TComponent class, the class helper needs some storage for the owner, the list of components, and the component name. As a class helper cannot define fields, Delphi for .NET relies on a TComponentSite object managed using the ISite interface of the FCL Component class (more on component containers and site later in this chapter in the section "The Component Class").

In the TComponent class of Delphi for .NET there are also some new features like the Change ComponentName and SetComponentParent class methods, the global routines SendNotification and DelegatesEqual, and a new definition of the Tag property, now of type Variant.

NOTE   The Tag property in the VCL for Win32 is of type Integer; in the VCL for .NET it is of type Variant, and in WinForms it is of type System.Object. These three alternatives can cause some confusion and compatibility problems when moving Delphi code from one library to another. Keep in mind that a Variant in Delphi for .NET is defined as System.Object, so the VCL for .NET and WinForms alternatives are actually quite similar.

Base Class Library (BCL)

The .NET Framework Class Library (FCL) is a large collection of classes covering many different areas, ranging from low-level techniques to user interface and web development. Microsoft generally uses the term Base Class Library (BCL) to refer to some of the core classes of the FCL. The BCL includes the namespaces listed in Table 9.2.

TABLE 9.2:   BCL Namespaces

NAMESPACE	INCLUDES
System	Base types, environmental support, and math functions among many others
System.CodeDom	Support for creating code, compiling, and running it on the fly
System.Collections	Container classes such as lists and hash tables
System.Diagnostics	Event logging, performance counters, and the like
System.Globalization	Support for globalizing .NET applications
System.IO	Support for streams based on file system or serial ports
System.Resources	Help with the translation of applications
System.Text	Support for string encoding and the string builder class
System.Text. RegularExpressions	Parsing and regular expressions support

This is the area of the FCL I'm focusing on in this section. There is no way I can describe (or even list) the classes of the BCL in this book, as you can easily write an entire volume of the subject. The System namespace alone defines slightly over 100 classes, and there is a detailed reference in the .NET Framework SDK and directly available from the Delphi 2005 IDE. My goal is to cover only a few relevant classes, comparing them with the corresponding Delphi RTL solution.

The *System.Object* Class

The Object class is the base class of every FCL (or Delphi for .NET) class. Its role corresponds to the TObject class in Delphi for Win32. You have already seen that TObject in Delphi for .NET is an alias of System.Object, but you haven't seen the features provided by this class.

Of the core methods of System.Object, only GetType has a correspondence in Delphi's TObject, while the others relate to object comparison and representation:

◆ The ReferenceEquals method compares the two references passed as parameters to verify whether they refer to the same object (that is, the same memory address). This corresponds to using the = symbol on variables containing object references.

◆ The Equals method is used to compare the content of the actual objects, field by field, to determine whether the data of the objects is the same, regardless of the fact the two objects are in different memory locations. This is a virtual method that nontrivial derived classes should override.

◆ The GetType method returns the type of the object. The result is a System.Type you can operate on using the Reflection API.

◆ The ToString method converts the object to a string representation, describing the specific instance and its data. This is another virtual you should override often in your own classes.

◆ The GetHashCode method returns a hash code identifying the object and used in hash tables. Again, this is a virtual you'll override often.

To demonstrate some of these methods, in particular the object comparisons, I wrote the FclSystemObject example. One of the buttons of the example calls the various methods of the System.Object class for the button itself, producing the output you can see in Figure 9.1. The second button is a showcase of the difference between Equals and ReferenceEquals. The program defines a custom class, which overrides the ToString and Equals methods:

```
type
  AnyObject = class
  private
    Value: Integer;
    name: string;
  public
    constructor Create (aName: string; aValue: Integer);
    function Equals(obj: TObject): Boolean; override;
    function ToString: string; override;
  end;
```

```
function AnyObject.Equals(obj: TObject): Boolean;
begin
  Result := (obj.GetType = Self.GetType) and
    ((obj as AnyObject).Value = Value);
end;

function AnyObject.ToString: string;
begin
  Result := Name;
end;
```

As you can see, the class provides a custom display (its name) and a custom comparison (involving one field and not the other). The string display is used when the program adds a few of these objects to two combo boxes when the program starts:

```
procedure TWinForm.TWinForm_Load(
    sender: System.Object; e: System.EventArgs);
begin
  ao1 := AnyObject.Create ('ao1', 10);
  ao2 := AnyObject.Create ('ao2 or ao3', 20);
  ao3 := ao2;
  ao4 := AnyObject.Create ('ao4', 20);

  ComboBox1.Items.Add(ao1);
  ComboBox1.Items.Add(ao2);
  ComboBox1.Items.Add(ao3);
  ComboBox1.Items.Add(ao4);
  // same for ComboBox2
```

FIGURE 9.1

The effect of pressing the Base button of the Fcl-SystemObject is to call the core System.Object methods for the same button component.

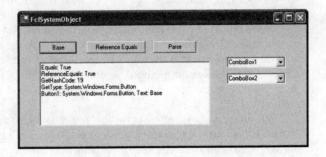

The other overridden method, Equals, is called when the Reference Equals button is pressed, after selecting two objects from the combo boxes:

```
TextBox1.AppendText ('Equals: ' +
  ComboBox1.SelectedItem.Equals (
  ComboBox2.SelectedItem).ToString + sLineBreak);
TextBox1.AppendText ('ReferenceEquals: ' +
  ReferenceEquals (ComboBox1.SelectedItem,
  ComboBox2.SelectedItem).ToString + sLineBreak);
```

Notice that Equals is a method of the object and receives as parameter a second object to compare, while ReferenceEquals is a static class method with the two objects to compare as parameters.

Finally, notice that while many classes define or override ToString, many classes and base types also have an opposite method (a static class method) to convert a string back into a value. This method is called Parse. This means that if you have a Double and a string, you can convert them back and forth with code like this:

```
var
  DoubleVal: Double;
  DoubleStr: string;
begin
  DoubleVal := 345.23;
  DoubleStr := DoubleVal.ToString;
  DoubleVal := System.Double.Parse(DoubleStr);
```

The *StringBuilder* Class

While discussing strings in .NET in Chapter 4, I mentioned that when you need to concatenate strings you should use the StringBuilder class, because in .NET string are immutable and adding data to an existing string means making a copy of the entire string. The StringConcatSpeed example of Chapters 4 highlighted the problem while showing possible solutions.

The System.Text.StringBuilder class, is also relevant in other circumstances, as it can provide ways to build strings out of different data types (with the heavily overloaded Append method and with the AppendFormat method). This class allows you to append characters but also to efficiently remove (with the Remove method), replace (with the Replace method), or insert (Insert method) them. When you are done, you can grab the string data of the object using the standard ToString method.

Again, the reason to use the StringBuilder class can be the speed difference and the different impact on the GC, because when modifying strings you keep creating new objects in memory, while when using the StringBuilder class you keep modifying the same object. This should be clear from looking at the two following code snippets, extracted from the StringBuilderDemo example, that remove a character from the string and insert another one taken from a different position of the same string:

```
// str: string
nPos := I mod str.Length;
str := str.Remove(nPos, 1);
str := str.Insert(nPos, str [(I*2) mod str.Length + 1]);
```

```
// strB: StringBuilder
nPos := I mod strB.Length;
strB.Remove(nPos, 1);
strB.Insert(nPos, strB [(I*2) mod strB.Length]);
```

NOTE In the preceding code snippets there's a relevant difference in the access to a character of the string using the [] notation between a string object and a `StringBuilder` object. In the former case, although in .NET positions are 0-based, Delphi shifts them to be 1-based for compatibility with existing Delphi for Win32 code. The `StringBuilder` class instead uses the standard .NET approach and its index is indeed 0-based.

The StringBuilderDemo program (see Figure 9.2), which is a WinForms application, has a couple of sample strings, a shorter one and a longer one. You can pick a string with the radio button and push the buttons to run the code snippets over one million times and see the required time. For a short string (about 20 characters) the difference is very limited, but when the string grows (about 200 characters), the `StringBuilder` version becomes twice as fast.

Container Classes

The BCL includes a very nice set of container classes, certainly more complete than those found in the Delphi native RTL. Classes range from generic arrays of objects that can dynamically grow (`ArrayList`) to low-level operations like manipulation of bits within an integer (`BitArray`), from fast-access containers like a `HashTable` to containers with specific behaviors like stacks and queues.

NOTE Version 2 of the .NET Framework should introduce generics to the architecture (and the C# language, with Delphi expected to follow soon). This technology will have a relevant impact on container classes, as you'll be able to have a container holding elements of specific types. In .NET 1.1, containers hold generic objects, which can be of any type. You can use the techniques demonstrated in Chapter 5 for Delphi containers to constrain them to a specific data type, but this is often a time-consuming operation.

Here, as usual I'll focus on only a couple of classes, comparing them to corresponding native Delphi solutions. The `ArrayList` class is somewhat similar to the `TList` (in fact, the `TList` in Delphi for .NET is based on an `ArrayList`, as described earlier in this chapter). There are some relevant differences, though.

FIGURE 9.2
The StringBuilderDemo program shows the speed difference between operations on a plain string or using the `StringBuilder` class.

The one I find most striking is that there is no way to sort elements in a list or efficiently do a Find operation. In fact, in this case you need to use a separate class, SortedList. The same is true if you are looking for a container of strings (like a TStringList), as the ArrayList does a good job replacing this class as well.

As an example, again including a test to compare speed, I wrote the StringListSpeedNet VCL application. This shows code difference and speed difference in looking for a string in an array of strings, stored in one of the two containers:

```
SourceList: TStringList;
SourceArray: ArrayList;
```

The two buttons toward the top of the form (see Figure 9.3 for the form of the .NET version) populate the lists with random strings. Here the code is almost identical and the speed advantage is similar as well:

```
// TStringList
for i := 1 to nPopItems do
  sourceList.Add (NewRandomString);

// ArrayList
for i := 1 to nPopItems do
  sourceArray.Add (NewRandomString);
```

There are two find operations: a plain call to Find over the unsorted list, or a copy of the strings in the list to a sorted list and a find on the sorted elements. In the latter case, the following code snippets are used to make the copies:

```
// TStringList: copy then sort
sSorted := TStringList.Create;
sSorted.AddStrings (sourceList);
sSorted.Sorted := True;
RepeatFind (sSorted);

// ArrayList: copy then sort
sSorted := ArrayList.Create;
sSorted.AddRange(SourceArray);
sSorted.Sort;
// True for "use BinarySearch"
RepeatFindNet (sSorted, True);
```

Again, the code is not very different. What is relevant, though, is that you use a different class for the ArrayList version. Moreover, you'll have to call a different method to search for the string, as indicated by the extra parameter. The *repeat* methods you see called in the preceding code perform the actual *find* operation a thousand times, and this is their core code:

```
// TStringList
for i := 1 to 1000 do
  if sList.IndexOf(sList [
      random (sList.Count)]) >= 0 then
    Inc (Result);
```

```
// ArrayList
for i := 1 to 1000 do
begin
  if not fSorted then
  begin
    if sList.IndexOf(sList [
        random (sList.Count)]) >= 0 then
      Inc (Result);
  end
  else
  begin
    if sList.BinarySearch (sList [
        random (sList.Count)]) >= 0 then
      Inc (Result);
  end;
end;
```

I don't particularly like having to call a different method on an inherited class, but if you try to call IndexOf on the SortedList you are back to a slow sequential search. On the positive side, the native .NET solution is much faster than the Delphi RTL code. The difference is quite significant, with the TStringList version taking about three times as long, both for the plain find and the search in a sorted list. This is due to a much better optimization of the underlying code and the fact it was written specifically for the .NET Framework. If you build a similar program for Win32, the speed of Delphi's RTL code will be on par with the ArrayList implementation on .NET.

NOTE   This very limited comparison can be interpreted as a proof that the slowness of .NET code is often a myth. CPU and memory-bound programs in .NET are fast. It is when a program starts calling the Windows API or other Win32 functions that a .NET application can slow down when compared to native Win32 version.

Another very useful .NET container you can use to speed up the search of elements in a list (including a string list) is a HashTable. This class works like a *dictionary*, in that it uses a key to refer to an element and an actual object (or a value). When looking for the keys (which can be objects of any type), the HashTable class extracts the hash code of the object, a feature build into the System.Object class, as you saw earlier.

FIGURE 9.3
The VCL-based String-ListSpeedNet application with some of the timing results

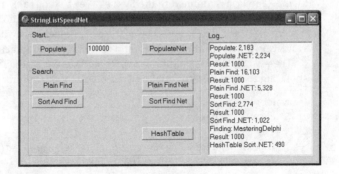

These are two code snippets from the StringListSpeedNet application:

```
var
  sHashed: HashTable;
  I, nSkipped: Integer;
begin
  sHashed := HashTable.Create;
  // copy (ignore sort, use hash, skip duplicates!)
  for i := 0 to sourceArray.Count - 1 do
    if not sHashed.ContainsKey(sourceArray[i]) then
      sHashed.Add (sourceArray[i], nil)
    else
      Inc (nSkipped);
  RepeatFindHash (sHashed);


// from RepeatFindHash
var
  i: Integer;
  akey: string;
begin
  for i := 1 to 1000 do
  begin
    akey := sourceArray [random
      (sourceArray.Count)].ToString;
    if sList.ContainsKey (akey) then
      Inc (Result);
  end;
```

On a list of 100,000 strings, the HashTable takes half the time of the sorted list (and about one tenth of the plain search), although it is true that some of the strings are duplicates and cannot be inserted in the hash table.

Regular Expressions

There are so many classes in the Base Class Library portion of the FCL that it is very hard to pick only a few interesting ones. It is certainly worth mentioning the support for regular expressions, provided by the Regex class (defined in the System.Text.RegularExpressions namespace). Regular expressions are a very powerful (but not easy) way to search for information within a string using complex pattern matching. The Regex class of the BCL, however, can be used for many different purposes, like validating input, splitting strings, and searching and replacing substrings.

The AssortedBCL example shows three different cases. The first is the check for text input corresponding to a credit card number, four blocks of four digits separated by a hyphen:

```
var
  regex1: Regex;
begin
  regex1 := RegEx.Create ('^\d{4}-\d{4}-\d{4}-\d{4}$');
  if regex1.IsMatch (TextInput.Text) then
```

```
TextLog.AppendText(TextInput.Text +
    ': regex match' + sLineBreak);
```

A second button of the demo splits the same string into its four parts using the Split method that returns an array of strings:

```
var
  regex1: Regex;
  lines: array of string;
  str: string;
begin
  regex1 := RegEx.Create ('-');
  lines := regex1.Split(TextInput.Text);
  for str in lines do
    TextLog.AppendText(str + sLineBreak);
```

Notice the use of the for..in loop. The third button of the demo related to regular expressions searches for a given character in the string. It looks for a single match first and then for all of the matches. Notice that in the first case the Match method invariably returns an object of the Match class, with a flag indicating success or failure. In the second case, if there is no match the Matched method returns an empty collection. Here is the relevant code:

```
var
  regex1: Regex;
  match1: Match;
  multiMatch:  MatchCollection;
begin
  regex1 := RegEx.Create ('3');
  match1 := regex1.Match(TextInput.Text);
  if match1.Success then
    TextLog.AppendText('Found at ' +
      match1.Index.ToString + sLineBreak)
  else
    TextLog.AppendText('Not Found' + sLineBreak);

  multiMatch := regex1.Matches(TextInput.Text);
  for match1 in multiMatch do
    TextLog.AppendText('Multi-Found at ' +
      match1.Index.ToString + sLineBreak)
```

Regular expressions have no real correspondence in the Delphi RTL, although there is a simplified version provided by the TMask class in the Masks unit.

.NET Streams

An area in which you might want to stick with Delphi native support is the management of files with stream classes. Still, .NET has a similar concept you might want to use when writing native applications you have no interest in compiling on Win32. This is the case, for example, of Win-Forms applications.

When you work with .NET streams, you can use classes specialized in reading and writing various data structures (strings, numbers, and so on) or rely on the generic read and write of byte arrays provided by the stream classes themselves. When working with files, in most cases you can simply use the `StreamReader` and `StreamWriter` classes for text files and the `BinaryReader` and `BinaryWriter` classes for binary files.

NOTE   This is similar to what happens in Delphi RTL with the low-level `TReader` and `TWriter` classes, which are mostly used to read and write properties to a DFM-like stream.

As an example, the AssortedBCL demo allows you to save the content of the log to a local file:

```
var
  sw1: StreamWriter;
begin
  sw1 := StreamWriter.Create ('temp.txt');
  try
    sw1.WriteLine(TextLog.Text);
  finally
    sw1.Close;
  end;
```

Similarly, you could have used a `StreamReader` object to reload the file, but this time I wrote the more detailed code that creates the file stream and assigns it to the reader:

```
var
  sr1: StreamReader;
  fs: FileStream;
begin
  fs := FileStream.Create ('temp.txt',
    FileMode.Open, FileAccess.Read);
  try
    sr1 := StreamReader.Create (fs);
    TextLog.Text := sr1.ReadToEnd;
  finally
    fs.Close;
  end;
end;
```

The only real difference is that in this case you explicitly assign the file access permissions and can fine-tune them to your specific needs.

The Component Class

Another class worth a look is the base class of the component library, which is the `System.Component` class. As described earlier, in Delphi for .NET `TComponent` is an alias of this class, with the `TComponentHelper` providing extra features to mimic the component class in the VCL for Win32. In both cases, the `Component/TComponent` class is the base class of all visual and nonvisual components you can work with at design time in the development environment. In .NET, the Component class has a second relevant role: it is remotable.

In the VCL components are containers (or owners) of other components, not visually but logically (visual containment is defined by the `Parent` property). The most relevant effect of components ownership is that the owner is responsible for destroying the owned objects, as you saw in Chapter 6.

In the .NET FCL, instead, object destruction is the realm of the GC. Still, a relationship among components is necessary at design time. This is why you can define component containers, add components to them, and reference the container interface (`IContainer`) through the component by means of its `Container` property. (There is also a `Site` property you can use to refer to an `ISite` interface, which is set up by the container as well and allows to you access to further design-time information.)

Although these properties are meant for design-time support, I think it is nice to be able to replace the Components list of the VCL with a similar capability. This technique is demonstrated by the CompContain example. At startup this program adds a few components to a newly created container:

```
procedure CompContainForm.TWinForm_Load(
  sender: System.Object; e: System.EventArgs);
var
  container1: System.ComponentModel.Container;
begin
  container1 := System.ComponentModel.Container.Create;
  container1.Add (Panel1);
  container1.Add (btnParent);
  container1.Add (Self);
```

Even if you don't save the container object, you can access it through any of the objects added to it, as in this code that shows the `ToString` representation of the container itself, the number of components it holds, and some data for each of those components:

```
procedure CompContainForm.btnContain_Click(
  sender: System.Object; e: System.EventArgs);
var
  comp: Component;
begin
  if (btnParent.Container <> nil) then
  begin
    txtLog.AppendText ('Container: ' +
      TObject(btnParent.Container).ToString + sLineBreak);
    txtLog.AppendText ('Container components count: ' +
      btnParent.Container.Components.Count.ToString +
      sLineBreak);
    for Comp in btnParent.Container.Components do
      txtLog.AppendText ('Container components: ' +
        Comp.ToString + sLineBreak);
  end;
```

The same method in the example also shows information about the Site, producing the output of Figure 9.4. Adding several related components to a container might be the way to compensate for the loss of a very interesting technique of the VCL components, the call of the `Notification` method. In Win32, knowing when another component is removed from a designer or at run time is vital information because you have to set to `nil` any reference to the object being destroyed. However, this technique is also used to manage references among objects, even between different designers, a feature that has no direct replacement in .NET.

FIGURE 9.4

The CompContain demo demonstrates the effect of adding components to a container.

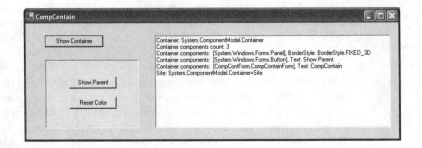

NOTE A protected property relevant only for component writers is `DesignMode`, which corresponds to the csDesigning flag of the `ComponentState` property of the VCL. Another is the list of events held by the `Events` property, of which there is no equivalent in the VCL.

WinForms

The last area of the FCL I want to delve into here is the visual portion of the library based on the traditional Windows GUI. The WinForms library is similar to the visual portion of the VCL and works parallel to it. Unlike the RTL portion, however, Borland hasn't tried to merge the two libraries and has kept the VCL as an alternative to Microsoft's WinForms. Both end up calling the Win32 API.

No DFM, Code Only

Like the VCL, WinForms include forms and visual controls, with comparable properties, methods, and events. One of the most important differences is that WinForms has nothing like a DFM file. Similar to Java, in fact, the operations you do on a form (or another visual container) at design time are reflected automatically in a portion of the source code of the program. The code generated is rather long, but I think it is worth it to list it once in the book, as you can see in Listing 9.1.

LISTING 9.1: The constructor and initialization code of the CompContain example

```
constructor CompContainForm.Create;
begin
  inherited Create;
  InitializeComponent;
end;

procedure CompContainForm.InitializeComponent;
begin
  Self.btnContainer := System.Windows.Forms.Button.Create;
  Self.Panel1 := System.Windows.Forms.Panel.Create;
  Self.btnColor := System.Windows.Forms.Button.Create;
  Self.btnParent := System.Windows.Forms.Button.Create;
  Self.txtLog := System.Windows.Forms.TextBox.Create;
  Self.Panel1.SuspendLayout;
  Self.SuspendLayout;
```

```
//
// btnContainer
//
Self.btnContainer.Location :=
  System.Drawing.Point.Create(40, 24);
Self.btnContainer.Name := 'btnContainer';
Self.btnContainer.Size :=
  System.Drawing.Size.Create(120, 23);
Self.btnContainer.TabIndex := 0;
Self.btnContainer.Text := 'Show Container';
Include(Self.btnContainer.Click, Self.btnContain_Click);
//
// Panel1
//
Self.Panel1.BackColor :=
  System.Drawing.SystemColors.ControlLight;
Self.Panel1.BorderStyle :=
  System.Windows.Forms.BorderStyle.Fixed3D;
Self.Panel1.Controls.Add(Self.btnColor);
Self.Panel1.Controls.Add(Self.btnParent);
Self.Panel1.Location :=
  System.Drawing.Point.Create(40, 72);
Self.Panel1.Name := 'Panel1';
Self.Panel1.Size :=
  System.Drawing.Size.Create(192, 136);
Self.Panel1.TabIndex := 1;
//
// btnColor
//
Self.btnColor.Location :=
  System.Drawing.Point.Create(48, 72);
Self.btnColor.Name := 'btnColor';
Self.btnColor.Size := System.Drawing.Size.Create(96, 23);
Self.btnColor.TabIndex := 1;
Self.btnColor.Text := 'Reset Color';
Include(Self.btnColor.Click, Self.btnColor_Click);
//
// btnParent
//
Self.btnParent.Location :=
  System.Drawing.Point.Create(48, 32);
Self.btnParent.Name := 'btnParent';
Self.btnParent.Size :=
  System.Drawing.Size.Create(96, 23);
Self.btnParent.TabIndex := 0;
Self.btnParent.Text := 'Show Parent';
Include(Self.btnParent.Click, Self.btnParent_Click);
//
```

```
  // txtLog
  //
  Self.txtLog.Location :=
    System.Drawing.Point.Create(264, 24);
  Self.txtLog.Multiline := True;
  Self.txtLog.Name := 'txtLog';
  Self.txtLog.Size := System.Drawing.Size.Create(480, 184);
  Self.txtLog.TabIndex := 2;
  Self.txtLog.Text := '';
  //
  // CompContainForm
  //
  Self.AutoScaleBaseSize :=
    System.Drawing.Size.Create(5, 13);
  Self.BackColor :=
    System.Drawing.SystemColors.Control;
  Self.ClientSize :=
    System.Drawing.Size.Create(760, 230);
  Self.Controls.Add(Self.txtLog);
  Self.Controls.Add(Self.Panel1);
  Self.Controls.Add(Self.btnContainer);
  Self.Name := 'CompContainForm';
  Self.Text := 'CompContain';
  Include(Self.Load, Self.TWinForm_Load);
  Self.Panel1.ResumeLayout(False);
  Self.ResumeLayout(False);
end;
```

As you can see in the listing, the constructor calls the InitializeComponent method. This method starts by creating all of the components involved so that they can (in most cases) reference one another regardless of the initialization order. In the first portion of the code there are also methods to temporarily stop repainting the form (the SuspendLayout method). Then comes the definition of the properties for each of the components, followed by the definition of the properties of the form and the activation of painting (the ResumeLayout method).

The initialization of each control includes its addition to the Controls property of the component that contains it. In this example, most components are added to the form and two to the panel (btnColor and btnParent). To connect events to their handlers, the initialization code uses the Include routine: as you might know or remember from Chapter 4, .NET uses multicast events, so multiple handlers can refer to a single event that *includes* a list of methods to call.

False Friends and Other Differences

One of the problems you might experience when moving from the VCL to .NET is that although many concepts are similar, there are also many false friends that might mislead you. For example, if you know about docking support in the VCL you'll be surprised to discover that this doesn't exist in

WinForms, although there is a `Dock` property that corresponds to the `Align` property of many VCL controls. Another naming difference relates to the events, which are called with the plain name in .NET (such as `Click` or `KeyPress`), while in the VCL they are preceded by *On* (such as `OnClick` and `OnKeyPress`). Having to pick one of the existing notations, in this case Microsoft has chosen the standard Visual Basic naming rules. To make things a little more complicated, `OnClick` actually exists and is the name of the virtual method that fires the `Click` event (just as in the VCL `Click` is the virtual method that fires the `OnClick` event).

Other relevant differences include:

◆ The `Caption` property (at times called `Text` as in a `TEdit`) is invariably called `Text` in Win-Forms. Having a single name is a good idea, but you'll have to get used to it.

◆ The `Color` of a control or form is called `BackColor` in WinForms. There is also a `ForeColor` property you set to determine the color of the text (which in the VCL is set in the `Font.Color` property).

◆ As I already mentioned, the `Tag` property is of the `System.Object` type.

◆ All controls are inherently data-aware (or data-bound). There are no separate Edit and DBEdit controls as in the VCL, but there is a single TextBox control that can be bound to data. The property you use is `DataBindings`, as you'll see in more detail in Chapter 16, which covers ADO.NET.

◆ There is a general `CauseValidation` property and two related events (`Validating` and `Validated`) related to the fact all controls can be data bound.

◆ There is support for low-vision or blind users through the accessibility properties: `AccessibleDescription`, `AccessibleName`, and `AccessibleRole`.

◆ The `PopupMenu` property of the VCL is called `ContextMenu` in WinForms.

◆ To show a simple message box instead of a global routine (`ShowMessage`), you use one of the many overloaded class methods of the `MessageBox` class, like `MessageBox.Show`.

◆ The WinForms `Application` class has a `DoEvents` method that replaces the `ProcessMessages` method of the VCL `TApplication` class. The two classes have a very similar role and corresponding features.

WinForms Controls

As in the VCL, components in WinForms can be divided into two broad categories: visual components, generally called controls, and nonvisual components. The main difference is that at design time the nonvisual components are not placed on the form with an icon but are added to a separate design area at the bottom of the form. This helps making forms less cluttered.

WinForms has no notion of graphical control (`TGraphicControl` in the VCL), which means that each control has a related Windows handle you can refer to with the `Handle` property.

Controls have a `Parent` control and a list of child `Controls` exactly like in the VCL. They have state attributes like `Enabled`, `Focused`, and `Visible` and positional properties like `Size` and `Location` (which replace `Left`, `Top`, `Height`, and `Width`).

In the CompContain example, some of the controls on the form are actually placed inside a panel, which becomes their parent control. One of the buttons of the program is used to display some of the parent-child relationships. The output of the code below is in Figure 9.5:

```
procedure CompContainForm.btnParent_Click(
  sender: System.Object; e: System.EventArgs);
var
  ctrl: Control;
begin
  txtLog.AppendText ('btnContainer.Parent: ' +
    btnContainer.Parent.ToString + sLineBreak);
  txtLog.AppendText ('btnParent.Parent: ' +
    btnParent.Parent.ToString + sLineBreak);
  for ctrl in Self.Controls do
    txtLog.AppendText ('Form controls: ' +
      ctrl.ToString + sLineBreak);
  for ctrl in Panel1.Controls do
    txtLog.AppendText ('Panel controls: ' +
      ctrl.ToString + sLineBreak);
end;
```

The VCL uses `ParentXxx` properties to indicate that a property should take the value of the same property of the parent control (an example is given by the `Color` and `ParentColor` properties). Win-Forms, instead, uses ambient properties (including `Cursor`, `Font`, `BackColor`, and `ForeColor`) that, if not defined, take the parent values. You can revert back to the parent/ambient property by emptying the specific value. For example, the panel of the CompContain example has a lighter color. If you want to set it to the same color of the form instead of copying the same color, you can set the specific color to the special value `Empty`:

```
procedure CompContainForm.btnColor_Click(
  sender: System.Object; e: System.EventArgs);
begin
  Panel1.BackColor := Color.Empty;
end;
```

FIGURE 9.5

Some of the parent-child relationships displayed by the CompContain example

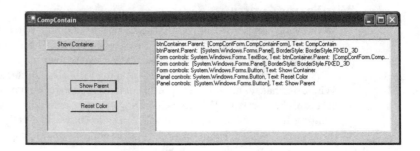

Methods and events of control classes in WinForms are very similar to their VCL counterpart. The GetStyle and SetStyle methods replace the TControl.ControlStyle property.

Looking at the specific set of controls available by default, there are again many similarities but a few differences worth mentioning. Of course, the common ground is the set of native Windows controls (Button, ListBox, TextBox, and so on) and extended Win32 common controls (TreeView, List-View, RichEdit, and so on).

In this group, a relevant difference is that there is no Memo control, as a memo in Windows is actually a multiline edit box. This is why to have a memo in WinForms you use a TextBox control and set its MultiLine property to True. Another difference is that the HotKey, Animate, HeaderControl, and PageScroller common controls are missing in WinForms.

Of course, all of the Borland-specific controls are also missing. The list includes RadioGroup, StringGrid, MaskEdit, Bevel, ValueListEditor, PaintBox, and MediaPlayer. WinForms provides its own custom controls, including LinkLabel and PropertyGrid, among others.

From GDI to GDI+

A very notable difference between VCL and WinForms is the way the two libraries paint on screen (or any other device). VCL uses the classic GDI library, while WinForms uses the newer GDI+. GDI+ has many new features compared to GDI: device contexts are gone, GDI objects (like pens and brushes) are passed as parameters to the painting functions, the coordinate system is based on universal transformations and uses floating point coordinates, brushes support gradients, there is support for alpha blending built into the Color structure, there is native support for more image formats (such as GIF, JPEG, TIFF, and PNG), and much more. The only drawback of GDI+ is that if your operating system doesn't include an optimized driver for it, it can be slower than traditional GDI. This is particularly true when working with fonts and text.

NOTE You might wonder why Borland hasn't updated the VCL to support GDI+. It turns out that GDI+ is compiled in a library with a C++ interface, while Delphi can bind to C-language DLLs or COM libraries. This makes it quite difficult (although not impossible) to support it from Delphi for Win32. Of course, support on .NET is available through WinForms.

As I mentioned in the preceding list of features, GDI+ doesn't use device contexts. You don't have to select a pen in a device context and than draw a line using the current pen. You simply draw a line passing a pen as parameter. In other words, GDI+ is stateless. The difference is that drawing methods use either a pen or a brush but not both at the same time, while a call to the GDI Rectangle function would have used both the current pen for the border and the current brush to fill the rectangle surface.

As an example, I wrote a simple application capable of drawing random alpha-blended lines and some text with a gradient brush. The WinFormLines example has a menu with two related commands. Notice that the WinForm designer allows you to preview the menu and create it in place, unlike the VCL designer. You can see the WinForms designer in the Delphi 2005 IDE in Figure 9.6.

FIGURE 9.6

The menu designer
for WinForms

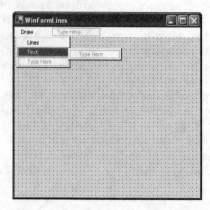

The code used for painting the lines (notice that the image created is not persistent, as it will be emptied in case of a repaint operation) is a loop repeated thousands of times:

```
procedure TLinesForm.MenuItem2_Click(
  sender: System.Object; e: System.EventArgs);
var
  I: Integer;
  aPen: Pen;
  g: Graphics;
begin
  aPen := Pen.Create (Color.Blue);
  g := Self.CreateGraphics;
  try
    for I := 1 to nTimes do
    begin
      Application.DoEvents;
      aPen.Color := Color.FromArgb (80,
        Random (255), Random (255), Random (255));
      g.DrawLine (aPen, Random (Width), Random (Height),
        Random (Width), Random (Height));
    end;
  finally
    aPen.Free;
    g.Dispose;
  end;
end;
```

Inside the loop, the program changes the pen color and draws a line passing the pen as parameter. Notice that the color is defined by the alpha channel followed by the three RGB values. Of course, you should remember to Free (that is, call Dispose) the pen and the Graphics class object returned by the CreateGraphics method of the form.

The other menu item of the program shows some text in a large font with a gradient brush (see Figure 9.7 for the output). The code is not too difficult to figure out—the only trouble is figuring out the proper class names and parameters:

```
uses
  System.Drawing.Drawing2D;

procedure TLinesForm.MenuItem3_Click(
  sender: System.Object; e: System.EventArgs);
var
  aBrush: System.Drawing.Brush;
  aFont: System.Drawing.Font;
  g: Graphics;
begin
  aBrush := LinearGradientBrush.Create (
    Self.ClientRectangle,
    Color.Aquamarine, Color.BlueViolet,
    LinearGradientMode.ForwardDiagonal);
  aFont := System.Drawing.Font.Create (
    'Arial Black', 25, GraphicsUnit.Millimeter);
  g := Self.CreateGraphics;
  try
    g.DrawString('Delphi for .NET', aFont,
      aBrush, 10, 10);
  finally
    aBrush.Free;
    aFont.Free;
    g.Dispose;
  end;
end;
```

NOTE   It is better to dispose of GDI+ objects directly (calling Free in Delphi for .NET) rather than replying on the finalization from the GC because graphic objects are a scarce resource in Windows and should be treated with extra care.

FIGURE 9.7
The gradient text painted by the WinFormLines example

The Forms Class

Another close match among the two libraries is the class that defines forms, although there are more difference in the naming of form properties, methods, and events. Some of the differences are shown in Table 9.3, and do not include common naming differences already discussed for generic controls (since a form is a special type of control).

The Form class in WinForms offers a few extra features compared to the VCL counterpart. There is (among others) a BackgroundImage property to set a sort of wallpaper for the form, a Language property that activates translation support, and a ShowInTaskBar that simplifies the support for taskbar. Of course, you should add to this the GDI+ support available when painting directly on a form.

NOTE   Forms in WinForms offer MDI support, which is quite odd considering that Microsoft declared this type of user interface obsolete with the release of Windows 95. You can use the IsMdiContainer property to set the MDI parent form and the MdiParent property to refer to that parent form from the MDI child forms.

TABLE 9.3:   Name Differences for Properties, Methods, and Events of Forms from VCL to WinForms

TFORM (VCL)	FORMS (WINFORMS)
OnCreate event	Load event
Contraints property	MaximumSize and MinimumSize properties
Button.Default property	AcceptButton property
BorderIcons property	ControlBox property
AlphaBlend and AlphaBlendValue properties	Opacity property
TransparentColor and TransparentColorValue properties	TransparencyKey property
fsStayOnTop value of the FormStyle property	TopMost property
OnClick event of the main menu	MenuStart event (there is also a MenuComplete event)
SelectNext method	GetNextControl and SelectNextControl methods

VCL Features Not in WinForms

Despite all the nice features added to WinForms, there are areas in which there is no correspondence for some relevant features of the VCL. Without getting too much into the details, I really miss the idea of actions provided by the ActionList component and the related architecture. As this is a very nice feature, some third-party component vendors with a Delphi background fill this gap by selling components that include similar architectures. An example is the CommandMaster package by Component Science, www.componentscience.net.

Another feature I miss is a nonvisual container like the data module, which comes in very handy for database applications, as you can share the same data access backend from multiple forms (more on this issue in the section covering Delphi's database architecture, starting with Chapter 13).

Two areas in which the differences are relevant, and I tend to prefer the VCL solution, are the use of frames (VCL) or user controls (WinForms) and the way you can obtain visual form inheritance. For these technologies, Delphi takes advantage of the form streaming and properties management, something totally different on WinForms. Still, I don't want to give a wrong impression: very similar features are indeed available in both libraries.

Finally, a minor issue that I find annoying when using WinForms is how you remove an event handler, possibly one added by mistake by clicking a component in the designer. In fact, you cannot just leave it empty, as in a VCL application, but you have to remove the method declaration and its definition, and disconnect the event handler in the designer-generated code.

What's Next

In this chapter we covered the core libraries available in Delphi for .NET, starting with the port to .NET of the Delphi native RTL library and then moving to the Framework Class Library (FCL) provided by Microsoft as part of the .NET SDK. I briefly covered some of the core classes of the FCL (part of the BCL), and I introduced the user interface portion of the library (WinForms).

The presentation was geared to existing Delphi developers, so rather than covering all of the features of these libraries extensively (a daunting task, considering their breadth), I focused on differences and specific features.

This chapter doesn't end the coverage of the .NET FCL, of course. We still have to focus on ADO.NET (in Chapter 16), HTML and Internet support (Chapter 19), web development with ASP.NET (Chapter 21), and XML and SOAP development (Chapters 22 and 23). Some of these chapters are specific to .NET (like the ADO.NET and the ASP.NET chapters). Other chapters mentioned offer coverage of both Win32 and .NET with a focus on Win32 and cross-platform features as well as some coverage of specific features of the FCL.

Part 2

Delphi Object-Oriented Architectures

In this section:

- Chapter 10: Refactoring and Unit Testing
- Chapter 11: Dynamic Architectures (with Libraries, Packages, and Assemblies)
- Chapter 12: COM and .NET Interoperability

Refactoring and Unit Testing

Among its many new features, the Delphi 2005 IDE introduces two technologies that have become relevant for programmers over the last few years. One is support for refactoring source code, while the other is the inclusion of two unit-testing frameworks. Although the two topics are not strictly bound one to the other, they are indeed used in conjunction and are part of the same approach to programming that we can summarize under the two terms of agile methodologies and extreme programming (XP).

Because these are relatively recent concepts in programming, particularly for Delphi developers, I've provided a little theory on the two topics, in addition to discussing them in practice in the Delphi IDE. I've also provided a very short introduction to the agile and XP worlds, mostly providing links to a few relevant sources. Don't worry about getting too much theory, though. Most of the text of this chapter covers the features provided by Delphi and shows practical examples.

Finally, the main reason these topics were not covered in Chapter 1, which discusses the IDE, is that understanding them requires a little more knowledge of the language and the libraries than is assumed in Chapter 1.

In addition to the general discussions on agile methodologies and extreme programming, this chapter delves specifically into refactoring in Delphi, covers other IDE code helpers, and discusses unit testing in Delphi with DUnit and NUnit.

Beyond RAD

If Delphi roots are in Rapid Application Development (RAD) or visual development, you have seen that Delphi at the same time fully supports and embraces object-oriented programming. You can indeed forget about visual designer and simply write your code, following all of the sound OOP approaches. Granted, this is not always the fastest way to get an application running, but certainly the structure of your program will be more flexible and robust in spite of the change.

OOP approaches to programming have been popular for a few years now, but more recently there has been a lot of discussion (and hype) about some specific approaches to programming that are often based on or that complement the OOP approach. On the coding side, the most relevant approach that complements OOP is the use of design patterns, a relevant movement of the industry that has also reached Delphi. You can find several articles and websites covering this topic, for which, regretfully, I don't have enough space in this book.

On the project lifecycle side, assumptions of traditional programming models include the prominent role of analysis and design in programming and the need for a very formal development process. Extreme programming and agile methodologies reverse the role of programmers, putting them at the center of the software development process; agile methodologies in general dispel the need for cumbersome processes.

There are entire books devoted to these topics, and a one-page summary won't do any justice to them, so I'll just try to highlight a few elements and give you my personal view.

The following sections cover a list of somewhat unrelated techniques that I feel are worth mentioning, even if I don't have enough space to cover them all in detail. I've provided some references to websites and books for further reading, though.

Agile Methodologies

If design and coding are two relevant steps of the development of a program, there are many more in terms of other activities spawning from requirements analysis to application testing. At the beginning, software development was more of a creative art; in the past decade and for large projects, the use of a formal development process and methodology has become the norm. However, not only are programmers generally at odds with these extra formal efforts, but methodologists have also found out they are often counterproductive.

This is why toward the end of the 1990s a new family of methodologies or software development processes started to appear and gain consistent ground. Although there are several approaches, the common trait of the new methodologies is that they promote simplicity over complexity, flexibility over structure (in a world of ever-changing requirements), and people over processes. That's why the term more commonly used to refer to them is *agile methodologies*. This term became particularly relevant when in 2001 a group of software development gurus published the Agile Manifesto, which you can find online at http://agilemanifesto.org.

One of the best online sources offering an overview of agile methodologies and a list of the proposals, with dozens of interesting references to books and web pages, is a paper by Martin Fowler, which can be found at:

www.martinfowler.com/articles/newMethodology.html

It is not my intention to get into the details on the various agile methodologies, as this is outside of the scope of this book. The next section describes one of them briefly because this methodology promotes the use of refactoring more than others and has introduced the notion of unit testing.

Extreme Programming

The idea behind extreme programming (XP, nothing to do with Windows XP, which stands for Windows eXPerience) is to give programmers a prominent role, as they use to have in small shops but rarely in large enterprises. Although XP can be viewed as a collection of best practices that have been experimented with success and can guide you in picking your development model, its proponents picture it more as a comprehensive methodology, a deliberate and disciplined approach to software development.

XP was formally introduced by Kent Beck and Ward Cunningham around 1996 as an alternative way to built software in all of its aspects. XP, in fact, doesn't focus only on programming (meaning writing code) but covers the entire software development process, from requirement analysis to testing.

Some of the base assumptions are the empowerment of the developers, the involvement of the customer in the working team along with managers and developers, and the flexibility in responding to requirement changes. XP focuses on communication, simplicity, feedback, and courage. In practice,

XP projects are based on frequent incremental releases; developers work in pairs and test their code from the start up. There are many XP techniques (or techniques formalized by XP), including:

User stories   Are written by the customer and replace a formal requirements document and provide a short description of what the application should do in the words of its users in a nontechnical format.

Release planning   Is done by estimating the time it should take to implement each user story, and it is later broken down into iteration plans for each iteration; XP, in fact, is based on iterative development and a release should be broken down into about a dozen iterations; keeping up with the iterations schedule helps measure the overall progress of the project.

Small releases   Are made frequently and given to the customer to start experimenting with to provide the team with valuable feedback from the user point of view.

Simple design   Is better than complex design. Even though everyone knows this, some methodologies tend to push in different directions with large and complex designs before coding even starts. A key to simple design is to avoid adding unneeded functionality in the core system.

CRC cards   (Class, Responsibilities, and Collaboration cards) are used to design the system in an object-oriented way. Each card represents a class, described by a set of responsibilities and a list of other collaborating classes.

Merciless refactoring   Means you'll rewrite and improve existing code even if it works (contrary to the common rule of not touching code that does work) to improve the overall design and make the code more understandable and manageable. (Refactoring is also the topic of a specific section in this chapter.)

Pair programming   Is the idea of always having two developers writing code in front of a computer, alternating the use of the keyboard. Pair programming pushes the idea of collective code ownership (another pillar of XP) and makes the project less dependent on a specific developer; moreover, contrary to what one might think, it can speed up the development process considerably, specifically in the most complex areas.

Test-driven development   Indicates both the use of unit testing (testing at the class/method level) and the writing of the test code before the actual code, as a way to make testing more robust and helping you write better code (I'll discuss this later in more details).

Acceptance tests   Are based on the user stories and indicate if the story has been implemented completely and correctly. These tests are part of the quality assurance (QA) effort and might be done by a specific team; the results of an acceptance test are published and are a key measure of the project progress.

Continuous integration   Of the code written by the pairs of programmers into a release means code is integrated often, but it should also be integrated by one team at a time, running the entire test suite after each integration effort.

Other relevant elements are the use of coding standards (to help developers share code), the idea of leaving optimizations to the very last (and only after measuring the speed bottlenecks), avoiding overtime, collective code ownership…but there is much more to XP than I can cover here.

There are many sources of information on XP, including the classic book by Kent Beck, *Extreme Programming Explained* (Addison-Wesley, 1999), recently republished in a second edition (Addison-Wesley, 2004). A good introduction to XP can be found at www.extremeprogramming.org; another interesting site is at www.xprogramming.com.

Some proponents of XP tend to say that you cannot just pick some of these techniques but must embrace them fully and use all of them for your projects to succeed. To me, this seems like an excuse to avoid accounting for failures. I find all of the XP techniques interesting, but I don't think they are the best practice nor that they have to be applied literally under every circumstance. The approach to individual projects and to large systems involving hundreds of programmers has to be very different. Also, the development tools, the target platform, the project scope, the physical distance among developers, and many other factors have to be considered when picking a development methodology.

Proponents of other agile methodologies are often upset by the high popularity of XP, as it has somewhat dwarfed other very interesting agile approaches. This is partly due to the efforts of Kent Beck to promote XP and mostly to its very strong nature. XP is often promoted with a sort of religious fervor, and this makes it a highly debated topic among its proponents and the skeptical. Software development methodologies are generally somewhat more *dry* and are simply considered tools.

Again, a lot can be said and has been written on the topic of agile methlodogies in general and XP in particular. Here I want to focus only on some specific areas, such as unit testing and refactoring. The reason is simple: Delphi 2005 provides direct support for them, and I thought it was unfair to cover these subjects without giving at least some background information to help you understand their role and scope.

Refactoring

While writing new code, how should you treat the existing code of the program you are working on? As I mentioned earlier, there is a tendency in the industry to avoid touching anything that isn't broken. However, as you keep adding new methods to a class, you cannot avoid from time to time updating the class structure and eventually modifying the relationship among the various classes.

Refactoring is an approach to modifying existing code. Its core idea is that you refactor when you change the internal structure of one or more related classes without changing the external behavior of the program. Another key idea is that even when you have to make large changes to the code, you apply a series of refactorings, each having a specific and somewhat limited scope. You want to keep the program working properly not only after the entire set of transformations, but also after each refactoring.

In addition to describing an overall approach and giving some relevant guidelines, refactoring helps give a commonly understood name to some changes in code, exactly like design patterns help give a common name to code structures. Refactoring can be applied not only when you are given code or projects by other developers, but also when maintaining your own code. Of course, it makes little sense to use refactoring when you start writing a program. The reference for this discipline is the book by Martin Fowler and others, *Refactoring: Improving the Design of Existing Code* (Addison-Wesley, 1999).

There are many different refactorings. As examples of refactoring not covered by Delphi, consider Hide Method, which suggests turning a method private if it is not called from outside of a class; Preserve Whole Objects, which suggests passing an object as a single parameter instead of passing several of its fields; or Replace Exception with Test, which suggests removing exceptions that might be triggered by wrong method parameters and replacing them with plain conditional statements. You can find an up-do-date list of refactorings (maintained by Martin Fowler himself) at:

```
www.refactoring.com/catalog/index.html
```

As you'll see in a moment, Delphi implements only a few refactorings from this list and uses the term in a sort of lousy way to denote other code writing helpers that do not fall in the refactoring approach.

Unit Testing

Unit testing is an interesting technique for testing the implementation of a class that is spreading rapidly among programmers using different tools and programming languages. A unit test is not a test of the outcome of the application but rather a low-level test related to a given method call.

The aim of unit testing is twofold. It is certainly used to test that the code you have written behaves properly and will keep behaving properly as you add new code or change the existing one (using refactoring). However, unit testing is also used up front to define some of the details of the requirements, particularly if you follow the XP suggestion of building the unit test before you actually write the application code.

In both cases, you should not *overtest*, writing test conditions for each possible border case, but rather focus on the core functionality and write specific test for bugs you've actually encountered during the development.

The idea promoted by XP and other agile methodologies is to embrace change, and that's why testing both the new and old code often is very relevant. Not only should every test succeed before you release a version, but every test should succeed before a developer incorporates changes into the application, so that every incremental version passes the tests. The extreme approach to unit testing denies developer's their right to go home in the evening until all tests pass. In other words, the work should end with code passing all tests every day.

Refactoring and Unit Testing Combined

It is relevant to notice that refactoring and unit testing are generally used together. Particularly when you refactor code written by other developers, you must be sure you're not changing the effect of the code and only changing how that effect is obtained. That's basically what unit testing is for.

Given an existing program, if you introduce unit testing before starting to change the code, you can then feel free to refactor the code often because you can easily check that you're not introducing new bugs or resurfacing old ones. If there is no unit testing support in an existing program and you plan to refactor it a lot (maybe because you are getting on board an existing development effort), you should first write unit tests as a way to check what the code does and help you understand its architecture. Only with the testing framework in place should you start refactoring the code.

Having said this, I'll not specifically use refactoring and unit testing combined in my presentation of how Delphi supports these techniques because I'll try to stick to simple demos.

Refactoring in Delphi 2005

Although there have been third-party plug-ins providing similar capabilities, Delphi 2005 adds official refactoring support to the Delphi IDE for the first time. Refactoring in Borland Developer Studio is based on a complete analysis of the source code done with the .NET CodeDOM technology, which is why, if you totally remove .NET support on your system, you lose Delphi's refactoring capabilities.

Refactorings have a specific menu item both in the main menu and in the context menu of the editor. Although the former is called Refactor and the latter Refactoring, the two menu items have the same content that depends on the symbol or code selected in the editor. As I've already mentioned, not all Delphi refactorings relate to the formal definition of this technique, but they include some generic coding helpers such as the Declare Variable refactoring.

But I'm getting ahead of myself. Before I describe each of the refactorings (real or fake) available in Delphi, let me emphasize that all refactorings have specific Undo support, which is handy as some of them perform a large number of editing operations at once, as in the case of a Rename.

Declare Refactoring

Delphi has two declare refactoring options. With one keystroke combination (Ctrl+Shift+V) you can declare a local variable, while with another (Ctrl+Shift+D) you can declare a field in the current class. The purpose of these two operations is to let you add new storage without changing the coding position, so that you can almost keep typing. All you have to do is fill (if the defaults are not correct) and accept a dialog box.

Besides letting you produce the code faster, this has the advantage of not interrupting your thoughts to jump around the source code. You don't have to move to the begin of the method, manually adding a var section if it is not already there (to add a local variable) or jump to the class of the method (to declare a field). You can stay focused on the code you are writing.

Both these helpers suggest a type for the new variable of field declaration using the available context, like the right-hand side of an assignment, the type of the parameter of a method, or the expression context.

For example, the declare variable is very handy when writing a for loop, as you don't have to declare manually the loop variable. All you have to do it type something like:

```
for i := 0 to
```

go back to the position of the i symbol, and activate the declare variable (by means of the shortcut key, the main menu, or the context menu). You'll see a dialog box like the one in Figure 10.1. Notice that if you don't add the := and a value, the IDE won't be able to pick up your intention and suggest a proper type.

Notice that you can also use this technique to declare an array (using the corresponding check box) and that you can provide an initial value for the variable. In this case, Delphi will add a new line of code with the corresponding assignment statement at the beginning of the method or procedure.

Declaring a field works in a very similar way. This time, however, the dialog box has one more option, the ability to select the visibility of the variable providing an access specifier (including the new strict private and strict protected specifiers), as shown in Figure 10.2.

FIGURE 10.1
The Declare Variable
dialog box

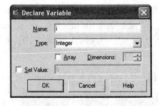

FIGURE 10.2
The Declare New
Field dialog box

In these dialog boxes you can also try to rename the symbol, modifying the original text selected in the editor. If you do so, notice that a cute flashing error symbol appears on the side of the name edit box if the symbol is illegal. If you want to see this error indicator, define an illegal identifier by entering a space within the name or adding a number at the beginning. However, if you modify the identifier name, the declaration will use the new name but the selected text in the editor will remain unchanged; you'll have to edit it manually. This seems quite odd to me.

The Declare Variable and Declare New Field refactoring included in Delphi are not part of the official list of refactorings by Fowler. However, they can be used to more easily implement some of the standard refactoring, including:

- Introduce Explaining Variable
- Consolidate Conditional Expression
- Push Down Field and Pull Up Field
- Move Field

Extract to Resource String

A second refactoring included in Delphi 2005 is a simplified way to move a constant string to a resource string. Resource strings are relevant as they are not compiled into the code segment of the application but are kept in the separate resource block. This can help save some memory, but it is particularly useful for translating an application.

The translation manager provided by Delphi, for example, extracts all the resource strings from a program and lets you create a DLL with their translation. At run time Delphi can pick up the proper language depending on the locale of the computer the program is running on. Something similar happens on the .NET Framework. Having a separate set of strings, or one per unit, rather than having constant strings dispersed throughout the code, helps make the messages to the user more coherent, as they are all listed in one place and can be checked for consistency more easily.

The problem is that using resource strings has always been quite tedious, as you have to copy a string, move from the editing position to a block earlier in the code or a different unit, paste the string there, declare the resource string, and finally, go back to the original editing position and paste the string name. All of this work can now be done with a single command, Ctrl+Shift+L.

This means that if you have a method like this:

```
procedure TForm1.Button1Click(Sender: TObject);
var
  strTest: string;
begin
  strTest := 'Hello';
```

You can move to the string (no need to select the entire string, just move the editor cursor within the quotes) and activate the refactoring you'll see the dialog box in Figure 10.3 and (by accepting the defaults) you'll get the following:

```
resourcestring
  StrHello = 'Hello';
...
procedure TForm1.Button1Click(Sender: TObject);
```

```
var
  strTest: string;
begin
  strTest := StrHello;
end;
```

The name of the resource string is suggested by the system using the actual text and an "Str" prefix. Unfortunately, there is no way to customize the name prefix (such as using lowercase "str", which I'd like better).

If the string is very long, Delphi will pick up only the first few words and capitalize them. For example, if you type on a single line:

```
strTest := 'This is a very long string that won''t even fit in
  a line of code after I refactor it';
```

after calling Extract Resource String and accepting the defaults, it becomes (second and third lines fit on one line in the editor):

```
resourcestring
  StrThisIsAVeryLong = 'This is a very long string that won''t
    even fit in a' +
  ' line of code after I refactor it';
```

Again, the Extract Resource String refactoring is not part of the official refactoring list, probably only because most of the official refactoring comes from the Java and C++ worlds.

FIGURE 10.3

The Extract Resource
String refactoring
dialog box

Rename Refactoring

The Rename refactoring (Ctrl+Shift+E) of Delphi 2005 is probably the most important refactoring included in the IDE and is one of those from the official refactoring list. Rename is very powerful and can work on different entities: variables, procedures, types (including classes), fields, and methods. You can see an example of its dialog box in Figure 10.4. After accepting this dialog box, if you keep the View references box checked, you'll get a list of changes in the Refactorings window (by default a pane docked to the bottom of the editor). You can review them and accept or reject the changes (see Figure 10.5, later).

Rename is a sort of context-sensitive search and replace and is very powerful as it can figure out when the same symbol name actually refers to a different symbol. Consider a type name declared in two different units: Delphi will change all of the references to the entity you refactor and keep the others unchanged.

In fact, the beauty of the Rename refactoring is that it affects not only the declaration and definition of a class or method, but also all of the references to it within the current project. You can rename a symbol for an entire project, but Delphi works also on independent projects within a project group.

In other words, if a project references an assembly or a package, the rename will work for the package declaring the symbol and the project using it at the same time (with a single rename operation).

Another example of the difference from a search and replace operation is that overloaded methods are renamed one at a time, so that you can use this refactoring to avoid excessive overloading or, conversely, to introduce it. Similarly, if you rename a virtual method in an ancestor class, Delphi will also rename the redefined methods in descendant classes.

Although this can get tricky at times, the Rename refactoring also works with symbols referenced in DFM files (such as form class names, component names). For example, if you rename a component, in the Refactorings window you'll get a list of changes that includes some "VCL Designer Updates." You can see an example in Figure 10.5.

What doesn't work as you might expect is the refactoring of a property name: the getter and setter methods, if any, won't be modified automatically. You'll have to refactor each of them separately.

There is an extra possible use of the Rename refactoring: fixing inconsistent case usage. If the same symbol is often spelled in different ways, you can use Rename to make it consistent. However, because Rename won't allow you to rename a symbol with the same name unless it uses a different capitalization, you have to use one of the two following tricks. The first is to rename the symbol twice, making all references wrong the first time and fixing them all the second time. The second approach is to use wrong cases in the original definition, then invoke Rename on it (or any other occurrence of the same symbol, as the dialog box uses the symbol name exactly as it is defined).

FIGURE 10.4

The Rename field
dialog box

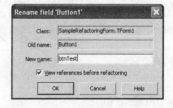

FIGURE 10.5

The Refactorings window, after the rename of
a visual component

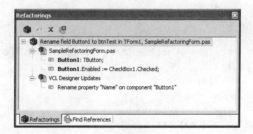

Extract Method

Another official refactoring, possibly the one producing more code on your behalf, is the Extract Method refactoring (Ctrl+Shift+M). The idea of Extract Method is to turn a snippet of code into a method. You might want to do this when the method is getting too complex to understand or because you need to use the same code from another method. What's interesting in the Extract Method refactoring is that variables used in the code snippets are automatically passed as parameters to the method. (Notice you are not asked for the visibility of the new method, as this is invariably private; when you apply an Extract Method refactoring, you don't want to change the interface of the class.)

In this case, the dialog box provides a preview of the effect of the refactoring, as you can see in Figure 10.6, a very simple case. In this confirmation dialog box, you can provide a proper name for the new method. For example, the core within the following for loop is turned into the method highlighted in the figure:

```
procedure TForm1.Button1Click(Sender: TObject);
var
  i: Integer;
  outStr: string;
begin
  for i := 1 to 10 do
  begin
    outStr := IntToStr (i);
    ListBox1.Items.Add (outStr);
  end;
end;
```

In this case the for loop counter variable i is passed as parameter to the method, while the other local variable is moved to the new method, as it is not used anymore in the original code. The complete effect of the refactoring is the following code:

```
procedure TForm1.NumberToString(i: Integer);
var
  outStr: string;
begin
  begin
    outStr := IntToStr(i);
    ListBox1.Items.Add(outStr);
  end;
end;

procedure TForm1.Button1Click(Sender: TObject);
var
  i: Integer;
begin
  for i := 1 to 10 do
    NumberToString(i);
end;
```

Aside from the extra unneeded begin end block in the new method, the effect is quite nice, particularly if you consider the time that manually editing the code in a similar way would take.

You cannot turn just any code fragment into a method. The code must be error-free, and it cannot include with statements, local procedures, or inherited calls. Also, Extract Method will invariably generate a procedure, never a function, although it can use var parameters where required. The Extract Method refactoring can also suggest the proper method parameters in some complex situations.

FIGURE 10.6
The Extract Method dialog box with the preview of the refactoring

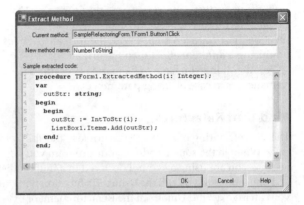

For example, if you have this code:

```
procedure TForm1.Button2Click(Sender: TObject);
var
  i: Integer;
  nTotal: Integer;
begin
  nTotal := 0;
  for i := 1 to 10 do
  begin
    nTotal := nTotal + i;
    ListBox1.Items.Add (IntToStr (i));
  end;
  ListBox1.Items.Add (IntToStr (nTotal));
end;
```

the Extract Method refactoring will add a reference parameter to the method, as the internal code of the for loop affects an external variable:

```
procedure TForm1.AddToList(i: Integer; var nTotal: Integer);
begin
  nTotal := nTotal + I;
  ListBox1.Items.Add(IntToStr(i));
end;

procedure TForm1.Button2Click(Sender: TObject);
var
  i: Integer;
  nTotal: Integer;
begin
  nTotal := 0;
  for i := 1 to 10 do
    AddToList(i, nTotal);
  ListBox1.Items.Add (IntToStr (nTotal));
end;
```

In the preceding code, if you use `Inc (nTotal, I)` instead of the assignment statement listed, the Delphi refactoring engine won't realize that there is a side effect on `nTotal`, as `Inc` is a compiler magic function that does a few tricks. With the `Inc` call, the `nTotal` parameter won't be passed by reference, producing a different effect than the original code. The fix is easy, though.

Another thing you have to fix manually at times is the use of `const` parameters for increased performance, as in case of string parameters.

Find Unit Refactoring

The last refactoring of Delphi 2005 provides the ability to add a unit to a `uses` statement automatically. When in the source code of your program you have an undeclared symbol, it might be simply because you are using a symbol declared in a unit not listed in the `uses` clause.

For example, if you call the `MinuteOf` function without having DateUtils listed in the `uses` clause, you can invoke Find Unit from the Refactor menu or by using Ctrl+Shift+A. You'll see a list with possible references, like the one in Figure 10.7. From here you can pick a specific function from a unit (or a type, in other cases), choose whether to place the `uses` statement in the interface or implementation portion of the unit, and enter it automatically. Again, one of the positive things is that you will be less distracted from your flow of thoughts and won't have to move around the code to do this operation.

Although this feature seems very nice, the problem lies with its limitations. As with other refactoring, Delphi works on the CodeDOM. This means that the unit you are looking for must already be referenced from within the project or project group. As this includes indirect references (like units used by VCL units you use), there is a good chance that Delphi can find the proper unit, but there are also cases in which this doesn't happen. Actually in Delphi for .NET, in which you refer to entire namespaces with a `uses` statement, the Find Unit refactoring tends to work better than on Win32.

FIGURE 10.7

The dialog box of the Uses Unit refactoring

Find References

Another new feature of the Delphi 2005 IDE closely related to refactoring, because it is based on the same architecture, is the ability to find references to a symbol within the code. This is the base on which the Rename refactoring is based, but at times it is handy to find references to modify one or more of them and not rename them all.

In the second section of the Search menu and under the Find menu item of the context menu of the editor, you can see three new commands:

Find References   Allows you to find all of the references to a given symbol (class, method, function, type, etc.) in the current project. For a method, for example, this would include the method declaration in the class, the method definition, and all of the calls to the method in the program. You can see the effect of a simple find reference for a library function in Figure 10.8; in this case you get only the list of source code locations where the function is called, not where it is defined.

Find Local References   Filters the Find References search to the current unit only.

Find Declaration Symbol   Finds where a given symbol is declared. You can often obtain the same effect by Ctrl-clicking the symbol, as discussed in Chapter 1.

FIGURE 10.8
The Find References window after a search

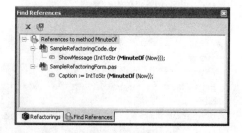

Unit Testing in Delphi 2005

I already introduced unit testing in theory and as part of XP programming earlier in this chapter when I covered the Test First approach and described what unit testing is for. I also discussed why unit testing and refactoring are two closely tied techniques. Now it is time to focus specifically on the unit testing support available in the Delphi 2005 IDE.

Delphi embeds two different unit testing frameworks, one specifically for Delphi and the other specifically for .NET. The first is DUnit (`http://dunit.sourceforge.net`), which works for Delphi both in Win32 and .NET, and the other is NUnit (`www.nunit.org`), which works in .NET for both the Delphi and C# languages. In other words, in Delphi for .NET projects you have a choice; otherwise you simply pick the available framework.

NOTE   By the time you read this, an updated version of the DUnit shipping with Delphi 2005 should have been made available by its developers. As both frameworks are under continuous evolution, check the respective websites for updates.

A relevant feature offered by Delphi besides the integration of the testing framework is the availability of a wizard to set up the test project and create test skeletons for methods of specific classes. I'll try to show you a couple of examples in the following sections, although it is very hard to demonstrate unit testing without an actual (large) project to work with. Notice—and this is a key feature of unit testing as compared to other testing techniques—that all of the test code is part of a different project from the one you are testing. There is no intermixed project code and test code. This is a huge benefit, as the testing has no impact on the actual source code of the application nor its compiled executable.

Using the wizards seems impossible in the case of the Test First approach. In practice, however, you can write a dummy class, create the tests for its methods, and then start writing the actual code of the class. Finally, these unit-testing frameworks can be used for functional tests involving multiple classes or layers, and they can also be used for some efficiency measurement, as they indicate the times taken by each test. On the other hand, it is very hard to use unit testing for UI testing; this area is certainly not in the scope of this technology.

DUnit

The reason I tend to prefer DUnit to NUnit for unit testing is simple: I still have a lot of Win32 code, and code compatibility is relevant to a good number of my .NET projects as well. Your mileage might vary, of course. DUnit was first developed by Juanco Añez as a port of JUnit to the Delphi language, although over the last few years the DUnit development has really become a team effort. DUnit is released under MPL license.

To demonstrate how DUnit works I wrote a sample program, UnitTestDemo. The main project contains the following sample class:

```
type
  TMyTest = class
  private
    FNumber: Integer;
    procedure SetNumber(const Value: Integer);
  public
    property Number: Integer read FNumber write SetNumber;
    function Text: string;
    procedure Add (n: Integer);
  end;
```

After writing this unit and a trivial form using the class, I used the File ➤ New ➤ Other menu command (or the corresponding Tool Palette button) to activate the New Items dialog box and selected the Test Project Wizard in the Unit test page. This wizard (visible in Figure 10.9) allows you to define a name and a location for the test project. The second page allows you to pick a test framework (only in the case of a Delphi for .NET project) and to pick the type of test runner application (GUI or console).

Once the test project has been set up, you can start adding tests to it. Again, you can select the Test Case Wizard (in the same page of the New Items dialog or in the same tab of the Tool Palette), and the corresponding dialog will guide you through a couple of steps and produce the structure of the test code on your behalf. In the case of my sample project, the Test Case Wizard lets me pick the methods of the TMytest class, as you can see in Figure 10.10.

FIGURE 10.9
The Test Project Wizard is used to set up a unit test project.

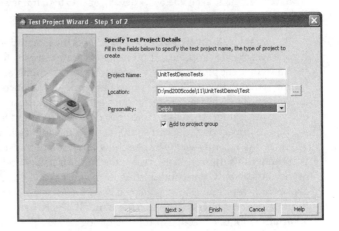

FIGURE 10.10
The Test Case Wizard al-
lows you to pick the
methods you want to
write tests for.

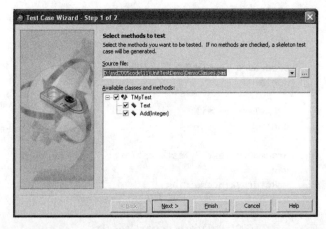

The following page of the wizard lets you determine the name of the test class and of the unit where you want to save it. Its effect is to produce a unit with the code in Listing 10.1 (with some of the stock comments removed).

LISTING 10.1:   The TestDemoClasses unit generated by the Test Case Wizard

```
unit TestDemoClasses;

interface

uses
  TestFramework, DemoClasses;

type
  // Test methods for class TMyTest
  TestTMyTest = class(TTestCase)
  strict private
    FMyTest: TMyTest;
  public
    procedure SetUp; override;
    procedure TearDown; override;
  published
    procedure TestText;
    procedure TestAdd;
  end;

implementation

procedure TestTMyTest.SetUp;
```

```
begin
  FMyTest := TMyTest.Create;
end;

procedure TestTMyTest.TearDown;
begin
  FMyTest.Free;
  FMyTest := nil;
end;

procedure TestTMyTest.TestText;
var
  ReturnValue: string;
begin
  ReturnValue := FMyTest.Text;
  // TODO: Validate method results
end;

procedure TestTMyTest.TestAdd;
var
  n: Integer;
begin
  // TODO: Setup method call parameters
  FMyTest.Add(n);
  // TODO: Validate method results
end;

initialization
  // Register any test cases with the test runner
  RegisterTest(TestTMyTest.Suite);
end.
```

As you can see in the listing, the initialization code lets the framework know about the class by calling RegisterTest over the TTestSuite returned by the base method Suite. This method is defined by the TTestCase base class.

The test class defines an object that is initialized in the SetUp method and destroyed in the TearDown method. These two methods are invoked automatically from the framework when you execute the tests. Testing the class (or running the class test suite, to be more precise) involves the execution of each of the published methods of the class, representing the single tests. By default, the wizard defines a test for each method, but you can add as many tests (that is, published methods) as you want.

Within this test method you can operate on the target object and then call one of the testing methods, which include checking values (Check, CheckEquals, CheckNotEquals, CheckNull, CheckNotNull, CheckIs, ...), checking for exceptions (CheckException), or causing a failure (Fail, FailEquals, FailNotSame...).

For example, this is a simple test for the Add method:

```
procedure TestTMyTest.TestAdd;
begin
  FMyTest.Number := 10;
  FMyTest.Add(5);
  CheckEquals(15, FMyTest.Number);
end;
```

As the code of the method raises an exception in the case of a negative parameter, another test for this method will be to check if in such a case an exception is indeed raised. To accomplish this, you have to write a nonpublished method that raises the exception and pass it to CheckException:

```
procedure TestTMyTest.TestAddException; // published test
begin
  FMyTest.Number := 10;
  CheckException (AddNegativeValue, Exception);
end;

procedure TestTMyTest.AddNegativeValue; // public helper method
begin
  FMyTest.Add(-5);
end;
```

Notice that if you run the test in the debugger, it will stop on the exception, as usual. Of course, if you use a specific exception you can tell the Delphi IDE not to break on it, or you can run the test suite outside of the debugger.

Finally, I wrote a bogus test for the TestText test method so that it will invariably fail. With this code in place you can actually run the test program. You'll get the user interface of the test framework (see Figure 10.11), which allows you to run the tests and see the result.

FIGURE 10.11
The user interface of the DUnit test framework main window, along with the tests defined in the UnitTestDemo project

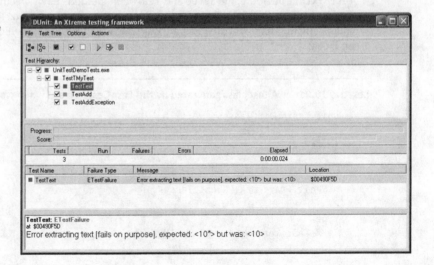

If you add new methods to the target class of the test, you can invoke the Test Class Wizard again to have new tests added to the test class. If you select a method for which there is an existing test, the code of this test won't be modified and no new test will be generated for the method.

I have to say, however, that although the wizards are handy at the beginning, after you get used to DUnit (or other unit testing frameworks), writing the tests directly is very easy, so you'll use the wizard less and less.

NOTE   Delphi 2005 Update 2 adds support in the Test Case Wizard for generating test cases for interfaces and for considering protected methods.

NUnit

As I mentioned, DUnit test projects are available on Win32 but can also be ported on .NET without changing the code. This is very handy if you want to create VCL applications ready for .NET that are still Win32 compatible, along with their tests. When you are working exclusively on the .NET platform, however, you can pick the NUnit framework. NUnit was initially ported verbatim from JUnit, as are most unit testing frameworks. Later, however, it was completely redesigned to take advantage of some core features of the .NET architecture, such as reflection in general and custom attributes in particular. NUnit works with any .NET language, including Delphi, of course.

As an example of the use of NUnit and a way to compare the two engines (from a very general perspective), I moved the previous example to .NET and rebuilt the test project from scratch using NUnit. The result of this work is in the NUnitDemo folder of this chapter's code.

To create the new project I used the same two wizards. The effect, though, is quite different. Where the DUnit test program is an executable file, the NUnit test project is a library assembly. This assembly can be *executed* by specifying as host program the NUnit interface program, which is called `nunit-gui.exe` and is installed by default under the `bin` folder of NUnit. This setup is provided automatically by the Test Project wizard.

Also, the test code looks quite different as it relies on reflection and custom attributes rather than suite registration and published properties. In particular, the test class is marked with the `TestFixture` attribute, the `SetUp` and `TearDown` methods have specific attributes, and each test case method is marked with the `Test` attribute. You can see the generated class (before I added any custom code) in Listing 10.2. You can compare this code with Listing 10.1, which showed a similar class based on DUnit.

LISTING 10.2:   A test class generated by the Test Case Wizard when working with NUnit

```
unit TestNDemoClasses;

interface

uses
  NUnit.Framework, NDemoClasses;

type
  // Test methods for class TMyTest
```

```delphi
  [TestFixture]
  TestTMyTest = class
  strict private
    FMyTest: TMyTest;
  public
    [SetUp]
    procedure SetUp;
    [TearDown]
    procedure TearDown;
  published
    [Test]
    procedure TestText;
    [Test]
    procedure TestAdd;
  end;

implementation

procedure TestTMyTest.SetUp;
begin
  FMyTest := TMyTest.Create;
end;

procedure TestTMyTest.TearDown;
begin
  FMyTest := nil;
end;

procedure TestTMyTest.TestText;
var
  ReturnValue: string;
begin
  ReturnValue := FMyTest.Text;
  // TODO: Validate method results
end;

procedure TestTMyTest.TestAdd;
var
  n: Integer;
begin
  // TODO: Setup method call parameters
  FMyTest.Add(n);
  // TODO: Validate method results
end;

end.
```

Now, you can start again to write the code for the tests, which follows a very similar approach. To implement the tests with NUnit, instead of using methods of the base class, you use class methods of a couple of specific classes defined in the NUnit.Framework namespace. In particular, you use the Assert class, which has methods such as IsTrue, IsFalse, AreEqual, IsNotNull, IsNull, and AreSame. In other words, for example, you use Assert.AreEqual instead of CheckEquals. The code of a test looks like:

```
procedure TestTMyTest.TestAdd;
begin
  FMyTest.Number := 10;
  FMyTest.Add(5);
  Assert.AreEqual(15, FMyTest.Number);
end;
```

The user interface of the GUI version of the NUnit framework is conceptually similar to the one in DUnit (and to any other unit testing framework); you can see it in action in Figure 10.12. Again, I left a testing error in the sample application to show what a test failure looks like.

The way NUnit tests for expected exceptions is really neat. Instead of the call with the method parameter of DUnit, you simply write the test with the code that raises the exception, such as:

```
procedure TestTMyTest.CheckException;
begin
  FMyTest.Add(-5); // raises exception
end;
```

You mark the fact you are expecting a given exception with another attribute, so that the method declaration (in the TestTMyTest class) becomes:

```
[Test, ExpectedException(typeof(Exception))]
procedure CheckException;
```

FIGURE 10.12

The user interface of the NUnit framework

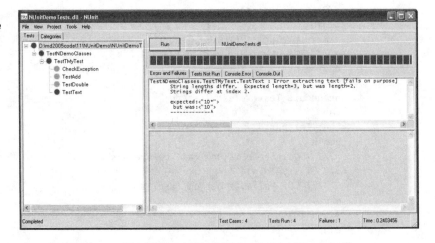

Again, this is far from a complete introduction to NUnit, but it should at least get you started with this unit testing framework. Notice that unlike the Delphi-specific DUnit, which is covered in only a few articles, there is a lot of documentation on the Web for NUnit and even entire books covering it because it has been adopted by many .NET developers across languages and development environments.

More Unit Testing Tips

Now that you have seen the practical presentation of the key features of the two unit testing frameworks available in the Delphi 2005 IDE, I will provide some more information about unit testing in general. Consider this a simple collection of tips from my experience and that of other unit testing users I've spoken with.

Unit testing, not memory checking   It is not a common practice to test constructors and destructors, nor to test the lifetime of the objects in general; looking for memory leaks requires specific tools.

Unit testing is not for the UI   Although you can try to test for the status of visual components, this is not what unit testing is for. Despite several proposals in this area, it seems that this is (again) the wrong tool for the job. What you can do is test the logic behind a visual component, but in general it is better if you actually split this code in two with a class providing the logic for the UI element. In this case, of course, you can and should test the class behind the UI control.

Test database access and logic   You can use unit testing to check for consistency in database access and database logic if you have business rules connected with field objects, for example, of dataset components. I have to say this falls more into the functional testing category than the unit testing idea, but you can still use unit testing frameworks to accomplish similar tasks.

Do not test too much   As I already said earlier, do not test every obvious condition; if an assignment operation doesn't set the proper value, you'd better find another compiler! Testing trivial operations is mostly useless. Testing every possible case is generally a waste. Add some general tests. Add tests for bugs you've actually run into. Add tests for conditions specifically relevant to the requirements. Look for enough tests, not a complete set.

Tests as documentation   A good set of tests can be readable enough to provide extra documentation to the classes you are writing. According to some developers, tests can even replace documentation, as they indicate what methods of a class should do.

Test percentages help track progress   If you write tests first, the percentage of tests passed can help you track the development progress, although if tests do not cover every area of the program, this is not a precise indication. If you add functional tests to your suite, they will provide a much better indication of the project completion.

Tests work better with OOP than RAD   If you use an OOP framework for database access, for example, an object-relational mapping layer, you can perform much better tests than if you hook user interface controls directly to database access components. The more OOP you use, the more you can have unit tests for it.

Use unit tests when refactoring heavily   As I've already mentioned, if you have to work on existing code and plan on refactoring it a lot, you should write unit testing against the current code base before refactoring it. If the tests work at first and keep working after your changes, you'll have more confidence that the refactoring you applied didn't change the behavior of the program.

Time test execution   With a good suite of tests, possibly repeating the call of methods inside loops, you can check if your refactoring or other changes in code produce a positive or negative effect on speed. A unit testing framework doesn't replace a good profiler but can come in handy to give you a rough estimate of the slowest method calls in your code and let you see large-grained differences among different implementations. For the fine-tuning, though, look elsewhere.

What's Next

In this chapter you started to see that there is much more than visual development in Delphi 2005. Delphi, in fact, is a full object-oriented language supporting all of the more recent OOP approaches and methodologies, including the use of design patterns and extreme programming. In practice, Delphi 2005 adds ready-to-use support for many recent techniques, such as refactoring and unit testing. Although Delphi support in this area doesn't rival some of tools that have had refactoring support for a while, such as Borland's own JBuilder, Delphi 2005 offers a very promising start in this direction.

Regardless of the theoretical approach, in fact, Delphi's official refactoring and other coding helpers based on the same architecture *do* speed up development considerably. This is the key point, in my opinion.

Now that you've been introduced to OOP architectures, we can delve into other related areas of the product. In particular, I'll cover the structure of flexible and dynamic application architectures and the use of COM and Win32 code from .NET. Later on, in the database portion of the book, I'll get back to more application design approaches, including Model Driven Architecture (MDA).

Chapter 11

Dynamic Architectures (with Libraries, Packages, and Assemblies)

Windows executable files come in two flavors: *programs* and *dynamic link libraries* (DLLs). *Dynamic linking* can take place when the application starts (static linking of the DLL) or at run time by loading the library and accessing it (dynamic linking of the DLL). Dynamic applications are made possible by loading DLLs dynamically. This feature is readily available to applications that call global functions but requires extra support if you want a DLL that exposes classes and methods. As you'll see, this extra support is available for Delphi packages or .NET assemblies. Before getting to this discussion, however, the chapter covers traditional DLLs, which are the foundation for the topic.

One of the relevant features of the .NET architecture is its ability to split an application into multiple assemblies, an executable assembly, and a few library assemblies. These can be linked directly to the application and loaded at startup or loaded dynamically as required. A similar architecture was and is also still possible with Delphi packages on Win32. This is the preferred approach for building dynamic applications in Delphi, as I'll demonstrate in this chapter.

DLLs in Win32

In Chapter 2 I highlighted a few elements of the architecture of the Win32 operating system, including the relevant role of DLLs. Here my aim is to provide a few more technical details before delving into the development of DLLs in Delphi.

What Is Dynamic Linking?

First, it is important to fully understand the difference between static and dynamic linking of functions or procedures. When a subroutine is not directly available in a source file, the compiler adds the subroutine to an internal table. Of course, the Delphi compiler must have seen the declaration of the subroutine and know about its parameters and type, or it will issue an error.

After compilation of a normal—*statically linked*—subroutine, the linker fetches the subroutine's compiled code from a Delphi compiled unit (or static library) and adds it to the program's code. The resulting executable file includes all the code of the program and of the units involved. The Delphi linker is smart enough to include only the minimum amount of code from the program's units and to link only the functions and methods that are actually used. This is why it is called "smart linker."

NOTE   A notable exception to this rule is the inclusion of virtual methods. The compiler cannot determine in advance which virtual methods the program will call, so it has to include them all. For this reason, programs and libraries with many virtual functions tend to generate larger executable files. While developing the VCL, the Borland developers had to balance the flexibility obtained with virtual functions against the reduced size of the executable files achieved by limiting the virtual functions.

In the case of dynamic linking, which occurs when your code calls a DLL-based function, the linker uses the information in the external declaration of the subroutine to set up an import table in the executable file. When Windows loads the executable file in memory, first it loads all the required DLLs, and then the program starts. During this loading process, Windows fills the program's import table with the addresses of the DLL functions in memory. If for some reason the DLL is not found or a referenced routine is not present in a DLL that is found, the program won't even start.

Each time the program calls an external function, it uses this import table to forward the call to the DLL code (which is now located in the program's address space). Note that this scheme does not involve two different applications. The DLL becomes part of the running program and is loaded in the same address space. All the parameter passing takes place on the application's stack (because the DLL doesn't have a separate stack) or in CPU registers. Because a DLL is loaded into the application's address space, any memory allocations of the DLL or any global data it creates reside in the address space of the main process. Thus, data and memory pointers can be passed directly from the DLL to the program and vice versa.

There is another approach to using DLLs that is even more dynamic than the one I just discussed: at run time, you can load a DLL in memory, search for a function (provided you know its name), and call the function by name. This approach requires more complex code and takes some extra time to locate the function. The execution of the function, however, occurs with the same speed as calling an implicitly loaded DLL. On the positive side, you don't need to have the DLL available to start the program. You will use this approach in the DynaCall example in this chapter and to build dynamic architectures based on packages later on.

What Are DLLs For?

Now that you have a general idea of how DLLs work, we can focus on the reasons for using them in Win32 development. Similar concepts apply for .NET library assemblies. The first advantage is that if different programs use the same DLL, the DLL is loaded in memory only once, thus saving system memory. DLLs are mapped into the private address space of each process (each running application), but their code is loaded in memory only once.

NOTE   To be more precise, the operating system will try to load the DLL at the same address in each application's address space (using the preferred base address specified by the DLL). If that address is not available in a particular application's virtual address space, the DLL code image for that process will have to be relocated—an operation that is expensive in terms of both performance and memory use, because the relocation happens on a per-process basis, not system-wide. This doesn't apply to the .NET world, in which a DLL contains IL for the JIT compiler.

Another interesting feature is that you can provide a different version of a DLL, replacing the current one, without having to recompile the application using it. This approach will work, of course, only if the functions in the DLL have the same parameters as the previous version. If the DLL has new functions, it doesn't matter. Problems may arise only if a function in the older version of the DLL is missing in the new one or if a function takes an object reference and the classes, base classes, or even compiler versions don't match.

This second advantage is particularly applicable to complex applications. If you have a very big program that requires frequent updates and bug fixes, dividing it into several executables and dynamic libraries allows you to distribute only the changed portions instead of a single large executable. Doing so makes sense for Windows system libraries in particular: you generally don't need to recompile your code if Microsoft provides an updated version of Windows system libraries—for example, in a new version of the operating system or a service pack. Using libraries to create flexible applications has been further pushed in .NET with specific and improved support for dynamic loading, versions management, and security support.

Another common technique is to use dynamic libraries to store nothing but resources. You can build different versions of a DLL containing strings for different languages and then change the language at run time, or you can prepare a library of icons and bitmaps and then use them in different applications. The development of language-specific versions of a program is particularly important, and both the VCL library and .NET include support for it. The Delphi IDE helps you with its Integrated Translation Environment (ITE).

Another key advantage is that DLLs are independent of the programming language. Most Windows programming environments, including most macro languages in end-user applications, allow a programmer to call a function stored in a DLL. This flexibility applies only to the use of functions, though. There are many troubles caused by differences in languages when you want to share classes and objects. For example, calling a DLL written in C++ can result in problems with the name mangling of parameters. To share objects in a library across programming languages, Microsoft promoted first the COM infrastructure and now the .NET architecture, which were both designed from the ground up to deal with and share objects in a language-independent way.

Rules for Delphi DLL Writers

Delphi DLL programmers on Win32 need to follow several rules:

♦ The declaration of the project of a DLL is indicated by the `library` keyword, which replaces the `program` keyword. A further alternative is `package`. In .NET, both library and package projects produce library assemblies, with packages being the preferred approach for generic code sharing.

♦ A DLL function or procedure to be called by external programs must be listed in the DLL's `exports` clause. This makes the routine visible to the outside world.

♦ Exported functions should also be declared as `stdcall`, to use the standard Win32 parameter-passing technique instead of the optimized `register` parameter-passing technique (which is the default in Delphi). The exception to this rule is if you want to use these libraries only from other Delphi applications. Of course, you can also use another calling convention, provided the other compiler understands it (such as `cdecl`, which is the default on C compilers).

♦ The types of a DLL's parameters should be the default Windows types (mostly C-compatible data types), at least if you want to be able to use the DLL within other development environments. There are further rules for exporting strings, as you'll see in the FirstDLL example.

◆ A DLL can use global data that won't be shared by different calling applications. Each time an application loads a DLL, it stores the DLL's global data in its own address space, as you will see in the DllMem example.

◆ Delphi libraries should trap all internal exceptions, unless you plan to use the library only from other Delphi programs.

Using Existing DLLs

You have already used existing DLLs in examples in this book, when calling Windows API functions. As you might remember, all the API functions are declared in the system Windows unit (in Delphi for Win32). Functions are declared in the `interface` portion of the unit, as shown here:

```
function PlayMetaFile(DC: HDC; MF: HMETAFILE): BOOL; stdcall;
function PaintRgn(DC: HDC; RGN: HRGN): BOOL; stdcall;
function PolyPolygon(DC: HDC; var Points; var nPoints; p4: Integer):
  BOOL; stdcall;
function PtInRegion(RGN: HRGN; p2, p3: Integer): BOOL; stdcall;
```

Then, in the `implementation` portion, instead of providing each function's code, the unit refers to the external definition in a DLL:

```
const
  gdi32 = 'gdi32.dll';

function PlayMetaFile; external gdi32 name 'PlayMetaFile';
function PaintRgn; external gdi32 name 'PaintRgn';
function PolyPolygon; external gdi32 name 'PolyPolygon';
function PtInRegion; external gdi32 name 'PtInRegion';
```

The external definition of these functions refers to the name of the DLL they use. The name of the DLL must include the .DLL extension, or the program will not work under Windows NT/2000/XP (although it will work under Windows 9x). The other element is the name of the DLL function. The name directive is not necessary if the Delphi function (or procedure) name matches the DLL function name (which is case sensitive).

To call a function that resides in a DLL, you can provide its declaration in the interface section of a unit and external definition in the implementation section, as shown earlier, or you can merge the two in a single declaration in the implementation section of a unit if it's only needed locally in that unit. Once the function is properly defined, you can call it in your Delphi application code just like any other function.

TIP   Delphi includes the Delphi language translation of a large number of Windows APIs, as you can see in the many files available in Delphi's source\Win32\rtl\win folder. More Delphi units referring to other APIs are available as part of the Delphi Jedi project at www.delphi-jedi.org.

As you saw in Chapter 9, Delphi for .NET declares the Windows API functions in a similar way but at times with different parameters and uses the DLLImport attribute rather than the external definition. You'll see more on DLLImport and PInvoke in the next chapter.

Building a Win32 DLL in Delphi

In addition to using DLLs written in other environments, you can use Delphi to build DLLs that can be used by Delphi programs or with any other development tool that supports DLLs. Building DLLs in Delphi is so easy that you might overuse this feature. In general, I suggest you try to build packages instead of plain DLLs. As I'll discuss later in this chapter, packages often contain components, but they can also include plain noncomponent classes, allowing you to write object-oriented code and reuse it effectively. Of course, packages can contain also simple routines, constants, variables, etc.

As I already mentioned, building a DLL is useful when a portion of a program's code is subject to frequent changes. In this case, you can often replace the DLL, keeping the rest of the program unchanged. Similarly, when you need to write a program that provides different features to different groups of users, you can distribute different versions of a DLL to those users.

As a starting point in exploring the development of DLLs in Delphi, I'll show you a library built in Delphi. To start, choose the DLL Wizard option in the Delphi Projects page of the New Items dialog box. Doing so creates a very simple source file that begins with the `library` keyword, indicating that you want to build a DLL instead of an executable file.

Now you can add routines to the library and list them in an `exports` statement. In Listing 11.1 you can see a simplified version of the code of the FirstDll example (the actual example code is much more complex, as described in the following sections).

LISTING 11.1:   The code of a preliminary version of the FirstDll library

```
library Firstdll;

uses
  SysUtils, Windows;

function Triple (N: Integer): Integer; stdcall;
begin
  try
    Result := N * 3;
  except
    Result := -1;
  end;
end;

function Double (N: Integer): Integer; stdcall;
begin
  try
    Result := N * 2;
  except
    Result := -1;
  end;
end;

exports
  Triple, Double;
```

In general (and in the companion code), the main project file includes only the uses and exports statements, whereas the function declarations are placed in a separate unit. In the FirstDll example, I wanted to change the preceding code slightly to show a message each time a function is called. You can accomplish this in many ways; the example either uses the Dialogs unit and calls the ShowMessage function or uses the Windows unit and calls the MessageBox function.

If you refer to the Dialogs unit, Delphi has to link a lot of VCL code into the application. If you statically link the VCL into this DLL, the resulting size will be almost 400 KB. The reason is that the ShowMessage function displays a VCL form that contains VCL controls and uses VCL graphics classes; those indirectly refer to things like the VCL streaming system and the VCL application and screen objects. In this case, a better alternative is to show the messages using direct API calls, using the Windows unit and calling the MessageBox function, so that the VCL code is not required. This code change brings the size of the application down to about 40 KB.

If you run a test program like the CallFrst example (described later) using the API-based version of the DLL, its behavior won't be correct. In fact, you can click the buttons that call the DLL functions several times without first closing the message boxes displayed by the DLL. This happens because the first parameter of the MessageBox API call is zero. Its value should instead be the handle of the program's main form or the application form—information you don't have at hand in the DLL.

Exporting Strings from a DLL

In general, functions in a DLL can use any type of parameter and return any type of value. There are two exceptions to this rule:

◆ If you plan to call the DLL from other programming languages, you should try using Windows native data types instead of Delphi-specific types. For example, to express color values, you should use integers or the Windows ColorRef type instead of the Delphi native TColor type, doing the appropriate conversions. For compatibility, you should avoid using some other Delphi types, including objects (which cannot be used by other languages) and Delphi strings (which can be replaced by PChar strings). In other words, every Windows development environment must support the basic types of the API, and if you stick to them, your DLL will be usable with other development environments. (This partially explains the language interoperability troubles .NET overcomes.)

◆ Even if you plan to use the DLL only from a Delphi application, you cannot pass Delphi strings (and dynamic arrays) across the DLL boundary without taking some precautions. This is due to how Delphi manages strings in memory—allocating, reallocating, and freeing them automatically. The solution to the problem is to include the ShareMem system unit both in the DLL and in the program using it. This unit must be included as the first unit of each of the projects. Moreover, you have to deploy the BorlndMM.DLL file (the name stands for Borland Memory Manager) along with the program and the specific library.

In the FirstDLL example, I've included both approaches: one function receives and returns a Delphi string, and another receives as parameter a PChar pointer that is then filled by the function. The first function is written as usual in Delphi, and I won't list it here—it is trivial as it concatenates the string with a separator.

The second function is slightly more complex because PChar strings don't have a simple + operator and have less automatic memory management, so you have to use some of the specific support functions. Here is the complete code; it uses input and output PChar buffers, which are compatible with any Windows development environment:

```
function DoublePChar (BufferIn, BufferOut: PChar;
  BufferOutLen: Cardinal; Separator: Char): LongBool; stdcall;
var
  SepStr: array [0..1] of Char;
begin
  try
    // if the buffer is large enough
    if BufferOutLen > StrLen (BufferIn) * 2 + 2 then
    begin
      // copy the input buffer in the output buffer
      StrCopy (BufferOut, BufferIn);
      // build the separator string (value plus null terminator)
      SepStr [0] := Separator;
      SepStr [1] := #0;
      // append the separator
      StrCat (BufferOut, SepStr);
      // append the input buffer once more
      StrCat (BufferOut, BufferIn);
      Result := True;
    end
    else
      // not enough space
      Result := False;
  except
    Result := False;
  end;
end;
```

This second version of the code is certainly more complex, but the first can be used only from Delphi. Moreover, the first version requires you to include the ShareMem unit and to deploy the file BorlndMM.DLL, as discussed earlier.

Calling the Delphi DLL

How can you use the library you just built? You can call it from within another Delphi project or from other environments. As an example, I built the CallFrst project (stored in the FirstDLL directory). To access the DLL functions, you must declare them as external. You can copy and paste the definition of the functions from the source code of the Delphi DLL, adding the external clause, as follows:

```
function Double (N: Integer): Integer;
  stdcall; external 'FIRSTDLL.DLL';
```

Once they are declared as `external`, the functions of the DLL can be used as if they were local functions. Here are two examples, with calls to the string-related functions (an example of the output is visible in Figure 11.1):

```
procedure TForm1.BtnDoubleStringClick(Sender: TObject);
begin
  // call the DLL function directly
  EditDouble.Text := DoubleString (EditSource.Text, ';');
end;

procedure TForm1.BtnDoublePCharClick(Sender: TObject);
var
  Buffer: string;
begin
  // make the buffer large enough
  SetLength (Buffer, 1000);
  // call the DLL function
  if DoublePChar (PChar (EditSource.Text), PChar (Buffer), 1000, '/') then
    EditDouble.Text := Buffer;
end;
```

Changing Library Names

For a library, as for a standard application, you end up with a library name matching a Delphi project filename. Delphi has special compiler directives you can use in libraries to determine their executable filename. Two of them ($LIBPREFIX, which adds a word in front of the library name, and $LIBVERSION, which adds a version number after the extension) make more sense on Linux than on Windows. A third, $LIBSUFFIX, adds text after the library name and before the extension and is also commonly used on Windows for changing the executable file name when versioning libraries and packages. These directives can be set in the IDE from the Application page of the Project Options dialog box, as you can see in Figure 11.2. As an example, consider the following directives, which generate a library called MarcoNameTest60.dll:

```
library NameTest;
{$LIBPREFIX 'Marco'}
{$LIBSUFFIX '60'}
```

FIGURE 11.1
The output of the Call-Frst example, which calls the DLL you built in Delphi

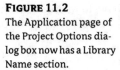

FIGURE 11.2
The Application page of
the Project Options dia-
log box now has a Library
Name section.

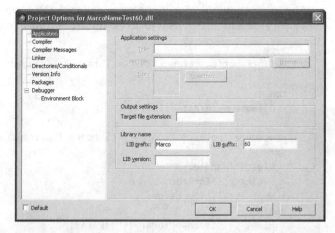

Delphi packages use the $LIBSUFFIX directive extensively. The VCL package in Delphi 2005 generates the VCL.DCP file and the VCL90.BPL file. The advantage of this approach is that you won't need to change the requires portions of your packages for every new version of Delphi. At the same time, you can deploy multiple versions of the compiled package on the same computer in separate executable files. Each program loads the version is was compiled for.

NOTE   The .BPL extension stands for Borland Package Library. This is in essence a DLL with some extra custom features.

Calling a DLL Function at Run Time

I mentioned earlier that you can delay the loading of a DLL until the moment it is needed, so you can use the rest of the program even if the DLL is not available. Dynamic loading of a DLL in Windows is accomplished by calling the LoadLibrary API function, which searches for the DLL in the program folder, in the folders on the path, and in some system folders. If the DLL is not found, Windows will show an error message, something you can skip by calling Delphi's SafeLoadLibrary function. This function has the same effect as the API it encapsulates, but it suppresses the standard Windows error message and should be the preferred way to load libraries dynamically in Delphi.

If the library is found and loaded (something you know by checking the return value of LoadLibrary or SafeLoadLibrary), a program can call the GetProcAddress API function, which searches the DLL's exports table, looking for the name of the function passed as a parameter. If GetProcAddress finds a match, it returns a pointer to the requested procedure. Now you can cast this function pointer to the proper type and call it.

Whichever loading function you used, don't forget to call FreeLibrary at the end, so that the DLL can be properly released from memory. In fact, the system uses a reference-counting technique for libraries, releasing them when each loading request has been matched by a freeing request.

The example I built to show dynamic DLL loading is named DynaCall. It uses the FirstDLL library built earlier in this chapter (to make the program work, you have to copy the DLL from its source folder into the same folder as the DynaCall example). Instead of declaring the Double and Triple functions and using them directly, this example obtains the same effect with somewhat more complex code. The advantage, however, is that the program will run even without the DLL.

Also, if new *compatible* functions are added to the DLL, you won't have to revise the program's source code and recompile it to access those new functions. Here is the core code of the program:

```
type
  TIntFunction = function (I: Integer): Integer; stdcall;

const
  DllName = 'Firstdll.dll';

procedure TForm1.Button1Click(Sender: TObject);
var
  HInst: THandle;
  FPointer: TFarProc;
  MyFunct: TIntFunction;
begin
  HInst := SafeLoadLibrary (DllName);
  if HInst > 0 then
  try
    FPointer := GetProcAddress (HInst,
      PChar (Edit1.Text));
    if FPointer <> nil then
    begin
      MyFunct := TIntFunction (FPointer);
      SpinEdit1.Value := MyFunct (SpinEdit1.Value);
    end
    else
      ShowMessage (Edit1.Text + ' DLL function not found');
  finally
    FreeLibrary (HInst);
  end
  else
    ShowMessage (DllName + ' library not found');
end;
```

WARNING   Because the library uses the Borland Memory Manager, the program dynamically loading it must do the same. So you need to have the ShareMem unit in the project of the DynaCall example.

How do you call a procedure in Delphi once you have a pointer to it? One solution is to convert the pointer to a procedural type and then call the procedure using the procedural-type variable, as in the previous listing. Notice that the procedural type you define must be compatible with the definition of the procedure in the DLL. This is the Achilles' heel of this method—there is no actual check of the parameter types.

What is the advantage of this approach? In theory, you can use it to access any function of any DLL at any time. In practice, it is useful when you have different DLLs with compatible functions or a single DLL with several compatible functions, as in this case. You can call the Double and Triple functions by entering their names in the edit box. Now, if someone gives you a DLL with a new function receiving an integer as a parameter and returning an integer, you can call it by entering its name in the edit box. You don't even need to recompile the application.

With this code, the compiler and the linker ignore the existence of the DLL. When the program is loaded, the DLL is not loaded immediately. You might make the program even more flexible and use an INI or another configuration file to hold the names of the DLLs to use. In some cases, this is a great advantage. A program may switch DLLs at run time, something the direct approach does not allow.

Only a system based on a compiler and a linker, such as Delphi, can use the direct approach, which is generally more reliable and also a little faster. In my opinion, the indirect loading approach of the DynaCall example is useful only in special cases, but it can be extremely powerful. On the other hand, I see a lot of value in using dynamic loading for packages including forms, as you'll see toward the end of this chapter.

NOTE   Needless to say, the situation changes radically in .NET. In this platform you can use unmanaged libraries with PInvoke, optionally preceded by a LoadLibrary call (as covered in the next chapter), but you can also create managed DLL assemblies. The .NET platform supports dynamic loading of assemblies, as discussed in the last part of the chapter.

Win32 DLLs in Memory: Code and Data

Before I discuss packages, I want to focus on a technical element of dynamic libraries: how they use memory. Let's start with the code portion of the library; then we'll focus on its global data. When Windows loads the code of a library, as with any other code module, it has to do a *fixup* operation. This fixup consists of patching addresses of jumps and internal function calls with the actual memory address where they've been loaded. The effect of this operation is that the code-loaded memory depends on where it has been loaded.

This is not an issue for executable files but might cause a significant problem for libraries. If two executables load the same library at the same base address, there will be only one physical copy of the DLL code in the RAM (the physical memory) of the machine, thus saving memory space. When a library is loaded and its memory address is already in use, it needs to be *relocated*, that is, moved with a different fixup applied. So you'll end up with a second physical copy of the DLL code in RAM.

You can use the dynamic loading technique, based on the GetProcAddress API function, to test which memory address of the current process a function has been mapped to. The code is as follows:

```
Label1.Caption := Format ('Address: %p', [
  GetProcAddress (HDLLInst, 'SetData')]);
```

This code displays, in a label, the memory address of the function, within the address space of the calling application. If you run two programs using this code, they'll generally both show the same address. This technique demonstrates that the code is loaded only once at a common memory address.

Another technique to get more information about what's going on is to use Delphi's Modules window, which shows the base address of each library referenced by the module and the address of each function within the library, as shown in Figure 11.3.

It's important to know that in Delphi the base address of a DLL is something you can request by setting the Image Base value in the linker page of the Project Options dialog box. In the DllMem library, for example, I set it to $00800000. You need to have a different value for each of your libraries, verifying that it doesn't clash with any system library or other library (like a package) used by the executable. Again, this is something you can figure out using the Modules window of the debugger.

FIGURE 11.3
Delphi's Modules Window opens up in the main pane of the IDE.

Although this doesn't guarantee a unique placement, the likelihood of the DLL being relocated is much lower than not setting a base address. In this case the base address defaults to $400000, which is where executables are loaded, thereby guaranteeing a relocation.

TIP You can also use Process Explorer from www.sysinternals.com to examine any process on any machine. This tool even has an option to highlight relocated DLLs. Check the effect of running the same program with its libraries on different operating systems (Windows 2000, Windows XP, and Windows Me) and settle on an unused area.

This is the case for the DLL code, but what about the global data? Basically, each copy of the DLL has its own copy of the data in the address space of the calling application. However, it is possible to share global data between applications using a DLL. The most common technique for sharing data is to use memory-mapped files. I'll use this technique for a DLL, but it can also be used to share data directly among applications.

This example is called DllMem for the library and UseMem for the demo application. The DLL code has a project file that exports four subroutines:

```
library dllmem;

uses
  SysUtils,
  DllMemU in 'DllMemU.pas';
```

```
exports
  SetData, GetData,
  GetShareData, SetShareData;
end.
```

The actual code is in the secondary unit (DllMemU.PAS), which contains the code for the four routines that read or write two global memory locations. These memory locations hold an integer and a pointer to an integer. Here are the variable declarations and the two Set routines:

```
var
  PlainData: Integer = 0; // not shared
  ShareData: ^Integer; // shared

procedure SetData (I: Integer); stdcall;
begin
  PlainData := I;
end;

procedure SetShareData (I: Integer); stdcall;
begin
  ShareData^ := I;
end;
```

Sharing Data with Memory-Mapped Files

For the data that isn't shared, there isn't anything else to do. To access the shared data, however, the DLL has to create a memory-mapped file and then get a pointer to this memory area. These operations require two Windows API calls:

- CreateFileMapping requires as parameters the filename (or $FFFFFFFF to use a virtual file in memory), some security and protection attributes, the size of the data, and an internal name (which must be the same to share the mapped file from multiple calling applications).

- MapViewOfFile requires as parameters the handle of the memory-mapped file, some attributes and offsets, and the size of the data (again).

Here is the source code of the initialization section, which is executed every time the DLL is loaded into a new process space (that is, once for each application that uses the DLL):

```
var
  hMapFile: THandle;

const
  VirtualFileName = 'ShareDllData';
  DataSize = sizeof (Integer);

initialization
  // create memory mapped file
  hMapFile := CreateFileMapping ($FFFFFFFF, nil,
```

```
    Page_ReadWrite, 0, DataSize, VirtualFileName);
  if hMapFile = 0 then
    raise Exception.Create ('Error creating memory-mapped file');

  // get the pointer to the actual data
  ShareData := MapViewOfFile (
    hMapFile, File_Map_Write, 0, 0, DataSize);
```

When the application terminates and the DLL is released, it has to free the pointer to the mapped file and the file mapping:

```
finalization
  UnmapViewOfFile (ShareData);
  CloseHandle (hMapFile);
```

The UseMem demo program's form has four edit boxes (two with an UpDown control connected), five buttons, and a label. The first button saves the value of the first edit box in the DLL data, getting the value from the connected UpDown control:

```
SetData (UpDown1.Position);
```

If you click the second button, the program copies the DLL data to the second edit box:

```
Edit2.Text := IntToStr(GetData);
```

The third button is used to display the memory address of a function, with the line of code shown at the beginning of this section. The last two buttons have basically the same code as the first two, but they call the SetShareData procedure and the GetShareData function.

If you run two copies of this program, you will see that each copy has its own value for the plain global data of the DLL, whereas the value of the shared data is common. Set different values in the two programs and then get them in both, and you'll see what I mean. This situation is illustrated in Figure 11.4.

FIGURE 11.4

If you run two copies of the UseMem program, you'll see by comparing the data from the two instances (on the left and on the right) that the global data in its DLL (the edit box near the Get button) is not shared, while the data from the memory mapped file is the same (the edit box near the GetShare button).

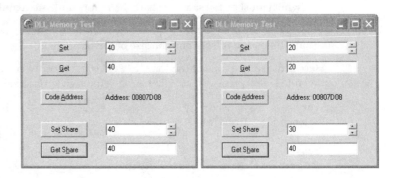

WARNING   Memory-mapped files reserve a minimum of a 64 KB range of virtual addresses and consume physical memory in 4 KB pages. The example's use of 4-byte Integer data in shared memory is rather expensive, especially if you use the same approach for sharing multiple values. If you need to share several variables, you should place them all in a single shared memory area (accessing the different variables using pointers or building a record structure for all of them).

Delphi Packages

In Delphi for Win32, component packages are an important type of DLL. Packages allow you to bundle a group of components and then link the components either statically (adding their compiled code to the executable file of your application) or dynamically (keeping the component code in a DLL, the run-time package that you'll distribute with your program, along with all other packages you will need).

Using Run-Time Packages

There are some advantages and disadvantages to the two forms of linking for a package. You need to keep many elements in mind:

◆ Using a run-time package makes the executable files much smaller.

◆ Linking the package units into the program allows you to distribute only part of the package code. The size of the executable file of an application plus the size of the required package DLLs is always much bigger than the size of the statically linked program. The linker includes only the code used by the program, whereas a package must link in all the functions and classes declared in the `interface` sections of all the units contained in the package.

◆ If you distribute several Delphi applications based on the same packages, you might end up distributing less code because the run-time packages are shared. In other words, once the users of your application have the standard Delphi run-time packages, you can ship them very small programs.

◆ If you run several Delphi applications based on the same packages, you can save some memory space at run time; the code of the run-time packages is loaded in memory only once among the multiple Delphi applications.

◆ Don't worry too much about distributing a large executable file. Keep in mind that when you make minor changes to a program, you can use any of various tools to create a *patch file*, so that you distribute only a file containing the differences, not a complete copy of the files.

◆ If you place a few of your program's forms in a run-time package, you can share them among programs. When you modify these forms, however, you'll generally need to recompile the main program as well and distribute both of them again to your users. There are techniques you can use to bypass this problem, as discussed later in this chapter.

◆ A package is a collection of compiled units (including classes, types, variables, routines), which don't differ at all from the units inside a program. The only difference is in the build process. The code of the package units and that of the units of the main program using them remains identical. This is arguably one of the key advantages of packages over DLLs.

Creating Design-Time and Run-Time Packages

Packages come in two flavors: design-time packages used by the Delphi IDE and run-time packages optionally used by applications. The designtime-only or runtime-only package option determines the package's type. When you attempt to install a package, the IDE checks whether it has the designtime-only or runtime-only flag, and decides whether to let the user install the package and whether it should be added to the list of run-time packages. Because there are two nonexclusive options, they can also be combined, so there are three different kinds of component packages (as indicated by the three radio buttons in the Description page of the Project Options dialog box for a package):

♦ Design-time-only component packages (having in the source code the {$DESIGNONLY} directive) can be installed in the Delphi environment. These packages usually contain the design-time parts of a component, such as its property editors and the registration code. Often they also contain the components themselves, although this is not the most professional approach. The code of a design-time package's components is usually statically linked into the executable file, using the code of the corresponding .DCU files. Keep in mind, however, that it is also technically possible to use a design-only package as a run-time package.

♦ Run-time-only component packages (having in the source code the {$RUNONLY} directive) are used by Delphi applications at run time. They cannot be installed in the Delphi environment, but they are automatically added to the list of run-time packages when they are required by a design-time package you install. Run-time packages usually contain the code of the component classes but no design-time support (this is done to minimize the size of the component libraries you ship with your executable file). Run-time packages are important because they can be freely distributed with applications, but other Delphi programmers won't be able to install them in the environment to build new programs.

♦ Design-time and run-time packages (having none of the two package directives in the source code) can be installed and are automatically added to the list of run-time packages. Usually these packages contain components requiring little or no design-time support (apart from the limited component registration code).

Writing and Compiling Packages

The structure of a package is visible in the project manager (as the Package Editor from previous Delphi versions is not available anymore) and has two parts:

♦ The Contains list indicates the units included in the package.

♦ The Requires list indicates the packages required by this package. Your package will generally require the rtl and vcl packages (the main run-time library package and core VCL package), but it might also need the vcldb package (which includes most of the database-related classes) if the code in your package does any database-related operations.

When you compile a package, you produce both a DLL with the compiled code (the .BPL file) and a file with only symbol information (a .DCP file) that includes no compiled machine code. The Delphi compiler uses the latter file to gather symbol information about the units that are part of the package without having access to the unit (.DCU) files, which contain both the symbol information and the compiled machine code. This process reduces compilation time and allows you to distribute just the packages without the precompiled unit files. The precompiled units are still required to statically link the package units into an application.

Package Versioning

A very important and often misunderstood element is the distribution of updated packages. When you update a DLL, you can ship the new version, and the executable programs requiring this DLL will still work (unless you've removed existing exported functions or changed some of their parameters).

When you distribute a Delphi package, however, if you update the package and modify the `interface` portion of any unit of the package, you may need to recompile all the applications that use the package. This step is required if you add methods or properties to a class, but not if you add new global symbols (or modify anything not used by client applications). There is no problem if you make changes affecting only the `implementation` section of the package's units.

A DCU file in Delphi has a version tag based on its timestamp and a checksum computed from the interface portion of the unit. When you change the `interface` portion of a unit, every other unit based on it should be recompiled. The compiler compares the timestamp and checksum of the unit from previous compilations with the new timestamp and checksum and decides whether the dependent unit must be recompiled. For this reason, you must recompile each unit when you get a new version of Delphi that has modified system units.

When packages were first introduced, the compiler added an extra entry function to the package library named with a checksum of the package, obtained from the checksum of the units it contained and the checksum of the packages it required. This checksum function was then called by programs using the package so that an older executable would fail at startup.

Recent versions of Delphi have relaxed the run-time constraints of the package. (The design-time constraints on DCU files remain identical, though.) The checksum of the package is no longer checked, so you can directly modify the units that are part of a package and deploy a new version of the package to be used with the existing executable file. Because methods are referenced by name, you cannot remove any existing method that is called by the main program. You cannot even change method parameters because of name-mangling techniques that protect a package's method against changes in parameters.

Removing a method referenced from the calling program will stop the program during the loading process. If you make other changes, however, the program might fail unexpectedly during its execution. For example, if you replace a component placed on a form compiled in a package with a similar component, the calling program might still be able to access the component at the given memory offset, although it is now different!

If you decide to follow this treacherous road of changing the interface of units in a package without recompiling all the programs that use it, you should at least limit your changes. When you add new properties or nonvirtual methods to the form, you should be able to maintain full compatibility with existing programs already using the package. Also, adding fields and virtual methods might affect the internal structure of the class, leading to problems with existing programs that expect a different class data and virtual method table (VMT) layout.

WARNING   Here I'm referring to the distribution of compiled programs divided between .EXE files and packages, not to the distribution of components to other Delphi developers. In this latter case the versioning rules are more stringent, and you must take extra care in package versioning.

Having said this, I recommend never changing the interface of any unit exported by your packages. To accomplish this, you can add to your package a unit with form-creation functions and use it to access another unit, which defines the form. Although there is no way to *hide* a unit that is linked into a package, if you never directly use the class defined in a unit but use it only through other routines, you'll have more flexibility in modifying it. You can also use form inheritance to modify a form within a package without affecting the original version.

The most stringent rule for packages is the following used by component writers: For long-term deployment and maintenance of code in packages, plan on having a major release with minor maintenance releases. A major release of your package will require all client programs to be recompiled from source; the package file should be renamed with a new version number, and the interface sections of units can be modified. Maintenance releases of that package should be restricted to implementation changes to preserve full compatibility with existing executables and units, as is generally done by Borland with its update packs.

Dynamic Architectures with Packages

At first sight, you might believe that Delphi packages are solely a way to distribute components to be installed in the environment. However, you can also use packages as a way to structure your code in a dynamic fashion that, unlike when you use plain DLLs, retains the full power of Delphi's OOP. Consider this: a package is a collection of compiled units, and your program uses several units. The units the program refers to will be compiled inside the executable file, unless you ask Delphi to dynamically link to them within their packages. As discussed earlier, the ease with which you can switch between static and dynamic linking is one of the main reasons for using packages.

An Application with Run-Time Packages

To set up an application so that its code is split among one or more packages and a main executable file, you only need to compile some of the units in a package and then set up the options of the main program to dynamically link this package. For example, I created a color selection form (visible at design time in Figure 11.5) and placed it in the PackWithForm package of the PackForm folder. You can see the Project Manager window with the structure of the package (with the Contains and Requires sections) in the screenshot.

FIGURE 11.5

The packaged form at design time (left) and the structure of the package project hosting it (right)

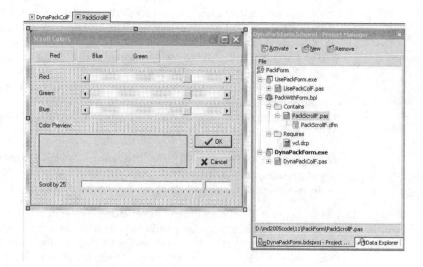

These sections are also reflected in the package project source code file after a rather long list of settings that I've mostly omitted here:

```
package PackWithForm;

{$R *.RES}
{$ALIGN OFF}
{$ASSERTIONS ON}
{$...}

{$IMPLICITBUILD OFF}

requires
  vcl;

contains
  PackScrollF in 'PackScrollF.pas' {FormScroll};

end.
```

By default, Delphi 2005 places all the compiled package files in the Borland Studio `Projects\Bpl` subfolder of the My Documents folder. It does this so the IDE can easily locate the files (as that folder is also added to the global path), and the location creates no particular problem when you are using packages for creating new components. When you want to link your code to the package or load it dynamically, your package will be always available, even from many different applications. For an easy deployment of the application and the packages it uses, though, having the compiled packages in the application folder might be much handier.

For this reason, before compiling this package, you should change its default output directories to refer to the current folder. To do this, go to the Directories/Conditional page of the package Project Options and set the current directory (a single dot, for short) for the Output directory of the .BPL file and DCP output directory. Then compile the package and do not install it in Delphi—there's no need to.

At this point, you can create a normal application and write the standard code you'd use in any program to show a secondary form, as in the following listing:

```
uses
  PackScrollF;

procedure TForm1.BtnChangeClick(Sender: TObject);
var
  FormScroll: TFormScroll;
begin
  FormScroll := TFormScroll.Create (Application);
  try
    // initialize the data
    FormScroll.SelectedColor := Color;
    // show the form
    if FormScroll.ShowModal = mrOK then
      Color := FormScroll.SelectedColor;
```

```
    finally
      FormScroll.Free;
    end;
  end;


  procedure TForm1.BtnSelectClick(Sender: TObject);
  var
    FormScroll: TFormScroll;
  begin
    FormScroll := TFormScroll.Create (Application);
    // initialize the data and UI
    FormScroll.SelectedColor := Color;
    FormScroll.BitBtn1.Caption := 'Apply';
    FormScroll.BitBtn1.OnClick := FormScroll.ApplyClick;
    FormScroll.BitBtn2.Kind := bkClose;
    // show the form
    FormScroll.Show;
  end;
```

If you compile this program, the unit of the form will be bound to the program. To keep the form's unit in the package, you'll have to use run-time packages for the application and manually add the PackWithForm package to the list of run-time packages (this is not suggested by the Delphi IDE, because you have not installed the package in the development environment).

Once you've performed this step, compile the program; it will behave as usual. But now the form is in a DLL package, and you can modify the form in the package, recompile just the package project, and run the application to see the effects. Notice, though, that for most changes affecting the interface portion of the package's units (for example, adding a component or a method to the form), you should also recompile the executable program calling the package.

Loading Packages at Run Time

In the previous example, I indicated that the PackWithForm package is a run-time package to be used by the application. This means the package is required to run the application and is loaded when the program starts, just as with the typical use of DLLs. (You can see this clearly if you rename the .BPL file and try running the program again.) You can avoid both aspects by loading the package dynamically, as you've done with DLLs. The resulting program will be more flexible, start more quickly, and use less memory. There is a drawback, though: you need to change the way you write the code!

An important element to keep in mind is that you'll need to call the LoadPackage and UnloadPackage Delphi functions rather than the LoadLibrary/SafeLoadLibrary and FreeLibrary Windows API functions. The functions provided by Delphi load the packages, but they also call their proper initialization and finalization code.

NOTE Delphi for .NET doesn't include LoadPackage and the like because it relies on .NET Framework services for assemblies to accomplish the same operation. I'll discuss a .NET program very similar to the current one in the section "From Packages to Assemblies."

In addition to this important element—which is easy to use once you know about it—the program will require some extra code because you cannot refer from the main program to the unit hosting the form. You cannot use the form class directly, nor access its properties or components—at least, not with the standard Delphi code. Both issues, however, can be solved using class references, class registration, and RTTI (run-time type information). Another option is to use interfaces, as I'll show in the next section.

Let me begin with the first approach. In the form unit, in the package, I added this initialization code:

```
initialization
  RegisterClass (TFormScroll);
```

As the package is loaded, the main program can use Delphi's GetClass function to get the class reference of the registered class and then call the Create constructor for this class reference.

To solve the second problem, I made the SelectedColor property of the form in the package a published property, so that it is accessible via RTTI. Then I replaced the code accessing this property (FormScroll.Color) with the following:

```
SetPropValue (FormScroll, 'SelectedColor', Color);
```

Summing up all these changes, here is the code used by the main program (the DynaPackForm application) to show the modal form from the dynamically loaded package:

```
procedure TForm1.BtnChangeClick(Sender: TObject);
var
  FormScroll: TForm;
  FormClass: TFormClass;
  HandlePack: HModule;
begin
  // try to load the package
  HandlePack := LoadPackage ('PackWithForm.bpl');
  if HandlePack > 0 then
  begin
    FormClass := TFormClass(GetClass ('TFormScroll'));
    if Assigned (FormClass) then
    begin
      FormScroll := FormClass.Create (Application);
      try
        // initialize the data
        SetPropValue (FormScroll, 'SelectedColor', Color);
        // show the form
        if FormScroll.ShowModal = mrOK then
          Color := GetPropValue (FormScroll, 'SelectedColor');
      finally
        FormScroll.Free;
      end;
    end
    else
      ShowMessage ('Form class not found');
    UnloadPackage (HandlePack);
  end
  else
    ShowMessage ('Package not found');
end;
```

Notice that the program unloads the package as soon as it is done with it. This step is not compulsory. I could have moved the UnloadPackage call in the OnDestroy handler of the form and avoided reloading the package after the first time.

Now you can try running this program without the package available. You'll see that it starts properly, only to complain that it cannot find the package as you click the Change button. In this program, the PackWithForm package doesn't need to be listed in the run-time packages. However, you must use run-time packages for it to work at all, or else your program will include VCL global variables (such as the Application object) and the dynamically loaded package will include another version because it will refer to the run-time VCL packages anyway.

WARNING   When a program that loads a package dynamically is closed, you may experience access violations. Frequently, they occur because an object whose class is defined in the package is kept in memory even after the package is unloaded. When the program shuts down, it may try to free that object by calling the Destroy method of a nonexistent VMT and thus cause the error. Having said this, I know by experience that these types of errors are very difficult to track and fix. I suggest that you make sure to destroy all the objects before unloading the package.

Using Interfaces in Packages

Accessing forms' classes by means of methods and properties is much simpler than using RTTI all over the place. To build a larger application, I suggest you definitely use interfaces. An example cannot really do justice to this type of architecture, which becomes relevant for a large program, but I tried to build a program to show how this idea can be applied in practice.

NOTE   If you don't know much about interfaces, refer to the related portion of Chapter 3 before reading this section.

To build the IntfPack project, I used three packages plus a demo application. Two of the three packages (IntfFormPack and IntfFormPack2) define alternative forms used to select a color. The third package (IntfPack) hosts a shared unit used by both other packages. This unit includes the definition of the interface. I couldn't add it to both other packages because you cannot load two packages that each have a unit with the same name (even if they are loaded at run-time).

The IntfPack package's only file is the IntfColSel unit, displayed in Listing 11.2. This unit defines the common interface (you'll probably have a number of them in real-world applications) plus a list of registered classes; it mimics Delphi's RegisterClass approach but makes available the complete list so that you can easily scan it.

LISTING 11.2:   The IntfColSel unit of the IntfPack package

```
unit IntfColSel;

interface

uses
  Graphics, Contnrs;

type
  IColorSelect = interface
```

```
  ['{3F961395-71F6-4822-BD02-3B475FF516D4}']
    function Display (Modal: Boolean = True): Boolean;
    procedure SetSelColor (Col: TColor);
    function GetSelColor: TColor;
    property SelColor: TColor
      read GetSelColor write SetSelColor;
  end;

procedure RegisterColorSelect (AClass: TClass);

var
  ClassesColorSelect: TClassList;

implementation

procedure RegisterColorSelect (AClass: TClass);
begin
  if ClassesColorSelect.IndexOf (AClass) < 0 then
    ClassesColorSelect.Add (AClass);
end;

initialization
  ClassesColorSelect := TClassList.Create;

finalization
  ClassesColorSelect.Free;
end.
```

Once you have this interface available, you can define forms that implement it, as in the following example taken from IntfFormPack:

```
type
  TFormSimpleColor = class(TForm, IColorSelect)
    ...
  private
    procedure SetSelColor (Col: TColor);
    function GetSelColor: TColor;
  public
    function Display (Modal: Boolean = True): Boolean;
```

The two access methods read and write the value of the color from some components of the form (a ColorGrid control in this case), whereas the Display method internally calls either Show or ShowModal, depending on the parameter:

```
function TFormSimpleColor.Display(Modal: Boolean): Boolean;
begin
  Result := True; // default
  if Modal then
```

```
    Result := (ShowModal = mrOK)
  else
  begin
    BitBtn1.Caption := 'Apply';
    BitBtn1.OnClick := ApplyClick;
    BitBtn2.Kind := bkClose;
    Show;
  end;
end;
```

As you can see from this code, when the form is modeless, the OK button is turned into an Apply button. Finally, the unit has the registration code in the initialization section so that it is executed when the package is dynamically loaded:

```
RegisterColorSelect (TFormSimpleColor);
```

The second package, IntfFormPack2, has a similar architecture but a different form. You can look it up in the source code (I don't discuss the second form here because its code doesn't add much to the structure of the example).

With this architecture in place, you can build a rather elegant and flexible main program that is based on a single form. When the form is created, it defines a list of packages (HandlesPackages) and loads them all. The packages could be searched for on disk, but I've preferred to use a configuration file (an .INI file named like the executable) to list them:

```
[packages]
IntfFormPack.bpl=
IntfFormPack2.bpl=
```

After loading the packages, the program shows the registered classes in a list box. This is the code of the LoadDynaPackage and FormCreate methods:

```
procedure TFormUseIntf.FormCreate(Sender: TObject);
var
  I: Integer;
  IniFile: TMemIniFile;
  sList: TStringList;
begin
  // loads all runtime packages
  HandlesPackages := TList.Create;

  // get packages list form INI file and load them
  IniFile := TMemIniFile.Create (
    ChangeFileExt (Application.ExeName, '.ini'));
  try
    sList := TStringList.Create;
    try
      IniFile.ReadSection('packages', sList);
      for I := 0 to sList.Count - 1 do
        LoadDynaPackage (sList[I]);
```

```
    finally
      sList.Free;
    end;
  finally
    IniFile.Free;
  end;

  // add class names and select the first
  for I := 0 to ClassesColorSelect.Count - 1 do
    lbClasses.Items.Add (ClassesColorSelect [I].ClassName);
  lbClasses.ItemIndex := 0;
end;


procedure TFormUseIntf.LoadDynaPackage(PackageName: string);
var
  Handle: HModule;
begin
  // try to load the package
  Handle := LoadPackage (PackageName);
  if Handle > 0 then
    // add to the list for later removal
    HandlesPackages.Add (Pointer(Handle))
  else
    ShowMessage ('Package ' + PackageName + ' not found');
end;
```

The main reason for keeping the list of package handles is to be able to unload them all when the program ends. You don't need these handles to access the forms defined in those packages; the runtime code used to create and show a form uses the corresponding component classes. This is a snippet of code used to display a modeless form (an option controlled by a check box):

```
var
  AComponent: TComponent;
  ColorSelect: IColorSelect;
begin
  AComponent := TComponentClass
    (ClassesColorSelect[LbClasses.ItemIndex]).Create (Application);
  ColorSelect := AComponent as IColorSelect;
  ColorSelect.SelColor := Color;
  ColorSelect.Display (False);
```

The program uses the Supports function to check that the form really does support the interface before using it, and it also accounts for the modal version of the form; but its essence is properly depicted in the preceding four statements.

By the way, notice that the code doesn't require a form. A nice exercise would be to add to the architecture a package with a component encapsulating the color selection dialog box or inheriting from it.

WARNING The main program refers to the unit hosting the interface definition but should not link this file in. Rather, it should use the run-time package containing this unit, as the dynamically loaded packages do. Otherwise the main program will use a different copy of the same code, including a different list of global classes. It is this list of global classes that should not be duplicated in memory.

The Structure of a Package

You may wonder whether it is possible to know if a unit has been linked in the executable file or if it's part of a run-time package. Not only is this possible in Delphi, but you can also explore the overall structure of an application. A component can use the undocumented ModuleIsPackage global variable, declared in the SysInit unit (a unit that, like System, is implicitly linked into all Delphi units). You should never need this variable, but it is technically possible for a component to have different code depending on whether it is packaged. The following code extracts the name of the run-time package hosting the component, if any:

```
var
  fPackName: string;
begin
  // get package name
  SetLength (fPackName, 100);
  if ModuleIsPackage then
  begin
    GetModuleFileName (HInstance, PChar (fPackName),
      Length (fPackName));
    fPackName := PChar (fPackName) // string length fixup
  end
  else
    fPackName := 'Not packaged';
```

In addition to accessing package information from within a component (as in the previous code), you can also do so from a special entry point of the package libraries, the GetPackageInfoTable function. This function returns some specific package information that Delphi stores as resources and includes in the package DLL. Fortunately, you don't need to use low-level techniques to access this information because Delphi provides some high-level functions to manipulate it.

You can use two functions to access package information:

◆ GetPackageDescription returns a string that contains the description of the package. To call this function, you must supply the name of the module (the package library) as the only parameter.

◆ GetPackageInfo doesn't directly return information about the package. Instead, you pass it a function that calls for every entry in the package's internal data structure. In practice, GetPackageInfo will call your function for every one of the package's contained units and required packages. In addition, GetPackageInfo sets several flags in an Integer variable.

These two function calls allow you to access internal information about a package, but how do you know which packages your application is using? You could determine this information by looking at an executable file using low-level functions, but Delphi helps you again by supplying a simpler approach. The EnumModules function doesn't directly return information about an application's modules, but it lets you pass it a function that it calls for each module of the application, the main executable file, and each of the packages the application relies on.

To demonstrate this approach, I built a program that displays the module and package information in a TreeView component. Each first-level node corresponds to a module; within each module I built a subtree that displays the contained and required packages for that module, as well as the package description and compiler flags (`RunOnly` and `DesignOnly`). You can see the output of this example in Figure 11.6.

In addition to the TreeView component, I added several other components to the main form but hid them from view: a DBEdit, a Chart, and a FilterComboBox. I added these components simply to include more run-time packages in the application beyond the ubiquitous Vcl and Rtl packages. The only method of the form class is `FormCreate`, which calls the module enumeration function:

```
procedure TForm1.FormCreate(Sender: TObject);
begin
    EnumModules(ForEachModule, nil);
end;
```

FIGURE 11.6

The output of the PackInfo example with details of the packages it uses

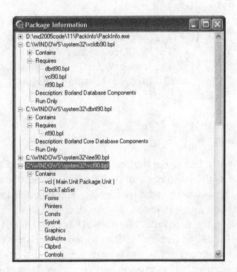

The `EnumModules` function accepts two parameters: the callback function (in this case, `ForEachModule`) and a pointer to a data structure that the callback function will use (in this case, `nil`, because you don't need this). The callback function must accept two parameters—an `HInstance` value and an untyped pointer—and must return a Boolean value. The `EnumModules` function will, in turn, call your callback function for each module, passing the instance handle of each module as the first parameter and the data structure pointer (`nil` in this example) as the second:

```
function ForEachModule (HInstance: Longint;
    Data: Pointer): Boolean;
var
    Flags: Integer;
    ModuleName, ModuleDesc: string;
    ModuleNode: TTreeNode;
```

```
begin
  with Form1.TreeView1.Items do
  begin
    SetLength (ModuleName, 200);
    GetModuleFileName (HInstance,
      PChar (ModuleName), Length (ModuleName));
    ModuleName := PChar (ModuleName); // fixup
    ModuleNode := Add (nil, ModuleName);

    // get description and add fixed nodes
    ModuleDesc := GetPackageDescription (PChar (ModuleName));
    ContNode := AddChild (ModuleNode, 'Contains');
    ReqNode := AddChild (ModuleNode, 'Requires');

    // add information if the module is a package
    GetPackageInfo (HInstance, nil, Flags, ShowInfoProc);
    if ModuleDesc <> '' then
    begin
      AddChild (ModuleNode, 'Description: ' + ModuleDesc);
      if Flags and pfDesignOnly = pfDesignOnly then
        AddChild (ModuleNode, 'Design Only');
      if Flags and pfRunOnly = pfRunOnly then
        AddChild (ModuleNode, 'Run Only');
    end;
  end;
  Result := True;
end;
```

As you can see in the preceding code, the ForEachModule function begins by adding the module name as the main node of the tree (by calling the Add method of the TreeView1.Items object and passing nil as the first parameter). It then adds two fixed child nodes, which are stored in the ContNode and ReqNode variables declared in the implementation section of this unit.

Next, the program calls the GetPackageInfo function and passes it another callback function, ShowInfoProc (which I'll discuss shortly) to provide a list of the application's or package's units. At the end of the ForEachModule function, if the module is a package the program adds more information, such as its description and compiler flags (the program knows it's a package if its description isn't an empty string).

Earlier, I mentioned passing another callback function (the ShowInfoProc procedure) to the GetPackageInfo function, which in turn calls the callback function for each contained or required package of a module. This procedure creates a string that describes the package and its main flags (added within parentheses) and then inserts that string under one of the two nodes (ContNode and ReqNode), depending on the type of the module. You can determine the module type by examining the NameType parameter. Here is the complete code for the second callback function:

```
procedure ShowInfoProc (const Name: string; NameType: TNameType;
  Flags: Byte; Param: Pointer);
var
  FlagStr: string;
```

```
begin
  FlagStr := ' ';
  if Flags and ufMainUnit <> 0 then
    FlagStr := FlagStr + 'Main Unit ';
  if Flags and ufPackageUnit <> 0 then
    FlagStr := FlagStr + 'Package Unit ';
  if Flags and ufWeakUnit <> 0 then
    FlagStr := FlagStr + 'Weak Unit ';
  if FlagStr <> ' ' then
    FlagStr := ' (' + FlagStr + ')';
  with Form1.TreeView1.Items do
    case NameType of
      ntContainsUnit: AddChild (ContNode, Name + FlagStr);
      ntRequiresPackage: AddChild (ReqNode, Name);
    end;
end;
```

From Packages to Assemblies

In Chapter 2 I discussed the role of assemblies in the .NET Framework. In Delphi for .NET, you create an assembly with a package project. To put it in a different perspective, if you recompile a package in Delphi for .NET, you end up with a managed assembly in a DLL. In other words, assemblies and packages share many features.

In .NET the use of assemblies is similar to the use of a run-time package, but you don't generally have the option of a static linking (including the package code into your executable file). However, in Delphi for .NET this is possible, although it is limited to assemblies written in Delphi itself.

As you have already seen some theory on assemblies, let me get to a practical example. To show you a demo I took the projects in the PackForm folder (a package with a form, a program referring to it, and a program loading it dynamically) and converted everything to .NET in the PackFormNet folder. Notice that these programs are based on VCL for .NET.

Writing and Using a Managed DLL

The package is almost identical to its Win32 counterpart. The only difference is in the requires statement of the package project:

```
requires
  System.Drawing,
  Borland.Delphi,
  Borland.Vcl,
  Borland.VclRtl;

contains
  PackScrollF in 'PackScrollF.pas' {FormScroll};
```

The code of the form unit remains identical. The program using the assembly is quite similar as well. Only this time instead of listing a set of run-time packages (including the one just built), you use the Add Reference dialog box, selecting some of the system .NET assemblies and adding the local assembly you just built.

The project source code should have some references like these (where I've omitted the paths):

```
{%DelphiDotNetAssemblyCompiler
  '$(SystemRoot)\...\System.Drawing.dll'}
{%DelphiDotNetAssemblyCompiler
  'c:\program files\...\Borland.Delphi.dll'}
{%DelphiDotNetAssemblyCompiler
  'c:\program files\...\Borland.Vcl.dll'}
{%DelphiDotNetAssemblyCompiler
  'c:\program files\...\Borland.VclRtl.dll'}
{%DelphiDotNetAssemblyCompiler 'PackWithFormNet.dll'}
```

That's all. Again no changes in the source code. You recompile the program and it will use the local assembly as it starts. If you remove or rename the local assembly, you'll get a rather ugly (and far from clear) error message:

Dynamically Loading a Managed DLL

Dynamically loading an assembly requires some changes compared to the Win32 program that loads the run-time package dynamically, but the approach remains similar. Basically, you have to replace the call to LoadPackage, which returns a handle to its module, with the call to the Load static method of the Assembly class, which returns an Assembly object. The parameter you pass to Load is the fully qualified assembly name (name, version, culture, hash), but for local assemblies the plain name alone will do as well. You can also use the similar LoadFile and LoadFromPartialName methods.

Once you have loaded an assembly dynamically, you can grab one of its types by name (with the GetType and GetTypes methods, demonstrated in the upcoming code) or create an instance one of its types directly with the CreateInstance method, passing the type name to its string parameter. In a VCL application, you can instead convert the System.Type object to a class references and create the instance using the virtual constructor of the class.

In the code of the example, instead of using Delphi's GetClass to retrieve the class reference to the class of the form inside the package, I used the GetType method of the Assembly object. If you need to know the name of the type (which includes its namespace), you can write some code to list all of them:

```
var
  allTypes: array of System.Type;
  aPack: Assembly;
  aType: System.Type;
begin
  aPack := Assembly.Load ('PackWithFormNet');
  allTypes := aPack.GetTypes;
  for aType in allTypes do
    ShowMessage (aType.ToString);
```

NOTE In Delphi for Win32 there isn't a similar way to list all of the types defined in a package; you can only get registered classes and other types with specific RTTI support. In this case, the extensive support for reflection of .NET comes in very handy.

Finally, there is no way (and no need) to unload the assembly DLL when you are done with it. Summing all these changes, the core code of the DynaPackFormNet example becomes:

```
uses
  System.Reflection, Variants;

procedure TForm1.BtnChangeClick(Sender: TObject);
var
  FormScroll: TForm;
  FormClass: TFormClass;
  aPack: Assembly;
  aType: System.Type;
begin
  // load the assembly and get the type
  aPack := Assembly.Load ('PackWithFormNet');
  aType := aPack.GetType('PackScrollF.TFormScroll');
  FormClass := TFormClass(aType);
  FormScroll := FormClass.Create (Application);
  try
    // initialize the data
    SetPropValue (FormScroll, 'SelectedColor', Color);
    // show the form
    if FormScroll.ShowModal = mrOK then
      Color := TColor (GetPropValue (FormScroll, 'SelectedColor'));
  finally
    FormScroll.Free;
  end;
end;
```

As with Win32 packages, rather than using RTTI, it is better to build a dynamic architecture using interfaces. I could port the IntfPack example to .NET as I did with this demo, but this wouldn't add much to the book.

From Loading to Downloading

In addition to loading an assembly from the local file system, you can load it from your local network or even from the Internet. Technically it is only a matter of replacing the call to `Assembly.Load` with another appropriate call, like `Assembly.LoadFrom`. This method has a URL parameter you can use to refer to a local assembly or one downloaded from a web server on the LAN or on the Internet. The CLR will use the Internet security settings and other information to determine the permission of the assembly, which by default will be reduced.

In the DynaPackFormNet example, I actually modified the previous code snippets to load the assembly locally or from the Web (there is a copy on my website you can refer to), depending on the initial status of a check box (cbWeb):

```
procedure TForm1.LoadAssembly;
var
  ev1: Evidence;
begin
  if not Assigned (aPack) then
  begin
    if not cbWeb.Checked then
      aPack := Assembly.Load ('PackWithFormNet')
    else
    begin
      ev1 := Evidence.Create;
      ev1.AddHost (Url.Create('http://www.marcocantu.com'));
      aPack := Assembly.LoadFrom (
        'http://www.marcocantu.com/code/' +
        'md2005/test/PackWithFormNet.dll', ev1);
    end;
    // after loading disable option
    cbWeb.Enabled := False;
  end;
end;
```

In case of a web download, the program created an Evidence object to permit downloading from the website. It doesn't provide any extra permissions, though, so the downloaded assembly will have a limited set of features. If you get the list of available types, the program will behave correctly. If you try to create the dialog to change the color, you'll get the following error message indicating the assembly is not allowed to work with user interface elements (lacking a user interface permission, or UIPermission):

WARNING If executed in the shipped version of Delphi 2005, this program can crash the IDE when raising the security error. The Delphi 2005 Update 2 has fixed the problem.

Dynamic Architecture with Assemblies

With the technical elements discussed in this section, you should now be able to create complex architectures based on assemblies. These can be even more powerful than those based on packages because .NET assemblies include rich metadata you can browse, like the list of available types discussed earlier.

Again, there are many ways for referring to objects of dynamically loaded classes; my preference is the use of interfaces, as demonstrated earlier for packages. The option to download assemblies from a local server or the Web makes the architecture more flexible. To fully exploit this feature, however, you need to learn about the security subsystem of .NET, which is beyond the scope of this book.

Inspecting Assemblies

As we did with packages, you can write an application that explores its own architecture. I built one with WinForms, but the same code also works with VCL for .NET, provided you modify the way the program interacts with the TreeView component used for the output.

The program inspects its own assemblies, that is, the assemblies of its own application domain

```
AppDomain.CurrentDomain.GetAssemblies
```

and proceeds as you saw, extracting the types from the assembly. For each type, the program looks at the fields, the methods, the events, and the subtypes. The complete code used to populate the tree is in Listing 11.3. This code takes a while because the tree is filled with a lot of information, as you can see by looking at the small excerpt of the tree visible in Figure 11.7.

LISTING 11.3:   The core method of the AssemblyInfo example

```
procedure TWinForm.btnPopulate_Click(
  sender: System.Object; e: System.EventArgs);
var
  assemblyList: array of Assembly;
  assembly1: Assembly;
  assemblyNode, typeNode: TreeNode;
  typesList: array of System.Type;
  type1, type2: System.Type;
  event1: EventInfo;
  field1: FieldInfo;
  method1: MethodInfo;
begin
  TreeView1.BeginUpdate;
  try
    // get the list of assemblies of the application
    assemblyList := AppDomain.CurrentDomain.GetAssemblies;
    for assembly1 in assemblyList do
    begin
      assemblyNode := TreeNode.Create(assembly1.FullName, -1, -1);
      TreeView1.Nodes.Add(assemblyNode);
      typesList := assembly1.GetTypes;
      for type1 in typesList do
      begin
        typeNode := TreeNode.Create(type1.FullName, -1, -1);
        assemblyNode.Nodes.Add (typeNode);
        for field1 in type1.GetFields do
          typeNode.Nodes.Add (field1.ToString);
        for method1 in type1.GetMethods do
          typeNode.Nodes.Add (method1.ToString);
        for event1 in type1.GetEvents do
          typeNode.Nodes.Add (event1.ToString);
```

```
        for type2 in type1.GetNestedTypes do
          typeNode.Nodes.Add (type2.ToString);
      end;
    end;
  finally
    TreeView1.EndUpdate;
  end;
end;
```

FIGURE 11.7

The AssemblyInfo program, in which I've expanded data related with the AssemblyInfo assembly itself

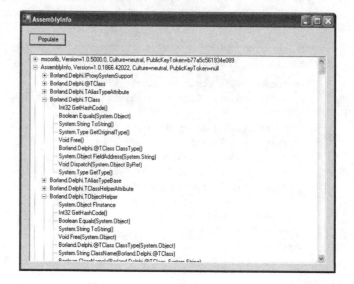

What's Next?

In this chapter, you saw how you can call functions that reside in DLLs and how to create DLLs using Delphi. After discussing dynamic libraries in general, I focused on Delphi packages, covering in particular how to place forms and other classes in a package. This is a handy technique for dividing a Delphi application into multiple executable files. While discussing packages, I explained how advanced techniques including RTTI and interfaces can be used to obtain dynamic and flexible application architectures.

In the final part of the chapter, I discussed how these techniques apply to assemblies in .NET, discussing direct linking, dynamic loading, and the extended RTTI (called Reflection) provided by .NET. What this chapter didn't focus on is how .NET applications can call into unmanaged DLLs; this is one of the topics discussed in the next chapter, along with COM and .NET/COM interoperability.

Chapter 12

COM and .NET Interoperability

For a number of years, COM has been an important aspect of Windows programming, inasmuch as it allows reusable components of code to be built and consumed from a variety of languages. Indeed, to aid adoption of COM, Microsoft saturated its own products with COM usage. For example, the Windows shell and Microsoft Office both offer an extensibility and programmability model based on the COM model.

Many Windows developers have added COM development to their repertoire, and COM development has become normal practice. As a consequence, there is a large investment in COM libraries in the development community, which warrants some thought given the recent push toward .NET.

Fortunately, Microsoft foresaw this issue and put much effort into ensuring there were ways of building "mix and match" applications out of .NET modules and Win32 modules (including COM objects). Existing Win32 applications can consume portions of .NET functionality, and .NET applications can consume COM objects and DLLs.

In this chapter, we'll look at all these areas. You'll build a simple COM object, sticking to the basic elements to help maintain clarity without confusing the issue by delving into the more complicated details. We'll continue by discussing Automation and the role of type libraries, and you'll see how to work with Delphi data types in Automation servers and clients. Having looked at COM itself, we can then move along to the support .NET offers to build applications that mix managed (.NET) code and unmanaged (Win32) code. We'll examine COM Interop as well as interoperability support for non-COM Win32 code using the Platform Invocation Service and Delphi's specific feature based on this called VLI.

The first part of this chapter covers COM, GUIDs and class factories, Delphi interfaces and COM, the VCL COM-support classes, creating and using automation servers, and using type libraries. The second part of the chapter covers COM objects in .NET, Win32 DLLs in .NET, .NET objects in COM applications, and .NET routines in Win32 applications.

NOTE   This chapter has been written by Brian Long, who was also the Technical Editor of the entire book. Since leaving Borland, Brian has spent the last 10 years as an independent consultant busy mainly with training, trouble-shooting, advising and mentoring with Borland's Delphi and C++Builder development tools. Over recent years this focus has extended to include Microsoft .NET technologies using Delphi and C#. In his spare time, Brian actively researches and employs strategies for the convenient identification, isolation and removal of malware. Besides writing a Pascal problem-solving book in 1994, Brian has contributed chapters to a couple of books, has written countless magazine articles over the last decade and acts as an occasional Technical Editor for Sybex. He has many online articles that can be found at http://blong.com.

A Short History of COM and .NET

So what is COM? Basically, COM, or the Component Object Model, is a technology that defines a standard way for a client module and a server module to communicate through interfaces. The implementation details of the interfaces are abstracted away and COM focuses on the interfaces themselves. Here, *module* indicates an application or a library (a DLL); the two modules may execute on the same computer or on different machines connected via a network (the latter being handled by Distributed COM or DCOM). The notion is that an interface implements some form of "service" to a client, so a COM object can implement as many interfaces as the requirements on it dictate. COM objects reside in the server modules referred to as COM servers, and all COM objects share some common capabilities thanks to the requirement that all COM interfaces be based on the IUnknown interface (which corresponds to the Delphi-specific IInterface introduced in Chapter 3).

The good news is that Delphi for Win32 is fully COM-compliant. When Delphi 3 was released, its COM support was much easier to work with than the support of C++ or other languages at the time, to the extent that there were reports of programmers on the Windows R&D team commenting, "We should have done COM the way Delphi does COM." This simplicity mainly derives from the incorporation of interface types into the Delphi language and Delphi's automatic code generation to support the lifetime management of interfaces.

As mentioned, the purpose of COM interfaces is to communicate between software modules, which can be executable files or DLLs. Implementing COM objects in DLLs is generally simpler, because in Win32, a program and the DLL it uses reside in the same memory address space. This means that if the program passes a memory address to the DLL, the address remains valid. When you use two executable files, COM has a lot of work to do behind the scenes to let the two applications communicate. This mechanism is called *marshaling* (which, to be accurate, is also required by DLLs if the client is multithreaded). Note that a DLL implementing COM objects is described as an *in-process* server (or in-proc server), whereas when the server is a separate executable, it is called an *out-of-process* server (or out-of-proc server). However, when DLLs are executing on another machine (DCOM) or inside a host environment (COM+), they are also out-of-process.

Moving forward, .NET is now an entire programming platform running in a virtual machine called the CLR (Common Language Runtime) with integrated security, versioning, hardware independence, and so forth. While it is a markedly different beast from the relatively humble beginnings of COM, .NET actually started life as several Microsoft projects that ended up amalgamating into what is now .NET, one of which was a continuation of the COM project. Originally, the seed of COM+ was to be grown into a run time where all the tedious repetitive tasks performed by COM developers to get COM systems up and running would be handled by the run time itself, along with a host of other additional enhancements. This new version was planned to be the Component Object Runtime (COR). You can see the remnants of this name in many of the CLR binary names, such as mscorlib.dll, mscoree.dll and mscorjit.dll. Additionally, the Microsoft acquisition of Colusa Software in 1996 gave Microsoft a language-neutral virtual machine, originally called OmniVM, which was ultimately developed into the CLR infrastructure.

Implementing *IUnknown*

Before we begin looking at an example of COM development, I'll introduce a few COM basics. Every COM object must implement the IUnknown interface, also dubbed IInterface in Delphi for non-COM usage of interfaces (as you saw in Chapter 3). This is the base interface from which every Delphi interface inherits, and Delphi provides a couple of different classes with ready-to-use implementations of IUnknown/IInterface, including TInterfacedObject and TComObject. The first can be used to create an internal object unrelated to COM, and the second is used to create objects that can be exported by servers. There are also other classes that inherit from TComObject and provide support for more interfaces required by Automation servers (TAutoObject from the ComObj unit) or ActiveX controls (TActiveXControl in the AxCtrls unit).

The IUnknown interface has three methods: _AddRef, _Release, and QueryInterface. Here is the definition of the IUnknown interface (extracted from the System unit):

```
type
  IUnknown = interface
    ['{00000000-0000-0000-C000-000000000046}']
    function QueryInterface(const IID: TGUID;
      out Obj): Integer; stdcall;
    function _AddRef: Integer; stdcall;
    function _Release: Integer; stdcall;
  end;
```

The _AddRef and _Release methods are used to implement lifetime management through reference counting. The QueryInterface method handles interface querying.

NOTE   In the previous code, you can see an example of an out parameter, a parameter passed back from the method to the calling program but without an initial value passed by the calling program to the method. The out parameter modifier was added to the Delphi language to support COM but can be used anywhere you wish to make the information direction clearer and can, in some cases, make parameter passing more efficient (such as with interfaces, strings, and dynamic arrays). It's also important to note that although Delphi's language definition for the interface type is designed for compatibility with COM, Delphi interfaces do not require COM. This was already highlighted in Chapter 3, where I built an interface-based example with no COM support.

You don't usually need to implement these methods because you can inherit from one of the Delphi classes already supporting them. The most important class is TComObject, defined in the ComObj unit. When you build a COM server, you'll generally inherit from this class.

TComObject implements the IUnknown interface (mapping its methods to ObjQueryInterface, ObjAddRef, and ObjRelease) and the ISupportErrorInfo interface (through the InterfaceSupportsErrorInfo method). Notice that the implementation of reference counting for the TComObject class is thread-safe because it uses the InterlockedIncrement and InterlockedDecrement API functions instead of the plain Inc and Dec procedures.

As you would expect if you remember the discussion of reference counting in Chapter 3, the _Release method of TInterfacedObject destroys the object when there are no more references to it. The TComObject class does the same. Also keep also in mind that Delphi automatically adds the required reference-counting calls to the compiled code when you use interface-based variables, meaning that the objects implementing those interfaces get destroyed as appropriate.

The interface querying role of QueryInterface is based around the principle that a COM object can implement as many interfaces as you want. When accessing the object through an interface reference of one type you can query whether the object implements another specified interface using the TGUID parameter. If so, QueryInterface usually returns a pointer to the object, using its reference output parameter (Obj).

Globally Unique Identifiers

The QueryInterface method has a parameter of the TGUID type. This type represents a unique ID used to identify COM object classes (in which case the GUID is called CLSID), interfaces (in which case you'll see the term IID), and other COM and system entities. When you want to know whether an object supports a specific interface, you ask the object whether it implements the interface that has a given IID (which is determined by Microsoft for the default COM interfaces). Another ID is used to indicate a specific class or CLSID. The Windows Registry stores this CLSID with indications of the related DLL or executable file. The developers of a COM server define the class identifier.

Both of these IDs are known as GUIDs, or *globally unique identifiers*. If each developer uses a number to indicate its COM server, how can you be sure these values are not duplicated? The short answer is that you cannot. The real answer is that a GUID is such a long number (16 bytes, or 128 bits—a number with 38 digits!) that it is almost impossible to come up with two random numbers having the same value. Moreover, programmers should use the specific API call CoCreateGuid (directly or through their development environment) to come up with a valid GUID that reflects some system information.

GUIDs created on machines with network cards are guaranteed to be unique because network cards contain unique serial numbers that form a base for the GUID creation. GUIDs created on machines with CPU IDs (such as the Pentium III) should also be guaranteed unique, even without a network card. With no unique hardware identifier, GUIDs are unlikely to ever be duplicated.

WARNING   Be careful not to copy the GUID from someone else's program (which can result in two different COM objects using the same GUID). You should also not make up your own ID by entering a casual sequence of numbers. To avoid any problem, press Ctrl+Shift+G in the Delphi editor, and you will get a new, properly defined, truly unique GUID.

In Delphi, the TGUID type (defined in the System unit) is a record structure, which is quite odd but required by Windows. Thanks to some Delphi compiler magic, which is typically available to make tedious or time-consuming tasks more straightforward, you can assign a value to a GUID using the standard hexadecimal notation stored in a string, as in this code fragment:

```
const
  Class_ActiveForm1: TGUID = '{1AFA6D61-7B89-11D0-98D0-444553540000}';
```

You can also pass an interface identified by an IID where a GUID is required, and again Delphi will magically extract the referenced IID. If you need to generate a GUID manually and not in the Delphi environment, you can call the CoCreateGuid Windows API function, as demonstrated by the NewGuid example. This example is so simple that I decided not to list its code. Note that to handle GUIDs, Delphi provides the GUIDToString function and the opposite StringToGUID function.

The Role of Class Factories

When you have registered the GUID of a COM object in the Windows Registry, you can use one of a handful of routines to create the object, such as CreateComObject from the ComObj unit, which itself is a wrapper around the CoCreateInstance API:

```
function CreateComObject (const ClassID: TGUID): IUnknown;
```

When called, the API function will look in the Registry, find the server registering the object with the given GUID, load it, and, if the server is a DLL, call the `DLLGetClassObject` method of the DLL. This is a function every in-process server must provide and export:

```
function DllGetClassObject (const CLSID, IID: TGUID;
  var Obj): HResult; stdcall;
```

This API function receives as parameters the requested class and interface, and it returns an object in its reference parameter. The object returned by this function is a *class factory*.

As the name suggests, a class factory is an object capable of creating other objects. Each server can implement multiple COM objects. The server exposes a class factory for each of the COM objects it can create. One of the many advantages of the Delphi simplified approach to COM development is that the system can provide a class factory for you. For this reason, I didn't add a custom class factory to my example.

The call to the `CreateComObject` API doesn't stop at the creation of the class factory, however. After retrieving it, `CreateComObject` calls the `CreateInstance` method of the `IClassFactory` interface implemented by the class factory. This method creates the requested object and returns an interface reference to it. If no error occurs, this object becomes the return value of the `CreateComObject` API.

By setting up this mechanism (including the class factory, the `DLLGetClassObject` call, and the simple function `CreateComObject` that hides complex behavior), Delphi makes it simple to create COM objects. What's great in Delphi is that many complex COM mechanisms are handled for you by the RTL. Let's begin looking in detail at how Delphi makes COM easy to master.

For each of the core VCL COM classes, Delphi also defines a class factory. The class factory classes form a hierarchy and include `TComObjectFactory`, `TTypedComObjectFactory`, `TAutoObjectFactory`, and `TActiveXControlFactory`. Class factories are important, and every COM server requires them. Usually Delphi programs use class factories by creating an object in the initialization section of the unit defining the corresponding server object class.

A First COM Server

There is no better way to understand COM than to build a simple COM server hosted by a COM server DLL. A library hosting a COM object is indicated in Delphi as an ActiveX library. For this reason, you can begin the development of this project by selecting File ➤ New ➤ Other, moving to the Delphi Projects/ActiveX page, and selecting the ActiveX Library option. Doing so generates a project file I saved as FirstCom among the book demos. Here is its complete source code:

```
library FirstCom;

uses
  ComServ;

exports
  DllGetClassObject,
  DllCanUnloadNow,
```

```
    DllRegisterServer,
    DllUnregisterServer;

{$R *.RES}

begin
end.
```

The four functions exported by the DLL are implemented in the ComServ RTL unit and are required for COM compliance. They are used by the system as follows:

- To access the class factory (DllGetClassObject)

- To check whether the server has destroyed all its objects and can be unloaded from memory (DllCanUnloadNow) when a programmer calls CoFreeUnusedLibraries

- To add or remove information about the server in the Windows Registry (DllRegisterServer and DllUnregisterServer)

COM Interfaces and Objects

Now that the structure of your COM server is in place, you can begin developing it. The first step is to define the interface you want to implement in the server. Here is the definition of a simple interface type, which you should add to a separate unit (called NumIntf in the example):

```
type
  INumber = interface
    ['{B4131140-7C2F-11D0-98D0-444553540000}']
    function GetValue: Integer; stdcall;
    procedure SetValue (New: Integer); stdcall;
    procedure Increase; stdcall;
  end;
```

After declaring the custom interface, you can add the object to the server. To accomplish this, you can use the COM Object Wizard (available in the Delphi Projects/ActiveX page of the File ➤ New ➤ Other dialog box once an ActiveX library project is active), as shown in Figure 12.1. Enter a name to identify the COM object where it says Class Name (referred to as the COM object's coclass) and a description. I disabled the generation of the Type Library (in which case the wizard disables the interface) to avoid introducing too many topics at once. However, it is common for a COM server to include a Type Library and for the COM interfaces to be found defined via the information found in the Type Library. You should also choose an instancing and a threading model, as described in the related sidebar.

The code generated by the COM Object Wizard is quite simple. You'll need to add the name of the interface into the definition of the class in the interface section of the unit and add NumIntf into the uses clause:

```
type
  TNumber = class(TComObject, INumber)
  protected
  end;
```

FIGURE 12.1
The COM Object Wizard

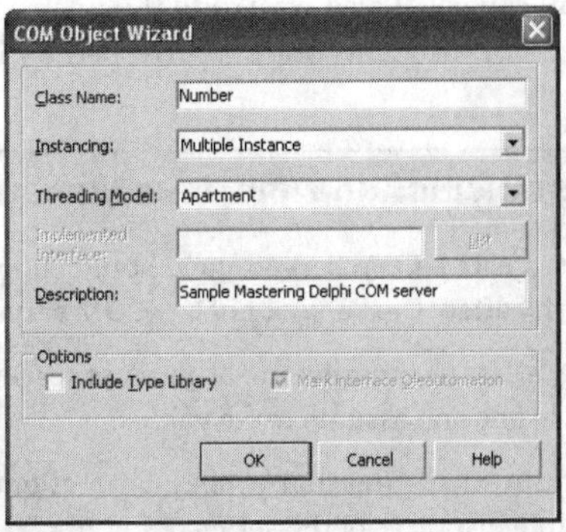

In addition to the GUID for the server (saved in the `Class_Number` constant), there is also code in the `initialization` section of the unit, which uses most of the options you set up in the wizard's dialog box:

```
initialization
  TComObjectFactory.Create(ComServer, TNumber, Class_Number, 'Number',
    'Sample Mastering Delphi COM Server', ciMultiInstance, tmApartment);
```

This code creates an object of the `TComObjectFactory` class, passing as parameters the global `ComServer` object, a class reference to the class you just defined, the GUID for the class, the server name, the server description, and the instancing and threading models you want to use.

The global `ComServer` object, defined in the ComServ unit, is a manager of the class factories available in the server library. It uses its own `ForEachFactory` method to look for the class supporting a given COM object request, and it keeps track of the number of allocated objects. As you've already seen, the ComServ unit implements the functions required by the DLL to be a COM library.

Having examined the source code generated by the wizard, you can now complete it by adding to the TNumber class the methods required for implementing the `INumber` interface and writing their code, and you'll have a working COM object in your server.

Initializing the COM Object

If you look at the definition of the TComObject class, you will notice it has a nonvirtual constructor. Actually it has multiple constructors, each calling the virtual `Initialize` method. For this reason, to set up a COM object properly, you should not define a new constructor (which will never be called) but instead override its `Initialize` method, as I did in the TNumber class. Here is the final version of this class:

```
type
  TNumber = class(TComObject, INumber)
  private
    fValue: Integer;
  protected
    function GetValue: Integer; stdcall;
    procedure SetValue (New: Integer); stdcall;
    procedure Increase; stdcall;
  public
    procedure Initialize; override;
    destructor Destroy; override;
  end;
```

As you can see, I also overrode the destructor of the class because I wanted to test the automatic destruction of the COM objects provided by Delphi.

COM INSTANCING AND THREADING MODELS

When you create a COM server, you should choose a proper instancing and threading model, which can significantly affect the behavior of the COM server.

Instancing affects primarily out-of-process servers (any COM server in a separate executable file, rather than a DLL) and can assume three values:

Multiple   Indicates that when several client applications require the COM object, the system starts multiple instances of the server.

Single   Indicates that, even when several client applications require the COM object, there is only one instance of the server application; it creates multiple internal objects to service the requests.

Internal   Indicates that the object can only be created inside the server; client applications cannot ask for one (this specific setting affects also in-process servers).

The second decision relates to the COM object's thread support, which is only applicable to in-process servers (DLLs). The threading model is a joint decision of the client and the server application: if both sides agree on one model, it is used for the connection. If no agreement is found, COM can still set up a connection using marshaling, which can slow down the operations. Also keep in mind that a server must not only publish its threading model in the Registry (as a result of setting the option in the wizard); it must also follow the rules for that threading model in the code. Here are the key highlights of the various threading models:

Single Model   No real support for threads. The requests reaching the COM server are serialized so the client can perform one operation at a time.

Apartment Model, or "Single-Threaded Apartment"   Only the thread that created the object can call its methods. This means the requests for each server object are serialized, but other objects of the same server can receive requests at the same time. For this reason, the server object must take extra care to access only global data of the server (using critical sections, mutexes, or some other synchronization techniques). This is the threading model generally used for ActiveX controls inside Internet Explorer.

Free Model, or "Multithreaded Apartment"   The client has no restrictions, which means multiple threads can use the same object at the same time. For this reason, every method of every object must protect itself and the nonlocal data it uses against multiple simultaneous calls. This threading model is more complex for a server to support than the Single and Apartment models because even access to the object's own instance data must be handled with thread-safe care.

Both   The server object supports both the Apartment model and the Free model.

Neutral   Introduced in Windows 2000 and available only under COM+. This model indicates that multiple clients can call the object on different threads at the same time, but COM guarantees that the same method is not invoked twice at the same time. Guarding for concurrent access to the object's data is required. Under COM, it is mapped to the Apartment model.

Testing the COM Server

Now that you've finished writing the COM server object, you can register and use it. Compile its code and then use the Run ➤ Register ActiveX Server menu command in Delphi. You do this to register the server on your own machine, updating the local Registry. A more automatic alternative is to enable the Auto Register Type Library option on the Linker page of the project options dialog. With this option enabled the IDE unregisters your server before every recompile and then reregisters it after a successful compilation. This ensures that no matter what you do with your COM objects in the project you won't end up littering the Registry with old interface or class IDs.

When you distribute this server, you should register it on the client computers. Given that target machines are unlikely to have Delphi installed on them, this is best done using the RegSvr32.exe utility that is included with Windows. On your development machine, as well as the IDE menu options, you can use a similar TRegSvr.exe utility that ships with Delphi. This is supplied in Delphi's Bin directory but the source is also supplied as a demo in the \Demos\DelphiWin32\VCLWin32\ActiveX\TRegSvr directory. Having registered the server, you can now turn to the client side of the example. This time, the example is called TestCom and is stored in a separate directory. The program loads the server DLL through the COM mechanism, thanks to the server information present in the Registry, so it's not necessary for the client to know which directory the server resides in.

The form displayed by this program is similar to the one you used to test some of the DLLs in Chapter 11. In the client program, you must include the source code file with the interface and redeclare the COM server GUID. The program starts with all the buttons disabled (at design time), and it enables them only after an object has been created. This way, if an exception is raised while creating one of the objects, the buttons related to the object won't be enabled:

```
procedure TForm1.FormCreate(Sender: TObject);
begin
  // create first object
  Num1 := CreateComObject (Class_Number) as INumber;
  Num1.SetValue (SpinEdit1.Value);
  Label1.Caption := 'Num1: ' + IntToStr (Num1.GetValue);
  Button1.Enabled := True;
  Button2.Enabled := True;

  // create second object
  Num2 := CreateComObject (Class_Number) as INumber;
  Label2.Caption := 'Num2: ' + IntToStr (Num2.GetValue);
  Button3.Enabled := True;
  Button4.Enabled := True;
end;
```

Notice in particular the call to CreateComObject and the following as cast. The call starts the COM object-construction mechanism I described earlier. This call also dynamically loads the server DLL. The return value is an IUnknown object. This object must be converted to the proper interface type before it is assigned to the Num1 and Num2 fields, which now have the interface type INumber as their data type.

WARNING   To downcast an interface from one type to another based on that type, *always* use the as cast (in favor of a hard cast), which for interfaces performs a QueryInterface call behind the scenes. Alternatively, you can do a direct QueryInterface or Supports call. In short, remember that to switch from one implemented interface to another you must perform some interface querying operation. Casting an interface pointer to another interface pointer directly is an error—never do it.

The program also has a button (toward the bottom of the form) with an event handler that creates a new COM object used to get the value of the number following 100. To see why I added this method to the example, click the button in the message showing the result. You'll see a second message indicating that the object has been destroyed. This demonstrates that letting an interface variable go out of scope invokes the object's _Release method and decreases the object's reference count, thereby destroying the object if its reference count reaches zero.

The same thing happens to the other two objects as soon as the program terminates. Even if the program doesn't explicitly do so, the two objects are indeed destroyed, as the message shown by their Destroy destructor clearly demonstrates. This happens because they were declared to be of an interface type, and Delphi will use reference counting for them. By the way, if you want to destroy a COM object reference with an interface, you cannot call a Free method (interfaces don't have Free) but can assign nil to the interface variable; this causes the removal of the reference and possibly the destruction of the object.

Using Interface Properties

As a further small step, you can extend the example by adding a property to the INumber interface. When you add a property to an interface, you indicate the data type and then the read and write directives. You can have read-only or write-only properties, but the read and write clauses must always refer to a method because interfaces don't have storage; they simply define functionality that can be implemented by one or more classes.

Here is the updated interface, which is part of the PropCom example:

```
type
  INumberProp = interface
    ['{B36C5800-8E59-11D0-98D0-444553540000}']
    function GetValue: Integer; stdcall;
    procedure SetValue (New: Integer); stdcall;
    property Value: Integer read GetValue write SetValue;
    procedure Increase; stdcall;
  end;
```

I gave this interface a new name and, even more important, a new interface ID. I could have inherited the new interface type from the previous one, but doing so would have provided no real advantage. COM by itself doesn't support inheritance, and from the perspective of COM all interfaces are different because they have different interface IDs. Needless to say, in Delphi you can use inheritance to improve the structure of the code of the interfaces and of the server objects implementing them.

In the PropCom example, I updated the server class declaration by referring to the new interface and providing a new server object ID. The client program (called TestProp) can now use the Value property instead of the SetValue and GetValue methods. Here is a small excerpt from the FormCreate method:

```
Num1 := CreateComObject (Class_NumPropServer) as INumberProp;
Num1.Value := SpinEdit1.Value;
Label1.Caption := 'Num1: ' + IntToStr (Num1.Value);
```

The difference between using methods and properties for an interface is only syntactical because interface properties cannot access private data as Delphi class properties can. By using properties, you can make the code a little more readable.

Automation

Up to now, you have seen that you can use COM to let an executable file and a library share objects. Another related technology is Automation, which offers the same facilities but opens up access from less capable languages, such as scripting languages that cannot express interface types. Scripting engines can take the required method calls and send the details of what is wanted across to the server at run time. The server looks at the requests and does its best to honor them. This late bound method dispatching process is achieved by the Automation server implementing a dedicated interface, IDispatch, declared in Delphi in the System unit as:

```
type
  IDispatch = interface(IUnknown)
    ['{00020400-0000-0000-C000-000000000046}']
    function GetTypeInfoCount(out Count: Integer): HResult; stdcall;
    function GetTypeInfo(Index, LocaleID: Integer;
      out TypeInfo): HResult; stdcall;
    function GetIDsOfNames(const IID: TGUID; Names: Pointer;
      NameCount, LocaleID: Integer; DispIDs: Pointer): HResult; stdcall;
    function Invoke(DispID: Integer; const IID: TGUID;
      LocaleID: Integer; Flags: Word; var Params;
      VarResult, ExcepInfo, ArgErr: Pointer): HResult; stdcall;
  end;
```

Controllers such as Delphi applications or scripting engines have innate knowledge of this single interface and take advantage of it by passing the requests at run time to its methods. The first two methods return type information; the last two are used to invoke an actual method. Actually, the invocation is performed only by the last method, Invoke, while GetIDsOfNames is used to determine the dispatch ID (required by Invoke) from the method name. When you create an Automation server in Delphi, all you have to do is define a Type Library and implement its interface. Delphi provides everything else through compiler magic and VCL code.

The role of IDispatch becomes more obvious when you consider that there are three ways a controller can call the methods exposed by an Automation server:

◆ It can ask for the execution of a method, passing its name in a string, in a way similar to the dynamic call to a DLL. This is what Delphi does when you use a variant (see the following note) to call the Automation server. This technique is easy to use, but it is rather slow and provides little compiler type-checking. It implies a call to GetIDsOfNames followed by one to Invoke.

◆ It can import the definition of a Delphi dispatch interface (`dispinterface`) for the object on the server and call its methods in a more direct way (dispatching a number, that is, calling `Invoke` directly as the `DispId` of each method is known at compile time). This technique is based on interfaces and allows the compiler to check the types of the parameters and produces faster code, but it requires a little more effort from the programmer (namely the use of a Type Library). Also, you end up binding your controller application to a specific version of the server.

◆ It can call the interface directly, through the interface *Vtable*, that is, treating it as a normal COM object. This works in most cases as most Automation server interfaces provide dual interfaces (they support both `IDispatch` and a plain COM interface).

In the following examples, you'll use these techniques and compare them further.

NOTE   You can use a variant to store a reference to an Automation object. In the Delphi language a variant is a *type-variant* data type, which means a variant variable can assume different data types as its value. Variant data types include the basic ones (such as Integers, strings, characters, and Boolean values, as well as arrays of these types) and also the `IDispatch` interface type. Variants are type-checked at run time when used for data storage, but the compiler lets you treat variants as if they were objects, thanks to its inherent support for late-bound Automation.

Dispatching an Automation Call

The most important difference between the three approaches is that the second generally requires a *Type Library*, one of the foundations of COM. A Type Library is basically a collection of type information, which also often accompanies regular COM objects. This collection generally describes all the elements (objects, interfaces, and other type information) made available by a generic COM server or an Automation server. The key difference between a Type Library and other descriptions of these elements (such as C or Pascal code) is that a Type Library is language-independent. The type elements are defined by COM as a subset of the standard elements of programming languages, and any development tool can use them. Why do you need this information? I mentioned earlier that if you invoke a method of an Automation object using a variant, the Delphi compiler doesn't validate the method at compile time. A small code fragment using Word's old Automation interface, registered as `Word.Basic`, illustrates how simple it is for a programmer:

```
var
  VarW: Variant;
begin
  VarW := CreateOleObject ('Word.Basic');
  VarW.FileNew;
  VarW.Insert ('Mastering Delphi by Marco Cantù');
```

NOTE   As you'll see later, recent versions of Word still register the `Word.Basic` interface, which corresponds to the historic WordBasic macro language, but they also register the new interface `Word.Application`, which corresponds to the VBA macro language. Delphi provides components that simplify the connection with Microsoft Office applications, introduced later in this chapter.

These three lines of code start Word (unless it was already running), create a new document, and add a few words to it. You can see the effect of this application in Figure 12.2.

Unfortunately, the Delphi compiler has no way to check whether the methods exist. Doing all the type checks at run time is risky because if you make even a minor spelling error in a function name, you get no warning about your error until you run the program and reach that line of code. For example, if you type **VarW.Isnert**, the compiler will not complain about the misspelling, but at run time you'll get an error. Because it doesn't recognize the name, Word assumes the method does not exist.

Although the IDispatch interface supports the approach you just saw, it is also possible—and safer—for a server to export the description of its interfaces and objects using a Type Library. This Type Library can then be converted by a specific tool (such as Delphi) into definitions written in the language you want to use to write your client or controller program (such as the Delphi language). This makes it possible for a compiler to check whether the code is correct and for you to use Code Completion and Code Parameters in the Delphi editor.

Once the compiler has done its checks, it can use either of two different techniques to send the request to the server. It can use a plain VTable (that is, an entry in an interface type declaration), or it can use a dispinterface (dispatch interface). You used an interface type declaration earlier in this chapter, so it should be familiar. A dispinterface is basically a way to map each entry in an interface to a number. Calls to the server can then be dispatched by number calling IDipatch.Invoke only, without the extra step of calling IDispatch.GetIDsOfNames. You can consider this an intermediate technique, in between dispatching by function name and using a direct call in the VTable.

NOTE   The term *dispinterface* is a keyword. A dispinterface is automatically generated by the type library editor for every interface. Along with dispinterface, Delphi uses other related keywords: dispid indicates the number to associate with each element; readonly and writeonly are optional specifiers for properties.

The term used to describe this ability to connect to a server in two different ways, using a more dynamic or a more static approach, is *dual interfaces*. When writing a COM controller, you can choose to access the methods of a server two ways: you can use late binding and the mechanism provided by the dispinterface, or you can use early binding and the mechanism based on the VTables, the interface types.

It is important to keep in mind that (along with other considerations) different techniques result in faster or slower execution. Looking up a function by name (and doing the type checking at run time) is the slowest approach, using a dispinterface is much faster, and using the direct VTable call is the fastest approach. You'll do this kind of test in the TLibCli example, later in this chapter.

FIGURE 12.2

The Word document is being created and composed by the WordTest Delphi application.

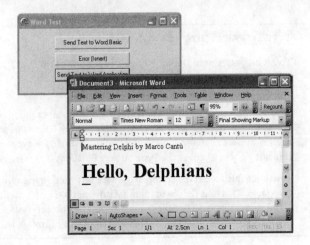

Writing an Automation Server

Let's begin by writing an Automation server. To create an Automation object, you can use Delphi's Automation Object Wizard. Begin with a new application, open the Object Repository by selecting File ➤ New ➤ Other, move to the ActiveX page, and choose Automation Object. You'll see the Automation Object Wizard:

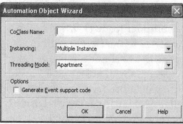

In this wizard, enter the name of the class (without the initial *T*, because it will be added automatically for you to the Delphi implementing class) and click OK. Delphi will now open the Type Library Editor.

TIP   Delphi can generate Automation servers that also export events. Select the corresponding check box in the wizard, and Delphi will add the proper entries in the Type Library and the source code it generates.

The Type Library Editor

You can use the Type Library Editor to define a Type Library in Delphi. Figure 12.3 shows its window after I added some elements to it. The Type Library Editor allows you to add methods and properties to the Automation server object you just created or to a COM object that was created using the COM Object Wizard. Once you add them, it can generate both the Type Library (TLB) file and the corresponding Delphi language source code stored in a unit called a Type Library import unit.

To build a first example, you can add a property and a method to the server by using the editor's corresponding toolbar buttons and typing their names either in the Tree View control on the left side of the window or in the Name edit box on the right side. You add these two elements to an interface, which I've called `IFirstServer`.

TYPE LIBRARY EDITOR SETTINGS

To get on better with Delphi's Type Library Editor there are some settings you can change. First, you can right-click the toolbar and turn on the Text Labels option to see captions in each toolbar button, which makes their purpose clearer.

Second, you can change other settings in the Type Library page of Delphi's Tools ➤ Options dialog box. Here you should switch the Language radio button from IDL to Pascal to make the method and parameter syntax display more understandable and make the list of data types more recognizable. I'll assume you changed this setting when I cover the Type Library Editor as it makes more sense to work with Pascal than IDL.

You should also select the option to use safecall function mapping on all Vtable interfaces rather than just dual interfaces. This tells Delphi to manufacture method implementations using the simpler safecall convention (see the next tip) for COM objects and Automation objects rather than just for Automation objects. This is wise unless you plan to return many custom error values through HRESULT values in your COM objects.

FIGURE 12.3
The Type Library Editor, showing the details of an interface

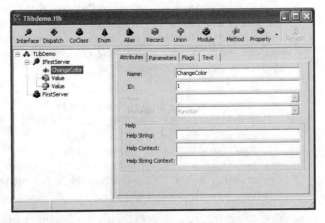

For the procedure, you can define the parameters in the Parameters page; for a function you can also specify its return type in the same page. In this specific case the ChangeColor method has no parameters and its Delphi definition is:

```
procedure ChangeColor; safecall;
```

NOTE   The methods contained in Automation interfaces in Delphi generally use the safecall calling convention. It wraps a try/except block around each method and provides a default return value indicating error or success. It also sets up a COM rich error object containing the exception message, so interested clients (such as Delphi clients) can re-create the server exception on the client side.

Now you can add a property to the interface by clicking the Property button on the Type Library Editor's toolbar. Again, you can type a name for it, such as **Value** and select a data type in the Type combo box. In addition to selecting one of the many types already listed, you can also enter other types directly, particularly interfaces of other objects.

The definition of the Value property of the example corresponds to the following elements of the Delphi interface:

```
function Get_Value: Integer; safecall;
procedure Set_Value(Value: Integer); safecall;
property Value: Integer read Get_Value write Set_Value;
```

Clicking the Refresh button on the Type Library Editor toolbar generates (or updates) the Delphi unit with the interface.

The Server Code

Now you can close the Type Library Editor and save the changes. This operation adds three items to the project: the Type Library file, a corresponding Delphi definition, and the declaration of the server object. The Type Library is connected to the project using a resource-inclusion statement added to the source code of the project file:

```
{$R *.TLB}
```

You can always reopen the Type Library Editor by using the View ➤ Type Library command or selecting the proper TLB file in Delphi's normal File Open dialog box.

As mentioned earlier, the Type Library is also converted into an interface definition and added to a new Delphi unit. This unit is quite long, so I listed in the book only its key elements. The most important part is the new interface declaration:

```
type
  IFirstServer = interface(IDispatch)
  ['{89855B42-8EFE-11D0-98D0-444553540000}']
  procedure ChangeColor; safecall;
  function Get_Value: Integer; safecall;
  procedure Set_Value(Value: Integer); safecall;
  property Value: Integer read Get_Value write Set_Value;
  end;
```

Then comes the dispinterface, which associates a number with each element of the IFirstServer interface:

```
type
  IFirstServerDisp = dispinterface
  ['{89855B42-8EFE-11D0-98D0-444553540000}']
  procedure ChangeColor; dispid 1;
  property Value: Integer dispid 2;
  end;
```

The last portion of the file includes a creator class, which is used to create an object on the server (and for this reason is used on the client side of the application, not on the server side):

```
type
  CoFirstServer = class
    class function Create: IFirstServer;
    class function CreateRemote(const MachineName: string): IFirstServer;
  end;
```

All the declarations in this file (I've skipped some others) can be considered internal, hidden implementation support. You don't need to understand them fully in order to write most Automation applications.

Finally, Delphi generates a file containing the implementation of your Automation object. This unit is added to the application and is the one you'll work on to finish the program. This unit declares the class of the server object, which must implement the interface you've just defined:

```
type
  TFirstServer = class(TAutoObject, IFirstServer)
  protected
    function Get_Value: Integer; safecall;
    procedure ChangeColor; safecall;
    procedure Set_Value(Value: Integer); safecall;
  end;
```

Delphi already provides the skeleton code for the methods, so you only need to complete the lines in between. In this case, the three methods refer to a property and two methods I added to the form. In general, you should not add code related to the user interface inside the class of the server object. I did it because I wanted to be able to change the `Value` property and have a visible side effect (displaying the value in an edit box).

Registering the Automation Server

The unit containing the server object has one more statement, added by Delphi to the `initialization` section:

```
initialization
  TAutoObjectFactory.Create(ComServer, TFirstServer, Class_FirstServer,
    ciMultiInstance);
end.
```

NOTE   In this case, I selected multiple instancing. For the various instancing styles possible in COM, see the sidebar "COM Instancing and Threading Models" earlier in this chapter.

This is not very different from the creation of class factories you saw at the beginning of this chapter. The ComServer unit hooks the `InitProc` system function to register all COM objects as part of the COM server application startup. The execution of this code is triggered by the `Application.Initialize` call, which Delphi adds by default to the project source code of any program.

You can add the server information to the Windows Registry by running this application on the target machine (the computer on which you want to install the Automation server) or by running it and passing to it the `/regserver` parameter on the command line (which will start the server, register it without displaying any of the UI, and then exit). You can do this by selecting Start ➢ Run, creating a shortcut in Explorer, or running the program within Delphi after you've entered a command-line parameter (using the Run ➢ Parameters command). Another command-line parameter, `/unregserver`, is used to remove this server from the Registry.

Writing a Client for the Server

Now that you have built a server, you can prepare a client program to test it. This client can connect to the server either by using variants or by using the new Type Library. This second approach can be implemented manually or by using Delphi techniques for wrapping components around Automation servers. You'll try all these approaches.

Create a new application—I called it TLibCli—and import the server's Type Library using the Component ➢ Import Component menu command of the Delphi IDE. This command shows the Import Wizard, and you should select Type Library from the list of choices. After clicking Next you are presented with the list of type libraries registered on the system, as you can see in Figure 12.4. You can add other type libraries to this list by clicking Add and browsing for the proper file module. The page you see when you click Next shows some details of the selected library (such as the list of server objects) and information about the Type Library import unit this dialog box is ultimately going to produce.

FIGURE 12.4
Delphi's Type Library
Import dialog box

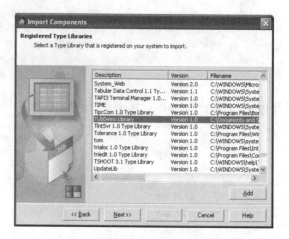

WARNING   Do not add the Type Library itself (the .tlb file) to the client application because you are writing the Automation controller, not a server. A controller's Delphi project should not include the Type Library of the server it connects to, but it should have definitions of the interfaces and so on represented by the Type Library, which is achieved through the import process.

The Type Library import unit is named by Delphi after the Type Library, with a _TLB at the end. In this case, the unit name is TlibdemoLib_TLB. I've already mentioned that one of the elements of this unit, also generated by the Type Library Editor, is the *creation* class. I showed you the interface of this class, but here is the implementation of the first of the two functions:

```
class function CoFirstServer.Create: IFirstServer;
begin
  Result := CreateComObject(Class_FirstServer) as IFirstServer;
end;
```

You can use it to create a server object (and possibly start the server application) on the same computer. As you can see in the code, the function is a shortcut for the CreateComObject call, which allows you to create an instance of a COM object if you know its GUID. As an alternative, you can use the CreateOleObject function, which requires as a parameter a ProgID, the registered name of the server. There is another difference between these two creation functions: CreateComObject returns an object of the IUnknown type, whereas CreateOleObject returns an object of the IDispatch type.

In this example, you'll use the CoFirstServer.Create shorthand. When you create the server object, you get as a return value an IFirstServer interface. You can use it directly or store it in a variant variable. Here is an example of the first approach:

```
var
  MyServer: Variant;
begin
  MyServer := CoFirstServer.Create;
  MyServer.ChangeColor;
```

This code, based on variants, is not very different from that of the first controller you built in this chapter (the one that used Microsoft Word). Here is the alternate code, which has the same effect:

```
var
  IMyServer: IFirstServer;
begin
  IMyServer := CoFirstServer.Create;
  IMyServer.ChangeColor;
```

The benefit here is that you get Code Completion and compile-time validation of what you type, unlike with the variant. You've seen how you can use the interface and the variant. What about the dispatch interface? You can declare a variable of the dispatch interface type, in this case:

```
var
  DMyServer: IFirstServerDisp;
```

Then you can use it to call the methods as usual, after you've assigned an object to it, by casting the object returned by the creator class:

```
DMyServer := CoFirstServer.Create as IFirstServerDisp;
```

INTERFACES, VARIANTS, AND DISPATCH INTERFACES: TESTING THE SPEED DIFFERENCE

As I mentioned in the section introducing type libraries, one of the differences between these approaches is speed. It is complicated to assess the exact performance of each technique because many factors are involved. I added a simple test to the TLibCli example among the demos for this chapter to give you an idea. The code for the test is a loop that accesses the Value of the server 100 times. The output of the program shows the timing, which is determined by calling the GetTickCount API function before and after executing the loop. (Two alternatives are to use Delphi's own time functions, which are slightly less precise, or to use the very precise Win32 timing functions, QueryPerformanceFrequency and QueryPerformanceCounter in the Windows unit or timeGetTime from MMSystem.)

With this program, you can roughly compare the output obtained by calling this method based on an interface, the corresponding version based on a variant, and a third version based on a dispatch interface. Looking at the timing of the example, you should see that interfaces are quicker and variants are slower, with dispatch interfaces falling in between but closer to interfaces.

The Scope of Automation Objects

Another important element to keep in mind is the *scope* of the Automation objects. Variants and interface objects use reference-counting techniques, so if a variable that is related to an interface object is declared locally in a method, then at the end of the method the object will be destroyed and the server may terminate (if all the objects created by the server have been destroyed). For example, writing a method with this code produces minimal effect:

```
procedure TClientForm.ChangeColor;
var
  IMyServer: IFirstServer;
```

```
begin
  IMyServer := CoFirstServer.Create;
  IMyServer.ChangeColor;
end;
```

Unless the server is already active, a copy of the program is created and the color is changed, but then the server is immediately closed as the interface-typed object goes out of scope. The alternative approach I used in the TLibCli example declares the object as a field of the form and creates the COM objects at startup, as in this procedure:

```
procedure TClientForm.FormCreate(Sender: TObject);
begin
  IMyServer := CoFirstServer.Create;
end;
```

With this code, as the client program starts, the server program is immediately activated. At program termination, the form is destroyed, the field therefore goes out of scope, has its reference decremented, and the server closes. A further alternative is to declare the object in the form but then create it only when it is used, as in these two code fragments:

```
// MyServerBis: Variant;
if varType (MyServerBis) = varEmpty then
  MyServerBis := CoFirstServer.Create;
MyServerBis.ChangeColor;

// IMyServerBis: IFirstServer;
if not Assigned (IMyServerBis) then
  IMyServerBis := CoFirstServer.Create;
IMyServerBis.ChangeColor;
```

NOTE   A variant is initialized to the varEmpty type when it is created. If you instead assign the value null to the variant, its type becomes varNull. Both varEmpty and varNull represent variants with no value assigned, but they behave differently in expression evaluation. The varNull value always propagates through an expression (making it a null expression), whereas the varEmpty value quietly disappears.

The Server in a Component

When creating a client program for your server or any other Automation server, you can use a better approach: wrapping a Delphi component around the COM server. If you look at the final portion of the TlibdemoLib_TLB file, you can find the declaration of a TFirstServer class inheriting from TOleServer. This is a component generated when importing the library, which the system registers in the unit's Register procedure.

If you add this unit to a package, the new server component will become available on the Delphi Component Palette. However, you have to choose a page in the Import Wizard, which shows (none) by default in the Palette Page entry. I created a new package, PackAuto, available in a directory of the same name. In this package, I added the directive LIVE_SERVER_AT_DESIGN_TIME in the Directories/ Conditionals page of the package's Project Options dialog box. This directive enables an extra feature that you don't get by default: at design time, the server component will have an extra property that lists as subitems all the properties of the Automation server:

WARNING   The LIVE_SERVER_AT_DESIGN_TIME directive should be used with care with the most complex Automation servers (including programs such as Word, Excel, PowerPoint, and Visio). Certain servers must be in a particular mode before you can use some properties of their Automation interfaces. Because this feature is problematic at design time for many servers, it is not active by default.

As you can see in the Object Inspector, the component has few properties. AutoConnect indicates when to activate the COM server. When the value is True the server object is loaded as soon as the wrapper component is created (both at run time and design time). When the AutoConnect property is set to False, the Automation server is loaded only the first time one of its methods is called. Another property, ConnectKind, indicates how to establish the connection with the server. It can always start a new instance (ckNewInstance), use the running instance (ckRunningInstance, which shows an error message if the server is not already running), or select the current instance or start a new one if none is available (ckRunningOrNew). Finally, you can ask for a remote server with ckRemote and directly attach a server in the code after a manual connection with ckAttachToInterface.

NOTE   To connect to an existing object, this needs to be registered in the Running Object Table (ROT). The registration must be performed by the server calling the RegisterActiveObject API function. Of course, only one instance for each COM server can be registered at a given time.

COM Data Types

COM dispatching doesn't support all the data types available in Delphi. This is particularly important for Automation, because the client and the server are often executed in different address spaces, and the system must move (or *marshal*) the data from one side to the other. Also keep in mind that COM interfaces should be accessible by programs written in any language.

COM data types include basic data types such as Integer, SmallInt, Byte, Single, Double, Wide-String, Variant, and WordBool (but not Boolean). In addition to the basic data types, you can use COM types for complex elements such as fonts, string lists, and bitmaps, using the IFontDisp, IStrings, and IPictureDisp interfaces. The following sections describe the details of a server that provides a list of strings and a font to a client.

EXPOSING STRINGS LISTS AND FONTS

The ListServ example is a practical demonstration of how you can expose two complex types, such as a list of strings and a font, from an Automation server written in Delphi. I chose these two specific types because they are both supported by Delphi.

The IFontDisp interface is provided by Windows and is available in the ActiveX unit. The AxCtrls Delphi unit extends this support by providing conversion methods like GetOleFont and SetOleFont. Delphi supports the IStrings interface in the StdVCL unit, and the AxCtrls unit provides conversion functions for this type (along with a third type I won't use here, TPicture).

WARNING To run this and similar applications, you must install and register the StdVCL library on the client computer. On your computer, it is registered during Delphi's installation.

The Set and Get methods of the complex types' properties copy information from the COM interfaces to the local data and from there to the form, and vice versa. The strings' two methods, for example, do this by calling the GetOleStrings and SetOleStrings Delphi functions. The client application used to demonstrate this feature is called ListCli. The two programs are complex; rather than list their details here I decided to leave the source code for your study, because Delphi programmers seldom use this advanced technique.

.NET Interoperability

The .NET Framework makes good contributions to helping build systems that are hybrids, using functionality written in .NET and functionality written in Win32. This is important when considering moving a project from Win32 to the .NET platform. While Delphi 2005 offers a strong code migration path with VCL for .NET, real applications do not move from one platform to another in one fell swoop. Sure, much of the VCL manipulation code can be taken across reasonably easily, with some effort put into taking account of the subtle changes that are found here and there, such as TList being a dynamic array of objects instead of pointers. However any real system will typically contain sections of code that contains a lot of pointer manipulation, such as character buffer logic using PChar variables to navigate through it, or perhaps memory block manipulation with pointers.

Even in small amounts, such code can present obstacles to smooth migration and so there is often a strong argument for isolating such code and leaving it in the form of a Win32 DLL or COM object and accessing it from the .NET system through the available interoperability support. In contrast, some developers take the approach of extending an existing system by writing new functionality in .NET and using it from Win32 systems. This allows them to build up experience of .NET development within the confines of a small part of a much larger system, leaving the full migration to a later point, if it happens at all. .NET objects can be exposed under the guide of COM wrappers, so they are readily consumed in a COM client.

There are also more advanced scenarios where .NET's interoperability support can be employed. .NET offers the ability to host a .NET session under program control in a Win32 application. This allows Win32 modules and .NET modules to coexist in a mixed mode process directly under the developer's control. This is, in fact, how the Borland Developer Studio operates. It is a Win32 process but hosts a CLR session and loads up many .NET assemblies as well as Win32 packages in order to offer development facilities for both platforms. However, this advanced level of interoperability is beyond the scope of this book.

The following sections will explore the support for building .NET applications that use COM objects and DLL exports and also extending Win32 systems with .NET functionality, either using objects or individual static methods.

NOTE The two COM interoperability permutations (.NET applications consuming COM objects and COM clients consuming .NET objects) are generically referred to as COM Interop.

Using COM in .NET

COM objects are different from .NET objects in various ways. First, COM objects reside in unmanaged code, whereas .NET objects are managed. This has implications on the different data types supported by the two types of objects. Second, COM objects are accessed solely through the interfaces they implement, whereas .NET objects can choose whether or not to implement interfaces and can be accessed through object references or through interface references. On top of this is the difference in lifetime management. COM objects are strictly reference counted; they destroy themselves when the reference counting method calls imply that no one else is making use of them. .NET objects are not reference counted. Instead, a garbage collector identifies objects whose usefulness has expired by following trails of references from given root points and identifying which objects are no longer reachable.

When using COM objects in .NET, all these differences must be reconciled for this marriage of disparate object models to work well, or indeed at all. Fortunately, the .NET Framework takes care of all this. To use COM objects from a COM server you first need a wrapper assembly based on the content of the COM server's Type Library. This wrapper assembly allows the CLR at run time to manufacture appropriate wrapper objects to hide and work with the differences between COM and .NET. Your .NET code works with the .NET wrapper objects just as it does with any other .NET objects.

INTEROP ASSEMBLIES AND RUNTIME CALLABLE WRAPPERS (RCWS)

You'll start with using a simple COM server. The project SimpleServer recreates a COM object like the one from the PropCom project, but it uses a Type Library to contain the description of the COM server's INumberProp interface. Figure 12.5 shows the Type Library Editor displaying the definition of the interface and the coclass, which is the name of the COM object as far as COM is concerned—the name you enter as the class name in the new COM Object Wizard (refer back to Figure 12.1). The goal is to create a .NET client application that looks like the TestProp COM client and uses the COM object.

The first task is to recreate the basic application UI, which in this case I did using VCL.NET, called RCWTest.

Some things that were not appropriate to leave in the form unit included the CLSID constant for the COM object and the reference to the old interface definition unit (remember, the interface is defined by the Type Library Editor and now resides in the SimpleServer_TLB Type Library import unit).

FIGURE 12.5

The simple COM object to be used in a .NET application

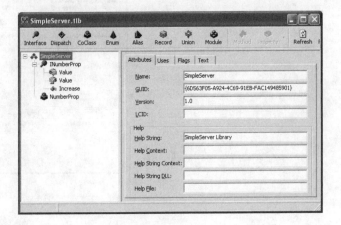

The first step to allowing .NET code to access the COM object is to manufacture an *Interop Assembly*. This assembly contains appropriate .NET metadata describing all the items exposed by the COM server and described in its Type Library. Making an Interop Assembly is a side effect of adding a reference to the Type Library into your .NET project.

NOTE An alternative to allowing the IDE to make your Interop Assembly is to use a tool that is part of the .NET Framework SDK, installed by default in the `C:\Program Files\Microsoft.NET\ SDK\v1.1` directory. The utility is a command-line tool called Tlbimp.exe, found in the SDK's bin directory, described by itself as the Microsoft (R) .NET Framework Type Library to Assembly Converter.

When you invoke the Add Reference dialog, either through the context menu of the project manager's References node or through the item on the main Project menu, you get a dialog with three tabs on it. The second tab allows you to choose a registered Type Library or locate an unregistered one, as shown in Figure 12.6.

When you add a reference to a COM server, the IDE makes light work of manufacturing an Interop Assembly using some prefabricated functionality in the depths of the .NET Framework. What you end up with is a ComImports subdirectory in your project directory containing the new Interop Assembly. Its name is based on the library name, as defined in the Type Library (the root node in the hierarchy shown in the Type Library Editor) and uses a fixed prefix to imply its role. In the case of a Delphi-generated COM server, the library name is the name of the project when the Type Library was added, so this Interop Assembly is called Interop.SimpleServer.dll.

NOTE You will also find a copy of this Interop Assembly in your project directory after compiling the project. This is because the Copy Local property of the Interop Assembly is set to True. If this were not the case, .NET would not be able to locate the Interop Assembly at runtime with it being in neither the GAC nor the project directory. Automatically having Copy Local set to True solves that issue by making sure it is copied into the same directory the executable is set to be written to.

FIGURE 12.6
Adding a COM reference
to a .NET project

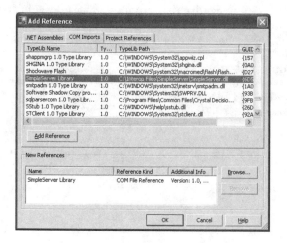

So what does the Interop Assembly contain? You'll find metadata describing various classes, interfaces, and types in Interop Assemblies all present so that .NET can use the information to dynamically manufacture special objects that sit in between your .NET code and the COM objects. These dynamic objects are called *Runtime Callable Wrappers* or *RCWs*, since they wrap the COM objects and enable them to be called from the .NET runtime.

You can browse the contents of the Interop Assembly using the built in Reflection window by right-clicking the assembly in the References list in the project manager and choosing Open. Reflection is available as a stand-alone tool on the Tools menu and in the Start menu group, but in this instance it is part of the IDE and creates an extra page in the editor illustrating the assembly's internals. In Figure 12.7 you can see that the Interop Assembly defines a class `NumberPropClass` that represents the original coclass `NumberProp`. This class implements the `INumberProp` interface, which has been carried through from the Type Library. Another interface, `NumberProp`, is also implemented, which is a helper interface. This collects together all the interfaces implemented by the original `NumberProp` coclass and includes extra support for COM events, which are not relevant in this case but which I will cover shortly in another example.

So you create an instance of `NumberPropClass` and store it in a variable declared either as `NumberPropClass` or as one of those two interface types. In a Win32 COM client you would use `INumberProp` (and this was the case in the original project), so stick with that for consistency. All the types are defined in the namespace SimpleServer (identified with the folder icon in Reflection), so SimpleServer needs to be added to the uses clause.

The one remaining change to the project needed to succeed with COM Interop is to update the calls that create the COM object. Instead of calling `CreateComObject` or other traditional approaches, you instead call the `NumberPropClass` constructor, for example:

```
Num1 := NumberpropClass.Create;
```

That's all that's needed; you are now using an RCW as defined in an Interop Assembly to access an unmanaged COM object.

NOTE In addition to adding a reference to a COM server's Type Library, registered or not, you can also add a reference directly to an already existing Interop Assembly for your COM server. This may exist because you have already gone through the process of calling a COM server from a .NET project before.

FIGURE 12.7
An Interop Assembly opened in the Reflection window

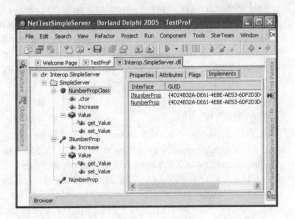

USING A REAL-WORLD COM SERVER

That works fine for a simple example, but what about a more realistic COM server? A usable server preinstalled on Windows XP is Microsoft's Speech API version 5. This API has an SDK available for download from www.microsoft.com/speech/download/SDK51 (it contains comprehensive documentation, but for our purposes here this will not be required). The Speech API allows you to use speech recognition as well as speech synthesis. To test how successfully you can use this COM server, you will implement some simple speech synthesis.

This time you will create a WinForms project for a change, and the example you are building up is called SAPIApp. To use SAPI, you have to reference the Type Library in the IDE, thereby creating an Interop Assembly as before. This time the Type Library is called Microsoft Speech Object Library and the created Interop Assembly is called Interop.SpeechLib.dll. The original COM server is called sapi.dll, but the Type Library defines the library as SpeechLib.

Inside the SpeechLib namespace in the Interop Assembly, you will find numerous entities. To get some speech out of the computer you need to use the SpVoiceClass class, which represents the original SAPI SpVoice coclass. If you were programming SAPI in a COM client, you would use the methods of the ISpeechVoice interface and could declare a variable of type ISpeechVoice and assign the RCW to it. However, as before the Interop Assembly defines another companion interface named after the coclass, SpVoice. Again, this replicates the methods from ISpeechVoice, but with this COM server you will see the benefit of this manufactured interface in the next section.

```
SAPIVoice: SpVoice;
```

To get some speech, you call the Speak method passing in the text to speak and one or more flags from the SpeechVoiceSpeakFlags enumerated type. For example, to get asynchronous speech where the speech is rendered in a separate thread and so does not make the UI freeze, you can use something like this:

```
SAPIVoice.Speak('Mastering Delphi 2005 by Marco Cantu',
    SpeechVoiceSpeakFlags.SVSFlagsAsync)
```

Clearly this can be readily extended to take text from a text box or anywhere else you can think of.

TIP   When an RCW becomes eligible for garbage collection, it releases the COM interface reference held within. This may occur later than you want so you may want a mechanism to deterministically release the COM object. Some references suggest calling GC.Collect followed by GC.WaitForPending-Finalizers (indeed, some references suggest calling this pair twice in succession). I urge against this approach because manual invocation of the garbage collector disables its self-tuning ability, an undesirable side effect. Instead, you should pass your RCW to the ReleaseComObject method of System.Runtime.InteropServices.Marshal class.

COM EVENTS IN .NET

The COM SpVoice coclass implements the ISpeechVoice interface (a normal interface, described as an incoming interface since the method calls come into the server from the client). However, it also implements a COM events interface (an outgoing interface) called _ISpeechVoiceEvents. This interface defines methods that are implemented in the client and can be called by SAPI when appropriate . COM events are somewhat tedious to set up in COM clients, but the Interop Assembly trivializes the whole situation by defining a helper interface with the same name but with an

`_Event` suffix (`_ISpeechVoiceEvents_Event` in this case). This interface contains events defined in terms of manufactured delegates to turn the convoluted COM events into straightforward .NET events. Each method in the original events interface has a delegate defined in the Interop Assembly that dictates the .NET event handler signature.

So what events can you play with in a SAPI application? With speech synthesis there are several of them. The `StartStream` event indicates when a stream of speech starts, and there is a corresponding `EndStream` event. Other noteworthy events include `Sentence`, triggered as each sentence is started; `Word`, which indicates individual words; and `Phoneme`, which breaks words down into individual sounds. There is also an `AudioLevel` event that reports how loud the current speech output is. Some of these events allow you to get some immediate visual feedback from the speech synthesis process.

The immediate question is how to correctly define the event handlers in your .NET code. In a Delphi Win32 COM client, it can be made a little easier with the component wrappers that get manufactured when importing the COM server. These component wrappers publish events so the IDE can readily set up the event handling framework. However, the Interop Assembly has not added any components to the Tool Palette, so this luxury is not available. Instead, you need to work out the appropriate definition some other way.

To automatically get event handlers set up for members of an events interface, you can take advantage of one of the Code Completion features that make themselves available in class declarations. The original event interface in this case that has been carried across to the Interop Assembly is called `_ISpeechVoiceEvents`. Temporarily adding this to the form class declaration as an implemented interface allows a neat shortcut to be employed. Pressing Ctrl+Space in an area where you could declare methods, such as the public section, brings up Code Completion, showing available methods to choose from that will be declared for you. Abstract methods (such as those in an interface) that require implementation are conveniently colored in red, and you can choose several at the same time, as shown in Figure 12.8. When Code Completion enters the declarations, you can invoke Class Completion (Ctrl+Shift+C) to get the implementations. Finally, don't forget to remove the interface from the form class implemented interface list before moving on.

FIGURE 12.8

Declaring COM event handlers in .NET

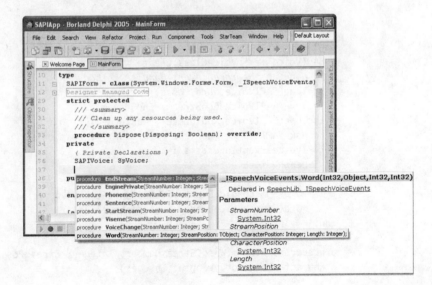

Now that you have the event handlers set up for the COM server, it's just a case of writing the rest of the code and hooking up the event handlers to the events. In order to connect the event handlers to the COM events, you use the extra .NET event properties conveniently added to the manufactured interface you are using. Since the SpVoice interface defines .NET event properties for all the voice object events, you can use the typical `Include/Exclude` syntax that Delphi offers.

The following code relies on a multiline textbox and a progress bar on the form.

```
type
  SAPIForm = class(System.Windows.Forms.Form)
  ...
  private
    SAPIVoice: SpVoice;
  public
    procedure AudioLevel(StreamNumber: Integer;
      StreamPosition: TObject; AudioLevel: Integer);
    procedure EndStream(StreamNumber: Integer;
      StreamPosition: TObject);
    procedure Word(StreamNumber: Integer; StreamPosition: TObject;
      CharacterPosition: Integer; Length: Integer);
  ...
  end;

procedure SAPIForm.SpeakButton_Click(sender: System.Object;
  e: System.EventArgs);
begin
  SAPIVoice.Speak(SpeechTextBox.Text,
    SpeechVoiceSpeakFlags.SVSFlagsAsync);
end;

procedure SAPIForm.SAPIForm_Load(sender: System.Object;
  e: System.EventArgs);
begin
  SAPIVoice := SpVoiceClass.Create;
  // Hook up the three event handler methods
  Include(SAPIVoice.Word, Word);
  Include(SAPIVoice.EndStream, EndStream);
  Include(SAPIVoice.AudioLevel, AudioLevel);
  // Ask SAPI to trigger the events of interest only
  SAPIVoice.EventInterests :=
    SpeechVoiceEvents(
      Ord(SpeechVoiceEvents.SVEWordBoundary) or
      Ord(SpeechVoiceEvents.SVEEndInputStream) or
      Ord(SpeechVoiceEvents.SVEAudioLevel));
end;

procedure SAPIForm.Word(StreamNumber: Integer; StreamPosition: TObject;
  CharacterPosition, Length: Integer);
```

```
begin
  SpeechTextBox.SelectionStart := CharacterPosition;
  SpeechTextBox.SelectionLength := Length; // highlight word
end;

procedure SAPIForm.EndStream(StreamNumber: Integer;
  StreamPosition: TObject);
begin
  // Reset VU meter
  AVProgressBar.Value := 0;
  // Highlight word being spoken in the text box
  SpeechTextBox.SelectionLength := 0;
  SpeechTextBox.SelectionStart := Length(SpeechTextBox.Text);
end;

procedure SAPIForm.AudioLevel(StreamNumber: Integer;
  StreamPosition: TObject; AudioLevel: Integer);
begin
  AVProgressBar.Value := AudioLevel;
end;
```

The code responds to the events to highlight each word as it is being spoken and have the progress bar act as a simple VU meter, as shown next. You can also see that SAPI understands various XML-like tags inserted in the text to control the way the speech is formed. This is a simple example of a SAPI application but demonstrates that you can access COM functionality from .NET applications through COM Interop.

PRIMARY INTEROP ASSEMBLIES (PIAS)

Each time you reference a COM library from a .NET application you get, by default, a new Interop Assembly manufactured in the COMImports subdirectory. The manufacture of this Interop Assembly is outside your control and follows the defaults that are chosen inside the import code invoked by the Delphi IDE. On commercial COM servers, the vendor can tweak its Interop Assembly to ensure best results with some of the trickier parameter combinations the vendor has chosen to use. This customized Interop Assembly may then be distributed by the vendor as a *Primary Interop Assembly* or PIA. When you add a reference to a COM server Delphi will check to see if a PIA has been installed for it before proceeding to make a fresh one for you. If a PIA is available, it gets used in preference.

You should find that recent versions of Microsoft Office have PIAs available. Indeed Office 2003 installs them (as a customizable option, which is disabled by default). Similarly, the COM-based ADO data access library has a PIA; on my machine it's installed as adodb.dll in the directory

C:\Program Files\Microsoft.NET\Primary Interop Assemblies. You need do nothing different; you still reference the appropriate Type Library from the second page of the Add Reference dialog, and Delphi does the checking and referencing as appropriate.

Using Win32 DLLs in .NET

As well as existing COM objects, there are many existing DLLs that contain functionality you still need to make use of. These could be third-party DLLs or the Win32 API, which is simply the combined exports of a collection of DLLs. The .NET platform offers a mechanism to call native code to achieve this called *Platform Invoke*, also known as *PInvoke* or sometimes *p/invoke*.

NOTE   The fact that PInvoke is a mainstay of the .NET platform is evidenced by it being part of the Common Language Infrastructure (CLI), the standard that the .NET platform is both an implementation and a superset of. The CLI standard has been ratified by the European Computer Manufacturers Association (ECMA) and the International Organization for Standardization (ISO).

This section looks at how Delphi gives you a way around the specifics of PInvoke and delves into the details of how you can build up PInvoke declarations. We'll finish this subject with a look at a Delphi-specific mechanism, called Virtual Library Interfaces. These allow DLLs to be treated like objects implementing interfaces, which offers consistency with operation in other areas of .NET in addition to other advantages.

USING PLATFORM INVOKE

A Win32 application has a special syntax for linking to routines that areexported from DLLs. This syntax employs the external directive to tell Delphi where each routine resides and what its exact name is. In Delphi for .NET, this same syntax can be used to create declarations for many DLL-based routines. Delphi will recognize the Win32 import syntax and render an appropriate PInvoke declaration in the generated executable during the compilation process. This convenience saves you the trouble of worrying about PInvoke declarations until you push the limit of what the traditional declaration syntax can muster.

We'll explore this using a Win32 DLL project called Win32DLL from the `PInvokeTest` directory. This DLL has a variety of routines declared in it and exported from it, as discussed in Chapter 11, that will let you test PInvoke. The first one is a simple routine that takes a couple of integers, returns the smaller of the two, and uses the typical Windows stdcall calling convention. The declaration of the routine in the DLL looks like this:

```
function Min(X, Y: Integer): Integer; stdcall;
```

There are two .NET client examples supplied that will make use of this and other Win32 routines. One is called PInvokeTestImplicit and uses this traditional Win32 DLL import syntax in .NET; the other explicitly uses the underlying .NET support for PInvoke via the `DllImportAttribute` attribute from the `System.Runtime.InteropServices` namespace. This way you get to see both sides of PInvoke support. The implicit test project has a unit containing the import declarations called Win32DLLImplicitImport.pas, and the explicit test project uses Win32DLLExplicitImport.

For `Min`, the implicit PInvoke import declaration looks like this:

```
function Min(X, Y: Integer): Integer; stdcall;
  external 'Win32DLL.dll' {name 'Min'};
```

This is typical syntax from previous Delphi versions, and it works just fine in the application. This example is straightforward because Integer is a type understood in Win32 and has the same implication in .NET—a 32-bit signed integral number. The explicit declaration is much the same, as Delphi will generate behind the scenes for the implicit declaration:

```
[DllImport('Win32DLL.dll', EntryPoint = 'Min',
  CallingConvention = CallingConvention.StdCall)]
function Min(X, Y: Integer): Integer; external;
```

In this case, the EntryPoint attribute parameter is not required because you are already specifying the correct name in the Pascal function declaration, but clearly this can be used to "alias" DLL routines by accessing them with other Delphi identifiers in your .NET code. This has the same effect as the optional name directive shown in a comment in the implicit declaration. You can see .NET provides an enumerated type that defines some of the common calling conventions.

WARNING   The CallingConvention enumerated type defines a Fastcall value that would be a close approximation to Delphi's default register calling convention. However, .NET documentation states this value is not supported. Another value, Winapi, is the same as StdCall in .NET on the Windows platform, but in fact equates to Cdecl in .NET Compact Framework on Windows CE. In summary, the only important values are StdCall and Cdecl.

The next two routines take textual parameters as input. They don't modify the text, but they use it to control the appearance of a message box they produce. As you can see, they both use the C calling convention, for a little variety. Also, ShowMsgA uses ANSI character strings whereas ShowMsgW uses wide character (Unicode) strings. Here are the original Win32 declarations of the functions in the DLL:

```
procedure ShowMsgA(const Msg, Caption: PAnsiChar); cdecl;
procedure ShowMsgW(const Msg, Caption: PWideChar); cdecl;
```

I named them with A and W suffixes solely because that's the way Win32 APIs that take textual parameters are named. On NT-based platforms (Windows NT/2000/XP/2003), you call whichever version you choose and get the appropriate behavior, whereas on Windows 95–based platforms (Windows 98/Me), the Unicode versions are typically stubs that chain onto the ANSI versions if they do anything at all.

NOTE   In Delphi for Win32, you are typically shielded from this naming convention and can call the API without either letter suffix; for example, you call CreateProcess rather than CreateProcessA or CreateProcessW. Delphi's Windows unit simply maps CreateProcess and similar APIs onto the ANSI version.

You have two options for creating import declarations in this case, both of which require a little explanation to understand fully. The issue arises due to .NET not having the distinction between ANSI and Unicode string encodings. .NET strings are Unicode, period. First, look at this .NET import declaration:

```
procedure ShowMsg(const Msg, Caption: String); cdecl;
  external 'Win32DLL.dll';
```

Notice that it is a single declaration named after the main part of the two DLL routines but without either suffix. However, because of the way Delphi creates the PInvoke declaration, this import this will work fine on all supported Windows platforms. Here is the equivalent attribute version:

```
[DllImport('Win32DLL.dll', CharSet = CharSet.Auto,
  CallingConvention = CallingConvention.Cdecl)]
procedure ShowMsg(const Msg, Caption: String); external;
```

The notable point here is the character marshaling parameter CharSet. The value of Auto causes different things to happen on different Windows platforms. On NT-based platforms it will first try and link to a routine ShowMsgW, and if that is not found it will try to link to ShowMsg and marshal .NET string parameters across as pointers to arrays of Unicode characters. On Windows 95–based platforms, it will first try to link to ShowMsg, and if that is not found it will seek ShowMsgA and marshal strings across as arrays of ANSI characters.

TIP   Using const to mark parameters that will not be changed is a good practice. Delphi marks the parameter with InAttribute when you do this. Similarly out parameters are marked with OutAttribute. Limiting the direction in which parameters travel can help the efficiency of the marshaling process. However, in Win32, nontrivial const parameters (records and arrays) are passed by reference as an implementation detail. This does not happen in .NET with const parameters, so if you want to mark a Win32 parameter as inbound only and to be passed by reference, mark it [In]var, for example: procedure Foo([In]var Rec: MyRecord);.

That's the first approach for calling these Win32 routines, but I mentioned there was another approach available. This allows you to explicitly target either routine and specify exactly which unmanaged type to marshal the strings to. You adorn each parameter of interest with the MarshalAsAttribute attribute, which is also defined in the System.Runtime.InteropServices namespace, passing in a value from the UnmanagedType enumerated type. Here are the implicit declarations specifying LPStr, which represents a pointer to an ANSI string of characters:

```
procedure ShowMsgA(
  [MarshalAs(UnmanagedType.LPStr)]const Msg: String;
  [MarshalAs(UnmanagedType.LPStr)]const Caption: String); cdecl;
  external 'Win32DLL.dll';
procedure ShowMsgW(
  [MarshalAs(UnmanagedType.LPWStr)]const Msg: String;
  [MarshalAs(UnmanagedType.LPWStr)]const Caption: String); cdecl;
  external 'Win32DLL.dll';
```

And here are the explicit ones to match:

```
[DllImport('Win32DLL.dll', CharSet = CharSet.Ansi,
  CallingConvention = CallingConvention.Cdecl)]
procedure ShowMsgA(const Msg, Caption: String); external;
[DllImport('Win32DLL.dll', CharSet = CharSet.Unicode,
  CallingConvention = CallingConvention.Cdecl)]
procedure ShowMsgW(const Msg, Caption: String); external;
```

In these cases, you instruct DllImportAttribute how to marshal all the string parameters it finds using values from the CharSet enumeration.

NOTE   Another member of the CharSet enumeration is None, but this value is obsolete (it was obsolete even in .NET 1.0) and is taken to imply CharSet.Ansi.

The string parameters in the preceding routines are all input parameters, and the target Win32 routines are not expected to modify them. When the Win32 routines expect a character buffer that they are free to fill with appropriate information, a parameter type of String is inappropriate in the .NET PInvoke declaration. This is because a String is an invariant type and does not support having its content changed. In regular .NET code, you can modify a String variable, but behind the scenes a new String is allocated and returned—the old one does not actually get changed, just copied and discarded. Instead of doing this, you should use a System.Text.StringBuilder, which is designed specifically to support acting as an editable string.

The next routine from the Win32 DLL has this signature:

```
function GetUser(Buf: PAnsiChar; var BufLen: Cardinal): Cardinal;
  stdcall;
```

This is designed to get the logged on user through a call to the Win32 GetUserName API. It expects an ANSI text buffer to be passed in that will be filled with the requested user name, whose capacity is passed as the second parameter. On return, the second parameter is updated with the number of characters returned in the buffer (plus one for the null terminator) if successful. Success is identified through the return value that is the Win32 error code from the API (zero means things went well). The appropriate nonattribute .NET import declaration looks like this:

```
function GetUser([MarshalAs(UnmanagedType.LPStr)]Buf: StringBuilder;
  var BufLen: Cardinal): Cardinal; stdcall; external Win32DLL;
```

Using an attribute changes it to this:

```
[DllImport('Win32DLL.dll',
  CallingConvention = CallingConvention.StdCall)]
function GetUser([MarshalAs(UnmanagedType.LPStr)]Buf: StringBuilder;
  var BufLen: Cardinal): Cardinal; external;
```

In the sample PInvoke application, the routine is used like this:

```
procedure TfrmMain.btnUserNameClick(Sender: TObject);
var
  UserName: StringBuilder;
  UserNameLen: Cardinal;
begin
  UserName := StringBuilder.Create(30);
  UserNameLen := UserName.Capacity;
  if GetUser(UserName, UserNameLen) = 0 then
    ShowMsg(UserName.ToString, 'User Name');
end;
```

VIRTUAL LIBRARY INTERFACES (VLI)

The idea behind VLI is twofold. First, it turns individual routines exposed from an unmanaged DLL into methods of a virtual interface that is "implemented" by the unmanaged library. This is good because interfaces support versioning readily by simply defining new interfaces based on old ones with extra methods. Second, the DLL you link to can be more flexibly located. Using PInvoke alone the Win32 DLL must be in one of the usual places: in the executable's directory, in the current directory, in the Windows directory, in the Windows system directory, or on the path. This isn't always convenient. You might want to have the DLL loaded from an application subdirectory. You might even want to choose between a number of different DLLs, perhaps by reading the fully qualified name from a configuration file.

You can achieve this second effect with regular PInvoke but only by explicitly using the Win32 API LoadLibrary (or LoadLibraryEx) in advance of the first call to a routine from the DLL, as demonstrated for Win32 dynamic DLLs in Chapter 11. The technique is sometimes described as dynamic PInvoke. However, the potential for versioning your DLLs through interfaces combined with the fact that the technique may be ported back to Win32 in some future version of Delphi makes VLI a nice approach to accessing unmanaged code.

The VLITest project has a unit called Win32DLLInterface.pas that defines an interface representing the functionality exposed by the Win32 DLL you have been using. Note that the interface needn't include all exposed routines, just those you want represented in the interface. You can see the dedicated LibraryInterfaceAttribute attribute used to communicate calling convention and text parameter marshaling rules.

```
uses
    Borland.Vcl.Win32, System.Runtime.InteropServices, System.Text;

type
  IWin32DLL = interface
    function Min(X, Y: Integer): Integer;
    [LibraryInterface(CallingConvention=CallingConvention.Cdecl,
      CharSet = CharSet.Ansi)]
    procedure ShowMsgA(const Msg, Caption: String);
    [LibraryInterface(CallingConvention=CallingConvention.Cdecl,
      CharSet = CharSet.Unicode)]
    procedure ShowMsgW(const Msg, Caption: String);
    function GetUser(Buf: StringBuilder;
      var BufLen: Cardinal): Cardinal;
  end;
```

To access the DLL routines, you need to define a variable using this type and then use a new version of the Supports function defined in Borland.Vcl.Win32. If all methods in the interface are found in the specified DLL, the passed-in interface reference variable is set up and Supports returns True.

```
var
  DLLStuff: IWin32DLL;
...
  if not Supports('Win32DLL.dll', TypeOf(IWin32DLL), DLLStuff) then
    ShowMessage('Unmanaged DLL not found');
...
  DLLStuff.ShowMsgA('Some message');
```

There are some downsides to VLI. For one, it does not support use of `MarshalAsAttribute` to specify custom marshaling for individual parameters. Indeed, the only attributes supported are the method attribute `SuppressUnmanagedCodeSecurityAttribute` and the parameter attributes `InAttribute` and `OutAttribute`. Additionally, the setup triggered by the `Supports` call is a little slower than a regular PInvoke call, but subsequent calls should be as quick as PInvoke.

Using .NET Objects in COM Clients

Earlier we looked at using COM objects in .NET applications. That is the most common COM Interop scenario, though there is also support for consuming .NET objects in Win32 COM applications. If new functionality is developed in .NET objects, these objects can be exposed in a suitable way to look like regular COM objects and contribute to the extension of an existing COM client application. For this to occur in a meaningful way, steps must be taken to request a special Type Library to be manufactured by .NET. This Type Library describes all the items from a given .NET library assembly that are being made available to COM clients through the COM Interop mechanism.

When a COM client imports the Type Library and creates a COM object described therein, .NET is invoked and uses the information in the Type Library and in the Windows Registry to create wrapper objects to stand in and take care of the differences between the two object models.

INTEROP TYPE LIBRARIES AND COM CALLABLE WRAPPERS (CCWs)

To prepare a managed assembly for consumption in Win32, you need to run it through a registration process. This can be achieved using a command-line utility supplied with Delphi called TRegSvr.exe, which has been extended in Delphi 2005 to handle .NET assembly registration over and above its traditional role of simply registering COM servers.

WARNING The TRegSvr utility dynamically loads a support DLL to perform the .NET Type Library generation and registration. This DLL, TRegAsm.dll was omitted from the product prior to Update Pack 2. If you try to register an assembly with the DLL not present, you will be informed that it failed to load the DLL and so will not do the job. This issue is remedied in Update Pack 2.

This registration process typically creates a Type Library containing descriptions of all the entities that are deemed to be suitable for COM consumption, referred to as an *Interop Type Library*. When a COM client asks COM to instantiate a coclass described in the Interop Type Library, .NET will dynamically create a COM wrapper object that allows access to the .NET class functionality. This wrapper object is called a *COM Callable Wrapper* or *CCW*.

WARNING The Delphi 2005 IDE has another option for importing a .NET assembly into a Win32 project in the guise of COM objects. This registration process is available through the Component ➤ Import Component Wizard by selecting Import .NET Assembly on the first page. However, it seems another glitch made its way into the release product (partially fixed by Update Pack 2). Essentially, the option doesn't work until you install Update Pack 2. After Update Pack 2 has been installed, things are much better but still not quite perfect. The required Interop Type Library is generated and the import unit for it is also created, but the IDE fails to open it and instead opens up the original assembly in the Reflection tool. This final issue is due to a defect in one of the IDE packages, compro90.bpl. This is rectified by an informal update to this package released by R&D member Chris Bensen at `http://blogs.borland.com/cbensen/archive/2005/03/29/3569.aspx`.

REGISTERING ASSEMBLIES WITH THE .NET SDK

The .NET Framework SDK installed with Delphi 2005 supplies its own tools to do the job as well. TlbExp.exe can manufacture a Type Library corresponding to the COM-exposed parts in the assembly. A separate and more useful utility is called RegAsm.exe. This will register the assembly for use with COM, optionally creating and registering a Type Library for you, as in this command line (the /v implies verbose output so you see which types are added to the Interop Type Library):

```
regasm /tlb /v YourAssembly.dll
```

The SDK utilities are not on the path, which is unfortunate. However, the SDK includes a batch file, sdk-vars.bat, in its bin directory. You can set up a shortcut on your desktop or in the Start menu to this batch file, but you have to do it carefully. By default, a batch file will run in a console window that immediately closes on you. To ensure the console window stays open you need to run the command prompt explicitly, passing it first the /K parameter and then the fully qualified batch file name. /K tells the command prompt not to close after running the supplied command. For example, this command line would be suitable for the shortcut, assuming default installation directories:

```
cmd /K "C:\Program Files\Microsoft.NET\SDK\v1.1\Bin\sdkvars.bat"
```

The default situation is that every public member in an assembly will be made visible to a COM client through some entry in the Interop Type Library, which typically isn't desirable. The attribute ComVisibleAttribute can be applied to types to control what will and what will not be exposed, and Delphi 2005 package and library assembly projects include an assembly-wide variant in the project source that sensibly defaults everything to being hidden from COM. The project file also contains a comment that suggests it is good practice when setting up an assembly to be accessed from COM to associate a GUID with the assembly using GuidAttribute, for example:

```
[assembly: ComVisible(False)]
[assembly: Guid('3A8BB32A-B785-460F-80E0-C364292D5584')]
```

Any types you wish to exposed need to be marked with [ComVisible(True)] to have them appear in the Interop Type Library. You should think carefully about specifically which types can be represented in a Type Library and the implications thereof. A Type Library's job is to describe the capabilities of a COM server, and COM works by making functionality accessible through interfaces. In other words, type libraries can contain descriptions of interfaces but not classes. If you built a number of classes that you want accessed from COM, it is important to consider how they will be accessed through interfaces.

By default, an exposed class Foo will have a coclass Foo defined in the Interop Type Library, implementing an interface _Foo. However, this interface is a memberless dispinterface that forces clients to use late-bound Automation to access any members. Indeed, if you registered your assembly using the .NET SDK's RegAsm tool without specifying the /tlb command-line switch, your assembly would be registered for use by COM clients without a Type Library manufactured. This is effectively the same situation as the functionality exposed by the assembly only being able to be accessed through Automation.

A better situation is obtained by marking your classes with ClassInterfaceAttribute. Without this attribute, the default value of ClassInterfaceType.AutoDispatch is assumed, which clearly does not help regular early bound COM programs be written against the .NET code. A potentially tempting value to choose is ClassInterfaceType.AutoDual, as this will add an IDispatch-based dual interface to the Interop Type Library containing all public members of the class. This will indeed allow COM clients to use the class via this manufactured interface; however, there are issues with this approach. Each time you modify your class and regenerate the Interop Type Library, the interface will be regenerated. Minor tweaks to the class will mean the interface definition will change, which breaks one of the cardinal rules of interfaces: once an interface has been defined and is in use, never change the interface definition or you break the code using it.

A better option is to define your own interface representing the functionality you want exposed and implement that interface in the class. You can then use the attribute value ClassInterfaceType .None on the class itself to ensure no automatic interface is generated from it, and you can then mark your own interface as visible to COM. This will also necessitate defining an interface identifier GUID in your interface, either using traditional Delphi syntax or again using GuidAttribute. Note that you can also add a GuidAttribute to your class that will fix the GUID associated with the coclass in the Interop Type Library. If you don't do this you may get different ClsIDs each time you regenerate the Type Library. The same applies to the assembly as a whole; you can apply an assembly-wide GUID to fix the Type Library's LibID value. In fact, there is a commented GuidAtribute in the project source waiting for you to do this.

WARNING Microsoft advises against using ClassInterfaceType.AutoDual as a value for Class-InterfaceAttribute on a class due to the inherent versioning issues of the auto-generated interface. Instead the recommended approach is to mark the class with ClassInterfaceType.None and implement an interface explicitly, which is made visible to COM.

To show you the steps required to get CCWs up and running, I made a simple .NET package project in the CCWTest directory called DotNetAssembly, which naturally generates an assembly called DotNetAssembly.dll. This contains a simple class Calc implemented in the Math namespace (thanks to being in a unit called Math.Utils) that performs various mathematical operations through its methods. All these methods are defined in an interface ICalc, which is implemented by the Calc class.

```
[ComVisible(True), Guid('9DB66430-5DC4-45E4-AD3C-D2D9375D6D87')]
ICalc = interface
  function Square(Num: Double): Double;
  function SquareRoot(Num: Double): Double;
  function Cube(Num: Double): Double;
  function CubeRoot(Num: Double): Double;
end;

[ClassInterface(ClassInterfaceType.None)]
[ComVisible(True)]
Calc = class(&Object, ICalc)
protected
  function Square(Num: Double): Double;
  function SquareRoot(Num: Double): Double;
  function Cube(Num: Double): Double;
  function CubeRoot(Num: Double): Double;
end;
```

Note the variety of syntax for marking a type with more than one attribute. You can either have a comma-separated list of attributes within a single set of square brackets or put individual attributes in their own square bracket pairs.

To register the assembly, you pass it to TRegSvr (assuming you have installed Update Pack 2; otherwise use RegAsm as described in the sidebar earlier):

```
tregsvr DotNetAssembly.dll
```

Now the assembly is registered and looks like any other COM server. You can see some of the Registry entries added by the registration process for the COM object in Figure 12.9. Notice that there is no path for the assembly name; it is just listed as the full name. As is usual with .NET, the assembly is assumed to be in the current directory or in the GAC. Also notice that the actual file specified as the in-proc server for this registered COM object is the main CLR DLL, mscoree.dll. When a COM object is requested, COM passes the request to mscoree.dll, which checks back in the Registry to see which assembly it is working with. It also looks up the Type Library and uses the information there to dynamically create CCWs.

The next step is to import this "COM server" into a regular Win32 project, such as the CCWTest project. As you saw earlier in the section on Automation, you import type libraries with Component ➤ Import Component. Once you've selected the Type Library and proceeded through the pages of the wizard, you can request the generated Type Library import unit to be added to your project as usual and then use the CCW like any other COM object.

```
procedure TfrmMain.btnCalcClick(Sender: TObject);
var
  Calc: ICalc;
  Num: Double;
begin
  Calc := CoCalc.Create;
  Num := StrToFloatDef(edtNum.Text, 0);
  edtSquare.Text := FloatToStr(Calc.Square(Num));
  edtSquareRoot.Text := FloatToStr(Calc.SquareRoot(Num));
  edtCube.Text := FloatToStr(Calc.Cube(Num));
  edtCubeRoot.Text := FloatToStr(Calc.CubeRoot(Num));
end;
```

FIGURE 12.9

A .NET assembly registered for COM use

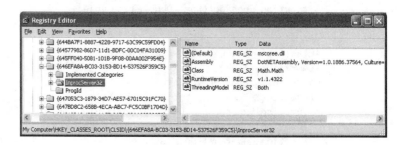

MARSHALASATTRIBUTE

If the .NET data types are not marshaled across to the right COM types, you can take control by applying `MarshalAsAttribute` to any parameters that need attention. You can also control the marshaling of function return values, but it is not obvious how. The obvious approach, based on how attributes are placed, simply causes compiler errors. For example, suppose you have a function that returns an Integer. However, you only need a COM client to see if the value is zero or nonzero, which is the typical implementation of the C bool data type. You could declare the method like this:

```
[result: MarshalAs(UnmanagedType.Bool)]
function Foo: Integer;
```

Using .NET Routines in Win32 Applications

This last interoperability permutation is probably the least useful when compared to the others, but it can still be usefully employed from time to time. The idea here is that you can write some logic in a .NET assembly, specifically a Delphi 2005 library project, and make that functionality available to Win32 applications through *managed exports*. A managed export is a way of taking a global routine (which, you may recall from Chapter 4 is not technically a global routine, but instead a static method of unit wrapper classes) and exporting it from the assembly to look like a regular DLL export. A Win32 application containing a suitable import declaration can call the routine and gain direct access to the functionality.

This is a technically admirable feat inasmuch as there are several steps that occur when the routine is called. If it is the first time the managed export has been called, some magic occurs behind the scenes to instantiate a CLR session within your process, loading up the standard .NET infrastructure so the assembly can be successfully used. After that the typical marshaling requirement and switching between managed and unmanaged code happens. Internally, the latter parts use the same infrastructure as the PInvoke mechanism but going in the other direction, which is why this technique is sometimes called *Inverse PInvoke*.

If you've ever written a Win32 DLL, you already know most of the syntax you need to create managed exports in a DLL since the exporting aspect is just the same as what you are used to. The key point to add is that when a .NET library assembly exports static methods in this way it automatically becomes unverifiable and requires you to assert your intention to generate unsafe code as discussed back in Chapter 4.

NOTE Unmanaged exports are supported only from Library projects. Generally, when building what are technically called library assemblies (.NET DLLs) you will actually create a Package project in Delphi 2005. Delphi Library projects are typically advised against for general use unless you are creating an ASP.NET application, which will always reside in a Library project. Their use outside of ASP.NET is intended just to host unmanaged exports.

This is a listing of a simple .NET library assembly that makes the trivial Max function available to Win32 applications. The sample project MEClient makes a call to this routine to prove the point.

```
library ManagedLibrary;

{$UNSAFECODE ON}

function Max(Val1, Val2: Integer): Integer;
begin
  if Val1 > Val2 then
    Result := Val1
  else
    Result := Val2
end;

exports
  Max;

begin
end.
```

What's Next?

In this chapter, I discussed applications of Microsoft's COM technology, including Automation. You saw how Delphi makes the development of Automation servers and clients reasonably simple. Delphi even enables you to wrap components around Automation servers, such as Word and Excel. We also looked at the support offered by .NET for mixing managed and unmanaged code together in a system through the various interoperability options that cater to reusing COM objects and unmanaged DLLs in .NET systems and .NET code in current Win32 systems.

I mentioned that if COM still has a key role in Windows, future versions of Microsoft's operating systems will downplay its role to push the .NET infrastructure. This is particularly true for Distributed COM (DCOM), which is being replaced by .NET remoting and even more by the use of SOAP and XML. But you'll have to wait until Chapter 23 for a complete discussion of Delphi SOAP support.

In the following chapters, in fact, we will focus on entirely different topics, namely the use of databases in Delphi applications and the development of client/server and multitier systems. This is an important area of Delphi programming, so you'll see a number of chapters on the topic that will include both VCL solutions (for both Win32 and .NET) and FCL solutions.

Part 3

Delphi Database-Oriented Architectures

In this section:

Chapter 13

Delphi's Database Architecture

Delphi's support for database applications is one of the programming environment's key features. Many programmers spend most of their time writing data-access code, which needs to be the most robust portion of a database application. This chapter provides an overview of Delphi's extensive support for database programming.

What you *won't* find in this chapter is a discussion of the theory of database design. I'm assuming that you already know the fundamentals of database design and have already designed the structure of a database. I won't delve into database-specific problems; my goal is to help you understand how Delphi supports database access.

I'll begin with an explanation of the alternatives Delphi offers in terms of data access, and then I'll provide an overview of the database components available in Delphi. This chapter focuses on the use of the TClientDataSet component for accessing local data; I'll defer all the client/server database access information to Chapter 14. Here I'll include an overview of the TDataSet class, an in-depth analysis of the TField components, and the use of data-aware controls. Chapter 14 follows up by providing information about more advanced database programming topics, particularly client/server programming with the use of the dbExpress library (and the InterBase Express components).

Finally, notice that almost everything discussed in this chapter is cross-platform. In particular, the examples can be ported to .NET by recompiling them. However, as this section focuses on Delphi's specific database architecture, I'll delay the coverage of the .NET standard data access technology (ADO.NET) until Chapter 16. To better understand this decision, consider that data access technologies and visual component architectures are strictly bound. You'll tend to use ADO.NET in WinForms programs and use Delphi's native database components with VCL applications.

This chapter covers Delphi's database components, database access alternatives, the use of data-aware controls, the DBGrid control, manipulating table fields, and database applications with standard controls.

Accessing a Database in Win32: dbExpress, Local Data, and Other Alternatives

The early incarnations of Delphi—immediately adopted as a tool for building database-oriented applications—could access a database only by means of the Borland Database Engine (BDE). Starting with Delphi 3, the portion of VCL related to database access was restructured to open it up to multiple database access solutions, which on Win32 currently include ADO, native InterBase components, the dbExpress library, and the BDE. On .NET all of these solutions are still available, plus you can use ADO.NET. There are also many third-party vendors that offer alternative database access mechanisms to a variety of data formats and still provide a solution integrated with Delphi's VCL, either directly or by extending the dbExpress technology with custom drivers.

TIP In .NET (specifically in ADO.NET) it is Borland that extends the standard technology with the Borland Data Provider (BDP). More on this topic and a broad discussion of data access alternatives in Delphi for .NET in Chapter 16. Notice also that in Kylix, Borland decided not to port the old BDE technology and focused instead only on dbExpress.

As a further solution, for simple applications you can use Delphi's ClientDataSet component, which has the ability to save tables to local files—something Borland touts with the name MyBase. Of course, you can still use the *outdated* BDE technology and use local Paradox or dBase tables, given that you can keep using these also on .NET.

The dbExpress Library

One of the most relevant new features of Delphi in recent years has been the introduction of the db-Express database library (DBX). I say *library* and not *database engine* because, unlike other solutions, dbExpress uses a lightweight approach and requires basically no configuration on end-user machines.

Being light and portable are the two key characteristics of dbExpress; Borland introduced it for those reasons. Compared to other powerhouses, dbExpress is very limited in its capabilities. It can access only SQL servers (no local files); it has no caching capabilities and provides only unidirectional access to the data; and it can natively work only with SQL queries and is unable to generate the corresponding SQL update statements.

At first, you might think these limitations make the library useless. On the contrary: these are *features* that make it interesting. Unidirectional datasets with no direct update are the norm if you need to produce reports, including generating HTML pages showing the content of a database. If you want to build a user interface to edit the data, however, Delphi includes specific components (the Client-DataSet and DataSetProvider, in particular) that provide caching and query resolution. These components allow your dbExpress-based application much more control than a separate (monolithic) database engine, which does extra things for you but often does them the way it wants to, not the way you would like.

dbExpress allows you to write an application that, aside from problems with different SQL dialects, can access many different database engines without much code modification. Supported RBDMSs include Borland's own InterBase database, Oracle database server, MySQL database (which is popular particularly on Linux), IBM Informix database, IBM's DB2, Microsoft SQL Server, SQL Anywhere, and Sybase. A more detailed description of dbExpress, the related VCL components, and many examples of its use will be provided in Chapter 14; the current chapter focuses on database architecture foundations.

The Borland Database Engine

Delphi still ships with the BDE, which allows you to access local database formats (like Paradox and dBase) as well as anything accessible through ODBC drivers. This was the standard database technology in early versions of Delphi, but Borland now considers it *obsolete*. This is particularly true for the use of the BDE to access SQL servers through the SQL Links drivers, which do not ship anymore with the product. Using the BDE to access local tables is still officially supported, simply because

Borland doesn't provide a direct migration path for this type of application. The.NET version of the BDE supports local tables only: the SQL Link drivers are not available.

In some cases, a local table can be replaced with the ClientDataSet component (MyBase) specifically for temporary and lookup tables. However, this approach won't work for larger local tables (hundreds of megabytes in size), because MyBase requires the entire table to be loaded in memory to access even a single record. The solution to this problem is to move larger tables to an database server installed on the client computer and then run a query to get the subset of data you require avoiding to waste memory space. InterBase, with its small footprint, is ideal in this particular situation.

Of course, if you have existing applications that use the BDE, you can continue using them. The BDE page of Delphi's Component Palette still has the Table, Query, StoredProc, and other BDE-specific components. I'd discourage you from developing new programs with this old technology, which is almost discontinued by its producer. Eventually, you should look to third-party engines to replace the BDE when your programs require a similar architecture (or you need compatibility with older database file formats).

InterBase Express

Borland has made available another set of database access components for Delphi: InterBase Express (IBX). These components are specifically tailored to Borland's own InterBase server. Unlike dbExpress, this is not a server-independent database engine, but a set of components for accessing a specific database server. If you plan to use only InterBase as your back-end database, using a specific set of components can give you more control over the server, provide the best performance, and allow you to configure and maintain the server from within a custom client application.

NOTE   The use of InterBase Express highlights the case of database-specific custom datasets, which are available from third-party vendors for many servers. (There are other dataset components for InterBase, just as there are for Oracle, local or shared dBase files, and many others.)

You can consider using IBX (or other comparable sets of components) if you are sure you won't change your database and you want to achieve the best performance and control at the expense of flexibility and portability. The down side is that the extra performance and control you gain may be limited. You'll also have to learn to use another set of components with a specific behavior, rather than learn to use a generic engine and apply your knowledge to different situations.

MyBase and the ClientDataSet Component

The ClientDataSet is a dataset that accesses data kept in memory. The in-memory data can be temporary (created by the program and lost as you exit it), loaded from a local file and then saved back to it, or imported by another dataset using a DataSetProvider component.

Borland uses the term *MyBase* to indicate the use of the ClientDataSet component mapped to a local file and that it can be considered a local database solution. I have trouble with the way Borland marketing has promoted this technology, but it has a place, as I'll discuss in the section "MyBase: Stand-Alone ClientDataSet."

Accessing data from a provider is a common approach both for client/server architectures (as you'll see in Chapter 14) and for multitier architectures (discussed in Chapter 17). The ClientDataSet component becomes particularly useful if the data-access components you are using provide limited or no caching, which is the case with the dbExpress engine.

dbGo for ADO

ADO (ActiveX Data Objects) is Microsoft's high-level interface for database access on Win32. ADO is implemented on Microsoft's data-access OLE DB technology, which provides access to relational and nonrelational databases as well as e-mail and file systems and custom business objects. ADO is an engine with features comparable to those of the BDE: database server independence supporting local and SQL servers alike, a heavyweight engine, and a simplified configuration (because it is not centralized). Installation should (in theory) not be an issue, because the engine is part of recent versions of Windows. However, the limited compatibility among versions of ADO will force you to upgrade your users' computers to the same version you used for developing the program. The size of the MDAC (Microsoft Data Access Components) installation, some compatibility problems, and the particular fact that it cannot be easily uninstalled, makes this operation far from trivial.

ADO offers definite advantages if you plan to use Access or SQL Server, because Microsoft's drivers for its own databases are of better quality than the average OLE DB providers. For Access databases, specifically, using Delphi's ADO components is a good solution. If you plan to use an database server other than SQL Server, first check the availability of a good-quality driver, or you might have some surprises. ADO is very powerful, but you have to learn to live with it—it stands between your program and the database, providing services but occasionally also issuing different commands than you may expect. On the negative side, do not even think of using ADO if you plan on future cross-platform development; this Microsoft-specific technology is not available on Linux or other operating systems.

In short, use ADO if you plan to work only on Windows, want to use Access or other Microsoft databases, or find a good OLE DB provider for each of the database servers you plan to work with (at the moment, this factor excludes InterBase and many other SQL servers).

ADO components (part of a package Borland calls dbGo) are grouped in the ADO page of the Component Palette. The three core components are ADOConnection (for database connections), ADOCommand (for executing SQL commands), and ADODataSet (for executing requests that return a result set). There are also three compatibility components—ADOTable, ADOQuery, and ADOStoredProc—that you can use to port BDE-based applications to ADO. Finally, the RDSConnection component lets you access data in remote multitier applications.

NOTE   ADO components were missing in Delphi 8 for .NET, but have been reintroduced in the .NET version of Delphi 2005 and are also still available on the Win32 version. Chapter 15 covers ADO and related technologies in detail.

Custom Dataset Components

As further alternatives, you can write your own custom dataset components or choose one of the many offerings available. Developing custom dataset components is one of the most complex issues of Delphi programming; I've covered it in past advanced Delphi books.

MyBase: Stand-Alone ClientDataSet

If you want to write a single-user database application in Delphi, the simplest approach is to use the ClientDataSet component and map it to a local file. This local file mapping is different from the traditional data mapping to a local file. The traditional approach is to read from the file a record at a time and possibly have a second file that stores indexes. The ClientDataSet maps an entire table (and possibly a master/detail structure) to the file in its entirety: when a program starts, the entire file is loaded in memory, and later everything is saved at once.

WARNING This explains why you cannot use this approach in a multiuser or multiapplication situation. If two programs or two instances of the same program load the same ClientDataSet file in memory and modify the data, the last table saved will overwrite changes made by other programs.

This support for persisting the content of a ClientDataSet was created a few years ago as a way to implement the so-called briefcase model. A user could (and still can) download data from its database server to the client, save some of the data, work disconnected (while traveling with a laptop computer, for example), and finally reconnect to commit the changes.

ADO.NET

Building on some of the ideas of ADO and fixing its limitations, Microsoft has a new data access technology in .NET, called ADO.NET. This is a highly flexible architecture comprising data access components and dataset management components, somehow similar to the combination of a ClientDataSet with the dbExpress components. This is so similar that the dbExpress drivers have been extended by Borland to be integrated in ADO.NET. They are part of an ADO.NET plug-in module indicated with the BDP acronym, for Borland Data Provider. As you'll see, WinForm controls bind directly to the ADO.NET data model (in WinForms, in fact, all controls are automatically data aware). This is not the case for VCL controls, nor is it the case for WinForm controls or (say) the ClientDataSet component because there is a natural fit of visual libraries with their data access technologies. Still, it is possible to mix solutions, for example using a special Delphi dataset that allows you to access to an ADO.NET dataset table. Chapter 16 covers ADO.NET in detail, including how to use ADO.NET from a VCL.NET application.

Connecting to an Existing Local Table

To map a ClientDataSet to a local file, you set its FileName property. To build a minimal program (called MyBase1 in the example), all you need is a ClientDataSet component hooked to a CDS file (there are a few in the Data folder available under \Program Files\Common Files\Borland Shared), a DataSource (more on this later), and a DBGrid control. Hook the ClientDataSet to the DataSource via the DataSource's DataSet property and the DataSource to the DBGrid via the grid's DataSource property, as in Listing 13.1. At this point turn on the Active property of the ClientDataSet and you'll have a program showing database data even at design time; see Figure 13.1.

As you make changes and close the application, the data will be automatically saved to the file. (You might want to disable the change log, as discussed later, to reduce the size of this data.) The dataset also has a SaveToFile method and a LoadFromFile method you can use in your code.

I also made another change: I disabled the ClientDataSet at design time to avoid including all of its data in the program's DFM file and in the compiled executable file; I want to keep the data in a separate file. To do this, close the dataset at design time after testing and add a line to the form's OnCreate event to open it:

```
procedure TForm1.FormCreate(Sender: TObject);
begin
  cds.Open;
end;
```

LISTING 13.1:   The DFM file of the MyBase1 sample program

```
object Form1: TForm1
  ActiveControl = DBGrid1
  Caption = 'MyBase1'
  OnCreate = FormCreate
  object DBGrid1: TDBGrid
    DataSource = DataSource1
  end
  object DataSource1: TDataSource
    DataSet = cds
  end
  object cds: TClientDataSet
    FileName = 'C:\...\Borland Shared\Data\customer.cds'
  end
end
```

From the MIDAS DLL to the MidasLib Unit

To run any application using the ClientDataSet component, you need to also deploy the `midas.dll` dynamic library referenced by the `DSIntf.pas` unit. The ClientDataSet component's core code is not directly part of the VCL and is not available in source code format. This is unfortunate, because many developers are accustomed to debugging the VCL source code and using it as the ultimate reference.

WARNING   The `midas.dll` library has no version number in its name. If a computer has an older version, your program will apparently run on it, but it may not behave properly.

FIGURE 13.1
A sample local table active at design time in the Delphi IDE

The MIDAS library is a C++-language library, but it can be bound directly into an executable by including the specific MidasLib unit (a special DCU assembled by Borland with compiled C/C++ code). In this case you won't need to distribute the library in the DLL format. This technique is available only in the Win32 personality of Delphi, not in the .NET one.

XML and CDS Formats

The ClientDataSet component supports two different streaming formats: the native format and an XML-based format. The `Borland Shared\Data` folder mentioned earlier holds versions of a number of tables in each of the two formats. By default, MyBase saves the datasets in CDS format, unless the extension of the file specified in the `FileName` property is .XML. The `SaveToFile` method has a parameter allowing you to specify the format, and the `LoadFromFile` method works automatically for both formats.

Using the XML format has the advantage of making the persistent data also accessible with an editor and with other programs not based on the ClientDataSet component. However, this approach implies converting the data back and forth, because the CDS format is close to the internal memory representation invariably used by the component, regardless of the streaming format. Also, the XML format generates large files because they are text based. On average, a MyBase XML file is twice the size of the corresponding CDS file.

TIP   While you have a ClientDataSet in memory, you can extract its XML representation by using the `XMLData` property without streaming out the data. The next example puts this technique into practice.

Defining a New Local Table

In addition to letting you hook to an existing database table stored in a local file, the ClientDataSet component allows you to create new tables easily. All you have to do is use its `FieldDefs` property to define the structure of the table. After doing this, you can physically create the file for the table with the Create DataSet command on the ClientDataSet component's shortcut menu in the Delphi IDE or by calling its `CreateDataSet` method at run time.

This is an extract from the MyBase2 example's DFM file, which defines a new local database table:

```
object ClientDataSet1: TClientDataSet
  FileName = 'mybase2.cds'
  FieldDefs = <
    item
      Name = 'one'
      DataType = ftString
      Size = 20
    end
    item
      Name = 'two'
      DataType = ftSmallint
    end>
  StoreDefs = True
end
```

Notice the `StoreDefs` property, which is automatically set to True when you edit the collection of field definitions. By default, a dataset in Delphi loads its metadata before opening. Only if a local definition is stored in the DFM file is this local metadata used (saving field definitions in the DFM file is also helpful to cache this metadata in a client/server architecture).

To account for the optional dataset creation, the disabling of the log (described later), and the display of the XML version of the initial data in a Memo control, the program's form class has the following `OnCreate` event handler:

```
procedure TForm1.FormCreate(Sender: TObject);
begin
  if not FileExists (cds.FileName) then
    cds.CreateDataSet;
  cds.Open;
  cds.MergeChangeLog;
  cds.LogChanges := False;
  Memo1.Lines.Text := StringReplace (
    cds.XMLData, '>', '>' + sLineBreak, [rfReplaceAll]);
end;
```

The last statement includes a call to `StringReplace` to provide a poor man's XML formatting: The code adds a new line at the end of each XML tag by adding a new line after the close angle bracket. You can see the table's XML display with a few records in Figure 13.2. You'll learn a lot more about XML in Delphi in Chapter 22.

Indexing

Once you have a ClientDataSet in memory, you can perform many operations on it. The simplest are indexing, filtering, and searching for records; more complex operations include grouping, defining aggregate values, and managing the change log. Here I'll cover only the simplest techniques; more complex material appears at the end of the chapter.

FIGURE 13.2

The XML display of a CDS file in the MyBase2 example. The table structure is defined by the program, which creates a file for the dataset on its first execution.

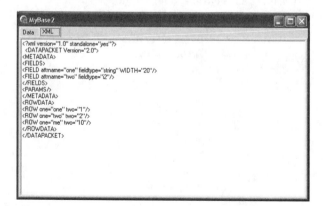

Indexing a ClientDataSet is a matter of setting the IndexFieldNames property. This is often accomplished when the user clicks the field title in a DBGrid component (firing the OnTitleClick event), as in the MyBase2 example:

```
procedure TForm1.DBGrid1TitleClick(Column: TColumn);
begin
  cds.IndexFieldNames := Column.Field.FieldName;
end;
```

Unlike other local databases, a ClientDataSet can have this type of dynamic index without any database configuration because indexes are computed in memory.

TIP   The component also supports indexes based on a calculated field, specifically an internally calculated field, available only for this dataset (as I'll describe later in this chapter). Unlike ordinary calculated fields, which are computed every time the record is used, values of internally calculated fields are calculated once and kept in memory. For this reason, indexes consider them plain fields.

In addition to assigning a new value to the IndexFieldNames property, you can define an index using the IndexDefs property. Doing so allows you to define several indexes and keep them in memory, switching from one to the other with a single line of code. Defining a separate index is also the only way to have a descending index, rather than an ascending index.

Filtering

As with any other dataset, you can use the Filter property to specify the inclusion in the dataset of portions of the data the component is bound to. The filtering operation takes place in memory after loading all the records, so this is a way to present less data to the user, not to limit the memory footprint of a large local dataset.

When you're working with a large amount of data, filtering locally with a ClientDataSet is far from an optimal choice. When you work in a client/server architecture, you should reduce the amount of data you work with by setting up a proper SQL query. Filtering up front in the server should generally be your first choice. With local data, you might consider splitting a large number of records into a set of different files, so you can load only those you need and not all of them.

Local filtering in the ClientDataSet can be useful, particularly because the filter expressions you can use with this component are much more extensive than those you can use with other datasets. In particular, you can use the following:

◆ The standard comparison and logical operators: for example, Population > 1000 and Area < 1000

◆ Arithmetic operators: for example, Population / Area < 10

◆ String functions: for example, Substring(Last_Name, 1, 2) = 'Ca'

◆ Date and time functions: for example, Year (Invoice_Date) = 2002

◆ Others, including a Like function, wildcards, and an In operator

These filtering capabilities are fully documented in the VCL Help file. You should look for the Filter property of the TClientDataSet class.

Locating Records

Filtering allows you to limit the records displayed to the program's user, but many times you want to display all the records and only move to a specific one. The Locate method does this. If you've never used Locate, at first sight the Help file won't be terribly clear. The idea is that you must provide a list of fields you want to search and a list of values, one for each field. If you want to match only one field, the value is passed directly, as in this case (where the search string is in the EditName component):

```
procedure TForm1.btnLocateClick(Sender: TObject);
begin
  if not cds.Locate ('LastName', EditName.Text, []) then
    MessageDlg ('"' + EditName.Text + '" not found', mtError, [mbOk], 0);
end;
```

If you search for multiple fields, you have to pass a variant array with the list of values you want to match. The variant array can be created from a constant array with the VarArrayOf function or from scratch using the VarArrayCreate call. This is a code snippet:

```
cds.Locate ('LastName;FirstName', VarArrayOf (['Cook', 'Kevin']), []);
```

Finally, you can use the same method to look for a record even if you know only the initial portion of the field you are looking for. All you have to do is to add the loPartialKey flag to the Options set parameter (the third) of the Locate call.

NOTE   Using Locate makes sense when you're working with a local table, but it doesn't port well to client/server applications. On a SQL server, similar client-side techniques imply moving all the data to the client application first (which is generally a bad idea) and then searching for a specific record. You should locate the data with restricted SQL statements. You can still call Locate after you retrieve a limited dataset. For example, you can search for a customer by name after you select all the customers of a given town or area, obtaining a result set of a limited size. There's more about this topic in Chapter 14, which is devoted to client/server development.

UNDO AND *SAVEPOINT*

As a user modifies the data in a ClientDataSet component, the updates are stored in a memory area called the delta. The reason for keeping track of user changes instead of holding the resulting table is due to the way the updates are handled in a client/server architecture. In this case, the program doesn't have to send the entire table back to the server, only a list of the user's changes (by means of specific SQL statements, as you'll see in Chapter 14).

Because the ClientDataSet component keeps track of changes, you can reject those changes, removing entries from the delta. The component has an UndoLastChange method to accomplish this. The method's FollowChange parameter allows you to *follow* the undo operation—the client dataset will move to the record that has been restored by the undo operation. Here is the code you can use to connect to an Undo button:

```
procedure TForm1.ButtonUndoClick(Sender: TObject);
begin
  cds.UndoLastChange (True);
end;
```

An extension of the undo support is the possibility of saving a sort of bookmark of the change log position (the current status) and restoring it later by undoing all successive changes. You can use the SavePoint property either to save the number of changes in the log or to reset the log to a past situation. However, you can only remove records from the change log, not reinsert changes. In other words, the SavePoint property refers to a position in a log, so it can only go back to a position where there were fewer records! This log position is a number of changes, so if you save the current position, undo some changes, and then do more edits, you won't be able to get back to the position you bookmarked.

TIP   Since Delphi 7, there has been a standard action mapped to the ClientDataSet's undo operation. Other recent actions include Revert and Apply, which you'll need when the component is connected to a dataset accessing a database.

ENABLING AND DISABLING LOGGING

Keeping track of changes makes sense if you need to send the updated data back to a server database. In local applications with data stored to a MyBase file, keeping this log around can become useless and consume memory. For this reason, you can disable logging with the LogChanges property. This will also stop the undo operations, though.

You can also call the MergeChangesLog method to remove all current editing from the change log and confirm the edits performed so far. Doing so makes sense if you want to keep the undo log around within a single session and then save the final dataset without the keeping the change log.

NOTE   The MyBase2 example disables the change log as discussed here: you can remove that code and re-enable it to see the difference in the size of the CDS file and in the XML text after editing the data.

Using Data-Aware Controls

Once you set up the proper data-access components, you can build a user interface to let a user view the data and eventually edit it. Delphi provides many components that resemble the usual controls but are data-aware. For example, the DBEdit component is similar to the Edit component, and the DBCheckBox component corresponds to the CheckBox component. You can find all these components in the Data Controls page of the Delphi Component Palette.

All these components are connected to a data source using the corresponding property DataSource. Some of them relate to the entire dataset, such as the DBGrid and DBNavigator components, and the others refer to a specific field of the data source, as indicated by the DataField property. Once you select the DataSource property, the DataField property editor will contain a list of available values.

Notice that all the data-aware components are unrelated to the data-access technology, provided the data-access component inherits from TDataSet. Thus your investment in the user interface is preserved when you change the data-access technology. However, some of the lookup components and extended use of the DBGrid (displaying a lot of data) make sense only when you're working with local data and should generally be avoided in a client/server situation, as you'll see in Chapter 14.

Data in a Grid

The DBGrid is a grid capable of displaying a whole table at once. It allows scrolling and navigation, and you can edit the grid's contents. It is an extension of the other Delphi grid controls. New to Delphi 2005 is DBGrid's support for mouse wheel operations, which in the past was totally lacking. In the new version of the VCL the grid manages mouse wheel events and also surfaces corresponding events.

You can customize the DBGrid by setting its `Options` property's various flags and modifying its `Columns` collection. The grid allows a user to navigate the data using the scrollbars as well as to perform all the major actions. A user can edit the data directly, insert a new record in a given position by pressing the Insert key, append a new record at the end by going to the last record and pressing the Down arrow key, and delete the current record by pressing Ctrl+Del.

The `Columns` property is a collection from which you can choose the table fields you want to see in the grid and set column and title properties (color, font, width, alignment, caption, and so on) for each field. Some of the more advanced properties, such as `ButtonStyle` and `DropDownRows`, can be used to provide custom editors for a grid's cells or a drop-down list of values (indicated in the column's `PickList` property).

DBNavigator and Dataset Actions

DBNavigator is a collection of buttons used to navigate and perform actions on the database. You can disable some of the DBNavigator control's buttons by removing some of the elements of the `VisibleButtons` set property.

The buttons perform basic actions on the connected dataset, so you can easily replace them with your own toolbar, particularly if you use an ActionList component with the predefined database actions provided by Delphi. In this case, you get all the standard behaviors and you'll also see the various buttons enabled only when their action is legitimate, as with the DBNavigator. The advantages of using the actions are that you can display the buttons in the layout you prefer, intermix them with other buttons of the application, and use multiple client controls, including main and pop-up menus.

TIP   If you use the standard actions, you can avoid connecting them to a specific DataSource component, and the actions will be applied to the dataset connected to the visual control that currently has the input focus. This way, a single toolbar can be used for multiple datasets displayed by a form, which can be very confusing to the user if not considered carefully.

Text-Based Data-Aware Controls

There are multiple text-oriented components:

DBText   Displays the contents of a field that cannot be modified by the user. It is a data-aware Label graphical control. It can be very useful, but users might confuse this control with the plain labels that indicate the content of each field-based control.

DBEdit   Lets the user edit a field (change the current value) using an Edit control. At times, you might want to disable editing and use a DBEdit as if it were a DBText but highlight the fact that this is data coming from the database.

DBMemo   Lets the user see and modify a large text field, eventually stored in a memo or BLOB (binary large object) field.

DBRichEdit Lets the user work with an RTF document, a fully formatted text generally saved in a BLOB field in the database. When you want to handle and display real text documents, this is often much better than using a DBMemo, which allows you to display the text only in a single font and supports no formatting options at all.

List-Based Data-Aware Controls

To let a user choose a value in a predefined list (which reduces input errors), you can use many different components. DBListBox, DBComboBox, and DBRadioGroup are similar, providing a list of strings in the Items property, but they do have some differences:

DBListBox Allows selection of predefined items (*closed selection*), but not text input, and can be used to list many elements. Generally it's best to show only about six or seven items to avoid using up too much space on the screen.

DBComboBox Can be used both for closed selection and for user input. The csDropDown style of the DBComboBox allows a user to enter a new value, in addition to selecting one of the available values. The component also uses a smaller area on the form because the drop-down list is usually displayed only on request.

DBRadioGroup Presents radio buttons (which permit only one selection), allows only closed selection, and should be used only for a limited number of alternatives. A nice feature of this component is that the values displayed can be those you want to insert in the database, but you can also choose to provide mapping. The values of the user interface (descriptive strings stored in the Items property) will map to corresponding values stored in the database (numeric or character-based codes listed in the Values property). For example, you can map numeric codes indicating departments to a few descriptive strings:

```
object DBRadioGroup1: TDBRadioGroup
  Caption = 'Department'
  DataField = 'Department'
  DataSource = DataSource1
  Items.Strings = (
    'Sales'
    'Accounting'
    'Production'
    'Management')
  Values.Strings = (
    '1'
    '2'
    '3'
    '4')
end
```

The DBCheckBox component is slightly different; it is used to show and toggle an option, corresponding to a Boolean field. It is a limited list because it has only two possible values plus the undetermined state for fields with null values. You can determine which are the values to send back to the database by setting the ValueChecked and ValueUnchecked properties of this component.

THE DBAWARE EXAMPLE

The DbAware example highlights the usage of a DBRadioGroup control with the settings discussed in the previous section and a DBCheckBox control. This example is not much more complex than earlier ones, but it has a form with field-oriented data-aware controls instead of a grid encompassing them all. You can see the example's form at design time in Figure 13.3.

As in the MyBase2 program, the application defines its own table structure, using the `FieldDefs` collection property of the ClientDataSet. Table 13.1 provides a short summary of the fields defined.

The program has some code to fill in the table with random values. This code is tedious and not too complex, so I won't discuss the details here, but you can look at the DbAware source code if you are interested.

Using Lookup Controls

If the list of values is extracted from another dataset, then instead of the DBListBox and DBComboBox controls you should use the specific DBLookupListBox or DBLookupComboBox components. These components are used every time you want to select a value for a field that corresponds to a record of another dataset (and not choose a different record to display!).

TABLE 13.1: The Dataset Fields in the DbAware Example

NAME	DATATYPE	SIZE
LastName	ftString	20
FirstName	ftString	20
Department	FtSmallint	
Branch	ftString	20
Senior	ftBoolean	
HireDate	ftDate	

FIGURE 13.3

The data-aware controls of the DbAware example at design time in Delphi

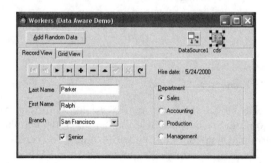

For example, if you build a standard form for taking orders, the orders dataset will generally have a field hosting a number indicating the customer who made the order. Working directly with the customer number is not the most natural way; most users will prefer to work with customer names. However, in the database, the customers' names are stored in a different table to avoid duplicating the customer data for each order by the same customer. To get around such a situation with local databases or small lookup tables, you can use a DBLookupComboBox control. (This technique doesn't port well to client/server architecture with large lookup tables, as discussed in the next chapter.)

The DBLookupComboBox component can be connected to two data sources at the same time: one source containing the data and a second containing the display data. I built a standard form using the `orders.cds` file from the Delphi sample data folder; the form includes several DBEdit controls.

You should remove the standard DBEdit component connected to the customer number and replace it with a DBLookupComboBox component (and a DBText component, to fully understand what is going on). The lookup component (and the DBText) is connected to the DataSource for the order and to the CustNo field. To let the lookup component show the information extracted from another file (`customer.cds`), you need to add another ClientDataSet component referring to the file, along with a new data source.

For the program to work, you need to set several properties of the DBLookupComboBox1 component. Here is a list of the relevant values:

```
object DBLookupComboBox1: TDBLookupComboBox
    DataField = 'CustNo'
    DataSource = DataSourceOrders
    KeyField = 'CustNo'
    ListField = 'Company;CustNo'
    ListSource = DataSourceCustomer
    DropDownWidth = 300
end
```

The first two properties determine the main connection, as usual. The next three properties determine the field used for the join (KeyField), the information to display (ListField), and the secondary source (ListSource). In addition to entering the name of a single field, you can provide multiple fields, as I did in the example. Only the first field is displayed as combo box text, but if you set a large value for the DropDownWidth property, the combo box's drop-down list will include multiple columns of data. You can see this output in Figure 13.4.

FIGURE 13.4

The output of the Cust-Lookup example with the DBLookupComboBox showing multiple fields in its drop-down list

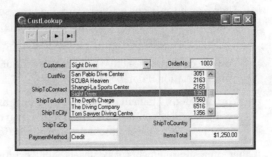

TIP *If you set the* IndexFieldNames *property of the ClientDataSet containing the customers data to the Company field, the drop-down list will show the companies in alphabetical order instead of customer-number order. I did this in the example.*

Graphical Data-Aware Controls

Delphi includes a graphical data-aware control: DBImage. It is an extension of an Image component that shows a picture stored in a BLOB field, provided the database uses a graphic format that the Image component supports.

Once you have a table that includes a BLOB storing an image with a compatible graphic format, hooking it to the component is trivial. If, instead, the graphic format requires a custom transformation in order to be displayed, it might be easier to use a standard non–data-aware Image component and write code so the image is updated each time the current record changes. Before I can discuss this subject, however, you need to know more about the TDataSet class and the dataset field classes.

There is actually a second graphical data-aware control, the DBChart, which is the data-aware version of the Chart component. Both components display business graphics (like pie charts, histograms, and so on). The data-aware version is capable of displaying the data of a record or showing in a graph the values of the same fields of the various records of a dataset. All it takes is setting up a few properties, and the result can indeed be very nice.

NOTE *The Chart and DBChart components have been in Delphi since the early versions but actually come from a third-party company, Steema Software (*www.steema.com*), which sells an extended version of the components called TeeChart Pro.*

The *TDataSet* Class

Instead of proceeding with the discussion of the capabilities of a specific dataset at this point, I prefer to devote some space to a generic introduction of the features of the TDataSet class, which are shared by all inherited data-access classes. The DataSet component is very complex, so I won't list all its capabilities—I will only discuss its core elements.

This component provides access to a series of records that are read from some source of data, kept in internal buffers (for performance reasons), and eventually modified by a user, with the possibility of writing back changes to the persistent storage. This approach is generic enough to be applied to different types of data (even nondatabase data), but it has a few rules:

- There can be only one active record at a time, so if you need to access data in multiple records, you must move to each of them, read the data, then move again, and so on. You'll find an example of this and related techniques in the section "Navigating a Dataset."

- You can edit only the active record. You cannot modify a set of records at the same time, as you can in a relational database.

- You can modify data in the active buffer only after you explicitly declare you want to do so by giving the Edit command to the dataset. You can also use the Insert command to create a new blank record and close both operations (insert or edit) by giving a Post command.

Other interesting elements of a dataset that I'll explore in the following sections are its status (and the status change events), its navigation and record positions, and the role of field objects. As a summary of the capabilities of the DataSet component, I included the public methods of its class in Listing 13.2 (the code has been edited and commented for clarity). Not all of these methods are directly used every day, but I kept them all in the listing.

LISTING 13.2: The public interface of the *TDataSet* class (excerpted)

```
TDataSet = class(TComponent, IProviderSupport)
...
public
  // create and destroy, open and close
  constructor Create(AOwner: TComponent); override;
  destructor Destroy; override;
  procedure Open;
  procedure Close;
  property BeforeOpen: TDataSetNotifyEvent...;
  property AfterOpen: TDataSetNotifyEvent...;
  property BeforeClose: TDataSetNotifyEvent...;
  property AfterClose: TDataSetNotifyEvent...;

  // status information
  function IsEmpty: Boolean;
  property Active: Boolean...;
  property State: TDataSetState read FState;
  function ActiveBuffer: PChar;
  property IsUniDirectional: Boolean...;
  function UpdateStatus: TUpdateStatus; virtual;
  property RecordSize: Word read GetRecordSize;
  property ObjectView: Boolean...;
  property RecordCount: Integer read GetRecordCount;
  function IsSequenced: Boolean; virtual;
  function IsLinkedTo(DataSource: TDataSource): Boolean;

  // datasource
  property DataSource: TDataSource read GetDataSource;
  procedure DisableControls;
  procedure EnableControls;
  function ControlsDisabled: Boolean;

  // fields, including blobs, details, calculated, and more
  function FieldByName(const FieldName: string): TField;
  function FindField(const FieldName: string): TField;
  procedure GetFieldList(List: TList; const FieldNames: string);
  procedure GetFieldNames(List: TStrings); virtual; //virtual since Delphi 7
  property FieldCount: Integer read GetFieldCount;
  property FieldDefs: TFieldDefs...;
  property FieldDefList: TFieldDefList read FFieldDefList;
  property Fields: TFields read FFields;
```

```
property FieldList: TFieldList read FFieldList;
property FieldValues[const FieldName: string]: Variant...; default;
property AggFields: TFields read FAggFields;
property DataSetField: TDataSetField...;
property DefaultFields: Boolean read FDefaultFields;
procedure ClearFields;
function GetBlobFieldData(FieldNo: Integer;
  var Buffer: TBlobByteData): Integer; virtual;
function CreateBlobStream(Field: TField;
  Mode: TBlobStreamMode): TStream; virtual;
function GetFieldData(Field: TField;
  Buffer: Pointer): Boolean; overload; virtual;
procedure GetDetailDataSets(List: TList); virtual;
procedure GetDetailLinkFields(MasterFields, DetailFields: TList); virtual;
function GetFieldData(FieldNo: Integer;
  Buffer: Pointer): Boolean; overload; virtual;
function GetFieldData(Field: TField; Buffer: Pointer;
  NativeFormat: Boolean): Boolean; overload; virtual;
property AutoCalcFields: Boolean...;
property OnCalcFields: TDataSetNotifyEvent...;

// position, movement
procedure CheckBrowseMode;
procedure First;
procedure Last;
procedure Next;
procedure Prior;
function MoveBy(Distance: Integer): Integer;
property RecNo: Integer read GetRecNo write SetRecNo;
property Bof: Boolean read FBOF;
property Eof: Boolean read FEOF;
procedure CursorPosChanged;
property BeforeScroll: TDataSetNotifyEvent...;
property AfterScroll: TDataSetNotifyEvent...;

// bookmarks
procedure FreeBookmark(Bookmark: TBookmark); virtual;
function GetBookmark: TBookmark; virtual;
function BookmarkValid(Bookmark: TBookmark): Boolean; virtual;
procedure GotoBookmark(Bookmark: TBookmark);
function CompareBookmarks(Bookmark1, Bookmark2: TBookmark):
  Integer; virtual;
property Bookmark: TBookmarkStr...;

// find, locate
function FindFirst: Boolean;
function FindLast: Boolean;
```

```pascal
function FindNext: Boolean;
function FindPrior: Boolean;
property Found: Boolean read GetFound;
function Locate(const KeyFields: string; const KeyValues: Variant;
  Options: TLocateOptions): Boolean; virtual;
function Lookup(const KeyFields: string; const KeyValues: Variant;
  const ResultFields: string): Variant; virtual;

// filtering
property Filter: string...;
property Filtered: Boolean...;
property FilterOptions: TFilterOptions...;
property OnFilterRecord: TFilterRecordEvent...;

// refreshing, updating
procedure Refresh;
property BeforeRefresh: TDataSetNotifyEvent...;
property AfterRefresh: TDataSetNotifyEvent...;
procedure UpdateCursorPos;
procedure UpdateRecord;
function GetCurrentRecord(Buffer: PChar): Boolean; virtual;
procedure Resync(Mode: TResyncMode); virtual;

// editing, inserting, posting, and deleting
property CanModify: Boolean read GetCanModify;
property Modified: Boolean read FModified;
procedure Append;
procedure Edit;
procedure Insert;
procedure Cancel; virtual;
procedure Delete;
procedure Post; virtual;
procedure AppendRecord(const Values: array of const);
procedure InsertRecord(const Values: array of const);
procedure SetFields(const Values: array of const);

// events related to editing, inserting, posting, and deleting
property BeforeInsert: TDataSetNotifyEvent...;
property AfterInsert: TDataSetNotifyEvent...;
property BeforeEdit: TDataSetNotifyEvent...;
property AfterEdit: TDataSetNotifyEvent...;
property BeforePost: TDataSetNotifyEvent...;
property AfterPost: TDataSetNotifyEvent...;
property BeforeCancel: TDataSetNotifyEvent...;
property AfterCancel: TDataSetNotifyEvent...;
property BeforeDelete: TDataSetNotifyEvent...;
```

```
property AfterDelete: TDataSetNotifyEvent...;
property OnDeleteError: TDataSetErrorEvent...;
property OnEditError: TDataSetErrorEvent...;
property OnNewRecord: TDataSetNotifyEvent...;
property OnPostError: TDataSetErrorEvent...;

// support utilities
function Translate(Src, Dest: PChar;
  ToOem: Boolean): Integer; virtual;
property Designer: TDataSetDesigner read FDesigner;
property BlockReadSize: Integer...;
property SparseArrays: Boolean...;
end;
```

The Status of a Dataset

When you operate on a dataset in Delphi, you can work in different states. These states are indicated by a specific State property, which can assume several different values:

dsBrowse   Indicates that the dataset is in normal browse mode; used to look at the data and scan the records.

dsEdit   Indicates that the dataset is in edit mode. A dataset enters this state when the program calls the Edit method or the DataSource has the AutoEdit property set to True and the user begins editing a data-aware control, such as a DBGrid or DBEdit. When the changed record is posted, the dataset exits the dsEdit state.

dsInsert   Indicates that a new record is being added to the dataset. This might happen when calling the Insert or Append methods, moving past the last row of a DBGrid, or using the corresponding command of the DBNavigator component.

dsInactive   Indicates a closed dataset.

dsCalcFields   Indicates that a field calculation is taking place (during a call to an OnCalcFields event handler).

dsNewValue, dsOldValue, and dsCurValue   Indicates that an update of the cache is in progress.

dsFilter   Indicates that a dataset is setting a filter (during a call to an OnFilterRecord event handler).

In simple examples, the transitions between these states are handled automatically, but it is important to understand them because many events refer to the state transitions. For example, every dataset fires events before and after any state change. When a program requests an Edit operation, the component fires the BeforeEdit event just before entering edit mode (an operation you can stop by raising an exception). Immediately after entering edit mode, the dataset receives the AfterEdit event. After the user has finished editing and requests to store the data by executing the Post command, the dataset fires a BeforePost event (which can be used to check the input before sending the data to the database); it fires an AfterPost event after the operation has been successfully completed.

Another more general state-change tracking technique involves handling the DataSource component's OnStateChange event. As an example, you can show the current status with code like this:

```
procedure TForm1.DataSource1StateChange(Sender: TObject);
var
  strStatus: string;
begin
  case cds.State of
    dsBrowse: strStatus := 'Browse';
    dsEdit: strStatus := 'Edit';
    dsInsert: strStatus := 'Insert';
  else
    strStatus := 'Other state';
  end;
  StatusBar.Panels[0].Text := strStatus;
end;
```

The code considers only the three most common states of a dataset component, ignoring the inactive state and other special cases.

The Fields of a Dataset

I mentioned earlier that a dataset has only one record that is current, or active. The record is stored in a buffer, and you can operate on it with some generic methods, but to access the data of the record you need to use the dataset field objects. This explains why field components (technically, instances of a class derived from the TField class) play a fundamental role in every Delphi database application. Data-aware controls are directly connected to these field objects, which correspond to database fields.

By default, Delphi automatically creates the TField components at run time, each time the program opens a dataset component. This is done after reading the metadata associated with the table or the query the dataset refers to. These field components are stored in the dataset's Fields array property. You can access these values by number (accessing the array directly) or by name (using the FieldByName method). Each field can be used to read or modify the current record's data by using its Value property or type-specific properties such as AsDate, AsString, AsInteger, and so on:

```
var
  strName: string;
begin
  strName := Cds.Fields[0].AsString;
  strName := Cds.FieldByName('LastName').AsString;
```

Value is a variant type property for the generic TField class, while it is of the specific type for its derived classes. Using the type-specific access properties for a generic TField object is a little more efficient. The dataset component also has a shortcut property for accessing the variant-type value of a field: the default FieldValues property. A *default property* means you can omit it from the code by applying the square brackets directly to the dataset:

```
strName := Cds.FieldValues ['LastName'];
strName := Cds ['LastName'];
```

Creating the field components each time a dataset is opened is only a default behavior. As an alternative, you can create the field components at design time, using the Fields Editor (double-click a dataset to see the Fields Editor in action, or activate the dataset's shortcut menu or that of the Structure View and choose the Fields Editor command). After creating a field for the LastName column of a table, for example, you can refer to its value by applying to it a specific method:

```
strName := CdsLastName.AsString;
```

In addition to being used to access the value of a field, each field object has properties for controlling visualization and editing of its value, including range of legitimate values and other validation settings, edit masks, display format, constraints, and more. These properties, of course, depend on the type of the field—that is, on the specific class of the field object. If you create persistent fields, you can set some properties at design time instead of writing code at run time (perhaps in the dataset's AfterOpen event).

NOTE   Although the Fields Editor is similar to the editors of the collections used by Delphi, fields are not part of a collection. They are components created at design time, listed in the published section of the form class and available in the drop-down combo box at the top of the Object Inspector.

As you open the Fields Editor for a dataset, it appears empty. You have to activate the shortcut menu of this editor or of the Fields pseudonode in the Structure View to access its capabilities. The simplest operation you can do is select the Add command, which allows you to add any other fields in the dataset to the list of fields. Figure 13.5 shows the Add Fields dialog box, which lists all the fields available in a table. These are the database table fields that are not already present in the list of fields in the editor.

The Fields Editor's New Field command lets you define a new calculated field, lookup field, or field with a modified type. In this dialog box, you can enter a descriptive field name, which might include blank spaces. Delphi generates an internal name—the name of the field component—which you can further customize. Next, select a data type for the field. If it is a calculated field or a lookup field, and not just a copy of a field redefined to use a new data type, select the proper radio button. You'll see how to define a calculated field and a lookup field in the sections "Adding a Calculated Field" and "Lookup Fields."

NOTE   A TField component has both a Name property and a FieldName property. The Name property is the usual component name. The FieldName property is either the name of the column in the database table or the name you define for the calculated field. It can be more descriptive than the Name, and it allows blank spaces. The FieldName property of the TField component is copied to the DisplayLabel property by default. You can change the field name to any suitable text. It is used, among other things, to search a field in the TDataSet class's FieldByName method and when using the array notation.

All the fields you add or define are included in the Fields Editor and can be used by data-aware controls or displayed in a database grid. If a field of the physical dataset is not in this list, it won't be accessible. When you use the Fields Editor, Delphi adds the declaration of the available fields to the form's class as new components (much as the Menu Designer adds TMenuItem components to the form). The components of the TField class (more specifically, its descendant classes) are fields of the form, and you can refer to these components directly in your program code to change their properties at run time or to get or set their value.

FIGURE 13.5

The Fields Editor with
the Add Fields dialog box

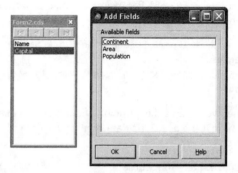

In the Fields Editor, you can also drag the fields to change their order. Proper field ordering is particularly important when you define a grid, which arranges its columns using this order (unless you override it in the grid's Columns collection).

TIP You can also drag the fields from the editor to the form to let the IDE create visual components for you. This is a handy feature that can save you a lot of time when you're creating database-related forms.

Using Field Objects

Before we look at an example, let's go over the use of the TField class. Don't underestimate the importance of this component: although it is often used behind the scenes, its role in database applications is fundamental. As I already mentioned, even if you do not define specific objects of this kind, you can always access the fields of a table or a query using their Fields array property, the FieldValues indexed property, or the FieldByName method. Both the Fields property and the FieldByName function return an object of type TField, so you sometimes have to use the as operator to downcast their result to its type (like TFloatField or TDateField) before accessing specific properties of these derived classes.

NOTE In Delphi 2005 you can also access the fields of the dataset using a for-in loop, thanks to the enumerator support provided by TDataset, as shown toward the end of this section.

The FieldAcc example has a form with three speed buttons in the Toolbar panel, which access various field properties at run time. The first button changes the formatting of the grid's population column. To do this, you have to access the DisplayFormat property, which is a specific property of the TFloatField class:

```
procedure TForm2.SpeedButton1Click(Sender: TObject);
begin
  (cds.FieldByName ('Population') as
    TFloatField).DisplayFormat := '###,###,###';
end;
```

When you set field properties related to data input or output, the changes apply to every record in the table. When you set properties related to the value of the field, however, you always refer to the current record only. For example, you can output the population of the current country in a message box by writing the following:

```
procedure TForm2.SpeedButton2Click(Sender: TObject);
begin
  ShowMessage (string (cds ['Name']) +': '+ string (cds ['Population']));
end;
```

When you access the value of a field, you can use a series of As properties to handle the current field value using a specific data type (if this data type is available; otherwise, an exception is raised):

```
AsBoolean: Boolean;
AsDateTime: TDateTime;
AsFloat: Double;
AsInteger: LongInt;
AsString: string;
AsVariant: Variant;
```

These properties can be used to read or change the value of the field. Changing the value of a field is possible only if the dataset is in edit mode. As an alternative to the As properties, you can access the value of a field by using its Value property .

Most of the other properties of the TField component, such as Alignment, DisplayLabel, DisplayWidth, and Visible, reflect elements of the field's user interface and are used by the various data-aware controls, particularly DBGrid. In the FieldAcc example, clicking the third speed button changes the Alignment of every field:

```
var
  Field: TField;
begin
  for Field in cds do
    Field.Alignment := taCenter;
```

This change affects the output of the DBGrid and of the DBEdit control I added to the toolbar, which shows the name of the country. You can see this effect, along with the new display format, in Figure 13.6.

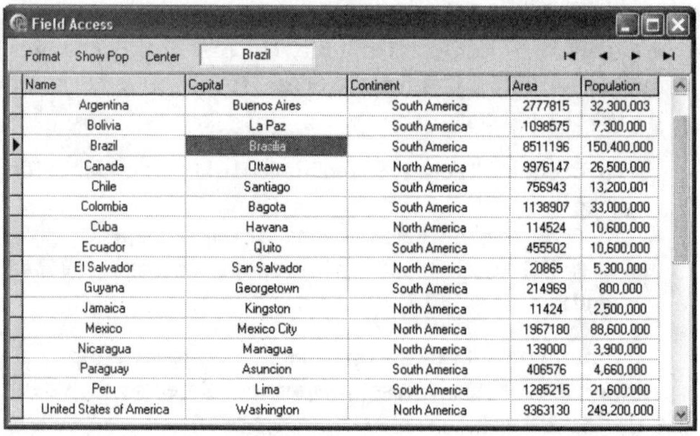

FIGURE 13.6

The output of the Field-Acc example after a user has clicked the Center and Format buttons

Name	Capital	Continent	Area	Population
Argentina	Buenos Aires	South America	2777815	32,300,003
Bolivia	La Paz	South America	1098575	7,300,000
Brazil	Brasilia	South America	8511196	150,400,000
Canada	Ottawa	North America	9976147	26,500,000
Chile	Santiago	South America	756943	13,200,001
Colombia	Bagota	South America	1138907	33,000,000
Cuba	Havana	North America	114524	10,600,000
Ecuador	Quito	South America	455502	10,600,000
El Salvador	San Salvador	North America	20865	5,300,000
Guyana	Georgetown	South America	214969	800,000
Jamaica	Kingston	North America	11424	2,500,000
Mexico	Mexico City	North America	1967180	88,600,000
Nicaragua	Managua	North America	139000	3,900,000
Paraguay	Asuncion	South America	406576	4,660,000
Peru	Lima	South America	1285215	21,600,000
United States of America	Washington	North America	9363130	249,200,000

A Hierarchy of Field Classes

The VCL includes a number of field class types. Delphi automatically uses one of them, depending on the data definition in the database, when you open a table at run time or when you use the Fields Editor at design time. Table 13.2 shows the complete list of derived classes of the TField class.

TABLE 13.2:   The Derived Classes of *TField*

DERIVED CLASS	BASE CLASS	DEFINITION
TADTField	TObjectField	An ADT (Abstract Data Type) field corresponding to an object field in an object relational database.
TAggregateField	TField	Represents a maintained aggregate. It is used in the ClientDataSet component and is discussed in this chapter.
TArrayField	TObjectField	An array of objects in an object relational database.
TAutoIncField	TIntegerField	A whole positive number connected with a Paradox table's auto-increment field (a special field automatically assigned a different value for each record). Note that Paradox AutoInc fields do not always work perfectly.
TBCDField	TNumericField	Real numbers with a fixed number of digits after the decimal point.
TBinaryField	TField	Generally not used directly. It is the base class of TBytesField.
TBlobField	TField	Binary data with no size limit (BLOB stands for binary large object). The theoretical maximum limit is 2 GB.
TBooleanField	TField	A Boolean value.
TBytesField	TBinaryField	Arbitrary data with a large (up to 64 KB characters) but fixed size.
TCurrencyField	TFloatField	Currency values with the same range as the Real data type.
TDataSetField	TObjectField	An object corresponding to a separate table in an object relational database.
TDateField	TDateTimeField	A date value.
TDateTimeField	TField	A date and time value.
TFloatField	TNumericField	Floating-point numbers (8 byte).

TABLE 13.2: The Derived Classes of *TField* (*CONTINUED*)

DERIVED CLASS	BASE CLASS	DEFINITION
TFMTBCDField	TNumericField	A true binary-coded decimal (BCD), as opposed to the existing TBCDField type, which converted BCD values to the Currency type. This field type is used automatically only by dbExpress datasets.
TGraphicField	TBlobField	A graphic of arbitrary length.
TGuidField	TStringField	A field representing a COM Globally Unique Identifier (part of the ADO support).
TIDispatchField	TInterfaceField	A field representing pointers to IDispatch COM interfaces (part of the ADO support).
TIntegerField	TNumericField	Whole numbers in the range of long integers (32 bits).
TInterfacedField	TField	Generally not used directly. This is the base class of fields that contain pointers to interfaces (IUnknown) as data.
TLargeIntField	TIntegerField	Very large integers (64 bit).
TMemoField	TBlobField	Text of arbitrary length.
TNumericField	TField	Generally not used directly. This is the base class of all the numeric field classes.
TObjectField	TField	Generally not used directly. This is the base class for fields providing support for object relational databases.
TReferenceField	TObjectField	A pointer to an object in an object relational database.
TSmallIntField	TIntegerField	Whole numbers in the range of integers (16 bits).
TSQLTimeStampField	TField	Supports the date/time representation used in dbExpress drivers.
TStringField	TField	Text data of a fixed length (up to 8192 bytes).
TTimeField	TDateTimeField	A time value.
TVarBytesField	TBytesField	Arbitrary data; up to 64 KB of characters. Very similar to the TBytesField base class.

TABLE 13.2:   The Derived Classes of *TField (CONTINUED)*

DERIVED CLASS	BASE CLASS	DEFINITION
TVariantField	TField	A field representing a variant data type (part of the ADO support).
TWideStringField	TStringField	A field representing a Unicode (16 bits per character) string.
TWordField	TIntegerField	Whole positive numbers in the range of words or unsigned integers (16 bits).

The availability of any particular field type and its correspondence with the data definition depends on the database in use. This is particularly true for the field types that provide support for object relational databases.

TIP   Validation support (with edit masks and valid ranges) depends on the field type, so using persistent fields makes it easier to set up user input validation.

Adding a Calculated Field

Now that you've been introduced to TField objects and have seen an example of their run-time use, I will build an example based on the declaration of field objects at design time using the Fields Editor and then adding a calculated field. In the country.cds sample dataset, both the population and the area of each country are available; you can use this data to compute the population density.

To build the new example, named Calc, follow these steps:

1. Add a ClientDataSet component to a form.

2. Open the Fields Editor. In this editor, right-click, choose the Add Fields command, and select some of the fields. (I included them all.)

3. Select the New Field command and enter a proper name and data type (Float, for a TFloatField) for the new calculated field, as shown in Figure 13.7.

FIGURE 13.7
The definition of a calculated field in the Calc example

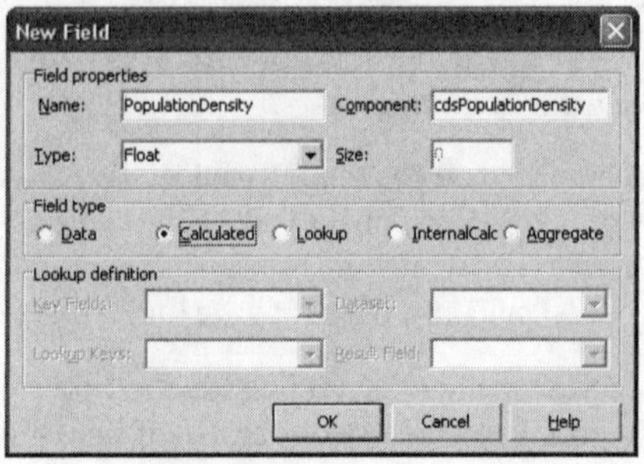

WARNING Obviously, because you create some field components at design time using the Fields Editor, the fields you skip won't get a corresponding object. As I already mentioned, the fields you skip will not be available even at run time with `Fields` or `FieldByName`. When a program opens a table at run time, if there are no design-time field components, Delphi creates field objects corresponding to the table definition. If there are some design-time fields, however, Delphi uses those fields without adding any extra field objects.

Of course, you also need to provide a way to calculate the new field. This is accomplished in the `OnCalcFields` event of the ClientDataSet component, which has the following code (at least in a first version):

```
procedure TForm2.cdsCalcFields(DataSet: TDataSet);
begin
  cdsPopulationDensity.Value := cdsPopulation.Value / cdsArea.Value;
end;
```

NOTE In general, calculated fields are computed for each record and recalculated each time the record is loaded in an internal buffer, invoking the `OnCalcFields` event over and over. For this reason, a handler of this event should be extremely fast to execute and cannot alter the status of the dataset by accessing different records. A more time-efficient (but less memory-efficient) version of a calculated field is provided by the ClientDataSet component with internally calculated fields: these fields are evaluated only once—when they are loaded—and the result is stored in memory for future requests.

Everything fine? Not at all! If you enter a new record and do not set the value of the population and area, or if you accidentally set the area to zero, the division will raise an exception, making it problematic to continue using the program. As an alternative, you could have handled every exception of the division expression and set the resulting value to zero:

```
try
  cdsPopulationDensity.Value := cdsPopulation.Value / cdsArea.Value;
except
  on Exception do
    cdsPopulationDensity.Value := 0;
end;
```

However, you can do even better: you can check whether the value of the area is defined—if it is not null—and whether it is not zero. It is better to avoid using exceptions when you can anticipate possible error conditions:

```
if not cdsArea.IsNull and (cdsArea.Value <> 0) then
  cdsPopulationDensity.Value := cdsPopulation.Value / cdsArea.Value
else
  cdsPopulationDensity.Value := 0;
```

The code for the `cdsCalcFields` method (in each of the three versions) accesses other fields directly, thanks to the use of persistent fields in the example.

Notice you won't see the value of each calculated field at design time; the field value will be available only at run time because it results from the execution of compiled Delphi code.

This example also takes advantage of persistent fields to customize some of the grid's visual elements. For example, to set a display format that adds a comma to separate thousands, I've used the ###,###,### value for the `DisplayFormat` property of some fields.

In the program, I also customized the DBGrid using its `Columns` property editor. I set the Population Density column to read-only and set its `ButtonStyle` property to cbsEllipsis to provide a custom editor. When you set this value, a small button with an ellipsis is displayed when the user tries to edit the grid cell. Clicking the button invokes the DBGrid's `OnEditButtonClick` event:

```
procedure TCalcForm.DBGrid1EditButtonClick(Sender: TObject);
begin
  MessageDlg (
    Format ('The population density (%.2n)'#13 +
      'is the Population (%.0n)'#13'divided by the Area (%.0n).'#13 +
      #13 + 'Edit these two fields to change it.',
      [cdsPopulationDensity.AsFloat, cdsPopulation.AsFloat,
      cdsArea.AsFloat]),
    mtInformation, [mbOK], 0);
end;
```

I haven't provided a real editor but rather a message describing the situation, as you can see in Figure 13.8, which shows the values of the calculated fields. To create an editor, you might build a secondary form to handle special data entries.

FIGURE 13.8

The output of the Calc example. Notice the Population Density calculated column and the ellipsis button displayed when you edit it.

Lookup Fields

As an alternative to placing a DBLookupComboBox component in a form (discussed earlier in this chapter in the section "Using Lookup Controls"), you can also define a lookup field, which can be displayed with a drop-down lookup list inside a DBGrid component. You've seen that to add a fixed selection to a DBGrid, you can edit the `PickList` subproperty of the `Columns` property. To customize the grid with a live lookup, however, you have to define a lookup field using the Fields Editor.

As an example, I built the FieldLookup program, which has a grid that displays orders; it includes a lookup field to display the name of the employee who took the order, instead of the employee's code number. To accomplish this functionality, I added to the data module a ClientDataSet component referring to the `employee.cds` dataset. Then I opened the Fields Editor for the orders dataset and added all the fields. I selected the EmpNo field and set its `Visible` property to False to remove it from the grid (you cannot remove it altogether, because it is used to build the cross-reference with the corresponding field of the employee dataset).

Now it is time to define the lookup field. If you followed the preceding steps, you can use the Fields Editor of the orders dataset and select the New Field command to open the New Field dialog box. The values you specify here will affect the properties of a new TField added to the table, as demonstrated by the DFM description of the field:

```
object cdsOrdersEmployee: TStringField
    FieldKind = fkLookup
    FieldName = 'Employee'
    LookupDataSet = cdsEmployee
    LookupKeyFields = 'EmpNo'
    LookupResultField = 'LastName'
    KeyFields = 'EmpNo'
    Size = 30
    Lookup = True
end
```

This is all that is needed to make the drop-down list work (see Figure 13.9) and to also view the value of the cross-reference field at design time. Notice that you don't need to customize the Columns property of the grid because the drop-down button and the value of seven rows for the list items are used by default. However, this doesn't mean you cannot use this property to further customize these and other visual elements of the grid.

This program has another specific feature. The two ClientDataSet components and the two DataSource components have not been placed on a form but rather on a special container for nonvisual components called a *data module* (see the sidebar "A Data Module for Data-Access Components"). You can obtain a data module from Delphi's File ➤ New ➤ Other dialog box. After adding components to it, you can link them from controls on other forms after enabling this feature by using the File ➤ Use Unit command.

FIGURE 13.9

The output of the FieldLookup example, with the drop-down list inside the grid displaying values taken from another database table

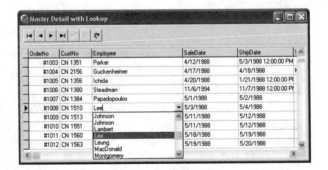

Handling Null Values with Field Events

In addition to a few interesting properties, field objects have a few key events. The OnValidate event can be used to provide extended validation of a field's value and should be used whenever you need a complex rule that the ranges and constraints provided by the field cannot express. This event is triggered before the data is written to the record buffer, whereas the OnChange event is fired soon after the data has been written.

Two other events—OnGetText and OnSetText—can be used to customize a field's output. These two events are extremely powerful: they allow you to use data-aware controls even when the representation of a field you want to display is different from the one Delphi will provide by default.

Handling null values provides an example of the use of these events. On SQL servers, storing an empty value for a field is a separate operation from storing a null value for a field. The latter tends to be more correct, but Delphi by default uses empty values and displays the same output for an empty or a null field. Although this behavior can be useful in general for strings and numbers, it becomes extremely important for dates, where it is hard to set a reasonable default value and if the user deletes the contents of the field you might have invalid input.

The NullDates program displays specific text for dates that have a null value and clears the field (setting it to the null value) when the user uses an empty string in input. Here is the relevant code of the field's two event handlers:

```
procedure TForm1.cdsShipDateGetText(Sender: TField;
  var Text: String; DisplayText: Boolean);
begin
  if Sender.IsNull then
    Text := '<undefined>'
  else
    Text := Sender.AsString;
end;

procedure TForm1.cdsShipDateSetText(Sender: TField; const Text: String);
begin
  if (Text = '') or (Text = '<undefined>') then
    Sender.Clear
  else
    Sender.AsString := Text;
end;
```

Figure 13.10 shows an example of the program's output, with undefined (or null) values for some shipping dates.

FIGURE 13.10
By handling the OnGet-Text and OnSetText events of a date field, the NullDates example displays specific output for null values.

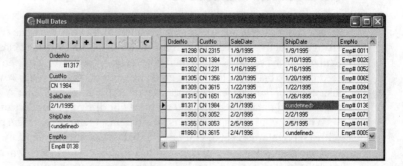

WARNING   The handling of null values in Delphi can be affected by changes in the way null variants work. As discussed in Chapter 5, in the section "The Variants and VarUtils Units," comparing a field that has a null value with another field will have a different effect in the latest versions of Delphi than in the past. As discussed in that section, in recent versions of Delphi you can use global variables to fine-tune the effect of comparisons involving variants.

A DATA MODULE FOR DATA-ACCESS COMPONENTS

To build a Delphi database application, you can place data-access components and the data-aware controls in a form. This approach is handy for a simple program, but having the user interface and the data access and data model in a single (often large) unit is far from a good idea. For this reason, Delphi implements the idea of a data module: a container of nonvisual components.

At design time, a data module is similar to a form, but at run time it exists only in memory. The TDataModule class derives directly from TComponent, so it is unrelated to the Windows concept of a window (and is fully portable among different operating systems). Unlike a form, a data module has just a few properties and events. So, it's useful to think of data modules as components and method containers.

Like a form or a frame, a data module has a designer. Delphi creates a specific unit for the definition of the data module's class and a form definition file that lists its components and their properties.

There are several reasons to use data modules. The simplest is that they let you share data-access components among multiple forms without associating the components with any given form, as I'll demonstrate at the beginning of Chapter 14. This technique works in conjunction with visual form linking—the ability to access components of another form or data module at design time (after using the File ➤ Use Unit command). The second reason is that data modules separate the data from the user interface, improving the structure of an application. Data modules in Delphi even exist in versions specific for multitier applications (remote data modules) and server-side HTTP applications (web data modules).

Finally, notice that the idea of a data module is unique to the VCL. The .NET Framework doesn't have a similar idea, so it is not available on WinForms. Similarly, in the .NET designers there is no way to refer to a component on another designer (or visual form linking).

Navigating a Dataset

You've seen that a dataset has only one active record; this active record changes frequently in response to user actions or because of internal commands given to the dataset. To move around the dataset and change the active record, you can use methods of the TDataSet class as you saw in Listing 13.2 (particularly in the section commented position, movement). You can move to the next or previous record, jump back and forth by a given number of records (with MoveBy), or go directly to the first or last record of the dataset. These dataset operations are available in the DBNavigator component and the standard dataset actions, and they are not difficult to understand.

What is not obvious, though, is how a dataset handles extreme positions. If you open any dataset with a navigator attached, you can see that as you move record by record the Next button remains enabled even when you reach the last record. Only when you try to move forward after the last record does the button become disabled (and the current record doesn't change). This happens because the Eof (end of file) test succeeds only when the cursor has been moved to a special position after the last record. If you jump forward with the Last button instead, you'll immediately be at the end. You'll encounter the same behavior for the first record (and the Bof test). As you'll soon see, this approach is handy because you can scan a dataset testing for Eof to be True and know at that point you've already processed the last record of the dataset.

In addition to moving record by record or by a given number of records, programs might need to jump to specific records or positions. Some datasets support the RecordCount property and allow movement to a record at a given position in the dataset using the RecNo property. You can use these properties only for datasets that support positions natively, which basically excludes all client/server architectures unless you grab all the records in a local cache (something you'll generally want to avoid) and then navigate on the cache. As you'll see in Chapter 14, when you open a query on a SQL server, you fetch only the records you are using, so Delphi doesn't know the record count (at least, not in advance).

You can use two alternatives to refer to a record in a dataset, regardless of its type:

◆ You can save a reference to the current record and then jump back to it after moving around. You do so by using bookmarks, either in the TBookmark or the more modern TBookmarkStr form. This approach is discussed in the section "Using Bookmarks."

◆ You can locate a dataset record that matches given criteria using the Locate method, already discussed in the section "Locating Records." This approach, which is presented in the next section, works even after you close and reopen the dataset because you're working at a logical (not physical) level.

The Total of a Table Column

So far in our examples, the user can view the current contents of a database table and manually edit the data or insert new records. Now you will see how you can change data in the table through the program code. The employee dataset you have already used has a Salary field, so a manager of the company can browse through the table and change the salary of a single employee. But what is the company's total salary expense? And what if the manager wants to give everyone a 10 percent salary increase (or decrease)?

The program, which also demonstrates the use of an action list for the standard dataset actions, has buttons to calculate the sum of the current salaries and change them. The total action lets you calculate the sum of the salaries of all the employees. Basically, you need to scan the table, reading the value of the cdsSalary field for each record:

```
var
  Total: Double;
begin
  Total := 0;
  cds.First;
  while not cds.EOF do
  begin
    Total := Total + cdsSalary.Value;
    cds.Next;
  end;
  MessageDlg ('Sum of new salaries is ' +
    Format ('%m', [Total]), mtInformation, [mbOk], 0);
end
```

This code works, as you can see from the output in Figure 13.11, but it has some problems. One problem is that the record pointer is moved to the last record, so the previous position in the table is lost. Another is that the user interface is refreshed many times during the operation.

FIGURE 13.11
The output of the Total program, showing the total salaries of the employees

Using Bookmarks

To avoid the two problems I just mentioned, you need to disable updates, store the current position of the record pointer in the table, and restore it at the end. You can do so using a *table bookmark*: a special variable that stores the position of a record in a database table. Delphi's traditional approach is to declare a variable of the TBookmark data type and initialize it while getting the current position from the table:

```
var
   Bookmark: TBookmark;
begin
   Bookmark := cds.GetBookmark;
```

At the end of the ActionTotalExecute method, you can restore the position and delete the bookmark with the following two statements (the second of which should be inside a finally block to ensure the pointer's memory is definitely freed):

```
cds.GotoBookmark (Bookmark);
cds.FreeBookmark (Bookmark); // inside a finally block
```

As a better (and more up-to-date) alternative, you can use the TDataset class's Bookmark property, which refers to a bookmark that is disposed of automatically. (The property is technically implemented as an *opaque string*—a structure subject to string lifetime management—but it is not a string with readable content, so you're not supposed to look at what's inside it.) This is how you can modify the previous code:

```
var
   Bookmark: TBookmarkStr;
begin
   Bookmark := cds.Bookmark;
   ...
   cds.Bookmark := Bookmark;
```

To avoid the other side effect of the program (you see the records scrolling while the routine browses through the data), you can temporarily disable the visual controls connected with the table. The dataset has a DisableControls method you can call before the while loop starts and an EnableControls method you can call at the end, after the record pointer is restored.

TIP   Disabling the data-aware controls connected with a dataset during long operations not only improves the user interface (because the output is not changing constantly), but also speeds up the program considerably. The time spent updating the user interface is much greater than the time spent performing the calculations.

You face some dangers from errors in reading the table data, particularly if the program is reading the data from a server using a network. If any problem occurs while retrieving the data, an exception takes place, the controls remain disabled, and the program cannot resume its normal behavior. To avoid this situation, you should use a try/finally block; to make the program 100 percent error-proof, use two nested try/finally blocks. Including this change and the two just discussed, here is the resulting code:

```
procedure TSearchForm.ActionTotalExecute(Sender: TObject);
var
  Bookmark: TBookmarkStr;
  Total: Double;
begin
  Bookmark := Cds.Bookmark;
  try
    cds.DisableControls;
    Total := 0;
    try
      cds.First;
      while not cds.EOF do
      begin
        Total := Total + cdsSalary.Value;
        cds.Next;
      end;
    finally
      cds.EnableControls;
    end
  finally
    cds.Bookmark := Bookmark;
  end;
  MessageDlg ('Sum of new salaries is ' +
    Format ('%m', [Total]), mtInformation, [mbOK], 0);
end;
```

NOTE   I wrote this code to show you an example of a loop to browse the contents of a dataset, but there is an alternative approach based on the use of a SQL query that returns the sum of the values of a field. When you use a SQL server, the speed advantage of a SQL call to compute the total can be significant because you don't need to move all the data of each field from the server to the client computer. The server sends the client only the final result. There is also a better alternative when you're using a ClientDataSet because totaling a column is one of the features provided by aggregates (discussed toward the end of this chapter). Here I discussed a generic solution, which should work for any dataset.

Editing a Table Column

The code of the increase action is similar to the action you just saw. The `ActionIncreaseExecute` method also scans the table, computing the total of the salaries, as the previous method did. Although it has just two more statements, there is a key difference: when you increase the salary, you change the data in the table. The two key statements are within the `while` loop:

```
while not cds.EOF do
begin
  cds.Edit;
  cdsSalary.Value := Round (cdsSalary.Value * SpinEdit1.Value) / 100;
  Total := Total + cdsSalary.Value;
  cds.Next;
end;
```

The first statement brings the dataset into edit mode, so that changes to the fields will have an immediate effect. The second statement computes the new salary, multiplying the old salary by the value of the SpinEdit component (by default, 105) and dividing it by 100. That's a 5 percent increase, although the values are rounded to the nearest dollar. With this program, you can change salaries by any amount with the click of a button.

WARNING The dataset enters edit mode every time the `while` loop is executed. This happens because in a dataset, edit operations can take place only one record at a time. You must finish the edit operation by calling `Post` or by moving to a different record, as in the previous code. Then, to change another record, you have to re-enter edit mode.

Customizing a Database Grid

Unlike most other data-aware controls, which have few properties to tune, the DBGrid control has many options and is more powerful than you might think. The following sections explore some of the advanced operations you can do using a DBGrid control. The first example shows how to draw in a grid, and the second shows how to use the grid's multiple-selection feature.

Painting a DBGrid

There are many reasons you might want to customize the output of a grid. A good example is to highlight specific fields or records. Another is to provide output for fields that usually don't show up in the grid, such as BLOB, graphic, and memo fields.

To thoroughly customize the drawing of a DBGrid control, you must set its `DefaultDrawing` property to False and handle its `OnDrawColumnCell` event. If you leave the value of `DefaultDrawing` set to True, the grid will display the default output before the method is called. In that case, all you can do is add something to the default output of the grid (unless you decide to draw over it, which will take extra time and cause flickering).

The alternative approach is to call the grid's `DefaultDrawColumnCell` method, perhaps after changing the current font or restricting the output rectangle. In this last case, you can provide an extra drawing in a cell and let the grid fill the remaining area with the standard output. This is what I did in the DrawData program.

The DBGrid control in this example, which is connected to the Borland's classic Biolife table, has the following properties:

```
object DBGrid1: TDBGrid
  Align = alClient
  DataSource = DataSource1
  DefaultDrawing = False
  OnDrawColumnCell = DBGrid1DrawColumnCell
end
```

The OnDrawColumnCell event handler is called once for each grid cell and has several parameters, including the rectangle corresponding to the cell, the index of the column you have to draw, the column itself (with the field, its alignment, and other subproperties), and the status of the cell. To set the color of specific cells to red, you change it in the special cases:

```
procedure TForm1.DBGrid1DrawColumnCell(Sender: TObject;
  const Rect: TRect; DataCol: Integer; Column: TColumn;
  State: TGridDrawState);
begin
  // red font color if length > 100
  if (Column.Field = cdsLengthcm) and (cdsLengthcm.AsInteger > 100) then
    DBGrid1.Canvas.Font.Color := clRed;
  // default drawing
  DBGrid1.DefaultDrawDataCell (Rect, Column.Field, State);
end;
```

The next step is to draw the memo and the graphics fields. For the memo, you can implement the memo field's OnGetText and OnSetText events. The grid will even allow editing on a memo field if its OnSetText event is not nil. Here is the code for the two event handlers. I used Trim to remove trailing nonprinting characters that make the text appear to be empty when editing:

```
procedure TForm1.cdsNotesGetText(Sender: TField;
  var Text: String; DisplayText: Boolean);
begin
  Text := Trim (Sender.AsString);
end;
```

```
procedure TForm1.cdsNotesSetText(Sender: TField; const Text: String);
begin
  Sender.AsString := Text;
end;
```

For the image, the simplest approach is to create a temporary TBitmap object, assign the graphics field to it, and paint the bitmap to the grid's Canvas. As an alternative, I removed the graphics field from the grid by setting its Visible property to False and added the image to the fish name, with the following extra code in the OnDrawColumnCell event handler:

```
var
  Picture: TPicture;
  OutRect: TRect;
  PictWidth: Integer;
begin
  // default output rectangle
  OutRect := Rect;

  if Column.Field = cdsCommon_Name then
  begin
    // draw the image
    Picture := TPicture.Create;
    try
      Picture.Assign(cdsGraphic);
      PictWidth := (Rect.Bottom - Rect.Top) * 2;
      OutRect.Right := Rect.Left + PictWidth;
      DBGrid1.Canvas.StretchDraw (OutRect, Picture.Graphic);
    finally
      Picture.Free;
    end;
    // reset output rectangle, leaving space for the graphic
    OutRect := Rect;
    OutRect.Left := OutRect.Left + PictWidth;
  end;
  // red font color if length > 100 (omitted - see above)
  // default drawing
  DBGrid1.DefaultDrawDataCell (OutRect, Column.Field, State);
```

As you can see in this code, the program shows the image in a small rectangle on the left of the grid cell and then changes the output rectangle to the remaining area before activating the default drawing. You can see the effect in Figure 13.12.

FIGURE 13.12

The DrawData program displays a grid that includes the text of a memo field and the ubiquitous Borland fish.

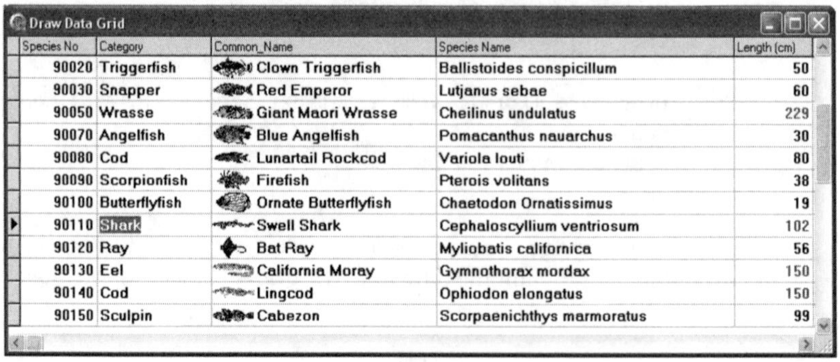

Species No	Category	Common_Name	Species Name	Length (cm)
90020	Triggerfish	Clown Triggerfish	Ballistoides conspicillum	50
90030	Snapper	Red Emperor	Lutjanus sebae	60
90050	Wrasse	Giant Maori Wrasse	Cheilinus undulatus	229
90070	Angelfish	Blue Angelfish	Pomacanthus nauarchus	30
90080	Cod	Lunartail Rockcod	Variola louti	80
90090	Scorpionfish	Firefish	Pterois volitans	38
90100	Butterflyfish	Ornate Butterflyfish	Chaetodon Ornatissimus	19
90110	Shark	Swell Shark	Cephaloscyllium ventriosum	102
90120	Ray	Bat Ray	Myliobatis californica	56
90130	Eel	California Moray	Gymnothorax mordax	150
90140	Cod	Lingcod	Ophiodon elongatus	150
90150	Sculpin	Cabezon	Scorpaenichthys marmoratus	99

A Grid Allowing Multiple Selection

The second example of customizing the DBGrid control relates to multiple selection. You can set up the DBGrid so that a user can select multiple rows (that is, multiple records). Doing so is easy, because all you have to do is toggle the dgMultiSelect element of the grid's Options property. Once you select this option, a user can keep the Ctrl key pressed and click with the mouse to select multiple grid rows (or use Shift + Up arrow and Shift + Down arrow), with the effect shown in Figure 13.13.

Because the database table can have only one active record, the grid keeps a list of bookmarks to the selected records. This list is available in the SelectedRows property, which is of type TBookmarkList. Besides accessing the number of objects in the list with the Count property, you can get to each bookmark with the Items property, which is the default array property. Each list item is of a TBookmarkStr type, which represents a bookmark pointer you can assign to the table's Bookmark property.

NOTE TBookmarkStr is a string type for convenience, but its data should be considered opaque and volatile. You shouldn't rely on any particular structure to the data you find if you peek at a bookmark's value, and you shouldn't hold on to the data too long or store it in a separate file. Bookmark data will vary with the database driver and index configuration, and it may be rendered unusable when rows are added to or deleted from the dataset (by you or by other users of the database).

To summarize the steps, here is the code for the MltGrid example, which is activated by clicking the button to move the Name field of the selected records to the list box:

```
procedure TForm1.Button1Click(Sender: TObject);
var
  I: Integer;
  BookmarkList: TBookmarkList;
  Bookmark: TBookmarkStr;
begin
  // store the current position
  Bookmark := cds.Bookmark;
  try
    // empty the list box
    ListBox1.Items.Clear;
    // get the selected rows of the grid
    BookmarkList := DbGrid1.SelectedRows;
    for I := 0 to BookmarkList.Count - 1 do
    begin
      // for each, move the table to that record
      cds.Bookmark := BookmarkList[I];
      // add the name field to the listbox
      ListBox1.Items.Add (cds.FieldByName ('Name').AsString);
    end;
  finally
    // go back to the initial record
    cds.Bookmark := Bookmark;
  end;
end;
```

FIGURE 13.13

The MltGrid example has a DBGrid control that allows the selection of multiple rows.

Dragging to a Grid

Another interesting technique is to use dragging with grids. Dragging *from* a grid is not difficult because you know which current record and column the user has selected. Dragging *to* a grid, however, is tricky to program. Recall that in Chapter 3 I mentioned the "protected hack"; I'll use this technique to implement dragging to a grid.

The example, called DragToGrid, has a grid connected to the country dataset, an edit box in which you can type the new value for a field, and a label you can drag over a grid cell to modify the related field. The problem is how to determine this field. The code is only a few lines, as you can see here, but it is cryptic and requires some explanation:

```
type
  TDBGHack = class (TDbGrid)
  end;

procedure TFormDrag.DBGrid1DragDrop(
  Sender, Source: TObject; X, Y: Integer);
var
  gc: TGridCoord;
begin
  gc := TDBGHack (DbGrid1).MouseCoord (x, y);
  if (gc.y > 0) and (gc.x > 0) then
  begin
    DbGrid1.DataSource.DataSet.MoveBy (gc.y - TDBGHack(DbGrid1).Row);
    DbGrid1.DataSource.DataSet.Edit;
    DBGrid1.Columns.Items [gc.X - 1].Field.AsString := EditDrag.Text;
  end;
  DBGrid1.SetFocus;
end;
```

The first operation determines the cell over which the mouse was released. Starting with the x and y mouse coordinates, you can call the protected MouseCoord method to access the row and column of the cell. Unless the drag target is the first row (usually hosting the titles) or the first column (usually hosting the indicator), the program moves the current record by the difference between the requested row (gc.y) and the current active row (the grid's protected Row property). The next step puts the dataset into edit mode, grabs the field of the target column (Columns.Items [gc.X - 1].Field), and changes its text.

Database Applications with Standard Controls

Although it is generally faster to write Delphi applications based on data-aware controls, this approach is not required. When you need precise control over the user interface of a database application, you might want to customize the transfer of the data from the field objects to the visual controls. My view is that doing so is necessary only in specific cases, because you can customize the data-aware controls extensively by setting the properties and handling the events of the field objects. However, trying to work without the data-aware controls should help you better understand Delphi's default behavior.

The development of an application not based on data-aware controls can follow two different approaches: you can mimic the standard Delphi behavior in code, possibly departing from it in specific cases, or you can go for a more customized approach. I'll demonstrate the first technique in the NonAware example and the latter in the SendToDb example.

Mimicking Delphi Data-Aware Controls

To build an application that doesn't use data-aware controls but behaves like a standard Delphi application, you can write event handlers for the operations that would be performed automatically by data-aware controls. Basically, you need to place the dataset in edit mode as the user changes the content of the visual controls and update the field objects of the dataset as the user exits from the controls, moving the focus to another element.

TIP   This approach can be handy for integrating a control that's not data-aware into a standard application.

The other element of the NonAware example is a list of buttons corresponding to some of the buttons in the DBNavigator control; these buttons are connected to five custom actions. I could not use the standard dataset actions for this example because they automatically hook to the data source associated with the control having the focus—a mechanism that fails with the example's non–data-aware edit boxes. In general, you could also hook a data source with each of the actions' DataSource property, but in this specific case we don't have a data source in the example.

The program has several event handlers I haven't used for past applications using data-aware controls. First, you have to show the current record's data in the visual controls (as in Figure 13.14) by handling the AfterScroll event of the dataset component:

```
procedure TForm1.cdsAfterScroll(DataSet: TDataSet);
begin
  EditName.Text := cdsName.AsString;
  EditCapital.Text := cdsCapital.AsString;
  ComboContinent.Text := cdsContinent.AsString;
  EditArea.Text := cdsArea.AsString;
  EditPopulation.Text := cdsPopulation.AsString;
end;
```

FIGURE 13.14

The output of the Non-Aware example in Browse mode. The program manually fetches the data every time the current record changes.

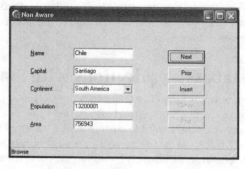

As there is not an OnStateChange event in the Dataset component, the program refreshes the dataset state in the status bar by handling most AfterXxx events. As the user begins typing in one of the edit boxes or drops down the combo box list, the program sets the table to edit mode:

```
procedure TForm1.EditKeyPress(Sender: TObject; var Key: Char);
begin
  if not (cds.State in dsEditModes) then
    cds.Edit;
end;
```

The dsEditModes is a set of states containing both dsEdit and dsInsert. This method is connected to the OnKeyPress event of the five components and is similar to the OnDropDown event handler of the combo box. As the user leaves one of the visual controls, the OnExit event handler copies the data to the corresponding field, as in this case:

```
procedure TForm1.EditCapitalExit(Sender: TObject);
begin
  if (cds.State in dsEditModes) then
    cdsCapital.AsString := EditCapital.Text;
end;
```

The operation takes place only if the table is in edit mode—that is, only if the user has typed in this or another control. This behavior is not ideal because extra operations are done even if the edit box's text didn't change; however, the extra steps happen fast enough that they aren't a concern. For the first edit box, you check the text before copying it, raising an exception if the edit box is empty:

```
procedure TForm1.EditNameExit(Sender: TObject);
begin
  if (cds.State in dsEditModes) then
    if EditName.Text <> '' then
      cdsName.AsString := EditName.Text
    else
    begin
      EditName.SetFocus;
      raise Exception.Create ('Undefined Country');
    end;
end;
```

An alternative approach for testing the value of a field is to handle the dataset's `BeforePost` event. Keep in mind that, in this example, the posting operation is not handled by a specific button but takes place as soon as a user moves to a new record or inserts a new one:

```
procedure TForm1.cdsBeforePost(DataSet: TDataSet);
begin
  if cdsArea.Value < 100 then
    raise Exception.Create ('Area too small');
end;
```

In each case, an alternative to raising an exception is to set a default value. However, if a field has a default value, it is better to set it up front so a user can see which value will be sent to the database. To accomplish this, you can handle the dataset's `AfterInsert` event, which is fired immediately after a new record has been created (I could have used the `OnNewRecord` event, as well):

```
procedure TForm1.cdsAfterInsert(DataSet: TDataSet);
begin
  cdsContinent.Value := 'Asia';
  RefreshStatus;
end;
```

Sending Requests to the Database

You can further customize your application's user interface if you decide not to handle the same sequence of editing operations as in standard Delphi data-aware controls. This approach allows you complete freedom, although it might cause some side effects (such as limited ability to handle concurrency, which I'll discuss in Chapter 14).

For this new example, I replaced the first edit box with another combo box and replaced all the buttons related to table operations (which corresponded to DBNavigator buttons) with two custom buttons that get the data from the database and send an update to it. Again, this example has no DataSource component.

The `GetData` method, connected to the corresponding button, gets the fields corresponding to the record indicated in the first combo box:

```
procedure TForm1.GetData;
begin
  cds.Locate ('Name', ComboName.Text, [loCaseInsensitive]);
  ComboName.Text := cdsName.AsString;
  EditCapital.Text := cdsCapital.AsString;
  ComboContinent.Text := cdsContinent.AsString;
  EditArea.Text := cdsArea.AsString;
  EditPopulation.Text := cdsPopulation.AsString;
end;
```

This method is called whenever the user clicks the button, selects an item in the combo box, or presses the Enter key while in the combo box:

```
procedure TForm1.ComboNameClick(Sender: TObject);
begin
```

```
    GetData;
  end;

  procedure TForm1.ComboNameKeyPress(Sender: TObject; var Key: Char);
  begin
    if Key = #13 then
      GetData;
  end;
```

To make this example work smoothly, at startup the combo box is filled with the names of all the countries in the table:

```
  procedure TForm1.FormCreate(Sender: TObject);
  begin
    // fill the list of names
    cds.Open;
    while not cds.Eof do
    begin
      ComboName.Items.Add (cdsName.AsString);
      cds.Next;
    end;
  end;
```

With this approach, the combo box becomes a sort of selector for the record, as you can see in Figure 13.15. Thanks to this selection, the program doesn't need navigational buttons.

The user can also change the values of the controls and click the Send button. The code to be executed depends on whether the operation is an update or an insert. You can determine this by looking at the name (although with this code, a wrong name can no longer be modified):

```
  procedure TForm1.SendData;
  begin
    // raise an exception if there is no name
    if ComboName.Text = '' then
      raise Exception.Create ('Insert the name');

    // check if the record is already in the table
    if cds.Locate ('Name', ComboName.Text, [loCaseInsensitive]) then
    begin
      // modify found record
      cds.Edit;
      cdsCapital.AsString := EditCapital.Text;
      cdsContinent.AsString := ComboContinent.Text;
      cdsArea.AsString := EditArea.Text;
      cdsPopulation.AsString := EditPopulation.Text;
      cds.Post;
    end
    else
    begin
      // insert new record
```

```
cds.InsertRecord ([ComboName.Text, EditCapital.Text,
  ComboContinent.Text, EditArea.Text, EditPopulation.Text]);
// add to list
ComboName.Items.Add (ComboName.Text)
end;
```

Before sending the data to the table, you can do any sort of validation test on the values. In this case, it doesn't make sense to handle the events of the database components because you have full control over when the update or insert operation is performed. Notice that the `InsertRecord` method, a much more efficient way to add a record, is easier to write but more error-prone.

FIGURE 13.15
In the SendToDb example, you can use a combo box to select the record you want to see.

Grouping and Aggregates

You've already seen that a ClientDataSet can have an index different from the order in which the data is stored in the file. Once you define an index, you can group the data by that index. In practice, a *group* is defined as a list of consecutive records (according to the index) for which the value of the indexed field doesn't change. For example, if you have an index by state, all the addresses within any particular state will fall in the group.

Grouping

The CdsCalcs example has a ClientDataSet component that extracts its data from the familiar Country dataset. The group is obtained, along with the definition of an index, by specifying a grouping level for the index:

```
object ClientDataSet1: TClientDataSet
  IndexDefs = <
    item
      Name = 'ClientDataSet1Index1'
      Fields = 'Continent'
      GroupingLevel = 1
    end>
  IndexName = 'ClientDataSet1Index1'
```

When a group is active, you can make it obvious to the user by displaying the grouping structure in the DBGrid, as shown in Figure 13.16. All you have to do is handle the `OnGetText` event for the grouped field (the Continent field in the example) and show the text only if the record is the first in the group:

```
procedure TForm1.ClientDataSet1ContinentGetText(Sender: TField;
  var Text: String; DisplayText: Boolean);
begin
  if gbFirst in ClientDataSet1.GetGroupState (1) then
    Text := Sender.AsString
  else
    Text := '';
end;
```

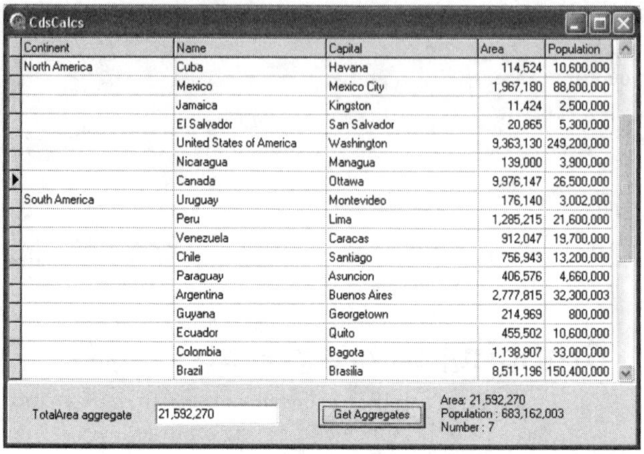

FIGURE 13.16

The CdsCalcs example demonstrates that by writing a little code, you can have the DBGrid control visually show the grouping defined in the ClientDataSet.

Defining Aggregates

Another feature of the ClientDataSet component is support for aggregates. An *aggregate* is a calculated value based on multiple records, such as the sum or average value of a field for the entire table or a group of records (defined with the grouping logic I just discussed). Aggregates are *maintained*; that is, they are recalculated immediately if one of the records changes. For example, the total of an invoice can be maintained automatically while the user types in the invoice items.

NOTE   Aggregates are maintained incrementally, not by recalculating all the values every time one value changes. Aggregate updates take advantage of the differences in the data tracked by the Client-DataSet. For example, to update a sum when a field is changed, the ClientDataSet subtracts the old value from the aggregate and adds the new value. Only two calculations are needed, even if there are thousands of rows in that aggregate group. For this reason, aggregate updates are instantaneous.

There are two ways to define aggregates. You can use the Aggregates property of the Client-DataSet, which is a collection, or you can define aggregate fields using the Fields Editor. In both cases, you define the aggregate expression, give it a name, and connect it to an index and a grouping level (unless you want to apply it to the entire table). Here is the `Aggregates` collection of the CdsCalcs example:

```
object ClientDataSet1: TClientDataSet
  Aggregates = <
    item
      Active = True
      AggregateName = 'Count'
      Expression = 'COUNT (NAME)'
      GroupingLevel = 1
      IndexName = 'ClientDataSet1Index1'
      Visible = False
    end
    item
      Active = True
      AggregateName = 'TotalPopulation'
      Expression = 'SUM (POPULATION)'
      Visible = False
    end>
  AggregatesActive = True
```

Notice in the last line of the previous DFM listing that you must activate the support for aggregates, in addition to activating each specific aggregate you want to use. Disabling aggregates is important because having too many of them can slow down a program.

The alternative approach, as I mentioned, is to use the Fields Editor, select the New Field command from its shortcut menu, and choose the Aggregate option (available, along with the Internal-Calc option, only in a ClientDataSet). This is the definition of an aggregate field:

```
object ClientDataSet1: TClientDataSet
  object ClientDataSet1TotalArea: TAggregateField
    FieldName = 'TotalArea'
    ReadOnly = True
    Visible = True
    Active = True
    DisplayFormat = '###,###,###'
    Expression = 'SUM(AREA)'
    GroupingLevel = 1
    IndexName = 'ClientDataSet1Index1'
  end
```

The aggregate fields are displayed in the Fields Editor in a separate group, as you can see in Figure 13.17. The advantage of using an aggregate field, compared to a plain aggregate, is that you can define the display format and hook the field directly to a data-aware control, such as a DBEdit in the CdsCalcs example. Because the aggregate is connected to a group, as soon as you select a record from a different group, the output is automatically updated. Also, if you change the data, the total immediately shows the new value.

FIGURE 13.17
The bottom portion of
a ClientDataSet's Fields
Editor displays aggregate
fields.

To use plain aggregates, you have to write a little code, as in the following example (notice that the
Value of the aggregate is a variant):

```
procedure TForm1.Button1Click(Sender: TObject);
begin
  Label1.Caption :=
    'Area: ' + ClientDataSet1TotalArea.DisplayText + #13'Population : '
    + FormatFloat ('###,###,###', ClientDataSet1.Aggregates[1].Value) +
    #13'Number : ' + IntToStr (ClientDataSet1.Aggregates[0].Value);
end;
```

Master/Detail Structures

Often, you need to relate tables that have a one-to-many relationship. This means that for a single
record in the master table, there are many detailed records in a secondary table. A classic example is
an invoice and the items of the invoice; another is a list of customers and the orders each customer has
placed.

These are common situations in database programming, and Delphi provides explicit support
with the master/detail structure. The TDataSet class has a DataSource property for setting up a master data source. This property is used in a detail dataset to hook to the current record of the master
dataset, in combination with the MasterFields property.

Master/Detail with ClientDataSets

The MastDet example uses the customer and orders sample datasets. I added a data source component for each dataset, and for the secondary dataset I assigned the MasterSource property to the data
source connected to the first dataset. Finally, I related the secondary table to a field of the main table,
using the MasterFields property's special editor. I did all this using a data module, as discussed in
the earlier sidebar "A Data Module for Data-Access Components."

The following is the complete listing (but without the irrelevant positional properties) of the data
module used by the MastDet program:

```
object DataModule1: TDataModule1
  OnCreate = DataModule1Create
  object dsCust: TDataSource
    DataSet = cdsCustomers
  end
```

```
object dsOrd: TDataSource
  DataSet = cdsOrders
end
object cdsOrders: TClientDataSet
  FileName = 'orders.cds'
  IndexFieldNames = 'CustNo'
  MasterFields = 'CustNo'
  MasterSource = dsCust
end
object cdsCustomers: TClientDataSet
  FileName = 'customer.cds'
end
end
```

In Figure 13.18, you can see an example of the MastDet program's main form at run time. I placed data-aware controls related to the master table in the upper portion of the form, and I placed a grid connected with the detail table in the lower portion. This way, for every master record, you immediately see the list of connected detail records—in this case, all orders placed by the current client. Each time you select a new customer, the grid below the master record displays only the orders pertaining to that customer.

FIGURE 13.18
The MastDet example at run time

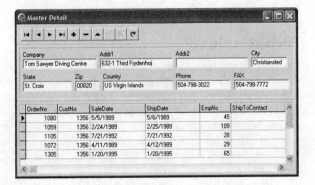

Handling Database Errors

Another important element of database programming is handling database errors in custom ways. Of course, you can let Delphi show an exception message each time a database error occurs, but you might want to try to correct the errors or show more details. You can use three approaches to handle database-related errors:

♦ Wrap a try/except block around risky database operations. This is not possible when the operation is generated by interaction with a data-aware control.

♦ Install a handler for the OnException event of the global Application object or for the ApplicationEvents component (which is a bit easier).

♦ Handle specific dataset events related to errors, such as OnPostError, OnEditError, OnDeleteError, and OnUpdateError.

Although most of the exception classes in Delphi deliver an error message, database exceptions often include error codes, native SQL server error codes and messages, and the like. The Client-DataSet adds only an error code to its exception class, EDBClient. I'll show you how to handle this, which will provide you with a guideline for other cases.

As an example, I built a database program that shows the details of the errors in a memo component (errors are automatically generated when the user clicks the program buttons). To handle all the errors, the DBError example installs a handler for the OnException event of the Application global object. The event handler logs some information in a memo showing the details of the database error if it is an EDBClient:

```
procedure TForm1.ApplicationError (Sender: TObject; E: Exception);
begin
  if E is EDBClient then
  begin
    Memo1.Lines.Add('Error: ' + (E.Message));
    Memo1.Lines.Add('   Error Code: ' +
      IntToStr(EDBClient (E).ErrorCode));
  end
  else
    Memo1.Lines.Add('Generic Error: ' + (E.Message));
end;
```

What's Next?

In this chapter, you saw examples of database access from Delphi programs. I covered the basic data-aware components, as well as the development of database applications based on standard controls. I explored the internal architecture of the TDataSet class and field objects and discussed many events and properties shared by all datasets and used by all database applications. Even though most of the examples used the ClientDataSet component accessing local data, the component is often also the gateway for data in a SQL server (in a client/server architecture) or in a remote application (in a three-tier architecture). I discussed calculated fields, lookup fields, customizations of the DBGrid control, and some advanced techniques.

I haven't delved into the database and data-access side of the picture, which depends on the type of database engine and server you're using. Chapter 14 will focus on this topic, with an in-depth overview of client/server development using the dbExpress library provided by Borland. I'll also cover InterBase and the IBX component, giving some elements of a real-world application.

Following chapters will continue to explore the database side of Delphi programming, discussing ADO connectivity and components, Borland's three-tier architecture (DataSnap, formerly MIDAS), the development of data-aware controls and custom dataset components, and reporting technologies. Another chapter will focus on ADO.NET, the specific data access technology that is part of the .NET Framework class library.

Chapter 14

Client/Server Development with the VCL Database Components

In the last chapter, we examined Delphi's support for database programming using local files (particularly using the ClientDataSet component, or MyBase) in most of the examples but not focusing on any specific database technology. This chapter moves on to the use of an RDBMS (relational database management system, often colloquially called database server or SQL server), focusing on client/server development with the dbExpress technology. A single chapter cannot cover this complex topic in detail, so I'll introduce it from the perspective of the Delphi developer and add some tips and hints.

For the examples I'll use InterBase, because the Delphi installation includes this Borland database server. I'll discuss InterBase from the Delphi perspective, without delving into its internal architecture. A lot of the information presented also applies to other SQL servers, so even if you've decided not to use InterBase, you may still find it valuable.

This chapter begins with an overview of client/server development and the elements of database design and then introduces InterBase. Next follow discussions of server-side programming: views, stored procedures, and triggers; the dbExpress library; caching with the ClientDataSet component; and the InterBase Express (IBX) components.

The Client/Server Architecture

The database applications presented in previous chapters used native components to access data stored in files on the local machine and loaded the entire file in memory. This is an extreme approach. More traditionally, the file is read record by record so that multiple applications can access it at the same time, provided write synchronization mechanisms are used.

When the data is on a remote server, copying an entire table in memory for processing it consumes time and bandwidth. As an example, consider taking a table like Employee (part of the InterBase sample database that ships with Delphi), adding thousands of records to it, and placing it on a networked computer working as a database server. If you want to know the highest salary paid by the company, you can open a dbExpress table component (EmpTable) or a query selecting all the records and run this code:

```
EmpTable.Open;
EmpTable.First;
MaxSalary := 0;
while not EmpTable.Eof do
```

```
begin
  if EmpTable.FieldByName ('Salary').AsCurrency > MaxSalary then
    MaxSalary := EmpTable.FieldByName ('Salary').AsCurrency;
  EmpTable.Next;
end;
```

The effect of this approach is to move all the data of the table from the networked computer to the local machine—an operation that might take minutes. In this case, the proper approach is to let the SQL server compute the result directly, fetching only this single piece of information. You can do so using a SQL statement like this:

```
select Max(Salary) from Employee
```

NOTE   The previous two code excerpts are part of the GetMax example, which includes code to time the two approaches. Using the Table component on the small Employee table takes about ten times longer than using the query, even if the InterBase server is installed on the computer running the program.

To store a large amount of data on a central computer and avoid moving the data to client computers for processing, the only solution is to let the central computer manipulate the data and send back to the client only a limited amount of information. This is the foundation of client/server programming.

In general, you'll use an existing program on the server (a database server) and write a custom client application that connects to it. Sometimes, however, you may want to write both a custom client and a custom server, as in three-tier applications. Delphi support for this type of program—which has been called the Middle-tier Distributed Application Services (MIDAS) architecture and is now dubbed DataSnap—is covered in Chapter 17.

The *upsizing* of an application—that is, the transfer of data from local files to a database engine—is generally done for performance reasons and to allow for larger amounts of data. Going back to the previous example, in a client/server environment the query used to select the maximum salary would be computed by the RDBMS, which would send back to the client computer only the final result: a single number. With a powerful server computer (such as a multiprocessor Sun Sparc-Station), the total time required to compute the result might be minimal.

However, there are other reasons to choose a client/server architecture. Such an architecture

◆   Helps you manage a larger amount of data because you don't want to store hundreds of megabytes in a local file.

◆   Supports the need for concurrent access to the data by multiple users at the same time. An RDBMS generally uses *optimistic locking*, an approach that allows multiple users to work on the same data and delays the concurrency control until users send back updates.

◆   Provides data integrity, transaction control, security, access control, backup support, and the like.

◆   Supports programmability—the possibility of running part of the code (stored procedures, triggers, table views, and other techniques) on the server, thereby reducing the network traffic and the workload of the client computers.

Having said this, we can begin focusing on particular techniques useful for client/server programming. The general goal is to distribute the workload properly between the client and the server and reduce the network bandwidth required to move information back and forth.

The foundation of this approach is good database design, which involves both table structure and appropriate data validation and constraints, or business rules. Enforcing the validation of the data on the server is important because the integrity of the database is one of the key aims of any program. However, the client side should include data validation as well, to improve the user interface and make the input and the processing of the data more user-friendly. It makes little sense to let the user enter invalid data and then receive an error message from the server, when you can prevent the wrong input in the first place.

Elements of Database Design

Although this is a book about Delphi programming, not databases, I feel it's important to discuss a few elements of good (and modern) database design. The reason is simple: If your database design is incorrect or convoluted, you'll have to either write terribly complex SQL statements and server-side code, or write a lot of Delphi code to access your data, possibly even fighting against the design of the TDataSet class.

Entities and Relations

The classic relational database design approach, based on the entity-relation (E-R) model, involves having one table for every entity you need to represent in your database, with one field for each data element you need plus one field for every one-to-one or one-to-many relation to another entity (or table). For many-to-many relations, you need a separate table.

As an example of a one-to-one relation, consider a table representing a university course. It will have a field for each relevant data element (name and description, room where the course is held, and so on) plus a single field indicating the teacher. The teacher data really should not be stored within the course data, but in a separate table, because it may be referenced from elsewhere.

The schedule for each course can include an undefined number of hours on different days, so they cannot be added in the same table describing the course. Instead, this information must be placed in a separate table that includes all the schedules, with a field referring to the class each schedule is for. In a one-to-many relation like this, *many* records of the schedule table point to the same *one* record in the course table.

A more complex situation is required to store information about which student is taking which class. Students cannot be listed directly in the course table because their number is not fixed, and the classes cannot be stored in the student's data for the same reason. In a similar many-to-many relation, the only approach is to create an extra table representing the relation—it lists references to students and courses.

Normalization Rules

The classic design principles include a series of so-called *normalization rules*. The goal of these rules is to avoid duplicating data in your database (partially to save space but mainly to avoid ending up with incongruous data). For example, you don't repeat all the customer details in each order but refer to a separate customer entity. This way you save memory, and when a customer's details change (for example, because of a change of address), all of the customer's orders reflect the new data. Other tables that relate to the same customer will be automatically updated as well.

Normalization rules imply using codes for commonly repeated values. For example, suppose you have a few different shipment options. Rather than include a string-based description for these options within the orders table, you can use a short numeric code that's mapped to a description in a separate lookup table.

The previous rule should not be taken to the extreme, to avoid having to join a large number of tables for every query. You can either account for some denormalization (leaving a short shipment description within the orders table) or use the client program to provide the description, again ending up with a formally incorrect database design. This last option is practical only when you use a single development environment (say, Delphi) to access this database.

From Primary Keys to OIDs

In a relational database, records are identified not by a physical position (as in Paradox and other local databases) but by the data within the record. Typically, you don't need the data from every field to identify a record, but only a subset of the data, forming the *primary key*. If the fields that are part of the primary key must identify an individual record, their value must be different for each possible record of the table.

NOTE Many database servers add internal record identifiers to tables, but they do so only for internal optimization; this process has little to do with the logical design of a relational database. These internal identifiers work differently in different database servers and may change among versions, so you shouldn't rely on them.

Early incarnations of relational theory dictated the use of *logical keys*, which means selecting one or more fields that indicate an entity without risk of confusion. This is often easier to say than to accomplish. For example, company names are not generally unique, and even the company name and its location don't provide a complete guarantee of uniqueness. Moreover, if a company changes its name (not an unlikely event, as Borland can teach us) or its location, and you have references to the company in other tables, you must change all those references as well and risk ending up with dangling references.

For this reason, and also for efficiency (using strings for references implies using a lot of space in secondary tables, where references often occur), logical keys have been phased out in favor of physical or surrogate keys:

Physical key A single field that identifies an element in a unique way. For example, each person in the U.S. has a Social Security Number (SSN) and almost every other country has a tax ID or other government-assigned number that identifies each person. The same is typically true for companies. Although these ID numbers are guaranteed to be unique, they can change depending on the country (creating troubles for the database of a company that sells goods abroad) or within a single country (to account for new tax laws). They are also often inefficient, because they can be quite large (Italy, for example, uses a 16-character code—letters and numbers—to identify people).

Surrogate key A number identifying a record, in the form of a client code, order number, and so on. Surrogate keys are commonly used in database design. However, in many cases, they end up being *logical identifiers*, with client codes showing up all over the place (not a great idea).

WARNING The situation becomes particularly troublesome when surrogate keys also have a meaning and must follow specific rules. For example, companies must number invoices with unique and consecutive numbers without leaving holes in the numbering sequence. This situation is extremely complex to handle programmatically, if you consider that only the database can determine these unique consecutive numbers when you send it new data. At the same time, you need to identify the record before you send it to the database—otherwise you won't be able to fetch it again. Practical examples of how to solve this situation are discussed at the end of this chapter in the section "Generators and IDs."

OIDs to the Extreme

An extension to the use of surrogate keys is the use of a unique Object Identifier (OID). An OID is either a number or a string with a sequence of numbers and digits; it's added to each record of each table representing an entity (and sometimes to records of tables representing relations). Unlike client codes, invoice numbers, SSNs, or purchase order numbers, OIDs are random: They have no sequencing rule and are never visible to the end user. This means you can use surrogate keys (if your company is used to them) along with OIDs, but all the external references to the table will be based on OIDs.

Another common rule suggested by the promoters of this approach (which is part of the theories supporting object-relational mapping) is the use of system-wide unique identifiers. If you have a table of client companies and a table of employees, you may wonder why you should use a unique ID for such diverse data. The reason is that you'll be able to sell goods to an employee without having to duplicate the employee information in the customer table—you can refer to the employee in your order and invoice. An order is placed by someone identified by an OID, and this OID can refer to many different tables.

Using OIDs and object-relational mapping is an advanced element of the design of Delphi database applications. I suggest that you investigate this topic before embracing medium or large Delphi projects because the benefit can be relevant (after some investment in studying this approach and building some basic support code).

External Keys and Referential Integrity

The keys identifying a record (whatever their type) can be used as external keys in other tables—for example, to represent the various types of relations discussed earlier. All database servers can verify these external references, so you cannot refer to a nonexistent record in another table. These referential integrity constraints are expressed when you create a table.

Besides not being allowed to add references to nonexistent records, you're generally prevented from deleting a record if external references to it exist. Some database servers go one step further: As you delete a record, instead of denying the operation, they can automatically delete all records that refer to it from other tables.

More Constraints

In addition to the uniqueness of primary keys and the referential constraints, you can generally use the database to impose more validity rules on the data. You can ask for specific columns (such as those referring to a tax ID or a purchase order number) to include only unique values. You can impose uniqueness on the values of multiple columns—for example, to indicate that you cannot hold two classes in the same room at the same time.

In general, simple rules can be expressed to impose constraints on a table, whereas more complex rules generally imply the execution of stored procedures activated by triggers (every time the data changes, for instance, or there is new data).

Again, there is much more to proper database design, but the elements discussed in this section can provide you with a starting point or a good refresher.

NOTE   For more information about SQL's Data Definition Language and Data Manipulation Language, see the chapter "Essential SQL" in the electronic book described in Appendix A.

Unidirectional Cursors

In local databases, tables are sequential files whose order is either the physical order or defined by an index. By contrast, database servers work on logical sets of data that aren't related to a physical order. A *relational* database server handles data according to the relational model: a mathematical model based on set theory.

For this discussion, it's important for you to know that in a relational database, the records (sometimes called *tuples*) of a table are identified not by position but exclusively through a primary key, based on one or more fields. Once you've obtained a set of records, the server adds to each of them a reference to the following record; thus you can move quickly from a record to the following one, but moving back to the previous record is extremely slow. For this reason, it is common to say that an RDBMS uses a *unidirectional* cursor. Connecting such a table or query to a DBGrid control is practically impossible, because doing so would make browsing the grid backward terribly slow.

Some database engines keep the data already retrieved in a cache to support full *bidirectional* navigation on it. In the Delphi architecture, this role can be played by the ClientDataSet component or another caching dataset. You'll see this process in more detail later, when we focus on dbExpress and the SQLDataset component.

NOTE   The case of a DBGrid used to browse an entire table is common in local programs but should generally be avoided in a client/server environment. It's better to filter out only part of the records and only the fields you are interested in. If you need to see a list of names, return all those starting with the letter *A*, then those with *B*, and so on, or ask the user for the initial letter of the name.

If proceeding backward might result in problems, keep in mind that jumping to the last record of a table is even worse; usually this operation implies fetching all the records! A similar situation applies to the RecordCount property of datasets. Computing the number of records often implies moving them all to the client computer. For this reason, the thumb of the DBGrid's vertical scrollbar works for a local table but not for a remote table. If you need to know the number of records, run a separate query to let the server (and not the client) compute it. For example, you can see how many records will be selected from the Employee table if you are interested in those records having a salary field higher than 50,000:

```
select count(*)
from Employee
where Salary > 50000
```

TIP Using the SQL instruction count(*) is a handy way to compute the number of records returned by a query. Instead of the * wildcard, you could use the name of a specific field, as in count(First_ Name), possibly combined with either distinct or all, to count only records with different values for the field or all the records having a non-null value.

Introducing InterBase

Although it has a limited market share, InterBase is a powerful RDBMS. In this section, I'll introduce the key technical features of InterBase (and the somewhat similar Firebird database) without getting into too much detail, because this is a book about Delphi programming. Most of the available material on InterBase is either in the documentation that accompanies the product or on a few websites devoted to it (your starting points for a search can be www.borland.com/interbase and www.ibphoenix.com).

InterBase was built from the beginning with a modern and robust architecture. Its original author, Jim Starkey, invented an architecture for handling concurrency and transactions without imposing physical locks on portions of the tables, something other well-known database servers can barely do even today. The InterBase architecture is called Multi-Generational Architecture (MGA); it handles concurrent access to the same data by multiple users, who can modify records without affecting what other concurrent users see in the database.

This approach naturally maps to the *Repeatable Read* transaction isolation mode, in which a user within a transaction keeps seeing the same data regardless of changes made and committed by other users. Technically, the server handles this situation by maintaining a different version of each accessed record for each open transaction. Even though this approach (also called *versioning*) can lead to larger memory consumption, it avoids most physical locks on the tables and makes the system much more robust in case of a crash. MGA also pushes toward a clear programming model— Repeatable Read—which other well-known database servers don't support without losing most of their performance.

In addition to the MGA at the heart of InterBase, the server has many other technical advantages:

◆ A limited footprint, which makes InterBase the ideal candidate for running directly on client computers, including portables. The disk space required by InterBase for a minimal installation is well below 10 MB, and its memory requirements are also incredibly limited.

◆ Good performance on large amounts of data.

◆ Availability on many different platforms (including 32-bit Windows, Solaris, and Linux), with totally compatible versions. Thus the server is scalable from very small to huge systems without notable differences.

◆ A very good track record, because InterBase has been in use for 15 years with few problems.

◆ A language complaint with the ANSI SQL standard.

◆ Advanced programming capabilities, including positional triggers, selectable stored procedures, updateable views, exceptions, events, generators, and more.

◆ Simple installation and management, with limited administrative headaches.

A SHORT HISTORY OF INTERBASE

Jim Starkey wrote InterBase for his Groton Database Systems company (hence the .GDS extension still used for InterBase files). The company was later bought by Ashton-Tate, which was then acquired by Borland. Borland handled InterBase directly for a while and then created an InterBase subsidiary, which was later reabsorbed into the parent company.

Since Delphi 1 an evaluation copy of InterBase has been distributed with the development tool, spreading the database server among developers. Although it doesn't have a large piece of the database server market, which is dominated by a handful of players, InterBase has been chosen by a few relevant organizations, from Ericsson to the U.S. Department of Defense, from stock exchanges to home banking systems.

InterBase history has a relevant change around the year 2000: Borland announced the release of InterBase 6 as an open-source database (December 1999), effectively released the source code to the community (July 2000), and made an officially certified version of InterBase 6 by Borland (March 2001). Between these events came announcements of the spin-off of a separate company to run the consulting and support business in addition to the open-source database. A group of former InterBase developers and managers (who had left Borland) formed IBPhoenix (www.ibphoenix.com) with the plan of supporting InterBase users.

At the same time, independent groups of InterBase experts started the Firebird open-source project to further extend InterBase. The project is hosted on SourceForge at the address http://sourceforge.net/projects/firebird/. For some time, SourceForge also hosted a Borland open-source project, but later the company announced it would continue to support only its proprietary version, dropping its open-source effort. In fact, Borland later released version 7 of InterBase (bundled also in Delphi 2005), with a traditional license.

In the meantime, Firebird is undergoing a more intensive development effort than InterBase. At the time of this writing, the current version is 1.5 and version 2.0 is at alpha stage. It will include a large number of new features to offer better performance and improved management of larger amounts of RAM. Firebird 2.0 will offer online incremental backups, global temporary tables, numerous optimizer improvements, and enhanced security features. At the same time, Jim Starkey himself is at work on a significant rewrite of Firebird for version 3 (called Vulcan), to better support multiprocessor architectures and 64-bit CPUs.

Using IBConsole

InterBase includes a front-end application called IBConsole. This full-fledged Windows program (built with Delphi) allows you to administer, configure, test, and query an InterBase server, whether local or remote.

IBConsole is a simple and complete system for managing InterBase servers and their databases. You can use it to look into the details of the database structure, modify it, query the data (which can be useful to develop the queries you want to embed in your program), back up and restore the database, and perform any other administrative tasks.

As you can see in Figure 14.1, IBConsole allows you to manage multiple servers and databases, all listed in a single configuration tree. You can ask for general information about the database and list its entities (tables, domains, stored procedures, triggers, and everything else), accessing the details of each. You can also create new databases and configure them, back up the files, update the definitions, check what's going on and who is currently connected, and so on.

The IBConsole application allows you to open multiple windows to look at detailed information, such as the tables window shown in Figure 14.2. In this window, you can see lists of the key properties of each table (columns, triggers, constraints, and indexes), see the raw metadata (the SQL definition of the table), access permissions, look at the data, modify the data, and study the table's dependencies. Similar windows are available for each of the other entities you can define in a database.

IBConsole embeds an improved version of the original Windows Interactive SQL application (see Figure 14.3). You can type a SQL statement in the upper portion of the window (without any help from the tool, unfortunately) and then execute the SQL query. As a result, you'll see the data as well as the access plan used by the database (which an expert can use to determine the efficiency of the query) and statistics about the operation performed by the server.

FIGURE 14.1

IBConsole lets you manage, from a single computer, InterBase databases hosted by multiple servers.

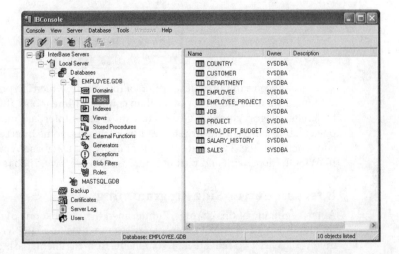

FIGURE 14.2

IBConsole can open separate windows to show you the details of each entity—in this case, a table.

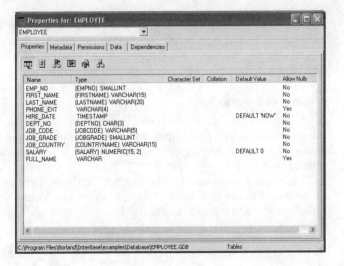

FIGURE 14.3
IBConsole's Interactive
SQL window lets you try
in advance the queries
you plan to include in
your Delphi programs.

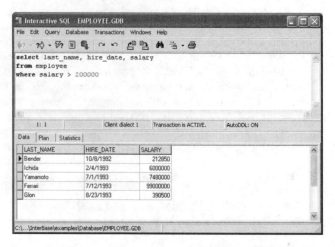

This has been a minimal description of IBConsole, which is a powerful tool (and the only one Borland includes with the server other than command-line tools). IBConsole is not the most complete tool in its category, though. Quite a few third-party InterBase management applications are more powerful, although not all are stable or user friendly. Some InterBase tools are shareware programs, and others are free. Two examples out of many are Database Workbench (`www.upscene.com`) and IB_WISQL (done with and part of InterBase Objects, `www.ibobjects.com`).

InterBase Server-Side Programming

At the beginning of this chapter, I underlined the fact that one of the objectives of client/server programming—and one of its problems—is the division of the workload between the computers involved. When you activate SQL statements from the client, the burden falls on the server to do most of the work. However, you should try to avoid `select` statements that return a large result set, jamming the network.

In addition to accepting DDL (Data Definition Language) and DML (Data Manipulation Language), most RDBMS servers allow you to create routines directly on the server using the standard SQL commands plus their own server-specific extensions (which generally are not portable). These routines typically come in two forms: stored procedures and triggers.

STORED PROCEDURES

Stored procedures are like the global functions of a Delphi unit and must be explicitly called by the client side. Stored procedures are generally used to define routines for data maintenance, to group sequences of operations you need in different circumstances, or to hold complex `select` statements.

Like Delphi procedures, stored procedures can have one or more typed parameters. Unlike Delphi procedures, they can have more than one return value. As an alternative to returning a value, a stored procedure can also return a result set—the result of an internal `select` statement or a custom fabricated one.

The following is a stored procedure written for InterBase; it receives a date as input and computes the highest salary among the employees hired on that date:

```
create procedure MaxSalOfTheDay (ofday date)
returns (maxsal decimal(8,2)) as
begin
  select max(salary)
  from employee
  where hiredate = :ofday
  into :maxsal;
end
```

Notice the use of the into clause, which tells the server to store the result of the select statement in the maxsal return value. To modify or delete a stored procedure, you can later use the alter procedure and drop procedure commands.

Looking at this stored procedure, you might wonder what its advantage is compared to the execution of a similar query activated from the client. The difference between the two approaches is not in the result you obtain but in its speed. A stored procedure is compiled on the server in an intermediate and faster notation when it is created, and the server determines at that time the strategy it will use to access the data. By contrast, a query is compiled every time the request is sent to the server. For this reason, a stored procedure can replace a very complex query, provided it doesn't change too often.

From Delphi, you can activate a stored procedure with the following SQL code:

```
select *
from MaxSalOfTheDay ('01/01/2003')
```

Triggers (and Generators)

Triggers behave more or less like Delphi events and are automatically activated when a given event occurs. Triggers can have specific code or call stored procedures; in both cases, the execution is done completely on the server. Triggers are used to keep data consistent, checking new data in more complex ways than a check constraint allows, and to automate the side effects of some input operations (such as creating a log of previous salary changes when the current salary is modified).

Triggers can be fired by the three basic data update operations: insert, update, and delete. When you create a trigger, you indicate whether it should fire before or after one of these three actions.

As an example of a trigger, you can use a generator to create a unique index in a table. Many tables use a unique index as a primary key. InterBase doesn't have an AutoInc field. Because multiple clients cannot generate unique identifiers, you can rely on the server to do this. Almost all database servers offer a counter you can call to ask for a new ID, which you should later use for the table. InterBase calls these automatic counters *generators*. Here is the sample InterBase code:

```
create generator cust_no_gen;
...
gen_id (cust_no_gen, 1);
```

The gen_id function extracts the new unique value of the generator passed as the first parameter; the second parameter indicates how much to increase (in this case, by one).

At this point you can add a trigger to a table (an automatic handler for one of the table's events). A trigger is similar to the event handler of the Table component, but you write it in SQL and execute it on the server, not on the client. Here is an example:

```
create trigger set_cust_no for customers
before insert position 0 as
begin
  new.cust_no = gen_id (cust_no_gen, 1);
end
```

This trigger is defined for the customers table and is activated each time a new record is inserted. The new symbol indicates the new record you are inserting. The position option indicates the order of execution of multiple triggers connected to the same event. (Triggers with the lowest values are executed first.)

Inside a trigger, you can write DML statements that also update other tables, but watch out for updates that end up reactivating the trigger and create endless recursion (although most servers raise an error when a trigger recurses too deeply, as a safety measure). You can later modify or disable a trigger by calling the alter trigger or drop trigger statement.

Triggers fire automatically for specified events. If you have to make many changes in the database using batch operations, the presence of a trigger can slow the process. If the input data has already been checked for consistency, you can temporarily deactivate the trigger. These batch operations are often coded in stored procedures, but stored procedures generally cannot issue DDL statements like those required for deactivating and reactivating the trigger. In this situation, you can define a view based on a select * from table command, thus creating an alias for the table. Then you can let the stored procedure do the batch processing on the table and apply the trigger to the view (which should also be used by the client program).

The dbExpress Library

Nowadays, the mainstream access to a database server in Delphi is provided by the dbExpress library. As mentioned in Chapter 13, this is not the only possibility but is certainly the mainstream approach. The dbExpress library, first introduced in Kylix and Delphi 6, allows you to access different servers. I provided a general overview of dbExpress compared with other solutions in Chapter 13, so here I'll skip the introductory material and focus on technical elements.

dbExpress in Delphi 2005 supports the most recent versions of several RDBMS, although most of the time previous versions are supported as well:

- InterBase 7.5

- Oracle 10g

- IBM DB2 UDB 8.x

- Microsoft SQL Server 2000

- IBM Informix 9.x

- SQL Anywhere 9

- MySQL 4.0.x

- Sybase 12.5

NOTE   The driver for Microsoft SQL Server, available since Delphi 7, is not implemented by interfacing the vendor library natively, as other dbExpress drivers do, but by interfacing Microsoft's OLEDB provider for SQL Server. (I'll talk more about OLEDB providers in Chapter 15.)

Working with Unidirectional Cursors

The motto of dbExpress could be "fetch but don't cache." The key difference between this library and BDE or ADO is that dbExpress can only execute SQL queries and fetch the results with a *unidirectional cursor*. As you just saw, in unidirectional database access you can move from one record to the next, but you cannot get back to a previous record of the dataset (except by reopening the query and fetching all the records again -1, an incredibly slow operation that dbExpress blocks). This is because the library doesn't store the data it has retrieved in a local cache, but only passes it from the database server to the calling application.

Using a unidirectional cursor might sound like a limitation, and it is—in addition to having problems with navigation, you cannot connect a database grid to a dataset. However, a unidirectional dataset is good for the following:

◆ You can use a unidirectional dataset for reporting purposes. In a printed report, as well as an HTML page or an XML transformation, you move from record to record, produce the output, and that's it—no need to return to past records and, in general, no user interaction with the data. Unidirectional datasets are probably the best option for web and multitier architectures. As you'll see in Chapter 16, this is the same model followed by connected data access in ADO.NET.

◆ You can use a unidirectional dataset to feed a local cache, such as the one provided by a ClientDataSet component. At this point, you can connect visual components to the in-memory dataset and operate on it with all the standard techniques, including the use of visual grids. You can freely navigate and edit the data in the in-memory cache and control it far better than with the BDE or ADO. As you'll see in Chapter 16, this is the same approach employed by disconnected data access in ADO.NET.

It's important to notice that, in these circumstances, avoiding the caching of the database engine saves time and memory. The library doesn't have to use extra memory for the cache and doesn't need to waste time storing data (and duplicating information). Over the last couple of years, many programmers moved from BDE-based cached updates to the ClientDataSet component, which provides more flexibility in managing the content of the data and updating information they keep in memory. However, using a ClientDataSet on top of the BDE (or ADO) exposes you to the risk of having two separate caches, which wastes a lot of memory.

Another advantage of using the ClientDataSet component is that its cache supports editing operations, and the updates stored in this cache can be applied to the original database server by the DataSetProvider component. This component can generate the proper SQL update statements and can do so in a more flexible way than the BDE (although ADO is powerful in this respect). In general, the provider can also use a dataset for the updates, but this isn't directly possible with the dbExpress dataset components.

Platforms and Databases

A key element of the dbExpress library is its availability for both Windows and Linux, in contrast to the other database engines available for Delphi (BDE and ADO), which are available only for

Windows. However, some of the database-specific components, such as InterBase Express, are also available on multiple platforms.

When you use dbExpress, you are provided with a common framework, which is independent of the SQL database server you are planning to use. dbExpress comes with drivers for MySQL, Inter-Base, Oracle, Informix, Microsoft SQL Server, and IBM DB2.

NOTE It is possible to write custom drivers for the dbExpress architecture. This is documented in detail in the paper "dbExpress Draft Specification," published on the Borland Community website. At the time of this writing, this document is at http://bdn.borland.com/article/ 0,1410,22495,00.html. You'll probably be able to find third-party drivers. For example, there is a free driver that bridges dbExpress and ODBC. A complete list is hosted in the article at http:// bdn.borland.com/article/0,1410,28371,00.html.

Driver Versioning Troubles

Technically, the dbExpress drivers are available as separate DLLs you have to deploy along with your program. The problem is, these DLLs' names haven't changed since the earlier versions of Delphi. So, if you install a Delphi compiled application on a machine that has the dbExpress drivers found in an older version of Delphi, the application will apparently work, open a connection to the server, but then it might fail when retrieving data. At that point you might see an error like "SQL Error: Error mapping failed." This is not a good hint that there is a version mismatch in the dbExpress driver!

To verify this problem, look at whether the DLL has proper version information—so you can figure out if you are working with the Delphi 2005 version (version 9), the Delphi 7 version, or (if version information is missing) the old and incompatible Delphi 6 driver. To make your applications more robust, you can provide a similar check within your code, accessing the version information using the related Windows APIs:

```
function GetDriverVersion (strDriverName: string): Integer;
var
  nInfoSize, nDetSize: DWord;
  pVInfo, pDetail: Pointer;
begin
  // the default, in case there is no version information
  Result := 6;
  // read version information
  nInfoSize := GetFileVersionInfoSize (pChar(strDriverName), nDetSize);
  if nInfoSize > 0 then
  begin
    GetMem (pVInfo, nInfoSize);
    try
      GetFileVersionInfo (pChar(strDriverName), 0, nInfoSize, pVInfo);
      VerQueryValue (pVInfo, '\', pDetail, nDetSize);
      Result := HiWord (TVSFixedFileInfo(pDetail^).dwFileVersionMS);
    finally
      FreeMem (pVInfo);
    end;
  end;
end;
```

This code snippet is taken from the DbxMulti example discussed later. The program uses it to raise an exception if the DLL version is too old (there should be no problem with future versions):

```
if GetDriverVersion ('dbexpint.dll') < 9 then
  raise Exception.Create (
    'Incompatible version of the dbExpress driver "dbexpint.dll" found');
```

If you try to put the driver found in bin folder of Delphi 6 or Delphi 7 in the application folder, you'll see the error. You'll have to modify this extra safety check to account for updated versions of the drivers or libraries, but this step should help you avoid the installation troubles dbExpress meant to solve in the first place.

You also have an alternative: you can statically link the dbExpress drivers' code into your application. To do so, include a given unit (like dbexpint.dcu or dbexpora.dcu) in your program, listing it in one of the uses statements. This feature is available in Delphi 2005 only in the Win32 personality.

The dbExpress Components

The VCL components used to interface the dbExpress library encompass a group of dataset components plus a few ancillary ones. To differentiate these components from other database-access families, the components are prefixed with the letters *SQL*, underlining the fact that they are used for accessing RDBMS servers.

These components include a database connection component, a few dataset components (a generic one; three specific versions for tables, queries, and stored procedures; and one encapsulating a Client-DataSet component), and a monitor utility.

The SQLConnection Component

The TSQLConnection class inherits from the TCustomConnection component. It handles database connections the same as its sibling classes (the Database, ADOConnection, and IBConnection components).

TIP   Unlike other component families, in dbExpress the connection is compulsory. In the dataset components you cannot specify directly which database to use and can only refer to a SQLConnection.

The connection component uses the information available in the drivers.ini and connections.ini files, which are dbExpress's only two configuration files (these files are saved by default under Common Files\Borland Shared\DBExpress). The drivers.ini file lists the available dbExpress drivers, one for each supported database. For each driver there is a set of default connection parameters. For example, the InterBase section reads as follows:

```
[Interbase]
GetDriverFunc=getSQLDriverINTERBASE
LibraryName=dbexpint.dll
VendorLib=GDS32.DLL
BlobSize=-1
CommitRetain=False
Database=database.gdb
Password=masterkey
RoleName=RoleName
```

```
ServerCharSet=ASCII
SQLDialect=1
Interbase TransIsolation=ReadCommited
User_Name=sysdba
WaitOnLocks=True
```

The parameters indicate the dbExpress driver DLL (the `LibraryName` value), the entry function to use (`GetDriverFunc`), the vendor client library, and other specific parameters that depend on the database. If you read the entire `drivers.ini` file, you'll see that the parameters are really database-specific. Some of these parameters don't make a lot of sense at the driver level (such as the database to connect to), but the list includes all the available parameters, regardless of their usage.

NOTE   To be picky, the default password is actually the eight-character "masterke" string. The last letter, y, is superfluous. Still, I tend to use the full word, which is very common and simpler to remember.

The `connections.ini` file provides the database-specific description. This list associates settings with a name, and you can enter multiple connection details for every database driver. The connection describes the physical database you want to connect to. As an example, this is the portion for the default `IBLocal` definition:

```
[IBLocal]
BlobSize=-1
CommitRetain=False
Database=C:\Program Files\Common Files\Borland Shared\Data\employee.gdb
DriverName=Interbase
Password=masterkey
RoleName=RoleName
ServerCharSet=ASCII
SQLDialect=1
Interbase TransIsolation=ReadCommited
User_Name=sysdba
WaitOnLocks=True
```

As you can see by comparing the two listings, this is a subset of the driver's parameters. When you create a new connection, the system will copy the default parameters from the driver; you can then edit them for the specific connection—for example, providing a proper database name. Each connection relates to the driver for its key attributes, as indicated by the `DriverName` property. Notice also that the database referenced here is the result of my editing, corresponding to the settings I'll use in most examples.

It's important to remember that these initialization files are used only at design time. When you select a driver or a connection at design time, the values of these files are copied to corresponding properties of the SQLConnection component, as in this example:

```
object SQLConnection1: TSQLConnection
  ConnectionName = 'IBLocal'
  DriverName = 'Interbase'
  GetDriverFunc = 'getSQLDriverINTERBASE'
  LibraryName = 'dbexpint.dll'
```

```
        LoginPrompt = False
        Params.Strings = (
          'BlobSize=-1'
          'CommitRetain=False'
          'Database=C:\Program Files\Common Files\Borland Shared\Data\employee.gdb'
          'DriverName=Interbase'
          'Password=masterkey'
          'RoleName=RoleName'
          'ServerCharSet=ASCII'
          'SQLDialect=1'
          'Interbase TransIsolation=ReadCommited'
          'User_Name=sysdba'
          'WaitOnLocks=True')
        VendorLib = 'GDS32.DLL'
      end
```

At run time, your program will rely on the properties to have all the required information, so you don't need to deploy the two configuration files along with your programs. In theory, the files will be required if you want to change the DriverName or ConnectionName properties at run time. However, if you want to connect your program to a new database, you can set the relevant properties directly.

When you add a new SQLConnection component to an application, you can proceed in different ways. You can set up a driver using the list of values available for the DriverName property and then select a predefined connection by selecting one of the values available in the ConnectionName property. This second list is filtered according to the driver you've already selected. As an alternative, you can begin by selecting the ConnectionName property directly; in this case it includes the entire list.

Instead of hooking up an existing connection, you can define a new one (or see the details of the existing connections) by double-clicking the SQLConnection component and launching the dbExpress Connections Editor (see Figure 14.4). This editor lists on the left all the predefined connections (for a specific driver or all of them) and allows you to edit the connection properties using the grid on the right. You can use the toolbar buttons to add, delete, rename, and test connections and to open the read-only dbExpress Drivers Settings window (also shown in Figure 14.4).

FIGURE 14.4

The dbExpress Connections Editor with the dbExpress Drivers Settings dialog box

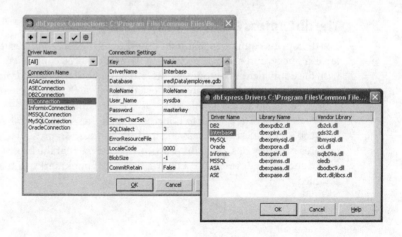

In addition to letting you edit the predefined connection settings, the dbExpress Connections Editor allows you to select a connection for the SQLConnection component by clicking the OK button. Note that if you change any settings, the data is immediately written to the configuration files—clicking the Cancel button doesn't undo your editing!

To define access to a database, editing the connection properties is certainly the suggested approach. This way, when you need to access the same database from another application or another connection within the same application, all you need to do is select the connection. However, because this operation copies the connection data, updating the connection doesn't automatically refresh the values within other SQLConnection components referring to the same named connection: you must reselect the connection to which these other components refer.

What really matters for the SQLConnection component is the value of its properties. Driver and vendor libraries are listed in properties you can freely change at design time (although you'll rarely want to do this), whereas the database and other database-specific connection settings are specified in the Params properties. This is a string list including information such as the database name, the username and password, and so on. In practice, you could set up a SQLConnection component by setting up the driver and then assigning the database name directly in the Params property, forgetting about the predefined connection. I'm not suggesting this as the best option, but it is certainly a possibility; the predefined connections are handy, but when the data changes, you still have to manually refresh every SQLConnection component.

To be complete, I have to mention that there is an alternative. You can set the LoadParamsOnConnect property to indicate that you want to refresh the component parameters from the initialization files every time you open the connection. In this case, a change in the predefined connections will be reloaded when you open the connection, at either design time or run time. At design time, this technique is handy (it has the same effect as reselecting the connection); but using it at run time means you'll also have to deploy the connections.ini file, which can be a good idea or inconvenient, depending on your deployment environment.

The only property of the SQLConnection component that is not related to the driver and database settings is LoginPrompt. Setting it to False allows you to provide a password among the component settings and skip the login request dialog box, both at design time and at run time. Although this is handy for development, it can reduce the security of your system. Of course, you should also use this option for unattended connections, such as on a web server.

The dbExpress Dataset Components

The dbExpress component's family provides four different dataset components: a generic dataset, a table, a query, and a stored procedure. The latter three components are provided for compatibility with the equivalent BDE components and have similarly named properties. If you don't have to port existing code, you should generally use the general SQLDataSet component, which lets you execute a query and also access a table or a stored procedure.

The first important thing to notice is that all these datasets inherit from a new special base class, TCustomSQLDataSet. This class and its derived classes represent unidirectional datasets, with the key features I already described. In practice, this means that the browse operations are limited to calling First and Next; Prior, Last, Locate, the use of bookmarks, and all other navigational features are disabled.

NOTE   Technically, some of the moving operations call the `CheckBiDirectional` internal function and eventually raise an exception. `CheckBiDirectional` refers to the public `IsUnidirectional` property of the `TDataSet` class, which you can eventually use in your own code to disable operations that are illegal on unidirectional datasets.

In addition to having limited navigational capabilities, these datasets have no editing support, so a lot of methods and events common to other datasets are not available. For example, there is no `AfterEdit` or `BeforePost` event.

As I mentioned earlier, of the four dataset components for dbExpress, the fundamental one is `TSQLDataSet`, which can be used both to retrieve a dataset and to execute a command. The two alternatives are activated by calling the `Open` method (or setting the `Active` property to True) and by calling the `ExecSQL` method.

The `SQLDataSet` component can retrieve an entire table, or it can use a SQL query or a stored procedure to read a dataset or issue a command. The `CommandType` property determines one of the three access modes. The possible values are ctQuery, ctStoredProc, and ctTable, which determine the value of the `CommandText` property (and also the behavior of the related property editor in the Object Inspector). For a table or stored procedure, the `CommandText` property indicates the name of the related database element, and the editor provides a drop-down list containing the possible values. For a query, the `CommandText` property stores the text of the SQL command, and the editor provides a little help in building the SQL query (in case it is a SELECT statement). You can see the editor in Figure 14.5. Notice that this editor's feature set has been expanded in Delphi 2005, making it easier to write queries and work with stored procedures.

When you use a table, the component will generate a SQL query for you, because dbExpress targets only SQL databases. The generated query will include all the fields of the table, and if you specify the `SortFieldNames` property, it will include an `order by` directive.

The three *specific* dataset components offer similar behavior, but you specify the SQL query in the SQL string list property, the stored procedure in the `StoredProcName` property, and the table name in the `TableName` property (as in the three corresponding BDE components).

FIGURE 14.5

The CommandText Editor used by the SQLDataSet component for queries has been significantly updated in Delphi 2005.

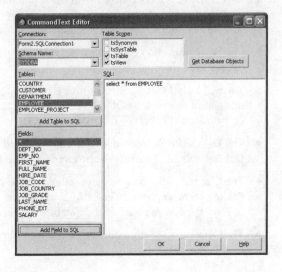

THE SIMPLEDATASET COMPONENT

The SimpleDataSet component is a combination of four existing components: SQLConnection, SQL-DataSet, DataSetProvider, and ClientDataSet. The component is meant to be a helper—you need only one component instead of four (which must also be connected). The component is basically a compound component that inherits from client dataset and embeds two subcomponents (the two dbExpress ones), plus a hidden provider. (The fact that the provider is hidden is odd, because it is created as a subcomponent.)

The component allows you to modify the properties and events of the subcomponents (besides the provider) and replace the internal connection with an external one, so that multiple datasets share the same database connection. In addition to problems caused by the hidden provider, the component has other limitations, including difficulty manipulating the dataset fields of the data access dataset (which is important for setting key fields and can affect the way updates are generated) and unavailability of some provider events. So, other than for simple applications, I don't recommend using the SimpleDataSet component.

NOTE Notice that this component was missing in Delphi 8 for .NET, but has been reintroduced in the .NET personality of Delphi 2005.

The SQLMonitor Component

The final component in the dbExpress group is SQLMonitor, which is used to log requests sent from dbExpress to the database server. This monitor lets you see the commands sent to the database and the low-level responses you receive, monitoring the client/server traffic at a low level.

A Few dbExpress Demos

Let's look at a demonstration that highlights the key features of these components and shows how to use the ClientDataSet to provide caching and editing support for the unidirectional datasets. Later, I'll show you an example of native use of the unidirectional query, with no caching and editing support required.

The standard visual application based on dbExpress uses this series of components:

◆ The SQLConnection component provides the connection with the database and the proper dbExpress driver.

◆ The SQLDataSet component, which is hooked to the connection (via the `SQLConnection` property), indicates which SQL query to execute or table to open (using the `CommandType` and `CommandText` properties discussed earlier).

◆ The DataSetProvider component, connected with the dataset, extracts the data from the SQL-DataSet and can generate the proper SQL update statements.

◆ The ClientDataSet component reads from the data provider and stores all the data (if its `PacketRecords` property is set to –1) in memory. You'll need to call its `ApplyUpdates` method to send the updates back to the database server (through the provider).

◆ The DataSource component allows you to surface the data from the ClientDataSet to the visual data-aware controls.

As I mentioned earlier, the picture can be simplified by using the SimpleDataSet component, which replaces the two datasets and the provider (and possibly even the connection). The Simple-DataSet component combines most of the properties of the components it replaces.

Using a Single Component or Many Components

For this first example, drop a SimpleDataSet component on a form and set the connection name of its Connection subcomponent. Set the CommandType and CommandText properties to specify which data to fetch, and set the PacketRecords property to indicate how many records to retrieve in each block. These are the key properties of the component in the DbxSingle example:

```
object SimpleDataSet1: TSimpleDataSet
  Connection.ConnectionName = 'IBLocal'
  Connection.LoginPrompt = False
  DataSet.CommandText = 'EMPLOYEE'
  DataSet.CommandType = ctTable
end
```

As an alternative, the DbxMulti example uses the entire sequence of components:

```
object SQLConnection1: TSQLConnection
  ConnectionName = 'IBLocal'
  LoginPrompt = False
end
object SQLDataSet1: TSQLDataSet
  SQLConnection = SQLConnection1
  CommandText = 'select * from EMPLOYEE'
end
object DataSetProvider1: TDataSetProvider
  DataSet = SQLDataSet1
end
object ClientDataSet1: TClientDataSet
  ProviderName = 'DataSetProvider1'
end
object DataSource1: TDataSource
  DataSet = ClientDataSet1
end
```

Both examples include some visual controls: a grid and a toolbar based on the action manager architecture.

APPLYING UPDATES

In every example based on a local cache, like the one provided by the ClientDataSet and Simple-DataSet components, it's important to write the local changes back to the database server. This is typically accomplished by calling the ApplyUpdates method. You can either keep the changes in the local cache for a while and then apply multiple updates at once, or you can post each change right away. In these two examples, I've gone for the latter approach, attaching the following event handler to the AfterPost (fired after an edit or an insert operation) and AfterDelete events of the ClientDataSet components:

```
procedure TForm1.DoUpdate(DataSet: TDataSet);
begin
  // immediately apply local changes to the database
  SQLClientDataSet1.ApplyUpdates(0);
end;
```

If you want to apply all the updates in a single batch, you can do so either when the form is closed or when the program ends, or you can let a user perform the update operation by selecting a specific command, possibly using the corresponding predefined action (of the TClientDataSetApply class). We'll explore this approach when discussing the update caching support of the ClientDataSet component in more detail later in this chapter.

MONITORING THE CONNECTION

Another feature I added to the DbxSingle and DbxMulti examples is the monitoring capability offered by the SQLMonitor component. In the example, the component is activated as the program starts. In the DbxSingle example, because the SimpleDataSet embeds the connection, the monitor cannot be hooked to it at design time, only when the program starts:

```
procedure TForm1.FormCreate(Sender: TObject);
begin
  SQLMonitor1.SQLConnection := SimpleDataSet1.Connection;
  SQLMonitor1.Active := True;
  SimpleDataSet1.Active := True;
end;
```

Every time a tracing string is available, the component fires the OnTrace event to let you choose whether to include the string in the log. If the LogTrace parameter of this event is True (the default value), the component logs the message in the TraceList string list and fires the OnLogTrace event to indicate that a new string has been added to the log.

The component can also automatically store the log into the file indicated by its FileName property, but I didn't use this feature in the example. All I did was handle the OnLogTrace event, adding the log string to the memo with the following code (producing the output shown in Figure 14.6):

```
procedure TForm1.SQLMonitor1LogTrace(Sender: TObject;
  CBInfo: pSQLTRACEDesc);
begin
  MemoLog.Lines.Add (CBInfo.pszTrace);
end;
```

In the VCL for .NET, the pointer parameter would cause some trouble so the method has to be replaced by the following (in the DbxMulti example I provide both in two IFDEF statements):

```
procedure TForm1.SQLMonitor1LogTrace(Sender: TObject;
  var CBInfo: SQLTRACEDesc);
```

FIGURE 14.6

A sample log obtained by the SQLMonitor in the DbxSingle example

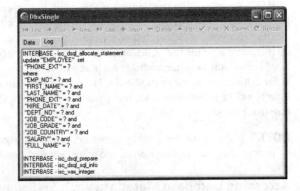

CONTROLLING THE SQL UPDATE CODE

If you run the DbxSingle program and change, for example, an employee's telephone number, the monitor will log this update operation:

```
update EMPLOYEE set
   PHONE_EXT = ?
where
   EMP_NO = ? and
   FIRST_NAME = ? and
   LAST_NAME = ? and
   PHONE_EXT = ? and
   HIRE_DATE = ? and
   DEPT_NO = ? and
   JOB_CODE = ? and
   JOB_GRADE = ? and
   JOB_COUNTRY = ? and
   SALARY = ? and
   FULL_NAME = ?
```

By setting the SimpleDataSet's properties there is no way to change how the update code is generated (this happens to be worse than with the SQLClientDataSet component, which had the UpdateMode you could use to tweak the update statements).

In the DbxMulti example, you can use the UpdateMode property of the DataSetProvider component, setting the value to upWhereChanged or upWhereKeyOnly. In this case you'll get the following two statements, respectively:

```
update EMPLOYEE set
   PHONE_EXT = ?
where
   EMP_NO = ? and
   PHONE_EXT = ?
```

```
update EMPLOYEE set
   PHONE_EXT = ?
where
   EMP_NO = ?
```

If you want more control over how the update statements are generated, you need to operate on the fields of the underlying dataset, which are also available when you use the all-in-one Simple-DataSet component (which has two field editors, one for the base ClientDataset component it inherits from and one for the SQLDataSet component it embeds). I made similar corrections in the DbxMulti example: after adding persistent fields for the SQLDataSet component I modified the provider options for some of the fields. To include them in the key I added the pfInKey flag in their `ProviderFlags` property and to exclude them from updates I've removed removing pfInUpdate flag from the same property.

NOTE   We'll discuss this type of problem again when we examine the details of the ClientDataSet component, the provider, the resolver, and other technical details later in this chapter and in Chapter 17.

Accessing Database Metadata with *SetSchemaInfo*

All RDBMS systems use special-purpose tables (generally called *system tables*) for storing metadata, such as the list of the tables, their fields, indexes, and constraints, and any other system information. Just as dbExpress provides a unified API for working with different database servers, it also provides a common way to access metadata. The SQLDataSet component has a SetSchemaInfo method that fills the dataset with system information. This SetSchemaInfo method has three parameters:

SchemaType   Indicates the type of information requested. Values include stTables, stSysTables, stProcedures, stColumns, and stProcedureParams.

SchemaObject   Indicates the object you are referring to, such as the name of the table whose columns you are requesting.

SchemaPattern   A filter that lets you limit your request to tables, columns, or procedures starting with the given letters. This is handy if you use prefixes to identify groups of elements.

For example, in the SchemaTest program, a Tables button reads into the dataset all of the connected database's tables:

```
ClientDataSet1.Close;
SQLDataSet1.SetSchemaInfo (stTables, '', '');
ClientDataSet1.Open;
```

The program uses the usual group of dataset provider, client dataset, and data source component to display the resulting data in a grid, as you can see in Figure 14.7. After you've retrieved the tables, you can select a row in the grid and click the Fields button to see a list of the fields of this table:

```
SQLDataSet1.SetSchemaInfo (stColumns,
  ClientDataSet1['Table_Name'], '');
ClientDataSet1.Close;
ClientDataSet1.Open;
```

In addition to letting you access database metadata, dbExpress provides a way to access its own configuration information, including the installed drivers and the configured connections. The unit DbConnAdmin defines a TConnectionAdmin class for this purpose, but the aim of this support is limited to dbExpress add-on utilities for developers (end users aren't commonly allowed to access multiple databases in a totally dynamic way).

FIGURE 14.7
The SchemaTest example allows you to see a database's tables and the columns of a given table.

RECNO	CATALOG_NAME	SCHEMA_NAME	TABLE_NAME	TABLE_TYPE
1	<NULL>	SYSDBA	COUNTRY	1
2	<NULL>	SYSDBA	CUSTOMER	1
3	<NULL>	SYSDBA	DEPARTMENT	1
4	<NULL>	SYSDBA	EMPLOYEE	1
5	<NULL>	SYSDBA	EMPLOYEE_PROJECT	1
6	<NULL>	SYSDBA	JOB	1
7	<NULL>	SYSDBA	PHONE_LIST	2
8	<NULL>	SYSDBA	PROJECT	1
9	<NULL>	SYSDBA	PROJ_DEPT_BUDGET	1
10	<NULL>	SYSDBA	SALARY_HISTORY	1
11	<NULL>	SYSDBA	SALES	1

NOTE The DbxExplorer demo included in Delphi shows how to access both dbExpress administration files and schema information. Also check the Delphi help file under "Fetching Metadata into a Unidirectional Dataset" (`ms-help://borland.bds3/bds3win32devguide/html/unifetchingmetadataintoaunidirectionaldataset.htm`).

A Parameterized Query

When you need slightly different versions of the same SQL query, instead of modifying the text of the query itself each time, you can write a query with a parameter and change the value of the parameter. For example, if you decide to have a user choose the employees in a given country (using the Employee table), you can write the following parameterized query:

```
select *
from employee
where job_country = :country
```

In this SQL clause, `:country` is a parameter. You can set its data type and startup value using the editor of the SQLDataSet component's `Params` property collection. When the `Params` collection editor is open, as shown in Figure 14.8, you see a list of the parameters defined in the SQL statement; you can set the data type and the initial value of these parameters in the Object Inspector.

FIGURE 14.8
Editing a query component's collection of parameters

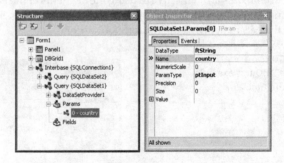

The form displayed by this program, called ParQuery, uses a combo box to provide all the available values for the parameters. Instead of preparing the combo box items at design time, you can extract the available contents from the same database table as the program starts. This is accomplished using a second query component with this SQL statement:

```
select distinct job_country
from employee
```

After activating this query, the program scans its result set, extracting all the values and adding them to the list box:

```
procedure TQueryForm.FormCreate(Sender: TObject);
begin
  SqlDataSet2.Open;
  while not SqlDataSet2.EOF do
  begin
    ComboBox1.Items.Add (SqlDataSet2.Fields [0].AsString);
    SqlDataSet2.Next;
  end;
  ComboBox1.Text := CombBox1.Items[0];
end;
```

The user can select a different item in the combo box and then click the Select button (Button1) to change the parameter and activate (or reactivate) the query:

```
procedure TQueryForm.Button1Click(Sender: TObject);
begin
  SqlDataSet1.Close;
  ClientDataSet1.Close;
  Query1.Params[0].Value := ListBox1.Items [Listbox1.ItemIndex];
  SqlDataSet1.Open;
  ClientDataSet1.Open;
end;
```

This code displays the employees from the selected country in the DBGrid, as you can see in Figure 14.9. As an alternative to using the elements of the Params array by position, you should consider using the ParamByName method to avoid any problem in case the query gets modified over time and the parameters end up in a different order.

FIGURE 14.9
The ParQuery example
at run time

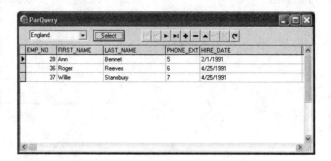

By using parameterized queries, you can usually reduce the amount of data moved over the wire from the server to the client and still use a DBGrid and the standard user interface common in local database applications.

TIP Parameterized queries are generally also used to obtain master-detail architectures with SQL queries—at least, this is what Delphi tends to do. The `DataSource` property of the SQLDataSet component automatically replaces parameter values with the fields of the master dataset having the same name as the parameter.

When One-Way Is Enough: Printing Data

You have seen that one of the key elements of the dbExpress library is that it returns unidirectional datasets. In addition, you can use the ClientDataSet component (in one of its incarnations) to store the records in a local cache. Now, let's discuss an example in which a unidirectional dataset is all you need.

Such a situation is common in *reporting*—that is, producing information for each record in sequence without needing any further access to the data. This broad category includes producing printed reports (via a set of reporting components or using the printer directly), sending data to another application such as Microsoft Excel or Word, saving data to files (including HTML and XML formats), and more.

I don't want to delve into HTML and XML, so I'll present an example of printing—nothing fancy and nothing based on reporting components, just a way to produce a draft report on your monitor and printer. For this reason, I used Delphi's most straightforward technique to produce a printout: assigning a file to the printer with the `AssignPrn` RTL procedure.

The example, called UniPrint, has a unidirectional SQLDataSet component hooked to an InterBase connection and based on the following SQL statement, which joins the Employee table with the Department table to display the name of the department where each employee works:

```
select d.DEPARTMENT, e.FULL_NAME, e.JOB_COUNTRY, e.HIRE_DATE
from EMPLOYEE e
inner join DEPARTMENT d on d.DEPT_NO = e.DEPT_NO
```

To handle printing, I wrote a somewhat generic routine, requiring as parameters the data to print, a progress bar for status information, the output font, and the maximum format size of each field. The entire routine uses file-print support and formats each field in a fixed-size, left-aligned string, to produce a columnar type of report. The call to the `Format` function has a parameterized format string that's built dynamically using the size of the field.

In Listing 14.1 you can see the code of the core `PrintOutDataSet` procedure, which uses three nested `try/finally` blocks to release all the resources properly.

LISTING 14.1: The core procedure of the UniPrint example

```
procedure PrintOutDataSet (data: TDataSet;
  progress: TProgressBar; Font: TFont; toFile: Boolean; maxSize: Integer = 30);
var
  PrintFile: TextFile;
  I: Integer;
  sizeStr: string;
```

```
  oldFont: TFontRecall;
begin
  // assign the output to a printer or a file
  if toFile then
  begin
    SelectDirectory ('Choose a folder', '', strDir);
    AssignFile (PrintFile,
      IncludeTrailingPathDelimiter(strDir) + 'output.txt');
  end
  else
    AssignPrn (PrintFile);
  // assign the printer to a file
  AssignPrn (PrintFile);
  Rewrite (PrintFile);

  // set the font and keep the original one
  oldFont := TFontRecall.Create (Printer.Canvas.Font);
  try
    Printer.Canvas.Font := Font;
    try
      data.Open;
      try
        // print header (field names) in bold
        Printer.Canvas.Font.Style := [fsBold];
        for I := 0 to data.FieldCount - 1 do
        begin
          sizeStr := IntToStr (
            min (data.Fields[i].DisplayWidth, maxSize));
          Write (PrintFile, Format ('%-' + sizeStr + 's',
            [data.Fields[i].FieldName]));
        end;
        Writeln (PrintFile);

        // for each record of the dataset
        Printer.Canvas.Font.Style := [];
        while not data.EOF do
        begin
          // print out each field of the record
          for I := 0 to data.FieldCount - 1 do
          begin
            sizeStr := IntToStr (
              min (data.Fields[i].DisplayWidth, maxSize));
            Write (PrintFile, Format ('%-' + sizeStr + 's',
              [data.Fields[i].AsString]));
          end;
          Writeln (PrintFile);
```

```
      // advance ProgressBar
      progress.Position := progress.Position + 1;
      data.Next;
    end;
  finally
    // close the dataset
    data.Close;
  end;
finally
  // reassign the original printer font
  oldFont.Free;
end;
finally
  // close the printer/file
  CloseFile (PrintFile);
end;
end;
```

The program invokes this routine when you click the Print All button. It executes a separate query (select count(*) from EMPLOYEE), which returns the number of records in the Employee table. This query is necessary to set up the progress bar (the unidirectional dataset has no way of knowing how many records it will retrieve until it has reached the last one). Then it sets the output font, possibly using a fixed-width font, and calls the PrintOutDataSet routine:

```
procedure TNavigator.PrintAllButtonClick(Sender: TObject);
var
  Font: TFont;
begin
  // set ProgressBar range
  EmplCountData.Open;
  try
    ProgressBar1.Max := EmplCountData.Fields[0].AsInteger;
  finally
    EmplCountData.Close;
  end;

  Font := TFont.Create;
  try
    Font.Name := 'Courier New';
    Font.Size := 9;
    PrintOutDataSet (EmplData, ProgressBar1, Font, cbFile.Checked);
  finally
    Font.Free;
  end;
end;
```

The Packets and the Cache

The ClientDataSet component reads data in packets containing the number of records indicated by the PacketRecords property. The default value of this property is –1, which means the provider will pull all the records at once (this is reasonable only for a small dataset). Alternatively, you can set this value to zero to ask the server for only the field descriptors and no data, or you can use any positive value to specify a number.

If you retrieve only a partial dataset, as you browse past the end of the local cache, if the FetchOnDemand property is set to True (the default value), the ClientDataSet component will get more records from its source. This property also controls whether BLOB fields and nested datasets of the current records are fetched automatically (these values might not be part of the data packet, depending on the dataset provider's Options value).

If you turn off this property, you'll need to fetch more records manually by calling the GetNextPacket method until the method returns zero. (You call FetchBlobs and FetchDetails for these other elements.)

WARNING   Notice, by the way, that before you set an index for the data, you should retrieve the entire dataset (either by going to its last record or by setting the PacketRecords property to –1). Otherwise you'll have an odd index based on partial data.

Manipulating Updates

One of the core ideas behind the ClientDataSet component is that it is used as a local cache to collect input from a user and then send a batch of update requests to the database. The component has both a list of the changes to apply to the database server, stored in the same format used by the ClientDataSet (accessible though the Delta property), and a complete update log that you can manipulate with a few methods (including an Undo capability).

TIP   The ClientDataSet component's ApplyUpdates and Undo operations are also accessible through predefined actions.

THE STATUS OF THE RECORDS

The component lets you monitor what's going on within the data packets. The UpdateStatus method returns one of the following indicators for the current record:

```
type TUpdateStatus = (usUnmodified, usModified, usInserted, usDeleted);
```

To easily check the status of every record in the client dataset, you can add a string-type calculated field to the dataset (I called it ClientDataSet1Status) and compute its value with the following OnCalcFields event handler:

```
procedure TForm1.ClientDataSet1CalcFields(DataSet: TDataSet);
begin
  ClientDataSet1Status.AsString := GetEnumName (TypeInfo(TUpdateStatus),
    Integer (ClientDataSet1.UpdateStatus));
end;
```

This method (based on the RTTI GetEnumName function) converts the current value of the TUpdateStatus enumeration to a string, with the effect you can see in Figure 14.10.

FIGURE 14.10

The CdsDelta program displays the status of each record of a Client-DataSet.

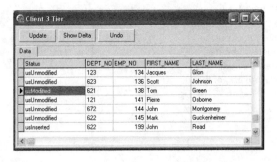

ACCESSING THE DELTA

Beyond examining the status of each record, the best way to understand which changes have occurred in a given ClientDataSet (but haven't been uploaded to the server) is to look at the *delta*—the list of changes waiting to be applied to the server. This property is defined as follows:

```
property Delta: OleVariant;
```

The format used by the Delta property is the same as that used for the data of a client dataset. You can add another ClientDataSet component to an application and connect it to the data in the Delta property of the first client dataset:

```
if ClientDataSet1.ChangeCount > 0 then
begin
  ClientDataSet2.Data := ClientDataSet1.Delta;
  ClientDataSet2.Open;
```

In the CdsDelta example, I added a data module with the two ClientDataSet components and a source of data: a SQLDataSet mapped to InterBase's Employee demo table. Both client datasets have the extra status calculated field, with a slightly more generic version than the code discussed earlier, because the event handler is shared between them.

TIP   To create persistent fields for the ClientDataSet hooked to the delta (at run time), I temporarily connected it at design time to the main ClientDataSet's provider. The delta's structure is the same as the dataset it refers to. After creating the persistent fields, I removed the connection.

The application's form has a page control with two pages, each of which has a DBGrid, one for the data and one for the delta. Code hides or shows the second tab depending on the existence of data in the change log, as returned by the ChangeCount method, and updates the delta when the corresponding tab is selected. The core of the code used to handle the delta is similar to the previous code snippet, and you can study the example source code to see more details.

Figure 14.11 shows the change log of the CdsDelta application. Notice that the delta dataset has two entries for each modified record (the original values and the modified fields) unless this is a new or deleted record, as indicated by its status.

TIP   You can filter the delta dataset (or any other ClientDataSet) depending on its update status, using the StatusFilter property. This property allows you to show new, updated, and deleted records in separate grids or in a grid filtered by selecting an option in a TabControl.

FIGURE 14.11

The CdsDelta example allows you to see the temporary update requests stored in the Delta property of the ClientDataSet.

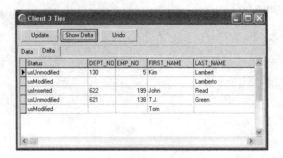

Updating the Data

Now that you have a better understanding of what goes on during local updates, you can try to make this program work by sending the local update (stored in the delta) back to the database server. To apply all the updates from a dataset at once, pass –1 to the ApplyUpdates method.

If the provider (or the Resolver component inside it) has trouble applying an update, it triggers the OnReconcileError event. This can take place because of a concurrent update by two different people. We tend to use optimistic locking in client/server applications, so this should be regarded as a normal situation.

The OnReconcileError event allows you to modify the Action parameter (passed by reference), which determines how the server should behave:

```
procedure TForm1.ClientDataSet1ReconcileError(DataSet: TClientDataSet;
  E: EReconcileError; UpdateKind: TUpdateKind; var Action: TReconcileAction);
```

This method has three parameters: the client dataset component (in case there is more than one client dataset in the current application), the exception that caused the error (with the error message), and the kind of operation that failed (ukModify, ukInsert, or ukDelete). The return value, which you'll store in the Action parameter, can be any one of the following:

```
type TReconcileAction = (raSkip, raAbort, raMerge, raCorrect, raCancel,
  raRefresh);
```

raSkip Specifies that the server should skip the conflicting record, leaving it in the delta (this is the default value)

raAbort Tells the server to abort the entire update operation and not to try to apply the remaining changes listed in the delta

raMerge Tells the server to merge the client data with the data on the server, applying only the modified fields of this client (and keeping the other fields modified by other clients)

raCorrect Tells the server to replace its data with the current client data, overriding all field changes already made by other clients

raCancel Cancels the update request, removing the entry from the delta and restoring the values originally fetched from the database (thus ignoring changes made by other clients)

raRefresh Tells the server to dump the updates in the client delta and to replace them with the values currently on the server (thus keeping the changes made by other clients)

To test a collision, you can launch two copies of the client application, change the same record in both clients, and then post the updates from both. We'll do this later to generate an error, but let's first see how to handle the `OnReconcileError` event.

Handling this event is not too difficult, but only because you'll receive a little help. Because building a specific form to handle an `OnReconcileError` event is common, Delphi provides such a form in the Object Repository (available with the File ➢ New ➢ Other menu command of the Delphi IDE). Go to the Delphi Projects/Delphi Files page and select the Reconcile Error Dialog item. This unit exports a function you can use directly to initialize and display the dialog box, as I did in the CdsDelta example:

```
procedure TDmCds.cdsEmployeeReconcileError (
  DataSet: TCustomClientDataSet; E: EReconcileError;
  UpdateKind: TUpdateKind; var Action: TReconcileAction);
begin
  Action := HandleReconcileError(DataSet, UpdateKind, E);
end;
```

WARNING   As the source code of the Reconcile Error Dialog unit suggests, you should use the Project Options dialog to remove this form from the list of automatically created forms (if you don't, an error will occur when you compile the project). Of course, you need to do this only if you haven't set up Delphi to skip the automatic form creation.

The `HandleReconcileError` function creates the dialog box form and shows it, as you can see in the code provided by Borland:

```
function HandleReconcileError(DataSet: TDataSet; UpdateKind: TUpdateKind;
  ReconcileError: EReconcileError): TReconcileAction;
var
  UpdateForm: TReconcileErrorForm;
begin
  UpdateForm := TReconcileErrorForm.CreateForm(
    DataSet, UpdateKind, ReconcileError);
  with UpdateForm do
  try
    if ShowModal = mrOK then
    begin
      Result := TReconcileAction(ActionGroup.Items.Objects[
        ActionGroup.ItemIndex]);
      if Result = raCorrect then
        SetFieldValues(DataSet);
    end
    else
      Result := raAbort;
  finally
    Free;
  end;
end;
```

The RecError unit, which hosts the Reconcile Error dialog (a window titled Update Error to be more understandable by end users of your programs), contains more than 350 lines of code, so I can't describe it in detail. However, you should be able to understand the source code by studying it carefully. Alternatively, you can use it without caring how everything works.

The dialog box will appear in case of an error, reporting the requested change that caused the conflict and allowing the user to choose one of the possible TReconcileAction values. You can see this form at run time in Figure 14.12.

TIP   When you call ApplyUpdates, you start a complex update sequence, which is discussed in more detail in Chapter 17 for multitier architectures. In short, the delta is sent to the provider, which fires the OnUpdateData event and then receives a BeforeUpdateRecord event for every record to update. These are two chances you have to look at the changes and force specific operations on the database server.

FIGURE 14.12
The Reconcile Error dialog provided by Delphi in the Object Repository and used by the CdsDelta example

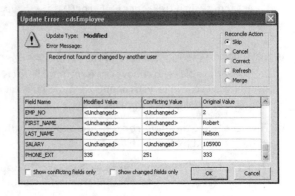

Using Transactions

Whenever you are working with a database server, you should use *transactions* to make your applications more robust. You can think of a transaction as a series of operations that are considered a single, "atomic" whole that cannot be split.

An example may help to clarify the concept. Suppose you have to raise the salary of each employee of a company by a fixed rate, as you did in the Total example in Chapter 13. A typical program would execute a series of SQL statements on the server, one for each record to update. If an error occurred during the operation, you might want to undo the previous changes. If you consider the operation "raise the salary of each employee" as a single transaction, it should either be completely performed or completely ignored. Or consider the analogy with financial transactions—if an error causes only part of the operation to be performed, you might end up with a missed credit or with some extra money.

Working with database operations as transactions serves a useful purpose. You can start a transaction and do several operations that should all be considered parts of a single larger operation; then, at the end, you can either commit the changes or *roll back* the transaction, discarding all the operations done up to that moment. Typically, you might want to roll back a transaction if an error occurred during its operations.

There is another important element to underline: transactions also serve a purpose when reading data. Until data is committed by a transaction, other connections and/or transactions should not see it.

Once the data is committed from a transaction, others should see the change when reading the data— that is, unless you need to open a transaction and read the same data over and over for data analysis or complex reporting operations. Different database servers allow you to read data in transaction according to some or all of these alternatives, as you'll see when we discuss transaction isolation levels.

Handling transactions in Delphi is simple. By default, each edit/post operation is considered a single *implicit* transaction, but you can alter this behavior by handling the operations explicitly. Use the following three methods of the dbExpress SQLConnection component (other database connection components have similar methods):

StartTransaction Marks the beginning of a transaction

Commit Confirms all the updates to the database done during the transaction

Rollback Returns the database to its state prior to starting the transaction

You can also use the InTransaction property to check whether a transaction is active. You'll often use a try block to roll back a transaction when an exception is raised, or you can commit the transaction as the last operation of the try block, which is executed only when there is no error. The code might look like this:

```
var
  TD: TTransactionDesc;
begin
  TD.TransactionID := 1;
  TD.IsolationLevel := xilREADCOMMITTED;
  SQLConnection1.StartTransaction(TD);
  try
    // -- operations within the transaction go here --
    SQLConnection1.Commit(TD);
  except
    SQLConnection1.Rollback(TD);
  end;
```

Each transaction-related method has a parameter describing the transaction it is working with. The parameter uses the record type TTransactionDesc and accounts for a transaction isolation level and a transaction ID. The transaction isolation level is an indication of how the transaction should behave when other transactions make changes to the data. The three most commonly used values are as follows:

xilDIRTYREAD Queries in a transaction of this type can see immediately see updates made within other transactions, even before they are committed. This is the only possibility in a few databases and corresponds to the behavior of databases with no transaction support.

xilREADCOMMITTED Queries can see updates made within other transactions only after those transactions have committed their changes, not updates made by ongoing transactions. This setting is recommended for most databases, to preserve efficiency.

xilREPEATABLEREAD Hides changes made by every transaction started after the current one, even if the changes have been committed. Subsequent repeat calls within a transaction will always produce the same result, as if the database took a snapshot of the data when the current transaction started. Only InterBase and a few other database servers work efficiently with this model.

TIP   As a general suggestion, for performance reasons, transactions should involve a minimal number of updates (only those strictly related and part of a single atomic operation) and should be kept short in time. You should avoid transactions that wait for user input to complete them, because the user might be temporarily gone, and the transaction might remain active for a long time. Caching changes locally, as the ClientDataSet allows, can help you make the transactions small and fast, because you can open a transaction for reading, close it, and then open a transaction for writing out the entire batch of changes.

The other field of the TTransactionDesc record holds a transaction ID. It is useful only in conjunction with a database server supporting multiple concurrent transactions over the same connection, like InterBase does. You can ask the connection component whether the server supports multiple transactions or doesn't support transactions at all, using the MultipleTransactionsSupported and TransactionsSupported properties.

When the server supports multiple transactions, you must supply each transaction with a unique identifier when calling the StartTransaction method:

```
var
  TD: TTransactionDesc;
begin
  TD.TransactionID := GetTickCount;
  TD.IsolationLevel := xilREADCOMMITTED;
  SQLConnection1.StartTransaction(TD);
  SQLDataSet1.TransactionLevel := TD.TransactionID;
```

You can also indicate which datasets belong to which transaction by setting the TransactionLevel property of each dataset to a transaction ID, as shown in the last statement.

To further inspect transactions and to experiment with transaction isolation levels, you can use the TranSample application. As you can see in Figure 14.13, radio buttons let you choose the various isolation levels and buttons let you work on the transactions and apply updates or refresh data. To get a real idea of the different effects, you should run multiple copies of the program (provided you have enough licenses on your InterBase server).

FIGURE 14.13

The form of the Tran-Sample application at design time. The radio buttons let you set different transaction isolation levels.

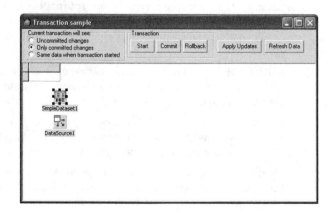

NOTE InterBase, like most database servers, doesn't support the "dirty read" mode that is typically used by simple local database engines (and was the only mode you could use in Paradox via the BDE). This means that in the TranSample program you cannot use the last option.

Using InterBase Express

The examples built earlier in this chapter were created with the new dbExpress database library. Using this server-independent approach allows you to switch the database server used by your application, although in practice doing so is often far from simple. If the application you are building will invariably use a given database, you can write programs that are tied directly to the API of the specific database server. This approach will make your programs intrinsically nonportable to other database servers.

Of course, you won't generally use these APIs directly, but rather base your development on dataset components that wrap these APIs and fit into Delphi and the architecture of its class library. An example of such a family of components is InterBase Express (IBX). Applications built using these components should work better and faster (even if only marginally), giving you more control over the specific features of the server. For example, IBX provides a set of administrative components specifically built for InterBase 6.

NOTE I'll examine the IBX components because they are tied to InterBase (the database server discussed in this chapter) and because they are the only set of InterBase-specific components available in the standard Delphi installation. Other similar sets of components (for InterBase, Oracle, and other database servers) are equally powerful and well regarded in the Delphi programmers' community. A good example (and an alternative to IBX) is InterBase Objects (www.ibobjects.com).

IBX Dataset Components

The IBX components include custom dataset components and a few others. The dataset components inherit from the base TDataSet class, can use all the common Delphi data-aware controls, and provide a field editor and all the usual design-time features. You can choose among multiple dataset components. Three IBX datasets have a role and a set of properties similar to the table/query/storedproc components in the dbExpress family:

◆ IBTable resembles the Table component and allows you to access a single table or view.

◆ IBQuery resembles the Query component and allows you to execute a SQL query, returning a result set. The IBQuery component can be used together with the IBUpdateSQL component to obtain a live (or editable) dataset.

◆ IBStoredProc resembles the StoredProc component and allows you to execute a stored procedure.

These components, like the related dbExpress ones, are intended for compatibility with older BDE components you might have used in your applications. For new applications, you should generally use the IBDataSet component, which allows you to work with a live result set obtained by executing a select query. It basically merges IBQuery with IBUpdateSQL in a single component.

Many other components in InterBase Express don't belong to the dataset category but are still used in applications that need to access to a database:

◆ IBDatabase acts like the DBX SQLConnection component and is used to set up the database connection. The BDE also uses the specific Session component to perform some global tasks done by the IBDatabase component.

◆ IBTransaction allows complete control over transactions. It is important in InterBase to use transactions explicitly and to isolate each transaction properly, using the Snapshot isolation level for reports and the Read Committed level for interactive forms. Each dataset explicitly refers to a given transaction, so you can have multiple concurrent transactions against the same database and choose which datasets take part in which transaction.

◆ IBSQL lets you execute SQL statements that don't return a dataset (for example, DDL requests, or update and delete statements) without the overhead of a dataset component.

◆ IBDatabaseInfo is used for querying the database structure and status.

◆ IBSQLMonitor is used for debugging the system, because the SQL Monitor debugger provided by Delphi is a BDE-specific tool.

◆ IBEvents receives events posted by the server. This last component is not available in the VCL for .NET.

This group of components provides greater control over the database server than you can achieve with dbExpress. For example, having a specific transaction component allows you to manage multiple concurrent transactions over one or multiple databases, as well as a single transaction spanning multiple databases. The IBDatabase component allows you to create databases, test the connection, and generally access system data, something the Database and Session BDE components don't fully provide.

TIP   IBX datasets let you set up the automatic behavior of a generator as a sort of auto-increment field. You do so by setting the GeneratorField property using its specific property editor. An example is discussed later in this chapter in the section "Generators and IDs."

IBX Administrative Components

The InterBase Admin page of Delphi's Component Palette hosts InterBase administrative components. Although your aim is probably not to build a full InterBase console application, including some administrative features (such as backup handling or user monitoring) can make sense in applications meant for power users.

Most of these components have self-explanatory names: IBConfigService, IBBackupService, IBRestoreService, IBValidationService, IBStatisticalService, IBLogService, IBSecurityService, IBServerProperties, IBInstall, and IBUninstall. (By the way, these last two components are not available in the VCL for .NET.) I won't build any advanced examples that use these components because they are focused more toward the development of server management applications than client programs. However, I'll embed a couple of them in the IbxMon example discussed later in this chapter.

Building an IBX Example

To build an example that uses IBX, you'll need to place in a form (or data module) at least three components: an IBDatabase, an IBTransaction, and a dataset component (in this case an IBQuery). Any IBX application requires at least an instance of the first two components. You cannot set database connections in an IBX dataset as you can do with other datasets, and at least a transaction object is required even to read the result of a query.

Here are the key properties of these components in the IbxEmp example:

```
object IBTransaction1: TIBTransaction
  Active = False
  DefaultDatabase = IBDatabase1
end
object IBQuery1: TIBQuery
  Database = IBDatabase1
  Transaction = IBTransaction1
  CachedUpdates = False
  SQL.Strings = (
    'SELECT * FROM EMPLOYEE')
end
object IBDatabase1: TIBDatabase
  DatabaseName = 'C:\Program Files\Common Files\' +
    'Borland Shared\Data\employee.gdb'
  Params.Strings = (
    'user_name=SYSDBA'
    'password=masterkey')
  LoginPrompt = False
  SQLDialect = 1
end
```

Now you can hook a DataSource component to `IBQuery1` and easily build a user interface for the application. I had to type in the pathname of the Borland sample database. However, not everyone has the `Program Files` folder, which depends on the local version of Windows, and the Borland sample data files could be installed elsewhere on the disk. You'll solve these problems in the next example.

WARNING   Notice that I embedded the password in the code, a naive approach to security. Not only can anyone run the program, but someone can extract the password by looking at the hexadecimal code of the executable file. I used this approach so I wouldn't need to keep typing my password while testing the program, but in a real application you should require your users to do so to ensure the security of their data.

Building a Live Query

The IbxEmp example includes a query that doesn't allow editing. To activate editing, you need to add an IBUpdateSQL component to the query, even if the query is trivial. Using an IBQuery that hosts the SQL `select` statement together with an IBUpdateSQL component that hosts the `insert`, `update`, and `delete` SQL statements is a typical approach from BDE applications. The similarities among these components make it easier to port an existing BDE application to this architecture. Here is the code for these components (edited for clarity):

```
object IBQuery1: TIBQuery
  Database = IBDatabase1
  Transaction = IBTransaction1
  SQL.Strings = (
    'SELECT Employee.EMP_NO, Department.DEPARTMENT, '
    ' Employee.FIRST_NAME, Employee.LAST_NAME, Job.JOB_TITLE, '
    ' Employee.SALARY, Employee.DEPT_NO, Employee.JOB_CODE, '+
    ' Employee.JOB_GRADE, Employee.JOB_COUNTRY'
    'FROM EMPLOYEE Employee'
    '  INNER JOIN DEPARTMENT Department'
    '  ON  (Department.DEPT_NO = Employee.DEPT_NO) '
    '  INNER JOIN JOB Job'
    '  ON (Job.JOB_CODE = Employee.JOB_CODE) '
    '  AND (Job.JOB_GRADE = Employee.JOB_GRADE) '
    '  AND (Job.JOB_COUNTRY = Employee.JOB_COUNTRY) '
    'ORDER BY Department.DEPARTMENT, Employee.LAST_NAME')
  UpdateObject = IBUpdateSQL1
end
object IBUpdateSQL1: TIBUpdateSQL
  RefreshSQL.Strings = (
    'SELECT Employee.EMP_NO, Employee.FIRST_NAME, Employee.LAST_NAME, '
    ' Department.DEPARTMENT, Job.JOB_TITLE, Employee.SALARY, '
    ' Employee.DEPT_NO, Employee.JOB_CODE, Employee.JOB_GRADE, '
    ' Employee.JOB_COUNTRY'
    'FROM EMPLOYEE Employee'
    'INNER JOIN DEPARTMENT Department'
    'ON (Department.DEPT_NO = Employee.DEPT_NO)'
    'INNER JOIN JOB Job'
    'ON (Job.JOB_CODE = Employee.JOB_CODE)'
    'AND (Job.JOB_GRADE = Employee.JOB_GRADE)'
    'AND (Job.JOB_COUNTRY = Employee.JOB_COUNTRY)'
    'WHERE Employee.EMP_NO=:EMP_NO')
  ModifySQL.Strings = (
    'update EMPLOYEE'
    'set'
    '  FIRST_NAME = :FIRST_NAME,'
    '  LAST_NAME = :LAST_NAME,'
    '  SALARY = :SALARY,'
    '  DEPT_NO = :DEPT_NO,'
    '  JOB_CODE = :JOB_CODE,'
    '  JOB_GRADE = :JOB_GRADE,'
    '  JOB_COUNTRY = :JOB_COUNTRY'
    'where'
    '  EMP_NO = :OLD_EMP_NO')
  InsertSQL.Strings = (
```

```
     'insert into EMPLOYEE'
     '  (FIRST_NAME, LAST_NAME, SALARY, DEPT_NO, JOB_CODE,'
     '  JOB_GRADE, JOB_COUNTRY)'
     'values'
     '  (:FIRST_NAME,:LAST_NAME,:SALARY,:DEPT_NO,:JOB_CODE,'
     '  :JOB_GRADE,:JOB_COUNTRY)')
  DeleteSQL.Strings = (
     'delete from EMPLOYEE '
     'where EMP_NO = :OLD_EMP_NO')
end
```

For new applications, you should consider using the IBDataSet component, which sums up the features of IBQuery and IBUpdateSQL. The differences between using the two components and the single component are minimal. Using IBQuery and IBUpdateSQL is a better approach when you're porting an existing application based on the two equivalent BDE components, even if porting the program directly to the IBDataSet component doesn't require much extra work.

In the IbxUpdSql example, I provided both alternatives so you can test the differences yourself. Here is the skeleton of the DFM description of the single dataset component:

```
object IBDataSet1: TIBDataSet
  Database = IBDatabase1
  Transaction = IBTransaction1
  DeleteSQL.Strings = (
     'delete from EMPLOYEE'
     'where EMP_NO = :OLD_EMP_NO')
  InsertSQL.Strings = (
     'insert into EMPLOYEE'
     '  (FIRST_NAME, LAST_NAME, SALARY, DEPT_NO, JOB_CODE, JOB_GRADE, ' +
     '  JOB_COUNTRY)'
     'values'
     '  (:FIRST_NAME, :LAST_NAME, :SALARY, :DEPT_NO, :JOB_CODE, ' +
     '  :JOB_GRADE, :JOB_COUNTRY)')
  SelectSQL.Strings = (...)
  UpdateRecordTypes = [cusUnmodified, cusModified, cusInserted]
  ModifySQL.Strings = (...)
end
```

If you connect the IBQuery1 or the IBDataSet1 component to the data source and run the program, you'll see that the behavior is identical. Not only do the components have a similar effect, but the available properties and events are also similar.

In the IbxUpdSql program, I also made the reference to the database a little more flexible. Instead of typing in the database name at design time, I extracted the Borland shared data folder from the Windows Registry (where Borland saves it while installing Delphi). Here is the code executed when the program starts:

```
uses
  Registry;

procedure TForm1.FormCreate(Sender: TObject);
```

```
var
  Reg: TRegistry;
begin
  Reg := TRegistry.Create;
  try
    Reg.RootKey := HKEY_LOCAL_MACHINE;
    Reg.OpenKey('\Software\Borland\Borland Shared\Data', False);
    IBDatabase1.DatabaseName :=
      Reg.ReadString('Rootdir') + '\employee.gdb';
  finally
    Reg.Free;
  end;
  EmpDS.DataSet.Open;
end;
```

Another feature of this example is the presence of a transaction component. As I've said, the Inter-Base Express components make the use of a transaction component compulsory, explicitly following a requirement of InterBase. Simply adding a couple of buttons to the form to commit or roll back the transaction would be enough, because a transaction starts automatically as you edit any dataset attached to it.

I also improved the program by adding an ActionList component. This component includes all the standard database actions and adds two custom actions for transaction support: Commit and Roll-back. Both actions are enabled when the transaction is active:

```
procedure TForm1.ActionUpdateTransactions(Sender: TObject);
begin
  acCommit.Enabled := IBTransaction1.InTransaction;
  acRollback.Enabled := acCommit.Enabled;
end;
```

When executed, they perform the main operation, but they also need to reopen the dataset in a new transaction (which can also be done by "retaining" the transaction context). CommitRetaining doesn't really reopen a new transaction, but it allows the current transaction to remain open. This way, you can keep using your datasets, which won't be refreshed (so you won't see edits already committed by other users), but will keep showing the data you've modified. Here is the code:

```
procedure TForm1.acCommitExecute(Sender: TObject);
begin
  IBTransaction1.CommitRetaining;
end;
```

```
procedure TForm1.acRollbackExecute(Sender: TObject);
begin
  IBTransaction1.Rollback;
  // reopen the dataset in a new transaction
  IBTransaction1.StartTransaction;
  EmpDS.DataSet.Open;
end;
```

WARNING   Be aware that InterBase closes any opened cursors when a transaction ends, which means you have to reopen them and refetch the data even if you haven't made any changes. When committing data, however, you can ask InterBase to retain the *transaction context*—not to close open datasets—by issuing a CommitRetaining command, as mentioned before. InterBase behaves this way because a transaction corresponds to a snapshot of the data. Once a transaction is finished, you are supposed to read the data again to refetch records that may have been modified by other users. InterBase includes a Rollback Retaining command, but I've decided not to use it because in a rollback operation, the program should refresh the dataset data to show the original values on screen, not the updates you've discarded.

The last operation refers to a generic dataset and not a specific one because I'm going to add a second alternate dataset to the program. The actions are connected to a text-only toolbar, as you can see in Figure 14.14. The program opens the dataset at startup and automatically closes the current transaction on exit, after asking the user what to do, with the following OnCloseQuery event handler:

```
procedure TForm1.FormCloseQuery(Sender: TObject;
  var Action: TCloseAction);
var
  nCode: Word;
begin
  if IBTransaction1.InTransaction then
  begin
    nCode := MessageDlg ('Commit Transaction? (No to rollback)',
      mtConfirmation, mbYesNoCancel, 0);
    case nCode of
      mrYes: IBTransaction1.Commit;
      mrNo: IBTransaction1.Rollback;
      mrCancel: CanClose := False; // don't close
    end;
  end;
end;
```

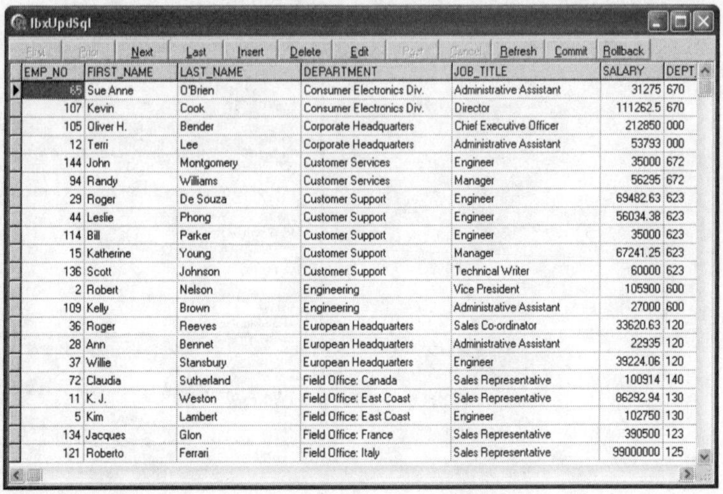

FIGURE 14.14
The output of the
IbxUpdSql example

EMP_NO	FIRST_NAME	LAST_NAME	DEPARTMENT	JOB_TITLE	SALARY	DEPT
65	Sue Anne	O'Brien	Consumer Electronics Div.	Administrative Assistant	31275	670
107	Kevin	Cook	Consumer Electronics Div.	Director	111262.5	670
105	Oliver H.	Bender	Corporate Headquarters	Chief Executive Officer	212850	000
12	Terri	Lee	Corporate Headquarters	Administrative Assistant	53793	000
144	John	Montgomery	Customer Services	Engineer	35000	672
94	Randy	Williams	Customer Services	Manager	56295	672
29	Roger	De Souza	Customer Support	Engineer	69482.63	623
44	Leslie	Phong	Customer Support	Engineer	56034.38	623
114	Bill	Parker	Customer Support	Engineer	35000	623
15	Katherine	Young	Customer Support	Manager	67241.25	623
136	Scott	Johnson	Customer Support	Technical Writer	60000	623
2	Robert	Nelson	Engineering	Vice President	105900	600
109	Kelly	Brown	Engineering	Administrative Assistant	27000	600
36	Roger	Reeves	European Headquarters	Sales Co-ordinator	33620.63	120
28	Ann	Bennet	European Headquarters	Administrative Assistant	22935	120
37	Willie	Stansbury	European Headquarters	Engineer	39224.06	120
72	Claudia	Sutherland	Field Office: Canada	Sales Representative	100914	140
11	K. J.	Weston	Field Office: East Coast	Sales Representative	86292.94	130
5	Kim	Lambert	Field Office: East Coast	Engineer	102750	130
134	Jacques	Glon	Field Office: France	Sales Representative	390500	123
121	Roberto	Ferrari	Field Office: Italy	Sales Representative	99000000	125

Monitoring InterBase Express

Like the dbExpress architecture, IBX also allows you to monitor a connection. You can embed a copy of the IBSQLMonitor component in your application and produce a custom log.

You can even write a more generic monitoring application, as I've done in the IbxMon example. I've placed in its form a monitoring component and a RichEdit control and written the following handler for the OnSQL event:

```
procedure TForm1.IBSQLMonitor1SQL(EventText: String);
begin
  if Assigned (RichEdit1) then
    RichEdit1.Lines.Add (TimeToStr (Now) + ': ' + EventText);
end;
```

The `if Assigned` test can be useful when receiving a message during shutdown, and it is required when you add this code directly inside the application you are monitoring.

To receive messages from other applications (or from the current application), you have to turn on the IBDatabase component's tracing options. In the IbxUpdSql example (discussed in the preceding section, "Building a Live Query"), I turned them all on:

```
object IBDatabase1: TIBDatabase
  ...
  TraceFlags = [tfQPrepare, tfQExecute, tfQFetch, tfError, tfStmt,
              tfConnect, tfTransact, tfBlob, tfService, tfMisc]
```

If you run the two examples at the same time, the output of the IbxMon program will list details about the IbxUpdSql program's interaction with InterBase, as you can see in Figure 14.15.

FIGURE 14.15

The output of the Ibx-Mon example, based on the IBSQLMonitor component

Getting More System Data

In addition to letting you monitor the InterBase connection, the IbxMon example allows you to query some server settings using the various tabs on its page control. The example embeds a few IBX administrative components, showing server statistics, server properties, and all connected users. You can see an example of the server properties in Figure 14.16. The code for extracting the users appears in the following code fragment.

```
// grab the user's data
IBSecurityService1.DisplayUsers;
// display the name of each user
for i := 0 to IBSecurityService1.UserInfoCount - 1 do
  with IBSecurityService1.UserInfo[i] do
    RichEdit4.Lines.Add (Format ('User: %s, Full Name: %s, Id: %d',
      [UserName, FirstName + ' ' + LastName, UserId]));
```

FIGURE 14.16

The server information displayed by the IbxMon application

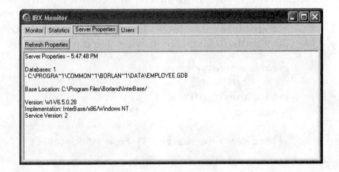

Real-World Blocks

Up to now, we've discussed specific techniques related to InterBase programming, but we haven't delved into the development of an application and the problems this presents in practice. In the following subsections, I'll discuss a few practical techniques, in no specific order.

Nando Dessena (who knows InterBase much better than I do) and I have used all of these techniques in a seminar discussing the porting of an internal Paradox application to InterBase. The application we discussed in the seminar was large and complex, and I trimmed it down to only a few tables to make it fit into the space I have for this chapter.

TIP   The database discussed in this section is called mastering.gdb. You can find it in the data subfolder of the code folder for this chapter. You can examine it using InterBase Console.

Generators and IDs

I mentioned earlier in this chapter (in the sidebar "OIDs to the Extreme ") that I'm a fan of using IDs extensively to identify the records in each table of a database.

NOTE   I tend to use a single sequence of IDs for an entire system, something often called an Object ID (OID) (discussed in a sidebar earlier in this chapter). In such a case, however, the IDs of the two tables must be unique. Because you might not know in advance which objects could be used in place of others, adopting a global OID allows you more freedom later. The drawback is that if you have lots of data, using a 32-bit integer as the ID (that is, having only 4 billion objects) might not be sufficient. For this reason, InterBase 6 supports 64-bit generators.

How do you generate the unique values for these IDs when multiple clients are running? Keeping a table with a *latest* value will create problems because multiple concurrent transactions (from different users) will see the same values. If you don't use tables, you can use a database-independent mechanism, including the rather large Windows GUIDs or the so-called *high-low technique* (the assignment of a base number to each client at startup—the high number—that is combined with a consecutive number—the low number—determined by the client).

Another approach, bound to the database, is the use of internal mechanisms for sequences, indicated with different names in each database server. In InterBase they are called *generators*. These sequences operate and are incremented outside of transactions so that they provide unique numbers even to concurrent users (remember that InterBase forces you to open a transaction to read data).

You already saw how to create a generator. Here is the definition for the one in my demo database, followed by the definition of the view you can use to query for a new value:

```
create generator g_master;

create view v_next_id (
  next_id
  ) as
select gen_id(g_master, 1) from rdb$database
  ;
```

Inside the RWBlocks application, I added an IBQuery component to a data module (because I don't need it to be an editable dataset) with the following SQL:

```
select next_id from v_next_id;
```

The advantage, compared to using the direct statement, is that this code is easier to write and maintain, even if the underlying generator changes (or you switch to a different approach behind the scenes). Moreover, in the same data module, I added a function that returns a new value for the generator:

```
function TDmMain.GetNewId: Integer;
begin
  // return the next value of the generator
  QueryId.Open;
  try
    Result := QueryId.Fields[0].AsInteger;
  finally
    QueryId.Close;
  end;
end;
```

This method can be called in the `AfterInsert` event of any dataset to fill in the value for the ID:

```
mydataset.FieldByName ('ID').AsInteger := data.GetNewId;
```

As I've mentioned, the IBX datasets can be tied directly to a generator, thus simplifying the overall picture. Thanks to the specific property editor (shown in Figure 14.17), connecting a field of the dataset to the generator becomes trivial.

Notice that both these approaches are much better than the approach based on a server-side trigger, discussed earlier in this chapter. In that case, the Delphi application didn't know the ID of the record sent to the database and so was unable to refresh it. Not having the record ID (which is also the only key field) on the Delphi side means it is almost impossible to insert such a value directly inside a DBGrid. If you try, you'll see that the value you insert gets lost, only to reappear in case of a full refresh.

Using client-side techniques based on the manual code or the `GeneratorField` property causes no trouble. The Delphi application knows the ID (the record key) before posting it, so it can easily place it in a grid and refresh it properly.

FIGURE 14.17

The editor for the GeneratorField property of the IBX datasets

Case-Insensitive Searches

An interesting issue with database servers in general, not InterBase specifically, has to do with case-insensitive searches. Suppose you don't want to show a large amount of data in a grid (which is a bad idea for a client/server application). You instead choose to let the user type the initial portion of a name and then filter a query on this input, displaying only the smaller resulting record set in a grid. I've done this for a table of companies.

This search by company name will be executed frequently and will take place on a large table. However, if you search using the `starting with` or `like` operator, the search will be case sensitive, as in the following SQL statement:

```
select * from companies
where name starting with 'win';
```

To make a case-insensitive search, you can use the `upper` function on both sides of the comparison to test the uppercase values of each string, but a similar query will be very slow, because it won't be based on an index. On the other hand, saving the company names (or any other name) in uppercase letters would be silly, because when you print those names, the result will be unnatural (even if common in old information systems).

If you can trade off some disk space and memory for the extra speed, you can use a trick: add an extra field to the table to store the uppercase value of the company name and use a server-side trigger to generate it and update it. You can then ask the database to maintain an index on the uppercase version of the name to speed the search operation even further.

In practice, the table definition looks like this:

```
create domain d_uid as integer;
create table companies
(
  id           d_uid not null,
  name         varchar(50),
  tax_code     varchar(16),
  name_upper   varchar(50),
constraint companies_pk primary key (id)
);
```

To copy the uppercase name of each company into the related field, you cannot rely on client-side code, because an inconsistency would cause problems. In a case like this, it is better to use a trigger on the server, so that each time the company name changes its uppercase version is updated accordingly. Another trigger is used to insert a new company:

```
create trigger companies_bi for companies
active before insert position 0
as
begin
  new.name_upper = upper(new.name);
end;

create trigger companies_bu for companies
active before update position 0
as
begin
  if (new.name <> old.name) then
    new.name_upper = upper(new.name);
end;
```

Finally, I added an index to the table with this DDL statement:

```
create index i_companies_name_upper on companies(name_upper);
```

With this structure behind the scenes, you can now select all the companies starting with the text of an edit box (edSearch) by writing the following code in a Delphi application:

```
dm.DataCompanies.Close;
dm.DataCompanies.SelectSQL.Text :=
  'select c.id, c.name, c.tax_code,' +
  ' from companies c ' +
  ' where name_upper starting with ''' +
  UpperCase (edSearch.Text) + '''';
dm.DataCompanies.Open;
```

TIP Using a prepared parameterized query, you might be able to make this code even faster.

As an alternative, you could create a server-side calculated field in the table definition, but doing so would prevent you from having an index on the field, which speeds up your queries considerably:

```
name_upper  varchar(50) computed by (upper(name))
```

Handling Locations and People

You might notice that the table describing companies is quite bare. It has no company address nor any contact information. The reason is that I want to be able to handle companies that have multiple offices (or locations) and list contact information about multiple employees of those companies.

Every location is bound to a company. Notice, though, that I decided not to use a location identifier related to the company (such as a progressive location number for each company) but rather a global ID for all the locations. This way, I can refer to a location ID (let's say, for shipping goods) without having to also refer to the company ID. This is the definition of the table that stores company locations:

```
create table locations
(
    id          d_uid not null,
    id_company  d_uid not null,
    address     varchar(40),
    town        varchar(30),
    zip         varchar(10),
    state       varchar(4),
    phone       varchar(15),
    fax         varchar(15),
constraint locations_pk primary key (id),
constraint locations_uc unique (id_company, id)
);

alter table locations add constraint locations_fk_companies
    foreign key (id_company) references companies (id)
    on update no action on delete no action;
```

The final definition of a foreign key relates the id_company field of the locations table with the ID field of the companies table. The other table lists names and contact information for people at specific company locations. To follow the database normalization rules, I should have added to this table only a reference to the location, because each location relates to a company. However, to make it simpler to change the location of a person within a company and to make my queries much more efficient (avoiding an extra step), I added to the people table both a reference to the location and a reference to the company.

The table has another unusual feature: one of the people working for a company can be set as the key contact. You obtain this functionality with a Boolean field (defined with a domain, because the Boolean type is not supported by InterBase) and by adding triggers to the table so that only one employee of each company can have this flag active:

```
create domain d_boolean as char(1)
    default 'F'
    check (value in ('T', 'F')) not null
```

```
create table people
(
    id              d_uid not null,
    id_company      d_uid not null,
    id_location     d_uid not null,
    name            varchar(50) not null,
    phone           varchar(15),
    fax             varchar(15),
    email           varchar(50),
    key_contact     d_boolean,
constraint people_pk primary key (id),
constraint people_uc unique (id_company, name)
);

alter table people add constraint people_fk_companies
    foreign key (id_company) references companies (id)
    on update no action on delete cascade;
alter table people add constraint people_fk_locations
    foreign key (id_company, id_location)
    references locations (id_company, id);

create trigger people_ai for people
active after insert position 0
as
begin
    /* if a person is the key contact, remove the
       flag from all others (of the same company) */
    if (new.key_contact = 'T') then
        update people
        set key_contact = 'F'
        where id_company = new.id_company
        and id <> new.id;
end;

create trigger people_au for people
active after update position 0
as
begin
    /* if a person is the key contact, remove the
       flag from all others (of the same company) */
    if (new.key_contact = 'T' and old.key_contact = 'F') then
        update people
        set key_contact = 'F'
        where id_company = new.id_company
        and id <> new.id;
end;
```

Building a User Interface

The three tables discussed so far have a clear master/detail relation. For this reason, the RWBlocks example uses three IBDataSet components to access the data, hooking up the two secondary tables to the main one. The code for the master/detail support is that of a standard database example based on queries, so I won't discuss it further (but I suggest you study the example's source code).

Each of the datasets has a full set of SQL statements to make the data editable. Whenever you enter a new detail element, the program hooks it to its master tables, as in the two following methods:

```
procedure TDmCompanies.DataLocationsAfterInsert(DataSet: TDataSet);
begin
  // initialize the data of the detail record
  // with a reference to the master record
  DataLocationsID_COMPANY.AsInteger := DataCompaniesID.AsInteger;
end;

procedure TDmCompanies.DataPeopleAfterInsert(DataSet: TDataSet);
begin
  // initialize the data of the detail record
  // with a reference to the master record
  DataPeopleID_COMPANY.AsInteger := DataCompaniesID.AsInteger;
  // the suggested location is the active one, if available
  if not DataLocations.IsEmpty then
    DataPeopleID_LOCATION.AsInteger := DataLocationsID.AsInteger;
  // the first person added becomes the key contact
  // (checks whether the filtered dataset of people is empty)
  DataPeopleKEY_CONTACT.AsBoolean := DataPeople.IsEmpty;
end;
```

As this code suggests, a data module hosts the dataset components. The program has a data module for every form (hooked up dynamically because you can create multiple instances of each form). Each data module has a separate transaction so that the various operations performed in different pages are totally independent. The database connection, however, is centralized. A main data module hosts the corresponding component, which is referenced by all the datasets. Each of the data modules is created dynamically by the form referring to it, and its value is stored in the form's dm private field:

```
procedure TFormCompanies.FormCreate(Sender: TObject);
begin
  dm := TDmCompanies.Create (Self);
  dsCompanies.Dataset := dm.DataCompanies;
  dsLocations.Dataset := dm.DataLocations;
  dsPeople.Dataset := dm.DataPeople;
end;
```

This way, you can easily create multiple instances of a form, with an instance of the data module connected to each of them. The form connected to the data module has three DBGrid controls, each tied to a data module and one of the corresponding datasets. You can see this form at run time, with some data, in Figure 14.18.

FIGURE 14.18
A form showing companies, office locations, and people (part of the RWBlocks example)

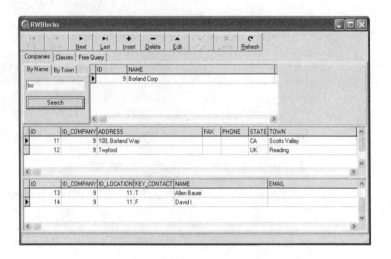

The form is hosted by a main form, which in turn is based on a page control, with the other forms embedded. Only the form connected with the first page is created when the program starts. The ShowForm method I wrote takes care of parenting the form to the tab sheet of the page control after removing the form border:

```
procedure TFormMain.FormCreate(Sender: TObject);
begin
  ShortDateFormat := 'dd/mm/yyyy';
  ShowForm (TFormCompanies.Create (Self), TabCompanies);
end;

procedure TFormMain.ShowForm (Form: TForm; Tab: TTabSheet);
begin
  Form.BorderStyle := bsNone;
  Form.Align := alClient;
  Form.Parent := Tab;
  Form.Show;
end;
```

The other two pages are populated at run time:

```
procedure TFormMain.PageControl1Change(Sender: TObject);
begin
  if PageControl1.ActivePage.ControlCount = 0 then
    if PageControl1.ActivePage = TabFreeQ then
      ShowForm (TFormFreeQuery.Create (Self), TabFreeQ)
    else if PageControl1.ActivePage = TabClasses then
      ShowForm (TFormClasses.Create (Self), TabClasses);
end;
```

The companies form hosts the search by company name (discussed in the previous section) plus a search by location. You enter the name of a town and get back a list of companies having an office in that town:

```
procedure TFormCompanies.btnTownClick(Sender: TObject);
begin
  with dm.DataCompanies do
  begin
    Close;
    SelectSQL.Text :=
      'select c.id, c.name, c.tax_code' +
      '  from companies c ' +
      '  where exists (select loc.id from locations loc ' +
      '  where loc.id_company = c.id and upper(loc.town) = ''' +
      UpperCase(edTown.Text) + ''' )';
    Open;
    dm.DataLocations.Open;
    dm.DataPeople.Open;
  end;
end;
```

The form includes a lot more source code. Some of it is related to closing permission (as a user cannot close the form while there are pending edits not posted to the database), and quite a bit relates to the use of the form as a lookup dialog, as described later.

Booking Classes

Part of the program and the database involves booking training classes and courses. (Although I built this program as a showcase, it also helps me run my own business.) The database includes a classes table that lists all the training courses, each with a title and the planned date. Another table hosts registration by company, including the classes registered for, the ID of the company, and some notes. Finally, a third table lists people who've signed up, each hooked to a registration for his or her company, with the amount paid.

The rationale behind this company-based registration is that invoices are sent to companies that book the classes for programmers and can receive specific discounts. In this case the database is more normalized, because the people registration doesn't refer directly to a class, but only to the company registration for that class. Here are the definitions of the tables involved (I omitted foreign key constraints and other elements):

```
create table classes
(
  id            d_uid not null,
  description   varchar(50),
  starts_on     timestamp not null,
constraint classes_pk primary key (id)
);
create table classes_reg
(
  id            d_uid not null,
```

```
  id_company  d_uid not null,
  id_class    d_uid not null,
  notes       varchar(255),
constraint classes_reg_pk primary key (id),
constraint classes_reg_uc unique (id_company, id_class)
);
create domain d_amount as numeric(15, 2);
create table people_reg
(
  id                d_uid not null,
  id_classes_reg    d_uid not null,
  id_person         d_uid not null,
  amount            d_amount,
constraint people_reg_pk primary key (id)
);
```

The data module for this group of tables uses a master/detail/detail relationship and has code to
set the connection with the active master record when a new detail record is created. Each dataset has
a generator field for its ID, and each has the proper update and insert SQL statements. These statements are generated by the corresponding component editor using only the ID field to identify existing records and updating only the fields in the original table. Each of the two secondary datasets
retrieves data from a lookup table (either the list of companies or the list of people). I had to edit the
RefreshSQL statements manually to repeat the proper inner join. Here is an example:

```
object IBClassReg: TIBDataSet
  Database = DmMain.IBDatabase1
  Transaction = IBTransaction1
  AfterInsert = IBClassRegAfterInsert
  DeleteSQL.Strings = (
    'delete from classes_reg'
    'where id = :old_id')
  InsertSQL.Strings = (
    'insert into classes_reg (id, id_class, id_company, notes)'
    'values (:id, :id_class, :id_company, :notes)')
  RefreshSQL.Strings = (
    'select reg.id, reg.id_class, reg.id_company, reg.notes, c.name '
    'from classes_reg reg'
    'join companies c on reg.id_company = c.id'
    'where id = :id')
  SelectSQL.Strings = (
    'select reg.id, reg.id_class, reg.id_company, reg.notes, c.name '
    'from classes_reg reg'
    'join companies c on reg.id_company = c.id'
    'where id_class = :id')
  ModifySQL.Strings = (
    'update classes_reg'
    'set'
    '  id = :id,'
```

```
    '  id_class = :id_class,'
    '  id_company = :id_company,'
    '  notes = :notes'
    'where id = :old_id')
  GeneratorField.Field = 'id'
  GeneratorField.Generator = 'g_master'
  DataSource = dsClasses
end
```

To complete the discussion of IBClassReg, here is its only event handler:

```
procedure TDmClasses.IBClassRegAfterInsert(DataSet: TDataSet);
begin
  IBClassReg.FieldByName ('id_class').AsString :=
    IBClasses.FieldByName ('id').AsString;
end;
```

The IBPeopleReg dataset has similar settings, but the IBClasses dataset is simpler at design time. At run time, this dataset's SQL code is dynamically modified using three alternatives to display scheduled classes (whenever the date is after today's date), classes already started or finished in the current year, and classes from past years. A user selects one of the three groups of records for the table with a tab control, which hosts the DBGrid for the main table (see Figure 14.19).

FIGURE 14.19

The RWBlocks example form for class registrations

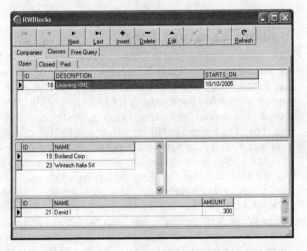

The three alternative SQL statements are created when the program starts or when the class registrations form is created and displayed. The program stores the final portion of the three alternative instructions (the where clause) in a string list and selects one of the strings when the tab changes:

```
procedure TFormClasses.FormCreate(Sender: TObject);
begin
  dm := TDmClasses.Create (Self);
  // connect the datasets to the data sources
  dsClasses.Dataset := dm.IBClasses;
```

```
dsClassReg.DataSet := dm.IBClassReg;
dsPeopleReg.DataSet := dm.IBPeopleReg;
// open the datasets
dm.IBClasses.Active := True;
dm.IBClassReg.Active := True;
dm.IBPeopleReg.Active := True;

// prepare the SQL for the three tabs
SqlCommands := TStringList.Create;
SqlCommands.Add (' where Starts_On > ''now''');
SqlCommands.Add (' where Starts_On <= ''now'' and ' +
  ' extract (year from Starts_On ) >= extract(year from current_timestamp)');
SqlCommands.Add (' where extract (year from Starts_On) < ' +
  ' extract(year from current_timestamp)');
end;

procedure TFormClasses.TabChange(Sender: TObject);
begin
  dm.IBClasses.Active := False;
  dm.IBClasses.SelectSQL [1] := SqlCommands [Tab.TabIndex];
  dm.IBClasses.Active := True;
end;
```

Building a Lookup Dialog

The two detail datasets of this class registration form display lookup fields. Instead of showing the ID of the company that booked the class, for example, the form shows the company name. You obtain this functionality with an inner join in the SQL statement and by configuring the DBGrid columns so they don't display the company ID. In a local application, or one with a limited amount of data, you could use a lookup field. However, copying the entire lookup dataset locally or opening it for browsing should be limited to tables with about 100 records at most, embedding some search capabilities.

If you have a large table, such as a table of companies, an alternative solution is to use a secondary dialog box to perform the lookup selection. For example, you can choose a company by using the form you've already built and taking advantage of its search capabilities. To display this form as a dialog box, the program creates a new instance of it, shows some hidden buttons already there at design time, and lets the user select a company to refer to from the other table.

To simplify the use of this lookup, which can happen multiple times in a large program, I added to the companies form a class function that has as output parameters the name and ID of the selected company. An initial ID can be passed to the function to determine its initial selection. Here is the complete code of this class function, which creates an object of its class, selects the initial record if requested, shows the dialog box, and finally extracts the return values:

```
class function TFormCompanies.SelectCompany (
  var CompanyName: string; var CompanyId: Integer): Boolean;
var
  FormComp: TFormCompanies;
begin
  Result := False;
```

```
    FormComp := TFormCompanies.Create (Application);
    FormComp.Caption := 'Select Company';
    try
      // activate dialog buttons
      FormComp.btnCancel.Visible := True;
      FormComp.btnOK.Visible := True;
      // select company
      if CompanyId > 0 then
        FormComp.dm.DataCompanies.SelectSQL.Text :=
          'select c.id, c.name, c.tax_code' +
          '  from companies c ' +
          '  where c.id = ' + IntToStr (CompanyId)
      else
        FormComp.dm.DataCompanies.SelectSQL.Text :=
          'select c.id, c.name, c.tax_code' +
          '  from companies c ' +
          '  where name_upper starting with ''a''';
    FormComp.dm.DataCompanies.Open;
    FormComp.dm.DataLocations.Open;
    FormComp.dm.DataPeople.Open;

    if FormComp.ShowModal = mrOK then
    begin
      Result := True;
      CompanyId := FormComp.dm.DataCompanies.
        FieldByName ('id').AsInteger;
      CompanyName := FormComp.dm.DataCompanies.
        FieldByName ('name').AsString;
    end;
  finally
    FormComp.Free;
  end;
end;
```

Another slightly more complex class function (available with the example's source code but not listed here) lets you select a person from a given company to register people for classes. In this case, the form is displayed after disallowing searching another company or modifying the company's data.

In both cases, you trigger the lookup by adding an ellipsis button to the column of the DBGrid—for example, the grid column listing the names of companies registered for classes. When this button is clicked, the program calls the class function to display the dialog box and uses its result to update the hidden ID field and the visible name field:

```
procedure TFormClasses.DBGridClassRegEditButtonClick(Sender: TObject);
var
  CompanyName: string;
  CompanyId: Integer;
begin
  CompanyId := dm.IBClassReg.FieldByName ('id_Company').AsInteger;
```

```
if TFormCompanies.SelectCompany (CompanyName, CompanyId) then
begin
  dm.IBClassReg.Edit;
  dm.IBClassReg.FieldByName ('Name').AsString := CompanyName;
  dm.IBClassReg.FieldByName ('id_Company').AsInteger := CompanyId;
end;
end;
```

Adding a Free Query Form

The program's final feature is a form in which a user can directly type and run a SQL statement. As a helper, the form lists in a combo box the available tables of the database, obtained when the form is created by calling

```
DmMain.IBDatabase1.GetTableNames (ComboTables.Items);
```

Selecting an item from the combo box generates a generic SQL query:

```
MemoSql.Lines.Text := 'select * from ' + ComboTables.Text;
```

The user (if an expert) can then edit the SQL, possibly introducing restrictive clauses, and then run the query:

```
procedure TFormFreeQuery.ButtonRunClick(Sender: TObject);
begin
  QueryFree.Close;
  QueryFree.SQL := MemoSql.Lines;
  QueryFree.Open;
end;
```

You can see this third form of the RWBlocks program in Figure 14.20. Of course, I'm not suggesting that you add SQL editing to programs intended for all your users—this feature is intended for power users or programmers. I basically wrote it for myself!

FIGURE 14.20

The free query form of the RWBlocks example is intended for power users.

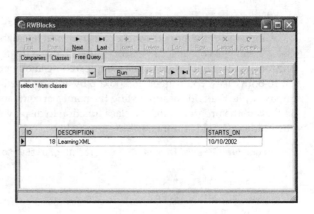

What's Next?

This chapter presented a detailed introduction to client/server programming with Delphi. We discussed the key issues and delved a little into interesting areas of client/server programming. After a general introduction, I discussed the use of the dbExpress database library. I also briefly covered the InterBase server and the InterBase Express (IBX) components. At the end of the chapter I presented a real-world example, going beyond the typical examples in the book to focus on a single feature at a time.

There is more I can say about client/server programming in Delphi. Chapter 15 will focus on Microsoft's ADO database engine. It's followed by a chapter on ADO.NET and one on Delphi's multitier architecture, DataSnap.

Chapter 15

Working with ADO

In the past chapter you saw that in the last few years Borland's database-independent access solution has moved from the *dated* BDE technology (it is about 10 years old) to the newer dbExpress architecture. The fact that BDE was more focused on local data while dbExpress supports only relational databases is a clear indication of an industry trend.

Meanwhile, Microsoft has kept promoting its own database-independent data access solutions, although Microsoft's *independent* proposals are often somewhat bound to the company database technologies, like Access or SQL Server. Microsoft started with Open Database Connectivity (ODBC), moved to OLE DB (a solution based on COM) and ActiveX Data Objects (ADO), and has now reworked the architecture on .NET with ADO.NET.

This chapter focuses specifically on the older but still viable ADO solution, which Delphi supports on both Win32 and on .NET (in Delphi 2005, as this feature was lacking in Delphi 8 for the Microsoft .NET Framework). All of the examples discussed in this chapter work equally under Delphi 2005 for Win32 and Delphi 2005 for .NET, using the VCL and the ADO components. See the next chapter for specific ADO.NET coverage.

NOTE   I wish to acknowledge and thank Guy Smith-Ferrier for originally writing this chapter for *Mastering Delphi 6* (Sybex, 2001). Guy is the author of *.NET Internationalization* (Addison-Wesley, due in 2005). He is the chief courseware architect for Courseware Online, a Microsoft Certified Professional developer, author, trainer, and speaker and has spoken at many European and U.S. conferences. He is the author of C#/.NET courseware and much of the official Borland courseware including courses on COM and ADO. Guy lives in England with his wife, his son, and his daughter.

This chapter covers ADO using *dbGo*—a set of Delphi VCL components initially called ADO-Express but renamed in Delphi 6 because Borland preferred to avoid the use of the Microsoft's branded term *ADO*. It is possible to use ADO in Delphi without using dbGo. By importing the ADO type library, you can gain direct access to the ADO interfaces; this is how Delphi programmers used ADO before the release of Delphi 5. However, this path bypasses Delphi's database infrastructure and doesn't let you make use of other Delphi technologies such as the data-aware controls or DataSnap. This chapter uses dbGo for all of its examples, not only because it is readily available and supported even in Delphi for .NET but also because it is a very viable solution. Regardless of your final choice, you will find the information here useful.

This chapter covers Microsoft Data Access Components (MDAC), Delphi's dbGo, Data Link files getting schema information, using the Jet engine, transaction processing, disconnected and persistent recordsets, the briefcase model, and deploying MDAC.

Microsoft Data Access Components (MDAC)

Microsoft started to replace ODBC with OLE DB in the mid-1990s with the success of the Component Object Model (COM). However, OLE DB is what Microsoft would classify as a *system-level* interface and is intended to be used by system-level programmers. It is very large, complex, and unforgiving. It makes greater demands on the programmer and requires a higher level of knowledge in return for lower productivity. ActiveX Data Objects (ADO) is a layer on top of OLE DB and is referred to as an *application-level* interface. It is considerably simpler than OLE DB and more forgiving. In short, it is designed for use by application programmers.

As you saw in Chapter 14, Borland replaced the BDE with dbExpress. ADO shares greater similarities with the BDE than with the lightweight dbExpress technology, however. BDE and ADO support navigation and manipulation of datasets, transaction processing, and cached updates (called *batch updates* in ADO), so the concepts and issues involved in using ADO are similar to those of the BDE.

NOTE   The BDE technology is not covered in this book. However, you can find an introduction to the BDE in Essential Delphi, as discussed in Appendix A.

ADO is part of a bigger picture called Microsoft Data Access Components (MDAC). MDAC is an umbrella for Microsoft's database technologies and includes ADO, OLE DB, ODBC, and RDS (Remote Data Services). Often you will hear people use the terms MDAC and ADO interchangeably —but incorrectly. Because ADO is only distributed as part of MDAC, we talk of ADO versions in terms of MDAC releases. The major releases of MDAC have been versions 1.5, 2.0, 2.1, and 2.5 to 2.8. Microsoft releases MDAC independently and makes it available for free download and virtually free distribution (there are distribution requirements, but most Delphi developers will have no trouble meeting them). MDAC is also distributed with most Microsoft products that have database content. Delphi 2005 ships with MDAC 2.8.

There are two consequences of this level of availability. First, it is highly likely that your users will already have MDAC installed on their machines. Second, whatever version your users have or you upgrade them to, it is also virtually certain that someone—you, your users, or other application software—will upgrade their existing MDAC to the current release of MDAC. You can't prevent this upgrade, because MDAC is installed with such commonly used software as Internet Explorer. Add to this the fact that Microsoft supports only the current release of MDAC and the release before it, and you arrive at this conclusion: Applications must be designed to work with the current release of MDAC or the release before it.

As an ADO developer, you should regularly check the MDAC pages on Microsoft's website at www.microsoft.com/data. From there you can download the latest version of MDAC for free. While you are on this website, you should take the opportunity to download the MDAC SDK (15 MB), if you do not already have it, or the Platform SDK (the MDAC SDK is part of the Platform SDK). The MDAC SDK is your bible: Download it, consult it regularly, and use it to answer your ADO questions. You should treat it as your first port of call when you need MDAC information.

OLE DB Providers

OLE DB providers enable access to a source of data. They are ADO's equivalent to the dbExpress drivers. When you install MDAC, you automatically install a series of the OLE DB providers, some of which are shown in Table 15.1.

◆ The ODBC OLE DB provider is used for backward compatibility with ODBC. As you learn more about ADO, you will discover the limitations of this provider.

◆ The Jet OLE DB providers support MS Access and other desktop databases. We will return to these providers later.

◆ The SQL Server provider supports SQL Server 7, SQL Server 2000, and Microsoft Database Engine (MSDE). MSDE is a reduced version of SQL Server, with most of the tools removed and some code added to deliberately degrade performance when there are more than five active connections. MSDE is important because it is free and it is fully compatible with SQL Server.

In addition to these MDAC OLE DB providers, Microsoft supplies other OLE DB providers with other products or with downloadable SDKs. For example the Active Directory Services OLE DB provider is included with the ADSI SDK; the AS/400 and VSAM OLE DB provider is included with SNA Server; and the Exchange OLE DB provider is included with Microsoft Exchange 2000. The OLE DB provider for Internet Publishing allows developers to manipulate directories and files using HTTP.

Still more OLE DB providers come in the form of *service providers*. As their name implies, OLE DB service providers provide a service to other OLE DB providers and are often invoked automatically as needed without programmer intervention. The Cursor Service, for example, is invoked when you create a client-side cursor, and the Persisted Recordset provider is invoked to save data locally.

MDAC includes many providers that I'll discuss, but many more are available from Microsoft and from the third-party market. It is impossible to reliably list all available OLE DB providers because the list is so large and changes constantly. In addition to independent third parties, you should consider most database vendors because the majority now supply their own OLE DB providers. For example, Oracle supplies the ORAOLEDB provider.

TABLE 15.1:   Some of the OLE DB Providers Included with MDAC

DRIVER	PROVIDER	DESCRIPTION
MSDASQL	ODBC drivers	ODBC drivers (default)
Microsoft.Jet.OLEDB.4.0	Jet 4.0	MS Access and other databases
SQLOLEDB	SQL Server	MS SQL Server databases
MSDAORA	Oracle	Oracle databases
SampProv	Sample provider	Example of an OLE DB provider for CSV files

TIP A notable omission from the vendors that supply OLE DB providers is InterBase. In addition to accessing it using the ODBC driver, you can use Dmitry Kovalenko's IBProvider (www.lcpi.lipetsk.ru/prog/eng/index.html). Also check Binh Ly's OLE DB Provider Development Toolkit (www.techvanguards.com/products/optk). If you want to write your own OLE DB provider, this tool is easier to use than most.

Using dbGo Components

Programmers familiar with dbExpress or IBExpress should recognize the set of components that make up dbGo. In Table 15.2 I compared the ADO components to the dbExpress equivalent components.

TABLE 15.2:   dbGo Components

DBGO COMPONENT	DESCRIPTION	DBEXPRESS COMPONENT
ADOConnection	Connection to a database	SQLConnection
ADOCommand	Executes an action SQL command	No equivalent
ADODataSet	All-purpose descendant of TDataSet	SQLDataSet
ADOTable	Encapsulation of a table	SQLTable
ADOQuery	Encapsulation of SQL SELECT	SQLQuery
ADOStoredProc	Encapsulation of a stored procedure	SQLStoredProc
RDSConnection	Remote Data Services connection	No equivalent

The four dataset components (ADODataSet, ADOTable, ADOQuery, and ADOStoredProc) are implemented almost entirely by their immediate ancestor class, TCustomADODataSet. This component provides the majority of dataset functionality, and its descendants are mostly thin wrappers that expose different features of the same component. As such, the components have a lot in common. In general, however, ADOTable, ADOQuery, and ADOStoredProc are viewed as "compatibility" components and are used to aid the transition of knowledge and code from their BDE counterparts. Be warned, though: These compatibility components are similar to their counterparts but not identical. You will find differences in any application except the most trivial. ADODataSet is the component of choice partly because of its versatility but also because it is closer in appearance to the ADO Recordset interface upon which it is based. Throughout this chapter, I'll use all the dataset components to give you the experience of using each.

A Practical Example

Enough theory; let's see some action. Drop an ADOTable onto a form. To indicate the database to connect to, ADO uses *connection strings*. You can type in a connection string by hand if you know what you are doing. In general, you'll use the connection string editor (the property editor of the ConnectionString property), shown in Figure 15.1.

This editor adds little value to the process of entering a connection string, so you can click Build to go straight to Microsoft's connection string editor, shown in Figure 15.2. This is a tool you need to understand. The first tab shows the OLE DB providers and service providers installed on your computer. The list will vary according to the version of MDAC and other software you have installed. In this example, select the Jet 4.0 OLE DB provider. Double-click Microsoft Jet 4.0 OLE DB Provider, and you will be presented with the Connection tab. This page varies according to the provider you select; for Jet, it asks you for the name of the database and your login details. You can choose an Access MDB file installed by Borland with Delphi 2005: the dbdemos.mdb file available in the shared data folder (by default, C:\Program Files\Common Files\Borland Shared\Data\dbdemos.mdb). Click the Test Connection button to test the validity of your selections.

The Advanced tab handles access control to the database; here you specify exclusive or read-only access to the database. The All tab lists all the parameters in the connection string. The list is specific to the OLE DB provider you selected on the first page. (You should make a mental note of this page because it contains many parameters that are the answers to many problems.) After closing the Microsoft connection string editor, you'll see in the Borland ConnectionString property editor the value that will be returned to the ConnectionString property (here split on multiple lines for readability):

```
Provider=Microsoft.Jet.OLEDB.4.0;
Data Source=C:\Program Files\Common Files\Borland Shared\Data\dbdemos.mdb;
Persist Security Info=False
```

FIGURE 15.1
Delphi's connection
string editor

FIGURE 15.2
The first page of
Microsoft's connec-
tion string editor

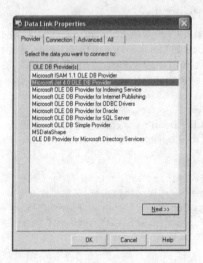

Connection strings are just strings with many parameters delimited by semicolons. To add, edit, or delete any of these parameter values programmatically, you must write your own routines to find the parameter in the list and amend it appropriately. A simpler approach is to copy the string into a Delphi string list and use its name/value pairs capability; this technique will be demonstrated in the JetText example covered in the section "Text Files Through Jet."

Now that you have set the connection string, you can select a table. Drop down the list of tables using the `TableName` property in the Object Inspector. Select the Customer table. Add a DataSource component and a DBGrid control and connect them all together; you are now using ADO in an actual—though trivial—program (available in the source code as FirstAdoExample). To see the data, set the `Active` property of the dataset to True or open the dataset in the `FormCreate` event (as in the example) to avoid design-time errors if the database is not available.

The ADOConnection Component

When you use an ADOTable component this way, it creates its own connection component behind the scenes. You do not have to accept the default connection it creates. In general, you should create your own connection using the ADOConnection component, which has the same purpose as the dbExpress SQLConnection component. It allows you to customize the login procedure, control transactions, execute action commands directly, and reduce the number of connections in an application.

Using an ADOConnection is easy. Place one on a form and set its `ConnectionString` property the same way you would for the ADOTable. Alternatively, you can double-click an ADOConnection component (or use a specific item of its component editor, in its shortcut menu) to invoke the connection string editor directly. With the `ConnectionString` set to the proper database, you can disable the login dialog box by setting `LoginPrompt` to False. To use the new connection in the previous example, set the `Connection` property of ADOTable1 to ADOConnection1. You will see ADOTable1's `ConnectionString` property reset because the `Connection` and `ConnectionString` properties are mutually exclusive. One of the benefits of using an ADOConnection is that the connection string is centralized instead of scattered throughout many components. Another more important benefit is that all the components that share the ADOConnection share a single connection to the database server. Without your own ADOConnection, each ADO dataset has a separate connection.

Data Link Files

So, an ADOConnection allows you to centralize the definition of a connection string within a form or data module. However, even though this is a worthwhile step forward from scattering the same connection string throughout all ADO datasets, it still suffers from a fundamental flaw: If you use a database engine that defines the database in terms of a filename, the path to the database file(s) is hard-coded in the .EXE. This makes for a fragile application. To overcome this problem, ADO uses Data Link files.

A Data Link file is a connection string in an .ini file. For example, Delphi's installation adds to the system the `dbdemos.udl` file, with the following text:

```
[oledb]
; Everything after this line is an OLE DB initstring
Provider=Microsoft.Jet.OLEDB.4.0;
Data Source=C:\Program Files\Common Files\
   Borland Shared\Data\dbdemos.mdb
```

Although you can give a Data Link file any extension, the recommended extension is .UDL. You can create a Data Link using any text editor, or you can right-click in Windows Explorer, select New ➢ Text Document, rename the file with a .UDL extension (assuming extensions are displayed in your configuration of Explorer), and then double-click the file to invoke the Microsoft connection string editor.

When you select a file in the connection editor, the ConnectionString property will be set to FILE NAME= followed by the actual filename, as demonstrated by the DataLinkFile example. You can place your Data Link files anywhere on the hard disk, but if you are looking for a common, shared location, you can use the DataLinkDir function in the ADODB Delphi unit. If you haven't altered MDAC's defaults, DataLinkDir will return the following:

```
C:\Program Files\Common Files\System\OLE DB\Data Links
```

Dynamic Properties

Imagine that you are responsible for designing a new database middleware architecture. You have to reconcile two opposing goals of a single API for all databases and access to database-specific features. You could take the approach of designing an interface that is the sum of all the features of every database ever created. Each class would have every property and method imaginable, but it would only use the properties and methods it had support for. It doesn't take much discussion to realize that this isn't a good solution. ADO has to solve these apparently mutually exclusive goals, and it does so using *dynamic properties*.

Almost all ADO interfaces and their corresponding dbGo components have a property called Properties that is a collection of database-specific properties. These properties can be accessed by their ordinal position, like this:

```
ShowMessage(ADOTable1.Properties[1].Value);
```

But they are more often accessed by name:

```
ShowMessage(ADOConnection1.Properties['DBMS Name'].Value);
```

Dynamic properties depend on the type of object and also on the OLE DB providers. To give you an idea of their importance, a typical ADO Connection or Recordset has approximately 100 dynamic properties. As you will see throughout this chapter, the answers to many ADO questions lie in dynamic properties.

TIP An important event related to the use of dynamic properties is OnRecordsetCreate, which is called immediately after the recordset has been created but before it is opened. This event is useful when you're setting dynamic properties that can be set only when the recordset is closed.

Getting Schema Information

In ADO, you can retrieve schema information using the ADOConnection component's OpenSchema method. This method accepts four parameters:

◆ The kind of data OpenSchema should return. It is a TSchemaInfo value: a set of 40 values including those for retrieving a list of tables, indexes, columns, views, and stored procedures.

◆ A filter to place on the data before it is returned. You will see an example of this parameter in a moment.

- A GUID for a provider-specific query. This parameter is used only if the first parameter is siProviderSpecific.
- An ADODataSet into which the data is returned. This parameter illustrates a common theme in ADO: Any method that needs to return more than a small amount of data will return its data as a Recordset or, in Delphi terms, an ADODataSet.

To use `OpenSchema`, you need an open ADOConnection. The following code (part of the OpenSchema example) retrieves a list of primary keys for every table into an ADODataSet:

```
ADOConnection1.OpenSchema(siPrimaryKeys,
  EmptyParam, EmptyParam, ADODataSet1);
```

Each field in a primary key has a single row in the result set, so a table with a composite key of two fields has two rows. The two `EmptyParam` values indicate that these parameters are given empty values and are ignored. The result of this code is shown in Figure 15.3 after resizing the grid with some custom code.

When `EmptyParam` is passed as the second parameter, the result set includes all information of the requested type for the entire database. For many kinds of information, you will want to filter the result set. You can, of course, apply a traditional Delphi filter to the result set using the `Filter` and `Filtered` properties or the `OnFilterRecord` event. However, doing so applies the filter on the client side in this example. Using the second parameter, you can apply a more efficient filter at the source of the schema information. The filter is specified as an array of values. Each element of the array has a specific meaning relevant to the kind of data being returned. For example, the filter array for primary keys has three elements: the catalog (*catalog* is ANSI-speak for the database), the schema, and the table name. This example returns a list of primary keys for the Customer table:

```
var
  Filter: OLEVariant;
begin
  Filter := VarArrayCreate([0, 2], varVariant);
  Filter[2] := 'CUSTOMER';
  ADOConnection1.OpenSchema(
    siPrimaryKeys, Filter, EmptyParam, ADODataSet1);
end;
```

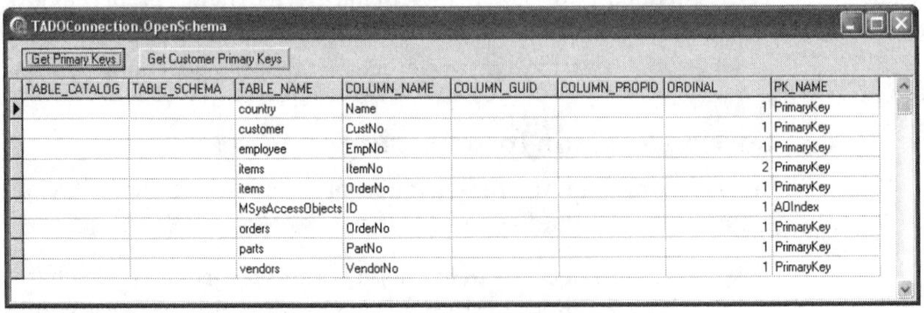
TADOConnection.OpenSchema
Get Primary Keys
Get Customer Primary Keys
TABLE_CATALOG TABLE_SCHEMA TABLE_NAME COLUMN_NAME COLUMN_GUID COLUMN_PROPID ORDINAL PK_NAME
country Name 1 PrimaryKey
customer CustNo 1 PrimaryKey
employee EmpNo 1 PrimaryKey
items ItemNo 2 PrimaryKey
items OrderNo 1 PrimaryKey
MSysAccessObjects ID 1 AOIndex
orders OrderNo 1 PrimaryKey
parts PartNo 1 PrimaryKey
vendors VendorNo 1 PrimaryKey

FIGURE 15.3
The OpenSchema example retrieves the primary keys of the database tables.

NOTE You can retrieve the same information using ADOX, and this warrants a brief comparison between OpenSchema and ADOX. ADOX is an additional ADO technology that allows you to retrieve and update schema information. It is ADO's equivalent to SQL's Data Definition Language (DDL—CREATE, ALTER, DROP) and Data Control Language (DCL—GRANT, REVOKE). ADOX is not directly supported in dbGo, but you can import the ADOX type library and use it successfully in Delphi applications. Unfortunately, ADOX is not as universally implemented as OpenSchema, so there are greater gaps. To only retrieve information and not update it, OpenSchema is usually a better choice.

Using the Jet Engine

Now that you have some of the MDAC and ADO basics under your belt, let's take a moment to look at the Jet engine. This engine is of great interest to some and of no interest to others. If you're interested in Access, Paradox, dBase, text, Excel, Lotus 1-2-3, or HTML, then this section is for you. If you have no interest in any of these formats, you can safely skip this section.

The Jet database engine is usually associated with Microsoft Access databases, and this is its forte. However, the Jet engine is also an all-purpose desktop database engine, and this lesser-known attribute is where much of its strength lies. Because using the Jet engine with Access is its default mode and is straightforward, this section mostly covers use of non-Access formats, which are not so obvious.

NOTE The Jet engine has been included in some (but not all) versions of MDAC. It is not included in version 2.8. There has been a long debate about whether programmers using a non-Microsoft development tool have the right to distribute the Jet engine. The official answer is positive, and the Jet engine is available as a free download (in addition to being distributed with many Microsoft software products, including the latest versions of the Windows operating system itself).

The Jet 4.0 OLE DB provider supports Access 97 (although the older Jet 3.51 OLE DB might work better with it), Access 2000, and Installable Indexed Sequential Access Method (IISAM) drivers. Installable ISAM drivers are those written specifically for the Jet engine to support access to ISAM formats such as Paradox, dBase, and text, and it is this facility that makes the Jet engine so useful and versatile. The complete list of ISAM drivers installed on your machine depends on what software you have installed. You can find this list by looking in the Registry at

```
HKEY_LOCAL_MACHINE\Software\Microsoft\Jet\4.0\ISAM Formats
```

However, the Jet engine includes drivers for Paradox, dBase, Excel, text, and HTML.

Paradox Through Jet

The Jet engine expects to be used with Access databases. To use it with any database other than Access, you need to tell it which IISAM driver to use. This is a painless process that involves setting the Extended Properties connection string argument in the connection string editor. Let's work through a quick example.

Add an ADOTable component to a form and invoke the connection string editor. Select the Jet 4.0 OLE DB Provider. Select the All page, locate the Extended Properties property, and double-click it to edit its value.

Enter **Paradox 7.x** in the Property Value, as illustrated in Figure 15.4, and click OK. Now go back to the Connection tab and enter the name of the directory containing the Paradox tables directly, because the Browse button won't help you (it lets you enter a filename, not a folder name). At this point you can select a table in the ADOTable's `TableName` and open it either at design time or at run time. You are now using Paradox through ADO, as demonstrated by the JetParadox example.

I have some bad news for Paradox users: Under certain circumstances, you will need to install the BDE in addition to the Jet engine. Jet 4.0 requires the BDE in order to be able to update Paradox tables, but it doesn't require the BDE just to read them. The same is true for most releases of the Paradox ODBC Driver. Microsoft has received justified criticism about this point and has made a new Paradox IISAM available that does not require the BDE; you can get these updated drivers from Microsoft Technical Support.

NOTE   As you learn more about ADO, you will discover how much it depends on the OLE DB provider and the database server in question. Although you can use ADO with a local file format, as demonstrated in this and following examples, the general suggestion is to install a local SQL engine whenever possible. Access and MSDE are good choices if you have to use ADO; otherwise, you might want to consider InterBase or Firebird as alternatives, as discussed in Chapter 14.

FIGURE 15.4
Setting extended properties

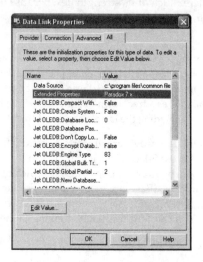

Excel Through Jet

Excel is easily accessed using the Jet OLE DB provider. Once again, you set the Extended Properties property, this time to Excel 8.0. Assume that you have an Excel spreadsheet called `ABCCompany.xls` with a sheet called Employees, and you want to open and read this file using Delphi. With a little knowledge of COM, you can do so by automating Excel. However, the ADO solution is considerably easier to implement and doesn't require Excel to be available on the computer.

TIP   You can also read an Excel file using the `XLSReadWrite` component (available from `www.axolot.com`). It doesn't require Excel to be available on the computer or the time to start it (as OLE Automation techniques do).

Ensure that your spreadsheet is not open in Excel, because ADO requires exclusive access to the file. Add an ADODataSet component to a form. Set its ConnectionString to use the Jet 4.0 OLE DB provider and set Extended Properties to Excel 8.0. In the Connection tab, set the database name to the full file and path specification of the Excel spreadsheet (or use a relative path if you plan to deploy the file along with the program).

The ADODataSet component works by opening or executing a value in its CommandText property. This value might be the name of a table, a SQL statement, a stored procedure, or the name of a file. You specify how this value is interpreted by setting the CommandType property. Set CommandType to cmd-TableDirect to indicate that the value in CommandText is the name of a table and that all columns should be returned from this table. Select CommandText in the Object Inspector, and you will see a drop-down arrow. Drop down the arrow and a single pseudo-table will be displayed: Employees$. (Excel workbooks are suffixed with a $.)

Add a DataSource and a DBGrid and connect them altogether, and you'll obtain the output of the JetExcel example, shown in Figure 15.5 at design time. By default it would be a little difficult to view the data in the grid, because each column has a width of 255 characters. You can change the field display size either by adding columns to the grid and changing their Width properties or by adding persistent fields and changing their Size or DisplayWidth properties.

Notice that you cannot keep the dataset open at design time and run the program, because the Excel IISAM driver opens the XLS file in exclusive mode. Close the dataset and add to the program a line of code to open it at startup. When you run the program, you will notice another limitation of this IISAM driver: You can add new rows and edit existing rows, but you cannot delete rows.

Incidentally, you could have used either an ADOTable or an ADOQuery component instead of the ADODataSet, but you need to be aware of how ADO treats symbols in things like table names and field names. If you use an ADOTable and drop down the list of tables, you will see the Employees$ table as you expect. Unfortunately, if you attempt to open the table, you will receive an error. The same is true for SELECT * FROM Employees$ in a TADOQuery. The problem lies with the dollar sign in the table name. If you use characters such as dollar signs, dots, or, more importantly, spaces in a table name or field name, then you must enclose the name in square brackets (for example, [Employees$]).

FIGURE 15.5

ABCCompany.xls in Delphi—a small tribute to Douglas Adams

Text Files Through Jet

One of the most useful IISAM drivers that comes with the Jet engine is the Text IISAM. This driver allows you to read and update text files of almost any structured format. We will begin with a simple text file and then cover the variations.

Assume you have a text file called NightShift.TXT that contains the following text:

```
CrewPerson ,HomeTown
Neo        ,Cincinnati
Trinity    ,London
Morpheus   ,Milan
```

Add an ADOTable component to a form, set its ConnectionString to use the Jet 4.0 OLE DB provider, and set Extended Properties to Text. The Text IISAM provider considers a directory a database, so you need to enter as the database name the directory that contains the NightShift.TXT file. If you look in the Object Inspector at the drop-down list of tables for the TableName property, you will notice that the dot in the filename has been converted to a hash, as in NightShift#TXT. Set Active to True, add a DataSource and a DBGrid and connect them altogether, and you will see the contents of the text file in a grid.

WARNING   If your computer's settings are such that the decimal separator is a comma instead of a period (so that 1,000.00 is displayed as 1.000,00), you will need to either change your operating system regional settings (select the Regional and Language Options icon in the Control Panel, click the Customize button of the Regional Options page, and edit the values in the Numbers page) or take advantage of SCHEMA.INI, described shortly.

The grid indicates that the widths of the columns are 255 characters. You can change these values just as you did in the JetExcel program by adding persistent fields or columns to the grid and then setting the relevant width property. Alternatively, you can define the structure of the text file more specifically using SCHEMA.INI.

In the JetText example, the database folder is determined at run time depending on the folder hosting the program. To modify the connection string at run time, first load it into a string list (after converting the separators) and then use the Values property to change only one of the elements of the connection string. This is the code from the example:

```
procedure TForm1.FormCreate(Sender: TObject);
var
  sl: TStringList;
begin
  sl := TStringList.Create;
  try
    sl.Text := StringReplace (ADOTable1.ConnectionString,
      ';', sLineBreak, [rfReplaceAll]);
    sl.Values ['Data Source'] := ExtractFilePath (Application.ExeName);
    ADOTable1.ConnectionString := StringReplace (sl.Text,
      sLineBreak, ';', [rfReplaceAll]);
    ADOTable1.Open;
  finally
    sl.Free;
  end;
end;
```

Text files come in all shapes and sizes. Often you do not need to worry about the format of a text file because the Text IISAM takes a peek at the first 25 rows to see whether it can determine the format for itself. It uses this information and additional information in the Registry to decide how to interpret the file and how to behave. If you have a file that doesn't match a regular format the Text IISAM can determine, then you can provide this information using a SCHEMA.INI file located in the same directory as the text files to which it refers. This file contains *schema* information, also called metadata, about any or all of the text files in the same directory. Each text file is given its own section, identified by the name of the text file, such as [NightShift.TXT].

Thereafter you can specify the format of the file; the names, types, and sizes of columns; any special character sets to use; and any special column formats (such as date/time or currency). Let's assume that you change your NightShift.TXT file to the following format:

```
Neo          |Cincinnati
Trinity      |London
Morpheus     |Milan
```

In this example, the column names are not included in the text file, and the delimiter is a vertical bar. An associated SCHEMA.INI file might look something like the following:

```
[NightShift.TXT]
Format=Delimited(|)
ColNameHeader=False
Col1=CrewPerson Char Width 10
Col2=HomeTown Char Width 30
```

Regardless of whether you use a SCHEMA.INI file, you will encounter two limitations of the Text IISAM: Rows cannot be deleted, and rows cannot be edited.

Importing and Exporting

The Jet engine is particularly adept at importing and exporting data. The process of exporting data is the same for each export format and consists of executing a SELECT statement with a special syntax. Let's begin with an example of exporting data from the Access version of the DBDemos database back to a Paradox table. You will need an active ADOConnection, called ADOConnection1 in the JetImport-Export example, which uses the Jet engine to open the database. The following code exports the Customer table to a Paradox Customer.db file:

```
SELECT * INTO Customer IN "C:\tmp" "Paradox 7.x;" FROM CUSTOMER
```

Let's look at the pieces of this SELECT statement. The INTO clause specifies the new table that will be created by the SELECT statement; this table must not already exist. The IN clause specifies the database to which the new table is added; in Paradox, this is a directory that already exists. The clause immediately following the database is the name of the IISAM driver to be used to perform the export. *You must include the trailing semicolon at the end of the driver name.* The FROM clause is a regular part of any SELECT statement. In the sample program, the operation is executed through the ADOConnection component and uses the program's folder instead of a fixed one:

```
ADOConnection1.Execute ('SELECT * INTO Customer IN "' +
  CurrentFolder + '" "Paradox 7.x;" FROM CUSTOMER');
```

TIP   As you cannot export to an already existing file, the JetImportExport program deletes each output file if it already exists before generating a new one. This happens for each of the three export drivers.

All export statements follow these same basic clauses, although IISAM drivers have differing interpretations of what a database is. Here, you export the same data to Excel:

```
ADOConnection1.Execute ('SELECT * INTO Customer IN "' +
   CurrentFolder + 'dbdemos.xls" "Excel 8.0;" FROM CUSTOMER');
```

A new Excel file called dbdemos.xls is created in the application's current directory. A workbook called Customer is added, containing all the data from the Customer table in dbdemos.mdb.

This last example exports the same data to an HTML file:

```
ADOConnection1.Execute ('SELECT * INTO [Customer.htm] IN "' +
   CurrentFolder + '" "HTML Export;" FROM CUSTOMER');
```

In this case, the database is the directory, as it was for Paradox but not for Excel. The table name must include the .HTM extension and, therefore, it must be enclosed in square brackets. Notice that the name of the IISAM driver is HTML Export, not just HTML, because this driver can only be used for exporting to HTML.

The last IISAM driver we'll look at in this investigation of the Jet engine is the partner to HTML Export: HTML Import. Add an ADOTable to a form, set its ConnectionString to use the Jet 4.0 OLE DB provider, and set Extended Properties to HTML Import. Set the database name to the name of the HTML file created by the export a few moments ago—that is, Customer.htm. Now set the TableName property to Customer. Open the table—you have just imported the HTML file. Bear in mind, though, that if you attempt to update the data, you'll receive an error because this driver is intended for import only. Finally, if you create your own HTML files containing tables and want to open these tables using this driver, remember that the name of the table is the value of the caption tag of the HTML table.

Working with Cursors

Two properties of ADO datasets have a fundamental impact on your application and are inextricably linked with each other: CursorLocation and CursorType. If you want to understand your ADO dataset behavior, you must understand these two properties.

Cursor Location

The CursorLocation property allows you to specify what is in control of the retrieval and update of your data. You have two choices: client (clUseClient) or server (clUseServer). Your choice affects your dataset's functionality, performance, and scalability.

A client cursor is managed by the ADO Cursor Engine. This engine is an excellent example of an OLE DB service provider: It provides a service to other OLE DB providers. The ADO Cursor Engine manages the data from the client side of the application. All data in the result set is retrieved from the server to the client when the dataset is opened. Thereafter, the data is held in memory, and updates and manipulation are managed by the ADO Cursor Engine. This is similar to using the ClientDataSet component in a dbExpress application. One benefit is that manipulation of the data, after the initial retrieval, is considerably faster. Furthermore, because the manipulation is performed in memory, the ADO Cursor Engine is more versatile than most server-side cursors and offers extra facilities. I'll examine these benefits later, as well as other technologies that depend on client-side cursors (such as disconnected and persistent recordsets).

A server-side cursor is managed by the database server. In a client/server architecture based on a database such as SQL Server, Oracle, or InterBase, this means the cursor is managed physically on the server. In a desktop database such as Access or Paradox, the "server" location is a logical location because the database is running on the desktop. Server-side cursors are often faster to load than client-side cursors because not all the data is transferred to the client when the dataset is opened. This behavior also makes them more suitable for very large result sets where the client has insufficient memory to hold the entire result set in memory. Often you can determine what kinds of features will be available to you with each cursor location by thinking through how the cursor works. Locking is a good example of how features determine the cursor type; I will discuss locking in more detail later. (To place a lock on a record requires a server-side cursor because there must be a conversation between the application and the database server.)

Another issue that will affect your choice of cursor location is scalability. Server-side cursors are managed by the database server; in a client/server database, this will be located on the server. As more users use your application, the load on the server increases with each server-side cursor. A greater workload on the server means that the database server becomes a bottleneck more quickly, so the application is less scalable. You can achieve better scalability by using client-side cursors. The initial hit on opening the cursor is often heavier because all the data is transferred to the client, but the maintenance of the open cursor can be lower. As you can see, many conflicting issues are involved in choosing the correct cursor location for your datasets.

Cursor Type

Your choice of cursor location directly affects your choice of cursor type. To all intents and purposes there are four cursor types, but one value is unused: a cursor type that means *unspecified*. Many values in ADO signify an unspecified value, and I will cover them all here and explain why you won't have much to do with them. They exist in Delphi because they exist in ADO. ADO was primarily designed for Visual Basic and C programmers. In these languages, you use objects directly without the assistance dbGo provides. As such, you can create and open *recordsets*, as they are called in ADO-speak, without having to specify every value for every property. The properties for which a value has not been specified have an unspecified value. However, in dbGo you use components. These components have constructors, and these constructors initialize the properties of the components. So from the moment you create a dbGo component, it will usually have a value for every property. As a consequence, you have little need for the unspecified values in many enumerated types.

Cursor types affect how your data is read and updated. As I mentioned, there are four choices: forward-only, static, keyset, and dynamic. Before we get too involved in all the permutations of cursor locations and cursor types, you should be aware that there is only one cursor type available for client-side cursors: the static cursor. All other cursor types are available only to server-side cursors. I'll return to the subject of cursor type availability after we look at the various cursor types, in increasing order of expense:

Forward-only cursor   The forward-only cursor is the least expensive cursor type and therefore the type with the best performance. As the name implies, the forward-only cursor lets you navigate forward. The cursor reads the number of records specified by CacheSize (default of 1); each time it runs out of records, it reads another CacheSize set. Any attempt to navigate backward through the result set beyond the number of records in the cache results in an error. This behavior is similar to that of a dbExpress dataset. A forward-only cursor is not suitable for use in the user interface where the user can control the direction through the result set. However, it is eminently suitable for batch operations, reports, and stateless web applications because these situations start at the top of the result set and work progressively toward the end, and then the result set is closed.

Static cursor A static cursor works by reading the complete result set and providing a window of CacheSize records into the result set. Because the complete result set has been retrieved by the server, you can navigate both forward and backward through the result set. However, in exchange for this facility, the data is static—updates, insertions, and deletions made by other users cannot be seen because the cursor's data has already been read.

Keyset cursor A keyset cursor is best understood by breaking *keyset* into the two words *key* and *set*. *Key*, in this context, refers to an identifier for each row. Often this will be a primary key. A keyset cursor, therefore, is a *set* of keys. When the result set is opened, the complete list of keys for the result set is read. If, for example, the dataset was a query like SELECT * FROM CUSTOMER, then the list of keys would be built from SELECT CUSTID FROM CUSTOMER. This set of keys is held until the cursor is closed. When the application requests data, the OLE DB provider reads the rows using the keys in the set of keys. Consequently, the data is always up to date. If another user changes a row in the result set, the changes will be seen when the data is reread. However, the set of keys is static; it is read only when the result set is first opened. If another user adds new records, these additions will not be seen. Deleted records become inaccessible, and changes to primary keys (you don't let your users change primary keys, do you?) are also inaccessible.

Dynamic cursor The most expensive cursor type, a dynamic cursor, is almost identical to a keyset cursor. The sole difference is that the set of keys is reread when the application requests data that is not in the cache. Because the default for TADODataSet.CacheSize is 1, such requests occur frequently. You can imagine the additional load this behavior places on the DBMS and the network and why this is the most expensive cursor. However, the result set can see and respond to additions and deletions made by other users.

Combining Cursor Locations and Types

Now that you know about cursor locations and cursor types, a word of warning: Not all combinations of cursor location and cursor type are possible. Usually, this limitation is imposed by the RDBMS and/or the OLE DB provider as a result of the functionality and architecture of the database. For example, client cursors always force the cursor type to static. You can see behavior this for yourself. Add an ADODataSet component to a form, set its ConnectionString to any database, and set the CursorLocation property to clUseClient and the CursorType property to ctDynamic. Now set Active to True and keep your eye on the CursorType; it changes to ctStatic. You learn an important lesson from this example: What you ask for is not necessarily what you get. Always check your properties after opening a dataset to see the actual effect of your requests.

Each OLE DB provider will make different changes according to different requests and circumstances, but here are a few examples to give you an idea of what to expect:

◆ The Jet 4.0 OLE DB provider changes most cursor types to keyset.

◆ The SQL Server OLE DB provider often changes keyset and static to dynamic.

◆ The Oracle OLE DB provider changes all cursor types to forward-only.

◆ The ODBC OLE DB provider makes various changes according to the ODBC driver in use.

No Record Count

ADO datasets sometimes return –1 for their `RecordCount`. A forward-only cursor cannot know how many records are in the result set until it reaches the end, so it returns –1 for the `RecordCount`. A static cursor always knows how many records are in the result set because it reads the entire set when it is opened, so it returns the number of records in its result set. A keyset cursor also knows how many records are in the result set because it has to retrieve a fixed set of keys when the result set is opened, so it also returns a useful value for `RecordCount`. A dynamic cursor does not reliably know how many records are in the result set because it is regularly rereading the set of keys, so it returns –1. You can avoid using `RecordCount` altogether and execute `SELECT COUNT(*) FROM tablename`, but the result will be an accurate reflection of the number of records in the database table—which is not necessarily the same as the number of records in the dataset.

Client Indexes

One of the many benefits of client-side cursors is the ability to create local, or *client*, indexes. Assuming you have an ADO client-side dataset for the DBDemos Customer table, which has a grid attached to it, set the dataset's `IndexFieldNames` property to CompanyName. The grid will immediately show that the data is in CompanyName order. There is an important point here: In order to index the data, ADO did not have to reread the data from its source. The index was created from the data in memory. So, not only is the index created as quickly as possible, but the network and the DBMS are not overloaded by transferring the same data over and over in different orders.

The `IndexFieldNames` property has more potential. Set it to `Country;CompanyName` and you will see the data ordered first by country and then, within country, by company name. Now set `IndexFieldNames` to CompanyName DESC. Be sure to write *DESC* in capitals (and not *desc* or *Desc*). The data is now sorted in descending order.

This simple but powerful feature allows you to solve one of the great bugbears of database developers. Users ask the inevitable and quite reasonable question, "Can I click the columns of the grid to sort my data?" Answers like replacing grids with non–data-aware controls such as ListView that have the sorting built into the control, or trapping the DBGrid's `OnTitleClick` event and reissuing the SQL SELECT statement after including an appropriate ORDER BY clause, are far from satisfactory.

If you have the data cached on the client side (as you've also seen in the use of the ClientDataSet component), you can use a client index computed in memory. Add the following `OnTitleClick` event to the grid (the code is available in the ClientIndexes example):

```
procedure TForm1.DBGrid1TitleClick(Column: TColumn);
begin
  if ADODataSet1.IndexFieldNames = Column.Field.FieldName then
    ADODataSet1.IndexFieldNames := Column.Field.FieldName + ' DESC'
  else
    ADODataSet1.IndexFieldNames := Column.Field.FieldName
end;
```

This simple event checks to see whether the current index is built on the same field as the column. If it is, then a new index is built on the column but in descending order. If not, then a new index is built on the column. When the user clicks the column for the first time, it is sorted in ascending order; when it is clicked for the second time, it is sorted in descending order. You could extend this functionality to allow the user to Ctrl+click several column titles to build up more complicated indexes.

NOTE All of this can be achieved using ClientDataSet, but that solution is not as elegant, because ClientDataSet does not support the DESC keyword—so you have to create an index collection item to obtain a descending index, something that requires more code.

Cloning

ADO is crammed with features. You can argue that *feature-rich* can translate into *footprint-rich*, but it also translates into more powerful and reliable applications. One such powerful feature is cloning. A cloned recordset is a new recordset that has all the same properties as the original from which it is cloned. First I'll explain how you can create and use a clone, and then I'll explain why clones are so useful.

NOTE The ClientDataSet also supports cloning; this feature was not discussed in Chapter 13.

You can clone a recordset (or, in dbGo-speak, a dataset) using the Clone method. You can clone any ADO dataset, but you will use ADOTable in this example. The DataClone example (see Figure 15.6) uses two ADOTable components, one hooked to database data and the other empty. Both datasets are hooked to a DataSource and grid. A single line of code, executed when the user clicks a button, clones the dataset:

```
ADOTable2.Clone(ADOTable1);
```

This line clones ADOTable1 and assigns the clone to ADOTable2. In the program, you'll see a second view of the data. The two datasets have their own record pointers and other status information, so the clone does not interfere with its original copy. This behavior makes clones ideal for operating on a dataset without affecting the original data. Another interesting feature is that you can have multiple different active records, one for each of the clones—functionality you cannot achieve in Delphi with a single dataset.

TIP A recordset must support bookmarks in order to be cloned, so forward-only and dynamic cursors cannot be cloned. You can determine whether a recordset supports bookmarks using the Supports method (for example, ADOTable1.Supports([coBookMark])). One of the useful side effects of clones is that the bookmarks created by one clone are usable by all other clones.

FIGURE 15.6

The DataClone example, with two copies of a dataset (the original and a clone)

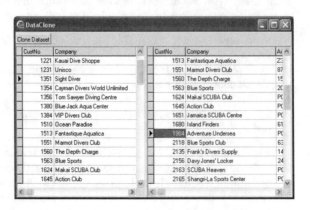

Transaction Processing

As you saw in the "Using Transactions" section of Chapter 14, transaction processing allows developers to group individual updates to a database into a single logical unit of work.

ADO's transaction processing support is controlled with the ADOConnection component, using the BeginTrans, CommitTrans, and RollbackTrans methods, which have effects similar to those of the corresponding dbExpress methods. To investigate ADO transaction processing support, you will build a test program called TransProcessing. The program has an ADOConnection component with the ConnectionString set to the Jet 4.0 OLE DB provider and the dbdemos.mdb file. It has an ADOTable component hooked to the Customer table and a DataSource and DBGrid for displaying the data. Finally, it has three buttons to execute the following commands:

```
ADOConnection1.BeginTrans;
ADOConnection1.CommitTrans;
ADOConnection1.RollbackTrans;
```

With this program, you can make changes to the database table and then roll them back, and they will be rolled back as expected. I emphasize this point because transaction support varies depending on the database and on the OLE DB provider you are using. For example, if you connect to Paradox using the ODBC OLE DB provider, you will receive an error indicating that the database or the OLE DB provider is not capable of beginning a transaction. You can find out the level of transaction processing support you have using the Transaction DDL dynamic property of the connection:

```
if ADOConnection1.Properties['Transaction DDL'].Value > DBPROPVAL_TC_NONE then
  ADOConnection1.BeginTrans;
```

If you are trying to access the same Paradox data using the Jet 4.0 OLE DB provider, you won't receive an error but you also won't be able to roll back your changes due to limitations of the OLE DB provider.

Another strange difference becomes evident when you're working with Access: If you use the ODBC OLE DB provider, you'll be able to use transactions—but not nested transactions. Opening a transaction when another is active will result in an error. Using the Jet engine, however, Access supports nested transactions.

Nested Transactions

Using the TransProcessing program, you can try this test:

1. Begin a transaction.

2. Change the Contact of the Unisco record from George Weathers to Dick Solomon.

3. Begin a nested transaction.

4. Change the Contact of the Sight Diver record from Phyllis Spooner to Sally Solomon.

5. Roll back the inner transaction.

6. Commit the outermost transaction.

The net effect is that only the change to the Unisco record is permanent. If, however, the inner transaction had been committed and the outer transaction rolled back, then the net effect would have been that *none* of the changes were permanent (even the changes in the inner transaction). This is as you would expect, with the only limit being that Access supports five levels of nested transactions.

ODBC does not support nested transactions, the Jet OLE DB provider supports up to five levels of nested transactions, and the SQL Server OLE DB provider doesn't support nesting at all. You might get a different result depending on the version of SQL server or the driver, but the documentation and my experiments with the servers seem to indicate that this is the case. Apparently only the outermost transaction decides whether all the work is committed or rolled back.

ADOConnection Attributes

There is another issue you should consider if you intend to use nested transactions. The ADOConnection component has an `Attributes` property that determines how the connection should behave when a transaction is committed or rolled back. It is a set of `TXActAttributes` that, by default, is empty. `TXActAttributes` contains only two values: xaCommitRetaining and xaAbortRetaining (this value is often mistakenly written as xaRollbackRetaining—a more logical name for it). When xaCommitRetaining is included in `Attributes` and a transaction is committed, a new transaction is automatically started. When xaAbortRetaining is included in `Attributes` and a transaction is rolled back, a new transaction is automatically started. Thus if you include these values in `Attributes`, a transaction will always be in progress, because when you end one transaction another will always be started.

Most programmers prefer to be in greater control of their transactions and not to allow them to be automatically started, so these values are not commonly used. However, they have a special relevance to nested transactions. If you nest a transaction and set `Attributes` to [`xaCommitRetaining, xaAbortRetaining`], then the outermost transaction can never be ended. Consider this sequence of events:

1. An outer transaction is started.

2. An inner transaction is started.

3. The inner transaction is committed or rolled back.

4. A new inner transaction is automatically started as a consequence of the `Attributes` property.

The outermost transaction can never be ended, because a new inner transaction will be started when one ends. The conclusion is that the use of the `Attributes` property and the use of nested transactions should be considered mutually exclusive.

Lock Types

ADO supports four different approaches to locking your data for update: ltReadOnly, ltPessimistic, ltOptimistic, and ltBatchOptimistic (there is also an ltUnspecified option, but for the reasons mentioned earlier, we will ignore unspecified values). The four approaches are made available through the dataset's `LockType` property. In this section I will provide an overview of the four approaches, and in subsequent sections we will take a closer look at them.

The ltReadOnly value specifies that data is read-only and cannot be updated. As such, there is effectively no locking control required, because the data cannot be updated.

PESSIMISTIC LOCKING

The words *pessimistic* and *optimistic* in this context refer to the developer's expectation of conflict between user updates. Pessimistic locking assumes that there is a high probability that users will attempt to update the same records at the same time and that a conflict is likely. In order to prevent such a conflict, the record is locked when the edit begins. The record lock is maintained until the update is completed or canceled. A second user who attempts to edit the same record at the same time will fail in their attempt to place their record lock and will receive a "Could not update; currently locked" exception.

This approach to locking will be familiar to developers who have worked with desktop databases such as dBase and Paradox. The benefit is that the user knows that if they can begin editing a record, they will succeed in saving their update. The disadvantage of pessimistic locking is that the user is in control of when the lock is placed and when it is removed. If the user is skilled with the application, then this lock could be as short as a couple of seconds. However, in database terms, a couple of seconds is an eternity. On the other hand, the user might begin an edit and go to lunch, and the record would be locked until the user returns. As a consequence, most proponents of pessimistic locking guard against this eventuality by using a timer or other such device to time out locks after a certain amount of keyboard and mouse inactivity.

Another problem with pessimistic locking is that it requires a server-side cursor. Earlier we looked at cursor locations and saw that they have an impact on the availability of the different cursor types. Now you can see that cursor locations also have an impact on locking types. Later in this chapter, we will discuss more benefits of client-side cursors; if you choose to take advantage of these benefits, then you'll be unable to use pessimistic locking.

To highlight how pessimistic locking works, I've built the PessimisticLocking example. It is similar to other examples in this chapter, but the `CursorLocation` property is set to clUseServer and the `LockType` property is set to ltPessimistic. To use it, run two copies from Windows Explorer or from the Delphi 2005 IDE using the Run ➤ Run Without Debugging command (Ctrl+Shift+F9) and attempt to edit the same record in both running instances of the program: You will fail because the record is locked by another user.

Updating the Data

One of the reasons people use the ClientDataSet component is to make a SQL join updatable. Consider the following SQL equi-join:

```
SELECT * FROM Orders JOIN Customer
ON Customer.CustNo=Orders.CustNo
```

This statement provides a list of orders and the customers that placed those orders. The result of this join could be considered read-only because inserting, updating, and deleting rows in a join is ambiguous. For example, should the insert of a row into the previous join result in a new order and also a new customer, or just a new order? The ClientDataSet/Provider architecture allows you to specify a primary update table and also customize the updates' SQL, as you partially saw in Chapter 14 and we'll further explore in Chapter 17.

ADO support to updates in memory is called *batch updates*, which are similar to using the `Delta` property of the ClientDataSet. In the next section we will take a closer look at ADO's batch updates, what they can offer you, and why they are so important. However, in this section you won't need them to solve the problem of updating a join because in ADO, joins are naturally updatable.

For example, the JoinData example is built around an ADODataset component that uses the previous SQL join. If you run it, you can edit one of the fields and save the changes (by moving off the record). No error occurs, because the update has been applied successfully. ADO has taken a practical approach to the problem. In an ADO join, each field object knows which underlying table it belongs to. If you update a field in the Orders table and post the change, then a SQL UPDATE statement is generated to update the field in the orders table. If you change a field in the orders table and a field in the Customers table, then two SQL UPDATE statements are generated, one for each table.

The insertion of a row into a join follows a similar behavior. If you insert a row and enter values for the Orders table only, then a SQL INSERT statement is generated for the Orders table. If you enter values for both tables, two SQL INSERT statements are generated, one for each table. The order in which the statements are executed is important, because the new order might relate to the new customer, so the new customer is inserted first.

The biggest problem with the ADO solution can be seen when a row in a join is deleted. The deletion attempt will appear to fail. The exact message you see depends on the version of ADO you are using and the database, but it will be along the lines that you cannot delete the row because other records relate to it. The error message can be confusing. In the current scenario, the error message implies that an order cannot be deleted because there are records that relate to the order, but the error occurs whether the order has any related records or not. The explanation can be found by following the same logic for deletions as for insertions. Two SQL DELETE statements are generated: one for the Customers table and then another for the Orders table. Contrary to appearances, the DELETE statement for the Orders table succeeds. It is the DELETE statement for the Customers table that fails, because the customer cannot be deleted while it still has dependent records.

TIP   If you are curious about the SQL statements that are generated, and you use SQL Server, you can see these statements using SQL Server Profiler.

Even if you understand how this process works, it's helpful to look at this problem through the users' eyes. From their point of view, when users delete a row in the grid, I would wager that 99 percent of them intend to delete just the order—not both the order and the customer. Fortunately, you can achieve this result using another dynamic property—in this case, the Unique Table dynamic property. You can specify that deletes refer to just the Orders table and not to Customers table using the following line of code:

```
ADOQuery1.Properties['Unique Table'].Value := 'Orders';
```

This value cannot be assigned at design time, so the next best alternative is to place this line in the form's OnCreate event.

Batch Updates

When you use batch updates, any changes you make to your records can be made in memory; later, the entire "batch" of changes can be submitted as one operation. This approach offers some performance benefits, but there are more practical reasons why this technology is a necessity: The user might not be connected to the database at the time they make their updates. This would be the case in a briefcase application (which we will return to in the section "The Briefcase Model"), but it can also be the case in web applications that use another ADO technology, Remote Data Services (RDS).

You can enable batch updates in any ADO dataset by setting LockType to ltBatchOptimistic before the dataset is opened. In addition, you will need to set the CursorLocation to clUseClient, because batch updates are managed by ADO's cursor engine. Hereafter, changes are all added to a *delta* (a list of changes). The dataset looks to all intents and purposes as if the data has changed, but the changes have only been made in memory; they have not been applied to the database. To make the changes permanent, use UpdateBatch (equivalent to cached updates' ApplyUpdates):

```
ADODataSet1.UpdateBatch;
```

To reject the entire batch of updates, use either CancelBatch or CancelUpdates. There are many similarities in method and property names between ADO batch updates and ClientDataSet. UpdateStatus, for example, can be used exactly the same way as for cached updates to identify records according to whether they have been inserted, updated, deleted, or unmodified. This approach is particularly useful for highlighting records in different colors in a grid or showing their status on a status bar. Some differences between the syntaxes are slight, such as changing RevertRecord to CancelBatch(arCurrent); others require more effort.

One useful cached update feature that is not present in ADO batch updates is the dataset's UpdatesPending property. This property is True if changes have been made but not yet applied. It's particularly useful in a form's OnCloseQuery event:

```
procedure TForm1.FormCloseQuery(
    Sender: TObject; var CanClose: Boolean);
begin
  CanClose := True;
  if ADODataSet1.UpdatesPending then
    CanClose := (MessageDlg('Updates are still pending' #13 +
      'Close anyway?', mtConfirmation, [mbYes, mbNo], 0) = mrYes);
end;
```

However, with a little knowledge and ingenuity you can implement a suitable ADOUpdatesPending function. The necessary knowledge is that ADO datasets have a property called FilterGroup, which is a kind of filter. Unlike a dataset's Filter property, which filters the data based on a comparison of the data against a condition, FilterGroup filters based on the status of the record. One such status is fgPendingRecords, which includes all records that have been modified but not yet applied. So, to allow the user to look through all the changes they have made so far, you need only execute two lines:

```
ADODataSet1.FilterGroup := fgPendingRecords;
ADODataSet1.Filtered := True;
```

Naturally, the result set will now include the records that have been deleted. The effect you will see is that the fields are left blank, which is not very helpful because you don't know which record has been deleted. (This was not the behavior in the first version of ADOExpress, which displayed the field values of deleted records.)

The ingenuity you need in order to solve the UpdatesPending problem involves clones, discussed earlier. The ADOUpdatesPending function will set the FilterGroup to restrict the dataset to only those changes that have not yet been applied. All you need to do is see whether there are any records in the dataset once the FilterGroup has been applied. If there are, then some updates are pending. However, if you do this with the actual dataset, then the setting of the FilterGroup will move the record pointer, and the user interface will be updated. The best solution is to use a clone:

```
function ADOUpdatesPending(ADODataSet: TCustomADODataSet): boolean;
var
  Clone: TADODataSet;
begin
  Clone := TADODataSet.Create(nil);
  try
    Clone.Clone(ADODataSet);
    Clone.FilterGroup := fgPendingRecords;
    Clone.Filtered := True;
    Result := not (Clone.BOF and Clone.EOF);
    Clone.Close;
  finally
    Clone.Free;
  end;
end;
```

In this function, you clone the original dataset, set the FilterGroup, and check to see whether the dataset is at both beginning of the file and also the end of the file. If it is, then no records are pending.

Optimistic Locking

Earlier we looked at the LockType property and saw how pessimistic locking works. In this section, we'll look at optimistic locking, not only because it is the preferred locking type for medium- to high-throughput transactions, but also because it is the locking scheme employed by batch updates.

Optimistic locking assumes there is a low probability that users will attempt to update the same records at the same time and that a conflict is unlikely. As such, the attitude is that all users can edit any record at any time, and you deal with the consequences of conflicts between different users' updates to the same records when the changes are saved. Thus, conflicts are considered an exception to the rule. This means there are no controls to prevent two users from editing the same record at the same time. The first user to save their changes will succeed; the second user's attempt to update the same record might fail. This behavior is essential for briefcase applications (discussed later in the chapter) and web applications, where there is no permanent connection to the database and, therefore, no way to implement pessimistic locking. In contrast with pessimistic locking, optimistic locking has the additional considerable benefit that resources are consumed only momentarily; therefore, the average resource usage is much lower, making the database more scalable.

Let's consider an example. Assume you have an ADODataSet connected to the Customer table of the dbdemos.mdb database, with LockType set to ltBatchOptimistic, and the contents are displayed in a grid. Assume that you also have a button to call UpdateBatch. Run the program twice (it is the BatchUpdates example, if you don't want to rebuild it) and begin editing a record in the first copy of the program. Although for the sake of simplicity I'll demonstrate a conflict using just a single machine, the scenario and subsequent events are unchanged when using multiple machines:

1. Choose a company change its name (the Company field).

2. Save the change, move off the record to post it, and click the button to update the batch.

3. In the second copy of the program, locate the same record, and change the company name to something else.

4. Move off the record and click the button to update the batch. It will fail.

As with many ADO error messages, the exact message you receive will depend not only on the version of ADO you are using but also on how closely you followed the example. In ADO 2.8, the error message is "Row cannot be located for updating. Some values may have been changed since it was last read." This is the nature of optimistic locking. The update to the record is performed by executing the following SQL statement:

```
UPDATE CUSTOMER
SET Company="Sight Diver Inc."
WHERE CustNo="1351" AND Company="Sight Diver"
```

The number of records affected by this UPDATE statement is expected to be one, because it locates the original record using the primary key and the contents of the CompanyName field as it was when the record was first read. In this example, however, the number of records affected by the UPDATE statement is zero. This result can occur only if the record has been deleted, the record's primary key has changed, or the field that you are changing was changed by someone else. Hence, the update fails.

If the "second user" had changed the ContactName field and not the CompanyName field, then the UPDATE statement would have looked like this:

```
UPDATE CUSTOMER
SET Contact="Erica Lee Norman"
WHERE CustNo="1221" AND Contact=" Erica Norman"
```

In the example scenario, this statement would have succeeded because the other user didn't change the primary key or the contact name. The Update Criteria dynamic property of the dataset can assume of the following values:

Constant	Locate Records By
AdCriteriaKey	Primary key columns only
AdCriteriaAllCols	All columns
AdCriteriaUpdCols	Primary key columns and changed columns only
AdCriteriaTimeStamp	Primary key columns and a timestamp column only

Don't fall into the trap of thinking that one of these settings is better than another for your whole application. In practice, your choice of setting will be influenced by the contents of each table. Say that the Customer table has just CustomerID, Name, and City fields. In this case, the update of any one of these fields is logically not mutually exclusive with the update of any of the other fields, so a good choice for this table is adCriteriaUpdCols (the default). If, however, the Customer table included a PostalCode field, then the update of a PostalCode field would be mutually exclusive with the update of the City field by another user (because if the city changes, then so should the postal code, and possibly vice versa). In this case, you could argue that adCriteriaAllCols would be a safer solution.

Another issue to be aware of is how ADO deals with errors during the update of multiple records. Using the ClientDataSet, you can use the OnUpdateError event to handle each update error as the error occurs and resolve the problem before moving on to the next record. In ADO, you cannot establish such a dialog. You can monitor the progress and success or failure of the updating of the batch using the dataset's `OnWillChangeRecord` and `OnRecordChangeComplete`, but you cannot revise the record and resubmit it during this process as you can with the ClientDataSet. There's more: If an error occurs during the update process, the updating does not stop. It continues to the end, until all updates have been applied or have failed. This process can produce an unhelpful and incorrect error message. If more than one record cannot be updated, or the single record that failed is not the last record to be applied, then the error message in ADO 2.8 is "Multiple-step OLE DB operation generated errors. Check each OLE DB status value, if available. No work was done." The last sentence is the problem; it states that "No work was done," but this is incorrect. It is true that no work was done on the record that failed, but other records were successfully applied, and their updates stand.

Resolving Update Conflicts

As a consequence of the nature of applying updates, the approach that you need to take to update the batch is to update the batch, let the individual records fail, and then deal with the failed records once the process is over. You can determine which records have failed by setting the dataset's `FilterGroup` to fgConflictingRecords:

```
ADODataSet1.FilterGroup := fgConflictingRecords;
ADODataSet1.Filtered := True;
```

For each failed record, you can inform the user of three critical pieces of information about each field using the following `TField` properties:

Property	Description
NewValue	The value this user changed it to
CurValue	The new value from the database
OldValue	The value when first read from the database

Users of the ClientDataSet component will be aware of the handy `ReconcileErrorForm` dialog, which wraps up the process of showing the user the old and new records and allows them to specify what action to take. Unfortunately, there is no ADO equivalent to this form, and `TReconcileErrorForm` has been written with ClientDataSet so much in mind that it is difficult to convert it for use with ADO datasets.

I'll point out one last gotcha about using these `TField` properties: They are taken straight from the underlying ADO Field objects to which they refer. This means, as is common in ADO, that you are at the mercy of your chosen OLE DB provider to support the features you hope to use. All is well for most providers, but the Jet OLE DB provider returns the same value for `CurValue` as it does for `OldValue`. In other words, if you use Jet, you cannot determine the value to which the other user changed the field unless you resort to your own measures. Using the OLEDB provider for SQL Server, however, you can access the `CurValue` only after calling the `Resync` method of the dataset with the `AffectRecords` parameter set to adAffectGroup and `ResyncValues` set to adResyncUnderlyingValues, as in the following code:

```
adoCustomers.FilterGroup := fgConflictingRecords;
adoCustomers.Filtered := true;
adoCustomers.Recordset.Resync(adAffectGroup, adResyncUnderlyingValues);
```

Disconnected Recordsets

This knowledge of batch updates allows you to take advantage of the next ADO feature: disconnected recordsets. A *disconnected recordset* is a recordset that has been disconnected from its connection. This feature is impressive because the user cannot tell the difference between a regular recordset and a disconnected one; their feature sets and behavior are almost identical. To disconnect a recordset from its connection, you must set the `CursorLocation` to clUseClient and the `LockType` to ltBatchOptimistic. You then tell the dataset that it no longer has a connection:

```
ADODataSet1.Connection := nil;
```

Hereafter, the recordset will continue to contain the same data, support the same navigational features, and allow records to be added, edited, and deleted. The only relevant difference is that you cannot update the batch because you need to be connected to the server to update the server. You can reconnect the connection (and use `UpdateBatch`) as follows:

```
ADODataSet1.Connection := ADOConnection1;
```

This feature is also available to other database access technologies by switching over to Client-DataSets, but the beauty of the ADO solution is that you can build your entire application using dbGo dataset components and be unaware of disconnected recordsets. When you discover this feature and want to take advantage of it, you can continue to use the same components you always used.

You might want to disconnect your recordsets for two reasons:

◆ To keep the total number of connections lower

◆ To create a briefcase application

I'll discuss keeping down the number of connections in this section and return to briefcase applications later.

Most regular client/server business applications open tables and maintain a permanent connection to their database while the table is open. However, there are usually only two reasons to be connected to the database: to retrieve data and to update data. Suppose you change your regular client/server application so that after the table is opened and the data is retrieved, the dataset is disconnected from the connection and the connection is dropped; your user will be none the wiser, and the application will not need to maintain an open database connection. The following code shows the two steps:

```
ADODataSet1.Connection := nil;
ADOConnection1.Connected := False;
```

The only other point at which a connection is required is when the batch of updates needs to be applied. The update code looks like this:

```
ADOConnection1.Connected := True;
ADODataSet1.Connection := ADOConnection1;
try
  ADODataSet1.UpdateBatch;
finally
  ADODataSet1.Connection := nil;
  ADOConnection1.Connected := False;
end;
```

If you followed this approach throughout the application, the average number of open connections at any one time would be minimal—the connections would be open only for the brief time they were required. The consequence of this change is scalability; the application can cope with significantly more simultaneous users than an application that maintains an open connection.

Connection Pooling

All this talk about dropping and reopening connections brings us to the subject of connection pooling. Connection pooling allows connections to a database to be reused once you have finished with them. This process happens automatically; if your OLE DB provider supports it and it is enabled, no action is necessary for you to take advantage of connection pooling.

There is a single reason to pool your connections: performance. The problem with database connections is that it can take time to establish a connection. In a desktop database such as Access, this time is typically brief. However, in a client/server database such as Oracle used on a network, this time could be measured in seconds. It makes sense to promote the reuse of such an expensive (in performance terms) resource.

With ADO connection pooling enabled, ADO Connection objects are placed in a pool when the application "destroys" them. Subsequent attempts to create an ADO connection will automatically search the connection pool for a connection with the same connection string. If a suitable connection is found, it is reused; otherwise, a new connection is created. The connections themselves stay in the pool until they are reused, the application closes, or they time out. By default, connections will time out after 60 seconds, but from MDAC 2.5 onward you can set this time-out period using the HKEY_ CLASSES_ROOT\CLSID\<ProviderCLSID>\SPTimeout Registry key. The connection pooling process occurs seamlessly, without the intervention or knowledge of the developer.

By default, connection pooling is enabled on all MDAC OLE DB providers for relational databases (including SQL Server and Oracle), with the notable exception of the Jet OLE DB provider. If you use ODBC, you should choose between ODBC connection pooling and ADO connection pooling, but you should not use both. From MDAC 2.1 on, ADO connection pooling is enabled and ODBC is disabled.

NOTE Connection pooling does not occur on Windows 95, regardless of the OLE DB provider.

To be comfortable with connection pooling, you need to see the connections being pooled and timed out. Unfortunately, no adequate ADO connection pool spying tools are available at the time of this writing; but you can use SQL Server's Performance Monitor, which can accurately spy on SQL Server database connections.

You can enable or disable connection pooling either in the Registry or in the connection string. The key in the Registry is OLEDB_SERVICES, which can be found at HKEY_CLASSES_ROOT\CLSID\ <ProviderCLSID>. It is a bit mask that allows you to disable several OLE DB services, including connection pooling, transaction enlistment, and the cursor engine. To disable connection pooling using the connection string, include ";OLE DB Services=-2" at the end of the connection string. To enable connection pooling for the Jet OLE DB provider, you can include ";OLE DB Services=-1" at the end of the connection string, which enables all OLE DB services.

Persistent Recordsets

The persistent recordset is a useful feature that contributes to the briefcase model (discussed in the next section). Persistent recordsets allow you to save the contents of any recordset to a local file, which can be loaded later. In addition to aiding with the briefcase model, this feature allows developers to create true single-tier applications—you can deploy a database application without having to deploy a database. This makes for a very small footprint on your client's machine.

You can "persist" your datasets using the `SaveToFile` method:

```
ADODataSet1.SaveToFile('Local.ADTG');
```

This method saves the data and its delta in a file on your hard disk. You can reload this file using the `LoadFromFile` method, which accepts a single parameter indicating the file to load. The format of the file is Advanced Data Table Gram (ADTG), which is a proprietary Microsoft format. It does, however, have the advantage of being very efficient. If you prefer, you can save the file as XML by passing a second parameter to `SaveToFile`:

```
ADODataSet1.SaveToFile('Local.XML', pfXML);
```

However, ADO does not have a built-in XML parser (as the ClientDataSet does), so it must use the MSXML parser. Your user must either install Internet Explorer 5 or later or download the MSXML parser from the Microsoft website.

If you intend to persist your files locally in XML format, be aware of a few disadvantages:

♦ Saving and loading XML files is slower than saving and loading ADTG files.

♦ ADO's XML files (and XML files in general) are significantly larger than their ADTG counterparts (XML files are typically twice as large as their ADTG counterparts).

♦ ADO's XML format is specific to Microsoft, like most companies' XML implementations. This means the XML generated in ADO is not readable by the ClientDataSet and vice versa. Fortunately this problem can be overcome using Delphi's XMLTransform component, which can be used to translate between different XML structures.

NOTE   More on XML processing in Delphi in Chapter 22.

If you intend to use these features solely for single-tier applications and not as part of the briefcase model, then you can use an ADODataSet component and set its `CommandType` to cmdFile and its `CommandText` to the name of the file. Doing so will save you the effort of calling `LoadFromFile` manually. However, you will still have to call `SaveToFile`. In a briefcase application this approach is too limiting, because the dataset can be used in two different modes.

The Briefcase Model

Using this knowledge of batch updates, disconnected recordsets, and persistent recordsets, you can take advantage of the *briefcase model*. The idea behind the briefcase model is that your users want to be able to use your application while they are on the road—they want to take the same application they use on their office desktops and use it on their laptops at client sites. Traditionally, the problem with this scenario is that when your users are at client sites, they are not connected to the database server, because the database server is running on the network back at their office. Consequently, there is no data on the laptop (and the data cannot be updated anyway).

This is where your newfound understanding comes in handy. Assume the application has been written; the user has requested a new briefcase enhancement, and you have to retrofit it into your existing application. You need to add a new option for your users to allow them to prepare the briefcase application by executing `SaveToFile` for every table in the database. The result is a collection of

ADTG or XML files that mirror the contents of the database. These files are then copied to the laptop, where a copy of the application has previously been installed.

The application needs to be sensitive to whether it is running locally or connected to the network. You can determine this by attempting to connect to the database and seeing whether the connection fails, by detecting the presence of a local briefcase file, or by creating a flag of your own design. If the application is running in briefcase mode, then it needs to use `LoadFromFile` for each table instead of setting `Connected` to True for the ADOConnections and `Active` to True for the ADO datasets. Thereafter, the briefcase application needs to use `SaveToFile` instead of `UpdateBatch` whenever data is saved. When the user returns to the office, they need to follow an update process that loads each table from its local file, connects the dataset to the database, and applies the changes using `UpdateBatch`.

TIP To see a complete implementation of the briefcase model, refer to the BatchUpdates example mentioned earlier.

What's Next?

This chapter described ActiveX Data Objects (ADO) and dbGo, the set of Delphi components for accessing the ADO interfaces. You saw how to take advantage of Microsoft Data Access Components (MDAC) and various server engines, and I described some of the benefits and hurdles you'll encounter in using ADO.

Although you can use dbGo in a VCL .NET application, you might also want to consider that .NET includes a rather different database access architecture that has little in common with ADO despite what the ADO.NET name might seem to imply. ADO.NET is used primarily in WinForms and ASP.NET applications, but it is technically possible to use it in VCL programs also, as you will find out in the next chapter. One certain advantage of the ADO plus VCL combination is the easy portability between Win32 and .NET, something you cannot achieve with ADO.NET.

Chapter 16

Using ADO.NET

In the last few chapters we explored a number of database access technologies available in Delphi for Win32 and in Delphi for .NET. One of the most relevant sections of the .NET Framework class library, though, is its System.Data namespace, which contains the support for ADO.NET.

The ADO.NET technology is quite different and much superior to ADO; they have little in common but the name. This is why I didn't just describe it in the chapter on ADO, but instead devote an entire chapter to it. ADO.NET is tied to the visual components of the FCL, so you'll generally use it with WinForms or ASP.NET. As you'll see, however, it is technically possible to also use it from a VCL for .NET application connecting VCL data-aware controls to an ADO.NET dataset.

As usual, I'll try to introduce and cover ADO.NET from the Delphi perspective, which is why I'll compare it to corresponding VCL components and stress the use of Borland's own extension to ADO.NET, the Borland Data Providers (BDP). While using BDP I'll try to stick to InterBase as database server, while for other examples I'll try to use local databases (to make it easier for you to test the demos), even if they are less relevant than full-blown client/server examples.

Needless to say, ADO.NET is available only on .NET and not on Win32, so this chapter focuses exclusively on the former.

The Architecture of ADO.NET

The architecture of ADO.NET is very flexible and lets programmers fully control how the data is fetched from the database and sent to them. ADO.NET allows you to write database and client/server applications fast and easily, but at the same time it lets you determine the exact behavior of an application and lets you plug in extra components in its open architecture.

ADO.NET has components falling in two different categories. There are components you use to connect to the database, issue commands to it, and retrieve the resulting data. These are known as *data-provider components*. Other components are used to process the data that has been fetched and cached in memory. These are called *content components*. Depending on how you use these two groups of components, your application falls in one of two different categories:

Connected mode   Indicates that you are working directly on the database data and are not caching it. This is often used when you are simply reading the data (that is, when you need a read-only forward cursor) or when you are processing the records one by one or in some custom way. The term *connected* here indicates you keep sending requests to the database.

Disconnected mode   Indicates that you are fetching the data into memory, displaying and processing the data, and eventually sending back cached updates to the database. The term *disconnected* here indicates you connect to the database to fetch the data but don't need to keep sending requests while displaying or processing the data (and don't even need to keep a database connection active).

NOTE In the .NET documentation and literature there are references to "connected dataset components" and "disconnected dataset components," but the same components can be used in both operating modes.

If you compare this with Delphi's own architecture, you can see the situation is similar to the use of dbExpress with the ClientDataSet component. The dbExpress datasets represent read-only and forward-only cursors, while the ClientDataSet is the in-memory and disconnected data cache. I'll keep referring to this Delphi architecture as a comparison because if you have a Delphi background you should find it understandable, although there are some relevant differences in the two approaches.

Working in Connected Mode

Regardless of the operating mode, you'll have to connect to a database to retrieve data (at least unless you are working with local files). ADO.NET has database connection components that indicate the type of database and the connection parameters. The two main operations you do on a connection are Open and Close. This is not dissimilar to Delphi's own SQLConnection or similar components, with the exception that transaction support is delegated to specific support classes. The database connections are used by commands, for direct execution of queries, or to fetch data in memory using data adapters.

Now, you might have noticed that in the last few sentences I used the plural (connections, commands, data adapters). This was done on purpose because ADO.NET doesn't define, for example, one specific connection component. There are as many connection components as there are connection types.

By default, the Data Components page of the Tool Palette of Delphi 2005 will list only one of these sets, made of the following components: SQLConnection, SQLDataAdapter, and SQLCommand, with the palette page also hosting the DataSet and DataView components:

NOTE The SQL data access components (like the SQLConnection class) of the FCL are specific to Microsoft SQL Server and not generic for any SQL server like Delphi's own SQL components (like the TSQLConnection class). This can be confusing at first if you come from Delphi for Win32 programming.

This is only because Delphi doesn't place in the Tool Palette all the data access components available in the FCL. If you open the Installed .NET Components dialog box with the corresponding command under the Component menu of the IDE, and you select the .NET Components page, you can see that there are four ODBC entries, four OleDb entries, and four Oracle entries that are not checked. (By the way, the easiest way to find them is to sort the assemblies by namespace, as these components belong to namespaces starting with System.Data).

If you enable them all, your Data Components page of the Tool Palette will have much more stuff in it; so much that I removed captions to avoid wasting too much space:

In version 1.1 of the .NET Framework there are four data connection namespaces, each containing a connection component, a command component, an adapter component, and many support classes. In Delphi for .NET there are five:

System.Data.OleDb   Lets you work with any OleDb data source, which is the same type of database driver used by ADO.

System.Data.Odbc   Is specifically intended to work with ODBC drivers, a format also supported by the OleDb components

System.Data.SqlClient   Is a set of components specifically tuned for Microsoft SQL Server, performing much better than a generic OleDb connection and offering some specific features. There is also a variation constituted by the SqlServerCE family of components, but they make sense only when working with the .NET Compact Framework for Windows CE handheld devices.

System.Data.OracleClient   Is a set of components for working natively with the Oracle database without passing thought the OleDb client.

Borland.Data.Provider   Is a fifth family of data access components (called BDP), not part of the .NET Framework but supplied by Borland. Advantages of these components include the ability to view live database data at design time and the option to work with different sources of data without having to change the components you use, but only the drivers they are hooked to. There is more on BDP later in this chapter.

As an example of the differences in coding for the various drivers and of the use of the low-level data access components, consider the simple applications of the following two sections.

Accessing Data via OleDbConnection

To better understand the use of the components described in the previous section, I built a couple of examples. The first uses an OleDbConnection component to read data from an Access database, the standard dbdemos.mdb provided by Borland.

To build it, create a new WinForms application and add to it two components, an OleDbConnection and an OleDbCommand. The connection is configured almost like an ADO connection. When you select the editor of the ConnectionString property, you'll see the Data Link Properties dialog box provided by the system and already shown in Figure 15.2 of the previous chapter. Once the connection has been defined, you can connect the OleDbCommand to it using the Connection property. At this point you can set the CommandType property (which can be Text for a SQL query, StoredProcedure, or TableDirect) and fill the CommandText property. As I plan on using the same OleDbCommand component for executing multiple queries, I did not fill this property at design time.

This is an extract from the InitializeComponents method showing the most relevant settings:

```
procedure TReadDataWinForm.InitializeComponent;
begin
  Self.OleDbCommand1 := System.Data.OleDb.OleDbCommand.Create;
  Self.OleDbConnection1 := System.Data.OleDb.OleDbConnection.Create;

  Self.OleDbCommand1.Connection := Self.OleDbConnection1;
  Self.OleDbConnection1.ConnectionString :=
    'Provider="Microsoft.Jet.OLEDB.4.0";' +
    'Data Source="...\Borland Shared\Data\dbdemos.mdb";';
end;
```

The user interface of the program is made of a list box and two buttons. Clicking the first button fills the list box with the names of the companies in the customers table. This is achieved by setting the SQL query and calling the `ExecuteReader` method, which returns an OleDbDataReader object you can use for browsing the data:

```
procedure TReadDataWinForm.btnGetData_Click(
  sender: System.Object; e: System.EventArgs);
var
  Reader: OleDbDataReader;
begin
  if OleDbConnection1.State = ConnectionState.Closed then
    OleDbConnection1.Open;
  OleDbCommand1.CommandText := 'select * from customer';
  Reader := OleDbCommand1.ExecuteReader;
  try
    while Reader.Read do
      lbCompanies.items.Add (Reader.Item ['Company']);
  finally
    Reader.Close;
  end;
end;
```

The OleDbDataReader component fetches one record at a time until there is no more data. The effect of this code is visible in Figure 16.1.

The OleDbCommand component (like other command components) has a method that returns a read-only cursor over a dataset (`ExecuteReader`); it also a method that returns a single value (`ExecuteScalar`) and one that doesn't return any data (`ExecuteNonQuery`, which actually returns the number of records affected by the query). By comparison, Delphi query components can generally execute a request without returning data (`ExecSql`) or return a dataset (`Open`), which might eventually contain a single value.

FIGURE 16.1

The list of companies retrieved with an OleDb-Command component by the AdoNetReadData application

As an example of the *scalar* result, consider the SQL count operation. This is demonstrated by the second button of the AdoNetReadData example:

```
procedure TReadDataWinForm.btnCount_Click(
    sender: System.Object; e: System.EventArgs);
var
    ObjResult: System.Object;
begin
    if OleDbConnection1.State = ConnectionState.Closed then
        OleDbConnection1.Open;
    OleDbCommand1.CommandText := 'select count(*) from customer';
    ObjResult := OleDbCommand1.ExecuteScalar;
    MessageBox.Show(ObjResult.ToString, 'Customer count');
end;
```

This example highlights the use of the "connected mode" approach, as the OleDbDataReader component fetches data from the database while the code browses it. The data is not fetched up front and cached, as in a disconnected architecture.

Accessing Data via ODBC

Now what if you decide to access the same dataset via ODBC rather than via OLEDB? You can, of course, use the OleDb family of components with an ODBC connection string, but what I want to explore here is the use of a specific set of components, such as the use of components for Microsoft SQL Server or Oracle. To build a program based on a different set of components you have to replace them and reassign their properties at design time. You can compare the following extract from the InitializeComponents method of the AdoNetReadDataOdbc example with the corresponding code snippet of the previous section to see what I mean:

```
procedure TReadDataWinForm.InitializeComponent;
begin
    Self.OdbcConnection1 := System.Data.Odbc.OdbcConnection.Create;
    Self.OdbcCommand1 := System.Data.Odbc.OdbcCommand.Create;

    Self.OdbcConnection1.ConnectionString :=
        'PageTimeout=5;MaxScanRows=8;DefaultDir=...\Borland Shared\Data;' +
        'FILEDSN=...\AdoNetReadDataOdbc\OdbcDataSource.dsn;' +
        'DriverId=25;DBQ=...\Borland Shared\Data\dbdemos.mdb;' +
        'UserCommitSync=Yes;FIL=MS Access;UID=admin;' +
        'Driver={Microsoft Access Driver (*.mdb)};MaxBufferSize=2048;' +
        'Threads=3;SafeTransactions=0';
    Self.OdbcCommand1.Connection := Self.OdbcConnection1;
    Self.Text := 'AdoNetReadDataOdbc';
end;
```

Changing the set of components is reasonable (although when you have multiple SQL queries set at design time the changes can takes a while), but the problem is that the code of the event handlers also changes. In fact, you have to refer to the proper components and use intermediate objects of the proper type, as in this code snippet, which you can compare with the version in the previous section:

```
var
   Reader: OdbcDataReader;
begin
   OdbcCommand1.CommandText := 'select * from customer';
   Reader := OdbcCommand1.ExecuteReader;
```

Of course, if you plan on using different sets of data access components there are better ways of writing this code to make it more generic. Don't look for a common base class for the various connection or command components, though, because there is none. The way to write generic code in .NET is often based on interfaces, and this case is no exception.

Generic Data Access Using Interfaces

It is worth demonstrating the use of interfaces to generalize the code of an ADO.NET application so that it is not tied to a specific set of connection and data access components. That's why I added to the AdoNetReadDataOdbc example a method (not an event handler) that shows data in the list box and works regardless of the type of connection and commands passed as parameters because it uses the IDbConnection, IDbCommand, and IDataReader interfaces:

```
procedure TReadDataWinForm.ReadData(
   Connection: IDbConnection; Command: IDbCommand);
var
   Reader: IDataReader;
begin
   if Connection.State = ConnectionState.Closed then
     Connection.Open;
   Command.CommandText := 'select * from customer';
   Reader := Command.ExecuteReader;
   try
     while Reader.Read do
       lbCompanies.items.Add (Reader.Item ['Company']);
   finally
     Reader.Close;
   end;
end;
```

The program has a button that calls this method from its Click event handler:

```
procedure TReadDataWinForm.btnIDataReader_Click(
   sender: System.Object; e: System.EventArgs);
begin
   ReadData (OdbcConnection1, OdbcCommand1);
end;
```

To have more flexibility you could place multiple sets of components in the program at design time, or even better, write interface-based code to initialize different types of components depending on the program configuration.

NOTE When you need custom and dynamic creation of components, instead of writing all of the code manually you can still use the designers to generate the base structure of the code. This way you can produce the component setup code faster and then copy this code from the InitializeComponents method (executed at startup) to a custom method (invoked if and when required).

Working in Disconnected Mode

As you have seen, a command component can use a data reader to fetch the result of a SQL query. The DataReader objects represent a forward-only, read-only recordset, exactly like a SQLDataset in dbExpress.

If you want to fetch data and store it in a dataset in memory, you use an alternative set of components (one for each type of database connection) called *data adapters*. Data adapters internally use commands and data readers. Data adapters have a role similar to Delphi's Provider component, along with the internal Resolver object.

For the dataset in memory, ADO.NET uses the DataSet component. This component is the same regardless of the database connection and of the other data access components you are using. The role of the DataSet corresponds to the ClientDataSet of the VCL, which holds data in memory and can be used with dbExpress as well as with other database connection components. Unlike the Client-DataSet, though, an ADO.NET DataSet can hold multiple tables. This means you can use multiple adapters to populate a single DataSet, as you'll see later in more detail. For the moment let's just build a simple example using disconnected mode.

Using an OleDbDataAdapter

I took the same connection component of the first example, AdoNetReadData, and added to it an Ole-DbDataAdapter component. This adapter holds a set of four OleDbCommand objects, one for each of the four SQL statements used to retrieve and update the data. Each command has its own CommandText and Connection property. This is the related initialization code from the AdoNetDisconnected example, which defines the details only for the SelectCommand property:

```
// from procedure TWinForm.InitializeComponent;
Self.oleDbSelectCommand1 := System.Data.OleDb.OleDbCommand.Create;
Self.oleDbInsertCommand1 := System.Data.OleDb.OleDbCommand.Create;
Self.oleDbUpdateCommand1 := System.Data.OleDb.OleDbCommand.Create;
Self.oleDbDeleteCommand1 := System.Data.OleDb.OleDbCommand.Create;
Self.OleDbDataAdapter1 := System.Data.OleDb.OleDbDataAdapter.Create;

Self.oleDbSelectCommand1.CommandText := 'select * from customer';
Self.oleDbSelectCommand1.Connection := Self.OleDbConnection1;

Self.OleDbDataAdapter1.DeleteCommand := Self.oleDbDeleteCommand1;
Self.OleDbDataAdapter1.InsertCommand := Self.oleDbInsertCommand1;
Self.OleDbDataAdapter1.SelectCommand := Self.oleDbSelectCommand1;
Self.OleDbDataAdapter1.UpdateCommand := Self.oleDbUpdateCommand1;
```

This is all it takes to set up an adapter. Next, you need to add a DataSet component to the form and connect it to the adapter. Quite surprisingly if you come from a Delphi background, you cannot connect the dataset to the adapter at design time; you have to add some extra initialization code, like the following:

```
procedure TWinForm.TWinForm_Load(
  sender: System.Object; e: System.EventArgs);
begin
  OleDbConnection1.Open;
  OleDbDataAdapter1.Fill(DataSet1);
end;
```

To show the data on-screen at this point you can place a DataGrid component in the form (the DataGrid component is the only one in the Data Controls page of the Tool Palette) and connect its DataSource property to the DataSet component (DataSet1 in the example).

NOTE The DataSource property in ADO.NET is of the DataSet type. There is no concept similar to that of the VCL TDataSource component.

With this code the program at startup will show an empty grid with a plus sign to get a list of the available tables:

Clicking the plus sign will expand the list of tables:

At this point you can select the given table and expand it in the grid to see the dataset data you have probably been expecting since the beginning. You can see the result in Figure 16.2.

The program can be modified to show a given table directly, of course, but I thought it was worth showing these steps to highlight two relevant features of the ADO.NET architecture. The first is that a DataSet can hold multiple tables; the second is that a DataGrid is connected to the entire DataSet and lets you navigate through all of the tables it contains. This is quite a different approach compared to the VCL, and there is more on these two topics later in the chapter.

NOTE The DataAdapter object defines a handy TableMappings collection. This collection determines how the names of the table fields in the database are mapped to the field names of the DataSet table. Using this collection can help you give more readable names to your columns in the code as well as slightly isolate the program from changes in the database structure.

FIGURE 16.2
The AdoNetDisconnect-
ed example with the
table visible in the
DataGrid

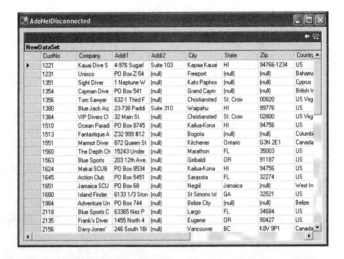

Creating a DataTable at Design Time

How do you modify the program to make it work as expected and show the table in the grid at startup? There are multiple ways to accomplish this. One of the simplest solutions is to create the table in
the DataSet at design time, connect the DataGrid to this table, and modify the call to the Fill method
to send data to this specific table, rather than creating a new one.

In practice, in the AdoNetTable example I first activated the editor of the Tables property of the
DataSet component and added a new table to it, giving it a readable name, as shown in Figure 16.3.
The effect of this setting on the startup code is quite relevant: there is a new DataTable object (called
CustomerTable as indicated in the Name property of the Design section of the Tables Collection Edi-
tor of Figure 16.3) that is added to an array of tables hooked to the DataSet:

```
procedure TWinForm.InitializeComponent;
type
  TArrayOfSystem_Data_DataTable = array of System.Data.DataTable;
begin
  Self.DataSet1 := System.Data.DataSet.Create;
  Self.CustomerTable := System.Data.DataTable.Create;

  Self.DataSet1.Tables.AddRange(
    TArrayOfSystem_Data_DataTable.Create(Self.CustomerTable));
  Self.CustomerTable.TableName := 'Customer';
```

Next, in the DataGrid I picked this table for the DataMember property (after setting the DataSource
property to the DataSet component), generating the following lines of the InitializeComponent
method:

```
Self.DataGrid1.DataMember := 'Customer';
Self.DataGrid1.DataSource := Self.DataSet1;
```

FIGURE 16.3
The Tables Collection
Editor of the ADO.NET
DataSet component

As an alternative, I could have selected the table (`CustomerTable`) in the `DataSource` property of the DataSet, leaving the `DataMember` property blank. Finally, I edited the startup code in the `Load` event handler of the form, as follows:

```
procedure TWinForm.TWinForm_Load(
  sender: System.Object; e: System.EventArgs);
begin
  OleDbConnection1.Open;
  OleDbDataAdapter1.Fill(DataSet1, 'Customer');
end;
```

Now as the program starts it automatically shows the data of that given table in the DataGrid, which is tied to it (so that you cannot browse the DataSet tables any more, certainly a good idea in this specific example). The output is not much different from what you already saw in Figure 16.2, but that was the effect of expanding the table in the grid. You can see the difference for yourself by running the two examples.

No Live Data at Design Time

As you build an ADO.NET application there is, by default, no way to see the database data in the visual controls, like the grid, at design time. This might come as a surprise, as this is common practice in Delphi as well as in other development tools. Seeing the data at design time is handy as you can check many elements of the application without having to compile and run it.

For example, you know right away that your SQL statements are correct if they give no errors when executed and you can see the proper result. Also, when building a field-oriented user interface, as well as when using a DataGrid, you can see right away how the application will look if there is enough space for larger fields and if shorter fields don't have too much empty space. It is faster to fix many of these issues visually at design time, rather than having to do multiple edit-compile-run-test cycles.

Consider also that the lack of data at design time is not a limitation of the ADO.NET architecture but of the adapters provided by the FCL. In fact, as you'll see shortly, the data adapter of the Borland Data Provider (BDP) fully supports live data at design time.

You can even use the Delphi-specific DataHub and DataSync components to obtain the same effect with the standard adapters so you can have live data at design time even with an OleDbDataAdapter. The idea is to add one or more data adapters to the `Providers` collection of the DataSync component, hook the DataHub to the local DataSync component (with the `DataPort` property), and set the `DataSource` property of the DataHub to the DataSet. As you activate the various components you'll see the design time data. If you want to make some experiments you can start from the AdoNetLocalHub example.

Using these components and their rather complex architecture for the sole purpose of having live data at design time seems like overkill to me, although in some cases it can really come in handy. I'll cover these components in the next chapter, as their primary role is to simplify ADO.NET remoting and multitier architectures.

Data Content Components

As you started to see in the previous examples, there are components used to store data in memory and provide access to it. These are often dubbed *disconnected components* because they are used when you work in disconnected mode.

The most relevant of these components is the DataSet. As you saw, this acts like a ClientDataSet and holds tables with data in memory. Unlike ClientDataSet, though, a DataSet has a collection of DataTable objects. Each DataTable has a collection of DataRow objects (the record of the table) and a collection of DataColumn objects (the fields of the table, including the calculated fields).

Other data content components include the DataView component, which is used for sorting and filtering the data of a table, and the DataRelation component, which is used to express parent/child (or master/detail) relationships among the tables included in a DataSet. We'll explore each of these components in the following sections.

Direct Access to DataSet Data

Once you have a DataTable with the data in memory, you can access the data in a fairly simple way, especially as compared to the VCL. The VCL still retains the Paradox and BDE architecture of having a cursor, so that you can access records only one at a time, and a status, so that you can modify data only when the dataset is in edit or insert mode. In ADO.NET, by contrast, the data of a table is like a matrix in memory, and you can access it directly by row and column. You can not only read data from a record without moving the cursor location, but also modify the data directly.

This difference is demonstrated by the following code snippets, part of the AdoNetFieldsAndRows example. The first code snippet shows the column names in a list box, using a `for..in` loop:

```
procedure TWinForm.btnColumns_Click(
  sender: System.Object; e: System.EventArgs);
var
  col1: DataColumn;
begin
  ListBox1.Items.Clear;
  for col1 in TableCustomer.Columns do
    ListBox1.Items.Add (col1.ColumnName +
      ' [' + col1.DataType.ToString + ']');
end;
```

Columns do not hold data, only the table definition, and they tend to be all of the same type. In VCL terms, they are more like FieldDefs than Fields (although in ADO.NET there really isn't a class corresponding to VCL TField objects).

The next code snippet adds to the same on-screen list box the values of a couple of rows. Once you have a row, you can access a field (or column) with the Item property passing a numeric index, a string with the column name, or a column object:

```
procedure TWinForm.btnCompanies_Click(
  sender: System.Object; e: System.EventArgs);
var
  row1: DataRow;
begin
  ListBox1.Items.Clear;
  for row1 in TableCustomer.Rows do
    ListBox1.Items.Add (row1[1].ToString +
      ' [' + row1.Item[0].ToString + ']');
end;
```

As this property is an indexer (or default property in Delphi terms), you can omit it as in the preceding first case. This means that to access the first field of the first record of a table you can write TableCustomer.Rows [0][0]. The third code snippet shows how you can edit the data directly. In this case the code renumbers the records so that all of the CustNo numbers form a progression starting with 1:

```
procedure TWinForm.btnRenumber_Click(
  sender: System.Object; e: System.EventArgs);
var
  i: Integer;
  colCustNo: DataColumn;
begin
  colCustNo := TableCustomer.Columns ['CustNo'];
  TableCustomer.Rows[0].Item[colCustNo] := 1
  for I := 1 to TableCustomer.Rows.Count - 1 do
    TableCustomer.Rows[i][colCustNo] :=
      Double(TableCustomer.Rows[i-1][colCustNo]) + 1;
end;
```

Changing the ID of a record is not a very good idea when you have other data structure referring to these records using that ID. Still, the example is interesting, as there is not an easy way to do the same thing with the VCL because in a cursor-oriented dataset you cannot move data from a record to another one directly in an expression.

Another operation the program does is add a new calculated field at run time. The following method defines such a field and then uses it:

```
procedure TWinForm.btnAddCol_Click(
  sender: System.Object; e: System.EventArgs);
var
  newCol: DataColumn;
begin
```

```
  newCol := TableCustomer.Columns.Add;
  newCol.ColumnName := 'TripleNo';
  newCol.Expression := 'CustNo * 3';
  // now get the value of the column for the first record
  MessageBox.Show(
    TableCustomer.Rows[0].Item[0].ToString + ' - ' +
    TableCustomer.Rows[0].Item[newCol].ToString);
  btnAddCol.Enabled := False;
end;
```

This event handler can be executed only once, which is why the program disables the corresponding button. You can also see the field was added by checking the list of columns before and after the operation.

The DataTable component has many other features, and I want to mention two more. First, there is a Compute method you can use to execute an expression over the table or a filtered set of records. In the following code I count the rows (count(CustNo)) after applying a filter to them (Country='US'):

```
procedure TWinForm.btnCompute_Click(
    sender: System.Object; e: System.EventArgs);
begin
  MessageBox.Show(TableCustomer.Compute(
    'count(CustNo)', 'Country=''US''').ToString, 'US Customers');
end;
```

The second relevant feature of the DataTable component is that it holds the data and the changes in memory. You can query a record for its update status and you can query a data item for its original value (before editing). Of course, you can also send the in-memory changes to the physical database, calling the AcceptChanges method or canceling them with RejectChanges. I'll later discuss in more detail how updates work in ADO.NET and how you can manage the list of changes.

Master/Detail in the DataSet Class

Now that I've discussed data tables with their columns and rows, I can say that a DataSet in ADO.NET is a collection of tables defining a subset of the database. Actually there is another relevant collection in a DataSet, Relations, which defines the relationship among the multiple tables. This is how you define, for example, a master/detail relationship.

As an example of a master/detail relationship in a DataSet component, I built the AdoNetMastDet example, based on the same OleDbConnection to the dbdemos.mdb sample database we've used in past example. This time, however, the program has three adapters, selecting three different tables. This is a summary of the design time properties set in the InitializeComponent method:

```
type
  TArrayOfSystem_Data_DataTable = array of System.Data.DataTable;
begin
  Self.DataSet1 := System.Data.DataSet.Create;
  Self.TableCustomers := System.Data.DataTable.Create;
  Self.TableOrders := System.Data.DataTable.Create;
  Self.TableItems := System.Data.DataTable.Create;
```

```
Self.DataSet1.Tables.AddRange(
  TArrayOfSystem_Data_DataTable.Create(
    Self.TableCustomers, Self.TableOrders, Self.TableItems));
Self.TableCustomers.TableName := 'Customers';
Self.TableOrders.TableName := 'Orders';
Self.TableItems.TableName := 'Items';
Self.oleDbSelectCommand1.CommandText := 'select * from customer';
Self.AdapterCustomer.SelectCommand := Self.oleDbSelectCommand1;
Self.oleDbSelectCommand2.CommandText := 'select * from orders';
Self.AdapterOrder.SelectCommand := Self.oleDbSelectCommand2;
Self.oleDbSelectCommand3.CommandText := 'select * from items';
Self.AdapterItem.SelectCommand := Self.oleDbSelectCommand3;
```

Notice in the preceding code (generated by the WinForms designer) the definition of a custom array type and its use with the call of its **Create** initializer, which receives as parameters the initial items of the array (in this case the three tables). I use a similar coding technique to initialize the primary key of the table in the handler of the Load event of the form. The TWinForm_Load method opens the connection, loads the three tables in the dataset, sets the primary key of the first, defines two master/detail relationships, and, finally, shows the main table in the DataGrid. Here is the complete code:

```
procedure TWinForm.TWinForm_Load(
  sender: System.Object; e: System.EventArgs);
type
  primaryKeyType = array of DataColumn;
var
  MdRelation1, MdRelation2: DataRelation;
begin
  OleDbConnection1.Open;
  AdapterCustomer.Fill (DataSet1, 'Customers');
  AdapterOrder.Fill (DataSet1, 'Orders');
  AdapterItem.Fill(DataSet1, 'Items');

  TableCustomers.PrimaryKey := primaryKeyType.Create(
    TableCustomers.Columns['CustNo']);

  MdRelation1 := DataRelation.Create ('CustomerOrders',
    TableCustomers.Columns['CustNo'],
    TableOrders.Columns['CustNo'], True);
  DataSet1.Relations.Add(MdRelation1);
  MdRelation2 := DataRelation.Create ('OrderItems',
    TableOrders.Columns['OrderNo'],
    TableItems.Columns['OrderNo'], False);
  DataSet1.Relations.Add(MdRelation2);

  DataGrid1.DataSource := TableCustomers;
end;
```

To set a master/detail relationship at run time you can create a DataRelation object and pass to its constructors its name plus the two columns it has to work with. You can either pass the DataColumn objects (as in the preceding code), or pass strings indicating the tables and columns names.

Now you can take advantage of the master/detail navigation capabilities of the DataGrid component to move from the main table to the secondary one and to its further details, as shown in the three screen snapshots of Figure 16.4.

NOTE The code that sets the primary key of the main table is not necessary for the example to work, but it is relevant (and I wanted to show it to you, anyway).

As you set up a master/detail relationship among tables, you can use the ChildRelations and ParentRelations properties of a DataTable to see the other tables this is connected with.

DataTables also have two different types of constraints. Constraints of the UniqueConstraint type enforce that the value of a field is and remains unique. Constraints of the ForeignKeyConstraint type are used along with master/detail relationship to determine the automatic *(cascaded)* update and delete operations.

FIGURE 16.4
The AdoNetMastDet lets you navigate from a master table (top) to its detail table (middle) to its further child (bottom).

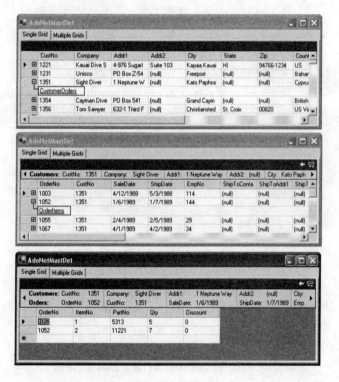

A DataSet in XML

One of the relevant features of ADO.NET is its support for data in XML format. XML will be covered in Chapter 22, but here I want to briefly introduce the support offered by the DataSet class in this area. There are basically four methods: WriteXml and ReadXml operate on the content of the dataset tables, while WriteXmlSchema and ReadXmlSchema work on the metadata. All of these methods can work on streams or on files.

The read/write capability of the ADO.NET DataSet is much more flexible than the VCL Client-DataSet component. First of all, XML data is structured in a node-oriented format and not an attribute-oriented format (as the ClientDataSet and ADO are structured). This is a snippet the XML produced by the AdoNetXml example:

```
<NewDataSet>
  <customers>
    <CustNo>1221</CustNo>
    <Company>Kauai Dive Shoppe</Company>
    <City>Kapaa Kauai</City>
    ...
  </customers>
  <customers>
    <CustNo>1231</CustNo>
    <Company>Unisco</Company>
    <City>Freeport</City>
    ...
  </customers>
  ...
</NewDataSet>
```

Furthermore, the DataSet can manage the tables' metadata in a standard format using XML Schemas. You can see an example of this format in Figure 16.5. The program uses a memory stream to save the output and a stream reader object to convert it into a string suitable for display in a multiline TextBox. The event handlers of the two buttons are almost identical; in the figure there is one of them.

```
procedure TWinForm.btnData_Click(
  sender: System.Object; e: System.EventArgs);
var
  strXml: System.IO.MemoryStream;
  reader: StreamReader;
begin
  strXml := MemoryStream.Create;
  DataSet1.WriteXml (strXml);
  strXml.Position := 0;
  reader := Streamreader.Create (strXml);
  textOut.Text := reader.ReadToEnd;
end;
```

Sorting and Filtering with a DataView

If you look at the DataTable and DataSet components' properties, one feature seems totally missing. There is apparently no way to sort the table in memory. That is because this feature is taken care of by a specific component called DataView. The idea behind this component is to let you create a subset of the data from a DataTable while avoiding duplicating the data in memory (in a somewhat similar way to a clone of an ADO dataset or a ClientDataSet component).

FIGURE 16.5

The AdoNetXml example can show the metadata of a table in XML Schema format.

A DataView component can perform multiple actions on the related data, including:

Filtering the data   Using the RowFilter property, which requires an expression ranging from the simple Country='US' (notice that literal values require single quotes that you'll have to double in the Delphi code) up to a more complex test for a null values like Isnull (TaxCol, 'Null Column')='Null Column'.

Filtering the records by status   Using the RowStateFilter property, which can assume values like DataViewRowState.Added, DataViewRowState.Deleted, or DataViewRowState.Modified Current, to name just a few. You might recall similar status filters for the ClientDataSet and the ADODataSet VCL components.

Sorting the data   Using the Sort property, which holds a comma-separated list of column names optionally followed by DESC indicating descending order (the opposite, ASC, is the default).

Once you have a DataView you can use the Item property to access a single row, much like a DataTable. You can also connect visual components directly to the DataView for setting to this component the DataSource property of a DataGrid control.

Generating Custom DataSet Classes

All of the code we have written so far accesses the in-memory data of the dataset in a dynamic way, accessing the columns by name. As an alternative, it is possible to generate a custom data set class that knows the specific structure of one or more tables it holds and lets you access their columns directly by property.

This makes the code faster and more robust but much less resilient to changes in the data structure. The comparable VCL technique is the generation of dataset fields at design time, but there are many relevant differences, including the fact that in .NET you don't add internal components but generate brand new classes at design time.

This is fairly simple to accomplish. As you've added a connection and an adapter to a form and configured them as usual (with the proper SQL Text for the SelectCommand), you can use the

Generate DataSet design-time command of the adapter at the bottom of the Object Inspector or on the component context menu as usual, as shown below:

In the next dialog box you can enter a new name for the table (*DataSetCustomers*), as shown in Figure 16.6. The table name can also be configured up front in the special TableMappings collection editor of the adapter.

FIGURE 16.6

The design time dialog box used to configure the generation of a custom dataset

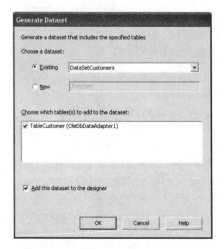

The .NET designers extract the table schema (as described in the section "A DataSet in XML") and then generate a new dataset class from the schema data. This is why, after you've done this operation, the Project Manager will list an XML Schema Document file (with the .xsd extension) with the Delphi unit below it:

In Listing 16.1 you can see a snippet of the declarations in the generated unit. This is a reduced version from which I omitted some of the details and part of the actual fields because the full listing of the interface portion of the unit is over 200 lines of code (with over 900 lines for the entire unit). As you can see, the DataSetCustomerUnit unit defined a DataSet descendant class, with nested classes for a custom data table and a custom data row.

LISTING 16.1:   The core elements of the code of a custom dataset (from the AdoNetCustom example)

```
type
  DataSetCustomers = class(DataSet)
  public
  type
    TableCustomerRow = class;
    TableCustomerDataTable = class(DataTable,
      System.Collections.IEnumerable)
    public
      function get_Item(index: Integer): TableCustomerRow;
      property Count: Integer read get_Count;
    protected
      property CustNoColumn: DataColumn read get_CustNoColumn;
      property CompanyColumn: DataColumn read get_CompanyColumn;
      property Addr1Column: DataColumn read get_Addr1Column;
      property CityColumn: DataColumn read get_CityColumn;
      property StateColumn: DataColumn read get_StateColumn;
      property ZipColumn: DataColumn read get_ZipColumn;
      property CountryColumn: DataColumn read get_CountryColumn;
    public
      property Item[index: Integer]: TableCustomerRow
        read get_Item; default;
      procedure AddTableCustomerRow(row: TableCustomerRow); overload;
      function AddTableCustomerRow(CustNo: System.Double;
        Company: string; Addr1: string City: string; State: string;
        Zip: string; Country: string; ...): TableCustomerRow; overload;
      function FindByCustNo(CustNo: System.Double): TableCustomerRow;
      function NewTableCustomerRow: TableCustomerRow;
    end;

    TableCustomerRow = class(DataRow)
    public
      property CustNo: System.Double read get_CustNo write set_CustNo;
      property Company: string read get_Company write set_Company;
      property Addr1: string read get_Addr1 write set_Addr1;
      property City: string read get_City write set_City;
      property State: string read get_State write set_State;
      property Zip: string read get_Zip write set_Zip;
      property Country: string read get_Country write set_Country;
    end;

  public
    constructor Create; overload;
    function get_TableCustomer: TableCustomerDataTable;
    property TableCustomer: TableCustomerDataTable
      read get_TableCustomer;
  end;
```

In addition to generating the source code for the custom dataset, Delphi will add to the form a new component corresponding to this local class:

```
procedure TWinForm.InitializeComponent;
begin
  Self.DataSetCustomers1 :=
    DataSetCustomersUnit.DataSetCustomers.Create;
  Self.DataSetCustomers1.DataSetName := 'DataSetCustomers';
  Self.DataSetCustomers1.Namespace :=
    'http://www.changeme.now/DataSetCustomers.xsd';
```

NOTE   It is possible to work with this component at design time only because its Pascal unit is compiled to an assembly behind the scenes. This assembly is compiled to an obj/Debug/TempPE subfolder of the current project folder and plays a relevant role. There is no need to deploy it, though, unless you really want to do so.

Of course you should instead fix the default namespace added to the program. The startup code of the program (in the Load event handler) can take advantage of the generated code:

```
OleDbDataAdapter1.Fill (DataSetCustomers1.TableCustomer);
```

But the real advantage comes when you need to process the dataset data at run time, as you can get access to the company name of the current record selected in the grid by writing:

```
DataSetCustomers1.TableCustomer.Item[
  DataGrid1.CurrentRowIndex].Company;
```

Similarly, you can add a new record and set some of its fields (including the record ID computed, increasing the current maximum value) with this code, again from the AdoNetCustom example:

```
procedure TWinForm.btnAdd_Click(
  sender: System.Object; e: System.EventArgs);
var
  newId: Double;
  newRow: DataSetCustomers.TableCustomerRow;
begin
  newId := Double (DataSetCustomers1.TableCustomer.
    Compute ('Max(CustNo)', ''));
  newId := newId + 1;
  newRow := DataSetCustomers1.TableCustomer.NewTableCustomerRow;
  newRow.CustNo := NewId;
  newRow.Company := 'Wintech Italia Srl';
  newRow.Country := 'Italy';
  DataSetCustomers1.TableCustomer.AddTableCustomerRow(newRow);
  // move grid to new record
  DataGrid1.CurrentRowIndex :=
    DataSetCustomers1.TableCustomer.Count - 1;
end;
```

Code like this is much more readable than the generic code you'd write without the custom data set. Finally, by generating table metadata at design time and connecting the DataSource of the DataGrid to the DataSetCustomers1.TableCustomer, you can see the table structure in the DataGrid at design time (even if not the table data).

Managing Cached Data and Updates

When you use the disconnected architecture of ADO.NET, with the adapter components moving tables to the DataSet component, the changes you make to the data are kept in a cache in memory. This is similar to other architectures like the ClientDataSet in the VCL. The DataSet class had five main members related to the list of changes in memory:

◆ The HasChanges method returns True if there are pending updates.

◆ The HasErrors property indicates whether tables have any errors. You can then proceed to checking individual tables.

◆ The GetChanges method creates a second DataSet with the changes to the original one. This can be handy for checking those changes or even displaying them on screen.

◆ The AcceptChanges method invokes the AcceptChanges method for each DataTable, which in turn calls the AcceptChanges method for each DataRow of the DataTable.

◆ The RejectChanges method rolls back the changes made to the data set since it was opened or since its data was last saved.

Most of these features are demonstrated by the AdoNetCache example, which has a tab with the actual data and another where you can see the changes (click the corresponding button to refresh them), as in Figure 16.7:

```
procedure TWinForm.Button1_Click(
  sender: System.Object; e: System.EventArgs);
begin
  DataGrid2.DataSource := DataSet1.GetChanges;
end;
```

FIGURE 16.7
The list of changes of a DataSet can be displayed in a grid, as the AdoNet-Cache program does.

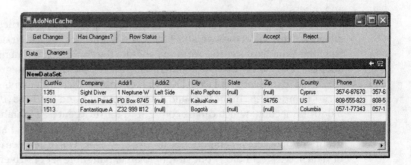

Notice that if you define only the `SelectCommand` on an adapter, the other three commands can be generated automatically from it, provided the query is simple enough (for example, if there is only one table in the SQL query and if the key fields are part of the result set). In any case, it is advisable to fill all of the four commands so that you have full control of what the program really does.

A Comparison with the ClientDataSet

Although I haven't exhaustively covered the features of the ADO.NET DataSet class and related classes, I hope I've given you a good overall picture and some details. Throughout the chapter I've often compared ADO.NET features to corresponding features of the VCL, in particular the ClientDataSet component. In this section I want to summarize the differences between the two.

First, I'll list what I consider advantages of ADO.NET: the way the ADO.NET DataSet manages related tables, the easy access to the data in memory (with no cursor), the simplified edit operations, the automatic XML mapping, and the related XSD support.

The ClientDataSet still retains some advantages, though. Among them is the way data is fetched in blocks of records (something you can partially achieve with the MaxRecords property of the BdpDataAdapter component described later in the section "Other Features of the BDP") and the delayed fetching of BLOBs and details (in the ClientDataSet master/detail architecture). Grabbing all of the data in memory, as the ADO.NET components tend to do, can be needlessly time- and bandwidth-consuming.

Regarding the management of updates, ADO.NET has an easy control over update SQL statements, as they are directly available in the adapter components (which is a large improvement over traditional ADO) and the ability to apply changes only for specific tables. On the other hand, when you apply the updates to a ClientDataSet, this automatically updates multiple tables in the correct order (deleting detailed records before the master and inserting the details after inserting the master), something not too easy to achieve with an ADO.NET DataSet.

Using the Borland Data Provider (BDP)

Having explored the ADO.NET architecture, you know its power but also some of its weaknesses. For example, the fact that you need to change the set of components in use when changing the database makes it difficult to have a single application targeting multiple servers. Another limitation is the lack of data at design time. Borland's BDP plug-in component for ADO.NET overcomes these limitations and others.

Another plus of the BDP is that it is tied to Delphi's IDE, in particular the Data Explorer. This view allows you to look at the available tables, their definition, and their data, as well as to drag those tables from the Data Explorer to a form to generate the proper components (including the connection, the adapter, and the various commands). This makes the development of applications even faster.

The BDP does not replace ADO.NET, of course; it complements it, providing a new set of data access components. In the `Borland.Data.Provider` and `Borland.Data.Common` namespaces there is a BdpConnection, which can be configured for different SQL databases; a BdpDataAdapter; a BdpDataReader; and a BdpCommand class. These four components have roles similar to those of other groups of data access components discussed earlier. The difference is that this set isn't tied to a server or data access technology but simply to an expandable set of drivers.

NOTE   The BDP is the counterpart of the dbExpress architecture. Behind the scenes these two technologies are very similar, although they are tied to different technologies (VCL DataSet and ADO.NET).

Configuring the BDP

Available database drivers for the BDP in Delphi 2005 include InterBase, Firebird, Microsoft's SQL Server and MSDE, Oracle, IBM's DB2, Sybase, and Microsoft's Access. As in dbExpress, in the BdpConnection component you select a driver and a database, using the settings provided by a local configuration file you don't need to deploy, as they are copied into the component's properties. The IDE uses this configuration file in the BDP Connections Editor, visible in Figure 16.8.

FIGURE 16.8

The Connections Editor of the Borland Data Provider (BDP)

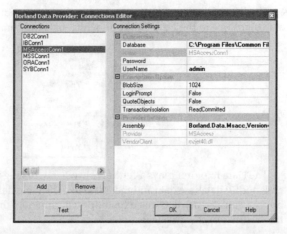

Behind the scenes, the BDP configuration is based on two files (much like the dbExpress configuration), one with a list of available drivers called BpdDataSources.xml and the other with a list of predefined connections called bpdConnections.xml. Here are two snippets from the two files related with the configuration of InterBase:

```
<!-- from BpdDataSources.xml -->
<provider name="Interbase"
  connectionStringType="Borland.Data.Interbase.IBConnectionString,
    Borland.Data.Interbase, Version=2.0.0.0, Culture=neutral,
    PublicKeyToken=91d62ebb5b0d1b1b">
  <objectTypes>
    <objectType>Tables</objectType>
    <objectType>Procedures</objectType>
    <objectType>Views</objectType>
  </objectTypes>
</provider>

<!-- from bpdConnections.xml -->
```

```
<BdpConnectionString xsi:type="IBConnectionString">
  <VendorClient>gds32.dll</VendorClient>
  <Assembly>
    Borland.Data.Interbase,Version=2.0.0.0,
    Culture=neutral,PublicKeyToken=91d62ebb5b0d1b1b
  </Assembly>
  <Name>IBConn1</Name>
  <Database>C:\Program Files\Borland\InterBase\examples\
    Database\EMPLOYEE.GDB</Database>
  <UserName>sysdba</UserName>
  <Password>masterkey</Password>
</BdpConnectionString>
```

The lists of available providers and of the connections available for each providers also show up at design time in the Data Explorer, which lists the connections under the respective providers:

The Data Explorer plays a central role when working with the BPD. Not only can you use it to view and modify database data and metadata like the table definitions (as already introduced in Chapter 1), but you can also use it to speed up the development of the database application considerably, making this a fully *visual* experience.

Visual Development with the BDP

In fact, simply by dragging tables to a .NET designer (WinForms or ASP.NET), the IDE will generate the corresponding BdpDataAdapter with a set of predefined commands and add a BdpConnection component if this is not already there. With a simple drag operation you end up with over 300 lines of initialization source code. The reason this code is so long is that it generates the proper parameter objects for the SQL queries of its commands and a set of table and column mappings. Here is a very short snippet (with many omissions even in the few lines listed, marked with an ellipsis):

```
procedure TWinForm.InitializeComponent;
type
  TArrayOfSystem_Data_Common_DataTableMapping =
    array of System.Data.Common.DataTableMapping;
  TArrayOfSystem_Data_Common_DataColumnMapping =
    array of System.Data.Common.DataColumnMapping;
begin
  // this is data copied from the connection configuration files
  Self.BdpConnection1.ConnectionOptions :=
    'transaction isolation=ReadCommitted;blobsize=1024';
```

```
Self.BdpConnection1.ConnectionString :=
  'database=C:\...\Borland Shared\Data\dbdemos.mdb;' +
  'assembly=Borland.Data.Msacc,...;' +
  'vendorclient=msjet40.dll;provider=MSAccess;' +
  'username=admin;password=';

// this is the data adapter with mappings
Self.BdpDataAdapter1.Active := False;
Self.BdpDataAdapter1.DeleteCommand := Self.bdpDeleteCommand1;
Self.BdpDataAdapter1.SelectCommand := Self.bdpSelectCommand1;
Self.BdpDataAdapter1.TableMappings.AddRange(
  TArrayOfSystem_Data_Common_DataTableMapping.Create(
    System.Data.Common.DataTableMapping.Create(
      'Table',
      'customer',
      TArrayOfSystem_Data_Common_DataColumnMapping.Create(
        System.Data.Common.DataColumnMapping.Create(
          'CustNo', 'CustNo'),
        System.Data.Common.DataColumnMapping.Create(
          'Company', 'Company'),
        // other columns omitted...
    )));

// this is a command with parameters
Self.bdpDeleteCommand1.CommandText :=
  'DELETE FROM customer WHERE CustNo = ? AND Company = ? AND ...';
Self.bdpDeleteCommand1.Connection := Self.BdpConnection1;
Self.bdpDeleteCommand1.ParameterCount := (SmallInt(13));
Self.bdpDeleteCommand1.Parameters.Add(
  Borland.Data.Common.BdpParameter.Create(
    'CustNoOriginal', Borland.Data.Common.BdpType.Double,
    Borland.Data.Common.BdpType.Unknown, 0,
    System.Data.ParameterDirection.Input, False,
    (Byte(0)), (Byte(0)), 0, 'CustNo',
    System.Data.DataRowVersion.Original, nil));
// other 12 parameters omitted...

// this is the select statement, with no parameters
Self.bdpSelectCommand1.CommandText := 'SELECT * FROM customer';
Self.bdpSelectCommand1.Connection := Self.BdpConnection1;
```

This is indeed quite handy. But there is more. Unlike other data adapters, the BdpAdapter has a DataSet property you can set to Fill a given dataset with the adapter on startup, without the need to write that standard line of code manually. This operation is performed as you turn the Active property of the BdpDataAdapter to True. Now, the interesting point is not that you have a line of code in the Initialization method instead of the Load event handler, but the fact that you can do all of these operations (setting the target DataSet, activating the adapter) at design time. Hook up a Data-Grid to the form, select the proper DataSource and DataMember, and you have live data at design time, as you can see in Figure 16.9.

FIGURE 16.9
The BDP supports live
data at design time.

NOTE   Long-time Delphi database developers generally take live data at design time for granted, as they've relied on this feature since Delphi 1. However, since the core FCL classes of .NET do not provide this feature, for which you need additional components like the BDP, it is not very common for .NET developers.

Although this example, called AdoNetBdpIntro, is quite simple, it could have no custom code at all. Everything could be set up at design time and end up in the Initialization method. However, as Delphi experience suggests, to avoid errors when opening a program in the IDE in case the database it refers to is missing from the computer, you should instead close the data adapter at design time and write a Load event handler with the single line:

```
BdpDataAdapter1.Active := True;
```

Other Features of the BDP

The Borland Data Provider offers a few more features in addition to the more obvious ones covered in the previous sections. Two relevant properties of the BdpDataAdapter are MaxRecord and StartRecord. The first indicates how many records to retrieve at most to avoid a very large query taking too much time to process and allocating too much memory, while the second sets the starting record. The first property can be used to limit the size of a dataset in memory, while the two combined can be used to paginate data in ASP.NET applications.

Another relevant feature (behind the scenes) of the BDP is that it maps logical database data types to native .NET types in a uniform way. This is not what you get when you use multiple providers to connect to different databases. There are also performance advantages, if we compare BDP with the OleDb solution, in that there is no need for COM Interop.

The BDP Schema Services

As I mentioned earlier, you saw in Chapter 1 that the Data Explorer in Delphi 2005 has many meta-data (or schema) services. You can define new tables or modify existing ones and also copy tables from a database to another, even of a different type. What might not be obvious at first is that all of these schema services are part of the BDP and can be leveraged in your code.

Schema services are defined in the `Borland.Data.Schema` namespace and can be accessed using the `GetMetaData` method of a BdpConnection component. This returns the `ISQLMetaData` interface, which allows you access to lists of tables or other database objects and lists of columns for the tables, not unlike the dbExpress components (as you saw in Chapter 14). What's new is that the `ISQLMeta Data` interface has a `GetSchemaCreate` method that returns yet another interface, `ISQLSchemaCreate`. As the name suggests, this second interface allows you to create and destroy (or drop) database objects, access their DDL definition, and so on.

Most of the methods of these interfaces return lists of elements as DataTable objects, so (for example) you can show this metadata in a grid with a single line of code, as in:

```
DataGrid1.DataSource := BdpConnection1.GetMetaData.
  GetTables('*', TableType.Table);
```

This code is taken from the AdoNetBdpSchema, which has only a BdpConnection component and a DataGrid, without any other data access component. The same example returns also the columns of a table:

```
DataGrid1.DataSource := BdpConnection1.GetMetaData.
  GetColumns(textTable.Text, '*', ColumnType.Default);
```

Finally, to complement these low-level interfaces, Delphi provides the BdpCopyTable component, which you can use to migrate both table structures, along with the primary keys and the actual data. You can copy tables from one database (or BdpConnection) to another. The source command cannot be based on a query, only on an entire table, because the only supported `CommandType` is `TableDirect`.

NOTE   BdpCopyTable can copy from one BDP data source to another, even if they refer to different database servers, but it cannot use other ADO.NET connections.

Using ADO.NET in a VCL Application

You saw in Chapters 13 to 15 that VCL applications can use a number of different database connection technologies, including dbExpress and ADO. A Delphi for .NET application based on the VCL, however, can also use ADO.NET for its database connectivity. Now the problem is that an ADO.NET DataSet cannot be connected directly to the VCL visual components.

The VCL for .NET includes two different components that inherit from `TDataSet` and surface an ADO.NET dataset as a VCL dataset. This means you can use these components to make VCL data-aware controls directly display data from an ADO.NET DataTable.

One of these two components, the ListConnector, has a `DataObject` property you can set to any .NET object supporting the `IList` interface. As the DataTable class doesn't support `IList`, you'll have to use a .NET DataView object connected to a DataSet or a DataTable.

The other component, the ADONETConnector, has a `DataTable` property you can set directly to a DataTable. This was the only solution available in Delphi 8, but in Delphi 2005 this component is not installed in the Tool Palette (I'm not sure why).

The only drawback of this approach, and it's a big one, is that you cannot work visually with the ADO.NET components in the VCL designer, so you'll have to write all of the code manually. To create a demo I placed the ADO.NET visual components in a WinForms application (similar to other applications we have built so far) and then copied all of the initialization code to the `OnCreate` event handler of a VCL for .NET program.

In the two programs I wrote, one for each VCL component, I added in the VCL designer a DBGrid and a DataSource. In the first demo, VclNetListConnector, I also added a ListConnector component, as well as this custom code to the code copied from the WinForms equivalent program:

```
OleDbConnection1.Open;
OleDbDataAdapter1.Fill(CustomerTable);
ListConnector1.DataObject := DataView1;
ListConnector1.Open;
```

The first two lines are standard in an ADO.NET program, while the latter two are specific for the VCL for .NET application that uses ADO.NET.

The VclNetAdoConnector example instead creates the `TADONETConnector` object dynamically, as this is not installed by default. The program has the following custom code (again, after the ADO.NET components initialization code copied from the WinForms equivalent program):

```
OleDbConnection1.Open;
OleDbDataAdapter1.Fill(CustomerTable);

ADONETConnector1 := TADONETConnector.Create (Self);
ADONETConnector1.DataTable := CustomerTable;
ADONETConnector1.Open;

DataSource1.DataSet := ADONETConnector1;
```

The effect of these two programs is almost identical. You can see the VclNetAdoConnector example at run time in Figure 16.10.

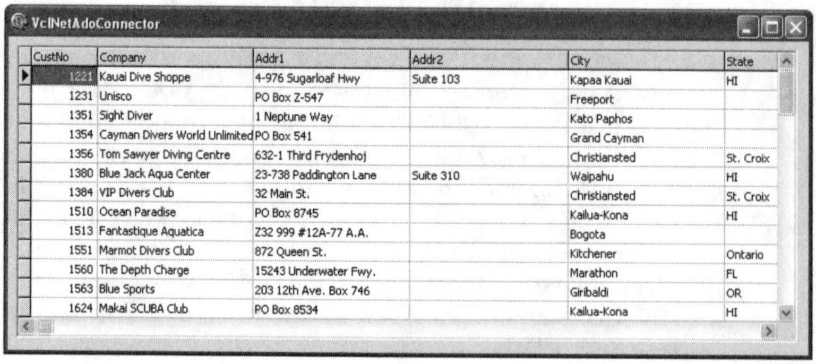

FIGURE 16.10

The VclNetAdoConnector is a VCL for .NET application that uses ADO.NET for database access and DBGrid for the user interface.

CustNo	Company	Addr1	Addr2	City	State
1221	Kauai Dive Shoppe	4-976 Sugarloaf Hwy	Suite 103	Kapaa Kauai	HI
1231	Unisco	PO Box Z-547		Freeport	
1351	Sight Diver	1 Neptune Way		Kato Paphos	
1354	Cayman Divers World Unlimited	PO Box 541		Grand Cayman	
1356	Tom Sawyer Diving Centre	632-1 Third Frydenhoj		Christiansted	St. Croix
1380	Blue Jack Aqua Center	23-738 Paddington Lane	Suite 310	Waipahu	HI
1384	VIP Divers Club	32 Main St.		Christiansted	St. Croix
1510	Ocean Paradise	PO Box 8745		Kailua-Kona	HI
1513	Fantastique Aquatica	Z32 999 #12A-77 A.A.		Bogota	
1551	Marmot Divers Club	872 Queen St.		Kitchener	Ontario
1560	The Depth Charge	15243 Underwater Fwy.		Marathon	FL
1563	Blue Sports	203 12th Ave. Box 746		Giribaldi	OR
1624	Makai SCUBA Club	PO Box 8534		Kailua-Kona	HI

What's Next

In this chapter I introduced you to the ADO.NET technology, a very modern database access application that is a key portion of the .NET Framework. Although I didn't get into low-level details, you saw the most relevant features of ADO.NET and built a number of examples. I also covered some of the extensions (or plug-ins) provided by Borland to this architecture, specifically the Borland Data Provider.

There is more about ADO.NET in the next two chapters. The first focuses on multitier architectures and covers both the Borland-specific DataSnap technology and ADO.NET remoting, along with the components provided by Delphi 2005 to simplify it.

The following chapter is focused on Enterprise Core Objects (ECO), an implementation of the Model Driven Architecture (MDA) available in the Architect version of Delphi 2005. The ECO chapter builds on the current one, because ECO uses ADO.NET for database access. Finally, you'll see some more demos that use ADO.NET in Chapter 21, which is devoted to ASP.NET.

Chapter 17

Multitier Architectures

Initially, database PC applications were client-only solutions: The program and the database files were on the same computer. Even if the database files were on a network file server, the client computers still hosted the application software and the database engine. The first big transition was to client/server development, embraced by Delphi since its first version. In the client/server world, the client computer requests the data from a server computer, which hosts both the database files and a database engine to access them.

The next logical step up from client/server was to keep some of the application logic on a server-side program and keep only the user interface portion in the client program. This is called a multitier architecture. Delphi 2005 supports different types of multitier architectures. In this chapter, I'll first cover DataSnap, Delphi's native multitier technology. This is a Win32 technology, but you can also use some of its client side components in Delphi for .NET. In the second part of this chapter, I'll move to ADO.NET remoting. In Chapter 23, I'll cover SOAP, a closely related technology.

NOTE You don't have to pay a deployment fee for DataSnap server applications, as Borland requested in early versions of the technology.

The Technical Foundation of DataSnap

Delphi generally pushes the idea of *logical* three-tier architecture with the use of data modules, nonvisual containers of data access components. To move from this approach to a physical multitier (specifically three-tier) architecture, you use a remote data module, which is compiled in a different executable. You'll run this program on a server, with the client application connecting to it to fetch the data from it (instead of connecting directly to the RDBMS). One of the advantages of the physical three-tier architecture, in fact, is that you don't need to install and configure the database access on the client computers. Because the client programs have only user interface code and are extremely simple to install, they now fall into the category of so-called *thin clients*.

DataSnap requires the installation of specific libraries on the server (actually the middle-tier computer), which provides your client computers with the data extracted from the SQL server database or other data sources. As you would expect, the client side of DataSnap is extremely thin and easy to deploy. The only file you need is `Midas.dll`, a small DLL that implements the ClientDataSet and

RemoteServer components and provides the connection to the application server. Notice that this DLL still has the older name of the DataSnap technology, MIDAS (Middle-tier Distributed Application Services).

NOTE   As an alternative to distributing midas.dll, you can embed the code of this library in your executable file by including the MidasLib unit in your uses statements, as discussed in Chapter 13. Again, MidasLib is not available in Delphi for .NET.

The *IAppServer* Interface

The two sides of a DataSnap application communicate using the IAppServer interface; this interface's definition in Delphi for Win32 appears in Listing 17.1. You'll seldom need to call the methods of the IAppServer interface directly, because Delphi includes components implementing this interface on the server-side applications and components calling the interface on the client-side applications. These components simplify the support of the IAppServer interface and at times even hide it completely. In practice, the server will make objects implementing this interface available to the client, possibly along with other custom interfaces.

LISTING 17.1:   The definition of the *IAppServer* interface in the Midas unit

```
IAppServer = interface(IDispatch)
  ['{1AEFCC20-7A24-11D2-98B0-C69BEB4B5B6D}']
  function AS_ApplyUpdates(const ProviderName: WideString;
    Delta: OleVariant; MaxErrors: Integer; out ErrorCount: Integer;
    var OwnerData: OleVariant): OleVariant; safecall;
  function AS_GetRecords(const ProviderName: WideString;
    Count: Integer; out RecsOut: Integer; Options: Integer;
    const CommandText: WideString; var Params: OleVariant;
    var OwnerData: OleVariant): OleVariant; safecall;
  function AS_DataRequest(const ProviderName: WideString;
    Data: OleVariant): OleVariant; safecall;
  function AS_GetProviderNames: OleVariant; safecall;
  function AS_GetParams(const ProviderName: WideString;
    var OwnerData: OleVariant): OleVariant; safecall;
  function AS_RowRequest(const ProviderName: WideString;
    Row: OleVariant; RequestType: Integer;
    var OwnerData: OleVariant): OleVariant; safecall;
  procedure AS_Execute(const ProviderName: WideString;
    const CommandText: WideString; var Params: OleVariant;
    var OwnerData: OleVariant); safecall;
end;
```

NOTE   A DataSnap server is a COM server that exposes an interface using a COM type library, a technology covered in Chapter 12.

The Connection Protocol

DataSnap defines only the higher-level architecture and can use different technologies for moving the data from the middle tier to the client side. DataSnap supports many different protocols, including the following:

Distributed COM (DCOM) and Stateless COM (MTS or COM+)   DCOM is directly available in Windows. DCOM is basically an extension of COM technology that allows a client application to use server objects that exist and execute on a separate computer. The DCOM infrastructure allows you to use stateless COM objects, available in the COM+ and in the older MTS (Microsoft Transaction Server) architectures. Both COM+ and MTS provide features such as security, component management, and database transactions and are available in Windows NT/2000/XP and in Windows 98/Me.

Due to the complexity of DCOM configuration and its problems in passing through firewalls, even Microsoft is abandoning DCOM in favor of SOAP-based solutions.

TCP/IP Sockets   These are available on most systems. Using TCP/IP, you might distribute clients over the Web, where DCOM cannot be taken for granted, and you'll have far fewer configuration headaches. To use sockets, the middle-tier computer must run the ScktSrvr.exe application provided by Borland, a single program that can run either as an application or as a service. This program receives the client requests and forwards them to the remote data module (executing on the same server) using COM. Sockets provide no protection against failure on the client side because the server is not informed and might not release resources when a client unexpectedly shuts down.

HTTP and SOAP   The use of HTTP as a transport protocol over the Internet simplifies connections through firewalls or proxy servers (which generally don't like custom TCP/IP sockets). You need a specific web server application, httpsrvr.dll, which accepts client requests and creates the proper remote data modules using COM. These web connections can also use SSL security. Finally, web connections based on HTTP transport can use DataSnap object-pooling support.

NOTE   The DataSnap HTTP transport can use XML as the data packet format, enabling any platform or tool that can read XML to participate in a DataSnap architecture. This is an extension of the original DataSnap data packet format, which is also platform independent. The use of XML over HTTP is also the foundation of SOAP. There's more on SOAP in DataSnap in Chapter 23.

Finally, notice that as an extension to this architecture, you can transform the data packets into XML and deliver them to a web browser. In this case, you basically have one extra tier: the web server gets the data from the middle tier and delivers it to the client. This architecture, called Internet Express, hasn't been updated from Borland in recent versions of Delphi, so it is not covered any more in this book.

Providing Data Packets

The entire Delphi multitier data-access architecture centers around the idea of *data packets*. In this context, a data packet is a block of data that moves from the application server to the client or from the client back to the server. Technically, a data packet is a sort of subset of a dataset. It describes the data it contains (usually a few records of data), and it lists the names and types of the data fields. Even more important, a data packet includes the constraints—that is, the rules to be applied to the dataset. You'll typically set these constraints in the application server, and the server sends them to the client applications along with the data.

The data exchange between the client and the server occurs by transmitting data packets. The provider component on the server manages the transmission of several data packets within a big dataset, with the goal of responding faster to the user. As the client receives a data packet in a ClientDataSet component, the user can edit the records it contains. As mentioned earlier, during this process the client also receives and checks the constraints, which are applied during the editing operations.

When the client has updated the records, it sends back a *delta* data packet, which tracks the differences between the original records and the updated ones, recording all the changes the client requested from the server (as you saw in Chapter 14). When the client asks to apply the updates to the server, it sends the delta to the server, and the server tries to apply each of the changes. I say *tries* because if a server is connected to several clients, the data may have changed already, and the update request may fail.

Because the delta packet includes the original data, the server can quickly determine if another client has already changed the data. If so, the server fires an OnReconcileError event. In other words, the three-tier architecture uses an update mechanism similar to the one Delphi uses for client/server applications based on the ClientDataSet component. The client can also save the data packets to the local disk and work offline, thanks to the MyBase support discussed in Chapter 13. Even error information moves using the data packet protocol, so it is truly one of the foundation elements of this architecture.

Delphi Support Components (Client-Side)

Now that we've examined the general foundations of Delphi's three-tier architecture, let's focus on the components that support it. For developing client applications, Delphi provides the ClientDataSet component, which provides all the standard dataset capabilities and embeds the client side of the IAppServer interface. In this case, the data is delivered through the remote connection.

The connection to the server application is made via another component you'll also need in the client application. You should use one of the three specific connection components (available in the DataSnap page of the Tool Palette):

◆ The DCOMConnection component can be used on the client side to connect to a DCOM and MTS server, located either on the current computer or on another computer indicated by the ComputerName property. The connection is with a registered object having a given ServerGUID or ServerName.

◆ The SocketConnection component can be used to connect to the server via a TCP/IP socket. You should indicate the IP address or the host name and the GUID of the server object (in the InterceptGUID property).

◆ The WebConnection component is used to handle an HTTP connection that can easily get through a firewall. You should indicate the URL where your copy of httpsrvr.dll is located and the name or GUID of the remote object on the server.

NOTE   In the WebServices page, you can also find the SoapConnection component, which requires a specific type of server and will be discussed in Chapter 23.

A few more client-side components are meant mainly for managing connections:

♦ The ConnectionBroker component can be used as an alias of an actual connection component, which is useful when you have a single application with multiple client datasets. To change the physical connection of each dataset, you only need to change the Connection property of the ConnectionBroker. You can also use the events of this virtual connection component in place of those of the actual connections, so you don't have to change any code if you change the data transport technology. For the same reason, you can refer to the AppServer object of the ConnectionBroker instead of the corresponding property of a physical connection.

♦ The SharedConnection component can be used to connect to a secondary (or child) data module of a remote application, piggybacking on an existing physical connection to the main data module. In other words, an application can connect to multiple data modules of the server with a single, shared connection.

♦ The LocalConnection component can be used to target a local dataset provider as the source of the data packet. The same effect can be obtained by hooking the ClientDataSet directly to the provider. However, using the LocalConnection, you can write a local application with the same code as a complete multitier application, using the IAppServer interface of the "fake" connection. Doing so will make the program easier to scale up, compared to a program with a direct connection.

Delphi Support Components (Server-Side)

On the server side (actually the middle tier), you can create either a standard VCL application or an ActiveX Library and you can add to it a remote data module, a special version of the TDataModule class. To add a remote data module you can pick the corresponding option in the Delphi Projects/ ActiveX page of the New Items dialog box (obtained from the File ➢ New ➢ Other menu).

The only specific component you need on the server side is the DataSetProvider component. You need one of these components for every dataset you want to make available to the client applications, which will then use a separate ClientDataSet component for every exported dataset. The DataSetProvider was already used as a local component in Chapter 14.

Building a Sample Application

Now you're ready to build a sample program. Doing so will let you observe in action some of the components I've just described and will also allow you to focus on some other problems, shedding light on other pieces of the Delphi multitier puzzle. I'll build the client and application server portions of a three-tier application in two steps. The first step will simply test the technology using a minimum of elements. These programs will be very simple.

From that point, I'll add more power to the client and the application server. In each example, I'll display data from a local InterBase table using dbExpress and set up everything to allow you to test the programs on a stand-alone computer.

The First Application Server

The server side of the basic example is easy to build. Simply create a new VCL application and add a remote data module to it using the corresponding icon in the Multitier page of the Object Repository. The Remote Data Module Wizard will ask you for a class name and the instancing style:

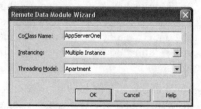

When you enter a class name, such as **AppServerOne** and click the OK button, Delphi will add a data module to the program. This data module will have the usual properties and events, but its class will have the following Delphi language declaration:

```
type
  TAppServerOne = class(TRemoteDataModule, IAppServerOne)
  private
    { Private declarations }
  protected
    class procedure UpdateRegistry(Register: Boolean;
      const ClassID, ProgID: string); override;
  public
    { Public declarations }
  end;
```

In addition to inheriting from the TRemoteDataModule base class, this class implements the custom IAppServerOne interface, which derives from the standard DataSnap interface (IAppServer). The class also overrides the UpdateRegistry method to add support for enabling the socket and web transports, as you can see in the code generated by the wizard. At the end of the unit, you'll find the class factory declaration, which should be clear if you read Chapter 12:

```
initialization
  TComponentFactory.Create(ComServer, TAppServerOne,
    Class_AppServerOne, ciMultiInstance, tmApartment);
end.
```

Now you can add a dataset component to the data module (I used the SQLDataSet), connect it to a database and a dataset, activate it, and finally add a DataSetProvider and hook it to the dataset component. You'll obtain a DFM file like this:

```
object AppServerOne: TAppServerOne
  object SQLConnection1: TSQLConnection
    ConnectionName = 'IBLocal'
    LoginPrompt = False
  end
```

```
  object SQLDataSet1: TSQLDataSet
    SQLConnection = SQLConnection1
    CommandText = 'select * from EMPLOYEE'
  end
  object DataSetProvider1: TDataSetProvider
    DataSet = SQLDataSet1
  end
end
```

The main form of this program is almost useless, so you can simply add a label to it indicating that it's the form of the server application. When you've built the server, you should compile it and run it once. This operation will automatically register it as an Automation server on your system, making it available to client applications. Of course, you should register the server on the computer where you want it to run, either the client or the middle tier.

The First Thin Client

Now that you have a working server, you can build a client that will connect to it. You'll again begin with a standard Delphi application and add a DCOMConnection component to it (or the proper component for the specific type of connection you want to test). This component defines a ComputerName property that you'll use to specify the computer that hosts the application server. If you want to test the client and application server from the same computer, you can leave this property blank.

Once you've selected an application server computer, you can simply display the ServerName property's combo box list to view the available DataSnap servers. This combo box shows the servers' registered names (the ProgID), by default the name of the executable file of the server followed by the name of the remote data module class, as in AppServ1.AppServerOne. Alternatively, you can enter the GUID of the server object as the ServerGUID property. Delphi will automatically fill this property as you set the ServerName property, determining the GUID by looking it up in the Registry.

At this point, if you set the DCOMConnection component's Connected property to True, the server form will appear, indicating that the client has activated the server. You don't usually need to perform this operation because the ClientDataSet component typically activates the Remote-Server component for you. I suggested this step simply to emphasize what's happening behind the scenes.

TIP You should generally leave the DCOMConnection component's Connected property set to False at design time so you can open the project in Delphi even on a computer where the DataSnap server is not already registered.

As you might expect, the next step is to add a ClientDataSet component to the form. You connect the ClientDataSet to the DCOMConnection1 component via the RemoteServer property and thereby to one of the providers it exports. You can see the list of available providers in the combo box for the ProviderName property. In this example, you'll be able to select only DataSetProvider1 because it is the only provider available in the server you just built. This operation connects the dataset in the client's memory with the dbExpress dataset on the server. If you activate the client dataset and add a few data-aware controls (or a DBGrid), you'll immediately see the server data appear in them, as illustrated in Figure 17.1.

FIGURE 17.1

When you activate a ClientDataSet component connected to a remote data module at design time, the data from the server becomes visible as usual.

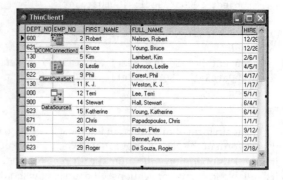

Here is the DFM file for the minimal client application ThinCli1:

```
object Form1: TForm1
  Caption = 'ThinClient1'
  object DCOMConnection1: TDCOMConnection
    ServerGUID = '{09E11D63-4A55-11D3-B9F1-00000100A27B}'
    ServerName = 'AppServ1.AppServerOne'
  end
  object ClientDataSet1: TClientDataSet
    ProviderName = 'DataSetProvider1'
    RemoteServer = DCOMConnection1
  end
  object DataSource1: TDataSource
    DataSet = ClientDataSet1
  end
  object DBGrid1: TDBGrid
    Align = alClient
    DataSource = DataSource1
  end
end
```

Obviously, the programs for this first three-tier application are quite simple, but they demonstrate how to create a dataset viewer that splits the work between two different executable files. At this point, the client is only a viewer. If you edit the data on the client, it won't be updated on the server. To accomplish this, you'll need to add more code to the client. However, before you do that, let's add some features to the server.

Building a .NET Client

You can build a .NET client based on the VCL for .NET library in a very similar way to how you would build a Win32 client. The only DataSnap client connection you can use, though, is the DCOM-ClientConnection. The lack of the socket connection is a problem, because it simplifies deployment by far, and it is the connection I prefer for real-world applications (along with the SOAP connection).

As an example, I built the ThinCliNet application, which is a brand-new example and not a port of the Win32 version. By creating a new application based on an NFM file, you can see right away in the Tool Palette which DataSnap components are available in the VCL for .NET. For the following clients, instead, I created a .NET project with the same form used by the Win32 VCL projects, as I've often done throughout the book.

WARNING   As DataSnap servers are based on COM, regardless of the client connection, it is not possible to create them in .NET. The only non-COM DataSnap server is the SOAP server, but Delphi's native flavor of SOAP is not available in Delphi for .NET either.

Adding Constraints to the Server

When you write a traditional data module in Delphi, you can easily add some of the application logic, or business rules, by handling the dataset events and by setting field object properties and handling their events. You should avoid doing this work on the client application; instead, write your business rules on the middle tier.

In the DataSnap architecture, you can send some constraints from the server to the client and let the client program impose those constraints during the user input. You can also send to the client some field properties, such as minimum and maximum values and the display and edit masks.

Field and Dataset Constraints

When the provider interface creates data packets to send to the client, it includes the field definitions, the table and field constraints, and one or more records (as requested by the ClientDataSet component). This implies that you can customize the middle tier and build distributed application logic by using SQL-based constraints.

The constraints you create using SQL expressions can be assigned to an entire dataset or to specific fields. The provider sends the constraints to the client along with the data, and the client applies them before sending updates back to the server. This process reduces network traffic, compared to having the client send updates back to the application server and eventually up to the SQL server, only to find that the data is invalid. Another advantage of coding the constraints on the server side is that if the business rules change, you need to update the single server application and not the many clients on multiple computers.

But how do you write constraints? You can use several properties:

◆ Each field object defines the CustomConstraint and ConstraintErrorMessage properties. There is also an ImportedConstraint property for constraints imported from the SQL server.

◆ Each field object has a DefaultExpression property, which can be used locally or passed to the ClientDataSet. This is not an actual constraint; it's only a suggestion to the end user.

The next example, AppServ2, adds a few constraints to a remote data module connected to the sample EMPLOYEE InterBase database. After connecting the table to the database and creating the field objects for it, you can set the following special properties:

```
object SQLDataSet1: TSQLDataSet
...

object SQLDataSet1EMP_NO: TSmallintField
  CustomConstraint = 'x > 0 and x < 10000'
  ConstraintErrorMessage =
    'Employee number must be a positive integer below 10000'
  FieldName = 'EMP_NO'
end
```

```
object SQLDataSet1FIRST_NAME: TStringField
  CustomConstraint = 'x <> '''
  ConstraintErrorMessage = 'The first name is required'
  FieldName = 'FIRST_NAME'
end
object SQLDataSet1LAST_NAME: TStringField
  CustomConstraint = 'not x is null'
  ConstraintErrorMessage = 'The last name is required'
  FieldName = 'LAST_NAME'
end
end
```

NOTE   In the preceding code I could have used the Required property instead of the Constraint x
<> '', but this would have worked only if I set the poIncFieldProps option as described in the next
section.

Including Field Properties

You can control whether the properties of the field objects on the middle tier are sent to the Client-
DataSet (and copied into the corresponding field objects of the client side) by using the poIncField-
Props value of the Options property of the DataSetProvider. This flag controls the download of the
field properties Alignment, DisplayLabel, DisplayWidth, Visible, DisplayFormat, EditFormat,
MaxValue, MinValue, Currency, EditMask, and DisplayValues, if they are available in the field.
Here is an example of another field of the AppServ2 example with some custom properties:

```
object SQLDataSet1SALARY: TBCDField
  DefaultExpression = '10000'
  FieldName = 'SALARY'
  DisplayFormat = '#,###'
  EditFormat = '####'
  Precision = 15
  Size = 2
end
```

With this setting, you can write your middle tier the way you usually set the fields of a standard
client/server application. This approach also makes it faster to move existing applications from a client/
server to a multitier architecture. The main drawback of sending fields to the client is that transmitting all the extra information takes time. Turning off poIncFieldProps can improve network performance of datasets with many columns.

A server can generally filter the fields sent to the client; it does so by declaring persistent field
objects with the Fields editor and omitting some of the fields. Because a field you're filtering out
might be required to identify the record for future updates (if the field is part of the primary key), you
can also use the field's ProviderFlags property on the server to send the field value to the client but
make it unavailable to the client ClientDataSet component (this provides some extra security, compared to sending the field to the client and hiding it there).

Field and Table Events

You can write middle-tier dataset and field event handlers as usual and let the dataset process the updates received by the client in the traditional way. In this case updates in the middle-tier are considered to be operations on the local dataset, exactly as if the user was directly editing, inserting, or deleting fields of the dataset locally in a client/server application.

This update process is requested by setting the `ResolveToDataSet` property of the `TDatasetProvider` component, again connecting either the dataset used for input or a second dataset used for the updates. This approach is possible with datasets supporting editing operations. These include ADO and IBX datasets but not those of the dbExpress architecture.

With this technique, the updates are performed by the dataset, which implies a lot of control (the standard events are being triggered) but generally slower performance. Flexibility is much greater, because you can use standard coding practices. Also, porting existing local or client/server database applications, which use dataset and field events, is much more straightforward with this model. However, keep in mind that the user of the client program will receive your error messages only when the local cache (the delta) is sent back to the middle tier. Saying to the user that some data prepared half an hour ago is not valid might be a little awkward. If you follow this approach, you'll probably need to apply the updates in the cache at every `AfterPost` event on the client side.

Finally, if you decide to let the dataset and not the provider do the updates, Delphi helps you a lot in handling possible exceptions. Any exceptions raised by the middle-tier update events (for example, `OnBeforePost`) are automatically transformed by Delphi into update errors, which activate the `OnReconcileError` event on the client side (more on this event later in this chapter). No exception is shown on the middle tier, but the error travels back to the client.

Adding Features to the Client

After adding some constraints and field properties to the server, let's return our attention to the client application. The first version was very simple, but now you can add several features to make it work well. In the ThinCli2 example (and in the ThinCli2Net version), I embedded support for checking the record status and accessing the delta information (the updates to be sent back to the server) using some of the ClientDataSet techniques already discussed in Chapter 13. The program also handles reconcile errors and supports the briefcase model.

Keep in mind that while you're using this client to edit the data locally, you'll be reminded of any failure to match the business rules of the application, which are set up on the server side using constraints. The server will also provide you with a default value for the Salary field of a new record and pass along the value of its `DisplayFormat` property. In Figure 17.2, you can see one of the error messages this client application can display. This message is received from the server with the data packet and is displayed when you're editing the data locally, not when you send the updates back to the server.

The Update Sequence

This client program includes a button to apply the updates to the server and a standard reconcile dialog. Here is a summary of the complete sequence of operations related to an update request and the possible error events:

1. The client program calls the `ApplyUpdates` method of a ClientDataSet.

2. The delta is sent to the provider on the middle tier. The provider fires the `OnUpdateData` event, where you have a chance to look at the requested changes before they reach the database

server. At this point you can modify the delta, which is passed in a format compatible with the data of a ClientDataSet.

3. The provider (technically, a part of the provider called the *resolver*) applies each row of the delta to the database server. Before applying each update, the provider receives a Before UpdateRecord event. If you've set the ResolveToDataSet flag, this update will eventually fire local events of the dataset in the middle tier.

4. In case of a server error, the provider fires the OnUpdateError event (on the middle tier) and the program has a chance of fixing the error at that level.

5. If the middle-tier program doesn't fix the error, the corresponding update request remains in the delta. The error is returned to the client side at this point or after a given number of errors have been collected, depending on the value of the MaxErrors parameter of the ApplyUpdates call.

6. The delta packet with the remaining updates is sent back to the client, firing the OnReconcile Error event of the ClientDataSet for each remaining update. In this event handler, the client program can try to fix the problem (possibly prompting the user for help), modifying the update in the delta, and later reissuing it.

FIGURE 17.2

The error message displayed by the ThinCli2 example when the employee ID is too large

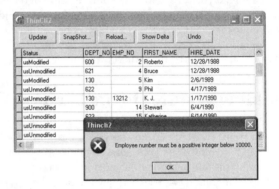

Refreshing Data

You can obtain an updated version of the data, which other users might have modified, by calling the Refresh method of the ClientDataSet. However, this operation can be done only if there are no pending update operations in the cache because calling Refresh raises an exception when the change log is not empty.

If only some records have been changed, you can refresh specific records by calling RefreshRecords. This method refreshes only the current record, but it should be used only if the user hasn't modified the current record. In this case, RefreshRecords leaves the unapplied changes in the change log. As an example, you can refresh a record every time it becomes the active one, unless it has been modified and the changes have not yet been posted to the server:

```
procedure TForm1.cdsAfterScroll(DataSet: TDataSet);
begin
  if cds.UpdateStatus = usUnModified then
    cds.RefreshRecord;
end;
```

When the data is subject to frequent changes by many users and each user should see changes right away, you should apply any change immediately in the `AfterPost` and `AfterDelete` methods and call `RefreshRecords` for the active record (as shown previously) or for each of the records visible inside a grid. This is demonstrated in the ClientRefresh example, connected to the AppServ2 server. For debugging purposes, the program also logs the EMP_NO field for each record it refreshes, as you can see in Figure 17.3.

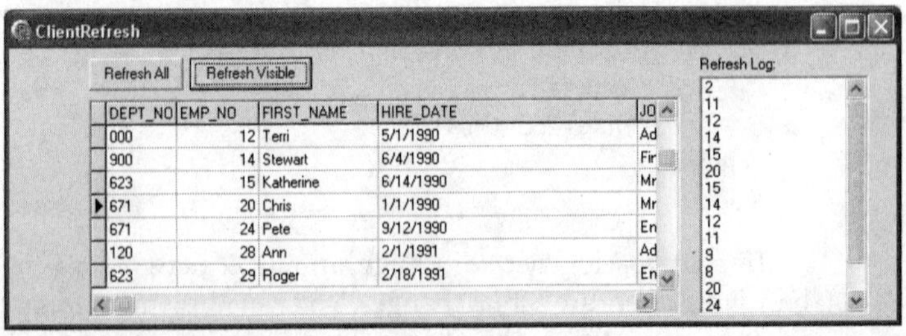

FIGURE 17.3

The form of the Client–Refresh example, which automatically refreshes the active record and allows more extensive updates by clicking the buttons

I did this by adding a button to the ClientRefresh example. The handler of this button moves from the current record to the first visible record of the grid and then to the last visible record. This is accomplished by noting that there are RowCount - 1 rows visible, assuming that the first row is the fixed one hosting the field names. The program doesn't call `RefreshRecord` every time because each movement will trigger an `AfterScroll` event with the code shown previously. The following code refreshes the visible rows, which might be triggered by a timer:

```
// protected access hack
type
  TMyGrid = class (TDBGrid)
  end;

procedure TForm1.Button2Click(Sender: TObject);
var
  i: Integer;
  bm: TBookmarkStr;
begin
  // refresh visible rows
  cds.DisableControls;
  // start with the current row
  i := TMyGrid (DbGrid1).Row;
  bm := cds.Bookmark;
  try
    // get back to the first visible record
    while i > 1 do
    begin
      cds.Prior;
      Dec (i);
    end;
    // return to the current record
    i := TMyGrid(DbGrid1).Row;
```

```
      cds.Bookmark := bm;
      // go ahead until the grid is complete
      while i < TMyGrid(DbGrid1).RowCount do
      begin
        cds.Next;
        Inc (i);
      end;
    finally
      // set back everything and refresh
      cds.Bookmark := bm;
      cds.EnableControls;
    end;
  end;
```

This approach generates a huge amount of network traffic, so you might want to trigger updates only when there are actual changes. You can implement this process by adding a callback technology to the server so that it can inform all connected clients that a given record has changed. The client can determine whether it is interested in the change and eventually trigger the update request.

Advanced DataSnap Features

DataSnap includes many more features than I've covered up to now. Here is a quick tour of some of the more advanced features of the architecture, partially demonstrated by the AppSPlus and Thin-Plus examples.

In addition to the features discussed in the following sections, the AppSPlus and ThinPlus examples demonstrate limited logging of events and updates on the server side and direct fetching of a record on the client side. The last feature is accomplished with this call:

```
procedure TClientForm.ButtonFetchClick(Sender: TObject);
begin
  ButtonFetch.Caption := IntToStr (cds.GetNextPacket);
end;
```

This allows you to get more records than are required by the client user interface (the DBGrid). In other words, you can fetch records directly without waiting for the user to scroll down in the grid. I suggest you study the details of these complex examples after reading the rest of this section.

Parameterized Queries

If you want to use parameters in a query or stored procedure, then instead of building a custom solution (with a custom method call to the server), you can let Delphi help you. First define the query on the middle tier with a parameter:

```
select * from employee
where job_code = :job_code
```

Use the Params property to set the type and default value of the parameter. On the client side, you can use the Fetch Params command from the ClientDataSet's shortcut menu after connecting the component to the proper provider. At run time, you can call the equivalent FetchParams method of the ClientDataSet component.

Now you can provide a local default value for the parameter through the Params property. The value of the parameter will be sent to the middle tier when you fetch the data. The ThinPlus example refreshes the parameter, using a value from a prepopulated combo box, with the following code:

```
procedure TFormQuery.btnParamClick(Sender: TObject);
begin
  cdsQuery.Close;
  cdsQuery.Params[0].AsString := ComboBox1.Text;
  cdsQuery.Open;
end;
```

Custom Method Calls

Because the server has a normal COM interface, you can add more methods or properties to it and call them from the client. Simply open the server's type library editor and use it as with any other COM server. In the AppSPlus example, I added a custom Login method with the following implementation:

```
procedure TAppServerPlus.Login(const Name, Password: WideString);
begin
  if Password <> Name then
    raise Exception.Create (
      'Wrong name/password combination received');
  ProviderDepartments.Exported := True;
  ServerForm.Add ('Login:' + Name + '/' + Password);
end;
```

The program performs a simple test instead of checking the name/password combination against a list of authorizations as a real application should do. If the test doesn't fail, it enables the provider that is disabled by default at startup. The client has a simple way to access the server: the AppServer property of the remote connection component. Here is a sample call from the ThinPlus example, which takes place in the AfterConnect event of the connection component:

```
procedure TClientForm.ConnectionAfterConnect(Sender: TObject);
begin
  ConnectionBroker1.AppServer.Login (Edit2.Text, Edit3.Text);
end;
```

Note that you can call extra methods of the COM interface through DCOM as well as by using a socket-based or HTTP connection. Because the program uses the safecall calling convention, the exception raised on the server is automatically forwarded and displayed on the client side. This way, when a user selects the Connect check box, the event handler used to enable the client datasets is interrupted, and a user with the wrong password won't be able to see the data.

NOTE   In addition to direct method calls from the client to the server, you can implement callbacks from the server to the client. You can use this approach, for example, to notify every client of specific events. COM events are one way to do this. As an alternative, you can add a new interface, implemented by the client, which passes the implementation object to the server. This way, the server can call the method on the client computer. Callbacks are not possible with HTTP connections, though.

Master/Detail Relations

If your middle-tier application exports multiple datasets, you can retrieve them using multiple Client-DataSet components on the client side and connect them locally to form a master/detail structure. This approach will create quite a few problems for the detail dataset unless you retrieve all the records locally. This solution also makes it quite complex to apply the updates; you cannot usually cancel a master record until all related detail records have been removed, and you cannot add detail records until the new master record is properly in place.

A completely different approach is to retrieve a single dataset that already includes the detail as a dataset field, a field of type TDataSetField. To accomplish this, you need to set up the master/detail relation on the server application:

```
object SQLDepartments: TSQLDataSet
  CommandText = 'select * from DEPARTMENT'
  SQLConnection = SQLConnection1
end
object SQLEmployees: TSQLDataSet
  CommandText = 'select * from EMPLOYEE where dept_no = :dept_no'
  DataSource = DataSourceDept
  Params = <
    item
      DataType = ftUnknown
      Name = 'dept_no'
      ParamType = ptInput
    end>
  SQLConnection = SQLConnection1
end
object DataSourceDept: TDataSource
  DataSet = SQLDepartments
end
object ProviderDepartments: TDataSetProvider
  DataSet = SQLDepartments
  OnUpdateData = ProviderDepartmentsUpdateData
  BeforeUpdateRecord = ProviderDepartmentsBeforeUpdateRecord
  BeforeGetRecords = ProviderDepartmentsBeforeGetRecords
end
```

On the client side, the detail table will show up as an extra field of the ClientDataSet, and the DBGrid control will display it as an extra column with an ellipsis button. Clicking the button will display a secondary form with a grid presenting the detail table (see Figure 17.4). If you need to build a flexible user interface on the client, you can then add a secondary ClientDataSet connected to the dataset field of the master dataset using the DataSetField property. Simply create persistent fields for the main ClientDataSet and then hook up the property:

```
object cdsDet: TClientDataSet
  DataSetField = cdsTableOrders
end
```

With this setting, you can show the detail dataset in a separate DBGrid placed as usual in the form (the bottom grid of Figure 17.4) or any other way you like. Note that with this structure, the updates relate only to the master table, and the server handles the proper update sequence even in complex situations. Specifically, it deletes detail records before the master record and inserts new master records before adding its detail records. This is accomplished with no need to add specific code on the programmer's part, as this process is managed automatically by the Resolver component.

FIGURE 17.4

The ThinPlus example shows how a dataset field can either be displayed in a grid in a floating window or extracted by a ClientDataSet and displayed in a second DBgrid. You'll generally do one of the two things, not both!

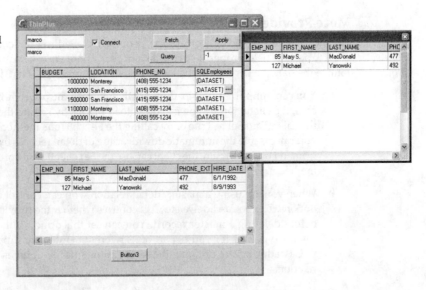

Using the Connection Broker

I already mentioned that the ConnectionBroker component can be helpful in case you might want to change the physical connection used by many ClientDataSet components of a single program. By hooking each ClientDataSet to the ConnectionBroker, you can change the physical connection of all the ClientDataSets by updating the physical connection of the broker.

The ThinPlus example uses these settings:

```
object DCOMConnection1: TDCOMConnection
  ServerGUID = '{E31849A9-4A82-11D3-B9F1-00000100A27B}'
  ServerName = 'AppSPlus.AppServerPlus'
end
object ConnectionBroker1: TConnectionBroker
  Connection = DCOMConnection1
  AfterConnect = ConnectionBroker1AfterConnect
end
object cds: TClientDataSet
  ConnectionBroker = ConnectionBroker1
end
```

```
// in the secondary form
object cdsQuery: TClientDataSet
  ConnectionBroker = ClientForm.ConnectionBroker1
end
```

That's basically all you have to do. To change the physical connection, drop a new DataSnap connection component to the main form and set the `Connection` property of the broker to it.

More Provider Options

I already mentioned the `Options` property of the DataSetProvider component, noting that you can use it to add the field properties to the data packet. There are several other options you can use to customize the data packet and the behavior of the client program. Here is a short list:

♦ You can minimize downloading BLOB data with the poFetchBlobsOnDemand option. In this case, the client application can download BLOBs by setting the `FetchOnDemand` property of the ClientDataSet to True or by calling the `FetchBlobs` method for specific records. Similarly, you can disable the automatic downloading of detail records by setting the poFetchDetailsOnDemand option. Again, the client can use the `FetchOnDemand` property or call the `FetchDetails` method.

♦ When you are using a master/detail relation, you can control cascades with either of two options. The poCascadeDeletes flag controls whether the provider should delete detail records before deleting a master record. You can set this option if the database server performs cascaded deletes for you as part of its referential integrity support. Similarly, you can set the poCascadeUpdates option if the server automatically updates key values of a master/detail relation.

♦ You can limit the operations on the client side. The most restrictive option, poReadOnly, disables any update. If you want to give the user a limited editing capability, use poDisableInserts, poDisableEdits, or poDisableDeletes.

♦ You can use poAutoRefresh to resend to the client a copy of the records the client has modified; doing so is useful in case other users have simultaneously made other, nonconflicting changes. You can also specify the poPropogateChanges option to send back to the client changes done in the `BeforeUpdateRecord` or `AfterUpdateRecord` event handler. This option is also handy when you are using auto-increment fields, triggers, and other techniques that modify data on the server or middle tier beyond the changes requested from the client tier.

♦ Finally, if you want the client to drive the operations, you can enable the poAllowCommandText option. It lets you set the SQL query or table name of the middle tier from the client using the `GetRecords` or `Execute` method.

The Simple Object Broker

The SimpleObjectBroker component provides an easy way to locate a server application among several server computers. You provide a list of available computers, and the client will try each of them in order until it finds one that is available.

Moreover, if you enable the LoadBalanced property, the component will randomly choose one of the servers; when many clients use the same configuration, the connections will be automatically distributed among the multiple servers. If this seems like a "poor man's" object broker, consider that some highly expensive load-balancing systems don't offer much more than this.

Object Pooling

When multiple clients connect to your server at the same time, you have two options. The first is to create a remote data module object for each of them and let each request be processed in sequence (the default behavior for a COM server with the ciMultiInstance style). Alternatively, you can let the system create a different instance of the server application for every client (ciSingleInstance). This approach requires more resources and more SQL server connections (and possibly licenses).

An alternate approach is offered by DataSnap's support for object pooling. All you need to do to request this feature is add a call to RegisterPooled in the overridden UpdateRegistry method. Combined with the stateless support built in to this architecture, the pooling capability allows you to share some middle-tier objects among a much larger number of clients. A pooling mechanism is built in to COM+, but DataSnap makes it available for HTTP and socket-based connections as well.

The users on the client computers will spend most of their time reading data and typing in updates, and they generally don't continue asking for data and sending updates. When the client is not calling a method of the middle-tier object, this same remote data module can be used for another client. Being stateless, every request reaches the middle tier as a brand-new operation, even when a server is dedicated to a specific client.

Customizing the Data Packets

There are many ways to include custom information within the data packet handled by the IAppServer interface. The simplest is to handle the OnGetDataSetProperties event of the provider. This event has a Sender parameter, a dataset parameter indicating where the data is coming from, and an OleVariant array Properties parameter, in which you can place the extra information. You need to define one variant array for each extra property and include the name of the extra property, its value, and whether you want the data to return to the server along with the update delta (the IncludeInDelta parameter).

Of course, you can pass properties of the related dataset component, but you can also pass any other value (extra fake properties). In the AppSPlus example, I pass to the client the time the query was executed and its parameters:

```
procedure TAppServerPlus.ProviderQueryGetDataSetProperties(
  Sender: TObject; DataSet: TDataSet; out Properties: OleVariant);
begin
  Properties := VarArrayCreate([0,1], varVariant);
  Properties[0] := VarArrayOf(['Time', Now, True]);
  Properties[1] := VarArrayOf(['Param',
    SQLWithParams.Params[0].AsString, False]);
end;
```

On the client side, the ClientDataSet component has a GetOptionalParameter method to retrieve the value of the extra property with the given name. The ClientDataSet also has the SetOptionalParameter method to add more properties to the dataset. These values will be saved to disk (in the briefcase model) and eventually sent back to the middle tier (by setting the `IncludeInDelta` member of the variant array to True). Here is a simple example of the retrieval of the dataset in the previous code:

```
Caption := 'Data sent at ' + TimeToStr (TDateTime (
  cdsQuery.GetOptionalParam('Time')));
Label1.Caption := 'Param ' + cdsQuery.GetOptionalParam('Param');
```

An alternative and more powerful approach for customizing the data packet sent to the client is to handle the `OnGetData` event of the provider, which receives the outgoing data packet in the form of a client dataset. Using the methods of this client dataset, you can edit data before it is sent to the client. For example, you might encode some of the data or filter out sensitive records.

Multitier Development in Microsoft .NET

The Microsoft .NET Framework supports distributed processing using a number of techniques, including what is called *.NET Remoting* and SOAP. I'll cover SOAP in Chapter 23. .NET remoting is based on sockets communication, and although I'll introduce sockets and HTTP in Chapter 19, I think it is relevant to give you an overview of .NET remoting in this chapter before discussing ADO.NET remoting. For more details on the technologies used here behind the scenes, refer to Chapters 19 and 23.

.NET Remoting Architecture

Given the extended flexibility for using types at run time and given the goals of .NET, it should come as no surprise that .NET has a very sophisticated support for calling objects living in other application domains, on the local computer, or on other computers of a network.

The remoting architecture of .NET is an RPC (Remote Procedure Call) system, similar to DCOM and other similar architectures. The system works by creating a local stub of the remote object, the *real* object. As you call the methods of the client (stub) object, these calls are sent over the wire to the remote object living in the server application domain. Once you set up the system, everything works behind the scenes and you don't need to change the way you write either the server code or the client code (although you might have to change the client setup code, the proxy creation, or use a configuration file for managing it). The only rule is that the object you want to be able to use remotely must inherit from the class `MarshalByRefObject` (or `TPersistent`, in Delphi equivalent terms).

NOTE   .NET remoting doesn't account for the automatic activation of the server program, a feature of other systems like DCOM called *client activation*. This means that for the client to connect the server must already be running. This happens with any TCP/IP based technology, as you'll see in Chapter 19.

As far as deployment is concerned, the good news is that there is no registry involved, which makes this much easier than a DCOM configuration. With .NET remoting you can pick two different transmission mechanisms, plain TCP over a custom port you choose or HTTP. Using standard and open protocols provides a distinct advantage over the DCOM solution, because you can, for example, add an encryption layer or install a different communication protocol. This is because the solution is completely open, unlike DCOM, which is completely closed.

So what do you need to set up this communication mechanism? Both the client and the server applications need to create a communication channel object (either a TCP-related object or an

HTTP-related object) and to register this channel. This is it for the communication. Than the server has to register the object it wants to make available to remote applications in the `RemotingConfiguration` object, using one of two possible methods, with different parameters, so that you end up having three activation models:

◆ The `RegisterActivatedServiceType` method defines a server object that is created at the same time the client stub is created and remains in memory to serve that specific stub object. This model is called *client activated*.

◆ The `RegisterWellKownServiceType` method with the `SingleCall` parameter defines a server object created to respond to method invocations, not when the stub is created. The `SingleCall` parameter indicates that the server object is created again for each method call, so that the object doesn't preserve state (it is a lightweight stateless object).

◆ The `RegisterWellKownServiceType` method with the `Singleton` parameter defines a server object that is kept in memory to server requests from different clients (possibly at the same time, so you should take care of synchronization).

.NET Remoting in Practice

To better understand this short introduction, I created an example featuring only one communication channel (TCP) and one activation mode (client activated). You can tweak the source code to do other tests (and some code snippets are already there). To create an application like this, the class with the object being shared is placed in a DLL assembly. The reason for this is that although this is used directly only by the server, the client application must have access to its metadata!

NOTE   Having the class as a shared assembly is not the only option to .NET remoting. For example, you could also share an interface to avoid sensitive information (that is, the class metadata and IL code) being deployed to the client.

For the demo I created three projects, all in the `RemotableTest` folder of this chapter's examples. The RemotableLib DLL assembly defines the remotable object; The RemotableTest project is a server WinForms application; and the RemotableClient project is the client WinForms application.

To define the RemotableLib assembly I created a Delphi for .NET package. This package includes only one unit, called RemotableUnit, which defines the object:

```
type
  TRemotableTest = class (MarshalByRefObject)
  private
    nValue: Integer;
  public
    class var RemotableObjCount: Integer;
    constructor Create;
    destructor Destroy; override;
    function GetValue: Integer;
    procedure SetValue (Value: Integer);
    procedure Increase;
    function ToString: string; override;
  end;
```

Notice the `RemotableObjCount` class data that keeps track of the number of objects and is increased and decreased by the constructor and the destructor. The remaining methods are self-explanatory.

The second step is to create the server project, a WinForms application. This program references the RemotableLib assembly and has the following startup code that creates a TCP communication channel over port 6066 and registers the type of the object for remoting (this last statement turns the program into a server):

```
procedure TWinForm.TWinForm_Load(
  sender: System.Object; e: System.EventArgs);
var
  aChannel: TcpServerChannel;
begin
  aChannel := TcpServerChannel.Create(6066);
  ChannelServices.RegisterChannel(aChannel);
  RemotingConfiguration.RegisterActivatedServiceType (
    typeof(TRemotableTest));
end;
```

The form of the program has a button and a list box, used to display the number of `TRemotableTest` objects in the server, obtained by accessing the `RemotableObjCount` class data.

NOTE   To compile the server and the client programs of this demo, you need to compile the library assembly first. This is why it is the first project in the project group. Notice also that each of the projects has a reference to the Borland.Delphi assembly.

Now let's move to the client program, which references the RemotableLib assembly as well (although only to access the type information). The client has a form with nothing more than a single button. Clicking this button activates the communication channel (the first time only), registers the remoting client, and then uses the object:

```
var
  test: TRemotableTest;
  I: Integer;
begin
  if not Assigned (aChannel) then
  begin
    aChannel := TcpClientChannel.Create;
    ChannelServices.RegisterChannel(aChannel);
    RemotingConfiguration.RegisterActivatedClientType(
      typeof(TRemotableTest), 'tcp://localhost:6066');
  end;

  test := TRemotableTest.Create;
  try
    test.SetValue(5);
    for I := 0 to 100 do
      test.Increase;
    MessageBox.Show(test.ToString);
```

```
  finally
    test.Free;
  end;
end;
```

NOTE The channel is not created in the Load event because the server might not be running yet (remember, there is no client-activation of the server in .NET remoting). The program delays the channel setup to the very last minute.

The preceding simple for loop seems trivial, but in fact each and every call is executed on the server, as the client application has only a stub object. This is not very easy to prove, but you can check that, while the message box is being displayed, the server has one object for each client with an active stub object (as you can see by clicking its button).

What is relevant to notice here is the use of deterministic finalization. The call test.Free activates the Dispose method of the client stub object, which causes the server object to have no more standing references so that is can be killed off as soon as possible. Without this call the client stub objects would remain active until the GC kicks in on the client side. This is not a problem for the client itself, but it can be for a server with many clients connected, as the server will keep around in memory potentially many unneeded objects (as their corresponding client stubs are not referenced any more). However, the server GC cannot dispose them until their client stubs are finalized.

As an alternative, the program also lets you experiment with stateless server-activated objects. Just replace the two registration calls with the following:

```
// server-side
RemotingConfiguration.RegisterWellKnownServiceType(
  typeof(TRemotableTest), 'tremotabletest',
  WellKnownObjectMode.SingleCall);
```

```
// client-side
RemotingConfiguration.RegisterWellKnownClientType(
  typeof(TRemotableTest), 'tcp://localhost:6066/tremotabletest');
```

Now if you run the program you might be in for a surprise, as the result of calling Increase a 100 times will be zero! The reason, you should now know, is that the server will create hundreds of different objects, one for each method invocation. If you make this change you should also remove the call to Free, as .NET won't like the call to Dispose the stub of a server-activated object.

ADO.NET Remoting with Delphi Components

The remoting techniques I just introduced can be used to create a multitier architecture for database access using ADO.NET. However, Delphi for .NET provides some ready-to-use components exactly for this purpose. These components are flexible, quite easy to use, and work even at design time. Therefore, I'll focus on the use of these Borland-specific components.

There are four components to consider, two used on the server side and two used on the client side:

◆ The DataSync component is used on the server side to synchronize and manage data from multiple data adapters. These data adapters are listed in its Provider collection property. As you saw in the last chapter, this component can also be used in stand-alone applications, but its key role is for a multitier architecture.

- The RemoteServer component is used on the server side to define the remoting channel (using the `ChannelType`, `Port`, and `URI` properties), and provide remote access to a DataSync component.

- The RemoteConnection component is used on the client side to refer to a RemoteServer component using aURL determined by matching `ChannelType`, `Port`, and `URI` properties.

- The DataHub component is used on the client side to access the connection (indicated in the `DataPort` property) and fill a local DataSet component with the data from the providers of the remote DataSync object.

If you look at this architecture from some distance, you can say you have a DataSet component that communicates (via the local DataHub) to a remote DataAdapter component (exposed by the Data-Sync) running in a different AppDomain, possibly on a different computer.

Looking at this architecture from a VCL perspective, the DataHub assumes a role similar to the provider, as in the ADO.NET client/server architecture; of course, the DataSet and the ClientDataSet play a similar role. There are other correspondences with the VCL architecture. For example, each item of the `Provider` collection of the DataSync has an `UpdateMode` property with a very familiar role. Still, compared to the DataSnap solution, this remoting architecture has fewer options you can control by means of properties and other settings (think for example of the provider options at the provider and field levels). On the other hand, the use of .NET remoting makes it very powerful and flexible in areas like installation and configuration, channels management, and integration with other languages and tools.

ADO.NET Remoting in Practice

Again, after some theory, let's have a look at an actual example. In the `AdoNetRemote` folder you can find two projects, AdoNetServer and AdoNetClient. The server uses a BdpConnection and the Data-Sync and RemoteServer components described in the previous section. These are their relevant settings (out of over 300 lines of code of the `InitializeComponent` method):

```
Self.BdpConnection1.ConnectionString :=
  'assembly=Borland.Data.Interbase,Version=2.0.0.0,...' +
  'database=C:\...\InterBase\examples\Database\EMPLOYEE.GDB';

Self.BdpDataAdapter1.Active := False;
Self.BdpDataAdapter1.SelectCommand := Self.bdpSelectCommand1;

Self.bdpSelectCommand1.CommandText := 'SELECT * FROM EMPLOYEE';
Self.bdpSelectCommand1.CommandType := System.Data.CommandType.Text;
Self.bdpSelectCommand1.Connection := Self.BdpConnection1;

Self.DataSync1.CommitBehavior :=
  Borland.Data.Provider.CommitBehaviorType.Atomic;
Self.DataSync1.Providers.Add(
  Borland.Data.Common.DataProvider.Create(
    'ProviderEmployee', Self.BdpDataAdapter1, 'EmployeeTable',
    Borland.Data.Common.BdpUpdateMode.Key, nil, nil));

Self.RemoteServer1.AutoStart := True;
```

```
Self.RemoteServer1.ChannelType :=
   Borland.Data.Remoting.ChannelType.Tcp;
Self.RemoteServer1.DataSync := Self.DataSync1;
Self.RemoteServer1.Port := 8000;
Self.RemoteServer1.URI := 'AdoNetServer';
Include(Self.RemoteServer1.OnGetDataProvider,
   Self.RemoteServer1_OnGetDataProvider);
```

The `OnGetDataProvider` event handler simply logs to a list box in the server form that some data has been retrieved. This allows you to figure out exactly when the data is fetched form the server.

On the client side there is a DataSet with a DataGrid, plus the combination of the RemoteConnection and DataHub components. Notably, there is no database connection! The RemoteConnection needs to specify the channel parameters plus the `ProviderType` property (which is easy to miss when you set it up):

```
Self.RemoteConnection1.ChannelType :=
   Borland.Data.Remoting.ChannelType.Tcp;
Self.RemoteConnection1.Host := 'localhost';
Self.RemoteConnection1.Port := 8000;
Self.RemoteConnection1.ProviderType := 'Borland.Data.Provider.DataSync';
Self.RemoteConnection1.URI := 'AdoNetServer';

Self.DataHub1.Active := False;
Self.DataHub1.DataPort := Self.RemoteConnection1;
Self.DataHub1.DataSet := nil;
```

As you can see, the DataHub is not tied to the DataSet at design time. If you do so, you'll see the data at design time. However, if you open up the project while the server is not running, you'll see an error. Similarly, if you keep the DataHub active and open the client application while the server is not active, you will then get an error and will have to close and restart the client application after executing the server application.

In other words, as in the previous remoting example, it is better to delay the connection to a specific event, such as clicking a button, unless you know the server is always running. As this is not the case for this example, it is better to finish the setup when the Open button of the client is clicked, by activating the DataHub and connecting the DataGrid to the proper table:

```
procedure TWinForm.btnOpen_Click(
   sender: System.Object; e: System.EventArgs);
begin
  DataHub1.DataSet := DataSet1;
  DataHub1.Active := True;
  DataGrid1.DataSource := DataSet1;
  DataGrid1.DataMember := 'EmployeeTable';
end;
```

The effect of these two programs is visible in Figure 17.5. There are a few advanced settings you can use but not as many as in a DataSnap application, as I mentioned earlier. What is very interesting in the use of the Borland remoting components is that the DataSync can be used to grab data from multiple DataAdapters. Therefore, you can use it as a conduit of data from multiple sources, including multiple databases.

FIGURE 17.5
The AdoNetServer and AdoNetClient programs at run time, after establishing the connection

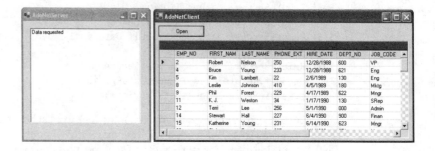

NOTE More information on the use of the DataSync and the other Delphi remoting components as data aggregators is described in a white paper available at www.borland.com/products/ white_papers/pdf/del2005_data_remoting.pdf.

What's Next?

Borland originally introduced its multitier technology in Delphi 3 and has kept extending it from version to version. Over the years the name was changed from MIDAS to DataSnap, and there were many updates including the introduction of SOAP support (explored in Chapter 23). However, the most relevant change was the introduction of a new licensing scheme in Delphi 7: *free deployment*. This paved the way for increased adoption of this technology.

It is certainly true, however, that in terms of remote communication and multitier architectures, the .NET platform and Delphi for .NET provide many goodies you don't get out of the box in the Win32 world (although Indy's socket support and SOAP support offer very interesting standard-based alternatives).

For the moment, we have another database-related topic to discuss: the Model Driven Architecture supported by the ECO framework, available in the Architect version of Delphi 2005, which we'll discuss in the next chapter.

Chapter 18

Using Enterprise Core Objects (ECO)

ECO (Enterprise Core Objects) is Borland's MDA (Model Driven Architecture) solution for .NET. What does that mean? It's essentially a framework that uses a UML model as the basis for your application at runtime. Why would you want to do that? The whole point of ECO is to improve the productivity of developers by raising the level of abstraction at which they work. ECO is for .NET, but it evolved from the Bold product for Win32 Delphi, which has been in production for many years. ECO II ships in the Architect version of Delphi 2005.

NOTE   This chapter was written by Malcolm Groves, Borland's Director of Products in Asia Pacific. Malcolm has been developing with Delphi since the beta of Delphi 1; he's spoken at developer conferences around the world and written numerous articles for developer magazines. You can get more ECO information from Malcolm on his blog at http://blogs.borland.com/malcolmgroves.

The aim of this chapter is to introduce you to enough aspects of ECO to get you started in your exploration of this very interesting technology. It won't make you an ECO guru, but it should serve to get you over the initial learning curve so that you can figure out if ECO is the right solution for your next project and start further exploration on your own.

I arranged this chapter into three distinct sections, following the separation of responsibility that ECO encourages:

Your Model (Business Logic)   Is where you define all the classes related to the problem you are trying to solve. For example, if you were building a CRM (Customer Relationship Management) application, you'd probably have classes like Company, Contact, Address, etc. Typically this layer has no knowledge of how these classes are presented to the user, nor how they are stored. It focuses solely on the operations of the business domain you are trying to model. Hence, it is often called the Domain Model.

Persistence (Data Access Logic)   Is the layer responsible for taking the objects defined in the model and storing them in some data store. It is also, of course, responsible for loading them from the data store again upon request. This data store will usually be a RDBMS, but does not have to be.

User Interface (Presentation Logic)   Is the layer responsible for taking the objects defined in the model and presenting them to the user. This could be via a WinForms client or via an ASP.NET client; however, exactly how the data is presented is of no concern to the classes in the model.

Although these are separate areas, there are times when I have to defer a more in-depth exploration of a topic until we've covered some other pieces. I'll give references to other places where you can get more information about ECO in the "What's Next" section at the end of this chapter so that you can take your exploration further. But for now, let's start with the model.

The Model

Quite often applications built using Delphi (or C#) are based heavily around a database. I suspect that part of the reason this is frequently the case is because the data-aware components and tools in these environments make it very easy to start at the database and build outward.

However, with ECO, the database becomes a secondary issue. The UML model of your application is the central piece upon which everything else is built. Your database is driven by the contents of your model, and even your user interface is based upon your model, not your database. As such, it becomes really, really important that you are comfortable creating models in ECO. Therefore, we'll devote the first and largest section of this chapter to the model.

WARNING   This chapter will not teach you UML. I'm assuming you know the basics of UML class diagrams already.

To work on a model, select File ➤ New ➤ Other in Delphi 2005 to bring up the New Items gallery. Select the Delphi for .NET Projects node and you'll see a few ECO related projects you can create:

◆   ECO ASP.NET Web Application

◆   ECO ASP.NET Web Service Application

◆   ECO WinForms Application

You'll be using the ECO WinForms Application type of project during the rest of this chapter, but once you've worked through Chapter 21 on ASP.NET, you should be able to also use ECO with ASP.NET. You can also create these same ECO project types with C#.

Select the ECO WinForms Application project and give the project a reasonable name; our example will be MyFirstECOApp. This will create a project with a few items in it:

WinForm1.pas   Is the main form of your ECO Application.

MyFirstECOAppEcoSpace.pas   Is the primary ECOSpace for you application (more on ECOSpaces later).

CoreClassesUnit.pas   Is the source file in which, by default, all your classes will be defined (later you'll look at how you can split these up over multiple files).

If you also bring up your Model View (View ➤ Model View), you'll see the top-level node has the same name as your project. Under that, you'll see a number of child nodes. One group of these has icons that look like small blue folders with curly braces next to them. In this example there are three of these, one for each of the three .pas files in the project. These are not ECO-specific but simply provide a way for you to get a UML visualization of any Pascal source code in your project.

You should also see an icon that looks like four colored squares on a sheet of paper. This icon represents a UML diagram, in this case a package diagram, but you'll see the same icon later for class diagrams. We'll look at UML packages later in this chapter as a way to logically arrange your model into different sections, but in this case the default package represents your entire application. Lastly, you should see an icon that looks like a gray folder, in this case named CoreClasses, and inside that a node representing the main class diagram of the CoreClasses file. As you create classes within your diagram, they will appear (by default) in the `CoreClassesUnit.pas` file and will be listed inside this CoreClasses folder.

Double-clicking the CoreClasses diagram node, as shown in Figure 18.1, should cause the CoreClasses class diagram to load into the IDE, although of course the diagram is empty at the moment. Selecting the diagram surface should cause the Tool Palette to display a bunch of UML-related items that you can drag and drop onto your diagram.

FIGURE 18.1

The Model View showing the CoreClasses diagram node

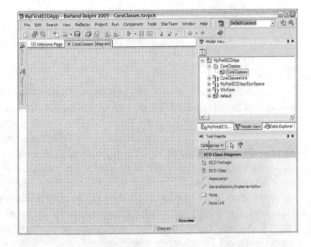

Classes

One of the first things you should do is create a class. Click the ECO class item in the Tool Palette and then click somewhere on the diagram surface. A UML representation of your class should appear. Type a name for the class (or select the class and change the Name property in the Object Inspector); in this case, I named my class `Person`.

Note that selecting the class causes its properties to be displayed in the Object Inspector, just like selecting a component on a form. Also, there is a live link between the classes you are designing on the diagram and the source code in the `CoreClassesUnit.pas` file. Now that you have set the name, right-click the class and select Go To Definition. This will take you to the definition of the class in your source code. If you jump back to the diagram and change the class name to something else, you should be able to see your changes already made in the source code While learning ECO, it's a good idea to make a habit of regularly looking at the source code ECO generates in response to your actions on the class diagram. It's always good to know what's going on under the cover.

Attributes

You have a class, but a class with a name and nothing else is not terribly useful. So let's add attributes to your class. An attribute in this case is not a .NET attribute, but rather a UML concept that ECO implements using a .NET property. There are a number of different types of attributes, and we'll look at each in turn. First though, let's create a simple attribute.

Right-click the class in the diagram and select Add ➤ Attribute. By default you'll get one that looks like `+Attribute_1: Integer`, but you can edit it in place or select it and edit the various pieces of it in the Object Inspector. Give it a name of `Fullname` and a type of string. You can also set the visibility, but in this case, leave it as public.

Right-click it and select Go To Definition again. You should see that ECO has created a property on your class with the `Fullname` name and string type, along with a getter and a setter method. Once you are comfortable with ECO, it is worth looking at the other code generated for you by ECO, as it is not quite this simple, but for the time being this will do.

There is nothing magical about this attribute. It is a property, and it will accept values and return its value on request. You selected a simple data type, but it could equally have been a more complex type such as a class. However, there is a lot more that can be done with attributes, as you'll see later on. For now, we'll look at the basic pieces of our ECO class diagram, specifically operations and associations.

Operations

As you can probably guess, an operation is basically a method. Right-clicking the class in the diagram and selecting Add ➤ Operation will result in an operation that looks like `+Operation_1()` being added. As with your attribute, you can rename it in place or select it and rename it in the Object Inspector. You can also specify any parameters the operation expects and its return type (if any) and control whether it is Abstract, Virtual, an Override, etc. In addition, as with your Attribute, right-clicking and selecting Go To Definition will take you to the definition of your operation in source code. You won't immediately be using the operation you just created beyond looking in the source code to see what ECO created, so give it whatever name and parameters you like. Again, it is worth playing with these different options and seeing the resulting source code that is generated. ECO has created an empty method, and it is still your job as a developer to fill that method with whatever Delphi code you require.

Associations

Another of the most basic items you can add to your class diagram is an association. An association lets you create relationships between the classes in your application. Create another class on your diagram called `Appointment`. Then select the Association item on your Tool Palette and click and drag from your `Person` class to the `Appointment` class. This creates an association between the two classes, represented as a line between them. Select the line and look in the Object Inspector. As well as a `Name` property and a few other properties that we'll cover later, you'll note that toward the top you have `End1` and `End2` properties. These let you control the details of the association at each end (that is, at each class involved). If you dragged the association from the `Person` to the `Appointment`, `End1` would represent the `Person` end of the association and `End2` would represent the `Appointment` end. The most important properties in here are `Name` and `Multiplicity` (I'll cover the others later on).

The `Name` property determines how the class on one end of the association will refer to the other. In this case, setting `End1.Name` to Owner means that the `Appointment` class will be able to refer to an attribute called `Owner`, which will map to a `Person` object. Setting `End2.Name` to Appointments will mean that the `Person` object will be able to refer to an attribute called `Appointments` in order to get a reference to the `Appointment` class on the other end of the association. As before, try changing the names and look at the source code generated.

`Multiplicity` is the other property you'll want to frequently change. As the name suggests, this controls the number of allowed instances of the classes at either end of this association. In my model, a person can have multiple appointments and any appointment can only belong to a single person. However, I need to be more specific than that. It's okay for a person to have zero or more appointments, and a single appointment can belong to one and only one person (not zero). Given that, I should set the `Multiplicity` property on `End1` to 1, meaning that there is only ever one owner of an appointment. I should also set the `Multiplicity` of `End2` to 0..*, meaning that I can have zero, one, or more appointments for a single person. Refer to Figure 18.2 for clarification.

It can get confusing keeping track of `End1` and `End2`, so I suggest that you give meaningful names to all your associations as soon as you add them to the diagram. That way at least you can use the `Name` property of `End1` and `End2` to keep track of which is which.

You now know the basics of building models in ECO. However, as I hinted at before, there is much, much more that you can do beyond these simple pieces. Let's look at a few of the more useful features of models in ECO.

FIGURE 18.2
The Object Inspector showing the properties of the selected association

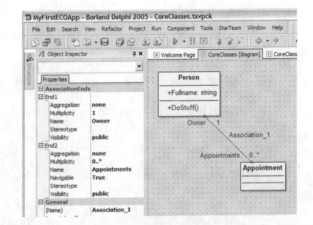

Derived Attributes: OCL

The `Fullname` attribute you defined on your `Person` class earlier was pretty straightforward. You can set a value into it and upon request it will return that value. However, sometimes an attribute's value is the result of a calculation. A simple example would be a class that represented a rectangle. You could have attributes that held the width and the height and also the area. However whenever you changed the width or height, you would also have to remember to change the value in the area attribute. It's possibly better to calculate the value on demand, by multiplying the width and height values. To use ECO terminology, area is a derived attribute, as its value can be derived when needed. Think calculated fields in Delphi database terminology, except these are attributes on a class, not fields in a dataset.

There are a couple of variants of derived attributes: those whose value is calculated using OCL (Object Constraint Language) defined in the model and those whose value is calculated using Pascal source code. There are also reverse derived attributes, which allow you to assign a value to a derived attribute and deconstruct that back to the various attributes from which it was originally derived. I'll cover using OCL to derive an attribute's value here, and in the following sections we'll look at the others.

Before we proceed, however, you need to know what OCL is. OCL is a language defined as part of the UML specification and, as the name suggests, was originally devised as a way to define constraints on the value of attributes in an object. ECO, however, uses OCL extensively, both as a way to express more of your business domain in your model and as a way to link your user interface to your model, as you'll see later in the chapter. OCL is not a difficult language to learn, and in this chapter you'll see a number of examples of its use.

NOTE There is an excellent OCL reference available at www.viewpointsa.com/bold_resources/getting_started_with_bold/Part3-OCL.html. While this was written for Bold, the predecessor of ECO, it applies equally well to ECO.

Back to our example. in Figure 18.3 you can see a very simple model: two classes, Order and OrderItem, and an association between them. The order class is associated with 0..* OrderItem classes; the OrderItem class is associated with only one order class. In addition, the OrderItem class has two attributes, Quantity and UnitPrice. Go ahead and replicate this simple model in your Project.

Now you're going to add an attribute to the OrderItem class called TotalPrice, which represents the total price of the OrderItem. The value of this attribute can be calculated by multiplying Quantity by UnitPrice, so create TotalPrice as an OCL-based derived attribute.

Right-click OrderItem and select Add ➤ Attribute. In the Object Inspector, set the name to TotalPrice, the type to Double, and derived to True. You should also note that changing derived to True has automatically set the Persistence property to Transient (meaning it won't be stored in the data store).

Now you need to specify how this attribute gets its value. This is where you use OCL. Enter the following OCL into the DerivationOCL property of the attribute:

```
UnitPrice * Quantity
```

That's it. Now when you access this TotalPrice attribute or update the Quantity or UnitPrice attributes, whether via code or via your application's user interface, the ECO framework will ensure your TotalPrice value will be calculated. As your TotalPrice, Quantity, and UnitPrice attributes are all part of the same class, you can just reference them by name in the OCL.

Now we'll look at using attributes from other classes.

Let's add another attribute, this time a ShippingQuantity attribute on the Order class. This is going to represent the total of all Quantity attributes for all OrderItems associated with this order. As before, set Name to ShippingQuantity, Type to Integer, and derived to True. In the DerivationOCL property in the Object Inspector, enter the following OCL:

```
Items.Quantity->sum
```

FIGURE 18.3
A simple class diagram
showing two classes
and an association
between them

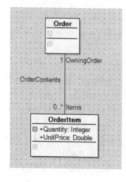

Basically this says that the result is the sum of all the `Quantity` attributes from the `OrderItem` classes associated with this order. Note the context is the `Order` class, so `Items` maps down to the end name of the association. It might be clearer to think of this as `Self.Items.Quantity->sum`, where `Self` is my `Order` object. Figure 18.4 shows the completed attribute. Again, any time this attribute is accessed in code or via the UI, it will return the calculated value.

OCL is a fairly powerful language. You can have such things as conditional branching and iterators. There are many built-in methods to aggregate values, sort, filter, etc. However, it is nowhere near as powerful as Delphi. Don't get too carried away trying to express all your logic as OCL. A general rule is put what is easy to represent in OCL in the model, and use code for those things not easily represented as OCL or that are tricky enough to require some serious debugging.

That said, there are still some big productivity and stability gains to be had by representing more of your logic in your model, letting the ECO framework to take care of more of the boring plumbing code and allowing you to focus on the more interesting, tricky business logic, where you truly add value.

FIGURE 18.4
The Object Inspector showing the properties of the derived attribute

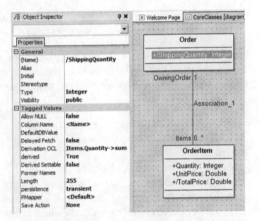

Derived Attributes: Code

We just looked at adding attributes to our ECO classes where the value of those attributes was calculated at runtime using OCL. It is possible to embed some fairly rich logic into your model using this language.

But let's not kid ourselves. Delphi is a much richer language than OCL, so there will come a time when either it's not possible to calculate your attribute's value using OCL, or when you are more comfortable doing it in code. That said, let's look at code-derived attributes.

In Figure 18.5, I added some attributes to the `Appointment` class I created earlier. It has a `Start` attribute of type `DateTime`, which represents the start time of the appointment, and a `Duration` attribute of type `Integer`, which is the length of the appointment in minutes. I also created a derived attribute called `Finish`, also of type `System.DateTime`. Just as before, I set its `derived` property to True. However, unlike before, I have not specified any OCL to calculate the value.

FIGURE 18.5

The Appointment
class with the derived
attribute Finish

When the ECO framework finds a derived attribute that has no OCL, it uses reflection to look for a method of a particular signature and name:

```
function <Attribute Name>DeriveAndSubscribe(
  ReevaluateSubscriber, ResubscribeSubscriber:
  ISubscriber): System.Object;
```

In this case, my attribute is called Finish, so it looks for a method called:

```
function FinishDeriveAndSubscribe(ReevaluateSubscriber,
  ResubscribeSubscriber: ISubscriber): System.Object;
```

If it finds this method, it executes it and uses the return value as the attribute's value. It's your job inside this method to do whatever you need to calculate the attribute's value. In my case, I want to add the Duration in minutes to my Start time, so my method looks like this:

```
function Appointment.FinishDeriveAndSubscribe(
  reevaluateSubscriber, resubscribeSubscriber:
  ISubscriber): system.object;
begin
  AsIObject.Properties['Start'].
    SubscribeToValue(reevaluateSubscriber);
  AsIObject.Properties['Duration'].
    SubscribeToValue(reevaluateSubscriber);
  Result := Start.AddMinutes(Duration);
end;
```

You will also need to add Borland.Eco.Subscription to the uses clause, as this is where the ISubscriber interface referenced in the parameter list is defined. The last line of code makes sense, but what are the first two lines doing? Let's step back a bit. ECO does not actually derive the value of your attribute every time someone asks for it. Instead it caches the value of the attribute after it is first calculated and returns this cached value on subsequent requests, provided the attribute is not marked as being out of date. How would our attribute get marked as out of date? That's where the first two lines of the preceding code come in. I subscribed to be notified whenever the values of Start or Duration change. When I am notified, the ECO framework will flag my Finish attribute as out of date. Then, when the next request for its value is made, before the cached value is returned, this flag will be checked and the value of the attribute will be recalculated.

It's not quite as easy as using OCL, but it's much more powerful, as you now have full access to the entire .NET Framework to use in calculating your attribute's value.

Reverse Derived Attributes

If you take a look at source code for the Finish derived attribute declaration from the previous model, you'll note it looks like this (a read-only property):

```
property Finish: DateTime read get_Finish;
```

I hope this makes sense, given what you now know about derived attributes. If the value of my attribute is calculated, the framework by itself cannot figure out how to undo it—that is, it doesn't know how to tear apart the value into the original parts used to calculate it in the first place. This may not even be algorithmically possible.

However, sometimes it is possible, and in these cases we use a Reverse-Derived Attribute to tell the ECO framework how to do it. In the Appointment example, the Finish time was derived by taking the Start time and adding the number of minutes held in the Duration attribute. In my case, if someone assigns a new value to the Finish attribute, I'll change the Duration to reflect the difference between my Start time and this new Finish value.

To do this, select the Finish attribute in your model and, in the Object Inspector, set the DerivedSettable property to True. Notice in the source code for the Finish declaration, a setter method (called set_Finish) has been added. You'll add your logic to recalculate the Duration in this setter method, but first you need to tell ECO that you are changing the logic in here and to leave it alone in the future. You do this by removing the ECOAutoMaintained attribute from the property declaration in your source code (don't worry, there is a comment reminding you to do this in the generated setter method). Your new set_Finish method should look like this:

```
procedure Appointment.set_Finish(Value: DateTime);
begin
  { If you add user code here, please remove the
    [EcoAutoMaintained] attribute from the property
    declaration in the interface section }
  Duration := Convert.ToInt32(
    Value.Subtract(Start).TotalMinutes);
end;
```

The new value for Finish is passed in as the Value parameter. I subtract from this the Start time and use the difference in minutes to set the value of the Duration attribute. This means that not only can I set the Start and Duration and it will calculate the Finish, but I can also set the Finish and it will calculate a new Duration.

Derived Associations

Look at the model in Figure 18.6. There's a Person class and an Appointment class, with an association between them where an appointment can belong to only one person and a person can have zero to many appointments. Note however, that the appointment has a Confirmed attribute. You may decide that you need to deal with only confirmed appointments so often that you want another association between these two classes that displays only appointments that have the Confirmed attribute set.

However, this isn't really a new association, as it should be possible to calculate the collection of confirmed appointments from the existing association. If you're thinking that sounds a little like derived attributes, you're right. You can define a new association and use OCL to derive the collection of appointments you want to appear as part of this association.

Go ahead and define a new association between these two classes. Set it to be a one-way association by setting the `Navigable` property on the `Appointment` end (End2) to False. This association is for navigating from the person down to the appointment. In this scenario, you can still use the existing association to get from the appointment back up to the person. Whether an appointment is confirmed or not does not change the person who owns it.

Also set the association's `derived` property to True, and the `Persistence` property to Transient. Lastly, specify some OCL in the `End1TaggedValue.DerivationOCL` property. This is the OCL that is going to determine which `Appointment` objects appear as part of this association:

```
Appointments->select(Confirmed)
```

This OCL is basically saying: from all appointments associated with this person, select the subset where the `Confirmed` attribute is True.

Figure 18.7 shows the two associations at run time. `Person.Appointments` shows all appointments for a specific person (the second grid from the top), while `Person.ConfirmedAppointments` (the bottom grid) shows only those appointments for a specific person that have the `Confirmed` attribute set to True. Don't worry too much at this stage how I built this interface; I'll cover that later in the chapter.

FIGURE 18.6
The model before you
add a derived association

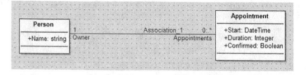

FIGURE 18.7
The user interface showing the derived association working at run time

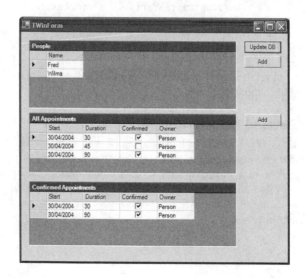

Association Classes

Let's forget ECO for a second and talk about why you might want Association classes in general. Think of the model you just looked at in the derived association example in the last section. There's a Person class and an Appointment class, and a relationship between them. The Appointment class has attributes for Start, Duration, and one for whether or not it is confirmed. It's this Confirmed attribute I want to focus on.

While at first it may seem obvious that the Confirmed attribute belongs on the Appointment class, that's actually not a very accurate model of our domain. You don't usually confirm an appointment, you confirm your participation in the appointment. While this might seem like a subtle difference, let me explain where it becomes important. Consider the case of a meeting with multiple attendees. You need to allow for the fact that some people will attend and some won't. This example doesn't support multiple persons per appointment, but it would be reasonable to expect this to occur in a real-world application. So in the case of multiple attendees per meeting, where does the Confirmed attribute belong if not on the Appointment class? It doesn't belong on the Person class. As I mentioned earlier, if you do not confirm an appointment, but rather you confirm a person's participation in an appointment, then Confirmed actually becomes an attribute of the association between the person and the appointment. This can be difficult to grasp at first, but remember, you are not just modeling classes. Equally important are the associations between those classes. So once we accept that associations can have attributes, the solution to allowing multiple people to attend multiple meetings becomes much simpler.

Let's think of another example. If you have a Person class and a Company class and an association between them that indicates employment, where would you put the start date of the employment? You wouldn't put it on the Person class (what if a person has multiple jobs?) and you wouldn't put it on the Company class (what if a company has multiple employees?). StartDate is really an attribute of the employment itself, which in this case is an association between the two classes.

So, how do you create an attribute on an association? Not surprisingly, you use an association class. You create a class and relate it to your association. Any attributes you want to add to the association, you add to your association class instead. Let's look at how you might model the changes to Appointment that we just discussed.

I've removed the Derived Relationship for now, but we'll add it back later. You can see in Figure 18.8 that I removed the Confirmed attribute from the Appointment and added another class called Participancy, which contains the Confirmed attribute. This Participancy class is going to be the association class. An association class is just a standard ECO class; you don't do anything special when creating the class to make it an association class. Just select the association between the two classes and enter the name of the association class, in this case Participancy, into the AssociationClass attribute. Just to make it stand out, I also changed the foreground color of my Participancy class.

In the diagram in Figure 18.9, I tried to show what this arrangement looks like in source code. Note that I built this diagram manually purely to explain what is going on. Don't go looking for a picture like this in the IDE.

FIGURE 18.8

Assigning the association class, Participancy, to the association

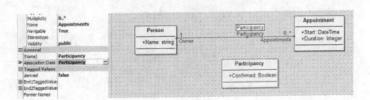

As you can see, there is still an association between `Person` and `Appointment`, and you can navigate that with absolutely no reference to the association class. However, there is also a path between `Person` and `Appointment` that goes via the association class. This effectively gives you two ways of navigating from `Person` to `Appointment`: you can use the existing direct association, or you can go via the association class.

From a `Person` object, there's an association to a collection of `Participancy` objects, one for each `Appointment` there is an association with. From an `Appointment` object, there's an association back to a single `Participancy` object. This makes sense, as an appointment is only associated with a single person.

In other words, this means that I can navigate from `Person` to `Appointment` (or vice versa) a few ways. Starting at the `Person` object, I can still use `self.Appointments`, which will return a collection of `Appointment` objects, but I can also use OCL as in Figure 18.10.

FIGURE 18.9
A conceptual model of our association class

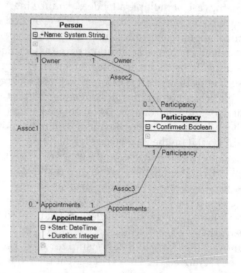

FIGURE 18.10
The OCL Expression Editor showing the OCL and the expected return value, in this case, a collection of `Participancy` objects

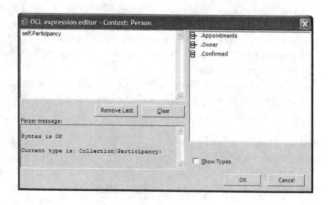

Notice my context (in the caption bar) is still `Person`. As it says at the bottom, `self.Participancy` will return a collection of `Participancy` objects. Also note on the right-hand side that each of these `Participancy` objects have the `Confirmed` attribute as well as an `Appointments` collection and `Owner` association.

If you reference the `Appointments` attribute of the `Participancy` object by using OCL as in Figure 18.11, it will return a collection of `Appointment` objects with the correct attributes (but note, as mentioned, the `Appointment` class now has a `Participancy` attribute as well).

If you use OCL as in Figure 18.12, it will return a collection of `Participancy` objects but only those where the `Confirmed` attribute is True. To complete the set, if you use OCL as in Figure 18.13, it will return a collection of all appointments for this person that are confirmed.

Of course, there's no black magic going on: you can access these same attributes in a similar way from Delphi code, as the attributes are there in code.

I hope this gives you some feeling for accessing the attributes of an association class. However, my model is still broken: I need to put back the derived relationship. This time I can use the association class. This is pretty easy now, as the last OCL example I showed is exactly the OCL I need. So, as before, create a one-way association between `Person` and `Appointment`, set it as Derived and Transient, and enter the following OCL in the `DerivationOCL` property:

```
self.Participancy->select(Confirmed).Appointments
```

FIGURE 18.11
OCL using the
`Association` class
to get to the
`Appointments`

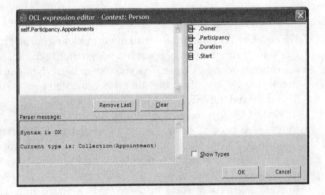

FIGURE 18.12
Using the `Select` operator, you can get back
only those `Participancy`
objects that have been
confirmed.

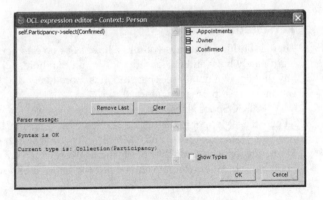

FIGURE 18.13

The last step, getting back the Appointment objects that have been confirmed via the association class. Note the expected return type is a collection of Appointment objects.

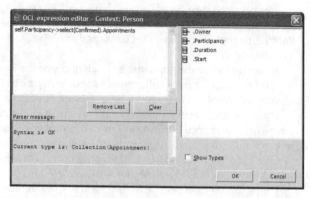

Now the model is restored and the ConfirmedAppointments derived relationship should work as before. However, by using the association class, we have more correctly modeled the true nature of the system. In addition, you probably realize that the Participancy class, while an association class, is still just a class, so it can have attributes, methods and even associations with other classes. Think about that last one for a while and you might start to see some interesting applications for association classes.

The ECOSpace

We've looked at different features of the modeling surface in ECO, but what actually happens with all this stuff at run time? A big part of understanding the answer to that question is first understanding the concept of an ECOSpace. As you remember, when you created your ECO application at the start of this chapter, one of the files that was generated for you was called MyFirstECOAppEcoSpace.pas. This is the default ECOSpace for your application.

An ECOSpace is responsible for managing all of your ECO classes in your application. It will create instances as needed, destroy them as needed, and importantly, also take care of loading and saving these objects to whatever data store you have selected (more on that in the next section).

If it makes it easier, think of an ECOSpace as a container for your objects at run time. Similar in concept to an EJB Container or a COM+ Container, it manages the objects for you, giving out references to objects as needed. You'll be using the ECOSpace quite a lot in the rest of this chapter, especially in the next section on persistence.

Persistence

There is nothing that says you must have your objects persist to a data store in ECO. You can quite legitimately have an ECO-based application that holds all of its objects in memory and never saves any of them to a database. That said, it is more likely that you'll need to save and load your objects to some sort of permanent storage.

Your ECOSpace is responsible for the persistence of your objects, and it uses a component called a PersistenceMapper to do this. ECO ships with PersistenceMapper components for SQL Server, BDP (Borland Data Providers), and XML files. As you'll see, the details of making your objects persist are kept quite separate from the objects themselves, which is a good thing. Your objects can be concerned about your business domain and be mostly ignorant of how, where, and even if they are stored. You can also change fairly easily from one data store to another simply by changing the Persistence-Mapper component used.

In this example, you'll be letting ECO have full control over the database. It can structure the tables and relationships between the tables however it sees fit. But this may not always be possible. Maybe you have to work with an existing database structure and cannot easily change it. ECO will also deal with this situation, allowing you to fully control the mapping between your object model and the database structure. Further, if you wish, it will even reverse-engineer the database structure into an object model that you can use as the starting point for your application. I will not be covering these topics in this introductory chapter, but if you follow the references at the end of the chapter you'll find material covering these and more.

Using ECO with Databases

ECO is natively designed to use an RDBMS as its primary choice of object storage. ECO handles the generation of the database schema, storage, and retrieval of application data, as well as maintaining database integrity by using transactions. In this example, you'll use InterBase, but the steps are similar for other PersistenceMapper components.

Open the `MyFirstECOAppEcoSpace` file and make sure the Design tab is selected in the editor. Drop a PersistenceMapperBDP component, from the Enterprise Core Objects category of the Tool Palette, on the design surface. Add a BDPConnection component by selecting the relevant InterBase database you wish to use from the Data Explorer window and dragging it on to the ECOSpace. If you haven't already, you may need to create an empty InterBase database and add it to the Data Explorer window.

Ensure that the following properties are set (shown here in code, but you may set these by using the Object Inspector):

```
persistenceMapperBDP1.Connection := BDPConnection1;
MyFirstECOAppEcoSpace.PersistenceMapper := persistenceMapperBDP1;
```

NOTE   Don't forget this last one, where you set the ECOSpace's `PersistenceMapper` property to the new persistence mapper component. Access this by clicking the blank area of the design surface. This will ensure ECO knows which persistence mapper to use to store you objects.

You will also need to right-click the PersistenceMapperBDP component and select the InterBase [dialect 3] setup menu item. This automatically sets a bunch of properties under the `sqlDatabaseConfig` property.

Creating the Database Schema

ECO can generate the database schema for the application based on its knowledge of your model. On the bottom-left corner of the design surface for the ECO Space, there is a Generate Schema button. Ensure that your application has been compiled since the most recent changes to the model (as ECO will use reflection to gather the metadata needed to know what tables to create, and so on), then click this button. A dialog box appears showing a list of tables that must be deleted and/or recreated. This list will be empty for the first schema generation. Click OK to proceed with the schema generation. If the database contains any data, that data will be lost.

The Delphi message window indicates the result of the process. In this example the database was being created for the first time, but quite frequently you will make changes to the model and want to update the database to take into account those changes. Clicking the next button, Evolve Database, will allow you to change the database to handle your new model while maintaining as much data as possible.

Okay, you've configured ECO to be able to persist your objects to InterBase, but how do you let the user actually invoke this persistence? I'll cover user interfaces and ECO in the "User Interfaces" section, but for now, realize that simply calling the `UpdateDatabase` method on your ECOSpace will cause the ECO framework to determine which objects in the database have changed and generate the necessary calls to the data store, in this case InterBase, to persist those changes.

That's all you have to do to save your data. Think about what you just achieved, and compare that to the code (both Delphi and SQL) that you would have had to write to persist your objects, not to mention the time you'd have had to take to create the database structure. Again, this emphasizes the fact that the main focus of attention in an ECO application is the model. The data store is just a place to save objects when they are not in use.

Optimistic Locking

When you have multiple users accessing the same application across a network, you need to consider the issue of collisions, i.e., if two people edit the same object at the same time, whose changes should be stored? This is where optimistic locking comes in. Let me give you an example.

Using my ECO application, I load a particular `Person` object from the database and start editing values. Meanwhile, my coworker Damien, who's running the same application, loads up the same `Person` object. Given that I have not yet persisted my changes to the database, when Damien loads his instance, he gets the data from the database. He then changes the `Firstname` property. I persist my changes to the database, and all is fine. However, at some point Damien is going to try and persist his changes to the database. Should his changes overwrite mine? Should his attempt to persist the changes fail? What if I didn't change the `Firstname` attribute? Should it still fail?

What happens when he tries to persist his changes depends on how you, the developer of this app, have configured optimistic locking.

Let's look at where you set up optimistic locking, then we'll look at what the different options mean. First, you need to turn optimistic locking on. Bring up your ECOSpace, click an empty area of the designer so that the Object Inspector shows the properties of the ECOSpace. You should see a Boolean property called `OptimisticLocking`. Set it to True.

But that's not all. Second, you need to specify the type of optimistic locking you want to occur for each class in your system. Bring up one of your class diagrams, select a class (make sure it's the class you have selected and not one of its attributes or methods) and look in the Object Inspector. You should see a property called `OptimisticLocking`. The default value of this is, appropriately enough, Default, but you can also choose Off, ModifiedMembers, AllMembers, or Timestamp. In the rest of this section we'll be looking at what happens when Damien tries to persist his changes to the `Person` object, depending on which of these values you selected.

OPTIMISTICLOCKING SET TO OFF

Setting `OptimisticLocking` to Off on your class means that no checks are performed before this object is persisted. So when Damien persists his changes, the following SQL is executed:

```
update Person
  set Firstname = 'Barney'
  where BOLD_ID = 3
```

Not surprisingly, this will overwrite any changes I may have made to the Firstname attribute for this person. Maybe that's what you want. Certainly it will execute faster than some of the other settings I'll mention shortly, but will quite possibly lead to lost information.

OPTIMISTICLOCKING SET TO DEFAULT

Default means that the OptimisticLocking behavior is determined by this class's ancestor. So, if Person descended from some other class, say a Contact class, then how Damien's Person class behaves in this situation depends on the value of Contact's OptimisticLocking property.

OPTIMISTICLOCKING SET TO MODIFIEDMEMBERS

As the name suggests, this value means that before ECO persists the Person object, it will check to see if any of the attributes that have been changed on the class have also been changed in the database. What this means, in the case of the Person object where Damien edited the Firstname property, is that the following SQL will be executed first:

```
SELECT B.BOLD_ID, B.BOLD_TYPE, B.Firstname
   FROM Person B
   WHERE B.BOLD_ID = 3
```

ECO will then check to see if the returned value for Firstname is the same as the value in the class before Damien edited it. If it's the same, ECO assumes that this field has not been changed in the database and proceeds to execute this SQL:

```
UPDATE Person
   SET Firstname = 'Barney'
   WHERE BOLD_ID = 3
```

However, if after executing the select, it finds that the value returned is different from the Firstname field prior to Damien's changes, it throws a Borland.Eco.Internal.BoldSystem. EBoldOperationFailedForObjectList exception with the message "Optimistic locking failed for 1 objects".

OPTIMISTICLOCKING SET TO ALLMEMBERS

I hope that by now you can guess what this one means. As with the previous example, ECO will check the database to see if the values are the same as when the Person object was first loaded, but this time it will check all attributes on the class, not just those that have been changed. So, in our example it will first execute SQL like this:

```
SELECT B.BOLD_ID, B.BOLD_TYPE, B.Firstname, B.Lastname
   FROM Person B
   WHERE B.BOLD_ID = 3
```

If all fields have the same value as the attributes of Person did prior to Damien's changes, it will then execute the following SQL:

```
UPDATE Person
   SET Firstname = 'Barney'
   WHERE BOLD_ID = 3
```

Note that it still only updates the fields that Damien changed, even though it first checks all fields.

PITSTOP

So far I don't think any of these examples have been very difficult to grasp. One way to look at them is that each setting gradually increases the requirements that must be satisfied in order for an object to be persisted successfully.

We started with no requirements (Off), then we went to the requirement that any attributes that are changed must not have been changed by anyone else (ModifiedMembers). We then stepped up a level again, requiring that none of the attributes of the class can have changed (AllMembers). The last setting (Timestamp) increases the strictness of these requirements another level again but does it in a slightly different way.

OPTIMISTICLOCKING SET TO TIMESTAMP

If you set OptimisticLocking to Timestamp on one or more of you classes, you'll need to go out to your PersistenceMapper component (in your ECOSpace) and change the SqlDatabaseConfig. UseTimestamp property to True. You'll also need to invoke the Evolve Database function so that ECO can create you a new table called ECO_TIMESTAMP. This table contains a single field called BOLD_TIME_STAMP, which despite its name, is an Integer field (at least in the InterBase example I built here).

Sticking with the same Person object example above, if OptimisticLocking is set to Timestamp, here's what happens when Damien tries to persist his Person object. First, ECO will execute the following SQL:

```
UPDATE ECO_TIMESTAMP
  SET BOLD_TIME_STAMP = BOLD_TIME_STAMP + 1
```

This does two things. It increments the Timestamp field and also returns the current value. ECO can then check that this value has not changed since this objects' fields were loaded from the database. If this value is the same, ECO will then execute this SQL to persist the object:

```
UPDATE Person
  SET Firstname = 'Barney'
  WHERE BOLD_ID = 3
```

If it finds the Timestamp field has been changed since this object was loaded (that is, the value in the field is greater than the one stored with the object) it will, like the other OptimisticLocking settings, throw a Borland.Eco.Internal.BoldSystem.EBoldOperationFailedForObjectList exception with the message "Optimistic locking failed for 1 objects".

Now, obviously this is a very simplistic example, but it should give you a feel for how optimistic locking works. The ability to assign different locking settings to different classes offers quite a bit of flexibility. You might have noticed that each setting gradually increases the potential scope that ECO will check before persisting an object: from nothing, to changed fields of an object, to all fields of an object, and finally, with Timestamp, to potentially other classes. If you want even more control, ECO has a feature called Regions, but exploration of that is beyond the scope of this introductory chapter.

User Interface

While it's perfectly possible to write an ECO application that does not have a GUI, many times you will want to connect a GUI to your ECO application. In this chapter, you'll be using WinForms-based GUIs, but, as I mentioned before, ECO also supports web-based user interfaces using ASP.NET. Once you can handle a WinForms-based ECO app, moving on to ASP.NET will not be difficult.

First, step back and think about what you need to do. You have the ECOSpace, which is managing the instances of all your objects. At the risk of over-simplifying, you can think of this as a container full of objects. As we've discussed, the objects in your ECOSpace know nothing about the user interface. Given all of that, from your user interface, at minimum you need to be able to do a few things:

◆ Select a subset of those objects from the container. That subset might be based on the type of object, the value of some of its properties, its status (whether it has been saved to the database or not), or many other combinations. Whatever your criteria for selection, you need to be able to retrieve a subset of objects. In the following sections on handles, we'll look at a few different ways to do this.

◆ Once you have that subset of objects, you may want to display them to the user. The section on databinding will cover this.

◆ You may not always know the criteria you want to use to select your subset until runtime, so the section on variables will show how to dynamically select that subset based on input from the user.

Handles

There are a number of nonvisual components you can use to create a WinForms GUI for your ECO app, and chief among these are handles. There are a few different sorts of handles, but at the risk of generalizing, a handle is a way to grab hold of one or more objects from your ECOSpace, or even your ECOSpace as a whole. Thinking of them as a GUI-version of a variable in source code is probably not a bad starting point. Let's look at a few different handles in turn, and I think it'll start to make sense.

ReferenceHandle

The ReferenceHandle is probably the first handle you'll come across, although possibly one of the least interesting. A ReferenceHandle serves as a connection point between other components on your form and your ECOSpace. If you've used the ECO Windows Form Application Wizard of the New Items dialog box to create an application, you'll note that it puts a ReferenceHandle on your main form automatically and calls it rhRoot. It also adds code to the form's constructor to ensure that the ReferenceHandle has a valid reference to the ECOSpace:

```
constructor TWinForm1.Create;
begin
  inherited Create;
  // Required for Windows Form Designer support
  InitializeComponent;


  FEcoSpace := TMyFirstECOAppEcoSpace1.Create;
  rhRoot.EcoSpace := FEcoSpace;


  // The line below will automatically activate the ECO Space on form create.
  // Remove the line if you wish to activate it manually

  FEcoSpace.Active := True;
end;
```

Most of the time, the only thing you'll do with your ReferenceHandle is connect other Handles to it. However, it's worth looking through its properties and methods once you are comfortable with the rest of this chapter to see whether they spark any creative ideas.

ExpressionHandle

Probably the handle you will use most often is the ExpressionHandle. Typically you will use an ExpressionHandle when you want to display one or more objects from your ECOSpace on your form. It has a `RootHandle` property that points to another handle that supplies the context for this Expression-Handle (I'll explain this in a second); it also has an `Expression` property that holds the OCL that will be executed in order to return the one or more objects you wish to access via this handle. It also implements the `IDataList` interface required by WinForms databinding so that standard .NET data bound controls can display objects from your ECOSpace rather than data sets from a database.

Let's have a look at an example. Assuming you have the `Person` class you've used before in the model, and you have your `rhRoot` ReferenceHandle component connected to your ECOSpace, you can drop down an ExpressionHandle, set its `RootHandle` property to `rhRoot`, and set the `Expression` property to the following OCL:

```
Person.allInstances
```

What this means is that your OCL will be evaluated and a reference to a collection of all the `Person` objects in your ECOSpace will be returned. It's quite possible the ECOSpace did not contain instances of all `Person` objects in memory and had to generate the SQL needed to load the others from the database. That's not your concern; let the ECOSpace worry about that. More than not being your concern, it highlights one of the real strengths of ECO: it encourages a nice clean separation between your business model, your user interface code, and your data-access logic. Of course, you could use different OCL to get different results.

NOTE By the end of this chapter you will have seen a few different OCL statements. To learn more, there is an excellent OCL tutorial (specifically for Bold, but it applies to ECO as well) at www .viewpointsa.com/bold_resources/getting_started_with_bold/Part3-OCL.html.

We'll come back to other Handles in a second, but I think it is worth talking about databinding at this point, so that you can complete this example and understand what I meant before when I said "It has a `RootHandle` property that points to another handle that supplies the context for this ExpressionHandle."

Databinding

One of the great features of ECO is that you can leverage all the power of WinForms databinding against your ECOSpace. Doing so is almost exactly as you would expect it to be. Your Expression-Handles (and other handles) show up as DataSources in the `DataSource` property of your .NET data bound controls, such as the DataGrid, and you can drill down into the attributes of you classes when binding other component properties.

If it was that easy, this would be a very short section. To a certain extent, databinding in ECO is just like "normal" databinding in .NET, once you get used to the fact that the data you are binding against comes from your objects, not from a result set. If you are coming from a VCL world and are used to VCL data-aware controls, then it won't take long to get used to .NET databinding.

That said, there is one concept you need to get used to if you are not already: CurrencyManagers.

CurrencyManagerHandle

One thing you'll probably find yourself doing fairly early in your .NET databinding career is to bind a DataGrid to an `IDataList`. As I mentioned before, the ExpressionHandle in ECO implements the `IDataList` interface, as does the DataSet. So, what's a CurrencyManager? Put out of your mind that it is anything to do with money or currencies. A CurrencyManager is essentially a cursor into your `IDataList`, which keeps track of the current item in the `IDataList`. Note this is a .NET concept, not an ECO concept.

Because ECO needs to play nicely in the .NET databinding world, it needs to deal with Currency-Managers. Let's say you used the example before in which you have an ExpressionHandle with `Person.allInstances` as the OCL and a DataGrid bound to the ExpressionHandle: the grid should display all your Person objects. You can even drop down a text box and bind its Text property to `ExpresionHandle1.Firstname`, and it will display the `Firstname` attribute of whichever `Person` object is currently selected in the grid. All great, and all done with no knowledge on your part of CurrencyManagers.

However, let's say you want to display a master/detail relationship on your form, for example, the `Person` and `Appointment` example from earlier (shown in Figure 18.14). If you just drop down another ExpressionHandle, set its `Name` to `ehAppointments`, set its `RootHandle` property to `rhRoot`, its `Expression` property to `Appointments.allInstances`, and bind another DataGrid to this ExpressionHandle, there will be absolutely no connection between the grid showing your `Person` objects and the grid showing the `Appointment` objects. All appointments will be displayed, not only the appointments for the selected person.

Instead of using `Appointments.allInstances` in your OCL, you really want to use "Appointments.allInstances for the currently selected Person." That isn't valid OCL, so you'll need to find another way.

Remember back when we were talking about ExpressionHandles, I said "It has a `RootHandle` property that points to another handle that supplies the context for this ExpressionHandle"? What you need to do is make your `ehAppointments` ExpressionHandle's context equal to whatever `Person` object is currently selected. In other words, you need to somehow connect the `RootHandle` property of your ExpressionHandle to the CurrencyManager being used by the grid displaying the `Person` objects.

So, how do you do it? Pretty easily actually. First you drop down another type of handle, a CurrencyManagerHandle. Next, set its `RootHandle` property to point to the ExpressionHandle that has `Person.allInstances` as its OCL and that has the DataGrid bound to it displaying all the `Person` objects. Also, set its `BindingContext` property to point to the DataGrid I just mentioned. This essentially gives you a Handle component that is connected to the CurrencyManager that points to the currently selected `Person` object. From here, you can use this CurrencyManagerHandle as the `RootHandle` property of your `ehAppointment` ExpressionHandle. However, when you bring up the Property Editor for the Expression property, as in Figure 18.15, you'll notice a couple of things.

FIGURE 18.14

The simple Person\
Appointments class
model

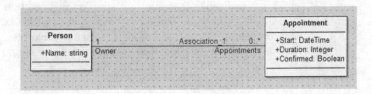

FIGURE 18.15

OCL that references the Appointments association of the Person object. Note the current context in the caption bar.

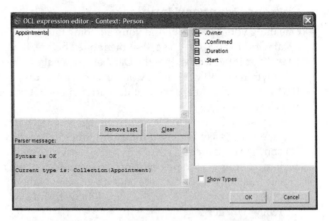

First, the caption shows that the context is now set to Person, which means the RootHandle property of our ExpressionHandle controls the context. In this case it is connected, via the Currency-ManagerHandle, to the currently selected Person object, so this makes sense. Second, the OCL doesn't have to say Appointments.allInstances. Instead, the OCL can reference the Appointments association of our Person class. This is really the same as saying self.Appointments, where the type of "self" is determined by your context, in this case, Person.

Also, now that you have changed your ExpressionHandle, your grid should behave correctly, displaying only the appointments related to the currently selected person.

OCLPSHandle

So far I've been ignoring the issue of performance. I've been behaving as if my application will perform identically whether I have 10 objects or 1,000,000 objects. Obviously, this is absurd, so let's look at one of the most direct ways ECO provides to deal with this issue, the OCLPSHandle.

Look at the following OCL, for example

```
Person.allInstances->select(Age < 18)
```

You should recognize that this OCL will return a collection of all Person objects that have the value of their Age attribute less than 18. If you use an ExpressionHandle to execute this OCL, as you have been doing in all the examples so far, a few things could happen. First, let's assume that your ECOSpace is empty, so any Person object you wish to access will need to be loaded from the database (we'll deal later with the case where your ECOSpace is not empty).

How can you see what happens when you request this OCL to be executed? There are a couple of tools that I find useful in this type of situation. One is some sort of SQL monitor so that I can view the actual SQL being executed by the ECO framework. The other is the OptimizeIt Profiler for .NET, a CPU and Memory Profiler that ships with the Architect edition of Delphi. The Memory Profiler in OptimizeIt allows you to peer inside you ECOSpace and see exactly what objects are in memory.

Back to the example, the behavior you'll get using an ExpressionHandle is that the preceding select filter will be executed by the ECOSpace. Assuming there are no Person objects in your ECOSpace when you execute this OCL using an ExpressionHandle, a number of SQL statements are executed. The example uses SQL Server, and in this case, ECO first executes this:

```
SELECT BOLD_ID, BOLD_TYPE
    FROM Person
```

Then the BOLD_IDs returned from this statement are used in the following SQL, to return the complete objects:

```
SELECT BOLD_ID, BOLD_TYPE, Firstname, Lastname, Age
    FROM Person
    WHERE BOLD_ID IN (...)
```

where the list of BOLD_IDs are inserted between the braces after the IN statement.

Think about this for a moment. This means that all your Person objects will be loaded from your database into your ECOSpace, and then the ECOSpace will filter out the correct Person objects and return your collection. While this might be fine for a small number of objects, what if you have 10,000 objects, or 100,000, or 1,000,000? This will rapidly become a problem. Just to be sure, the screenshot from OptimizeIt in Figure 18.16 shows that the ECOSpace after this statement is executed holds nine Person objects, even though the grid in Figure 18.17 only displays the two that match the select statement. Obviously, this is not very efficient.

How can you exercise some control over this? This is where you can use a component called OCLPSHandle. The PS in the name stands for Persistent Store because this component will attempt to convert the OCL into a SQL statement so that the filtering in this case will be executed by the back-end database rather than the ECOSpace. So, the same OCL as before except that it's loaded into an OCLPSHandle rather than an ExpressionHandle, results in the following SQL being executed:

```
SELECT BOLD_ID
    FROM Person
    WHERE (Age < 18)
```

Note the very important WHERE clause, which means the database will do the heavy lifting and only return the records that match the OCL filter. ECO can then request the full data only for the required objects. Again, using OptimizeIt will show you that after this OCL is executed, only the two matching objects exist in your ECOSpace, while the end result in your grid is the same.

FIGURE 18.16

Optimizelt profiler showing the number of active objects in the ECOSpace. Note the filter at the bottom of the screen to show only objects in the CoreClassesUnit namespace.

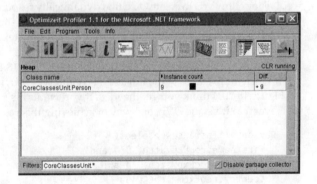

FIGURE 18.17
The results in the UI of
using the Expression-
Handle to filter

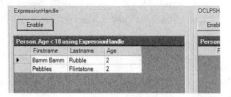

This is obviously much more efficient over the network and in terms of memory, and as a result, it also executes a lot faster. There are a couple of downsides you should be aware of, however. Whereas an ExpressionHandle will execute its OCL automatically, you need to call the `OCLPSHandle.Execute` method for it to execute the OCL and return the result. Still, it's a small price to pay for such improved performance.

Second, the OCLPSHandle, by its very nature, can only return objects that are stored in the database. If there was a `Person` object in memory that matched your OCL filter but that had not yet been persisted to the database, the OCLPSHandle would not by default include that in the resulting collection.

TIP   This can be worked around, and Christophe Floury in his excellent "Unleashing Enterprise Models" white paper at www.borland.com/products/white_papers/del_unleashing_ enterprise_models_with_delphi_for_dotnet.html shows example source for this very issue. Basically, he uses the OCLPSHandle as just discussed, then interrogates the ECOSpace and adds any `Person` objects to the resulting collection that have not yet been saved and that match the filter.

Taking this relatively simple step will result in applications that continue to perform well when the number of objects in your database grow.

Variables

If you've done any Delphi database programming, think about the SQL statements you've used. Have you always known all the SQL you want to use at design time? I'm guessing the answer is no. You quite often know most of the statement, but maybe at run time you have to substitute in some parameters for your Where clause, for example.

It's the same thing with OCL. So far we've been assuming we know all the OCL we intend to use at design time. Far more common is needing the same ability to use parameters in your OCL as you do with SQL. However, in ECO they are called variables rather than Parameters, but it's the same concept. They allow you to create OCL that dynamically responds to changes at run time. Let me give you an example. Say you want a search screen, like the one shown in Figure 18.18.

The figure shows a grid of `Person` objects and some text boxes above each field. I'd like to be able to start typing in one or more of the text boxes and have the grid only display the objects that match. So, if I type J in the first box, my grid looks like Figure 18.19.

If I then jump across to the third text box and type a U, my grid narrows further to the one shown in Figure 18.20. I think you get the idea. If you want this type of behavior, how are you going to achieve it? With static OCL, one way of achieving this result would be with OCL like this:

```
Person.allInstances->select(
  Firstname.regExpMatch("J") and
  Lastname.regExpMatch("") and
  Country.regExpMatch("U"))
```

FIGURE 18.18
A simple search screen where you can limit the number of objects displayed by entering text you want the attributes to match

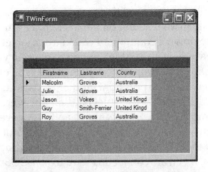

FIGURE 18.19
The search filter further refined

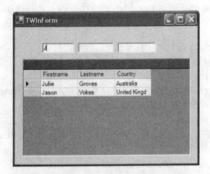

FIGURE 18.20
And I found the Person I'm after.

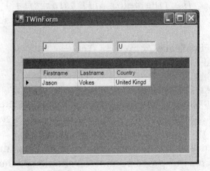

Note that you're using the select operator, which returns a collection of Person objects that match the Boolean expression inside the brackets. In this case, you're doing Regular Expression matching on each of the fields in order to return this Boolean expression. While it is true that this will work, you really want to be able to substitute in the values to match against at run time. You could build up this string dynamically, but another way is to use variables. Let's look at how you do it.

Apart from the preceding DataGrid and text boxes, you'll have a ReferenceHandle pointing at your ECOSpace and an ExpressionHandle connected up to the ReferenceHandle. The DataGrid is connected to your ExpressionHandle. If you've worked your way through the rest of this chapter, all of that should not be terribly difficult. Don't worry about what OCL to put in the ExpressionHandle just yet. What you need to do is to take the text entered into the text boxes and get it into some OCL. Start with just searching on the Firstname attribute, then look at what to do to search on all three.

Drop down a component called a VariableHandle. The VariableHandle is responsible for holding the value of a variable you wish to use in your OCL. Name it vhFirstname and drop down the ECOSpaceType property and select the type of the ECOSpace you are using. Why do you do this? Think about an ExpressionHandle. It connects to a ReferenceHandle that it uses to "reach into" your ECOSpace. A VariableHandle, however, does not connect to a ReferenceHandle. Strictly speaking, you can use it without an ECOSpace at all, although the situations where you will want to do this are fairly limited. Because it does not connect to a ReferenceHandle, you need to tell it the type of the ECOSpace to use (if any) by setting its ECOSpaceType property. Also, like a ReferenceHandle, if you are connecting it up to an ECOSpace, you need to make sure it has a reference to your ECOSpace. The wizard that created your ECO WinForm did this automatically for our ReferenceHandle, but you need to add the VariableHandle. Have a look in the form's constructor, and add the vhFirstname.EcoSpace := fEcoSpace line as follows:

```
constructor TWinForm1.Create;
begin
  inherited Create;
  // Required for Windows Form Designer support
  InitializeComponent;

  FEcoSpace := TMyFirstECOAppEcoSpace1.Create;
  rhRoot.EcoSpace := FEcoSpace;
  vhFirstname.EcoSpace := fEcoSpace;

  // The line below will automatically activate the ECO Space on form create.
  // Remove the line if you wish to activate it manually

  FEcoSpace.Active := True;
end;
```

You also need to specify the type of this variable. In this case, it's a string, but it could be a number, a date or time value, etc. Unlike SQL Parameters, it could be even more than this. Your variable could be a collection of strings, dates, an object, or even a collection of objects! Think about the flexibility that would provide.

So, to specify the type of our variable, use the StaticValueTypeName property. Click the ellipsis button for this property and you should see the Type Name Selector dialog shown in Figure 18.21, which allows you to select the simple type or class or collection of either that you want this VariableHandle to hold. In this case, select System.String.

Now that you have a VariableHandle to hold the value entered into the text box, how do you get the value in there? Go to the TextBox component and put the following code into its TextChanged event:

```
vhFirstname.Element.AsObject := txtFirstname.Text;
```

FIGURE 18.21
The list of types in the
ECO application. In
this case you want the
variable to be of type
System.String.

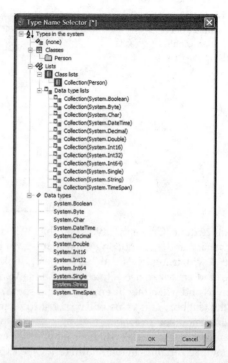

Now whenever the user changes the text in the text box, your VariableHandle component will be updated with the new value. You can replicate this for the other attributes you want to search on: drop down two more VariableHandles, set their `ECOSpaceType` and `StaticValueTypeName` properties, add the relevant code to the `get_ECOSpace` method, and set up `TextChanged` events on the relevant text boxes so that the VariableHandles get updated as the user changes the search text.

That's great, but you still have no connection between the VariableHandles and the OCL in your ExpressionHandle. To hook them up, you need to drop down an OCLVariables component. This component is responsible for holding a collection of variables used in OCL and the relevant Variable-Handles from which their values should be retrieved. Select the OCLVariable component and bring up the property editor for the OclVariablesCollection property. Add three members to the collection and, for each one, set the `ElementHandle` and `VariableHandle` properties. In Figure 18.22, you can see how I set the first one.

This screenshot shows that I created a connection between the vhFirstname VariableHandle component and a variable called vFirstname. I did the same for LastName and Country.

The last piece is to connect the ExpressionHandle that is connected to your DataGrid to your OCLVariables component using the ExpressionHandle's `Variables` property. Then, enter the following OCL into your ExpressionHandle:

```
Person.allInstances->select(
    Firstname.regExpMatch(vFirstname) and
    Lastname.regExpMatch(vLastname) and
    Country.regExpMatch(vCountry))
```

FIGURE 18.22
Connecting the Variable-Handles to the variable names used in the OCL

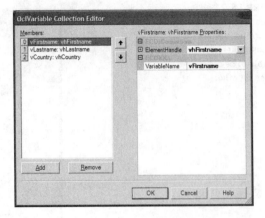

You're done. Conceptually, when the OCL is evaluated, the OCL parser will come across vFirstname and, not knowing what that is, will go out to the ExpressionHandle and request the value. It will, using its Variables property, look in the OCLVariables component and see that the value of vFirstname needs to come from the VariableHandle called vhFirstname. This value will be retrieved and will either be empty or hold some string value that was assigned when the user typed into the text box. This value will be substituted into the OCL. The same happens for the other two variables, and you're away.

A few things to realize: In this case you're using strings and the regExpMatch OCL function, but you can use variables in many different OCL expressions and with many different types. Also, as I mentioned before, your variable could contain a collection or an object (or a collection of objects) and, provided that type was valid where you were placing your variable in your OCL, that's fine. Once you have this sample up and running, try changing around the OCL and even changing the types of your variables and see what you can come up with.

ECO in Code

No matter how many components you drag and drop, how much UML you design, and how much OCL you write, the reality is that you still will end up writing Delphi or C# code in your ECO applications. Some of that code is "inside" your ECO model (the code in methods of your ECO objects) and some of it is "outside" your ECO model (button click events and so on). Either way, you need to know how to interact with ECO from code.

The developers of ECO have gone out of their way to make writing code in an ECO app very similar to any other object-oriented application. Code "inside" your ECO model looks especially very similar to code inside any other object model. Code "outside" can look a little different, given that it tends to interact with the ECO API more frequently and that it needs to get "inside" the ECO model more frequently (for example, to call a method on an ECO object). So, let's look at a few examples.

Creating Objects Part 1

In the click event of a button, you may want to create an instance of an ECO object and place it into your ECOSpace. This is fairly straightforward:

```
procedure TWinForm.Button1_Click(
  sender: System.Object; e: System.EventArgs);
var
  tmpPerson : Person;
begin
  tmpPerson := Person.Create(EcoSpace);
end;
```

This is really no different from creating an instance of a class in a non-ECO Delphi app. The only real difference is that the constructor takes a reference to the ECOSpace that should be responsible for managing this object. In this case, you're passing in the EcoSpace property of your form.

Getting a Reference to the Currently Selected Object

You learned earlier that you use a CurrencyManagerHandle when you want to reference the currently selected object in, say, a DataGrid. Sometimes you may want to reference that same object from code:

```
Text := (cmhPerson.Element.AsObject as Person).Name;
```

The code above uses the cmhPerson CurrencyManagerHandle and references its Element property, which represents the currently selected object's IElement interface. However, you don't want that object's IElement interface, you want a reference to the actual object. IElement provides the AsObject method, which returns a System.Object. You can then cast this to the specific type, in this case Person, and reference the Person class's methods, properties, and so on. This is essentially an example of getting from "outside" the ECO model to "inside." Once you can get a reference to an IElement, you can get down to the ECO object itself, and from there you are inside the model. You'll find yourself using this pattern again and again.

Creating Objects Part 2

Think back to the Person and Appointment example earlier, where we displayed a master/detail relationship. In that example, if you were creating a new Appointment object, you would not only want to add it to the ECOSpace, but you'd need to connect it to the correct Person object. Now that you've seen the previous two examples, this should not be very hard:

```
procedure TWinForm.Button5_Click(
  sender: System.Object; e: System.EventArgs);
var
  tmpAppointment : Appointment;
begin
  tmpAppointment := Appointment.Create(EcoSpace);
  tmpAppointment.Owner :=
    (cmhPerson.Element.AsObject as Person);
end;
```

Executing OCL from Code

As you saw, you can use an ExpressionHandle to execute OCL against your ECOSpace, but this is really only necessary if you want to display the result of that OCL using data binding. Sometimes, you may just want to execute some OCL and operate on the result in code:

```
procedure TWinForm.Button1_Click(
  sender: System.Object; e: System.EventArgs);
var
  OCLResult : IElement;
  ObjList : IObjectList;
  i : Integer;
begin
  OCLResult := ECOSpace.OclService.EvaluateAndSubscribe(
    nil, 'Person.AllInstances', nil, nil);
  if OCLResult is IObjectList then
  begin
    ObjList := IObjectList(OCLResult);
    for i := 0 to ObjList.Count - 1 do
    begin
      MessageBox.Show(
        Person(ObjList.Item[i].AsObject).Name);
    end;
  end;
end;
```

In the preceding example, you use the `OclService` property of your ECOSpace to call `EvaluateAndSubscribe` with the OCL `Person.allInstances`. This returns an `IElement`, which you can then test to see if it is a collection of objects or, more specifically, an `IObjectList`. You then iterate over the collection, grabbing each `Item` property, which again is an `IElement`, using `AsObject` and casting it as a `Person` to reference its attributes and methods. Again, this last bit is the same pattern you saw in the last example.

These are only a few samples, but they should give you a feeling for how to interact with ECO from code. They also introduced one of the ECO Services, the OclService. ECO exposes much of its API via Services. It's well worth your time, once you are comfortable with the contents of this chapter, to look at some of the other services exposed via the ECOSpace, such as the PersistenceService, DirtyList-Service, UndoService, TypeSystemService, ObjectFactoryService, and the VariableFactoryService.

NOTE I will be exploring some of these services in more detail in future entries on my blog (http:// blogs.borland.com/malcolmgroves). In addition, the Borland ECO Center referenced at the end of this chapter contains links to a number of white papers that include coverage of these services as well.

What's Next

This chapter provided you with an introduction to the ECO framework available in Delphi 2005 Architect. You should now have an appreciation for how ECO works and how you may be able to use it to very quickly build well-structured, model-based applications.

You saw that in ECO the model becomes the most important piece of the application. I covered a number of tools you can use to express yourself clearly in the model, kind of like a vocabulary for modeling. We then looked at some of ECO's powerful support for Object Persistence. You saw how you can leave ECO to manage the details of the database, allowing you to focus on the model. Last, we looked at how to present your model to the user and the productivity ECO gives in this area by leveraging .NET databinding.

ECO has many more capabilities than I've covered here, and the time you invest to become familiar with ECO will pay you back in application quality and development productivity in short order. I find the best way to learn about ECO is to get in and write some applications using it. I hope I've given you enough grounding in the basics that that exploration will be easier. For further information, visit Borland's ECO Center at www.borland.com/delphi/architect/eco/ and read the sections under borland.public.delphi.modeldrivenarchitecture of Borland's newsgroup.

This chapter ends the third part of the book, devoted to database technologies. The next part will be devoted to Internet programming techniques. We'll start in Chapter 19 with the coverage of the HTTP protocol and the dynamic generation of HTML and move in the following chapters to the various web development frameworks available in Delphi, WebSnap, IntraWeb, and ASP.NET.

Part 4

Delphi and the Internet

In this section:

Chapter 19

HTML and HTTP Development

In recent years, writing programs for the Web has become commonplace, so I've devoted the last portion of the book to discussing various technologies related to the HTTP protocol. These technologies include HTML, CGI and web server extensions, XML, SOAP, and the frameworks commonly used for web development in Delphi (WebSnap, IntraWeb, and ASP.NET). This first chapter introduces low-level socket programming and Internet protocols and then focuses on core Delphi technologies for server-side web programming.

I'll begin by looking at sockets technology in general; then I'll move to the use of the Internet Direct (Indy) components supporting both low-level socket programming and the most common Internet protocols. I will introduce some elements of the HTTP protocol, leading up to building HTML files from database data. Next, you will learn how to integrate the dynamic generation of HTML documents within a server.

WARNING   To test some of the examples in this chapter, you'll need access to a web server. The simplest solution is to use the version of Microsoft's IIS already installed on your computer (or Personal Web Server if you have Windows 9x). As an alternative to ASP.NET you can use Cassini server, described in Chapter 21. My personal preference, however, is to use the free open-source Apache Web Server available at www.apache.org. I won't spend much time giving you details of the configuration of your web server to enable the use of dynamic applications; you can refer to the documentation of the specific server for this information.

Building Socket Applications

Delphi 2005 ships with two sets of TCP components—Indy socket components (IdTCPClient and IdTCPServer) and native Borland components, which are hosted in the Internet page of the Component palette. The Borland components, TcpClient and TcpServer, were developed to replace the ClientSocket and ServerSocket components available in past versions of Delphi. However, now that the Client-Socket and ServerSocket components have been declared obsolete, Borland suggests using the corresponding Indy components instead.

In this chapter I'll focus on using Indy during my discussion of low-level socket programming, as well as in the coverage of high-level Internet protocols. To learn more about the Indy project, refer to the sidebar "Internet Direct (Indy) Open Source Components"; keep reading to see how you can use these components for low-level socket programming.

Before I present an example of a low-level socket-based communication, let's take a tour of the core concepts of TCP/IP so you understand the foundations of the most widespread networking technology.

INTERNET DIRECT (INDY) OPEN SOURCE COMPONENTS

Delphi ships with a collection of open-source Internet components called Internet Direct (Indy). The Indy components are built by a group of developers led by Chad Hower. They are available for Win32, .NET, and Linux. You can find more information and the most recent versions of the components at www.indyproject.org.

Delphi 2005 ships with both Indy 9 and Indy 10, although only one set of components is installed in the IDE (a setting you pick during Delphi installation); you should check the website for updated versions. The components are free and are complemented by many examples and a reasonable help file. Indy 10 marks the full .NET version of Indy, which can also be used with other .NET programming languages.

With more than 150 components installed on Delphi's palette, Indy has an enormous number of features, ranging from the development of client and server TCP/IP applications for various protocols to encoding and security. You can recognize Indy components from the Id prefix. Rather than list the various components here, I'll touch on a few of them throughout this chapter.

BLOCKING AND NONBLOCKING CONNECTIONS

When you're working with sockets in Windows, reading data from a socket or writing to it can happen asynchronously, so that it does not block the execution of other code in your network application. This is called a *nonblocking connection*. The Windows socket support sends a message when data is available. An alternative approach is the use of *blocking connections,* where your application waits for the reading or writing to be completed before executing the next line of code. When you're using a blocking connection, you must use a thread on the server, and you'll generally also use a thread on the client.

The Indy components use blocking connections exclusively. Because of this, any client socket operation that might be lengthy should be performed within a thread or by using Indy's IdAntiFreeze component as a simpler but limited alternative. Using blocking connections to implement a protocol has the advantage of simplifying the program logic because you don't have to use the state-machine approach of nonblocking connections.

All the Indy servers use a multithreaded architecture that you can control with the IdThreadMgrDefault and IdThreadMgrPool components. The first is used by default; the second supports thread pooling and should provide for faster connections.

Foundations of Socket Programming

To understand the behavior of the socket components, you need to understand several terms related to the Internet in general and to sockets in particular. The heart of the Internet is the *Transmission Control Protocol/Internet Protocol (TCP/IP)*, a combination of two separate protocols that work together. In brief, IP is responsible for defining and routing the *datagrams* (Internet transmission units) and specifying the addressing scheme. TCP is responsible for higher-level transport services.

ADDRESSES AND PORTS

Each computer on a TCP/IP network has an assigned IP address, usually written as four numbers separated by dots (as in 192.168.0.0). Instead of IP addresses you can refer to computers by a domain name. How does the IP address map to a domain name? On the Internet, the client program looks up the values on a domain name server, but it is also possible to have a local `Hosts` file, a text file you can easily edit to provide local mappings.

You may wonder whether to use an IP or a domain name in your programs. Domain names are easier to remember and won't require a change if the IP address changes (for whatever reason). On the other hand, IP addresses don't require any resolution, whereas domain names must be resolved (a time-consuming operation if the lookup takes place on the Web).

Each TCP connection takes place though a *port*, which is represented by a 16-bit number. Different processes running on the same machine cannot use the same port.

Some TCP ports have a standard usage for specific high-level protocols. You should use those port numbers only when implementing those services, which include:

Protocol	Port
HTTP (Hypertext Transfer Protocol)	80
FTP (File Transfer Protocol)	21
SMTP (Simple Mail Transfer Protocol)	25
POP3 (Post Office Protocol, version 3)	110
Telnet	23

The `Services` file (a text file similar to the `Hosts` file) lists the standard ports used by services. Client sockets always specify the port number or the service name of the server socket to which they want to connect.

SOCKET CONNECTIONS

To begin communication through a socket, the server program starts running first, but it simply waits for a request from a client. The client program requests a connection indicating the server it wishes to connect to. When the client sends the request, the server can accept the connection, starting a specific server-side socket, which connects to the client-side socket.

To support this model, there are three types of socket connections:

♦ *Client connections* are initiated by the client and connect a local client socket with a remote server socket. Client sockets must describe the server they want to connect to by providing its hostname (or its IP address) and its port.

♦ *Listening connections* are passive server sockets waiting for a client. Once a client makes a new request, the server spawns a new socket devoted to that specific connection and then gets back to listening. Listening server sockets must indicate the port that represents the service they provide. (The client will connect through that port.)

♦ *Server connections* are activated by servers; they accept a request from a client.

These different types of connections are important only for establishing the link from the client to the server. Once the link is established, both sides are free to make requests and to send data to the other side.

Using Indy's TCP Components

To let two programs communicate over a socket (either on a local area network or over the Internet), you can use the IdTCPClient and IdTCPServer components of the Indy library. As I mentioned earlier, there are two versions of Indy available with Delphi, Indy 9 and Indy 10. If you have existing applications based on Indy, you might want to stick with Indy 9, as the new version has been redesigned and has many incompatibilities at the low level. The differences are particularly relevant for the low-level components (like the IdTCPClient and IdTCPServer components used in this section), while few elements change for the higher level protocols. In this book I upgraded the examples from Indy 9 to Indy 10, something that took me much more time than I expected. My goal, though, was to have examples I could build both on Win32 and .NET, and Indy 10 allowed me to achieve it.

NOTE   When you install Delphi, you pick up the version of Indy you want to see enabled at design time. If you later want to switch your Indy version, you can follow the detailed steps provided in the Readme.html file of Delphi 2005. Basically, you have to change the set of installed design time packages and fix the Win32 Library Path to include either $(BDS)\lib\Indy9 or $(BDS)\lib\Indy10. A further change relates to the Browsing path.

To create a client and a server application based on Indy sockets, you use the two components just mentioned. Place one of them on a program form and the other on another form in a different program; then, make them use the same port, let the client program refer to the host of the server program, and you'll be able to open a connection between the two applications. For example, you can use these settings:

```
// server program
object IdTCPServer1: TIdTCPServer
  DefaultPort = 1050
end
// client program
object IdTCPClient1: TIdTCPClient
  Host = 'localhost'
  Port = 1050
end
```

At this point, in the client program you can connect to the server by executing

```
IdTCPClient1.Connect;
```

The server program has a list box used to log information. When a client connects or disconnects, the program lists the IP of that client along with the operation, as in the following OnConnect event handler:

```
procedure TFormServer.IdTCPServer1Connect(AThread: TIdPeerThread);
begin
  lbLog.Items.Add ('Connected from: ' +
    AThread.Connection.Socket.Binding.PeerIP);
end;
```

Now that you have set up a connection, you need to make the two programs communicate. Both the client and server sockets have read and write methods you can use to send data. Notice, though, that the client-side syntax for writing directly on the socket has changed from

```
IdTCPClient1.WriteLn('execute');
```

of Indy 9 to the following Indy 10 code:

```
IdTCPClient1.IOHandler.WriteLn('execute');
```

In particular, when the client connects to this server, the server sends back a greeting message, so the client code should look like:

```
procedure TFormClient.btnConnectClick(Sender: TObject);
begin
  IdTCPClient1.Connect;
  ShowMessage (IdTCPClient1.IOHandler.ReadLn);
end;
```

NOTE   If some data is sent over the socket you *must* read it right away; otherwise you'll receive it within the result of the following command.

Writing a multithreaded server that can receive many different commands (usually based on strings) and operate differently on each of them is far from trivial. For this reason, on the server side you can use the IdCmdTCPServer component, which provides easy to use management of commands. In Indy 9 the two components were combined in the class TIdTCPServer. In Indy 10, the command management capability has been moved to the inherited class TIdCmdTCPServer.

This command architecture simplifies the development of a server. In a server, you can define a number of commands, which are stored in the CommandHandlers collection. In the IndySock1 example the server has three handlers, all implemented differently to show you some of the possible alternatives.

The first server command, called test, is the simplest one, because it is fully defined in its properties. I set the command string, a numeric code, and a string result in the NormalReply property of the command handler:

```
object IdTCPServer1: TIdTCPServer
  CommandHandlers = <
    item
      CmdDelimiter = ' '
      Command = 'test'
      Disconnect = False
      Name = 'TIdCommandHandler0'
      NormalReply.Code = '100'
      NormalReply.Text.Strings = (
        'Hello from your Indy Server')
      ParamDelimiter = ' '
      ParseParams = False
      Tag = 0
    end
```

The client code used to execute the command and show its response is as follows:

```
procedure TFormClient.btnTestClick(Sender: TObject);
begin
  IdTCPClient1.SendCmd ('test');
  ShowMessage (IdTCPClient1.LastCmdResult.TextCode + ' : ' +
    IdTCPClient1.LastCmdResult.Text.Text);
end;
```

For more complex cases, you should execute code on the server and read and write directly over the socket connection. This approach is shown in the second command of the trivial protocol I came up with for this example. The server's second command is called **execute**, is defined in a command handler similar to the previous one, and also has the following OnCommand event handler:

```
procedure TFormServer.IdTCPServer1TIdCommandHandler1Command(
  ASender: TIdCommand);
begin
  lbLog.Items.Add ('Execute command from: ' +
    ASender.Context.Connection.Socket.Binding.PeerIP);
  ASender.SendReply;
  ASender.Context.Connection.IOHandler.WriteLn (
    'This is a dynamic response');
end;
```

As you can see, the server logs the request, sends back the header of the reply, and finally writes directly on the socket. The corresponding client code writes the command name to the socket connection and then reads the header and the single-line response:

```
procedure TFormClient.btnExecuteClick(Sender: TObject);
begin
  IdTCPClient1.SendCmd ('execute');
  ShowMessage (IdTCPClient1.LastCmdResult.Code + ' : ' +
    IdTCPClient1.LastCmdResult.Text.Text);
  ShowMessage (IdTCPClient1.IOHandler.ReadLn);
end;
```

A more interesting extension is provided by the third and last command in the example, which allows the client program to request a bitmap file from the server (in a sort of file-sharing architecture). The server command has parameters (the filename) and is defined as follows:

```
object IdTCPServer1: TIdTCPServer
  CommandHandlers = <
    item
      CmdDelimiter = ' '
      Command = 'getfile'
      Disconnect = False
      Name = 'TIdCommandHandler2'
      NormalReply.Code = '200'
      NormalReply.Text.Strings = (
        'OK for getfile')
```

```
    ParamDelimiter = ' '
    Tag = 0
    OnCommand = IdTCPServer1TIdCommandHandler2Command
  end>
```

The code uses the first parameter as a filename and returns it in a stream. In case of error, it raises an exception, which will be intercepted by the server component, which in turn will terminate the connection (not a very realistic solution but a safe approach and a simple one to implement). The normal flow, instead, is made of a standard header, followed by a string with the stream size, and then the stream itself:

```
procedure TFormServer.IdTCPServer1TIdCommandHandler2Command(
  ASender: TIdCommand);
var
  filename: string;
  aStream: TFileStream;
  aIdStream: TIdStreamVCL;
begin
  if Assigned (ASender.Params) then
    filename := TIdUri.URLDecode (ASender.Params [0]);
  lbLog.Items.Add ('File request [' + filename + '] from: ' +
    ASender.Context.Connection.Socket.Binding.PeerIP);
  if not FileExists (filename) then
  begin
    lbLog.Items.Add ('File not found: ' + filename);
    raise EIdTCPServerError.Create ('File not found: ' + filename);
  end
  else
  begin
    ASender.SendReply;
    aStream := TFileStream.Create(filename,
      fmOpenRead or fmShareDenyWrite);
    try
      ASender.Context.Connection.IOHandler.Writeln (
        IntToStr (aStream.Size));
      aIdStream := TIdStreamVCL.Create(aStream, False);
      try
        ASender.Context.Connection.IOHandler.
          Write (aIdStream, aIdStream.Size);
        lbLog.Items.Add ('File returned: ' + filename +
          ' (' + IntToStr (aIdStream.Size) + ')');
      finally
        aIdStream.Free;
      end;
    finally
      aStream.Free;
    end;
  end;
end;
```

The call to the TIdUri.URLDecode utility function on the parameter is required to decode a pathname that includes spaces as a single parameter; at the reverse the client program calls TIdUri.URLEncode or TIdUri.ParamsEncode. As you can see, the server also logs the files returned and their sizes or an error message. In Indy 10 the stream operations are based on the TIdStream class, a generic class that caters to stream differences between the VCL on Win32 and the FCL on .NET. Specific derived classes, like TIdStreamVCL, are wrappers of the platform streams.

The client program reads the stream and copies it into an Image component to show it directly (see Figure 19.1):

```
procedure TFormClient.btnGetFileClick(Sender: TObject);
var
  wrapperStream: TIdStreamVCL;
  realStream: TMemoryStream;
  strSize: string;
  nSize: Integer;
begin
  IdTCPClient1.SendCmd('getfile ' +
    TIdUri.ParamsEncode (edFileName.Text));
  ShowMessage (IdTCPClient1.LastCmdResult.Code + ' : ' +
    IdTCPClient1.LastCmdResult.Text.Text);
  strSize := IdTCPClient1.IOHandler.ReadLn;
  nSize := StrToInt (strSize);
  realStream := TMemoryStream.Create;
  wrapperStream := TIdStreamVCL.Create (realStream, False);
  try
    IdTCPClient1.IOHandler.ReadStream (wrapperStream, nSize);
    realStream.Position := 0;
    Image1.Picture.Bitmap.LoadFromStream (realStream);
  finally
    realStream.Free;
    wrapperStream.Free;
  end;
end;
```

FIGURE 19.1

The client program of the IndySock1 example

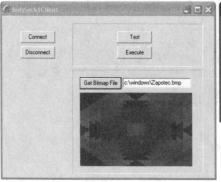

This simple example can be extended supporting the exchange of larger files and of database data, but in general it is better to build similar programs on top of HTML, possibly using the SOAP technology.

Now that you have a basic understanding of sockets, we can jump to the core topic of the chapter, which is the use of the HTTP protocol.

NOTE   Not only can you compile the source code in Delphi for .NET, you can also use the Win32 client with the .NET server and the .NET client with the Win32 server.

Working with HTTP

There are several Internet protocols that are interesting such as handling mail messages with SMTP and POP3. Handling mail protocols in client applications with the Indy component is relatively simple, and there are ready-to-use examples that ship with Indy itself.

NOTE   You'll have to download the Indy demos because the Indy 9 examples are not installed with Delphi and there are only two Indy 10 examples in the folder BDS\3.0\Demos\Indy10. The Indy demos area is available on www.indyproject.org/Demos.

The other popular protocol is HTTP, which is used by web servers and web browsers. To show a web page from your application you can use the TWebBrower control, which is a wrapper around the Internet Explorer ActiveX control, or you can activate the browser installed on the user's computer—for example, opening an HTML page by calling the ShellExecute method (defined in the ShellApi unit):

```
ShellExecute (Handle, 'open', FileName, '', '', sw_ShowNormal);
```

Using ShellExecute, you can simply execute a document, such as a file. Windows will start the program associated with the .htm or .html extensions using the action passed as the parameter (in this case, open, although passing nil would have invoked the standard action producing the same effect). You can use a similar call to view a website by using a string such as 'http://www.example.com' instead of a filename. In this case, the system recognizes the *http* section of the request as requiring a web browser and launches it.

On the server side, you generate and make available the HTML pages or graphic files. At times it may be enough to have a way to produce static pages, occasionally extracting new data from a database table to update the HTML files as needed. In other cases, you'll need to generate pages dynamically based on a request from a user.

As a starting point, I'll discuss HTTP by building a simple but complete client and server; then I'll move on to discuss HTML producer components. After this introduction, I'll move from this "core technology" level to the RAD development style for the Web supported by Delphi, introducing the web server extension technologies (CGI, ISAPI, and Apache modules) and discussing the WebBroker architecture.

Grabbing HTTP Content with the IdHTTP Component

As an example of the use of the HTTP protocols, I wrote a specific search application. The program hooks onto the Google website, searches for a keyword, and retrieves the first 100 sites found. Instead of showing the resulting HTML file, the program parses it to extract only the URLs of the related sites to a list box. The description of these sites is kept in a separate string list and displayed as you click a list-box item. The program demonstrates two techniques at once: retrieving a web page and parsing its HTML code.

To demonstrate how you should work with blocking connections, such as those used by Indy, I implemented the program using a background thread for the processing. This approach also gives you the advantage of being able to start multiple searches at once. The thread class used by the WebFind application receives as input a URL to look for, strUrl. For more information about multi-threading in Delphi, see the sidebar "Threads in Delphi."

THREADS IN DELPHI

When you need to perform background operations or any processing not strictly related to the user interface, you can follow the technically most correct approach: spawn a separate thread of execution within the process. Multithreaded programming might seem like an obscure topic, but it really isn't that complex, even if you must consider it with care. It is worth knowing at least the basics of multithreading, because in the world of sockets and Internet programming, there is little you can do without threads.

THE *TTHREAD* CLASS

Delphi's RTL library provides a TThread class that will let you create and control threads. This class is also available in Delphi for .NET, where it encapsulates the System.Threading.Thead class of the FCL. You will never use the TThread class directly because it is an abstract class—a class with a virtual abstract method. To use threads, you always subclass TThread and use the features of this base class.

The TThread class has a constructor with a single parameter (CreateSuspended) that lets you choose whether to start the thread immediately or suspend it until later. If the thread object starts automatically or when it is resumed, it will run its Execute method until it is done. The class provides a protected interface, which includes the two key methods for your thread subclasses:

```
procedure Execute; virtual; abstract;
procedure Synchronize(Method: TThreadMethod);
```

The Execute method, declared as a virtual abstract procedure, must be redefined by each thread class. It contains the thread's main code—the code you would typically place in a *thread function* when using the system functions.

The Synchronize method is used to avoid concurrent access to VCL components. The VCL code runs inside the program's main thread, and you need to synchronize access to VCL to avoid re-entry problems (errors from re-entering a function before a previous call is completed) and concurrent access to shared resources. The only parameter of Synchronize is a method that accepts no parameters, typically a method of the same thread class. Because you cannot pass parameters to this method, it is common to save some values within the data of the thread object in the Execute method and use those values in the *synchronized* methods.

Delphi includes two versions of Synchronize that allow you to synchronize a method with the main thread without calling it from the thread object. Both the overloaded Synchronize and StaticSynchronize are class methods of TThread and require a thread as parameter.

Another way to avoid conflicts is to use the synchronization techniques offered by the operating system. The SyncObjs unit defines a few VCL classes for some of these low-level synchronization objects, such as events (with the TEvent class and the TSingleEvent class) and critical sections (with the TCriticalSection class). (Synchronization events should not be confused with Delphi events, as the two concepts are unrelated.)

AN EXAMPLE OF THREADING

For an example of a thread, you can refer to the BackTask example (which also shows other background processing techniques not discussed here). This example spawns a secondary thread for computing the sum of the prime numbers. The thread class has the typical Execute method, an initial value passed in a public property (Max), and two internal values (FTotal and FPosition) used to synchronize the output in the ShowTotal and UpdateProgress methods. The following is the complete class declaration for the custom thread object:

```
type
  TPrimeAdder = class(TThread)
  private
    FMax, FTotal, FPosition: Integer;
  protected
    procedure Execute; override;
    procedure ShowTotal;
    procedure UpdateProgress;
  public
    property Max: Integer read FMax write FMax;
  end;
```

The Execute method has the same algorithm executed directly by other methods of the BackTask example, not discussed here. The only difference is in the calls to Synchronize, as you can see in the following two fragments:

```
procedure TPrimeAdder.Execute;
var
  I, Tot: Integer;
begin
  Tot := 0;
  for I := 1 to FMax do
  begin
    if IsPrime (I) then
      Tot := Tot + I;
    if I mod (fMax div 100) = 0 then
    begin
      FPosition := I * 100 div fMax;
      Synchronize(UpdateProgress);
    end;
  FTotal := Tot;
  Synchronize(ShowTotal);
end;
```

```
procedure TPrimeAdder.ShowTotal;
begin
  ShowMessage ('Thread: ' + IntToStr (FTotal));
end;


procedure TPrimeAdder.UpdateProgress;
begin
  Form1.ProgressBar1.Position := fPosition;
end;
```

The thread object is created when a button is clicked and is automatically destroyed as soon as its Execute method is completed:

```
procedure TForm1.Button3Click(Sender: TObject);
var
  AdderThread: TPrimeAdder;
begin
  AdderThread := TPrimeAdder.Create (True);
  AdderThread.Max := Max;
  AdderThread.FreeOnTerminate := True;
  AdderThread.Resume;
end;
```

Instead of setting the maximum number using a property, it would have been better to pass this value as an extra parameter of a custom constructor; I avoided doing so only to remain focused on the example of using a thread. By the way, this example is also available in Delphi for .NET.

The class has two output procedures, AddToList and ShowStatus, to be called inside the Synchronize method. The code of these two methods sends some results or some feedback to the main form, respectively adding a line to the list box and changing the status bar's SimpleText property. The key method of the thread is Execute. Before we look at it, however, here is how the thread is activated by the main form:

```
const
  strSearch = 'http://www.google.com/search?as_q=';

procedure TForm1.BtnFindClick(Sender: TObject);
var
  FindThread: TFindWebThread;
begin
  // create suspended, set initial values, and start
  FindThread := TFindWebThread.Create (True);
```

```
  FindThread.FreeOnTerminate := True;
  // grab the first 100 entries
  FindThread.strUrl := strSearch + EditSearch.Text +'&num=100';
  FindThread.Resume;
end;
```

The URL string is made of the main address of the search engine, followed by some parameters. The first, as_q, indicates the words you are looking for. The second, num=100, indicates the number of sites to retrieve; you cannot use numbers at will but are limited to a few alternatives, with 100 being the largest possible value.

WARNING   The WebFind program works with the server on the Google website at the time this book was written and tested. The custom software on the site can change, however, which might prevent WebFind from operating correctly. For example, a version of this program in a past edition of *Mastering Delphi* was later blocked by a change in the Google engine. The reason is that the original code was lacking the user agent HTTP header. If you are serious about doing searches based on the Google engine, you should instead use the SOAP interface provided for this purpose by Google, after subscribing on their site.

The thread's Execute method, activated by the Resume call, calls the two methods doing the work (shown in Listing 19.1). In the first, GrabHtml, the program connects to the HTTP server using a dynamically created IdHttp component and reads the HTML with the result of the search. The second method, HtmlToList, extracts the URLs referring to other websites from the result, the strRead string.

LISTING 19.1:   The *TFindWebThread* class (of the WebFind program)

```
unit FindTh;

interface

uses
  Classes, IdComponent, SysUtils, IdHTTP;

type
  TFindWebThread = class(TThread)
  protected
    Addr, Text, Status: string;
    procedure Execute; override;
    procedure AddToList;
    procedure ShowStatus;
    procedure GrabHtml;
    procedure HtmlToList;
    procedure HttpWork (Sender: TObject;
      AWorkMode: TWorkMode; AWorkCount: Integer);
  public
    strUrl: string;
    strRead: string;
  end;
```

```
implementation

{ TFindWebThread }

uses
  WebFindF, IdURI;

procedure TFindWebThread.AddToList;
begin
  if Form1.ListBox1.Items.IndexOf (Addr) < 0 then
  begin
    Form1.ListBox1.Items.Add (Addr);
    Form1.DetailsList.Add (Text);
  end;
end;

procedure TFindWebThread.Execute;
begin
  GrabHtml;
  HtmlToList;
  Status := 'Done with ' + StrUrl;
  Synchronize (ShowStatus);
end;

procedure TFindWebThread.GrabHtml;
var
  Http1: TIdHTTP;
begin
  Status := 'Sending query: ' + StrUrl;
  Synchronize (ShowStatus);
  // encode extended characters
  strUrl := TIdUri.URLEncode(StrUrl);
  Http1 := TIdHTTP.Create (nil);
  try
    Http1.Request.UserAgent := 'User-Agent: NULL';
    Http1.OnWork := HttpWork;
    strRead := Http1.Get (StrUrl);
  finally
    Http1.Free;
  end;
end;

procedure TFindWebThread.HtmlToList;
var
  strAddr, strText: string;
  nText: integer;
  nBegin, nEnd: Integer;
```

```
begin
  Status := 'Extracting data for: ' + StrUrl;
  Synchronize (ShowStatus);
  strRead := LowerCase (strRead);
  nBegin := 1;
  repeat
    // find the initial part HTTP reference
    nBegin := PosEx ('href=http', strRead, nBegin);
    if nBegin <> 0 then
    begin
      // find the end of the HTTP reference
      nBegin := nBegin + 5;
      nEnd := PosEx ('>', strRead, nBegin);
      strAddr := Copy (strRead, nBegin, nEnd - nBegin);
      // move on
      nBegin := nEnd + 1;
      // add the URL if 'google' is not in it
      if Pos ('google', strAddr) = 0 then
      begin
        nText := PosEx ('</a>', strRead, nBegin);
        strText := copy (strRead, nBegin, nText - nBegin);
        // remove cached references and duplicates
        if (Pos ('cached', strText) = 0) then
        begin
          Addr := strAddr;
          Text := strText;
          AddToList;
        end;
      end;
    end;
  until nBegin = 0;
end;

procedure TFindWebThread.HttpWork(Sender: TObject;
  AWorkMode: TWorkMode; AWorkCount: Integer);
begin
  Status := 'Received ' + IntToStr (AWorkCount) + ' for ' + strUrl;
  Synchronize (ShowStatus);
end;

procedure TFindWebThread.ShowStatus;
begin
  Form1.StatusBar1.SimpleText := Status;
end;

end.
```

The program looks for subsequent occurrences of the `href=http` substring, copying the text up to the closing > character. If the found string contains the word *google*, or its target text includes the word *cached*, it is omitted from the result. For each link it finds, the program grabs the URL and the description (the content of the *anchor* tag) and copies them to the list box and a string list of the form, as you can see in the `AddToList` method of the thread class in the listing.

When a user clicks a list box item, this description is displayed in a memo component at the bottom, as you can see in Figure 19.2. Double-clicking the list opens the given URL in the default browser, with a call to `ShellExecute`, which uses an `IFDEF` directive to compile with both Delphi for Win32 and Delphi for .NET:

```
procedure TForm1.ListBox1DblClick(Sender: TObject);
var
{$IFDEF CLR}
  strTarget: string;
{$ELSE}
  strTarget: PChar;
{$ENDIF}
begin
  strTarget := {$IFNDEF CLR}PChar{$ENDIF}
    (ListBox1.Items[ListBox1.ItemIndex]);
  ShellExecute (Handle, 'open', strTarget, '', '', sw_ShowNormal);
end;
```

Finally, remember that given the multithreaded nature of the program, you can start multiple searches at the same time, but be aware that the results will be added to the same memo component.

FIGURE 19.2
The WebFind application can be used to search for a list of sites on the Google search engine.

The WinInet API (Win32)

When you need to use the FTP and HTTP protocols, as alternatives to using particular VCL components, in Delphi for Win32 you can use a specific API provided by Microsoft in the WinInet DLL. This library is part of the core operating system and implements the FTP and HTTP protocols on top of the Windows sockets API.

With just three calls—InternetOpen, InternetOpenURL, and InternetReadFile—you can retrieve a file corresponding to any URL and store a local copy or analyze it. Other simple methods can be used for FTP; I suggest you look for the source code of the WinInet.pas Delphi unit, which lists all the functions.

The InternetOpen function establishes a generic connection and returns a handle you can use in the InternetOpenURL call. This second call returns a handle to the URL that you can pass to the InternetReadFile function in order to read blocks of data. In the following sample code, the data is stored in a local string. When all the data has been read, the program closes the connection to the URL and the Internet session by calling the InternetCloseHandle function twice:

```
var
  hHttpSession, hReqUrl: HInternet;
  Buffer: array [0..1023] of Char;
  nRead: Cardinal;
  strRead: string;
  nBegin, nEnd: Integer;
begin
  strRead := '';
  hHttpSession := InternetOpen ('FindWeb', INTERNET_OPEN_TYPE_PRECONFIG,
    nil, nil, 0);
  try
    hReqUrl := InternetOpenURL (hHttpSession,
      PChar(StrUrl), nil, 0,0,0);
    try // read all the data
      repeat
        InternetReadFile (hReqUrl, @Buffer, sizeof (Buffer), nRead);
        strRead := strRead + string (Buffer);
      until nRead = 0;
    finally
      InternetCloseHandle (hReqUrl);
    end;
  finally
    InternetCloseHandle (hHttpSession);
  end;
end;
```

The *WebClient* Class of the FCL (.NET)

The FCL of .NET includes a number of low-level classes that can help you rewrite the WebFind example in a cleaner way. In particular, the WebClient class of the System.Net namespace allows you to retrieve data from the Web. It does spawn a background thread for you, as you can see if you debug the WebFindFcl example.

The program is a WinForms application similar to the previous example (although in this case I do not extract the textual description within the anchor). In addition to downloading the HTML page, the program uses regular expressions to grab the hyperlinks and to filter out those referring back to the Google website (see the introduction to regular expressions in Chapter 9). The core code of the demo is in Listing 19.2 and a sample output is shown in Figure 19.3.

FIGURE 19.3

The output of the
WebFindFcl WinForms
example

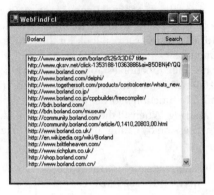

LISTING 19.2: The core code of the WebFindFcl WinForms example

```
uses
  System.Net, System.Text, System.Text.RegularExpressions;

const
  strSearch = 'http://www.google.com/search?as_q=';

procedure TWinForm.Button1_Click(
  sender: System.Object; e: System.EventArgs);
var
  wc: WebClient;
  buffer: array of byte;
  strDoc: string;
  rex: RegEx;
  rex2: RegEx;
  matches: MatchCollection;
  aMatch: Match;
begin
  // get the HTML result
  wc := WebClient.Create;
  buffer := wc.DownloadData (strSearch + tbSearch.Text +
    '&num=100'); // grab the first 100 entries
  strDoc := Encoding.Default.GetString (buffer);
  // now process the string
  rex := RegEx.Create ('http://\"*[^\">]*');
  matches := rex.Matches(strDoc);
  // now grab all the strings not referring back to google
  rex2 := RegEx.Create ('google|cache');
  for aMatch in matches do
    if not rex2.Match(aMatch.ToString).Success then
      ListBox1.Items.Add(aMatch);
end;
```

A Simple HTTP Server

The situation with the development of an HTTP server is quite different. Building a server to deliver static pages based on HTML files is far from simple, although one of the Indy demos provides a good starting point. However, a custom HTTP server might be interesting when building a totally dynamic site, something I'll focus on in more detail in second part of this chapter.

To show you how to begin the development of a custom HTTP server, I built the HttpServ example. This program has a form with a list box used for logging requests and an IdHTTPServer component (again from Indy 10) with these settings:

```
object IdHTTPServer1: TIdHTTPServer
  Active = True
  DefaultPort = 8088
  OnCommandGet = IdHTTPServer1CommandGet
end
```

The server uses port 8088 instead of the standard port 80 so that you can run it alongside another web server. All the custom code is in the OnCommandGet event handler, which returns a fixed page plus some information about the request:

```
procedure TForm1.IdHTTPServer1CommandGet(AContext: TIdContext;
  ARequestInfo: TIdHTTPRequestInfo; AResponseInfo:TIdHTTPResponseInfo);
var
  strHtml: String;
begin
  // log
  Listbox1.Items.Add (ARequestInfo.Document);
  // respond
  strHtml := '<h1>HttpServ Demo</h1>' +
    '<p>This is the only page you''ll get from this example.</p><hr>' +
    '<p>Request: ' + ARequestInfo.Document + '</p>' +
    '<p>Host: ' + ARequestInfo.Host + '</p>' +
    '<p>Params: ' + ARequestInfo.UnparsedParams + '</p>' +
    '<p>The headers of the request follow: <br>' +
    ARequestInfo.RawHeaders.Text + '</p>';
  AResponseInfo.ContentText := strHtml;
end;
```

NOTE   This code changed slightly from Indy 9. The first parameter used to be a TIdThread and is now a TIdContext, while the other two parameters were called RequestInfo and ResponseInfo, without the initial A. In cases like this, SyncEdit comes handy!

By passing a path and some parameters in the command line of the browser, you'll see them reinterpreted and displayed. For example, Figure 19.4 shows the effect of this command line:

```
http://localhost:8088/test?user=marco
```

FIGURE 19.4
The page displayed by
connecting a browser to
the custom HttpServ
program

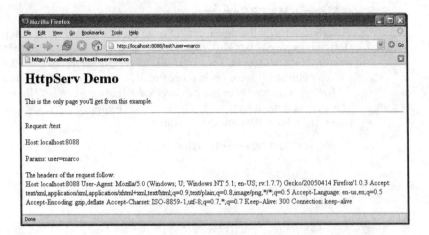

If this example seems too trivial, you'll see a slightly more interesting version in the next section, where I discuss the generation of HTML with Delphi's producer components. An interesting feature of this program is that you can recompile it in Win32 and .NET without any change in the source code. This means you can build your own (simple) managed web server for .NET with a limited effort.

Generating HTML

The Hypertext Markup Language, better known by its acronym HTML, is the most widespread format for content on the Web. HTML is the format web browsers typically read; it is a standard defined by the W3C (World Wide Web Consortium, www.w3.org), which is one of the bodies controlling the Internet. The HTML standard document is available on www.w3.org/MarkUp along with some interesting links.

Delphi's HTML Producer Components

Delphi's HTML producer components (on the Internet page of the Component Palette) can be used to generate the HTML files and particularly to turn a database table into an HTML table. Many developers believe that the use of these components makes sense only when writing a web server extension. Although they were introduced for this purpose and are part of the WebBroker technology, you can still use three out of the five producer components in any application in which you must generate a static HTML file.

NOTE   The producer components are available only in Delphi for Win32, not in Delphi for .NET. Although they are somewhat platform independent, their code depends on some of the WebBroker units, which were not ported to .NET and have low-level code that is not straightforward to convert. There are alternative techniques for producing HTML in .NET, but these simple components would have also been helpful in .NET programs.

Before looking at the HtmlProd example, which demonstrates the use of these HTML producer components, let me summarize their role:

◆ The simplest HTML producer component is the PageProducer, which manipulates an HTML file in which you've embedded special tags. The HTML can be stored in an external file or an internal string list. The advantage of this approach is that you can generate such a file using the HTML editor you prefer. At run time, the PageProducer converts the special tags to HTML code, giving you a straightforward method for modifying sections of an HTML document. The special tags have the basic format <#tagname>, but you can also supply named parameters within the tag. You'll process the tags in the OnTag event handler of the PageProducer.

◆ The DataSetPageProducer extends the PageProducer by automatically replacing tags corresponding to field names of a connected data source.

◆ The DataSetTableProducer component is generally useful for displaying the contents of a table, query, or other dataset. The idea is to produce an HTML table from a dataset, in a simple yet flexible way. The component has a nice preview, so you can see how the HTML output will look in a browser directly at design time.

◆ The QueryTableProducer and the SQLQueryTableProducer components are similar to the DataSetTableProducer, but they are specifically tailored for building parametric queries (for the BDE or dbExpress, respectively) based on input from an HTML search form. These components make little sense in a stand-alone program, and for this reason I'll delay covering these components until after introducing WebBroker, later in this chapter in the section "Queries and Forms."

Producing HTML Pages

A very simple example of using tags (introduced by the # symbol) is creating an HTML file that displays fields with the current date or a date computed relative to the current date, such as an expiration date. If you examine the HtmlProd example, you'll find a PageProducer1 component with internal HTML code, specified by the HTMLDoc string list:

```
<html>
  <head>
    <title>Producer Demo</title>
  </head>
<body>
  <h1>Producer Demo</h1>
    <p>This is a demo of the page produced by the
      <b><#appname></b>  application on
      <b><#date></b>.
    </p>
    <hr>
    <p>The prices in this catalog are valid until
      <b><#expiration days=21></b>.
    </p>
  </body>
</html>
```

WARNING If you prepare this file with an HTML editor (something I suggest you do), it may automatically place quotes around tag parameters, as in days="21", because this format is required by HTML 4 and XHTML. The PageProducer component has a `StripParamQuotes` property you can activate to remove those extra quotes when the component parses the code (before calling the `OnHTMLTag` event handler).

The Demo Page button copies the PageProducer component's output to the `Text` of a Memo. As you call the `Content` function of the PageProducer component, it reads the input HTML code, parses it, and triggers the `OnTag` event handler for every special tag. In the handler for this event, the program checks the value of the tag (passed in the `TagString` parameter) and returns a different HTML text (in the `ReplaceText` reference parameter), producing the output shown in Figure 19.5.

```
procedure TFormProd.PageProducer1HTMLTag(Sender: TObject;
  Tag: TTag; const TagString: String; TagParams: TStrings;
  var ReplaceText: String);
var
  nDays: Integer;
begin
  if TagString = 'date' then
    ReplaceText := DateToStr (Now)
  else if TagString = 'appname' then
    ReplaceText := ExtractFilename (Forms.Application.Exename)
  else if TagString = 'expiration' then
  begin
    nDays := StrToIntDef (TagParams.Values['days'], 0);
    if nDays <> 0 then
      ReplaceText := DateToStr (Now + nDays)
    else
      ReplaceText := '<i>{expiration tag error}</i>';
  end;
end;
```

FIGURE 19.5
The output of the Html-Prod example, a simple demonstration of the PageProducer component, when the user clicks the Demo Page button

Notice in particular the code I wrote to convert the last tag, #expiration, which requires a parameter. The PageProducer places the entire text of the tag parameter (in this case, *days=21*) in a string that's part of the TagParams list. To extract the value portion of this string (the portion after the equal sign), you can use the Values property of the TagParams string list and search for the proper entry at the same time. If it can't locate the parameter or if the parameter's value isn't an integer, the program displays an error message.

TIP The PageProducer component supports user-defined tags, which can be any string you like, but you should first review the special tags defined by the TTags enumeration. The possible values include tgLink (for the link tag), tgImage (for the img tag), tgTable (for the table tag), and a few others. If you create a custom tag, as in the PageProd example, the value of the Tag parameter to the OnTag event handler will be tgCustom.

Producing Pages of Data

The HtmlProd example also has a DataSetPageProducer component, which is connected with a database table and with the following HTML source code:

```html
<html>
  <head>
    <title>Data for <#name></title>
  </head>
  <body>
    <h1>
      <center>Data for <#name></center>
    </h1>
    <p>Capital: <#capital></p>
    <p>Continent: <#continent></p>
    <p>Area: <#area></p>
    <p>Population: <#population></p><hr>
    <p>Last updated on <#date>
      <br>HTML file produced by the program <#program>.
    </p>
  </body>
</html>
```

By using tags with the names of the connected dataset's fields (the usual country.cds database table), the program automatically gets the value of the current record's fields and replaces them automatically. This produces the output shown in Figure 19.6; the browser is connected to the HtmlProd example working as an HTTP server, as I'll discuss later. In the source code of the program related to this component, there is no reference to the database data:

```pascal
procedure TFormProd.DataSetPageProducer1HTMLTag(Sender: TObject;
  Tag: TTag; const TagString: String; TagParams: TStrings;
  var ReplaceText: String);
begin
  if TagString = 'program' then
    ReplaceText := ExtractFilename (Forms.Application.Exename)
  else if TagString = 'date' then
    ReplaceText := DateToStr (Date);
end;
```

FIGURE 19.6
The output of the Html-Prod example for the Print Line button

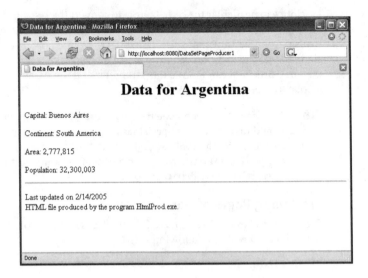

Producing HTML Tables

The third button in the HtmlProd example is Print Table. This button is connected to a DataSetTable-Producer component, again calling its Content function and copying its result to the Text of the Memo. By connecting the DataSet property of the DataSetTableProducer to ClientDataSet1, you can produce a standard HTML table.

The component by default generates only 20 rows, as indicated by the MaxRows property. If you want to get all of the table's records, you can set this property to –1—a simple but undocumented setting.

TIP The DataSetTableProducer component starts from the current record rather than from the first one, so the second time you click the Print Table button, you'll see no records in the output. Adding a call to the dataset's First method before calling the producer component's Content method fixes the problem.

To make the output of this producer component more complete, you can perform two operations. The first is to provide some Header and Footer information (to generate the HTML heading and closing elements) and add a Caption to the HTML table. The second is to customize the table by using the setting specified by the RowAttributes, TableAttributes, and Columns properties. The property editor for the columns, which is also the default component editor, allows you to set most of these properties, providing at the same time a nice preview of the output, as you can see in Figure 19.7. Before using this editor, you can set up properties for the dataset's fields using the Fields editor. This is how, for example, you can format the output of the population and area fields to use thousands separators.

You can use three techniques to customize the HTML table, and it's worth reviewing each of them:

♦ You can use the table producer component's Column's property to set properties, such as the text and color of the title, or the color and the alignment for the cells in the rest of the column.

♦ You can use the TField properties, particularly those related to output. In the example, I set the DisplayFormat property of the ClientDataSet1Area field object to ###,###,###. This is the approach to use if you want to determine the output of each field. You might go even further and embed HTML tags in the output of a field.

◆ You can handle the DataSetTableProducer component's OnFormatCell event to customize the output further. In this event, you can set the various column attributes uniquely for a given cell, but you can also customize the output string (stored in the CellData parameter) and embed HTML tags. You can't do this using the Columns property.

In the HtmlProd example, I used a handler for this event to turn the text of the Population and Area columns to bold font and to a red background for large values (unless it is the header row). Here is the code:

```
procedure TFormProd.DataSetTableProducer1FormatCell(
  Sender: TObject; CellRow, CellColumn: Integer;
  var BgColor: THTMLBgColor; var Align: THTMLAlign;
  var VAlign: THTMLVAlign; var CustomAttrs, CellData: String);
begin
  if (CellRow > 0) and
    (((CellColumn = 3) and (Length (CellData) > 8)) or
    ((CellColumn = 4) and (Length (CellData) > 9))) then
  begin
    BgColor := 'red';
    CellData := '<b>' + CellData + '</b>';
  end;
end;
```

The rest of the code is summarized by the settings of the table producer component, including its header and footer, as you can see by opening the source code of the HtmlProd example.

FIGURE 19.7

The editor of the DataSetTableProducer component's Columns property provides you with a preview of the final HTML table (if the database table is active).

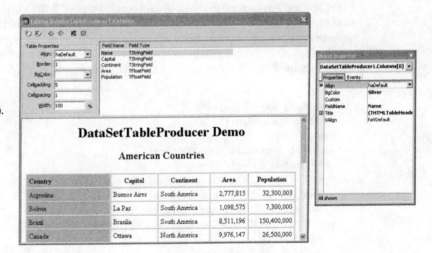

Using Style Sheets

The latest incarnations of HTML include a powerful mechanism for separating content from presentation: Cascading Style Sheets (CSS). Using a style sheet, you can separate the formatting of the HTML (colors, fonts, font sizes, and so on) from the text displayed (the content of the page). This approach makes your code more flexible and your website easier to update. In addition, you can separate the task of making the site graphically appealing (the work of a web designer) from automatic content generation (the work of a programmer). Style sheets are a complex technique, in which you give formatting values to the main types of HTML sections and to special "classes" (which have nothing to do with OOP). Again, see an HTML reference for the details.

You can update table generation in the HtmlProd example to include style sheets by providing a link to the style sheet in the `Header` property of a second DataSetTableProducer component:

```
<link rel="stylesheet" type="text/css" href="test.css">
```

You can then update the code of the `OnFormatCell` event handler with the following action (instead of the two lines changing the color and adding the bold font tag):

```
CustomAttrs := 'class="highlight"';
```

The style sheet I provided (`test.css`, available in the source code of the example) defines a highlight style, which has the bold font and red background that were hard-coded in the first DataSetTableProducer component.

The advantage of this approach is that now a graphic artist can modify the CSS file and give your table a nicer look without touching its code. When you want to provide many formatting elements, using a style sheet can also reduce the total size of the HTML file. This is an important element that can reduce download time.

Dynamic Pages from a Custom Server

The HtmlProd component can be used to generate static HTML files; it doubles as a web server, using an approach similar to that demonstrated in the HttpServ example but in a more realistic context. The program accesses the request of one of the possible page producers, passing the name of the component in a request. This is a portion of the IdHTTPServer component's `OnCommandGet` event handler, which uses the `FindComponent` method to locate the proper producer component:

```
var
  strReq, strHtml: String;
  Comp: TComponent;
begin
  strReq := RequestInfo.Document;
  if strReq[1] = '/' then
    strReq := Copy (strReq, 2, 1000); // skip '/'
  Comp := FindComponent (strReq);
  if (strReq <> '') and Assigned (Comp) and
    (Comp is TCustomContentProducer) then
  begin
    ClientDataSet1.First;
    strHtml := TCustomContentProducer (Comp).Content;
```

```
      end;
      ResponseInfo.ContentText := strHtml;
    end;
```

In case the parameter is not there (or is not valid), the server responds with an HTML-based menu of the available components:

```
strHtml := '<h1>HtmlProd Menu<h1><p><ul>';
for I := 0 to ComponentCount - 1 do
  if Components[i] is TCustomContentProducer then
    strHtml := strHtml + '<li><a href="/' + Components[i].Name + '">' +
      Components[i].Name + '</a></li>';
strHtml := strHtml + '</ul></p>';
```

Finally, if the program returns a table that uses CSS, the browser will request the CSS file from the server; so I added some specific code to return it. With the proper generalizations, this code shows how a server can respond by returning files and also how to indicate the MIME type of the response (ContentType):

```
if Pos ('test.css', Req) > 0 then
begin
  CssTest := TStringList.Create;
  try
    CssTest.LoadFromFile(ExtractFilePath(
      Application.ExeName) + 'test.css');
    ResponseInfo.ContentText := CssTest.Text;
    ResponseInfo.ContentType := 'text/css';
  finally
    CssTest.Free;
  end;
  Exit;
end;
```

Dynamic Web Pages

When you browse a website, you generally download static pages—HTML-format text files—from the web server to your client computer. As a web developer, you can create these pages manually, but for most businesses, it makes more sense to build the static pages from information in a database (a SQL server, a series of files, and so on). Using this approach, you're basically generating a snapshot of the data in HTML format, which is reasonable if the data isn't subject to frequent changes.

As an alternative to static HTML pages, you can build dynamic pages. To do this, you extract information directly from a database in response to the browser's request, so that the HTML sent by your application displays current data, not an old snapshot of the data. This approach makes sense if the data changes frequently.

As mentioned earlier, there are a couple of ways you can program custom behavior at the web server, and these are ideal techniques you can use to generate HTML pages dynamically. In addition to script-based techniques, which are very popular, two common protocols for programming web servers are CGI (the Common Gateway Interface) and the web server APIs.

> **NOTE**   Keep in mind that Delphi's WebBroker technology flattens the differences between CGI and server APIs by providing a common class framework. This way, you can easily turn a CGI application into an ISAPI library or integrate it into Apache.

An Overview of CGI

CGI is a standard protocol for communication between the client browser and the web server. It's not a particularly efficient protocol, but it is widely used and is not platform specific. This protocol allows the browser to both ask for and send data, and it is based on the standard command-line input and output of an application (usually a console application). When the server detects a page request for the CGI application, it launches the application, passes command-line data from the page request to the application, and then sends the application's standard output back to the client computer.

You can use many tools and languages to write CGI applications, and Delphi is only one of them. CGI is a low-level technique because it uses the standard command-line input and output along with environment variables to receive information from the web server and pass it back. To build a CGI program without using support classes, you can create a Delphi console application, remove the typical project source code, and replace it with the following statements:

```
program CgiDate;
{$APPTYPE CONSOLE}

uses SysUtils;

begin
  writeln ('content-type: text/html');
  writeln;
  writeln ('<html><head>');
  writeln ('<title>Time at this site</title>');
  writeln ('</head><body>');
  writeln ('<h1>Time at this site</h1>');
  writeln ('<hr>');
  writeln ('<h3>');
  writeln (FormatDateTime('"Today is " dddd, mmmm d, yyyy,' +
      '"<br> and the time is" hh:mm:ss AM/PM', Now));
  writeln ('</h3>');
  writeln ('<hr>');
  writeln ('<i>Page generated by CgiDate.exe</i>');
  writeln ('</body></html>');
end.
```

CGI programs produce a header followed by the HTML text using the standard output. If you execute this program directly, you'll see the text in a terminal window. If you run it instead from a web server and send the output to a browser, the formatted HTML text will appear, as shown in Figure 19.8.

Building advanced applications with plain CGI requires a lot of work. For example, to extract status information about the HTTP request, you need to access the relevant environment variables, as in the following:

```
// get the pathname
GetEnvironmentVariable ('PATH_INFO', PathName, sizeof (PathName));
```

FIGURE 19.8
The output of the Cgi-
Date application, as seen
in a browser

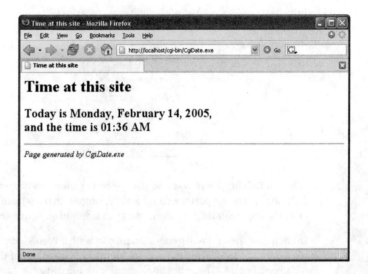

FIGURE 19.8
The output of the Cgi-
Date application, as seen
in a browser

Using Dynamic Libraries

A completely different approach is the use of the web server APIs: the popular ISAPI (Internet Server API, introduced by Microsoft), the less common NSAPI (Netscape Server API), or the Apache API. These APIs allow you to write a library that the server loads into its own address space and keeps in memory. Once it loads the library, the server can execute individual requests via threads within the main process, instead of launching a new .exe for every request (as it must in CGI applications).

When the server receives a page request, it loads the DLL (if it hasn't done so already) and executes the appropriate code, which may launch a new thread or use an existing one to process the request. The library then sends the appropriate HTTP data back to the client that requested the page. Because this communication generally occurs in memory, this type of application tends to be faster than CGI.

Delphi's WebBroker Technology

The CGI code snippet I showed you demonstrates the plain, direct approach to this protocol. I could have provided similar low-level examples for ISAPI or Apache modules, but in Delphi it's more interesting to use the WebBroker technology. This comprises a class hierarchy within VCL and a specific type of data modules called *WebModules*.

NOTE The WebBroker technology is only in Delphi for Win32, not in Delphi for .NET. If you are interested in Linux compatibility for CGI and Apache modules, the same technology is available in Kylix.

Using the WebBroker technology, you can begin developing an ISAPI or CGI application easily. On the Delphi Projects/WebBroker page of the New Items dialog box, select the Web Server

Application icon. The subsequent dialog box will offer you a choice among ISAPI, CGI, and the Web App Debugger:

NOTE In Delphi 7 there was also the option to generate a project for Apache. While the low-level units for Apache support are still there, the support in the wizard is missing, so you'll have to write all of the code manually. I'll show you an example of an Apache module later.

In each case, Delphi will generate a project with a WebModule, which is a nonvisual container similar to a data module. This unit will be identical, regardless of the project type; only the main project file changes. For a CGI application, it will look like this:

```
program Project2;

{$APPTYPE CONSOLE}

uses
  WebBroker,
  CGIApp,
  Unit1 in 'Unit1.pas' {WebModule1: TWebModule};

{$R *.res}

begin
  Application.Initialize;
  Application.CreateForm(TWebModule1, WebModule1);
  Application.Run;
end.
```

Although this is a console CGI program, the code looks similar to that of a standard Delphi application. However, it uses a trick—the Application object used by this program is not the typical global object of class TApplication but an object of a new class. This Application object is of class TCGIApplication or another class derived from TWebApplication, depending on your web project type.

The most important operations take place in the WebModule. This component derives from TCustomWebDispatcher, which provides support for all the input and output of your programs. The TCustomWebDispatcher class defines Request and Response properties, which store the client request and the response you're going to send back to the client. Each of these properties is defined using a base abstract class (TWebRequest and TWebResponse), but an application initializes them using a specific object (such as the TISAPIRequest and TISAPIResponse subclasses). These classes make available all the information passed to the server, so you have a single approach to accessing all the information. The same is true of a response, which is easy to manipulate. The key advantage of this approach is that the code written with WebBroker is independent of the type of application (CGI, ISAPI, Apache module); you'll be able to move from one to the other, modifying the project file or switching to another one, but you won't need to modify the code written in a WebModule.

This is the structure of Delphi's framework. To write the application code, you can use the Actions editor in the WebModule to define a series of actions (stored in the `Actions` array property) depending on the *pathname* of the request. This pathname is a portion of the CGI or ISAPI application's URL, which comes after the program name and before the parameters, such as `path1` in the following URL:

```
http://www.example.com/scripts/cgitest.exe/path1?param1=date
```

By providing different actions, your application can easily respond to requests with different pathnames, and you can assign a different producer component or call a different `OnAction` event handler for every possible pathname. Of course, you can omit the pathname to handle a generic request. Also consider that instead of basing your application on a WebModule, you can use a plain data module and add a WebDispatcher component to it. This is a good approach if you want to turn an existing Delphi application into a web server extension.

WARNING   The WebModule inherits from the base WebDispatcher class and doesn't require it as a separate component. Unlike WebSnap applications, WebBroker programs cannot have multiple dispatchers or multiple web modules. Also note that the actions of the WebDispatcher have nothing to do with the actions stored in an ActionList or ActionManager component of the VCL.

When you define the accompanying HTML pages that launch the application, the links will make page requests to the URLs for each of those paths. Having a single library that can perform different operations depending on a parameter (in this case, the pathname) allows the server to keep a copy of this library in memory and respond much more quickly to user requests. The same is partially true for a CGI application: the server has to run several instances but can cache the file and make it available more quickly.

In the `OnAction` event, you write the code to specify the *response* to a given *request*, the two main parameters passed to the event handler. Here is an example:

```
procedure TWebModule1.WebModule1WebActionItem1Action(Sender: TObject;
  Request: TWebRequest; Response: TWebResponse; var Handled: Boolean);
begin
  Response.Content :=
    '<html><head><title>Hello Page</title></head><body>' +
    '<h1>Hello</h1>' +
    '<hr><p><i>Page generated by Marco</i></p></body></html>';
end;
```

In the `Content` property of the `Response` parameter, you enter the HTML code you want users to see. The only drawback of this code is that the output in a browser will be correctly displayed on multiple lines but, looking at the HTML source code, you'll see a single line corresponding to the entire string. To make the HTML source code more readable by splitting it onto multiple lines, you can insert the #13 newline character (or, even better, the cross-platform and more readable `sLineBreak` value).

To let other actions handle this request, you set the last parameter, `Handled`, to False. The default value is True; if this value is set, then once you've handled the request with your action, the WebModule assumes you're finished. Most of a web application's code will be in the `OnAction` event handlers for the actions defined in the WebModule container. These actions receive a request from the client and return a response using the `Request` and `Response` parameters.

When you're using the producer components, your `OnAction` event often returns as `Response.Content` the `Content` of the producer component, with an assignment operation. You can shortcut this code by assigning a producer component to the `Producer` property of the action, and you won't need to write these event handlers any more (but don't do both things, because it might get you into trouble).

TIP   As an alternative to the `Producer` property, you can use the `ProducerContent` property. This property allows you to connect custom producer classes that don't inherit from the `TCustomContentProducer` class but implement the `IProduceContent` interface. The `ProducerContent` property is *almost* an interface property: it behaves the same way, but this behavior is due to its property editor and is not based on Delphi's support for interfaced properties.

Debugging with the Web App Debugger

Debugging web applications written in Delphi is often difficult. You cannot simply run the program and set breakpoints in it; you must convince the web server to run your CGI program or library within the Delphi debugger. You can do so by indicating a host application in Delphi's Run Parameters dialog box, but this approach implies letting Delphi run the web server (which is often a Windows service, not a stand-alone program).

To solve these issues, Borland has developed a specific Web App Debugger program. This program, which is activated by the corresponding item on the Tools menu, is a web server that waits for requests on a port you can set up (8081 by default). When a request arrives, the program can forward it to a stand-alone executable. In Delphi 2005 this communication is based on Indy sockets and the program use VCL for its user interface. (In Delphi 7, the Web App Debugger was instead a CLX application for Kylix compatibility, while in earlier versions it used COM techniques instead of Indy sockets for communication.) Using this tool means you can run the web server application from within the Delphi IDE, set all the breakpoints you need, and then (when the program is activated through the Web App Debugger) debug the program as you would a plain executable file.

The Web App Debugger does a good job of logging all the received requests and the responses returned to the browser, as you can see in Figure 19.9. The program also has a Statistics page that tracks the time required for each response, allowing you to test the efficiency of an application in different conditions.

WARNING   Because the Web App Debugger uses Indy sockets, your application will receive frequent exceptions of type `EidConnClosedGracefully`. For this reason, this exception is automatically disabled by default in the Delphi 2005 IDE (see Debugger Options/Borland Debuggers/Language Exceptions page in the Options dialog box).

By using the corresponding option in the New Web Server Application dialog, you can easily create a new application compatible with the debugger. This option defines a standard project, which creates both a main form and a web module. The (useless) form includes code for providing initialization code and adding the application to the Windows Registry:

```
initialization
  TWebAppSockObjectFactory.Create('program_name');
```

The Web App Debugger uses this information to get a list of the available programs. It does so when you use the default URL for the debugger, indicated in the form as a link, as you can see (for example) in Figure 19.10. The list includes all the registered servers, not only those that are running, and can be used to activate a program. This is not a good idea, though, because you have to run the program within the Delphi IDE to be able to debug it. (Notice that you can expand the list by clicking View Details; this view includes a list of the executable files and many other details.)

The data module for this type of project includes initialization code:

```
uses WebReq;

initialization
  if WebRequestHandler <> nil then
    WebRequestHandler.WebModuleClass := TWebModule2;
```

FIGURE 19.9
The logging capability of the Web App Debugger can be used to follow the low-level flow of HTTP requests and responses.

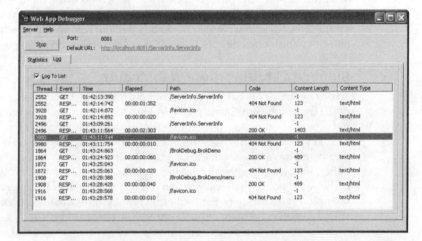

FIGURE 19.10
A list of applications registered with the Web App Debugger is displayed when you hook to its home page.

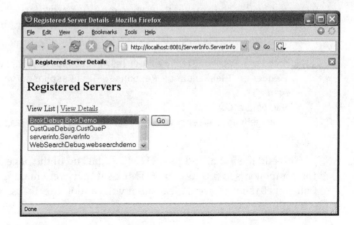

The Web App Debugger should be used only for debugging. To deploy the application, you should use one of the other options. You can create the project files for another type of web server program and add to the project the same web module as the debug application.

The reverse process is slightly more complex. To debug an existing application, you have to create a program of this type, remove the web module, add the existing one, and patch it by adding a line to set the WebModuleClass of the WebRequestHandler, as in the preceding code snippet.

WARNING   Although in most cases you'll be able to move a program from one web technology to another, this is not always the case. For example, in the CustQueP example (discussed later), I had to avoid the request's ScriptName property (which is fine for a CGI program) and use the InternalScriptName property instead.

There are two other interesting elements involved in using the Web App Debugger. First, you can test your program without having a web server installed and without having to tweak its settings. In other words, you don't have to deploy your programs to test them—you can try them right away. Second, instead of doing early development of an application as CGI, you can begin experimenting with a multithreaded architecture immediately without having to deal with the loading and unloading of libraries (which often implies shutting down the web server and possibly even the computer).

Building a Multipurpose WebModule

To demonstrate how easily you can build a feature-rich server-side application using Delphi's support, I created the BrokDemo example. I built this example using the Web App Debugger technology but provided alternative project files for the various technologies.

A key element of the WebBroker example is the list of actions. The actions can be managed in the Actions editor or directly in the Object TreeView. Actions are also visible in the Designer page of the editor, so you can graphically see their relationship with database objects. If you examine the source code, you'll notice that every action has a specific name. I also gave meaningful names to the OnAction event handlers. For instance, TimeAction as a method name is much more understandable than the WebModule1WebActionItem1Action name automatically generated by Delphi.

Every action has a different pathname, and one is marked as default and executed even if no pathname is specified. The first interesting idea in this program is the use of two PageProducer components, PageHead and PageTail, which are used for the initial and final portion of every page. Centralizing this code makes it easier to modify, particularly if it is based on external HTML files. The HTML produced by these components is added at the beginning and the end of the resulting HTML in the web module's OnAfterDispatch event handler:

```
procedure TWebModule1.WebModule1AfterDispatch(Sender: TObject;
  Request: TWebRequest; Response: TWebResponse; var Handled: Boolean);
begin
  Response.Content :=
    PageHead.Content + Response.Content + PageTail.Content;
end;
```

You add the initial and final HTML at the end of the page generation because doing so allows the components to produce the HTML as if they were making all of it. Starting with HTML in the OnBeforeDispatch event means that you cannot directly assign the producer components to the actions, or the producer component will override the Content you've already provided in the response.

The PageTail component includes a custom tag for the script name, replaced by the following code, which uses the current request object available in the web module:

```
procedure TWebModule1.PageTailHTMLTag(Sender: TObject;
  Tag: TTag; const TagString: String;
  TagParams: TStrings; var ReplaceText: String);
begin
  if TagString = 'script' then
    ReplaceText := Request.ScriptName;
end;
```

This code is activated to expand the <#script> tag of the PageTail component's HTMLDoc property.

The code for the time and date actions is straightforward. The really interesting part begins with the Menu path, which is the default action. In its OnAction event handler, the application uses a for loop to build a list of the available actions (using their names without the first two letters, which are always Wa in this example), providing a link to each of them with an anchor (an <a> tag):

```
procedure TWebModule1.MenuAction(Sender: TObject; Request: TWebRequest;
  Response: TWebResponse; var Handled: Boolean);
var
  I: Integer;
begin
  Response.Content := '<h3>Menu</h3><ul>'#13;
  for I := 0 to Actions.Count - 1 do
    Response.Content := Response.Content + '<li> <a href="' +
      Request.ScriptName + Action[I].PathInfo + '"> ' +
      Copy (Action[I].Name, 3, 1000) + '</a>'#13;
  Response.Content := Response.Content + '</ul>';
end;
```

The BrokDemo example also provides users with a list of the system settings related to the request, which is useful for debugging. It is also instructive to learn how much information (and exactly what information) the HTTP protocol transfers from a browser to a web server and vice versa. To produce this list, the program looks for the value of each property of the TWebRequest class, as this snippet demonstrates:

```
procedure TWebModule1.StatusAction(Sender: TObject;
  Request: TWebRequest; Response: TWebResponse; var Handled: Boolean);
var
  I: Integer;
begin
  Response.Content := '<h3>Status</h3>'#13 +
    'Method: ' + Request.Method + '<br>'#13 +
    'ProtocolVersion: ' + Request.ProtocolVersion + '<br>'#13 +
    'URL: ' + Request.URL + '<br>'#13 +
    'Query: ' + Request.Query + '<br>'#13 + ...
```

Dynamic Database Reporting

The BrokDemo example defines two more actions, indicated by the /table and /record pathnames. For these last two actions, the program produces a list of names and then displays the details of one record, using a DataSetTableProducer component to format the entire table and a DataSetPage-Producer component to build the record view. Here are the properties of these two components:

```
object DataSetTableProducer1: TDataSetTableProducer
  DataSet = dataEmployee
  OnFormatCell = DataSetTableProducer1FormatCell
end
object DataSetPage: TDataSetPageProducer
  HTMLDoc.Strings = (
    '<h3>Employee: <#LastName></h3>'
    '<ul><li> Employee ID: <#EmpNo>'
    '<li> Name: <#FirstName> <#LastName>'
    '<li> Phone: <#PhoneExt>'
    '<li> Hired On: <#HireDate>'
    '<li> Salary: <#Salary></ul>')
  OnHTMLTag = PageTailHTMLTag
  DataSet = dataEmployee
end
```

To produce the entire table, you connect the DataSetTableProducer to the Producer property of the corresponding actions without providing a specific event handler. The table is made more powerful by adding internal links to the specific records. The following code is executed for each cell of the table but a link is created only for the first column and not for the first row (the one with the title):

```
procedure TWebModule1.DataSetTableProducer1FormatCell(Sender: TObject;
  CellRow, CellColumn: Integer; var BgColor: THTMLBgColor;
  var Align: THTMLAlign; var VAlign: THTMLVAlign;
  var CustomAttrs, CellData: String);
begin
  if (CellColumn = 0) and (CellRow <> 0) then
    CellData := '<a href="' + ScriptName + '/record?LastName=' +
      dataEmployee['Last_Name'] + '&FirstName=' +
      dataEmployee['First_Name'] + '"> '
      + CellData + ' </a>';
end;
```

You can see the result of this action in Figure 19.11. When the user selects one of the links, the program is called again, and it can check the QueryFields string list and extract the parameters from the URL. It then uses the values corresponding to the table fields used for the record search (which is based on the FindNearest call):

```
procedure TWebModule1.RecordAction(Sender: TObject;
  Request: TWebRequest; Response: TWebResponse; var Handled: Boolean);
begin
  dataEmployee.Open;
  // go to the requested record
```

```
    dataEmployee.Locate ('LAST_NAME;FIRST_NAME',
      VarArrayOf([Request.QueryFields.Values['LastName'],
      Request.QueryFields.Values['FirstName']]), []);
    // get the output
    Response.Content := Response.Content + DataSetPage.Content;
  end;
```

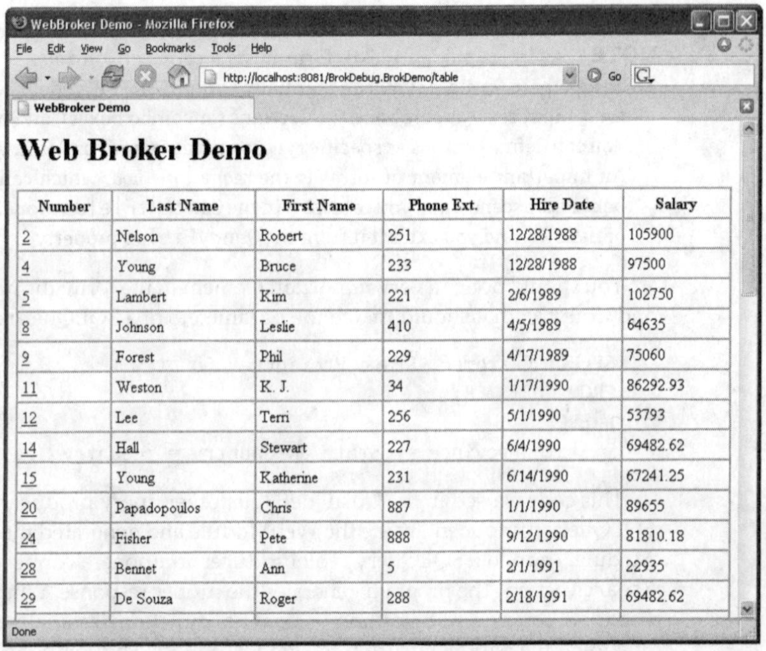

FIGURE 19.11

The output corresponding to the table path of the BrokDemo example, which produces an HTML table with internal hyperlinks

Queries and Forms

The previous example used some of the HTML producer components introduced earlier in this chapter. This group includes another component you haven't used yet: QueryTableProducer (for the BDE) and its sister SQL QueryTableProducer (for dbExpress). As you'll see in a moment, this component makes building even complex database programs a breeze.

Suppose you want to search for customers in a database. You might construct the following HTML form (embedded in an HTML table for better formatting):

```
<h4>Customer QueryProducer Search Form</h4>
<form action="<#script>/search" method="POST">
  <table>
    <tr>
      <td>State:</td>
      <td><input type="text" name="State"></td>
    </tr>
    <tr>
      <td>Country:</td>
```

```
       <td><input type="text" name="Country"></td>
     </tr>
     <tr>
      <td></td>
      <td><center><input type="Submit"></center></td>
     </tr>
    </table>
   </form>
```

NOTE As in Delphi, an HTML form hosts a series of controls. There are visual tools to help you design these forms, or you can manually enter the HTML code. The available controls include buttons, input text (or edit boxes), selections (or combo boxes), and input buttons (or radio buttons). You can define buttons as specific types, such as Submit or Reset, which imply standard behaviors. An important element of forms is the *request method,* which can be either POST (data is passed behind the scenes, and you receive it in the ContentFields property) or GET (data is passed as part of the URL, and you extract it from the QueryFields property).

You should notice a very important element in the form: the names of the input components, State and Country, that should match the parameters of a SQLQuery component:

```
SELECT Customer, State_Province,  Country
FROM CUSTOMER
WHERE
  State_Province = :State OR Country = :Country
```

This code is used in the CustQueP (customer query producer) example. To build it, I placed a SQLQuery component inside the WebModule and generated the field objects for it. In the same Web-Module, I added a SQLQueryTableProducer component connected to the Producer property of the /search action. The program generates the proper response. When you activate the SQLQueryTable-Producer component by calling its Content function, it initializes the SQLQuery component by obtaining the parameters from the HTTP request. The component can automatically examine the request method and then use either the QueryFields property (if the request is a GET) or the ContentFields property (if the request is a POST).

One problem with using a static HTML form as you did earlier is that it doesn't tell you which states and countries you can search for. To address this issue, you can use a selection control instead of an edit control in the HTML form. However, if the user adds a new record to the database table, you'll need to update the element list automatically. As a final solution, you can design the ISAPI DLL to produce a form on the fly, and you can fill the selection controls with the available elements.

You'll generate the HTML for this page in the /form action, which you connect to a PageProducer component. The PageProducer contains the following HTML text, which embeds two special tags:

```
<h4>Customer QueryProducer Search Form</h4>
<form action="<#script>/search" method="POST">
<table>
  <tr>
    <td>State:</td>
    <td>
      <select name="State">
        <option></option>
```

```
        <#State_Province>
      </select>
    </td>
  </tr>
  <tr>
    <td>Country:</td>
    <td>
      <select name="Country">
        <option></option>
        <#Country>
      </select>
    </td>
  </tr>
  <tr>
    <td></td>
    <td><center><input type="Submit"></center></td>
  </tr>
  </table>
</form>
```

You'll notice that the tags have the same name as some of the table's fields. When the Page-Producer encounters one of these tags, it adds an <option> HTML tag for every distinct value of the corresponding field. Here's the OnTag event handler's code, which is generic and reusable:

```
procedure TWebModule1.PageProducer1HTMLTag(Sender: TObject;
  Tag: TTag; const TagString: String;
  TagParams: TStrings; var ReplaceText: String);
begin
  ReplaceText := '';
  SQLQuery2.SQL.Clear;
  SQLQuery2.SQL.Add ('select distinct ' + TagString +
    ' from customer');
  try
    SQLQuery2.Open;
    try
      SQLQuery2.First;
      while not SQLQuery2.EOF do
      begin
        ReplaceText := ReplaceText +
          '<option>' + SQLQuery2.Fields[0].AsString + '</option>'#13;
        SQLQuery2.Next;
      end;
    finally
      SQLQuery2.Close;
    end;
  except
    ReplaceText := '{wrong field: ' + TagString + '}';
  end;
end;
```

This method uses a second SQLQuery component, which I manually placed on the form and connected to a shared SQLConnection component. It produces the output shown in Figure 19.12.

FIGURE 19.12
The form action of the CustQueP example produces an HTML form with a selection component dynamically updated to reflect the current status of the database.

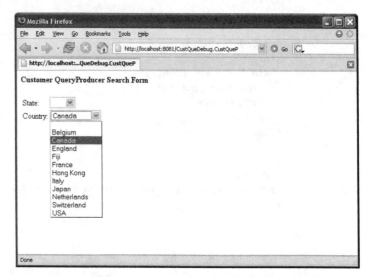

This web server extension, like many others, allows the user to view the details of a specific record. As in the previous example, you can accomplish this by customizing the output of the first column (column zero), which is generated by the QueryTableProducer component:

```
procedure TWebModule1.QueryTableProducer1FormatCell(
  Sender: TObject; CellRow, CellColumn: Integer;
  var BgColor: THTMLBgColor; var Align: THTMLAlign;
  var VAlign: THTMLVAlign; var CustomAttrs, CellData: String);
begin
  if (CellColumn = 0) and (CellRow <> 0) then
    CellData := '<a href="' + Request.ScriptName +
      '/record?Company=' + CellData +'">' + CellData + '</a>'#13;
  if CellData = '' then
    CellData := ' ';
end;
```

TIP   When you have an empty cell in an HTML table, most browsers render it without the border. For this reason, I added a *nonbreaking space* symbol ( ) in each empty cell. You'll have to do this in each HTML table generated with Delphi's table producers.

The action for this link is /record, and you pass a specific element after the ? parameter (without the parameter name, which is slightly nonstandard). The code you use to produce the HTML tables for the records doesn't use the producer components as you've been doing; instead, it shows the data of every field in a custom-built table:

```
procedure TWebModule1.RecordAction(Sender: TObject;
  Request: TWebRequest; Response: TWebResponse; var Handled: Boolean);
var
  I: Integer;
begin
  if Request.QueryFields.Count = 0 then
    Response.Content := 'Record not found'
  else
  begin
    Query2.SQL.Clear;
    Query2.SQL.Add ('select * from customer ' +
      'where Company="' + Request.QueryFields.Values['Company'] + '"');
    Query2.Open;
    Response.Content :=
      '<html><head><title>Customer Record</title></head><body>'#13 +
      '<h1>Customer Record: ' + Request.QueryFields[0] + '</h1>'#13 +
      '<table border>'#13;
    for I := 1 to Query2.FieldCount - 1 do
      Response.Content := Response.Content +
        '<tr><td>' + Query2.Fields [I].FieldName + '</td>'#13'<td>' +
        Query2.Fields [I].AsString + '</td></tr>'#13;
    Response.Content := Response.Content + '</table><hr>'#13 +
      // pointer to the query form
      '<a href="' + Request.ScriptName + '/form">' +
      ' Next Query </a>'#13 + '</body></html>'#13;
  end;
end;
```

Working with Apache

If you plan to use Apache instead of Microsoft's Internet Information Services (IIS) or another web server, you can take advantage of the CGI technology to deploy your applications on almost any web server. However, using CGI means reduced speed and some trouble handling state information (because you cannot keep any data in memory). This is a good reason to write an ISAPI application or a dynamic Apache module. Using Delphi's WebBroker technology, you can also easily compile the same code for both technologies, so that moving your program to a different web platform becomes much simpler. You can also recompile a CGI program or a dynamic Apache module with Kylix and deploy it on a Linux server.

As I've mentioned, Apache can run traditional CGI applications but also has a specific technology for keeping the server extension program loaded in memory at all times for faster response. To build such a program in Delphi, you have to write the complete code, as in Delphi 2005 the New Web Server Application dialog box no longer includes Apache.

The structure of an Apache module is not very complex, so all you have to do is to write a similar project source code:

```
library Apache1;

uses
  WebBroker,
  ApacheApp,
  ApacheWm in 'ApacheWm.pas' {WebModule1: TWebModule};

{$R *.res}

exports
  apache_module name 'apache1_module';

begin
  Application.Initialize;
  Application.CreateForm(TWebModule1, WebModule1);
  Application.Run;
end.
```

Notice in particular the exports clause, which indicates the name used by Apache configuration files to reference the dynamic module. In the project source code, you can add two more definitions—the module name and the content type—in the following way:

```
ModuleName := 'Apache1_module';
ContentType:= 'Apache1-handler';
```

If you don't set these values, Delphi will assign them defaults, which are built adding the _module and -handler strings to the project name (resulting in the two names I used here).

An Apache module is generally not deployed within a script folder but rather within the modules subfolder of the server. You have to edit the http.conf file, adding a line to load the module, as follows:

```
LoadModule apache1_module modules/apache1.dll
```

Finally, you must indicate when the module is invoked. The handler defined by the module can be associated with a given file extension (so that your module will process all the files having a given extension) or with a physical or virtual folder. In the latter case, the folder doesn't exist, but Apache pretends it is there. This is how you can set up a virtual folder for the Apache1 module:

```
<Location /Apache1>SetHandler Apache1-handler</Location>
```

Because Apache is inherently case sensitive (because of its Linux heritage), you also might want to add a second, lowercase virtual folder:

```
<Location /apache1>SetHandler Apache1-handler</Location>
```

Now you can invoke the sample application with the URL http://localhost/Apache1. A great advantage of using virtual folders in Apache is that a user doesn't really distinguish between the physical and dynamic portions of your site, as you can see by experimenting with the Apache1 example (which includes the code discussed here).

As another example of an Apache module I created a project of this type for the BrokDemo example. The source file of the BrokApache project is almost identical to that of the Apache1 example I just listed.

Working with IIS

Another alternative, particularly suited for the Windows platform, is the use of Microsoft's own Internet Information Services (IIS). This server has a public interface called Internet Server API (or ISAPI, for short). This API allows you to write a DLL loaded in the address space of the server, exactly like Apache does for a module.

The WebBroker architecture simplifies working with IIS, as the wizard can generate the proper project file for you. Before I show you an example, though, I think it is worth looking at a low-level example, just as we have done with CGI. In Listing 19.3 you can see the complete code of a DLL you can install in IIS.

LISTING 19.3:   The complete source code of the IsapiDem example

```delphi
library IsapiDem;

uses
  SysUtils, Classes, Windows, Isapi2;

function GetExtensionVersion (
  var Ver: THSE_VERSION_INFO): BOOL; stdcall;
begin
  with Ver do
  begin
    dwExtensionVersion := $00010000;
    StrCopy (lpszExtensionDesc, 'Low-level Isapi Demo');
  end;
  Result := True;
end;

function HttpExtensionProc (
  var ECB: TEXTENSION_CONTROL_BLOCK): DWORD; stdcall;
var
  OutStr: string;
  StrLength: Cardinal;
begin
  with ECB do
  begin
    OutStr :=
      '<html><head><title>First Isapi Demo</title></head><body>' +
      '<h2><center>First Isapi Demo</center></h2>' +
```

```
      '<p>Hello Mastering Delphi Readers...</p><hr>' +
      '<p><b>Activated by ' + PChar(@lpszPathInfo[1]) + '</b></p>' +
      '<p><i>From IsapiDLL on ' + DateToStr(Now) + ' at ' +
      TimeToStr(Now) + '</i></p></body></html>';
    StrLength := Length (OutStr);
    WriteClient(ConnID, PChar (OutStr), StrLength, 0);
  end;
  Result := HSE_STATUS_SUCCESS;
end;


exports
  GetExtensionVersion,
  HttpExtensionProc;


end.
```

This ISAPI DLL exports two functions: `GetExtensionVersion`, which is called when the DLL is first loaded by IIS, and `HttpExtensionProc`, which is called for each page request. The parameters of these functions are complex data structures holding input data and sever methods you can call to produce the result. All the program does is to display some information about the request.

If you want to create a more complex ISAPI library in Delphi you should instead use the WebBroker architecture and the page producer components. In this case, you can use the New Web Server Application dialog box and pick the ISAPI option. The project file will look like the following (extracted by the BrokIsa version of the BrokDemo example):

```
library BrokIsa;

uses
  WebBroker,
  ISAPIApp,
  BrokWm in 'BrokWm.pas';

{$R *.RES}

exports
  GetExtensionVersion,
  HttpExtensionProc,
  TerminateExtension;

begin
  Application.Initialize;
  Application.CreateForm(TWebModule1, WebModule1);
  Application.Run;
end.
```

Practical Examples

After this general introduction to developing server-side applications with WebBroker, I'll end this chapter with two practical examples. The first is a classic web counter. The second is an extension of the WebFind program presented earlier, which produces a dynamic page instead of filling a list box.

A Graphical Web Hit Counter

The server-side applications you've built up to now were based only on text. Of course, you can easily add references to existing graphics files. What's more interesting, however, is to build server-side programs capable of generating graphics that change over time.

A typical example is a *page hit counter*. To write a web counter, you save the current number of hits to a file and then read and increase the value every time the counter program is called. To return this information, all you need is HTML text with the number of hits. The code is straightforward:

```
procedure TWebModule1.WebModule1WebActionItem1Action(Sender: TObject;
  Request: TWebRequest; Response: TWebResponse; var Handled: Boolean);
var
  nHit: Integer;
  LogFile: Text;
  LogFileName: string;
begin
  LogFileName := 'WebCont.log';
  System.Assign (LogFile, LogFileName);
  try
    // read if the file exists
    if FileExists (LogFileName) then
    begin
      Reset (LogFile);
      Readln (LogFile, nHit);
      Inc (nHit);
    end
    else
      nHit := 0;
    // saves the new data
    Rewrite (LogFile);
    Writeln (LogFile, nHit);
  finally
    Close (LogFile);
  end;
  Response.Content := IntToStr (nHit);
end;
```

WARNING   This simple file handling does not scale. When multiple visitors hit the page at the same time, this code may return false results or fail with a file I/O error because a request in another thread has the file open for reading while this thread tries to open the file for writing. To support a similar scenario, you'll need to use a mutex (or a critical section in a multithreaded program) to let each subsequent thread wait until the thread currently using the file has completed its task.

It's more interesting to create a graphical counter that can be easily embedded into any HTML page. There are two approaches to building a graphical counter: You can prepare a bitmap for each digit up front and then combine them in the program, or you can let the program draw over a memory bitmap to produce the graphic you want to return. In the WebCount program, I chose the second approach.

Basically, you can create an Image component that holds a memory bitmap, which you can paint on with the usual methods of the TCanvas class. Then you can attach this bitmap to a TJpegImage object. Accessing the bitmap through the JpegImage component converts the image to the JPEG format. Then, you can save the JPEG data to a stream and return it. As you can see, there are many steps, but the code is not complicated:

```
// create a bitmap in memory
Bitmap := TBitmap.Create;
try
  Bitmap.Width := 120;
  Bitmap.Height := 25;
  // draw the digits
  Bitmap.Canvas.Font.Name := 'Arial';
  Bitmap.Canvas.Font.Size := 14;
  Bitmap.Canvas.Font.Color := RGB (255, 127, 0);
  Bitmap.Canvas.Font.Style := [fsBold];
  Bitmap.Canvas.TextOut (1, 1, 'Hits: ' +
    FormatFloat ('###,###,###', Int (nHit)));
  // convert to JPEG and output
  Jpeg1 := TJpegImage.Create;
  try
    Jpeg1.CompressionQuality := 50;
    Jpeg1.Assign(Bitmap);
    Stream := TMemoryStream.Create;
    Jpeg1.SaveToStream (Stream);
    Stream.Position := 0;
    Response.ContentStream := Stream;
    Response.ContentType := 'image/jpeg';
    Response.SendResponse;
    // the response object will free the stream
  finally
    Jpeg1.Free;
  end;
finally
  Bitmap.Free;
end;
```

The three statements responsible for returning the JPEG image are the two that set the ContentStream and ContentType properties of the Response and the final call to SendResponse. The content type must match one of the possible MIME types accepted by the browser, and the order of these three statements is relevant. The Response object also has a SendStream method, but it should be called only after sending the type of the data with a separate call. Here you can see the effect of this program:

To embed the program in a page, add the following code to the HTML:

```
<img src="http://localhost/scripts/webcount.exe" border="0"
  alt="hit counter">
```

Searching with a Web Search Engine

I discussed earlier in this chapter the use of the Indy HTTP client component to retrieve the result of a search on the Google website. Let's extend the example, turning it into a server-side application. The WebSearcher program, available as a CGI application or a Web App Debugger executable, has two actions: The first returns the HTML retrieved by the search engine; and the second parses the HTML filling a client data set component, which is hooked to a table page producer for generating the final output. Here is the code for the second action:

```
const
  strSearch = 'http://www.google.com/search?as_q=borland+delphi&num=100';

procedure TWebModule1.WebModule1WebActionItem1Action(Sender: TObject;
  Request: TWebRequest; Response: TWebResponse; var Handled: Boolean);
var
  I: integer;
begin
  if not cds.Active then
    cds.CreateDataSet
  else
    cds.EmptyDataSet;
  for i := 0 to 5 do // how many pages?
  begin
    // get the data form the search site
    GrabHtml (strSearch + '&start=' + IntToStr (i*100));
    // scan it to fill the cds
    HtmlStringToCds;
  end;
  cds.First;
  // return producer content
  Response.Content := DataSetTableProducer1.Content;
end;
```

The GrabHtml method is identical to the WebFind example. The HtlStringToCds method is similar to the corresponding method of the WebFind example (which adds the items to a list box); it adds the addresses and their textual descriptions by calling

```
cds.InsertRecord ([0, strAddr, strText]);
```

The ClientDataSet component is set up with three fields: the two strings plus a line counter. This extra empty field is required in order to include the extra column in the table producer. The code fills the column in the cell-formatting event, which also adds the hyperlink:

```
procedure TWebModule1.DataSetTableProducer1FormatCell(Sender: TObject;
    CellRow, CellColumn: Integer; var BgColor: THTMLBgColor;
    var Align: THTMLAlign; var VAlign: THTMLVAlign;
    var CustomAttrs, CellData: String);
begin
  if CellRow <> 0 then
  case CellColumn of
    0: CellData := IntToStr (CellRow);
    1: CellData := '<a href="' + CellData + '">' +
          SplitLong(CellData) + '</a>';
    2: CellData := SplitLong (CellData);
  end;
end;
```

The call to SplitLong is used to add extra spaces in the output text to avoid having grid columns that are too large—the browser won't split the text on multiple lines unless it contains spaces or other special characters. The result of this program is a rather slow application (because of the multiple HTTP requests it must forward) that produces output like that shown in Figure 19.13.

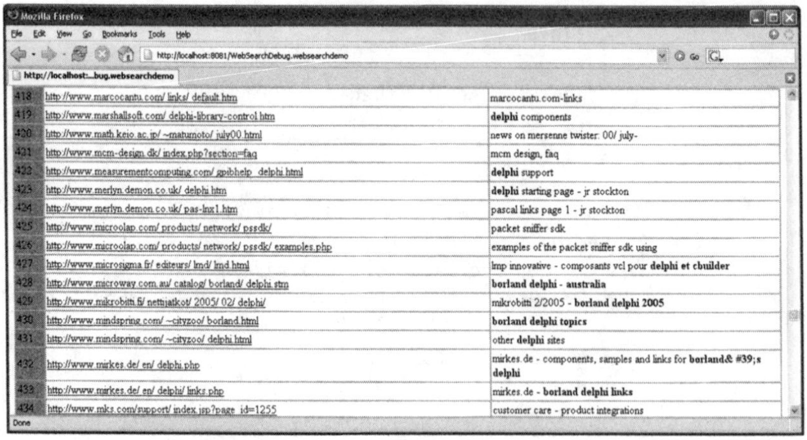

FIGURE 19.13
The WebSearcher program shows the result of multiple searches done on Google.

What's Next?

In this chapter, I focused on some core Internet technologies, including the use of sockets and core Internet protocols. I discussed the main idea and showed a few examples of using the HTTP protocol. You can find many more examples that use the Indy components in the demos written by their developers. The next topic was the generation of HTML, particularly out of database data.

Then I covered web server applications based on WebBroker. This wasn't an in-depth presentation because one could write an entire book on this topic alone. It was intended as a starting point, and (as usual) I tried to make the core concepts clear rather than building complex examples.

WebBroker is a core technology that provides very little help in the layout of the web pages and in the management of users and sessions. Delphi 2005 provides many other web development techniques we'll explore in the next two chapters: Borland's WebSnap, AToZed's IntraWeb, and Microsoft's ASP.NET. A further approach to the development of web applications is represented by XML technologies, covered in Chapter 22. Furthermore, Chapter 23 describes a related technology, web services (and SOAP).

Chapter 20

WebSnap and IntraWeb

In the last chapter you saw how you can use Delphi to create client and server applications for the HTTP protocol. Although Delphi's core web development support is given by the WebBroker framework discussed in the previous chapter, there are higher-level solutions available. Two Delphi web technologies (WebSnap and IntraWeb) are discussed in this chapter, while support for ASP.NET is covered in Chapter 21.

WebSnap is a higher-level framework supporting limited visual design of HTML pages, scripting support, a good separation of HTML from the code behind it, and ready-to-use components for managing users, sessions, and other standard chores. WebSnap hides some of the Web's complexity, but it is not visual in nature.

If you are looking for visual development of web applications similar to traditional Delphi programs, IntraWeb might be the right solution for you. This framework, currently developed by Atozed software, in the words of its chief architect Chad Z. Hower, is for "building web applications, not websites."

In this chapter I cannot cover every detail of WebSnap and IntraWeb—together they add almost one hundred components to Delphi's IDE. My plan is to cover their foundations so that you can choose whether to use it for your forthcoming projects, or for portions of those projects, as appropriate.

WebSnap

The WebSnap framework is built on the solid foundation offered by WebBroker. A WebSnap application can be a CGI program or an ISAPI library (or optionally an Apache module) and can be debugged using the Web App Debugger. WebSnap has a few definite advantages over WebBroker, such as allowing for multiple web modules each corresponding to a page, integrating server-side scripting, and XSL (this last element will be covered in Chapter 22). Moreover, many ready-to-use components are available for handling common tasks, such as user logins, session management, and so on. Instead of listing all the features of WebSnap, though, I decided to cover them in a sequence of simple and focused applications. I built these applications using the Web App Debugger for testing purposes, but you can easily deploy them using one of the other available technologies.

NOTE   The WebSnap technology is available only in Delphi for Win32, not in Delphi for .NET. Alternative options for web development in Delphi for .NET are IntraWeb (covered in the second half of this chapter) and ASP.NET (covered in the next chapter).

When you're developing a WebSnap application, the starting point is a dialog box you can invoke either in the WebSnap page of the New Items dialog box (File ≻ New ≻ Other) or using the Internet toolbar in the IDE (which is not visible by default):

The resulting dialog box, shown in Figure 20.1, allows you to choose the type of application (as in a WebBroker application) and to customize the initial application components (you'll be able to add more later). The bottom portion of the dialog determines the behavior of the first page (usually the default or home page of the program). A similar dialog box is displayed for subsequent pages.

If you choose the defaults and type in a name for the home page, the dialog box will create a project and open a `TWebAppPageModule`. This module contains the components you've chosen, by default:

♦   A WebAppComponents component is a container for all the centralized services of the Web-Snap application, such as the user list, core dispatcher, session services, and so on. Not all of its properties must be set up because an application might not need all the available services.

♦   One of these core services is offered by the PageDispatcher component, which (automatically) holds a list of the application's available pages and defines the default page.

♦   Another core service is given by the AdapterDispatcher component, which handles HTML form submissions and image requests.

♦   The ApplicationAdapter is the first component you encounter from the adapters family. These components offer fields and actions to the server-side scripts evaluated by the program. Specifically, the ApplicationAdapter is a field adapter that exposes the value of its own `ApplicationTitle` property. If you enter a value for this property, it will be made available to the scripts.

♦   The module hosts a PageProducer that includes the HTML code of the page—in this case, the program's default page. Unlike in WebBroker applications, the HTML for this component is not stored inside its `HTMLDoc` string list property or referenced by its `HTMLFile` property. The HTML file is an external file, stored by default in the folder hosting the project's source code and referenced from the application using a comment that somewhat resembles a resource include statement: `{*.html}`.

♦   Because the HTML file included by the PageProducer is kept as a separate file (the Locate-FileService component will eventually help you for its deployment), you can edit it to change the output of a page of your program without having to recompile the application. These possible changes relate not only to the fixed portion of the HTML file but also to some of its dynamic content, thanks to the support for server-side scripting. The default HTML file, based on a standard template, already contains some scripting.

WARNING   The similarity between resource inclusion and a comment with an HTML reference is based mostly on the fact that in both cases the asterisks (*) are used to indicate a file named like the current unit, but with a different extension. The HTML reference in a comment is used only for the design-time location of the file, with no inclusion of the file into the executable.

FIGURE 20.1
The options offered by
the New WebSnap Appli-
cation dialog box include
the type of server and a
button that lets you select
the core application
components.

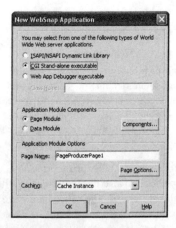

You can view the HTML file in the Delphi editor thanks to that directive (with reasonably good syntax highlighting) by selecting the corresponding lower tab. The editor also has pages for a Web-Snap module, including by default an HTML Result page where you can see the HTML generated after evaluating the scripts, and a Preview page hosting what a user will see in a browser. The Delphi editor for a WebSnap module includes a powerful HTML editor with rich syntax highlighting and code completion.

The standard HTML template used by WebSnap adds to any page of the program its title and the application title, using script lines such as these:

```
<h1><%= Application.Title %></h1>
<h2><%= Page.Title %></h2>
```

We'll get back to the scripting in a while; you'll begin developing the WSnap1 example in the next section by creating a program with multiple pages. But first, I'll finish this overview by showing you the source code for a sample web page module:

```
type
  Thome = class(TWebAppPageModule)
    ...
  end;

function home: Thome;

implementation

{$R *.dfm} {*.html}

uses WebReq, WebCntxt, WebFact, Variants;

function home: Thome;
```

```
begin
  Result := Thome(WebContext.FindModuleClass(Thome));
end;

initialization
  if WebRequestHandler <> nil then
    WebRequestHandler.AddWebModuleFactory(
      TWebAppPageModuleFactory.Create(Thome, TWebPageInfo.Create(
        [wpPublished {, wpLoginRequired}], '.html'), caCache));
end.
```

The module uses a global function instead of a form's typical global object to support page caching. This application also has extra code in the initialization section (particularly registration code) to let the application know the role of the page and its behavior.

Managing Multiple Pages

The first notable difference between WebSnap and WebBroker is that instead of having a single data module with multiple actions eventually connected to producer components, WebSnap has multiple data modules, each corresponding to an action and having a producer component with an HTML file attached to it. You can add multiple actions to a page/module, but the idea is that you structure applications around pages rather than actions. As is the case with actions, the name of the page is indicated in the request path.

As an example, I added two more pages to the WebSnap application (which was built with default settings). For the first page, in the New WebSnap Page Module dialog (see Figure 20.2), choose a standard page producer and name it date. For the second, choose a DataSetPageProducer and name it country. After saving the files, you can begin testing the application. Thanks to some of the scripting I'll discuss later, each page lists all the available pages (unless you've unchecked the Published check box in the New WebSnap Page Module dialog).

The pages will be rather empty, but at least you have the structure in place. To complete the home page, you'll edit its linked HTML file directly. For the date page, use the same approach as a WebBroker application. Add some custom tags to the HTML text, like the following:

```
<p>The time at this site is <#time>.</p>
```

I also added code to the producer component's OnTag event handler to replace this tag with the current time. For the third page (the country page, shown in Figure 20.3), modify the HTML to include tags for the various fields of the country table, as in:

```
<h3>Country: <#name></h3>
```

Then attach the ClientDataSet to the page producer:

```
object DataSetPageProducer: TDataSetPageProducer
  DataSet = cdsCountry
end
object cdsCountry: TClientDataSet
  FileName = 'C:\...\Borland Shared\Data\country.cds'
end
```

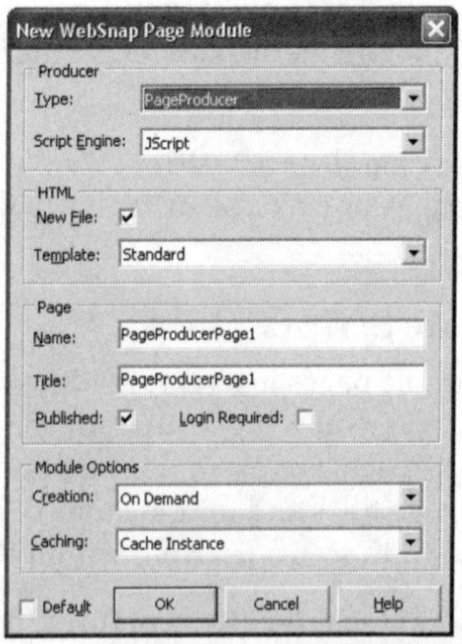

FIGURE 20.2
The New WebSnap Page
Module dialog box

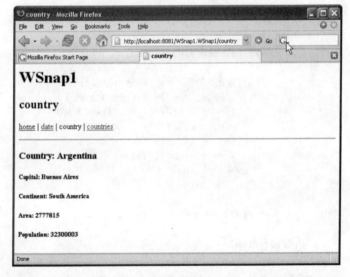

FIGURE 20.3
The country page of the
WebSnap1 example

To open this dataset when the page is first created and reset it to the first record in further invocations, you handle the OnBeforeDispatchPage event of the web page module, adding this code to it:

```
cdsCountry.Open;
cdsCountry.First;
```

The fact that a WebSnap page can be very similar to a portion of a WebBroker application (basically, an action tied to a producer) is important if you want to port existing WebBroker code to this new architecture. You can even port your existing DataSetTableProducer components to the new architecture. Technically, you can generate a new page, remove its producer component, replace it with a DataSetTableProducer, and hook this component to the PageProducer property of the web page module. In practice, this approach would cut out the HTML file of the page and its scripts.

In the WSnap1 program, I used a better technique. I added a custom tag (`<#htmltable>`) to the HTML file and used the `OnTag` event of the page producer to add to the HTML the result of the dataset table:

```
if TagString = 'htmltable' then
  ReplaceText := DataSetTableProducer1.Content;
```

Server-Side Scripts

Having multiple pages in a server-side program—each associated with a different page module—changes the way you write a program. Having the server-side scripts at hand offers an even more powerful approach. For example, the standard scripts of the WSnap1 example account for the application and page titles and for the index of the pages. This index is generated by an enumerator, the technique used to scan a list from within WebSnap script code. Let's look at it:

```
<table cellspacing="0" cellpadding="0"><td>
<% e = new Enumerator(Pages)
   s = ''
   c = 0
   for (; !e.atEnd(); e.moveNext())
   {
     if (e.item().Published)
     {
       if (c > 0) s += ' | '
       if (Page.Name != e.item().Name)
         s += '<a href="' + e.item().HREF + '">' +
           e.item().Title + '</a>'
       else
         s += e.item().Title
       c++
     }
   }
   if (c>1) Response.Write(s)
%>
</td></table>
```

NOTE Typically, WebSnap scripts are written in JavaScript, an object-based language common to Internet programming because it is the only scripting language generally available in browsers (on the client side). JavaScript (technically indicated as ECMAScript) borrows the core syntax of the C language and has almost nothing to do with Java. WebSnap uses Microsoft's ActiveScripting engine, which supports both JScript (a variation of JavaScript) and VBScript.

Inside the single cell of this table (which, oddly enough, has no rows), the script outputs a string with the `Response.Write` command. This string is built with a `for` loop over an enumerator of the application's pages, stored in the `Pages` global entity. The title of each page is added to the string only if the page is published. Each title uses a hyperlink with the exclusion of the current page. Having this code in a script, instead of hard-coded into a Delphi component, allows you to pass it to a good web designer, who can turn it into something a more visually appealing.

TIP   To publish or unpublish a page, don't look for a property in the web page module. This status is controlled by a flag of the AddWebModuleFactory method called in the web page module initialization code. You can comment or uncomment this flag to obtain the desired effect.

As a sample of what you can do with scripting, I added to the WSnap2 example (an extension of the WSnap1 example) a demoscript page. The page's script can generate a full table of multiplied values with the following scripting code (see Figure 20.4 for its output):

```
<table border=1 cellspacing=0>
<tr>
  <th> </th>
  <% for (j=1;j<=5;j++) { %>
  <th>Column <%=j %></th>
  <% } %>
</tr>
<% for (i=1;i<=5;i++) { %>
<tr>
  <td>Line <%=i %></td>
  <% for (j=1;j<=5;j++) { %>
  <td>Value= <%=i*j %></td>
  <% } %>
</tr>
<% } %>
</table>
```

In this script, the <%= symbol replaces the longer Response.Write command. Another important feature of server-side scripting is the inclusion of pages within other pages. For example, if you plan to modify the menu, you can include the related HTML and script in a single file, instead of changing it and maintaining it in multiple pages. File inclusion is generally done with a statement like this:

```
<!-- #include file="menu.html" -->
```

FIGURE 20.4

The WSnap2 example features a plain script and a custom menu stored in an include file.

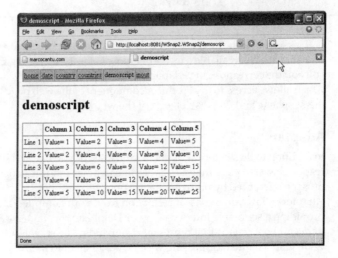

In Listing 20.1, you can find the complete source code of the include file for the menu, which is referenced by all of the project's other HTML files. Figure 20.4 shows an example of this menu, which is displayed across the top of the page using the table-generation script mentioned earlier.

LISTING 20.1:   The *menu.html* file included in each page of the WSnap2 example

```
<html>
  <head>
  <title><%= Page.Title %></title>
  </head>
<body>
  <h2><%= Application.Title %></h2>
  <table cellspacing="0" cellpadding="2" border="1" bgcolor="#c0c0c0">
    <tr>
<%  e = new Enumerator(Pages)
    for (; !e.atEnd(); e.moveNext())
    {
      if (e.item().Published)
      {
        if (Page.Name != e.item().Name)
          Response.Write ('<td><a href="' + e.item().HREF + '">' +
            e.item().Title + '</a></td>')
        else
          Response.Write ('<td>' + e.item().Title + '</td>')
      }
    }
%>
    </tr>
  </table>
  <hr>
  <h1><%= Page.Title %></h1>
```

This script for the menu uses the Pages list and the Page and Application global scripting objects. WebSnap makes available a few other global objects, including EndUser and Session objects (in case you add the corresponding adapters to the application), the Modules object, and the Producer object, which allows access to the Producer component of the web page module. The script also has available the Response and Request objects of the web module.

Adapters

In addition to these global objects, within a script you can access all the adapters available in the corresponding web page module. (Adapters in other modules, including shared web data modules, must be referenced by prefixing their name with the Modules object and the corresponding module.) Adapters allow you to pass information from your compiled Delphi code to the interpreted script, providing a scriptable interface to your Delphi application. Adapters contain fields that represent data and host actions that represent commands. The server-side scripts can access these values and issue these commands, passing specific parameters to them.

ADAPTER FIELDS

For simple customizations, you can add new fields to specific adapters. For instance, in the WSnap2 example, I added a custom field to the application adapter. After selecting this component, you can either open its Fields editor (accessible via its shortcut menu) or work in the Structure View. After adding a new field (called `AppHitCount` in the example), you can assign a value to it in its `OnGetValue` event. Because you want to count the hits (or requests) on any page of the web application, you can also handle the `OnBeforePageDispatch` event of the global PageDispatcher component to increase the value of a local field, `HitCount`. Here is the code for the two methods:

```
procedure Thome.PageDispatcherBeforeDispatchPage(Sender: TObject;
  const PageName: String; var Handled: Boolean);
begin
  Inc (HitCount);
end;

procedure Thome.AppHitCountGetValue(Sender: TObject;
  var Value: Variant);
begin
  Value := HitCount;
end;
```

Of course, you could use the page name to also count hits on each page (and you could add support for persistency, because the count is reset every time you run a new instance of the application). Now that you've added a custom field to an existing adapter (corresponding to the `Application` script object), you can access it from within any script, like this:

```
<p>Application hits since last activation:
<%= Application.AppHitCount.Value %></p>
```

ADAPTER COMPONENTS

In the same way, you can add custom adapters to specific pages. If you need to pass along a few fields, use the generic Adapter component. Other custom adapters (besides the global ApplicationAdapter you've already used) include these:

◆ The PagedAdapter component has built-in support for showing its content over multiple pages.

◆ The DataSetAdapter component is used to access a Delphi dataset from a script and is covered in the section "Using the DataSetAdapter."

◆ The StringValuesList holds a list of name/value pairs, such as a string list, and can be used directly or to provide a list of values to an adapter field. The inherited DataSetValuesList adapter has the same role but grabs the list of name/value pairs from a dataset, providing support for lookups and other selections.

◆ User-related adapters, such as the EndUser, EndUserSession, and LoginForm adapters, are used to access user and session information and to build a login form for the application that is automatically tied to the users list. I'll discuss these adapters in the section "Sessions, Users, and Permissions" later in this chapter.

USING THE ADAPTERPAGEPRODUCER

Most of these components are used in conjunction with an AdapterPageProducer component. The AdapterPageProducer can generate portions of script after you visually design the desired result. As an example, I added to the WSnap2 application the inout page, which has an adapter with two fields, one standard and one Boolean:

```
object Adapter1: TAdapter
  OnBeforeExecuteAction = Adapter1BeforeExecuteAction
  object TAdapterActions
    object AddPlus: TAdapterAction
      OnExecute = AddPlusExecute
    end
    object Post: TAdapterAction
      OnExecute = PostExecute
    end
  end
  object TAdapterFields
    object Text: TAdapterField
      OnGetValue = TextGetValue
    end
    object Auto: TAdapterBooleanField
      OnGetValue = AutoGetValue
    end
  end
end
```

The adapter also has a couple of actions that post the current user input and add a plus sign (+) to the text. The same plus sign is added when the Auto field is enabled. Developing the user interface for this form and the related scripting would take some time using plain HTML. But the Adapter-PageProducer component (used in this page) has an integrated HTML designer, which Borland calls Web Surface Designer. Using this tool, you can visually add a form to the HTML page and add an AdapterFieldGroup to it. Connect this field group to the adapter to automatically display editors for the two fields. Then you can add an AdapterCommandGroup and connect it to the AdapterField-Group to provide buttons for all of the adapter's actions. You can see an example of this designer in Figure 20.5.

To be more precise, the fields and buttons are automatically displayed if the AddDefaultFields and AddDefaultCommands properties of the field group and command group are set. The effect of using these visual operations to build this form are summarized in the following DFM snippet:

```
object AdapterPageProducer: TAdapterPageProducer
  object AdapterForm1: TAdapterForm
    object AdapterFieldGroup1: TAdapterFieldGroup
      Adapter = Adapter1
      object FldText: TAdapterDisplayField
        FieldName = 'Text'
      end
      object FldAuto: TAdapterDisplayField
        FieldName = 'Auto'
      end
```

```
    end
    object AdapterCommandGroup1: TAdapterCommandGroup
      DisplayComponent = AdapterFieldGroup1
      object CmdPost: TAdapterActionButton
        ActionName = 'Post'
      end
      object CmdAddPlus: TAdapterActionButton
        ActionName = 'AddPlus'
      end
    end
  end
end
```

Now that you have an HTML page with some scripts to move data back and forth and issue commands, let's look at the source code required to make this example work. First, you must add to the class two local fields to store the adapter fields and manipulate them, and you need to implement the OnGetValue event for both, returning the field values. When each button is clicked, you must retrieve the text passed by the user, which is not automatically copied into the corresponding adapter field. You can obtain this effect by looking at the ActionValue property of these fields, which is set only if something was entered (for this reason, when nothing is entered you set the Boolean field to False). To avoid repeating this code for both actions, place it in the OnBeforeExecuteAction event of the web page module:

```
procedure Tinout.Adapter1BeforeExecuteAction(Sender, Action: TObject;
  Params: TStrings; var Handled: Boolean);
begin
  if Assigned (Text.ActionValue) then
    fText := Text.ActionValue.Values [0];
  fAuto := Assigned (Auto.ActionValue);
end;
```

FIGURE 20.5

The Web Surface Designer for the inout page of the WSnap2 example at design time

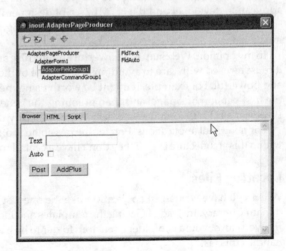

Notice that each action can have multiple values (in case components allow multiple selections); but this is not the case here, so you can grab the first element. Finally, here is the code for the OnExecute events of the two actions:

```
procedure Tinout.AddPlusExecute(Sender: TObject; Params: TStrings);
begin
  fText := fText + '+';
end;

procedure Tinout.PostExecute(Sender: TObject; Params: TStrings);
begin
  if fAuto then
    AddPlusExecute (Self, nil);
end;
```

As an alternative, adapter fields have a public EchoActionFieldValue property you can set to get the value entered by the user and place it in the resulting form. This technique is typically used in case of errors to let the user change the input starting with the values already entered.

NOTE   The AdapterPageProducer component has specific support for Cascading Style Sheets (CSS). You can define the CSS for a page using either the StylesFile property or the Styles string list. Any element of the editor of the producer's items can define a specific style or choose a style from the attached CSS. You accomplish this last operation (which is the suggested approach) using the StyleRule property.

SCRIPTS RATHER THAN CODE?

Even this example of the combined use of an adapter and an adapter page producer, with its visual designer, shows the power of this architecture. However, this approach also has a drawback: By letting the components generate the script (in the HTML, you have only the <#SERVERSCRIPT> tag), you save a lot of development time, but you end up mixing the script with the code so changes to the user interface require updating the program. The division of responsibilities between the Delphi application developer and the HTML/script designer is lost. And, ironically, you end up having to run a script to accomplish something the Delphi program could have done right away, possibly much faster.

In my opinion, WebSnap is a powerful architecture and a huge step forward from WebBroker, but it must be used with care to avoid misusing some of these technologies just because they are simple and powerful. For example, it might be worth using the AdapterPageProducer designer to generate the first version of a page, and then grabbing the generated script and copying it to a plain Page-Producer's HTML, so that a web designer can modify the script with a specific tool.

For nontrivial applications, I prefer the possibilities offered by XML and XSL, which are available within this architecture even if they don't have a central role. You'll find more on this topic in Chapter 22.

Locating Files

When you have written an application like the one just described, you must deploy it as a CGI or dynamic library. Instead of placing the templates and include files in the same folder as the executable file, you can devote a subfolder or custom folder to host all the files. The LocateFileService component handles this task.

The component is not intuitive to use. Instead of having you specify a target folder as a property, the system fires one of this component's events any time it has to locate a file. (This approach is much more powerful.) There are three events: `OnFindIncludeFile`, `OnFindStream`, and `OnFindTemplateFile`. The first and last events return the name of the file to use in a var parameter. The `OnFindStream` event allows you to provide a stream directly, using one you already have in memory or that you've created on the fly, extracted from a database, obtained via an HTTP connection, or gotten any other way you can think of. In the simplest case of the `OnFindIncludeFile` event, you can write code like the following:

```
procedure TPageProducerPage2.LocateFileService1FindIncludeFile(
  ASender: TObject; AComponent: TComponent; const AFileName: String;
  var AFoundFile: String; var AHandled: Boolean);
begin
  AFoundFile := DefaultFolder + AFileName;
  AHandled := True;
end;
```

Using the DataSetAdapter

Delphi has always shone in the area of database programming. For this reason, it is not surprising to see a lot of support for handling datasets within the WebSnap framework. Specifically, you can use the DataSetAdapter component to connect to a dataset and display its values in a form or a table using the AdapterPageProducer component's visual editor.

As an example, I built a new WebSnap application (called WSnapTable) with an AdapterPage-Producer as its main page to display a table in a grid and another AdapterPageProducer in a secondary page to show a form with a single record. I also added to the application a WebSnap Data Module as a container for the dataset components. The data module has a ClientDataSet that's wired to a dbExpress dataset through a provider and based on an InterBase connection, as you've already seen many times.

A Web Interface for a DataSetAdapter

Now that you have a dataset available, you can add a DataSetAdapter to the first page and connect it to the web module's ClientDataSet. The adapter automatically makes available all of the dataset's fields and several predefined actions for operating on the dataset (such as Delete, Edit, and Apply). You can add them explicitly to the `Actions` and `Fields` collections to exclude some of them and customize their behavior, but this step is not always required.

Like the PagedAdapter, the DataSetAdapter has a `PageSize` property you can use to indicate the number of elements to display in each page. The component also has commands you can use to navigate among pages. This approach is particularly suitable when you want to display a large dataset in a grid. These are the adapter settings for the main page of the WSnapTable example:

```
object DataSetAdapter1: TDataSetAdapter
  DataSet = WebDataModule1.ClientDataSet1
  PageSize = 6
end
```

The corresponding page producer has a form containing two command groups and a grid. The first command group (displayed above the grid) has the predefined commands for handling pages: CmdPrevPage, CmdNextPage, and CmdGotoPage. The last command generates a list of numbers for the pages, so that a user can jump to each of them directly. The AdapterGrid component has the default columns plus an extra column hosting Edit and Delete commands. The bottom command group provides a button used to create a new record. You can see an example of the table's output in Figure 20.6 and the complete settings of the AdapterPageProducer in Listing 20.2.

LISTING 20.2:   AdapterPageProducer settings for the WSnapTable main page

```
object AdapterPageProducer: TAdapterPageProducer
  object AdapterForm1: TAdapterForm
    object AdapterCommandGroup1: TAdapterCommandGroup
      DisplayComponent = AdapterGrid1
      object CmdPrevPage: TAdapterActionButton
        ActionName = 'PrevPage'
        Caption = 'Previous Page'
      end
      object CmdGotoPage: TAdapterActionButton...
      object CmdNextPage: TAdapterActionButton
        ActionName = 'NextPage'
        Caption = 'Next Page'
      end
    end
    object AdapterGrid1: TAdapterGrid
      Adapter = DataSetAdapter1
      AdapterMode = 'Browse'
      object ColCUST_NO: TAdapterDisplayColumn
      ...
      object AdapterCommandColumn1: TAdapterCommandColumn
        Caption = 'COMMANDS'
        object CmdEditRow: TAdapterActionButton
          ActionName = 'EditRow'
          Caption = 'Edit'
          PageName = 'formview'
          DisplayType = ctAnchor
        end
        object CmdDeleteRow: TAdapterActionButton
          ActionName = 'DeleteRow'
          Caption = 'Delete'
          DisplayType = ctAnchor
        end
      end
    end
    object AdapterCommandGroup2: TAdapterCommandGroup
      DisplayComponent = AdapterGrid1
      object CmdNewRow: TAdapterActionButton
```

```
        ActionName = 'NewRow'
        Caption = 'New'
        PageName = 'formview'
      end
    end
  end
end
```

There are a couple of things to notice in this listing. First, the grid's `AdapterMode` property is set to Browse (other possibilities are Edit, Insert, and Query). This dataset display mode for adapters determines the type of user interface (text or edit boxes and other input controls) and the visibility of other buttons (for example, Apply and Cancel buttons are only present in the edit view; the opposite is true for the Edit command—it is only available when you are not in the edit view). You can also modify the adapter mode by using server-side script and accessing `Adapter.Mode`.

Second, I modified the display of the commands in the grid using the ctAnchor value for the `DisplayType` property instead of the default button style. Similar properties are available for most components of this architecture to tweak the HTML code they produce.

FIGURE 20.6

The page shown by the WSnapTable example at startup includes the initial portion of a paged table.

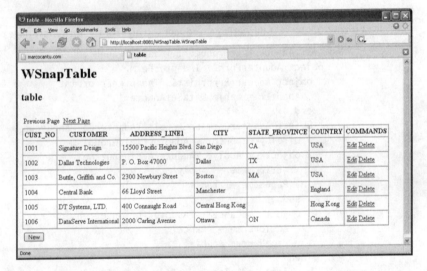

EDITING THE DATA IN A FORM

Some of the commands are connected to a different page, which will be displayed after the commands are invoked. For example, the Edit command's `PageName` property is set to formview. This second page of the application has an AdapterPageProducer with components hooked to the same DataSet-Adapter as of the other table, so that all the requests will be automatically synchronized. If you click the Edit command, the program will open the secondary page that displays the data of the record corresponding to the command.

Listing 20.3 shows the details of the page producer for the program's second page. Again, building the HTML form visually using the Delphi-specific designer (see Figure 20.7) was a very fast operation.

FIGURE 20.7

The formview page shown by the WSnap-Table example at design time in the Web Surface Designer (or Adapter-PageProducer editor)

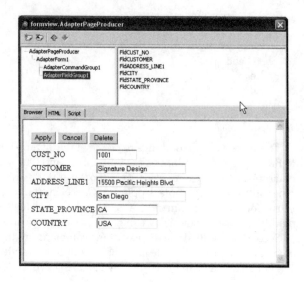

LISTING 20.3: AdapterPageProducer settings for the formview page

```
object AdapterPageProducer: TAdapterPageProducer
  object AdapterForm1: TAdapterForm
    object AdapterErrorList1: TAdapterErrorList
      Adapter = table.DataSetAdapter1
    end
    object AdapterCommandGroup1: TAdapterCommandGroup
      DisplayComponent = AdapterFieldGroup1
      object CmdApply: TAdapterActionButton
        ActionName = 'Apply'
        PageName = 'table'
      end
      object CmdCancel: TAdapterActionButton
        ActionName = 'Cancel'
        PageName = 'table'
      end
      object CmdDeleteRow: TAdapterActionButton
        ActionName = 'DeleteRow'
        Caption = 'Delete'
        PageName = 'table'
      end
    end
    object AdapterFieldGroup1: TAdapterFieldGroup
      Adapter = table.DataSetAdapter1
      AdapterMode = 'Edit'
      object FldCUST_NO: TAdapterDisplayField
        FieldName = 'CUST_NO'
      end
```

```
      object FldCUSTOMER: TAdapterDisplayField
        ...
    end
  end
end
```

In the listing, you can see that all the operations send the user back to the main page and that the `AdapterMode` is set to Edit, unless there are update errors or conflicts. In this case, the same page is displayed again, with a description of the errors obtained by adding an AdapterErrorList component at the top of the form:

formview

- Invalid value for field 'CUST_NO'

[Apply] [Cancel] [Delete]

CUST_NO   [   ]

The second page is not published because selecting it without referring to a specific record would make little sense. To unpublish the page, you comment the corresponding flag in the initialization code. Finally, to make the changes to the database persistent, you can call the `ApplyUdpates` method in the `OnAfterPost` and `OnAfterDelete` events of the ClientDataSet component hosted by the data module.

This program has a problem: the database server assigns the ID of each customer, so that when you enter a new record the data in the ClientDataSet and in the database are no longer aligned. This situation can cause Record Not Found errors.

MASTER/DETAIL IN WEBSNAP

The DataSetAdapter component has specific support for master/detail relationships between datasets. After you've created the relationship among the datasets, as usual, define an adapter for each dataset and then connect the `MasterAdapter` property of the detail dataset's adapter. Setting up the master/detail relationship between the adapters makes them work in a more seamless way. For example, when you change the work mode of the master or enter new records, the detail automatically enters into Edit mode or is refreshed.

The WSnapMD example uses a data module to define such a relationship. It includes two ClientDataSet components, each connected to a SQLDataSet through a provider. The data access components each refer to a table, and the ClientDataSet components define a master/detail relationship. The same data module hosts two dataset adapters that refer to the two datasets and again define the master/detail relationship:

```
object dsaDepartment: TDataSetAdapter
  DataSet = cdsDepartment
end
object dsaEmployee: TDataSetAdapter
  DataSet = cdsEmployee
  MasterAdapter = dsaDepartment
end
```

WARNING   I originally tried to use a SimpleDataSet component to avoid cluttering the data module, but this approach didn't work. The master/detail portion of the program was correct, but moving from a page to the next or a previous page with the related buttons kept failing. The reason is that if you use a SimpleDataSet, a bug closes the dataset at each interaction, losing the status information.

This WebSnap application's only page has an AdapterPageProducer component hooked to both dataset adapters. The page's form has a field group hooked to the master and a grid connected with the detail. Unlike with other examples, I tried to improve the user interface by adding custom attributes for the various elements. I used a gray background, displayed some of the grid borders (HTML grids are often used by Web Surface Designer), centered most of the elements, and added spacing. Notice that I added extra spaces to the button captions to prevent them from being too small. You can see the related code in the following detailed excerpt and the effect in Figure 20.8:

```
object AdapterPageProducer: TAdapterPageProducer
  object AdapterForm1: TAdapterForm
    Custom = 'Border="1" CellSpacing="0" CellPadding="10" ' +
      'BgColor="Silver" align="center"'
    object AdapterCommandGroup1: TAdapterCommandGroup
      DisplayComponent = AdapterFieldGroup1
      Custom = 'Align="Center"'
      object CmdFirstRow: TAdapterActionButton...
      object CmdPrevRow: TAdapterActionButton...
    end
    object AdapterFieldGroup1: TAdapterFieldGroup
      Custom = 'BgColor="Silver"'
      Adapter = WDataMod.dsaDepartment
      AdapterMode = 'Browse'
    end
    object AdapterGrid1: TAdapterGrid
      TableAttributes.BgColor = 'Silver'
      HeadingAttributes.BgColor = 'Gray'
      Adapter = WDataMod.dsaEmployee
      AdapterMode = 'Browse'
      object ColEMP_NO: TAdapterDisplayColumn...
      object ColFIRST_NAME: TAdapterDisplayColumn...
      object ColLAST_NAME: TAdapterDisplayColumn...
      ...
    end
  end
end
```

WebSnap Sessions, Users, and Permissions

Another interesting feature of the WebSnap architecture is its support for sessions and users. Sessions are supported using a classic approach: temporary cookies. These cookies are sent to the browser so that following requests from the same user can be acknowledged by the system. By adding data to a session instead of an application adapter, you can have data that depends on the specific session or user (although a user can run multiple sessions by opening multiple browser windows on the same computer). For supporting sessions, the server application keeps session data in memory, so this feature is not available in CGI programs.

FIGURE 20.8
The WSnapMD example shows a master/detail structure and has some customized output.

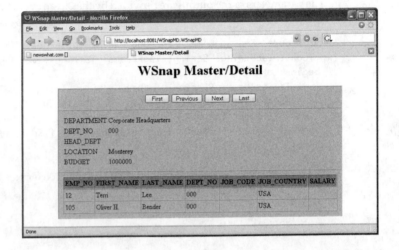

Using Sessions

To underline the importance of this type of support, I built a WebSnap application with a single page showing both the total number of hits and the total number of hits for each session. The program has a SessionService component with default values for its MaxSessions and DefaultTimeout properties. For every new request, the program increases both an nHits private field of the page module and the SessionHits value of the current session:

```
procedure TSessionDemo.WebAppPageModuleBeforeDispatchPage(
  Sender: TObject; const PageName: String; var Handled: Boolean);
begin
  // increase application and session hits
  Inc (nHits);
  WebContext.Session.Values ['SessionHits'] :=
    Integer (WebContext.Session.Values ['SessionHits']) + 1;
end;
```

NOTE The WebContext object (of type TWebContext) is a thread variable created by WebSnap for each request. It provides thread-safe access to other global variables used by the program.

The associated HTML displays status information by using both custom tags evaluated by the OnTag event of the page producer and script evaluated by the engine. Here is the core portion of the HTML file:

```
<h3>Plain Tags</h3>
<p>Session id: <#SessionID>
<br>Session hits: <#SessionHits></p>
```

```
<h3>Script</h3>
<p>Session hits (via application): <%=Application.SessionHits.Value%>
<br>Application hits: <%=Application.Hits.Value%></p>
```

The parameters of the output are provided by the `OnTag` event handler and the fields' `OnGetValue` events:

```
procedure TSessionDemo.PageProducerHTMLTag(Sender: TObject; Tag: TTag;
  const TagString: String; TagParams: TStrings; var ReplaceText: String);
begin
  if TagString = 'SessionID' then
    ReplaceText := WebContext.Session.SessionID
  else if TagString = 'SessionHits' then
    ReplaceText := WebContext.Session.Values ['SessionHits']
end;

procedure TSessionDemo.HitsGetValue(Sender: TObject;
  var Value: Variant);
begin
  Value := nHits;
end;

procedure TSessionDemo.SessionHitsGetValue(Sender: TObject;
  var Value: Variant);
begin
  Value := Integer (WebContext.Session.Values ['SessionHits']);
end;
```

The effect of this program is visible in Figure 20.9, where I activated two sessions in two different browsers.

TIP   In this example, I used both the traditional WebBroker tag replacement and the newer Web-Snap adapter fields and scripting so that you can compare the two approaches. Keep in mind that they are both available in a WebSnap application.

Requesting Login

In addition to generic sessions, WebSnap also has specific support for users and login-based authorized sessions. You can add to an application a list of users (with the WebUserList component), each with a name and a password. This component is rudimentary in the data it can store. However, instead of filling it with your list of users, you can keep the list in a database table (or in another proprietary format) and use the WebUserList component's events to retrieve your custom user data and check the user passwords.

You'll generally also add to the application the SessionService and EndUserSessionAdapter components. At this point, you can ask the users to log in, indicating for each page whether it can be viewed by everyone or only by logged-in users. This is accomplished by setting the wpLogin-Required flag in the constructor of the TWebPageModuleFactory and TWebAppPageModuleFactory classes in the web page unit's initialization code.

FIGURE 20.9

Two instances of the browser operate on two different sessions of the same WebSnap application.

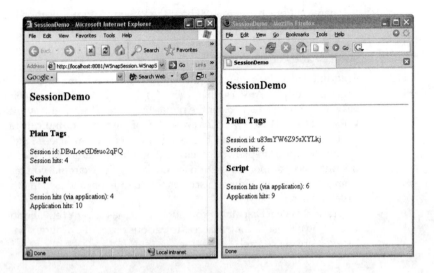

NOTE　Rights and publication information is included in the internal module factory object rather than in the WebPageModule because the program can check the access rights and list the pages even without loading the module.

When a user tries to see a page that requires user identification, the login page indicated in the EndUserSessionAdapter component is displayed. You can create such a page easily by creating a new web page module based on an AdapterPageProducer and adding to it the LoginFormAdapter. In the page's editor, add a field group within a form, connect the field group to the LoginFormAdapter, and add a command group with the default Login button. The resulting login form will have fields for the username and its password and also for the requested page. This last value is automatically filled with the requested page, in case this page required authorization and the user wasn't already logged in. This way, a user can immediately reach the requested page without being bounced back to a generic menu.

The login form is typically not published because the corresponding Login command is already available when the user isn't logged in to the system; when the user logs in, it is replaced by a Logout command. This command is obtained by the standard script of the web page module, particularly the following:

```
<% if (EndUser.Logout != null) { %>
<%   if (EndUser.DisplayName != '') { %>
  <h1>Welcome <%=EndUser.DisplayName %></h1>
<%   } %>
<%   if (EndUser.Logout.Enabled) { %>
  <a href="<%=EndUser.Logout.AsHREF%>">Logout</a>
<%   } %>
<%   if (EndUser.LoginForm.Enabled) { %>
  <a href=<%=EndUser.LoginForm.AsHREF%>>Login</a>
<%   } %>
<% } %>
```

There isn't much else to say about the WSnapUsers application because it has almost no custom code and settings. This script for the standard template demonstrates the access to the user data.

SINGLE PAGE ACCESS RIGHTS

In addition to making pages require a login for access, you can give specific users the right to see more pages than others. Any user has a set of rights separated by semicolons or commas. The user must have all the rights defined for the requested page. These rights, which are generally listed in the ViewAccess and ModifyAccess properties of the adapters, indicate respectively whether the user can see the given elements while browsing or can edit them. These settings are granular and can be applied to entire adapters or specific adapter fields (notice I'm referring to the adapter fields, not the user interface components within the designer). For example, you can hide some of a table's columns from given users by hiding the corresponding fields (and also in other cases, as specified by the HideOptions property).

The global PageDispatcher component also has OnCanViewPage and OnPageAccessDenied events, which you can use to control access to various pages of a program within the program code, allowing for even greater control.

IntraWeb

IntraWeb is a web development framework produced by Atozed Software (www.atozedsoftware.com) and included in Delphi 2005. The Professional edition includes the limited Professional version of IntraWeb, called the page edition, which contains all functionality for developing using Page Mode (a technique described later in this chapter) and an evaluation capability for Application Mode. The Enterprise and Architect editions of Delphi include the full version of IntraWeb for Borland VCL. In both cases, IntraWeb works both in Delphi for Win32 and Delphi for .NET.

Delphi 2005 includes IntraWeb 7.2.14, but you are entitled to download from Atozed Software and install newer updates up to the last version before version 7.5. Notice that a bug in the version shipping with Delphi 2005 reverts applications back to evaluation mode when they are deployed outside of the IDE. This is why I recommend that you update your copy of IntraWeb if you plan to go beyond a simple evaluation (even though the process takes a while because you need to ask Atozed Software for a permission key).

Although Delphi 7 was the first version of the Borland IDE to include this set of components, IntraWeb has been around for several years; it has received appraisal and support, including the availability of several third-party components. IntraWeb third-party components include IWChart by Steema (the makers of TeeChart), IWOpenSource, IWTranslator, IWDialogs, IWDataModulePool by Arcana, IW Component Pack by TMS, and IWGranPrimo by GranPrimo.

Although you don't have the source code for the core library (available on request and upon a specific payment), the IntraWeb architecture is fairly open, and the full source code of the components is readily available. A relevant feature is that this architecture works on three different platforms: Win32, .NET, and Linux.

From Websites to Web Applications

As I mentioned earlier, the idea behind IntraWeb is to build web applications rather than websites. When you work with WebBroker or WebSnap, you think in terms of web pages and page producers, and you work closely at the HTML generation level. When you work with IntraWeb, you think in terms of components, their properties, and their event handlers, as you do in Delphi visual development.

To create a new IntraWeb application, select File ➤ New ➤ Other, move to the Delphi Projects/ IntraWeb page (or the Delphi for .NET Projects/IntraWeb page) of the New Items dialog box, and choose IntraWeb Application Wizard (or IntraWeb Application Wizard for Delphi for .NET). In the dialog box of the wizard (shown in Figure 20.10 in the Win32 version) you can choose the type of application, the name and the directory of the project, and a few other parameters. For the first example (called IWSimpleApp), I kept the StandAlone Application option and checked the Create User Session check box.

NOTE   When the wizard creates a new IntraWeb project, it adds to it a deployment configuration file for Delphi's Deployment Manager . I'll describe this tool at the end of the chapter.

Before we examine the architecture of the code generated by the wizards, let's complete the example. To build it, after using the wizard, follow these steps:

1. Move to the main form of the program and add to it a button, an edit box, and a list box from the IW Standard page of the Tool Palette. That is, don't add the VCL components from the Standard page of the palette—instead, use the corresponding IntraWeb components: IWButton, IWEdit, and IWListbox.

2. Slightly modify their properties as follows:

```
object IWButton1: TIWButton
  Caption = 'Add Item'
end
object IWEdit1: TIWEdit
  Text = 'four'
end
object IWListbox1: TIWListbox
  Items.Strings = (
    'one'
    'two'
    'three')
end
```

FIGURE 20.10
The IntraWeb Application Wizard helps you getting started with a web application.

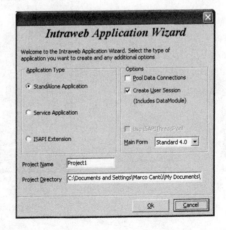

3. Handle the OnClick event of the button by double-clicking the component at design time as usual and writing this familiar code:

```
procedure TMainForm.IWButton1Click(Sender: TObject);
begin
  IWListBox1.Items.Add (IWEdit1.Text);
end;
```

That's all it takes to create a web-based application capable of adding text to a list box, as you can see in Figure 20.11 (which shows the final version of the program, with a couple more buttons). The important thing to notice when you run this program is that every time you click the button, the browser sends a new request to the application, which runs the Delphi event handler and produces a new HTML page based on the new status of the components on the form.

As you execute the application, you won't see the program output in the browser, but rather IntraWeb's controller form, shown in Figure 20.12. A stand-alone IntraWeb application is a full-blown HTTP server, as you'll see in more detail in the next section. The form you see is managed by the IWRun call in the project file created by default in each stand-alone IntraWeb application. The debug form allows you to select a browser and run the application through it or copy the URL of the application to the Clipboard, so you can paste it within your browser. It's important to know that the application will by default use port 8888, while it uses a random port number different for each execution when in evaluation mode. You can modify the port by selecting the server controller's designer (similar to a data module) and setting the port property. In the example I left the standard 8888, but any other value will do.

IntraWeb code is mainly server side, but IntraWeb also generates JavaScript to control some application features; you can also execute extra code on the client side. You do so by using specific client-side IntraWeb components or by writing your own custom JavaScript code. As a comparison, the two buttons in the bottom right corner of the form in the IWSimpleApp example show a message box using two different approaches.

FIGURE 20.11

The IWSimpleApp program in a browser

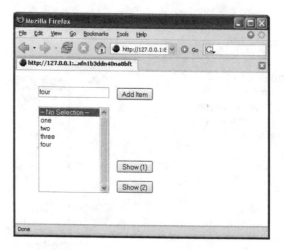

FIGURE 20.12
The controller form of a
stand-alone IntraWeb
application

The first of these two buttons (`IWButton2`) shows a message using a server-side event, with this Delphi code:

```
procedure TMainForm.IWButton2Click(Sender: TObject);
var
  nItem: Integer;
begin
  nItem := IWListbox1.ItemIndex;
  if nItem >= 0 then
    WebApplication.ShowMessage (IWListBox1.Items [nItem])
  else
    WebApplication.ShowMessage ('No item selected');
end;
```

The second of these two buttons (`IWButton3`) uses JavaScript, which is inserted in the Delphi program by setting the proper JavaScript event handler in the special property editor for the `ScriptEvents` property:

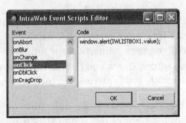

A First Look Behind the Scenes

You saw that creating an IntraWeb application is as simple as creating a Delphi form-based program: You place components on a form and handle their events. Of course, the effect is rather different because the application runs in a browser. To give you a feel for what's going on, let's briefly look behind the scenes of this simple program. Doing so should help you understand the effect of setting the component properties and of working with them in general.

This is a browser-based program, so there is no better way to understand it than by looking at the HTML it sends to the browser. Open the source of the IWSimpleApp program's page (not listed here because it would waste too much book space) and you'll notice it is divided into three main sections. The first is a list of styles (based on the HTTP style tag) with lines like the following:

```
.IWEDIT1CSS {position:absolute;left:48;top:32;
  z-index:100;width:145;height:21;font-style:normal;
  font-size:13px;text-decoration: none;text-align:left;}
```

IntraWeb uses styles to determine not only the visual appearance of each component such as its font and color, but also the component's position, using default absolute positioning. Each style is affected by a number of the IntraWeb component's properties, so you can easily experiment if you have some knowledge of style sheets. If you aren't familiar with style sheets, just use the properties and trust that IntraWeb will do its best to render the components in the web page.

The second block consists of JavaScript scripting. The main script block contains initialization code and the code of client-side event handlers for the components, like the following:

```
function IWBUTTON1_onclick (ASender) {
  return SubmitClickConfirm('IWBUTTON1','', true, '');
}
```

This handler invokes the corresponding server-side code. If you've provided the JavaScript code directly in the IntraWeb application, as discussed earlier, you'll see this code:

```
function IWBUTTON3_onclick(ASender) {
  window.alert(ASender.value);
}
```

The scripting section of the page also has references to other files required by the browser and made available by IntraWeb. Some of these files are generic; others are tied to the specific browser: IntraWeb detects the browser being used and returns different JavaScript code and base JavaScript files.

NOTE   Because JavaScript is not identical on all browsers, IntraWeb has specific support for many of them, including Microsoft Internet Explorer, Netscape Navigator, Mozilla Firefox, Opera, and Safari. See the SupportedBrowsers property of the IntraWeb form. Keep in mind that a browser can fake its identity: for example, Opera and Firefox can be set to identify themselves as Internet Explorer for some sites to work, but this can prevent IntraWeb from making a proper identification.

The third part of the generated HTML is the definition of the page structure. Inside the body tag are two form tags. One form tag defines the actual structure of the form and hosts the specific user interface components. The other form tag contains the real command to be executed on a mirror set of hidden fields, which are filled by the JavaScript code :

```
<form onsubmit="return FormDefaultSubmit();">
  <input value="Add Item" name="IWBUTTON1" type="button"
    class="IWBUTTON1CSS" id="IWBUTTON1">
  <input type="TEXT" name="IWEDIT1" value="four"
    class="IWEDIT1CSS" id="IWEDIT1">
  <!-- more controls -->
</form>
```

```
<form method="POST" name="SubmitForm" action="/EXEC/1/
  0yyohu91h2tlma0zs4afc1q0va7y">
  <input type="HIDDEN" name="IWBUTTON1">
  <input type="HIDDEN" name="IWEDIT1">
<!-- more controls -->
  <input type="HIDDEN" name="IW_FormName" value="MainForm">
  <input type="HIDDEN" name="IW_FormClass" value="TMainForm">
</form>
```

The form also has a few hidden components that IntraWeb uses to pass information back and forth. However, the URL is the most important way to pass information in IntraWeb; in the program it looks like this:

```
http://127.0.0.1:88888/EXEC/1/0yyohu91h2tlma0zs4afc1q0va7y
```

That is, the first part is the IP address and port used by the stand-alone IntraWeb application (it changes when you use a different architecture to deploy the program), followed by the EXEC command, a progressive request number, and a session ID. We'll get back to sessions later on, but suffice to say that IntraWeb uses a URL token instead of cookies to make its applications available regardless of browser settings. If you prefer, you can use cookies instead of URLs by changing the TrackMode property in the server controller.

The Source Code of the IntraWeb Application

If you've used IntraWeb in the past (for example, the version included in Delphi 7), you might remember some very unusual project source code with the call to a global IWRun function. More recent versions of IntraWeb have a standard project source code that creates the controller form already shown in Figure 20.12. This is the IntraWeb project code in Delphi 2005:

```
program IWSimpleApp;

{%DeployDocTool 'IWSimpleAppDeployment.bdsdeploy'}

uses
  Forms,
  IWMain,
  // specific units…

begin
  Application.Initialize;
  Application.CreateForm(TformIWMain, formIWMain);
  Application.Run;
end.
```

As the project source code doesn't indicate the main web form of the project, this is set in the initialization section of the unit of the main form itself, with the code (extracted from IWSimpleAppForm.pas):

```
initialization
  TMainForm.SetAsMainForm;
```

Building the Delphi for .NET Version of IWSimpleApp

Unlike with VCL applications, in an IntraWeb project you cannot have a single source code file shared by the Win32 and the .NET version of the program. This is also the case for the IWSimpleApp program. Some of the properties of the IntraWeb components, in fact, are different, so if you load the form description of a Win32 IntraWeb application in a .NET IntraWeb application this will fail. There are also some minor differences in the source code, so that trying to use IFDEFs to compile for Win32 and .NET with a single source might become quite difficult.

As a demo I created the IWSimpleAppNet program, in its own specific folder, and recreated almost the same program. Among the two applications there are differences in the main project file and in the initialization code of the main form:

```
initialization
  TMainForm.SetAsMainForm(typeof(TMainForm)); // .NET
  TMainForm.SetAsMainForm; // Win32
```

There are many other similar subtle differences, as you can see by generating a project with the .NET version of the IntraWeb Application Wizard.

NOTE   The following IntraWeb demos of this chapter remain in their Win32 version, as showing both Win32 and .NET versions of each would provide little extra insight into IntraWeb architecture. Everything discussed for Win32 also applies to the .NET side of IntraWeb.

IntraWeb Architectures

Before I write more examples to demonstrate the use of some other IntraWeb components, let's discuss another key element of IntraWeb: the different architectures you can use to create and deploy applications based on this library. You can create IntraWeb projects in Application mode (which makes available all of the features of IntraWeb) or Page mode (which is a simplified version you can plug into existing Delphi WebBroker or WebSnap applications). Application mode applications can be deployed as ISAPI libraries or by using IntraWeb Stand-alone mode (a variation of the Application mode architecture). Page mode programs can be deployed as any other WebBroker application (ISAPI, Apache module, CGI, etc.). IntraWeb features three different but partially overlapping architectures:

Stand-alone mode   Provides you with a custom web server, as in the first example you built. This is handy for debugging the application (because you can run it from the Delphi IDE and place breakpoints anywhere in the code). You can also use Stand-alone mode to deploy applications on internal networks (intranets) and to let users work in offline mode on their own computers with a web interface. If you run a stand-alone IntraWeb program with the -install flag, it will run as a service, and the dialog box won't appear. Stand-alone mode gives you a way to deploy an Application mode IntraWeb program using IntraWeb itself as web server.

Application mode   Allows you to deploy an IntraWeb application on a commercial server, building an IIS library. Application mode includes session management and all the IntraWeb features and is the preferred way to deploy a scalable application for use on the Web. To be precise, Application mode IntraWeb programs on Win32 can be deployed as stand-alone programs or ISAPI libraries.

Page mode   Opens a way to integrate IntraWeb pages in WebBroker and WebSnap applications. You can add features to existing programs or rely on other technologies for portions of a dynamic site based on HTML pages, while providing the interactive portions with IntraWeb. Page mode is the only choice for using IntraWeb in CGI applications, but it lacks session-management features. Stand-alone IntraWeb servers do not support Page mode.

NOTE   As you saw last chapter, in Delphi for .NET there is no support for WebBroker. Atozed software, however, has licensed this technology from Borland and ported it to .NET to support Page mode development in Delphi for .NET. So you could say that WebBroker is indeed available in .NET, although not in a way officially supported by Borland.

In the examples in the rest of the chapter, I'll use Stand-alone mode for simplicity and easier debugging, but I'll also cover Page mode support.

Building IntraWeb Applications

When you build an IntraWeb application, a number of components are available. For example, if you look at the IW Standard page of Delphi's Component Palette, you'll see an impressive list of core components, from the obvious button, check box, radio button, edit box, list box, memo, and so on to the intriguing tree view, menu, timer, grid, and link components. I won't list each component and describe its use with an example—instead I'll use some of the components in a few demos and underline the architecture of IntraWeb rather than specific details.

I built an example (called IWTree) showcasing the menu and tree view components of IntraWeb and also featuring the creation of a component at run time. The IWMenu component makes available in a dynamic menu the content of a standard Delphi menu by referring its `AttachedMenu` property to a `TMainMenu` component:

```
object MainMenu1: TMainMenu
  object Tree1: TMenuItem
    object ExpandAll1: TMenuItem
    object CollapseAll1: TMenuItem
    ...
  end
  object About1: TMenuItem
    object Application1: TMenuItem
    object TreeContents1: TMenuItem
  end
end
object IWMenu1: TIWMenu
  AttachedMenu = MainMenu1
  Orientation = iwOHorizontal
  ItemSpacing = itsNone
  AutoSize = mnaNone
end
```

Be aware that some of the settings of the `AutoSize` and `ItemSpacing` properties cause the pull-down menus to be transparent, at least in the IntraWeb version shipping with Delphi 2005. If the menu items handle the `OnClick` event in the code, they become links at run time. You can see an example of a menu in a browser in Figure 20.13. The example's second component is a tree view with a set of predefined nodes. This component has a lot of JavaScript code to let you expand and collapse nodes directly in the browser (with no need to call back the server). At the same time, the menu items allow the program to operate on the tree by expanding or collapsing nodes and changing the font. Here is the code for a couple of event handlers:

```
procedure TMainForm.ExpandAll1Click(Sender: TObject);
var
  i: Integer;
begin
  for i := 0 to IWTreeView1.Items.Count - 1 do
    IWTreeView1.Items [i].Expanded := True;
end;

procedure TMainForm.EnlargeFont1Click(Sender: TObject);
begin
  IWTreeView1.Font.Size := IWTreeView1.Font.Size + 2;
end;
```

Thanks to the similarity of IntraWeb components to standard Delphi VCL components, the code is easy to read and understand.

The menu has two submenus, which are slightly more complex. The first displays the application ID, which is an application execution/session ID. This identifier is available in the AppID property of the WebApplication global object. The second submenu, Tree Contents, shows a list of the first tree nodes of the main level along with the number of direct subnodes. What's interesting, though, is that the information is displayed in a memo component created at run time (see again Figure 20.13), exactly as you'd do in a VCL application:

```
procedure TMainForm.TreeContents1Click(Sender: TObject);
var
  i: Integer;
begin
  with TIWMemo.Create(Self) do
  begin
    Parent := Self;
    Align := alBottom;
    for i := 0 to IWTreeView1.Items.Count - 1 do
      Lines.Add (IWTreeView1.Items [i].Caption + ' (' +
        IntToStr (IWTreeView1.Items [i].SubItems.Count) + ')');
  end;
end;
```

TIP   Alignment in IntraWeb works similarly to its VCL counterpart. For example, this program's menu uses alTop alignment, the tree view has alClient alignment, and the dynamic memo is created with alBottom alignment. As you resize the browser window, the components will adjust themselves with no need to call back the server. As an alternative, you can use anchors (again working as in the VCL): You can create bottom-right buttons or components in the middle of the page with all four anchors set. See the following demos for examples of this technique.

FIGURE 20.13

The IWTree example features a menu, a tree view, and the dynamic creation of a memo component.

Writing Multipage Applications

All the programs you have built so far have had a single page. Now let's create an IntraWeb application with a second page. As you'll see, even in this case, IntraWeb development resembles standard Delphi development and is different from most other Internet development libraries. This example will also serve as an excuse to delve into some of the source code automatically generated by the IntraWeb Application Wizard.

Let's start from the beginning. The main form of the IWTwoForms example features an IntraWeb grid. This powerful component allows you to place within an HTML grid both text and other components. In the example, the grid content is determined at startup (in the OnCreate event handler of the main form):

```
procedure TTwoMainForm.IWAppFormCreate(Sender: TObject);
var
  i: Integer;
  link: TIWURL;
begin
  // set grid titles
  IWGrid1.Cell[0, 0].Text := 'Row';
  IWGrid1.Cell[0, 1].Text := 'Owner';
  IWGrid1.Cell[0, 2].Text := 'Web Site';
  // set grid contents
  for i := 1 to IWGrid1.RowCount - 1 do
  begin
    IWGrid1.Cell [i,0].Text := 'Row ' + IntToStr (i+1);
    IWGrid1.Cell [i,1].Text := 'IWTwoForms by Marco Cantu';
    link := TIWURL.Create(Self);
```

```
      link.Text := 'Click here';
      link.URL := 'http://www.marcocantu.com';
      IWGrid1.Cell [i,2].Control := link;
    end;
  end;
```

The effect of this code is shown in Figure 20.14. In addition to the output, there are a few interesting things to notice. First, the grid component uses Delphi anchors (all set to False) to generate code that keeps it centered in the page, even if a user resizes the browser window. Second, I added an IWURL component to the third column, but you could add any other component (including buttons and edit boxes) to the grid.

The third and most important consideration is that an IWGrid is translated into an HTML grid, with or without a frame around it. Here is a snippet of the HTML generated for one of the grid rows:

```html
<table id="IWGRID1" border="1" cellpadding="0" cellspacing="0"
  width="979" class="IWGRID1CSS">
  <CAPTION>IWGrid1</CAPTION>
  <SUMMARY>This is a grid</SUMMARY>
...
<tr>
  <td valign="middle" align="left" NOWRAP>
    <font style="font-size:13px;">Row 2</font>
  </td>
  <td valign="middle" align="left" NOWRAP>
    <font style="font-size:13px;">IWTwoForms by Marco Cantu</font>
  </td>
  <td valign="middle" align="left" NOWRAP>
    <a href="#TIWURL1"
      onclick="parent.LoadURL('http://www.marcocantu.com')"
      title="http://www.marcocantu.com"
      id="TIWURL1" name="TIWURL1"
      style="z-index:100;font-style:normal;font-size:13px;
        text-decoration:underline;">
      Click here</a>
  </td>
</tr>
```

NOTE   In the previous listing, the linked URL is activated via JavaScript, not with a direct link. This happens because all actions in IntraWeb allow for extra client-side operations, such as validations, checks, and submits. For example, if you set the Required property for a component, if the field is empty the data won't be submitted, and you'll see a JavaScript error message (customizable by setting the descriptive FriendlyName property).

The core feature of the program is its ability to show a second page. To accomplish this, you first need to add a new IntraWeb page to the application, using the New Form option on the IntraWeb page of Delphi's New Items dialog box (File ➤ New ➤ Other). In the resulting New Form Wizard, pick the default Application Form:

Add to this page a few IntraWeb components, as usual, and then add to the main form a button or other control you'll use to show the secondary form (with the reference anotherform stored in a field of the main form):

```
procedure TTwoMainForm.btnShowGraphicClick(Sender: TObject);
begin
  anotherform := TAnotherForm.Create(WebApplication);
  anotherform.Show;
end;
```

Even though the program calls the Show method, it can be considered like a ShowModal call because IntraWeb considers visible pages a stack. The last page displayed is on the top of the stack and is displayed in the browser. By closing this page (hiding or destroying it), you redisplay the previous page. In the program, the secondary page closes itself by calling the Release method, which as in the VCL is the proper way to dispose of a currently executing form. You can also hide the secondary form and then display it again to avoid re-creating it each time (particularly if doing so implies losing the user's editing operations).

FIGURE 20.14

The IWTwoForms example uses an IWGrid component with embedded text and IWURL components.

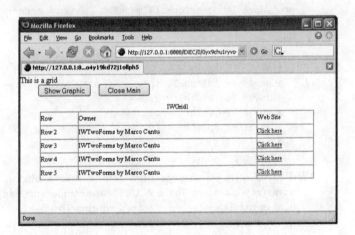

NOTE In the program I added a Close button to the main form. It should not call `Release`, but rather should invoke the `WebApplication` object's `Terminate` method, passing the output message, as in `WebApplication.Terminate('Goodbye!')`. The demo uses an alternative call: `TerminateAndRedirect`.

The secondary form of the IWTwoForms example shows another interesting feature of IntraWeb: its extensive graphics support. The form has a graphical component with the classic Delphi Athena image. This is accomplished by loading a bitmap into an IWImage component: IntraWeb converts the bitmap into a JPEG, and returns a reference to it, with the following HTML:

```
<img src="/Cache/user/0nw1np40ibun18109yw8w03sx0wk/JPGEA.tmp" name="IWIMAGE1"
border="0" class="IWIMAGE1CSS" id="IWIMAGE1">
```

The image is cached and there is one for each user because a user can modify this image. The extra feature provided by IntraWeb and exploited by the program, in fact, is that a user can click the image with the mouse to modify the image by launching server-side code. In this program, the effect is to draw small green circles.

This effect is obtained with the following code:

```
procedure Tanotherform.IWImage1MouseDown(ASender: TObject;
  const AX, AY: Integer);
var
  aCanvas: TCanvas;
begin
  aCanvas := IWImage1.Picture.Bitmap.Canvas;
  aCanvas.Pen.Width := 8;
  aCanvas.Pen.Color := clGreen;
  aCanvas.Ellipse(Ax - 10, Ay - 10, Ax + 10, Ay + 10);
end;
```

WARNING The painting operation takes place on the bitmap canvas. Do not try to use the Image canvas (as you can do with the VCL's TImage component), and do not try to use a JPEG in the first place, or you'll see either no effect or a run-time error.

Sessions Management

If you've done any web programming, you know that session management is a complex issue. IntraWeb provides predefined session management and simplifies the way you work with sessions. If you need session data for a specific form, all you have to do is add a field to that form. The IntraWeb forms and their components have an instance for each user session. For example, in the IWSession example, I've added to the form a field called FormCount. As a contrast, I've also declared a global unit variable called GlobalCount, which is shared by all the instances (or sessions) of the application.

To increase your control over session data and let multiple forms share it, you can customize the TIWUserSession class that the IntraWeb Application Wizard places in the UserSessionUnit unit (it was in the ServerController unit in the version of IntraWeb 5 included in Delphi 7), if you selected the corresponding check box in the wizard. In the IWSession example, I customized the class as follows:

```
type
  TIWUserSession = class (TIWUserSessionBase)
  public
    UserCount: Integer;
  end;
```

IntraWeb creates an instance of this object for each new session, as you can see in the IWServerControllerBaseNewSession method of the TIWServerController class in the default ServerController unit:

```
procedure TIWServerController.IWServerControllerBaseNewSession(
  ASession: TIWApplication; var VMainForm: TIWBaseForm);
begin
  ASession.Data := TIWUserSession.Create(nil);
end;
```

In an application's code, the session object can be referenced by accessing the Data field of the WebApplication global variable, used to access the current user's session. As a helper, the Server-Controller unit defines a UserSession function, as follows:

```
function UserSession: TIWUserSession;
begin
  Result := TIWUserSession(WebApplication.Data);
end;
```

Because most of this code is generated for you, after adding data to the TIWUserSession class you simply use it through the UserSession function, as in the following code extracted from the IWSession example. When you click a button, the program increases several counters (one global and two session-specific) and shows their values in labels:

```
procedure TformMain.IWButton1Click(Sender: TObject);
begin
  InterlockedIncrement (GlobalCount);
  Inc (FormCount);
```

```
    Inc (UserSession.UserCount);

    IWLabel1.Text := 'Global: ' + IntToStr (GlobalCount);
    IWLabel2.Text := 'Form: ' + IntToStr (FormCount);
    IWLabel3.Text := 'User: ' + IntToStr (UserSession.UserCount);
  end;
```

Notice that the program uses Windows' `InterlockedIncrement` call to avoid concurrent access to the global shared variable by multiple threads. Alternative approaches include using a critical section or Indy's `TIdThreadSafeInteger` (found in the IdThreadsafe unit).

Figure 20.15 shows the output of the program (with two sessions running in two different browsers). The program has also a check box that activates a timer. Odd as it sounds, in an IntraWeb application, timers work almost the same as in Windows. When the timer interval expires, code is executed. Over the Web, this means refreshing the page by triggering a refresh in the JavaScript code:

```
    IWTop().IWTIMER1_ID=setTimeout(
      'IWTop().SubmitClickConfirm("IWTIMER1","", false,"")',
      5000);
```

FIGURE 20.15

The IWSession application has both session-specific and global counters, as you can see by running two sessions in two different browsers (or even in the same browser).

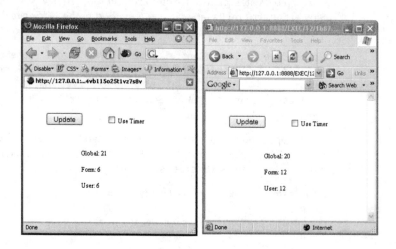

Integrating with WebBroker (and WebSnap)

Up to now, you have built stand-alone IntraWeb applications. When you create an IntraWeb application in a library to be deployed on IIS, you are basically in the same situation. Things change considerably, however, if you want to use IntraWeb Page mode, which is integrated in an IntraWeb page in a WebBroker (or WebSnap) Delphi application.

NOTE   One of the reasons for discussing IntraWeb Page mode is that this is the only option available to owners of Delphi 2005 Professional. As already mentioned, this also works on Delphi for .NET despite the lack of an official version of WebBroker form Borland.

The bridge between the two worlds is the IWPageProducer component. This component hooks to a WebBroker action like any other page producer component and has a special event you can use to create and return an IntraWeb form:

```
procedure TWebModule1.IWPageProducer1GetForm(ASender: TIWPageProducer;
  AWebApplication: TIWApplication; var VForm: TIWPageForm);
begin
  VForm := TMainForm.Create(AWebApplication);
end;
```

With this single line of code (plus the addition of an IWModuleController component in the web module), the WebBroker application can embed an IntraWeb page, as the CgiIntra program does. The IWModuleController component provides core services for IntraWeb support but has no specific properties and events. A component of this type must exist in every project for IntraWeb to work properly.

Here is a summary of the DFM of the example program's web module:

```
object WebModule1: TWebModule1
  Actions = <
    item
      Default = True
      Name = 'WebActionItem1'
      PathInfo = '/show'
      OnAction = WebModule1WebActionItem1Action
    end
    item
      Name = 'WebActionItem2'
      PathInfo = '/iwdemo'
      Producer = IWPageProducer1
    end>
  object IWModuleController1: TIWModuleController
  object IWPageProducer1: TIWPageProducer
    OnGetForm = IWPageProducer1GetForm
  end
end
```

The default action generates some plain HTML text with a link to the action hosting the IntraWeb page:

```
procedure TWebModule1.WebModule1WebActionItem1Action(Sender: TObject;
  Request: TWebRequest; Response: TWebResponse; var Handled: Boolean);
begin
  Response.Content := '<h1>Hello</h1>' +
    '<p>This is a WebBroker page, click ' +
    '<a href="CgiIntra/iwdemo">here</a> for an IntraWeb page</p>';
end;
```

Because this is a Page mode CGI application, it has no session management. Moreover, the status of the components in a page is not automatically updated by writing event handlers, as in a standard IntraWeb program. To accomplish the same effect you need to write specific code to handle further parameters of the HTTP request. It should be clear even from this simple example that Page mode does less for you than Application mode, but it's more flexible. In particular, IntraWeb Page mode allows you to add visual RAD design capabilities to your WebBroker and WebSnap applications.

Controlling the Layout

The CgiIntra program features another interesting technology available in IntraWeb: the definition of a custom layout based on HTML. (This topic isn't really related, because HTML layouts also work in Application mode—but I happened to use these two techniques in a single example.) In the programs built so far, the resulting page is the mapping of a series of components placed at design time on a form, in which you can use properties to modify the resulting HTML. But what if you want to embed a data-entry form within a complex HTML page? Building the entire page contents with IntraWeb components is awkward, even if you can use the IWText component to embed a custom piece of HTML within an IntraWeb page.

The alternative approach is represented by the use of IntraWeb's layout managers. In IntraWeb you invariably use a layout manager; the default is the IWLayoutMgrForm component. The other two alternatives are IWTemplateProcessorHTML for working with an external HTML template file and IWLayoutMgrHTML for working with internal HTML.

This second component includes a powerful HTML editor you can use to prepare the generic HTML as well as embed the required IntraWeb components (something you'll have to do manually with an external HTML editor). Moreover, as you select an IntraWeb component from this editor (which is activated by double-clicking an IWLayoutMgrHTML component), you'll be able to use Delphi's Object Inspector to customize the component's properties. As you can see in Figure 20.16, the HTML Layout Editor available in IntraWeb is a powerful visual HTML editor; the HTML text it generates is available in a separate page.

FIGURE 20.16

IntraWeb's HTML Layout Editor is a full-blown visual HTML editor.

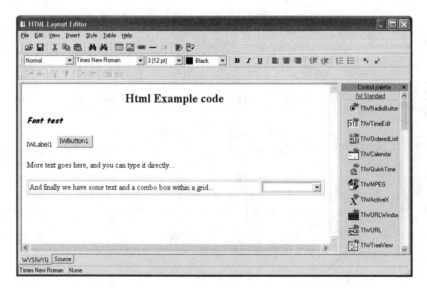

In the generated HTML, the HTML defines the structure of the page. The components are marked only with a special tag based on curly braces, as in the following HTML lines taken from the example:

```
<TABLE cellSpacing=2 cellPadding=1 width="100%" border=1>
  <TR>
    <TD width="100%">
      And finally...
    </TD>
    <TD width="100%">
      {%IWComboBox1%}
    </TD>
  </TR>
</TABLE>
```

TIP When you're using HTML, the components don't use absolute positioning but flow along with the HTML. Thus the form becomes only a component holder, because the size and position of the form's components are ignored.

Needless to say, the HTML you see in the visual designer of the HTML Layout Editor corresponds almost perfectly to the HTML you'll see when running the program in a browser.

Web Database Applications

As in Delphi's libraries, a significant portion of IntraWeb's available controls relates to the development of database applications. When you select the check box Create User Session in the IntraWeb Application Wizard, this will create a UserSessionUnit unit (as mentioned earlier), which is a data module—a good starting point for the development of a database application. As the TIWUser Session object is a data module, the application's predefined code creates an instance of the data module for each session, saving it in the session's data. (Notice that the code behind the user session and the session data module has changed considerably since IntraWeb 5, which was included in Delphi 7.)

This means you can refer to a dataset in the data module by writing UserSession.SimpleDataSet1. Instead of accessing a global data module, you are using the current session's data module.

In the first sample program featuring database data, called IWScrollData, I added to the data module a SimpleDataSet component and to the main form an IWDBGrid component with the following configuration:

```
object IWDBGrid1: TIWDBGrid
  Anchors = [akLeft, akTop, akRight, akBottom]
  UseFrame = False
  UseSize = True
  DataSource = DataSource1
  FriendlyName = 'IWDBGrid1'
  FromStart = False
  Options = [dgShowTitles]
  RefreshMode = rmAutomatic
  RowLimit = 10
```

```
      RowAlternateColor = clWebSILVER
      RowCurrentColor = clWebTEAL
   end
```

The most important settings are the removal of a frame hosting the control with its own scroll bars (the UseFrame property set to False), the fact that the data is displayed from the current dataset position (the FromStart property set to False), and the number of rows to be displayed in the browser (the RowLimit property). In the user interface, I removed vertical lines and colored alternate rows. I also had to set up a color for the current row (the RowCurrentColor property); otherwise, the alternate colors wouldn't appear to work properly since the current row is the same color as the background rows, regardless of its position (set the RowCurrentColor property to clNone to see what I mean). These settings produce the effect you can see in Figure 20.17 or by running the IWScrollData example.

The program opens the dataset when the form is created, using the dataset hooked to the current data source:

```
procedure TMainForm.IWAppFormCreate(Sender: TObject);
begin
  DataSource1.DataSet := UserSession.SimpleDataSet1;
  DataSource1.DataSet.Open;
end;
```

The example's relevant code is in the button code, which can be used to move through the data showing the following page or returning to the previous one. Here is the code for one of the two methods (the other is omitted because it's very similar):

```
procedure TMainForm.btnNextClick(Sender: TObject);
var
  i: Integer;
begin
  nPos := nPos + 10;
  if nPos > DataSource1.DataSet.RecordCount - 10 then
    nPos := DataSource1.DataSet.RecordCount - 10;
  DataSource1.DataSet.First;
  for i := 0 to nPos do
    DataSource1.DataSet.Next;
end;
```

Linking to Details

The grid of the IWScrollData example shows a single page of a table's data; buttons let you scroll up and down the pages. An alternative grid style in IntraWeb is offered by framed grids, which can move larger amounts of data to the web browser within a screen area of a fixed size using a frame and an internal scroll bar, as a Delphi ScrollBox control does. This is demonstrated by the IWGridDemo example.

The example customizes the grid in a second powerful way: It sets the Columns collection property of the grid. This setting allows you to fine-tune the output and behavior of specific columns, for example, by showing hyperlinks or handling clicks on items or title cells. In the IWGridDemo example, one of the columns (the last name) is turned into a hyperlink; the employee number is passed as a parameter to the follow-up command, as you can see in Figure 20.18.

FIGURE 20.17
The data-aware grid of the IWScrollData example

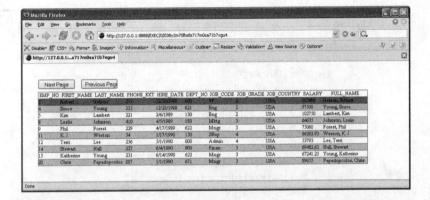

FIGURE 20.18
The main form of the IWGridDemo example uses a framed grid with hyperlinks to the secondary form.

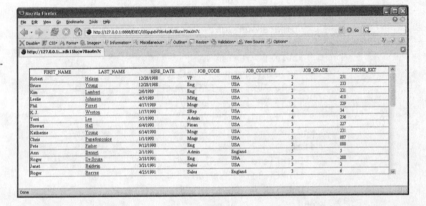

Listing 20.4 shows a summary of the grid's key properties. Notice in particular the last name column, which as mentioned has a linked field (which turns the cell's text into a hyperlink) and an event handler responding to its selection. In this method, the program creates a secondary form in which a user can edit the data:

```
procedure TGridForm.IWDBGrid1Columns1Click(ASender: TObject;
  const AValue: String);
begin
  with TRecordForm.Create (WebApplication) do
  begin
    StartID := AValue;
    Show;
  end;
end;
```

LISTING 20.4: Relevant properties of the IWDBGrid component in IWGridDemo

```
object IWDBGrid1: TIWDBGrid
  Anchors = [akLeft, akTop, akRight, akBottom]
  CellPadding = 1
  UseFrame = True
  UseSize = True
  ScrollToCurrentRow = False
  Columns = <
    item
      Alignment = taLeftJustify
      DoSubmitValidation = True
      Header = False
      VAlign = vaMiddle
      Visible = True
      Wrap = False
      CompareHighlight = hcNone
      DataField = 'FIRST_NAME'
      RawText = False
      Title.Alignment = taCenter
      Title.Text = 'FIRST_NAME'
      Title.VAlign = vaMiddle
      Title.Visible = True
    end
    item
      DataField = 'LAST_NAME'
      LinkField = 'EMP_NO'
      OnClick = IWDBGrid1Columns1Click
    end
    item
      DataField = 'HIRE_DATE'
    end
    ...>
  DataSource = DataSource1
  FriendlyName = 'IWDBGrid1'
  Options = [dgShowTitles]
end
```

By setting the second form's `StartID` property, you can locate the proper record. This is the code used by the secondary form:

```
procedure TRecordForm.SetStartID(const Value: string);
begin
  FStartID := Value;
  DataSource1.DataSet.Locate('EMP_NO', Value, []);
end;
```

TIP   The IWDBGrid columns also have an `OnTitleClick` event you can handle to sort the data or perform other operations on the column.

The secondary form is hooked to the same data module as the main form. So, after the database data is updated, you can see the modified data in the grid (but the updates are kept only in memory, because the program doesn't have an `ApplyUpdates` call to send back the in-memory data to the database). The secondary form uses a few edit controls and a navigator, provided by IntraWeb. You can see this form at run time in Figure 20.19.

FIGURE 20.19

The secondary form of the IWGridDemo example allows a user to edit the data and navigate through records.

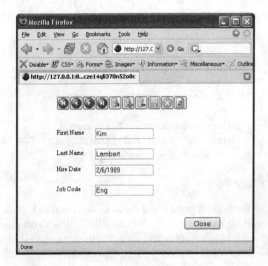

Moving Data to the Client Side

The IWDBGrid component invariably produces HTML with the database data embedded in the cells, but it cannot then work on the data once it is on the client side. A different component (or a set of IntraWeb components) allows you to follow a different model. The data is sent to the browser in a custom format, and the JavaScript code on the browser populates a grid and operates on the data, moving from record to record without asking for more data from the server.

NOTE   This architecture is similar to Delphi's native Internet Express architecture, which was introduced in Delphi 5 and is still available in Delphi 2005 but hasn't been improved in recent versions and is becoming obsolete. Therefore, I decided not to cover it, although I did like it a lot when it was first introduced.

You can use several IntraWeb components for a client-side application, but these are the most important ones:

IWClientSideDataSet   An in-memory dataset you define by setting the `ColumnNames` and `Data` properties within your program's code. In future updates, you will be able to edit client-side data, sort it, filter it, define master/detail structures, and more.

IWClientSideDataSetDBLink   A data provider you can connect to any Delphi dataset, connecting it with the `DataSource` property.

IWDynGrid   A dynamic grid component connected to one of the two previous components using the `Data` property. This component moves all the data to the browser and can operate on it on the client via JavaScript.

There are other client-side components in IntraWeb, such as IWCSLabel, IWCSNavigator, and IWDynamicChart. As an example of using client-side components , I built the IWClientGrid example. The program has little code because there is a lot available in the components being used. Here are the core elements of its main form:

```
object formMain: TformMain
  OnCreate = IWAppFormCreate
  object IWDynGrid1: TIWDynGrid
    Align = alClient
    Data = IWClientSideDatasetDBLink1
  end
  object DataSource1: TDataSource...
  object IWClientSideDatasetDBLink1: TIWClientSideDatasetDBLink
    DataSource = DataSource1
  end
end
```

The dataset from the data module is hooked to the DataSource when the form is created. The resulting grid, shown in Figure 20.20, allows you to sort the data on any cell (using the small arrow *after* the column title) and filter the data displayed on one of the field's possible values. In the figure, for example, I filtered the employees with 'Eng' in the job code field and sorted them by last name.

FIGURE 20.20

The grid of the IWClient-Grid example supports custom sorting and filtering without refetching the data on the web server.

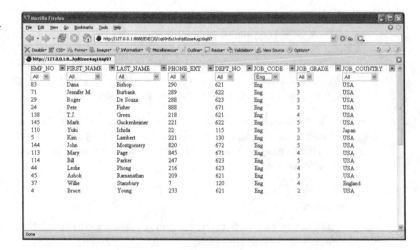

This functionality is possible because the data is moved to the browser within the JavaScript code. Here is a snippet of one of the scripts embedded in the page's HTML:

```
<script language="Javascript1.2">
  var IWDYNGRID1IWCL = null;
  var CSDSFieldNames_IWCLIENTSIDEDATASETDBLINK1 =
    ["EMP_NO","FIRST_NAME","LAST_NAME","PHONE_EXT",
    "DEPT_NO","JOB_CODE","JOB_GRADE","JOB_COUNTRY"];
  var CSDSDataArray_IWCLIENTSIDEDATASETDBLINK1 = new Array();
  CSDSDataArray_IWCLIENTSIDEDATASETDBLINK1[0] =
    [2,'Robert','Nelson','251','600','VP',2,'USA'];
  CSDSDataArray_IWCLIENTSIDEDATASETDBLINK1[1] =
    [4,'Bruce','Young','233','621','Eng',2,'USA'];
  CSDSDataArray_IWCLIENTSIDEDATASETDBLINK1[2] =
    [5,'Kim','Lambert','221','130','Eng',2,'USA'];
```

Delphi 2005 Deployment Manager

One of the significant new features of Delphi 2005 for Internet development is the availability of a Deployment Manager (also called Deployment Wizard) you can use to move the relevant files from the development folder to a local web server or to a remote server using the FTP protocol. The wizard has two panes in which you see relevant local files (not the source code, of course) and the files in the remote folder. With a single click you can deploy your new or updated web application to the server. An example of the Deployment Manager's window is visible in Figure 20.21.

As you select a file, you can see the version and the date both of the local and the remote file. With the context menu for each file (or group) you can perform some core operations on it (or on each of the files of the group). These operations include copying files to the remote destination, removing them, and changing the remote file name. To be sure no relevant file is skipped, you can select the Show Ignored Groups and Files command and you'll be able to see a long list of files (every file in that folder) and optionally enable some of them. Conversely, you can mark a file to be ignored.

FIGURE 20.21

Delphi 2005's new Deployment Manager

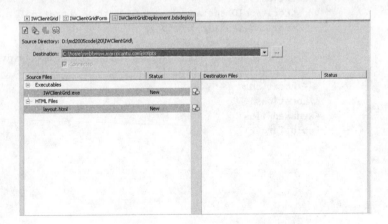

IntraWeb applications tend to be rather monolithic, although you can use external HTML template files and external images. This is why the Deployment Manager is handy but not as much as in an ASP.NET application, which tends to require the deployment of many files. In any case, the deployment data is saved in a file with the .bdsdeploy extension, which has an XML format. Here is a simplified version of the file deployment file of the IWClientGrid example:

```xml
<?xml version="1.0"?>
<DeployTarget>
  <Rules>
    <Rule>
      <Title>Executables</Title>
      <Filter>*.exe</Filter>
      <Ignored>0</Ignored>
    </Rule>
    <Rule>
      <Title>HTML Files</Title>
      <Filter>*.html;*.htm;*.css;*.js</Filter>
      <Ignored>0</Ignored>
    </Rule>
    <Rule>
      <Title>Image Files</Title>
      <Filter>*.jpg;*.bmp;*.dib;*.png;*.tiff;*.gif</Filter>
      <Ignored>0</Ignored>
    </Rule>
    <Rule>
      <Title>Other Files</Title>
      <Filter>*.*</Filter>
      <Ignored>1</Ignored>
    </Rule>
  </Rules>
  <Locations>
   <Location>
      <LocationID>Borland.Studio.Directory</LocationID>
      <Borland.Studio.Directory>
        <Active>1</Active>
        <Directory>C:\home\web\www.marcocantu.com\scripts</Directory>
      </Borland.Studio.Directory>
    </Location>
  </Locations>
  <RenamedFiles/>
</DeployTarget>
```

What's Next?

In this chapter, I covered web server applications using multiple techniques and two different frameworks: WebSnap and IntraWeb. This wasn't an in-depth presentation because one could write an entire book on this topic alone. It was intended as a starting point, and (as usual) I tried to make the core concepts clear rather than building complex examples.

If you want to learn more about the WebSnap framework and see examples in action, refer to the extensive Delphi demos in the `Demos\DelphiWin32\VCLWin32\WebSnap` folder. Some other options, relating to XML, XSL, and client-side scripts, will be examined in Chapter 22.

This chapter's description of IntraWeb's features is far from complete, but my aim was mainly to let you evaluate this technology so you can choose whether to use it in your forthcoming Delphi projects. IntraWeb is so powerful that you now have a good reason to build web applications in Delphi, instead of resorting to other development tools.

Delphi's default installation includes the IntraWeb demos, including the extensive Features example that shows at once most of the features of this component library. Also refer to the IntraWeb website (`www.atozedsoftware.com`) for updates and further documentation and examples.

The next chapter focuses on a specific .NET technique, ASP.NET. This is the most significant and most used portion of the .NET Framework and it is worth exploring it with care. In Chapter 22, I cover another alternative cross-platform web development approach based on XML and XSLT. This chapter is a complete roundup of XML-related technologies from the Delphi perspective.

Chapter 21

The ASP.NET Architecture

Of the various technologies in the Microsoft .NET Framework, the one that is used most by developers is certainly ASP.NET. This is a significantly improved version of the Active Server Pages (ASP) technology that is available on the Win32 platform. Like IntraWeb, ASP.NET greatly simplifies the development of web applications, turning the process into a visual experience. Like WebSnap, ASP.NET pages are laid out using HTML plus some server-side scripting. Unlike IntraWeb and WebSnap, however, with ASP.NET the code used to process the pages is stored in assembly libraries loaded on demand by the web server.

In this chapter I'll cover the foundations of the ASP.NET architectures, similar to what I've done in the previous chapter for the other web technologies available in Delphi. Although I'll devote some extra space to the topic, including a description of Borland native add-in DBWeb components, this is by no means detailed coverage of ASP.NET.

Delphi support for ASP.NET is extensive. Unlike WinForms, the support for the web user interface includes custom HTML/ASP.NET designers, specific editors, and add-in components. Development of ASP.NET applications in Delphi 2005 (for both the Delphi and C# languages) is a more visual development experience than using any other IDE for .NET.

In this chapter you'll learn about ASP.NET foundations, the development of ASP.NET pages and of entire applications, session and user management, Borland's DBWeb controls, Delphi's Deployment Wizard for ASP.NET, and more.

ASP.NET Foundations

ASP.NET is the successor to Microsoft's ASP technology, a server-side scripting solution that could be empowered by connecting to the COM technology for server-side processing.

While ASP often mixes HTML and server-side scripting, frequently including SQL for database access, ASP.NET moves to a cleaner separation of the page layout from the server-side processing. Both elements can be saved in the same .aspx file, but in the preferred situation (called *code behind*) the page layout is stored in an .aspx file and the code is kept in a standard source code file and compiled to a .NET managed library you deploy. (An assembly is generated behind the scenes if you use a single .aspx file also containing the source code.) Notice that both Delphi 2005 and Microsoft's Visual Studio .NET support only the code behind model.

To further mark the difference in approach from ASP, ASP.NET uses WebForms rather than pages. As you can guess, WebForms (defined in the System.Web.UI namespace) are the web counterpart of WinForms and provide a similar RAD development approach. As you remember from the last chapter, using forms is what IntraWeb tends to do as well, but while IntraWeb moves away from standard HTML-like files (unless you use templates), an ASP.NET WebForm remains closely related to a web page.

ASP.NET and Web Servers

There is currently only one web server supporting the ASP.NET architecture, Microsoft's Internet Information Services (IIS). You can use the Cassini server, a demo server built by Microsoft in C# on .NET, but only while developing your applications and for simplified debugging; it cannot be used for deployment because it works only on the local machine.

NOTE A further option that is emerging is the use of Apache for hosting ASP.NET applications deployed on Mono (www.mono-project.com/ASP.NET), both for Linux and for Windows. This is quite an interesting evolution, as my impression is that having to deploy on IIS and on Windows servers is the biggest limitation of the ASP.NET technology.

IIS doesn't come automatically with ASP.NET support on Windows 2000 or Windows XP, but when you install the .NET Framework on a computer the setup process updates the IIS configuration properly. If you have IIS disabled, follow the steps provided by Delphi 2005's readme.htm file in the section "Internet and HTML Notes."

If you want to try the Cassini server, you don't need to download it as Delphi already installs its source code in the Demos folder, under the Cassini subfolder. In that folder you'll find a ready-to-use build.bat file. This batch file is easy to use from the command line, provided you have the folders of the .NET Framework executables in the path, available by default in the Windows\Microsoft .NET\Framework\v1.1.4322 folder, as well as those of the .NET SDK tools, available by default in the Program Files\Microsoft.NET\SDK\v1.1\Bin folder. (See the section "Interop Type Libraries and COM Callable Wrappers (CCWs)" in Chapter 12 to get these paths set up in a command prompt through an SDK batch file.)

In the book I tend to use Cassini for development, as this is fully supported by the Delphi IDE and has a simplified configuration and installation. It should also be easier for you to work with the provided examples with Cassini, as you won't have to modify IIS configuration to see them. To test that Cassini was properly compiled, simply run the CassiniWebServer.exe that is generated by the compilation. If you don't provide the required parameters for the application directory, the server port, and the virtual root, you'll get a window asking for them, as in Figure 21.1.

Once Cassini is compiled and ready, you can configure the Delphi IDE to use it by providing the folder it has been compiled to and the TCP/IP port you want to use for it. The setting is available in the ASP.NET page of the section related to HTML/ASP.NET Options of the Tools ➢ Options dialog box.

NOTE In the same ASP.NET page of the Options dialog box, you can also configure Delphi 2005 to use a browser other than Internet Explorer for debugging your ASP.NET applications.

FIGURE 21.1
Cassini Web Server, upon execution, will ask for the parameters you haven't provided on the command-line parameter; otherwise, the options will be grayed out.

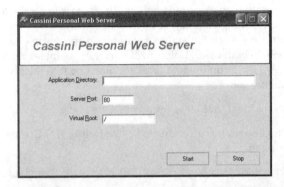

The web server you choose for debugging your application can be different from your deployment target, as your options don't affect the source code created by Delphi for a new ASP.NET application, but only some configuration settings. Regardless of the web server you use for development, toward the end of the chapter I'll discuss the ASP.NET deployment support provided by Delphi, which was already introduced in the last chapter for an IntraWeb example. With this wizard you can deploy your ASP.NET application to a different server from the development targets, which is relevant mostly for debugging purposes.

A Blank Page in Delphi

To check that the configuration is correct and to provide a starting point for the remaining part of the ASP.NET foundation coverage, let's start with a very limited example of ASP.NET support in Delphi. If you select the File ➢ New ➢ ASP.NET Web Application – Delphi for .NET, in the following dialog box you can pick the server you intend to use for development and a deployment folder:

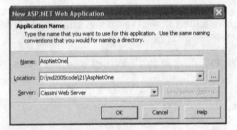

Once you accept this dialog box, Delphi will generate a brand new ASP.NET project for you with a project source code file, a WebForm1.aspx page, and the related WebForms1.pas file, plus a couple of configuration files (web.config, global.asax, and the corresponding global.pas). After generating the files, Delphi opens WebForm1 and you'll see a blank HTML page in the designer.

NOTE The web.config file is an application configuration file. Configuration files for normal applications are named like the program with an extra .config extension (as in myprogram.exe .config). Since ASP.NET projects are library assemblies, they use a different scheme: the configuration file is called web.config and resides in the virtual directory of the ASP.NET application.

You can simply type something and use the toolbar to set the font of the text and other visual elements. The resulting page can be opened in a browser by running the compiled program in the debugger (Run ➢ Run or F9) and as a stand-alone program (Run ➢ Run Without Debugging or Shift+Ctrl+F9). In both cases, Delphi will start the Cassini server (and you'll see its user interfaces, as in Figure 21.1) and run Internet Explorer directing it to the given page, in this case (and with my specific configuration):

```
http://localhost:8888/AspNetOne/WebForm1.aspx
```

As a starting point, I wrote some text in the Delphi HTML editor/designer, which resulted in the following .aspx file:

```
<!DOCTYPE HTML PUBLIC "-//W3C//DTD HTML 4.01 Transitional//EN">
<html>
  <head>
    <title>AspNetOne</title>
  </head>
  <body ms_positioning="GridLayout">
    <form runat="server"><font face="Verdana" size="5">This
      is the AspNetOne example.</font>
    </form>
  </body>
</html>
```

In the preceding HTML code, you can see that page is indeed a web form, as all of content defined in the designer ends up within a form tag. The runat attribute is an HTML extension used to ask for server-side processing. This means that the ASP.NET engine will process the HTML, create a control on the server to represent that tag, and ask the control to render itself by generating replacement HTML tags. For example, the runat attribute is removed by the process, as it makes no sense in HTML, but other attributes are added as well as a p tag. This is the HTML that the browser will receive with the preceding ASP.NET page code:

```
<!DOCTYPE HTML PUBLIC "-//W3C//DTD HTML 4.01 Transitional//EN">
<html>
  <head>
    <title>AspNetOne</title>
  </head>
  <body ms_positioning="GridLayout">
    <form name="_ctl0" method="post"
        action="WebForm1.aspx" id="_ctl0">
      <input type="hidden" name="__VIEWSTATE"
        value="dDwtMTI3OTMzNDM4NDs7PtGYtmOs9fPMySQ++m1o7wb0xUxA" />
      <p><font face="Verdana" size="5">This is
        the AspNetOne example.</font>
      </p>
    </form>
  </body>
</html>
```

I'll discuss the extra input tag called the __VIEWSTATE in the section "Introducing State Management." This is the simple output (the actual AspNetOne demo has a couple of more features):

The Scripting Technology

You saw that an ASP.NET web form (often still indicated as a page) is defined in an .aspx file, which is a text file based on HTML tags including controlling tags like directives and scripting blocks, in a fashion similar to the older ASP technology.

NOTE   There's nothing magic about the .aspx extension. You can pick another extension and configure IIS accordingly.

At the very beginning of the ASP.NET file there is a declaration with a Page directive (directives in ASP.NET are marked with the <%@ symbols), like the following from the AspNetOne demo:

```
<%@ Page Language="c#" Debug="true" Codebehind="WebForm1.pas"
AutoEventWireup="false" Inherits="WebForm1.TWebForm1"%>
```

This directive among other things sets the language used for the automatic code generation for the descendant page class that creates all the server-side controls. It also does some other housekeeping (Language attribute) such as indicating the associated compiled module and the class you want the generated descendant page class to inherit from (the CodeBehind and Inherits attributes, discussed in the next section).

In addition to a handful of directives, there are many other special blocks you can use, including ASP-like code declaration blocks (<script runat="server">), code-rendering blocks (marked with <% and %>), simple data-binding expressions (marked with <%# and %>), and extended HTML control syntax (as in <asp:button>).

Server-side scripting can be embedded directly anywhere in a page using one of the supported languages, such as C# and VB.NET, the same specified in the page directive with the Language attribute. The code you write is not much different from the WebSnap server-side scripts (usually based on JavaScript). For example, all I have to do to adapt the code of the script of the WSnap2 example of the last chapter was to add the variable type (int, for integer) within the for loops:

```
<table border="1">
  <tbody>
    <tr>
      <th><br></th>
      <% for (int j=1;j<=5;j++) { %>
      <th>
        Column <%=j %>
      </th>
```

```
      <% } %>
    </tr>
    <% for (int i=1;i<=5;i++) { %>
    <tr>
      <td>Line <%=i %></td>
      <% for (int j=1;j<=5;j++) { %>
      <td>Value= <%=i*j %></td>
      <% } %>
    </tr>
    <% } %>
  </tbody>
</table>
```

The effect of this code is visible in Figure 21.2, which also includes a button with a modified caption, as described in the following section.

NOTE   In theory it is possible to use Delphi as another ASP.NET scripting language, after installing the Delphi provider (something that the Borland license restricts), but in practice this is complex to achieve and is not directly supported by the IDE. As you'll see in the next section, Delphi favors the use of code behind, which is the primary and preferred solution for ASP.NET development in general; programmers using Microsoft development tools prefer it as well.

Understanding Code Behind

As you can see when you create a new ASP.NET application in Delphi, every form has an .aspx file with its HTML-like structure and an actual Delphi file with the declaration of the corresponding page class. As usual, you can switch from the Delphi file to the .aspx file using the F12 key (remember, as mentioned in Chapter 1, that you can also use the Alt+PgUp and Alt+PgDn key combinations to cycle through the tabs at the bottom of the Delphi editor).

FIGURE 21.2
The output of the AspNetOne example, which has some plain HTML text, a table based on server-side script, and an ASP button

As with GUI forms, the specific page class inherits from the generic one (the Page class) provided by the library. While WinForms uses initialization code to *create* the components and set their properties and VCL uses the DFM resource file to *load* the form data, ASP.NET generates an inherited class. When a page is requested, the system reads the .aspx file and dynamically creates a class that inherits from the corresponding page class, adding to it the proper initialization code.

Again this is driven by the Page directive discussed in the previous section and in particular by the following two attributes:

```
Codebehind="WebForm1.pas"
Inherits="WebForm1.TWebForm1"
```

You compile the Delphi code to a library assembly, placed (by default) in a bin directory under your web application virtual directory (which is the folder hosting the .aspx files). When the ASPX page is hit, the web server processes the .aspx file and loads the appropriate library assembly. In case of ASP controls, the .aspx file also contains their declaration, like the following (extracted again from the AspNetOne example):

```
<asp:Button
  id="Button1"
  style="Z-INDEX: 1; LEFT: 262px; POSITION: absolute; TOP: 302px"
  runat="server"
  text="Button">
</asp:Button>
```

Notice that the button uses a local style with absolute positioning (this is a default you can change, as you'll see) and again has a runat attribute set to server, implying this component has to be processed and modified by the server to become a standard HTML control. Executing the page, in fact, the button generates the following HTML:

```
<input
  type="submit"
  name="Button1"
  value="Button"
  id="Button1"
  style="Z-INDEX: 1; LEFT: 262px; POSITION: absolute; TOP: 302px" />
```

As you can see, the style remains unchanged (although this is not an absolute rule) while almost everything else is turned into standard HTML, including the input tag and the type, value, and name attributes. The code of the button click event resides in the Delphi source file, along with other startup and event handling code and doesn't generate HTML directly. Rather, you use code to modify control properties, which are reflected in the generated HTML.

If you look at the source code of the AspNetOne example (or any other simple web form), you can see a class declaration, like the following:

```
type
  TWebForm1 = class(System.Web.UI.Page)
  strict private
    procedure InitializeComponent;
    procedure Button1_Click(sender: System.Object;e: System.EventArgs);
```

```
strict private
  procedure Page_Load(sender: System.Object; e: System.EventArgs);
strict protected
  Button1: System.Web.UI.WebControls.Button;
  procedure OnInit(e: EventArgs); override;
end;
```

Unlike a WinForms application, the InitializeComponent method is called by the OnInit handler, while the Page_Load event handler by default is only an empty placeholder. This event handler is set up along with the Click event of the button in the InitializeComponent method:

```
procedure TWebForm1.InitializeComponent;
begin
  Include(Self.Button1.Click, Self.Button1_Click);
  Include(Self.Load, Self.Page_Load);
end;
```

Again, this is very different from a WinForms application. In fact, the initialization code doesn't create the components and doesn't set their properties. This information is already in the .aspx file, which is compiled into an inherited class of the local one (TWebForm1, in this example). The class does provide the event handlers, including the custom ones, like the minimal Click event handler I wrote for the button (the effect of clicking the button was already visible in Figure 21.2):

```
procedure TWebForm1.Button1_Click(
  sender: System.Object; e: System.EventArgs);
begin
  Button1.Text := Button1.Text + ' *';
end;
```

Having a Delphi source code file with the event handlers (and also the database access logic, as you'll see) and as a separate .aspx file with the definition of the web form layout certainly helps obtain a better separation of the application logic from the user interface. In other words, the advantage is that the .aspx file can be modified without having to touch or recompile the code behind assembly. At the same time, the application code is type checked at compile time and not late bound (with any type checking until execution). Still, most of the HTML will be generated dynamically, and this is particularly true for complex components, like grids, so there are many customizations a web designer cannot do on the .aspx file without an intervention of the developer on the code behind libraries.

This architecture is certainly much better than the older ASP technology, which had a single flow of scripts within a page encompassing everything, from the UI to the database access code. The ASP.NET approach should also be more familiar to RAD developers, including those with a VB or Delphi background.

Introducing State Management

The last technical element I want to introduce is state management. Since the HTTP protocol is stateless, how does the AspNetOne program keep track of how many times its button was clicked (or how many stars have already been added to the button's text)? By default, this information is not kept on the server but is sent back and forth between the server application and the client browser by means of the __VIEWSTATE hidden field mentioned earlier. This is the value of the field the first time the page of the AspNetOne example is rendered:

```
<input
  type="hidden"
  name="__VIEWSTATE"
  value="dDwtMTU3NTI5MDMzMzs7PiHiogZzBA15Uody+/E199QFnWs5" />
```

After clicking the button a couple of times, the information changes and the size of the data increases (to about 140 characters after clicking the button a couple of times and to about 200 bytes after clicking the button 20 times). The __VIEWSTATE hidden field keep track of the status of the ASP.NET form and of its controls. The value of __VIEWSTATE, in fact, represents the values of the controls in the page: All controls stream their state and the stream is encoded in base-64 to the __VIEWSTATE field. Although this base-64 value seems unreadable, it is quite easy to decode and open it. In fact, if you want to send data to a client in a more secure way you can set the EnableViewStateMac attribute of the Page directive, to use an encrypted __VIEWSTATE value or resort to the HTTPS protocol.

The advantage of not having server-side information is increased scalability and flexibility, as you can have multiple web servers responding to requests directed to a very popular site. Using the __VIEWSTATE field is only one of the possible options for an ASP.NET application, as you'll see in the section "Session Management." From within the code, this information is copied back to the proper controls, so if you inspect the Text property of the button you'll see the current value for the given user, not the initial value. This is why the simple event handler of the button (which adds a star to the current text) works as expected in both single-user and multiuser environments.

Building ASP.NET Pages

Now that I've introduced the foundations of an ASP.NET application, we can start focusing on some of the technologies involved. I'll start by looking at the classes used to represent controls and pages, and later I'll move on to applications involving multiple pages. Because the Control class is a base class of the Page class, as in the case of WinForms and VCL, I'll start with the former and provide an introduction to some of the available controls before looking to features related to pages (or web forms).

The *Control* Class

Like the WinForms technology, WebForms also have a Control class, which is the base class for all visual controls and their container. All controls share a number of relevant properties defined in the Control class. Each control has an ID that identifies the control in server-side code (like the Name of a WinForm or VCL control) and a ClientID that can be used in client-side scripts. Each control also has a Controls property with the list of child controls, as you'll see in the AspNetViewState example described in this section.

An important feature of controls is how they manage their state. The EnableViewState Boolean property determines whether the control will maintain its state when the page is refreshed due to a user operation on a control (the term generally used for this is *postback*). This property also affects any child controls of the control. The ViewState property defines name/value pairs that hold status information for the specific control. It is an instance of the StateBag class holding a number of StateItem objects. This ViewState property is what is streamed and encoded (for all of the control) in the __VIEWSTATE field of the page.

Because the ViewState management for controls is a significant feature and can present a challenge to understand, I wrote an example to explore it called AspNetViewState. This example also demonstrates the parent/child relationship among controls. Its form has two panels hosting two text boxes and two labels each, plus a few buttons and an output label. You can see its web form at design time in Figure 21.3.

This example has a Get Info button that does two things: It lists the classes and names of the child controls of the first panel and shows the ViewState entries of the first edit box. The output, which uses some <br> tags for minimal formatting, is saved in a StringBuilder object and then copied to a label, as you can see in its code:

```
procedure TWebForm1.btnGetInfo_Click(
  sender: System.Object; e: System.EventArgs);
var
  strOutput: StringBuilder;
  Ctrl: Control;
  key: string;
begin
  strOutput := StringBuilder.Create;
  strOutput.Append('Panel Child Controls Count: ');
  strOutput.Append(Panel1.Controls.Count);
  strOutput.Append('<br>');
  for Ctrl in Panel1.Controls do
  begin
    strOutput.Append(Ctrl.ToString); // long class name
    strOutput.Append(': ');
    strOutput.Append(Ctrl.ID);
    strOutput.Append('<br>');
  end;

  strOutput.Append('<br>');
  strOutput.Append('TextBoxOne.ViewState Count: ');
  strOutput.Append(TextBoxOne.ViewState.Count);
  strOutput.Append('<br>');
  for key in TextBoxOne.ViewState.Keys do
  begin
    strOutput.Append(key + ': ');
    strOutput.Append(TextBoxOne.ViewState.Item[key]);
    strOutput.Append('<br>');
  end;

  LabelOutput.Text := strOutput.ToString;
end;
```

FIGURE 21.3
The web forms of the
AspNetViewState
example in the design
view of the Delphi IDE

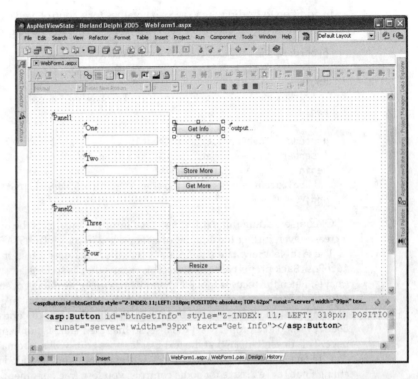

FIGURE 21.3
The web forms of the
AspNetViewState
example in the design
view of the Delphi IDE

The code iterates on the child controls of the panel first and on the viewstate keys of the first text box next. If you click the button as soon as the program starts, you'll get an output like this:

```
Panel Child Controls Count: 9
System.Web.UI.LiteralControl:
System.Web.UI.WebControls.TextBox: TextBoxOne
System.Web.UI.LiteralControl:
System.Web.UI.WebControls.TextBox: TextBoxTwo
System.Web.UI.LiteralControl:
System.Web.UI.WebControls.Label: Label1
System.Web.UI.LiteralControl:
System.Web.UI.WebControls.Label: Label2
System.Web.UI.LiteralControl:

TextBoxOne.ViewState Count: 0
```

Notice that the panel content also includes some literal text (the Panel1 text and the new lines and whites spaces between controls within the .aspx file). If you enter *some text* in the first text box, the final part of the output becomes:

```
TextBoxOne.ViewState Count: 1
Text: some text
```

In addition to reading the ViewState values for a control, you can add custom ones. The Store More button saves the text of the second edit box as part of the state of the first one (any text will do):

```
procedure TWebForm1.btnStoreMore_Click(
  sender: System.Object; e: System.EventArgs);
begin
  TextBoxOne.ViewState['More'] := TextBoxTwo.Text;
end;

procedure TWebForm1.btnGetMore_Click(
  sender: System.Object; e: System.EventArgs);
begin
  LabelOutput.Text := TextBoxOne.ViewState['More'].ToString;
end;
```

Of course, adding this extra ViewState information affects the output of the first button and increases even further the amount of data passed in the __VIEWSTATE hidden field of the form.

The AspNetViewState example has two more features. First, the second text box has the AutoPostBack property set to True. This means that as soon as a user finishes editing that text box (that is, when the focus is moved to another control) the data is posted to the server and the page is refreshed. There are cases in which this might be worthwhile, but in general this will only confuse the user and put an extra burden on the server. Finally, the text box controls in the second panel have the EnableViewState property set to False, so that their state is not kept when the server refreshes the page. This doesn't mean that the text inside those edits will not remain persistent when you post the data. In fact, that text is part of the form data even if it is not included in its ViewState. By instead disabling EnableViewState for some controls, you lose track of other properties, like their size. This is demonstrated by the use of the Resize button on the form that changes the size of the four edit boxes, two of which will keep the new setting while the others (with ViewState disabled) will return to the predefined size.

NOTE   Among the methods of the Controls class, there is a relevant Render method that lets you generate specific HTML for custom controls using the provided parameter of the HtmlTextWriter type.

The HtmlControls

If you look at the Tool Palette while the designer of an ASP.NET web form is active, you'll notice two sections offering some apparently overlapping components, WebControls and HTML Elements. The first page hosts the real ASP.NET controls, which are discussed in the next section. The second page hosts plain HTML tags, which in ASP.NET are generally called HtmlControls. These are server objects that map to plain HTML controls.

The HtmlControls use the standard HTML syntax, with a compulsory ID and a runat attribute that is removed during the processing. HtmlControls are used to define the layout of a page and are passed as they are to the browser with little processing. This is different from ASP.NET custom controls that generate some HTML equivalent at run time. While the HtmlControls are very lightweight, they are mostly programmed with client-side JavaScript, not with server-side Delphi code.

The WebControls

On the other hand, the WebControls family includes the real ASP.NET controls. Indeed, some of these controls (such as a TextBox or a Label) are similar to their HTML counterpart, but they are fully managed by ASP.NET and include features like state management and server-side events. Moreover, ASP.NET controls include some rich controls like calendars and grids, which are built out of complex collections of HTML tags.

WebControls are easy to spot on an ASPX page, as they use a custom syntax like this one extracted form the previous example:

```
<asp:Button
  id="btnGetInfo"
  style="Z-INDEX: 11; LEFT: 318px; POSITION: absolute; TOP: 62px"
  runat="server"
  width="99px"
  text="Get Info">
</asp:Button>
```

There are many WebControls you can use in your applications, including simple ones like the TextBox control for single and multiline editing, the RadioButton and RadioButtonList controls, the CheckBox and the CheckBoxList controls, and the DropDownList and LixtBox controls.

More complex controls include the AdRotator control, the Calendar control, and the Table control. Another interesting control is the Literal, which allows you to embed a portion of plain HTML within a page. To work on data tables, there are three specific controls, the DataGrid, the DataList, and the Repeater (which will be covered later in the section "Working with Databases" and in the AspNet-DataOne example).

The *Page* Class

As I already mentioned, the Page class derives from the Control class, just as the Form class derives from the Control class in WinForms (and TForm derives from TControl in the VCL). Aside from the base class properties shared with any other control, the Page class has a few relevant properties of its own, including the ErrorPage property to indicate the page to which the browser is redirected in case of an error, the IsPostBack property to indicate whether this is not the first time a page is hit, and the Validators collection with all validation server controls on the page.

The page also has direct access to the current HTTP request and response through a set of objects familiar to ASP programmers, such as Application, Server, Session, Request, and Response, as well as a few new ones like the Cache, User, and Trace.

The AspNetReqResp example shows how you can directly access the Request and Response objects. This application is a sort of extreme case, as it uses no ASP.NET controls at all. The page is empty and the only event handler (for the Load event) writes directly to the HTML output:

```
procedure TWebForm1.Page_Load(
  sender: System.Object; e: System.EventArgs);
var
  str: string;
begin
  Response.Write('<h2>AspNetReqResp</h2>');
```

```
// description omitted...

for str in Request.QueryString do
begin
  Response.Write('<p>');
  Response.Write(str); // name
  Response.Write(' = ');
  Response.Write(Request.QueryString[str]); // value
  Response.Write('</p>');
end;
end;
```

BROWSER TRICKS WITH ASP.NET CONTROLS

In theory, server controls are browser independent. However, many of them use the Browser property of the Request object to figure out the actual browser of the user and generate HTML matching its capabilities. The trouble is that ASP.NET seems to have little knowledge of (or little desire to support) some of the new browsers outside of the Microsoft realm. It's not that it doesn't support their specific features, which would be unusual, but that if such a browser is encountered the generated HTML misses some of its standard features.

To see an example, try out the last demo (AspNetViewState) with Mozilla's Firefox and you'll see that all of the text boxes within the panel are messed up:

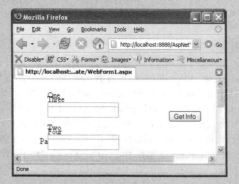

At first sight you might think this is a problem with Firefox, but in fact it depends on the HTML generated by ASP.NET, which in turn depends on the user agent indicated in the HTTP request. If you change the user agent sent by Firefox to the server pretending it is Internet Explorer, the page will show up properly and everything in most ASP.NET applications will work smoothly. (By the way, changing the user agent is not one of the basic features of Firefox, but requires a plug-ins, like the User Agent Switcher Extension by Chris Pederick.)

Personally, I think this is quite a significant problem with ASP.NET. It is true that if you design your pages with care, keep them simple, and use third-party ASP.NET controls with good support for multiple browsers, you can create pages that behave properly in multiple browsers. However, this extra effort could be avoided if ASP.NET simply produced standard HTML for each browser.

Another interesting feature (for developers) is enabling the trace support. To accomplish this you can add the `Trace="true"` attribute to the `<%@ Page` declaration in the .aspx file. With this setting, the page will be decorated with a lot of detailed information about the page execution (including a detailed trace with timings, as you can see in Figure 21.4), the HTTP parameters, and so on. Moreover, you can use the `Trace` property to add custom information to the trace. This is what I did in the Asp-NetTrace demo, with the effect visible in the figure.

You can also get the same effect by setting to True the `pageOutput` attribute of `trace` node of the `web.config` file:

```
<trace enabled="true" pageOutput="true"/>
```

FIGURE 21.4

The output of the AspNetTrace demo includes detailed trace information (with custom trace information highlighted).

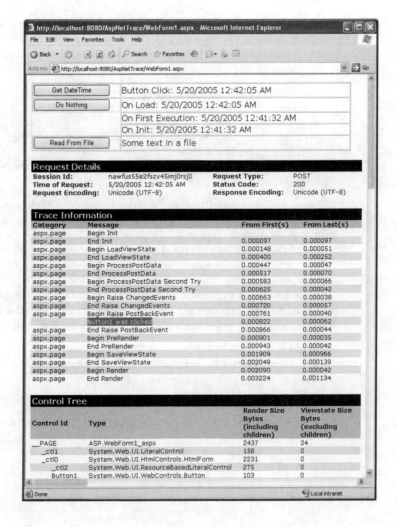

A further alternative is to add the node but leave this attribute set to False so that the tracing data won't show up in the page but will be visible by pointing the browser to a special `trace.axd` URL in the same path as your ASP.NET application.

In the demo, the custom tracing is added to the program when the first button is clicked:

```
procedure TWebForm1.Button1_Click(
  sender: System.Object; e: System.EventArgs);
begin
  Label1.Text := 'Button Click: ' + DateTime.Now.ToString;
  Trace.Write('Button1 was clicked');
end;
```

The second button of the program does nothing (there is no event handler), but still causes a refresh of the page when it is clicked. This is useful for seeing the different times written to the labels by the Load event handler, which use IsPostBack to change some of the data only at the first execution of the page:

```
procedure TWebForm1.Page_Load(
  sender: System.Object; e: System.EventArgs);
begin
  Label2.Text := 'On Load: ' + DateTime.Now.ToString;
  if not IsPostback then
    Label3.Text := 'On First Execution: ' + DateTime.Now.ToString;
end;
```

The fourth label is modified in the OnInit method, which is executed only the first time and not for each postback operation (providing an alternative to the use of IsPostBack). In other words, the OnInit method is executed when the page and its controls are created (like VCL's Loaded method), while the Load event is executed for each request even in case of a postback (and you can test IsPostBack to avoid needless reinitialization). Finally, you might want to use the Unload method to free any resources you allocated during initialization.

The example has a further button showcasing a particular method of the Page class, MapPath, which can be used to compute a path relative to the virtual folder hosting the page. So, for example, you can access a file in the same folder of the .aspx file with this code:

```
procedure TWebForm1.Button3_Click(
  sender: System.Object; e: System.EventArgs);
var
  strReader: StreamReader;
begin
  strReader := StreamReader.Create(MapPath('.') + '/demo.txt');
  try
    Label5.Text := strReader.ReadToEnd;
  finally
    strReader.Free; // dispose
  end;
end;
```

Not having a reference to a specific folder but only a relative path helps you deploy the application.

There is one further element to consider about this example, and it is the way the controls are arranged in the web page. In fact, I added a grid to the page as well as various controls to the grid cells. This means that even if the page uses the standard grid layout (with the body tag attribute ms_positioning set to GridLayout), the page is actually using a layout based on the table. The designer helps a lot because it snaps the controls into the grid cells when you drag the controls over the cells. There are also many other designer helpers, starting with the grid creation tool, that allow you to use grids and obtain nice and portable user interfaces for your web pages.

The grid layout uses an absolute position for each element of the page, which is very easy to use but can cause problems because it doesn't adapt very well to different sizes of the browser window. This problem is becoming even more relevant with small devices. ASP.NET offers an alternative layout for page controls, the standard HTML flow layout. You can change the layout in the Object Inspector after selecting the DOCUMENT object, and the body tag will have its ms_positioning attribute set to FlowLayout. As the AspNetTrace example is based on a table, I could change the layout to the flow layout without any problem.

TIP   Using tables to host controls helps you design pages that adapt better to different browsers and to different sizes of the browser window. Another relevant technique you should consider is using an external Cascading Style Sheet (CSS) connected to each page of an ASP.NET application.

Validating Controls Content

ASP.NET has specific support for managing the validation of the input provided by a user. This is important, as validation in a stateless web application is much more complex than in a GUI-based program. Support for validation in ASP.NET is based on a set of controls that perform different types of validation (such as a range check or a regular expression test). These are controls that show the error message (or nothing if the test passes) and are connected to a target control with their ControlToValidate property.

The actual validation is performed after editing each TextBox and moving to the next because the EnableClientScript property is True by default. You can activate the validation process directly by calling the Validate method of the Page class. To demonstrate the use of validation controls with a simple practical example, I created a form with five text boxes and five different validation controls. You can see the form at design time in Figure 21.5.

WARNING   This JavaScript-based validation (like the one demonstrated by the AspNetValidate example) uses specific extensions provided by Internet Explorer and doesn't work in other browsers I've tried. Not everything is lost, though: In other browsers the validation will still take place but on the server side—for example, when a button control is clicked.

The simplest validation control is the RequiredFieldValidator, which has an InitialValue indicating the text you set at the beginning in the text and which the user has to modify. You can enter a text like *[name]*, within square brackets to indicate that the user must enter the name. Setting the same string for InitialValue makes it compulsory for the user to enter something, but the user can also remove the text and leave it empty, something I find quite odd. If you leave the text box and the

`InitialValue` property empty, everything works as expected. This is the definition of this validator in the ASPX code of the AspNetValidate example:

```
<asp:RequiredFieldValidator
  id="RequiredFieldValidator1"
  controltovalidate="TextBox1"
  errormessage="Required Field">
</asp:RequiredFieldValidator>
```

In the RangeValidator control you have to set a minimum and a maximum value as well as the data type used for the comparison (a property that's easy to forget):

```
<asp:RangeValidator
  id="RangeValidator1"
  controltovalidate="TextBox2"
  errormessage="Must be between 10 and 100"
  minimumvalue="10"
  maximumvalue="100"
  type="Integer">
</asp:RangeValidator>
```

FIGURE 21.5
The web form of the AspNetValidate example at design time

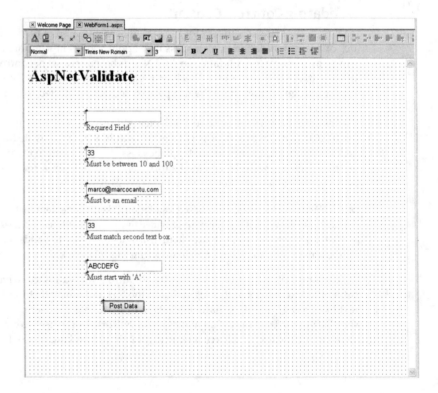

The RegularExpressionValidator, on the other hand, needs a regular expression for the `ValidationExpression` property (notice that the corresponding property editor has a few predefined ones):

```
<asp:RegularExpressionValidator
    id="RegularExpressionValidator1"
    controltovalidate="TextBox3"
    errormessage="Must be an email"
    validationexpression="\w+([-+.]\w+)*@\w+([-.]\w+)*\.\w+([-.]\w+)*">
</asp:RegularExpressionValidator>
```

The CompareValidator can have two text boxes with the same value (useful for asking a user to type a password or an e-mail twice in the same page), or a small and large text box, or other combinations. The example requires the same value in two text boxes:

```
<asp:CompareValidator
    id="CompareValidator1"
    controltovalidate="TextBox4"
    errormessage="Must match second text box"
    controltocompare="TextBox2"
    type="Integer">
</asp:CompareValidator>
```

Finally, there is a CustomValidator control that lets you provide a validation function either in client-side JavaScript code or handling a server-side event. These are the controls in the .aspx file and its custom event handler, which checks that the strings begin with an uppercase 'A':

```
<asp:CustomValidator
    id="CustomValidator1"
    controltovalidate="TextBox5"
    errormessage="Must start with 'A'">
</asp:CustomValidator>
```

```
procedure TWebForm1.CustomValidator1_ServerValidate(
  source: System.Object;
  args: System.Web.UI.WebControls.ServerValidateEventArgs);
begin
  args.IsValid := args.Value[1] = 'A';
end;
```

Data Access in ASP.NET

All the simple applications we have built so far lack a fundamental feature because they do not store any of their data. In many cases, you'll instead write web applications connected to a database. ASP.NET controls can be bound to an ADO.NET dataset in a fairly direct way, but you have to write some code to fill the dataset and connect the data to the controls by calling their DataBind method. In contrast, Borland's own DBWeb controls can be attached directly and visually to a dataset. Let's progress through the proper steps, starting with the simpler technique.

NOTE   Using the Borland Data Provider (BDP) for ADO.NET can help you obtain live data at design time for ASP.NET web pages.

Before I cover some of the ASP.NET controls you can use to display data, there is a relevant feature of the ASPX scripts that I have mentioned but not described yet: simple data binding expressions. These expressions use the <%#...%> notation to access data from the page definition. For example, to show the value of a page property called MyData in an HTML paragraph or an ASP.NET label control you could write the following two lines of code, and add in the source code a call to the DataBind method for the control (or the entire page):

```
<p><%# MyData %></p>
<asp:Label text='<%# MyData %>' runat=server/>
```

A similar technique can be used to access database data with the DataBinder.Eval expression, as in the following snippet extracted from the next example:

```
<span><%# DataBinder.Eval (Container.DataItem, "Company") %></span>
```

Working with Databases

As in WinForms, in WebForms data binding works for all controls. There are, however, some specific controls that make sense only in the context of data binding. In fact, the DataGrid, DataList, and Repeater controls are bound to an entire table of data, not a single field like simpler controls. This is a very short summary of their features, which are more understandable if you look at Figure 21.6, with the output of an example that showcases all three controls:

DataGrid   Is the counterpart of a DataGrid (or DBGrid) in a WinForm (or VCL) application. A DataGrid shows all or a set of columns of the table. There are many ways to customize the output of each column with the only constraint being the table-based structure. Each table item shows the text data by default but can be customized to show a link, a button, or some custom HTML based on a template.

DataList   Is, like the VCL DBCtrlGrid component, a container of other controls, repeated for each row of the database table. The DataList uses a table for its overall structure with a cell for each row. This means you can have a single cell for each row or multiple columns each showing different data. This is obtained by modifying the RepeatColumns property. For each item you define a template containing HTML output or ASP.NET controls.

Repeater   Is a more flexible but less powerful component. It is based on an HTML template that is repeated for each item, but there is no fixed structure (like a table) hosting these items. This means that in the simplest form you define a paragraph of text with the information extracted from the rows of the table.

FIGURE 21.6
The output of the Asp-
NetDataOne example,
which uses multiple
data-bound controls to
show the same data

There are many properties available to customize the styles of the various elements of a DataGrid or a DataList. There are also some predefined color schemes available through the Auto Format command at the bottom of the Object Inspector, which opens up the following dialog box:

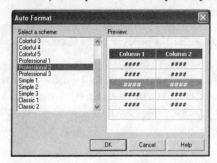

I used this dialog box to customize the output of the controls in the AspNetDataOne example, which uses all three controls. The example is based on an HTML table, with the first cell hosting the Repeater controls with its colspan set to 2 to take the entire row, and the second row hosting the other two controls in the two cells. The program uses an OleDbConnection and the related OleDbAdapter to fetch the data. I also created a `DataTable` object at design time called `CustomerTable`. Here are the most relevant properties for these components, which are set in the `InitializeComponent` methods of the web form:

```
Self.OleDbConnection1.ConnectionString :=
  'Provider="Microsoft.Jet.OLEDB.4.0";' +
  'Data Source="C:\..\Borland Shared\Data\dbdemos.mdb"';
Self.oleDbSelectCommand1.Connection := Self.OleDbConnection1;
Self.oleDbSelectCommand1.CommandText :=
  'select Company, City, State from customer where Country="US"';
Self.OleDbDataAdapter1.SelectCommand := Self.oleDbSelectCommand1;
Self.DataSet1.Tables.AddRange(
  TArrayOfSystem_Data_DataTable.Create(Self.CustomerTable));
Self.CustomerTable.TableName := 'CustomerTable';
```

The database access setup is completed in the Load event handler of the page by opening the connection, moving the data to the table, and binding the visual controls to the dataset:

```
procedure TWebForm1.Page_Load(
  sender: System.Object; e: System.EventArgs);
begin
  if not IsPostBack then
  begin
    OleDbConnection1.Open;
    OleDbDataAdapter1.Fill(CustomerTable);
    DataGrid1.DataBind;
    Repeater1.DataBind;
    DataList1.DataBind;
  end;
end;
```

TIP   As an alternative to calling the `DataBind` method for each control connected to a dataset, you can call the `DataBind` method of the page. This will call the `DataBind` method of each control and also trigger the substitution of simple data binding expressions in the page. In general, the single `DataBind` method call to the page is preferable over the call to the method for each control. Here I left the specific calls to underline the behavior of these data-enabled controls in ASP.NET.

All three visual controls, in fact, have their `DataSource` property set to the `DataSet1` object and their `DataMember` property set to the `CustomerTable` object. The grid doesn't have any special settings aside from one of the standard color schemes. It is worth looking once at its ASPX code, though. This should explain what I meant when I said that code behind helps with the separation of the user interface code from the application logic, but you have limited control on the generated HTML when using complex ASP.NET controls:

```
<asp:DataGrid id="DataGrid1"
  style="Z-INDEX: 2"
  datamember="CustomerTable"
  datasource="<%# DataSet1 %>"
  cellpadding="3"
  backcolor="White"
  bordercolor="#999999"
  borderwidth="1px"
  gridlines="Vertical"
  borderstyle="None">
  <FooterStyle
    forecolor="Black"
    backcolor="#CCCCCC">
  </FooterStyle>
  <HeaderStyle
    font-bold="True"
    forecolor="White"
    backcolor="#000084">
  </HeaderStyle>
  <PagerStyle
    horizontalalign="Center"
    forecolor="Black"
    backcolor="#999999"
    mode="NumericPages">
  </PagerStyle>
  <SelectedItemStyle
    font-bold="True"
    forecolor="White"
    backcolor="#008A8C">
  </SelectedItemStyle>
  <AlternatingItemStyle
    backcolor="#DCDCDC">
  </AlternatingItemStyle>
  <ItemStyle
    forecolor="Black"
    backcolor="#EEEEEE">
  </ItemStyle>
</asp:DataGrid>
```

In fact, the HTML code generated by the control looks quite different (here is a small excerpt), although many HTML attributes are indeed generated from ASP.NET control's attributes:

```
<table id="DataGrid1" style="z-index: 2;" bgcolor="White" border="1"
  bordercolor="#999999" cellpadding="3" cellspacing="0" rules="cols">
```

```
<tbody>
  <tr bgcolor="#000084">
    <td><font color="White"><b>Company</b></font></td>
    <!-- more headers -->
  </tr>
  <tr bgcolor="#eeeeee">
    <td><font color="Black">Kauai Dive Shoppe</font></td>
    <td><font color="Black">Kapaa Kauai</font></td>
    <td><font color="Black">HI</font></td>
  </tr>
  <!-- more lines -->
```

The customization of the DataList is slightly less intuitive. As you drop such a component into a web form in the Delphi IDE you get a placeholder with a description of the operations you have to do:

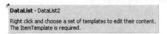

In fact, the context menu for this component has extra commands (notice that you don't select them at the bottom of the Object Inspector as usual). If you pick Item Templates, the control will paint a template editor where you can indeed start entering information:

In the small template area you can type fixed output text or place HTML or ASP.NET controls by dragging them over the area. For example, I added an ASP.NET Label control to the template and set the following value for the DataBinding property (in the corresponding special editor):

```
DataBinder.Eval (Container.DataItem, "Company")
```

The container in this case is the DataList itself. You can also customize this and other templates directly in the source code, which is required for connecting plain HTML elements to the database data. This is a trimmed version of the ASPX code for the DataList in the AspNetDataOne example:

```
<asp:DataList
  id="DataList1"
  datamember="CustomerTable"
  datasource="<%# DataSet1 %>"
  repeatdirection="Horizontal"
  repeatcolumns="3">
  <ItemStyle
    forecolor="Black"
    backcolor="#DEDFDE">
```

```
    </ItemStyle>
    <ItemTemplate>
      <asp:Label
        id="Label1"
        text='<%# DataBinder.Eval (Container.DataItem, "Company") %>'>
      </asp:Label>
      <div>
        <%# DataBinder.Eval (Container.DataItem, "City") %>
        [<%# DataBinder.Eval (Container.DataItem, "State") %>]
      </div>
    </ItemTemplate>
  </asp:DataList>
```

As you can see within the template node, there is the `asp:Label` followed by a `div` tag hosting some direct HTML with two data binding expressions. Notice also that the DataList has three columns for each row (the `repeatcolumns` attribute) and uses a horizontal flow (the `repeatdirection` attribute); you set up these attributes in the Object Inspector by editing the corresponding properties.

Editing the HTML directly is what you have to do when you use the Repeater control, for which there is almost no design-time support, as you can see in Figure 21.7. Similar to the DataList, as you place it on the form you'll see a message describing what you must do, which is basically open the .aspx file and type the HTML directly in there. The code is not very different from what you just saw:

```
<asp:Repeater
  id="Repeater1"
  datamember="CustomerTable"
  datasource="<%# DataSet1 %>">
  <ItemTemplate>
    <span>
      <%# DataBinder.Eval (Container.DataItem, "Company") %>
      [<%# DataBinder.Eval (Container.DataItem, "State") %>],
    </span>
  </ItemTemplate>
</asp:Repeater>
```

FIGURE 21.7
The final form of the AspNetDataOne example at design time

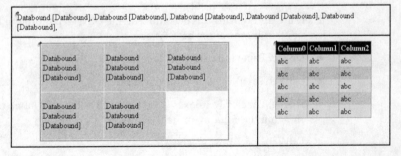

AspNetDataOne

Notice that in this case the HTML generated by the control has no external structure (no table and not even a `div` placeholder), so it becomes a repetition of the template with the actual data:

```
<span>Kauai Dive Shoppe [HI], </span>
<span>Blue Jack Aqua Center [HI], </span>
<span>Ocean Paradise [HI], </span>
```

The good news is that you have fine control of the HTML. The bad news is that you need to make a great effort to obtain a nice user interface, something the DataList and especially the DataGrid help you achieve.

Using Borland's DBWeb Components

If you want to further simplify and speed up the development of database-driven ASP.NET applications, you can use a set of controls provided by Borland called DBWeb controls. These components have an architecture reminiscent of Delphi's VCL data-aware controls, with a *data source* object acting as a broker between the dataset and the visual controls.

There are some advantages to using the DBWeb controls over the standard ASP.NET ones, including the ability (when combined with the use of the BDP ADO.NET components) to view the data at design time and work on a page very similar to what the user will actually see. In fact, with the DBWeb controls you can avoid the call to `DataBind` in the code. Other advantages include the ability to post changes back to dataset automatically.

A key feature of the DBWeb controls is that using the DBWebDataSource component the web form maintains a current row position on a per-session basis. This component also has a list of changes to the data, which can be undone by the user. Finally, the DBWebGrid has complete support for paging (similarly to the DataGrid) for local editing and provides many other features with no coding.

THE AVAILABLE COMPONENTS

Borland's DBWeb components comprise a rich set of controls and a nonvisual component, the DBWebDataSource, which acts as a bridge between the data-aware controls and the dataset. A DBWebDataSource links to a DataTable or DataView and has the role of tracking the current record for each session/user connected to the application. The component also has specific XML data support, as you'll see in the next chapter.

NOTE   While the core DBWeb technology was already available in Delphi 8 for .NET, some of the controls are new in Delphi 2005, including the audio and video controls, the aggregate, and the navigator extender.

There are different groups of controls in the DBWeb page of the Tool Palette. A first group lets you access single columns of the base types:

◆ DBWebLabel is a read-only label.

◆ DBWebTextBox is a standard text box.

◆ DBWebLabeledTextBox is a text box with a standard label (not a DBWebLabel), automatically showing the column (or field) name.

◆ DBWebCheckBox is a check box.

- DBWebCalendar is a calendar you can use to edit a date.

- DBWebAggregateControl is a text box that displays aggregate values (sum, max, min, average, count) from a specified column and has a caption.

There are also controls capable of showing rich content, from a BLOB field of a database or from a file:

- DBWebMemo is a multiline editor you can connect to a memo field.

- DBWebImage is an image control.

- DBWebSound is a sound control that activates the default media player on the user's system.

- DBWebVideo is a video control that activates the default media player as well.

Another group represents selection controls, which can be used to implement a lookup field (as I'll do in the AspNetEmployee example) or to provide a selection among a fixed list of choices:

- DBWebRadioButtonList shows a group of radio buttons.

- DBWebListBox is a list box.

- DBWebDropDownList is a combo box.

Finally, there are controls that work on the table as a whole and not on specific columns:

- DBWebGrid is a powerful and flexible data grid.

- DBWebNavigator is a customizable navigation bar.

- DBWebNavigationExtender is a helper to make standard web controls behave like the data-aware navigation buttons.

A First Demo: Using the DBWebGrid

To help you better understand the capabilities and the advantages of using the DBWeb controls, there is nothing better than to build a simple demo step by step. As you'll see, it is only a matter of dragging components and setting properties (mostly to connect those components), as no code is required.

After creating a new ASP.NET application, you can speed up the development by dragging the table you want to show in the web form from the Data Explorer. In this example, I dragged the Employee table of the demo InterBase database Delphi installs in the `Common Files/Borland Shared/Data` folder. By dragging the table you should have a BdpConnection and a BdpDataAdapter. Remember to prefix the connection string property of the BdpConnection with `localhost:` in front of the actual path (otherwise the ASP.NET program will work at design time but will have problems when deployed). Now add a DataSet component and set it as target of the BdpDataAdapter in its `DataSet` property. At this point, if everything is properly set up, you should be able to activate the BdpDataAdapter (`Active` property set to True) with no error. You should be able to see the employee table (or any other table you've selected) in the `Tables` collection of the dataset.

Now that you have finished the database side of the program, let's move to the user interface. Add to the designer a DBWebDataSource component and connect its `DataSource` property to the table (in the drop-down list you'll see the dataset itself and the tables it defines). Place a DBWebGrid on the web form and set its two key properties: the DBDataSource property should refer to the DBWebData-Source component and the TableName property to the table. Finally, apply one of the standard formatting styles for the grid (using the editor at the bottom of the Object Inspector). You should now be able to see at design time the grid with the live database data, as in the Figure 21.8, which shows the web form of the AspNetDBTable example I built with these steps.

This application has a few interesting features readily available. The first is paging of the table data. The DBWebGrid control has an AllowPaging Boolean property that toggles automatic support for paging through the data (it is active by default) and a PageSize property you can use to determine how many records you'll see for each page (the default is 10). At the bottom of the grid, the controls show the numbers of the pages you can jump to or some simple navigation controls, depending on the PagerStyle property (and its Mode attribute, in particular).

A second feature of the DBWebGrid is that it supports direct editing of the database data within the grid (unless the ReadOnly property is set to True). To make this work properly, however, you need to add a second component to the form, a DBWebNavigator control. Again, set its DBDataSource and TableName properties, and pick up one of the ByttonType options (I used ButtonText in the demo). This will turn the web form into a complete editor of the data in the dataset. A user will be able to edit data for the current record, change the current record, insert new records, delete records, undo any of the changes done so far, and refresh the original data of the table.

The only feature missing is the ability to update the data in the actual database, as the Apply To Server button invariably remains grayed out until you write some code for the handler of the OnApplyUpdateChanges (and not OnApplyChanges as listed in some of the help pages) of the DBWeb-DataSource component. If you are using the BDP, you can write some very simple code for this event handler:

```
procedure TWebForm1.DBWebDataSource1_OnApplyChangesRequest(
    sender: System.Object; e: Borland.Data.Web.WebControlEventArgs);
begin
    BdpDataAdapter1.AutoUpdate;
end;
```

BUILDING A FORM

For editing the data it is much better to use a form-based layout rather than a grid-based one. In the AspNetEmployeeForm example, I used the same database access components, adding also a second table (the Departments table) to be used for a lookup control. I changed the user interface, providing a set of DBWebLabeledTextBox controls as text boxes for the various fields, plus a DBWebCalendar for the hire date, a DBWebListBox as a lookup field, a DBWebAggregateControl to show the total salary, and a DBWebNavigator for moving from a record to another. You can see the form of the example at run time in Figure 21.9.

For those data-aware controls showing a single column, in addition to the DBDataSource and TableName properties, you have to set the ColumnName property. Lookup controls also require the LookupTableName, the DataTextField, and the DataValueField properties.

FIGURE 21.8
The web form of the
AspNetDBTable
example shows live
data at design time.

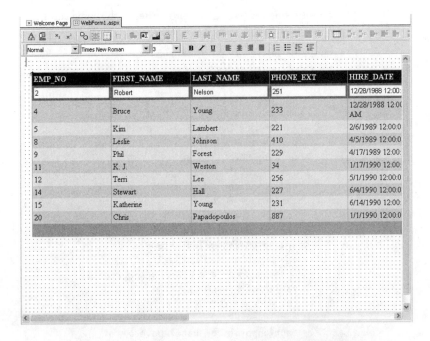

FIGURE 21.9
The AspNetEmployee-
Form example at
run time

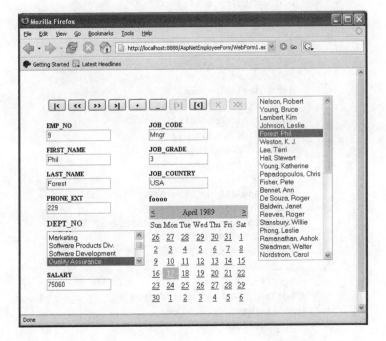

Here is a small excerpt of the properties of the some controls of different types (with styles and positions omitted) from the .aspx file:

```
<body ms_positioning="GridLayout">
  <form runat="server">
    <borland:DBWebNavigator
      id="DBWebNavigator1"
      dbdatasource="<%# DBWebDataSource1 %>"
      tablename="EMPLOYEE">
    </borland:DBWebNavigator>
    <borland:DBWebCalendar
      id="DBWebCalendar1"
      dbdatasource="<%# DBWebDataSource1 %>"
      tablename="EMPLOYEE"
      columnname="HIRE_DATE">
    </borland:DBWebCalendar>
    <borland:DBWebLabeledTextBox
      id="DBWebLabeledTextBox1"
      dbdatasource="<%# DBWebDataSource1 %>"
      tablename="EMPLOYEE"
      columnname="EMP_NO"
      caption="EMP_NO"
      captionposition="LabelAbove">
    </borland:DBWebLabeledTextBox>
    <borland:DBWebListBox
      id="DBWebListBox1"
      dbdatasource="<%# DBWebDataSource1 %>"
      tablename="EMPLOYEE"
      columnname="DEPT_NO"
      datavaluefield="DEPT_NO"
      datatextfield="DEPARTMENT"
      lookuptablename="DEPARTMENT">
    </borland:DBWebListBox>
    <borland:DBWebAggregateControl
      id="DBWebAggregateControl1"
      caption="TOTAL SALARY"
      captionposition="LabelAbove"
      aggregatetype="aggSum"
      dbdatasource="<%# DBWebDataSource1 %>"
      tablename="EMPLOYEE"
      columnname="SALARY"
      enableviewstate="False"
      ignorenullvalues="True">
    </borland:DBWebAggregateControl>
    <asp:ListBox
      id="ListBox1"
```

```
          datavaluefield="EMP_NO"
          datatextfield="FULL_NAME"
          rows="20"
          datasource="<%# DataTable1 %>">
      </asp:ListBox>
    </form>
  </body>
```

As you can see at the end of the list, the program also uses a standard ListBox control, which is not used as a lookup but only to display the list of the available records. This component grabs the data directly from the table of the dataset, and needs the standard ASP.NET data binding code:

```
procedure TWebForm1.Page_Load(
  sender: System.Object; e: System.EventArgs);
begin
  if not IsPostBack then
  begin
    ListBox1.DataBind;
    ListBox1.SelectedIndex := 0;
  end;
end;
```

At the beginning the program selects the first item of the list box. While the user moves among the records, the selection is updated with the proper element. This operation requires the use of one of the many custom interfaces supported by the DBWebDataSource component and documented sparingly, if at all. In this case you can use the IDBDataSource interface, which has a GetCurrentRow method returning the index of the current row:

```
procedure TWebForm1.DBWebDataSource1_OnScroll(
  sender: System.Object; e: Borland.Data.Web.OnScrollEventArgs);
var
  iDataSource: Borland.Data.Web.IDBDataSource;
begin
  iDataSource := Borland.Data.Web.IDBDataSource (DBWebDataSource1);
  ListBox1.SelectedIndex := iDataSource.
    GetCurrentRow (Self, 'EMPLOYEE');
end;
```

The program also does the opposite: If you select an element of the list box, you can jump to that record by selecting the Goto button, which uses another undocumented interface, IDBPostStateManager, to change the position of the current record. Before doing that, however, it has to clear the current record information saved in the session data, or the current record will override the default setting:

```
procedure TWebForm1.Button1_Click(
  sender: System.Object; e: System.EventArgs);
var
  iStateManager: Borland.Data.Web.IDBPostStateManager;
begin
```

```
    DBWebDataSource1.ClearSessionChanges(Self);
    iStateManager := Borland.Data.Web.IDBPostStateManager (DBWebDataSource1);
    iStateManager.SetCurrentRow (
      Self, 'EMPLOYEE', ListBox1.SelectedIndex);
  end;
```

Building ASP.NET Applications

Up to now you have built ASP.NET applications with a single page. In general, however, applications will have multiple pages. This is why this section starts by exploring how to move data among pages and then moves on to session data and session management and to user login and management. With all of this information you'll be able to move from the development of single pages to entire applications.

Moving Data Between Pages

You have seen that ASP.NET simplifies the management of the data the user is working on in a specific page with the ViewState collection. However, this technique does not help when a user moves from a web page to another one of the same application (or virtual folder).

If you need to pass data from one page to another, there are many different techniques you can use, each with advantages and disadvantages. In the AspNetMultipage example, I explored three different approaches: the use of URL parameters (query parameters), the access to the *handler* page, and the use of session parameters. The first page of the program has a TextBox and four LinkButton controls, while the second form has a table with several Label controls in which the program copies (with different techniques, not all working at the same time) the text of the TextBox of the first page. You can see the two pages in Figure 21.10.

FIGURE 21.10

The two pages of the AspNetMultipage example after moving same data with the session and using the redirection of the URL

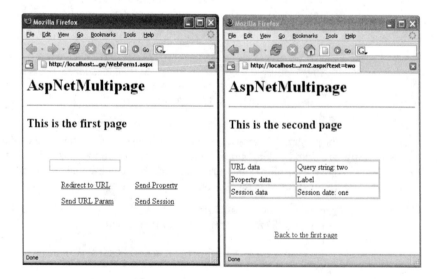

The simplest approach is the use of a URL to pass the parameter in a further request made to the application (redirection works by returning a special HTTP response that will ask the browser to request a different page, as indicated by the *redirection* URL). The Redirect to URL link of the first form has the following code:

```
Response.Redirect('WebForm2.aspx?text=' + TextBox1.Text);
```

This URL parameter is passed to the second page within the query parameters of the new HTTP request. The page can read this parameter, with the following code in its Page_Load event handler:

```
var
  strText: string;
begin
  strText := Request.Params.Item['text'];
  if strText <> '' then
    Label1.Text := 'Query string: ' + strText;
```

A similar technique is also used by the second LinkButton control, Send URL Param, which activates the second page directly, without a further request from the browser:

```
Server.Transfer('WebForm2.aspx?text=' + TextBox1.Text);
```

The difference is that in this second case you won't see the destination URL, but you'll still see the URL of the first page, with no parameter. Using this link button, the second parameter passing mechanism is triggered as well. The third link button, in fact, has some very similar code:

```
Server.Transfer('WebForm2.aspx');
```

In both of these cases, the second form is *called* by the code of the first one, directly (without a further HTTP request like in the Response.Redirect call described earlier). This means that the form being invoked can refer to the caller object by using the Context.Handler property:

```
var
  wf1: TWebForm1;
begin
  wf1 := TWebForm1 (Context.Handler);
  if Assigned (wf1) then
    Label2.Text := 'Form data: ' + wf1.Text;
```

The fourth and last button copies the TextBox input to a session parameter, which is therefore available to any other page or request made in the same session. This is the code executed by the Link-Button (I use Response.Redirect only to avoid triggering the previous technique as well):

```
Session.Add('Text', TextBox1.Text);
Response.Redirect('WebForm2.aspx');
```

The Session object is a list that can be accessed by index by the second form:

```
var
  strText: string;
  obj: System.Object;
```

```
begin
  obj := Session.Item ['Text'];
  if Assigned (obj) then
  begin
    strText := obj.ToString;
    if strText <> '' then
      Label3.Text := 'Session date: ' + strText;
  end;
```

This last technique is probably the most flexible and robust, although passing parameters by URL or grabbing the data from the other form are more lightweight, and I'd rather avoid saving too much data in each session of a website with many hits.

Session Management

While using the Session object is relatively simple, as you saw in the last example, session management in ASP.NET is flexible and powerful. Without changing the source the code, in fact, you can configure ASP.NET to manage sessions in radically different ways. This is very nice, as the changing scalability of the application and its deployment might require modifying the local web.config file but won't affect the code you write.

In particular, the sessionState element of the web.config file defines where the session data is stored (locally, on a remote state server, or on a SQL Server), whether you want to use a cookie or not, and the session timeout; it also provides the configuration for the optional external server. These are the default settings for a Delphi ASP.NET application:

```
<sessionState
  mode="InProc"
  stateConnectionString="tcpip=127.0.0.1:42424"
  sqlConnectionString="data source=127.0.0.1;user id=sa;password="
  cookieless="false"
  timeout="20"/>
```

Forms Authentication

Another setting you'll find in the web.config file relates to user authentication. The default generated by the Delphi IDE is

```
<authentication mode="Windows" />
```

This means the Windows login is used. If you want to manage login with a specific page, use the Forms mode. Also if you deny the use of the application by users not logged in, instead of writing specific code in each page you can add to the web.config file an authorization section. These are the settings of the AspNetLogin example:

```
<authentication mode="Forms">
  <forms loginUrl="WebForm2.aspx" name=".authToken"/>
</authentication>
<authorization>
  <deny users="?"/>
</authorization>
```

The program has only a main form (with a useless calendar in it), but this form cannot be accessed until you log in. As you try to access the form, you'll be automatically redirected to the login form specified in the preceding settings. This login form has the classic text boxes for the name and the password and a login button, with this code:

```
procedure TWebForm2.btnLogin_Click(
  sender: System.Object; e: System.EventArgs);
begin
  if textName.Text = textPassword.Text then
    FormsAuthentication.RedirectFromLoginPage(
      textName.Text, false);
end;
```

While the test in this case is trivial (you'll generally have to look up the name and password in a database), the following statement that calls RedirectFromLoginPage plays a significant role. This method returns control to the page the user was trying to see before the login page was displayed and passes to the system the name of the user. This name will be available in the application using the Context.User object, as the following snippet taken from the main form of the program shows:

```
procedure TWebForm1.Page_Load(
  sender: System.Object; e: System.EventArgs);
begin
  labelHello.Text := 'Hello, ' + Context.User.Identity.Name;
end;
```

Caching in ASP.NET

Another key feature of ASP.NET applications I want to mention (however briefly) is caching support. This comes in two different forms. The first, called *output caching*, is the caching of the HTML text generated by the system for pages (or portions of pages). If you know the data of a page won't change for some time, regardless of the user seeing it, you can add in the page a declaration like:

```
<%@ OutputCache duration="300" varbyparam="none" %>
```

This specific directive indicates to keep the cached data for five minutes and return it regardless of the parameters. At other times you'll want a copy of the cached data for each possible value of its URL parameters.

A totally different technique is represented by *application data caching*, that is, caching some data in memory that takes time to recreate or reload. For example, you might cache a database table or an XML document obtained from a remote server. In these cases you can use the Cache collection of the application, a series of items storing data with a priority, a duration, and some dependencies from other cache entries or files.

ASP.NET Applications Deployment

As I described in the last chapter when covering the deployment of IntraWeb applications, Delphi 2005 has a Deployment Manager that was introduced primarily for deploying ASP.NET applications.

If you select any ASP.NET project, you'll see a folder with an arrow and the Deployment name. Right-click it to select the New ASP.NET Deployment command, and it will generate a new .bdsdeploy file that opens the corresponding viewer. In the viewer you can select a destination folder (a local, network, or FTP location), and the wizard will list the files you need to deploy and check the version on the server, prompting you to copy only the modified files. You can see an example (for the AspNet-Multipage example) in Figure 21.11.

FIGURE 21.11
Delphi 2005 Deployment Manager for an ASP.NET application

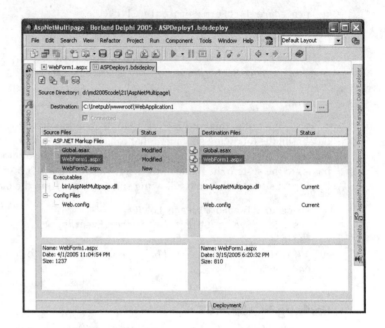

What's Next

In this chapter, you got an introduction to the ASP.NET technology. Even without going into too much depth, reading this chapter should have given you a feeling for development with this architecture and provided you with a starting point for your experiments or further reading. I hope that this chapter, combined with the previous two, has given you a good overview of the alternative web development technologies Delphi 2005 provides. We'll have more about ASP.NET in the next chapter, which is devoted to XML technologies. You'll see how to use XML and XSLT in an ASP.NET page and how to use XML files with DBWeb controls. In the chapter following that, devoted to web services, you'll continue to use .aspx files and ASP.NET related technologies.

Chapter 22

Using XML Technologies

Building applications for the Internet means using protocols and creating browser-based user interfaces, as you've done in the preceding three chapters, but it also opens an opportunity for exchanging business documents electronically. The emerging standards for this type of activity center around the XML document format and include the SOAP transmission protocol, XML schemas for the validation of documents, and XSLT for rendering documents as HTML.

In this chapter, I'll discuss the core XML technologies and the extensive support Delphi and .NET offer for them. Because XML knowledge is far from widespread, I'll provide a little introduction about each technology, but you should refer to books specifically devoted to them to learn more. In Chapter 23, I'll focus specifically on web services and SOAP.

This chapter includes coverage of the XML Document Object Model (DOM), Delphi XML interface mapping, parsing XML documents with SAX, .NET XmlReader and XmlWriter support, and using XSLT for web development.

Introducing XML

Extensible Markup Language (XML) is getting a lot of attention in the IT world. XML is a *markup language*, meaning it uses symbols to describe its own content—in this case, *tags* consisting of specially defined text enclosed in angle brackets. It is *extensible* because it allows for free markers (in contrast, for example, to HTML, which has predefined markers). The XML language is a standard promoted by the World Wide Web Consortium (W3C). The XML Recommendation is at www.w3.org/TR/REC-xml.

XML has been touted as the ASCII of the year 2000, to indicate a simple and widespread technology and also to indicate that an XML document is a plain-text file (generally using Unicode characters instead of plain ASCII text). The important characteristic of XML is that it is descriptive, because every tag has an almost human-readable name. Here is an example, in case you've never seen an XML document:

```
<book>
  <title>Mastering Borland Delphi 2005</title>
  <author>Cantu</author>
  <publisher>Sybex</publisher>
</book>
```

XML has a few disadvantages I want to emphasize from the beginning. The biggest is that without a formal description, a document is worth little. If you want to exchange documents with another company, you must agree on what each tag means and also on the semantic meaning of the content. (For example, when you have a quantity, you have to agree on the measurement system or include it in the document.) Another disadvantage is that XML documents are much larger than other formats; using strings for numbers, for example, is far from efficient, and the repeated opening and closing tags eat up a lot of space. The good news is that XML compresses well, for the same reason.

Core XML Syntax

A few technical elements of XML are worth knowing before we discuss its usage in Delphi. Here is a short summary of the key elements of the XML syntax:

- White space (including the space character, carriage return, line feed, and tabs) is generally ignored (as in an HTML document). It is important to format an XML document to make it readable by a human being, but your programs won't care much.

- You can add comments within `<!--` and `-->` markers, which are ignored by XML processors. There are also directives and processing instructions, enclosed within `<?` and `?>` markers.

- There a few special or reserved characters you cannot use in the text. The only two symbols you can *never* use are the less-than character (or left angle bracket, <, used to delimit a marker), which is replaced by `&lt;`, and the ampersand character (&), which is replaced by `&amp;`. Other optional special characters are `&gt;` for the greater-than symbol (right angle bracket, >), `&apos;` for the single quote ('), and `&quot;` for the double quote (").

- To add non-XML content (for example, binary information or a script), you can use a CDATA section, enclosed within `<![CDATA[` and `]]>`.

- All markers are enclosed by angle brackets, < and >. Markers are case sensitive (in contrast to HTML).

- For each opening marker, you must have a matching closing marker, denoted by an initial slash character:

  ```
  <node>value</node>
  ```

- Markers must not overlap—they must be *properly nested*, as in the first line here (the second line is not correct):

  ```
  <node>xx <nested>yy</nested> </node>   // OK
  <node>xx <nested>yy</node> </nested>   // WRONG
  ```

- If a marker has no content (but its presence is important), you can replace the opening and closing markers with a single marker that includes a final (*trailing*) slash: `<node/>`.

- Markers can have attributes, using multiple attribute names followed by a value enclosed within quotes:

  ```
  <node attrib1="aaa">
  ```

◆ Any XML node can have multiple attributes, multiple embedded tags, and only one block of text, representing the value of the node. It is common practice for XML nodes to have either a textual value or embedded tags, and not both. Here is an example of the full syntax of a node:

```
<node attrib1="aaa" attrib2="bbb">
  value1
  <child1>
    value2
  </child1>
</node>
```

◆ A node can have multiple child nodes with the same tag (tags need not be unique). Attribute names are unique for each node.

Well-Formed XML

The elements discussed in the previous section define the syntax of an XML document, but they are not enough. An XML document is considered syntactically correct, or *well formed,* if it follows a few extra rules. Notice that this type of check doesn't guarantee that the content of the document is meaningful—only that the tags are properly laid out.

Each document should have a prologue indicating that it is indeed an XML document, which version of XML it complies with, and possibly the type of character encoding. Here is an example:

```
<?xml version="1.0" encoding="UTF-8"?>
```

Possible encodings include Unicode character sets (such as UTF-8, UTF-16, and UTF-32) and some ISO encodings (such as ISO-10646-xxx or ISO-8859-xxx). The prologue can also include external declarations, the schema used to validate the document, namespace declarations, an associated XSLT file, and some internal entity declarations. Refer to XML documentation or books for more information about these topics.

An XML document is well formed if it has a prologue, has a proper syntax (see the rules in the previous section), and has a tree of nodes with a single root. Most tools (including Internet Explorer) check whether a document is well formed when loading it.

Working with XML

To get acquainted with the format of XML, you can use one of the existing XML editors available on the market (including Delphi itself and Context, a programmer's editor written in Delphi). When you load an XML document into Internet Explorer, Firefox, or another browser, you'll see it in a read-only tree-like structure.

The trouble when using a plain editor is that it doesn't tell you whether the XML is correct. To overcome this limitation, I built the simplest XML editor I could come up with—basically a memo with XML syntax-checking and a browser attached to it. The XmlEditOne example has a PageControl with two pages. The first page hosts a Memo control; the text of the XML file is loaded and saved by clicking the two toolbar buttons. As soon as you load the file, or each time you modify its text, its content is loaded into a DOM to let a parser check for its correctness (something that would be complex to do with your own code). To parse the code, I used the XMLDocument component available in Delphi, which is basically a wrapper around a DOM available on the computer and indicated by its DOMVendor property. I'll discuss the use of this component in more detail in the next section. For the moment, suffice it to say you can assign a string list to its XML property and activate it to let it parse the XML text and eventually report an error with an exception.

For this example, this behavior is far from good, because while typing the XML code you'll have temporarily incorrect XML. Still, I prefer not to ask the user to click a button to do the validation and instead to let it run continuously. Because it is not possible to disable the parse exception raised by the XMLDocument component, I had to work at a lower level, extracting the DOMPersist property (referring to the persistency interface of the DOM) after extracting the IXMLDocumentAccess interface from the XMLDocument component (called XmlDoc in this code). You can also extract the IDOMParseError interface from the document component to display any error message in the status bar:

```
procedure TFormXmlEdit.MemoXmlChange(Sender: TObject);
var
  eParse: IDOMParseError;
begin
  XmlDoc.Active := True;
  xmlBar.Panels[1].Text := 'OK';
  xmlBar.Panels[2].Text := '';
  (XmlDoc as IXMLDocumentAccess).DOMPersist.loadxml(MemoXml.Text);
  eParse := (XmlDoc.DOMDocument as IDOMParseError);
  if eParse.errorCode <> 0 then
    with eParse do
    begin
      xmlBar.Panels[1].Text := 'Error in: ' + IntToStr (Line) + '.' +
        IntToStr (LinePos);
      xmlBar.Panels[2].Text := SrcText + ': ' + Reason;
    end;
end;
```

You can see an example of the output of the program in Figure 22.1. The program also has a second tab hosting the XML tree. This second page of the program is built using the WebBrowser component, which embeds Internet Explorer's ActiveX control. Unfortunately, there is no direct and simple way to assign a string with the XML text to this control, so as you move to this second page the program saves the current content of the memo to a file and loads it in the browser.

NOTE I used this code as a starting point to build a full-fledged XML editor called XmlTypist. This free XML editor includes syntax highlighting, XSLT support, code completion for XSLT and schemas, and a number of extra features. It is available at www.xmltypist.com.

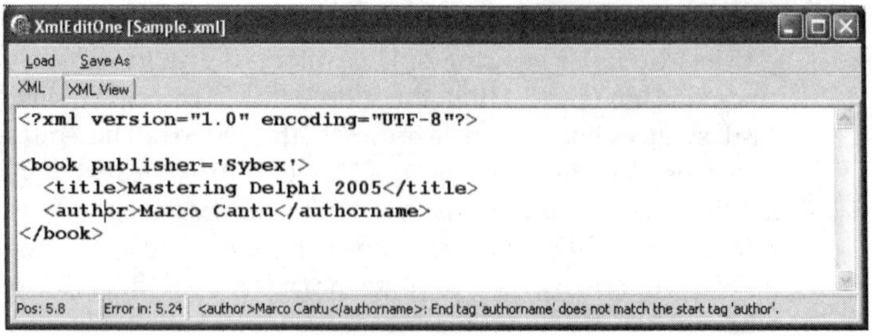

FIGURE 22.1
The XmlEditOne example allows you to enter XML text in a memo, indicating errors as you type.

FROM HTML TO XHTML

XML is more formal and precise than HTML. The W3C has published the XHTML standard that makes HTML documents XML compliant, for better processing with XML tools. The XHTML standard implies many changes in a typical HTML document, such as avoiding attributes with no values, adding all the closing markers (as in `</p>` and `</li>`), adding the slash to stand-alone markers (as `<hr/>` and `<img.../>`), the use of lowercase tags, the use of quotes for attributes, proper nesting, and much more.

If you are interested in converting existing HTML, a converter called HTML Tidy is hosted by the W3C website and is installed by default in the Delphi 2005 IDE. If you open any HTML page, and select the Edit ➢ HTML Tidy menu, you'll see the two submenus Format Document and Check Document for Errors. Notice that Internet Explorer 6 has some compatibility problems with XHTML, which limits the use of pure XHTML in websites, although most of the problems can be worked around.

XHTML 1 is a transitional version, retaining compatibility with HTML tags to a large extent. Version 2 poses some restrictions on tags, however, removing duplications like `<b>` and `<strong>`, with the former being deprecated. XHTML 2 also adds many interesting new technologies, like XForms, but because it requires specific browser support, it will take time before it is widely adopted.

Managing XML Documents in Delphi

Now that you know the core elements of XML, we can begin discussing how to manage XML documents in Delphi programs (or in programs in general; some of the techniques discussed here go beyond the language used). There are two typical techniques for manipulating XML documents: using a Document Object Model (DOM) interface or using the Simple API for XML (SAX). The two approaches are quite different:

◆ The DOM loads the entire document into a hierarchical tree of nodes, allowing you to read them and manipulate them to change the document. For this reason, the DOM is suitable for navigating the XML structure in memory and editing it or for creating new documents from scratch.

◆ The SAX parses the document, firing an event for each element of the document without building a structure in memory. Once parsed by the SAX, the document is lost, but this operation is generally much faster than the construction of the DOM tree. Using the SAX is good for reading a document once—for example, if you're looking for a portion of its data.

There is a third classic way to manipulate (and specifically create) XML documents: string management. Creating a document by adding strings is the fastest operation, particularly if you can do a single pass (and don't need to modify nodes already generated). Even reading documents by means of string functions is very fast, but this process can become difficult for complex structures.

Besides these classic XML processing approaches, which are also available for other programming languages, Delphi provides two more techniques you should consider. The first is the definition of interfaces that map the document structure and are used to access the document instead of the generic DOM interface. As you'll see, this approach makes for faster coding and more robust applications. The second technique is the development of transformations that allow you to read a generic XML document into a ClientDataSet component or save the dataset into an XML file of a given structure (not the specific XML structure natively supported by the ClientDataSet or MyBase).

Finally, .NET has specific support for XML, both with DOM and with a customized version of SAX, implemented by the XmlReader class. The .NET Framework also has an XmlWriter class, extensive support for XML in ADO.NET, and transformation components, as we'll see later in the section on XSLT.

I won't try to fully assess which option is better suited for each type of document and manipulation, but I will highlight some of the advantages and disadvantages while discussing examples of each approach in the following sections. At the end of the chapter, I'll discuss the relative speed of techniques for processing large files.

Programming with the DOM

Because an XML document has a tree-like structure, loading an XML document into a tree in memory is a natural fit. This is what the DOM does. The DOM is a standard interface, so when you have written code that uses a DOM, you can switch DOM implementations without changing your source code (at least, if you haven't used any noncustom extensions).

In Delphi, you can install several DOM implementations, available as COM servers, and use their interfaces. One of the most commonly used DOM engines on Windows is the one provided by Microsoft as part of the MSXML SDK that is also installed by Internet Explorer (and for this reason in all recent versions of Windows) and many other Microsoft applications. Other DOM engines directly available in Delphi include Apache Foundation's Xerces and the open-source OpenXML.

TIP OpenXML is a native open-source Delphi DOM available at www.philo.de/xml. Another native Delphi DOM was offered by TurboPower and is now freely available at http://sourceforge.net/projects/tpxmlpartner. An advantage to these solutions is that they don't require an external DLL for the program to execute. OpenXML is cross-platform and works with both Kylix and Linux. At the time of this writing, none of them were available in Delphi for .NET.

Delphi embeds the DOM implementations into a wrapper component called XMLDocument, which is available in both Delphi for Win32 and Delphi for .NET (although it wasn't in Delphi 8 for .NET). I used this component in the preceding example, but here I will examine its role in a more general way. The idea behind using this component instead of the DOM interface is that you remain more independent from the implementations and can work with some simplified methods, or helpers.

The DOM interface is complex to use. A *document* is a collection of nodes, each having a name, a text element, a collection of attributes, and a collection of child nodes. Each collection of nodes lets you access elements by position or search for them by name. Notice that the text within the tags of a node, if any, is rendered as a child of the node and listed in its collection of child nodes. The root node has some extra methods for creating new nodes, values, or attributes.

With Delphi's XMLDocument, you can work at two levels:

♦ At a lower level, you can use the DOMDocument property (of the IDOMDocument interface type) to access a standard W3C Document Object Model interface. The official DOM is defined in the xmldom unit and includes interfaces like IDOMNode, IDOMNodeList, IDOMAttr, IDOMElement, and IDOMText. With the official DOM interfaces, Delphi supports a lower-level but standard programming model. The DOM implementation is indicated by the XMLDocument component in the DOMVendor property.

♦ As a higher-level alternative, the XMLDocument component also implements the IXMLDocument interface. This is a custom DOM-like API defined by Borland in the XMLIntf unit and comprising interfaces like IXMLNode, IXMLNodeList, and IXMLNodeCollection. This Borland layer simplifies some of the DOM operations by replacing multiple method calls, which are repeated often in sequence, with a single property or method.

In the following examples (particularly the DomCreate demo), I'll use both approaches to give you a better idea of the practical differences between the two. I'll also show the .NET version of these programs, which is somewhat troublesome: As explained in the section "Using the XMLDocument Component in .NET," you need to use a few IFDEF statements to pick up the proper DOM mapper, MSXML on Win32 or the CLR XML support in .NET.

An XML Document in a TreeView

The starting point generally consists of loading a document from a file or creating it from a string, but you can also start with a new document. As a first example of using the DOM, I built a program that can load an XML document into a DOM and show its structure in a TreeView control. I also added to the XmlDomTree program (and the XmlDomTreeNet version, discussed later in some depth) a few buttons with sample code used to access the elements of a sample file, as an example of accessing the DOM data. Loading the document is simple, but showing it in a tree requires a recursive function that navigates the nodes and subnodes:

```
procedure TFormXmlTree.DomToTree (
  XmlNode: IXMLNode; TreeNode: TTreeNode);
var
  I: Integer;
  NewTreeNode: TTreeNode;
  NodeText: string;
  AttrNode: IXMLNode;
begin
  // skip text nodes and other special cases
  if XmlNode.NodeType <> ntElement then
    Exit;
  // add the node itself
  NodeText := XmlNode.NodeName;
  if XmlNode.IsTextElement then
    NodeText := NodeText + ' = ' + XmlNode.NodeValue;
  NewTreeNode := TreeView1.Items.AddChild(TreeNode, NodeText);
  // add attributes
  for I := 0 to xmlNode.AttributeNodes.Count - 1 do
  begin
    AttrNode := xmlNode.AttributeNodes.Nodes[I];
    TreeView1.Items.AddChild(NewTreeNode,
      '[' + AttrNode.NodeName + ' = "' + AttrNode.Text + '"]');
  end;
  // add each child node
  if XmlNode.HasChildNodes then
    for I := 0 to xmlNode.ChildNodes.Count - 1 do
      DomToTree (xmlNode.ChildNodes.Nodes [I], NewTreeNode);
end;
```

This code is interesting because it highlights some of the operations you can do with a DOM. First, each node has a `NodeType` property you can use to determine whether the node is an element, attribute, text node, or special entity (such as CDATA and others). Second, you cannot access the textual representation of the node (its `NodeValue`) unless it has a text element (notice that the text node will be skipped, as per the initial test). After displaying the name of the item and then the text value if available, the program shows the content of each attribute directly and of each subnode by calling the `DomToTree` method recursively (see Figure 22.2).

Once you have loaded the sample document that accompanies the XmlDomTree program into the XMLDocument component, you can use the various methods to access generic nodes, as in the previous tree-building code, or you can fetch specific elements. For example, you can grab the value of the attribute `text` of the root node by writing:

```
XMLDocument1.DocumentElement.Attributes ['text']
```

Notice that if there is no attribute called `text`, the call will fail with a generic error message, "Could not convert variant of type (Null) into type (String)," which helps neither you nor the end user to understand what's wrong. If you need to access to the first attribute of the root without knowing its name, you can use the following code:

```
XMLDocument1.DocumentElement.AttributeNodes.Nodes[0].NodeValue
```

To access the nodes, you use a similar technique, possibly taking advantage of the `ChildValues` array. This is a Delphi extension to the DOM, which allows you to pass as parameter either the name of the element or its numeric position:

```
XMLDocument1.DocumentElement.ChildNodes.Nodes[1].ChildValues['author']
```

This code gets the (first) author of the second book. You cannot use the `ChildValues['book']` expression, because there are multiple nodes with the same name under the root node.

FIGURE 22.2

The XmlDomTree example can open a generic XML document and show it inside a TreeView.

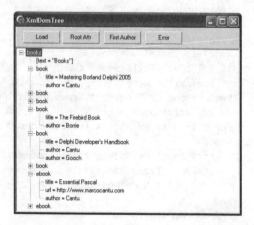

Using the XMLDocument Component in .NET

If you create a brand new VCL for .NET application with an NFM file, you can use the XMLDocument component in a very smooth way. By default it sets the DOMVendor property to the only option available in .NET, CLRXML. This option is not available if your VCL for .NET application uses a DFM file (because it was ported from Win32) or if you are trying to use both compilers from a single source, as I tend to do in this book.

In this case to create the .NET version of the example, called XmlDomTreeNet, I reset the value of the DOMVendor property of the XMLDocument1 component. The initialization takes place when the form is created using the proper DOM for Win32 or .NET, defined in the units alternatively included in the uses statement of the `interface` section:

```
uses
  Windows, Messages, SysUtils, ...
  {$IFDEF MSWINDOWS} MsXmlDom, {$ENDIF}
  {$IFDEF CLR} ClrXmlDom, {$ENDIF}
  StdCtrls;

procedure TFormXmlTree.FormCreate(Sender: TObject);
begin
{$IFDEF MSWINDOWS}
  XMLDocument1.DOMVendor := TMSDOMImplementationFactory.Create;
{$ENDIF}

{$IFDEF CLR}
  XMLDocument1.DOMVendor := TCLRDOMImplementationFactory.Create;
{$ENDIF}
end;
```

That's all it takes to port the program to .NET. Everything else works exactly as in the Win32 version.

WARNING   There is a problem when the DFM is reloaded: the DOMVendor property is automatically reset to the Microsoft DOM and as you compile or save the file a reference to the msxmldom unit is added automatically, even if there is another reference with an IFDEF statement. This means that every time you load the DFM you need to reset the DOMVendor property of the XmlDocument1 component and optionally remove the extra msxmldom reference. For this reason, you might consider using a single Delphi source code file with both a DFM and an NFM file referenced inside IFDEF statements.

Creating Documents Using the DOM

Although I mentioned earlier that you can create an XML document by chaining together strings, this technique is far from robust. Using a DOM to create a document ensures that the XML will be well formed. Also, if the DOM has a schema definition attached, you can validate the structure of the document while adding data to it.

To highlight different cases of document creation, I built the DomCreate example (and the Dom-CreateNet version as well). This program can create XML documents within the DOM, showing their text on a memo and optionally in a TreeView.

WARNING   The XMLDocument component uses the doAutoIndent option to improve the output of the XML text to the memo by formatting the XML in a slightly better way. You can choose the type of indentation by setting the NodeIndentStr property. To format generic XML text, you can also use the global FormatXMLData function.

The Simple button on the form creates simple XML text using the low-level, official DOM interfaces. The program calls the document's createElement method for each node, adding them as children of other nodes:

```
procedure TForm1.btnSimpleClick(Sender: TObject);
var
  iXml: IDOMDocument;
  iRoot, iNode, iNode2, iChild, iAttribute: IDOMNode;
begin
  // empty the document
  XMLDoc.Active := False;
  XMLDoc.XML.Text := '';
  XMLDoc.Active := True;

  // root
  iXml := XmlDoc.DOMDocument;
  iRoot := iXml.appendChild (iXml.createElement ('xml'));
  // node "test"
  iNode := iRoot.appendChild (iXml.createElement ('test'));
  iNode.appendChild (iXml.createElement ('test2'));
  iChild := iNode.appendChild (iXml.createElement ('test3'));
  iChild.appendChild (iXml.createTextNode('simple value'));
  iNode.insertBefore (iXml.createElement ('test4'), iChild);

  // node replication
  iNode2 := iNode.cloneNode (True);
  iRoot.appendChild (iNode2);

  // add an attribute
  iAttribute := iXml.createAttribute ('color');
  iAttribute.nodeValue := 'red';
  iNode2.attributes.setNamedItem (iAttribute);

  // show XML in memo
  Memo1.Lines.Text := FormatXMLData (XMLDoc.XML.Text);
end;
```

Notice that text nodes are added explicitly, attributes are created with a specific create call, and the code uses cloneNode to replicate an entire branch of the tree. Overall, the code is cumbersome to write, but after a while you may get used to this style. The effect of the program is shown (formatted in the memo and in the tree) in Figure 22.3.

FIGURE 22.3

The DomCreate example can generate various types of XML documents using a DOM.

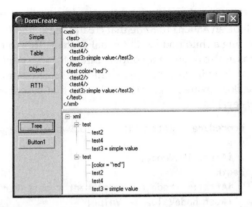

The second example of DOM creation relates to a dataset. I added to the form a dbExpress dataset component (but any other dataset would do). I also added to a button the call to my custom DataSetToDOM procedure, like this:

```
DataSetToDOM ('customers', 'customer', XMLDoc, SQLDataSet1);
```

The DataSetToDOM procedure creates a root node with the text of the first parameter, grabs each record of the dataset, defines a node with the second parameter, and adds a subnode for each field of the record, all using extremely generic code:

```
procedure DataSetToDOM (RootName, RecordName: string; XMLDoc: TXMLDocument;
  DataSet: TDataSet);
var
  iNode, iChild: IXMLNode;
  i: Integer;
begin
  DataSet.Open;
  DataSet.First;
  // root
  XMLDoc.DocumentElement := XMLDoc.CreateNode (RootName);

  // add table data
  while not DataSet.EOF do
  begin
    // add a node for each record
    iNode := XMLDoc.DocumentElement.AddChild (RecordName);
    for I := 0 to DataSet.FieldCount - 1 do
    begin
      // add an element for each field
      iChild := iNode.AddChild (DataSet.Fields[i].FieldName);
      iChild.Text := DataSet.Fields[i].AsString;
    end;
    DataSet.Next;
  end;
  DataSet.Close;
end;
```

The preceding code uses the simplified DOM access interfaces provided by Borland, which include an AddChild node that creates the subnode, and the direct access to the Text property for defining a child node with textual content. This routine extracts an XML representation of your dataset, also opening up opportunities for web publishing, as I'll discuss later in the section on XSLT.

Another interesting opportunity is the generation of XML documents describing Delphi objects. The DomCreate program has a button that describes a few properties of an object, again using the low-level DOM:

```
procedure AddAttr (iNode: IDOMNode; Name, Value: string);
var
  iAttr: IDOMNode;
begin
  iAttr := iNode.ownerDocument.createAttribute (name);
  iAttr.nodeValue := Value;
  iNode.attributes.setNamedItem (iAttr);
end;

procedure TForm1.btnObjectClick(Sender: TObject);
var
  iXml: IDOMDocument;
  iRoot: IDOMNode;
begin
  // empty the document
  XMLDoc.Active := False;
  XMLDoc.XML.Text := '';
  XMLDoc.Active := True;

  // root
  iXml := XmlDoc.DOMDocument;
  iRoot := iXml.appendChild (iXml.createElement ('Button1'));

  // a few properties as attributes (might also be nodes)
  AddAttr (iRoot, 'Name', Button1.Name);
  AddAttr (iRoot, 'Caption', Button1.Caption);
  AddAttr (iRoot, 'Font.Name', Button1.Font.Name);
  AddAttr (iRoot, 'Left', IntToStr (Button1.Left));
  AddAttr (iRoot, 'Hint', Button1.Hint);

  // show XML in memo
  Memo1.Lines := XmlDoc.XML;
end;
```

Of course, it is more interesting to have a generic technique capable of saving the properties of each Delphi component (or *persistent object*, to be more precise), recursing on persistent subobjects and indicating the names of referenced components. I did this in the ComponentToDOM procedure, which uses the low-level RTTI information provided by the TypInfo unit, including the extraction of the list of component properties not having a default value. Once more, the program uses the simplified Delphi XML interfaces:

```
procedure ComponentToDOM (iNode: IXmlNode; Comp: TPersistent);
var
  nProps, i: Integer;
  PropList: PPropList;
  Value: Variant;
  newNode: IXmlNode;
begin
  // get list of properties
  nProps := GetPropList (Comp.ClassInfo, PropList);
  try
    for i := 0 to nProps - 1 do
    begin
      Value := GetPropValue (Comp, PropList [i].Name);
      NewNode := iNode.AddChild(PropList [i].Name);
      NewNode.Text := Value;
      if (PropList [i].PropType^.Kind = tkClass) and (Value <> 0) then
        if TObject (Integer(Value)) is TComponent then
          NewNode.Text := TComponent (Integer(Value)).Name
        else
          // TPersistent but not TComponent: recurse
          ComponentToDOM (newNode,
            TObject (Integer(Value)) as TPersistent);
  finally
    FreeMem (PropList);
  end;
end;
```

These two lines of code, in this case, trigger the creation of the XML document:

```
XMLDoc.DocumentElement := XMLDoc.CreateNode(Self.ClassName);
ComponentToDOM (XMLDoc.DocumentElement, Self);
```

XML Data-Binding Interfaces

You have seen that working with the DOM to access or generate a document is tedious because you must use positional information and not logical access to the data. Also, handling series of repeated nodes of different possible types is far from simple. Moreover, you can create any well-formed document using a DOM, but (unless you use a validating DOM) you can add any subnode to any node, coming up with almost useless document, because no one else will be able to manage them.

To solve these issues, Borland added to Delphi for Win32 an XML Data Binding Wizard, which can examine an XML document or a document definition (a schema, a Document Type Definition, or another type of definition) and generate a set of interfaces for manipulating the document. These interfaces are specific to the document and its structure and allow you to have more readable code, but they are certainly less generic as far as the types of documents you can handle (and this is more positive than it might sound at first).

NOTE   The Data Binding Interface Wizard is listed only among the Win32 tools, but you can also use it for a .NET application. Provided you set the XmlDocument component to refer to the CLR XML and tweak the generated code a little (as described later), your program should be able to work in .NET as it does in Win32.

You can activate the XML Data Binding Wizard by using the corresponding icon in the Delphi Projects/XML page of the New Items dialog box. After a first page in which you can select an input file, this wizard shows you the structure of the document graphically, as you can see in Figure 22.4 for the sample XML used by some of the demos in this chapter. In this page, you can give a name to each entity of the generated interfaces, if you don't like the defaults suggested by the wizard. You can also change the rules used by the wizard to generate the names (an extended flexibility I'd like to have in other areas of the Delphi IDE). The final page gives you a preview of the generated interfaces and offers options for generating schemas and other definition files.

For the sample XML file with the author names, the XML Data Binding Wizard generates an interface for the root node, two interfaces for the elements lists of two different types of nodes (books and e-books), and two interfaces for the elements of the two types. Here are a few excerpts of the generated code, available in the XmlIntfDefinition unit of the XmlInterface example (and its XmlInterfaceNet counterpart):

```
type
  IXMLBooksType = interface(IXMLNode)
    ['{C9A9FB63-47ED-4F27-8ABA-E71F30BA7F11}']
    { Property Accessors }
    function Get_Text: WideString;
    function Get_Book: IXMLBookTypeList;
    function Get_Ebook: IXMLEbookTypeList;
    procedure Set_Text(Value: WideString);
    { Methods & Properties }
    property Text: WideString read Get_Text write Set_Text;
    property Book: IXMLBookTypeList read Get_Book;
    property Ebook: IXMLEbookTypeList read Get_Ebook;
  end;

  IXMLBookTypeList = interface(IXMLNodeCollection)
    ['{3449E8C4-3222-47B8-B2B2-38EE504790B6}']
    { Methods & Properties }
    function Add: IXMLBookType;
    function Insert(const Index: Integer): IXMLBookType;
    function Get_Item(Index: Integer): IXMLBookType;
    property Items[Index: Integer]: IXMLBookType
      read Get_Item; default;
  end;

  IXMLBookType = interface(IXMLNode)
```

```
['{26BF5C51-9247-4D1A-8584-24AE68969935}']
{ Property Accessors }
function Get_Title: WideString;
function Get_Author: IXMLString_List;
procedure Set_Title(Value: WideString);
{ Methods & Properties }
property Title: WideString read Get_Title write Set_Title;
property Author: IXMLString_List read Get_Author;
end;
```

For each interface, the XML Data Binding Wizard also generates an implementation class that provides the code for the interface methods by translating the requests into DOM calls. The unit includes three initialization functions, which can return the interface of the root node from a document loaded in an XMLDocument component (or a component providing a generic IXMLDocument interface), or return one from a file, or create a brand new DOM:

```
function Getbooks(Doc: IXMLDocument): IXMLBooksType;
function Loadbooks(const FileName: WideString): IXMLBooksType;
function Newbooks: IXMLBooksType;
```

After generating these interfaces using the wizard in the XmlInterface example, I repeated XML document access code that's similar to the XmlDomTree example but is much simpler to write (and to read). For example, you can get the attribute of the root node by writing

```
procedure TForm1.btnAttrClick(Sender: TObject);
var
   Books: IXMLBooksType;
begin
   Books := Getbooks (XmlDocument1);
   ShowMessage (Books.Text);
end;
```

FIGURE 22.4
Delphi's XML Data Binding Wizard can examine the structure of a document or a schema (or another document definition) to create a set of interfaces for simplified and direct access to the DOM data.

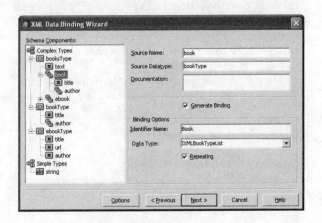

It is even simpler if you recall that while typing this code, Delphi's code insight can help by listing the available properties of each node, thanks to the fact that the parser can read in the interface definitions (although it cannot understand the format of a generic XML document). Accessing a node of one of the sublists is a matter of writing one of the following statements (possibly the second, with the default array property):

```
Books.Book.Items[1].Title  // full
Books.Book[1].Title        // further simplified
```

You can use similarly simplified code to generate new documents or add new elements, thanks to the customized Add method available in each list-based interface. Again, if you don't have a predefined structure for the XML document, as in the dataset-based and RTTI-based examples of the previous demonstration, you won't be able to use this approach.

NOTE   For the .NET version I had to tweak some of the generated code, as you can see by looking at the source code files of the example. In particular, you need to replace the type parameter of the CreateCollection calls, passing a type instead of an interface.

The XML Data Binding Wizard can work from existing schemas or generate a schema for an XML document. An XML document describes some data, but to exchange this data among companies, it must stick to some agreed structure. A schema is a document definition against which a document can be checked for correctness, an operation usually indicated with the term *validation*.

The first—and still widespread—type of validation available for XML used *document type definitions (DTDs)*. These documents describe the structure of the XML but cannot define the possible content of each node. Also, DTDs are not XML documents themselves but use a different, awkward notation. The W3C promotes a different approach based on XML *schemas*. An XML schema is an XML document that can validate both the structure of the XML tree and the content of the node. A schema is based on the use and definition of simple and complex data types, similar to what happens in an OOP language.

Using the Native XML DOM in .NET

I already showed you that in a VCL for .NET it is possible to use the XmlDocument component wrapping the XML DOM classes provided by the CLR. You can also use these classes directly. Of course, this is your only option in a WinForms application. Like other demos of this chapter, the WinFormDom example has a multiline TextBox control and a TreeView control to show the plain XML text and its hierarchical representation.

The program uses the System.XML namespace directly and declares among the private fields of the form an object of the XmlDocument class, initialized directly when the form is created:

```
private
  xmlDom: XmlDocument;

constructor TWinForm.Create;
begin
  xmlDom := XMLDocument.Create;
```

The Load button opens an XML file and populates both views by calling the ShowDocument helper method:

```
procedure TWinForm.btnLoad_Click(
  sender: System.Object; e: System.EventArgs);
begin
  if OpenFileDialog1.ShowDialog =
    System.Windows.Forms.DialogResult.OK then
  begin
    xmlDom.PreserveWhitespace := True;
    xmlDom.Load(OpenFileDialog1.FileName);
    ShowDocument;
  end;
end;


procedure TWinForm.ShowDocument;
begin
  TextBox1.Text := xmlDom.InnerXml;
  TreeView1.Nodes.Clear;
  DomToTree (xmlDom.DocumentElement, nil);
end;
```

The DomToTree recursive method is somewhat similar to the one you already saw for the IXmlNode interface, so I won't list it here. Notice, though, that the code is slightly more complex as it is a pure DOM and you have to navigate not only elements and attributes, but also text nodes.

Similar differences are also visible in the handler of the Click event of the second button, Create. As you can see in the following code, each object is created using the creation methods of the XmlDocument class itself and added to the proper position of the DOM tree. This is a more complex but more standard DOM approach, compared to Borland's simplified solution:

```
procedure TWinForm.btnCreate_Click(
  sender: System.Object; e: System.EventArgs);
var
  aXmlNode: XmlElement;
begin
  xmlDom.AppendChild(xmlDom.CreateElement('root'));
  xmlDom.DocumentElement.AppendChild(
    xmlDom.CreateElement('test'));

  aXmlNode := xmlDom.CreateElement('test2');
  xmlDom.DocumentElement.AppendChild(aXmlNode);
  aXmlNode.SetAttribute ('value', '100');
  aXmlNode.AppendChild(
    xmlDom.CreateElement('subnode'));

  xmlDom.DocumentElement.AppendChild(
    xmlDom.CreateElement('test3'));
  ShowDocument;
end;
```

The effect of this code is to create the following XML:

```
<root>
  <test />
  <test2 value="100">
    <subnode />
  </test2>
  <test3 />
</root>
```

Parsing XML

Even if the DOM interfaces provide a standard approach for reading and modifying an XML tree in memory, there are many times you want to use a different approach, parsing the document one node at a time as it is read from a stream and not loading it as a whole. The XML standard (although a very informal one) that uses this approach is the Simple API for XML (SAX), but there are many similar alternatives based on alternative XML streaming and parsing techniques.

SAX support isn't directly available in Delphi for Win32 nor in the .NET Framework. However, MSXML has SAX support, so it is easy to expose it in Delphi for Win32, and .NET provides similar nonstandard techniques in the XmlReader class.

Using the SAX API

The Simple API for XML (SAX) doesn't create a tree for the XML nodes but parses the node—firing events for each node, attribute, value, and so on. Because it doesn't keep the document in memory, using the SAX allows you to manage much larger documents. Its approach is also useful for one-time examination of a document or retrieval of specific information. This is a list of the most important events fired by the SAX:

- StartDocument and EndDocument for the entire document
- StartElement and EndElement for each node
- Characters for the text within the nodes

It is common to use a stack to handle the current path within the nodes tree and push and pop elements to and from the stack for every StartElement and EndElement event.

Delphi does not include specific support for the SAX interface, but you can import Microsoft's MSXML2 COM library, available on most computers in multiple versions (in fact, the MSXML2.dll filename is used for versions 2, 3, and 4 of the MSXML library). For the SaxDemo1 example I used version 4, which is required by Delphi 2005. This version is not widely available, so if you need to write an application for older versions of Windows you might want to stick with version 2. I generated a Pascal type library import unit from the type library, and the import unit is available within the source code of the program, but you must have that specific COM library registered on your computer to run the program successfully.

NOTE   Another example at the end of this chapter (LargeXml) demonstrates, among other things, the use of the SAX API with the OpenXML engine.

To use the SAX, you must install a SAX event handler within a SAX reader and then load a file and parse it. I used the SAX reader interface provided by MSXML for VB programmers. The official (C++)

interface had a few problems as the type library uses a nonstandard data type for strings and the Delphi type library importer converts them to the Word type. The main form of the SaxDemo1 example declares

```
sax: IVBSAXXMLReader;
```

In the FormCreate method, the sax variable is initialized with the COM object:

```
sax := CoSAXXMLReader.Create;
sax.ErrorHandler := TMySaxErrorHandler.Create;
```

The code also sets an error handler, which is a class implementing a specific interface (IVBSAXErrorHandler) with three methods that are called depending on the severity of the problem: error, fatalError, and ignorableWarning.

Simplifying the code a little, the SAX parser is activated by calling the parseURL method after assigning a content handler to it:

```
sax.ContentHandler := TMySaxHandler.Create;
sax.parseURL (filename)
```

So, the code ultimately resides in the TMySaxHandler class, which has the SAX events. Because I have multiple SAX content handlers in this example, I wrote a base class with the core code and a few specialized versions for specific processing. This base class implements both the IVBSAXContentHandler interface and the IDispatch interface the IVBSAXContentHandler interface is based on, as you can see in the source code of the example. All this base class does is emit information to a log when the parser starts (startDocument) and finishes (endDocument) and keep track of the current node and its parent nodes with a stack:

```
// TMySaxHandler.startElement
stack.Add (strLocalName);
// TMySaxHandler.endElement
stack.Delete (stack.Count - 1);
```

An implementation is provided by the TMySimpleSaxHandler class, which overrides the startElement event triggered for any new node to output the current position in the tree with the following statement:

```
Log.Add (strLocalName + '(' + stack.CommaText + ')');
```

Another method implemented by the TMySimpleSaxHandler class is the characters event, which is triggered when a node value (or a test node) is encountered and outputs its content (as you can see in Figure 22.5):

```
procedure TMySimpleSaxHandler.characters(var strChars: WideString);
var
  str: WideString;
begin
  inherited;
  str := RemoveWhites (strChars);
  if (str <> '') then
    Log.Add ('Text: ' + str);
end;
```

FIGURE 22.5
The log produced by
reading an XML docu-
ment with the SAX in
the SaxDemo1 example

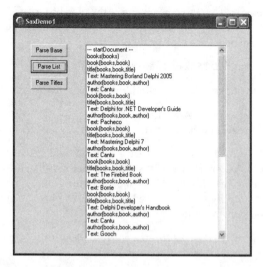

This is a generic parsing operation affecting the entire XML file. The second derived SAX content handler class refers to the specific structure of the XML document, extracting only nodes of a given type. In particular, the program looks for nodes of the *title* type. When a node has this type (in startElement), the class sets the isbook Boolean variable. The text value of the node is considered only immediately after a node of this type is encountered:

```
procedure TMyBooksListSaxHandler.startElement(
  var strNamespaceURI, strLocalName, strQName: WideString;
  const oAttributes: IVBSAXAttributes);
begin
  inherited;
  isbook := (strLocalName = 'title');
end;

procedure TMyBooksListSaxHandler.characters(var strChars: WideString);
var
  str: string;
begin
  inherited;
  if isbook then
  begin
    str := RemoveWhites (strChars);
    if (str <> '') then
      Log.Add (stack.CommaText + ': ' + str);
  end;
end;
```

Parsing XML in .NET

The XML classes of the FCL include full support for DOM but no support for SAX. As an alternative, the .NET Framework includes a class for parsing XML called XmlReader. There is also an XmlWriter class that helps produce XML in a very lightweight fashion (without having to use a DOM).

The XmlReader class is more similar to a token parser than to a SAX. You simply cycle on the tokens of the XML document and can produce an action depending on the type of node. If you want to know anything about the current position with the document you should use a stack-bases solution as I suggested for the previous example. Although this is a nonstandard solution, using the XmlReader class is simpler than using a SAX. In the following sample code, taken from the XmlReaderWriterNet project, I scan the usual XML file with books and authors looking for the author's names. What I look for is a text node that has an ancestor node (on the nodeStack array) called *author*:

```
var
  aReader: XmlTextReader;
  aStream: StreamReader;
  nodeStack: ArrayList;
begin
  aStream := StreamReader.Create ('books.xml');
  aReader := XmlTextReader.Create (aStream);
  nodeStack := ArrayList.Create;
  Textbox1.Clear;

  while aReader.Read do
  begin
    case aReader.NodeType of
      XmlNodeType.Element:
        nodeStack.Add (aReader.Name);
      XmlNodeType.EndElement:
        nodeStack.RemoveAt(NodeStack.Count-1);
      XmlNodeType.Text:
        if string(nodeStack.Item[NodeStack.Count-1])='author' then
          Textbox1.AppendText(aReader.Value + sLinebreak);
    end;
  end;
end;
```

The same example also shows how to use the XmlWriter class to produce an XML document. Using this class is certainly much easier than creating the XML using string concatenation, as you simply open nodes, place content inside and close nodes in a balanced way, without having to remember exactly which node you are closing. The following method creates an XmlWriter based on a file and writes to it a root node (books), with other nodes inside containing both elements and attributes:

```
var
  aWriter: XmlTextWriter;
begin
  aWriter := XmlTextWriter.Create('another.xml', ASCIIEncoding.Create);
  aWriter.Formatting := Formatting.Indented;
```

```
aWriter.Indentation := 2;
aWriter.WriteStartDocument;

aWriter.WriteStartElement('book');
aWriter.WriteStartElement('author');
aWriter.WriteString('Marco');
aWriter.WriteEndElement;
aWriter.WriteStartElement('title');
aWriter.WriteAttributeString('series', 'Mastering');
aWriter.WriteString('Mastering Delphi 2005');
aWriter.WriteEndElement;
aWriter.WriteStartElement('publisher');
aWriter.WriteString('Sybex');
aWriter.WriteEndElement;
aWriter.WriteEndElement;

aWriter.WriteEndDocument;
aWriter.Close;
end;
```

This is the resulting XML:

```
<?xml version="1.0" encoding="utf-8"?>
<book>
  <author>Marco</author>
  <title series="Mastering">Mastering Delphi 2005</title>
  <publisher>Sybex</publisher>
</book>
```

Using XSLT

When you have an XML document (a local file, some database data converted to XML...) you can process it in a web application by using the Extensible Stylesheet Language (XSL) or, to be more precise, its XSL Transformations (XSLT) subset. The aim of XSLT is to transform an XML document into another document, generally an XML document. One of the most frequent uses of the technology is to turn an XML document into an XHTML document (or even a plain HTML document) to be sent to a browser from a web server.

NOTE   The only other subset of XSL is XSL-FO (XSL Formatting Objects), which can be used to turn an XML document into a PDF or another *formatted* document.

An XSLT document is a well-formed XML document. The structure of an XSLT file requires a root node like the following:

```
<xsl:stylesheet version="1.0" xmlns:xsl="...">
```

The content of the XSLT file is based on one or more templates (or rules or functions), which will be processed by the engine. Their node is `xsl:template`, usually with a `match` attribute. In the simplest case, a template operates on nodes with a given name; you invoke the template by passing to it one or more nodes with an XPath expression, as explained in the following section:

```
<xsl:apply-templates select="node_name"/>
```

Within templates, you can find any of the other commands, such as the extraction of a value from an XML document (`xsl:value-of select`), looping statements (`xsl:for-each`), conditional expressions (`xsl:if`, `xsl:choose`), sorting requests (`xsl:sort`), and numbering requests (`xsl:number`), just to mention a few common XSLT commands.

Using XPath

XSLT uses another XML standard technology, XPath, to identify portions of documents. XPath defines a set of rules to locate one or more nodes within a document. The rules are based on a pathline structure of the node within the XML tree, so that `/books/book` identifies any *book* node under the *books* document root. XPath uses special symbols to identify nodes:

◆ A star (*) stands for any node; for example, `book/*` indicates any subnode under a *book* node.

◆ A dot (`.`) stands for the current node.

◆ The pipe symbol (`|`) indicates alternatives, as in `book|ebook`.

◆ A double slash (`//`) stands for any path, so that `//title` indicates all the title nodes, whatever their parent nodes, and `books//author` indicates any `author` node under a `books` node regardless of the nodes in between.

◆ The at sign (`@`) indicates an attribute instead of a node, as in the hypothetical `author/@lastname`.

◆ Square brackets can be used to choose only nodes or attributes having a given value. For example, to select all authors with a given first name attribute, you can use `author[@name="marco"]`.

There are many other cases (and a large set of available functions), but this short introduction to the rules of XPath should get you started and help you understand the following examples. An XSLT document is an XML document that works on the structure of a source XML document and generates in output another XML document, such as an XHTML document you can view in a web browser.

XSLT in Practice

Let's discuss a couple of examples. As a starting point, you should study XSL by itself, and then focus on its activation from within a Delphi application.

For your initial tests, you can connect an XSL file directly to an XML file. As you load the XML file in Internet Explorer, you will see the resulting XHTML transformation. The connection is indicated in the heading of the XML document with a command like this:

```
<?xml-stylesheet type="text/xsl" href="sampleembedded.xsl"?>
```

This is what I did in the `sample1embedded.xml` file available in the XslEmbed folder. The related XSL embeds various XSL snippets that I don't have space to discuss in detail. For example, it grabs the entire list of authors or filters a specific group of them with this code:

```
<h2>All Authors</h2>
<ul>
  <xsl:for-each select="books//author">
    <li><xsl:value-of select="."/></li>
  </xsl:for-each>
</ul>
<h3>E-Authors</h3>
<ul>
  <xsl:for-each select="books/ebook/author">
    <li><xsl:value-of select="."/></li>
  </xsl:for-each>
</ul>
```

More complex code is used to extract nodes only when a specific value is present in a subnode or attribute, regardless of the higher-level nodes. The following XSL snippet also has an `if` statement and produces an attribute in the resulting node, as a way to build an `href` hyperlink in the HTML:

```
<h3>Marco's works (books + ebooks)</h3>
<ul>
  <xsl:for-each select="books/*[author = 'Cantu']">
    <li> <xsl:value-of select="title"/>
        <xsl:if test="url">
          (<a><xsl:attribute name="href"><xsl:value-of select="url"/>
             </xsl:attribute>Jump to document</a>)
        </xsl:if>
    </li>
  </xsl:for-each>
</ul>
```

XSLT with WebSnap

Within the code of a program, you can execute the `TransformNode` method of a DOM node, passing to it another DOM hosting the XSL document. Instead of using this low-level approach, however, you can let WebSnap help you to create an XSL-based example. You can create a new WebSnap application (I built a CGI program called XslCust in this case) and choose an XSLPageProducer component for its main page to let Delphi help you begin the application code. Delphi also includes a skeleton XSL file for manipulating a ClientDataSet data packet and adds many new views to the editor. The XSL text replaces the HTML file; the XML Tree page shows the data, if any; the XSL Tree page shows the XSL within the Internet Explorer ActiveX; the HTML Result page shows the code produced by the transformation; and the Preview page shows what a user will see in a browser.

TIP   The Delphi editor provides full-blown code completion for XSLT, which makes editing this code in the editor as powerful as it is in some sophisticated and specific XML editors.

To make this example work, you must provide data to the XSLPageProducer component via its XMLData property. This property can be hooked up to an XMLDocument or directly to an XMLBroker component, as I did in this case. The broker takes its data from a provider connected to a local table attached to the classic `Customer.cds` table. The effect is that, with Delphi-generated XSL, you get (even at design time) the output shown in Figure 22.6.

NOTE The standard XSL template has been extended since the first time this technology become available because the original version didn't account for null fields omitted from the XML data packet. I presented several extensions to the original XSL code at the 2002 Borland Conference and some of my suggestions have been incorporated in the template.

This code generates an HTML table consisting of the expansion of field metadata and row data. The fields are used to generate the table heading, with a `<th>` cell for each entry in a single row. The row data is used to fill in the other rows of the table. Taking the value of each attribute (`select="@*"`) wouldn't be enough, because an attribute might be missing. For this reason, the list of fields and the current row are saved in two variables; then, for each field, the XSL code extracts the value of a row item having an attribute name (`@*[name()=...`) corresponding to the name of the current field stored in its *attrname* attribute (`@attrname`). This code is far from simple, but it is a compact and portable way to examine different portions of an XML document at the same time:

```
<xsl:template match="ROWDATA/ROW">
  <xsl:variable name="fieldDefs" select="//METADATA/FIELDS"/>
  <xsl:variable name="currentRow" select="current()"/>
  <tr>
    <xsl:for-each select="$fieldDefs/FIELD">
      <td>
        <xsl:value-of
          select="$currentRow/@*[name()=current()/@attrname]"/>
        <br/>
      </td>
    </xsl:for-each>
  </tr>
</xsl:template>
```

FIGURE 22.6
The result of an XSLT transformation generated at design time by the XSLPageProducer component in the XslCust example

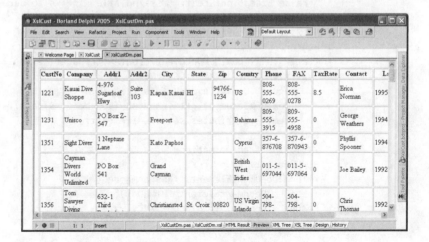

Direct XSL Transformations with the DOM

Using the XSLPageProducer can be handy, but generating multiple pages based on the same data just to handle different possible XSL styles with WebSnap isn't the best approach. I built a plain CGI application called CdsXslt that can transform a ClientDataSet data packet into different types of HTML, depending on the name of the XSL file passed as a parameter. The advantage is that I can modify the existing XSL files and add new XSL files to the system without having to recompile the program. Notice that Delphi also has a custom transformation technology, discussed in the section "Mapping XML with Transformations."

To obtain the XSL transformation, the program loads both the XML and the XSL files into two XMLDocument components called XmlDom and XslDom. Then it invokes the transformNode method of the XML document, passing the XSL document as a parameter and filling in a third XMLDocument component called HtmlDom:

```
procedure TWebModule1.WebModule1WebActionItem1Action(Sender: TObject;
  Request: TWebRequest; Response: TWebResponse; var Handled: Boolean);
var
  xslfile, xslfolder: string;
  attr: IDOMAttr;
begin
  // open the client dataset and load its XML in a DOM
  ClientDataSet1.Open;
  XmlDom.Xml.Text := ClientDataSet1.XMLData;
  XmlDom.Active := True;
  // load the requested xsl file
  xslfile := Request.QueryFields.Values ['style'];
  if xslfile = '' then
    xslfile := 'customer.xsl';
  xslfolder := 'xsl\';
  if FileExists (xslfolder + xslfile) then
    xslDom.LoadFromFile (xslfolder + xslfile)
  else
    raise Exception.Create('Missing file: ' + xslfolder + xslfile);
  XSLDom.Active := True;
  if xslfile = 'single.xsl' then
  begin
    attr := xslDom.DOMDocument.createAttribute('select');
    attr.value := '//ROW[@CustNo="' +
      Request.QueryFields.Values ['id'] + '"]';
    xslDom.DOMDocument.getElementsByTagName ('xsl:apply-templates').
      item[0].attributes.setNamedItem(attr);
  end;
  // do the transformation
  HTMLDom.Active := True;
  xmlDom.DocumentElement.transformNode (
    xslDom.DocumentElement, HTMLDom);
  Response.Content := HTMLDom.XML.Text;
end;
```

The code uses the DOM to modify the XSL document for displaying a single record, adding the XPath statement for selecting the record indicated by the id query field. This id is added to the hyperlink by the XSL with the list of records, but I'll skip listing more XSL files. They are available for study in the XSL subfolder of this example's folder.

NOTE To run this program, deploy the XSL files in a folder called XSL under the one where the script is located. You can find the demo files in the XSL subfolder folder of this example. To deploy these files in a different location, change the preceding code that extracts the XSL folder name from the program name available in the first command-line parameter.

XSLT in ASP.NET

XSLT can also be used as an alternative way to build ASP.NET applications. Instead of using the various components, you can basically have a page hosting a Literal control and fill it with the result of the transformation. The ASPX file will simply provide the page structure, and the page parameters can be used to modify the XML or pick a different XSL file, as in the previous example:

```
<form runat="server">
  <h1>AspNetAdoXstl</h1>
  <p><asp:Literal id="Literal1" runat="server"></asp:Literal></p>
</form>
```

The program uses a table of the dbdemos.gdb InterBase database available from the Data folder (under Common Files/Borland Shared), to mimic the previous example; it uses a style parameter where you can indicate the XSL file to use. The program uses the XmlDocument component for storing the data from the DataSet, an XslTransform component to load the XSL file and apply it, and a StringWriter for the output:

```
procedure TWebForm1.Page_Load(
    sender: System.Object; e: System.EventArgs);
var
  XmlDoc: XmlDocument;
  xslfile: string;
  XslDoc: XslTransform;
  writer: StringWriter;
begin
  // load XML
  XmlDoc := XmlDocument.Create;
  BdpDataAdapter1.Active := True;
  XmlDoc.LoadXml(DataSet1.GetXml);

  // load XSL
  XslDoc := XslTransform.Create;
  xslfile := Request.QueryString.Item ['style'];
  if xslfile = '' then
    xslfile := 'customer.xsl';
  XslDoc.Load(MapPath ('.') + '/' + xslfile);

  // produce output
```

```
    writer := StringWriter.Create;
    XslDoc.Transform (XmlDoc, nil, writer);
    Literal1.Text := writer.ToString;
  end;
```

By default the program uses a rather simple XSL file, based on the XML representation of an ADO.NET dataset already described in Chapter 16. This is a snippet of the XSL file that uses the nodes of one of the records to extract their names and build the table header and then scans the actual data (producing the output of Figure 22.7):

```
<xsl:template match="/">
  <h3>Customers List</h3>
  <p/>
  <table border="1" cellspacing="0" cellpadding="3">
    <tr>
      <xsl:for-each select="/NewDataSet/CUSTOMER[1]/*">
        <th><xsl:value-of select="name()"/></th>
      </xsl:for-each>
    </tr>
    <xsl:apply-templates select="/NewDataSet/CUSTOMER"/>
  </table>
</xsl:template>

<xsl:template match="CUSTOMER">
  <tr valign="top">
    <td align="left"><xsl:value-of select="CUSTNO"/></td>
    <td align="left"><xsl:value-of select="COMPANY"/></td>
    <!-- and so on -->
  </tr>
</xsl:template>
```

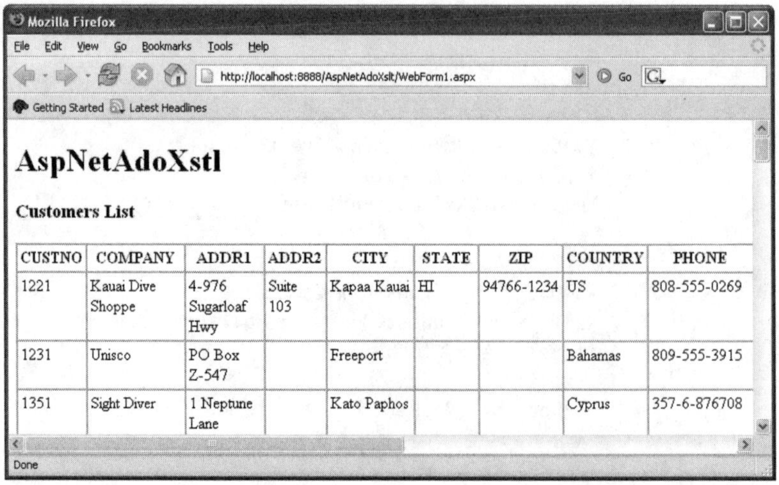

FIGURE 22.7
The output of the AspNetAdoXslt with the default XSL in a browser

Mapping XML with Transformations

You can use one more technique in Delphi to handle an XML document: You can create a *transformation* to translate the XML of a generic document into the format used natively by the ClientDataSet component when saving data to a MyBase XML file. In the reverse direction, another transformation can turn a dataset available within a ClientDataSet (through a DataSetProvider component) into an XML file of a required format (or schema).

Delphi includes a wizard to generate such transformations. Called XML Mapper, it can be invoked from the IDE's Tools menu or executed as a stand-alone application. The XML Mapper, shown in Figure 22.8, is a design-time helper that assists you in defining transformation rules between the nodes of a generic XML document and fields of the ClientDataSet data packet.

The XML Mapper window has three areas:

◆ On the left is the XML Document section, which displays information about the structure of the XML document in the Document View or an XML schema in the Schema View.

◆ On the right is the Datapacket section, which displays information about the metadata in the data packet. The XML Mapper can also open files in the native ClientDataSet format.

◆ The central portion is used by the mapping section. It contains two pages: Mapping, where you can see the correspondence between selected elements of the two sides that will be part of the mapping; and Node Properties, where you can modify the data types and other details of each possible mapping.

The Mapping page of the central pane also hosts the shortcut menu used to generate the transformation. The other panes and views have specific shortcut menus you can use to perform the various actions (in addition to the few commands in the main menu).

FIGURE 22.8
The XML Mapper shows the two sides of a transformation to define a mapping between them (with the rules indicated in the central portion).

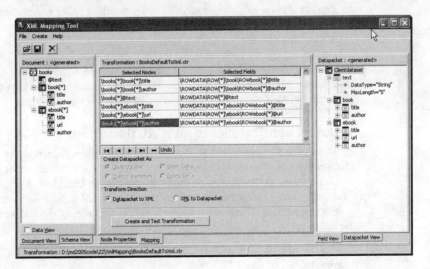

You can use XML Mapper to map an existing schema (or extract it from a document) to a new data packet, an existing data packet to a new schema or document, or an existing data packet into an existing XML document (if a match is reasonable). In addition to converting the data of an XML file into a data packet, you can also convert to a delta packet of the ClientDataSet. This technique is useful for merging a document to an existing table, as if a user had inserted the modified table records. In particular, you can transform an XML document into a delta packet for records to be modified, deleted, or inserted.

The result of using the XML Mapper is one or more transformation files, each representing a one-way conversion (so you need at least two transformation files to convert data back and forth). These transformation files are then used at design time and at run time by the XMLTransform, XMLTransformProvider, and XMLTransformClient components.

As an example, you can have a look at the XmlMapping folder and load in the available transformations (the .XTR files). The example uses a TransformProvider component with two transformation files attached to read in an XML document and make it available to a ClientDataSet. As the name suggests, the TransformProvider component is a dataset provider. The program allows you to edit the data of the various sublists of nodes within the grids, modifying them and adding or deleting records. As you apply the changes to the dataset (clicking the Save button, which calls `ApplyUdpates`), the transform provider saves an updated version of the file to disk.

A more traditional example, MapTable, turns the XML of a ClientDataSet into a plain XML document. In any case, due to the nonstandard nature of Delphi's XML Mapper transformations and their extreme slowness (when compared to XSLT), I'm not a strong supporter of this technology.

Processing Large XML Documents

As you have seen, there are often many different techniques to accomplish the same task with XML. In many cases you can choose any solution with the goal of writing less and more maintainable code; but when you need to process a large number of XML documents or very large XML documents, you must consider efficiency.

Discussing theory by itself is not terribly useful, so I built a Win32 example you can use (and modify) to test different solutions. The example is called LargeXml, and it covers a specific area: moving data from a database to an XML file and back. The example can open a dataset (using dbExpress) and then replicate the data many times in a ClientDataSet in memory.

From a ClientDataSet to an XML Document

Now that the program has a (large) dataset in memory, it provides three different ways to save the dataset to a file. The first is to save the `XMLData` of the ClientDataSet directly to a file, obtaining an attribute-based document. This Borland-specific attribute-based format is probably not the format you want, so the second solution is to apply an XmlMapper transformation with an XMLTransformClient component. The third solution involves processing the dataset directly and writing out each record to a file using a simple (but effective) support function to create XML nodes:

```
while not ClientDataSet1.EOF do
begin
  s := '';
  for i := 0 to ClientDataSet1.FieldCount - 1 do
    s := s + MakeXmlstr (ClientDataSet1.Fields[i].FieldName,
      ClientDataSet1.Fields[i].AsString);
```

```
  s := MakeXmlStr ('employeeData', s);
  str.Write(s[1], length (s));
  ClientDataSet1.Next
end;

function MakeXmlstr (node, value: string): string;
begin
  Result := '<' + node + '>' + value + '</' + node + '>';
end;
```

If you run the program, you can see the time taken by each operation. Saving the ClientDataSet data is the fastest approach, but you probably don't get the result you want. Custom streaming is only slightly slower; but you should consider that this code doesn't require you to first move the data to a ClientDataSet because you can apply it directly even to a unidirectional dbExpress dataset. You should forget using the code based on the XmlMapper for a large dataset, because it is hundreds of times slower, even for a small dataset (I haven't been able to try a large dataset because the process takes too long). For example, if I run this program on my computer and pick the medium dataset, custom streaming requires less than 100 milliseconds while transformation mapping takes over 5 seconds (over 50 times as much).

From an XML Document to a ClientDataSet

Once you have a large XML document, obtained by a program (as in this case) or from an external source, you need to process it. As you have seen, XmlMapper support is far too slow, so you are left with three alternatives: an XSL transformation, a SAX, or a DOM. XSL transformation will probably be fast enough, but in this example I opened the document with a SAX; it's the fastest approach and doesn't require much code. The program can also load a document in a DOM, but I haven't written the code to navigate the DOM and save the data back to a ClientDataSet.

In both cases, I tested the OpenXml engine versus the MSXML DOM. This allows you to see the two SAX solutions compared, because (unfortunately) the code is slightly different. I can summarize the results here: Using the MSXML SAX is slightly faster than using the OpenXml SAX (the difference is about 30 percent), whereas loading in the DOM marks a huge advantage in favor of MSXML.

The MSXML SAX code uses the same architecture discussed in the SaxDemo1 example, so I listed only the code of the handlers you use here. As you can see, at the beginning of an employeeData element you insert a new record, which is posted when the same node is closed. Lower-level nodes are added as fields of the current record. Here is the code:

```
procedure TMyDataSaxHandler.startElement(var strNamespaceURI, strLocalName,
  strQName: WideString; const oAttributes: IVBSAXAttributes);
begin
  inherited;
  if strLocalName = 'employeeData' then
    Form1.clientdataset2.Insert;
  strCurrent := '';
end;

procedure TMyDataSaxHandler.characters(var strChars: WideString);
```

```
begin
  inherited;
  strCurrent := strCurrent + RemoveWhites(strChars);
end;

procedure TMyDataSaxHandler.endElement(var strNamespaceURI, strLocalName,
  strQName: WideString);
begin
  if strLocalName = 'employeeData' then
    Form1.clientdataset2.Post;
  if stack.Count > 2 then
    Form1.ClientDataSet2.FieldByName (strLocalName).
      AsString := strCurrent;
  inherited;
end;
```

The code for the event handlers in the OpenXml version is similar. All that changes is the interface of the methods and the names of the parameters, as you can see by looking at the source code and comparing the two SAX implementations.

What's Next?

In this chapter I covered XML and related technologies, including DOM, SAX, XSLT, XML schemas, XPath, and a few more. You saw how Delphi simplifies DOM programming with XML access using interfaces and XML transformations. I also discussed the use of XSL for web programming, introducing the XSLT support of WebSnap. In addition, I introduced the VCL for .NET version of some of the programs and covered .NET-specific classes, including XmlReader and XmlWriter.

Chapter 23 will continue the discussion of XML with one of the most interesting and promising technologies of the last few years: web services. I'll cover SOAP and WSDL and also introduce UDDI and other related technologies.

Chapter 23

Web Services and SOAP

The rapidly emerging web services technology has the potential to change the way the Internet works for businesses. Browsing web pages to enter orders is fine for individuals (business-to-consumer [B2C] applications) but not for companies (business-to-business [B2B] applications). If you want to buy a few books, going to a book vendor website and punching in your requests is probably fine. But if you run a bookstore and want to place hundreds of orders a day, this is far from an efficient approach, particularly if you have a program that helps you track your sales and determine reorders. Grabbing the output of this program and reentering it into another application is ridiculous.

Web services are meant to solve this issue: The program used to track sales can automatically create a request and send it to a web service, which can immediately return information about the order. The next step might be to ask for a tracking number for the shipment. At this point, your program can use another web service to track the shipment until it is at its destination, so you can tell your customers how long they have to wait. As the shipment arrives, your program can send a reminder via SMS or pager to the people with pending orders, issue a payment with a bank web service, and…I could continue but I think I've given you the idea. Web services are meant for computer interoperability, much as the Web and e-mail let people interact.

The topic of web services is broad and involves many technologies and business-related standards. As usual, I'll focus on the underlying Delphi implementation and the technical side of web services, rather than discuss the larger picture and business implications. Delphi for Win32 offers some rather sophisticated support for web services and so does Delphi for .NET, relying on the extensive support for this technology available in the Microsoft .NET Framework. You'll see how to create a web service client and a web service server, using both technologies (in this case the code isn't portable) and also how to move database data over SOAP using the DataSnap technology. This chapter covers SOAP and WSDL, building web services clients and servers in Delphi for Win32 and Delphi for .NET, DataSnap over SOAP, the use of attachments, and more.

Web Service Technologies

The idea of a web service is rather abstract. When it comes to technologies, there are currently three solutions that are attracting developers. One is the use of the SOAP (Simple Object Access Protocol, www.w3.org/TR/soap/) standard, another is the use of a REST (Representational State Transfer) approach, and a third is the use of XML-RPC (XML-Remote Procedure Call). The latter two solutions are quite similar and at times are even confused one for the other.

NOTE   There isn't a formal REST standard. For a good introduction, see www.xfront.com/REST-Web-Services.html and for a good set of links see www.prescod.net/rest.

What is relevant to notice is that all three of these solutions generally use HTTP as the transmission protocol (although they do provide alternatives) and use XML for moving the data back and forth. By using standard HTTP, a web server can handle the requests, and the related data packets can pass though firewalls.

SOAP was originally developed by DevelopMentor (the training company run by COM expert Don Box) and Microsoft, to overcome weaknesses involved with using DCOM in web servers. Submitted to the W3C for standardization, it is being embraced by many companies, with a particular push from IBM. It is too early to know whether there will be standardization to let software programs from Microsoft, IBM, Sun, Oracle, and many others truly interoperate, or whether some of these vendors will try to push a private version of the standard. In any case, SOAP is a cornerstone of Microsoft's .NET architecture and also of the current platforms by Sun and Oracle.

SOAP replaces COM invocation, at least between different computers. Similarly, the definition of a SOAP service in the Web Services Description Language (WSDL) format will replace the IDL and type libraries used by COM and COM+. WSDL documents are another type of XML document that provides the metadata definition of a SOAP request. As you get a file in this format (generally published to define a service), you'll be able to create a program to call it.

The most significant difference among them is that while SOAP has a more formal and complex mechanism for passing parameters and receiving responses, the other two technologies use a more lightweight approach. A SOAP call returns a predefined data structure, while a REST call returns an XML document. While SOAP is tightly coupled (even minor changes in the resulting data structures require changes in the WSDL and in the calling application), REST and XML-RPC are more loosely coupled, as there is no strict definition for the documents returned.

Delphi Win32 SOAP Support

In this chapter I'll mostly focus on SOAP, because this is the technology directly supported by Delphi. In the section "The REST Architecture with Delphi," I'll provide an example of the REST approach. Specifically, Delphi for Win32 provides a bidirectional mapping between WSDL and interfaces. This means you can grab a WSDL file and generate an interface for it. You can then create a client program, embedding SOAP requests via these interfaces, and use a special Delphi component that lets you convert your local interface requests into SOAP calls (I doubt you want to manually generate the XML required for a SOAP request).

Conversely, you can define an interface (or use an existing one) and let a Delphi component generate a WSDL description for it. Another component provides you with a SOAP-to-Pascal mapping, so that by embedding this component and an object implementing the interface within a server-side program, you can have your web service up and running in a matter of minutes.

A SOAP Client: Stock Quotes

As a first example of the use of web services, I built a client for the Yahoo stock quote service. This is available as a web service through the XMethods website (www.xmethods.com), a site that has a few test services and hosts a large list of available web services written with many different languages and tools. The WSDL file for that specific web service is available at:

```
http://services.xmethods.net/soap/urn:xmethods-delayed-quotes.wsdl
```

This is the URL you can insert in Delphi's Web Services Importer, available in the Delphi Projects/WebServices page of the New Items dialog box. The wizard lets you preview the structure of the service (see Figure 23.1) and generate the proper Delphi-language interfaces in a unit like the following (with the interface name trimmed down from the lengthy automatically generated net_ xmethods_services_stockquote_StockQuotePortType and many of the comments removed):

```
unit xmethods_delayed_quotes;

interface

uses InvokeRegistry, SOAPHTTPClient, Types, XSBuiltIns;

type
  StockQuotePortType = interface(IInvokable)
  ['{844B8652-C1A5-7173-F44D-121210784988}']
    function  getQuote(const symbol: WideString): Single; stdcall;
  end;

function Get_StockQuotePortType (
  UseWSDL: Boolean=System.False; Addr: string='';
  HTTPRIO: THTTPRIO = nil): StockQuotePortType;

implementation

// omitted

initialization
  InvRegistry.RegisterInterface(
    TypeInfo(StockQuotePortType),
   'urn:xmethods-delayed-quotes', 'UTF-8', '',
    'net.xmethods.services.stockquote.StockQuotePortType');
  InvRegistry.RegisterDefaultSOAPAction(
    TypeInfo(StockQuotePortType),
    'urn:xmethods-delayed-quotes#getQuote');
end.
```

FIGURE 23.1
The WSDL Import
Wizard in action

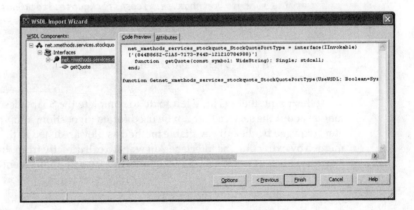

Notice that the interface inherits from the IInvokable interface. This interface doesn't add anything in terms of methods to Delphi's IInterface base interface, but it is compiled with the flag used to enable RTTI generation, {$M+}, like the TPersistent class. In the initialization section, you notice that the interface is registered in the global invocation registry (or InvRegistry), passing the type information reference of the interface type.

NOTE   Having RTTI information for interfaces is the most important technological advance underlying SOAP invocation. Not that SOAP-to-Pascal mapping isn't important—it is crucial to simplify the process—but having RTTI for an interface makes the entire architecture powerful and robust. As you'll see, this RTTI-based mapping is performed on the client side by the HTTPRIO component, described later in this section. A similar mapping is available on the server side through the HTTP-SoapPascalInvoker component, described in the next section.

The third element of the unit generated by the WSDL Import Wizard is a global function named after the service. This function helps simplify the code used to call the web service. The Get_StockQuotePortType function returns an interface of the proper type, which you can use to issue a call directly. For instance, the following code returns the last available value of Borland's stock:

```
Get_StockQuotePortType.getQuote('BORL')
```

WARNING   You might see a long delay or an error message (HTTP 500) from time to time. There are occasional problems with the web service due to the way it piggybacks on the Yahoo website.

If you look at the code for the Get_StockQuotePortType function, you'll see that it creates an internal invocation component of the class THTTPRIO to process the call. You can also place this component manually on the client form (as I did in the example program) to gain better control over its various settings (and handle its events).

This component can be configured in two basic ways: You can refer to the WSDL file or URL, import it, and extract from it the URL of the SOAP call; or, you can provide a direct URL to call. The example has two components that provide the alternative approaches (with exactly the same effect):

```
object HTTPRIO1: THTTPRIO
  WSDLLocation = 'http://services.xmethods.net/soap/' +
    'urn:xmethods-delayed-quotes.wsdl'
  Service = 'net.xmethods.services.stockquote.StockQuoteService'
  Port = 'net.xmethods.services.stockquote.StockQuotePort'
end
object HTTPRIO2: THTTPRIO
  URL = 'http://64.124.140.30:9090/soap'
end
```

At this point, there is little left to do to complete the SoapClientStocks project. You have information about the service that can be used for its invocation, and you know the types of the parameters required by the only available method as they are listed in the interface. The two elements are merged by extracting the interface you want to call directly from the HTTPRIO component, with an expression like HTTPRIO1 as StockQuotePortType. It might seem astonishing at first, but it is also outrageously simple. This are three different web service calls done by the example, one via the helper functions, one using the local HTTPRIO component, and one via the helper function passing the other HTTPRIO component to it:

```
procedure TForm1.btnCheckClick(Sender: TObject);
begin
  memoOutput.Lines.Add (edTicker.Text + ': ' + FloatToStr (
    Get_StockQuotePortType.getQuote(edTicker.Text)));
end;

procedure TForm1.btnRio1Click(Sender: TObject);
begin
  memoOutput.Lines.Add (edTicker.Text + ': ' + FloatToStr (
    (HTTPRIO1 as StockQuotePortType).getQuote(edTicker.Text)));
end;

procedure TForm1.btnRio2Click(Sender: TObject);
begin
  memoOutput.Lines.Add (edTicker.Text + ': ' + FloatToStr (
    Get_StockQuotePortType (False, '', HTTPRIO2).
      getQuote(edTicker.Text)));
end;
```

The program output lets you track a single stock option, but once you figure out the structure it is very easy to extend it with multiple stock quotes and continuous and automatic checks.

Building a Web Service in Delphi for Win32

If calling a web service in Delphi is straightforward, the same can be said of developing a service. If you go into the Delphi Projects/WebServices page of the New Items dialog box, you can see the SOAP Server Application option. Select it, and Delphi presents you with a list that's quite similar to what you see if you select a WebBroker application. A web service is typically hosted by a web server using one of the available web server extension technologies, CGI or ISAPI. You can also choose the Web App Debugger for your initial tests, as I did for this program.

When you click the OK button, the wizards asks you whether you want to create an interface for the SOAP module, and if you click Yes it shows the Add New WebService dialog box:

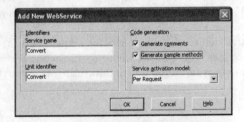

After completing this step, Delphi adds three components to the resulting web module, which is just a plain web module with no special additions:

◆ The HTTPSoapDispatcher component receives the web request, as any other HTTP dispatcher does. Its `WebDispatch` property has a `PathInfo` subproperty indicating the initial portion of the path used for SOAP requests, by default *soap*.

◆ The HTTPSoapPascalInvoker component does the reverse operation of the HTTPRIO component; it can translate SOAP requests into calls of Pascal interfaces (instead of shifting interface method calls into SOAP requests).

◆ The WSDLHTMLPublish component can be used to extract the WSDL definition of the service from the interfaces it supports and performs the opposite role of the Web Services Importer Wizard. Technically, this is another HTTP dispatcher. Its `WebDispatch` property again has a `PathInfo` subproperty indicating the initial portion of the path used for WSDL requests, by default *wsdl*.

A CURRENCY CONVERSION WEB SERVICE

Once you've got this framework in place—something you can also do by adding the three components listed in the previous section to an existing web module—you can begin writing a service. As an example, I took the Euro conversion example from Chapter 5 and transformed it into a web service called ConvertService. First, I added to the program a unit defining the interface of the service, as follows:

```
type
  IConvert = interface(IInvokable)
  ['{FF1EAA45-0B94-4630-9A18-E768A91A78E2}']
    function ConvertCurrency (Source, Dest: string;
      Amount: Double): Double; stdcall;
    function ToEuro (Source: string; Amount: Double): Double; stdcall;
    function FromEuro (Dest: string; Amount: Double): Double; stdcall;
    function TypesList: string; stdcall;
  end;
```

Defining an interface directly in code, without having to use a tool such as the Type Library Editor, provides a great advantage, as you can easily build an interface for an existing class and don't have to learn how to use a specific tool for this purpose. Notice that I gave a GUID to the interface as usual and used the `stdcall` calling convention because the SOAP converter does not support the default `register` calling convention.

In the same unit that defines the interface of the service, you should also register it. Because the registration of the interface is necessary on both the client and server sides of the program, you generally add it to the interface definition unit and include this unit in both programs:

```
uses InvokeRegistry;

initialization
  InvRegistry.RegisterInterface(TypeInfo(IConvert));
```

Now that you have an interface you can expose to the public, you have to provide an implementation for it, again by means of the standard Delphi code (and with the help of the predefined TInvokableClass class:

```
type
  TConvert = class (TInvokableClass, IConvert)
  protected
    function ConvertCurrency (Source, Dest: string;
      Amount: Double): Double; stdcall;
    function ToEuro (Source: string; Amount: Double): Double; stdcall;
    function FromEuro (Dest: string; Amount: Double): Double; stdcall;
    function TypesList: string; stdcall;
  end;
```

The implementation of these functions, which call the code of the Euro conversion system from Chapter 5, is not discussed here because it has little to do with the development of the service. However, it is important to notice that this implementation unit also has a registration call in its initialization section:

```
InvRegistry.RegisterInvokableClass (TConvert);
```

PUBLISHING THE WSDL

By registering the interface, you make it possible for the program to generate a WSDL description. The web service application displays a first page describing its interfaces and the detail of each interface and returns the WSDL file. By connecting to the web service via a browser, you'll see something similar to Figure 23.2.

FIGURE 23.2
The description of the ConvertService web service provided by Delphi components

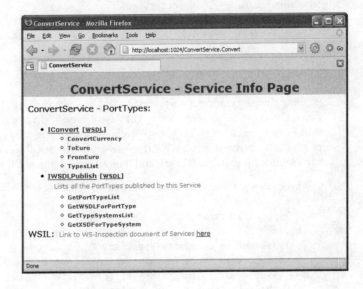

WARNING Although other web service architectures automatically provide you with a way to execute the web service from the browser, this technique is mostly meaningless because using web services makes sense in an architecture where different applications interoperate. If all you need to do is show data on a browser, you should build a website application, not a web service!

CREATING A CUSTOM CLIENT

Let's move to the client application that calls the service. I don't need to start from the WSDL file, because I already have the Delphi interface. This time the form doesn't even have the HTTPRIO component, which is created in code:

```
private
  Invoker: THTTPRio;

procedure TForm1.FormCreate(Sender: TObject);
begin
  Invoker := THTTPRio.Create(nil);
  Invoker.URL :=
    'http://localhost:1024/ConvertService.Convert/soap/iconvert';
  ConvIntf := Invoker as IConvert;
end;
```

As an alternative to using a WSDL file, the SOAP invoker component can be associated with a URL. In this case you have to type in the direct URL of the SOAP interface, which is obtained by concatenating the server URL, the dispatch path indicated in the HTTPSoapDispatcher component (by default *soap*), and the interface name. You can find this URL toward the end of the WSDL document in this example:

```
<service name="IConvertservice">
  <port name="IConvertPort" binding="tns:IConvertbinding">
    <soap:address location="http://localhost:1024/
      ConvertService.Convert/soap/IConvert"/>
  </port>
</service>
```

Once this association has been made and the required interface has been extracted from the component, you can begin writing straight Pascal code to invoke the service, as you saw earlier. In this sample program a user fills the two combo boxes, calling the TypesList method, which returns a list of available currencies within a string (separated by semicolons). You extract this list by replacing each semicolon with a line break and then assigning the multiline string directly to the combo items:

```
procedure TForm1.Button2Click(Sender: TObject);
var
  TypeNames: string;
begin
  TypeNames := ConvIntf.TypesList;
  ComboBoxFrom.Items.Text := StringReplace (
    TypeNames, ';', sLineBreak, [rfReplaceAll]);
  ComboBoxTo.Items := ComboBoxFrom.Items;
end;
```

After selecting two currencies, you can perform the conversion with this code (Figure 23.3 shows the result):

```
procedure TForm1.Button1Click(Sender: TObject);
begin
  LabelResult.Caption := Format ('%n', [
    (ConvIntf.ConvertCurrency(ComboBoxFrom.Text,
      ComboBoxTo.Text, StrToFloat(EditAmount.Text)))]);
end;
```

Debugging the SOAP Headers

One final note for this example relates to the use of the Web App Debugger for testing SOAP applications. Of course, you can run the server program from the Delphi IDE and debug it easily, but you can also monitor the SOAP headers passed on the HTTP connection. Although looking at SOAP from this low-level perspective can be far from simple, it is the ultimate way to check if something is wrong with either a server or a client SOAP application. As an example, in Figure 23.4 you can see the HTTP log of a SOAP request from the last example.

FIGURE 23.3
The Convert Caller client of the ConvertService web service shows how few German marks you used to get for so many Italian liras, before the Euro changed everything.

FIGURE 23.4
The HTTP log of the Web App Debugger includes the low-level SOAP request.

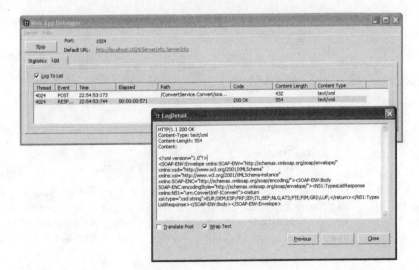

The Web App Debugger might not always be available, so another common technique is to handle the events of the HTTPRIO component, as the SoapClientStocksDebug example does. The program's form has two memo components in which you can see the SOAP request and the SOAP response:

```
procedure TForm1.HTTPRIO1BeforeExecute(const MethodName: String;
  var SOAPRequest: WideString);
begin
  MemoRequest.Text := SoapRequest;
end;

procedure TForm1.HTTPRIO1AfterExecute(const MethodName: String;
  SOAPResponse: TStream);
begin
  SOAPResponse.Position := 0;
  MemoResponse.Lines.LoadFromStream(SOAPResponse);
end;
```

Exposing an Existing Class As a Web Service

Although you might want to begin developing a web service from scratch, in some cases you may have existing code to make available. This process is not too complex, given Delphi's open architecture in this area. To try it, follow these steps:

1. Create a web service application or add the related components to an existing WebBroker project.

2. Define an interface inheriting from `IInvokable` and add to it the methods you want to make available in the web service (using the `stdcall` calling convention). The methods will be similar to those of the class you want to make available.

3. Define a new class that inherits from the class you want to expose and implements your interface. The methods will be implemented by calling the corresponding methods of the base class.

4. Write a factory method to create an object of your implementation class any time a SOAP request needs it.

This last step is the most complex. You could define a factory and register it as follows:

```
procedure MyObjFactory (out Obj: TObject);
begin
  Obj := TMyImplClass.Create;
end;

initialization
  InvRegistry.RegisterInvokableClass(TMyImplClass, MyObjFactory);
```

However, this code creates a new object for every call. Using a single global object would be equally bad: Many different users might try to use it, and if the object has state or its methods are not thread-safe, you might be in for big problems. So you're left with the need to implement some form of session management or object pooling. That is, unless your object is stateless.

The REST Architecture with Delphi

The Representational State Transfer (REST) approach dictates a more direct use of the existing web technologies (URLs, HTTP, XML) than you tend to use in SOAP. In particular the URL is used to indicate the *method* to execute (with its path) and its *parameters* (with further positional entries the path or with a query string).

A notable example of the REST approach is Amazon Web Service. Although it offers both SOAP and REST, a large majority of developers has ended up using the REST interface. For example, with the following URL you can request information about this book:

```
http://xml.amazon.com/onca/xml3?t=aaa&dev-t=bbb&
    AsinSearch=0782143423&type=heavy&f=xml
```

The path is the Amazon Web Service version, the first two parameters indicate the referral and a developer token (the system currently works with blank values, but is subject to require proper values any time), while the others indicate the book ID (or ASIN), the amount of data returned, and the format. The result of this URL is the detailed XML description of the book on the Amazon website, including price, user's rating, and so on.

NOTE Interestingly enough, because the Amazon Web Service has both SOAP and REST interfaces, it provides a good comparison of the two technologies. It turns out that 85 percent of the thousands of developers who use this web service have chosen the REST approach, including myself. For an example of an application that uses the Amazon Web Service, in fact, you can see mine at www.marcocantu.com/books/store.htm. This Kylix application applies some XSLT to the data of a predefined set of books, combining the result in a static HTML page, refreshed each hour.

REST Client Technologies

Because most actual web services require some developer token, as an example of a client application using REST, I wrote a very simple RSS client looking into Borland's Blog website (http://blogs .borland.com). Every time you access dynamic XML data by a URL and you can change the URL to access different data, you are using the REST approach.

The RssClient program uses an IdHttp component to grab the data from the Web. The XML is then added to an XmlDocument component. The code uses XPath expressions to extract some of the nodes. This requires the use of a custom interface of the Microsoft engine: hence the cast to extended interface IDOMNodeSelect. Finally, once I have the nodes I look for any child text node, using a getChildNodes helper function I wrote for this purpose, and add the data to a list box:

```
procedure TForm1.btnUpdateClick(Sender: TObject);
var
  strXml, title, author: string;
  I, J: Integer;
  IDomSel: IDOMNodeSelect;
  Node: IDOMNode;
begin
  strXml := IdHTTP1.Get ('http://blogs.borland.com/MainFeed.aspx');
  XMLDocument1.LoadFromXML(strXml);
  XMLDocument1.Active := True;
  IDomSel := (XMLDocument1.DocumentElement.DOMNode as IDOMNodeSelect);
  for I := 1 to 10 do
```

```
  begin
    Node := IDomSel.selectNode(
      '/rss/channel/item[' + IntToStr (i) + ']/title');
    title := getChildNodes (Node);
    Node := IDomSel.selectNode(
      '/rss/channel/item[' + IntToStr (i) + ']/source');
    author := getChildNodes (Node);
    ListBox1.Items.Add(title + ' -- ' + author);
  end;
end;
```

This is the effect of running the program:

Building a REST Server

Just as building a REST client is more straightforward and requires less support from the developer tool than building a SOAP client, the same can be said for the server. It is true that a SOAP server is a web server with an extra component for mapping requests to classes, but a REST server is a plain web server.

As an example, I ported the currency conversion SOAP server built in the previous section to this alternative architecture. I decided to use the same example to provide a better comparison. To build the RestConvertService project I created a standard web server using the WebApp Debugger technology. The web program has three actions. Two actions implement the actual operations of the web service and are called *typeslist* and *convertcurrency*. A third action (the default one) provides some HTML with the description and the links that can be used to test the other actions, in case someone hits the web service with a browser. In fact, unlike a SOAP server, the browser can be used directly to invoke the services via the proper URL.

The first action returns the list of available currency types, formatting them in an XML string, which is returned in the Content property of the Response along with setting the proper ContentType:

```
procedure TWebModule2.WebModule2actionTypesListAction(Sender: TObject;
  Request: TWebRequest; Response: TWebResponse; var Handled: Boolean);
var
  i: Integer;
  ATypes: TConvTypeArray;
  strXml: string;
```

```
begin
  strXml := '';
  GetConvTypes(cbEuroCurrency, ATypes);
  for i := Low(aTypes) to High(aTypes) do
    strXml := strXml + MakeXmlStr ('type',
      ConvTypeToDescription (aTypes[i]));
  strXml := MakeXmlStr ('typeslist', strXml);
  Response.Content := strXml;
  Response.ContentType := 'text/xml';
end;
```

You can see the result of this code directly in a browser by using a URL like the following, as you can see in Figure 23.5:

```
http://localhost:1024/RestConvertService.RestCurrency/typeslist
```

FIGURE 23.5
The data of the Rest-ConvertService can be seen directly in a browser.

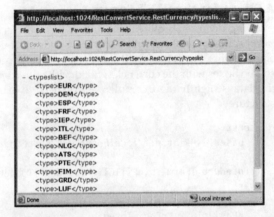

The second action is different because it has three parameters passed in its query string. This is a sample query string (it should be on a single line):

```
http://localhost:1024/RestConvertService.RestCurrency/convertcurrency?
  from=DEM&dest=ITL&amount=1000
```

The server handles this request by extracting and checking the parameters and then calling the internal Convert function with the proper parameters. The result is returned in a trivial XML document:

```
procedure TWebModule2.WebModule2actionConvertCurrencyAction(
  Sender: TObject; Request: TWebRequest; Response: TWebResponse;
  var Handled: Boolean);
var
  strFrom, strDest: string;
  nAmount, nResult: double;
  BaseType, DestType: TConvType;
```

```pascal
begin
  strFrom := Request.QueryFields.Values ['from'];
  strDest := Request.QueryFields.Values ['dest'];
  nAmount := StrToFloat(Request.QueryFields.Values ['amount']);

  if DescriptionToConvType (cbEuroCurrency, strFrom, BaseType) and
      DescriptionToConvType (cbEuroCurrency, strDest, DestType) then
    nResult := EuroConvert (nAmount, BaseType, DestType, 4)
  else
    raise Exception.Create ('Undefined currency types');

  Response.Content := MakeXmlStr ('result', FloatToStr (nResult));
  Response.ContentType := 'text/xml';
end;
```

A Client for the REST Server

Although you can browse the results of this web service online, this is for testing and debugging purposes only, as a user will query this service through a client application. Again, I adapted the client application of the SOAP convert service to the new architecture. The program retains the two combo boxes with the currencies, filled with data from the server by pressing a button. Processing the data is slightly more complex, as you need to extract the relevant information from the XML structure:

```pascal
const
  baseUrl = 'http://localhost:1024/RestConvertService.RestCurrency';

procedure TForm1.btnFillClick(Sender: TObject);
var
  strTypeNames: string;
  nPos, nInit, nEnd: Integer;
begin
  strTypeNames := IdHTTP1.Get(baseUrl + '/typeslist');
  ComboBoxFrom.Items.Clear;
  nPos := Pos ('<type>', strTypeNames);
  while nPos > 0 do
  begin
    nInit := nPos + 6;
    nEnd := PosEx ('</type>', strTypeNames, nPos);
    ComboBoxFrom.Items.Add (Copy (strTypeNames, nInit, nEnd - nInit));
    nPos := PosEx ('<type>', strTypeNames, nEnd);
  end;
  ComboBoxTo.Items := ComboBoxFrom.Items;
end;
```

When you have the lists of the currencies, you can enter an amount in the corresponding edit box and use the other button to do the conversion. This time the URL you have to invoke is more complex, while the data extraction process is much simpler:

```
const
  resultTag = '<result>';
  resTagLenght = Length (resultTag);

procedure TForm1.btnConvertClick(Sender: TObject);
var
  strResult: string;
begin
  strResult := IdHTTP1.Get(baseUrl +
    '/convertcurrency?from=' + ComboBoxFrom.Text +
    '&dest=' + ComboBoxTo.Text +
    '&amount=' + EditAmount.Text);
  LabelResult.Caption := copy (strResult, resTagLenght + 1,
    Length (strResult) - (resTagLenght * 2 + 1));
end;
```

Web Services in .NET

As I mentioned earlier, the Microsoft .NET Framework offers extensive support for SOAP, which can be considered one of the foundations of its entire architecture. In particular there is a rich System.Web.Services namespace, there is support for UDDI and other web service discovery features, and there is a command-line tool called wsdl that similar to Delphi's WSDL importer and can create a proxy class for the remote web service.

The starting point of this section will be the use of this tool (through the interface provided by the Delphi IDE) to create a WinForms client for the currency server I built in the previous section. Then I'll proceed to create a web server in .NET.

A .NET Web Service Client

To call a web service in Delphi for a .NET project, you create a project (of any type), move it to the Project Manager, select the project node, and use the Add Web Reference command of the context menu. The resulting dialog box hosts a customized browser you can use to navigate the Web looking for the proper WSDL file. To create a client for the previous server, type in the box above the browser the following URL:

```
http://localhost:1024/ConvertService.Convert
```

You should see a page similar to Figure 23.2. Now click on the WSDL link on the side of IConvert interface, inside the browser, and you should see the actual WSDL as in Figure 23.6. At this point the Add Reference button should be active, and you can click it to let the wizard generate the proper code for you.

FIGURE 23.6
The Add Web Reference dialog box of the Delphi .NET personality with the selected WSDL

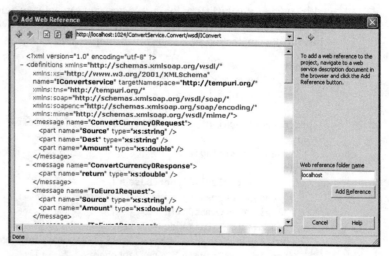

The Delphi wizard will run the wsdl utility of the .NET SDK to generate the Delphi source code for a proxy class for the web server. The generated code is quite complex, as you can see in the source code for the ConvertClientNet example. Each method of the class is decorated with a few attributes indicating its binding to the web service:

```
[System.Web.Services.Protocols.SoapRpcMethodAttribute(
  'urn:ConvertIntf-IConvert#ConvertCurrency',
  RequestNamespace='urn:ConvertIntf-IConvert',
  ResponseNamespace='urn:ConvertIntf-IConvert')]
[result: System.Xml.Serialization.SoapElementAttribute('return')]
function ConvertCurrency(
  Source: string; Dest: string; Amount: System.Double): System.Double;
```

Notice this is not an interface, as in Delphi for Win32, but an actual class with some code generated behind the scenes, like the following:

```
function IConvertservice.ConvertCurrency(Source: string;
  Dest: string; Amount: System.Double): System.Double;
type
  TArrayOfSystem_Object = array of System.Object;
var
  results: TArrayOfSystem_Object;
begin
  results := Self.Invoke('ConvertCurrency',
    TArrayOfSystem_Object.Create(Source, Dest, Amount));
  Result := (System.Double(results[0]));
end;
```

Because the support for the remote SOAP call is built into these classes and the related attributes, there is no need for a component like the VCL's HTTPRIO. If you stick with a synchronous invocation (see the sidebar "Asynchronous SOAP Calls" for an alternative approach) to invoke the remote service, you simply create an instance of the proxy class and call one of its methods. An example is in the following event handle of the ConvertClientNet project:

```
procedure TWinForm.btnList_Click(
  sender: System.Object; e: System.EventArgs);
var
  convert: IConvertservice;
  strCurr: string;
begin
  convert := IConvertservice.Create;
  strCurr := convert.TypesList;
  strCurr := StringReplace (strCurr, ';', sLineBreak, [rfReplaceAll]);
  TextBox1.Text := strCurr;
end;
```

ASYNCHRONOUS SOAP CALLS

The proxy class created in .NET by the wsdl command-line tool includes the standard synchronous methods calls (like the one I just used) as well as a set of two asynchronous method calls for each WSDL method. For example, for the TypeList method, there is also a BeginTypeList and an EndTypeList method:

```
function BeginTypesList(callback: System.AsyncCallback;

  asyncState: System.Object): System.IAsyncResult;

function EndTypesList(asyncResult: System.IAsyncResult): string;
```

Asynchronous method calls for SOAP invocations make sense because HTTP calls over the Internet can take time, and the amount of data returned can be quite large at times. To obtain asynchronous calls, you call the *begin* method, either passing a callback method to be executed, or waiting for the completion state of the IAsyncResult object it returns. Later on (when the state indicates completion or in the callback method), you'll call the matching *end* method to get the result. In practice, this is not much different from executing the SOAP call in a secondary thread, but certainly .NET helps you by providing a standard and ready-to-use implementation.

Building a .NET Server

In the Microsoft .NET Framework, web services are based on the same technology as web pages, namely ASP.NET. However, there is specific support for this technology in terms of attributes you use to decorate classes and methods you want to expose, as well as internal support code. To build a new managed web service Delphi has an ASP.NET Web Service Application option in the Delphi for .NET Projects page of the New Items dialog box. The dialog box that follows is similar to that of a plain ASP.NET project, with the request for the name, the location, and the web server (I picked Cassini as usual).

The wizard generates the skeleton of a web service application (or web service provider). This is based on an ASMX file that parallels the ASPX file of a visual ASP.NET application. If you don't add components to the designer, the file will have a content like this:

```
<%@ WebService Language="c#" Debug="true"
   Codebehind="WebService1.pas" Class="WebService1.TWebService1" %>
```

Of course, the ASMX file has a companion Delphi class, referenced in the preceding code. The generated class inherits from the WebService class and includes some designer-managed code, plus a Create constructor and a Dispose method. I replaced the dummy web service method entry with two functions and added the WebService namespace attribute at the very beginning. The resulting class (without the designer managed code) is listed here:

```
type
  [WebService(Namespace='http://marcocantu.com')]
  TWebService1 = class(System.Web.Services.WebService)
  strict protected
    procedure Dispose(disposing: boolean); override;
  public
    constructor Create;
    [WebMethod]
    function CrazyAdd (a, b: Integer): Integer;
    [WebMethod]
    function RemoteTime: string;
  end;
```

The code of the methods is not very relevant: the CrazyAdd function *approximately* adds the numbers (using some random corrections), while the RemoteTime function returns the time on the server.

At this point you can test your web service by running the application and looking at the descriptive pages added automatically by the system. The starting page should look like this:

WARNING If you debug the AspNetService1 application using the Cassini web server, it will stop on several exceptions at startup. The exceptions are of the class System.ArgumentException and the error message keeps saying "Error binding to target method". If you ignore exceptions of that type, the program will debug smoothly. Stand-alone execution has no problem, of course. You can also debug it and avoid disabling the exception but it keep running repeatedly pressing the Continue button after each of them (I counted 18).

Unlike the Delphi for Win32 server, the .NET server provides a ready to use interface for picking a web server method, entering the parameters, and viewing the result. An example of this page for the server I built before is in Figure 23.7.

FIGURE 23.7

FIGURE 23.7
The minimal web application generated automatically by the .NET Framework for testing a web service

TWebService1 Web Service - Mozilla Firefox

File   Edit   View   Go   Bookmarks   Tools   Help

TWebService1 Web Service

TWebService1

Click here for a complete list of operations.

CrazyAdd

Test

To test the operation using the HTTP POST protocol, click the 'Invoke' button.

Parameter	Value
a:	10
b:	20

[Invoke]

SOAP

The following is a sample SOAP request and response. The placeholders shown need to be replaced with actual values.

```
POST /AspNetService1/WebService1.asmx HTTP/1.1
Host: 127.0.0.1
Content-Type: text/xml; charset=utf-8
Content-Length: length
SOAPAction: "http://marcocantu.com/CrazyAdd"

<?xml version="1.0" encoding="utf-8"?>
<soap:Envelope xmlns:xsi="http://www.w3.org/2001/XMLSchema-instance" xmlns:xsd="http://www.w3.org/2001/XMLSchema" xmln
  <soap:Body>
    <CrazyAdd xmlns="http://marcocantu.com">
      <a>int</a>
      <b>int</b>
    </CrazyAdd>
  </soap:Body>
</soap:Envelope>
```

Done

If you click the Service Description link in the starting page you'll see the WSDL for the service. You might want to copy the URL of that page to be used when building a client application:

```
http://localhost:8080/AspNetService1/WebService1.asmx?WSDL
```

Instead of building a simple WinForms client for this server, I decided to create one in the VCL for Win32 to further demonstrate the interoperability of SOAP. After executing the web service outside of the debugger (with Shift+Ctrl+F9), I created a new VCL application, opened the WSDL Importer, inserted the preceding URL, and added the corresponding Delphi interfaces to the application.

In the form I added two edit boxes with attached UpDown controls, plus two buttons and two output labels. The calls to the web service are straightforward:

```
Label1.Caption := IntToStr (GetTWebService1Soap.
  CrazyAdd(UpDown1.Position, UpDown2.Position));
Label2.Caption := GetTWebService1Soap.RemoteTime;
```

The effect of these calls (which change over time) looks like this:

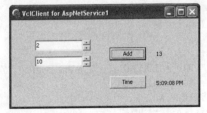

Database Data over SOAP

Now that you know the foundations of web services technologies and have explored the various techniques available in Delphi for Win32 and .NET, let's look at a more complex example, capable of accessing database data.

For this example, I built a web service (based on the Web App Debugger) capable of exposing data about employees of a company. This data is mapped to the EMPLOYEE table of sample InterBase database we've used so often throughout the book. The Delphi interface of the web service is defined in the SoapEmployeeIntf unit as follows:

```
type
  ISoapEmployee = interface (IInvokable)
    ['{77D0D940-23EC-49A5-9630-ADE0751E3DB3}']
    function GetEmployeeNames: string; stdcall;
    function GetEmployeeData (EmpID: string): string; stdcall;
  end;
```

The first method returns a list of the names of all the employees in the company, and the second returns the details of a given employee. The implementation of this interface is provided in the SoapEmployeeImpl unit with the following class:

```
type
  TSoapEmployee = class(TInvokableClass, ISoapEmployee)
  public
    function GetEmployeeNames: string; stdcall;
    function GetEmployeeData (EmpID: string): string; stdcall;
  end;
```

The implementation of the web service lies in the two previous methods and some helper functions to manage the XML data being returned. But before we get to the XML portion of the example, let me briefly discuss the database access section.

Accessing the Data

All the connectivity and SQL code in this example are hosted in a separate data module. Of course, I could have created some connection and dataset components dynamically in the methods, but doing so is contrary to the approach of a visual development tool like Delphi. The data module has the following structure:

```
object DataModule3: TDataModule3
  object SQLConnection: TSQLConnection
    ConnectionName = 'IBConnection'
    DriverName = 'Interbase'
  end
  object dsEmplList: TSQLDataSet
    CommandText = 'select EMP_NO, LAST_NAME, FIRST_NAME from EMPLOYEE'
    SQLConnection = SQLConnection
    object dsEmplListEMP_NO: TStringField
    object dsEmplListLAST_NAME: TStringField
```

```
    object dsEmplListFIRST_NAME: TStringField
  end
  object dsEmpData: TSQLDataSet
    CommandText = 'select * from EMPLOYEE where Emp_No = :id'
    Params = <
      item
        DataType = ftFixedChar
        Name = 'id'
        ParamType = ptInput
      end>
    SQLConnection = SQLConnection
  end
end
```

As you can see, the data module has two SQL queries hosted by SQLDataSet components. The first is used to retrieve the name and ID of each employee, and the second returns the entire set of data for a given employee.

Passing XML Documents

The problem is how to return this data to a remote client program. In this example, I used the approach I like best: I returned XML documents instead of working with complex SOAP data structures.

NOTE   Because of its remote procedure call (RPC) roots, SOAP uses XML as a data transport mechanism but defines its own data structures for conveying complex data. This approach adds extra complexity and makes interface dependable on data structure details. I find it odd that SOAP proponents don't see that XML is the perfect way to pass data around, something that can also be done in SOAP by using string parameters and returning values and passing complex XML documents within those strings. This approach is closer to the REST architecture than to classic SOAP.

In this example, the GetEmployeeNames method creates an XML document containing a list of employees, with their first and last names as values and the related database ID as an attribute, using two helper functions MakeXmlStr (already used in the last chapter) and MakeXmlAttribute (listed here):

```
function TSoapEmployee.GetEmployeeNames: string;
var
  dm: TDataModule3;
begin
  dm := TDataModule3.Create (nil);
  try
    dm.dsEmplList.Open;
    Result := '<employeeList>' + sLineBreak;
    while not dm.dsEmplList.EOF do
    begin
      Result := Result + '  ' + MakeXmlStr ('employee',
        dm.dsEmplListLASTNAME.AsString + ' ' +
```

```
              dm.dsEmplListFIRSTNME.AsString,
            MakeXmlAttribute ('id',
              dm.dsEmplListEMPNO.AsString)) + sLineBreak;
        dm.dsEmplList.Next;
      end;
      Result := Result + '</employeeList>';
    finally
      dm.Free;
    end;
end;


function MakeXmlAttribute (attrName, attrValue: string): string;
begin
  Result := attrName + '="' + attrValue + '"';
end;
```

You may wonder why the program creates a new instance of the data module each time. The negative side of this approach is that the program establishes a new connection to the database each time (a rather slow operation), but the plus side is that there is no risk related to the use of a multithreaded application. If two web service requests are executed concurrently, you can use a shared connection to the database, but you must use different dataset components for the data access. You could move the datasets in the function code and keep only the connection on the data module, or have a global shared data module for the connection (used by multiple threads) and a specific instance of a second data module hosting the datasets for each method call.

Let's now look at the second method, GetEmployeeData. It uses a parametric query and formats the resulting fields in separate XML nodes (using another helper function, FieldsToXml):

```
function TSoapEmployee.GetEmployeeData(EmpID: string): string;
var
  dm: TDataModule3;
begin
  dm := TDataModule3.Create (nil);
  try
    dm.dsEmpData.ParamByName('ID').AsString := EmpId;
    dm.dsEmpData.Open;
    Result := FieldsToXml ('employee', dm.dsEmpData);
  finally
    dm.Free;
  end;
end;


function FieldsToXml (rootName: string; data: TDataSet): string;
var
  i: Integer;
begin
  Result := '<' + rootName + '>' + sLineBreak;
  for i := 0 to data.FieldCount - 1 do
    Result := Result + '  ' + MakeXmlStr (
```

```
      LowerCase (data.Fields[i].FieldName),
      data.Fields[i].AsString) + sLineBreak;
  Result := Result + '</' + rootName + '>' + sLineBreak;
end;
```

The Client Program (Mapping to a ClientDataSet with XSLT)

The final step for this example is to write a test client program. You can do so as usual by importing the WSDL file defining the web service. In this case, you also have to convert the XML data you receive into something more manageable—particularly the list of employees returned by the GetEmployeeNames method. Since there's an XML to convert in the XML of a data packet for the ClientDataSet component, I could have used Delphi's XML Mapper. However, to have a more flexible solution and one you can easily port to ADO.NET as well, I used an XSL transformation instead.

To accomplish this, I first wrote the code to receive the XML with the list of employees and copied it into a memo component and from there to a file (employeeList.xml in the SoapEmployee folder of the example). Then, I opened the XML of a ClientDataSet component and used its structure to write the XSL document (mapper.xsl, in the same folder), available in Listing 23.1.

LISTING 23.1:   The XSLT used to convert custom XML data into the XML for the ClientDataSet

```
<?xml version="1.0" encoding="UTF-8"?>
<xsl:stylesheet version="1.0"
  xmlns:xsl="http://www.w3.org/1999/XSL/Transform">

  <xsl:template match="/employeeList">
    <DATAPACKET Version="2.0">
      <METADATA>
        <FIELDS>
          <FIELD attrname="id" fieldtype="i2" required="true"/>
          <FIELD attrname="fullname" fieldtype="string"
            required="true" WIDTH="45"/>
        </FIELDS>
        <PARAMS/>
      </METADATA>
      <ROWDATA>
        <xsl:apply-templates select="employee"/>
      </ROWDATA>
    </DATAPACKET>
  </xsl:template>

  <xsl:template match="employee">
    <ROW id="{@id}" fullname="{.}"/>
  </xsl:template>

</xsl:stylesheet>
```

The program applies this XSLT to the result of the web service call and feeds the ClientDataSet component with the resulting string:

```
procedure TForm1.btnGetListClick(Sender: TObject);
var
  strXml: string;
  strXmlOutput: WideString;
begin
  xmlDoc.Active := False;
  strXml := GetISoapEmployee.GetEmployeeNames;
  xmlDoc.XML.Text := strXml; // load the XML from the web service
  xmlDoc.Active := True;

  xslDoc.Active := True;
  xmlDoc.DocumentElement.transformNode (
    xslDoc.DocumentElement, strXmlOutput);
  ClientDataSet1.XmlData := strXmlOutput;
  ClientDataSet1.Open;
end;
```

With this code, the program can display the list of employees in a DBGrid, as you can see in Figure 23.8. When you retrieve the data for the specific employee, the program extracts the ID of the active record from the ClientDataSet and then shows the resulting XML in a memo:

```
procedure TForm1.btnGetDetailsClick(Sender: TObject);
begin
  Memo2.Lines.Text := GetISoapEmployee.GetEmployeeData(
    ClientDataSet1.FieldByName ('id').AsString);
end;
```

TIP   Again, the reason I used XSLT is that this approach can also be used to map the data into the ADO.NET XML format or any other XML data structure. You could use a similar approach to convert the XML of a ClientDataSet component into or from that of an ADO.NET dataset.

FIGURE 23.8
The client program of the SoapEmployee web service example

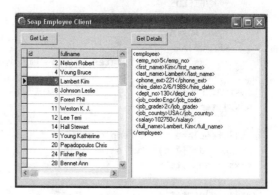

DataSnap over SOAP

Now that you have a reasonably good idea how to build a SOAP server and a SOAP client, let's look at how to use this technology in building a multitier DataSnap application. You'll use a Soap Server Data Module to create the new web service and the SoapConnection component to connect a client application to it.

BUILDING THE DATASNAP SOAP SERVER

Let's look at the server side first. Go to the Web Services page of the New Items dialog box and use the Soap Server Application icon to create a new web service and then use the Soap Server Data Module icon to add a DataSnap server-side data module to the SOAP server. I did this in the SoapDataServer example (which uses the Web App Debugger architecture for testing purposes). From this point on, all you do is write a normal DataSnap server (or a middle-tier DataSnap application), as discussed in Chapter 17. In this case, I added InterBase access to the program by means of dbExpress, resulting in the following structure:

```
object SoapTestDm: TSoapTestDm
  object SQLConnection1: TSQLConnection
    ConnectionName = 'IBLocal'
  end
  object SQLDataSet1: TSQLDataSet
    SQLConnection = SQLConnection1
    CommandText = 'select * from EMPLOYEE'
  end
  object DataSetProvider1: TDataSetProvider
    DataSet = SQLDataSet1
  end
end
```

The data module built for a SOAP-based DataSnap server defines a custom interface (so you can add methods to it) inheriting from IAppServerSOAP, which is defined as a published interface (even though it doesn't inherit from IInvokable).

TIP Delphi 6 used DataSnap's standard IAppServer interface for exposing data via SOAP. Since Delphi 7 this has been replaced with the inherited IAppServerSOAP interface, which is function-ally identical but allows the system to discriminate the type of call depending on the interface name. Older applications can still be called from a client built with newer versions of Delphi.

The implementation class, TSoapTestDm, is the data module, as in other DataSnap servers. Here is the code Delphi generated, with the addition of the custom method:

```
type
  ISampleDataModule = interface(IAppServerSOAP)
  ['{D47A293F-4024-4690-9915-8A68CB273D39}']
    function GetRecordCount: Integer; stdcall;
  end;

  TSampleDataModule = class(TSoapDataModule, ISampleDataModule,
    IAppServerSOAP, IAppServer)
```

```
      DataSetProvider1: TDataSetProvider;
      SQLConnection1: TSQLConnection;
      SQLDataSet1: TSQLDataSet;
    public
      function GetRecordCount: Integer; stdcall;
    end;
```

The base TSoapDataModule doesn't inherit from TInvokableClass. This is not a problem as long as you provide an extra factory procedure to create the object (which is what TInvokableClass does for you) and add it to the registration code (as discussed earlier, in the section "Exposing an Existing Class as a Web Service"):

```
    procedure TSampleDataModuleCreateInstance(out obj: TObject);
    begin
      obj := TSampleDataModule.Create(nil);
    end;
```

```
    initialization
      InvRegistry.RegisterInvokableClass(
        TSampleDataModule, TSampleDataModuleCreateInstance);
      InvRegistry.RegisterInterface(TypeInfo(ISampleDataModule));
```

The server application also publishes the IAppServerSOAP and IAppServer interfaces, thanks to the (little) code in the SOAPMidas unit.

TIP Web service applications can include more than one SOAP data module. To identify a specific SOAP data module, use the SOAPServerIID property of the SoapConnection component or add the data module interface name to the end of the URL.

The server has a custom method that uses a query with the select count(*) from EMPLOYEE SQL statement:

```
    function TSampleDataModule.GetRecordCount: Integer;
    begin
      // read in the record count by running a query
      SQLDataSet2.Open;
      Result := SQLDataSet2.Fields[0].AsInteger;
      SQLDataSet2.Close;
    end;
```

BUILDING THE DATASNAP SOAP CLIENT

To build the client application, called SoapDataClient, I began with a plain program and added a SoapConnection component to it (from the Web Services page of the palette), hooking it to the URL of the DataSnap web service and referring to the specific interface I was looking for:

```
    object SoapConnection1: TSoapConnection
      URL = 'http://localhost:1024/SoapDataServer.soapdataserver/' +
        'soap/Isampledatamodule'
```

```
    SOAPServerIID = 'IAppServerSOAP - ' +
      '{C99F4735-D6D2-495C-8CA2-E53E5A439E61}'
    UseSOAPAdapter = False
  end
```

Notice the last property, `UseSOAPAdapter`, which indicates you are working against a server built with Delphi 7 or Delphi 2005. Set it to True to call a server built with Delphi 6. From this point on, you proceed as usual, adding a ClientDataSet component, a DataSource, and a DBGrid to the program; choosing the only available provider for the client dataset; and hooking the rest. Not surprisingly, for this simple example, the client application has little custom code: a single call to open the connection when a button is clicked (to avoid startup errors) and an `ApplyUpdates` call to send changes back to the database.

SOAP VERSUS OTHER DATASNAP CONNECTIONS

Regardless of the apparent similarity of this program to all the other DataSnap client and server programs built in Chapter 17, there is a very important difference worth underlining: The SoapDataServer and SoapDataClient programs do not use COM to expose or call the `IAppServerSOAP` interface. Quite the opposite—the socket- and HTTP-based connections of DataSnap still rely on local COM objects and a registration of the server in the Windows Registry. The native SOAP-based support, however, allows for a totally custom solution that's independent of COM and that offers many more chances to be ported to other operating systems (Linux in particular, as Kylix supports this technology).

The client program can also call the custom method I added to the server to return the record count. This method can be used in a real-world application to show only a limited number of records and inform the user how many haven't yet been downloaded from the server. The client code to call the method relies on an extra HTTPRIO component:

```
    procedure TFormSDC.Button3Click(Sender: TObject);
    var
      SoapData: ISampleDataModule;
    begin
      SoapData := HttpRio1 as ISampleDataModule;
      ShowMessage (IntToStr (SoapData.GetRecordCount));
    end;
```

Handling Attachments

An important feature of Delphi's native SOAP implementation is the full support for SOAP attachments. Attachments in SOAP allow you to send data other than XML text, such as binary files or images. In Delphi, attachments are managed through streams. You can read or indicate the type of attachment encoding, but the transformation of a raw stream of bytes into and from a given encoding is up to your code. This process isn't too complex, though, if you consider that Indy includes a number of encoding components.

WARNING   Delphi Win32 SOAP attachments use MIME multipart encoding and are not compatible with .NET SOAP attachments (including those built with Delphi for .NET), that use DIME multipart encoding instead.

As an example of how to use attachments, I wrote a program that forwards the binary content of a ClientDataSet (which also hosts images) or one of the images alone. The server has the following interface:

```
type
  ISoapFish = interface(IInvokable)
  ['{4E4C57BF-4AC9-41C2-BB2A-64BCE470D450}']
    function GetCds: TSoapAttachment; stdcall;
    function GetImage(fishName: string): TSoapAttachment; stdcall;
  end;
```

The implementation of the GetCds method uses a ClientDataSet that refers to the classic BIOLIFE table, creates a BLOB stream for the graphic field, and then attaches the stream to the TSoapAttachment result:

```
function TSoapFish.GetCds: TSoapAttachment; stdcall;
var
  BlobStream: TStream;
begin
  Result := TSoapAttachment.Create;
  memStr := TMemoryStream.Create;
  BlobStream := WebModule2.cdsFish.CreateBlobStream(
    WebModule2.cdsFishGraphic, bmRead);
  Result.SetSourceStream (memStr, soOwned);
end;
```

Notice that the TSoapAttachment object created and returned by this function is destroyed automatically by the SOAP server. The SoapAttachment object, in turn, owns and destroys memory stream objects, because this is passed with soOwned ownership in the SetSourceStream method.

On the client side, I prepared a form with a ClientDataSet component connected to a DBGrid and a DBImage. All you have to do is grab the SOAP attachment, save it to a temporarily in-memory stream, and then copy the data from the memory stream to the local ClientDataSet:

```
procedure TForm1.btnGetCdsClick(Sender: TObject);
var
  sAtt: TSoapAttachment;
  memStr: TMemoryStream;
begin
  nRead := 0;
  sAtt := (HttpRio1 as ISoapFish).GetCds;
  try
    memStr := TMemoryStream.Create;
    try
      sAtt.SaveToStream(memStr);
      memStr.Position := 0;
      ClientDataSet1.LoadFromStream(MemStr);
    finally
      memStr.Free;
    end;
```

```
  finally
    DeleteFile (sAtt.CacheFile);
    sAtt.Free;
  end;
end;
```

At the other end of the SOAP transmission channel, the client program receives a newly created SoapAttachment object and must free it after it has finished using it, along with the temporary file used when receiving the attachment.

WARNING   By default, SOAP attachments received by a client are saved to a temporary file, referenced by the CacheFile property of the TSOAPAttachment object. If you don't delete this file it will remain in a folder that hosts temporary files.

This code produces the same visual effect as a client application loading a local file into a Client-DataSet, as you can see in Figure 23.9. In this SOAP client I used an HTTPRIO component explicitly to be able to monitor the incoming data (which could possibly be very large and slow); for this reason, I set a global nRead variable to zero before invoking the remote method. In the OnReceivingData event of the HTTPRIO object's HTTPWebNode property, you add the data received to the nRead variable. The Read and Total parameters passed to the event refer to the specific block of data sent over a socket, so they are almost useless by themselves to monitor progress:

```
procedure TForm1.HTTPRIO1HTTPWebNode1ReceivingData(
  Read, Total: Integer);
begin
  Inc (nRead, Read);
  StatusBar1.SimpleText := IntToStr (nRead);
  Application.ProcessMessages;
end;
```

FIGURE 23.9
The FishClient example receives a binary Client-DataSet within a SOAP attachment.

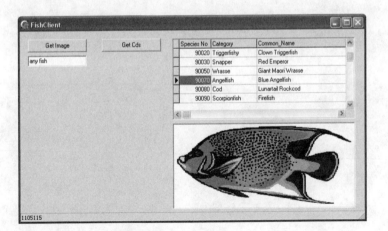

What's Next?

In this chapter, I focused on web services, covering SOAP and WSDL. Technically, I used the native Borland implementation available in Delphi Win32 and the support available in the .NET platform. I also introduced the REST approach with a couple of examples. For more information in the area of business-oriented web services, refer to the UDDI (www.uddi.org) and ebXML (www.ebxml.org) sites. Refer also to the Organization for the Advancement of Structured Information Standards (OASIS, www.oasis-open.org), an industry consortium that is helping standardize these and other XML technologies.

You should have noticed in this chapter that Delphi is strong player in the area of web services with a powerful, open architecture. You can use web services to interact with applications written for the Microsoft .NET platform as well as with applications for the Java platform and programs written in many other languages. Although web services are spreading much more slowly than some analysts predicted, their role is already relevant and growing significantly in many different sectors.

Just as Borland wants to provide the best tools to developers, I hope this book has helped you master Delphi, a development tool that, 10 years after its introduction, still has a very modern architecture and a rather large following of developers. Remember to check from time to time the reference, foundations, and advanced material I've collected on my website (www.marcocantu.com). Much of this material could not be included in this book because of space constraints: see Appendix A for more information.

Appendix B discusses some add-on tools for Delphi that I built and which are freely available on my site, as well as a few other notable free Delphi tools. Also, check my site for updates and integration of the material in the book, and feel free to use the newsgroups hosted there for your questions about the book and about Delphi in general.

Part 5

Appendices

In this section:
- ◆ **Appendix A: Learning the Foundations of Delphi**
- ◆ **Appendix B: Add-on Delphi Tools**

Appendix A

Learning the Foundations of Delphi

This is the eighth edition of *Mastering Delphi*, and I've also written other books, material for classes and conference presentations, and much more; so, in addition to the thousand or so pages this book can accommodate, I have a lot of other material about Delphi programming, particularly introductory material.

Over the last few years, I've turned this information into two electronic books, *Essential Pascal* and *Essential Delphi*, which I've made available on my website, while some of the more advanced material ended up in my *Delphi Power Book*. The two *Essential* books can be freely downloaded, but I do ask for a payment from the professional developers who benefit from them (see the details online). I'll ask for a small fee for the *Power Book* once it is complete.

This appendix outlines the titles and their contents, which complement *Mastering Delphi* by providing introductory information with a gentler learning curve. These e-books are hosted on www.marcocantu.com.

Essential Pascal

Essential Pascal (www.marcocantu.com/epascal) is an introduction to the foundations of the Pascal language. The 100-page book doesn't cover Borland's OOP extensions, but it does detail many features Turbo Pascal added to the core language over the years. The following is the current list of this e-book's chapters:

Chapter 1: "Pascal History"

Chapter 2: "Coding in Pascal"

Chapter 3: "Types, Variables, and Constants"

Chapter 4: "User-Defined Data Types"

Chapter 5: "Statements"

Chapter 6: "Procedures and Functions"

Chapter 7: "Handling Strings"

Chapter 8: "Memory (and Dynamic Arrays)"

Chapter 9: "Windows Programming"

Chapter 10: "Variants"

Chapter 11: "Programs and Units"

Chapter 12: "Files in the Pascal Language"

Appendix A: "Glossary of Terms"

Appendix B: "Examples"

Essential Delphi

Essential Delphi (www.marcocantu.com/edelphi) is an introduction to the use of Delphi as a RAD tool, with a detailed introduction to the VCL library. Most of the material comes from early editions of *Mastering Delphi* that I had to cut in order to make room for coverage of new features Borland has added over the years. Here is the table of contents (which is always under development):

Chapter 1: "A Form Is a Window"

Chapter 2: "Highlights of the Delphi Environment"

Chapter 3: "The Object Repository and the Delphi Wizards"

Chapter 4: "A Tour of the Basic Components"

Chapter 5: "Creating and Handing Menus"

Chapter 6: "Multimedia Fun"

Chapter 7: "Saving Settings: From INI Files to the Registry"

Chapter 8: "More on Forms"

Chapter 9: "Delphi Database 101 (with Paradox)"

Chapter 10: "Printing and Reporting"

Chapter 11: "Managing Files"

Appendix A: "Essential SQL"

Appendix B: "Common VCL Properties"

Delphi Power Book

Delphi Power Book (www.marcocantu.com/delphipowerbook) is not an introduction to Delphi but a collection of more advanced information that, though it is certainly worth good coverage, is not relevant enough to all developers to be included in this edition of *Mastering Delphi*. Unlike the free introductory book, only part of the material of the *Delphi Power Book* will be freely available, while the complete e-book will be sold online on a subscription basis. This is the planned structure:

Chapter 1: "Delphi Language Secrets"

Chapter 2: "Using Interfaces in Delphi"

Chapter 3: "RTL Secrets"

Chapter 4: "Delphi Persistency and Streaming"

Chapter 5: "RTTI in Depth"

Chapter 6: "VCL Secrets"

Chapter 7: "Graphics in Delphi"

Chapter 8: "Writing VCL Components"

Chapter 9: "Win32 VCL Components"

Chapter 10: "Data-Aware VCL Components"

Chapter 11: "Dataset-Derived VCL Components"

Chapter 12: "Writing Property Editors"

Chapter 13: "Writing Component Editors"

Chapter 14: "Wizards and other IDE Customizations"

Chapter 15: "Processes and Memory"

Chapter 16: "Multitasking and Multithreading"

Chapter 17: "Debugging Techniques"

Chapter 18: "Advanced Exceptions Management"

Chapter 19: "COM in Delphi"

Chapter 20: "COM Shell Extensions"

Chapter 21: "Sockets Programming (with Indy)"

Chapter 22: "Delphi and the World Wide Web"

Chapter 23: "From Delphi to Kylix"

Chapter 24: "CLX Secrets"

Chapter 25: "Kylix: Linux System Programming"

Chapter 26: "Delphi for .NET"

Chapter 27: "FCL Secrets"

Appendix B

Add-On Delphi Tools

This appendix highlights some free (mostly open source) Delphi add-on components and tools. As there are hundreds of free Delphi offerings available, many of which are of a high quality, I could only pick a few that are relevant to me, either because I wrote them or have used them extensively.

Marco's Own Tools

During the last few years I have developed a number of small components and Delphi add-in tools. Some of these tools were written for books or were the result of extending examples from books. Others were written as helpers for repetitive operations. All these tools are available for free, and some include the source code. Support for all these tools is available on my newsgroups (on http://delphi.newswhat.com).

CanTools Wizards

This is a set of wizards you can install in Delphi, either within an extra pull-down menu or as a submenu of the Tools menu. The wizards (freely available at www.marcocantu.com/cantoolsw) are unrelated and offer disparate features. Here is a selection of the available wizards:

List Template Wizard   Streamlines the development of strongly typed list-based classes, each dedicated to working with elements on a single type. Because it does a search-and-replace operation on a base source file, it can be used any time you need repeated code and the name of a class (or other entity) varies.

OOP Form Wizard   (Mentioned in Chapter 6, in the section "Hiding the Form Fields".) Allows you to hide the published components of a form, making your form more object-oriented and providing a better encapsulation mechanism. Start it when a form is active, and it will fill the OnCreate event handler. Then you must manually move part of the code into the unit initialization section.

Object Inspector Font Wizard   Lets you change the font of the Object Inspector (something particularly useful for presentations, because the Object Inspector's font is too small to be seen easily on a projection screen).

Rebuild Wizard   Allows you to rebuild all the Delphi projects in a given subfolder after loading each of them in sequence in the IDE. You can use this wizard to grab a series of projects (like those in a book) and open the one you are interested in by clicking the list. You can also automatically compile a given project or start a multiproject build without having to set up a project group.

Clip History Viewer   Keeps track of a list of text items you've copied to the Clipboard. A memo in the viewer's window shows the last 100 clipped lines. Editing the memo (and clicking Save) modifies this Clipboard history. If you keep Delphi open, the Clipboard will also get text from other programs (but only text, of course). I've seen occasional Clipboard-related error messages caused by this wizard.

VCL Hierarchy Wizard   Shows the (almost) complete hierarchy of the VCL, including third-party components you've installed, and allows you to search one class and see many details (base and derived classes, published properties, and so on).

Extended Database Forms Wizard   Does much more than the Database Forms Wizard available in the Delphi IDE (found in the Delphi Projects/Business page of the New Items dialog box): it allows you to choose the fields to place on a form and also to use datasets other than those based on the BDE.

Object Debugger

At design time, you can use the Object Inspector to set the properties of the components of your forms and other designers. Delphi also has a run-time Debug Inspector, which has a similar interface and shows similar information. Before Borland added this feature, I implemented a run-time clone of the Object Inspector meant for debugging programs, called Object Debugger and available at www.marcocantu.com/cantools.

It allows read-write access to all the published properties of a component and has two combo boxes that let you select a form and a component within the form. Some of the property types have custom property editors (lists and so on). You can place the Object Debugger component on a program's main form (or you can create it dynamically in code): It will appear in its own window. There is room for improvement, but even in its current form this tool is handy and has numerous users.

Memory Snap

There are many tools to track the memory status of a Delphi application. During the development of a project, I had to write such a tool, and afterward I made it available. I've written a custom memory manager that plugs into Delphi's default memory manager, keeping track of all memory allocations and de-allocations. In addition to reporting the total number (something Delphi also does now by default), it can save a detailed description of the memory status to a file.

Memory Snap (available at: www.marcocantu.com/cantools) keeps in memory a list of allocated blocks (up to a given total number, which can be easily varied), so that it can dump the contents of the heap to a file with a low-level perspective. This list is generated by examining each memory block and determining its nature with empirical techniques you can see in the source code (although they are not easy to understand).

Other Relevant Free Tools

Thousands of Delphi add-on components and tools are available on the market, ranging from simple freebies to large open-source projects, from shareware programs to highly professional components. This appendix provides a list of notable open-source projects, skipping those already discussed in the book such as Indy (www.nevrona.com/indy and www.atozedsoftware.com/indy) and Open XML (www.philo.de/xml).

Project JEDI

The Joint Endeavor of Delphi Innovators, better known as Project JEDI (`www.delphi-jedi.org`), is not a single project but rather the largest community of open-source Delphi developers. The site hosts its own projects plus others contributed and maintained by members on separate websites.

Project JEDI started as an effort to translate APIs for specific Windows libraries distributed by Microsoft or other companies. Making available the Delphi units with the declarations of those APIs allowed any Delphi developer to use them easily. More recently, the goals of Project JEDI have been extended with the definition of many subprojects and groups. In addition to an ever-growing API library, you can find projects including the JEDI Visual Component Library (JVCL), the JEDI Code Library (JCL, a set of utility functions and nonvisual classes, including a nice exception stack tracer), plus many projects in the area of graphics, multimedia, and game programming. Other activities range from a JEDI Version Control System client to the DARTH header conversion kit, from a programmer's editor to online tutorials.

GExperts

GExperts (`www.gexperts.org`) is probably the most widespread add-in for the Delphi IDE. Self-described as "a set of tools built to increase the productivity of Delphi and C++Builder programmers," it includes a large collection of wizards.

GExperts includes Procedure List, Clipboard History, Expert Manager, Grep Search, Grep Regular Expressions, Grep Results, Message Dialog, Backup Project, Set Tab Order, Clean Directories, Favorite Files, Class Browser, Source Export, Code Librarian, ASCII Chart, PE Information, Component Grid, IDE Menu Shortcuts, Project Dependencies, Perfect Layout, To Do List, and Code Proofreader.

InstantObjects

InstantObjects (`www.instantobjects.org`) is an object-relational mapping framework mostly designed following Scott Ambler's approach. Originally a paid tool, it has been released to open source and has an active community behind it that is extending InstantObjects to better support client/server architectures with large sets of data.

InstantObjects offers a *model realization* in the Delphi IDE via integrated two-way tools, *object persistence* for the most common relational databases, and *object presentation* via standard data-aware controls. One of the most relevant features of InstantObjects is its tight integration with the VCL and the Delphi IDE.

Index

Note to the Reader: Throughout this index **boldfaced** page numbers indicate primary discussions of a topic. *Italicized* page numbers indicate illustrations.

Visit Marco's Delphi Developer Website

This book's author, Marco Cantù, has created a site specifically for Delphi developers, at www.marcocantu.com. It's a great resource for all of your Delphi programming needs.

The site includes:

◆ The source code of the book

◆ Extra examples and tips

◆ Delphi components, wizards, and tools built by the author

◆ The online books Essential Pascal, Essential Delphi, and others

◆ Papers the author has written about Delphi, C++, and Java

◆ Extensive links to Delphi-related websites and documents

◆ Other material related to the author's books, the conferences he speaks at, and his training seminars

The site also hosts a newsgroup, which has a specific section devoted to the author's books, so that readers can discuss the book content with him and among themselves. Other sections of the newsgroup discuss Delphi programming and general topics. The newsgroup can also be accessed from a Web interface.

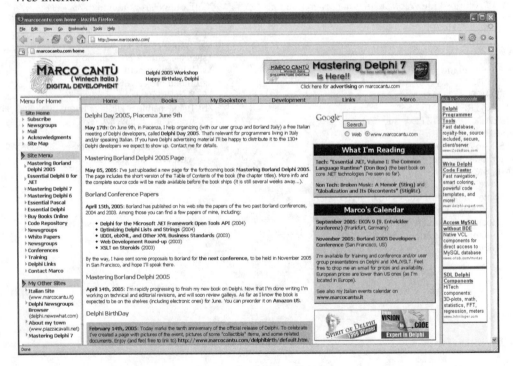